Introduction to Psychology

THIRD EDITION

Introduction to Psychology

THIRD EDITION

Rod Plotnik
San Diego State University

Interior Design
John Odam Design Associates

 Brooks/Cole Publishing Company
Pacific Grove, California

Brooks/Cole Publishing Company
A Division of Wadsworth, Inc.

Printed in the United States of America

10 9 8 7 6 5 4 3 2

Library of Congress Cataloging in Publication Data
Plotnik, Rod.
    Introduction to psychology / Rod Plotnik.—3rd ed.
      p.   cm.
    Includes bibliographical references and indexes.
    ISBN 0-534-16446-3
    1. Psychology. I. Title.
    [DNLM: 1. Psychololgy. BF 139 P729i]
BF121.P626   1993
150—dc20
DNLM/DLC
for Library of Congress   92-49217
                                     CIP

Managing Editor: Vicki Knight
Marketing Manager: Jim Brace-Thompson
Developmental Editor: Janet M. Hunter
Media Specialist: Pat Gadban
Editorial Associate: Heather L. Graeve
Production Coordinator: Joan Marsh
Production: Nancy Sjoberg, Del Mar Associates
Manuscript Editor: Jackie Estrada
Photo Research and Permissions: Linda Rill
Interior Design: John Odam
Cover Design: Katherine Minerva
Design Coordinator: Jonathan Parker
Interior Illustration: John Odam, Jill Malena Davis, Deborah Ivanoff, Jonathan Parker
Assignment Photographer: Craig McClain
Concept Illustrators: Max Seabaugh, Lisa Matzkin, Janet Ashford
Digital Typography: John Odam Design Associates and Del Mar Associates
Manufacturing Coordinator: Vena M. Dyer
Color Separation: Rainbow Graphic Arts Company Ltd.
Cover Printing: Lehigh Press Lithographers
Printing and Binding: R. R. Donnelley & Sons Company, Willard Manufacturing Division

For Sandy, Tiger, and Bear.

Thank you for being there
when the going got tough.

To the Instructor

For the past 15 years, I have been supervising graduate assistants who teach introductory psychology. In our weekly meetings we discuss a variety of topics, but we generally agree that one of our biggest challenges is how to present difficult concepts in new and exciting ways. To meet this challenge, we have been videotaping and analyzing our lectures to discover what works best and what interests today's students. We have found that three elements are especially useful in explaining concepts and capturing students' interest: (1) using interesting examples and real-life cases to bring concepts to life, (2) applying basic psychological principles to solving everyday problems, and (3) stimulating interest with clever graphics. It has become clear to me that the same elements that capture students' interest in lectures can be used to enliven material in a textbook. Thus, my goals for this edition have been to use interesting examples and cases to discuss concepts, to apply psychological principles to real-life problems, and to stimulate interest with intriguing graphics.

In addition, I wanted the graphics to be integrated with the text so that each would reinforce the other. However, integrating text and graphics in a textbook turns out to be no easy matter, because an author usually writes the manuscript first and then the graphics are added later. This process often results in graphics being placed some distance from the relevant text. To solve this problem, I had to insert the graphics as I wrote the text. The result is a new way of presenting concepts, holding student interest, and providing visual cues for remembering the material. Another major advantage of this integration of text and graphics is that each major concept is organized and explained in a one- or two-page spread. Thus, the third edition has an exciting format in that each one- or two-page spread discusses a concept that is integrated with its graphics.

Because of this new approach, I discovered that I had to rewrite almost all the text. As a result, 90% of the material and graphics in the third edition are not merely revised but new. Still, users of previous editions will discover that many popular features, such as the modular approach, Applying/Exploring sections, and mastery tests for students, have been kept and updated.

But enough of explanation. The proof is in the reading. Let me show you the features of the third edition. As you examine the following pages, notice that the traditional content is presented in a dramatically different and interesting way.

Modular Approach

According to users and reviewers, one of the most popular features of the first two editions was the modular approach. This approach continues in the third edition with one change. Each chapter is now divided into two modules, which permits greater continuity in presenting material but still allows for relatively short units.

What's the advantage?

The modular approach developed out of the needs of both students and professors. Students said that they prefer short chapters because that makes the material more manageable and allows students to test their mastery of the material before going on to a new module. In addition, research on the Personalized System of Instruction (PSI) has indicated that material is best mastered when presented in smaller units.

Professors said that they prefer the modular approach because it provides unique flexibility in planning and personalizing a course. You have the option of assigning or omitting material by using traditional chapter titles or by selecting individual modules. For example, in covering a traditional topic, such as biological bases of behavior, you could assign all of Chapter 2. If you wanted to cover only the basic anatomy and function of the brain, you could assign just Module 4. Similarly, if you wanted to cover the topic of perception in the traditional way, you would assign Chapter 4; but if you wanted to cover just basic perceptual processes, you could assign Module 7.

Thus, the third edition continues to use the modular approach but improves continuity by dividing the material into two modules per chapter.

Chapter *Four*
PERCEPTION

MODULE 7

BASIC PERCEPTUAL PROCESSES
Perceptual Thresholds
Sensations Versus Perceptions
Principles of Perceptual Organization
Depth Perception
Perceptual Constancies
Illusions: Fooling Our Perceptions
Applying/Exploring: Creating Perceptual Experiences

MODULE 8

INFLUENCES ON PERCEPTION
Studying Heredity and Experience
Effects of Restricted Experiences
Learning Influences
Perceptual Sets
Cultural Diversity: Culture and Perception
Applying/Exploring: Extrasensory Perception

122

Module Opener

Each module opener contains three elements. First, there is an interesting vignette to introduce the material, generate interest, and raise questions. Second, there is a definition of the module's major concept. Third, there is a paragraph, titled "What's Coming," that introduces the concepts that will be covered in the modules.

What's the purpose of the vignettes?
Besides catching the students' attention, the opening vignettes stimulate questions and discussions by presenting a wide range of people in diverse situations. For the third edition, 26 of the 32 vignettes are new. At the end of the course students often remember the vignettes and the points they make. Here's a sample of some of the vignettes and the questions they raise:

Module 1: A young boy is diagnosed as autistic. How do psychologists study this problem?

Module 2: Linus Pauling believes in the curative properties of vitamin C. How do we judge the evidence?

Module 8: A man regained his vision after 53 years. What did he see?

Module 9: Stefania lived underground for 130 days. What happened to her sleep-wake cycle?

Module 12: An adult Kodiak bear starred in a movie. What techniques were used to train the bear?

Module 13: A man named Rajan memorized over 33,000 numbers in order. How did he do it?

Module 17: Mark, a paraplegic, climbed a mountain. What motivated him?

Module 18: Eric, a surfer, was attacked by a shark. How did his emotions affect his physiological responses?

Module 21: A young teenager wants to be president. How do her thinking processes change through adolescence?

Module 24: Charles Dutton, a convicted felon, became a respected actor. What changed his personality?

Module 27: Mass murderer Jeffrey Dahmer was sentenced to prison. In what way was he abnormal?

Module 29: Anna O. could not drink a glass of water. Was her problem psychological?

Module 31: Dr. Fran Conley, neurosurgeon, charged her male colleagues with sexism. Why does sexism occur?

In addition to these opening vignettes, many other case studies are used throughout the text to illustrate concepts and maintain interest.

MODULE 9
CONSCIOUSNESS, SLEEP, AND DREAMS

Although 20 people had volunteered to live alone in an underground cave for four months, researchers selected Stefania for her inner strength and stamina. On the chosen day, she and her favorite books entered a 20-by-12-foot Plexiglas module 30 feet underground, sealed off from sunlight, radio, television, and other cues for time. During her first month underground, Stefania's concentration seemed to come and go. She appeared depressed, and she snapped at researchers when they asked her to do routine measurements. She had strange dreams, such as that her computer monitor had turned into a TV that was talking to her. After several months, however, she became more comfortable with her underground isolation. She followed a regular routine of taking her body temperature, heart rate, and blood pressure and typing the results into a computer monitor, her only link with the outside world.

She spent her time playing the guitar, cooking on a hot plate, reading books, dealing infinite hands of solitaire, and making friends with two mice that she named Giuseppe and Nicoletta. Without clocks, radio, television, or the sun, she found it difficult to keep track of time, which seemed to have slowed down. When told she could leave her underground apartment because her 130 days were up, she felt certain she had been underground only about 60 days. Her time underground, which was a women's record (the men's record is 210 days), allowed researchers to closely monitor her sleeping and waking behaviors in the absence of all time cues. (adapted from *Newsweek*, June 5, 1989)

How long is a day when you're living underground?

Stefania emerges after spending 130 days in an isolated underground cave.

About a half dozen men and women have voluntarily lived in underground caves so researchers could study sleep and wakefulness. These two states are part of **consciousness,** *which refers to various levels of awareness of one's thoughts and feelings, as well as of other internal and external stimuli and events.*

What's Coming
In this module, we'll discuss consciousness, mechanisms of sleep, meaning of dreams, and treatment of sleep problems. In the next module, we'll examine many aspects of hypnosis and the use and abuse of drugs. Let's begin with something that you are now experiencing—consciousness.

Step-by-Step Approach

The basic idea underlying the preparation of this edition was that the material would be organized into smaller units and assembled, with appropriate graphics, on a one- or two-page spread. This meant that each page was individually designed so that the material could be presented in the most understandable way. For example, the complex concept of storing memories (page 242) makes more sense when presented in small sequential steps.

What are the steps in encoding memories? Students often find it difficult to understand how a stimulus is encoded into long-term memory. As shown here, the text breaks down this encoding process into six steps, with an appropriate graphic for each. Through the use of graphics, students are given visual cues to help remember each step.

This technique of organizing and presenting material in small steps or in sequence has been used throughout the textbook. Here's a sample of such material:

Module 1: Six Approaches in Psychology
Module 2: Conducting an Experiment: Seven Steps
Module 3: Neuron Structure and Function
Module 4: The Human Brain: Three Major Divisions
Module 5: Pathway of Light Waves Through the Eye
Module 6: Structure and Function of the Ear
Module 7: Steps for Constructing a Perception
Module 9: Journey Through the Night
Module 11: Establishing Classical Conditioning
Module 12: Comparison: Classical Versus Operant Conditioning
Module 14: Network Theory
Module 16: Language Stages
Module 18: Peripheral Theories of Emotions
Module 19: Genetic Process
Module 20: Erikson's Psychosocial Stages
Module 21: Biological Changes During Puberty
Module 22: Levinson's Real-Life Stages
Module 23: Freud's Psychosexual Stages
Module 25: Activation of Fight-Flight Response
Module 30: Desensitization

The extensive use of this step-by-step approach will help students better understand the material, and the graphics will help them better remember it. This feature is new to the third edition.

Long-Term Memory: Storing

As you have just seen, when Norman lost an area of his brain, he also lost most of his ability to transfer information into long-term memory. Long-term memory stores enormous quantities of information for long periods of time.

To illustrate the process of transferring information into long-term memory, imagine strolling through the park on a summer's day. Around you are children yelling, dogs barking, jugglers juggling, and people talking. Among all these thousands of incoming auditory and visual stimuli are the notes of a familiar song. Suddenly, you pay attention to that particular auditory information—familiar notes. We'll trace the path these notes take to reach your long-term memory.

Steps in the Memory Process

1 *Sensory memory.* For a very brief period environmental information is held in sensory memory: iconic memory lasts about 1/4 second; echoic memory lasts 1–2 seconds. If you do not pay attention to the information in sensory memory, it disappears forever. If you do pay attention, such as by focusing on the familiar notes, that information is automatically transferred to short-term memory.

2 *Attention.* This is the process for controlling the transfer of information from sensory memory to short-term memory.

3 *Short-term memory.* Once information is in short-term memory, you have time for further analysis. However, if you do not pay attention, think about, or rehearse the song any further, the unrehearsed material will disappear from short-term memory in 2–30 seconds. If you further rehearse the material, such as by humming, singing along, or talking about the song and forming associations, information in short-term memory will be transferred or encoded into long-term memory.

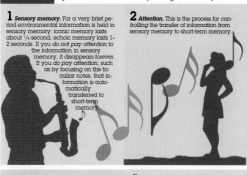

4 *Encoding.* Encoding is the process that controls the transfer of information from short-term memory into long-term memory. Encoding may involve deliberate effort, such as rehearsing, taking notes, or making associations between new and old information. Encoding may occur almost automatically, such as when something interests you. Because of your attention, interest, and thinking about this song, it may be encoded into long-term memory with little effort.

5 *Long-term memory.* Once information is placed or encoded in long-term memory, it may remain for your lifetime. Later, if you were to describe hearing the song to a friend, you would be retrieving the information from long-term memory and placing it back into short-term memory. This is an example of information being retrieved with little effort and almost automatically. In other cases (such as trying to remember who you were with when you first heard a particular song), you may have to search long and hard with deliberate effort to retrieve information from long-term memory. The fact that information is encoded in long-term memory does not guarantee that such information can always or easily be retrieved or remembered.

6 *Retrieving.* Retrieving is the process for selecting information from long-term memory and transferring it back into short-term memory. Retrieval may occur almost automatically or may require extensive searching. When we talk about remembering, we usually mean retrieving.

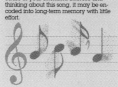

The last time I heard this song I was in New York

By knowing the difference between short-term and long-term memory and how information is transferred between them, we can explain a classic finding in memory research.

Side-by-Side Comparisons

One goal of an introductory course is to give students an appreciation of psychology's different approaches, theories, and points of view. Because of the third edition's flexible format, various theories or points of view can be presented in a side-by-side format with their own graphics.

What are three viewpoints of cognitive learning?

As shown here, three approaches to explaining cognitive learning—those of Skinner, Tolman, and Bandura—are presented in a side-by-side format with appropriate graphics. This format allows a clear comparison of these three viewpoints along with visual cues for remembering the viewpoints.

The ability to present competing viewpoints in a side-by-side format is one of the unique features of the third edition. Here's a sample of material presented in this way:

Module 1: Previous Approaches—Learning from History

Module 4: Autonomic Nervous System

Module 5: Two Theories of Color Vision

Module 8: Three Approaches to Studying Influences of Perception

Module 9: Continuum of Consciousness

Module 10: Two Explanations of Hypnosis

Module 11: Three Approaches to Learning

Module 12: Schedules of Reinforcement

Module 13: Three Kinds of Memory

Module 15: Approaches to Defining Intelligence

Module 17: Approaches to Motivation

Module 23: Divisions of the Mind

Module 24: Four Theories of Personality

Module 25: Three Stages of the General Adaptation Syndrome

Module 27: Three Approaches to Understanding Mental Disorders

Module 29: Background on Treatment of Mental Disorders

Module 30: Psychotherapy: Overview

The widespread use of this side-by-side format will help students better compare viewpoints, and the accompanying graphics will help them better remember them.

Cognitive Learning

Do you hate bugs?

Learning to detest bugs from watching someone's fearful reaction is an example of cognitive learning, the third approach that psychologists use to study learning. Recall from Module 11 that *cognitive learning* is a kind of learning that involves mental processes, such as attention and memory, and may not involve any external rewards or require the person to perform any observable behaviors. Although interest in cognitive learning was "reborn" in the 1960s, its roots extend back to the work of Wundt in the late 1800s and that of psychologist Edward Tolman in the 1930s. Today the concepts of cognitive learning have become popular in explaining animal and human behavior (Schwartz & Reisberg, 1991). We'll learn about various aspects of cognitive learning, including observational and insight learning, but first let's compare three different views on cognitive learning.

Three Viewpoints

B. F. Skinner—Against. Eight days before his death, B. F. Skinner was honored by the American Psychological Association (APA) with the first APA Citation for Outstanding Lifetime Contribution to Psychology. In his acceptance speech to over 1,000 friends and colleagues, Skinner spoke of how psychology was splitting between those who were studying feelings and cognitive processes and those who were studying observable behaviors. Repeating a thought he had expressed many times before, Skinner said, "As far as I'm concerned, cognitive science is the creationism [downfall] of psychology" (Vargas, 1991, p. 1).

Skinner's severe criticism of cognitive processes and mental events caused many in the audience to gasp and only a few to applaud (Vargas, 1991). Apparently, many in the audience, as well as throughout psychology today, believe that cognitive processes are not psychology's creationism (or, as Skinner implied, a step backward in knowledge). Instead, they believe that cognitive processes are a useful approach to understanding learning and behavior.

Edward Tolman—In Favor. In the 1930s, about the same time that Skinner was emphasizing observable behaviors, Tolman was exploring hidden mental processes. For example, he would place rats individually in a maze, such as the one shown above, and allow each rat time to explore the maze with no food present. Then, with food present in the maze's food box, he would retest the rat to see which path it took. The rat learned very quickly to take the shortest path. Next, Tolman blocked the shortest path to the food box. The first time the rat encountered the blocked shortest path, it selected the next shortest path to the food box. According to Tolman (1948), the rat selected the next shortest path because it had developed a cognitive map of the maze. A **cognitive map** *is a mental representation of the layout of an environment.*

In addition, Tolman showed that rats learned the layout of a maze without being reinforced, a position very different from Skinner's. Tolman's emphasis on cognitive processes in learning is continued today by Albert Bandura.

Albert Bandura—In Favor. Although Bandura began as a behaviorist in the Skinnerian tradition, he has gradually and almost entirely shifted to a cognitive approach. In many of his studies, Bandura (1986) has focused on how humans learn through observation. For example, Bandura would say that a child can learn to hate spiders simply by observing the behaviors of someone who exhibits a great dislike of spiders. This is an example of **observational learning,** *which is a form of learning that develops through watching and does not require the observer to perform any observable behavior or receive a reinforcer.* Just as Tolman found that learning occurred while rats were exploring, Bandura found that humans learned while observing and that much of human learning takes place through observation. Observational learning, which emphasizes cognitive processes, is 180 degrees from Skinner's position, which emphasizes observable, noncognitive behaviors.

We'll next describe one of Bandura's best-known studies on observational learning, which is one form of cognitive learning.

Cultural Diversity

Too often students accept the viewpoint that their culture is normal and that other cultures are deviant, or that their culture is advanced and other cultures need to catch up to theirs. One goal of an introductory psychology course is to broaden students' viewpoints with material from other cultures. To meet this goal, each chapter has a feature called "Cultural Diversity," which presents a viewpoint from another culture.

How do aborigines remember things?
One reason people in nonindustrial cultures score low on Western-style IQ tests is that such tests emphasize verbal information. As shown here, aborigines do poorly on Western-style IQ tests, which stress verbal information. However, aborigines excel at tests that emphasize visual information, which is critical to survival in their desert environment. These kinds of cultural differences raise many interesting questions for discussion.

Here are the topics discussed in the Cultural Diversity features:

The Cultural Diversity feature broadens students' views, challenges their provincial attitudes, and broadens their understanding of the world.

Aborigines' Memory Cues

You have spent a major part of 12 years of your life in various classrooms. In the academic world, your survival has depended to a large extent on your ability to store or encode enormous amounts of *verbal information*. In stark contrast to your academic world is the harsh, barren desert world of western Australia. Here live Aborigines, who for 30,000 years have followed a seminomadic lifestyle of hunting and gathering. In this desert world the Aborigines' survival depends on finding their way through vast stretches of unmapped country and remembering locations of water, food, and game. Their survival depends to a large extent on their ability to store or encode enormous amounts of environmental or *visual information*.

Psychologist Judith Kearins suggested that Aborigines, who scored low on Western verbal-style intelligence tests, might perform better on tests that took advantage of their ability to encode with visual cues. To test this idea, Kearins placed 20 objects on a board divided into 20 squares. Some objects were natural—stone, feather, leaf; others were manufactured— eraser, thimble, ring. Aborigine and white Australian children were told to study the board for 30 seconds. Then all the objects were heaped into a pile in the center of the board and the children were asked to replace the items in their original locations. Kearins found that the Aborigine children performed significantly better than the white Australian children in placing the objects into their original locations (Kearins, 1981). Kearins concluded that survival of the Aborigines in the harsh desert landscape had encouraged and rewarded their ability to store or encode information using visual retrieval cues. These interesting results suggest that survival needs may shape and reward a particular way of encoding information in memory.

Although we may accurately encode information, there are times when we misremember. One example of a situation in which people may misremember is eyewitness testimony, which we discuss in the following Applying/Exploring section.

Aborigines encode information using primarily visual cues, while Westerners use primarily verbal cues.

Concept/Glossary

One challenge for students taking an introductory psychology course is the hundreds of new terms and concepts that need to be learned. To help students identify and remember major terms, this text contains a pedagogical feature called the Concept/Glossary. This feature gives definitions and asks students to fill in the correct terms. As students answer the questions, they are essentially creating their own glossary. Thus, the Concept/Glossary serves three functions: it identifies the major terms and concepts in the module, tests students' mastery of the major concepts, and allows students to generate their own glossary.

As shown here, the Concept/Glossary gives definitions of about a dozen major concepts as well as provides visual cues to recall the correct terms.

What's unique about the Concept/Glossary? When each major concept is discussed in the text, it is linked to an appropriate graphic. These linked graphics offer visual cues for remembering the concept. Later, when students answer the Concept/Glossary questions, the graphics are placed next to their appropriate definitions. Thus, the Concept/Glossary is unique in that it facilitates remembering by providing visual cues linked to major concepts.

CONCEPT/ GLOSSARY: Cognitive Learning

1. A kind of learning that involves mental processes, such as attention and memory, and that may not require any external rewards or the performance of any observable behaviors is referred to as _____.

2. Tolman studied the behavior of rats that were allowed to explore a maze without any reward given. When food was present, rats quickly learned to select the next shortest path if a previously taken path was blocked. Tolman said the rats had developed a mental representation of the layout of their environment, which he called a _____.

3. Although an organism may learn a behavior through observation or exploration, the organism may not immediately demonstrate or perform the newly learned behavior. This phenomenon is known as the _____ distinction.

4. According to Bandura, one form of cognitive learning that develops through watching and that does not require the observer to perform any observable behavior or receive a reinforcer is called _____ learning.

5. Bandura's theory of observational learning involves four mental processes. The observer must pay (a)_____ to what the model says or does. The observer must then code the information and be able to retrieve it from (b)_____ to use it at a later time. The observer must be able to use the coded information to guide his or her (c)_____ in performing and imitating the model's behavior. Finally, the observer must be (d)_____ to perform the behavior, which involves some reason, reinforcement, or incentive.

6. In Köhler's study of problem solving in chimps, he identified a mental process marked by the sudden occurrence of a solution, which he termed _____.

7. Köhler's study of insightful problem solving, Bandura's theory of observational learning, and Tolman's idea of cognitive maps represent three kinds of _____ learning.

8. Learning may be either facilitated or inhibited by the structure of the organism's brain and body, which is referred to as (a)_____. When learning is inhibited by biological factors, it is called (b)_____.

9. The innate tendency of animals to be equipped to recognize, attend to, and store certain cues over others is referred to as (a)_____. An example of this tendency is observed in young geese who are preprogrammed to follow objects immediately after birth. This tendency in newborn birds is called (b)_____.

Answers: 1. cognitive learning; 2. cognitive map; 3. learning-performance; 4. observational; 5. (a) attention, (b) memory, (c) motor control, (d) motivation; 6. insight; 7. cognitive; 8. (a) biological factors, (b) biological restraint; 9. (a) prepared learning, (b) imprinting.

Applying/Exploring

One of the more popular features with students and reviewers is the Applying/Exploring section. This section discusses how psychologists apply basic principles to real-life problems, and it points out new or controversial findings. For example, here's part of the Applying/Exploring section from Module 11.

Why did Michelle become nauseous?
In this Applying/Exploring section, students learn that classical conditioning of nausea occurs in some patients undergoing chemotherapy in the doctor's office. The first page of this section, which is shown here, describes how patients are classically conditioned to be nauseous to cues in the doctor's office. On the second page (not shown here), students learn how a treatment based on classical conditioning—systematic desensitization—can be used to treat classically conditioned nausea.

Here's a sample of some of the Applying/Exploring topics that appear at the end of each module:

As these examples indicate, the Applying/Exploring feature gives students a different view of how psychology works.

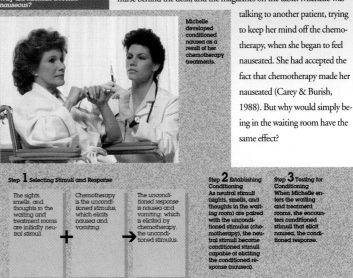

APPLYING/EXPLORING: CHEMOTHERAPY AND CONDITIONED NAUSEA

Just an hour earlier, Michelle had received her second chemotherapy treatment for breast cancer. Now she was feeling nauseated, a common side effect of the powerful anticancer drugs used in chemotherapy. Her nausea, which was accompanied by severe vomiting, would last for 6 to 12 hours. In Michelle's case, the medication she had been given to control the nausea was not working.

About a week later, Michelle arrived at the clinic for her third chemotherapy session and took her customary seat in the waiting room. As she looked around, she recognized the painting on the wall, the nurse behind the desk, and the magazines on the table. Michelle was talking to another patient, trying to keep her mind off the chemotherapy, when she began to feel nauseated. She had accepted the fact that chemotherapy made her nauseated (Carey & Burish, 1988). But why would simply being in the waiting room have the same effect?

Why did Michelle become nauseous?

Michelle developed conditioned nausea as a result of her chemotherapy treatments.

Step 1 Selecting Stimuli and Response

The sights, smells, and thoughts in the waiting and treatment rooms are initially neutral stimuli.

Chemotherapy is the *unconditioned stimulus*, which elicits nausea and vomiting.

The *unconditioned response* is nausea and vomiting, which is elicited by chemotherapy, the *unconditioned stimulus.*

Step 2 Establishing Conditioning
As neutral stimuli (sights, smells, and thoughts in the waiting room) are paired with the unconditioned stimulus (chemotherapy), the neutral stimuli become conditioned stimuli capable of eliciting the conditioned response (nausea).

Step 3 Testing for Conditioning
When Michelle enters the waiting and treatment rooms, she encounters conditioned stimuli that elicit nausea, the conditioned response.

CHAPTER 6: LEARNING

Summary/Self-Test

Researchers tell us that students are relatively poor judges of how well they know material, because they often lack specific feedback. For example, students may think they understand classical conditioning, but they need feedback on their knowledge of specific terms. To give students feedback on their mastery of the material, a Summary/Self-Test is provided at the end of each module. The Summary/Self-Test serves two functions: it reviews the material like a traditional summary, and it provides specific feedback by having students answer fill-in questions.

Critical Thinking Questions

We usually have two goals for our students: we want them to learn a body of information, and we also want them to think about and discuss the material. Students can judge how well they meet our first goal—learning specific terms and concepts—by answering the fill-in questions of the Summary/Self-Test. In addition, students can judge how well they meet our second goal—discussing the material—by answering the critical thinking question that appears at the end of each major heading in the Summary/Self-Test. Critical thinking questions can be used to generate classroom discussions or can be used as short essay questions. A separate supplement, called *Fostering Critical Thinking*, suggests ways to answer each of the critical thinking questions.

Thus, each module has two pedagogical aids—Concept/Glossary and Summary/Self-Test—that provide specific feedback and stimulate critical thinking.

Summary/Self-Test

THREE APPROACHES TO LEARNING

1. A relatively permanent change in behavior that results from experience is a definition of _____; one of its important functions is to help us adapt and adjust to our environments.
2. Psychologists have used three approaches to study learning. One approach had its beginning in Pavlov's well-known experiment in which a bell was sounded and then food was placed in a dog's mouth. Today, Pavlov's procedure for establishing conditioned reflexes is called _____.
3. A second approach to studying learning grew out of Thorndike's observations of cats learning to escape from a box. To explain a cat's goal-directed behavior of hitting a latch to get food, Thorndike formulated a principle of learning called the (a)_____. This law states that if certain random actions are followed by a pleasurable consequence or reward, such actions are strengthened and will likely occur in the future. Today, the law of effect has become part of the second approach to studying learning, called (b)_____.
4. A third approach is learning through observation or imitation, which occurs inside your head. This relatively newer approach, which involves mental processes without any external rewards, is called _____.
■ *As a psychologist, how would you study your friend's problem of being overweight?*

ESTABLISHING CLASSICAL CONDITIONING

5. Suppose you wanted to classically condition your roommate to salivate to the sight of a psychology textbook. One procedure for establishing classical conditioning would be to present two stimuli close together in time. The presentation of the two stimuli is called a *trial*. In our example, a typical trial would involve first presenting a psychology textbook, initially called the (a)_____, which does not elicit salivation. A short time later, you would present a piece of brownie, called the (b)_____ stimulus, which elicits salivation. Salivation, an innate, automatic, and involuntary physiological reflex, is called the (c)_____.
6. After giving your roommate about a dozen trials, you observe that as soon as you show him the psychology text, he begins to salivate. Because the sight of the psychology textbook itself elicits salivation, the psychology text has become a (a)_____. The roommate's salivation to the sight of the psychology book, presented alone, is called the (b)_____. You know that classical conditioning is established when the neutral stimulus becomes the (c)_____ and elicits the (d)_____. Compared to the unconditioned response, the conditioned response is usually similar in appearance but smaller in amount or magnitude.
■ *How do you explain why your heart pounds when you hear the words, "There will be a test next time"?*

OTHER CONDITIONING CONCEPTS

7. During classical conditioning there is a tendency for a stimulus similar to the original conditioned stimulus to elicit a response similar to the conditioned response. This tendency is called _____. Generally, the response will be stronger or larger the more similar the new stimulus is to the original conditioned stimulus.
8. During classical conditioning, an organism learns to make a particular response to some stimuli but not to others; this phenomenon is called _____.
9. If a conditioned stimulus is repeatedly presented without the unconditioned stimulus, there is a tendency for the conditioned stimulus to no longer elicit the conditioned response; this phenomenon is called (a)_____. For example, if

Supplements

For the third edition, existing supplements have been revised and several new ones added.

Instructor's Resource Manual

The *Instructor's Resource Manual* was written by Dr. Gary Poole of Simon Fraser University. Gary is the director of the Center for University Teaching and is active in training teaching assistants and conducting workshops for improving teaching skills. Drawing on his experience as director and as a classroom instructor, Gary has written a user-friendly instructor's manual. For example, Gary provides excellent classroom exercises, examples, and demonstrations that can be integrated into lectures. He also lists handouts, films, and videos to accompany the modules.

A special section has been included at the back of the *Instructor's Resource Manual* to help first-time instructors and teaching assistants. This section gives new instructors specific tips on what to include in a class syllabus, how to organize the course, and how to prepare lectures and stimulate discussion.

Fostering Critical Thinking

One aspect of Gary Poole's work on improving teaching skills has been the development of materials for critical thinking. Using his expertise in this area, he has developed a new supplement called *Fostering Critical Thinking*. In this supplement, Gary explains the goals of critical thinking and ways to foster it. Specific methods include using the more than 250 critical thinking questions included in the Summary/Self-Tests. For each question, Gary suggests answers that provide excellent jumping-off points for discussion. In addition, the critical thinking questions could be used as essay questions.

Test Bank

The *Test Bank* for the third edition has been written by Jeff Parsons of Jersey City State College. Professor Parsons has written hundreds of new test items that are divided between factual and applied. In addition, all the test items were reviewed by me and by Dr. Francene Evans of Worthington Community College, Minnesota.

The *Test Bank* is available for IBM-PCs and compatibles, Macintosh, and the Apple II series. This user-friendly testing system permits professors to select items in a variety of ways and to print them quickly and easily. It also allows users to create their own questions and to edit and customize those provided.

Visual Information

Three kinds of visual information are available to users of the third edition.

First, there is a complete set of transparencies or slides that can be used to illustrate major concepts in the text.

Second, there is a wide choice of updated video and film options for use in the classroom. The selection includes videos from three popular series: *The Brain, The Mind,* and *Discovering Psychology*.

Third, there is a videodisc that includes material and animations. For example, it provides animations of neural transmission for Chapter 2 and of sensory and perceptual processes for Chapters 3 and 4. The videodisc is new for the third edition and was developed by Pat Gadban, media specialist of Brooks/Cole.

Student Guide

The *Student Guide* was written by Matthew Enos of Harold Washington College. Professor Enos draws on his many years of teaching introductory psychology to provide excellent pedagogical aids for the students. Specific aids include short summaries, outlines of modules, and many multiple-choice, matching, and true-false questions and answers.

To help the increasing number of students who may have difficulty with English, the *Student Guide* contains a section for nonnative speakers written by Laurie Blass. This section, which appears at the end of the Student Organizer, provides numerous skill-building exercises for vocabulary and reading that will help students better understand the material.

Electronic Study Guide

The *Electronic Study Guide* is a user-friendly computer study guide. It provides questions and answers in an interactive format, reinforcing students for correct answers and providing helpful cues for incorrect answers. The *Electronic Study Guide* is new for the third edition.

To the Student

What am I in for?

You are about to begin a course that is one of the most popular on campus because it discusses so many aspects of your life. For example, introductory psychology discusses how your brain functions, what happens when you sleep, how you learned to be anxious during exams, what an IQ score means, why you develop psychosomatic symptoms, how your personality changes, what abnormal behaviors are, how you perceive others, and many more questions that affect your life. This course also discusses many techniques that psychologists have developed to deal with relatively common problems: how to improve study habits, reduce stress, overcome insomnia, relieve mild depression, treat phobias, improve memory, and reduce anger. As you can see, this course will help you better understand your behaviors as well as those of others.

Is this course mostly common sense?

I can guarantee that if you used just common sense, you would never pass this course. That's because much of our common sense about human behavior is just plain wrong. For example, using your common sense, decide whether the following statements are true (T) or false (F):

T F   You only use about 50% of your brain.

T F   IQ tests measure natural intelligence.

T F   The most common cause of colds is standing in a draft.

T F   The first five years of your life are critical for the development of your personality.

T F   Eyewitness testimony is the most accurate.

T F   You can learn a foreign language by listening to a recording during sleep.

T F   Psychosomatic problems are imaginary.

T F   The best way to get over an intense fear is to always avoid the feared thing.

Based on common sense, you may decide that some of these statements are true. Based on what psychologists have discovered

through systematic investigation, all of the statements are false. This course will introduce you to a system of discovery that psychologists use to understand behavior. Learning all the terms, concepts, and theories will be hard, but it will also be challenging and rewarding and will improve your common sense.

What's different about this textbook?
As you look through this text, you will immediately notice that it doesn't look like most textbooks. I'll point out the major features of this text and explain how they are designed to help you understand and better remember the material.

What are modules?
Each chapter is divided into two modules, which are relatively short, self-contained units. The advantage of the modular approach is that material is broken down into smaller, manageable units, making the material easier to master. You'll notice that each module begins with a real-life example that raises interesting questions that are answered in the module.

What's a Concept/Glossary?
Toward the end of each module, you'll discover a brief test called the Concept/Glossary. The Concept/Glossary presents short definitions and asks you to fill in the correct concept or term. As you fill in the blanks of the Concept/Glossary, you can test your mastery of the material as well as compose a glossary of important terms. To help you remember important terms, each item in the Concept/Glossary is linked to a graphic. By linking a definition to a visual cue you will have a better chance of remembering the term.

Should I complete the Summary/Self-Test?
One question you may have when finishing an assignment is how much you learned and remembered. A good way to answer this question is to test your mastery of the material by taking the Summary/Self-Test, which is at the end of each module. As you read and fill in the blanks of the Summary/Self-Test, you can review the information as well as test your memory of the major concepts and terms. If you find that you have forgotten some material, you can go back and restudy it until you are able to answer all the questions in the Summary/Self-Test. In addition, you'll find that each major section in the Summary/Self-Test contains a critical thinking question. These questions foster your ability to think critically about a variety of issues.

Where's the Glossary?
In addition to the Concept/Glossary, which is at the end of each module, there is a complete Glossary at the end of the book. It contains all the major terms and concepts with their definitions.

Do I need the Student Guide?
Students often ask about whether they should buy the separate *Student Guide* by Matthew Enos. If you would like or need additional help in mastering a module, the *Student Guide* is a useful tool. It contains outlines of each module, plus a variety of questions (multiple-choice, true-false, matching) that will give you many chances to test your mastery of the material.

If you are into computers, you can also purchase the *Electronic Study Guide,* which presents questions, rewards correct answers, and—if you make an error—prompts the correct answer.

Now that I've told you a little about the course and the textbook, you're ready to begin. Here's your chance to use 100% of your brain.

Acknowledgments

Working on this book with a remarkable group of creative people was one of the best experiences of my life. I would like to sincerely thank each one.

Publisher

Because of differing views on the direction of the textbook, I decided to change publishers for the third edition. My new publisher, Brooks/Cole, not only agreed to produce a radically different textbook but to provide an unprecedented amount of support, encouragement, and creative help. I am especially grateful to Bill Roberts, president of Brooks/Cole, for his financial faith in the third edition and to Craig Barth, vice president, editorial, for keeping the text on the philosophically right path.

Managing Editor

One of the most difficult things for me as an author is to change editors and develop a new creative working relationship. Imagine telling an editor that text and graphics would be interwoven, that each page had to be individually written and designed, and that the author should be involved throughout the production process. Any one of these demands would make most editors question the author's sanity. But such was not the case with Vicki Knight, my managing editor. From the very first meeting, Vicki agreed with the book's new direction, threw her editorial support behind the project, and gave me the creative freedom to complete the third edition. In addition, Vicki provided continual emotional support and encouragement when I thought that I could never finish. I am forever indebted to Vicki for giving me the chance to turn one of my lifetime writing dreams into reality.

Editorial Associate

Heather Graeve, editorial associate, made sure that everyone, especially the reviewers, was sent the correct chapters. Heather got married as the book came to an end, but I don't think there is any connection.

Captain

Our book team needed a captain, and that was Nancy Sjoberg of Del Mar Associates. Nancy used a velvet whip to keep everyone on schedule and make sure that, in the end, all the pieces came together. No one had more headaches than Nancy but no one handled them better. Once I learned how to deal with Nancy, which was to bring her cookies, my life became immeasurably easier.

Designer

One of my major joys in writing the third edition was working with John Odam. John was the creative force behind the book's unique and stunning interior design and illustration program. John has twinkly eyes, a panama hat, a mandolin, and one of the best senses for design in this universe. I would give John a page of manuscript and ideas for graphics and watch as he magically gave the page color and design and brought it to life. As it turns out, the third edition owes as much to John's design as it does to my writing.

Illustrators

The book is filled with wonderful illustrations by Jonathan Parker, Jill Malena Davis, and Deborah Ivanoff. They did an especially great job on Chapters 2 and 3. Jonathan, Jill, and Deborah spent more hours than they care to remember in designing illustrations, making corrections, and inserting final changes on each and every page.

Concept Illustrator

Many ideas and concepts simply do not lend themselves to photos. In these cases we would simply give Max Seabaugh and his assistant, Lisa Matzkin, an idea, and they would come up with unique and ingenious illustrations. In every chapter you'll discover Max's clever creations that range from a dog on a bicycle to fresh symbols for Freudian stages. Max's wonderful illustrations bring concepts to life and make them easier to remember.

Photographer

In some cases we needed specific or unusual photos, which were taken by Craig McClain. Craig created some very imaginative photos for this text. For example, check page 171 for a photo of Craig flying through the air like Superman.

Photo Researcher

Linda Rill was in charge of photo research and permissions. Linda has a wonderful sense of capturing the essence of an idea with a photo.

I gave her some impossible photo requests and she always came through. For example, if you want to hear a long story, call Linda and ask her how she finally found a photo of Phineas Gage's death mask. As you look through the text, you'll have a chance to appreciate Linda's work firsthand.

Developmental Editor

Janet Hunter, my developmental editor, made sure that concepts were clearly defined and that ideas were intelligently organized. Jan was wonderfully diplomatic in suggesting changes and removing some of my favorite sentences that now reside in a file of that name. Jan is married to Billy Bud, whose name is the title of one of Herman Melville's stories and one of my favorite classic movies. What a small world it is.

Manuscript Editor

Jackie Estrada needed the biblical patience of Job in her role as manuscript editor. Jackie had to go over each and every page several times to mark the manuscript for design as well as correct any and all errors. Her task was made doubly difficult by the design that interwove text and graphics. We also turned to her when we wanted ideas for graphics or an answer to a design problem. Jackie has a wonderful cat with whom I developed an intimate friendship as I delivered and picked up manuscripts.

Production

A number of people at Brooks/Cole were involved in the book's production. Joan Marsh, who drives one of the oldest running VWs, was in charge of the schedule and keeping everything on track. Like her car, Joan was very reliable.

Vena Dyer and Bill Bokermann made sure that the pages were properly produced and that the color was great. My only concern about Bill was his relationship to the unusual tropical plant in his office. It could star in a horror movie, but Bill seemed to like it.

Marketing

Several people at Brooks/Cole have been involved in the marketing program. The grand overseer is Adrian Perenon, who directs an extremely competent staff. Jim Brace-Thompson put together and carried out one of the most impressive marketing plans that any publisher has ever done. Jim has a great sense of humor and likes desserts, which I consider important in someone marketing my book.

Another member of the marketing team is Margaret Parks, who is always full of enthusiasm and writes great advertising copy. In addition, Margaret and Jean Thompson were responsible for planning and sending out clever mailers. Together, Adrian, Jim, Margaret, and Jean have done an exceptional job in publicizing the book's features.

Supplements

Among the many talented people who worked on the supplements, I want to especially thank Gary Poole, who worked with me on the first two editions as well as the third. Gary wrote the *Instructor's Resource Manual* and *Fostering Critical Thinking*. The latter was Gary's idea, which he turned into a great supplement. Many thanks go to Matthew Enos, who was not only a great reviewer but also did a fantastic job on the *Student Guide*. Additional thanks go to Jeff Parsons, who took on the difficult task of writing the *Test Bank* and did such a thorough job.

Teaching Assistants

Many of my ideas for the third edition came from regular meetings with my enthusiastic and highly motivated teaching assistants. I wish to thank my current group of Ann, Debbie, Matt, Leigh, Susyn, Leif, Bev, Becky, Amie, Richard, John, Stephanie, and Karen. They are wonderful teachers full of great ideas.

Research Assistants

Special thanks go to my four research assistants at San Diego State University: Tawyna Bowlan, Duncan Macdonell, Michele Australie, and Peter Matsos. They worked long and hard getting materials from the library, making photocopies, and organizing materials for the instructor's manual. They are especially remarkable for never grumbling about doing some fairly tedious work.

Colleague

Most special thanks go to my friend and colleague Sandy Mollenauer, who provided emotional support, encouragement, and understanding. There were many times when working on the book was overwhelming and I needed someone to talk to and get a little help and sympathy. I could always rely on Sandy. She also has two wonderful fuzzy dogs that became my biggest fans.

Reviewers

I especially want to thank the following reviewers who put in an amazing amount of time and energy to review multiple chapters. Their continuing input resulted in a much improved third edition.

Peter Caprioglio
Middlesex Community College

Matthew Enos
Harold Washington College

Francene Evans
Worthington Community College

William Ford
Bucks County Community College

Albert Gorman,
Suffolk County Community College

Frank Hager
Allegany Community College

Sanford Lopater
Christopher Newport College

I also wish to thank the following reviewers whose suggestions for individual chapters greatly improved the manuscript:

Gina Agostinelli
University of New Mexico

Roger Baily
East Tennessee State University

Nyla Branscombe
University of Kansas

Lewis Clariece
Sacramento City College

Kathleen Connor
Concord College

R. H. Defran
San Diego State University

Nolan Embry
Lexington Community College

Terry Hines
Pace University

James Reid Jones
Delta State University

Patricia Kariger
San Diego State University

Sandra Mollenauer
San Diego State University

Robert Osterhouse
Prince George's Community College

Anthony Pratkanis
University of California at Santa Cruz

Steve Reid
San Diego State University

Joanne Smythe
Mendocino College

Edwin Stefan
Findlay College

Finally, I want to thank the reviewers of the second edition whose efforts laid the groundwork for this edition:

David Bernstein
Grand Valley State College

Larry Brandstein
Berkshire Community College

Lynn Brokaw
Portland Community College

Robert C. Brown, Jr.
Georgia State University

Samuel Clarke
North Adams State College

Lorry Cology
Owens College

Tom Eckle
Modesto Junior College

Julie Felender
Fullerton Junior College

John Foust
Parkland College

Grace Galliano
Kennesaw College

Mike Garzo
Brookhaven College

Marvin Goldstein
Rider College

Albert Gorman
Suffolk Community College

Arthur Gutman
Florida Institute of Technology

William Hills
Coastal Carolina College

Bruce Jaeger
USAF Academy

Judy Keith
Tarrant County Junior College

Elinor MacDonald
Quinebaug Valley Community College

Roger Mellgren
University of Oklahoma

Steve Mewaldt
Marshall University

William Owen
Virginia Western Community College

Alan Schultz
Prince George's Community College

Janet Shaban
California State University

Jim Smrtic
Mohawk Valley Community College

Adolf Streng
Eastfield College

Marilynn Thomas
Prince George's Community College

Michael Zeller
Mankato State University

Brief Contents

Contents

CHAPTER NINE MOTIVATION AND EMOTION 312

CHAPTER TEN CHILD DEVELOPMENT 354

Introduction to Psychology

THIRD EDITION

Chapter *One*
DISCOVERING PSYCHOLOGY

MODULE 1
WHAT PSYCHOLOGY IS

Why doesn't Patrick open his birthday presents?

Mary and Channing tried to convince themselves that their son, Patrick, was all right. They tried to ignore the facts that Patrick was very slow to talk and babbled much of the time, that he woke frequently during the night and seemed to need only a few hours' sleep, that he sometimes laughed hysterically, that he did not enjoy his birthday party or play with the other children or show any interest in opening his presents. Finally, when they could ignore Patrick's unusual behaviors no longer, they had him evaluated by a team of experts in childhood problems. After conducting sensory, psychological, and brain tests, the head of the team told Mary and Channing what all parents dread to hear: "Your son has a serious problem. Patrick is autistic."

Earlier definitions of psychology did not include the study of abnormal behavior, such as autism.

Autistic children typically have some degree of mental retardation, poorly developed language skills that may or may not improve with age, and unusual repetitive behaviors, such as rocking or unexplained laughing. Sometimes they possess a special skill at which they excel, such as art, music, or memory feats. Most require some sort of supervision their entire lives.

Upon first meeting, Patrick appears rather ordinary, with clear white skin and big blue eyes. However, he has a peculiar gaze that looks right past you, as if you weren't there. Five-year-old Patrick is considered a "high-functioning" autistic child because he knows the whole alphabet and the numbers from 1 to 50, has a relatively good memory, speaks in simple five- or six-word sentences, and recognizes shapes and objects. Because of these skills, Patrick's parents are trying to have him admitted to a regular grade school so that he can take advantage of his potential to learn and benefit from social interactions with other children. (adapted from *Los Angeles Times Magazine*, February 24, 1991)

When Mary and Channing were first told that Patrick was autistic, their questions poured out. "What caused his autism? How can we help him? What kind of life will he have? Will he be able to get a job some day? Will he become more sociable?" To answer these questions, psychologists study a wide range of behaviors, touching on topics in each of the 18 chapters of this text.

What's Coming

In this module, we'll explore the major approaches of psychology and its historical roots, current areas, and careers. In the next module, we'll discuss methods psychologists use to answer questions, especially how they conduct experiments. Let's begin with a definition of psychology.

Defining Psychology

We can define **psychology** *as the systematic, scientific study of behaviors and mental processes.* The term *behavior* refers to observable actions or responses in both humans and animals. Behaviors might include eating, speaking, laughing, avoiding, sleeping, and hundreds of others. *Mental processes,* which are not directly observable, include planning, thinking, imagining, coping, dreaming, and many others. As you will see, this definition of psychology developed out of the ideas, discussions, and arguments among the early psychologists.

Goals of Psychology

What caused Patrick's autism? Why does Patrick have difficulty learning? How can we help Patrick make friends and develop social relationships?

These questions that Patrick's parents asked reflect the three goals of psychology:

1. Psychologists' first goal is to *explain* or *understand* why organisms behave in certain ways. In Patrick's case, psychologists want to explain the causes of Patrick's autism and his difficulties in paying attention, learning, and forming friendships.

Five-year old Patrick is considered a "high-functioning" autistic child because he knows the whole alphabet and the numbers from 1 to 50.

2. The second goal is to *predict* how organisms will behave in the future. Psychologists would like to be able to predict how Patrick would learn in a normal classroom, how he would get along with other students, and how he would meet the challenges of being a teenager and adult.

3. Some psychologists would include a third goal, to *control* behavior. Psychologists would like to be able to control Patrick's behavior so that he could function well in many situations. The idea of control has both positive and negative sides. The positive side is that psychologists can help people learn to control anger, depression, overeating, smoking, poor study habits, and even the difficulties that accompany autism. The negative side is that people's behaviors might be controlled without their knowledge or intention. In Module 2, we'll discuss the strict guidelines that psychologists have established to prevent potential abuse of the "control" aspect of their field and to protect the rights and privacy of individuals, patients, and subjects in experiments.

As you can see, all three of psychology's goals—to explain, predict, and control—apply in Patrick's case. At the time of this writing, Patrick was making sufficient progress that his parents were trying to have him admitted to a regular grade school. We'll return to Patrick in Module 12, when we explain the methods that psychologists use to teach autistic children academic and social skills.

Let's now use a problem that many students have—test anxiety—as an example of how psychologists study a problem using a number of different approaches.

Modern Approaches to Psychology

Why do I feel so much test anxiety?

Faced with answering difficult and complex questions, such as those involving autism or test anxiety, psychologists follow a general plan of attack. They divide the behavior into many subareas, study each subarea separately, and then combine information from all the subareas into an explanation of the total behavior. For example, psychologists might subdivide test anxiety into study habits, thinking processes, memory abilities, stressful feelings, personality traits, unconscious fears, and psychological problems. Psychologists use various **approaches to understanding behavior**, *each of which has a different focus or perspective that may involve a different method or technique.* We'll summarize six commonly used approaches:

1 The *psychobiological approach* focuses on how our genes, hormones, and nervous system interact with our environments to influence learning, personality, memory, motivation, emotions, and coping techniques.

2 The *cognitive approach* examines how we process, store, and use information, and how this information influences what we notice, perceive, and remember.

3 The *behavioral approach* studies how organisms learn new behaviors or modify existing ones depending on whether events in their environments reward or punish these behaviors.

4 The *psychoanalytic approach* stresses the influence of unconscious fears, desires, and motivations on thoughts, behaviors, and the development of later personality traits and psychological problems.

> Why am I so anxious when I take exams?

5 The *humanistic approach* emphasizes that each individual has great freedom in directing his or her future, a large capacity for personal growth, a considerable amount of intrinsic worth, and enormous potential for self-fulfillment.

6 The *cross-cultural approach* examines the influence of cultural and ethnic similarities and differences on psychological and social functioning.

These six approaches show that psychologists study a problem from many different viewpoints. We'll discuss each approach in more detail and show how each would give a different answer to our question: "What causes test anxiety?"

Modern Approaches to Psychology

Test Anxiety. From psychobiological research, we know that many stressors, including taking exams, cause increased body arousal that may interfere with concentration, memory, and thought processes, thereby decreasing performance. One way to reduce test anxiety is to learn a method of relaxation to decrease body arousal.

Psychobiological Approach

Why does my heart pound during exams?

During an exam, a typical student experiences a pounding heart, sweaty palms, dry mouth, tense muscles, and a feeling of anxiety. These kinds of physiological responses are the focus of the psychobiological approach.

The **psychobiological approach** *examines how our genes, hormones, and nervous system interact with our environments to influence learning, personality, memory, motivation, emotions, coping techniques, and other traits and abilities.* For example, psychobiologists and medical doctors have used newly developed techniques (discussed in Module 4) to examine the living brains of autistic children like Patrick. For the first time, they have discovered that some autistic children have a deficit in one area of the brain (the cerebellum) (Courchesne et al., 1988). Such information, if confirmed, will make it possible to diagnose autism earlier and to develop better treatment programs.

Psychobiologists are finding that the mind greatly influences the functions of the body and vice versa. Many studies show that having a negative state of mind, such as being depressed, worrying, or being in a bad mood, makes the body less able to fight off toxic agents, viruses, and bacteria (Hoon et al., 1991; Kamarck & Jennings, 1991; Vollhardt, 1991). In a very real sense, psychobiologists are working on solving one of the oldest puzzles in psychology: how the mind, brain, and body interact.

Studies of twins indicate that genes influence the development of personality traits and intellectual abilities.

Cognitive Approach

I thought I knew the material, so why did I miss so many questions on the exam?

This kind of question illustrates the **cognitive approach,** *which studies how we process, store, and use information and how this information influences what we notice, perceive, and remember.* Cognitive psychologists study remembering and forgetting, such as why it's so easy to remember every word of a conversation but so hard to remember a list of terms memorized for an exam. They investigate how people form stereotypes, how stereotypes affect their perceptions of others, and how people's moods influence the things they notice and remember. Cognitive psychologists have analyzed the differences between skills of graduate and beginning students with the hope of improving problem-solving abilities. They have also probed the thinking of master chess players with the goal of writing computer programs that approximate human thought processes. Many psychologists agree that over the past ten years the cognitive approach has become a major force in psychology.

Test Anxiety. Cognitive psychologists find that students may misjudge how well they know material because they focus on general information rather than on specific details. In the Applying/Exploring section of this module, we'll discuss several ways to more accurately judge one's mastery of studied material and, as a result, prepare better for exams and reduce test anxiety.

Cognitive psychologists try to duplicate human thinking in computer chess programs.

Behavioral Approach

What's wrong with the way I study?

When faced with reading a chapter, some students first count the number of pages,

then read as fast as they can, underline almost every sentence, take a break in the middle to call a friend, and skip some material toward the end. These kinds of study habits could be greatly improved by following guidelines from the **behavioral approach,** *which analyzes how organisms learn new behaviors or modify existing ones depending on whether events in their environment reward or punish these behaviors.* Behavioral principles have been used to help students change poor study habits; to teach severely retarded people to feed and dress themselves; to toilet train young children; to teach people to be more assertive, less shy, or less depressed; to help people stop smoking or drinking or to lose weight; and to help people overcome extreme fears. Psychologists have also used behavioral principles to train animals to press levers, discriminate between colors and shapes, and even use symbols to communicate.

Largely through the creative work and original ideas of B. F. Skinner, the behavioral approach has grown into a major force in psychology. Skinner (1989) insisted that psychologists analyze in a rigorous and scientific way how environmental events influence and determine observable behaviors. Skinner's ideas stress the study of observable behaviors, the importance of environmental reinforcers, and the exclusion of mental processes. His ideas, often referred to as *strict behaviorism,* continue to have an impact on psychology.

Some behaviorists, such as Albert Bandura (1989), disagree with strict behaviorism and have formulated a theory that includes mental or cognitive processes in addition to observable behaviors. According to Bandura's *social learning approach,* our behaviors are influenced not only by environmental events and reinforcers but also by observation, imitation, and thought processes. Bandura believes that many of our behaviors are learned through observation and imitation and that it is possible for us to reinforce our own behaviors by thinking positive (rewarding) or negative (punishing) thoughts.

Test Anxiety. Strict behaviorists believe that changing reinforcing events in your environment will change your study habits. For instance, behaviorists would suggest that you can improve concentration by having a particular place for study that eliminates distractions; that you can lengthen your study time by providing some reward; and that you can better prepare for exams by giving yourself regular feedback through constant quizzes.

Social learning behaviorists would agree with all the above suggestions and would suggest converting negative thoughts and beliefs about studying to positive ones. For instance, a habit of thinking negative or punishing thoughts ("It doesn't matter," "It's too late," "I'll never get this," "I can't remember things") will decrease motivation and increase your test anxiety. On the other hand, substituting positive or rewarding thoughts will increase your motivation and study time as well as help you better prepare for exams and decrease test anxiety.

In later modules, we'll discuss many examples of how behavioral principles are used to modify both thought processes and observable behaviors.

B. F. Skinner stressed the study of observable behaviors.

According to his parents, 3-year-old Dusty first watched and then imitated skateboarders. The social learning approach believes that much of human learning occurs through observation and imitation.

Modern Approaches to Psychology

Psychoanalytic Approach

Do unconscious fears underlie test anxiety?

The **psychoanalytic approach** *focuses on the influence of unconscious fears, desires, and motivations on thoughts, behaviors, and the development of later personality traits and psychological problems.* Proposed by Sigmund Freud in the 1880s, the idea of an unconscious force influencing human thought and behavior was revolutionary. Freud, a physician at the time, arrived at this idea from analyzing patients with various psychological problems. He reasoned that thoughts or feelings that make us feel fearful or guilty, that threaten our self-esteem, or that come from unresolved sexual conflicts are automatically pushed deep into our unconscious. As a result, these unconscious, threatening thoughts or feelings give rise to anxiety, fear, or other psychological problems.

Sigmund Freud

Because Freud's patients could not readily tap their unconscious fears, he developed several techniques to bring hidden fears to the surface. One technique, which he called *free association,* involves talking about anything that comes into one's mind, perhaps including fears from one's unconscious. A second technique is the *interpretation of dreams,* which Freud believed contain symbols that disguise one's unconscious fears. With Freud's guidance, patients used these techniques to bring up, expose, and slowly resolve their formerly unconscious fears.

Test Anxiety. The psychoanalytic approach suggests that unconscious feelings or fears may contribute to a student's increased level of anxiety. For example, suppose that a student is angry at his father for making him choose an undesirable major or is jealous of his sister, who earned better grades. In the psychoanalytic view, such angry or jealous feelings that threaten the student's self-concept would automatically be pushed into the unconscious, where they would generate anxiety. A therapist using the psychoanalytic approach would first help the student uncover the unconscious fears. The therapist would then assist the student in resolving the unconscious fears, thereby reducing the level of anxiety.

Many of Freud's beliefs, such as the existence of unconscious feelings and fears that influence thoughts and behaviors, have survived intact, while other ideas have been revised. Some contemporary psychoanalysts believe that our conscious thoughts and feelings are more significant and have a larger influence than Freud believed. Others, such as Erik Erikson (1968), disagreed with Freud's insistence that the first five years of life shape a person's adult personality or that child-parent sexual interactions are the major determinants of adult personality. Instead, Erikson emphasized a longer period of psychological development, well into young adulthood, and child-parent social interactions.

Humanistic Approach

Why can't I get more excited about my classes?

At the end of her freshman year, Carol had a great grade point average and was looking forward to her sophomore year. Yet a year later, she was doing below-average work in most of her classes and was thinking about dropping out for a year. Her problem is sometimes referred to as the "sophomore blues," which includes a drop in motivation for college, a lack of interest in classes, and an uncertainty about what to do with one's life.

These concerns illustrate the focus of the **humanistic approach**, *which emphasizes that each individual has great freedom in directing his or her future, a large capacity for achieving personal growth, a considerable amount of intrinsic worth, and enormous potential for self-fulfillment.* Humanists believe that you have control of your fate and are free to become whatever you are capable of being. The humanistic approach emphasizes the positive side of human nature, along with its creative and constructive tendencies and its inclination to build caring relationships. This concept of human nature is the most distinctive feature of the humanistic approach and sets it far apart from the behavioral and psychoanalytic approaches (DeCarvalho, 1990).

Abraham Maslow

Humanists disagree with the psychoanalytic approach, which emphasizes how unconscious fears and feelings influence or control one's destiny, and with the behavioral approach, which stresses how the environment determines or manipulates one's behaviors. Because of its concept of human nature and its lack of rigorous experimental methods, many behaviorists regard the humanistic approach as more of a philosophy of life than a science of human behavior.

Test Anxiety. Humanists believe that individuals have the ability to choose, direct, and change the guiding forces in their lives and that individuals must take ultimate responsibility for their lives. The humanistic approach to dealing with test anxiety would be to search for whatever is blocking and preventing the student from reaching his or her full potential. The student would also be counseled about having to take responsibility for studying, attending classes, and completing activities that relate directly to exams. Finally, the student may be asked to explain his or her future plans and goals and to describe how college fits into these plans.

The humanistic approach officially began in the early 1960s with the publication of the *Journal of Humanistic Psychology.* One of the major figures behind establishing the journal and the humanistic approach was Abraham Maslow, who had become dissatisfied with the behavioral and psychoanalytic approaches. To paraphrase Maslow (1968), the humanistic approach was to be a new way of perceiving and thinking about the individual's capacity, freedom, and potential for growth. At the time, Maslow admitted that the behavioral and psychoanalytic approaches were the two major forces, but he hoped that the humanistic approach would become the third major force in psychology. Although it is too early to judge whether the humanistic approach has achieved Maslow's goal, many of humanism's ideas have been incorporated into approaches for counseling and psychotherapy.

Modern Approaches to Psychology

Test Anxiety. In several studies on test anxiety, researchers have found that Mexican, Chilean, and black American inner-city grade school children report higher levels of test anxiety than do white American students (Guida & Ludlow, 1989). The researchers suggest that higher test anxiety in black inner-city children results from their special educational problems and that higher test anxiety in Mexican and Chilean students results from having fewer educational opportunities than their white American counterparts. Because higher test anxiety is associated with poorer educational achievement, cross-cultural studies highlight potential problems that must be addressed to raise achievement.

Cross-Cultural Approach

Do students from different cultures have different problems?
The following conversations I've had with students illustrate the focus of the cross-cultural approach:

"You're doing very well, Maria," I said, "but I wonder why you never volunteer to answer questions, even when you know the answer."

Maria replied, in her quiet voice, "It's not part of me to speak up in public." And then she added, "Especially for a woman."

"You're doing pretty well, Tony, but you could raise your grade a full letter if you put in more study time."

Tony looked straight at me and said, "Man, it's hard to take books home and study 'cause none of my friends go to school. They make fun of me reading all the time."

"You're doing excellent, Chi, but I wonder why you speak so quietly in class and never laugh at any of my jokes, especially the bad ones."

Chi looked off to the side and said, in his soft way, "In my country it is not polite to speak loudly in front of strangers and it is certainly impolite to laugh."

These student differences arose from cultural and ethnic differences. The **cross-cultural approach** *studies the influence of cultural and ethnic similarities and differences on psychological and social functioning.* Researchers study the individual's cultural experience from two perspectives: from experiments conducted under controlled laboratory conditions, such as giving different cultural groups the same test, and from observations in the field, such as recording how individuals respond and behave in their own culture or ethnic group (Kagitcibasi & Berry, 1989). Of the six approaches that we have discussed, the cross-cultural one is the "newest" and is certainly growing. Many interesting cross-cultural studies will be highlighted throughout this text and will be indicated by the symbol of the world.

Watch for this symbol wherever cultural diversity topics occur

One Question, Many Approaches

We began with a single but complex question: "What causes test anxiety?" We discussed how each of the six approaches—psychobiological, cognitive, behavioral, psychoanalytic, humanistic, and cross-cultural—provides answers from a different perspective. Psychologists are less interested in which approach gives the best answer and more concerned with how pieces of information from all six approaches can be assembled to give the most complete answer.

African American   Asian

Hispanic   Native American

By the year 2000 these four ethnic groups will make up about one-third of all citizens in the United States under the age of 17. The cross-cultural approach seeks to understand their similarities and differences.

Discrimination in Psychology

For the first 75 of its little over 100 years of existence, American psychology was dominated by white males, who discriminated both intentionally and unintentionally against women and other minorities.

Women in Psychology

As an example of discrimination, let's look at the difficulties faced by Mary Calkins, who established a laboratory in psychology at Wellesley College in 1891. After several years at Wellesley, she returned to Harvard to complete her studies for a Ph.D. By 1894 she had completed all requirements and had been recommended for a doctorate by her professors, but the Harvard administration declined to grant it because she was a woman (Furumoto, 1989). It was not until 1908 that a woman, Margaret Washburn, was awarded a Ph.D. in psychology.

Even after women began obtaining doctorates, the only positions open to them were teaching jobs at women's colleges or normal schools (Furumoto & Scarborough, 1986). During the past 25 years, women have made great progress in the field; currently about equal percentages of men and women obtain Ph.D.'s in psychology.

Mary Calkins was denied a Ph.D. because she was a woman.

Minorities in Psychology

In psychology's early days, only a few Northern white American universities accepted and encouraged black students, while all Southern white universities denied admission to black students. The first black person to receive a Ph.D. in psychology was Ruth Howard, who graduated from the University of Minnesota in 1934. She had a successful career as a clinical psychologist and school consultant. Between 1920 and 1966, only 8 Ph.D.'s were awarded to black students, compared to 3,767 doctorates to whites (Guthrie, 1976). During the same time period, few degrees were awarded to Hispanics. One early exception was George Sanchez, who conducted pioneering work on the cultural bias of intelligence tests given to minority students. The many problems faced by minorities are well documented by Robert Guthrie in his book *Even the Rat Was White*.

From the founding of the American Psychological Association in 1892 up until 1990, its cumulative membership was 128,000. Of these members, only 700 were black (African American), 700 were Hispanic, and 70 were Native American. This limited minority membership indicates how much further psychology must go to remedy its earlier discriminatory practices.

It was not until 1934 that the first black woman, Ruth Howard, obtained a Ph.D. in psychology.

George Sanchez, Hispanic, overcame discrimination to obtain a Ph.D. and contribute to psychology.

Trying to Right the Wrongs

Almost every major university and college now has a program to recruit, aid, and help minority students complete degrees in psychology. The American Psychological Association has recognized the need to recruit minority members and has formed a special group to carry out this goal. In addition, groups such as the Association of Black Psychologists and the Asian American Psychological Association and an increasing number of journals (*Psychology of Women Quarterly, Hispanic Journal of Behavioral Science,* and *Journal of Black Psychology*) are promoting the causes of women and minorities and are fighting the remnants of discrimination in the field.

Previous Approaches—Learning from History

Psychology is a relatively young science, about the same age as the oldest living human being (100 years plus). During psychology's early development, a series of approaches were tried, criticized, rejected, and replaced. This process of criticizing old and developing new approaches is the key to understanding how psychology has evolved.

1879

Wilhelm Wundt

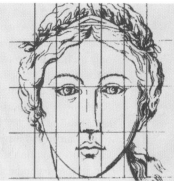

1890

William James

Structuralism— Elements of the Mind

What's in the mind?

The very first psychology laboratory was established by Wilhelm Wundt in Leipzig, Germany, in 1879. In this laboratory, the heavily bearded Wundt (considered the father of psychology) would ask subjects to break down mental structures, such as triangles, circles, and squares, into smaller and smaller units, in an effort to understand how sensations and images were formed. Wundt and his followers were called *structuralists* and their approach was called *structuralism.* **Structuralism** *was the study of conscious elements—sensations, images, and feelings—of the normal human mind.* Just as you might assemble pieces of a jigsaw puzzle into a complete picture, structuralists studied how the mind's elements or building blocks were assembled into complete conscious experiences. To explore and identify the elements of the mind, Wundt developed the method of **introspection**, *which required subjects to look inward and observe and report on the workings of their minds.* For example, after looking at a triangle, subjects would be asked to introspect and report on the elements that made up the experience of seeing a triangle. Introspection was later criticized as an unscientific method because it was solely dependent on subjects' self-reports rather than on objective measurements.

Approximately 90 years later, Wundt's emphasis on the study of mental events was revived and transformed into the current cognitive approach. However, today's cognitive psychologists use different scientific methods and have much broader interests than those of Wundt and the structuralists.

Functionalism— Functions of the Mind

How does the mind work?

If you were allowed to take one psychology book to a desert island, you would do well to choose *Principles of Psychology,* published in 1890 by the first important American psychologist, William James. One hundred years later, a virtual who's who of psychologists held a symposium to pay tribute to James's *Principles* and to discuss its enormous influence on psychology (Estes, 1990).

Unlike Wundt, who divided the mind into distinct elements, James viewed mental activity as a continuous flow that evolves and adapts to input from the environment. Unlike Wundt, who was interested in the mind's structural pieces, James was interested in the mind's goals, purposes, and functions, an approach called *functionalism.* **Functionalism** *was the study of the function, use, and adaptability of the mind to one's changing environment.* His view that mental processes are inseparable from brain processes makes James one of the fathers of the psychobiological approach. His work on classifying memory also makes him one of the fathers of the cognitive approach. In fact, there are so many original ideas in *Principles* that James is credited with being the father of many areas of psychology (Estes, 1990). Functionalism did not last as a unique approach, but many of its ideas were absorbed by other approaches.

Gestalt Approach—
Perceptions of the Mind

Is what you perceive more than what's there?
Each time you see an advertisement or road hazard sign with flashing lights that seem to move, you are observing a phenomenon that was first studied in 1912. Three

Behaviorism—
Observable Behaviors

Is what you see what you study?
In 1913, John B. Watson published a landmark paper titled "Psychology as a Behaviorist Views It." In it, he rejected Wundt's structuralism and its study of mental

1912

Max
Wertheimer

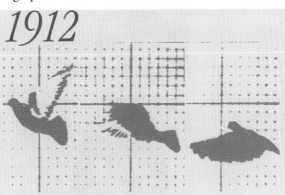

1913

John B. Watson

psychologists, Max Wertheimer, Wolfgang Köhler, and Kurt Koffka, reported that they had created the perception of movement by briefly flashing one light and then, a short time later, a second one. Although the two bulbs were fixed, the light actually appeared to move from one to the other, which they called the *phi phenomenon* and that today is known as *apparent motion.*

Wertheimer and his colleagues believed that the perception of apparent motion cannot be explained by adding together sensations from two fixed lights. Instead, they argued that perceptual experiences result from analyzing a "whole pattern," or, in German, a *Gestalt.* The **Gestalt approach** *emphasized that perception is more than the sum of its parts and studied how sensations are assembled into meaningful perceptual experiences.* The Gestalt approach is still alive and well. In fact, we'll discuss some of the Gestalt principles of perception in Module 7.

elements and conscious processes. He rejected introspection as a psychological technique because its results could not be scientifically verified by other psychologists. Instead, Watson boldly stated that psychology should be considered an objective, experimental science whose goal should be the analysis of observable behaviors and the prediction and control of those behaviors. It is a small step from these ideas to Watson's famous boast, which I have updated to read, "Give me a dozen healthy infants and I will raise them to become doctors, secretaries, lawyers, computer programmers, assembly-line workers, or marathon runners." Watson's paper and ideas marked the beginning of the **behavioral approach,** *which emphasized the objective, scientific analysis of observable behaviors.*

As you already know, psychologist B. F. Skinner expanded and developed Watson's ideas into modern-day behaviorism, which is a major force in psychology.

Popularity of Approaches. It is interesting to trace the rise and fall of approaches in psychology. Because he was the first "official psychologist," Wundt and his approach were easy targets for criticism. William James and his colleagues criticized structuralism for omitting the goals and purposes of the mind, and they championed their new approach of functionalism. Max Wertheimer, Wolfgang Köhler, Kurt Koffka, and their colleagues criticized structuralism for omitting how sensations are assembled and began the Gestalt approach. John Watson criticized structuralism, functionalism, and the Gestalt approach as too concerned with mental events and pushed hard for behaviorism. Developing largely in parallel to these approaches, Sigmund Freud's psychoanalytic approach emphasized how unconscious processes influence the development of personality, emotions, and later psychological problems. These continual discussions, criticisms, and heated arguments among early psychologists helped broaden psychology and guide its growth into the scientific field it is today.

1. The systematic, scientific study of behaviors and mental processes is called _____.

2. The three goals of psychology are to (a)_____ why organisms behave, to (b)_____ how organisms will behave in new situations, and to (c)_____ behavior.

3. The approach that focuses on how one's nervous system, hormones, and genes interact with the environment is called the _____.

4. The approach that studies how people think, solve problems, and process information is called the _____.

5. The approach that analyzes how environmental rewards and punishments shape, change, or motivate behavior is called the _____.

6. The approach that stresses the influence of unconscious feelings, fears, or desires on the development of behavior, personality, and psychological problems is called the _____.

7. The approach that emphasizes freedom of choice, self-fulfillment, and attaining one's potential is called the _____.

8. The newest approach, which focuses on cultural and ethnic influences on behavior, is called the _____.

9. Wundt studied the elements that made up the conscious mind and called this approach (a)_____. Subjects were asked to observe the workings of their minds, a technique that Wundt called (b)_____.

10. Reacting to Wundt, William James emphasized the functions, goals, and purposes of the mind and its adaptation to the environment; he called this approach _____.

11. Disagreeing with Wundt, some psychologists focused on how perceptions are more than the sum of many individual sensations; they called their approach _____.

Answers: *1.* psychology; *2.* (a) understand or explain, (b) predict, (c) control; *3.* psychobiological approach; *4.* cognitive approach; *5.* behavioral approach; *6.* psychoanalytic approach; *7.* humanistic approach; *8.* cross-cultural approach; *9.* (a) structuralism, (b) introspection; *10.* functionalism; *11.* Gestalt approach.

Careers in Psychology

What are you planning to do in psychology?

When I ask this question of beginning psychology majors, the majority seem to be most interested in the areas of counseling and therapy. In fact, many students think that psychologists are primarily counselors and therapists, even though advanced degrees in psychology are awarded in a dozen different areas. Obtaining an advanced degree in psychology requires that one finish college and spend about two to three years in postgraduate study to obtain a master's degree and four to five years in postgraduate study to obtain a Ph.D. Some careers or work settings require that one have a master's degree, while others need someone with a Ph.D.

Some students are confused about the difference between a psychologist, a clinical psychologist, and a psychiatrist. A **psychologist** *is usually someone who has completed four to five years of postgraduate education and has obtained a Ph.D. in psychology.* Some states permit individuals with master's degrees to call themselves psychologists. A **clinical psychologist** *has a Ph.D., has specialized in the subarea of clinical, and has spent an additional year in a supervised therapy setting to gain experience in diagnosing and treating a wide range of abnormal behaviors.* Clinical psychologists do not assess physical or neurological causes of mental problems or prescribe drugs. A **psychiatrist** *is a medical doctor who has spent several years in clinical training, which includes diagnosing possible physical and neurological causes of abnormal behaviors and treating these behaviors, often with prescription drugs.*

Students entering psychology today have a wide and exciting range of career choices, some of which are highlighted in the next section.

Where Do Psychologists Work?

1 The largest percentage (46%) of psychologists work as clinical psychologists in either a *private practice or therapy setting,* such as a psychological or psychiatric clinic, a mental health center, a psychiatric, drug, or rehabilitation ward of a hospital, or a private office. The duties of clinical psychologists might involve doing individual or group therapy; helping patients with drug, stress-related, weight, sleep, or chronic pain problems; designing "wellness" programs; or testing patients for psychological or neurological problems.

2 The second largest percentage (34%) of psychologists work in the *academic settings of universities and colleges.* Academic psychologists may engage in some combination of classroom teaching and research in their areas of interest.

3 The third largest percentage (12%) of psychologists work in *industrial settings,* such as businesses, corporations, and consulting firms. These psychologists, often called industrial/organizational psychologists, may work at selecting personnel, increasing production, or improving job satisfaction and employer-employee relations.

4 The smallest percentage (8%) work in *secondary schools and other settings.* For example, secondary school psychologists conduct academic and career testing and provide counseling for minor psychological problems.

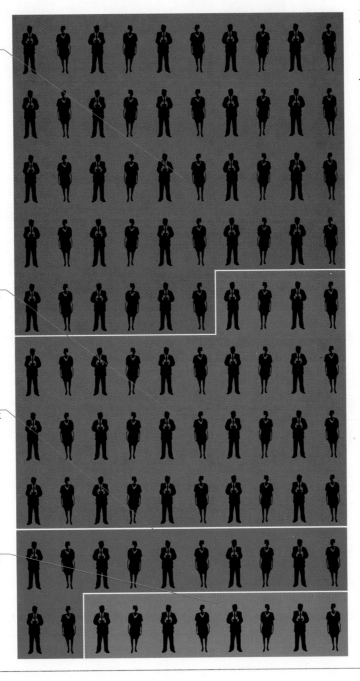

Research Areas in Psychology

If you enter graduate school in psychology, you will be expected to specialize in one of the half-dozen subareas into which psychology has been divided. Each subarea encompasses an enormous amount of information and is a kingdom unto itself.

How important are first impressions? How does one develop a certain personality? Do other people perceive me the way I see myself?

How does day care affect a young child? How does a child learn right from wrong? When does a child know to "act" like a boy or like a girl?

How is an animal conditioned to press a bar to obtain food? Do different learning principles apply more to animals than to humans? What motivates organisms? What is an emotion?

These questions interest psychologists in the areas of **personality and social psychology,** *who study social interactions, stereotypes, prejudices, attitudes, conformity, group behaviors, aggression, personality development, personality change and assessment, and abnormal behaviors.* About 30% of psychologists choose one of these two specialties.

Those who study **developmental psychology** examine these kinds of questions. Psychologists in this area study *moral, social, emotional, and cognitive development during the life span.* Some concentrate on changes in infancy and childhood, while others trace changes through adolescence, adulthood, and old age. About 24% of psychologists choose this specialty.

These kinds of questions interest **experimental psychologists,** *whose research includes areas of sensation, perception, learning, motivation, and emotion.* Much of their research is conducted under carefully controlled laboratory conditions, with both animal and human subjects. About 19% of psychologists specialize in experimental psychology.

Decisions, Decisions. If you decide to become a psychologist, a number of decisions await you. You must decide whether to obtain a master's degree or a Ph.D., which of the half-dozen or more subareas of psychology to specialize in, and which career setting to choose.

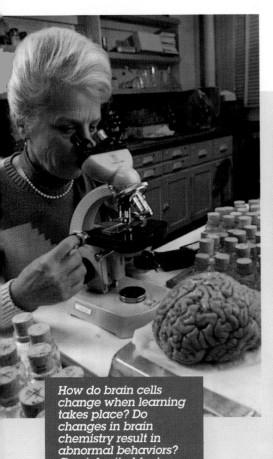

How do brain cells change when learning takes place? Do changes in brain chemistry result in abnormal behaviors? Can inherited factors increase chances for mental problems?

Physiological psychologists, or psychobiologists, *answer questions about how our genetic makeup and nervous system interact with our environments and influence our behaviors.* They search for the physiological basis of learning and memory, the effects of brain damage, the causes of sleep and wakefulness, the basis of hunger, thirst, and sex, the effects of stress on the body, and the ways in which drugs influence behavior. About 8% of psychologists choose this subarea.

What was unique about Einstein's thought processes? Why could he solve so many "unsolvable" problems? Did he have a super memory?

Such questions interest **cognitive psychologists,** *who study how we process, store, and retrieve information.* Their research includes areas of memory, thinking, language, creativity, and decision making. Newer areas, such as artificial intelligence, combine knowledge of the brain's functions with computer programming in an attempt to duplicate "human" thinking and intelligence. About 5% of psychologists select this subarea.

What do college entrance tests prove? What career best fits my abilities? How do tests measure abnormal behavior?

These questions introduce the area of **psychometrics,** *which focuses on the measurement of people's abilities, skills, intelligence, personality, and abnormal behaviors.* To undertake such measurement, psychologists develop a wide range of tests that must be continually updated and checked for cultural biases. These tests are used not only to assess people's abilities but also to predict their performance in certain situations, such as college. About 5% of psychologists select this subarea.

As a student you are no doubt interested in two topics that psychologists study: test anxiety and study skills. We have already discussed various approaches to handling test anxiety. Now we turn to suggestions that psychologists have on improving your study skills.

APPLYING/ EXPLORING: STUDY SKILLS

Preparing for an Exam

Do you remember the six modern approaches discussed earlier?

Suppose you answer, "I'm sure I know the six approaches." Well, researchers have found almost no relationship between how well you *think* you know material and how well you *perform* on a test of that material (Pressley et al., 1987). The reason students tend to be poor judges of what they know is that they base their judgments more on what they know *generally* rather than on what they *specifically remember* (Glenberg et al., 1987). For example, you might generally remember reading about the six approaches. However, on an exam you will be asked specific information, such as names and definitions. One of the best ways to judge how prepared you are for an exam is to test yourself and get feedback from answering specific questions. For instance, can you list the six approaches and their definitions? Because answering specific questions is one way to judge your learning, we have built specific questions and answers into this text. You can test yourself by answering questions in the Concept/Glossary sections within modules and by answering questions in the Summary/Self-Test at the end of each module.

Setting Goals

1 Which of the following goals do you think would make your study time more efficient and improve your test performance? Set a **time goal**, such as studying ten hours a week or more, and then keep track of your study time during the semester.

A good way to keep awake and interested in class is to ask questions.

> **Remember:** To judge how prepared you are for an exam, ask yourself specific questions about the material, such as by taking the tests built into this text.

2 Set a **general goal**, such as trying to study hard and stay on schedule, and then try to reach this goal during the semester.

3 Set a **specific performance goal**, such as answering at least 80% of the Concept/Glossary questions correctly for each module.

To determine which of these goals leads to more effective studying, researchers told three different groups of students to follow time goals, general goals, or specific performance goals when they studied on their own. The researchers found that students who set *specific performance goals* did significantly better on the final exam than students who set time or general goals (Morgan, 1985). Thus, if you want to improve your study skills, you should worry less about the total time you study and concentrate more on reaching specific performance goals every week. For example, the first week your goal might be to correctly answer 80% of the Concept/ Glossary questions and 80% of the Summary/Self-Test questions. Once you have reached this goal, you can aim for answering 90% of the questions correctly.

> **Remember:** One way to make your study time more efficient is to set specific performance goals and to keep track of your progress.

Rewarding Yourself

When you reach a specific goal, such as answering 80% of the questions correctly, give yourself a reward. It might be a special treat (such as a record, meal, movie, or time with friends) or a positive statement (such as "I'm doing really well" or "I'm going to get a good grade on the test"). Giving yourself a reward (self-reinforcement) is an effective way to improve performance (Hayes et al., 1986).

Remember: *Immediately after you reach a specific goal, give yourself a reward, which will both maintain and improve your motivation.*

Taking Notes

Students generally make two kinds of mistakes in taking notes. One is to try to write down everything the instructor says, which is impossible and leads to confusing notes. The other is to mechanically copy down terms or concepts that they do not understand but hope to learn by sheer memorization, which is difficult. Researchers have several suggestions for taking good notes:

Remember: *Take lecture notes in your own words and try to associate the new, unfamiliar information with information you already know.*

1 Write down the information in your own words. This approach will ensure that you understand the material and will increase your chances of remembering it.

2 Use headings or an outline format. This method will help you better organize and remember the material.

3 Try to associate new lecture or text material with material that you already know. It's easier to remember new information if you can relate it to your existing knowledge. That is the reason we have paired terms in the Concept/Glossary section with illustrations, drawings, and photos that you are familiar with from earlier in the text.

Procrastinating

How do I get started?
Some students find the task of reading several assignments or writing a paper so daunting that they cannot bring themselves to begin. There are three things you can do to get started.

1 *Stop thinking or worrying* about the final goal—reading several assignments—which may seem too overwhelming.

2 Break the final assignment down into a number of *smaller goals* that are less overwhelming and easier to accomplish. Work on the first small goal, and when you finish it go on to the next small goal. Continue until you have completed all the small goals.

3 Write down a *realistic schedule* for reaching each of your smaller goals. This schedule should indicate the time and place for study and what you will accomplish that day. Use a variety of self-reinforcements to stay on your daily schedule and accomplish your specific goals.

Remember: *One of the most effective ways to start a large assignment is to break it down into a series of smaller ones and work on each one of them separately.*

Get started by breaking a long assignment into smaller ones.

Summary/Self-Test

DEFINING PSYCHOLOGY

1. The broad definition of psychology is the systematic, scientific study of (a) _behavior_ and (b) _mental process_. The term in (a) refers to observable responses of animals and humans, and the term in (b) refers to processes that are not directly observable, such as thoughts, ideas, and dreams.

2. All psychologists agree that the first two goals of psychology are to (a) _understand_ why organisms behave as they do and to (b) _predict_ how they will respond in the future and in different situations. Some psychologists add a third goal, which is to (c) _control_ behavior and thus curb or eliminate psychological and social problems.

■ *Everyone knows that seatbelts save lives, yet 20%–40% of drivers do not wear them. How do the three goals of psychology apply to people who don't wear seatbelts?*

MODERN APPROACHES TO PSYCHOLOGY

3. Because behavior is often so complex, psychologists study it using six different approaches. The approach that focuses on how one's genetic makeup, hormones, and nervous system interact with the environment to influence a wide range of behaviors is called the (a) _psychobiology_ approach. The approach that studies how organisms learn

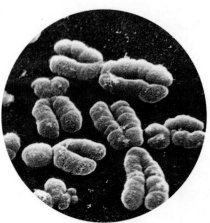

new behaviors or change or modify existing ones in response to influences from the environment is called the (b) _behaviorist_ approach. There are two versions of this approach. One that primarily studies observable behaviors and excludes mental events is called (c) _Behavior_ and is best expressed by the ideas of B. F. Skinner; the other, which includes observable behaviors plus cognitive processes, is called the (d) _social learning_ approach and is expressed by the ideas of Albert Bandura and his colleagues.

4. An approach that examines how one's unconscious fears, desires, and motivations influence behaviors, thoughts, and personality and cause psychological problems is called the (a) _psychoanalytical_ approach. Sigmund Freud developed this approach as well as two techniques—free association and dream interpretation—to bring unconscious ideas to the surface. The approach that investigates how people process, store, and use information in solving problems, remembering, and creating is called the (b) _free association_ approach. An approach that emphasizes people's capacity for personal growth, freedom in choosing one's future, and potential for self-fulfillment is called the (c) _humanist_ approach. One of the founders of this approach was Abraham Maslow. The approach that studies how cultural and ethnic similarities and differences influence the psychological and social functioning of its members is called the (d) _cross cultural_ approach.

■ *You're interested in whether alcoholism runs in families. How would psychologists use the six modern approaches to study this problem?*

DISCRIMINATION IN PSYCHOLOGY

5. During the first 75 of its over 100 years of existence, the field of psychology discriminated against (a) _woman_ and (b) _minorities_, as indicated by the very limited number of these individuals who were granted Ph.D.'s or offered positions in major universities. During the past 25 years, the American Psychological Association, minority organizations, and most universities and colleges have been actively recruiting and helping minorities enter the field of psychology.

■ *Imagine being a black woman in the early days of psychology. What kinds of problems would you have faced?*

PREVIOUS APPROACHES: LEARNING FROM HISTORY

6. Considered the father of psychology, Wilhelm Wundt developed an approach called (a) _Structulism_. It studied the elements of the conscious mind by using a technique of self-report, called (b) _Structism_. Wundt's approach was the beginning of today's cognitive approach. Disagreeing with Wundt's approach, William James said that it was important to study functions rather than elements of the mind. Accordingly, James studied how mental processes continuously flow and adapt to input from the environment, an approach called (c) _Functionalist_ James's ideas contributed to the modern cognitive and psychobiological approaches.

7. Also disagreeing with Wundt's approach was a group of psychologists, led by Wertheimer, Köhler, and Koffka, who stated that perceptions cannot be explained by breaking them down into individual elements or sensations. Instead, they believed that perceptions are more than the sum of individual sensations, an idea called the _Gestalt_ approach.

8. Another psychologist who disagreed with Wundt's approach was John B. Watson. He stated that psychology should use scientific principles to study only observable behaviors and not mental events, an approach called _Behaviorism_. Watson's approach gave rise to the modern behavioral approach.

■ *Suppose you met one of Wundt's students who had been frozen in 1895 and had only recently "thawed out." How would you explain what has happened in psychology since Wundt's time?*

CAREERS IN PSYCHOLOGY

9. There are four major settings in which psychologists work and establish careers. The largest percentage of psychologists work in private practice or (a) _Therapy_ settings, where they diagnose and help clients with psychological problems. The second largest group work in (b) _acdamic_ settings, doing a combination of teaching and research. The third largest group work in (c) _industrial_ settings, where they are involved in selecting personnel, increasing job satisfaction, and improving worker-management relations. The fourth largest group work in other settings, such as (d) _Secondary School_ where they do academic testing and counseling.

■ *You're talking to a friend about a career in psychology. Your friends asks, "So, what are the possibilities?" What would you answer?*

RESEARCH AREAS IN PSYCHOLOGY

10. There are six common subareas in which psychologists specialize. Those who are interested in prejudice, attitudes, group behaviors, or personality development and change specialize in (a) _Personality_ psychology. Those interested in social, emotional, and cognitive changes across the life span specialize in (b) _Social_ psychology. Those interested in studying sensation, perceptions, learning, and motivation, often under laboratory conditions, specialize in (c) _Experimental_ psychology. Those interested in the interaction among genes, nervous system, and the environment choose (d) _Psychobiology_ Those interested in how people process, store, and retrieve information choose (e) _Cognitive_ psychology, and those who are interested in measurement and testing of skills, abilities, personality, and mental problems specialize in (f) _Psychometrics_

■ *Imagine receiving your letter of acceptance for graduate school. Since your main interest is in helping people reduce stress, which of the six subareas of psychology should you specialize in?*

APPLYING/EXPLORING: STUDY HABITS

11. A good way to judge how prepared you are for an exam is to ask yourself specific (a) _Questions_ rather than to trust your judgment about what you think you know. A good way to make your study time more efficient is to set specific (b) _time frames_ and keep track of your progress. Immediately after you reach a specific performance goal, give yourself a (c) _reward_, which will both maintain and improve your motivation. To improve your lecture notes, take them in your own words and try to (d) _associate_ the new, unfamiliar information with information you already know. One of the most effective ways to overcome (e) _Realistic Schedule_ is to break down a large assignment into a series of smaller goals and work on each goal separately.

■ *You're working part-time and never seem to have enough time to study. How could you best use your time in class and study most efficiently?*

MODULE 2
WHAT SCIENCE IS

Is he a misunderstood genius?

Why do some scientists criticize Linus Pauling's beliefs about the benefits of taking large doses of vitamin C?

Each day Linus Pauling takes an amount of vitamin C that is equivalent to drinking 260 glasses of orange juice, or 300 times above the recommended daily dose. One reason this makes the newspapers is that Linus Pauling is a renowned scientist: he won the Nobel prize for his work on chemical bonding in 1954 and the Nobel prize for peace in 1962. Pauling turned 90 in 1991 and partly attributed his good health, avoidance of cancer, lack of colds, and remarkable longevity to his daily megadose of vitamin C. Some assume that when Linus Pauling speaks about vitamin C, one should listen; others wonder how a Nobel laureate can come so close to being a quack.

For example, most mainstream scientists shake their heads in disbelief at Pauling's claims that high doses of vitamin C can cure colds, lengthen the lives of AIDS patients, and prevent cancer and heart disease. Physician Victor Herbert, author of *The Mount Sinai School of Medicine Complete Book of Nutrition,* characterizes Pauling as "a believer, rather than a scientist in this area. There is no value in a megadose, and there is no study showing that people who take megadoses of vitamin C live longer than people who don't take megadoses. Linus just believes what he wants to believe." According to Jim Enstrom, who is associate research professor at UCLA School of Public Health and has published with Pauling on vitamin C, "Pauling is not doing his scientific reputation any good. He's not following the scientific methods." Ahmed Zewail, the Linus Pauling Professor of Chemical Physics at Caltech, calls Pauling a misunderstood genius and says, "As a chemist, Pauling has to be one of the greatest scientists of the 20th century. Whether or not he is right on vitamin C needs experimentation and proof." (adapted from *Los Angeles Times,* February 26, 1991)

What's Coming

In the first part of this module, we'll explore the methods that psychologists use to gather data and answer questions. In the second part we'll focus on one particular method of answering questions—conducting an experiment—that minimizes the chances of error and bias. Let's begin with the general method of science.

Methods of Science

Linus Pauling stuck very closely to the scientific method in his creative work on chemical bonding. Scientists obtain proof by following the **scientific method,** *which is a set of rules and procedures on how to study, observe, or conduct experiments and minimize the effects of error, bias, and chance occurrences.* However, Pauling's work on vitamin C has been another matter. Critics charge that Pauling has not followed the scientific method in his research on vitamin C and that he has reached conclusions before completing the research. If it is true that Pauling's studies have not been based in the scientific method, his conclusions would be open to error and bias.

Let's look at various ways that scientists might gather information about vitamin C.

Three Methods to Obtain Information

Compared with other professionals, what distinguishes scientists are their *goals* of gathering information, answering questions, and obtaining proof by using the scientific method. Scientists prefer to use the scientific method because two other popular methods for gathering information, case studies and surveys, have greater potential for error and bias. We'll compare how these three methods would approach the following question: Can large doses of vitamin C cure colds?

Do large doses of vitamin C cure colds?

Testimonial: Vitamin C cures colds.
Scientific evidence: Vitamin C does not cure colds.

1 *Case study:* "I had a cold and took large doses of vitamin C. My cold went away, proving that vitamin C really worked."

This method of answering questions is based on a **case study,** *in which information is obtained through an in-depth analysis of the thoughts, feelings, beliefs, or behaviors of a single person.* In this case study, the person is expressing a particular belief, or giving a testimonial, about vitamin C. A **testimonial** *is a statement in support of a particular viewpoint based on one's personal experience.*

Potential for error and bias: High.

2 *Survey:* When 25 people were asked whether taking large doses of vitamin C helped cure their colds, 75% replied that it had.

This method of answering questions is called a **survey,** *in which information is obtained by asking many individuals to answer written or oral questions.* A survey is useful for obtaining information from a large number of people.

Potential for error and bias: High.

3 *Experiment:* Researchers gave sugar pills to one group of people with colds and megadoses of vitamin C to another group. They analyzed differences between rates of recovery between the two groups, found no differences, and concluded that large doses of vitamin C do not cure the common cold.

This method of answering questions is called an **experiment,** *in which information is obtained by following the rules and guidelines of the scientific method.* If possible, scientists prefer to use experiments to obtain information.

Potential for error and bias: Low.

Each of the three methods—case study, survey, and experiment—may provide information and answer questions, but only the experimental method takes special precautions to eliminate error and bias. Although case studies (testimonials) and surveys indicate the popularity of taking large doses of vitamin C for colds, the experimental method has generally found that vitamin C has no effect on curing colds and has perhaps a slight effect on preventing colds (Briggs, 1984). We'll examine the advantages and disadvantages of each of the three methods, beginning with case studies.

Case Study: Testimonials

Does powdered rhino horn increase sexual stamina and cure headaches?

Testimonial: Especially in China, Thailand, South Korea, and Taiwan, millions of people believe and report that rhino horn is an aphrodisiac that will increase sexual desire and stamina or a cure for everything from headaches and nosebleeds to high fevers and typhoid. **Scientific evidence:** The basic ingredient of rhino horn, keratin, has been shown to have no proven medicinal powers. This information has not changed the beliefs of its many users (*Sierra*, Nov./Dec. 1989). Many concerned with the rhino's extinction have recommended substituting water buffalo horn, which is essentially the same substance, but users believe that only rhino horn has special medicinal properties.

Three Sources of Error and Bias in Testimonials

Although scientific evidence questions the medicinal value of rhino horn or the curative value of vitamin C, the believer's personal experience may give rise to testimonials that override such evidence. I'll use a testimonial from Greg, one of my students, to demonstrate three potential sources of error and bias.

> **Greg's testimonial:** I raised my grades by listening to a subliminal tape called "Improving One's Memory."

In the late 1970s, some 65,000 two-ton black rhinos roamed Africa; by the early 1990s, high-powered rifles of poachers had reduced that number to a pathetic 3,500. A single rhino horn, which is essentially a compacted mass of hair (keratin) weighing about 4 to 5 pounds, will bring from $25,000 to $50,000 on the black market. Rhino horns are highly valued in China as a vital ingredient in patent medicines. According to the U.S. Fish and Wildlife Service, more than $5 million worth of medicines containing rhino horn slip into the United States illegally each year (*Sierra*, Nov./Dec. 1989).

1 Personal beliefs. If we believe strongly in something, it may bias our perception and cause us to credit an unrelated treatment or event as the reason for some change. Greg believes strongly in the effectiveness of subliminal tapes; as a result, his *personal beliefs* may have biased his perception and caused him to credit his improved grades to listening to the tape. Because of his biased perception, Greg may be unaware of other ways that he may have changed, such as having increased his study time, improved his note taking, or developed better attitudes.

2 Self-fulfilling prophecy. If we strongly believe that something is going to happen, we may unknowingly behave in a way to make it happen. This phenomenon, called **self-fulfilling prophecy**, *involves making a prophecy or statement about a future behavior and then acting, usually unknowingly, to fulfill it.* For example, Greg told me that he bought the subliminal memory tape because his roommate had used it with great success. As a result, Greg believed that the tape would improve his memory and he may have been unaware that he was also studying harder and fulfilling his own prophecy.

3 Confounded causes. Because personal experiences involve many ongoing behaviors, thoughts, and feelings, it is usually impossible to identify which one is the primary cause of some change. For example, at least four ongoing behaviors may have been responsible for an improvement in Greg's grades: listening to subliminal tapes, unknowingly studying harder, attending more classes, or taking better notes. *Since all four behaviors were tangled up with each other, they are said to have been* **confounded**. It is impossible for Greg to separate the four confounded behaviors and identify one (or more) as the cause of his improved grades.

Let's return to Greg's testimonial and see whether his belief was supported by experimental evidence.

Evaluating Greg's Testimonial on Subliminal Tapes

Subliminal tapes usually contain clearly audible music and brief inaudible messages that are slightly below the normal threshold for hearing. Such verbal messages are called ***subliminal messages***. Advertisements for subliminal tapes claim that subliminal messages can help listeners change or improve a wide range of behaviors, such as increasing motivation, raising self-esteem, losing weight, and improving memory. In addition, there are testimonials from users like Greg who claim the subliminal messages have changed their behaviors.

To evaluate the effectiveness of subliminal "motivational" tapes, researcher Anthony Greenwald and his colleagues (1991) made two tapes: one containing soothing music with subliminal messages to improve self-esteem and a second containing soothing music with subliminal messages to improve memory. Subjects were asked to listen to the tapes for several weeks and then judge improvement in their behaviors. Half of the subjects who had listened to the tape labeled "Improve Self-Esteem" reported improved self-esteem. Half of the subjects who had listened to the tape labeled "Improve Memory" reported improved memory.

Unknown to the listener, the subliminal tapes actually contained messages that did not match the labels on the tapes.

This 50% improvement rate would suggest that subliminal tapes are reasonably effective in changing behavior. But there's a hitch: the subjects did not know that their tape label did not match their subliminal messages. The tape labeled "Improve Self-Esteem" actually contained subliminal messages to improve memory, whereas the tape labeled "Improve Memory" actually contained subliminal messages to improve self-esteem. Subjects reported improvements in what the label said, rather than based on the tape's subliminal messages.

A popular use of testimonials is for a well-known person to promote a particular product.

Greenwald concluded that the messages in subliminal "motivational" tapes did not affect the behavior they were designed to change. Instead, any changes in behavior resulted from the listeners' beliefs that the tapes would be effective. The listeners' beliefs created ***self-fulfilling prophecies,*** which apparently accounted for any improvements or changes in behaviors.

Greenwald's study is an excellent example of how the scientific method can answer questions with less error and bias than testimonials can.

In some cases, testimonials provide useful information and may promote worthwhile social causes. In other cases, testimonials may promote products, treatments, or cures that later prove to be suspect. The *advantages* of testimonials are that they may provide useful information and offer cues and explanations that scientists might follow up. Their main *disadvantage* is their high potential for error and bias.

Surveys

Do you think it is easier to be a man or a woman?
In a telephone survey, the majority of both men and women answered that it is easier to be a man (see graph). When psychologists want to sample the attitudes, beliefs, and behaviors of a large number of individuals, they use a survey. In a **survey,** *which can be conducted person-to-person, by telephone, or by mail, individuals are asked to respond to a fixed set of questions.* Perhaps the most famous survey of all times was the original Kinsey report, which asked about the sexual behaviors of Americans in the 1940s (Kinsey, Pomeroy, & Martin, 1948). We can use this Kinsey report to show the disadvantages and advantages of surveys.

A man may be tempted to give socially desirable answers to questions asked by a woman interviewer.

Among the *advantages* of surveys are that psychologists can quickly and efficiently collect information on the beliefs, attitudes, and behaviors of a large sample of people and can compare answers from various ethnic, age, socioeconomic, and cultural groups. When the Kinsey report was published, it was the first time the sexual attitudes, beliefs, and practices of a large sample of Americans had been reported. The report shocked many people, who thought such information should be kept private. Nevertheless, Kinsey's report served to open up discussion of sexual attitudes and behaviors, whether or not people agreed or disagreed with the findings or approach.

Among the *disadvantages* of surveys are that the sample may be biased because some part of the population is overrepresented or underrepresented, that people may not answer questions truthfully, that questions may be worded to influence the results, that people may not remember accurately and thus may make up answers, that people may answer in a way that they think is more socially desirable, and that people may not accurately predict how they will behave in an actual situation, such as how they will vote when they enter the polling booth.

In Kinsey's research, interviews were conducted face to face, with guarantees of confidentiality; this made it difficult to judge the truthfulness of the respondents' answers. But the major criticism of Kinsey's method was his use of a biased sample, which was composed almost entirely of white, middle-class, college-educated males and females, with few minorities and people from the working classes. Despite potential problems, psychologists continue to use surveys to assess the beliefs, attitudes, and behaviors of large numbers of people.

Do you think it is easier to be a man or a woman?

	Females		Males
To be a woman	30%		21%
To be a man	59%		65%

In a telephone survey, the majority of men and women answered that it is easier to be a man than a woman. The sample was 505 Americans ages 18 to 24.

Who should be the next president of the United States?

Respondents' top four choices in order were TV's Mr. Rogers, singer-dancer Janet Jackson, film star Arnold Schwarzenegger, and Vanna White, co-host of the *Wheel of Fortune* TV game show. Playskool, a toy manufacturer, conducted this survey among preschoolers in five American cities. The respondents' interesting and unusual answers indicate what may happen when a survey uses a very biased sample (*Newsweek*, February 18, 1991).

Preschoolers' picks for president:

1 Mister Rogers

2 Janet Jackson

3 Arnold Schwarzenegger

4 Vanna White

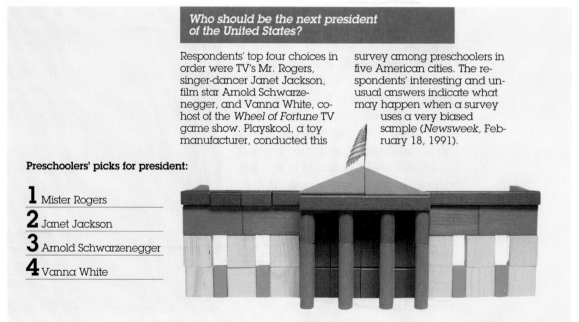

Correlation

Does drinking regular coffee promote sexual activity in people over age 60?
Researchers studied 800 subjects age 60 and older and found that 62% who drank regular coffee still enjoyed active sex lives, compared to only 37% of non-coffee drinkers (*Los Angeles Times*, September 18, 1990).

Does drinking coffee increase sexual activity?

Does this study therefore indicate that coffee drinking increases sexual activity in those over 60? If we carefully read the entire study, we would discover that these two events are linked together. *A linkage or relationship between the occurrence of two or more events is called a* **correlation.** *The strength of this relationship or correlation is indicated by a number called the* **correlation coefficient.** We'll take the liberty of adjusting the results of the coffee study so that we can explain the meaning of correlation coefficients, which range from −1.00 to +1.00.

Explanation of correlational coefficients (hypothetical) between two events: drinking coffee and sexual activity over age 60.

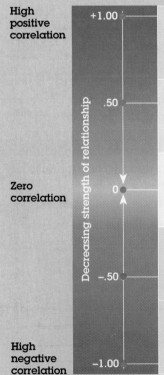

Decreasing strength of relationship

High positive correlation — +1.00

If 20 subjects drank three cups of coffee a day and all reported increased sexual activity, the correlation coefficient would be positive and perfect, which would be indicated by a +1.00 correlation coefficient. A **perfect positive correlation coefficient** means that an increase in one event is always matched by an increase in a second event.

.50

Any **positive correlation coefficient** between 0 and +1.00, such as +.50, indicates that as one event tends to increase, the second event sometimes but not always increases. As the coefficient decreases, it indicates a lessening in the strength of the relationship.

Zero correlation — 0

If 20 subjects drank three cups of coffee a day and some reported increases, some reported decreases, and some reported no changes in sexual activity, there would be no correlation. This is called a **zero correlation** and is expressed as 0.

−.50

Any **negative correlation coefficient** between −1.00 and 0, such as −.50, indicates that as one event increases a second sometimes but not always decreases. As the coefficient increases, it indicates a lessening in strength of the relationship.

High negative correlation — −1.00

If 20 subjects drank three cups of coffee a day and all reported a complete lack of sexual interest, the correlation coefficient would be said to be negative and perfect, indicated by a −1.00 correlation coefficient. A **perfect negative correlation coefficient** means that an increase in one event is always matched by a decrease in a second event (or vice versa).

Correlation

Correlation Versus Causation

We know there is a correlation between drinking coffee and enjoying sex, but we do not know whether one event causes the other, because correlations do not identify the cause or effect. Can you think of a reason having nothing to do with coffee drinking that might explain why coffee drinkers may be reporting more sex? Perhaps people who are over 60 years old and in good health have not been advised to stop consuming caffeine. Thus, the increased or decreased sexual activity may be caused by subjects' relative health (good or poor), which is also correlated with their consumption of coffee.

To illustrate how even a perfect positive correlation cannot show cause and effect, consider the following example. From the years 1972 to 1985, there was a perfect positive correlation (+1.00) between which league won the Super Bowl (NFL or AFL) and whether stock market prices rose or fell that year. Since a Super Bowl winner cannot *cause* a stock market trend, we realize that correlation says nothing about cause and effect.

Although correlations do not indicate causation, they do serve two useful purposes: they help predict behavior and they point to *possible* causes of behavior.

Correlation and Prediction

Psychologists use relatively high correlations *to predict behavior*, which is one of psychology's goals. This is one reason that grade school students are given IQ tests. The correlation between IQ scores and performance in academic settings is as high as +.60 to +.70. This is a relatively high correlation, meaning that these two behaviors are strongly linked together. In comparison, the correlation between IQ scores and mental health is relatively low, indicating that IQ scores are only moderately useful in making predictions about people's corresponding mental health. (We discuss the advantages and disadvantages of IQ tests in Module 15.)

Correlations as Clues

Can correlations help solve one of the most perplexing problems in psychology?
During the past ten years, researchers have used newly developed brain-imaging techniques to study chemical sites in brains of living patients with schizophrenia. Some of these researchers have found a correlation between the presence of abnormal chemical sites in the brain and the occurrence of this mental disorder (Wong et al., 1986). Although this research is far from complete, it provides researchers with clues in their investigation into the causes of mental illness.

In answering a question, psychologists may conduct a survey or an experiment or look for clues through correlations. In doing so they may use a number of research techniques and settings, which we'll turn to next.

SURGEON
GENERAL'S
WARNING:
CIGARETTE
SMOKING
MAY CAUSE
LUNG CANCER

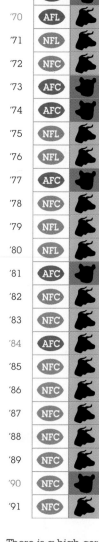

There is a high correlation between who wins the Super Bowl and the goings on of the stock market. A win by the AFC (American Football Conference) is most often followed by a bear market (decrease), while a win by the NFC (National Football Conference) is most often followed by a bull market (increase).

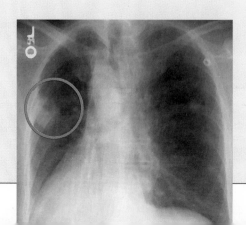

A success story in the use of correlational research involves studies of cigarette smoking. For many years, smoking was shown to be positively correlated with lung cancer, but it was unknown whether smoking was the *cause* of cancer. Acting on the theory that some ingredient of cigarette smoke might trigger the development of lung cancer, researchers rubbed tar, an ingredient of cigarette smoke, on the skin of animals. After repeated applications over a period of time, the animals developed cancerous growths. This research proved that tar could cause cancer and provides an example of how correlations are useful in pinpointing potential causes.

1. One of the chief differences between science and other professions is the scientists' use of a set of rules and procedures to minimize error and bias in gathering information, answering questions, and obtaining proof; this set of rules is called the (a)_____. When psychologists gather information by following the rules and guidelines of the scientific method, they are obtaining information by conducting an (b)_____. If possible, psychologists prefer to use this method to obtain information because it has the lowest potential for error and bias.

2. Psychologists can use three methods to obtain information. If they obtain information through an in-depth analysis of the thoughts, feelings, beliefs, or behaviors of a single person, this method is called a (a)_____. If a person expresses a belief or feeling in support of a particular viewpoint based on his or her's personal experience, such a statement is called a (b)_____. Although this kind of statement can provide useful information, it has a high potential for error and bias.

3. There are three sources of error and bias in testimonials. If people believe strongly in something, their (a)_____ may bias their perceptions. If people believe strongly that something will happen, they may unknowingly behave in such a way to make it happen, a phenomenon called (b)_____. Because a personal experience usually involves several or more ongoing thoughts, behaviors, and feelings, it is often difficult to identify the real cause of certain results because all these factors are said to be linked together or (c)_____.

4. If psychologists gather information by asking many individuals to answer questions about their attitudes, beliefs, and behaviors, they are using a _____. One advantage of this method is that it samples information from a large number of people. One disadvantage of this method is that the people's answers may be biased.

5. Psychologists describe the association, relationship, or linkage among two or more events as a (a)_____. They describe the strength of such a relationship by a number called the (b)_____, which may vary from –1.00 to +1.00. If an increase in one event is associated with an increase in a second event, this relationship is called a (c)_____ correlation. If an increase in one event is associated with a decrease in a second event, this relationship is called a (d)_____ correlation. Finding that two or more events are linked together does not prove that one event (e)_____ the other. However, finding that one event is related to another may help psychologists (f)_____ future behavior or may provide (g)_____ as to where to look for answers.

Answers: 1. (a) scientific method, (b) experiment. 2. (a) case study, (b) testimonial. 3. (a) personal beliefs, (b) self-fulfilling prophecy, (c) confounded. 4. survey. 5. (a) correlation, (b) correlation coefficient, (c) positive, (d) negative, (e) causes, (f) predict, (g) clues.

Decisions about Doing Research

Suppose you're a psychologist interested in studying some aspect of schizophrenia, one of the more prevalent and serious mental disorders. Once you have decided on this topic, you need to answer two questions about doing research:

1. *How will you obtain information?* This question involves choosing from a number of research techniques. We'll explain five common techniques.

2. *Where will you study the subjects?* This question involves choosing a place or setting. We'll examine two common settings.

Choosing a Research Technique

1 Questionnaires and Interviews

Does a schizophrenic think differently?
You could answer this question by using interviews or questionnaires. In **interviews**, *psychologists ask questions, ranging from opened ended to highly structured, about a subject's behaviors and attitudes, usually in a one-on-one situation.* With **questionnaires**, *which are similar to highly structured interviews, subjects are asked to read a list of written questions and then mark specific answers.* For instance, through interviews psychologists have found that schizophrenics have a disorganized and disturbed thought pattern.

2 Standardized Tests

How do schizophrenics differ from normals?
One way to obtain this kind of information is by giving standardized tests. **Standardized tests** *are psychological tests that have been given to hundreds of people and shown to reliably measure thought patterns, personality traits, emotions, or behaviors.* Using standardized tests, psychologists have found that schizophrenics differ from others in a number of personality traits, emotional reactions, and behaviors.

3 Laboratory Experiment: Behaviors

Does a schizophrenic have trouble paying attention?
A good technique to use to answer this question would be a laboratory experiment: Present two stimuli at the same time and measure whether schizophrenics can attend to one and not the other. In a **laboratory experiment,** *psychologists study behavior in a controlled environment that permits the careful manipulation of some treatment and the measurement of the treatment's effects on behavior.* From laboratory experiments, psychologists have found that schizophrenics have a deficit in attention, such as being unable to select relevant stimuli from irrelevant ones.

4 Laboratory Experiment: Physiological/Neurological Responses

Do schizophrenics have chemical deficits in their brains?
Besides studying observable behaviors in the laboratory, you could measure internal physiological or neurological responses in schizophrenics. **Physiological/ neurological responses** *include changes in the body—such as in blood pressure, heart rate, or hormonal secretions—as well as in the brain, such as electrical and chemical changes.* Psychobiologists have identified several unusual biochemical deficits in the brains of people with schizophrenia.

5 Research Using Animals

Can new drugs to treat schizophrenia be tested on animals first?
Many drugs now used to treat schizophrenia were first tested for safety and potential therapeutic value on animals. Psychologists may also use animals in their research to develop an animal model for some condition. An **animal model** *involves testing animals on a behavioral task or physiological condition that closely approximates some human problem, disease, or condition.* For example, psychobiologists have used rats to test the sleep-inducing properties of antischizophrenic drugs.

After psychologists decide which research techniques to use, they next decide where to conduct their studies.

Choosing the Setting for Studying Behavior

There are two common *settings* in which psychologists conduct their studies: in a laboratory or in a more naturalistic environment. We'll explain each setting and compare their advantages and disadvantages.

Naturalistic Setting

What happens to the homeless?

In a **naturalistic setting**, *psychologists gather information by observing individuals' behaviors in their environments, without attempting to change or control the situation.* Psychologists study behaviors in many naturalistic settings, including schools, workplaces, college dormitories, bars, sports arenas, and homeless shelters. For example, in New York City, an enormous building shelters 700 homeless each night. Of these 700, an estimated 25% are mentally ill. Caseworkers have found that after weeks, months, and even years in the shelter, the mentally ill often become worse and lose all motivation, but they have no place else to go (*Los Angeles Times,* May 6, 1991). Naturalistic observations of the homeless mentally ill point up the critical need for psychological treatment facilities in large cities.

The *advantage* of naturalistic observations is that psychologists can study behaviors in real-life situations and environments, which cannot or would not be duplicated in the laboratory. The *disadvantage* is that the psychologists' own beliefs or values may bias their observations and cause them to misperceive or misinterpret behaviors.

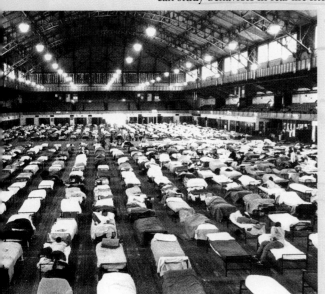

In New York City, an enormous building shelters 700 homeless each night.

In some cases, a single individual may be studied in his or her natural environment. In a *case study,* psychologists study a single individual in great depth to understand the person's unique personality, motivations, emotions, fears, beliefs, attitudes, or psychological problems. The case study approach is often used in clinical psychology to understand the development of a personality or psychological problem or in developmental psychology to examine a person's behavior across the life span.

The *advantage* of case studies is that psychologists can obtain detailed descriptions and insights into many aspects of an individual's complex life and behaviors. The *disadvantage* is that the information obtained is unique to an individual and may not apply to or help understand the behaviors of others.

Laboratory Setting

Could you be hypnotized to pick up a deadly snake?

If psychologists answer questions by *studying individuals under systematic and controlled conditions, with many of the real-world influences eliminated,* they are using a **laboratory setting.** Psychologists study a wide range of behaviors in the laboratory, including motivation, emotion, learning, sleep, brain mechanisms, and physiological responses, so they can carefully control the situations and prevent interference from outside sources. For example, if you were hypnotized, would you reach into a box and pick up a deadly snake? To study this potentially dangerous situation, researchers examined it in the laboratory. They asked subjects, some of whom had been hypnotized and some who had not, to reach into a box and pick up a snake (Rowland, 1939). In the next section we'll explain the interesting results of this laboratory study and the precautions the researchers used to avoid any harm to the subjects.

The *advantage* of the laboratory setting is that psychologists can carefully control and manipulate one or more treatment conditions while preventing interference from other situational or environmental factors. The *disadvantage* is that the setting may be so controlled or artificial that its results are not always transferable to or meaningful for real-life situations.

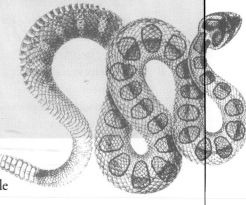

Now that you are familiar with research techniques and settings, we'll focus on one particular research technique and setting and show how psychologists have tried to answer the question of whether people can be hypnotized to do something dangerous.

Experiments: Scientific Method

Can people be hypnotized to perform dangerous acts?

In the 1930s, there were press reports of people being hypnotized and made to perform dangerous behaviors, such as robbery and attempted murder. Because press reports were inconclusive, one researcher, Dr. Rowland, decided to answer the question "Does hypnosis cause one to perform dangerous behaviors?" in a laboratory setting. He conducted an **experiment**, *which is a procedure for delivering a treatment, observing its effects on behavior, and analyzing the results using statistical procedures.* In conducting an experiment, researchers follow the scientific method to minimize error, bias, and chance occurrences.

We will divide the scientific method's guidelines into seven steps and observe how closely they were followed in Rowland's experiment.

Murder Suspect Claims to Have Been Hypnotized

In the 1930s the press reported people performing dangerous acts such as robbery and attempted murder under hypnosis.

Conducting an Experiment: Seven Steps

Step 1: Ask one or more specific questions, which are called hypotheses. A **hypothesis** *is an educated guess about some phenomenon and is stated in precise, concrete language to rule out any confusion or error in the meaning of its terms.* Researchers develop hypotheses from observations or previous research.

Following this first step, Rowland changed his general question, "Does hypnosis cause one to perform dangerous behaviors?" into very concrete terms: "Will hypnosis cause a person to pick up a poisonous snake?" "Will hypnosis cause a person to throw acid into the researcher's face?"

Step 2: Identify the treatment that will be administered to the subjects and the behavior(s) of the subjects that will be used to measure the effects of the treatment. *The treatment is something the researcher controls or manipulates; it is called the* **independent variable.** *The affected behaviors of the subjects are called* **dependent variables**, because they are "dependent" on the treatment.

Independent variable

Dependent variable

The independent variable may include a wide range of treatments or various levels of the same treatment. The dependent variable can be any of a wide range of behaviors, including observable responses, cognitive processes obtained through self-reports, and various responses of the body and brain obtained by physiological recordings.

Rowland's independent variable was administering a hypnotic procedure to one group of subjects. His dependent variable, an easily measured observable behavior, was picking up a snake.

Random selection
of subjects.

Step 3: # Choose subjects through random selection. **Random selection** *means that each subject in a sample population, such as all students on a college campus, has an equal chance of being selected to participate in the experiment.*

By randomly selecting subjects, researchers reduce potential error that may arise from their unknowingly wanting to choose the "best subjects" for their experiment. There are many ways to select randomly, such as taking every tenth student from a college campus (sample population).

Rowland did not randomly select subjects, which was a potential source of error.

Step 4: # Assign subjects randomly to different groups. *The group that will receive the treatment is called the* **experimental group.** *The group that undergoes everything the experimental group does except receiving the treatment is called the* **control group.**

By randomly assigning subjects to experimental and control groups, researchers control for many extraneous and potentially influential factors, such as intelligence, social class, economic level, age, personality variables, and genetic differences.

Rowland did not randomly assign his subjects, another potential source of error.

Experimental group

Control group

Step 5: # Manipulate the independent variable by administering the treatment (or one level of a treatment) to the experimental group while the control group receives similar conditions but no treatment (or different levels of the treatment).

Rowland manipulated the independent variable by inducing hypnosis in the 4 subjects who made up his experimental group. He did not hypnotize the 42 subjects in his control group but only asked them to participate voluntarily in the experiment.

Step 6: # Measure the effects of the independent variable (treatment) on behaviors that have been selected as the dependent variables.

Rowland hypnotized 2 subjects and told each to reach into a box and pick up a rattlesnake. Without any hesitation, both reached for the snake, but their hands struck a glass panel that separated and protected them from the snake. Rowland asked 42 other people, none of whom had been hypnotized, to pick up the rattlesnake, which was behind invisible glass. Only one attempted to do so, admitting later that he thought the snake was artificial.

The experimental subjects picked up the snake.   The control group did not.

Experiments: The Scientific Method

Step 7: Analyze differences between the behaviors of subjects in the experimental and control groups. Researchers use various **statistical procedures** (see Appendix) to determine whether differences are due to independent variables (treatment) or to error or chance occurrence.

When Rowland compared the behaviors of the experimental and control groups, he found that all 4 subjects in the experimental group performed potentially dangerous behaviors (picking up a snake) but only 1 out of 42 subjects in the control group performed a dangerous behavior. On the basis of these results, he concluded that hypnosis could motivate potentially dangerous behavior in the safe laboratory setting (Rowland, 1939).

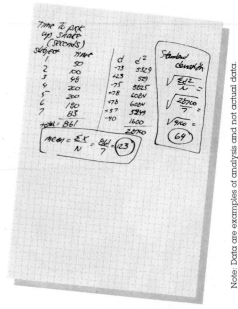

Note: Data are examples of analysis and not actual data.

The Effects of the Laboratory Setting

Results from other experiments suggested that subjects in a laboratory setting may feel compelled to cooperate with researchers and make the experiment work. Following this idea, one group of researchers hypothesized that subjects who were told to *pretend* to be hypnotized would comply with instructions to perform potentially dangerous behaviors (Orne & Evans, 1965). They asked hypnotized subjects in the experimental group and nonhypnotized subjects in the control group to perform potentially dangerous behaviors. Members of a third group were asked to behave as though they were hypnotized and try to fool the experimenter into thinking that they had been hypnotized. Researchers found that subjects in this third group behaved similarly to hypnotized subjects in their willingness to perform "dangerous" acts; subjects in the control group usually refused. The researchers concluded that the laboratory setting creates an atmosphere in which subjects feel compelled to comply with experimenters' demands (Orne & Evans, 1965). Because such demands do not usually exist in the world outside the laboratory, it is unlikely that people could be motivated with hypnosis or other instructions to perform potentially dangerous behaviors.

Subjects in the real world behave differently from those in the laboratory.

Conclusion

We know that the scientific method provides guidelines for answering questions with a minimum of error, bias, and chance occurrence. We know that answering one question may raise another and that answering a question in a controlled laboratory setting does not automatically give an answer that would apply to the real world. Finally, we know that researchers function much like detectives as they sort out clues and solve scientific mystery stories. This kind of detective work makes a career in science interesting, exciting, and rewarding.

After the Concept/Glossary, we'll discuss two related questions about doing research—use of human subjects and the use of animals in research.

1. After selecting a topic to study, psychologists can use at least five common research techniques to gather information. They can ask subjects oral or written questions by using (a) _Survey_ and (b) _questionnaire_. They might ask subjects to answer questions on established tests, which are called (c) _standrize_ tests. They might measure *behaviors* in a controlled environment, called a (d) _Experiment_. They could study *internal responses* of the body, such as (e) _Neurological/Responses_ responses. They could study the problem in animals by developing an (f) _animal model_ that closely approximates the human condition.

2. Psychologists conduct research in two common settings. If they study individuals in their real-life environments, without trying to control the situation, they are using a (a) _naturlistic_ setting. A variation of this approach is to study a single individual in great depth in his or her own environment, which is called a (b) _Case Study_. If psychologists study individuals under carefully controlled conditions, they are using a (c) _labortory_ setting.

3. The scientific method's guidelines can be divided into seven steps. Step 1 is to *ask* specific questions in very concrete terms: these scientific questions are called (a) _Hypothesis_. Step 2 is to *identify* the treatment, which is called the (b) _indepent_; and to choose the behaviors or responses that will be observed to judge the effectiveness of the treatment. These behaviors or responses are called the (c) _Varible_. Step 3 is to *choose* subjects through a process called (d) _random selection_, which gives everyone in a sample population an equal chance of being selected. Step 4 is to *assign* subjects to different groups by random selection. The group that will receive the treatment is called the (e) _experiment_ and the group that undergoes everything but the treatment is called the (f) _control_. Step 5 is to *manipulate* the (g) _independent_ by administering it to the experimental but not the control group. Step 6 is to *measure* the effects of the independent variable on behaviors that have been selected as the (h) _dependent Variable_. Step 7 is to *analyze* the difference between the experimental and control groups by using (i) _Statistical_.

APPLYING/ EXPLORING: HUMAN SUBJECTS AND ANIMAL RESEARCH

Before you graduate, there is a good possibility that you will be asked to participate in a psychology experiment. For example, the above "Subjects Wanted" notices recently appeared on the Experimenter's Bulletin Board at my university, reflecting the demand for college students to serve as subjects in psychological research. Even if you are not going to be a subject, you may wonder what kinds of safeguards are used to protect subjects' rights and privacy.

Commonly Asked Questions about Being a Subject

Can partici- pating in an experi- ment cause me harm?

Will the experiment cause me harm or make me look dumb or foolish? It is unlikely that Rowland's experiments on hypnosis and potentially dangerous behaviors could be conducted today. That is because all experiments, especially those with the potential for causing psychological or physical harm, are now carefully screened by research committees. Experiments are not approved unless any potential damaging effects can be eliminated or counteracted. Counteracting potential harmful effects is usually done by thoroughly debriefing the subjects following the experiment. ***Debriefing*** includes explaining the purpose and method of the experiment, asking the subjects their feelings about having been in the experiment, and helping the subjects deal with possible doubts or guilt arising from their behaviors in the experiment.

Will I be fooled by the experi- menter?

Is it true that the experiment is never about what it says? The results of an experiment may be biased by subjects' expectations or self-fulfilling prophecies or by their efforts to make themselves look good or to please the experimenter. One way that researchers control for such biases is to use bogus procedures or instructions that prevent subjects from learning the experiment's true purpose. Another way to avoid bias from expectations is to keep both the researcher and the subject in the dark about the experiment's purpose. This is called a ***double-blind technique,*** which means that both researcher and subject are "blind" to the experiment's treatment or purpose.

Will my privacy be re- spected by the experi- menter?

How do I know that what I say or do will be kept private? The American Psychological Association (1981) has established a set of ethical guidelines that ensure a subject's right to privacy. Anything the subject says or does during the experimental procedure must be treated as strictly confidential and must never be made public without the subject's consent. When researchers publish data, they report numbers, not names. Ethical guidelines on the use of human subjects protect the rights, welfare, and privacy of subjects.

Pros and Cons of Using Animal Subjects

Besides using human subjects, psychologists use animals in research, primarily rats and mice (90%) and a very small percentage of other animals (cats, dogs, monkeys, birds) (Mesirow, 1984). We'll examine the justification of animals in research and the protection of their rights.

Are research animals mistreated? You may have seen a disturbing photo or heard about a laboratory animal being mistreated. The fact is, however, that of the millions of animals used in research, only a few cases of animal mistreatment have been confirmed. That is because scientists know that proper care and treatment of their laboratory animals is vital to the success of their research. To abolish the use of all laboratory animals because of one or two isolated cases of mistreatment would be like abolishing all medical practice because of isolated cases of malpractice. Instead, researchers suggest balancing the rights of animals with the needs for advancing the medical, physiological, and psychological health of humans.

Why should animals be used in research? According to Frederick King (King et al., 1988), the former chair of the American Psychological Association's Committee on Animal Research and Experimentation, animal research has resulted in major medical advances, the discovery of treatments for human diseases, and a better understanding of human disorders. Animal research led to the discovery of insulin and the development of virtually all modern vaccines against infectious diseases such as polio, measles, and hepatitis B. Researchers are currently using animals to study epilepsy, Huntington's disease, Parkinson's disease, fetal alcohol syndrome, schizophrenia, AIDS, and transplantation of brain tissue, none of which is possible with human subjects.

Who watches over the care and treatment of animals? Numerous government and university regulations ensure the proper care and humane treatment of laboratory animals. For example, the U. S. Department of Agriculture conducts periodic inspections of all animal research facilities to ensure proper housing and to oversee experimental procedures that might cause pain or distress. Universities hire veterinarians to regularly monitor the care and treatment of laboratory animals. Finally, universities have animal subject committees with authority to decide whether sufficient justification exists for using animals in specific research projects.

Should animals be used in research? There is continuing discussion among psychologists over the use of animals in research (Johnson, 1990, Ulrich, 1991). One of the basic issues is how to strike the right balance between animal rights and research needs. Based on past, present, and potential future benefits of animal research, many experts in the scientific, medical, and mental health communities believe that the *conscientious* use of animals in research is justified and should continue.

Thanks to animal research, they'll be able to protest 20.8 years longer.

According to the U.S. Department of Health and Human Services, animal research has helped extend our life expectancy by 20.8 years. Of course, how you choose to spend those extra years is up to you.

Foundation for Biomedical Research

The concerns raised by animal rights protestors need to be balanced against the health and medical benefits obtained from animal research.

Summary/Self-Test

METHODS OF SCIENCE

1. In answering a question or obtaining proof, at least three methods can be used. One method of obtaining proof is to collect statements that are based on an individual's personal experience and that support a certain viewpoint. These statements are called (a)_____. A second method of obtaining proof is to ask opinions of a large number of individuals; this procedure is called a (b)_____. A third method of obtaining proof is to conduct (c)_____ in a controlled laboratory setting or make observations according to the guidelines of the scientific method.

■ **One of your friends asks whether drinking coffee (caffeine) helps you study better? How could you answer this question?**

CASE STUDY: TESTIMONIALS

2. Testimonials have three potential sources of error and bias. One source comes from people's believing strongly or having a personal stake in something so that their (a)_____ may bias their perceptions and keep them unaware of other contributing factors. A second source of error comes from believing strongly that something will happen and then unknowingly acting in such a way to make that something occur; a phenomenon called (b)_____. A third source of error arises from many ongoing behaviors, thoughts, and feelings occurring together and becoming so tangled or (c)_____ that we cannot identify the significant one.

■ **Some people insist that they get hungry when their blood sugar drops. What are the problems with this statement?**

SURVEYS

3. One method psychologists use to measure the attitudes, beliefs, and behaviors of a large sample of individuals is by conducting a _____, which asks individuals to respond to a set of questions. One advantage of this method is that psychologists can quickly and efficiently collect information about a large number of people.

One disadvantage is that people may answer in a way that they think is more socially desirable.

■ **Suppose a recent survey found that people never lie to their best friends. Would you believe the survey?**

CORRELATION

4. If two or more events are associated or linked together, they are said to be (a)_____. The strength of this association is indicated by a number called the (b)_____, which has a range from –1.00 to +1.00. If there were a perfect association between two events such that when one increased, the other did also, this association would be called a (c)_____. If an increase in one event is usually but not always accompanied by an increase in a second event, this would be called a (d)_____. If an increase in one event is always accompanied by a decrease in a second event, this is called a (e)_____. If an increase in one event is usually, but not always, accompanied by a decrease in a second event, this is called a (f)_____.

5. Although a correlation indicates that two or more events are occurring in some pattern, a correlation does not identify which event may _____ the other(s).

■ **Your friend is convinced that every time she takes vitamins, she has more energy. What would you tell her?**

DECISIONS ABOUT DOING RESEARCH

6. Depending on the topic, psychologists may study it by using one or more of five commonly used research techniques. If psychologists ask questions about people's attitudes and behaviors, usually in a one-on-one situation, they are using (a)_____. If psychologists ask subjects to read a list of questions and indicate a specific answer, they are using a (b)_____. If they ask subjects to complete established tests that measure personality, intelligence, or other behaviors, they are using (c)_____. If psychologists study subjects' *behaviors* under carefully controlled conditions, they are conducting a (d)_____. If psychologists study the *internal responses* of the body or brain, they are recording (e)_____. Psychologists can study a problem using animals by developing an (f)_____, which closely approximates the human condition.

7. Psychologists conduct research in two common settings. If they answer questions by observing an individual's behaviors in his or her environment, without attempts to control or manipulate the situation, they would be using _____. The *advantage* of this method is that it gives information that would be difficult to obtain or duplicate in a laboratory. The *disadvantage* of this method is that the psychologists' own beliefs or values may bias their observations and cause them to misinterpret the behaviors under observation.

8. If psychologists study a single individual in considerable depth in his or her own environment, they are using a _____. The *advantage* of this method is that it results in detailed descriptions and insights into many aspects of an individual's life. The *disadvantage* is that the information obtained may be so unique that it does not apply to others.

9. If psychologists want to study individuals under controlled and systematic conditions, with many of the real-life factors removed, they use a _____. The *advantage* of this setting is that it permits great control and manipulation of many conditions while ruling out possible contaminating factors. The *disadvantage* of this setting is that it may be too artificial or controlled so that its results may not necessarily apply to real-life situations.

■ *You want to find out whether schizophrenia runs in families. How would you go about answering this question?*

EXPERIMENTS: SCIENTIFIC METHOD

10. The scientific method offers a set of rules or guidelines on how to conduct research with a minimum of error or bias. We have divided these guidelines into the seven steps. Step 1 is to ask a question in precise, concrete terms. Each question is called a (a)_____. Step 2 is to identify the treatment, which is called the (b)_____, and select the behaviors, which are called the (c)_____, that will be used to assess the effects of the treatment. Step 3 is to choose subjects so that each one in a sample has an equal chance of being selected. One procedure for doing so is called (d)_____. Step 4 is to assign subjects randomly to one of two groups. The group that will receive the treatment is called the (e)_____ and the group that will undergo everything but the treatment is called the (f)_____. Step 5 is to manipulate the (g)_____ by administering it (or one level of it) to the experimental group but not to the control group. Step 6 is to measure the effects of the independent variable on behaviors that have been selected as the (h)_____. Step 7 is to analyze differences between behaviors of subjects in the experimental group with those in the control group by using various (i)_____, which determine whether differences were due to the treatment or to chance occurrences.

■ *What's the best way to study for an exam? Should you cram material the night before the exam, or study during the week preceding the exam?*

APPLYING/EXPLORING: HUMAN SUBJECTS AND ANIMAL RESEARCH

11. One method of counteracting potential harmful effects to experimental subjects is by thoroughly _____ them. This includes explaining the purpose and method of the experiment, asking subjects about their feelings, and helping subjects deal with possible doubts or problems arising from the experiment.

12. The justification for using _____ in research is that it has resulted in major medical advances, treatments for diseases, and understanding of human disorders.

■ *What concerns might a student have about volunteering to be a subject in an experiment?*

Chapter *Two*
BIOLOGICAL BASES OF BEHAVIOR

MODULE 3
BUILDING BLOCKS OF THE BRAIN

Can a psychophysiologist read your mind?

Specific brain activity indicates when you are deciding to move a finger.

Imagine hearing the following boast: "In some sense, we have indeed been able to read our subjects' minds" (Coles, 1989, p. 262). You would expect this kind of statement to be made at a parapsychology meeting, not at the annual meeting of the Society for Psychophysiological Research. Members of this society, who study the relationship between psychological and physiological events, recognized this statement by their president, Michael Coles, as something unusual. Coles, a serious researcher, was not claiming extrasensory powers. Rather, he was claiming the ability to predict, with great accuracy, whether or not a person is thinking about moving a finger.

Coles discovered that immediately before you decide to make a voluntary movement, such as moving a finger, a burst of electrical activity occurs in your brain and signals that you are about to move your hand. Coles calls this electrical signal the *readiness potential*, which he thinks reflects specific brain activity related to "deciding to move" one's hand. (adapted from Coles, 1989)

What is happening when you are "deciding to move"?
What is fascinating about the readiness potential is that it occurs while you are "deciding to move" but milliseconds before you actually move. Although the readiness potential raises many interesting questions, at this point we focus on one: How do brain cells produce electrical activity? In answering this question, we journey inside a brain cell and explore its structure and function.

What's Coming

In this module we'll examine two groups of cells that are the building blocks of the brain and explain their structure and function. In the next module, we'll discuss the structure and function of the entire brain.

However, before we examine individual brain cells, it will help if you get the big picture and learn a little about the entire human brain.

The Big Picture: The Human Brain

One is both shocked and intrigued at first seeing a human brain, a structure that once contributed to someone's intelligence, humor, creativity, personality, and all that we value as human. The brain, which has a pinkish-white color, is a relatively small, melon-shaped structure that weighs about 1400 grams (less than 3 pounds) and has the consistency of firm Jell-O. One is surprised to learn that this structure, small enough to be cradled in two hands and fueled primarily by sugar (glucose), can surpass the thinking of highly sophisticated computers.

Brain and Mind

Is the mind the same as the brain?

This is one of the oldest questions in science. The **mind,** *which is not directly observable, is often defined as mental activities, such as feeling, thinking, learning, imagining, and dreaming.* The **brain,** *which is directly observable, is defined as a physical structure composed of membranes, fluids, and chemicals.* Some experts believe that the mind and the brain are totally separate entities that do not interact. Others believe that there is only the physical brain but that it has two aspects—electrochemical reactions and mental functions—that interact and influence each other. This text favors the latter definition and assumes an interaction between the mind's mental functions and the brain's physical functions.

Substance of the Brain

What is the brain made of?

If you were to look at a section of the human brain under a powerful microscope, you would observe hundreds of different-shaped cells. These cells can be divided into two groups—neurons and glial cells—that have different structures and functions.

Although neurons and glial cells can be considered the building blocks of the brain, we'll focus on neurons because of their key role in psychological functioning. Neurons allow us to receive sensory information and are involved in controlling muscles, regulating digestion, and secreting hormones, as well as in carrying out mental processes, such as thinking, imagining, dreaming, and remembering.

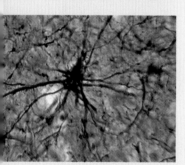

Neurons. One group of cells, called **neurons,** *have specialized extensions for the reception and transmission of electrical signals.* Neurons generate and transmit electrical signals over distances from a fraction of an inch to over 3 feet. We'll examine the neuron's structure and its ability to generate electrical signals that can race along at 200 miles per hour.

Glial cells. The second group of brain cells, called **glial cells,** *have at least three functions: they provide scaffolding to guide the growth of developing neurons and support mature neurons, they wrap themselves around neurons and form a kind of insulation to prevent interference from other electrical signals, and they release chemicals that influence a neuron's growth and function.* Of the approximately 100 billion brain cells, there are about ten times more glial cells than neurons.

Is the mind the same as the brain?

Development of Neurons

How do neurons begin?

Imagine that we place a single grain of sand on your desk and insist that inside this speck we have inserted a microscopic book with a million pages. A fertilized egg, which is about the size of a grain of sand, does contain the equivalent of a million pages of chemically coded instructions. Following these instructions, this single-celled fertilized egg will develop into billions of cells that grow into the human body and brain. From a single cell will develop the 100 billion neurons and glial cells that make up the mature human brain.

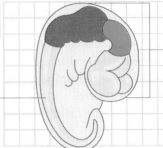

This tiny 3/8 inch curved structure is the approximate size of a 6-week-old human brain and spinal cord.

Spinal cord

This strange shape (greatly enlarged) will eventually develop into a mature brain containing 100 billion cells.

Can neurons be replaced?

Since we do know that neurons are indispensable to our physical and mental functioning, it would be comforting to know that we could always replace or regrow a damaged or diseased neuron. It would be comforting—but is it true?

Neurobiologist Fernando Nottebohm (1989) had always been fascinated by the song patterns of canaries. He knew that a mature male canary learns to sing a "breeding" song in the spring but that when breeding season is over, the song disappears from the canary's repertoire. During the next autumn, the canary must relearn the breeding song, which is accompanied by changes to its brain. During this relearning, two areas of the bird's brain that control singing increase dramatically—50% or more. The increase in size results from the formation of new neurons in the mature brain.

In these two areas of the mature canary's brain a 50% or more increase in size occurs because of growth of new neurons.

This remarkable discovery in canaries raised an interesting question: Do mature brains of primates (humans, chimpanzees, and monkeys) have the ability to develop new neurons? Pakso Rakic (1985) answered this question by studying neural growth and development in monkeys' brains, which are similar in development, structure, and function to human brains. He concluded that the primate brain, which includes that of monkeys, chimpanzees, gorillas, and humans, has developed the vast majority of its neurons by birth and that there is little growth of new neurons in the mature primate brain (Rakic, 1985).

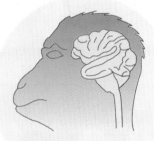

Neurons do not regrow in the mature primate brain.

The fact that the vast majority of neurons in the mature human brain are not replaced or regrown after damage explains why lasting behavioral deficits often follow brain damage or disease.

Now let's get a close-up view of some neurons, whose functions are critical to all our physical and mental functions.

Neuron Structure and Function

What do neurons look like?

Although neurons develop into wondrous shapes and many sizes, almost all share three basic structures.

1 A *cell body* keeps the neuron in working order and has specialized extensions that arise from it.

2 The *dendrites*, one group of extensions, receive information from the environment or from other neurons.

3 The *axon*, a single extension, transmits electrical signals to neighboring neurons, organs, or muscles.

Electrical activity from many thousands of neurons contributes to the distinct electrical activity that is associated with "deciding to move a hand." To help you visualize and understand the neuron's structure and function, we will examine each part of the neuron.

We'll look at a relatively large motor neuron because it clearly illustrates all three structures. Motor neurons make contact with and control muscles. As you turn the pages of this text, you are using thousands of motor neurons.

Dendrites (DEN-drites) *are branchlike extensions that arise from the cell body; they receive signals from other neurons, muscles, or sense organs and pass these signals to the cell body.* At the time of birth, a neuron has few dendrites. After birth, dendrites undergo dramatic growth that accounts for much of the increase in brain size. As dendrites grow, they make connections and form communication networks between neurons and other cells or organs.

The **axon** (AXE-on) *is a single threadlike structure that extends from and carries signals away from the cell body.* Here the axon is indicated by a line inside a tube. Axons vary in length from less than a hair's breadth to as long as 3 feet (from your spinal cord to your toes). The axon conducts electrical signals to a neighboring neuron, an organ, or, in our example, a muscle fiber.

The **cell body (or soma)** *is a relatively large, egg-shaped structure that provides fuel, manufactures chemicals, and maintains the entire neuron in working order.* In the center of the cell body is a small oval shape representing the **nucleus,** which contains the instructions (in the form of DNA) for the manufacture of chemicals and regulation of the neuron.

The **myelin** (MY-lin) **sheath** *is a tubelike structure of fatty material that wraps around and insulates an axon.* The myelin sheath prevents interference from electrical signals generated in adjacent axons. The axons of most large neurons, including motor neurons, have myelin sheaths. You may have heard the brain described as consisting of gray and white matter. Gray is the color of cell bodies, while white is the color of myelin sheaths.

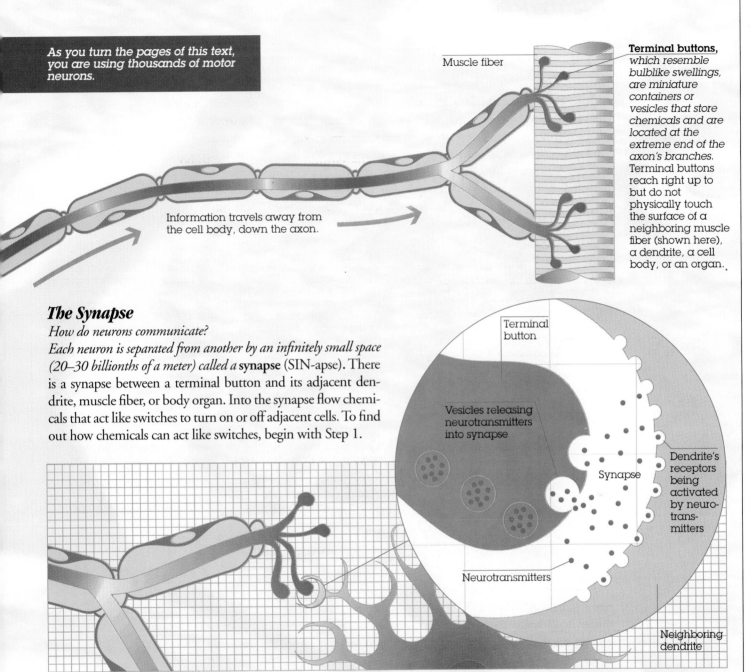

Muscle fiber

Terminal buttons, *which resemble bulblike swellings, are miniature containers or vesicles that store chemicals and are located at the extreme end of the axon's branches.* Terminal buttons reach right up to but do not physically touch the surface of a neighboring muscle fiber (shown here), a dendrite, a cell body, or an organ.

Information travels away from the cell body, down the axon.

The Synapse

How do neurons communicate?

Each neuron is separated from another by an infinitely small space (20–30 billionths of a meter) called a **synapse** *(SIN-apse). There is a synapse between a terminal button and its adjacent dendrite, muscle fiber, or body organ. Into the synapse flow chemicals that act like switches to turn on or off adjacent cells. To find out how chemicals can act like switches, begin with Step 1.*

Terminal button

Vesicles releasing neurotransmitters into synapse

Synapse

Dendrite's receptors being activated by neurotransmitters

Neurotransmitters

Neighboring dendrite

Step 1. Imagine thinking about moving your hand. At that moment, neurons in your brain are being excited. We'll focus on a single excited neuron to discover how it can excite a neighboring neuron.

Step 2. Electrical signals that began in the dendrites and cell body speed down the entire length of the axon and reach the terminal buttons.

Step 3. As you have just learned, terminal buttons contain tiny sacs or *vesicles* that are filled with chemicals. *Because these chemicals are produced by neurons and transmit information between neurons, they are called* **neurotransmitters.** When electrical signals reach the vesicles, they spill their neurotransmitters into the synapse.

Step 4. Once released, neurotransmitter molecules flow across the synapse and coat the surface of the adjacent muscle fiber, body organ, or (in our example) dendrite. Specialized areas on the surface of a dendrite, called *receptors*, are highly sensitive to the action of neurotransmitters. There are several kinds of neurotransmitters with different kinds of action. Some neurotransmitters turn on or *excite* receptors; others turn off or *inhibit* receptors. Most neurons secrete only one kind of neurotransmitter, either an excitatory or an inhibitory one. Thus, neurotransmitters act like chemical switches, either exciting or inhibiting adjacent neurons, muscle fibers, or body organs.

In the next section, we'll use this basic knowledge of the neuron's structure and function to explain a response that you have no doubt experienced—the instant withdrawal of your hand after touching a hot object.

Reflex Responses

Sequence: Reflex Triggered by Touching a Painful Stimulus

Why does your hand move without thinking?

If you accidentally touched a very hot kettle, your hand would instantly jerk away, without conscious thought or effort on your part. *This kind of unlearned, involuntary reaction to a stimulus is called a* **reflex.** You are born with a number of reflexes, such as the constriction of your pupil in response to a bright light, the jerk of your leg in response to a sharp tap below the knee, and the turning of your head in response to a loud noise, to name a few. In many cases, reflexes protect the body from harm. The fact that reflexes occur even in newborns indicates that certain neurons have been prewired to execute an automatic response to a certain stimulus. Let's examine some of the steps that go into executing a common reflex.

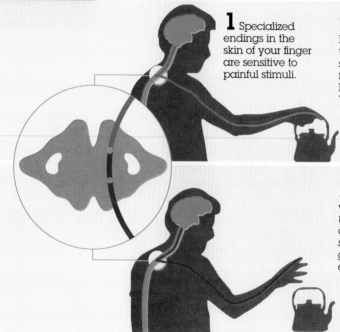

1 Specialized endings in the skin of your finger are sensitive to painful stimuli.

2 These endings are part of long dendritelike extensions that travel all the way to your spinal cord, a distance of 2 to 3 feet. When you touch a hot kettle, these extensions carry "pain" information, actually electrical signals, to the spinal cord. *Neurons that carry information from the senses to the spinal cord are called* **afferent** *(AFF-er-ent) or* **sensory neurons.** We'll use the term *sensory neuron.*

3 *Neurons that carry information away from the spinal cord and are involved in producing some response in muscles or organs are called* **efferent** *(EFF-er-ent) or* **motor neurons.** In our example, the motor neuron has a 2- to 3-foot-long axon that carries "movement information," actually electrical signals, back to the muscle from the spinal cord.

Here is the actual sequence: electrical signals travel down the axon and strike the terminal buttons, which spill their neurotransmitter into the synapse. The neurotransmitter flows across the synapse and switches on the receptors in the muscle fiber, causing the muscle to contract and the hand to withdraw from the hot kettle.

How fast are your reflexes?

The entire reflex, from touching the kettle to withdrawing your hand, occurs in a fraction of a second. The hand-withdrawal reflex occurs so quickly because it involves transferring information between only three neurons. In comparison, it takes much longer before you can yell "Ouch!" By the time you can yell (which requires transferring information between many thousands of neurons), your hand has already withdrawn from the hot kettle.

In trying to make the reflex response easy to understand, we took the liberty of referring to "pain" and "movement" information traveling in neurons. In fact, neurons carry only electrical signals. In the next section we will look inside an axon to see how it generates tiny electrical signals. In Module 5 we will explain how electrical signals must reach the brain and be interpreted before one can experience sensations of "pain" or "movement."

1

3 4

2

Check your knowledge of the neuron's structure and function by filling in the appropriate terms.

Neuron Structures

1. _____   5. _____
2. _____   6. _____
3. _____   7. _____
4. _____   8. _____
                     9. _____

neighboring dendrite.
transmitter; 9. receptor of
6. vesicle; 7. synapse; 8. neuro-
elin sheath; 5. terminal button;
body or soma; 3. axon; 4. my-
***Answers:** 1. dendrites; 2. cell*

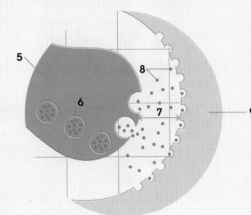

5

8

6

7

9

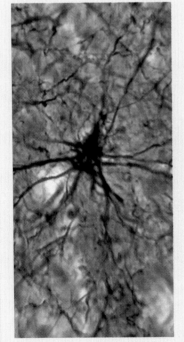

Neuron Functions

1. The structure that nourishes and maintains the entire neuron is the _____.

2. Branchlike extensions that receive signals from senses and environment are called _____.

3. A single threadlike extension that speeds signals away from the cell body toward a neighboring cell is the _____.

4. A tubelike structure that insulates the axon from interference of neighboring signals is the _____.

5. Tiny swellings at the very end of the axon are called _____.

6. Tiny packets that store neurotransmitters and are located at the very end of the axon are _____.

7. Between the terminal buttons of one neuron and the dendrites or cell body of a neighboring neuron is an extremely small space called the _____.

8. Into the synapse, vesicles release chemicals or _____, which excite or inhibit neighboring receptors.

9. If you touch a sharp object, your hand automatically withdraws because of a reflex response. Neurons that carry "painful" information into the spinal cord are called (a)_____ neurons. Neurons that carry information away from the spinal cord to muscles or organs are called (b)_____.

7. synapse; 8. neurotransmitters; 9. (a) sensory or afferent, (b) motor or efferent.
***Answers:** 1. cell body or soma; 2. dendrites; 3. axon; 4. myelin sheath; 5. terminal buttons; 6. vesicles;*

Axon Structure and Function

How does an axon, a microscopic threadlike extension, generate an electrical signal that can travel distances exceeding 3 feet at speeds approaching 200 miles per hour?

The answer involves tiny charged particles that move through the axon's membrane and generate a miniature electrical current. Let's examine this specialized membrane of the axon.

The Axon Membrane

Imagine the axon as a tubelike structure. The walls of the tube are composed of a thin membrane that is filled with and surrounded by a watery fluid. The axon's thin membrane has chemical gates that can be opened or closed by electrical current. For many complex reasons, some of the axon's "gates" are open and some are closed, allowing some chemical particles to enter and others to be kept out.

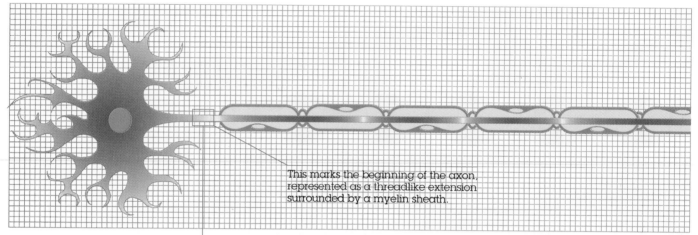

This marks the beginning of the axon, represented as a threadlike extension surrounded by a myelin sheath.

Think of the axon's membrane as having gates that can open and close to control the flow of chemical particles.

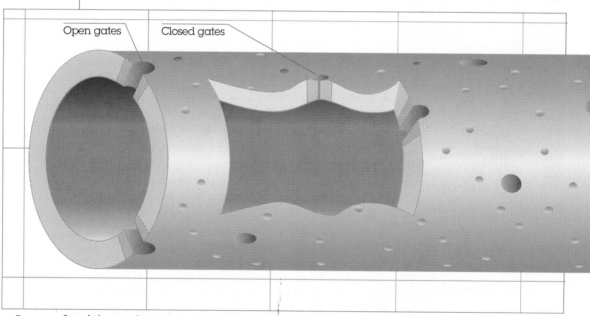

Open gates   Closed gates

Because of its ability to selectively regulate the flow of chemical particles, the membrane is said to be **semipermeable**. A common example of a semipermeable membrane is plastic wrap. If you have ever wrapped leftover pizza in plastic wrap and left it in your refrigerator overnight, your refrigerator no doubt smelled like pizza the next day. That's because plastic wrap seals in some molecules but lets out others.

Now, let's examine the chemical particles that are present in the fluid.

Ions

Ions *are chemical particles that have electrical charges.* The behavior of ions follows two ironclad rules: opposite-charged ions attract and like-charged ions repel. If you had magnetic toys when you were a child, you witnessed similar rules at work: toys with magnets of opposite forces were attracted and those with like forces were repelled.

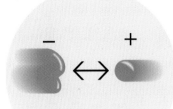

Oppositely charged ions are attracted.

Although the fluid inside the axon contains a number of different ions, we can explain its function by focusing on two ions: sodium ion, which has a positive charge and is abbreviated Na^+, and the larger protein ion, which has a negative charge and is abbreviated P^-.

Where are the ions?

Normally, an axon's fluid contains a number of ions, but we can more clearly explain how the axon produces an electrical signal by using only sodium and protein ions. Inside the axon are negative protein ions that are much too large to leave through the open membrane gate. Since negative protein ions are trapped inside, the *inside* of the membrane has a *negative charge*.

Outside the axon are numerous sodium ions that obey one of the ironclad rules: opposite charges attract. Following this rule, sodium ions are greatly attracted to the negatively charged proteins. However, working against this attraction, almost all the sodium ions are pumped outside the membrane by a process called the *sodium pump*. Because positive sodium ions are kept outside, the *outside* of the membrane has a *positive charge*.

Ready and Waiting: The Resting State

If the outside of the membrane has a positive charge, which is chiefly due to sodium ions, and the inside has a negative charge, which is due to protein ions, then an axon is said to be in the *resting state*. In the resting state, the axon is ready but is not actually generating an electrical signal. Think of the resting state as the buildup of an enormous positive force of sodium ions eager and waiting to enter the negatively charged interior. In the resting state the axon is similar to a fully charged battery that is not connected to anything. As soon as the positive and negative ends of the battery are connected, a current will flow. Similarly, as soon as something breaks open the axon's sodium gates, the sodium ions will rush inside.

Imagine that some sensory stimulus, such as touching a hot kettle, has started electrical signals that will eventually reach the neuron's axon. The axon in its resting state has a certain set point, or *threshold*. If electrical signals are strong enough to reach the axon's threshold, the axon will be activated. Think of the axon's threshold as like the setting on the thermostat of an air conditioner. Only if the temperature rises above the setting, or threshold, will the air conditioner come on.

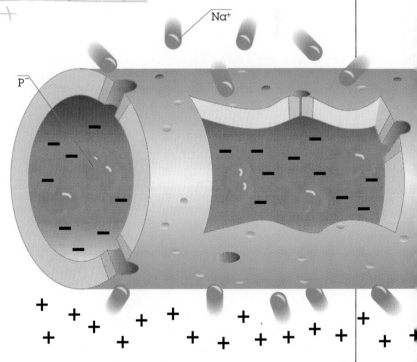

Because the outside of the axon's membrane has a positive (plus) charge and the inside has a negative (minus) charge, we know that the axon is in the resting state.

Axon Structure and Function

Conducting: The Action Potential and Nerve Impulse

Action potential

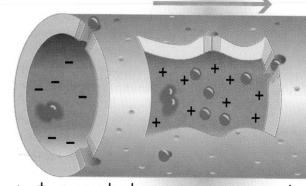

If the axon's threshold is reached, a tremendous amount of activity begins. All the sodium gates are opened, and many thousands of positively charged sodium ions that were kept outside now rush into the negatively charged interior. This great inward surge of sodium ions does two things: *it causes the inside of the axon to reverse its charge and become positive, and it generates a tiny electrical current that is called the* **action potential**. As the action potential travels down the axon, it is called a *nerve impulse*. Just as current flows when you connect the poles of a battery, current flows when sodium ions rush through the opened sodium gates.

The action potential is like a battery discharging. Notice that the outside of the membrane changes to negative and the inside to positive.

If you lit the beginning of a three-foot-long firecracker fuse, the flame would speed down the entire length. *In a similar fashion, an impulse starts in a small segment at the very beginning of the axon and, once begun, continues full strength to the very end; this phenomenon is referred to as the* **all-or-none law**. The all-or-none law applies only to the axon, since there is a gradual decrease in the strength of electrical signals as they spread across the dendrites and cell body.

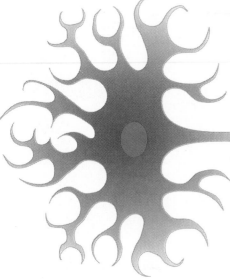

1 The nerve impulse starts in the beginning segment of axon. According to the all-or-none law, once started, the impulse speeds down the axon to its very end.

2 Notice that the myelin sheath has regular breaks where the axon is bare and uninsulated. It is at these bare points that the gates of the axon open and the impulse is generated.

3 The impulse literally jumps from break to break as it moves swiftly down the entire length of the axon. By this jumping action, an impulse can reach speeds approaching 200 miles per hour.

Why does a dentist give you an injection of novocaine?

The answer is that novocaine interfers with the conduction of the impulse in the neuron. Let's see how this happens.

If you were to have a tooth drilled without first having an injection of novocaine, you would experience varying degrees of pain. Signals from your tooth would travel along sensory nerves to your brain; once these signals reached your brain, they would be interpreted as pain. Rather than require you to tough it out, your dentist injects your gums with novocaine. Novocaine acts by blocking the membrane's sodium gates, thereby preventing sodium ions from entering the membrane. You feel relatively little pain because the novocaine essentially prevents pain signals from reaching the brain. Novocaine is classified as a local anesthetic, which means that it will reduce pain only in the area of injection.

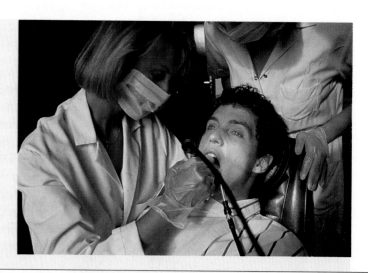

Neurotransmitters and Receptors

Much as a flame reaching the end of a fuse causes a firecracker to explode, a nerve impulse reaching the end of an axon causes a terminal button to explode. Steps 1 through 5 below explain what happens after the explosion.

In many ways, the action of a neurotransmitter on a receptor is similar to the action of a key in a lock. Just as a specific key fits only a matched lock, a specific neurotransmitter fits only a matched receptor. As an example, a specific neurotransmitter key released by a motor neuron's terminal button fits into the receptor's matching lock on a muscle fiber. If the neurotransmitter key opens the receptor's lock, the neurotransmitter is said to be *excitatory;* if the neurotransmitter key closes or blocks the receptor's lock, the neurotransmitter is said to be *inhibitory.* By opening or closing the receptor's lock, the muscle fiber is excited to or inhibited from contracting. All this action at the synapse occurs in less time than an eyeblink. It is through the secretion of specific neurotransmitter keys and their actions on matching receptors' locks that neurons are able to excite or inhibit other neurons, muscles, or body organs.

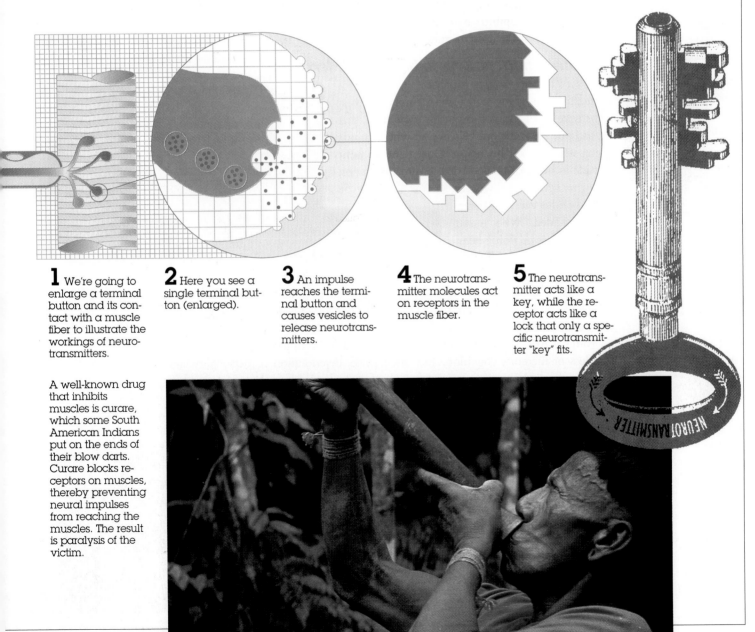

1 We're going to enlarge a terminal button and its contact with a muscle fiber to illustrate the workings of neurotransmitters.

2 Here you see a single terminal button (enlarged).

3 An impulse reaches the terminal button and causes vesicles to release neurotransmitters.

4 The neurotransmitter molecules act on receptors in the muscle fiber.

5 The neurotransmitter acts like a key, while the receptor acts like a lock that only a specific neurotransmitter "key" fits.

A well-known drug that inhibits muscles is curare, which some South American Indians put on the ends of their blow darts. Curare blocks receptors on muscles, thereby preventing neural impulses from reaching the muscles. The result is paralysis of the victim.

Neurotransmitters and Receptors

Neurotransmitters by the Dozen

How many different neurotransmitter keys does the brain use in unlocking the receptors of dendrites, cell bodies, muscles, or organs?

So far researchers have identified about a dozen chemicals that have all the characteristics of neurotransmitters and another 40 to 50 chemicals that influence communication between neurons but do not have all the characteristics of true neurotransmitters. Researchers continue to discover new neurotransmitters in the brain. Whatever the final count, each neurotransmitter has a single function: it either excites or inhibits adjacent neurons, muscles, or organs.

A neurotransmitter's ability to excite or inhibit makes possible different and even opposite reactions. For example, one neurotransmitter increases heart rate, another decreases it; some neurotransmitters are involved in sleeping, others are involved in waking; some in feelings of hunger, others in feelings of fullness; and so on. One of the newly discovered neurotransmitters, called endorphin, is a powerful painkiller that functions like morphine. We will discuss endorphins in Module 9.

For now, let's examine what happens when a part of the brain is deprived of its normal supply of a neurotransmitter.

Neurotransmitters: Keys to Brain Disorders

Why did Tom forget who he was?

Something was wrong with Tom's memory. The first signs were that he forgot to put his tools away, that he had put the kettle on the stove, or where he was going when he left his house. One night he went outside in his pajamas and tried to direct traffic on the street. Most terrifying of all was the time he turned on his wife of 40 years and demanded, "Who are you and what are you doing here? This is my house." His wife

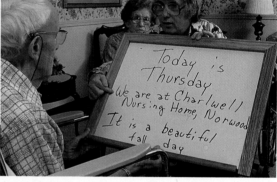

Why did Tom forget what day it was?

answered, "Honey, I'm your wife, and I have a right to be here." Tom said, "No, you are not my wife." As Tom's condition worsened, he had to be hospitalized. Now, at age 73, he lies on his back in a hospital bed, not recognizing his wife or his doctor and unaware of who he is (*San Diego Union*, August 9, 1981).

Due to loss of neurotransmitters, a patient in the advanced stages of Alzheimer's disease may not know the day, place, or season.

Tom has Alzheimer's (ALTS-hi-mers) disease, whose symptoms include a progressive loss of memory, cognition, and intelligence, deterioration of personality, and eventual death. Alzheimer's is not the result of normal aging but rather is caused by a number of problems in the brain. One such problem is a steady reduction in the supply of a particular neurotransmitter (acetylcholine) from a particular brain area (the hippocampus). As a result, there are fewer and fewer neurotransmitter keys to open receptors' locks. In turn, there is a progressive decline in communication between neurons and increased behavioral, cognitive, and personality problems. This disease affects 5%–15% of people over the age of 65, including half of all nursing home residents, and is now the nation's fourth largest killer (about 100,000 deaths per year). Researchers are searching for causes of and cures for Alzheimer's disease (Selkoe, 1990).

A new technique with great potential for treating neurotransmitter deficits is the transplant of healthy brain tissue, which is discussed at the end of this module. Much hope rides on brain transplants because neurons in the brain do no regrow or regenerate if damaged. However, you will discover that other nerves in the body are remarkably good at regeneration.

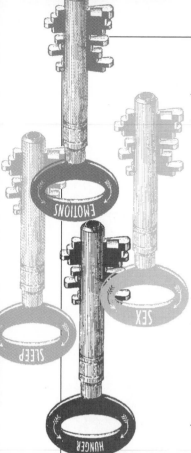

Neurotransmitters function like keys that open receptors' locks. Different neurotransmitters are involved in different behaviors, such as hunger, sleep, emotions, and sex.

CONCEPT/ GLOSSARY:
Neuron States and Neurotransmitters

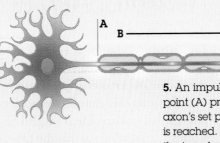
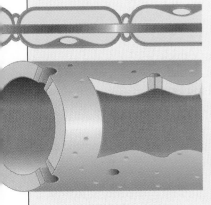

1. The axon's membrane has gates that can be opened or closed to regulate the flow of chemicals. Chemicals that have electrical charges are called (a)___ions___, which obey two rules: opposite charges attract and like charges repel. Because the membrane has gates that selectively regulate the flow of chemicals, the membrane is said to be (b)___semipermeable___.

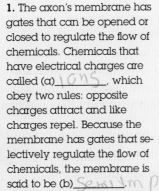

2. The fluid of the axon contains a number of ions, but we have focused on only two. A negatively charged ion that is given the symbol "P" is (a)___protein___. A positively charged ion that is given the symbol "Na" is (b)___sodium___.

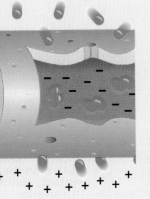

3. If the axon membrane is like a charged battery, it is said to be in the (a)___resting___. During this state, the outside of the membrane has a positive charge because most of the ions outside the membrane are positively charged (b)___sodium___ ions; the inside of the membrane has a negative charge because of the negatively charged (c)___protein___ ions. In the resting state, the axon is not conducting the impulse.

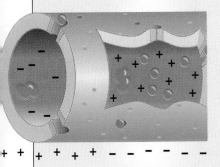

4. If the axon membrane is like a battery discharging, it is said to have an (a)___action___. During this state, all the (b)___sodium___ gates have opened, allowing positively charged ions to rush inside. This inrush generates a tiny (c)___current___ and also gives the inside of the membrane a (d)___positive___ charge while the outside of the membrane has a (e)___negative___ charge. As the action potential moves down the axon, is it called an (f)___impulse___.

5. An impulse usually begins at point (A) provided that the axon's set point or (a)___threshold___ is reached. Once this occurs, the impulse travels full strength from the beginning to the end of the axon; this phenomenon is referred to as the (b)___all-or-none___. This law applies only to the axon, not to the cell body or dendrites.

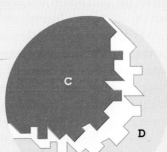

6. Structure (C) is a key that represents a specific (a)___NT___, which can open matching lock (D). Lock (D) represents a (b)___recept___, which may be located on the surface of a dendrite, a cell body, a muscle, or an organ.

7. A neurotransmitter is said to be (a)___excit___ if it opens a receptor's lock; a neurotransmitter is said to be (b)___inhib___ if it blocks a receptor's lock.

8. Researchers have identified about a dozen chemicals that have all the characteristics of _____ and another 40 to 50 chemicals that influence communication between neurons. Each of the dozen chemicals has a single function: either to excite or to inhibit adjacent neurons, muscles, or organs.

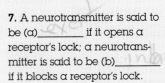
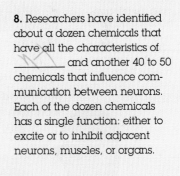

Answers: 1. (a) ions, (b) semipermeable; 2. (a) protein, (b) sodium; 3. (a) resting state, (b) sodium, (c) protein; 4. (a) action potential, (b) sodium, (c) current, (d) positive, (e) negative, (f) impulse or nerve impulse; 5. (a) threshold, (b) all-or-none law; 6. (a) neurotransmitter, (b) receptor; 7. (a) excitatory, (b) inhibitory; 8. neurotransmitters.

Neurons, Nerves, and the Nervous System

Is that really a toe?

I was tired and grumpy as I waited for the plane to take off. The man next to me said, "Hi, I'm Herb," and didn't stop talking for the next ten minutes. "I've just come from my doctor and I'm flying home and I'm real proud of my new thumb."

Still grumpy but now interested, I looked at his new thumb. It looked a little thick but not that unusual. Herb wiggled his thumb and continued, "Well, it's not actually a thumb, it's my big toe that the Doc transplanted. I cut off my thumb and the Doc said my toe would do almost as well. Just look at what I can do. I can move it, hold things, and got almost all my feeling back."

The reason that the doctor was able to replace Herb's severed thumb with a big toe has to do with the difference between neurons and nerves. As you know, neurons are cells that have specialized extensions that can generate electrical signals and transmit information to adjacent neurons, muscles, or organs. *Neurons are located in the brain and spinal cord, which together are called the* **central nervous system**. One unfortunate characteristic of neurons is their inability to regrow or regenerate if they are damaged or diseased. For this reason, individuals with brain damage or spinal cord injury often sustain lasting physical or psychological deficits.

However, researchers are currently developing new ways to stimulate the regeneration of neurons in the central nervous system. For example, axons that had been damaged and would normally wither and die have been made to regrow and make new connections when provided with tubes that guide their growth or if injected with growth-producing chemicals (Aguayo, 1985; Davis et al., 1987). Stimulating the growth of neurons in the central nervous system is an exciting new area that holds hope for treating brain and spinal cord damage.

In contrast to neurons, **nerves** *are stringlike bundles of axons and dendrites that are held together by connective tissue. Nerves are located throughout the body and make up the* **peripheral nervous system**. Nerves carry information from the senses, skin, muscles, and body's organs *to* the brain and spinal cord, and they carry information *from* the brain and spinal cord to regulate muscles, organs, and glands throughout the body.

One amazing characteristic of nerves is their ability to regrow, regenerate, or reattach if severed or damaged. Because of this characteristic, severed fingers can be successfully reattached, and Herb's big toe could be used to replace his severed thumb. Since nerves in the peripheral nervous system can regrow, both movement and feeling return to reattached fingers, as occurred with Herb's transplanted toe.

You will learn much more about nerves and the nervous system in the next module. With your current knowledge, you can understand an uncomfortable experience that you've probably had and a potentially dangerous eating experience that you'll wish to avoid.

Both of John Thompson's arms were torn off in a farm accident. He managed to pull himself to the farmhouse and dial for help with a pencil clenched in his teeth. Doctors reattached both arms, and John is already able to raise his left arm about a month after surgery. That's because nerves in the peripheral nervous system have the capacity to regrow.

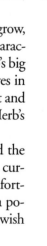

Neurons located in the brain and spinal cord do not normally have the capacity to regrow if damaged.

Nerves, which are located outside the brain and spinal cord, have the capacity to regrow if damaged.

What causes my leg to fall asleep?

Let's imagine that you are engrossed in a thrilling movie and do not realize that you are holding your legs tightly crossed. When the movie ends and you try to move, one of your legs has no feeling. What has happened? Holding your legs tightly crossed has put pressure on the nerves that travel near the surface of the leg. This pressure prevents electrical signals in the dendrites and axons from reaching the spinal cord; thus, your leg has "no feeling" and is difficult to move. A few seconds after removing the pressure, electrical signals flow to your spinal cord and you experience intense tingling in your leg as it "wakes up."

Can eating fish kill you?

Various organs of the Japanese puffer fish contain a deadly poison (tetrodotoxin). In preparing the fish for human consumption (cost of meal in American dollars: $160 to $450), a chef must carefully remove these organs so that none of the poison infects

Will this fish poison you?

the part of the fish to be eaten. If you were to eat a puffer fish whose poison-containing organs had not been properly removed, the effect would be numbness, paralysis of respiratory muscles—and almost certain death. This particular poison acts to block sodium gates in nerves controlling the respiratory muscles; as a result, respiratory muscles stop functioning, breathing stops, and death results.

Certain species of puffer fish have organs that contain a deadly poison that affects nerves that control respiratory muscles. Shortly after consuming the poison, you would experience numbness, paralysis of respiratory muscles, and almost certain death.

We began this module by discussing the readiness potential and asking how brain cells can generate electrical activity. Remember that the readiness potential is electrical activity that occurs while you are "deciding to move" but some milliseconds before you actually move a finger or hand. With what you now know of the neuron's structure and function, you can explain how electrical activity is generated. The process of "deciding to move" involves activity in many thousands of neurons, each one generating a tiny electrical current. The combined electrical activity from the dendrites, cell bodies, and axons of thousands of neurons results in a particular kind of brain wave called the readiness potential. When we discuss different kinds of electrical brain waves recorded during sleep and wakefulness in Module 9, you will know that these waves represent the electrical activity coming from millions of neurons.

APPLYING/ EXPLORING: BRAIN TRANSPLANT— NEW TREATMENT FOR PARKINSON'S DISEASE

The tremors started in his right arm, but Charles shrugged them off. Perhaps he had pulled a muscle. He was 49 years old and in good health, so why worry about some muscle shakes? Besides, the problem was only with his right arm. But he did begin to worry when his arm became rigid and unmovable for short periods of time. He worried more when rarely a day went by without some tremors or periods of rigidity in his arm. Then, as if a nightmare were coming true, the symptoms became worse and spread throughout his body. One moment Charles would be in what is called an "on" period: he would be able to move and control his limbs. The next moment he might be in an "off" period: he would be rigid and frozen in time and space. There was no doubt about his problem. Charles had all the symptoms of Parkinson's disease, including the rigidity and tremors in his right arm and, worst of all, the sudden switch from an on to an off period, from mobility to rigidity. Charles was placed on medication, called L-dopa, that controls but does not cure the symptoms of Parkinson's.

Even on his medication, Charles's symptoms grew worse. During the on periods, Charles moved about in a relatively normal way. Then, without warning, Charles would enter an off period and become rigid. For almost a year before his operation, Charles spent 40% to 50% of his day in off periods, frozen and immobile. His medication was not controlling his symptoms and his life had become a nightmare. (adapted from Lindvall et al., 1990)

In Parkinson's disease, there are "on" periods during which the person moves in a relatively normal fashion. Then, without warning, comes an "off" period during which the person becomes rigid and immobile, as if frozen in time and space.

Charles had **Parkinson's disease,** *which results in movement problems when neurons in an area of the forebrain, called the basal ganglia, do not receive a sufficient supply of the neurotransmitter dopamine (DOPE-ah-mean).* Without dopamine, the basal ganglia can no longer regulate muscles; the result is "on" and "off" periods of muscle tremors and rigidity.

Because medication no longer controlled his symptoms, Charles chose an experimental operation that had proved successful in reducing Parkinson-like symptoms in rats and monkeys. Using animal models, researchers had established that fetal brain cells survive, grow, and function when transplanted into adult animals (Bjorklund & Stenevi, 1979; Gage et al., 1984; Norman et al., 1989; Redmond et al., 1988). Charles's operation involved taking healthy nervous tissue from the basal ganglia of a fetal brain and transplanting it into the basal ganglia of his brain.

Human Fetal Brain Transplant

A Swedish research team, headed by Ollie Lindvall, has published the first complete report describing a significant reduction in Parkinson's symptoms following a human fetal brain transplant (Lindvall et al., 1990). Lindvall's research team dissected dopamine-producing cells from the midbrain of a fetus that had been aborted. Using the procedure that we will describe, Lindvall's team transplanted the human fetal cells into the basal ganglia of Charles's brain.

Procedure. The procedure used to transplant fetal cells into a precise location in either animal or human brains is called the **stereotaxic procedure.** In this procedure the neurosurgeon fixed Charles's head inside a holder, as shown below. Next, the surgeon removed part of the skull and exposed the top of Charles's brain. The surgeon attached a syringe to the holder (far left) that contained fetal tissue. A thin needle or cannula extended down from the syringe and entered Charles's brain. The surgeon had previously calculated the location of the left basal ganglia in the brain. Using these measurements, the surgeon lowered the cannula into that area. Finally, the surgeon injected the

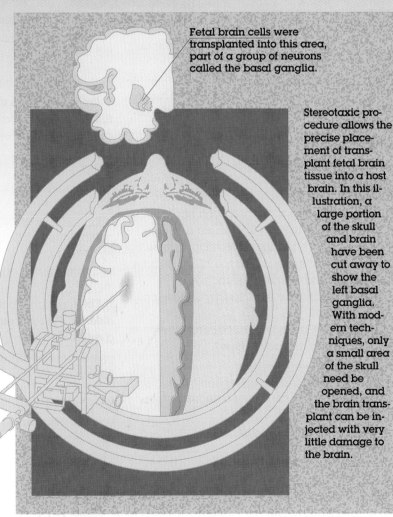

Fetal brain cells were transplanted into this area, part of a group of neurons called the basal ganglia.

Stereotaxic procedure allows the precise placement of transplant fetal brain tissue into a host brain. In this illustration, a large portion of the skull and brain have been cut away to show the left basal ganglia. With modern techniques, only a small area of the skull need be opened, and the brain transplant can be injected with very little damage to the brain.

human fetal cells into the left basal ganglia. The advantages of the stereotaxic procedure are that it causes relatively little damage to

the brain and that it pinpoints locations in the brain that can either be injected or, in other cases, destroyed.

Results. Before surgery, Charles had suffered severe rigidity in his right arm. Five months after transplant surgery, Lindvall and his colleagues reported that Charles had experienced significantly reduced rigidity and increased mobility in his right arm. Before surgery, Charles had spent 40% to 50% of his day in the immobile or off period. Five months after surgery, Charles had only one or two off periods per day. In addition, a PET scan revealed an increased amount of dopamine in the basal ganglia of Charles's brain, which indicated that the transplanted fetal cells were producing dopamine. Lindvall concluded that human fetal neurons can survive, grow, and restore lost dopamine, all of which contribute to a decrease in Parkinson's symptoms. Lindvall will follow Charles's progress to determine how long the fetal cells will survive and function.

Significance. As you know, diseased or damaged neurons in the adult human brain do not usually regrow or regenerate. The use of fetal brain transplants represents one of the few ways that diseased or damaged neurons can be replaced in the mature human brain. If fetal brain transplant proves successful, it will open up a new way of treating currently incurable brain diseases, such as Parkinson's.

Summary/Self-Test

THE BIG PICTURE: THE HUMAN BRAIN

1. The brain is composed of millions of cells that can be divided into two groups. In one group are cells that have specialized extensions for receiving and transmitting information. These cells, which are called (a)_____, are involved in communicating with other neurons, receiving sensory information, and regulating muscles, glands, and organs. The other group of cells provide the scaffolding to guide and support neurons, insulate neurons, and release chemicals that influence neuron functions. These cells are much more numerous than neurons and are called (b)_____.

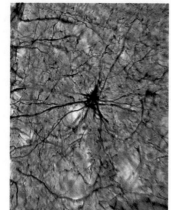

■ *You are given a tiny piece of tissue. How would you know whether the tissue came from brain or muscle?*

DEVELOPMENT OF NEURONS

2. There is a major difference between the growth of neurons in a human brain and in the brain of a bird. The mature (a)_____ brain is generally not capable of developing new neurons and has almost all its neurons present at the time of birth. The mature (b)_____ brain has the capacity to develop new neurons.

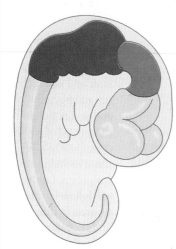

■ *Why is having a car with airbags for driver and passenger a real advantage?*

NEURON STRUCTURE AND FUNCTION

3. Although neurons come in wondrous shapes and sizes, they all share three structures. The structure that maintains the entire neuron in working order, manufactures chemicals, and provides fuel is called the (a)_____. The structure that has many branchlike extensions that receive signals from other neurons, muscles, or organs and conducts these signals to the cell body is called a (b)_____. The single threadlike extension that leaves the cell body and carries signals to other neurons, muscles, or organs is called the (c)_____. At the very end of this structure are individual swellings that are called (d)_____; they contain tiny vesicles filled with (e)_____.

4. Surrounding most axons is a fatty material called the (a)_____. This material acts like (b)_____ and prevents interference from electrical signals traveling in neighboring axons.

5. Neurons do not make physical contact with one another or with other organs. Instead, there is an infinitely small space between a neuron's terminal buttons and neighboring dendrites, cell body, or other organs. This space is called the (a)_____. When an axon's terminal buttons secrete a neurotransmitter, it flows across this space and affects the (b)_____ on the neighboring membrane.

■ *From your Brain Catalog, you want to order all the parts to make a 3-foot-long neuron. What should you order?*

REFLEX RESPONSES

6. The movement of automatically withdrawing your hand after touching a hot plate is called a (a)_____, which involves several or more neurons. Information is carried to the spinal cord by the (b)_____ neuron. Information is carried from the spinal cord to the muscle by the (c)_____ neuron.

■ *The tennis instructor says that you have quick reflexes. Can you explain what happens during a reflex?*

AXON STRUCTURE AND FUNCTION

7. If the axon is ready but not conducting an impulse, the axon is said to be in the (a)_____ state. In this state, most of the positively charged (b)_____ ions are on the outside of the membrane and all the negatively charged (c)_____ ions are trapped inside. Because the membrane can regulate the flow of ions by opening and closing gates, the membrane is said to be (d)_____. In the resting

state, the outside of the membrane has a (e)_____ charge compared to the (f)_____ charge on the inside.

8. If a stimulus activates a neuron's dendrites, the excitation will spread to the cell body and then to the axon. If the excitation is strong enough to reach the axon's (a)_____, an impulse will start in this beginning segment. Once this happens, all the sodium gates open, sodium ions rush inside, and this inrush generates a tiny electrical current called the (b)_____. During an impulse, the inside of the axon's membrane has a (c)_____ charge compared to the (d)_____ charge on the outside.

9. Once the impulse starts in the beginning segment of the axon, it will continue full strength to its very end. This phenomenon is called the

_____.

■ *How is the structure and function of the axon like that of a battery?*

NEUROTRANSMITTERS AND RECEPTORS

10. When the impulse reaches the terminal buttons at the end of the axon, it causes the terminal buttons to secrete (a)_____ that was stored in the vesicles. The neurotransmitter functions like a key to unlock the (b)_____ on neighboring neurons, muscles, or other organs. The brain contains about a dozen different neurotransmitters. Neurotransmitters are said to be (c)_____ if they activate neighboring cells or organs; they are said to be (d)_____ if they decrease activity in neighboring cells or organs. Because of these different actions, neurotransmitters can cause different and even opposite actions in neurons, muscles, or organs.

■ *One of the more scary and deadly weapons of war is nerve gas. How do you suppose nerve gas works?*

NEURONS, NERVES, AND THE NERVOUS SYSTEM

11. There are major differences between neurons and nerves. Neurons are cells with specialized extensions and are located in the brain and spinal cord. The brain and spinal cord together are referred to as the (a)_____ nervous system. Nerves are stringlike bundles of (b)_____ and (c) _____, which are held together by connective tissue. Nerves, which are located outside the brain and spinal cord, are part of the (d)_____ nervous system. Nerves carry information back and forth between the body and the brain and spinal cord. In the central nervous system, if a neuron is damaged, it does not have the capacity to (e)_____. In the peripheral nervous system, if a (f)_____ is cut or damaged, it has the capacity to regrow or regenerate.

■ *The headline read, "Chimp brain transplanted into human skull." Is this possible or pure fiction?*

APPLYING/EXPLORING: BRAIN TRANSPLANT—NEW TREATMENT FOR PARKINSON'S DISEASE

12. In a new, experimental operation, fetal brain cells were transplanted into a host brain by using a technique called the (a)_____ procedure. Unlike cells from a mature brain, cells from fetal brains will grow and make connections when transplanted into a host brain. It is hoped that transplanted brain tissue will prove effective in treating diseases of the nervous system, such as (b)_____, which is caused by progressive destruction of neurons in the basal ganglia.

■ *Why is there so much hope and excitement for developing methods to transplant brain tissue?*

Answers: 1. (a) neurons, (b) glial cells; 2. (a) human, (b) bird; 3. (a) cell body or soma, (b) dendrite, (c) axon, (d) terminal buttons, (e) neurotransmitter; 4. (a) myelin sheath, (b) insulation; 5. (a) synapse, (b) receptors; 6. (a) reflex or reflex response, (b) sensory or afferent, (c) motor or efferent; 7. (a) resting, (b) sodium, (c) protein, (d) semipermeable, (e) positive, (f) negative; 8. (a) threshold, (b) impulse or action potential, (c) positive, (d) negative; 9. all-or-none law; 10. (a) neurotransmitter, (b) receptors, (c) excitatory, (d) inhibitory; 11. (a) central, (b) axons (c) dendrites, (d) peripheral, (e) regrow or regenerate, (f) nerve; 12. (a) stereotaxic, (b) Parkinson's disease.

MODULE 4
THE INCREDIBLE NERVOUS SYSTEM

I can see the clock but why can't I tell the time?

Something happened to Steve's brain that prevented him from telling time.

As I walked into the hotel, I felt an incredible pain in my head. I am 28 years old, a successful journalist, in excellent health, but something terrible is happening. It takes great effort to talk to the registration clerk. My room isn't ready and I'll have to wait. I move slowly across the hotel lobby and sit in a high-backed chair. When will my room be ready? I glance at the clock on the wall. I can see the hands of the clock, but no matter how hard I stare at the hands I cannot figure out the time. Like a small child, I say out loud to myself, "The big hand is on twelve and the little hand is on eight." As I hear myself describing the position of the hands, I figure out that it is 8 o'clock. I am startled to discover that I can tell time by sound but not by sight.

"Steve Fishman!" The registration clerk calls my name and it means my room is ready. I glance down to pick up my suitcase and notice that one of my shoelaces is untied. As I have done a thousand times, I reach down and pick up the loose laces. For some reason, when I look at my fingers, I can't make them move in the right sequence to tie my shoes. I close my eyes to try to calm myself. Without looking at my fingers, I try again. Somehow my fingers move automatically in the right sequence and my shoelaces are tied. I can tie my shoelaces by touch but not by sight. (adapted from Fishman, 1988)

Why were some of Steve's behaviors intact and others strangely disrupted? Why was he unable to tell time or tie his shoelaces by sight but able to hear, walk, talk, touch, and see? We will answer these questions as we investigate the many structures and functions of the brain.

We tend to think of the brain, and perhaps the spinal cord, as the nervous system. However, the human nervous system is much more complex. As you look at the diagram on the left, notice that the nervous system has two major divisions, the central and peripheral nervous systems. In turn, the peripheral nervous system has four subdivisions. Later we'll explain each nervous system and division, but for now you should just note its organization.

What's Coming

In this module, we'll explain the structure and function of the entire brain. As we do, you'll understand why some of Steve's behaviors were intact while others were strangely disrupted.

Organization of the human nervous system.

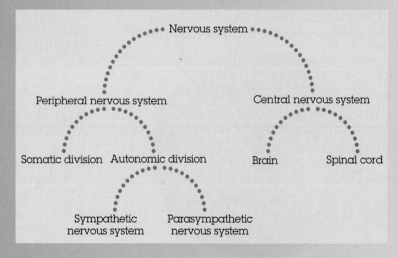

Nervous system

Peripheral nervous system

Central nervous system

Somatic division   Autonomic division

Brain   Spinal cord

Sympathetic nervous system   Parasympathetic nervous system

The Central and Peripheral Nervous Systems

The Central Nervous System

You are capable of some highly complex responses—thinking, imagining, conversing, being conscious of your own existence—and of hundreds of more ordinary responses—moving, sensing, perceiving—because of the brain and spinal cord. *The brain and spinal cord make up one major part of the nervous system,* the **central nervous system**. Later in this module, we'll explain the structure and function of the brain. The *spinal cord* is about as thick as a big thumb (1 inch in diameter) and about 16 to 18 inches long. Inside the spinal cord are neurons and bundles of axons and dendrites that carry information back and forth between the brain and the body. Extending from the spinal cord are a series of spinal nerves that belong to the second major part of the nervous system, the peripheral nervous system.

Dancer Bill T. Jones illustrates the incredible functions of the human nervous system.

The Peripheral Nervous System

You are able to move your muscles, receive sensations from your body, and perform many other responses because of the peripheral nervous system. The **peripheral nervous system** *includes all the nerves outside the brain and spinal cord.* The peripheral nervous system in turn comprises two parts: the somatic and autonomic systems.

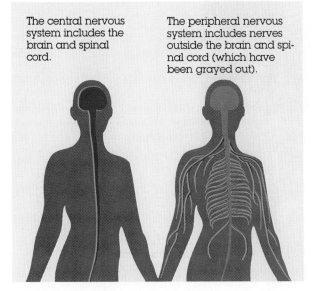

The central nervous system includes the brain and spinal cord.

The peripheral nervous system includes nerves outside the brain and spinal cord (which have been grayed out).

One part of your peripheral nervous system, called the **somatic nervous system**, *consists of a network of ropelike nerves that are connected either to sensory receptors or to muscles that you can move voluntarily, such as muscles in your limbs, back, neck, and chest.* Nerves in the somatic nervous system usually contain two kinds of fibers. *Afferent fibers* carry information from sensory receptors in the skin, muscles, and other organs to the spinal cord and brain. *Efferent fibers* carry information from the brain and spinal cord to the muscles.

It is the somatic nervous system that allows dancer Bill Jones to control the muscles in his arms, legs, and body and execute his complex leaps and turns.

The Central and Peripheral Nervous Systems

The Autonomic Nervous System

The second part of the peripheral nervous system, called the **autonomic nervous system,** *regulates heart rate, breathing, blood pressure, digestion, secretion of hormones, and other functions.* Much of the time the autonomic nervous system functions without any conscious effort or thought on your part. In fact, only a few responses controlled by the autonomic nervous system can also be controlled voluntarily, such as eyeblink and breathing.

The autonomic nervous system also consists of two parts: the sympathetic and parasympathetic nervous systems.

The Sympathetic Nervous System

Imagine 6-foot 6-inch, 195-pound Michael Jordan in the heat of a playoff game making one of his outrageous layup shots. Michael's heart is pounding, his blood pressure is up, his mouth is dry, his breathing is fast and shallow, and his entire body is aroused by the secretion of excitatory hormones from his adrenal glands. All these responses, which put Michael's body in a state of heightened physiological arousal, are controlled by the part of his autonomic nervous system called the sympathetic nervous system. The **sympathetic nervous system,** *which is triggered by threatening or challenging physical or psychological stimuli, increases the body's physiological arousal.*

We can guess that the sympathetic system originally helped cave people fight or flee when threatened by saber-toothed tigers. The **fight-or-flight response,** *which is increased physiological arousal caused by activation of the sympathetic system, helps people cope with and survive threatening situations.* Although there are no saber-toothed tigers around today, our sympathetic systems can be triggered by threatening or challenging physical situations, such as sporting events or automobile accidents, and by threatening or challenging psychological stimuli, such as exams or disagreements.

The Parasympathetic Nervous System

Some time after a basketball game, Michael Jordan's breathing, heart rate, and blood pressure return to normal, his palms stop sweating, his mouth becomes moist, and digestion becomes possible. The **parasympathetic nervous system,** *which is the other part of the autonomic nervous system, returns the body to a calmer, relaxed state and is involved in digestion.* When you are feeling relaxed and peaceful, your parasympathetic system is functioning. Various techniques to induce relaxation are actually methods to activate the parasympathetic system, which in turn calms your body.

The "adrenaline rush" is produced by the sympathetic nervous system.

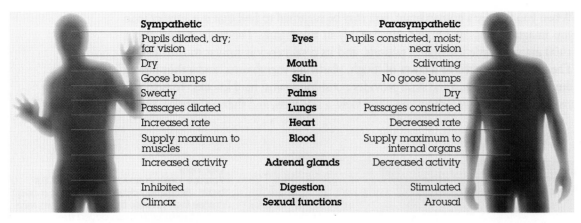

	Sympathetic		Parasympathetic
	Pupils dilated, dry; far vision	**Eyes**	Pupils constricted, moist; near vision
	Dry	**Mouth**	Salivating
	Goose bumps	**Skin**	No goose bumps
	Sweaty	**Palms**	Dry
	Passages dilated	**Lungs**	Passages constricted
	Increased rate	**Heart**	Decreased rate
	Supply maximum to muscles	**Blood**	Supply maximum to internal organs
	Increased activity	**Adrenal glands**	Decreased activity
	Inhibited	**Digestion**	Stimulated
	Climax	**Sexual functions**	Arousal

Homeostasis

Throughout the day, whether you are awake or sleeping, the sympathetic and parasympathetic divisions work together to keep your internal organs working at optimum levels, a mechanism called homeostasis. **Homeostasis** (ho-me-oh-STAY-sis) *is the tendency of the autonomic nervous system to maintain the body's internal environment in a balanced state of optimum functioning.* An example of the autonomic nervous system maintaining homeostasis is seen in the unusual and tragic case of Karen Ann Quinlan.

Although she was in a coma, part of Karen Ann Quinlan's nervous system kept her alive for ten years.

The sympathetic nervous system, which is one part of the autonomic nervous system, increases heart rate and blood pressure and releases excitatory hormones from the adrenal glands. These responses arouse the body and prepare it for fight or flight.

The parasympathetic nervous system, which is another part of the autonomic nervous system, decreases heart rate and blood pressure, stimulates digestion, and so on. These responses return the body to a calmer state.

What kept her alive for ten years?

What keeps a person in a coma alive?

After taking some aspirin and a mild tranquilizer, Karen Ann Quinlan had stopped to have several drinks. For reasons that have never been determined, Karen lapsed into a coma. After extensive tests, her doctors concluded that the young woman would never recover any of her cognitive functions because most of her brain was not functioning. Based on this information, her parents asked for and received permission from the State Supreme Court of New Jersey to disconnect her from the respirator that was thought to be keeping her alive. Although the respirator was turned off, Karen continued breathing on her own. She remained in a complete coma until she died of respiratory failure almost ten years later (*Time*, June 24, 1985).

Although Karen remained in a coma for nearly ten years, her sympathetic and parasympathetic systems continued to regulate her body's heart rate, blood pressure, breathing, and other responses. With most of her brain nonfunctional, her autonomic nervous system kept her body in a state of homeostasis.

We will return to the functions of the autonomic nervous system when we discuss emotions and stress in later modules.

Steve Fishman's Problem
We opened this module with a discussion of Steve's unusual symptoms. Let's review the divisions of the nervous system to discover which one might have been damaged. The somatic nervous system, which controls muscles throughout the body and brings in sensory information, seems to be intact, since Steve could hear, walk, talk, touch, and see. The autonomic nervous system, which maintains the body's internal environment, appears undamaged, since Steve's heart rate, blood pressure, and other functions were normal. However, the central nervous system, which is involved in thinking and perceiving, seemed to be damaged, since Steve could not tell time or tie his shoelaces by sight. As we examine the structure and function of the human brain, we will be able to pinpoint the location of Steve's brain damage.

The Human Brain

When you first see a human brain, you may be surprised to find that it is smaller than you imagined and can be held comfortably in two hands. The brain weighs about 1400 grams, a little less than 3 pounds, and its consistency is similar to firm Jell-O. The brain is protected by a cover of tough, plasticlike membranes, and a thin film of fluid between the brain and skull provides a cushion against hard knocks. To help you visualize the brain, we'll show you a top view, a side view, and then an internal view.

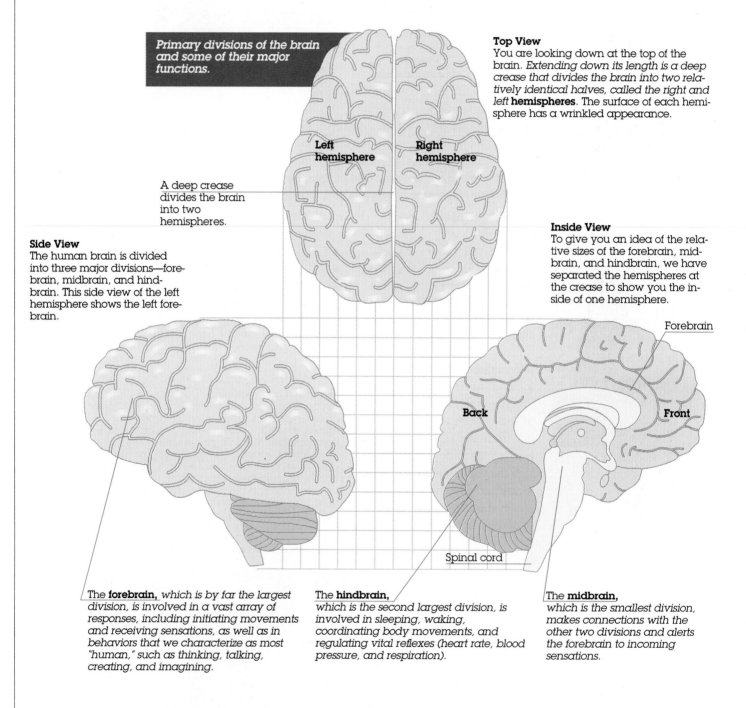

Primary divisions of the brain and some of their major functions.

Top View
You are looking down at the top of the brain. *Extending down its length is a deep crease that divides the brain into two relatively identical halves, called the right and left* **hemispheres**. The surface of each hemisphere has a wrinkled appearance.

Left hemisphere

Right hemisphere

A deep crease divides the brain into two hemispheres.

Side View
The human brain is divided into three major divisions—forebrain, midbrain, and hindbrain. This side view of the left hemisphere shows the left forebrain.

Inside View
To give you an idea of the relative sizes of the forebrain, midbrain, and hindbrain, we have separated the hemispheres at the crease to show you the inside of one hemisphere.

Forebrain

Back

Front

Spinal cord

The **forebrain,** *which is by far the largest division, is involved in a vast array of responses, including initiating movements and receiving sensations, as well as in behaviors that we characterize as most "human," such as thinking, talking, creating, and imagining.*

The **hindbrain,** *which is the second largest division, is involved in sleeping, waking, coordinating body movements, and regulating vital reflexes (heart rate, blood pressure, and respiration).*

The **midbrain,** *which is the smallest division, makes connections with the other two divisions and alerts the forebrain to incoming sensations.*

Now that you have an overall view of the brain, we'll take you through the brain and explain its structure and function in more detail.

The Forebrain. You are looking at the inside of the right hemisphere. Everything shown in the dashed oval at the top is the forebrain. Among animals, humans have one of the largest forebrains. The functions of the forebrain most contribute to your being a person. Without a forebrain, you would be in a vegetative coma, similar to that of Karen Ann Quinlan. We'll return to the forebrain's structures and functions a little later.

The Midbrain. The tiny area near the bottom middle of the brain is the midbrain. If you could peer down the center of the midbrain, you would see a long column of neurons extending down into the hindbrain. *The neurons form the* **reticular formation,** *which alerts and arouses the forebrain to incoming sensory information.* For example, sensory information from your visual system stimulates the reticular formation, which in turn arouses the forebrain so it is prepared to receive and process the incoming visual information. If your reticular formation were seriously damaged, you would go into a coma because the forebrain could not be aroused.

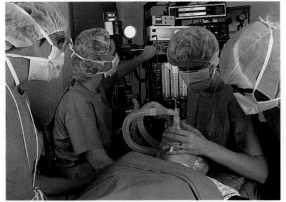

General anesthesia depresses the reticular formation.

What causes people to lose consciousness?
Before undergoing major surgery, patients are given a general anesthetic, which temporarily depresses the reticular formation and produces unconsciousness. As long as the anesthetic keeps the reticular formation depressed, the forebrain will not be alerted or aroused, the patient will be unconscious, and he or she will not be aware of any sensory information, including painful sensations from the operation.

How do you go to sleep?
Scientists believe that the reticular formation is one of several areas involved in the sleep-wake cycle. In order for you to go to sleep, other areas of your brain temporarily suppress the reticular formation, resulting in a temporary state of unconsciousness that you experience as sleep.

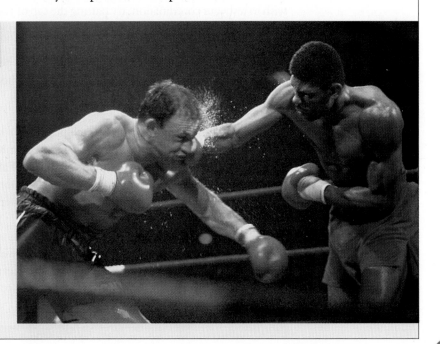

What makes a knockout punch?

A sharp blow to a boxer's jaw causes his head to twist and snap back. This violent motion can temporarily depress the reticular formation and contributes to a "knockout," or unconsciousness. Blows to the head also cause the gelatinlike brain to smash against the concretelike boney skull. After years of boxing, men may show signs of permanent brain damage. In fact, about one-third of professional boxers have symptoms of slowed motor reactions, clumsiness, tremors, memory deficits, and personality changes, apparently due to the punishment their brains take during fights.

The Human Brain

The Hindbrain. The structures and functions of the hindbrain are interesting because they have remained constant through millions of years of evolution. For example, the hindbrain of the primitive alligator brain is similar in structure and function to that of the human brain. Let's examine the three distinct structures of the hindbrain: the pons, medulla, and cerebellum.

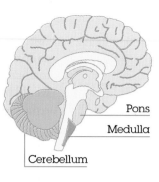

Pons

Medulla

Cerebellum

The **pons,** *which in Latin means "bridge," serves as a bridge that connects the spinal cord with the brain and parts of the brain with one another.* The pons also has a significant role in sleep: some of its cells manufacture chemicals that are involved in sleep. For example, researchers have learned that if an animal's pons is damaged, it will sleep much less.

Every now and then you will read a tragic story about someone who drank an enormous amount of hard alcohol and then died shortly after. The cause of death in such cases involves the medulla. The **medulla** *has groups of cells that control vital reflexes, such as respiration, heart rate, and blood pressure.* If these groups of cells are depressed by an extremely large dose of alcohol or other depressant drugs (heroin, sleeping pills), the result can be death from respiratory or heart failure.

If it were possible for you to take a microscopic trip through the brain, you would discover that the **cerebellum,** *which is involved in coordination, resembles an enchanted forest, with millions of rows of elaborate treelike structures formed by neurons (Purkinje cells).*

When you initiate a voluntary movement, such as reaching for a glass of water on the counter, your hand makes one continuous, fluid motion to reach out and pick up the glass. The cerebellum does not initiate such voluntary movements but rather coordinates and makes them smooth and graceful. If you wish to test your coordination, try patting the top of your head with your right hand while at the same time using your left hand to rub your belly with circular motions.

Damage to the cerebellum makes it difficult to perform coordinated movements, as happens with some alcoholics.

Why do some alcoholics have a shuffling step?
Heavy, long-term drinking can produce permanent brain damage, including damage to the cerebellum. As a result, some alcoholics have difficulty keeping their balance and coordinating their walking movements. To compensate for this difficulty, they hold their feet wide apart and take small, shuffling steps.

The cerebellum is involved in coordination.

We have completed our overview of the three divisions of the brain—forebrain, midbrain, and hindbrain. In a moment we'll return to the forebrain and explore its structures in greater detail. But now, let's see how earlier researchers tried to make a case for who had the biggest and most intelligent brain.

Racial Myths about Brain Size

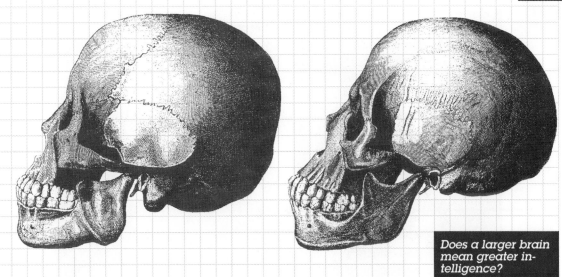

Does a larger brain mean greater intelligence?

Skull Size and Intelligence

Which race had the biggest brain?

When he died in 1851, *The New York Times* said that Samuel George Morton, scientist and physician, had one of the best reputations among scholars throughout the world. Morton had spent his lifetime collecting skulls of different races to determine which race had the biggest brain. During Morton's time, it was generally accepted that a bigger brain meant greater intelligence and innate mental ability.

Morton estimated the size of a brain by pouring tiny lead pellets (the size of present-day BBs) into each skull and then measuring the number of pellets. Using this procedure, he arrived at the following ranking of brain size in different races, from biggest to smallest: white (Caucasian), yellow (Mongolian), brown (American Indian), and black (Negro). Along with his racial ranking of decreasing brain size, Morton noted a corresponding decrease in behavioral and cognitive skills. For instance, Morton wrote that Mongolians were close in feeling and action to the monkey race, that American Indians were incapable of reasoning on abstract subjects, and that Negroes were the nearest approximation to animals (Morton, 1839, in Gould, 1981).

A hundred and thirty years later, Stephen Jay Gould, a renowned evolutionary biologist, reanalyzed Morton's data on brain size. Gould discovered that Morton had made a number of errors but had not deliberately lied or faked his data. One of Morton's errors was to include skulls that matched his personal expectations and to omit skulls that tended to refute his beliefs. Gould found that Morton's own data showed no significant size differences among races. Gould concluded that Morton's strong white biases had unknowingly swayed his scientific judgment to fit the racial notions of the time (Gould, 1981).

Interest in skull size as an indication of intelligence declined and was replaced by a new interest: brain size.

Brain Size and Intelligence

Whose brain is the smartest?

One of the most famous surgeons of the late 1800s, Paul Broca, declared that there was a remarkable relationship between size of brain and development of intelligence (Broca, 1861; in Gould, 1981).

However, a number of scientists have reported findings that disagree with Broca's conclusions. For example, if we take 1400 grams as average brain size, two famous 19th-century figures greatly exceeded that size: writer Ivan Turgenev's brain weighed 2000 grams, and naturalist Georges Cuvier's brain weighed 1883 grams. However, the brain of American poet Walt Whitman weighed in at only 1282 grams, and that of French writer Anatole France weighed only 1017 grams. Broca's ideas about brain size and intelligence died out by the beginning of the 20th century. (Watch for Broca's name later in this module.)

In short, as has been shown repeatedly, there is no correlation between the brain size of *normal* individuals and their level of intelligence.

The Master Control Center: The Brain

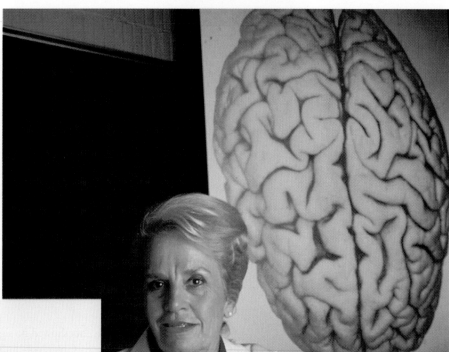

Dr. Marian Diamond is holding a preserved human brain, which has been cut down the middle and spread open to reveal its two almost identical sides. Behind her is an enlarged view of the top of the human brain, showing its characteristic creases and folds.

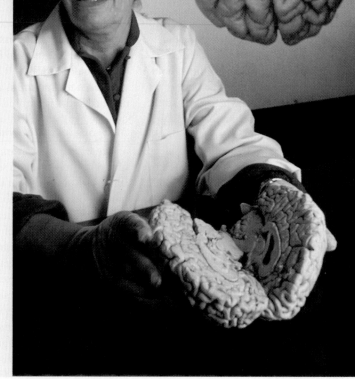

What's as big as a TV screen?

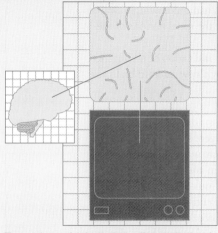

The cortex, which contains the majority of the forebrain's neurons, is a thin layer of cells that covers the entire forebrain. If the cortex were unfolded as shown here, it would form a square about 18 inches on each side, about the size of a TV screen. Through evolution, this large cortical square has been folded until it fits inside a small oval skull.

Where do you put 100 billion cells?

About 4 million years ago, our early ancestors walked the world with brains that weighed about 450 grams—close to 1 pound. At present, humans walk the world with brains that weigh about 1400 grams—a little over 3 pounds. With this more than threefold increase in brain size, primarily of the forebrain, came an enormous problem: how to fit billions of new neurons into a relatively small, oval-shaped human skull.

Most of the neurons, between 50 and 100 billion, are located in the **cortex**, *a thin layer of cells that essentially covers the entire surface of the forebrain.* If the cortex were spread out like a sheet of paper, it would form a square about 18 inches on each side (Hubel & Wiesel, 1979). Obviously, an 18-inch square does not fit inside a small, oval-shaped skull. In the same way that you can crinkle a large sheet of paper to fit inside your palm, the evolutionary process has folded and crinkled the cortex until it fits snugly inside the human skull. The result is a cortex with many folds and creases, which is much easier to carry around than a large square head.

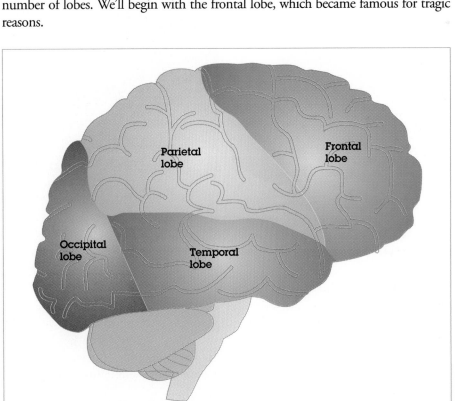

This side view of the human forebrain reveals a surface marked by creases and folds. More folds indicate more surface area and a more highly developed brain. The less developed rat's brain has a smooth, wrinkle-free surface.

The cortex is divided into four separate areas or lobes: frontal, parietal (pear-ree-ITE-all), occipital (ock-SIP-pih-tull), and temporal (TEM-purr-all). If some unknown virus were to suddenly destroy these four lobes, you would be unable to move, talk, see, hear, perceive, understand, think, or write—to name but a few of the functions.

Some responses, such as moving and seeing, are primarily located in specific areas of a single lobe. Other responses, such as perceiving and thinking, involve areas in a number of lobes. We'll begin with the frontal lobe, which became famous for tragic reasons.

Each side of the cortex is divided into four separate areas, or lobes.

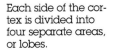

Parietal lobe

Frontal lobe

Occipital lobe

Temporal lobe

The Master Control Center: The Brain

The Frontal Lobe

The **frontal lobe**, *which is a relatively large cortical area in the front part of the brain, is involved in many of our social-emotional behaviors, such as behaving normally in social and emotional situations, maintaining a healthy personality, and making and carrying out plans.* To illustrate the functions of the frontal lobe, let's examine the case of a young lawyer who suffered a frontal lobe tumor.

Can a brain tumor ruin one's career?

Larry, who had graduated from a very good law school, had just started working for a law firm. His first symptoms were terrible headaches that interfered with his work. When the headaches continued, Larry underwent a number of neurological tests that revealed a tumor in his frontal lobe. After the tumor was removed, Larry tried to continue working. However, when he was sent to the law library to research previous legal rulings, he would begin working on one case only to become distracted and find himself working on a totally different case. He would try to start over but would soon lose his train of thought. This kind of haphazard searching continued all afternoon. He finally returned to his office without having accomplished any of the research. Because he was unable to make and carry out plans, he had to abandon his law career. Instead he had to take a simple job with a set routine: making postal deliveries on a fixed route. Larry tested high on IQ tests and could still carry on conversations, read books, watch and understand television, and even make jokes. He was lucky because his relatively small tumor did not greatly affect his social, emotional, and personal behaviors. As you'll see, however, significant damage to the frontal lobe can greatly change a person's personality and social behaviors.

Damage to Larry's frontal lobe prevented him from carrying out library research.

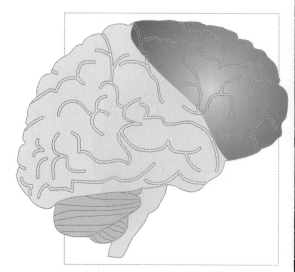

The frontal lobe is involved in social-emotional behaviors and in making and carrying out plans.

Why can't this person do library research?

Can someone's personality be changed in an instant?
The accident occurred at about half past four on the afternoon of September 13, 1848, near the small town of Cavendish, Vermont. The railroad crewmen were about to blast a rock that blocked their way. Foreman Phineas Gage took charge of the delicate business of pouring gunpowder into a deep, narrow hole drilled in the rock. The powder in place, he rammed in a long iron rod to tamp down the charge before covering it with sand. But the tamping iron rubbed against the side of the shaft and a spark ignited the powder. The massive rod, 3½ feet long, 1¼ inches in diameter, weighing 13 pounds, shot from the hole under the force of the explosion. It struck Gage just beneath his left eye and tore through his skull. It shot out the top of his head and landed some 50 yards away (Blakemore, 1977).

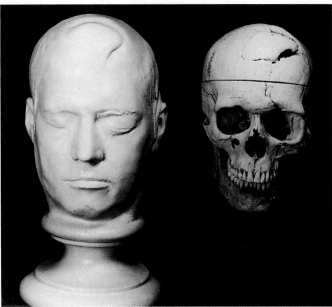

The skull and death mask of Phineas Gage show where an iron rod damaged his brain.

The Phineas Gage who miraculously recovered from this terrible accident was not the same man his friends had known. The old Phineas had been a considerate, efficient, and capable foreman. The new Phineas was capricious, impatient, incapable of completing a project, given to cursing his workers, and unconcerned about the social propriety of his actions. The iron rod had extensively damaged Phineas's frontal lobe, and this damage had changed his personality forever. Phineas had suffered a crude and massive form of frontal lobotomy.

What is a frontal lobotomy?
The **frontal lobotomy** *is an operation in which the front part of the frontal lobe is cut away and thus separated from the rest of the brain.* The actual operation is relatively simple and easy to perform. The patient, often awake, is placed in a chair, and his or her eyelids are anesthetized and rolled back. A tool resembling an ice pick is inserted above the eyes and pushed into the front part of the frontal lobe. As the tool is moved back and forth, it severs the front part of the frontal lobe.

In the 1930s and 1940s neurosurgeons performed about 18,000 frontal lobotomies. Since the frontal lobe was known to be involved in social and emotional behaviors, doctors hoped that severing the frontal lobe would curb uncontrollable emotional behaviors in mental patients.

Why are lobotomies no longer performed?

Frontal lobotomy involves cutting off this part of the frontal lobe.

Did lobotomies turn people into vegetables?
A frontal lobotomy did not necessarily turn people into vegetables, as some movies and novels suggest. Some patients who underwent the operation did become less violent, but improvements in this area of behavior were often accompanied by serious problems in other areas. For example, patients had difficulty making and carrying out plans, adjusting to new social demands, or knowing which emotional responses were appropriate.

For two reasons, few frontal lobotomies have been performed since the early 1950s. First, the success of lobotomies in relieving social-emotional problems proved to be little better than chance. Second, in the early 1950s came the discovery of antipsychotic drugs, which had significant success in reducing social-emotional problems (Valenstein, 1986). (Unfortunately, as you will find out in Modules 29 and 30, antipsychotic drugs may also produce serious side effects.)

Now let's examine the back edge of the frontal lobe to discover why you are able to turn the pages of this book.

The Master Control Center: The Brain

Frontal Lobe: The Motor Cortex

If my grandfather had a stroke on the right side of his brain, why is his left arm paralyzed?

The answer has to do with the peculiar way that the brain is "wired" to the body. For unknown reasons, the left hemisphere is wired to the opposite side of the body—the right side—and the right hemisphere is wired to the left side of the body. If a stroke destroyed part of your grandfather's right hemisphere, it would affect movement on his left side.

Why was my grandfather's left arm paralyzed but not his left leg?

The answer lies in the organization of the **motor cortex,** *which is a strip of cortex located on the back edge of the frontal lobe that is involved in the initiation of all voluntary movements.* Your grandfather had paralysis in his arm but not in his leg because the area controlling the leg is located in a different area of the motor cortex and was not damaged by the stroke.

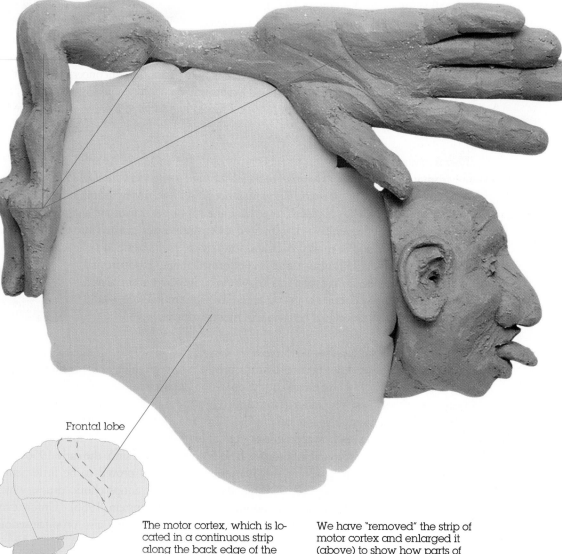

Two things to remember about the motor cortex:

1 Separate areas. Each part of the body is represented on a different area of the motor cortex. This means that the control of each part of the body is separate from control of the other parts.

2 Motor homunculus. Each body part is represented on a smaller or larger area on the motor cortex depending on whether that part controls fewer or more muscles. If we draw each body part smaller or larger according to how much area it takes up on the motor cortex, we will produce a very distorted body. *This distorted body, which shows the location of the body's parts along the motor strip, is called* **the motor homunculus** (*homunculus* means "little man"). For example, the motor homunculus shows a very large hand, indicating a large area on the motor cortex.

Frontal lobe

The motor cortex, which is located in a continuous strip along the back edge of the frontal lobe, controls the movement of voluntary muscles.

We have "removed" the strip of motor cortex and enlarged it (above) to show how parts of the body are represented.

Parietal Lobe: The Somatosensory Cortex

How does grandfather feel things?

The answer to this question lies in the **parietal lobe**, *which is located directly behind the frontal lobe.* Along the front edge of the parietal lobe is a narrow strip of cortex called the **somatosensory cortex**, *which receives sensations, such as touch, pain, and temperature, from receptors in the skin and joints.* The somatosensory cortex is wired like the motor cortex: the left hemisphere receives sensory information from the right side of the body, and the right hemisphere receives information from the left side of the body. In a real sense, your grandfather feels things when sensory information is processed by the somatosensory cortex.

If my grandfather's arm is totally paralyzed, why can he still feel things?

Although your grandfather's arm is paralyzed (motor cortex), his somatosensory cortex is intact and, thus, can still feel things.

Two things to remember about the somatosensory cortex:

1 **Separate areas.** Each part of the body is represented on a different area on the somatosensory cortex. This means that sensory information from each part of the body is separate from the other parts.

2 **Sensory homunculus.** Each body part is represented by a smaller or larger area on the somatosensory cortex depending on how sensitive it is to external stimuli. If we draw each part of the body smaller or larger according to how much area it takes up on the somatosensory cortex, we produce another distorted body. *This distorted body, which shows the location of the body's parts along the somatosensory strip, is called the* **sensory homunculus.** For example, the sensory homunculus has a very large tongue, indicating a proportionately large area on the somatosensory cortex.

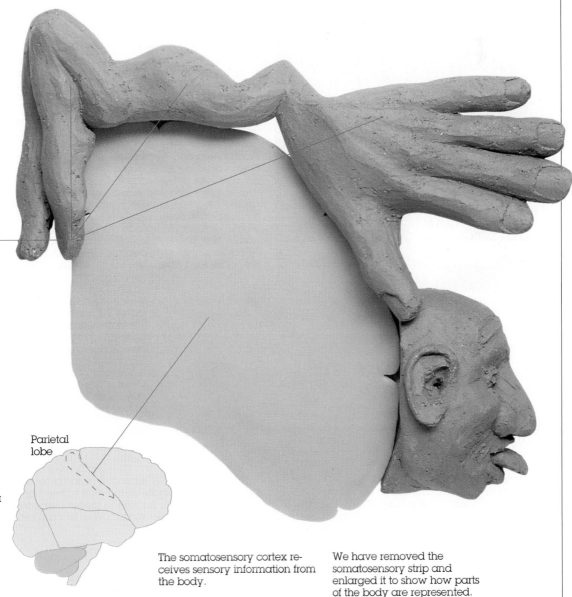

Parietal lobe

The somatosensory cortex receives sensory information from the body.

We have removed the somatosensory strip and enlarged it to show how parts of the body are represented.

The Master Control Center: The Brain

The Temporal Lobe

How does my grandfather hear things?

We can answer this question by pointing to the **temporal lobe,** *which is located directly below the parietal lobe and is critical to hearing and speech.* The temporal lobe has a number of functions, so we'll begin with its role in hearing. The **primary auditory cortex,** *which is a relatively small area located in each temporal lobe, receives and begins processing sensory information that originates in the auditory receptors of the ears.* The primary auditory cortex transforms sensory information into auditory sensations, such as "meaningless" sounds, clicks, or hums. However, for these meaningless sounds to become meaningful words and sentences, these sounds must be relayed to another area of the temporal lobe.

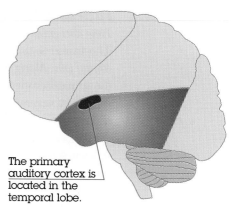

The primary auditory cortex is located in the temporal lobe.

Why was grandfather fortunate to have had his stroke on the right rather than left side of his brain?

Wernicke's Area and Wernicke's Aphasia

Why was grandfather fortunate to have had his stroke on the right rather than left side of his brain? For 95% of right-handed people and 70% of left-handed people, an area in the left temporal lobe is necessary for understanding and speaking coherently. (In about 5% of right-handed individuals and about 15% of left-handed people, this area is located in the right temporal lobe.)

Wernicke's area, *which is usually located in the left temporal lobe, is necessary for understanding speech and speaking in coherent sentences.* If Wernicke's area were damaged, your grandfather would have one type of aphasia, or a loss of the

ability to use or understand words. **Wernicke's aphasia** *is a difficulty in understanding spoken or written words and in putting words into meaningful sentences.* Here's how one patient with Wernicke's aphasia spoke: "I'm awful nervous, you know, once in a while I get caught up, I mention the tarripoi, a month ago, quite a little, I've done a lot well, I impose a lot, while, on the other hand, you know what I mean" (Gardner, 1976, p. 68).

In addition to Wernicke's area in the temporal lobe, an area in the frontal lobe is involved in speaking.

Broca's Area and Broca's Aphasia

Broca's area, *which is located in the frontal lobe, is necessary for producing and arranging words into meaningful sentences.* **Broca's aphasia,** *which is caused by damage to Broca's area, results in an inability to speak in fluent sentences but does not interfere with understanding written or spoken words.* For example, a person with Broca's aphasia was asked, "What have you been doing in the hospital?" The patient answered, "Yes, sure. Me go, er, uh, P.T. non o'cot, speech . . . two times . . . read . . . wr . . . ripe, er, rike, er, write . . . practice . . . get-ting better" (Gardner, 1976, p. 61). The patient was trying to say "I go to P.T. (physical therapy) at one o'clock to practice speaking, reading, and writing and I'm getting better."

In real life, patients rarely have pure forms of Wernicke's or Broca's aphasia but rather a part or combination of the two, depending on site and amount of damage in the left hemisphere.

You can now understand why your grandfather was "fortunate" to have a stroke on the right rather than the left side of the brain. A stroke in the left hemisphere might have damaged Wernicke's or Broca's area, causing speech difficulties.

Broca's area

Wernicke's area

Sometimes minor accidents may temporarily disturb one's brain and provide unusual experiences, as happened to a good friend of mine.

The Occipital Lobe

Why did I see stars when I hit my head?

Recently a friend of mine tried roller-skating after not having been on skates for ten years. He laced his skates, stood up, took off, gained speed, hit a crack, lost his balance, fell over backward, and struck his head on the concrete sidewalk. As he recovered his breath and pride, he rubbed the back of his head and asked me why he had "seen stars." The answer involves the **occipital lobe,** *which is located at the very back of the brain and is involved in vision.* The **primary visual cortex,** *a small area located at the back of each occipital lobe, receives sensory information from visual receptors in the eyes and transforms that information into visual sensations.* The reason my friend saw stars was that his primary visual cortex had been stimulated when he hit the back of his head on the sidewalk.

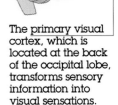

The primary visual cortex, which is located at the back of the occipital lobe, transforms sensory information into visual sensations.

Association Areas

What's in the rest of the cortex?

The areas of the cortex that we have discussed—motor cortex, somatosensory cortex, primary auditory cortex, and primary visual cortex—take up only about 20% of the total cortex. The remaining cortex, called **association areas,** *is involved in adding meaning or associations to sensory stimuli.* Each of the senses has one or more association areas, in which basic sensations are transformed into complex perceptions. For example, visual sensations, such as lights, shadows, or textures, are relayed to visual association areas, which transform these sensations into visual perceptions so that you can recognize, for example, a friend's face, your car, family pictures, and advertisements. Similarly, auditory sensations, such as sounds, hums, and squeaks, are relayed to the auditory association areas, which transform them into auditory perceptions such as your favorite song, a police siren, or a dog barking. Association areas occur in each of the four lobes and are involved in recognition, interpretation, and complex thought processes and in social-emotional behaviors.

After the Concept/Glossary section, we'll return to Steve Fishman's visual problem. Because he could see the hands of the clock but could not tell time, you might guess that his visual association area was damaged. We'll see whether you guessed right when we explain how doctors and researchers study the living brain.

When visual stimuli arrive in the primary projection area, the result is sensations of lines, angles, contours, textures, and colors, but no organized image.

Association areas in the primary visual cortex put sensations together into an organized pattern.

Techniques for Studying the Living Brain

Why was Steve Fishman able to see, hear, touch, walk, and think but unable to look at a clock and tell time?

Suppose you guessed that Steve had experienced damage to the visual association area. To diagnose and treat a problem such as Steve's, neurologists must pinpoint the location and type of damage involved. A number of techniques are available that permit a look inside the living, functioning brain. Let's examine three of these techniques, the first of which was used to pinpoint the cause of Steve's problem.

CAT Scans

Computerized axial tomography (CAT), *which is one technique used to study the structure of the brain, measures the amount of radiation absorbed by brain cells.* We'll describe Steve's CAT scan.

The technician instructed Steve to lie on his back on a narrow board while straps were placed around his chest and legs to help keep him motionless. His head was positioned on a foam pad and also taped to the board. The board was moved slowly forward until Steve's head was in the center of the huge donut-shaped CAT machine. The machine rotated slowly around his head and delivered a small amount of radiation.

A CAT machine emits a low-level radiation that is absorbed by brain cells. As this radiation passes through brain tissue, it is absorbed in differing amounts depending on

How can we look inside a living brain?

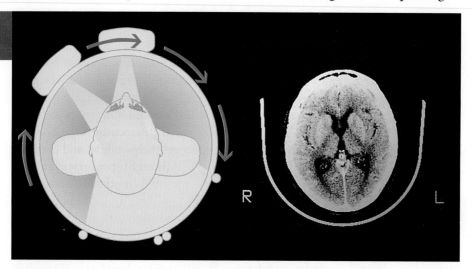

R   L

This CAT scan shows a visual slice of a living human brain and provides a relatively detailed image of the structures inside the brain.

the density of the tissue. The denser the brain tissue, the more radiation that will be absorbed, and vice versa. The machine measures how much radiation the cells absorb and translates this into an image such as the one shown here. Although the CAT machine emits a low-level dose of radiation, this procedure is considered relatively harmless to the brain.

During Steve's CAT scan, slice-by-slice images of his brain appeared on a television screen. Suddenly, standing out from the normal grayish image of a brain slice, was an unusual whitish area about the size of a quarter. This area was on the right side of Steve's occipital lobe and indicated the presence of abnormal blood and fluid. After examining all the CAT scans, the neurologist concluded that Steve had suffered bleeding or hemorrhaging that had destroyed a small part of his right occipital lobe. Because the hemorrhage had destroyed only a small area, it had disrupted only a few visual functions and spared many others.

The next technique gives an even more detailed picture of the living brain.

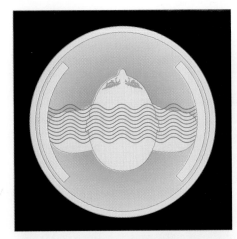

MRI Scans

Magnetic resonance imaging (MRI)—*sometimes referred to as nuclear magnetic-resonance (NMR) imaging—is another technique for studying the structure of the brain; it measures nonharmful signals passing through brain cells.*

During an MRI scan, the patient lies with his or her head in the center of a giant donut-shaped machine that makes a dull drumming sound as it emits a combination of nonharmful magnetic fields and radio frequencies. The MRI machine measures how these signals interact with brain cells. A computer translates these signal changes in brain cells into an image such as the one presented here.

The MRI image gives a more detailed view of the structures inside the living brain than does the CAT scan. MRI uses no radiation and produces a much clearer and more detailed image than a CAT scan.

Both CAT and MRI are used primarily to study the *structure* of the brain. When researchers want to investigate the *function* of the brain, they use other recently developed methods, such as PET scans.

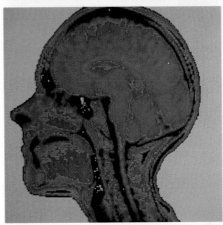

This MRI scan shows a slice of living brain.

PET Scans

Positron emission tomography (PET) *is a technique used to study the function of the brain by measuring the brain cells' absorption of radioactive substances.* During a PET scan, subjects are first injected with a relatively harmless radioactive glucose, which is taken up and used as fuel by the brain. Brain areas that are more active use more fuel and thus take up more radioactive glucose than those that are less active. In medicine, PET scans help doctors identify brain tumors, which show up as very active areas, or brain damage, which shows up as inactive areas. In research, psychobiologists use PET scans to study how the brain processes information. For example, in the PET scan on the right, you can see activity in various areas of the brain during processing of various types of stimuli.

The advent of the CAT, MRI, and PET techniques has given researchers the tools for studying the living brain. With these tools, they are able to explore normal brain functioning, the development of physical and mental disorders, and the effects of drug treatments (Andreasen, 1988).

These techniques are used to study the surface of the brain as well as structures deep inside. Now we'll go deep inside the human forebrain and show you structures whose origins can be traced back to the ancient alligator brain.

These PET scans show the areas of the brain that were most active when subjects were seeing, hearing, speaking, or thinking of a word (yellow areas indicate most activity). Notice that as the task changed, so did the most active areas in the brain.

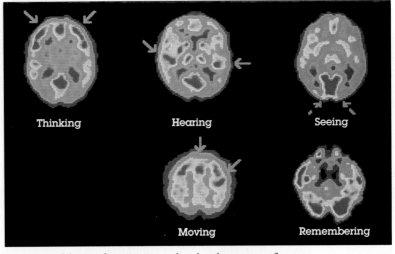

Thinking   Hearing   Seeing

Moving   Remembering

1. The human nervous system has two major divisions. The major division that includes the brain and spinal cord is called the (a)_____. The brain is divided into three major parts: (b)_____, _____, and _____.

2. All the nerves outside the brain and spinal cord make up the second major division of the nervous system, called the (a)_____. In turn, this system has two parts. One part is a network of nerves that are connected either to sensory receptors or to muscles that you can move voluntarily, such as muscles in your limbs, back, neck, and chest; this part is called the (b)_____. Another part of the peripheral nervous system regulates heart rate, breathing, blood pressure, digestion, secretion of hormones, and other functions; this part is called the (c)_____.

3. The part of the autonomic nervous system that is triggered by threatening or challenging physical or psychological stimuli and that responds by increases the body's physiological arousal is called the (a)_____. The part of the autonomic nervous system that is primarily responsible for returning the body to a calm or relaxed state and is involved in digestion is called the (b)_____. These two parts work together to keep the body in an optimum state of functioning, which is called (c)_____.

The number on the drawing matches the number of the question.

4. The cortical area that controls voluntary movements is called the (a)_____ and is located in the (b)_____ lobe. If the body parts are drawn so that their sizes match their cortical areas, the result is called a (c)_____.

5. The cortical area that receives input from sensory receptors in the skin, muscles, and joints is called the (a)_____ and is located in the (b)_____ lobe. If the body parts are drawn so that their sizes match their cortical areas, the result is called a (c)_____.

6. The cortical area that receives input from sensory receptors in the ears is called the (a)_____ and is located in the (b)_____ lobe.

7. The cortical area that receives input from sensory receptors in the eyes is called the (a)_____ and is located in the (b)_____ lobe.

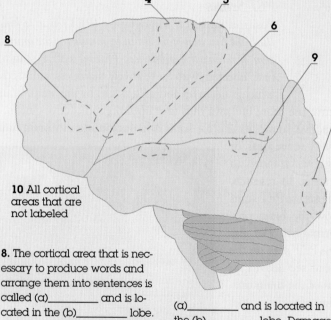

10 All cortical areas that are not labeled

8. The cortical area that is necessary to produce words and arrange them into sentences is called (a)_____ and is located in the (b)_____ lobe.

9. The cortical area that is necessary for understanding spoken and written words and putting words into meaningful sentences is called (a)_____ and is located in the (b)_____ lobe. Damage to speech areas result in difficulties in speaking or understanding, which are called (c)_____.

10. Cortical areas that add meaning to stimuli and are involved in thinking and conceptual processes are called _____.

11. The technique that measures the amount of radiation absorbed by brain cells and shows the brain's structure is called the (a)_____ scan. The technique that measures nonharmful signals passing through brain cells and also shows the brain's structure is called the (b)_____ scan. The technique that measures how low-level radioactive substances are absorbed by brain cells and shows the brain's function is called the (c)_____ scan.

Answers: 1. (a) *central nervous system*, (b) *forebrain, midbrain, hindbrain*; 2. (a) *peripheral nervous system*, (b) *somatic nervous system*, (c) *autonomic nervous system*; 3. (a) *sympathetic nervous system*, (b) *parasympathetic nervous system*, (c) *homeostasis*; 4. (a) *motor cortex*, (b) *frontal*, (c) *motor homunculus*; 5. (a) *somatosensory cortex*, (b) *parietal*, (c) *sensory homunculus*; 6. (a) *primary auditory cortex*, (b) *temporal*; 7. (a) *primary visual cortex*, (b) *occipital*; 8. (a) *Broca's area*, (b) *frontal*; 9. (a) *Wernicke's area*, (b) *temporal*, (c) *aphasias*; 10. *association areas*; 11. (a) *CAT*, (b) *MRI*, (c) *PET*.

Inside the Forebrain

If the thin layer of cortex were peeled away, you would look down on dozens of variously shaped structures located throughout the forebrain and hundreds of neural pathways that interconnect these structures with the midbrain, hindbrain, and spinal cord. We'll focus here on one particular group of structures that are involved in many motivational and emotional behaviors.

The Limbic System

Have you ever been accused of behaving like an animal?

There may be some truth to the accusation that you have "behaved like an animal." In the center of your forebrain is a group of structures that together are referred to as the "animal brain," or limbic system. The **limbic system** *consists of about half a dozen interconnected structures that are involved in many motivational and emotional behaviors.* The term *animal brain* comes from the fact that these same structures are found in the brains of evolutionarily ancient animals, such as the alligator.

The limbic system in an alligator's brain has the same structures as those found in the human brain. However, in the alligator brain, the limbic system makes up essentially the entire forebrain. In the human brain, the limbic system forms a central core around which has evolved a highly developed forebrain with its large, folded cortex and billions of additional neurons. In the alligator, the limbic system is heavily involved in smell, which plays an important role in defending territory, fighting for mates, hunting, and eating prey. In humans, the limbic system is much less involved in smell and much more involved in motivation and emotional behaviors.

The alligator's limbic system is involved primarily in "smell behaviors."

Limbic System Functions

What distinguishes the human brain from that of animals is the phenomenal development of the forebrain on top of and around the animal brain. As our massive forebrain evolved around the limbic system, it increased its regulation and control over the limbic system's functions. These functions include motivational behaviors, such as obtaining food, drink, and sex, and organizing emotional behaviors such as fear, anger, and aggression.

The main structures that make up the limbic system are outlined below.

Limbic System Structures and Functions

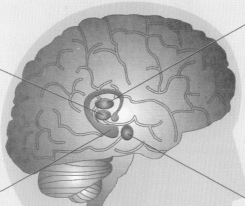

The **hypothalamus,** which is located near the bottom middle of the brain, is involved in many motivational and emotional behaviors. It has a role in eating, drinking, sexual behavior, regulation of the autonomic nervous system (fight, flight), and control of secretion of many hormones.

The **hippocampus,** which lies inside the temporal lobe, is involved in putting memories into permanent storage. Here's a great mnemonic device for remembering the function of the hippocampus: a hippo came to campus and tried to remember where the snack bar was.

The **thalamus,** which is relatively large and located in the middle of the forebrain, is involved in receiving sensory information, doing some initial processing, and then relaying the sensory information to areas of the cortex (the somatosensory cortex, primary auditory cortex, and primary visual cortex).

The **amygdala** (ah-MIG-duh-la), which is located in the tip of the temporal lobe, is involved in emotional behaviors.

You have just seen that one structure of the limbic system, the hypothalamus, has a role in regulating a complex hormonal system. Next we examine the regulation of hormones in more detail.

The Endocrine System

There are two major systems for regulating the body and the brain's many structures. As you know, one is the nervous system, which uses neurons, nerves, and neurotransmitters to communicate and to regulate responses. The second major system is the **endocrine system,** *whose glands secrete chemicals, called* **hormones,** *that affect organs, muscles, and glands throughout the body.* As you study the following diagram, notice the location and functions of the various glands of the endocrine system.

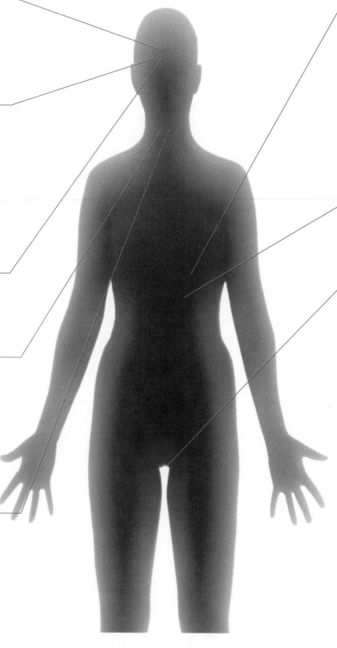

Hypothalamus. In many ways, the hypothalamus is the control center of the endocrine system. The hypothalamus controls much of the endocrine system by regulating the pituitary gland, which is located directly below it.

Anterior pituitary. The front part of the pituitary regulates growth through secretion of growth hormone and produces hormones that control the adrenal cortex, pancreas, thyroid, and gonads. *Dysfunction:* Too little growth hormone produces dwarfism; too much causes gigantism. Other problems in the pituitary cause problems in the glands it regulates.

Posterior pituitary. The rear portion of the pituitary regulates water and salt balance. *Dysfunction:* Lack of hormones causes a less common form of diabetes.

Thyroid. This gland in the neck regulates metabolism through secretion of hormones. *Dysfunction:* Hormone deficiency during development leads to stunted growth and mental retardation. Undersecretion during adulthood leads to reduction in motivation. Oversecretion results in high metabolism, weight loss, and nervousness.

Parathyroids. These glands, attached to the thyroid, produce hormones that regulate the amount of calcium in the bloodstream. *Dysfunction:* Lack of calcium may result in psychotic symptoms and in nerve and muscle problems that may cause tremors and lockjaw.

Adrenal glands. The adrenal cortex (the outside part) secretes hormones that regulate sugar and salt balances and help the body resist stress. The adrenal medulla (the inside part) secretes two hormones, epinephrine (adrenaline) and norepinephrine (noradrenaline), that arouse the body to deal with stress and emergencies. *Dysfunction:* With a lack of cortical hormones, the body's responses are unable to cope with stress.

Pancreas. This organ regulates the level of sugar in the bloodstream by secreting insulin. *Dysfunction:* Lack of insulin results in the more common form of diabetes.

Gonads. In females, the ovaries produce hormones that regulate sexual development, ovulation, and growth of sex organs. In males, the testes produce hormones that regulate sexual development, production of sperm, and growth of sex organs. *Dysfunction:* Lack of sex hormones during puberty results in lack of secondary sexual characteristics (facial and bodily hair, muscles in males, breasts in females).

Up to this point, we have examined the structure and function of individual parts that make up the human brain and nervous system. Now we turn to the brain's amazing organization that allows it to perform, often simultaneously, many thousands of motor, sensory, cognitive, emotional, and motivational behaviors.

Organization of the Brain

Do I use all of my brain?

It may help to understand the organization of the brain if you think of it as having hundreds of separate but interconnected programs, such as sensory programs to smell, taste, touch, see, and hear; motor programs to walk, reach, and climb; cognitive programs to read, write, and understand language; emotional programs to interpret, express, and intensify feelings; and so on. *The idea that your brain has hundreds of these programs located in many different areas is referred to as* **localization of function.** However, to perform even simple tasks, such as to read and understand the word *smile,* the brain combines a number of programs located in several or more areas (Posner et al., 1988). Even though programs are localized, we are able to carry out sensory, motor, social, emotional, and cognitive behaviors by combining programs from many areas. Thus, it's a good guess that you use all of your brain.

Let's look at three questions that always come up about the brain.

Am I "left-brained" or "right-brained"?

It is a popular notion that some of us primarily use the programs in our right hemispheres, which are characterized as involving images, creativity, and intuition, while others primarily use the programs in their left hemisphere, which are characterized as involving language, reason, and logic.

According to Jerre Levy (1985), who has devoted her career to studying how the brain's hemispheres interact, these characterizations and distinctions are much too simple. She believes that we are constantly using both hemispheres, since each hemisphere is specialized for processing certain kinds of information. For example, when reading this paragraph, you are probably using programs in the left hemisphere that allow you to understand language in written form. But at the same time, you are using programs in the right hemisphere to keep track of the overall story, appreciate humor and emotional content, and interpret diagrams and illustrations. Levy concludes that there is no activity in which only one hemisphere is involved. Instead of using programs in a single hemisphere, we use and combine programs from both hemispheres to accomplish our goals.

Popular media portray the left hemisphere as logical and rational and the right hemisphere as artsy-craftsy.

Which hemisphere is more dominant?

At one time the left hemisphere was considered to be the more important and dominant one because it contains the programs for speech and language. However, we now know that each hemisphere has its own expertise, skills, intelligence, and ways of thinking and analyzing (Levy, 1983). The original idea of dominance has given way to the current idea of *specialization:* the hemisphere that is more active at any given moment will be the one specialized for the task at hand.

Does the left hemisphere always know what the right is thinking?

This is the most controversial question. Roger Sperry (1974, 1982), who received the Nobel prize in 1982 for his work in this field, and Michael Gazzaniga (1985), who has studied the topic for many years, argue that each hemisphere may indeed have its own motivations, goals, and thoughts. If that is true, it would mean that one hemisphere may not always know what the other is thinking. This question generally remains unanswered because it is so difficult to research.

Now that you understand how the brain is organized, let's see what would happen if the brain were literally split in two.

APPLYING/ EXPLORING: SPLIT-BRAIN RESEARCH

When she was 6 years old, Victoria had both measles and scarlet fever. Shortly afterward she began to have terrible, recurring seizures. During the seizures she would lose consciousness, she would fall to the floor, and her muscles would jerk. She took anti-convulsant medicine and had no more seizures until she was 18. At that time, the seizures resumed with greater intensity, and to her dismay anticonvulsant medication no longer had any effect. Finally, when she was 27, she had to make a difficult decision. The best chance she had of reducing her frightening, uncontrollable seizures was to have an operation that had a high probability of producing serious side effects. In this operation, a neurosurgeon would sever the major connection between her right and left hemispheres, leaving her with what is called a "split brain." Choosing between a future of uncontrollable seizures and the potential problems of having a split brain, Victoria chose the operation (Sidtis et al., 1981).

In addition to Victoria (identified as V.P. in published reports), about 30 people have been treated for severe, uncontrollable seizures by having the hemispheres of their brains disconnected in what is called a *split-brain* operation. During this operation, doctors open the top of the skull, expose the brain, and then carefully cut the *corpus callosum.* This structure consists of some 200 million nerve fibers that form the major connection between the left and right hemispheres. Severing the corpus callosum not only disrupts the major pathway between the hemispheres but, to a large extent, leaves each hemisphere functioning independently. In many split-brain patients, severing the

Why did Victoria agree to have her brain split in two?

1 In a split-brain operation, the neuro-surgeon opens the patient's skull and separates the two hemispheres by cutting the corpus collosum.

2 After cutting the corpus callo-sum, which is the major nerve connection between the two hemispheres, the right and left hemispheres function relatively independently.

Left hemisphere

Right hemisphere

corpus callosum prevented the spread of seizures from one hemisphere to another and thus reduced their frequency and occurrence.

Can a split-brain person carry on a normal conversation?
Four months after her operation, Victoria was alert and talked easily about past and present events. She could read, write, reason, and perform everyday functions such as eating, dressing, and walking, as well as carry on normal conversations. For Victoria with her split brain, as well as for most of us with normal brains, *only* the left hemisphere can express itself through the spoken word (Springer & Deutsch, 1989). If the speech area is in the left hemisphere, then the right hemisphere is mute. (For a small percentage of left-handers, the speech area is in the right

hemisphere and the left hemisphere is mute.) Thus, one reason a split-brain person appears normal in casual conversation is that only one hemisphere is directing speech.

Split-Brain Testing Procedure
What did you see?
Suppose we ask Victoria to stare at the black dot between *HE* and *ART* as the word *HEART* is displayed on a screen. Because Victoria's hemispheres are split, information from each side of the black dot will go only to the opposite hemisphere. Victoria's left hemisphere will see only the word *ART* and her right hemisphere will see only the word *HE.*

Now we ask, "What did you see?" Victoria says that she saw "ART." If you trace the visual nerves that carry the word

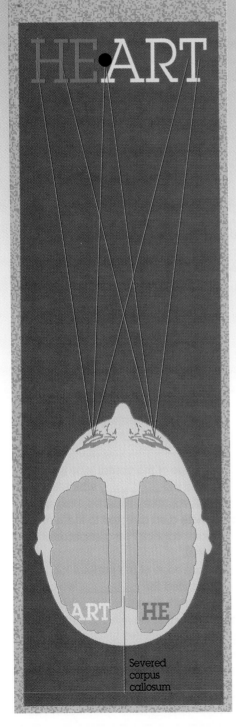

Things that appear on the left side of our vision, such as the word HE, go to our right hemisphere. Things that appear on the right side of our vision, such as the word ART, go to our left hemisphere.

HE•ART

Severed corpus callosum

ART, you'll notice that they end in the left hemisphere, which has the ability to speak.

Although Victoria's right hemisphere saw the word *HE*, it is mute and cannot orally relate what it saw. However, Victoria can point with her left hand to a photo of a man (HE), indicating that the right hemisphere understood the question and saw the word *HE*. (Victoria points with her left hand because her right hemisphere controls the left side of the body.)

Although the right hemisphere cannot utter a sound, we know from tests like this that the right hemisphere is conscious, can see and understand pictures, and can hear and follow instructions.

Specialization of the Hemispheres

Based on similar kinds of tests with split-brain patients, researchers have discovered the locations of many other programs in the brain. We now know that each hemisphere has specialized programs for certain functions, excels at particular tasks, and appears to process information in its own unique way. These specializations are summarized below.

Although separate cognitive functions or programs are located in each hemisphere, it is necessary to combine several or more programs in order to read, write, perceive, recognize, feel, calculate, and perform our many human behaviors.

Left Hemisphere	Right Hemisphere
Verbal. Is location of major programs for language-related skills: speaking, understanding language, carrying on a conversation, reading, writing, spelling.	**Nonverbal.** Although mute, has a childlike ability to read, write, and understand speech (Gazzaniga, 1983; Sperry, 1982; Zaidel, 1983). For example, when spoken to, the right hemisphere can understand simple sentences and read simple words.
Mathematical. Is location of programs for mathematical skills: adding, subtracting, multiplying, dividing, solving complex problems in calculus, physics, etc. Generally, the right hemisphere can perform simple addition and subtraction but not more complex mathematics (Sperry, 1974).	**Spatial.** Is location of programs for solving spatial problems, such as arranging blocks to match a geometric design.
Analytic. Has a program for processing information by analyzing each separate piece that makes up a whole. For example, the left hemisphere would "see" a face by analyzing piece by piece its many separate parts—nose, eyes, lips, cheeks, and so on (Levy & Trevarthen, 1976).	**Holistic.** Has a program for processing information by combining parts into a meaningful whole. For example, the right hemisphere "sees" a face as a whole and, for this reason, is better at recognizing and identifying faces (Levy et al., 1972). There is also evidence that the right hemisphere is involved in recognizing emotional expressions and in producing them (Springer & Deutsch, 1989).

Summary/Self-Test

THE CENTRAL AND PERIPHERAL NERVOUS SYSTEMS

1. The human nervous system is divided into two major parts. The brain and spinal cord make up the (a)_____. The network of nerves outside the brain and spinal cord make up the (b)_____.

2. The peripheral nervous system in turn has two parts. One part is made up of a network of nerves that either carry messages to muscles and organs throughout the body or carry input from sensory receptors to the spinal cord; this is called the (a)_____. The second part of the peripheral nervous system, which regulates heart rate,  breathing, digestion, secretion of hormones and related responses, is called the (b)_____. In turn, this nervous system is divided into two parts.

3. The part of the autonomic nervous system that arouses the body, increases physiological responses (such as heart rate and blood pressure), and prepares the body for the fight-or-flight response is called the (a)_____. The part of the autonomic nervous system that calms down the body and aids digestion is called the (b)_____. These two parts work together to keep the body's internal organs in a balanced physiological state, which is called (c)_____.

■ *How can the organization of the nervous system be compared to the structure of a pyramid?*

THE HUMAN BRAIN

4. The human brain has three subdivisions. The largest, which is involved in responses that we characterize as most "human," is called the (a)_____, which is divided into right and left hemispheres. The next largest division, which is involved in sleeping, waking, and coordinating body movements, is called the (b)_____. The smallest division, which is involved in alerting the brain to incoming sensations, is called the (c)_____.

5. Beginning in the midbrain and extending downward is a long column of cells called the_____ that alerts the forebrain to incoming sensory information.

6. The hindbrain consists of three structures. The structure that serves as a "bridge" to connect the brain and body and also manufactures chemicals involved in sleep is called the (a)_____. The structure that controls vital reflexes, such as heart rate, blood pressure, and respiration, is called the (b)_____. The structure that is involved in coordinating body movements is called the (c)_____.

■ *Suppose you had to give up one of the human brain's three divisions. Which one would you choose to give up?*

CULTURAL DIVERSITY: RACIAL MYTHS ABOUT BRAIN SIZE

7. In the 1800s, one scientist measured actual brain size and concluded that a larger brain indicated more intelligence. As has been shown repeatedly, there is no _____ between skull size or brain size of normal individuals and intelligence.

■ *Why do you think that some scientists wanted to find a relationship between brain size and intelligence?*

THE MASTER CONTROL CENTER: THE BRAIN

8. The thin layer of cells that has a wrinkled look and covers almost the entire forebrain is called the (a)_____. This layer of cells is divided into four separate areas or lobes: (b)_____, _____, _____, and _____.

9. The lobe that is involved in social-emotional behaviors, maintaining a healthy personality, and making and carrying out plans is called the _____ lobe.

10. At the back edge of the frontal lobe is a continuous strip called the _____, which controls the movement of voluntary muscles. Larger body parts indicate more area devoted to them on this cortex and greater capacity for complicated muscle movement.

11. Along the front edge of the parietal lobe is a continuous strip called the _____, which receives sensations from the body. Larger body parts indicate more area devoted to them on this cortex and greater sensitivity.

12. A small cortical area in the upper middle of the temporal lobe receives sensations from receptors in the ears. This area is called the (a)_____. For most individuals, an area in the left temporal lobe is involved in understanding and speaking coherently; it is called (b)_____ area. Damage to it results in being unable to understand spoken and written speech or to speak coherently. This speech problem is called (c)_____. Related to speech, an area in the frontal lobe, called (d)_____, is necessary for producing and arranging words into fluent sentences. If this area is damaged, the result is a speech problem called (e)_____.

13. A small area at the very back of the occipital lobe, called the _____, receives information from sensory receptors in the eyes.

14. The vast majority of cortex in the four lobes, called _____, is involved in adding meaning and associations to sensory stimuli, recognition and interpretation, and complex thought processes.

■ *Which brain areas would you need to duplicate in a robot so that it could perform most of the sensory and motor functions of a human brain?*

TECHNIQUES FOR STUDYING THE LIVING BRAIN

15. Two techniques are used to study the *structure* of the living human brain. One technique, which measures the amount of radiation absorbed by brain cells, is called a (a)_____; a second technique, which measures how nonharmful signals interact with brain cells, is called (b)_____. A technique to study the *function* of the living brain that measures how much radioactive glucose is taken up by brain cells is called (c)_____.

■ *A patient can understand speech but has trouble forming words and sentences. How would you locate this patient's problem?*

INSIDE THE FOREBRAIN

16. Inside the forebrain is a central core of interconnected structures called the "animal brain," or more technically, the _____, which is involved in motivational and emotional behaviors.

■ *What would happen if you replaced your friend's limbic system with one from an alligator?*

THE ENDOCRINE SYSTEM

17. Besides the nervous system, there is a network of glands that regulate organs through the secretion of hormones. This chemical system is called the (a)_____. A major gland that controls other glands in this system is the (b)_____ gland, which has an anterior and posterior part.

■ *Can you explain the following: tall basketball players, short jockeys, physical changes in adolescent girls; diabetes, dealing with stress, and the hormone control center?*

ORGANIZATION OF THE BRAIN

18. The idea that your brain has hundreds of programs located in many different areas is referred to as _____. However, to perform even simple tasks, such as to read and understand the word *smile*, the brain combines a number of programs located in several or more areas.

■ *Is there any truth to the statement that most of the time you use only 20% of your brain?*

APPLYING/EXPLORING: SPLIT-BRAIN RESEARCH

19. The two hemispheres are connected by a major bundle of fibers that is called the _____. From studying patients who had this structure severed, which is called a split brain, researchers have discovered that each hemisphere generally processes information in a different way.

20. For most individuals, the left hemisphere has language and speech programs while the right hemisphere is mute and has minimal language skills. The left hemisphere has programs for performing complex mathematics while the right hemisphere has programs for solving spatial problems. The left hemisphere processes information in a more (a)_____ way, compared to the right hemisphere's more (b)_____ approach.

■ *If you were supposed to act like a person with a split brain, what would you do differently?*

Answers: 1. (a) central nervous system, (b) peripheral nervous system; 2. (a) somatic nervous system, (b) autonomic nervous system; 3. (a) sympathetic nervous system, (b) parasympathetic nervous system, (c) homeostasis; 4. (a) forebrain, (b) hindbrain, (c) midbrain; 5. (a) reticular formation; 6. (a) pons, (b) medulla, (c) cerebellum; 7. correlation, or relationship; 8. (a) cortex, (b) frontal, parietal, temporal, occipital; 9. frontal; 10. motor cortex; 11. somatosensory; 12. (a) primary auditory cortex, (b) Wernicke's, (c) Wernicke's aphasia, (d) Broca's area, (e) Broca's aphasia; 13. primary visual cortex; 14. association areas; 15. (a) CAT scan, (b) MRI scan, (c) PET scan; 16. limbic system; 17. (a) endocrine system, (b) pituitary; 18. localization of function; 19. corpus callosum. (b) split-brain; 20. (a) analytic, (b) holistic.

Chapter *Three*
THE SENSES

MODULE 5
VISION

Can Craig see without using his eyes?

It was the kind of accident that changes one's life forever. Craig remembered the gunshot, the searing pain as the bullet passed through his skull, and then darkness. The bullet destroyed the nerves that send visual information from Craig's eyes to his brain: he was left totally blind.

Until recently, this story would have ended here. But today, with the help of an experimental surgical procedure, Craig is at least able to see flashes of light. To accomplish this medical miracle, doctors implanted a plate with 64 miniature wires on top of the visual area in the occipital lobe of Craig's brain. When tiny, nonharmful electrical currents pass through these wires, brain cells are activated and Craig sees flashes of light.

Craig has learned a kind of visual Braille in which flashes at various locations stand for different letters of the alphabet. After considerable practice, he is now able to identify a flash of light on the far left as the letter *A,* a flash in a different location as the letter *B,* and so on through the alphabet. Craig is even able to read simple words, such as *cat,* by using his flash alphabet. (author's files)

Although Craig is blind, he can experience visual sensations when his visual cortex is electrically stimulated. The fact that Craig "sees" flashes of light when his brain is electrically stimulated raises an interesting question: Do you "see" with your eyes or with your visual cortex? The answer may surprise you, since you have probably assumed that you "see" with your eyes.

No one mistakes an eye for an ear or a nose for a tongue, because they look so different. Despite their external differences, all the sense organs share three characteristics:

1 Our sense organs have one primary function, which is to transform stimuli into impulses. **Transduction** *refers to the process by which a sense organ changes or transforms particular physical stimuli into impulses.* For example, the eye transforms light waves into impulses, while the ear transforms sound waves into impulses.

2 Our sense organs have built-in mechanisms that reduce responding if stimulation continues. **Adaptation** *in sense organs refers to a decrease in responding with prolonged or continuous stimulation.* Because of adaptation, a "hot" shower seems less hot after a short period. Some sense organs adapt very quickly and some very slowly. However, sense organs do not adapt to intense forms of stimulation because such stimulation may cause physical damage. Instead, intense stimulation may cause pain that warns us of impending damage.

3 Our sense organs do not really "sense" anything. A **sensory experience**, *which is a psychological experience of some physical stimuli,* occurs after impulses are processed by the brain. For example, our ears do not hear. Rather, we have the sensory experience of hearing when certain areas of our brain are activated.

What's Coming

Because humans rely so heavily on visual information, that is the topic of this module. In the next module we'll explain the other major senses: hearing, taste, smell, touch, and balance.

Stimulus: Light Waves

Why can't you see X rays?

The last time you watched the sun set in the western sky, you probably saw an orange-red ball of light sink slowly into the horizon. This ball of light was a form of electromagnetic energy, in this case light waves. Besides light waves, there are many other forms of electromagnetic energy, such as X rays, TV waves, radio waves, and radar waves. What distinguishes one form of electromagnetic energy from another is the length of its waves, which varies from very short to very long.

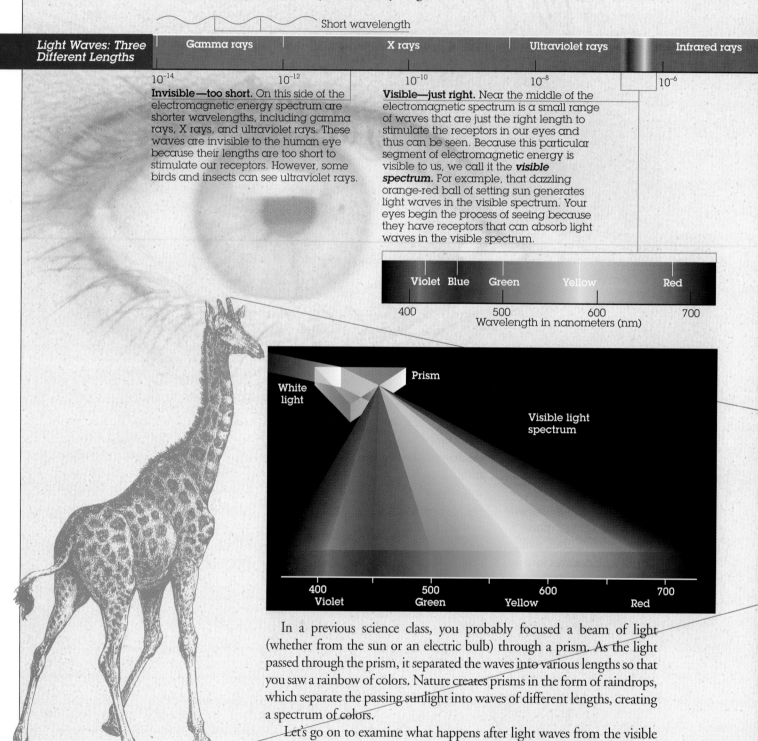

Short wavelength

Light Waves: Three Different Lengths

Gamma rays	X rays	Ultraviolet rays	Infrared rays

10^{-14} 10^{-12} 10^{-10} 10^{-8} 10^{-6}

Invisible—too short. On this side of the electromagnetic energy spectrum are shorter wavelengths, including gamma rays, X rays, and ultraviolet rays. These waves are invisible to the human eye because their lengths are too short to stimulate our receptors. However, some birds and insects can see ultraviolet rays.

Visible—just right. Near the middle of the electromagnetic spectrum is a small range of waves that are just the right length to stimulate the receptors in our eyes and thus can be seen. Because this particular segment of electromagnetic energy is visible to us, we call it the **visible spectrum.** For example, that dazzling orange-red ball of setting sun generates light waves in the visible spectrum. Your eyes begin the process of seeing because they have receptors that can absorb light waves in the visible spectrum.

Violet	Blue	Green	Yellow	Red

400   500   600   700
Wavelength in nanometers (nm)

White light

Prism

Visible light spectrum

400	500	600	700
Violet	Green	Yellow	Red

In a previous science class, you probably focused a beam of light (whether from the sun or an electric bulb) through a prism. As the light passed through the prism, it separated the waves into various lengths so that you saw a rainbow of colors. Nature creates prisms in the form of raindrops, which separate the passing sunlight into waves of different lengths, creating a spectrum of colors.

Let's go on to examine what happens after light waves from the visible spectrum enter the eye.

Structure and Function of the Eye

How do you see a giraffe?
Suppose a 16-foot-tall giraffe were standing in front of you. For you to see the giraffe, your eyes must gather, focus, absorb, and transform light waves into impulses. We'll follow the path of light waves from the giraffe to the back of your eyes.

Long wavelength

Radar		FM	TV	Shortwave		AM		AC electricity	

10^{-2} 1 10^2 10^4 10^6 10^8

Wavelength in meters (m)

Invisible—too long. On this side of the electromagnetic spectrum are longer wavelengths, such as infrared rays, radar, and radio and television waves. These waves are invisible to the human eye because their lengths are too long to stimulate our receptors. The fact that waves generated by radar guns are undetected by these receptors is part of what makes them effective in catching speeding motorists.

Pathway of Light Waves Through the Eye

1 Light waves. As light waves strike an object, such as a giraffe, they are reflected back in a broad, straight beam. For you to see the giraffe, your eye must change this beam of light into a narrow, focused one. To do so, your eye has two structures, the cornea and the lens, that bring an image into focus, much as the structures in a camera bring an image into focus.

2 Cornea. The broad beam of light reflected from the giraffe passes first through the **cornea,** *the rounded, transparent covering over the front of your eye. As the light waves pass through the cornea's curved surface, they are bent or focused into a narrower beam.*

3 Pupil. After passing through the cornea, light waves next go through the **pupil,** *which is a round opening at the front of your eye.*

4 Iris. The **iris** *is a circular muscle that surrounds the pupil and controls the amount of light entering the eye. The iris muscle contains the pigment that gives your eye its characteristic color.*

In dim light, the iris relaxes, allowing more light to enter; in bright light, it constricts, allowing less light to enter. If you look in a mirror in bright light, you will see that the iris is constricted and that your pupil—the black dot in the center of your eye—is very small.

5 Lens. A short distance beyond your pupil, light passes through the **lens,** *a transparent, oval structure whose curved surface functions to bend and focus light waves into an even narrower beam.* Muscles attached to the lens can change its shape, depending on the distance between the eye and the object being viewed. When an object is farther away, such as a person across the street, light waves reflected from it need less bending, and muscles automatically stretch the lens so its surface is less curved. When an object is close, such as a word on this page, light reflected from it needs more bending, so the muscles relax and the lens becomes rounder and its surface more curved. By adjusting its shape, the lens can bend light waves into a narrow beam and perfectly focus them on the back surface of the eye, called the retina.

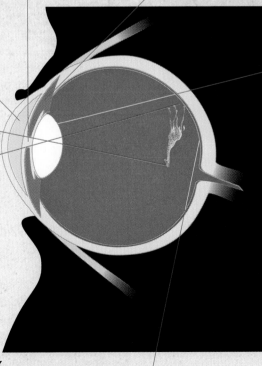

6 Retina. At the very back of the eye is a layer of cells that are extremely sensitive to light.

Structure and Function of the Eye

Kinds of Vision

Variations in the shape of the eyeball are one reason that some of us have almost perfect vision and others have poorer vision.

Normal Vision. If light waves reflected from a scene are perfectly focused on the back of your retina, both the near objects and distant ones will appear clear and sharp. If this is the case, you have good vision.

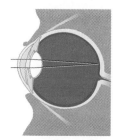

Nearsightedness. If the light waves from a scene are not perfectly focused on the back of your retina, you see a blurry image. **Nearsightedness**, *in which near objects are clear but distant objects appear blurry, may be caused by an eyeball that is too long.* If the eyeball is too long, light from distant objects focuses at a point slightly in front of the retina. As a result, light waves must travel somewhat farther to reach the retina itself. In traveling farther, the light waves scatter a little and distant objects appear blurry.

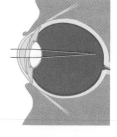

Farsightedness. On the other hand, **farsightedness**, *in which distant objects are clear but near objects are blurry, is often caused by the eyeball being too short.* As a result, light from near objects focuses at a point slightly behind the retina, and thus the light from these objects is not yet focused when it strikes the retina.

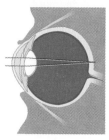

A common treatment for nearsightedness and farsightedness is to wear glasses or contact lenses to help bend and focus incoming light directly on the retina itself.

Cataracts. In the elderly, increasingly poor vision may signal the development of *cataracts,* in which an opaque film grows slowly over or inside the lens. This film may eventually block all light from passing through the lens, resulting in blindness. This once devastating condition can now be successfully treated with a relatively safe surgical procedure in which the damaged lens is removed and is replaced with a plastic one.

So far, we know that light waves must be perfectly focused on the retina. Let's discover what the retina does.

The Retina: A Miniature Computer

The retina functions much like a miniature computer as it transforms light waves into impulses, a process that you know as *transduction*. Here's how transduction occurs.

1 Light waves reflected by an object such as a giraffe enter the eye and are focused precisely on the retina. The **retina** *is a thin film that lines the back of the eye and contains several layers of cells that perform transduction—that is, change light waves into impulses.*

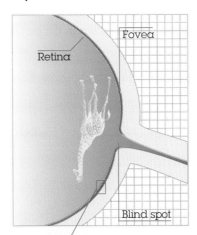

Retina

Fovea

Blind spot

2 The very back layer of the retina contains **photoreceptors,** *which are cells that can absorb light waves.* There are two kinds of photoreceptors, rods and cones, so named to describe their relative shapes. A human eye contains about 3 million cones, concentrated primarily in a small circular area in the center of the retina called the *fovea* (FOH-vee-ah). Each eye contains about 60 million rods, concentrated primarily along the periphery of the retina. If we enlarge the retina, you can see its layers of cells, especially the rods and cones.

Layers of Cells in the Retina

Light waves pass through cells to reach the back of the eye.

The front layer of the retina contains nerve fibers that carry impulses to the brain.

The middle layer of the retina contains ganglion cells in which impulses begin.

The back layer of the retina contains photoreceptors called rods and cones, which begin the process that creates impulses.

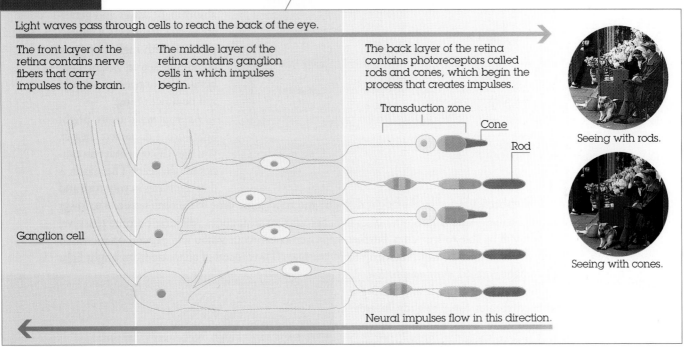

Transduction zone

Cone

Rod

Ganglion cell

Seeing with rods.

Seeing with cones.

Neural impulses flow in this direction.

3 **Rods** *are photoreceptors that contain a single chemical, called **rhodopsin** (row-DOP-sin), that is activated by small amounts of light.* With rods we see in dim light and we see only black, white, and shades of gray, with no colors. Most birds have no rods and thus see poorly at night, when they usually roost.

4 **Cones** *are photoreceptors that contain three chemicals called **opsins** (OP-sins), which are activated in bright light and allow us to see color.* Each of the three opsins is most sensitive to one of the three wavelengths that make up the three primary colors: red, green, and blue. By mixing the three primary colors, your visual system makes all other colors. Some animals, such as rats, dogs, cats, and cattle, have few, if any, cones and little, if any, color vision.

5 Here is where **transduction** occurs. As light waves are absorbed by the rods or cones, their chemicals are broken down. This chemical breakdown generates a tiny electrical force that, if large enough, triggers impulses in neighboring cells.

6 Light waves pass through the first several layers of retinal cells to reach the back layer of rods and cones. Neural impulses flow in the opposite direction, from the back layer through intermediary cells to the front layer of the retina, which contains nerve fibers. These fibers exit the back of the eye to form the **optic nerve,** which carries impulses toward the brain. The point of exit, which has neither rods nor cones, is called the **blind spot,** which you will "see" in the Applying/Exploring section.

Besides being involved in transduction, the retina performs several other amazing functions.

The Retina: A Miniature Computer

Seeing Details

How can you discriminate the tiny difference between the letter *i* and the letter *l*? Your ability to see such fine details is due primarily to an important difference in how rods and cones are connected to neighboring ganglion cells, as shown in the box below.

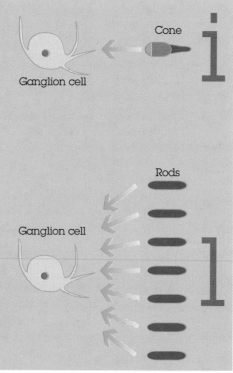

Cones. Each cone sends visual input, including information about fine details, to a single ganglion cell. Because of this almost one-to-one arrangement between cone and ganglion cell, information about fine details is preserved by the ganglion cell and sent on to the brain. Since only one cone usually connects with or converges on a single ganglion cell, cones are said to have very little **convergence.** Because of this limited averaging of information, cones can "see" fine details and can easily distinguish an *i* from an *l*.

Rods. Notice that many rods send their visual input to a single ganglion cell. Because of this arrangement, visual information is combined and averaged by a ganglion cell; in the process, fine details are lost. In contrast to the minimal convergence of cones, rods undergo a great deal of convergence. As a consequence of this extensive averaging of information, rods cannot process or "see" fine details and cannot distinguish an *i* from an *l*.

> **How can you discriminate the tiny difference between the letter i and the letter l?**

Adaptation to Light

Rods and cones are both important to our ability to adapt to changing patterns of light. As one example, people with **night blindness,** which is difficulty seeing at night, are often found to have vitamin A deficiencies. Vitamin A is needed to manufacture rhodopsin, without which rods cannot absorb light waves and generate electrical forces. Of course, a person with night blindness could still see in bright light because his or her cones would still be functioning.

As you walk from bright light into a darkened theater, you may discover that you cannot see the seats. The reason is that chemicals in your rods and cones have been affected by the bright daylight and need some time to become sensitive to lower light intensities. After about 5 minutes, the chemicals in your cones will have become sensitive, and you will be able to see better. Further improvement in your vision will depend on increased sensitivity of your rods, which takes up to 30 minutes. The process of adapting from bright light to dim light is called *dark adaptation.*

After watching a movie and leaving a darkened theater for a brightly lit area, the light may seem blinding. Having adapted to the dark, your rods and cones are now extremely sensitive and will need time to adapt to the bright light. The process of adapting from dim light to bright light is called *light adaptation.*

After the Concept/Glossary, we'll follow impulses as they travel in the optic nerve to the brain. You'll discover how the brain interprets millions of impulses as a bright red apple.

As we go from bright light into dim light, our visual system undergoes dark adaptation.

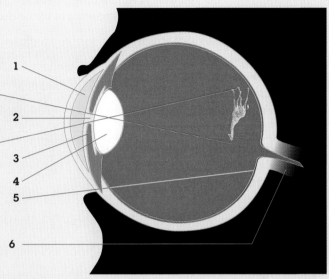

The numbers on the diagrams refer to the numbers of the questions.

1. A transparent, curved structure at the front of the eye, called the _____, focuses or bends light waves into a more narrow beam.

2. A round opening at the front of the eye that allows varying amounts of light to enter the eye is called the _____.

3. A circular, pigmented muscle that dilates or constricts, thus increasing or decreasing the size of the pupil, is called the _____.

4. The function of the transparent, oval structure called the _____ is to bend light waves into a more narrow beam of light and focus the beam precisely on a layer of cells in the very back of the eye.

5. Lining the back of the eye is a filmlike layer called the (a)_____, which contains several layers of cells. The back layer of cells has two kinds of photoreceptors, called (b)_____ and (c)_____.

6. This band of nerve fibers, called the (a)_____, exits from the back of the eye and carries impulses to the brain. The point at which this nerve exits is called the (b)_____ because it contains no rods or cones.

7. The photoreceptor that functions in dim light, called a (a)_____, contains a chemical called (b)_____, which is partly made from vitamin A.

8. The photoreceptor that functions in bright light, called a (a)_____, contain chemicals called (b)_____, which are involved in seeing color.

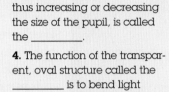
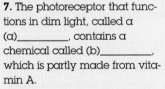
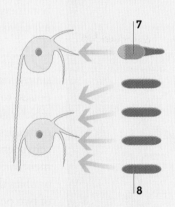

9. Rods do not transmit details because they have a great deal of (a)_____. This means that many rods send their information to a single ganglion cell, which averages and loses some of the information (details). In contrast, cones transmit details because they usually send their information to a single (b)_____ cell.

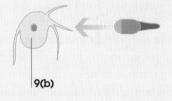

9(b)

10. If you walk from a brightly lit area into a darkened one, your visual system undergoes a process called _____.

Answers: 1. *cornea;* 2. *pupil;* 3. *iris;* 4. *(a) lens;* 5. *(a) retina,* (b) *rods,* (c) *cones;* 6. *(a) optic nerve,* (b) *blind spot;* 7. *(a) rod,* (b) *rhodopsin;* 8. *(a) cone,* (b) *opsins;* 9. *(a) convergence,* (b) *ganglion;* 10. *dark adaptation.*

The Visual Pathway: Eye to Brain

How are light waves turned into performers?
If you were to see this image in real life, your visual system would transform light waves into the sensory experience of seeing these two performers.

1 The sequence of a visual sensory experience begins when light waves reflected from an object enter your eyes, are focused precisely on the retinas, and are transformed into nerve impulses.

2 The impulses exit from the back of the eye and travel via the *optic nerve* to the right and left hemispheres.

3 The place where branches of the optic nerve cross is called the *optic chiasm* (kye-AS-em).

4 At the very back of each occipital lobe lies a *primary visual cortex,* which transforms nerve impulses into simple visual sensations, such as texture, shadow, line, movement, and color. Transformation of simple sensations into meaningful images happens later.

From the Nobel Prize–winning research of David Hubel and Torsten Wiesel (1962, 1979), we know that cells in the primary visual cortex respond to specific stimuli in the visual fields. For example, some cortical cells respond best when a line of a particular width is flashed in the visual field. Other cells respond best to a line oriented at a particular angle, or to a line that is moving, often in a particular direction, and so forth. These "feature-detecting" cortical cells respond to and transform different stimuli into simple visual sensations, such as shadows, lines, textures, or angles. Although cells in the primary visual cortex produce many kinds of visual sensations, these sensations are unassembled, like the pieces of a jigsaw puzzle. To assemble these sensations into a meaningful image, such as two performers, these sensations must be relayed to other cortical areas.

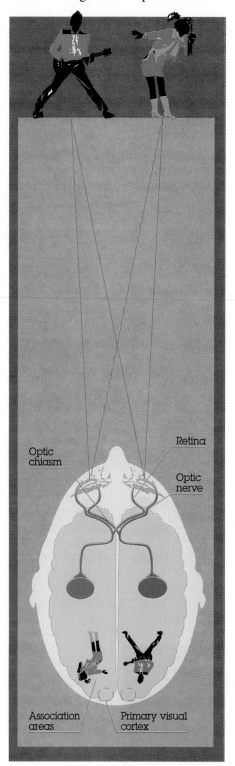

Optic chiasm

Retina

Optic nerve

Association areas

Primary visual cortex

At the beginning of this module, we told you about Craig, who had 64 tiny wires implanted into his primary visual cortex. Craig could see flashes of light when electricity was passed through these wires to stimulate neurons. He did not see complete images because neurons in the primary visual cortex produce only simple visual sensations. Unlike Craig's primary visual cortex, which can be stimulated at only 64 points, the over 100 million cells of your primary visual cortex can be stimulated; this explains why you can see images in such incredible detail and color.

If part of your primary visual cortex were to be damaged, you would have a blind spot in the visual field, similar to looking through glasses with a tiny black spot painted on the lens. Damage to the entire primary visual cortex in both hemispheres would result in almost total blindness, perhaps leaving the ability to tell night from day.

5 The primary visual cortex sends simple visual sensations (actually, impulses) to neighboring *association areas,* which add meaning or "associations." In our example, the association area receives sensations of texture, line, movement, orientation, and color and assembles them into a meaningful image of two performers.

If part of your visual association area were to be damaged, you would experience **visual agnosia,** *which is difficulty in assembling simple visual sensations into more complex, meaningful images.* A person with visual agnosia might have difficulty in recognizing or naming objects or faces.

You probably noticed that the performers are dressed in colorful outfits, which fits in with our last topic: how we see color.

Color Vision

Color is not in the apple but in the brain.

What would it be like to suddenly see color?

Debra was born with congenital cataracts that made her almost totally blind. For the first 28 years of her life, she could tell night from day but could see little else. Then she

underwent a newly developed operation in the hope that, for the first time in her life, she would be able to see. When the bandages were removed from her eyes, she cried with delight as she looked around her room and saw things she had only imagined. "Colors were a real surprise to me," Debra said. "They were so bright. You can't conceive what colors are until you've seen them. They are my favorite things in the world, and red is my very favorite color. I couldn't imagine what a red apple looked like and now I can hold one and actually see red" (San Diego *Tribune*, April 3, 1984).

Colors and Wavelengths

Isn't an apple really red?

Like Debra, most of us assume that a red apple is really red, but you are about to discover otherwise. Objects do not have colors. Rather, objects such as a red apple reflect light waves whose different lengths are transformed by your visual system into your experience of color. To help convince you that "colors" are wavelengths, let's make colors out of light waves.

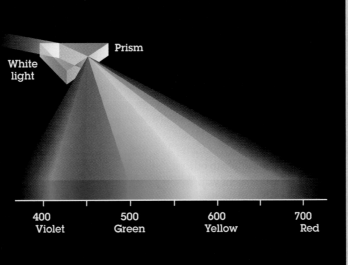

Making Colors from Wavelengths

1. A ray of sunlight is called **white light** because it contains all the light waves in the visible spectrum.

2. As white light is passed through a prism, it separates into light waves of differing lengths.

3. Our visual system transforms light waves of various lengths into different colors. For example, we see shorter wavelengths as shades of violet, blue, and green, and longer wavelengths as shades of yellow, orange, and red.

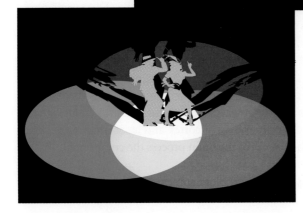

An apple is not really red but rather reflects back certain wavelengths that your visual system transforms into the sensation of red. Let's examine how you see red as well as all the colors of the rainbow.

The three primary colors of light are red, green, and blue. By mixing red and green we produce yellow, and by mixing all three colors (that is, mixing all light waves) we produce white. Black is the result of an absence of all light waves.

Color Vision

Theories of Color Vision

How does 3 plus 2 equal all the colors of the rainbow?
It has taken hundreds of years of research and two different but complementary theories to explain how we see color.

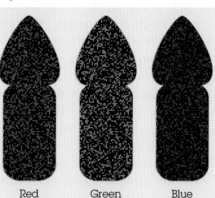

According to the trichromatic theory, each cone contains one of three opsins that are especially responsive to each of the three primary colors: red, green, and blue.

Red cone   Green cone   Blue cone

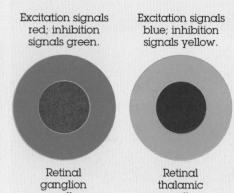

Excitation signals red; inhibition signals green.

Excitation signals blue; inhibition signals yellow.

According to the opponent-process theory of color, retinal ganglion and thalamic cells respond in "opposing" ways (excitation or inhibition) to pairs of colors—red-green and yellow-blue.

Retinal ganglion cell   Retinal thalamic cell

Trichromatic Theory

Two hundred years ago the work of American chemist John Young laid the basis for one theory of color. Young's idea became known as the **trichromatic** (TRI-crow-MAH-tic) **theory,** *which says that cones in the retina are most responsive to three primary colors—blue, green, and red—from which all other colors can be mixed.* Following up on Young's idea, researchers eventually found three different light-sensitive chemicals, called *opsins,* which are present in the cones. Each cone contains one of the three opsins, and each opsin responds most to one of Young's three primary colors (Nathans et al., 1986).

According to the trichromatic theory, we see color because the three light-sensitive chemicals in the cones respond most to one of the three primary colors.

The trichromatic theory explains how *cones in the retina* transform light waves into colors. However, it does not apply to other parts of the nervous system that code color in a different way. To understand how coding of colors occurs in the brain, we need the opponent-process theory of color vision.

Opponent-Process Theory

An interesting visual experience is an **afterimage,** *which is a visual sensation that continues after the original stimulus is removed.* For example, if you stare at a red square and then look at a white piece of paper, you'll see an afterimage of a green square. Similarly, if you stare at a blue square, you'll see a yellow afterimage. Based on his work with afterimages, physiologist Ewald Hering suggested that the visual system codes color by using two complementary pairs—red-green and blue-yellow. Hering's idea became known as the **opponent-process theory,** *which says that ganglion cells in the retina and cells in the thalamus of the brain respond to two pairs of colors, red-green and blue-yellow; when these cells are excited, they respond to one color of the pair and when inhibited, they respond to the complementary pair.* Although researchers now question whether the opponent-process theory explains afterimages, you can experience afterimages in the Applying/Exploring section.

Let's see how the trichromatic and opponent-process theories work together. According to the trichromatic theory, cones in the retina respond primarily to one of the three primary colors. Next, the cones send their information to cells in the ganglion and thalamus. The ganglion and thalamic cells follow the opponent-process theory and signal one color of a pair if excited and the other color if inhibited. For example, some ganglion and thalamic cells respond to the red-green pair by signaling "red" when excited and "green" when inhibited; other cells respond to the yellow-blue pair by signaling "blue" when excited and "yellow" when inhibited.

If we combine the trichromatic theory of the cones with the opponent-process theory of the ganglion and thalamic cells, we can explain how light waves are transformed into "color signals." In turn, these color signals are relayed to the primary visual cortex and association areas in the occipital lobe of the brain. It is only after these areas of the brain process the color signals that we "see" colors.

Although most of us are very good at discriminating colors, some people have varying degrees of color blindness.

Color Blindness

Would a bank president wear yellow striped slacks and a green plaid shirt?

A bank president might if he or she had **color blindness**, *which is the inability to distinguish two or more shades in the color spectrum.* There are several kinds of color blindness. **Monochromats** (MOHN-oh-crow-mats) *have total color blindness, and their world looks like a black-and-white movie.* This kind of color blindness is rare and results from individuals having only rods or only one kind of functioning cone (instead of three). **Dichromats** (DIE-crow-mats) *usually have trouble distinguishing red from green because they have just two kinds of cones.* This is an inherited condition, found mostly in males (Nathans et al., 1986b).

You might think that color-blind people would quickly discover that they have a problem. In fact, many do not find out until quite late in life; they assume that others see the world exactly as they do.

A dog might appear green to a dichromat.

Have you ever seen a green dog?

One boy's dichromatic condition was first discovered when he told his mother that he was chased home by a big green dog. But for his encounter with a "green dog," this boy might not have discovered that he was color blind until much later in life.

People in some occupations, such as electrical technicians, are screened for color blindness because they must identify different colored wires or parts. A quick test for color blindness appears in the Applying/Exploring section.

CONCEPT/ GLOSSARY: Transforming Light Waves into Sensations

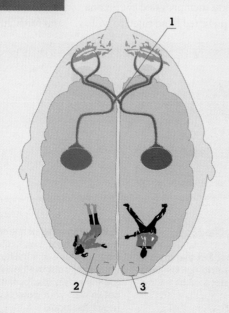

1. The optic nerve carries visual information to the brain. The point where branches of the optic nerve cross is called the _____.

2. Visual information is sent to an area in the back of each occipital lobe called the (a)_____. Cells in this area respond to specific features of stimuli in the visual field. This area transforms nerve impulses into simple (b)_____, such as lines, textures, shadows, and angles.

3. This area, which assembles and transforms simple sensations into meaningful images, is called an (a)_____ area. Damage to parts of this area causes difficulties in producing a complete, meaningful image, a problem that is called visual (b)_____.

4. According to one theory of color vision, the retina contains three types of cones, each of which contains one of three opsins that responds to one of the three primary colors; this is called the _____ theory.

5. According to the second theory of color vision, the retinal ganglion and thalamic cells respond with opposing responses, by becoming excited or inhibited when stimulated by a color in a pair of colors; this is called the _____ theory.

Answers: 1. optic chiasm; 2. (a) primary visual cortex, (b) sensations; 3. (a) association, (b) agnosia; 4. trichromatic; 5. opponent-process.

APPLYING/ EXPLORING: VISUAL EXPERIENCES

Here's your chance to identify your preferred eye, find your blind spot, see an afterimage, and take a quick test for color blindness.

Preferred Eye

Take a piece of paper, roll it into a tube, and look through the tube at some object. The eye you look with is your preferred eye—that is, the eye you use for precise sighting.

For a more dramatic demonstration of your preferred eye, hold your thumb at arm's length and, using both eyes, line up your thumb with the corner of a room. Next, look at your thumb through one eye and then the other. When you look with your nonpreferred eye, your thumb will appear to jump several inches to one side. When looking with your preferred eye, your thumb will not jump to the side. This demonstrates that even though you thought that you had lined up your thumb with both eyes, you had used only your preferred eye.

Knowing the location of one's preferred eye is especially important to baseball players. José Portal (1988) reported that good hitters have their preferred eye on one side and their preferred hand (used to write

with or pick things up) on the other. For example, a good right-handed hitter has a keen left eye turned toward the pitcher and a well-practiced right hand to guide the swing. In contrast, a poor hitter has the preferred eye and preferred hand on the same side. Portal's advice to baseball players is to select their batting side according to the location of their dominant eye. If right-eyed, they should bat left-handed, and vice versa. His research also explains why switch-hitters always have a higher average on one side, the side opposite the preferred eye.

Blind Spot

At the point where the optic nerve exits from the back of the eye, a small circular "hole" occurs in the retina. Since that hole has neither rods nor cones, it is literally a **blind spot,** which you can "see" by following the instructions below.

Normally you are unaware of your blind spot because your eyes constantly move back and forth, filling in the area that is lost.

Why does a switch-hitter always have a better batting average on one side?

__Finding the Blind Spot__

1. Close your left eye and stare at the mitt (on the left). Be careful not to shift your gaze.

2. While staring at the mitt, move the book back and forth, about 8 to 9 inches from your eye, until the baseball (on the right) disappears. Try not to shift your gaze as you move the book.

3. The baseball will completely disappear when it falls on your blind spot.

Afterimage

You can easily produce an afterimage by staring at a color and then shifting your gaze to a white surface. For example, if you stare at a red square, you will see a green afterimage; similarly, if you stare at a blue square, you will see a yellow afterimage. Because the afterimage complements or completes the color pair (red-green, yellow-blue), these images are called *complementary afterimages.* To see complementary afterimages, follow the instructions in the figure.

Because afterimages remain for only a brief time, you may need to repeat steps 1 and 2 to see all four complementary colors.

Color Blindness

Individuals who are suspected of having some form of color blindness are shown a number of charts similar to those presented here. The individual is asked to read the number (in contrasting colored dots) embedded in each chart. Can you read the numbers in these charts?

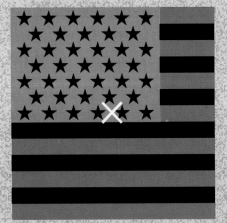

1. Place this page under a bright light and, without moving your eyes, stare at the X in the middle of the colors. Keep staring while you slowly count to 45.

2. Immediately after you reach 45, shift your gaze to the X on the right. You will now see complementary afterimages of each of the colors.

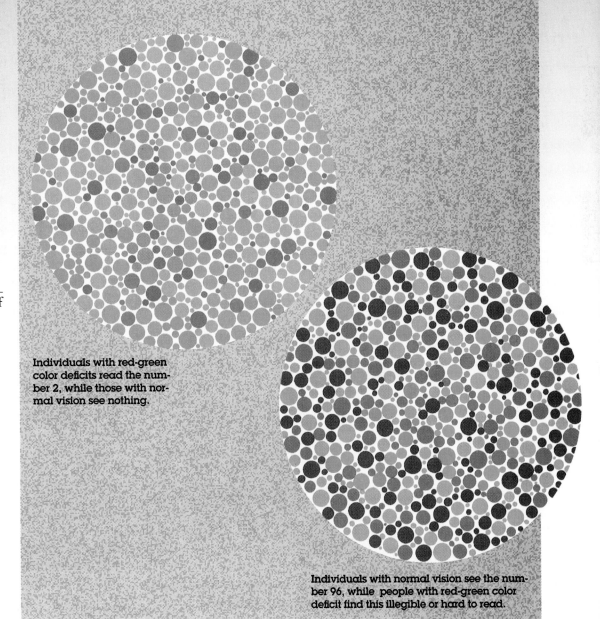

Individuals with red-green color deficits read the number 2, while those with normal vision see nothing.

Individuals with normal vision see the number 96, while people with red-green color deficit find this illegible or hard to read.

Summary/Self-Test

STIMULUS: LIGHT WAVES

1. Electromagnetic energy is composed of (a)_____ of varying lengths. Shorter waves, such as X rays, and longer waves, such as radio waves, are invisible because they cannot be absorbed by the human eye. Waves in about the middle of the electromagnetic spectrum are visible because they can be absorbed by the human eye. These waves make up the (b)_____.

■ *Your radio has no difficulty receiving radio waves, so why can't you see them?*

STRUCTURE AND FUNCTION OF THE EYE

2. Upon entering the eye, light waves pass first through a curved, thin, transparent structure called the (a)_____, whose function is to bend or focus light waves into a narrower beam. Next, light waves pass through an opening in the eye called the (b)_____. Around this opening is a circular, pigmented muscle called the (c)_____; its function is to dilate or constrict, thus increasing or decreasing the amount of entering light. Finally, light waves pass through a transparent, oval structure called the (d)_____, whose function is to further focus light waves precisely on the photosensitive back surface of the eye, which is called the (e)_____.

3. If light waves are perfectly focused on the retina, the image will be clear and sharp and result in normal vision. If an eyeball is too long and light waves are focused slightly in front of the retina, the result is a condition known as (a)_____. If an eyeball is too short and light waves are focused slightly behind the retina, the result is a condition known as (b)_____. If an opaque (nontransparent) film grows over or inside the lens, (c)_____ have developed.

■ *What parts would you need to build a miniature eye that can be used in robots?*

THE RETINA: A MINIATURE COMPUTER

4. The retina has several layers of cells, but only the very back layer contains photoreceptors. The photoreceptors that lie primarily along the retina's periphery are called (a)_____. Those that lie primarily in the center of the eye are called (b)_____, and the center area is called the (c)_____. When rods absorb light waves, their chemical, which is called (d)_____, breaks down and in turn generates tiny electrical forces that trigger (e)_____ in neighboring cells. Similarly, when cones absorb light waves, their chemicals, which are called (f)_____, break down and generate tiny electrical forces.

5. Photoreceptors that are used to see in dim light and that transmit only black, white, and shades of gray are called (a)_____. These receptors do not transmit fine detail because they undergo a great amount of (b)_____ with neighboring retinal ganglion cells. If a person's diet lacks vitamin A, these receptors are without the chemical (c)_____, resulting in a condition known as (d)_____. Photoreceptors that are used to see in bright light and transmit colors are called (e)_____. These receptors can pick up fine details because they undergo very little (f)_____ with retinal ganglion cells.

■ *If you examined a piece of retina under a microscope, how would you know whether it came from a bird, a dog, or a human?*

THE VISUAL PATHWAY: EYE TO BRAIN

6. Nerve impulses generated in the eye travel along fibers that combine to form the (a)_____ nerve. This nerve exits from the back of the eye in an area called the (b)_____. The point where the branches of the optic nerve cross is called the (c)_____. Impulses eventually reach an area in the back of each occipital lobe called the (d)_____.

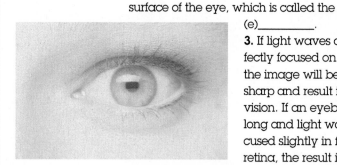

7. The primary visual cortex transforms nerve impulses into simple visual (a)_____, such as lines, shadows, colors, and textures. Similar to the cells in the retinal ganglia and thalamus, the primary visual cortex also has cells that detect (b)_____, such as movement, direction, thickness of a line, and the onset or offset of light. If the primary visual cortex is partially damaged, the usual result is a blind spot in the field of vision; if it is totally damaged, the person is essentially blind, perhaps being able to distinguish night from day.

8. For simple sensations to be transformed into complete, meaningful images, the primary visual cortex must relay its information to other areas, called (a)_____. These cortical areas assemble separate sensations into a complete, meaningful image. If parts of these cortical areas are damaged, the person experiences difficulty in adding meaning to visual experiences, a condition called (b)_____.

■ *Why could a patient clearly see individual parts and pieces of an object but not recognize the whole object?*

COLOR VISION

9. When we talk about seeing colors, we are actually talking about our eyes absorbing light waves of different (a)_____, which are transformed by the visual system into our experience of seeing colors. To explain how light waves are transformed into colors, we distinguish between the function of the cones, which involves the (b)_____ theory, and the function of the ganglion and thalamic cells, which involves the (c)_____ theory of color.

10. According to the trichromatic theory, the cones contain three kinds of chemicals, called opsins, that absorb light waves associated with the three primary colors, (a)_____, _____, and _____. The primary colors of light can be mixed to form all other colors. According to the opponent-process theory, the ganglion and thalamic cells respond in opposite ways, by either being excited or inhibited, when stimulated by one color in a pair of colors. There are two pairs of colors, (b)_____ and _____. It is not until information about "color" reaches the primary visual cortex and association areas that we actually have the experience of seeing colors.

11. There are several kinds of color blindness. A person who has only rods or only one kind of functioning cone is totally color blind and is called a (a)_____, which is a rare condition. A person who has only two kinds of cones is called a (b)_____, which often involves a difficulty in distinguishing red from green. This condition is inherited and primarily affects males.

■ *How would you explain the fact that a rainbow has no colors?*

APPLYING/EXPLORING: VISUAL EXPERIENCES

12. One reason baseball players hit better from one side of the plate is the location of their (a)_____. One reason we can stare at objects and make them disappear is that the objects are falling on our (b)_____. The experience of staring at a color and then staring at a blank white surface and seeing its complementary color is called an (c)_____.

■ *As you look around, why don't objects get lost in your blind spot?*

MODULE 6
HEARING AND OTHER SENSES

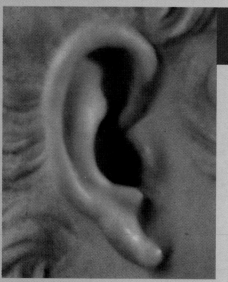

What made a yell sound like a whisper?

One sunny morning Dave was in the kitchen making the usual pot of get-me-up coffee. Just as he finished, his wife walked in and Dave poured her a cup. She added her usual enormous amounts of milk and sugar, tasted it, nodded her approval, and began to talk excitedly about her new project. After several minutes Dave's face took on a puzzled and frightened look. He could see that her lips were moving, but for some reason he couldn't hear a word she was saying. At first he thought his wife must be playing that old joke of mouthing the words without making any sounds. But he watched her face more closely and saw that she was too earnest to be joking. As he tried to figure out why he couldn't hear, a wave of panic swept over him. He grabbed his wife by the shoulders and shook her to get her attention. Then with both hands he pointed to his ears as he shook his head wildly from side to side, indicating "No," he couldn't hear her. Totally bewildered by Dave's strange behavior, his wife yelled, "What's wrong?" From her exaggerated facial movements, Dave could see that she was yelling. He heard only a faint whisper and blurted out, "I can't hear anything!"

Leaving his wife standing in the middle of the kitchen, he ran into the living room. He grabbed a music tape, stuck it into the player, turned up the volume, and waited for the sound to shake the walls. He heard only a faint murmur of distant music. He cupped his ears several times, hoping to get rid of whatever stopped his hearing, but that didn't help. Exasperated, he sat down on the couch and stared at the tape player, which he knew must be blaring loudly. After 32 years of normal hearing, he had suddenly become almost totally deaf. (adapted from the *Los Angeles Times*, May 14, 1984)

What's Coming

We usually think of people as having five senses—*seeing, hearing, tasting, smelling,* and *feeling*. However, physiologists would explain that there are several more senses, such as information from *positioning* of body. In this module, we'll examine five senses: hearing, taste, smell, touch, and position.

Let's begin with hearing and where sound comes from. The reason for Dave's tragic loss of hearing will become clear as we explain the structure and function of the ear.

Hearing

Stimulus: Sound Waves

What happens when you snap your fingers?

Your quick finger movements cause air to be compressed and expanded into a sequence of traveling waves, called *sound waves.* These sound waves are the stimuli for hearing, or audition. If we could make sound waves visible, they would resemble ripples of different sizes. Similar to ripples on a pond, sound waves have varying heights and speeds. *Height, which is the distance from the bottom to the top of a sound wave, is called* **amplitude;** *speed, which is the number of sound waves that occur within one second, is called* **frequency.** These characteristics, as interpreted by our auditory system, determine the quality of what we hear.

Amplitude and Loudness. With every sound we hear, our auditory system transforms the physical stimuli of the height or amplitude of sound waves into the subjective experience of *loudness.* We perceive a yell as loud because it produces high-amplitude waves that are transformed into loud-sounding sensations. In contrast, we perceive a whisper as soft because it produces low-amplitude waves.

A yell produces high-amplitude sounds that we interpret as loud. Notice that amplitude is indicated by the height of the sound waves.

A whisper produces low-amplitude sounds that we interpret as soft. Notice the low height of the sound waves.

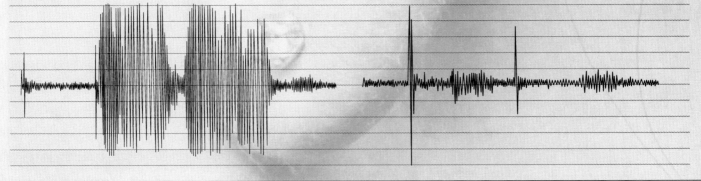

Hearing

PLEASE DO NOT TALK
ABOVE 30 DECIBELS

If this sign were posted in the library, it would refer to loudness, which is measured in units called *decibels*. As you can see in the table, a whisper is about 30 decibels, while the sound from a live rock band is 120 decibels (measured near the speakers). Constant exposure to loud sounds in the 90–100 decibel range and above can permanently damage auditory receptors in the ears. That is why people who work around jet engines, jackhammers, or amplified musical instruments should wear protective ear covers.

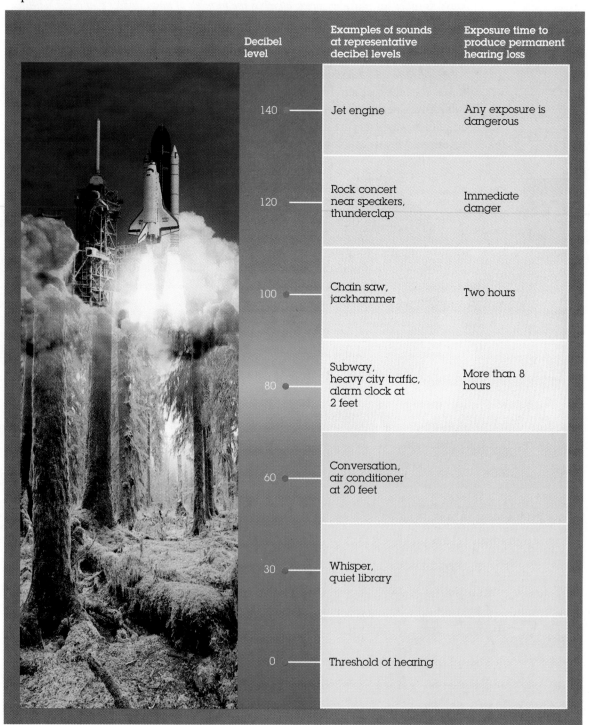

Decibel level	Examples of sounds at representative decibel levels	Exposure time to produce permanent hearing loss
140	Jet engine	Any exposure is dangerous
120	Rock concert near speakers, thunderclap	Immediate danger
100	Chain saw, jackhammer	Two hours
80	Subway, heavy city traffic, alarm clock at 2 feet	More than 8 hours
60	Conversation, air conditioner at 20 feet	
30	Whisper, quiet library	
0	Threshold of hearing	

Frequency and Pitch. We interpret a sound as being high or low, which is called ***pitch***, based on the speed or frequency of its sound waves. The frequency of sound waves is measured in cycles, which refers to how many sound waves occur within one second. For example, a soprano produces sound waves with a fast frequency (many cycles per second) that results in higher sounds or pitch; a bass singer produces sound waves of slower frequency (fewer cycles per second) that results in lower pitch.

Frequency is measured in cycles, which refer to the number of waves that occur per second.

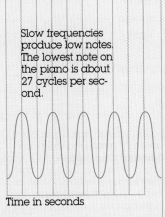

Slow frequencies produce low notes. The lowest note on the piano is about 27 cycles per second.

Time in seconds

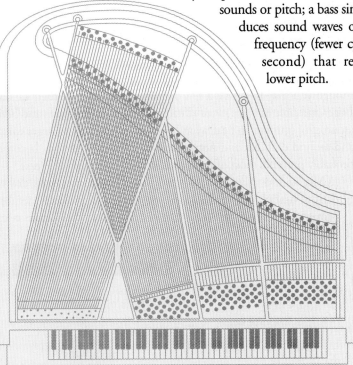

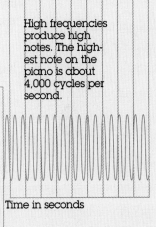

High frequencies produce high notes. The highest note on the piano is about 4,000 cycles per second.

Time in seconds

Adult:
Frequency range: 30 to 18,000 cps

Baby:
Frequency range: 20 to 20,000 cps

Hearing Range. Infants have the widest range of human hearing. They can hear frequencies from 20 to 20,000 cycles per second. Because of the effects of normal aging, by the time infants become college students, they have a slightly smaller range of hearing, from perhaps 30 to 18,000 cycles per second. With progressive aging of the auditory system, we lose the ability to detect the very highest frequencies. For example, by the age of 70, many people have trouble hearing sounds above 6,000 cycles.

Some animals, such as elephants and whales, can produce and hear very low sounds (down to about 14 cycles per second) that are far below the range of human hearing. These very low frequency sounds, which can travel several miles, allow the animals to communicate over the large areas in which they roam (Payne, 1989). Other animals, such as bats and porpoises, can produce and hear very high sounds (up to 100,000 cycles per second), far above our range of hearing. These ultrahigh sounds bounce off objects, and the animals use the returning echoes to locate objects in space. Thus, in a very literal sense, bats and porpoises "see" with sound waves.

Now that you know what sound is and how it is measured, let's see how we transform sound waves into auditory sensations.

Structure and Function of the Ear

How do you turn sound waves into a song?

In explaining the ear, we'll divide it into three parts: the outer ear, the middle ear, and the inner ear. You'll see that each part plays its own critical role in hearing.

The Outer Ear: External Ear, Auditory Canal, and Tympanic Membrane

The two oval-shaped projections attached to each side of your head are part of the **outer ear**, which also includes the auditory canal and the tympanic membrane. The only function of the external ear's funnel-like shape is to gather sound waves. Unlike some animals, such as dogs and deer, humans have relatively small, nonmovable outer ears (although you may have met a few people who can wiggle their ears). Animals with larger, movable ears can more efficiently gather sound waves and better locate the sources of sounds. To hear what it would be like to have larger ears, cup one hand around each ear and notice how much louder sounds become. Vanity probably prevents most of us from wanting larger, movable ears.

Once sound waves are gathered into the ear, they pass down a short narrow tunnel, called the **auditory canal,** and strike a membrane that covers the end of the tunnel. This thin, taut membrane is called the

Outer Ear

External ear

Auditory canal

Tympanic membrane

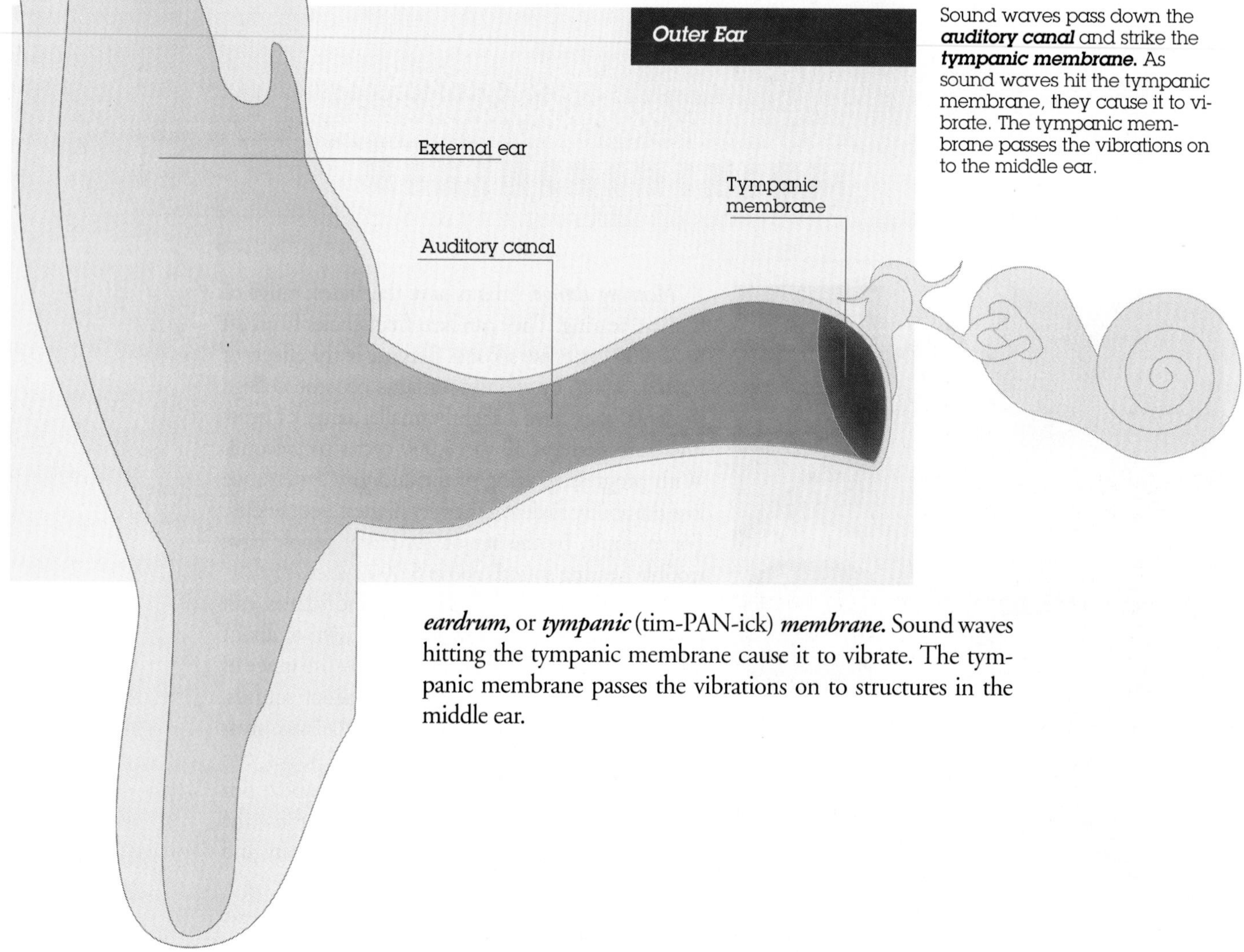

Sound waves pass down the **auditory canal** and strike the **tympanic membrane.** As sound waves hit the tympanic membrane, they cause it to vibrate. The tympanic membrane passes the vibrations on to the middle ear.

eardrum, or **tympanic** (tim-PAN-ick) **membrane.** Sound waves hitting the tympanic membrane cause it to vibrate. The tympanic membrane passes the vibrations on to structures in the middle ear.

The Middle Ear: Ossicles and Oval Window

Attached to the back of the tympanic membrane is the first of three small bones, which together are called *ossicles* (AHS-sick-culls). The vibrations of the tympanic membrane are picked up by the first ossicle (hammer), which passes the vibrations on to the other two ossicles (anvil and stirrup). Each ossicle acts as a lever that increases the pressure on the next, until the pressure exerted by the third ossicle is many times greater than that exerted by the first. The function of the middle ear is to transform vibrations of the tympanic membrane into mechanical movements or vibrations of the ossicles.

The third ossicle (stirrup) is attached to another thin, taut membrane, called the *oval window.* Because the oval window is much smaller than the tympanic membrane

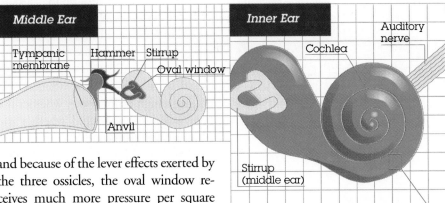

and because of the lever effects exerted by the three ossicles, the oval window receives much more pressure per square millimeter than the tympanic membrane does. This increased pressure is needed to move fluid in the next chamber, the inner ear, which begins at the oval window.

The Inner Ear: Cochlea

The inner ear contains two main structures: the cochlea, which is involved in hearing, and the vestibular system, which is involved in perceiving movement and motion. We'll discuss the vestibular system later; here we will focus on the cochlea.

The coiled, fluid-filled apparatus of the inner ear is called the *cochlea* (KOCK-lee-ah). With its membranes, fluids, and miniature cells that resemble fine hairs, the cochlea can perform the amazing feat of turning vibrations into nerve impulses.

Attached to the oval window is a long, narrow tube that is constructed from membranes and filled with fluid. As the oval window vibrates, so, too, does the fluid in the cochlea. The bottom membrane of the cochlea is called the *basilar* (BAZ-ih-lahr) *membrane.* From this membrane rise fine hairlike cells, which are the auditory receptors.

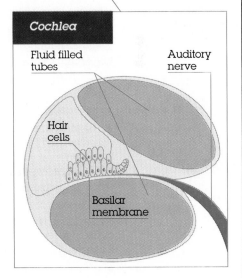

Vibration of fluid in the cochlear tube causes movement of the basilar membrane, which literally bends the hair cells. The mechanical bending of the hair cells generates miniature electrical forces that, if large enough, trigger *nerve impulses.* Now the cochlea has completed its role, which is to transform vibrations into nerve impulses. From the cochlea, these impulses travel to the brain on a band of fibers called the *auditory nerve.*

Structure and Function of the Ear

Neural Pathways to the Brain

As you listen to a favorite song, many thousands of nerve impulses are streaming out of your cochleas, speeding down the auditory nerves toward your brain. Eventually these impulses reach the *primary auditory cortex* in the temporal lobe. Here the electrical impulses are transformed into sensations of simple, rather meaningless sounds and tones of various pitches and loudness. Next, the sound and tone impulses are relayed to neighboring *association areas,* which transform and assemble them into meaningful melodies, songs, words, or sentences. It is surprising to realize that, although your outer, middle, and inner ear transform sound waves into impulses, you actually "hear" with your brain.

In the next section we examine a number of interesting auditory experiences. For example, if you were listening to a guitar, how would you—that is, how would your brain—know whether it is playing a high or low note, whether the note is loud or soft, and whether the guitar is playing on your right or left side?

Primary auditory cortex in temporal lobe

Association areas in temporal lobe

CONCEPT/ GLOSSARY: Structure and Function of the Auditory System

Numbers on illustration match the numbers of the questions.

1. The funnel-like structure called the _____ gathers in sound waves from the environment.

2. The short tunnel called the _____ carries sound waves that strike a membrane.

3. The thin, taut membrane at the end of the auditory canal, called the _____, transforms sound waves into vibrations.

4. The three small bones (hammer, anvil, and stirrup), called the (a)_____, are part of the middle ear. They transform vibrations of the tympanic membrane into mechanical movements, which in turn vibrate a second membrane, called the (b)_____.

5. The coiled, fluid-filled structure called the (a)_____ is one part of the inner ear. It contains auditory receptors called (b)_____ that are attached to the basilar membrane.

6. The band of fibers called the _____ carries nerve impulses from the cochlea to the brain.

7. Located in the temporal lobe is an area that transforms nerve impulses into simple, rather meaningless sensations of sound and tone, with different pitches and loudness; this area is called the _____.

8. Neighboring brain areas transform and assemble simple auditory sensations into meaningful melodies, sounds, and words; these areas are called _____.

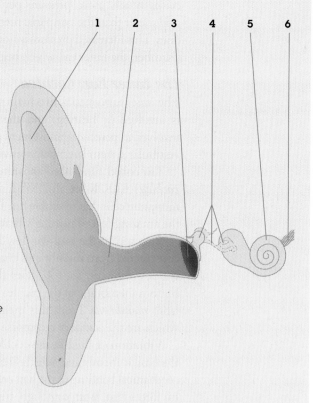

1   2   3   4   5   6

Answers: 1. external ear; 2. auditory canal; 3. tympanic membrane (eardrum); 4. (a) ossicles, (b) oval window; 5. (a) cochlea, (b) hair cells; 6. auditory nerve; 7. primary auditory cortex; 8. association areas.

Direction, Loudness, and Pitch

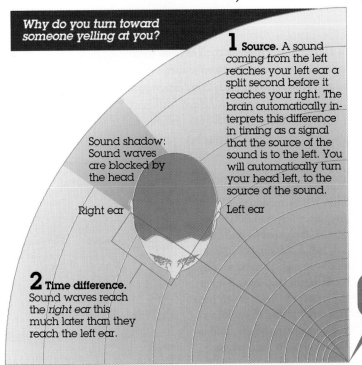

1 Source. A sound coming from the left reaches your left ear a split second before it reaches your right. The brain automatically interprets this difference in timing as a signal that the source of the sound is to the left. You will automatically turn your head left, to the source of the sound.

Sound shadow: Sound waves are blocked by the head

Right ear

Left ear

2 Time difference. Sound waves reach the *right ear* this much later than they reach the left ear.

When you hear your name mentioned, you know—without looking—whether the person who said it is shouting angrily across the room or talking happily beside you. How is it that you can know so much from sound waves?

Direction

What do you do when someone yells, "Watch out!"?

If someone yelled "Watch out!" you would automatically turn toward the source of the yell. You can locate the direction of sounds in space because sound waves reach each of your ears at slightly different times, since your ears are about six inches apart.

WATCH OUT!

If you have difficulty telling where a sound is coming from, the sound is probably arriving at both ears simultaneously. To locate the direction, you can turn your head from side to side, causing the sound to reach one ear before the other.

Loudness

Was that a yell or a whisper?

The subjective sensations of loudness are measured by presenting sounds of various decibels and asking listeners to rate and compare how loud or soft these sounds seem to them. Curiously, a threefold increase in the physical intensity of a sound usually results in only a twofold increase in the subjective experience of loudness. Because there is not a one-to-one relationship between physical intensity and the subjective experience of loudness, we must conclude that our auditory system is actively involved in interpreting and transforming physical stimuli into experiences of loudness.

To discover how the auditory system transforms intensities of sound waves into the subjective experiences of a soft whisper or a loud yell, we must look inside the cochlea.

Lower-intensity sound waves, such as those produced by a whisper, set off a chain of events: fewer vibrations of the tympanic membrane, less movement of fluid in the cochlea, less movement of the basilar membrane, fewer bent hair cells, less electrical force, and finally, fewer nerve impulses triggered and sent to the brain. The brain transforms *rate of impulses* into sensations of loudness. For example, the brain interprets a slower rate of impulses as a softer tone (whisper) and a faster rate as a louder tone (yell).

Higher-intensity sound waves, such as those produced by a yell, set off a chain of events that are opposite those produced by a whisper. Higher-intensity sound waves will generate faster rates of impulses that the brain interprets as louder sounds. In a yelling contest held yearly in Japan, one contestant bellowed at 115 decibels, as loud as the music coming out of the speakers at a rock concert. A 115-decibel yell would generate a very fast rate of impulses that the brain would interpret as an incredibly loud sound.

Direction, Loudness, and Pitch

Pitch

Was that a growl or a scream?

Imagine the the low, menacing growl of a lion and then the high screech of fingernails on the blackboard. Your auditory system transforms *frequency of sound waves*, which is the physical stimulus produced by a growl or a screech, into the subjective experience of low or high tones, called *pitch*. By combining two different theories—frequency theory and place theory—we are able to explain the transformation of frequency into pitch.

Why does a growl sound different from a scream?

Frequency Theory

Was that a lion's growl?

Here is how low-frequency waves, such as a lion's growl, are transformed into low-pitched sounds.

If a lion produces sound waves of 25, 500, or 1,000 cycles per second, neurons will fire impulses at roughly the same rate: 25, 500, or 1,000 impulses per second. In turn, the brain transforms *rate of impulses* into sensations of low-pitched sounds. According to the **frequency theory,** *low-frequency sound waves are transformed directly into rates of impulses, as long as the sound waves are 1,000 cycles or less.* Neurons cannot fire faster than 1,000 times per second.

If the lion makes sound waves above 1,000 cycles per second, a number of different *groups* of neurons fire in rounds, or "volleys." For example, if a growl produces sound waves at 3,000 cycles per second, four groups of neurons could each fire a round or volley of 750 times per second. The four rounds or volleys would add up to 3,000 cycles per second, matching the frequency of the sound wave. Another part of the frequency theory is the *volley theory,* which says that above 1,000 cycles per second, neurons fire in volleys and the brain "adds" volleys and creates the sensation of a low-pitched sound.

But the frequency theory explains only how you hear low sounds. To understand how you hear a high-pitched screech, we need the place theory.

Place Theory

Was that a baby's scream?

Here is how medium- to high-frequency waves (5,000 to 20,000 cycles per second), such as a baby's scream, become medium- to high-pitched sounds.

First, the middle and inner ear transform medium- to high-frequency sound waves into vibrations that move the fluid in the cochlea. As fluid moves back and forth in the tubelike structure of the cochlea, it generates a miniature wave. This wave grows in size and finally peaks at a particular place along the basilar membrane's length.

As the miniature wave crests, it literally flexes the basilar membrane and activates hair cells. According to the **place theory,** *the place on the basilar membrane where the wave crests determines the pitch: nearer the oval window results in medium-pitched sensations and farther away from the oval window results in higher-pitched sensations.*

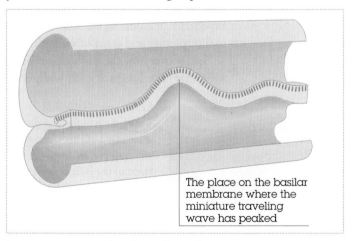

The place on the basilar membrane where the miniature traveling wave has peaked

By combining the place and frequency theories, we can explain how the auditory system transforms frequencies of sound waves ranging from 20 to 20,000 cycles per second into sensations of pitch ranging from very low growls to very high screams.

Various things can happen to the auditory system and interfere with its ability to discriminate loudness, pitch, and direction. For example, what causes deafness?

Deafness: Causes and Treatments

There are two general kinds of deafness—conduction and neural—that have different causes and treatments.

Conduction Deafness

It is not uncommon to see older people wearing hearing aids, often used to treat **conduction deafness**, *which can be caused by wax in the auditory canal, injury to the tympanic membrane, or malfunction of the ossicles.* All of these conditions interfere with transmitting vibrations from the tympanic membrane to the fluid of the cochlea. If simple cleaning of the ear canal does not restore normal hearing, conduction deafness can usually be treated with a hearing aid, which essentially replaces the function of the middle ear.

Neural Deafness

At the beginning of this module, we told you about Dave, who started to go deaf when he was 32. For the next 20 years, Dave lived in a world of garbled noises, muffled sounds, and unintelligible conversations. Finally, at age 52, Dave agreed to a surgical procedure in which a thin wire cable was implanted inside his cochlea. With this device, Dave can hear sounds more clearly, understand some conversation, and feel much better about the quality of his life (*Los Angeles Times*, May 14, 1984).

Dave has **neural deafness**, *which can be caused by damage to the auditory receptors (hair cells), preventing the triggering of impulses, or by damage to the auditory nerve, preventing impulses from reaching the brain.* Since neither hair cells nor auditory nerve fibers regenerate, neural deafness was generally untreatable up until recently. However, in 1984 the U.S. Food and Drug Administration approved the use of a miniature electronic device, called a cochlear implant, that is surgically implanted into the cochlea. If the auditory nerve is intact, the cochlear implant can be used to treat neural deafness caused by damaged hair cells, which is the problem for about 90% of those with hearing impairment. As you proceed step by step through the next illustration, you'll see how a cochlear implant triggers nerve impulses.

Cochlear Implant: How It Works

1&2 A microphone, which is worn behind the ear, gathers and sends sound waves to a sound processor, which is usually worn on the belt. The sound processor transforms sound waves into electrical signals, which are sent to four tiny transmitters implanted in the skin.

Transmitters

3 A receiver, which is implanted in the bony skull, receives the electrical signals and sends them along a thin wire cable to the cochlea.

4 A thin cable is threaded into a fluid-filled tube of the cochlea until it makes contact with the auditory nerve. When the receiver sends electrical signals through the wire cable, the signals trigger impulses in the auditory nerve.

5 The auditory nerve carries the "manufactured" impulses to the auditory areas in the brain, which interpret and transform impulses into auditory sensations.

Outer ear

Cochlea

Auditory canal

How well can Dave hear?

Although Dave's cochlear implant has greatly improved his hearing, it cannot begin to duplicate normal hearing. With a cochlear implant, only a small number of wires (typically 1 to 8) are implanted into the cochlea compared to a normal ear with about 15,000 hair cells. For this reason, Dave cannot make out more than one voice at a time, and he understands up to 70% of the words in a conversation by using clues from his implant, the content of the conversation, and facial expressions. Researchers report a 20%–90% success in recognizing words and sentences with cochlear implants; the higher success rates are due to patients using extra clues, as Dave does (Loeb, 1985; Nadol & Eddington, 1988). Even so, the cochlear implant is a major breakthrough for many people who have neural deafness.

Earlier, we mentioned that there were two main structures in the inner ear, the cochlea and the vestibular organs. If you have ever stood on your head or gotten seasick, you have firsthand experience with the vestibular organs.

The Vestibular System

Where does that sick feeling come from?

For most of my childhood years, I hated drives on curvy roads. I now hate bumpy flights in airplanes. After about an hour, I get a cold, sweaty feeling. Then come nausea, dizziness, and an extreme desire to lie down anywhere—stationary. Along with about 25% of the population, I experience moderate to severe signs of motion sickness. About 55% of people experience only mild symptoms, while the remaining 20% are lucky, since they rarely experience motion sickness (Dobie et al., 1987). Researchers think that motion sickness is a side effect of the functioning of the vestibular organs.

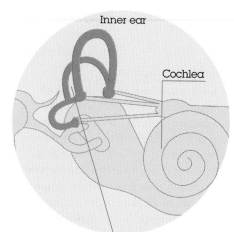

Inner ear

Cochlea

Which end is up?

In the inner ear, above the cochlea, sit the **vestibular organs,** *three archlike structures set at different angles that provide feedback on your body's position in space.* Movement of your head or body causes movement of the fluid in these three arches. In turn, the moving fluid triggers impulses that the brain transforms into sensations of movement and position. The vestibular organs indicate which end is up by providing information on whether you are standing on your feet or hands, are lying on your stomach or back, are losing your balance, or need to initiate a movement to regain or correct your balance. Under certain conditions, however, the vestibular organs are also involved in motion sickness.

Vestibular organs, shaped like three miniature arches set at different angles, are involved in perceiving movement and position.

Vestibular organs signal the position of your body.

Motion Sickness

Apparently, motion sickness arises when your vestibular system sends signals to the brain that you are bouncing around in the seat of a car or plane but your eyes report that objects in the distance look fairly steady. Many movie watchers feel queasy when they experience the reverse of this situation: their eyes report the sharp turning and twisting of a speeding car across the screen while their vestibular system reports that they are sitting very still in their seats. Researchers believe that if your vestibular system sends information that conflicts with that reported by your eyes, the sensory mismatch can result in motion sickness. Studies have shown that vestibular information is more important than visual information in causing motion sickness (Matsnev et al., 1987).

A number of drugs are available that reduce the symptoms of motion sickness (Attias et al., 1987). As an alternative to drugs, a significant reduction in motion sickness was reported by fliers who had completed a behavioral training program that taught them to per-

form relaxation responses, think positive thoughts, or use calming images at the first sign of symptoms. Of 53 fliers who had been grounded because of chronic, severe motion sickness, 49 were able to overcome their problem and start flying again after completing the behavioral program (Jones et al., 1985).

If you suffer from motion sickness, you may need a few minutes to relax before beginning the next topic, which involves tasting and smelling food.

Chemical Sense: Taste

What does your tongue know?

Throughout the day, you put thousands of chemicals (food and drink) into your mouth. However, your tongue has receptors for only four basic tastes: sweet, salty, sour, and bitter. The reason **taste** *is called a chemical sense is that the stimuli are chemicals.*

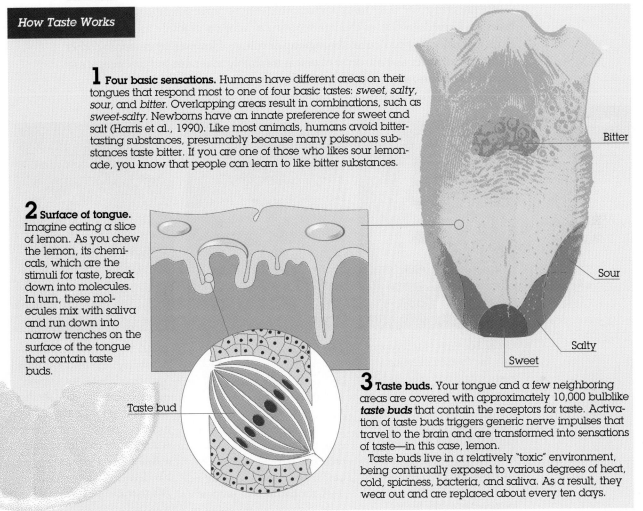

How Taste Works

1 **Four basic sensations.** Humans have different areas on their tongues that respond most to one of four basic tastes: *sweet, salty, sour,* and *bitter*. Overlapping areas result in combinations, such as *sweet-salty*. Newborns have an innate preference for sweet and salt (Harris et al., 1990). Like most animals, humans avoid bitter-tasting substances, presumably because many poisonous substances taste bitter. If you are one of those who likes sour lemonade, you know that people can learn to like bitter substances.

2 **Surface of tongue.** Imagine eating a slice of lemon. As you chew the lemon, its chemicals, which are the stimuli for taste, break down into molecules. In turn, these molecules mix with saliva and run down into narrow trenches on the surface of the tongue that contain taste buds.

Taste bud

Bitter

Sour

Salty

Sweet

3 **Taste buds.** Your tongue and a few neighboring areas are covered with approximately 10,000 bulblike **taste buds** that contain the receptors for taste. Activation of taste buds triggers generic nerve impulses that travel to the brain and are transformed into sensations of taste—in this case, lemon.

Taste buds live in a relatively "toxic" environment, being continually exposed to various degrees of heat, cold, spiciness, bacteria, and saliva. As a result, they wear out and are replaced about every ten days.

Taste and Smell

If your taste receptors are sensitive to only four basic tastes, how can you tell the difference between two sweet tastes (a brownie and vanilla ice cream, for example) or between two sour ones (lemon juice and vinegar)? The truth is that a considerable percentage of the sensations we attribute to "taste" are actually contributed by our sense of smell. Thus, if you hold your nose, which requires you to rely totally on your tongue's taste receptors, you would probably not be able to differentiate between the two "sweet" tastes of cola and 7-Up, for example. When we combine sensations of taste and smell we are experiencing *flavor.* You have probably experienced the limitations of your taste buds when you had a cold and lived with blocked nasal passages. Foods taste bland indeed when your sense of smell is impaired.

Our sense of taste is not always limited to our tongues. Many of us dislike the taste of unusual foods or may even refuse to taste a food that we have not grown up with. Following is a sample of some different cultural "tastes" in food.

Different Tastes

Individuals across cultures use a common facial expression to indicate disgust: closing of the eyes, narrowing of the nostrils, downward curling of the lips, and sometimes sticking out the tongue. Children begin to show this disgust expression between the ages of 2 and 4, a time when they are learning which foods in their culture are judged edible and which are considered repugnant (Farb & Armelagos, 1980). Besides an innate preference for sweet tastes and an avoidance of bitter substances, most of our tastes are learned. In fact, as children we learn to adopt a relatively narrow range of tastes that reflect our particular ethnic group or culture. However, by examining other cultures we discover that our sense of taste is incredibly adaptable and that people can learn to like an amazing variety of substances.

Bon appétit!

Grubs. For most North Americans, the thought of eating a worm would be totally unthinkable. For the Asmat of New Guinea, however, a favorite delicacy is the plump, white, two-inch larva or beetle grub. The natives harvest dozens of the grubs, put them on bamboo slivers, and roast them. A photographer from the United States who did a story on the Asmat tried to eat a roasted grub but his American tastes would not let him swallow it (Kirk, 1972).

Fish Eyes and Whale Fat. Although some Americans have developed a taste for raw fish (sushi), a common dish in Japan, most would certainly gag at the thought of eating raw fish eyes. Yet for some Eskimo children, raw fish eyes are like candy. Here you see a young girl using the Eskimo's all-purpose knife to gouge out the eye of an already-filleted Arctic fish.

Eskimos also hunt a type of whale (the narwhal) that provides much of their protein. They consider the layer of fat under the skin (*mukluk*) a delicacy, and they eat it raw or dried.

Blood. Several tribes in East Africa supplement their diet with fresh blood that is sometimes mixed with milk. They obtain the blood by puncturing a cow's jugular vein with a sharp arrow. A cow can be bled many times and suffer no ill effects. The blood-milk drink provides a rich source of protein and iron.

What Tastes Good and What Tastes Bad

Depending on whether you were raised in North America, Japan, New Guinea, Greenland, or Africa, your preferred tastes dramatically reflect your culture. These examples illustrate the powerful influences that culture has on our sense of what tastes good and what tastes bad. When we refer to how things taste, what we mean to a large extent is how they smell, which is our next topic.

Chemical Sense: Smell

Like taste, **smell (olfaction)** *is called a chemical sense because its stimulus is chemical.* And, as we have seen, smell greatly influences our sense of taste. In fact, the sense of smell is 10,000 times more sensitive than that of taste (Reyneri, 1984).

If you walked into a room with an irritated skunk, you would immediately identify its smell. The skunk's spray gives off thousands of molecules, which are carried by the air and drawn into your nose as you breathe. You can greatly increase the number of molecules entering your nose by sniffing (not recommended here).

How We Smell Things

1 Stimulus. The reason you can smell substances such as a skunk spray is that they are **volatile**, which means they give off molecules at room temperature. A rose can be smelled because it is volatile (gives off molecules); glass, on the other hand, is not volatile and cannot be smelled.

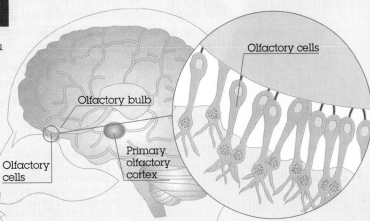

Olfactory cells

Olfactory bulb

Primary olfactory cortex

Olfactory cells

3 Sensations. Nerve impulses travel to the **olfactory bulb**, which is a tiny wiener-shaped area in the brain that lies directly above the olfactory cells. From here, impulses are relayed to the **primary olfactory cortex**, located underneath the brain. This cortex transforms nerve impulses into **olfactory sensations** of a skunk or a rose. In contrast to taste, which is limited to four basic sensations, people can identify as many as 10,000 different odors. We do find it difficult to give these odors exact names and often resort to saying, "It smells like . . ."

2 Receptors. As you breathe, a small percentage of the total air entering your nose reaches the uppermost surface of your nasal passages. Here are located two one-inch-square patches of tissue that are covered with mucus, a thick, gluey film into which skunk odor molecules dissolve. Underneath the mucus is a layer of olfactory cells, which are the **receptors** for smell (olfaction). As molecules dissolve in the mucus, they stimulate the olfactory cells, which trigger nerve impulses that travel to the brain. People can lose their sense of smell through a virus or inflammation that destroys their olfactory cells or by a blow to the head damaging the neural network that carries impulses to the brain.

The Function of Olfaction

As you already know, one function of smell is to intensify the taste of food. Another is to warn us away from potentially dangerous foods; the repulsive odor of spoiled or rotten food does this very effectively. A third function is to elicit strong memories, often associated with emotional feelings, such as the smell of pumpkin reminding you of a festive family gathering (Schab, 1991). For many animals, such as cats and dogs, smell also functions to locate food, mates, and territory.

Why does her nose earn over $100,000?

Sophia Grojsman, one of only a dozen master perfumers in the United States, is responsible for creating some of the best-known perfumes. Known in the trade as a "nose," she earns over $100,000 a year because there is no scientific/computer substitute for her "nose's" ability to identify, remember, and mix fragrances. To create a perfume, she often samples from over 400 vials containing both natural and manufactured fragrances. One reason a computerized nose has not yet replaced a human nose is that scientists do not fully understand which of smell's molecular qualities (weight, shape) determine its odor.

Humans may learn to increase their smell sensitivity but cannot match that of a good hounddog. A dog has an olfactory receptor area the size of a small handkerchief; a human's is the size of a postage stamp. However, studies indicate that people who work with perfumes and wines develop incredible abilities to detect subtle differences in odors (Cain, 1977).

Sense of Touch

What does fur feel like?

If you were to draw your hand across the surface of this cat, you would have the sensations of touching something soft and "furry." These sensations are produced by the sense of **touch**, *which includes pressure, temperature, and pain.* If you were to examine the surface of your skin, you would see a relatively smooth membrane, covered in some places with hair. If you could look beneath the outer layer of skin, you would discover the locations of a half-dozen miniature sensors that are the receptors for the sense of touch. The sensors in skin with hair follicles (the backs of your arms) are slightly different from those in skin without hair (your palms). Let's examine some of these miniature sensors and explain how they function.

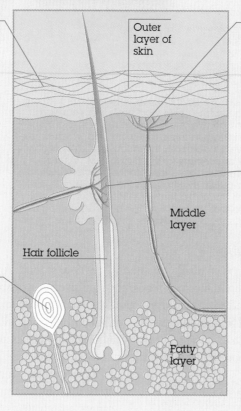

Outer layer of skin

Middle layer

Hair follicle

Fatty layer

Skin. The outermost layer of skin is a thin film of dead cells containing no receptors. Immediately below the dead layer are the first receptors, which look like groups of threadlike extensions. In the middle and fatty layers of skin are a variety of receptors with different shapes and functions. We're going to pull out several representative touch receptors and explain their functions.

Pacinian corpuscle. In the fatty layer of skin is the largest touch sensor, called the *Pacinian corpuscle* (pa-SIN-ee-in core-PUS-sole). This receptor, which has distinctive layers like a slice of onion, is highly sensitive to touch, is the only receptor that responds to vibration, and adapts very quickly.

Free nerve endings. Near the bottom of the outer layer of skin is a group of threadlike extensions called *free nerve endings* because they have nothing protecting or surrounding them. One puzzling feature of free nerve endings is that the same receptor can transmit information about both temperature and pain. Researchers think that different patterns of neural activity may signal different sensations, such as slow bursts of firing for temperature and fast bursts for pain.

Hair receptors. In the middle layer are free nerve endings that are wrapped around the base of each hair follicle; these are called *hair receptors.* Hair receptors respond or fire with a burst of activity when hairs are first bent. However, if hairs remain bent for a period of time, the receptors cease firing, a phenomenon called *adaptation.* For example, when you first put on a watch, it bends hairs, causing hair receptors to fire; your brain interprets this firing as "pressure on your wrist." If you keep the watch on and it remains in place, keeping the hairs bent, the hair receptors adapt or cease firing and you no longer feel pressure from your watch, even though it is still there. Your skin contains some receptors that adapt rapidly (hair receptors) and others that adapt slowly. Adaptation prevents your sense of touch from being overloaded. Thanks to adaptation, you are not aware of the continual pressure from your clothes, socks, or shoes—until I point them out.

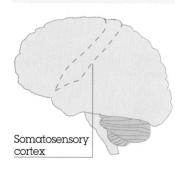

Somatosensory cortex

As the receptors in your skin are stimulated by touch, temperature, or pain, they trigger "generic" nerve impulses that eventually reach the *somatosensory cortex* located in the parietal lobe. As we explained in Module 4, different parts of the body are represented on different parts of this cortex. The more sensitive the body part (lips), the larger the area on the somatosensory cortex; the less sensitive the area (trunk), the smaller the area. The somatosensory cortex transforms generic impulses into sensations of touch, temperature, and pain.

After the Concept/Glossary, we'll discuss pain and its treatment.

CONCEPT/
GLOSSARY:
Vestibular System,
Chemical Senses,
and Sense of
Touch

1. The inner ear contains a group of structures shaped like three tiny arches set at different angles. These structures signal body movement and position and are called _____.

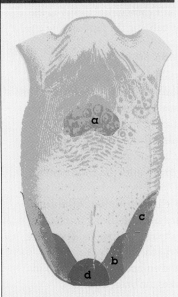

2. Various areas of the tongue respond most to one of the four basic tastes. The middle back area of the tongue responds most to (a)_____; the sides of the tongue near the middle respond most to (b)_____; the sides of the tongue nearer the front respond most to (c)_____; and the very middle front of the tongue responds most to (d)_____.

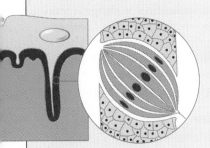

3. The receptors for taste, called _____, are located in narrow, deep trenches on the surface of the tongue.

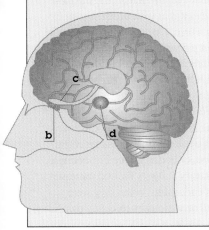

4. If a substance gives off molecules at room temperature, it is said to be (a)_____ and thus can be smelled. Molecules from these substances are drawn into the nose, dissolve in mucus, and activate the receptors, which are called (b)_____. Olfactory receptors trigger generic impulses that go to the (c)_____ and then to (d)_____, which transforms generic impulses into olfactory sensations.

5. The sense of touch is actually made up of three different sensations: (a)_____, (b)_____, and (c)_____.

6. When a receptor stops firing impulses even though the stimulus is still present, the receptor is said to show _____.

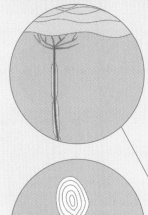

7. This touch receptor, called a _____, is fast adapting.

8. This touch receptor, called a _____, is fast adapting.

9. This touch receptor, called a _____, responds to both touch and vibration.

10. Nerve impulses from touch receptors are transformed into sensations of touch, temperature, and pain by the _____, which is located in the parietal lobe.

APPLYING/ EXPLORING: THE EXPERIENCE OF PAIN

How does pain differ from the other senses? If you have ever banged a finger, you are familiar with two different kinds of pain sensations. At first, you feel a *sharp, localized pain,* which is shortly replaced by a *dull, more generalized pain.* Intense pressure or tissue damage (which releases pain-producing chemicals) activates free nerve endings, which are the *receptors* for pain. These pain receptors trigger generic impulses that travel to your brain, where they are transformed into pain *sensations.*

The sense of pain differs from the other senses in two interesting ways. First, while each of the other senses responds primarily to a single stimulus, pain results from many *different stimuli.* For example, besides intense pressure or tissue damage, pain can be produced by very loud noises, bright lights, chemicals (in peppers), and intense heat or cold (which may or may not cause tissue damage). Second, the *intensity* of the painful sensation depends not only on the intensity of the stimulus but also on a number of psychological factors, including attentional or emotional states. Let's look at how these factors affect your experience of pain.

Gate Control Theory

Why does it help to rub a banged finger? After banging a finger, you may partially reduce the pain by gently rubbing the hurt area. According to the **gate control theory** (Melzack & Wall, 1965), rubbing the area triggers nonpainful nerve impulses that compete with pain impulses as they enter the spinal cord. This competition creates a neural gate that allows only nonpainful impulses to pass through and reach the brain. The neural gate is not an actual gate but rather a description of what happens when nerve impulses from two different sources (painful versus nonpainful) compete for entrance to the brain. With the neural gate closed, fewer painful impulses reach the

Two Steps in Gate Control

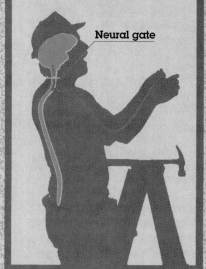

Neural gate

Impulses carrying pain signals from an injured area try to enter the spinal cord. Competition between painful and nonpainful impulses creates a neural gate, which prevents painful impulses from reaching the brain.

brain, and you feel less pain from the hurt area. The next time you bump or bruise yourself, put the gate control theory to the test by gently rubbing the surrounding area.

Attention and Emotion

If you have mildly bruised, bumped, or cut yourself while being thoroughly involved in something, you may have not noticed the injury or felt any pain until later. An extreme example is the football player who may play for hours with a broken bone and not feel any "pain" until the game is over (Warga, 1987).

Ronald Melzack, coauthor of the gate control theory, uses this theory to explain how intense distraction can block pain. He believes that the football player's intense attentional and emotional involvement in the game causes the brain to send nonpainful impulses that close neural gates in the spinal cord. The closed neural gates block pain impulses from reaching the brain and thus prevent feelings of pain. Sometime later, when the game is over and the player's attentive and emotional states calm down, neural gates open, impulses from the broken bone reach his brain, and he feels pain.

Endorphins

Someone who has experienced a serious injury will usually report that at first the pain was bearable but that with time the pain grew much worse. One reason for this initial reduction in pain is that *the brain makes its own pain-reducing chemicals, called* **endorphins** (en-DOOR-fins), *that have the same pain-reducing properties as morphine, a powerful painkilling drug* (Terenius & Wahlstrom, 1975). The brain produces endorphins in situations that evoke great fear, anxiety, stress, or bodily injury. For example, in the laboratory, subjects showed increased secretion of endorphins when they were made fearful or anxious by receiving painful

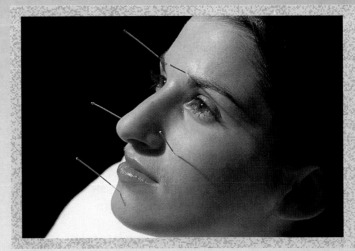

During acupuncture, thin needles are inserted and rotated or electrically stimulated.

electric shock or by holding their hands in ice water (Millan, 1986). In real life, patients show increases in endorphins when having their tooth pulp touched (very painful) or having bandages removed from badly burned areas of the body (Szyfelbein, Osgood, & Carr, 1985). Such studies indicate that the brain produces endorphins to help us cope with periods of intense physical stress. In addition, endorphins seem to explain how acupuncture reduces pain.

Acupuncture

Initially, scientists trained in the rigorous methods of the West (United States) expressed great doubt that an ancient Oriental procedure called *acupuncture* could produce relief of pain. One reason for disbelief was the procedure itself: the practitioner inserted thin needles into various points on the body's surface and then manually twirled or electrically stimulated the needles. After such stimulation for 10 to 20 minutes, patients often reported a reduction in pain.

The mysterious part of this procedure was that the points of insertion were mapped over a thousand years ago and were often far removed from the site of pain. Today, however, modern scientists have explained some of the mystery surrounding acupuncture. First, the points of needle insertion, which seem unrelated to the point of injury, are actually very close to known pathways that conduct pain (Chen, Li, & Jiang, 1986). Second, stimulation of these points causes secretion of endorphins, which we know can reduce pain (Chen, Li, & Jiang, 1986). If patients are first given a drug (naloxone) that blocks secretion of endorphins, acupuncture does not reduce pain. There is now considerable evidence that acupuncture may relieve acute or short-lived pain—and, in some cases, chronic or long-lasting pain—by causing secretion of endorphins (Richardson & Vincent, 1986; Kreitler, Kreitler, & Carasso, 1987).

In response to injury or great stress, the brain produces powerful pain-reducing chemicals called endorphins.

Summary/Self-Test

1. The stimuli for hearing or audition are (a)_____, which have several physical characteristics that the auditory system transforms into psychological or subjective experiences. For example, the physical characteristic of amplitude or height of sound waves is transformed into the subjective experience of (b)_____, which is measured in units called (c)_____. The frequency of sound waves (cycles per second) is transformed into the subjective experience of (d)_____, which for humans ranges from about 20 to 20,000 cycles per second.

■ *A new stereo is advertised as having a special frequency range of 1,000 to 5,000 cycles per second. Should you buy it?*

STRUCTURE AND FUNCTION OF THE EAR

2. On each side of your head are two funnel-like shapes called (a)_____, whose function is to gather sound waves. These waves travel down a short tunnel called the (b)_____. At the end of this tunnel, sound waves strike a thin, taut membrane called the (c)_____, whose function is to transform sound waves into (d)_____.

3. Attached to the back of the tympanic membrane are three tiny bones, the hammer, anvil, and stirrup, which together are called (a)_____ and are located in the (b)_____. Vibrations in the tympanic membrane produce mechanical movements in these bones. The third and last of these bones (the stirrup) is attached to another thin membrane, called the (c)_____, which is made to vibrate.

4. Of several structures in the inner ear, one is a coiled, fluid-filled, tubelike apparatus called the (a)_____. This structure contains the auditory receptors, called (b)_____, which are located on the (c)_____. Movement of the fluid in the tube causes movement of the membrane, which in turn causes bending of the hair cells, generating a tiny (d)_____. If this is large enough, it will trigger nerve impulses, which leave the cochlea via the (e)_____ and travel to the brain.

5. Nerve impulses travel to the brain and eventu-ally reach the (a)_____, which is located in the temporal lobe. There, nerve impulses are transformed into rather simple, meaningless auditory sensations. These sensations are finally relayed to (b)_____, which assemble and transform them into meaningful and complete melodies, songs, words, or sentences.

■ *You're going to build an ear that can be used in robots. What parts would you need?*

DIRECTION, LOUDNESS, AND PITCH

6. To tell the direction or source of a sound, the brain analyzes the difference in time between _____ arriving from the left and right ears.

7. Different intensities of sound waves result in our experiencing different degrees of (a)_____. The brain uses (b)_____ of impulses as the signal for different degrees of loudness.

8. To produce low-pitched tones, the auditory system transforms low-frequency sound waves into low-frequency vibrations that in turn are transformed into a (a)_____ of neurons or groups of neurons firing impulses. This method of coding low frequencies according to rate of firing is referred to as the (b)_____ theory. The method of coding medium to high frequencies according to where the basilar membrane is bent is called the (c)_____ theory.

9. There are two basic causes of deafness. If the cause is wax in the auditory canal, injury to the tympanic membrane, or malfunction of the ossicles, it is called (a)_____ deafness. If the cause is damage to hair cells in the cochlea or to the auditory nerve, it is called (b)_____ deafness.

■ *Your grandmother complains that she can hear low sounds but not high sounds. What could be the problem?*

THE VESTIBULAR SYSTEM

10. Besides the cochlea, the inner ear contains three arch-shaped, fluid-filled structures called _____. The movement of fluid in these organs provides signals that the brain interprets as movement and position of the head and body.

■ *Advertisement: Permanently cure motion sickness by removing the vestibular organs. Why is this too good to be true?*

CHEMICAL SENSE: TASTE

11. Different areas on our tongues respond most to one of four basic tastes. The middle back of the tongue responds most to (a)_____; the middle sides of the tongue respond to (b)_____; the middle front sides of the tongue respond to (c)_____; and the very front center of the tongue responds to (d)_____. The sense of taste is called a chemical sense because the stimuli for different tastes are (e)_____.

12. Chewing food breaks it down into molecules that dissolve in saliva, which runs along the surface of the tongue into narrow trenches that contain (a)_____, which are the receptors for taste. These receptors trigger nerve impulses that travel to the brain, which then transforms them into the sensations of taste. Because our sense of taste is limited to four basic tastes and their combinations, a considerable amount of what we think of as coming from our sense of taste is actually contributed by our sense of (b)_____.

■ *You want to build an artificial tongue that can be used to taste new food products. What parts would you need?*

CULTURAL DIVERSITY: DIFFERENT TASTES

13. Besides an innate preference for sweet tastes and avoidance of bitter substances, most of our tastes are _____. Examples of different tastes from around the world indicate the powerful influences that culture has on our sense of taste.

■ *After eating a new food in China, an American tourist finds out that the food was rat. Predict what happens next.*

CHEMICAL SENSE: SMELL

14. If a substance is to be smelled, it must be able to give up molecules at room temperature; that is, it must be (a)_____. These airborne molecules, which are drawn into the nose by regular breathing or by sniffing, dissolve in a thin sticky film or mucus, which lies at the top of the nose cavity. Underneath the layer of mucus are layers of receptors for smell, which are called (b)_____. These receptors trigger impulses that travel to an area underneath the brain called the (c)_____. This area transforms generic impulses into hundreds of different odors.

■ *Explain what happens after you "scratch" a scratch-and-sniff magazine advertisement.*

SENSE OF TOUCH

15. The sense of touch actually provides information on three different kinds of stimuli: _____, _____, and _____. The various layers of skin contain different kinds of touch receptors.

16. Receptors for the sense of touch trigger generic impulses that travel to an area in the brain called the _____. This area transforms generic impulses into sensations of pressure, temperature, and pain. The more sensitive the area of the body is to touch, the larger its area on this cortex.

■ *You are developing an artificial skin that can be used with burn victims. What kinds of sensors does your artificial skin need?*

APPLYING/EXPLORING: THE EXPERIENCE OF PAIN

17. After an injury, you feel two different kinds of pain sensations: at first there is sharp, localized pain, which is followed by a duller, more generalized pain. The receptors for pain are (a)_____, which respond to pressure and to pain-producing chemicals released during tissue damage. Rubbing an injured area may reduce the pain because, according to the (b)_____, impulses coming from nonpainful stimuli (rubbing) compete with and prevent impulses coming from painful stimuli (injury) from reaching the brain. We may feel reduced pain immediately following great fear, anxiety, or physical injury because the brain produces pain-reducing chemicals called (c)_____.

■ *You just stubbed your toe. Predict what will happen next.*

Chapter *Four*
PERCEPTION

MODULE 7
BASIC PERCEPTUAL PROCESSES

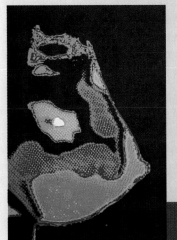

The cancerous breast tumor has been computer enhanced to stand out as a white spot (middle of photo).

When is it cancer?

Helen was very upset and I was trying to think of something reassuring to say. "When will you know for sure?"

"I always thought that one just had a mammogram and the doctor said you either did or didn't have breast cancer." Helen stopped and tried to hold back her tears. "I won't know for sure for a couple of days."

"What did the doctor actually say?"

"My doctor said there was an area that looked suspicious on the mammogram, but at this point she couldn't be absolutely sure it was cancer. When the doctor showed me the spot on the mammogram, I could barely make it out. She said that it takes a trained eye, one that has seen literally hundreds of mammograms, to find suspicious-looking spots."

"What happens next?"

"My doctor said that we should repeat the mammogram to make sure the spot is still there. I'm having that done next Thursday. I'm just hoping that the spot will be gone." Helen was drying her eyes. "I know this has happened to others but I never thought it would happen to me."

Helen's doctor must first detect tissue change in the mammogram and then decide whether the change is great enough to signal the presence of a cancerous tumor. The doctor's task is similar to three experimental questions that are basic to perception:

1 At what point are we aware of a stimulus?

2 At what point do we know a stimulus intensity has increased (or decreased)?

3 At what point do bits of sensory information (sensations) change into a pattern or meaningful image (perceptions)?

The answer to the first question involves the concept of stimulus **threshold**: *a point above which a stimulus is perceived and below which it is not perceived.* For Helen's doctor, the stimulus threshold is the point at which a potentially cancerous tumor can be detected by a change in the tissue's appearance on a mammogram.

What's Coming

In this module we'll look at the basic processes involved in perception, such as the differences between sensation and perception, principles of how we organize our perceptions, and illusions. In the next module we'll examine how various factors, such as heredity, experience, learning, and culture, influence our perceptions.

Let's start with a very basic question, "How do psychologists decide whether we have perceived something?"

Perceptual Thresholds

Absolute Threshold

Imagine taking the following test to check your range of hearing. You will be presented with a series of tones that slowly increase in intensity; you are to press a button when you first hear a tone. You may think that there is a certain intensity (loudness), or absolute point, at which you will first hear a tone. This idea of there being an absolute threshold was initially proposed by Gustav Fechner, an important historical figure in perceptual research. He defined *absolute threshold* as the smallest amount of stimulus energy (such as sound or light) that can be observed or experienced. According to this idea, if your hearing were always measured under exactly the same conditions, your absolute threshold would always remain the same. Although

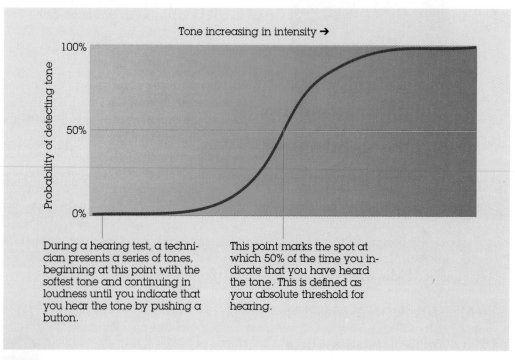

Tone increasing in intensity →

Probability of detecting tone

100%

50%

0%

During a hearing test, a technician presents a series of tones, beginning at this point with the softest tone and continuing in loudness until you indicate that you hear the tone by pushing a button.

This point marks the spot at which 50% of the time you indicate that you have heard the tone. This is defined as your absolute threshold for hearing.

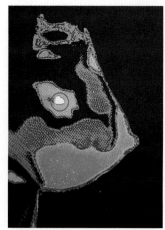

Doctors use various procedures to achieve a high accuracy rate in identifying tumors.

Fechner tried various methods to identify absolute thresholds, he found that an individual's threshold was not absolute and in fact differed depending on various conditions, such as the state of the subject and the test situation. Because of this variability, researchers had to redefine **absolute threshold** *as the intensity level that a person detects 50% of the time*, which is the definition of absolute threshold that is used today. A stimulus that is detected less than 50% of the time is called a ***subliminal stimulus.***

In the case of Helen's doctor, an accuracy rate of only 50% (absolute threshold) in identifying signals for cancerous tumors would be potentially deadly for her patients. To increase accuracy, doctors recommend regular checkups so they can compare tests (in Helen's case, mammograms) across time and ask other experienced colleagues to read the tests. If there is some doubt, doctors perform a *biopsy*, surgically removing a tiny amount of suspected tissue for microscopic examination.

The answer to our first question, "At what point are we aware of a stimulus?" is answered in an experimental way by measuring the absolute threshold. To illustrate the answer to our second question, "At what point do we know a stimulus intensity has increased (or decreased)?" we'll use a common parent-child perceptual problem.

Just Noticeable Difference and Weber's Law

Why must loud music be turned way down before it sounds softer?

The answer to this question is based on the historical work of E. H. Weber, a famous figure in perceptual research. He developed the concept of a **just noticeable difference,** *which is an increase or decrease in the intensity of a stimulus that a person can just manage to detect.* Weber asked people to compare stimuli of varying intensities and indicate when they could detect a difference between them. He discovered that if he presented two stimuli with very low intensities (for example, a 2-ounce weight versus a 3-ounce weight), people could easily detect small differences between them. If, however, he presented stimuli with high intensities (a 40-pound weight versus a 41-pound weight), people could no longer detect small differences. For higher-intensity stimuli, a much larger difference in intensity was required for the difference to be noticed.

Such observations formed the basis for **Weber's law,** *which states that the amount of increase in intensity of a stimulus needed to produce a just noticeable difference grows in proportion to the intensity of the initial stimulus.* Experience you've had with your parents asking you to turn down the stereo may confirm Weber's law and the concept of just noticeable differences. If you are playing your stereo very softly, you must increase the volume only slightly in order to detect a just noticeable difference in loudness. But if you are playing your stereo loudly, you must turn it down a great deal (much more than you think) for your parents to detect a just noticeable decrease in volume.

Why is it difficult to notice a decrease in the volume of loud music?

Understanding Weber's Law

1 The same height of each step illustrates your ability to detect "one sensory unit" of a just noticeable difference between two weights.

2 The narrow width of this step indicates that you need only a small difference in weight in order to detect a just noticeable difference between two weights. According to Weber's law, when judging stimuli of lower intensity, such as lighter weights, only a small difference in intensity is required for you to detect a just noticeable difference.

3 The wide width of this step indicates that you need a larger difference in weight in order to detect a just noticeable difference between two weights. According to Weber's law, when judging stimuli of higher intensity, such as heavier weights, a larger difference in intensity is required for you to detect a just noticeable difference.

Lighter → Heavier

Now that we have answered our first two questions about perception—at what point we are aware of a stimulus and at what point we know a stimulus intensity has changed—let's turn to the third: How do sensations differ from perceptions?

Sensations Versus Perceptions

Sensations

What am I looking at?

One way to experience the difference between sensations and perceptions is to look (for only a few seconds) at the illustration on the right. At first glance, you see only meaningless blotches of color randomly arranged on a background. For purposes of illustration, let's consider each of these meaningless blotches a sensation. A **sensation** *is our first awareness of some outside stimulus; the stimulus activates sensory receptors, which in turn produce signals that are transformed by the brain into a sensory experience.*

Sensations are meaningless bits of information that will eventually be organized and assembled into meaningful images. For example, you can create "raw" sensations by gently rubbing the outside of your closed eyelids. This results in random flashes and splashes of light that have no pattern or meaning and thus are good examples of sensations.

For a moment, return to the photo and see whether you can transform these meaningless blotches of color into an ultrasound photo of a fetus in the womb. The fetus is lying on its back with its rounded tummy on the left and its head on the right. Above the head is the right arm, and the fetus is sucking on its thumb. As soon as you see the fetus, it means that you have transformed thousands of sensations into a meaningful pattern, a perception.

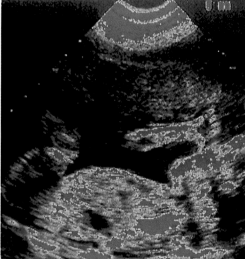

Do you see the fetus?

Perceptions

How many sensations make up a dog?

Perception occurs when meaningless stimuli are organized into the image of a very colorful dog.

As you look at this dog, your brain initially processes many thousands of sensations, such as textures, shadows, lines, colors, and curves. A **perception** *is the experience of a meaningful pattern or image that our brain assembles from thousands of individual sensations; a perception is normally changed, biased, colored, or distorted by one's unique set of experiences.* Because the transformation of sensations into a perception, such as a puppy, is largely an unconscious, instantaneous process, we rarely experience "raw" sensations. Instead, most of our sensory experiences are composed of meaningful patterns and images that we call perceptions.

Your perceptions are rarely exact copies of the real world, because they are influenced by a wide range of experiences that may change, bias, and, in some cases, distort reality. For example, if you grew up with a pet dog or cat, that experience may bias your current perception of pets in the direction of "wonderful-desirable." In contrast, if your family members disliked and complained about the neighbor's pets or if you were attacked by a neighbor's pet, that experience may bias your current perception of pets in the direction of "bothersome-undesirable." We will discuss developmental, learning, and cultural influences on perception in Module 8.

Steps for Constructing a Perception

In reviewing how a perception is constructed, we have simplified the process by making each step follow the preceding one. In real life, there is interaction between some of these steps.

1 A *stimulus* is any change of energy in the environment (light, sound, pressure) that activates your sense receptors (eyes, ears, skin). In this example, the stimuli are light waves reflecting from fur on a dog.

2 Once *sense organs* are activated, they trigger electrical signals or impulses that travel to the brain. Sense organs, such as the eye, do not produce sensations but rather only transform energy into electrical signals.

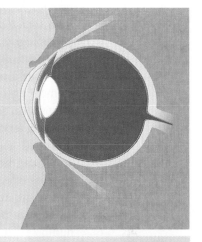

3 Initially, your *brain* transforms electrical signals into sensations. An area in the occipital lobe produces visual sensations.

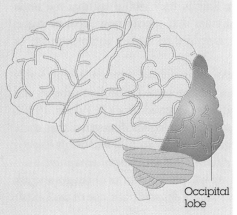

Occipital lobe

4 *Sensations* represent your first experiences with outside stimuli. Sensations consist of meaningless bits of sensory information. For example, sensations would be similar to seeing meaningless blobs of color.

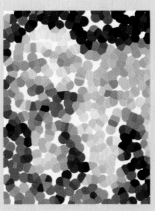

5 Each of us has a unique set of *experiences* that may automatically add meanings, feelings, or memories to our perceptions. As a result, we are most likely to perceive a changed, biased, or distorted copy of the real world. For example, former pleasant experiences with dogs will influence future perceptions of dogs.

6 Your brain assembles the many thousands of individual sensations into a meaningful pattern or image, which is a perception. In this case, the meaningless blobs of color are assembled into the image of a dog. However, depending on your previous experience with dogs, you may perceive the dog as cute and lovable or as noisy and demanding. We can define *perceptions* as experiences of meaningful patterns or images that have been changed, biased, colored, or distorted by your unique set of experiences.

Psychologists have a long history of studying the inherited and learned processes that transform and organize sensations into perceptions. We will show you a variety of images that will allow you to use some of these processes and experience how they change, organize, bias, or distort reality.

Principles of Perceptual Organization

How many parts make up a whole?

If you had lived in the early 1900s, you could have followed an interesting debate over how perceptions are formed. As you may recall from Module 1, one group of psychologists, the **structuralists,** *argued that we can understand how perceptions are formed by breaking them down into smaller and smaller units and then analyzing these basic units.* The other group, the **Gestalt psychologists,** *argued that perceptions cannot be understood by simply breaking them down into individual units, structures, or elements because our perceptual experience involves something more than simply adding individual units.* This "something more" results from a pattern or organization that the brain imposes on sensations. The Gestalt psychologists believed that the brain follows a set of rules that specify how individual pieces are to be assembled, organized, and constructed to form a meaningful pattern or perception.

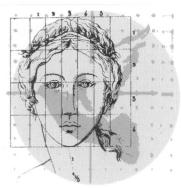

We can bring this debate to life by asking you to study the figure on the left, noticing especially that it is composed entirely of individual dots of different colors.

The structuralists would argue that your image or perception of the woman and her umbrella is formed by simply combining all these dots, as you might add a string of numbers. The Gestalt psychologists would counter by saying that this perception is more than the simple combination of dots. Rather, they would say that the brain forms this perception by following a set of rules that specify how separate pieces

(sensations) are organized and assembled to form a complex image or perception.

The Gestalt psychologists won this debate through a remarkably detailed series of studies in which they presented stimuli to subjects and then asked them to describe what they perceived (Rock & Palmer, 1990). Based on subjects' reports, Gestalt psychologists discovered that there were indeed **principles of organization,** *which are rules that specify how our brains organize separate pieces or elements into meaningful perceptions.*

Similar to the Gestalt studies, we will present a series of images and ask you to describe what you see. Each image demonstrates one of the Gestalt principles of organization.

This is a detail of a famous painting by Georges Seurat. He achieved his effects by using many thousands of individual dots of various colors. Do you see the woman and umbrella by simply adding all the dots?

How many dots make up an image?

Perceptual Rules for Grouping Stimuli

According to the Gestalt principles of organization, you (your brain) automatically arrange or group visual stimuli according to a number of perceptual rules.

Figure-ground

If you look at this figure for about ten seconds, you are initially likely to see a white vase standing out against a black background. *Your experience of automatically identifying a figure, which has more detail, standing out against a background, which has less detail, is called the* **figure-ground principle** and is one of the

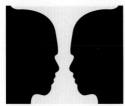

most basic principles of perceptual organization. There is some evidence that your ability to separate figure from ground is an innate response. For example, individuals who were blind from early on and had their sight restored as adults, often by removal of cataracts, were able to distinguish between figure and ground with little or no training (Senden, 1960). As you continue to stare at this image, you will suddenly see the figure and ground reverse. The black background becomes the figure, and you see two silhouetted profiles facing each other against a white background. With continued staring, you can often make the figure reverse at will because the images are essentially equal in importance. In the real world, we usually encounter nonreversible images, or detailed images, clearly standing out against a background.

Closure

You can easily see the dog, although the lines are incomplete. This illustrates the principle of **closure**, *which says that we have a tendency to fill in any missing parts of a figure and see the figure as complete.* You may have more difficulty "closing" the other form, since there are fewer clues. But once you are told that it is an elephant, you can make a deliberate effort to fill in the missing parts and see it.

Simplicity

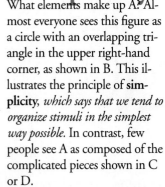

What elements make up A? Almost everyone sees this figure as a circle with an overlapping triangle in the upper right-hand corner, as shown in B. This illustrates the principle of **simplicity**, *which says that we tend to organize stimuli in the simplest way possible.* In contrast, few people see A as composed of the complicated pieces shown in C or D.

Similarity

As you look at this circle filled with white and black smaller circles, you see a black numeral 2. The principle of **similarity** *says that we tend to group elements together that appear similar; in this case, we group the black circles.* The

principle of similarity is so powerful here that it is impossible for us to see the figure as a random arrangement of black and white circles.

Proximity

Notice that although there are exactly eight black circles in each horizontal line, you do not perceive each line as having this similar feature. Instead, you see the black circles in groups depending on how they are spaced. This illustrates the principle of **proximity**, *which says that we tend to group objects that are physically close together.*

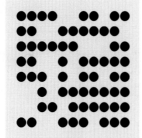

Continuity

As you scan this figure, keep track of the path that your eyes follow. If you are like most people, your eyes will move from left

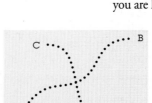

to right in a continuous line, following the path from A to B or from C to D. This illustrates the principle of **continuity**, *which says that we tend to perceive a series of points or lines along a smooth or continuous path.* For example, this principle would predict that you do not see a line that begins at A and then turns abruptly to C or to D.

Throughout the day, your brain uses these principles to organize and give meaning to the millions of sensations that you process. In fact, at this very moment, you are using these principles to organize the marks on this page into words, sentences, paragraphs, and figures.

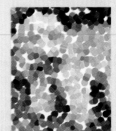

1. This figure illustrates the concept of the _____, which is defined as the intensity level of a stimulus that a person detects 50% of the time it is presented.

2. In this figure, the height of each step illustrates the concept of (a)_____, which is the amount of increase or decrease in the intensity of a stimulus that a person can just manage to detect. The width of each step illustrates (b)_____ law, which states that the amount of increase in intensity of a stimulus needed to produce a just noticeable difference grows in proportion to the intensity of the initial stimulus.

3. Our first experience with sensory information in the form of meaningless bits of information is called a _____.

4. When many bits of sensory information have been assembled into a meaningful image or pattern that has been changed, biased, or distorted by our unique set of experiences, the result is called a _____.

5. The _____ psychologists demonstrated the existence of a set of rules or principles that we use automatically to group or arrange stimuli into perceptual experiences.

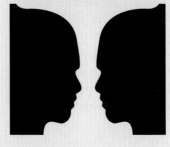

6. You automatically separate an image into a more dominant, detailed figure and a less detailed background according to the rule of _____.

7. You see this image as formed by a circle and over lying triangle because of the rule of _____.

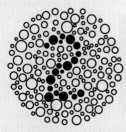

8. You see this black 2 instead of white and black circles because of the rule of _____.

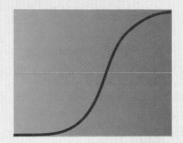

9. You divide each line into separate groups of objects according to the rule of _____.

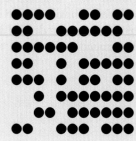

10. You see a continuous line from A to B, rather than a line from A to C, following the rule of _____.

11. You fill in missing parts to form a complete image as a result of the rule of _____.

Answers: 1. *absolute threshold.* 2. (a) *just noticeable difference.* (b) *Weber's;* 3. *sensation;* 4. *perception;* 5. *Gestalt;* 6. *figure-ground;* 7. *simplicity;* 8. *similarity;* 9. *proximity;* 10. *continuity;* 11. *closure.*

Depth Perception

How do you see in three dimensions?

When you look at a photo or television screen, you perceive an image that has only two dimensions, height and width. One goal of engineers who design cameras and televisions is to enable you to see a third dimension in images: depth. Visual images are initially projected onto your retinas in only two dimensions, height and width; depth is added by your visual system.

It is almost impossible for most of us to imagine a world without depth, since we constantly rely on depth to move about and locate objects in space. Let's examine the two kinds of cues—*binocular cues*, which are built into the visual system, and *monocular cues*, some of which are built into the visual system and some of which are produced by the arrangement of objects in space—to see how depth is added to our visual experiences.

As her eyes turn inward or converge to see the fly on her nose, they provide a binocular cue for her perception of depth.

Can you see the end of your nose?

Binocular Depth Cues

How far away is your nose?

When you have an eye exam, the doctor may ask you to extend your arm in front of you and then slowly bring it toward you until your finger touches your nose. This is a test for **convergence**, *which occurs when muscles move both eyes inward to focus on a near object; in turning your eyes inward, the muscles provide signals that your brain interprets as cues for depth.* For example, the more your eyes turn inward or converge, the nearer the object. If you looked at a fly on your nose, the extreme convergence of your eyes would signal that the fly is very close indeed. Convergence cues are *binocular,* meaning that they depend on the movement of both eyes. If you had only one eye, you would lack convergence cues for depth.

If you had one eye in the middle of your forehead, you would lose retinal disparity, which is an important cue for depth. *Because your two eyes are separated by several inches, each eye actually receives a slightly different image, which is called* **retinal disparity.** The greater the retinal disparity, or difference between the images of the two eyes, the closer you perceive the object. The smaller the retinal disparity, the farther away you perceive the object to be.

With only one eye, you would lose depth cues created by retinal disparity.

A 3D movie adds the dimension of depth by using retinal disparity. Two slightly different images are projected onto the screen. You wear special glasses that allow one of these images to be seen by your right eye and the other to be seen by your left. As your brain processes the separate images, it adds depth and you experience the illusion of a spear coming right out of the movie screen.

By staring at these two photos with your eyes crossed, like the woman above left, you can make the two images overlap to form a 3D image.

Depth Perception

Monocular Depth Cues

How can a person with one eye land an airplane?

Because a person with one good eye can land an airplane, there must be a way to judge the distance to the approaching runway that does not rely solely on binocular cues for depth and distance.

Monocular cues *for depth, which are produced by signals from a single eye, most commonly result from how objects are positioned in the environment.* Here are some of the most common monocular cues.

Interposition
If you see one object (cheese) partially overlapping another (wine bottle), the overlapping object will appear closer. This depth cue is called *interposition.*

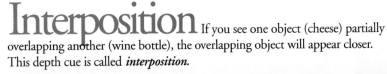

Linear perspective
As you look down a long stretch of highway, the receding sides of the road form parallel lines that appear to come together at a far point and create a sense of distance. The depth cue provided by the convergence of parallel lines is called *linear perspective.*

Relative size
If you expect two images to be the same size and they are not, the larger of the two will appear closer and the smaller will appear farther away. This depth cue is called *relative size.*

Atmospheric perspective
The presence of dust, smog, or water vapor gives far objects a hazy look and makes them appear farther away. This depth cue is called *atmospheric perspective.*

Texture gradient
As you look at this textured surface, the closest area has a sharp and detailed texture while the area in the background has less sharpness and detail. This depth cue, called the *texture gradient,* creates the impression that the cracked ground is receding into the distance.

Light & shadow
Notice how the interplay of lights and shadows gives these tubes a three-dimensional look. The faces of the tubes appear to stand out, and the spaces between appear to recede. It is no surprise that this depth cue is called *light and shadow.*

Motion parallax
If you look out the window of a moving train or car, objects that are near (cars, trees, shrubs) appear to be whizzing by compared to objects in the distance (telephone poles, houses) that seem to be barely moving. This depth cue, called *motion parallax,* refers to your transforming the speed of moving objects into signs of distance.

Although people with only one good eye lack binocular depth cues, such as convergence and retinal disparity, they have all these monocular cues to perceive depth and distance accurately. Because of monocular depth cues, people with one good eye can perform tasks requiring precise depth judgments, such as landing an airplane.

Perceptual Constancies

Size, Shape, Brightness, and Color Constancies

Why don't cars shrink as they drive away?

Although you live in an ever-changing world, you perceive many things as remaining constant. For example, cars do not grow smaller as they speed away, colors appear the same under very different lighting, and doors look rectangular even though when they open and close the shapes they project on the retinas change drastically. *The tendency to perceive sizes, shapes, brightness, and colors as remaining the same even though they are constantly changing is called* **perceptual constancy,** which can be broken down into several separate constancies.

Size constancy. As a car comes nearer, its image on your retina grows larger and larger until it becomes gigantic. However, from your experience with moving objects, you have learned that things do not grow just because they move closer. Your tendency to perceive objects as remaining the same size even when their images on the retina are continually growing or shrinking is called **size constancy**.

Shape constancy. As you look at this rectangular book in the near position, it projects a rectangular shape on your retinas. If you move the book farther away, it projects trapezoid shapes on your retinas, but you still perceive the book as rectangular. The tendency to see an object as retaining its same shape no matter what angle it is viewed from is called **shape constancy**.

Brightness and color constancy. Whether you read this book in dim or bright light, the pages will appear similar in brightness. The tendency to perceive brightness as remaining the same in changing illumination is called **brightness constancy.** Whether you search for a red shirt in a brightly lit room or a dimly lit closet, the red color remains approximately the same (even though in dim light, red is almost grayish). The tendency to perceive colors as remaining stable despite differences in lighting is called **color constancy**.

How do things change and still stay the same?

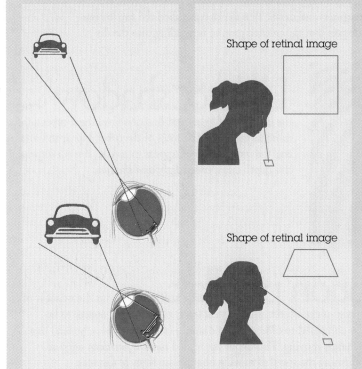

Shape of retinal image

Shape of retinal image

Do we need perceptual constancies?

If you lacked perceptual constancies, you would have the impression that your house was shrinking as you drove away, that your books were constantly changing shapes as you moved them, and that your clothes were changing colors as you went from sunlight to shadow. Perceptual constancies transform a potentially ever-changing, chaotic world into one with reassuring stability.

Illusions: Fooling Our Perceptions

Can we always believe what we see?

We have discussed a number of perceptual cues and constancies that function to organize and stabilize our views of the world. And, much of the time, our perceptions are reasonably accurate reflections of reality (remembering that perceptions are influenced by our previous experiences). *If perceptual cues are changed so that we (our brains) can no longer interpret the cues correctly, we perceive a distorted image of reality, which is called an* **illusion**. As you encounter the following visual illusions, notice that you may continue to see the illusion even after you know it is a distorted image.

Ames Room. The boy on the right appears to be twice as tall as the one on the left, but they are actually the same height. You see the boys' heights as distorted because you rely more on your assumptions about shape constancy (that the room is rectangular) than on size constancy (that boys about the same age are similar in height). This illusion was produced by placing the two boys in a distorted room, called the *Ames room,* after its inventor, Adelbert Ames.

From previous experience, you assume this room is rectangular, but in fact it is an odd trapezoid-like shape with a sharply angled back wall. The result is that the boy in the right near corner of the room appears very tall and the boy in the far left corner appears much shorter. To obtain the greatest illusion and distortion in heights, subjects view the Ames room with one eye through a peep-

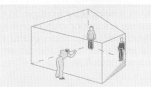

hole, which greatly reduces cues about size and depth. If subjects are allowed to view the Ames room with two eyes and to move their heads, the illusion is greatly reduced but still remains (Gehringer & Engel, 1986).

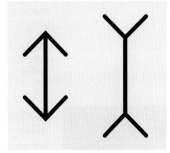

Müller-Lyer Illusion. The left arrow appears to be shorter than the right arrow, but if you measure them, you'll prove that they are of equal length. One explanation for this distortion in length, called the Müller-Lyer illusion, is that you are relying on previous experience with corners of rooms. For example, a corner of a room that extends outward appears closer and therefore shorter; a corner of a room that recedes inward appears farther away, and thus longer. Similarly, you interpret the left arrow as shorter (similar to an outward corner) and the right arrow as longer (similar to an inward corner) (Eijkman, Jongsma, & Vincent, 1981).

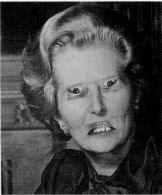

Thatcher Illusion. As you look at Margaret Thatcher's face upside down, she appears to have a fairly normal facial expression. But notice what happens when you turn her face right side up. Researchers suggest that our difficulty in interpreting an upside-down mouth and eyes is what creates the Thatcher illusion (Parks & Coss, 1986).

Illusions: Fooling Our Perceptions

Impossible Figures. Because the two figures below seem to defy basic geometric laws, they are called *impossible figures.* Yet they do exist here, and you can trace your finger along their impossible outlines. One reason they seem impossible is that our previous experience with line drawings makes us interpret these figures as three-dimensional objects. Unfortunately, it is almost impossible to draw these figures as three-dimensional objects because the depth cues are ambiguous.

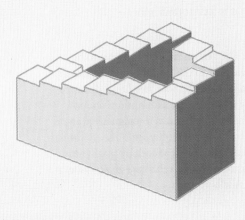

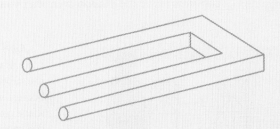

The book title *Up the Down Staircase* perfectly describes this impossible figure. As your eye follows the steps, they seem to reverse directions, sometimes going up and sometimes going down.

As you look at this figure, it almost magically changes from a two-pronged object to a three-pronged one. The middle prong seems impossible because it appears out of nowhere. It is interesting that Africans with no formal education can draw this figure from memory because they perceive it as a pattern of flat lines (two dimensions), which is very easy to draw. In contrast, people with formal education, who have spent years looking at three-dimensional representations in books, perceive this object as having three dimensions, a pattern that is almost impossible to draw (Coren & Ward, 1989).

Moon Illusion. All the illusions we've discussed so far have been created to deceive, but some illusions occur naturally. One such illusion that has intrigued people for centuries is the fact that a full moon appears to be as much as 50% larger when it is near the horizon than when it is overhead, even though its size on our retinas remains the same. The explanation for the moon illusion is complex and not fully understood, but it does involve misinterpreting cues for size constancy (Coren & Ward, 1989).

Moon illusion: the moon appears 50% larger near the horizon.

What do we learn from illusions?

Illusions remind us that perception is an active process. We are continually making assumptions and interpretations about the size, shape, and color of objects in our environment. Illusions demonstrate how our rather reliable perceptual process can be fooled when constancy cues are distorted. For example, many of us pay good money to see movies, which are actually clever illusions in which things seem to move across the screen. In the Applying/Exploring section, we'll explain how the movie illusion occurs.

1. Cues for depth perception that depend on both eyes are called (a)_____ cues. Cues for depth perception that depend on a single eye are called (b)_____ cues.

4. If you watch a car speed into the distance, you know that the car is not getting smaller, because of _____.

2. The binocular cue that occurs when your eyes move inward to track a fly landing on your nose is called (a)_____. It explains how you know that a fly on your nose is very close. The binocular cue that occurs when each eye receives a slightly different image is called (b)_____.

5. If you move a book from your desk to a shelf, you know the form of the book is not changing, because of _____.

3. All the following cues are monocular.

(a) The cue for depth that is produced when one object overlaps another and appears nearer is called _____.

(b) The cue for depth that is produced when two parallel lines converge in the distance and seem farther away is called _____.

(c) The cue for depth that arises when you expect two images to be similar in size and the larger one appears closer is called _____.

(d) The depth cue that is produced by the presence of dust and smog that makes distant objects appear hazy and farther away is called _____.

(e) The depth cue that arises when we are moving and perceive nearer objects to be moving faster than farther objects is called _____.

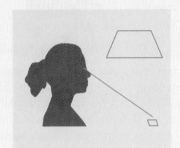

6. If you reach for a green shirt in a dimly lit closet, you still recognize the color green because of _____.

7. If perceptual cues are so changed that we (our brains) can no longer interpret the cues correctly and we perceive a distorted image of reality, it is called an _____.

Answers: 1. (a) *binocular,* (b) *monocular;* 2. (a) *convergence,* (b) *retinal disparity;* 3. (a) *interposition,* (b) *linear perspective,* (c) *relative size,* (d) *atmospheric perspective,* (e) *motion parallax;* 4. *size constancy;* 5. *shape constancy;* 6. *color constancy;* 7. *illusion.*

APPLYING/ EXPLORING: CREATING PERCEPTUAL EXPERIENCES

Creating Movies

What makes horses run?

If you are at a horse race, you are seeing live horses run—*real motion*, which is defined as stimuli (horses) actually moving in space (around the track). If you watched a replay of the same race, you would be seeing *apparent motion*, which is created by a series of stationary images that are rapidly presented (24 frames per second) to create the illusion of motion. How does your visual system transform the rapidly presented still pictures into apparent motion?

The basis for apparent motion is deceptively simple. Each successive movie frame shows a horse in a slightly different posture or position. When you view these frames one after the other, your brain fills in the blanks (principle of closure) and creates the continuous illusion of a horse racing around the track. This same principle is used to create apparent motion in movies, television, or flip books.

The principle for creating movies becomes obvious if you examine the position of the horse's feet in the above movie frames. From frame to frame, there is only a slight change in the positions of the horse's legs. However, if these movie frames are presented rapidly, we see the illusion of a galloping horse.

In a series of ingenious experiments, researchers discovered that our visual system has several built-in complex mechanisms that detect cues for producing the illusion of apparent motion (Ramachandran & Anstis, 1986).

Creating Your Own Reality

The invention of the movie camera was revolutionary because it created a new perceptual experience: the illusion of still pic-

tures moving. We are about to see the marketing of another revolutionary invention, *virtual reality,* that produces the illusion that you are creating your own reality. Similar to the difference between real and apparent motion, the difference between real and virtual reality is that the latter is an illusory experience of reality that is computer generated. If the promises of virtual reality come true, players will be able to enter a video game and become the main characters; doctors will be able to enter a copy of the body

to search for tumors or damaged nerves; and biology students will be able to experience, observe, and interact with dinosaurs.

One company (Lasko-Harvill) makes it possible for you to dive into a computer-created ocean and swim along with the whales and dolphins. Researchers at the University of North Carolina have created a program for architects that allows their clients a computerized walk through a proposed home or office, and another program for biochemists allows them to ride on top of a mol-

To experience virtual reality, you put on special goggles that produce a three-dimensional image, a glove that serves as a pointer, and a body suit with sensors, all connected to a supercomputer.

A "moving" traffic arrow is based on an old principle of perception.

1. This gold-painted face mask has a convex shape, similar to all faces you have seen.

2. As we slowly rotate the convex mask, you can see a concave blue face painted on the inside.

3. With the gold mask turned 180 degrees, you now see the complete blue face. Even though you know that the blue face is painted on a concave surface, you perceive it as convex. You automatically transform the face into a convex shape, presumably because that is the only face shape that you have experienced.

ecule as they explore the structure of a chemical compound. The technology for virtual reality, which is in its infancy, promises to create new perceptual experiences that will allow us to blend our present reality with one that we create.

Creating Moving Lights

The father of modern flashing traffic arrows was a distinguished Gestalt psychologist named Max Wertheimer, who experimented with flashing lights in the early 1900s. In a darkened room, Wertheimer flashed first one light and then a second light that was some distance away. If the time between flashes was just right, the two flashes were perceived as a moving spot of light instead of two separate flashes. Wertheimer called this illusion of movement *phi movement*, which today we refer to as apparent motion. Each time you pass a traffic arrow composed of flashing lights or see a "moving" string of lights on a neon sign, you are witnessing the application of Wertheimer's phi movement.

Changing Reality

From previous experience, you know that every human face has a convex shape, which means that it bulges outward like the outside of a bowl. If you are shown a face that is concave (bulges inward like the inside of a bowl), will you see it as concave, or will your previous learning experiences transform the concave face to convex? To answer this question, follow the steps on the left.

This sequence of photos illustrates how we perceive reality as we think it *should be* rather than as it exists. In fact, try as you can, it is virtually impossible to see the blue face with a concave shape. This example demonstrates the principle that our perceptions are, at best, *reflections* and not copies of reality.

Summary/Self-Test

1. We discussed three basic questions that psychologists ask about perception. Our first question, "At what point are we aware of a stimulus?" can be answered by measuring a stimulus's threshold, which is a point above which a stimulus is perceived and below which it is not. If a stimulus is perceived 50% of the time that it is presented, this is called the _____.

2. Our second question, "At what point do we know a stimulus intensity has increased (or decreased)?" can be answered by measuring the smallest increase or decrease in the intensity of a stimulus that a person can detect; this is called (a)_____. Related to this concept is a law that says the amount of increase in stimulus intensity needed to produce a just noticeable difference increases in proportion to the intensity of the initial stimulus; this is called (b)_____ law. Applied to real life, this law says that you could detect small differences in flashes of light of low intensity in a darkened room but would need large differences in flashes of higher intensity in order to detect just noticeable differences.

■ *How does Weber's law apply to diagnosing diseases?*

3. Our third question, "At what point do sensations change into perceptions?" can be answered by analyzing our own perceptual experiences. Our first awareness of some outside stimulus is

called a (a)_____. This awareness results when some change in energy activates sensory receptors, which produce signals that in turn are transformed by the brain into sensory experiences. When many individual sensations are assembled into a meaningful experience, image, or pattern, it is called a (b)_____. The latter is not an exact replica of the real world but rather a copy that has been changed, biased, or distorted by our unique set of (c)_____.

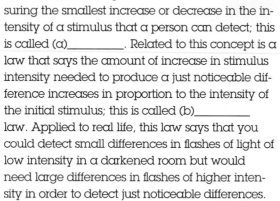

4. The structuralists argued that perceptions are composed of individual elements; the (a)_____ psychologists replied that perceptions are more than individual elements and that the brain has rules for assembling perceptions, which they called principles of (b)_____. According to one of these principles, the first thing we do is automatically separate an image into two parts: the more detailed feature of an image becomes (c)_____ and the less detailed background becomes (d)_____.

■ *How is putting together a 1,000-piece jigsaw puzzle similar to explaining sensations and perceptions?*

5. Many of the principles of perceptual organization concern rules for grouping stimuli. According to the rule of (a)_____, stimuli tend to be organized in the most basic, elementary way. According to the rule of (b)_____, stimuli that appear the same tend to be grouped together. According to the rule of (c)_____, stimuli that are near one another tend to be grouped together. According to the rule of (d)_____, stimuli that are arranged in a smooth line or curve tend to be perceived as forming a continuous path. According to the rule of (e)_____, we tend to fill in the missing parts of a figure and perceive it as complete.

■ *Why can you still read the message on a faded and torn billboard sign?*

6. The visual system transforms the two-dimensional image (height and width) of stimuli projected on the retina into a three-dimensional experience by adding depth. Cues for depth that are dependent on both eyes are called (a)_____; cues for depth that are dependent only on a single eye are called (b)_____. The binocular cue for depth that arises from muscles turning your eyes inward is called (c)_____. The binocular cue for depth that comes from a slightly different image of each eye reaching the brain is called (d)_____.

7. There are a number of monocular cues for depth. If an object appears closer because it overlaps another, the cue is called (a)_____. If parallel lines seem to stretch to a point at the horizon and create a sense of distance, the cue is called (b)_____. If two figures are expected to be of the same size but one is larger and thus appears closer, the cue is called (c)_____. If dust or smog makes objects appear hazy and thus farther away, the cue is called (d)_____. As texture changes from sharp and detailed to dull and monotonous it creates the impression of distance; this cue is called (e)_____. The play of lights and shadows gives objects a three-dimensional look, a cue that is called (f)_____. As you ride in a car, the impression that near objects are speeding by and far objects are barely moving is called (g)_____.

■ *Would a one-eyed pitcher have any particular problems playing baseball?*

PERCEPTUAL CONSTANCIES

8. Although the size, shape, brightness, and color of objects are constantly changing, we tend to see them as remaining the same, a phenomenon that is called (a)_____. A person walking away does not appear to grow smaller, even though the image on the retina is decreasing in size, because of (b)_____ constancy. Even though the image of a door that is opened and closed changes on the retina from a rectangle to a trapezoid, we see it as retaining its rectangular outline because of (c)_____ constancy. Even though the color and brightness of a car changes when we drive from bright into dim light, we tend to see the color and brightness remaining the same because of (d)_____ and _____ constancy.

■ *By some quirk of nature, you are born without any constancies. What particular problems would you have?*

ILLUSIONS: FOOLING OUR PERCEPTIONS

9. For much of the time, our perceptions are relatively accurate reflections of the world (except for anything added by attentional, motivational, or emotional filters). However, if perceptual cues that we have learned to use and rely on are greatly changed, the result is a distorted image that is called an _____. Although illusions are extreme examples, they illustrate that our perceptual process is an active, ongoing one in which we use past experiences to interpret current sensory experiences.

■ *Your friend says, "Everything I see is real." What would you reply?*

APPLYING/EXPLORING: CREATING PERCEPTUAL EXPERIENCES

10. When you view objects moving in space, it is called (a)_____ motion. When you view images of stationary objects that are rapidly presented, it is called (b)_____ motion, which is the basic principle used to create movies. The illusion that stationary lights are moving can be traced to the work of Max Wertheimer, who called this phenomenon (c)_____ movement. A perceptual experience that is created by allowing the viewer to enter and participate in computer-generated images is called (d)_____ reality, which breaks down some of the traditional boundaries between reality and fantasy.

■ *How would you explain how movies work to a young child?*

MODULE 8
INFLUENCES ON PERCEPTION

Is that car real or a toy?

Sam's hospital room was four stories up, but he believed it was only a few feet above the ground. Having no fear, he crawled out on the window ledge to get a better look at those tiny objects on the street below. Thankfully, a nurse appeared to rescue Sam and explain that those tiny objects were regular-sized cars.

Sam had been blind since he was 10 months old and now, at age 53, his vision had been restored with corneal transplants. When he first regained his sight, Sam could make out the image of his doctor and separate it from the wall of the room. However, he made many errors in distinguishing between simple sizes and shapes of objects, as well as in figuring out the meaning of complex stimuli. For example, Sam had trouble keeping track of the hospital staff entering and leaving his room because he couldn't recognize and identify the complex shapes of different faces. Similarly, he had no idea whether his doctor was smiling or frowning when she entered his room because Sam could not "read" facial expressions.

Sam felt rather hopeless when he failed very simple visual tests, such as being asked to describe how two objects differed. He could see the objects, for which he was very happy, but he had to count the sides to decide that one object was a square and the other was a triangle. However, his visual skills increased rapidly, and within six months he could recognize faces and objects, draw pictures of triangles and squares, and even accomplish the difficult perceptual task of safely crossing a busy street. (adapted from Gregory, 1974)

From Sam's unusual visual experience, we can guess at some of the factors that influence perception. We know that immediately after his vision was restored, Sam had no trouble distinguishing his doctor from a wall. We would guess that this ability to separate figure from ground was perhaps *inherited*—that is, it existed from birth. On the other hand, he had trouble identifying faces, recognizing facial expressions, distinguishing a triangle from a square, and judging distance and depth. We would guess that some of the perceptual processes involving size and shape constancies and perceiving depth would require *learning experiences*.

These guesses raise a general question: How do the influences of heredity and learning interact to produce our complex perceptual processes? As we discuss the contributions and influences of heredity and learning on perception, please keep in mind that, in real life, there is a constant interaction between these two processes.

What's Coming

In the first part of this module we'll focus on how heredity and learning (experience) interact to produce our complex perceptual processes. In the second part, we'll explain how societal and cultural values influence our perceptions. But first, let's examine the approaches that psychologists use to study perceptual influences.

Studying Heredity and Experience

Psychologists use three approaches—developmental, experimental, and case study—to examine the interaction of heredity and learning in perception.

Three Approaches for Studying Influences on Perception

1 In the *developmental approach,* psychologists study the normal development of perceptual processes through infancy and childhood. Because there is an ongoing interplay between an infant's inherited and learned experiences, this approach primarily tells us the age at which a perceptual process first appears.

Would a baby creep off a cliff?
A more scientific way of asking this question is, "When does an infant develop depth perception?" Eleanor Gibson, a well-known child researcher, answered this question by designing an apparatus called the *visual cliff.* The visual cliff is a glass tabletop with a checkerboard patterned surface on one side; on the other side is clear glass with a checkerboard pattern several feet below, creating the illusion of a clifflike drop to the floor. If a 6-month-old infant is placed on the checkerboard pattern side and encouraged to creep off the "cliff," the infant will hesitate at the clear glass "drop off," indicating he or she has depth perception. These experiments indicate that infants do not develop clear signs of depth perception until about 6 months of age.

2 In the *experimental approach,* psychologists either restrict or experimentally change an organism's sensory experience and then assess effects on later perceptual processes. The experimental approach has the advantage of identifying cause-and-effect relationships in perceptual processes and the disadvantage of having to generalize results across species or situations.

What would happen if an animal saw only vertical stripes?
Using the experimental approach, researchers raised animals in an environment composed entirely of vertical stripes. Later, they tested the animals' ability to see vertical and horizontal stripes. Their response to horizontal stripes (described on page 144) will surprise you.

3 In the *case-study approach,* psychologists study perceptual processes in patients who, like Sam, had severely restricted sensory experiences or had some form of brain damage that greatly changed their perceptual processes. Although the results from these patients are of great interest, the complexity of their conditions makes it difficult to disentangle inherited influences from learned experiences.

How long before Sam could recognize facial expressions?
When Sam's vision was first restored at age 53, he was unable to decipher facial expressions. It required six months of exposure to faces and learning about facial expressions before he was able to identify and distinguish between them.

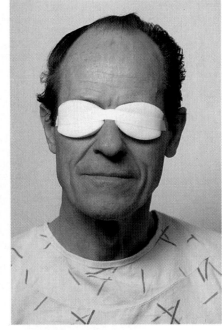

Each approach has advantages and disadvantages. Together they help answer our general question: How do the influences of heredity and learning (experience) interact to produce our complex perceptual processes?

To show how learning experiences interact with inherited processes, let's turn to some interesting findings on restricting early perceptual experiences.

Effects of Restricted Experiences

In this section, we'll describe several experiments and case studies that illustrate how perceptual processes are influenced by the interaction between environment and heredity.

In the experimental approach, psychologists either restrict or change an organism's sensory experience and then assess these effects on later perception. We'll explain three rather unusual studies that use this approach: kittens living in a vertical world, salamanders starving in a land of plenty, and humans coping in an upside-down world.

Developing Animals: Experience Necessary

When a kitten is born, the neurons in its visual cortex are already wired to respond to visual stimuli (such as flashes of light or movement of lights) very much like cells in the brains of adult cats are (Hubel & Wiesel, 1979). These findings indicate that heredity plays the key role in the development of the visual system prior to birth. After birth, however, the functioning of these brain cells can be greatly altered by either restricting or eliminating the animal's visual experience.

If visual experience is eliminated by raising a newborn animal in total darkness for many weeks, the cells in its visual cortex become much less responsive, indicating that these cells require early experience with visual stimuli to develop and function normally (Mower, Christen, & Caplan, 1983). From experiments such as this, we have learned that a minimal amount of visual experience is necessary for the normal development of cat, monkey, ape, and—presumably—human visual systems.

What would happen if an animal's visual experiences weren't totally eliminated but were greatly restricted? To answer this question, researchers placed a kitten for several hours a day in an apparatus that allowed the kitten to see only vertical stripes. (A fanned neck collar prevented the kitten from seeing its own body.) After weeks in which the kitten was exposed to a world composed entirely of vertical stripes, researchers recorded the electrical responses of the kitten's brain cells to vertical and horizontal stripes.

When the kitten viewed a vertical stripe, with which it had previous experience, its brain cells responded with increased activity, which indicated normal cell functioning.

When the kitten viewed a horizontal stripe, with which it had no previous experience, its brain cells made no response, which indicated abnormal cell functioning.

From these restricted-experience studies, we have learned two things. First, it is possible to permanently alter the responsiveness of brain cells by restricting sensory experience. Second, there is a "window" of time, called the **critical period,** during which brain cells are especially vulnerable to changes or restrictions in sensory experience. If a restriction occurs outside the critical period, it will have little or no effect on the responsiveness of brain cells (Hirsch & Spinelli, 1970; Mitchell, 1980). These studies demonstrate that organisms need a wide range of *particular* sensory experiences for the development of normal perceptual processes.

A Lesson from Salamanders

We can change visual perception in newborn kittens, but what about in adults? In the two examples that we present next, we will examine how much adults' perceptual systems can adapt to incredible changes in their environments.

Salamander Perceptual Puzzle

We'll provide two pieces of a perceptual puzzle. See if you can answer the questions before we provide the third.

First Piece: Some animals, such as salamanders, are born with depth perception for which cues come primarily from the location of an image on the animal's retina. For example, if an image of a fly were projected near the top of the retina, it would be a cue that the object is located up. Acting on this up cue, the salamander would jump up to seize the fly and have its lunch.

Jumps up

Eyes rotated 180 degrees

180°

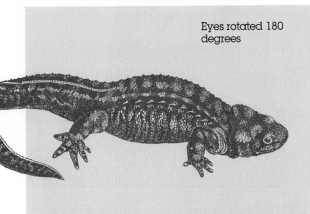

Second Piece: Imagine that the salamander's eyes have been surgically rotated 180 degrees (this is possible), so that objects projected on the animal's retina are actually reversed 180 degrees: a fly located "up" would thus be projected on the bottom of the retina (and vice versa).

Puzzle: If a salamander with its eyes rotated 180 degrees sees the retinal image of a fly located "up," will it jump upward or downward to seize the fly?

Jumps up
Jumps down

?

Eyes rotated 180 degrees

180°

Third Piece: In a clever series of experiments, Roger Sperry (1943) found that salamanders with rotated eyes would jump downward because the fly depth cue on their retinas indicated down. Alas, even after many errors and missed lunches, salamanders never learned to *adapt* to the new world in which depth cues had been reversed. **Adaptation** refers to the ability of an organism to change its responses based on new sensory or perceptual experiences.

Salamanders cannot adapt to the rotation of their eyes. They "see" the fly as located "down," so they jump down and miss the fly, which is actually located "up."

Jumps down

These experiments demonstrate that, in some animals, perceptual processes are set in stone by heredity and no amount of learning experiences can alter the fixed processes. Now, let's compare the perceptual adaptability of salamanders with that of humans.

Effects of Restricted Experiences

Seeing the World Upside Down

Could you ride a bike upside down?

With a few changes, we're going to repeat the salamander experiment using human subjects. Instead of rotating human subjects' eyes (which is not possible and certainly unethical), we'll have them wear goggles that rotate the world 180 degrees. Similar to the salamander's experience with rotated eyes, human subjects will experience a world that is turned upside down; that is "up" and "down" are completely reversed. Here's our puzzle: Will a human adapt to an upside-down world and learn to perform complex behaviors, such as reaching for a glass and even riding a bike?

In actual experiments, humans wore the upside-down goggles for several weeks. At first, they reported that their world was very unstable and seemed to turn as their heads turned. They had difficulty walking and needed help to perform simple tasks, such as pouring water into a glass. However, one subject adapted so well to his upside-down world that he learned to ride a bike after three days and to ski after a few weeks.

Even more surprising, subjects reported that some events were perceived as right-side up. For instance, water pouring from a pitcher and smoke rising from a cigarette were perceived as occurring in the normal, upright direction (Kohler, 1962). These experiments convincingly demonstrate that humans have a great capacity for *perceptual adaptation*—changing behaviors in response to new sensory experiences.

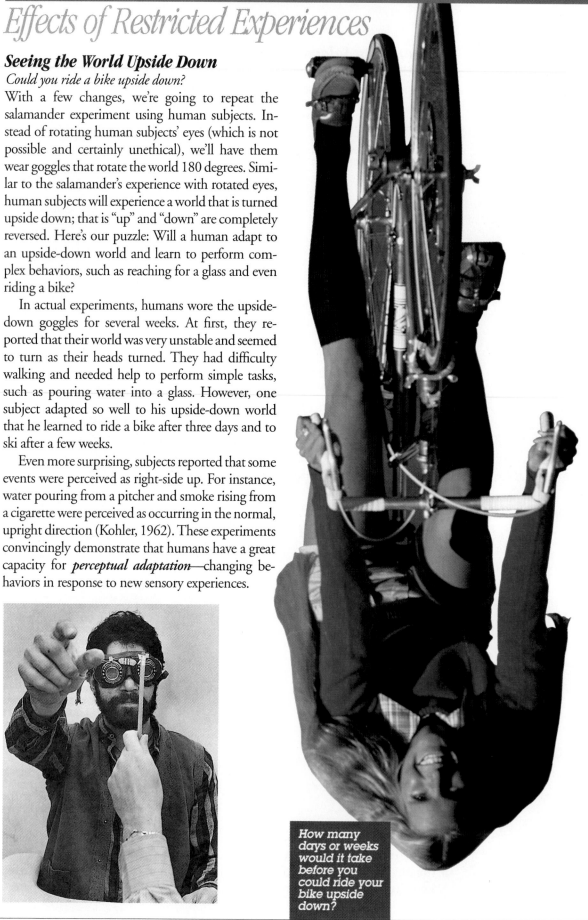

How many days or weeks would it take before you could ride your bike upside down?

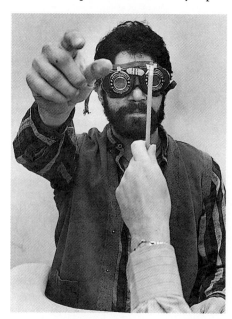

Wearing special goggles caused the world to look upside down.

Adults with Brain Damage

We have just described studies that restricted sensory input by changing the *external environment*, such as by raising animals in a "vertical" world or wearing upside-down goggles. Now we turn to studies on perceptual changes that occur when *internal environments*, subjects' brains, are damaged. We will use the case-study approach to illustrate these often tragic perceptual changes.

How does brain damage affect perception?

Gary was talking to his physical therapist about his rehabilitation program for a previous injury to his brain. In the middle of their conversation, Gary suddenly realized that he could no longer recognize his therapist's face. He knew she was sitting there because he could hear her voice and see her body, but could not recognize her face. The therapist tried to calm Gary, for she guessed that he had just had a stroke that further damaged his brain (Lhermitte et al., 1972).

Gary's frightening perceptual experience illustrates how a blockage of blood supply in the brain (a stroke), a severe blow to the head, or a brain tumor can produce damage that may alter perception, often permanently. Damage to the brain may affect perception in two ways. First, brain damage may restrict the *input* of sensory experiences that, in turn, interferes with perception. We discussed these sensory and perceptual problems (blindness, deafness) in Modules 5 and 6. Second, brain damage may interfere not with the input of sensory information but rather with *processing and assembling* sensory information into meaningful images and patterns, such as Gary's inability to see but not recognize a familiar face. Gary's deficit is called *agnosia* (ag-NO-zee-ah), which means that he can receive bits of sensory information but cannot assemble them into a meaningful pattern or image. We'll concentrate on examples of agnosia in the visual system, although brain damage can produce agnosia in each of the five major senses (seeing, hearing, touching, smelling, and tasting).

What happened to your face?

Agnosia for Faces. During the first part of his conversation with the therapist, Gary was able to receive bits of sensory information and assemble them into the meaningful image of the therapist's face. Following his stroke, he had agnosia for faces (called *prosopagnosia*—pro-so-pag-NO-zee-ah), which means that he could still receive visual bits of information but could not assemble them into a face. Patients with agnosia for faces, which is very rare, have the greatest difficulty recognizing and naming familiar faces but may also have varying degrees of difficulty in recognizing and naming common objects in their environment. Gary could identify most objects in the room, had depth perception, had the use and understanding of language, and had good memory for past and present events. But because of his agnosia for faces, Gary could recognize his therapist only by the sound of her voice.

Agnosia for Objects. Patients with agnosia for objects can see the object's parts, but they have great difficulty identifying even familiar objects, apparently because they cannot assemble the parts into a meaningful whole or image. Agnosia for objects and faces is caused by damage to *association areas* in the brain and are involved in transforming bits of sensory information into meaningful images.

A patient with agnosia for objects was shown a familiar drawing of a horse and asked to make a close copy.

Here is the patient's copy or perception of the horse. Notice that the copy is essentially a "list" of the horse's separate parts, which the patient was unable to assemble into a complete image of a horse.

Effects of Restricted Experiences

Agnosia for One Side: The Neglect Syndrome. If you were watching a patient with agnosia for one side, you would notice that he shaves the right side of his face but not his left, adjusts his clothes on the right side but not the left, eats food from the right side of his plate but not the left, and tells time from the right side of the clock and not the left. A patient with agnosia for the left side, called ***neglect syndrome***, essentially neglects everything on the left side. Neglect syndrome on the left side of the body is usually caused by extensive damage to association areas in the brain's right hemisphere.

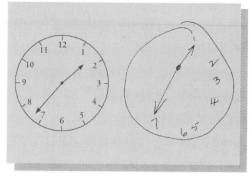

A patient with left-sided neglect syndrome was asked to make a copy of this clock.

Notice that the patient essentially copied only the right side of the clock, indicating that he perceived only the right side of his world and neglected his left.

We have examined how restrictions in our external environment (sensory input) and damage to our internal environment (the brain) affect perceptual processes. Together, these studies and observations point out that our complex perceptual processes, which include everything from being able to ride a bike to recognizing familiar faces, depend not only on the interaction between inherited processes and learned experiences but also on the interaction between our internal (brain) and external (sensory input) environments.

CONCEPT/GLOSSARY: Effects of Restricting Environments

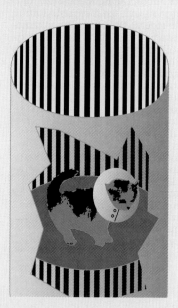

1. During the developmental process, there are certain "windows" of time, called _____, when brain cells are especially sensitive to restrictions in environmental stimuli.

2. The fact that a salamander cannot adjust to an upside-down world but a human can indicates that the human perceptual system has a great capacity for _____, which is the ability to show new responses to changes in environmental stimuli.

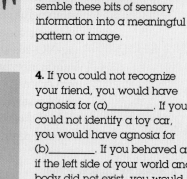

3. If you were shown a baseball and could see it but not identify it as a baseball, you would have a deficit that is called _____, which is being able to receive sensory input but being unable to assemble these bits of sensory information into a meaningful pattern or image.

4. If you could not recognize your friend, you would have agnosia for (a)_____. If you could not identify a toy car, you would have agnosia for (b)_____. If you behaved as if the left side of your world and body did not exist, you would have agnosia for one side, which is called the (c)_____.

Answers: 1. *critical periods;* 2. *perceptual adaptation;* 3. *agnosia;* 4. (a) *faces,* (b) *objects,* (c) *neglect syndrome.*

Learning Influences

At 5 feet, 6 inches and 180 pounds, this woman is 21 pounds overweight (according to a weight chart). Because of media pressure on women to watch their weight, college women perceive themselves as being overweight much more frequently than college men, who rarely admit to being overweight (even when they are).

From experiments and case studies, we have seen how restricting animals' experiences can influence their perceptions and how brain damage can alter humans' perceptions. Now we'll see how our perceptions are influenced by a wide variety of factors in the real world.

Media Pressures

Am I overweight?

You can answer this question in two ways: one based on objective data and one based on personal perception. The objective answer comes from comparing your weight with the numbers on a standard weight chart: is it more or less than the "standard" weight for your height? The personal answer comes from whether you perceive yourself as overweight. This answer may or may not be related to objective data.

At 5 feet, 1½ inches and 104 pounds, this woman is very close to normal weight (according to a weight chart). However, if this woman had a history of eating problems, she would probably perceive herself as too heavy and choose a lower weight as her ideal weight.

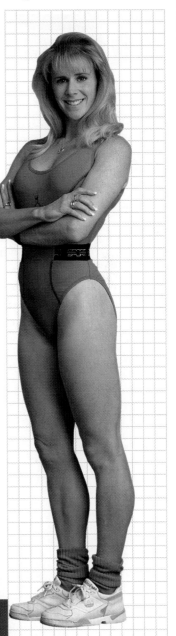

One factor that influences personal perceptions of being overweight is pressure from the media (television, movies, magazines, and advertisements). There is much more media pressure on women than on men to watch their weight. This may make women more critical and less tolerant of being overweight. For example, researchers found that a higher percentage of college women in the United States reported that weight was important to their self-concept and that many of them were currently overweight. In contrast, almost no college men said that weight was important to their self-concept, and very few admitted to being overweight (Markus, Hamill, & Sentis, 1987).

Because women reported that weight was very important to their self-concept, we would expect women to be more accurate in perceiving their weight than men. And in fact, overweight college women were much more accurate in perceiving their weight than were college men, who underestimated their weight by an average of 23 pounds (Klesges, 1983). Not surprisingly, women with a history of eating problems perceived their normal weight as "too heavy" and chose an ideal weight lower than their current normal weight (Williamson et al., 1985).

Although weight can be measured objectively, one's perception of what is "normal" or "overweight" is based partly on one's personal feelings. These are in turn influenced by media pressures or experiences with eating problems. In the United States, media pressures influence women's perceptions of weight more than men, so women may actually "perceive" themselves as being heavier than they really are.

What is "normal" weight?

Learning Influences

Gender Differences

The finding that males perceive their weights differently than females illustrates a perceptual difference based on sex, or gender. Let's look at some other *gender differences* in perception.

Ambiguous Objects. Before reading further, please look briefly at these three figures and decide what each looks like.

Most females see this figure as a comb or teeth. Males tend to perceive it as a brush, centipede, or caterpillar.

Most females see this object as a dinner plate; males perceive it as a target or bull's-eye. However, both sexes equally report that it looks like a ring or a tire.

Most females see this as a cup; males perceive it as a head.

Because an identical figure is perceived as one object by males and another by females, we assume this perceptual difference results from differences in gender. One explanation for this gender difference is that males are exposed to, play with, and talk about different objects than do females. For example, if boys are exposed more to caterpillars and girls more to combs, it follows that these differential learning experiences will bias their interpretations of these ambiguous figures.

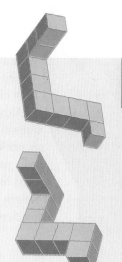

Visual-Spatial Problem: Rotating Figures

Another interesting gender difference is that males are generally better than females at solving a certain kind of visual-spatial problem called *rotating figures*. Solving this visual-spatial problem requires a number of abilities, such as being able to perceive and rotate objects in space.

Here's an example of a specific kind of visual-spatial problem that is called a *rotating figure*. Look at the target figure and then find the same figure, but with a different orientation, among options shown here.

In solving a rotating-figure problem, you must first accurately perceive the target figure and then rotate its image in your mind until it matches the orientation of one of the alternative figures. (The correct answer is the third figure.)

Target

As a group, males are reported to be either faster or more accurate than women in solving rotating-figure problems, and women report this task as being more difficult than males report (Bryden et al., 1990). However, on other kinds of spatial problems, there is little or no gender difference (Caplan et al., 1985). Psychologist Diane Halpern (1986) concluded that any gender differences found in spatial-perceptual skills are due to an interaction between physiological factors (perhaps hormonal) and psychological factors (perhaps experience with objects).

Perceptual Sets

Do you see what you want to see?

From our previous experiences with images and objects, we develop certain expectations about what we see or perceive. **Perceptual sets,** *which are learned, are expectations that automatically add information or feelings to our perceptions and thus change or bias our perceptions.* For example, as you look at this bodybuilder, you perceive a heavily muscled male body and you automatically add other physical characteristics, such as weight and height. You may also add personal feelings (such as like-dislike, approve-disapprove).

How large is this bodybuilder?

Based on past experiences, you "expect" bodybuilders to be large, so you probably guessed his height at about 6 feet and his weight at around 250 pounds. In fact, he is only 5 feet, 2 inches tall and weighs 182 pounds. One function of perceptual sets is to automatically fill in information or add feelings that change or bias our perceptions of images or objects.

Guess the weight of this bodybuilder (answer in text).

Because perceptual sets are formed from previous experiences, we should be able to create different perceptual sets by giving people different experiences.

Experience 1. Candidates who complete police training spend a great deal of time talking about, learning to recognize, and dealing with potentially violent and dangerous situations. This concentrated experience in violence recognition might create a perceptual set so that candidates are more likely to expect and thus to perceive situations or images as more violent.

Experience 2. In contrast, college students spend a great deal of time talking about, learning to recognize, and dealing with material that may show up on exams. Their nonviolent experience might create a perceptual set to expect and perceive situations as less violent.

In an experiment using police candidates and college students

as subjects, all subjects were shown the two images below simultaneously, one to each eye. Images were drawn to be somewhat ambiguous to maximize the potential influence of different perceptual sets.

Results. When all subjects were simultaneously shown these two images, police candidates recalled seeing the violent image more than twice as often as did college students (Toch & Schulte, 1961). These findings are not meant to criticize police training but to illustrate the powerful influence of perceptual sets, which often cause us to perceive what we expect.

When our brain sees two conflicting images, it resolves the conflict by automatically suppressing awareness of one image. As a result, we focus on and remember one image and forget the other.

Violent image: A man holding a smoking gun, standing over a slain victim, was shown to the left eye.

Nonviolent image: Simultaneously, an image of a man pushing a plow was shown to the right eye.

Function of Perceptual Sets

These studies show that the major *function of perceptual sets* is to automatically add information, meaning, or emotional feelings to images or objects that we are perceiving. Because of the function of perceptual sets, we may rarely perceive social or physical stimuli without their being changed or biased in some way.

Culture and Perception

How much does your culture influence what you see?

We are usually unaware of cultural influences on people until we visit ethnic sections of large American cities, such as "Chinatown," "Little Italy," or "Old Germany." **Cultural influences** *are persuasive pressures that encourage members of a particular society to conform to shared values.* Besides affecting social and personal values, cultural influences can also affect our perception of cues, images, depth, constancy, and motion. Cultural anthropologists, who go into the field to study behaviors in other cultures, have reported many intriguing examples of cultural experiences influencing perceptual processes. As you'll see, one's cultural experience can affect perceptual cues in surprising ways.

Perception of Images

Why couldn't African natives recognize these two familiar animals?

An anthropologist showed African natives a black-and-white photo of a cow and a dog, animals the natives were very familiar with. But the natives looked puzzled and their expressions suggested that the anthropologist was lying to them. The anthropologist then showed the natives a color photograph of the same animals. The natives smiled and nodded in recognition and pointed to the cow and dog (Deregowski, 1980).

Because the people of this tribe had never seen black-and-white photos, they had no experience in recognizing animals in this format. But when they were shown color photographs, which presented a world more similar to the one they experienced, they immediately recognized the cow and dog. Presumably, they drew on their everyday experiences with objects in full color and could relate what they saw in the photo to what they saw in the real world. This is an example of how cultural experiences can influence relatively basic perceptual processes, such as recognizing familiar images presented in different pictorial formats.

Perception of Constancy and Depth

Is that a herd of insects?

A researcher was studying a tribe of African pygmies who lived in a dense jungle that limited their visual experiences to relatively short distances. One day the researcher took Kenge, one of the pygmies, out of the forest for the first time. As they were driving across a broad plain, Kenge looked to the distance where a herd of about a hundred buffalo were grazing and asked what kind of insects they were. The researcher replied that they were not insects but very large buffalo (Turnbull, 1961).

Why did pygmies see large animals as insects?

If we assume that the "hardware" or wiring of Kenge's visual system is virtually identical to ours, then the most likely reason for his poorly developed size constancy and depth perception was his limited visual experience with seeing objects in the far distance. If you had spent your entire life in a dense jungle, where vision is limited to distances measured in feet, you, too, would be perplexed by your first sight of objects miles away.

Let's turn to a common example in our culture to show that what you take for granted people in other cultures find strange.

Perception of Motion

As you look at this car, dog, and dancer you immediately perceive what is happening: the car is speeding along, the dog is wagging its tail, and the dancer is spinning. Through our Western cultural experience with drawings of this sort, we have learned a set of conventions to depict movement. We are so accustomed to seeing these conventions that the car, tail, and dancer really do seem to be in motion. In comparison, people from non-Western cultures, who have no experience with these conventions for movement, perceive our indicators of motion for exactly what they are—squiggly lines on a page (Friedman & Stevenson, 1980).

Why don't people from non-Western cultures perceive these cartoon figures as "moving"?

We began our discussion of perception by stating that we rarely perceive the world as an exact copy but rather as a changed, biased, or distorted copy. In this module we examined various learning experiences, gender differences, perceptual sets, and cultural differences that change our experiences.

Psychologists are in general agreement about the functions of and influences on basic perceptual processes. In the Applying/Exploring section, we turn to a more controversial topic in perception: ESP.

CONCEPT/ GLOSSARY: Learning Influences on Perception

1. Although body weight can be measured objectively on a scale, one's _____ of one's own weight can be influenced by a variety of factors, such as media pressures or a history of eating problems.

2. When differences in perception are attributed primarily to differences between the sexes, they are called _____ differences.

3. When our previous experiences (thoughts, feelings, observations) result in our developing certain expectations about what we will perceive, these expectations are called _____ and they may change and bias our perceptions.

4. Pressures that encourage members of a particular society to conform to shared values are called _____ influences, which have been shown to affect a number of perceptual processes.

Answers: 1. perception; 2. gender; 3. perceptual sets; 4. cultural.

APPLYING/ EXPLORING: EXTRASENSORY PERCEPTION

Why hasn't someone won the $10,000 challenge?

For nearly 20 years, magician James Randi (known as the Amazing Randi) has offered $10,000 to anyone who can read the contents of a sealed envelope, move objects without touching them, or read someone's mind. Since Randi has accomplished these feats using trickery, he requires all challengers to perform these feats under his scrutiny. Nearly 600 have inquired: 57 have taken the test. So far all have failed.

According to Randi and others acquainted with magic, much of what passes for extrasensory perception is actually done through trickery (Gardner, 1981). For example, to show how easily people may be fooled, Randi sent two young magicians to a lab that studied psychic phenomena. Instead of admitting they were magicians, the pair claimed to have psychic powers and to perform "psychic feats," such as mentally bending keys and making images on film. After 120 hours of testing, the lab's researchers concluded that the two did indeed have genuine psychic abilities.

Randi's studies demonstrate that it is difficult for people untrained in recognizing trickery to distinguish between psychic feats and skillful tricks. For this reason, claims of psychic abilities must stand the scrutiny of scientific investigation.

What Is ESP?

We take for granted the ability to see, hear, and perceive the world through normal sensory channels (our eyes, ears, nose, and skin). Yet, about 50% of American adults claim to have had psychic experiences: perception outside normal sensory channels (Marks & Kammann, 1980; Myers, 1981). Extrasensory percep-

How do people prove they have psychic powers?

tion (ESP) *is a group of psychic experiences that involve perceiving or sending information (images) outside normal sensory processes or channels.* Three general abilities are included in ESP. The ability to transfer one's thoughts to another or to read the thoughts of others is called *telepathy.* The ability to foretell events is called *precognition.* The ability to perceive events or objects that are out of sight is called *clairvoyance.*

Besides these categories of ESP, people report two other psychic experiences. One is

These two young magicians (pictured with Randi) fooled researchers into believing that they had "psychic" powers.

the ability to exert mind over matter, such as moving objects without touching them, which is called *psychokinesis.* A second is *out-of-body experiences,* which have been claimed by some people who have been near death. In out-of-body experiences, people claim to perceive the world from a location outside of their physical body (Blackmore, 1987a; Moody, 1976). Perhaps you're among the adults who feel they have had a psychic experience; or perhaps you're part of the large percentage of college-age students who believe in ESP. Stay with us then as we discuss the ESP controversy.

Sample ESP Experiment

"As I sat in one room, my brother was in a neighboring room and was concentrating on a particular picture. Later I was shown a number of pictures and told to select the one that I thought my brother had been concentrating on. I selected a picture that resembled lakes, mountains, and people fishing. This image happened to be similar to the one that my brother had been concentrating on" (adapted from Blackmore, 1987b).

The subject in this study is Susan Blackmore, a well-known researcher in ESP. She had correctly identified a picture that was similar to the one that her brother was concentrating on in a neighboring room. Was this an example of telepathy, or just a coincidence? To answer that question, the procedure was repeated many times. Except for her first correct selection, Blackmore's overall success rate in other studies was no better than chance and therefore offered no evidence for telepathy (Blackmore, 1987b). Blackmore's studies illustrate a major and continuing problem in psychic research: the inability to repeat positive results (Alcock, 1987; Blackmore, 1985). With this problem in mind, let's review the debate over psychic abilities.

Debate: Is There Convincing Evidence for ESP?

Pro Argument

There must be a good reason why a relatively small group of researchers believe in and have been investigating psychic experiences for over a hundred years.

Charles Honorton (1985), a respected researcher and believer in psychic phenomena, acknowledges that some psychic studies have had flaws. However, because some ESP studies have shown positive findings, Honorton believes that the positive findings were produced by psychic phenomena rather than error or chance. Similarly, in a review of ESP experiments, researchers Rao & Palmer (1987) have argued that sensory cues, machine bias, cheating by subjects, and experimenter error or incompetence cannot reasonably account for the positive results. They suggest that there is now sufficient and convincing evidence to support the existence of psychic abilities.

Con Argument

There must be a good reason why the vast majority of scientists and researchers either do not believe in or seriously question psychic and extrasensory experiences.

Ray Hyman (1985), a respected critic of psychic phenomena (often called psi phenomena), concluded that many psychic (ganzfeld) studies have contained flaws in their design, execution, or analysis. For example, some studies have not randomized the procedure for choosing and selecting images. As a result, Hyman concludes that we cannot rule out the possibility that these flaws, and not psychic phenomena, have produced the positive findings (Hyman & Honorton, 1986). Similarly, a committee report for the U.S. Army has concluded that there is little or no scientific evidence to support extrasensory perceptual abilities (Swets & Bjork, 1990).

Because psychic phenomena occur outside the realm of normal sensory channels, researchers demand proof that must pass three rigorous tests: the proof must be free from human error, it must be unbiased by a researcher's expectations, and it must be repeatable in other laboratories and by other researchers. At present, the majority of scientists are not convinced that psychic proof passes these three tests. Thus, they do not believe in or seriously question the existence of psychic abilities or ESP.

Summary/Self-Test

STUDYING HEREDITY AND EXPERIENCE

1. In studying the interaction of heredity and learning on perception, psychologists use three approaches. The study of perceptual processes in patients with restricted sensory input or brain damage is an example of the (a)_____ approach. The study of the normal development of perceptual processes through infancy and childhood is an example of the (b)_____ approach. The study of how the restriction of sensory experiences affects perceptual processes is an example of the (c)_____ approach.

■ *A friend believes that males like to look more at objects but females like to look more at people. How would you study this problem?*

EFFECTS OF RESTRICTED EXPERIENCES

2. If newborn kittens were totally deprived of visual experiences, the brain cells in their

(a)_____ would become less responsive to visual stimulation. In the development of brain cells, there is a window of time, called the (b)_____, when brain cells are especially responsive to restrictions or changes in sensory experiences. If newborn kittens were exposed to only vertical stripes during the critical period, their "visual" brain cells would be less responsive when exposed to stripes with a (c)_____ orientation. When the eyes of salamanders were rotated 180 degrees, they were unable to change their behaviors in response to new sensory or perceptual experiences. In comparison, humans adjusted to wearing goggles that made their world upside down, indicating that the perceptual system of humans has a great capacity for (d)

_____.

3. Damage to the brain may affect perceptual processes in two ways. If a person experiences deficits in receiving sensory stimuli, damage to the brain has interfered with the (a)_____ of sen-

sory stimuli. If a person experiences no deficits in receiving sensory stimuli but has difficulty assembling sensory information into meaningful images or patterns, damage to the brain has produced a deficit called (b)_____. If a person can see objects but cannot identify them, the deficit is called (c)_____. If a person can see but not recognize a familiar face, the deficit is called (d)_____. If patients behave as if they do not perceive one side of their bodies or one side of their world, the deficit is called (e)_____.

■ *Is it true that heredity is the most important influence on the perceptual processes of animals while learning is the most important influence on the perceptual processes of humans?*

LEARNING INFLUENCES

4. Different kinds of learning and experience can influence, change, or sensitize one's perceptions. For example, apparently because of (a)_____, overweight college women were much more aware of and accurate in estimating their weight than were college men. Women

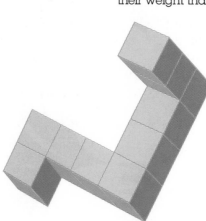

who were normal weight but had a history of (b)_____ chose a lower, subnormal weight as their "ideal weight," apparently because their former problem had biased their perceptions of "normal" weight.

5. Differences in perception that are attributed to differences between the sexes are called (a)_____ differences. One such difference is that males generally perform faster and more accurately in solving a set of problems called (b)_____.

■ *In every major department store, why is the women's clothing section always much larger than the men's section?*

PERCEPTUAL SETS

6. An expectation that is based on previous experience (thoughts, feelings, and so on) and that automatically influences one's perception is called a (a)_____. An important function of perceptual sets is that they automatically add (b)_____ to some stimulus, and this added "something" changes or biases our perceptions.

■ *What would you think if you discovered a new tribe in which the female of a couple is always taller than the male?*

CULTURAL DIVERSITY: CULTURE AND PERCEPTION

7. Experiences that are typical of and shared by other members of a society are called (a)_____ influences. These influences have been show to have a significant effect on a number of perceptual processes. For example, because African natives lacked experience with viewing black-and-white photos, they could not perceive familiar (b)_____ when they were presented in this pictorial format. In other cultures, natives who viewed animals from a great distance perceived them as insects because their dense

jungle environment had limited their development of (c)_____. When people from non-Western cultures view Western cartoon drawings as "squiggly lines," they do not perceive objects as having (d)_____.

■ *List as many things as you can that illustrate how your American culture has influenced your perceptions.*

APPLYING/EXPLORING: EXTRASENSORY PERCEPTION

8. The perceiving or sending of thoughts or images by way of other than normal sensory channels is referred to as psychic experiences or abilities. Three general categories of psychic abilities are included in ESP, which stands for (a)_____. The ability to transfer one's thoughts to another or read another's thoughts is called (b)_____. The ability to foretell events is called (c)_____. The ability to perceive events or objects that are out of sight is called (d)_____. Other psychic experiences include the ability to move objects without touching them, which is called (e)_____, and the experience of viewing the world from outside one's body, which is called (f)_____.

9. A relatively small group of researchers believe that reported positive results in psychic studies are free enough from error, bias, and trickery to support the existence and acceptance of ESP and other psychic experiences. However, a large majority of researchers argue that past and current psychic studies do not meet three very rigorous tests; thus, they either question or do not believe in ESP and psychic experiences. The three tests are that evidence or proof must be free from (a)_____, unbiased by a researcher's (b)_____, and (c)_____ in other laboratories and by other researchers.

■ *Suppose you thought that you had a psychic experience. How would you know whether it was due to ESP or to chance?*

Answers: 1. (a) case study, (b) developmental, (c) experimental; 2. (a) visual cortex, (b) critical period, (c) horizontal, (d) adaptation; 3. (a) input, (b) agnosia, (c) object agnosia, (d) facial agnosia, (e) neglect syndrome; 4. (a) media pressures, (b) eating problems; 5. (a) gender, (b) rotating figures; 6. (a) perceptual set, (b) information, meaning, emotion; 7. (a) cultural, (b) images, (c) size constancy, (d) motion; 8. (a) extrasensory perception, (b) telepathy, (c) precognition, (d) clairvoyance, (e) psychokinesis, (f) out-of-body experience; 9. (a) human error, (b) expectations, (c) repeatable.

Chapter *Five*
STATES OF CONSCIOUSNESS

MODULE 9
CONSCIOUSNESS, SLEEP, AND DREAMS

Although 20 people had volunteered to live alone in an underground cave for four months, researchers selected Stefania for her inner strength and stamina. On the chosen day, she and her favorite books entered a 20-by-12-foot Plexiglas module 30 feet underground, sealed off from sunlight, radio, television, and other cues for time. During her first month underground, Stefania's concentration seemed to come and go. She appeared depressed, and she snapped at researchers when they asked her to do routine measurements. She had strange dreams, such as that her computer monitor had turned into a TV that was talking to her. After several months, however, she became more comfortable with her underground isolation. She followed a regular routine of taking her body temperature, heart rate, and blood pressure and typing the results into a computer monitor, her only link with the outside world.

She spent her time playing the guitar, cooking on a hot plate, reading books, dealing infinite hands of solitaire, and making friends with two mice that she named Giuseppe and Nicoletta. Without clocks, radio, television, or the sun, she found it difficult to keep track of time, which seemed to have slowed down. When told she could leave her underground apart-

How long is a day when you're living underground?

ment because her 130 days were up, she felt certain she had been underground only about 60 days. Her time underground, which was a women's record (the men's record is 210 days), allowed researchers to closely monitor her sleeping and waking behaviors in the absence of all time cues. (adapted from *Newsweek*, June 5, 1989)

Stefania emerges after spending 130 days in an isolated underground cave.

About a half dozen men and women have voluntarily lived in underground caves so researchers could study sleep and wakefulness. These two states are part of **consciousness,** *which refers to various levels of awareness of one's thoughts and feelings, as well as of other internal and external stimuli and events.*

What's Coming

In this module, we'll discuss consciousness, mechanisms of sleep, meaning of dreams, and treatment of sleep problems. In the next module, we'll examine many aspects of hypnosis and the use and abuse of drugs. Let's begin with something that you are now experiencing—consciousness.

The Continuum of Consciousness

In everyday conversation, we divide our world into being either awake and conscious or being asleep and unconscious. However, there is actually a *continuum of consciousness,* which ranges from being acutely aware and alert to being totally unaware and unresponsive. As we examine various activities along this continuum, notice the different levels of consciousness.

What's the secret of a great tennis serve?

What am I eating?

What would you rather be doing?

Why don't I feel any pain?

Controlled Processes

One secret is the ability to focus all of one's attention on the ball. *Activities that require full awareness, alertness, and concentration to reach some goal and that interfere with other ongoing activities are called* **controlled processes.** Controlled processes, which include serving a tennis ball, taking an exam, or playing chess, represent our most alert states of consciousness. Another characteristic of controlled processes is that their performance disrupts other ongoing activities. For example, concentrating on answering test questions will disrupt thinking about making plans for the weekend.

As we begin to learn a new task, such as playing tennis, we try to focus our complete attention on the task. As we become more skilled at a task, some of our responses may become more habitual or automatic.

Automatic Processes

Although this lady's attention is primarily on reading an important report, she is also eating the donut that she holds in her hand. *Activities that require little awareness, take minimal attention, and do not interfere with other ongoing activities are called* **automatic processes.** Examples of automatic process are eating while reading or watching television or driving a car along a familiar route while listening to the radio or thinking of something else. Although we seem to concentrate less during automatic processes, at some level we are conscious of what is occurring. For instance, people who are driving on automatic pilot are, at some level, conscious of neighboring cars and road conditions and can respond to emergencies.

Daydreaming

An activity that requires a low level of awareness and often occurs during automatic processes is fantasizing or engaging in "awake" dreaming, or *daydreaming.* We may begin daydreaming in a relatively conscious state and then drift into a state between sleep and wakefulness. Usually we daydream in situations that require little attention or during activities that are repetitious or boring. Having a daydream is like taking a mental side trip. Most daydreams are rather ordinary, such as thinking about getting one's hair cut, planning on where to eat, pondering some problem, or fantasizing a date. These kind of daydreams serve to remind us of important things in our future. Few daydreams are out-and-out gratification, such as escaping to a secret island or winning the lottery, and few are actually romantic or sexual. Although you might guess otherwise, men's and women's daydreams are remarkable similar in frequency, vividness, and realism (Klinger, 1987).

Altered States

One way to decrease responsiveness to pain is through self-hypnosis, which some consider an altered state. *Altered states* of consciousness represent a change from normal awareness; they may be produced by a number of procedures, including meditation, drugs, hypnosis, or sensory isolation. In this photo an Indian holy man is using meditation to reach an altered state of consciousness in which he can focus all his attention on a single word or thought.

From the self-observations of neuropsychologist John Lilly (1972), we know the drug LSD can produce unusual, incredible, bizarre, and frightening altered-state experiences. Some people who have been near death report having been awake and able to perceive the world from a location outside their physical body in the altered state known as out-of-body-experiences (Moody, 1976). In altered states, however they are produced, we perceive our internal and external environments in ways very different from normal perception.

How much sleep do you need?

Are there things I don't know about myself?

What's the goal of every boxer?

Sleep and Dreams

This infant will sleep about 16 hours a day as compared to the average 8 hours that most adults sleep. During *sleep*, we pass through five different stages that involve different levels of consciousness, awareness, and responsiveness as well as different levels of physiological arousal. Thus, although we think of sleep as being one continuous state, sleep is actually composed of different states of awareness. As you will learn, during the initial stage of sleep we are often aware of stimuli in our environment; in very deep sleep, we may be unaware of sleeptalking or sleepwalking and are very difficult to awaken.

During another sleep stage, our body is in a state of increased physiological arousal and most of our *dreams* occur. People often ask how long dreams last, since some seem to go on forever. Sleep researchers tell us that dreams that occur during sleep last about as long as daydreams we experience during waking. A large part of this module is devoted to sleep and dreams.

The Unconscious

As you may remember, one of Sigmund Freud's revolutionary ideas was the notion of the *unconscious*, a mental place into which we pushed secret or sexual desires that threatened our self-esteem. Once in the unconscious, these menacing desires give rise to anxiety and guilt, which in turn can influence conscious behaviors and thoughts. According to Freud, we can become aware of our unconscious thoughts only through a process of free association or dream interpretation, both of which will be explained in Module 12.

Freud's theory of the unconscious has been greatly modified by modern cognitive psychologists, such as John Kihlstrom (1987). Kihlstrom uses the term **cognitive unconscious** *to refer to mental structures and processes of which we are unaware but that influence our conscious thoughts and behaviors.* For example, we perform many practiced motor patterns, such as tying our shoes or riding a bike, by using memories stored in the cognitive unconscious. The reason we cannot easily explain how we tie our shoes or ride a bike is that memories in our cognitive unconscious are not accessible to our conscious mind. According to Kohlstrom, the current idea of the cognitive unconscious, which emphasizes the influence of many different kinds of "normal" memories, is very different from Freud's unconscious, which emphasized the influence of threatening memories.

Unconsciousness

A boxer's goal is to use a quick and hard blow to knock out the opponent, producing a temporary state of unconsciousness. The state of **unconsciousness**, which can result from a blow to the head or from general medical anesthesia, results in a total loss of awareness and responsiveness.

Different levels of unconsciousness can also result from trauma to the brain, which is called a *coma*. When we hear the word *coma* most of us think of a person who appears to be asleep and has absolutely no awareness or responsiveness. This kind of coma, which is called a vegetative state, is usually caused by such extensive damage to the forebrain that the person is considered to be brain dead. The term *brain dead* usually means that a person is in a coma with no human functions because the forebrain is permanently damaged. As you may remember from Module 4, Karen Ann Quinlan, whose forebrain was dead, remained unconscious and in a vegetative coma for almost ten years.

Rhythms of Sleeping and Waking

After people spend several weeks in an underground cave with no time cues, their day becomes 25 hours long.

Would you like a longer day?

From studies on underground cave dwellers such as Stefania we have learned that when people are deprived of all time cues, their day (the total time for one sleep-wake cycle) lasts closer to 25 hours than 24 (Wever, 1989). The timing of many physiological responses is accomplished by ***biological clocks*** that are genetically set for different periods of time, varying from hours to a single day to many days (menstrual cycle). *When a biological clock, such as the sleep-wake cycle, is set for about a 24- to 25-hour period (one day), it is called a* **circadian** *(sir-KAY-dee-un)* **rhythm.** Circadian rhythms control the rise and fall of physiological responses such as temperature, as well as the start and stop of responses such as going to sleep and awakening.

Because the industrialized world has standardized a day as exactly 24 hours, the natural 25-hour circadian rhythm of the sleep-wake cycle must be set back about one hour each day (Moore-Ede & Czeisler, 1984). Let's examine the miniature biological clock that controls the sleep-wake cycle.

Biological Clocks

In the middle of the brain lies a group of cells collectively called the hypothalamus. Researchers have found that in hamsters, one part of the hypothalamus, the ***suprachiasmatic*** (SUE-pra-kye-as-MAT-ick) ***nucleus,*** is actually a sophisticated biological clock that controls a number of circadian rhythms, including the sleep-wake cycle. This nucleus receives input from the eyes and is highly responsive to changes in light. Hamsters have suprachiasmatic clocks that are genetically set for either a 22- or 24-hour circadian rhythm, depending on the breed. Researchers have been able to replace the 22-hour suprachiasmatic clock from animals of one breed with the 24-hour suprachiasmatic clocks removed from animals of another breed (Ralph et al., 1990). They have also discovered that only light at dawn and dusk, but not during the day, stimulates the suprachiasmatic nucleus to fine-tune the length of its circadian rhythm. Researchers assume that human circadian rhythms are also controlled by a suprachiasmatic nucleus.

What controls the sleep-wake cycle?

Hamsters have a biological clock.

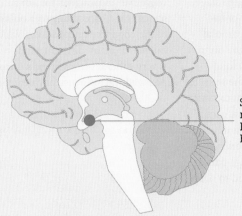

Suprachiasmatic nucleus (greatly enlarged) in human brain

Incidents of early morning accidents may involve out of sync circadian rhythms, including a severe plane mishap that occurred at 2:14 A.M., a head-on train crash that occurred at 3:58 A.M., a train that was struck from behind at 4:56 A.M., a cargo ship that went aground at 2:15 A.M., and a bus accident that occurred at 4:15 A.M. (Lauber & Kayten, 1988).

Can Circadian Rhythms Be a Problem?

Although our sleep-wake cycle is regulated by a natural circadian rhythm set to a 25-hour day, most of us easily set it back by one hour to match the 24-hour day. Researchers assume that this resetting is accomplished when light stimulates the suprachiasmatic nucleus, which functions like a biological clock. When the circadian rhythm must be reset by three, four, or more hours—as required when flying across time zones or changing from day to night shift—the sleep-wake cycle may be disrupted until the resetting process is accomplished.

The problem is that resetting the biological clock is a slow process, and each hour of resetting requires about one day. For example, if you flew from Los Angeles to New York, a three-hour time difference, you would need about three days for your circadian rhythm to be in step with New York clock time.

Having one's circadian rhythm out of step with clock time produces *jet lag*, a feeling of fatigue, disorientation, and lack of concentration that is common to travelers. Workers on night shifts experience a similar feeling. In fact, a number of plane, automobile, ship, and job accidents have been partly attributed to the lack of concentration, fatigue, and human error that occurred in the early hours of the morning when a night shift worker's circadian rhythm was out of sync with the clock time (Lauber & Kayten, 1988).

Jet lag occurs when one's circadian rhythm is out of sync with local clock time.

Can We Reset Circadian Rhythms?

Until recently, no one had suspected that the human circadian rhythm can be changed or reset simply by exposing individuals to light. But researcher Charles Czeisler and his colleagues (1989) have found that by exposing individuals to either bright light or room light for a certain period of time and at a particular point in the circadian rhythm they can reset circadian rhythms. These results have implications for treating jet lag and problems associated with shift work and insomnia. For example, if you flew from New York to Sydney, Australia, you would be 14 hours ahead of New York time and your circadian rhythm would be greatly out of step with local clock time. If you went to work every day and were exposed only to regular indoor lighting, your biological clock would take ten days to fully adapt. If, however, you spent 6 to 8 hours of the first two days outside in bright sunlight, you would reset your biological clock and cause your circadian rhythm to be on local clock time (Kronauer, 1989).

Night shift workers' biological clocks were reset by exposure to bright light.

Light. To test this idea on workers, Czeisler and colleagues (1990) exposed workers who had been shifted to night work to periods of bright light. The result? The periods of bright light reset the workers' biological clocks, matched their circadian rhythms to the new clock time, and improved both alertness and performance. Widespread use of this treatment in industry has enormous potential for improving shift workers' quality of life as well as decreasing their chances of accidents.

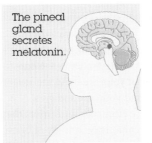

The pineal gland secretes melatonin.

Melatonin. Near the center of the human brain is an oval-shaped group of cells collectively called the *pineal gland.* These cells secrete a hormone called *melatonin*, which in many animals plays a major role in the regulation of circadian rhythms (Armstrong, 1989). In humans, the function of melatonin is less clear, and its role in the human sleep-wake cycle is under study. When researchers gave melatonin to flyers, it reduced the effects of jet lag (Petrie et al., 1989). At this point, we do not know whether the melatonin reduced jet lag by acting like a sleeping pill or by modifying the circadian rhythm.

The World of Sleep

Some of us dream about reducing our time asleep so that we can have more time to do things. According to legend, Leonardo da Vinci made more time for his creative work by taking a 15-minute nap every 4 hours; at this rate he averaged only 1.5 hours of sleep a day. A recent volunteer replicated part of Leonardo's sleep legend by taking six 15-minute naps and averaging about 2.7 hours of sleep a day for nine days. This individual's performance on tests of memory, logical reasoning, and mathematical calculations was not significantly reduced—but he did not create any great paintings, either (Stampi, 1990). Solo ocean racers typically take short naps throughout the day and average only 5 hours of sleep a day (Stampi, 1990). Under most circumstances, however, we all need an average of almost 8 hours of sleep a night to avoid feeling grumpy and fatigued the next day.

Researchers have been studying sleep to answer some of our commonly asked questions: Are there different kinds of sleep? Why do I sleep? Why do I dream? What causes insomnia? We address these questions in the rest of this section.

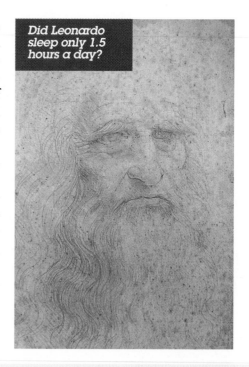

Did Leonardo sleep only 1.5 hours a day?

How Sleep Is Measured

Imagine that you are a subject in a sleep experiment and that the technician is describing the procedure for recording brain waves during sleep.

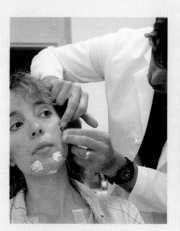

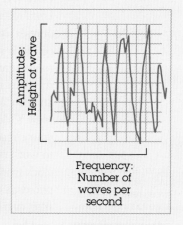

Amplitude: Height of wave

Frequency: Number of waves per second

1 *The sleep technician explains:* I am gluing small metal disks or electrodes to the outside of your skull and the area around your jaw and eyes. These electrodes are sensors that detect electrical activity of brain cells, measure muscle tension in the jaw, and record your eye movements.

2 Then I will connect the electrodes to a machine that detects and magnifies the activity of muscles in the jaw and eyes and of nerve cells located primarily in the cortex (covering) of the brain. The machine writes out patterns of electrical activity from nerve cells (and muscle cells). This tracing is called an *electroencephalogram* (ee-LECK-trow-en-SEF-ul-la-gram), or *EEG.*

3 EEGs consist of wavy lines that represent the averaged activity of many thousands of brain cells. The height of a single wave is called its *amplitude,* and the number of waves that occur in 1 second is called its *frequency.* A change in the amplitude and frequency of your brain waves and muscle activity provides an excellent indication of your stage of sleep and whether you are dreaming.

Stages of Sleep

Imagine lying on a laboratory bed, and despite all the electrodes and wires attached to you, you are waiting (and hoping) to go to sleep. For approximately the next 8 hours you will first pass through a relaxed, drowsy state and then through five stages of sleep, each with its characteristic brain-wave activity. Passage through these stages is gradual and probably unnoticeable to you, but it is clearly visible in your EEG activity.

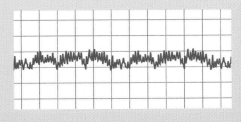

Alpha waves. As you become relaxed and drowsy and close your eyes, your EEG shows *alpha waves,* which are low amplitude and fast frequency.

Non-REM sleep, *which includes stages 1-4, makes up about 80% of an adult's sleep time. (Non-REM stands for non-rapid eye movement, also abbreviated NREM).*

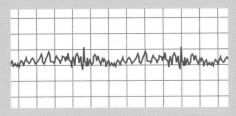

Stage 1. This stage lasts from 1 to 7 minutes and is a transition from wakefulness to sleep. In it, you gradually lose responsiveness to stimuli and experience drifting thoughts and images. Although this period is usually labeled a stage of sleep, some individuals who are aroused from it feel as if they have been awake. Stage 1 is marked by the presence of *theta waves,* which are lower in amplitude and slower in frequency (3 to 7 cycles per second) than alpha waves.

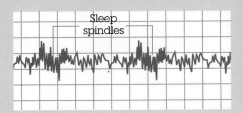

Sleep spindles

Stage 2. As you pass through stages 2, 3, and 4, your muscle tension, heart rate, respiration, and temperature gradually decline, and it becomes more difficult for you to be awakened. If you were awakened from stage 2, you would report having been asleep. EEG tracings show fast-frequency bursts of brain activity called *sleep spindles.*

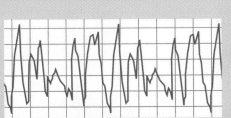

Stages 3 and 4. About 30 to 45 minutes after drifting off, you pass through stage 3 and then enter into stage 4, which has high-amplitude and low-frequency *delta waves* (shown here). Stage 4 is often considered the deepest stage of sleep because it is the most difficult from which to be awakened. During stage 4, heart rate, respiration, temperature, and blood flow to the brain are reduced, and there is a marked secretion of growth hormone, which controls many aspects of metabolism, physical growth, and brain development (Shapiro, 1981). After spending a few minutes to an hour in stage 4, you will return to the lighter sleep of stage 2 and from here pass into a new stage, called REM sleep.

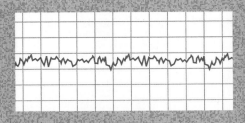

REM sleep. About every 30 to 90 minutes throughout the night, you pass from stage 2 into REM sleep. The EEG tracing for REM sleep looks exactly like that for the fast-frequency, low-amplitude beta waves that are observed when you are wide awake and alert. You remain in REM sleep an average of 15 minutes, although later REM periods tend to be longer (up to an hour).

REM (rapid eye movement) sleep, *which makes up the remaining 20% of one's sleep time, is so called because during it one's eyes move rapidly back and forth behind closed eyelids.*

Journey Through the Night

To understand what happens during the night, follow the bicycle from the top left and continue up and down the mountainous road until you reach the upper right.

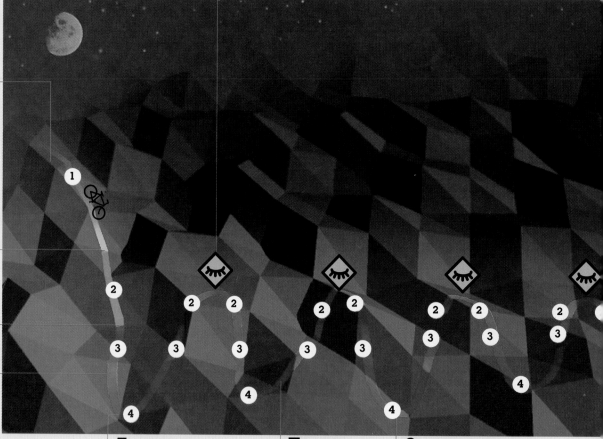

6 REM: Instead of returning to stage 1 and then awakening, you enter REM sleep. You remain in REM for 20 to 40 minutes. During REM you experience dreams. Then you go back down through stages 2, 3, and 4. During REM, your body is in a high state of arousal. Nightmares occur during REM sleep.

1 As you go to sleep, you go through a series of stages that have different brain waves, body arousal, and thoughts (dreams).

2 NREM Stage 1: You become drowsy. This is the transition stage between awake and asleep.

3 NREM Stage 2: First stage of real sleep. You may experience short, fragmented thoughts.

4 NREM Stage 3: Deeper stage of sleep.

5 NREM Stage 4: Slow-wave or delta sleep, the hardest stage to be awakened from. You remain in stage 4 for several minutes to an hour before going back to stages 3 and 2.

7 You remain in stage 4 for a period before again going back up the stages to your second REM period of the night. In children, night terrors occur during stage 4 sleep. The next morning, children do not remember having them.

8 It is during NREM stage 4 that people sleepwalk. Activities performed during stage 4 or when partially awakened from stage 4, such as turning off the alarm or getting up to go to the bathroom, are not remembered.

9 Throughout the night, you go in and out of REM sleep five or six times, with each period becoming a little longer.

10 When your alarm goes off, you leave whatever sleep stage you are in and slowly return to being alert.

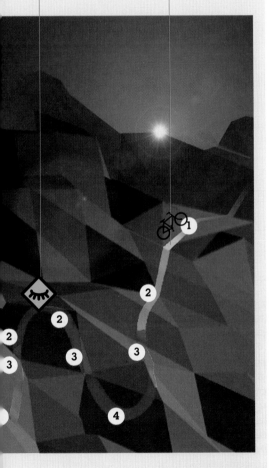

Characteristics of REM Sleep

During REM sleep, your body is in a state of physiological arousal, with increased heart rate, breathing, and oxygen consumption and a rapid back-and-forth movement of your eyes. Although many physiological responses are greatly increased, muscle tension (tonus) is lost in your neck and limbs, probably to prevent you from thrashing about and injuring yourself. REM sleep is often called ***paradoxical sleep*** because although you are asleep, your body is in a general state of physiological arousal and your brain waves are identical to those recorded when awake and alert.

When do dreams occur?

Are you dreaming?
About 80% of the time subjects are awakened from a REM period, they report having a vivid, well-organized, and relatively long dream. In the late 1950s, many psychologists believed that if people were prevented from entering REM sleep and were therefore not allowed to dream, they might suffer harmful effects to their personalities and behaviors. Since that time, many volunteer subjects have been deprived of REM sleep and dreaming by being awakened whenever their physiological signs show they are starting a REM period. Such subjects have shown no obvious ill effects (Cohen, 1979). However, suppression of REM sleep on one night does produce an increased percentage of time spent in REM on the following night, a phenomenon called ***REM rebound.***

A short time after you awaken, EEG tracings show fast-frequency, low-amplitude beta waves, which are associated with being wide awake and alert. Notice that beta waves look very similar to waves that occur during REM sleep.

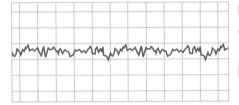

After the Concept/Glossary, we'll discuss why we sleep and dream.

1. The various levels of awareness of one's thoughts and feelings, as well as of other internal and external stimuli, are referred to as (a)_____. This experience varies on a continuum from very aware and alert to totally unaware and unresponsive. Activities that require full awareness and alertness and may interfere with other ongoing endeavors are called (b)_____. In comparison, activities that require little awareness and minimal attention and that do not interfere with other ongoing endeavors are called (c)_____.

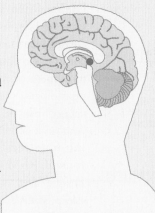

4. Near the center of the human brain is an oval-shaped group of cells, collectively called the pineal gland, that secrete a hormone called _____. In many animals, this hormone plays a major role in the regulation of circadian rhythms.

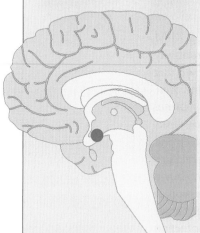

2. The biological clock that is set for a 24- to 25-hour day is called a (a)_____. This rhythm regulates our sleep-wake cycle, which is set to a 25-hour day and must be set back by one hour to match the 24-hour day. In hamsters, and probably humans, this clock is located in a part of the hypothalamus called the (b)_____.

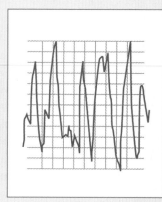

5. The recording of electrical activity primarily from nerve cells in the brain's cortex during sleep and waking is called an (a)_____. Brain waves are discussed in terms of two characteristics: the height of the wave is called its (b)_____ and the number of waves that occur per second is called the (c)_____.

3. If one's circadian rhythm is out of step with local time, one may feel fatigued and disoriented, a traveler's complaint called _____. Researchers have reset circadian rhythms by exposing subjects and night workers to periods of bright light.

6. During a night's sleep, one gradually passes through five stages. Stage 1, which is a transition between waking and sleeping, has brain waves known as (a)_____. Stage 2 has brain waves with bursts of activity that are called (b)_____. Stage 3 and especially stage 4 are marked by high-amplitude, low-frequency (c)_____. Stage 4 is often considered the deepest stage of sleep because it is the most difficult from which to be awakened. During stage 4, heart rate, respiration, temperature, and blood flow to the brain are (d)_____. Together, stages 1, 2, 3, and 4 are referred to as (e)_____, in which we spend about 80% of our sleep time. About five or six times throughout the night, we enter a paradoxical state called (f)_____, in which we spend the remaining 20% of our sleep time. During this stage, there is increased physiological arousal, "alert and awake" brain waves, and vivid dreaming.

Answers: 1. (a) *consciousness,* (b) *controlled processes,* (c) *automatic processes;* 2. (a) *circadian rhythm,* (b) *suprachiasmatic nucleus;* 3. *jet lag;* 4. *melatonin;* 5. (a) *electroencephalogram (EEG),* (b) *amplitude,* (c) *frequency;* 6. (a) *theta waves,* (b) *sleep spindles,* (c) *delta waves,* (d) *reduced,* (e) *non-REM or NREM sleep,* (f) *REM sleep.*

Why We Sleep

Causes of Sleep and Wakefulness

Most of us fall asleep within 15 to 30 minutes after going to bed and sleep an average of 8 hours. How and why this happens involves a number of neurotransmitters and areas of the brain.

The *reticular formation*, which is a column of cells that stretches the length of the brain stem, alerts the forebrain and prepares it to receive information from all the senses. The reticular formation is important to keeping our brains alert and us awake. When it is stimulated in sleeping animals, they awaken; when it is seriously damaged in animals or humans, they lapse into a permanent coma.

Researchers have identified several *neurotransmitters* that are involved in the control of REM sleep but have been less successful in discovering those that control non-REM sleep. Researchers have located areas in the *pons* (one of several structures in the hindbrain) that secrete various neurotransmitters: one neurotransmitter (acetylcholine) is involved in initiating REM sleep and two other neurotransmitters (serotonin and norepinephrine) are involved in inhibiting REM sleep (Carlson, 1991).

Although some researchers believe that circulating *chemicals* in the blood are involved in controlling non-REM and REM sleep, such chemicals have not yet been identified to the satisfaction of all (Krueger, Pappenheimer, & Karnovsky, 1982; Maugh, 1982).

We do know that *body temperature*, which is controlled by the hypothalamus, is important in regulating the sleep-wake cycle. We usually go to sleep several hours after our body temperature drops, and we get up when our body temperature starts to rise (Lewy et al., 1980; Moore-Ede & Czeisler, 1984; Sewitch, 1987).

These data indicate that a combination of physiological factors (temperature), brain areas (pons, reticular formation), neurotransmitters, and possibly chemicals in the blood control our going to sleep and awakening.

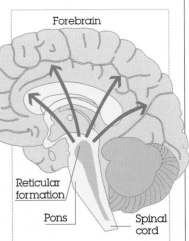

The reticular formation prepares the forebrain to receive information from all the senses.

Sleep across the Lifetime

From birth to old age, a gradual change occurs in the total time we spend sleeping, the percentage of time we spend in REM sleep, and the kinds of sleep problems we experience.

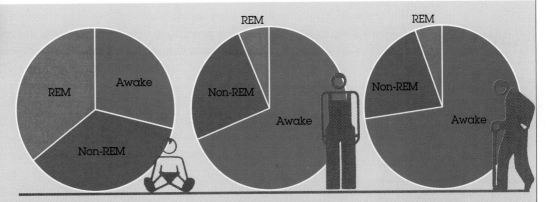

Infancy and childhood. From infancy to adolescence, the total amount of time spent in sleep and the percentage spent in REM gradually decline. For example, a newborn sleeps about 17 hours a day, and 50% of that time is spent in REM; a 4-year-old sleeps about 10 hours, and 25%–30% of that time is spent in REM.

Adolescence and adulthood. From adolescence (puberty) to old age (60s), we maintain the same amount of total sleep time, approximately 7.5 hours a day, and the same percentage of REM sleep, about 20% or less. After age 35, people report more difficulties in getting to sleep.

Old age. Upon reaching the 60s, total sleep time drops to about 6.5 hours a day, but the percentage of REM sleep remains about the same (20%). This age group is more likely to nap throughout the day and to report difficulties in sleeping through the night.

Why We Sleep

Reasons for Sleeping

How much sleep do I need?

A healthy young adult sleeps an average of 7.5 hours each night. About 95% of us sleep somewhere between 6.5 and 8.5 hours. For the remaining 5%, some are short sleepers, requiring less than 6.5 hours, and some are long sleepers, requiring more than 8.5 hours.

Researchers suggest worrying less about sleep averages and more about satisfying the body's need for sleep. If that need is not satisfied, you will likely feel fatigued, have trouble concentrating, and be generally grumpy. There are two different theories to explain why we sleep.

Two Theories of Why We Sleep

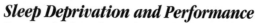

The **repair theory** *suggests that activities during the day deplete key factors in our brain or body that are replenished or repaired by sleep.* In support of this theory is the finding that during stage 4 sleep there is a marked secretion of growth hormone, which controls many aspects of metabolism, physical growth, and brain development (Shapiro, 1981). But as logical as the theory seems, it is not supported by data on humans who have gone without sleep for 60 to 264 hours (11 days) with no apparent damage to body or brain.

The **adaptive theory** *suggests that sleep evolved because it prevented early humans and animals from wasting energy and exposing themselves to the dangers of nocturnal predators.* According to Wilse Webb (1983), a prominent sleep researcher, sleep is a behavioral trait that evolved and endured because it helped our ancestors survive (and keep their heads). Some organisms protected themselves by evolving nighttime sleep, while others evolved daytime sleep.

The adaptive theory focuses on how sleep once had survival value; it is not at odds with the repair theory, which emphasizes underlying biological factors.

Sleep Deprivation and Performance

People who have been deprived of sleep for one or more days have been observed carefully for physical and behavioral changes. Their heart rate, blood pressure, and hormone secretions appear normal, as do their reflexes. They rarely experience hallucinations or illusions, and they never do so before reaching 60 hours of deprivation. When confronted with boring tasks that require vigilance (such as picking out a certain kind of blip on a radar screen), they do less well than usual. But when confronted with complex and interesting tasks (such as playing a mechanical baseball game), they may show remarkably little drop in mental or physical performance (Deaconson et al., 1988; Naitoh, 1976).

Does being on call and going without sleep affect a medical intern's performance?

To test for a link between sleep deprivation and performance, for 18 days researchers studied a group of medical interns who were on call every other night and who usually obtained less than 4 hours of continuous sleep when they were on call. The interns' diaries revealed that when they had less than 4 hours of sleep, they reported increased fatigue and decreased motivation. However, their performance on a variety of cognitive and coordination tasks did not show a significant decrease following a fitful night of sleep. Researchers concluded that the traditional hospital on-call schedules, which produce sleep deprivation, did not significantly affect the staff's performance (Deaconson et al., 1988). We do not know, however, whether the researchers' tests adequately assessed the kinds of medical judgments, decisions, and diagnoses performed by staff under real-world medical conditions.

The World of Dreams

Do you dream every night?

Although some people insist that they never dream, research suggests that everyone dreams during the night, even though many have forgotten their dreams by morning. In sleep laboratories, people awakened from REM periods report they've been dreaming 80% to 100% of the time (Foulkes, 1983).

Some dream of flying.

What do you dream about?

Researchers collected hundreds of dream descriptions from people who had just been aroused from REM sleep. They found that dreams usually have several characters, involve motion such as running or walking, are more likely to take place indoors than out, and are more often unpleasant than pleasant. Oddly enough, although most dreams are filled with visual sensations, few involve the sensations of taste, smell, or pain. Dreams often seem bizarre because they disregard physical laws and the ways we normally behave. We also have dreams of experiences we would never have in real life, such as flying or jumping to the top of a building. The majority of college students reported recurrent dreams, such as being threatened, being pursued, or trying to hide (Robbins & Houshi, 1983). Also, if dream reports can be believed, we rarely dream about sexual encounters and almost never about sexual intercourse (Hall & Van de Castle, 1966; Kiester, 1980).

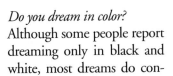

Some dream of falling.

Do you dream in color?

Although some people report dreaming only in black and white, most dreams do contain color, even though you may not remember the color on awakening. There is no evidence that a certain color, such as red, always has a certain meaning, such as danger.

Some dream about unusual combinations of events.

Do dreams come true?

A friend may have told you how she dreamt one night about meeting a certain person and then it happened the next afternoon. It is rare, but not unheard of, for part of a dream to "come true." When you consider that each night our dreams contain many hundreds of themes, ideas, and actions, sooner or later one of these dream aspects may "come true" by chance alone.

Do animals dream?

Pet owners often report that during sleep, their animals' legs move as if running. Are their dogs or cats dreaming about chasing squirrels or mice? Researchers do know that animals have REM sleep but can't yet get answers about whether animals dream (Winson, 1990).

The World of Dreams

Interpretation of Dreams

I am in an elevator sitting by myself against the wall. A girl comes in, and I say, "Come sit by me," and she sits by me (I don't even know her). I lean over and try to kiss her, and she says, "No, don't do that." I say, "How come?" and she says something about her acne, and I say it doesn't matter and she laughs and we end up kissing and stuff on the elevator. Then these parents get on and the elevator is real shaky, and I think that the elevator will crash or get stuck (adapted from Cohen, 1979).

Let's look at three theories about what this dream might mean.

Three Theories: Meaning of Dreams

According to **Freud's theory**, we dream for wish fulfillment—to satisfy unconscious desires or wishes, especially those involving sex or aggression. These wishes cannot be fulfilled during waking hours because they would create too much guilt or anxiety. Freud believed that dreams contain experiences of preceding days as well as memories of early childhood.

Because dreams may contain wishes that make us anxious, Freud (1900) held that we disguise these wishes with symbols. For instance, he thought that long objects, such as an elevator shaft or a cigar, represented male genitals and that circular objects or cavities, such as a peach or the inside of an elevator, represented female genitals. He saw the therapist's task as interpreting these symbols and helping the client discover his or her fearful and unconscious desires, needs, and feelings. According to Freudian theory, the "elevator dream," suggests that the young man may have difficulties with sexual and parental relationships.

Many therapists agree with Freud that dreams can represent past, present, or future concerns, fears, or worries. However, therapists disagree over how much of a dream's content is symbolic of disguised wishes and desires.

Disagreeing completely with Freud, researchers J. Alan Hobson and Robert W. McCarley (1977) proposed their **activation-synthesis theory**, which says that dreaming is nothing more than random and meaningless activity of nerve cells in the brain. According to their idea, an area in the pons sends millions of random nerve impulses to the cortex. In turn, the cortex tries to make sense of these random signals by creating feelings, imagined movements, perceptions, changing scenes, and meaningless images that we define as dreams. From their viewpoint, there would be no reason to interpret the elevator dream, since it represents random activity of neurons and not unconscious wishes or desires.

Hobson (1988) has revised this dream theory to acknowledge that dreams may have deep personal significance. He now believes that the images and feelings that our cortex imposes on millions of incoming neural signals reflect our past memories and own personal view of the world.

Agreeing partly with Freud, many therapists and sleep-dream researchers believe that dreams are **extensions of waking life**, including thoughts and concerns, especially emotional ones. Rosalind Cartwright (1988) says, "The problem most therapists face is that patients' dream material is sparse and incomplete. People simply don't remember their dreams very well. The therapist's task is often like trying to reconstruct a 500-page novel from just the last page. But dreams collected from a single night in the sleep lab read like chapters in a book. They illuminate current concerns and the feelings attached to them" (p. 36).

For example, she found that the dreams of people undergoing divorce seem to reflect being stuck in the rut of the past (marital problems); in contrast, the dreams of those who are happily married reflect many themes. In one sense, Cartwright is updating Freud's idea that dreams are the "royal road to the unconscious." She studies dreams in a sleep laboratory, and like Freud, she would see the elevator dream as providing clues to the person's problems, concerns, and emotions.

CHAPTER 5: STATES OF CONSCIOUSNESS

Lucid Dreaming

Most of the time we are unaware of the fact that we are dreaming. Some individuals, however, during REM sleep become mentally aware of the fact that they are dreaming, a phenomenon called *lucid dreaming*. Lucid dreamers report that they are conscious of dreaming, and they experience their dreams with remarkable clarity and vividness. In the sleep laboratory, only 1%–2% of all subjects' dreams are lucid, but Stephen LaBerge (1988) believes that lucid dreaming is a skill that can be improved with practice. Researchers speculate that the purpose of lucid dreaming is to make us notice something, such as what it is like to be awake and to be asleep (Moffitt et al., 1988). Lucid dreaming is one of the newer areas of dream research.

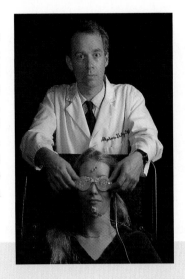

Researcher Stephen LaBerge is adjusting a subject's goggles that will detect eye movements during REM sleep and trigger a pulsing red light. The red light serves to remind the subject that he or she is dreaming and will perhaps increase lucid dreaming.

CONCEPT/GLOSSARY: Sleeping and Dreaming

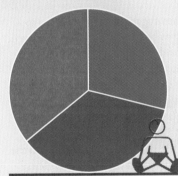

1. From birth through old age, there is a decrease in total sleep time, from about 17 hours in newborns to 6.5 hours after age 60. In addition, one stage of sleep, called _____, decreases from 50% of sleep time in infancy to 20% in adulthood.

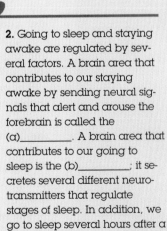

2. Going to sleep and staying awake are regulated by several factors. A brain area that contributes to our staying awake by sending neural signals that alert and arouse the forebrain is called the (a)_____. A brain area that contributes to our going to sleep is the (b)_____; it secretes several different neurotransmitters that regulate stages of sleep. In addition, we go to sleep several hours after a fall in body (c)_____ and get up when it starts to rise. This physiological response is controlled by an area in the brain called the (d)_____.

3. There are two different but not incompatible theories of why we sleep. The theory that says the purpose of sleep is to restore factors depleted throughout the day is the (a)_____. The theory that says sleep is based on an evolutionary need to conserve energy and escape nocturnal harm is the (b)_____.

4. There are three theories of what dreams mean. The theory that says dreams are an attempt to fulfill unconscious desires, which are often disguised in symbols, is (a)_____. The theory that says dreams are the result of random and meaningless activity of millions of neurons is the (b)_____. This theory has been recently revised to acknowledge that dreams may have a personal significance. The theory that is in partial agreement with Freud and is held by many therapists and researchers is that dreams represent (c)_____. A newer area of dream research involves our awareness that we are dreaming, a phenomenon called (d)_____.

Answers: 1. REM sleep; 2. (a) reticular formation, (b) pons, (c) temperature, (d) hypothalamus; 3. (a) repair theory, (b) adaptive theory; 4. (a) Freudian theory, (b) activation-synthesis theory, (c) extensions of waking thoughts and concerns, (d) lucid dreaming.

APPLYING/ EXPLORING: SLEEP PROBLEMS AND TREATMENTS

Insomnia

The most common sleep problem is **insomnia**, *which is difficulty in going to sleep or staying asleep through the night.* About 20% to 40% of adult Americans report bouts of insomnia; 17% consider the problem serious, and sufferers spend half a billion dollars a year on medications (Gillin & Byerley, 1990; Hopson, 1986).

Psychological causes of insomnia include worrying about getting to sleep, experiencing an overload of stressful events, worrying about personal or job-related problems, grieving over a loss or death, and dealing with mental health difficulties.

Physiological causes include changing to night-shift work that upsets circadian rhythms, having medical problems or chronic pain, and abusing alcohol or other substances (sedatives), all of which disrupt the sleep stages. A common cause of insomnia is a change in sleep schedule, such as staying up late Saturday night and sleeping late on Sunday morning. Sunday night you will not be tired and ready for sleep at your usual time. This "Sunday night insomnia" may make you irritable and grumpy on Monday morning.

A less common physiological cause of insomnia is *sleep apnea,* in which a sleeping person literally stops breathing and then wakes up to start breathing again. Sleep apnea has been found to occur in about 40% of elderly people; it is less common in younger adults (Coleman et al., 1981). Some sufferers can tolerate a device that fits like a mask over their noses and keeps the airways open, allowing them to breath normally. In severe cases, sleep apnea can be treated by surgically enlarging the upper airway passages in the nose (Fujita, 1990).

Depending on the cause and severity, doctors may treat insomnia by prescribing medication (benzodiazepines), or psychologists may treat it by using a number of nondrug, behavioral treatments, such as those described below.

How can I deal with insomnia?

Although behavioral treatments for insomnia differ in method, they all have the same goal: to stop the person from excessive worrying and tension, which are major psychological causes of insomnia. The three behav-

Insomnia is the most common sleep problem.

ioral methods we describe (or a combination of them) have proved successful in dealing with insomnia.

The ***stimulus control method*** helps the insomniac make the act of getting into bed a stimulus for getting to sleep rather than starting to worry. Instructions for making "going to bed" a stimulus for sleep include doing something relaxing before going to bed, going to bed only when you are relaxed or sleepy, and getting out of bed after a relatively short time (10 to 20 minutes) if you are unable to fall asleep, going to another room to do something relaxing to distract yourself, and returning to the bedroom only when you feel sleepy. These instructions helped a group of chronic insomniacs reduce their time for falling asleep from an average of 85 minutes to only 36 (Bootzin & Nicassio, 1978).

How do I stop worrying and get to sleep?

The ***progressive relaxation method*** teaches insomniacs to relax and relieve body tension by completing a series of muscle tensing and relaxing exercises. These exercises involve sitting or lying in a comfortable position and focusing one's thoughts on the feelings that come from contracting and relaxing the major muscle groups in the body.

The ***visual imagery method*** has subjects practice imagining an object in great detail for several minutes, once during the day and immediately before trying to go to sleep. Engaging in pleasant visual images distracts one from worries and helps one relax. Insomniacs who tried progressive relaxation or visual imagery showed a significant improvement in getting to sleep (Nicassio & Bootzin, 1974; Woolfolk & McNulty, 1983).

Although night terrors are frightening experiences, they are not remembered.

Night Terrors and Nightmares

Children sometimes experience *night terrors*, which arise during delta sleep. They usually start with a piercing scream, followed by sudden waking in great distress. The child experiences rapid breathing and a twofold to fourfold increase in heart rate. The child is difficult to calm and, even if severely shaken, requires several minutes to regain full awareness (Hauri, 1982). The next morning, the child has no memory of the fright. Fortunately, children usually grow out of night terrors.

Unlike night terrors, nightmares arise during REM sleep and are usually experienced by adults. *Nightmares* contain emotionally charged images that provoke fear and anxiety, all of which may be vividly remembered. Persistent nightmares suggest a more serious problem that may need the attention of a therapist.

Sleepwalking

A man was acquitted of murdering his mother-in-law after saying he had been sleepwalking when he drove 15 miles to her house and hit her with an iron bar (*Los Angeles Times,* May 28, 1988). If the jury decided correctly, this is a tragic case of sleepwalking (somnambulism). *Sleepwalking* usually begins in delta sleep and consists of walking in one's sleep as well as carrying out routine behaviors, such as dressing, eating, performing bathroom functions, and even driving a car. When sleepwalking, people generally have poor coordination and unintelligible speech; they are clumsy but can avoid objects. Occasional sleepwalking is considered normal in children; frequent sleepwalking in adults may be caused by increased stress or mental problems. Sleepwalking can be a serious problem because of the potential of injury and harm to oneself and others.

Narcolepsy

Narcolepsy (NAR-ku-lep-see) is a relatively rare condition (affecting about .05% of the population) that consists of irresistible attacks of sleepiness and often muscle paralysis (cataplexy), which are commonly triggered by laughing (Scharf & Fletcher, 1989). Narcoleptics enter REM sleep immediately, without going through the normal NREM stages. Narcolepsy runs in families, its cause is unknown, and its standard treatment is stimulant drugs.

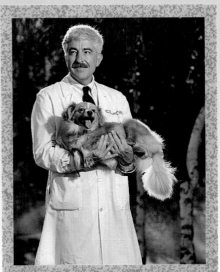

Renowned sleep researcher William Dement holds a dog named Tucker, who is alert and awake.

Tucker is totally limp from a sleep attack brought on by the sight of food. Dement is studying sleep attacks in dogs as a model to understand narcolepsy in humans.

Summary/Self-Test

THE CONTINUUM OF CONSCIOUSNESS

1. The awareness of our own thoughts and feelings, as well as of other internal and external stimuli, is called (a)_____, which occurs on a continuum from being very alert to being very unresponsive. Those activities that require our full awareness and concentration to reach some goal are called (b)_____. Those activities that require little awareness and minimal attention and that do not interfere with other ongoing activities are called (c)_____.

2. Engaging in fantasizing or "awake" dreaming often occurs during automatic processes and is called (a)_____. Perceiving our internal and external environments in ways different from normal because of drugs, meditation, or hypnosis is referred to as (b)_____. Sigmund Freud suggested that we push unacceptable wishes or desires into our (c)_____. A blow to the head or general anesthesia can produce complete loss of awareness, which is called (d)_____. Being in a vegetative state with absolutely no responsiveness is one kind of a (e)_____.

■ *How many different states of consciousness have you been in today?*

RHYTHMS OF SLEEPING AND WAKING

3. A biological clock that is set to run on a 24- to 25-hour time cycle is called a (a)_____. In animals (and probably humans) the biological clock for the sleep-wake cycle is located in a part of the hypothalamus called the (b)_____.

4. If we travel across time zones and our circadian rhythm gets out of phase with the local clock time, we experience difficulty in going to sleep and getting up at normal times, a condition known as (a)_____. Researchers have been able to reset circadian rhythms in workers by exposing them to (b)_____ during certain periods.

5. In the center of the animal and human brain is a small group of cells that are collectively called the pineal gland, which secretes the hormone _____. This hormone has a major role in regulating the sleep-wake cycle in animals, but its role in humans is less clear.

■ *Suppose we discovered a tribe who never slept. How might their biological rhythms and brains be different from ours?*

THE WORLD OF SLEEP

6. Researchers study sleep and wakefulness by recording activity of brain cells and muscles. Electrical brain activity is recorded in tracings called an (a)_____. The height of a wave is called its (b)_____ and the number of wave cycles that occur in one second is called the (c)_____.

7. If one is awake and alert, one's brain waves have a very fast frequency and low amplitude and are called (a)_____ waves. Closing one's eyes and becoming relaxed and drowsy is associated with brain waves that remain low amplitude but that decrease slightly in frequency; these are called (b)_____ waves. Researchers divide sleep into five stages. Stage 1 is the transition from wakefulness to sleep and is marked by (c)_____ waves and a feeling of gradually losing responsiveness to the outside world. Stage 2 represents the first real phase of sleep and is marked by fast-frequency bursts of brain activity called (d)_____. In stage 3 and especially stage 4, there are enormous high-amplitude, low-frequency brain waves called (e)_____. Stage 4 may be considered the deepest stage of sleep since it is the most difficult from which to wake someone. Together, stages 1, 2, 3, and 4 are referred to as (f)_____ sleep, which makes up about 80% of one's sleep time.

8. About every 30 to 90 minutes throughout sleep, one leaves stage 4 (delta sleep) and progresses upward to stage 2. From stage 2, one enters a new stage of sleep that is marked by fast-frequency, low-amplitude brain waves that look identical to (a)_____ waves. This stage is called (b)_____ sleep, because one's eyes

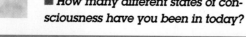

are rapidly moving back and forth underneath closed eyelids. During this stage one is asleep and loses muscle tension in the neck and limbs. However, one's brain waves are like those when awake and alert, and there is increased arousal of many physiological responses. When awakened from this stage, people report that they have been (c)_____ about 80% of the time.

■ *How would we know whether astronauts in space were awake, asleep, or dreaming?*

WHY WE SLEEP

9. The control of wakefulness involves a column of cells (reaching from medulla to pons and midbrain) collectively known as the (a)_____. This structure alerts the forebrain and prepares it for receiving information from the senses. The control of sleep involves an area of the brain called the (b)_____. This structure secretes chemicals or (c)_____ that are involved in the regulation of non-REM sleep. Additionally, the regulation of sleep-wake cycles involves changes in body temperature, since we fall asleep after our body temperature drops and wake up when it begins to rise.

10. From infancy through old age, there is a gradual reduction in total (a)_____ time, from about 17 to 6.5 hours, and a reduction in the percentage of (b)_____ sleep, from about 50% to 20%.

11. The theory that says we sleep because we use up vital factors during the day that must be replaced at night is called the (a)_____ theory. The theory that says that we sleep to conserve energy and avoid potential harm and injury from nocturnal predators is called the (b)_____ theory.

12. Although we usually sleep an average of almost eight hours, individuals have gone without any sleep for many days at a time with no lasting injury or harm to _____ responses.

■ *Your friend says that we sleep because we have to. What's your reply?*

THE WORLD OF DREAMS

13. According to Freud's theory, dreams represent (a)_____, which involves satisfying unconscious desires, especially those involving sex and aggression, that cannot be fulfilled during waking hours because they would create too much guilt or anxiety. According to Hobson and McCarley's original theory, called the (b)_____, dreaming has no meaning because it results from the random and meaningless activity of millions of neurons. According to many therapists and sleep-dream researchers, such as Cartwright, dreams are (c)_____ of waking thoughts and concerns, especially emotional ones, and provide clues to a person's problems.

■ *How could you be absolutely sure about what your dreams mean?*

APPLYING/EXPLORING: SLEEP PROBLEMS AND TREATMENTS

14. The most common sleep problem is (a)_____, which may be difficulty in going to sleep or remaining asleep throughout the night. Insomnia caused when one stops breathing and then wakes up is called (b)_____. If children wake up screaming and in a great fright, they have experienced (c)_____ but will remember nothing the next morning. When adults experience emotionally charged, frightening images during their dreams, they are having (d)_____. If a person walks or carries out other behaviors during sleep, it is called (e)_____, which may be caused by increased stress. A relatively rare condition that involves irresistible attacks of sleepiness and often muscle paralysis is called (f)_____.

■ *If you worked in a clinic that treated sleep problems, what kinds of symptoms would your patients have?*

MODULE 10
HYPNOSIS AND DRUGS

Why would a reluctant friend get on stage and pretend he was Elvis?

Why would anyone get on stage and do something foolish?
One night a friend and I were sitting in the front row of one of the longest-running nightclub acts in San Diego. A psychologist-turned-performer entertained locals and tourists by hypnotizing volunteers from the audience and asking them to perform funny, strange, and somewhat embarrassing acts on a public stage. Before the hypnotist appeared, my friend Paul repeated for the tenth time that nothing would get him up on that stage.

Finally the lights dimmed and the hypnotist appeared. He was a very good performer and soon had the audience laughing at his jokes and believing that he was a wonderful, trustworthy human being.

"Now we come to the interesting part," the hypnotist said in a low, soothing voice. "Just sit back and relax, and if you wish, follow my suggestions." The hypnotist slowly repeated a list of suggestions: "You cannot bend your right arm . . . you cannot close your eyes . . . your left arm will become rigid and slowly rise above your head." As I looked around the dimly lit room, a number of rigid left arms were slowing rising. To my surprise, one of those arms was Paul's. (I could not or would not raise my arm for fear that some of my students were in the audience and would never let me forget.)

At the end of the show, we all filed out. Paul said nothing until we were in the car. Then he turned and asked, "Why did you let me get on that stage and be hypnotized? You better not tell anyone."

I smiled and replied, "You were terrific. That was the best imitation of Elvis Presley ever done by a reluctant friend." Then I added, "I might have been tempted to try Mick Jagger."

Although I have changed Paul's name and minor details to protect his pride and reputation, his story is essentially true and illustrates some of the strange effects that hypnosis seems to produce. For over 200 years, psychologists have puzzled over what hypnosis really is.

What's Coming

In the first part of this module we'll discuss what hypnosis is, how one is hypnotized, what one does under hypnosis, and how hypnosis is used. In the second part, we'll explore the use and abuse of drugs in our society.

Hypnosis: Definition and Process

What is hypnosis?

In the late 1700s, Anton Mesmer promised to cure a variety of symptoms by passing a force into the patient's body, a force that he called "animal magnetism." So many patients testified to the success of animal magnetism as a treatment that a committee of the French Academy of Science was appointed to investigate. The committee concluded that many of Mesmer's patients were indeed cured (of various psychosomatic problems), but they banned the future use of animal magnetism because Mesmer's claims about its existence could not be verified. To this day, we use the term *mesmerized* to mean hypnotized or captivated.

Although we know that Paul was not a victim of animal magnetism, he did engage in strange and unusual behaviors after he was "hypnotized." We can define **hypnosis** *as an altered state of awareness, attention, and alertness, during which a person is usually much more open to the suggestions of a hypnotist or therapist.*

Can I be hypnotized?

Only about 15% of the population can be easily and deeply hypnotized, about 75% can be hypnotized to some extent, and the remaining 10% show little if any susceptibility to hypnosis. However, individuals who originally scored low on a test of susceptibility to hypnosis have been made more hypnotizable by removing negative misconceptions and creating positive attitudes toward hypnosis and being encouraged to engage in mental imagery (Spanos et al., 1987; Spanos, Lush, & Gwynn, 1989).

Are you susceptible?

You may not know your degree of hypnotizability without taking a test for susceptibility or actually being hypnotized. The best-known test is the Stanford Hypnotic Susceptibility Scale, which asks the individual to carry out both simple suggestions (such as that your arm is moving up) and complex suggestions (such as that your body is heavy and you cannot stand up). Individuals who score high on this scale are usually easily hypnotized, retain their susceptibility across time, and have a greater ability to engage in imaginary activities (Piccione, Hilgard, & Zimbardo, 1989).

One suggestion in a hypnotic susceptibility scale is "Your left arm is weightless and moving up."

How is a person hypnotized?

The media's portrayal of a person being hypnotized by staring at a pocketwatch swinging back and forth is only partly true. Although hypnotists use slightly different procedures, they generally use the following four steps to induce hypnosis:

How is hypnosis induced?

1. The hypnotist establishes a sense of trust so that the subject feels comfortable in the situation.

2. The hypnotist suggests that the subject concentrate on something, such as the sound of the hypnotist's voice or an image.

3. The hypnotist suggests what the subject will experience during hypnosis, such as becoming relaxed, feeling sleepy, or having a floating feeling.

4. The hypnotist closely observes the subject and suggests specific behaviors that are known to occur, such as the subject's eyes closing or head falling forward. As the subject actually experiences these behaviors, he or she will think that they are being caused by "hypnosis." This further increases the subject's suggestibility.

Now that we know how hypnosis is accomplished, let's examine how individuals behave under hypnosis.

Behaviors under Hypnosis

What might people do under hypnosis?

Hypnotizing subjects and asking them to return or regress to an earlier age is called ***age regression.*** During age regression, hypnotized subjects may act out early life experiences, such as playing with a favorite toy or attending a birthday party. Some researchers maintain that during age regression subjects do not behave like real children but like adults who are attempting to *act* like children (Nash, 1987).

When a hypnotized subject responds to the suggestion that there is a fly buzzing around her head by swatting at the fly, this is called an ***imagined perception,*** which is experiencing sensations or perceiving stimuli that do not exist.

If the hypnotist tells the subject that when she "wakes up" she will not remember what took place during hypnosis and she subsequently can't recall what happened, it is called ***posthypnotic amnesia.*** One explanation is that the person forgets because the experiences have been repressed and made unavailable to normal consciousness. Another explanation is that the subjects can remember what happened but that they inhibit verbally reporting these suggestions because they have been "forbidden" to report them (Huesmann, Gruder, & Dorst, 1987; Spanos, 1986).

Telling the subject during hypnosis that she will perform a certain behavior when she "wakes up" is called a ***posthypnotic suggestion.*** Some researchers contend that subjects who follow posthypnotic suggestions are acting automatically in response to some predetermined cue, such as sneezing when they hear the word *student.* Other researchers believe that subjects are performing a certain goal-directed behavior in response to the demands and pressures of the hypnotist and the situation (Spanos et al., 1987).

If the hypnotist suggests that the subject will not feel pain and the subject subsequently reports little pain, this reduced sensitivity to pain is called ***hypnotic analgesia*** (an-nahl-GEEZ-ee-ah). For example, hypnotized subjects will hold their hands significantly longer in ice water (which is painful but not damaging) and report less pain than control subjects (Tenenbaum, Kurtz, & Bienias, 1990). Hypnotic analgesia has been widely used in dentistry and medicine to help patients cope with painful procedures or treatments.

Researchers generally agree that hypnosis motivates people to perform a variety of behaviors, but they disagree about why hypnosis works. In fact, the question of why hypnosis works is answered by two very different theories.

When Paul responded to the suggestion "You're singing and playing the guitar just like Elvis Presley," he was experiencing an imagined perception. Paul later confessed that one of his secret fantasies was to play Elvis on stage.

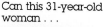

Can this 31-year-old woman . . .

. . . return to age 3?

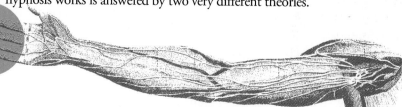

Hypnosis reduces pain.

Explanations of Hypnosis

Why did Paul perform on a public stage?
Two theories try to explain why highly susceptible individuals, after being hypnotized, close their eyes, appear to fall asleep, and then follow the hypnotist's suggestions in a robotlike fashion.

Two Theories: Special Process Versus Sociocognitive

Was Paul in a special trancelike state?

One explanation for hypnosis is the **special process theory,** *which says that a hypnotized individual is in a special state (a trance); as a result, hypnotic behaviors are different from normal waking behaviors.* For example, hypnotic reactions, such as raising an arm, are involuntary, while waking behaviors are voluntary. Hypnotic cognitive responses, such as induced amnesia, result when mental barriers are set up to produce loss of memory.

To explain how hypnosis might produce this special state, psychologist Ernest Hilgard (1977) has developed the hidden observer concept. According to this idea, hypnosis divides consciousness into two different parts. There is a hypnotized part that can communicate with and carry out suggestions of the hypnotist, but there is also an unhypnotized part, called the **hidden observer,** that "observes" all that is happening; it is "hidden" or unavailable for communication until called on through a special procedure.

So that you can experience the hidden observer phenomenon, we'll place you in an experiment. Imagine being hypnotized and told that your consciousness is divided into two parts. Your hypnotized part will feel little or no pain and can answer questions orally. Your unhypnotized part will feel normal pain sensations; it cannot answer questions orally but can answer by tapping your finger— once for yes and twice for no. Now the hypnotist asks you to plunge one hand in ice water (painful but not injurious) with the suggestion that you will not feel pain. When asked "Do you feel pain?" the voice controlled by your hypnotized part answers, "No." But the finger controlled by your unhypnotized, hidden part taps once, indicating "Yes" (Hilgard, 1979). Findings from such experiments support the idea of the hidden observer and suggest that hypnosis creates a special state or process.

Was Paul pressured to perform?

Another group of researchers disagree completely with the idea of hypnosis as a special state. Instead, they propose the **sociocognitive theory,** *which states that hypnosis works by creating powerful pressures that make subjects want to conform and, as a result, want to perform behaviors suggested by the hypnotist.* According to this theory, Paul was motivated to act like Elvis because of audience pressures that he conform to the hypnotist's suggestion.

The sociocognitive theory states that hypnotized subjects are awake, that they do not lose voluntary control or suffer memory loss, and that their suggested behaviors are similar to other *social behaviors* that occur during conformity or obedience (Sarbin & Coe, 1972; Spanos, 1986, 1988). Essentially, this theory says that good hypnotic subjects are neither in a special state nor faking their behaviors. Rather, hypnotized subjects are caught up in playing a role that involves voluntarily performing supposedly "involuntary behaviors."

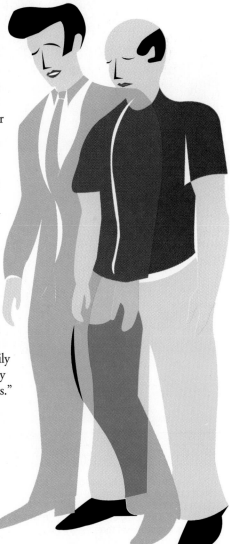

The two explanations for how hypnosis works remain miles apart and widely debated. Even so, we'll see that hypnosis has proved useful in a number of treatments and settings.

Applications of Hypnosis

How is hypnosis used?

We'll examine the major uses of hypnosis in medical, dental, and behavioral-change settings, as well as in police work, which is more controversial.

(*Top*) A woman who is anxious about undergoing a painful dental procedure is about to be hypnotized. (*Bottom*) The hypnotist has hypnotized the woman and suggested that as she relaxes she will feel less pain.

Medical and Dental Uses

One major use of hypnosis is helping patients deal with psychological difficulties that accompany medical and dental treatment. For example, hypnosis may be used to control pain by producing hypnotic analgesia, to reduce fear and anxiety by helping individuals relax, or to help patients deal with a terminal disease by motivating them to make the best of a difficult situation. In rare cases, hypnosis has been used as a primary anesthetic during general surgery (Silberner, 1986). Hypnosis may work best when combined with other behavioral programs. In one study, hypnosis alone was not effective in reducing headaches in children and adolescents but was useful when combined with other behavioral programs (Smith, Womack, & Chen, 1989). One of the major advantages of hypnosis in medical and dental settings is that patients who learn self-hypnosis can gain considerable benefits without suffering unwanted side effects of drugs. In a presidential address to the American Society of Clinical Hypnosis, Alexander Levitan (1991) predicted a continued role for hypnosis in medical and dental settings, especially in the area of hypnotic analgesia.

Police Investigations

You have probably heard stories of people under hypnosis being able to recall details of a crime they witnessed, such as remembering a license plate number. Because hypnosis has been reported to improve memory, it has been used in police investigations. However, there are at least two good reasons why our courts have been reluctant to admit the testimony of witnesses questioned under hypnosis (Morris, 1989). First, subjects under hypnosis are usually so eager to please and so suggestible that they may make up or agree with erroneous information or lie or misremember important details. Second, hypnosis has a tendency to fix or "cement" erroneous memories in a witness's mind, so that in later testimony the witness may repeat the error as fact. For these reasons, evidence obtained under hypnosis has questionable accuracy, and many states and courts have limited the admissibility of such testimony (Morris, 1989).

Behavioral Change

Because hypnosis makes some people more suscep-tible to suggestions, it has been used to help people quit smoking, overeating, and drinking, overcome insomnia, or decrease fear and anxiety, especially in competitive situations. For example, researchers com-pared the effectiveness of hypnosis with two other treatments in helping people stop smoking. One group of subjects were hypnotized and given sugges-tions to stop smoking; a second group were given health education, such as being told about the ad-verse health effects of smoking; and a third group received behavior modification, which involved re-cording when and where they smoked and substitut-ing deep breathing or relaxation for smoking. As seen in the graph, hypnosis was no more or less

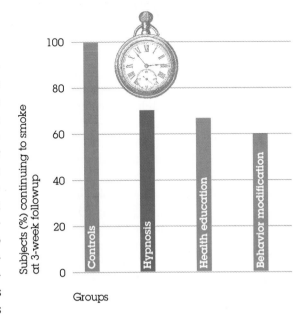

effective in motivating people to stop smoking than was health education or behavior modification (Rabkin et al., 1984). The general conclusion about the usefulness and effectiveness of hypnosis in behavior change is that, by itself, it is not a miracle treatment. Rather, hypnosis is a useful technique best used in combination with other behavioral or cognitive programs for behavioral change (Smith, Womack, & Chen, 1989).

Hypnosis by itself was not more effec-tive than other pro-grams for quitting smoking.

CONCEPT/ GLOSSARY: Hypnosis

1. A procedure that produces an altered state of awareness, attention, and alertness and that increases suggestibility is called _____.

2. Under hypnosis, individuals may return to an earlier age in life, which is called (a)_____; they may experi-ence a reduction in pain, an ef-fect that is called (b)_____; or they may experience loss of memory, called (c)_____. Subjects of hypnosis may per-ceive stimuli that do not exist; this is called (d)_____. They may perform some behavior af-ter "waking"; this is called (e)_____.

3. According to the (a)_____ theory, hypno-tized subjects perform sug-gested behaviors because they are in a special state. According to the (b)_____ theory, hypnotized subjects perform suggested behaviors because they feel pressures to conform.

4. Hypnosis has been used in a variety of medical and dental settings, especially to control _____. The reason courts do not usually permit testimony taken under hypnosis is that such testimony may be unreli-able.

Answers: 1. hypnosis; 2. (a) age regression, (b) hypnotic analgesia, (c) posthypnotic amnesia, (d) imagined perception, (e) posthypnotic suggestion; 3. (a) special process, (b) sociocognitive; 4. pain.

Drugs: Important Terms

Can you guess the name of this famous theorist?

When he was 38, his heartbeat was so irregular that he was told to stop smoking. Although he tried to cut down, he was soon back to smoking his usual 20 cigars a day. When his heart problems got worse, he stopped smoking and experienced such severe withdrawal symptoms that he started smoking again. When he was 67, small sores were discovered in his mouth and diagnosed as cancers. During the next 16 years, he had 33 operations for cancer on his mouth and jaw but continued smoking. By age 79, most of his jaw had been removed and replaced by an artificial one. He was in continual pain, barely able to swallow or talk. However, he continued to smoke an endless series of cigars. In 1939, at age 83, he died of cancer caused by 45 years of heavy smoking (Brecher, 1972; Jones, 1953).

Although a recognized genius and the father of psychoanalysis, Sigmund Freud had a personal drug problem that he tried but was unable to control. We can use Freud's lifetime struggle with smoking to define four important terms related to drug use.

Definition of Terms

1 Tolerance *means that the brain and body react to regular drug use by building up a resistance, which results in the person having to take larger doses of the drug to achieve the same behavioral effect.* One reason Freud smoked 20 cigars daily was that he had developed a tolerance to nicotine and needed a large dose of it to produce the desired behavioral effect.

2 Addiction *means that the brain and body develop a physical need for a drug in order to function normally. In addition, the addict develops an intense craving for the drug.* One reason Freud could not give up smoking was that he was heavily addicted to nicotine. Another reason was that each time he stopped smoking, he experienced severe withdrawal symptoms.

3 Withdrawal symptoms *are painful physical and psychological symptoms that occur when an addicted person stops using a drug. If the brain and body have become dependent on an outside drug, suddenly stopping use of the drug results in withdrawal symptoms.* After one of his attempts to stop smoking, Freud resumed because he could not bear his depressed mood, images of dying, and a tortured feeling that he felt was beyond human power to bear (Jones, 1953).

4 Psychological dependency *refers to the strong psychological need or desire to use a drug to deal with some situation or problem. Unlike addiction, which refers to a physical need, this type of dependency is a psychological need.* Freud was most likely both physically addicted to nicotine and psychologically dependent on cigar smoking. This combination made stopping doubly difficult.

Why Use Drugs?

Although we do not know why Freud first used nicotine, his biographer describes why Freud had tried cocaine. At age 28, Freud was poverty stricken and suffering from depression, chronic fatigue, and other neurotic symptoms. He tried cocaine and "found it turned the bad mood he was in into cheerfulness, giving him the feeling of having dined well" (Jones, 1953, vol. 1, p. 80). We will see that Freud later stopped using cocaine.

According to drug researcher Ronald Siegel (1989), people use drugs to obtain pleasure, joy, ecstasy, and self-understanding; to achieve altered states of consciousness; or to escape and avoid pain. Because humans have used drugs continually for at least 6,000 years, Siegel calls the urge to use drugs the "fourth drive." However, unlike the three drives necessary for our survival—hunger, thirst, and sex—Siegel believes that drug usage is an acquired drive. He also believes that it is likely to persist for another 6,000 years.

In a recent review of 200 years of drug use in the United States, psychiatry professor David Musto (1991) noted that our society has gone through tolerant and intolerant cycles of illegal drug usage. Because history tends to repeat itself, Musto warns that our society will continue to face physical and psychological problems related to drugs.

Drug Usage and Effects

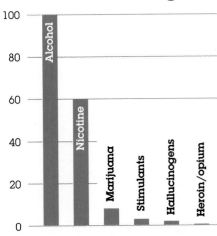

100 — Alcohol
80 —
60 — Nicotine
40 —
20 — Marijuana | Stimulants | Hallucinogens | Heroin/opium
0 —

Percentage of Americans reporting using various drugs.

In the rest of this chapter we'll discuss a number of commonly used psychoactive drugs, including stimulants, marijuana, hallucinogens, opiates, and alcohol. **Psychoactive drugs** *are chemicals that affect our nervous system and, as a result, may alter consciousness and awareness, influence sensations and perceptions, or modify moods and cognitive processes.*

Drug Usage

A survey of people age 12 and older indicated that the psychoactive drugs they used were, in order of popularity, alcohol, nicotine, marijuana, stimulants, hallucinogens, and heroin/opium (National Institute of Drug Abuse, 1990). Although the use of marijuana, stimulants (such as cocaine and amphetamines), and sedatives (downers) has declined in high school students, college students, and young adults, the United States continues to have the highest rates of drug use among the industrialized nations (Newcomb & Bentler, 1989).

The history of legal and illegal drug use in the United States (and worldwide) indicates that the popularity and usage of a specific drug rises or falls depending on availability, government support or suppression, black-market profit, crackdown on other drugs, advertising/marketing, and medical/health campaigns. For example, the history of stimulant usage reveals that amphetamine's popularity will rise and cocaine's will fall (or vice versa) if cocaine is targeted in "a war on drugs." The Office of National Drug Control estimates that over $40 billion was spent on illegal drugs in the United States in 1990 (*USA Today,* June 20, 1991).

Drug Effects on the Nervous System

How do drugs change behavior?

In Module 4, we discussed the structure and function of neurons, which are cells specialized for communication. The box at the right presents four ways that drugs can influence neurons and thus produce various psychological and physiological effects. A particular drug may act by one or more of these four mechanisms (as well as by more complex mechanisms that we have not discussed).

How Drugs Change Behavior

1 *Drugs increase the release of neurotransmitters.* Neurons manufacture and secrete neurotransmitters, which are chemicals that either excite or inhibit the receptors on neighboring neurons. One of the ways that some stimulants (amphetamines and cocaine) increase arousal is by causing more neurotransmitter (dopamine) to be released from neurons in the brain. Because having additional neurotransmitters provides more "keys" to "unlock" more receptors, the result is increased activation of neurons. This, in turn, produces increased arousal and other effects.

2 *Drugs mimic the action of neurotransmitters.* Some drugs, such as morphine, closely resemble the structure of naturally occurring neurotransmitters

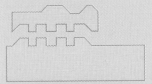

Neurotransmitter acts like a key.

Receptor acts like a lock that only a specific neurotransmitter "key" fits.

(such as endorphins). As a result of this similarity, drugs can duplicate the action of neurotransmitters by functioning as chemical keys to open and excite the locks of neighboring neurons and produce various perceptual and sensory changes.

3 *Drugs block the locks of receptors.* Some drugs, such as alcohol, block or plug the receptors' locks; as a result, neurotransmitter keys can neither open these locks nor excite these neurons. Drugs that block receptors' locks cause neurons to be inhibited or depressed. This is why alcohol is classified as a depressant drug.

4 *Drugs block the removal of the neurotransmitter.* A short time after neurons secrete neurotransmitters into the synapse, the neurotransmitters are reabsorbed back into the neuron. The action by which neurotransmitters are removed from the synapse through reabsorption is called **reuptake**. If reuptake did not occur, neurotransmitters would remain in the synapse and neurons would be continually stimulated. Both cocaine and amphetamines slow down reuptake and, as a result, cause increased stimulation.

Stimulants

"Two pills beat a month's vacation."

This marketing slogan was used to sell amphetamines in Sweden in the 1940s. It resulted in epidemic usage that peaked in the mid-1960s. About this same time, billions of doses of amphetamines were being used in the United States. By the early 1970s, both countries had brought amphetamine usage under control through a combination of measures, including regulation of prescriptions, decrease in supply, and stiffer penalties.

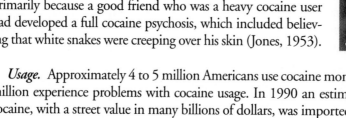

This crackdown on amphetamine usage in the United States was, however, partly responsible for the increased popularity of cocaine and the resulting cocaine epidemic of the 1980s. In turn, the federal "war on cocaine" in the late 1980s and early 1990s has been partly responsible for an upsurge in amphetamine usage.

All **stimulants**, *including cocaine, amphetamine, caffeine, and nicotine, increase activity of the nervous system and result in heightened alertness, arousal, and euphoria and decreased appetite and fatigue.* Dose for dose, cocaine and amphetamines are considered powerful stimulants because they produce a strong effect with a small dose; caffeine and nicotine are considered mild stimulants.

Caution. When humans or monkeys have unlimited access to pure cocaine, they will use it continually to the point of starvation and death. Only extreme shock will reduce an addicted monkey's use of cocaine, and only extreme health, legal, or personal problems will reduce an addicted human's intake.

Cocaine

Why did Freud stop using cocaine?

For centuries, the ancient Incas and their descendants, the current native Andean Indians of Peru, have chewed coca leaves as they made demanding journeys through the high mountains. Some minutes after chewing the leaves, which contain cocaine, they reported feeling more vigor and strength and less fatigue, hunger, thirst, and cold. Few problems are observed in present-day Indians who chew coca leaves, but many problems are observed among those who have switched to the white powder that is more concentrated cocaine (Siegel, 1989).

In a letter to his fiancée, Sigmund Freud wrote that during his previous severe depression he had taken cocaine and it had lifted him to new and wonderful heights. He added that he was preparing a song of praise for cocaine, which he published in 1884. Three years later, however, Freud stopped using cocaine, primarily because a good friend who was a heavy cocaine user had developed a full cocaine psychosis, which included believing that white snakes were creeping over his skin (Jones, 1953).

Coca leaves have been used for about 3,000 years.

Sigmund Freud used cocaine to ease his depressed mood but later quit.

Usage. Approximately 4 to 5 million Americans use cocaine monthly, and about 1 million experience problems with cocaine usage. In 1990 an estimated 190 tons of cocaine, with a street value in many billions of dollars, was imported into the United States.

Effects. Cocaine can be sniffed or snorted. More concentrated forms (crack) can be smoked or injected. One of cocaine's major effects on the nervous system is to increase the amount of neurotransmitters that arouse the brain and body.

In *moderate doses,* cocaine is short acting (the high lasts 10 to 30 minutes) and produces bursts of energy, arousal, and alertness. Users tend to feel euphoric, self-

confident, and certain that they are thinking more clearly. Under cocaine's influence, users usually overestimate their own capacities or the quality of their work.

In *heavy doses,* cocaine can result in addiction and serious physical and psychological problems, which may include hallucinations and feelings of bugs crawling under the skin. Heavy users often require professional help.

Physical problems associated with cocaine abuse can include increased blood pressure, elevated body temperature, lack of appetite, insomnia, irritation and damage to cartilage of the nose (if snorted), heart irregularity, convulsions, and death. Heavy usage may also cause physical addiction.

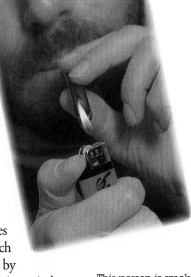

User's Vicious Circle. As cocaine effects wear off, the user experiences depression, fatigue, and an intense craving for more cocaine, which causes the user to seek another dose. Taking another dose is followed by depression and craving for more, which in turn continues the user's vicious circle.

According to researcher Frank Gawin (1991), dependency and addiction to cocaine are especially difficult to treat because continued and long-term use of cocaine may decrease the capacity of the nervous system to experience pleasure. As a result, Gawin suggests the need to develop new techniques for treating cocaine abuse.

This person is smoking crack, a more concentrated and addicting form of cocaine.

Amphetamines

During the 1960s, billions of amphetamine pills were legally produced in the United States and were heavily prescribed for fatigue, depression, mood problems, and weight loss. Heavy amphetamine (speed) users, called "speed freaks," often exhibited true paranoid psychotic symptoms. Finally, in the mid-1970s the federal government outlawed prescribing amphetamines except for hyperactivity and narcolepsy.

In the late 1980s and early 1990s, a crackdown on cocaine has been matched by a resurgence of amphetamine use in the form of "crystal meth" or "ice."

Effects of Ice. Ice, a pure form of methamphetamine that can be smoked, has

arousing and euphoric effects similar to but longer lasting than those of cocaine. In 1990 ice had become the number one drug problem in Hawaii (replacing cocaine) and the most widely produced illicit drug (Cho, 1990).

Heavy users of ice, as well as of amphetamine in other forms, show periods of aimless and restless activity, performance of repetitive behaviors, and development of true paranoid feelings in which they believe people are talking about or plotting against them. Because of its risk for addiction and dependency, as well as physical and psychological problems, ice/amphetamine is a very dangerous drug.

In the 1960s, billions of amphetamine pills per year were legally produced in the United States.

Next we turn to two legal drugs, caffeine and nicotine, that are the most widely used stimulants.

Stimulants

Caffeine

Caffeine is the most widely used psychoactive drug in the world. The average amount consumed in the United States translates into 220 milligrams per person per day (it's 400 milligrams in Sweden and England). One cup of regular coffee, two cups of regular tea, one No-Doz tablet, two diet colas, and four regular-sized chocolate bars all contain about 100 milligrams of caffeine. References to the use of caffeine go back two thousand years.

What does caffeine do?

In *moderate doses* (2–3 cups of coffee per day), caffeine affects brain receptors (adenosine receptors) and produces mild arousal and *psychological feelings* of decreased fatigue and drowsiness, increased reaction time, and a mild feeling of alertness or arousal (Zahn & Rapoport, 1987). *Physical symptoms* include increased heart rate, dilation of blood vessels, increased production of urine, and increased secretion of acid in the stomach. Because of the latter effect, people with ulcers are advised to avoid caffeine.

Heavy doses (500 milligrams or 5 or more cups of coffee per day), which is referred to as caffeinism, can result in physical addiction, psychological dependency, and feelings of depression, tension, anxiety, and fatigue due to insomnia. Individuals consuming these high levels of caffeine often report chronic fatigue, partly because of their increasing periods of insomnia.

Caffeine, a major chemical in coffee beans, is the most widely used drug in the world.

What happens if you suddenly stop consuming caffeine?

If you have been consuming small to moderate doses of caffeine, you may experience few or minimal withdrawal symptoms. However, if you have been consuming heavy doses, for as little as one or two weeks, abruptly stopping the consumption of caffeine will result in a number of discomforting *withdrawal symptoms,* including chronic headache, irritability, fatigue, and an intense craving for caffeine. These symptoms peak about two days after stopping and disappear within five to seven days.

Why has coffee drinking been decreasing?

Coffee drinking among adults in the United States declined from 75% of adults in 1962 to 52% in 1985, primarily because of well-publicized information about potential health risks of caffeine. These risks include worsening heart and blood pressure problems, increasing symptoms of ulcers, contributing to insomnia, and increasing feelings of anxiety in people with anxiety disorders (Schuckit, 1989).

How does caffeine produce a buzz?

Coffee drinkers often report feeling a *buzz,* or the stimulating effects of caffeine, shortly after finishing a cup or two. However, caffeine takes about an hour to reach peak levels in the blood and takes about two hours to reach peak levels in the brain. Because of this delay, the immediate stimulating effects of caffeine probably result from either a placebo effect or the effects of sugar in the coffee.

After reaching the brain, caffeine affects a number of neurotransmitters. A major brain effect of caffeine is blocking the neurotransmitter adenosine, which is a naturally occurring depressant. It is this blocking that produces the caffeine buzz or feeling of arousal.

Nicotine

How does nicotine produce opposite effects?

After caffeine, nicotine is the world's most widely used psychoactive drug. In the United States, tobacco is responsible for the greatest number of drug-related deaths. Besides cigarette smoking causing an estimated 460,000 deaths per year, secondhand exposure to cigarettes (passive smoking) is estimated to cause an additional 3,700 cases of lung cancer and 37,000 cases of fatal heart disease in nonsmokers yearly. The U.S. Surgeon General has declared that cigarette smoking is the single largest avoidable cause of death in our society and the most important public health issue of our time (U.S. Department of Health and Human Services, 1982).

Psychological and Physical Effects. One reason nicotine is so popular is that some of the time smokers light up to reduce stress and soothe themselves while at other times they light up to be stimulated. Initially, nicotine stimulates receptors in the brain and produces arousal. With continued usage, nicotine blocks receptors and produces calming. Nicotine is reported to improve attention, concentration, mental performance, and memory.

Besides affecting the brain, nicotine stimulates the sympathetic nervous system, which is responsible for arousing and alerting the body by increasing heart rate, blood pressure, and secretion of stimulating hormones.

Health Risks. Nicotine increases the risk of heart attack because it activates the heart muscle while at the same time reduces its oxygen supply. Besides nicotine, cigarette smoke contains tar and gases that contribute to bronchitis (inflammation of passages to lungs), emphysema, and lung cancer.

Quitting. Because nicotine is a highly addicting drug, quitting causes withdrawal symptoms, which range in severity and may include nervousness, irritability, difficulty in concentrating, sleep disturbances, and a craving for the drug. By 1986 almost half of all persons in the United States who reported ever smoking had quit, and most had done so by stopping on their own (Fiore et al., 1990). As the result of antismoking laws and campaigns, cigarette smoking among American adults is now at its lowest rate (29%) since 1944.

The best-selling brand of cigarettes in the United States carries a variety of health warnings.

SURGEON GENERAL'S WARNING: Smoking By Pregnant Women May Result in Fetal Injury, Premature Birth, And Low Birth Weight.

SURGEON GENERAL'S WARNING: Cigarette Smoke Contains Carbon Monoxide.

SURGEON GENERAL'S WARNING: Smoking Causes Lung Cancer, Heart Disease, Emphysema, And May Complicate Pregnancy.

Marijuana

How dangerous is marijuana?

Since you've already learned that a crackdown on one drug often results in increased use of another, it may not surprise you that Prohibition resulted in increased use of marijuana. In the 1920s, after the Eighteenth Amendment restricted the use of alcohol and raised its price, marijuana soared in popularity (Brecher, 1972). Later, during the 1940s and 1950s, the effects of marijuana were exaggerated: there was talk of "killer weed" and "reefer madness."

Despite a series of increasingly restrictive laws, marijuana grew in popularity, and in the 1970s it became the most popular illegal (recreational) drug in America. At present, marijuana is estimated to be fourth in overall popularity, behind caffeine, nicotine, and alcohol. However, surveys of high school seniors indicate that the monthly use of marijuana declined from 37% in 1978 to 26% in 1985 (Kozel & Adams, 1986).

Smoking 3 to 4 joints of marijuana is equal to smoking 20 cigarettes.

Psychological/Social Effects and Dangers

The primary active ingredient in marijuana is THC (tetrahydrocannabinol), which can be smoked or eaten (such as baked into desserts). The average marijuana cigarette (joint) contains 2.5 to 5.0 mg of THC, which is a tenfold increase over the amount of THC found in marijuana in the 1970s. The THC is rapidly absorbed by the lungs and in five to ten minutes produces a "high" that lasts for several hours. The type of high is closely related to the dose: low doses produce mild euphoria, moderate doses produce perceptual and time distortions, and high doses produce hallucinations, delusions, and distortions of body image (Palfai & Jankiewicz, 1991). Because marijuana's "high" depends partly on the user's initial mood and state of mental health, marijuana can heighten or distort unpleasant experiences, moods, or feelings.

There are three major psychological/social dangers of marijuana. First, marijuana greatly hinders one's ability to drive a car, boat, or plane because it decreases reaction time, judgment, and use of peripheral vision (Schuckit, 1990). Second, researchers have found that marijuana and pregnancy are a dangerous mix, since babies born to marijuana-using mothers are significantly lower in birth weight (Zuckerman et al., 1989). Third, at high doses, marijuana may cause toxic psychoses, including delusions, paranoia, and feelings of terror.

Physical Effects and Dangers

Marijuana causes many of the same kinds of respiratory problems as smoking tobacco, including bronchitis and asthma attacks. Because marijuana smoke contains 50% more cancer-causing substances and users hold smoke in their lungs longer, the effects of smoking 3 to 4 joints of marijuana are similar to those of 20 cigarettes. A panel of scientists reviewed the marijuana literature and concluded that although marijuana produces temporary changes in brain functioning, there is no conclusive evidence that prolonged marijuana usage causes permanent changes to the brain, nervous system, or genetic makeup (Relman, 1982). Although regular use of marijuana may result in psychological dependency, it is unclear whether it is addicting or whether withdrawal symptoms occur.

Is marijuana more concentrated today?

A group of scientists at the National Institute of Mental Health recently discovered a receptor in the brain that responds specifically to THC (Matsuda et al., 1990). Because THC is not normally found in the brain, the existence of a "marijuana" receptor suggests that the brain may make a marijuana-like chemical that affects these receptors.

Looking back, we discover that the potential dangers of marijuana were greatly exaggerated in the 1940s and seriously underestimated in the 1970s. Currently, researchers conclude that marijuana is a relatively dangerous illegal drug because of its risk for psychological dependency, as well as its involvement in a number of health and social problems (Schuckit, 1990).

Hallucinogens

Why were these drugs used in religious ceremonies?
Around the world, some six different species of plants containing potent hallucinogenic drugs have been used to produce visions as part of cultural or religious experiences. Western Caucasians rarely used hallucinogens until the 1950s and 1960s, when these drugs gained popularity as part of the hippie subculture.

Hallucinogens *are drugs that act on the brain (and body) to produce perceptual, sensory, and cognitive experiences that are not occurring in reality.* Such nonreality-based experiences are called **hallucinations**. We'll focus on three of the more commonly used hallucinogens: LSD, psilocybin (mushrooms), and mescaline (peyote).

The user's current state of mind, mood, and mental health, as well as feelings about the safety of the setting, all interact to exaggerate the effects of hallucinogenic drugs. As a result, hallucinogens may produce a terrifying experience, or "bad trip." In addition, some time after using a hallucinogenic drug, a user may suddenly have a frightening drug-related experience called a *flashback.*

In the 1960s Timothy Leary advocated the use of hallucinogenic drugs for spiritual purposes.

LSD

In the late 1980s, there was a reported upsurge in LSD usage. An incredibly small dose of LSD (.03 mg) is capable of producing powerful hallucinogenic experiences of great sensory, emotional, perceptual, and psychological impact that usually last eight to ten hours. At the peak of the LSD "trip," the user often has the experience of entering into the hallucinations. It is like the dreamer becomes part of the dream.

Why are hallucinogens used in religious ceremonies?

Physical Effects. Although the exact mechanisms of LSD action are unknown, the drug is believed to affect several neurotransmitter systems (including serotonin and dopamine). There have been no reports of physical addiction to LSD or death from overdose, but users do quickly develop a tolerance to LSD.

Dangers. Users, especially novices, may experience bad trips, which if severe may lead to psychotic reactions (especially paranoid feelings) that require hospitalization. Users may experience frightening flashbacks. Additionally, LSD is illegal and is often mixed with unknown and possibly dangerous agents.

Psilocybin (Magic Mushrooms)

The active ingredient in magic mushrooms is *psilocybin,* which is chemically related to LSD. The psychological experience produced by psilocybin is related to its dose. At a low dose, users report pleasant, relaxed feelings, with minimal body sensations. Medium to higher doses produce distortion in time and space, perceptual changes, and possibly hallucinations. In addition, higher doses may trigger body arousal (activate the sympathetic system) that includes increased heart rate, increased respiration, and related responses.

Use of "magic mushrooms" dates back to 500 B.C.

Hallucinogens

Ancient Aztec Indians used peyote in religious ceremonies, and today peyote has been accepted for sacramental usage by the Native American Church of North America.

Mescaline (Peyote Cactus)

The peyote cactus contains *mescaline*. Because mescaline does not easily cross into the brain, users must take high doses to achieve desired effects. In fact, it may take hours for effective levels to be reached in the brain. During this time, mescaline activates body arousal (the sympathetic system) and may cause increased heart rate and temperature (sweating), dilated pupils, and vomiting. Mescaline produces profound sensory and perceptual distortions that may last six to eight hours without interfering with intellect. Users report profound visual hallucinations, such as latticework, cobweb figures, tunnels, and spirals, which appear in various colors and intense brightness.

Users can experience severe headaches and hangovers. In very high doses, there have been reports of death following convulsions and cessation of breathing.

Designer Drugs

The mid-1980s marked the appearance of *designer drugs*, synthetic drugs that are variations of known psychoactive drugs (amphetamines, heroin) and are manufactured in home laboratories. Two illegal designer drugs, PCP (angel dust) and MDMA (ecstasy), are partly hallucinogenic.

PCP (phencyclidine) acts as a sedative, because it reduces activity, and as an analgesic, because it reduces pain. Although it is not a true hallucinogen, PCP is often classified as one because it produces distortions in body image, such as feeling like a rubber doll. PCP is considered highly dangerous because at moderate and high doses it produces sensory overload, agitation, violence, aggression, and psychotic reactions.

MDMA (ecstasy) closely resembles both amphetamine and a natural hallucinogen that is found in nutmeg. It appeared on the streets in the early 1980s as a "love drug" that reportedly increased communication, feelings of intimacy, and sexual sensations. Because of growing popularity and unknown effects, MDMA was put into the same classification as heroin: it cannot be prescribed or used in research. Although a few human studies have reported positive mood changes and visual experiences, since MDMA cannot now be used in research, these studies cannot be replicated. MDMA is illegally manufactured.

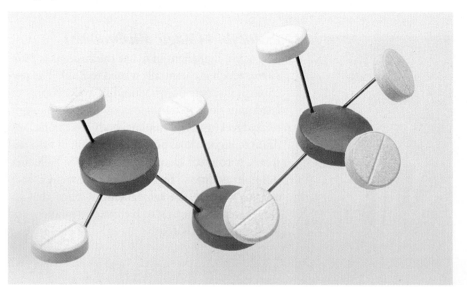

Designer drugs are manufactured to produce psychoactive effects.

Opiates

What's one of the oldest drugs on record?

From 6000 B.C. to today, opiates have been used around the world. In the early 1800s, the active ingredient in the juice of the opium poppy was found to be morphine, and in the late 1800s morphine was chemically altered to make heroin. Law enforcement agencies usually refer to opiates as *narcotics*. In the early 1900s the sale and use of narcotics (opium, morphine, and heroin) were made illegal, which gave rise to a lucrative world-wide opium black market. In spite of restrictive laws and billions of dollars spent on enforcement, the Unites States has been unable to eliminate the importation and use of opiates.

What powerful drugs come from flowers?

The source of opium is a beautiful flower, the opium poppy.

Effects

Opiates *are drugs that produce three primary effects: analgesia, which is a reduction in pain; opiate euphoria, which is often described as a twilight state between waking and sleeping; and constipation, which means that opiates have been used to treat diarrhea.* Continued use of opiates results in tolerance, physical addiction, and an intense craving for the drug. If the user cannot obtain the drug, he or she will experience painful but not life-threatening withdrawal symptoms. In the 1970s researchers discovered that the brain not only has its own opiate receptors but also produces its own morphinelike chemicals. These chemicals, which function like neurotransmitters, are called *endorphins* and are found to have the same analgesic properties as morphine.

Opiates are extremely addictive and users must administer one or more doses daily to prevent the occurrence of withdrawal symptoms. Opiates obtained on the black market may contain other hazardous substances or may vary in strength and lead to an overdose. In high doses, opiates depress the neural control of breathing that may cause death.

Although all three opiates—opium, morphine, and heroin—produce similar effects, users generally prefer to inject heroin because it reaches the brain more quickly and produces the biggest "rush," which users liken to a whole body sexual experience. Users pay a high price for the rush in having to support an expensive habit and in living with the constant fear of not obtaining their daily fix and going into withdrawal symptoms.

We have seen that for many thousands of years, humans have had a desire to change their consciousness, mood, and perception by using psychoactive drugs. After the Concept/Glossary, we'll examine a widely used and abused legal drug: alcohol.

1. When the brain and body react to a particular drug by building up a resistance so that the user must increase the dosage to achieve the same behavioral effect, it is called (a) _____. When the brain and body require an outside drug for normal functioning and the person has an intense craving for the drug, it is called (b)_____. An addicted person who stops using a drug will experience a number of painful physical and upsetting psychological symptoms that are called (c)_____. If a regular user of a drug is not addicted but has developed a strong need for the drug to deal with a particular situation, this need is referred to as (d)_____.

5. The primary psychoactive substance in marijuana is _____, which produces a "high" that may include intensified sensations and changed perceptions and moods.

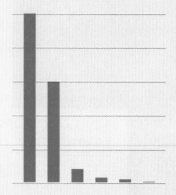

2. Drugs that affect the nervous system and result in altered awareness and consciousness, as well as changes in mood, cognition, and perception, are called _____.

6. Drugs that produce perceptual, sensory, and cognitive experiences that are not occurring in reality are called (a)_____. One of the most powerful of these drugs, which can cause trips that last up to eight hours, is (b)_____. A drug that is found in certain mushrooms is (c)_____; one that is found in peyote cactus is (d)_____. All of these drugs may produce terrifying experiences, which are called (e)_____, as well as a drug-related experience when one is no longer taking the drug, which is called a (f)_____.

3. Four of the more common ways that psychoactive drugs affect the nervous system are by increasing the neurons to release more (a)_____; by duplicating the actions of naturally occurring (b)_____; by blocking the locks of (c)_____ so that the neurotransmitters' chemical keys have no effect; and by preventing the neuron's reabsorption of neurotransmitter by slowing down a process called (d)_____.

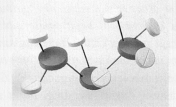

7. Synthetic drugs that are variations of known psychoactive drugs and are manufactured in illegal laboratories are called _____.

4. Drugs that increase the activity of the nervous system and result in increased arousal, alertness, and euphoria are called (a)_____. The potent stimulant that comes from a plant, can be sniffed, smoked, or injected, and produces short-acting alertness and euphoria is (b)_____. The potent stimulant that is a form of amphetamine, is smoked, and produces longer-lasting alertness and euphoria is (c)_____. The world's most widely used stimulant, which produces mild arousal and alertness, is (d)_____. The drug that is the single largest avoidable cause of death in the United States and has both stimulating and calming properties is (e)_____.

8. Drugs that have three primary effects—analgesia, euphoria, and constipation—are called (a)_____. Continued use of these drugs causes the user to become (b)_____; if the user stops using the drug, he or she will experience painful (c)_____.

Answers: 1. (a) tolerance, (b) addiction, (c) withdrawal symptoms, (d) psychological dependency; 2. psychoactive drugs; 3. (a) neurotransmitters, (b) neurotransmitters, (c) receptors, (d) reuptake; 4. (a) stimulants, (b) cocaine, (c) crack or ice, (d) caffeine, (e) nicotine; 5. THC or tetrahydrocannabinol; 6. (a) hallucinogens, (b) LSD, (c) psilocybin, (d) mescaline, (e) bad trips, (f) flashback; 7. designer drugs; 8. (a) opiates, (b) addicted, (c) withdrawal symptoms.

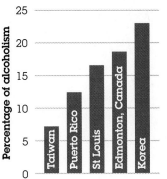

Risks for Alcoholism

Asians are more likely than Caucasians to respond to alcohol with facial flushing.

Cultural Responses to Alcohol

After the very first drink of alcohol, some individuals respond with a sudden reddening of the face. This reaction is called *facial flushing* and is caused by the absence of a liver enzyme involved in metabolizing alcohol. Facial flushing to alcohol, which is a genetic trait, rarely occurs in Caucasians (whites) but does occur in about 30% to 50% of Asians (Koreans, Taiwanese, Chinese, and Japanese) tested. Researchers report that Asians who show facial flushing tend to drink less; as a result, they may be at less risk for alcoholism than Asians who lack this response (Johnson & Nagoshi, 1990).

Rates of Alcoholism

According to Marcus Grant, World Health Organization senior scientist dealing with alcohol and other drugs, alcohol abuse and alcoholism are beginning to have a devastating effect on Third World countries, just as they have in American and European populations (*San Diego Union*, July 21, 1991). **Alcoholism** *is usually defined as a problem in which a person has drunk heavily for a long period of time, is addicted to and has an intense craving for alcohol, and has problems in two or three major life areas (such as social, personal, financial, medical, legal, or business areas) that are caused by drinking.*

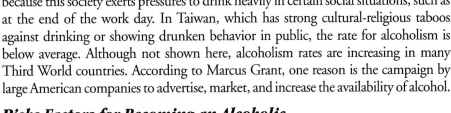

As this graph shows, the alcoholism rate varies across cultures. For example, in two large North American cities (St. Louis, Missouri, and Edmonton, Alberta, Canada) that have typical big-city stressors, the alcoholism rate averages between 10% and 20%. In Korea, alcoholism is above average in males because this society exerts pressures to drink heavily in certain social situations, such as at the end of the work day. In Taiwan, which has strong cultural-religious taboos against drinking or showing drunken behavior in public, the rate for alcoholism is below average. Although not shown here, alcoholism rates are increasing in many Third World countries. According to Marcus Grant, one reason is the campaign by large American companies to advertise, market, and increase the availability of alcohol.

Risks Factors for Becoming an Alcoholic

Am I at risk for becoming an alcoholic?

We have known for some time that one's risk for becoming an alcoholic is increased three to four times if members of one's family were alcoholics. Researchers have discovered that this increased risk, which exists across cultures, may result from both environmental and genetic factors.

Environmental risk factors include a number of psychological and emotional traits that are learned by being in a family with one or more alcoholic members. Examples of environmental risk facts, which occur in children of alcoholic parents, include difficulties in showing trust, overdependency in relationships, and exaggerated reaction to events out of their control. When faced with these and other problems, children of alcoholic parents may turn to alcohol and abuse it as did their parents.

Genetic risk factors, which are inherited predispositions that increase the potential for alcoholism, have been identified by Robert Cloninger (1987) and his associates. They report that children of alcoholic parents, even when adopted by nonalcoholics, are three or four times more likely to become alcoholics than children born to nonalcoholics.

It is important to remember that not every child of an alcoholic parent becomes an alcoholic. Thus, other environmental variables, such as support in childhood, quality of home life, and successful coping with stress, apparently decrease the risk of alcoholism (Zucker & Gomberg, 1986).

Next we'll focus on the effects of alcohol and the treatment of alcoholism and drug abuse.

APPLYING/ EXPLORING: ALCOHOL EFFECTS AND TREATMENT FOR DRUG ABUSE

Alcohol Abuse

The first brewery appeared in Egypt in 3700 B.C., making alcohol the oldest drug to be made by humans (Palfai & Jankiewicz, 1991). Because of alcohol's enormous popularity, there have been continuing problems with drunkenness and abuse over the ages. In the 1920s, the U.S. Congress reacted to alcohol abuse by passing the Eighteenth Amendment, which prohibited the sale and manufacture of alcohol. However, Ameri-

cans' desire for alcohol was so deeply ingrained that Prohibition failed and was later repealed.

Alcohol abuse is a major contributor to personal problems, fatal traffic accidents, birth defects, homicides, assaults, date rape, and suicide. About 10%–15% of drinkers become alcoholics. Because it is associated with so many serious problems, alcohol is considered to be one of our most dangerous drugs.

What happens as one drinks?

Alcohol is a *depressant*, which means that it decreases the activity of the nervous system and depresses many behavioral and psychological functions. The behavioral and psy-

The party begins.
I can drive when I drink.
2 drinks later.
I can drive when I drink
After 4 drinks.
I can drive when I drunk.
After 5 drinks.
I can driv whnd driv
7 drinks in all.
I can drink drive

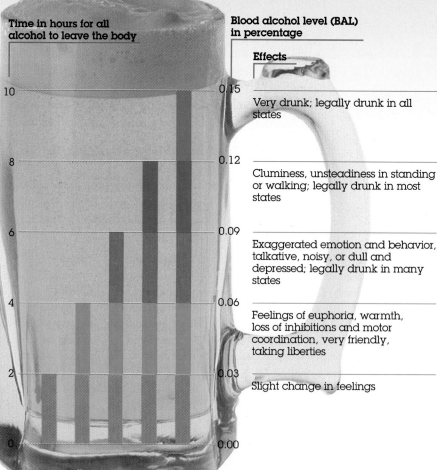

Number of drinks

| **Time in hours for all alcohol to leave the body** | **Blood alcohol level (BAL) in percentage** | **Effects** |

5 cocktails (1¼ ounces of whiskey each)
25 oz. of wine
5 12 oz. bottles of beer

10 — 0.15 — Very drunk; legally drunk in all states

4 cocktails
20 oz. of wine
4 12 oz. bottles of beer

8 — 0.12 — Clumsiness, unsteadiness in standing or walking; legally drunk in most states

3 cocktails
15 oz. of wine
3 12 oz. bottles of beer

6 — 0.09 — Exaggerated emotion and behavior, talkative, noisy, or dull and depressed; legally drunk in many states

2 cocktails
10 oz. of wine
2 12 oz. bottles of beer

4 — 0.06 — Feelings of euphoria, warmth, loss of inhibitions and motor coordination, very friendly, taking liberties

1 cocktail
5 oz. of wine
1 12 oz. bottle of beer

2 — 0.03 — Slight change in feelings

0 — 0.00

chological effects of alcohol depend on the dosage: at low doses, alcohol causes euphoria, friendliness, and loss of inhibitions. At higher doses, alcohol seriously impairs motor coordination, cognitive abilities, decision making, and speaking and causes sleep, stupor, and, in very high doses, death.

The chart on the left shows the relationship between number of drinks and amount of alcohol in the blood, which is called the *blood alcohol level,* or BAL. The numbers are for an average 150-pound male with an empty stomach. The numbers may be different for women, who have been found to metabolize alcohol more slowly and as a result to reach higher blood alcohol levels than men (after accounting for weight and number of drinks) (Frezza et al., 1990).

Some think that alcohol is a stimulant because at lower blood alcohol levels (about 0.05%) they feel relaxed, happy, talkative, and friendly. However, with continued drinking the depressant effects of alcohol become clear as drinkers become moody and sleepy.

The majority of 100 million or more Americans who use alcohol do so in moderation, with few harmful effects. However, about 10%–15% of those who use alcohol—beer, wine, or whiskey—become alcoholics and need professional help and treatment. We'll discuss a program for the treatment of alcoholism. Many elements of this program are used in the treatment of all drug abuse.

Drug Treatment Programs

What do I do if I have a drug problem?
For most individuals, treatment for drug abuse involves going through a number of steps. We'll follow Jeff, an alcoholic, through a process that is typical of most drug treatment programs.

Step 1. Admitting to a Drug Problem

The first step in getting help is admitting that one has a drug problem. Although this step appears obvious, in reality it represents a hurdle that many drug abusers have a difficult time getting over. What happens is that a drug user believes that drugs are the solution to his or her problems, fears, insecurities, and worries. In fact, the opposite is true.

Heavy drug use has become the problem, and the user refuses to admit it. Convincing a heavy drug user to seek treatment often requires the efforts of his or her family, loved ones, employer, or doctor.

Step 2. Entering a Treatment Program

Although Jeff entered a treatment center for alcoholics, its approach is typical of drug treatment programs.

After being admitted, Jeff was given a complete medical checkup and went

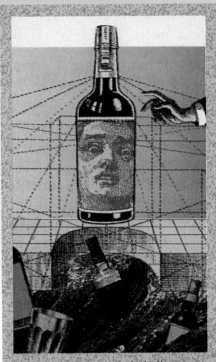

Treatment programs help individuals resist the temptations of drugs and substitute nondrug methods to help them deal with their problems.

through a two-week period of detoxification. When he was free of drugs, a treatment team consisting of a physician, a psychologist, a counselor, and a nurse discussed the program with Jeff. One goal of the program was to help Jeff face up to and deal with academic, personal, and social problems that may have contributed to or intensified his drug abuse, such as shyness, unassertiveness, procrastination, or poor social skills. A second goal was getting Jeff to substitute relaxation exercises and other enjoyable activities

(sports, hobbies) for the escape and enjoyment that alcohol had provided. A third goal was to provide Jeff with an opportunity to share his experiences in group therapy. Group sessions helped Jeff realize that he was not suffering alone, that it was important for him make plans for the future, and that he might have to make new, nondrinking friends once he left the program. A fourth goal was to help Jeff work out problems with his family and learn to alter behavior patterns that triggered his drinking.

Some programs use *aversive conditioning,* in which drinking alcohol is associated with nausea and vomiting, so that these unpleasant sensations are evoked whenever the client takes a drink. Although aversive conditioning has a long history, its effectiveness is still debated (Elkins, 1991; Wilson, 1991).

Step 3. Preventing Relapse

Once Jeff left the treatment center, he needed an aftercare plan to give him support for remaining sober. Aftercare might include referrals to Alcoholics Anonymous (AA) or personal or family therapy. Some programs require that after inpatient treatment is completed, the client must return at least a half-dozen times for additional sessions of evaluation, counseling, and aversive conditioning. Involvement in Alcoholics Anonymous has been reported to help recovering alcoholics stay sober and enjoy a better quality of life (Cross et al., 1990). The prevention of relapse is increasingly being considered the central problem in treatment of alcoholism and other substance abuse (Annis, 1990).

Step 4. Measuring Success

Usually the success of a drug treatment program is measured by how many clients remain abstinent (do not use drugs) for a period of one year. Drug treatment programs range in success from about 30% for most program to 54% for a few (Holden, 1987; Neubuerger et al., 1982). The goal of alcohol treatment programs is usually total abstinence because it is questionable whether alcoholics can learn to drink socially or in moderate amounts (Ojehagen & Berglund, 1989).

Summary/Self-Test

HYPNOSIS: DEFINITION AND PROCESS

1. Hypnosis is defined as an altered state of awareness, attention, and alertness, during which a person is usually much more open to the _____ of a hypnotist or therapist. About 15% of the population are easily hypnotized, 75% can be to some extent, and the remaining 10% show very little inclination.

■ *Could a television hypnotist hypnotize you as you watched in your living room?*

BEHAVIORS UNDER HYPNOSIS

2. Under hypnosis, subjects will experience or perform the following _____: age regression, imagined perception, posthypnotic amnesia, posthypnotic suggestions, and hypnotic analgesia.

■ *Could you tell if someone were performing a suggested behavior because of being hypnotized or because of just pretending?*

EXPLANATIONS OF HYPNOSIS

3. According to the (a)_____ theory, a hypnotized individual is in a special state; as a result, hypnotic behaviors are different from waking behaviors. According to the (b)_____ theory, hypnosis is not a special state but rather a procedure that creates powerful pressures, which in turn make subjects want to conform and carry out the hypnotist's suggestions.

■ *A friend who was hypnotized said that she did things in a dreamlike state. What's another possibility?*

APPLICATIONS OF HYPNOSIS

4. In dental and medical settings, hypnosis is used to help patients deal with painful procedures by producing (a)_____. In behavioral change settings, hypnosis is used in combination with other behavioral and cognitive treatments to help individuals overcome (b)_____. Testimony taken under hypnosis in police investigations is not usually permitted in courts because such testimony may be (c)_____.

■ *If you had a badly sprained ankle and were allergic to painkillers, why might you learn self-hypnosis?*

DRUGS: IMPORTANT TERMS

5. Regular use of a drug usually results in one or more of the following. If the brain/body builds up a resistance to the drug so that a user must take larger dosages to achieve the same behavioral result, a user is said to have developed a (a)_____ or the drug. If the nervous system grows accustomed to having the drug and the body needs the drug for normal functioning, the user is said to have developed an (b)_____. If a habitual user suddenly stops taking the drug, he or she will experience unpleasant or painful (c)_____. If a user has developed a strong psychological need to use the drug to deal with certain situations, the user is said to have developed a (d)_____.

■ *Your father, who smokes a pack of cigarettes a day, says that he is addicted. What would you reply?*

DRUG USAGE AND EFFECTS

6. Drugs that affect the nervous system to alter consciousness, awareness, sensations, perceptions, mood, and cognitive processes are called _____ drugs.

7. Drugs affect the nervous system by altering the action of chemicals in the brain that are called _____. For example, some drugs (such as amphetamines) cause neurons to release more neurotransmitters; drugs such as morphine act like or mimic the action of naturally occurring neurotransmitters; drugs such as alcohol block the action of neurotransmitters; and drugs such as cocaine interfere with the reuptake of neurotransmitter back into the neuron.

■ *A new snake venom is discovered that has hallucinogenic effects. How could it affect the nervous system?*

STIMULANTS

8. A class of drugs that increase activity of the nervous system and result in heightened alertness, arousal, and euphoria and decreased appetite and fatigue are called _____.

9. In moderate doses, cocaine produces a short-lived feeling of _____. In heavy doses, it can produce addiction; serious psychological effects, such as frightening hallucinations; and serious physical problems, such as heart irregularity, convulsions, and death.

10. Ice, which has become a major drug problem of the 1990s, is a pure form of _____.

11. The most widely used legal psychoactive drug in the world is _____, which affects brain receptors and, depending on the dose, produces physiological arousal, a mild feeling of alertness or arousal, increased reaction time, and decreased fatigue and drowsiness.

12. A legal drug that is second to caffeine in world-wide usage is _____, which has both stimulating and calming properties.

■ *Your mother says that coffee is not a drug but cocaine is. What's your reply?*

MARIJUANA

13. After caffeine, nicotine, and alcohol, the fourth most popular psychoactive drug in the United States is (a)_____. In low doses it produces mild euphoria, in moderate doses it produces distortions in perception and time, and in high doses it may produce hallucinations and delusions. Researchers recently discovered that the brain has (b)_____ that respond to marijuana.

■ *A regular user of marijuana says that he can drive just fine after he smokes. What's he overlooking?*

HALLUCINOGENS

14. Drugs that act on the brain (and body) to produce perceptual, sensory, and cognitive experiences that are not occurring in reality are called (a)_____. Some time after using a hallucinogenic drug, a user may suddenly have a frightening drug-related experience called a (b)_____. Examples of hallucinogenic drugs are LSD, psilocybin, and mescaline.

■ *Why have some groups used hallucinogens in their religious ceremonies?*

OPIATES

15. All opiates produce three primary effects: a reduction in pain, which is called (a)_____; a twilight state between waking and sleeping, which is called (b)_____; and a treatment for diarrhea because opiates cause (c)_____. With continued use of opiates, users develop tolerance, addiction, and an intense craving for the drug. The brain also produces its own morphinelike chemicals, which are called (d)_____.

■ *Why do you think the brain makes its own morphinelike substance?*

CULTURAL DIVERSITY: RISKS FOR ALCOHOLISM

16. About 10%–15% of drinkers become _____, which are people who have drunk heavily for a long period of time, are addicted to and have an intense craving for alcohol, and have problems in two or three major life areas caused by drinking.

17. One's risk for becoming an alcoholic increases three to four times if members of one's family were alcoholics. Factors such as difficulties in showing trust, being overdependent in relationships, and having related problems that increase the risk for alcoholism are called (a)_____ factors. The risk for alcoholism is also increased by the inheritance of predispositions for alcoholism, which is called the (b)_____ factor.

■ *Do you think people should be informed as children that they may have an increased risk for alcoholism?*

APPLYING/EXPLORING: ALCOHOL EFFECTS AND TREATMENT FOR DRUG ABUSE

18. Alcohol is classified as a _____ because it decreases the activity of the nervous system and depresses many behavioral and psychological functions. Alcohol abuse is a major contributor to personal problems, fatal traffic accidents, birth defects, homicides, assaults, date rape, and suicide.

19. Steps in the treatment of alcoholism and in most drug abuse programs include the following. The first step is admitting that one has a (a)_____. The second step is entering a (b)_____, which has several components that help the individual stay free of drugs. The third step is preventing (c)_____, which is a major problem in the treatment of alcoholism and other forms of drug abuse. The fourth step is measuring (d)_____, which is usually defined as being drug-free for one year.

■ *What do you say to someone who says that alcohol must be all right since it is legal?*

Chapter *Six*
LEARNING

MODULE 11
CLASSICAL CONDITIONING

Why would going to the dentist make her cancel a magazine subscription?

The first thing I noticed about Carla was her smile and her perfect set of white teeth.

"What a great smile," I said. "Did you have to spend a lot of time in the dentist's chair?"

"I like my teeth now, but they cost my parents a lot of money and me a lot of grief. In fact, my teeth made me cancel my subscription to *Zoo World.*"

"I've heard of people canceling magazine subscriptions for a lot of reasons, but never because of their teeth," I replied.

Carla continued, "I'm interested in photography and used to love *Zoo World* because it has the best color photos of animals. Now I get anxious every time I read or hold *Zoo World.* That's why I canceled my subscription."

I couldn't help asking, "What does *Zoo World* have to do with your teeth?"

"One of the best things about my dentist was that she had *Zoo World* in the waiting room. When it was my turn in the chair, I took *Zoo World* with me and read it between drillings, fillings, and cappings. Without realizing it, every time I felt pain I automatically rolled up the copy of *Zoo World* and held on tight. I made a lot of trips to the dentist and clutched a lot of *Zoo Worlds.* Now, I've got perfect teeth, but I can't read, hold, or even think about *Zoo World* without feeling anxious."

Like Carla, many of us have had peculiar experiences connected with going to the dentist. Some report feeling anxious when they open the office door or enter the office and smell the antiseptic odor. Almost everyone reports a surge of anxiety when they see the dentist reach for a syringe or hear the drill's high-pitched sound. These examples illustrate a certain kind of learning that takes place in the dentist's office.

In fact, some kind of learning is going on in almost every situation, whether in the library, in the classroom, in the gymnasium, at a party, or simply while watching others. We'll explain how learning occurs in these situations. But first let's define learning. We can use Carla's *Zoo World* experience to illustrate two characteristics shared by all learning. First, learning is a relatively permanent change in behavior. In Carla's case, the relatively permanent change is her feeling of anxiety every time she thinks about or reads *Zoo World.* The second characteristic of learning is that it occurs as a result of experience. Carla's experiences at the dentist's office resulted in her anxiety response to reading *Zoo World.* These two characteristics are included in the formal definition of **learning,** *which is a relatively permanent change in behavior (both mental events and overt behaviors) that results from experience.* One important function of learning is to help us adapt and adjust to our environment.

What's Coming

In this module, we'll examine three approaches psychologists use to study learning, and then we'll focus on one particular approach: classical conditioning. In the next module, we'll discuss the other two approaches—operant conditioning and cognitive learning—that psychologists use to study learning.

Three Approaches to Learning

Learning is at the heart of psychology, since in almost all situations we have the potential for some kind of learning. From the beginning of psychology as a science, psychologists have searched for principles to explain how learning occurs. In their search, they have primarily used three approaches to study learning: classical conditioning, operant conditioning, and the newest approach, cognitive learning.

Classical Conditioning

Imagine that it is the early 1900s and that you are working as a technician in the laboratory of Ivan Pavlov. He has already won a Nobel prize for his studies on the reflexes involved in digestion. For example, he found that when food is placed in a dog's

What does salivation have to do with learning?

mouth, the food triggers the reflex of salivation.

As a lab technician, your task is to place various kinds of food in a dog's mouth and measure the amount of salivation. But soon you encounter a problem. After you have placed food in a dog's mouth on a number of occasions, the dog begins to salivate merely at the sight of the food.

At first Pavlov considered this sort of anticipatory salivation to be a bothersome problem. Later, in one of the great moments of science, he reasoned that the dog's salivation at the sight of food was also a reflex, but one that the dog had somehow *learned*. In a well-known experiment, Pavlov rang a bell before putting food in the dog's mouth. After a number of instances of hearing a bell paired with food, the dog salivated at the sound of the bell alone, a phenomenon that Pavlov called a *conditioned reflex*. Conditioned reflexes were an important discovery because they allowed Pavlov to study learning in an objective way. Pavlov is credited with the discovery of **classical conditioning**, *a kind of learning in which a neutral stimulus acquires the ability to produce a response that was originally produced by a different stimulus.*

Law of Effect/Operant Conditioning

It is still the early 1900s, and you have sailed to America to work in the laboratory of the American psychologist E. L. Thorndike. Your task is to place a cat in a box with a door that can be opened from the inside by hitting a simple latch. Outside the box is a fish on a dish. You are to record the time it takes the cat to hit the latch, open the door, and get the fish.

How does a cat learn to escape?

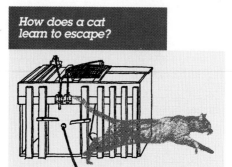

On the first trial, the cat sniffs around the box, sticks its paw in various places, accidentally hits the latch, opens the door, and gets the fish. You place the cat back into the box for another trial. Again the cat moves around, accidentally strikes the latch, and gets the fish. After many such trials, the cat learns to spend its time around the latch. Finally, it learns to hit the latch and get the fish in very short time.

To explain the cat's goal-directed behavior, Thorndike formulated the **law of effect:** *if some random actions are followed by a pleasurable consequence or reward, such actions are strengthened and will likely occur in the future.* Thorndike's law of effect was important because it identified a learning process different from Pavlov's conditioned reflex. Today, the law of effect has become part of **operant conditioning**, *a kind of learning in which the consequences that follow some behavior increase or decrease the likelihood of that behavior occurring in the future.* We will discuss operant conditioning in Module 12.

Cognitive Learning

In Pavlov's lab, you learned that reflexes can be conditioned. Then in Thorndike's lab, you learned that according to the law of effect, certain behaviors can be strengthened and thus made more likely to occur in the future. Yet these two principles cannot explain how learning occurs in all situations.

Can I learn by watching a chess game?

Without making any observable responses, you can learn to play chess simply by observing others play. In this situation, neither conditioned reflexes nor the law of effect seems to be operating. In fact, the entire learning process appears to take place internally, inside your head. These internal learning processes are part of cognitive learning, which is a relatively new approach that began in the 1960s. **Cognitive learning** *is a kind of learning that involves mental processes, such as attention and memory, and may not involve any external rewards or require the person to perform any observable behaviors.* For example, learning through imitation or observation is an example of cognitive learning. We will discuss some aspects of cognitive learning in Modules 12 and other aspects in Modules 13 and 14.

Let's begin our study of learning by returning to Pavlov's laboratory and examining his work on conditioned reflexes in greater detail.

Establishing Classical Conditioning

Imagine that you are back in Pavlov's laboratory and that your task is to establish classical conditioning (a conditioned reflex) in a big scruffy dog named Russ. You will follow a procedure, developed by Pavlov, that will eventually make Russ salivate to a tone. The first thing to do is to select the stimuli and response that will be used in conditioning.

Step 1. Selecting Stimuli and Response

Neutral stimulus. During classical conditioning, Russ will be conditioned to salivate to a **neutral stimulus,** *which is a stimulus that causes some reaction, such as being seen, heard, or smelled, but does not produce the reflex being tested (in this case, salivation).* Your neutral stimulus will be a tone (represented here by a bell), which affects the dog (via its hearing) but does not produce the reflex of salivation.

Unconditioned stimulus. You will choose an **unconditioned stimulus (UCS),** *which triggers or elicits some physiological reflex, such as salivation.* Your unconditioned stimulus will be food, which will elicit the reflex of salivation.

Unconditioned response. The **unconditioned response (UCR)** *is an unlearned, innate, involuntary physiological reflex that is elicited by the unconditioned stimulus.* For example, salivation is an unconditioned response that is elicited by food, the unconditioned stimulus.

Step 2. Establishing Classical Conditioning

A common procedure for establishing classical conditioning is to pair the neutral stimulus with the unconditioned stimulus. Each pairing is called a **trial,** and you will give Russ a number of trials.

Neutral stimulus. In a typical trial, the *neutral stimulus,* the tone, is paired with the unconditioned stimulus, the food.

+

Unconditioned stimulus. Several seconds after the tone begins, you present the *unconditioned stimulus,* a piece of food, which elicits salivation.

→

Unconditioned response. The unconditioned stimulus, the food, elicits the *unconditioned response,* salivation.

Step 3. Testing for Conditioning

After many trials that pair tone with food, you can test for conditioning by presenting the tone alone, without the food.

Conditioned stimulus. At the presentation of the tone alone, Russ shows salivation, because the tone has become a conditioned stimulus. A **conditioned stimulus (CS)** *is a formerly neutral stimulus that has acquired the ability to elicit a response that was previously elicited by the unconditioned stimulus.*

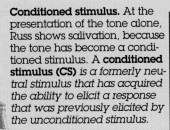

→

Conditioned response. Russ salivates to the tone (CS), but the amount of salivation is less than that elicited by food. The **conditioned response (CR),** *which is elicited by the conditioned stimulus, is similar to the unconditioned response.* The conditioned response is usually similar in appearance to but is smaller in amount or magnitude than the unconditioned response.

We know that classical conditioning has occurred when the formerly neutral stimulus becomes a conditioned stimulus and acquires the ability to elicit the conditioned response.

Now that you know how classical conditioning is established, we can return to the example of Carla and her problem with *ZooWorld.*

Classical Conditioning: An Example

Why does reading ZooWorld *cause Carla to feel anxious?*
During many trips to her dentist, Carla unknowingly experienced classical conditioning. Let's examine how she was conditioned to feel anxious when reading *ZooWorld*.

Step 1. Identifying the Stimuli and the Response

The *neutral stimulus* was a copy of *ZooWorld*, which Carla held tightly while experiencing pain in the dentist's chair. *ZooWorld* has two characteristics that make it a neutral stimulus: it affected Carla (she held it) and it did not initially produce feelings of anxiety. In fact, initially Carla greatly enjoyed reading *ZooWorld*.

The *unconditioned stimulus* was pain caused by the dental procedures (injection, drilling, and filling). The unconditioned stimulus (pain) elicited the unconditioned response (anxiety).

The *unconditioned response* was a feeling of anxiety, which is a combination of physiological reflexes (increased heart rate, blood pressure, and rapid breathing) and emotional reactions.

Step 2. Establishing Classical Conditioning

One procedure for establishing classical conditioning is to present the neutral stimulus and follow it close in time with the unconditioned stimulus.

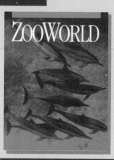

In Carla's case, the *neutral stimulus* was holding a copy of *ZooWorld*.

Carla's many trips to the dentist caused the neutral stimulus (*ZooWorld*) and *unconditioned stimulus* (pain) to be repeatedly presented close together in time.

The pain elicited the *unconditioned response*, anxiety.

Step 3. Testing for Conditioning

One test for classical conditioning is to determine whether the neutral stimulus has become a conditioned stimulus and can elicit the conditioned response.

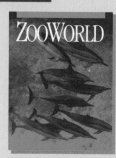

When Carla held a copy of *ZooWorld* in the dentist's office, she felt anxious. *ZooWorld*, formerly a neutral stimulus, had now become a *conditioned stimulus* eliciting anxiety, the conditioned response.

The *conditioned response*, feeling anxious, was elicited by holding *ZooWorld*, the conditioned stimulus. The anxiety elicited by *ZooWorld* was similar to but not as great as the anxiety Carla felt during the actual dental procedures.

Carla's experience of classical conditioning in the dentist's chair is not uncommon. If you think about visits to the dentist, you can probably identify a number of your own conditioned stimuli that elicit anxiety, such as entering the office, smelling antiseptic odor, sitting in the dentist's chair, or hearing the sound of the drill. Partly because of classical conditioning, approximately 6% of the population have developed such an intense fear or phobia of dental procedures that they entirely avoid dental treatment (Bernstein & Kleinknecht, 1982; Johnson, Mayberry, & Meglynn, 1990). These individuals may require psychological treatment to decondition their phobias, a procedure we discuss in the Applying/Exploring section. Now, let's return to our example of Russ and examine other concepts of classical conditioning.

Other Conditioning Concepts

What else happens during classical conditioning?

During classical conditioning, Russ not only learned to salivate to a tone but simultaneously learned a number of other things. We'll explain four other phenomena—generalization, discrimination, extinction, and spontaneous recovery—that Pavlov identified as being a part of the classical conditioning procedure.

Generalization

Why does Russ also salivate to a phone ringing?

During Russ's conditioning trials, the conditioned stimulus was a tone, which eventually elicited the conditioned response, salivation. However, other sounds, such as a phone ringing, would also elicit salivation in Russ. Salivation to a whistle is an example of **generalization,** *which is the tendency for a stimulus that is similar to the original conditioned stimulus to elicit a response that is similar to the conditioned response.* The dog's salivation to other, similar stimuli will not be as strong as that elicited by the tone, the original conditioned stimulus. Generally, the response will be stronger or larger the more similar the new stimulus is to the original conditioned stimulus.

In the case of Carla, the anxious feeling she experiences when reading *Zoo World* may generalize to similar magazines, such as *National Geographic.*

Sounds similar to the tone, such as a phone ringing, may elicit the conditioned response.

Discrimination

Why doesn't Russ salivate to the sound of a slamming door?

If Russ would salivate to the sound of a phone, why wouldn't he salivate to the sound of a slamming door? **Discrimination** *occurs during classical conditioning when an organism learns to make a particular response to some stimuli but not to others.* While Russ was being classically conditioned, you presented food after the tone and not after other sounds, such as a slamming door. Through this procedure, Russ learned to differentiate or discriminate between the sound of a tone and the sound of a slamming door.

Carla has also learned discrimination: she does not feel anxious reading magazines that are quite different from *Zoo World,* such as *Time* and *People.*

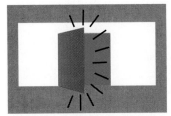

Dissimilar sounds, such as a slamming door, do not elicit the conditioned response.

Extinction

How would Russ respond if the tone was not followed by food?

Suppose that after Russ had been conditioned to salivate to the tone, you presented the tone but did not follow it with food. After a number of such tone-only trials, Russ would stop salivating to the tone. This is an example of **extinction:** *If a conditioned stimulus is repeatedly presented without the unconditioned stimulus, there is a tendency for the conditioned stimulus to no longer elicit the conditioned response.*

If the conditioned stimulus (tone) is not followed by the unconditioned stimulus (food), extinction occurs.

Spontaneous Recovery

What happens after extinction?

After you repeatedly presented the tone without food, Russ's conditioned response of salivation underwent extinction and no longer occurred. Suppose that two days later you brought Russ back into the lab and again presented the tone without food. To your surprise, Russ showed the conditioned response (salivation). This is an example of the conditioned response showing spontaneous recovery. **Spontaneous recovery** *is the tendency for the conditioned response to reappear even though there are no further conditioning trials.* Spontaneous recovery of the conditioned response will not persist for long. If the conditioned stimulus (tone) is not again paired with the unconditioned stimulus (food), the spontaneously recovered conditioned response will undergo extinction and cease to occur.

After extinction, the conditioned response (salivation) may spontaneously recover.

Now that you are familiar with the procedure and terms of classical conditioning, we can discuss why classical conditioning occurs.

Classical Conditioning: Two Explanations

Why does classical conditioning work?

According to Robert Rescorla (1987, 1988), one of the prominent researchers in classical conditioning, the modern explanation of why Russ salivates to a tone is very different from the traditional one. We'll let you compare the traditional and modern explanations of why classical conditioning occurs.

Traditional Explanation

Tone **substitutes** for food.

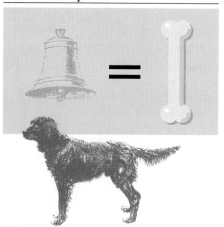

Modern Explanation

Tone **predicts** food.

Does Russ learn to substitute one stimulus for another?

Pavlov's traditional explanation of classical conditioning is called stimulus substitution. According to **stimulus substitution,** *a bond or association forms between the conditioned stimulus and unconditioned stimulus so that the conditioned stimulus eventually substitutes for the unconditioned stimulus.* Stimulus substitution theory would explain that Russ learns to salivate to a tone because the tone (the conditioned stimulus) becomes bonded in the nervous system to the food (the unconditioned stimulus). Because of this bond or association, the tone begins to substitute for the food so that eventually the tone itself can elicit salivation (the conditioned response).

Does Russ learn that one stimulus predicts another?

Rescorla's modern explanation of classical conditioning focuses on stimulus information rather than on stimulus substitution. According to the **information theory of classical conditioning,** *an organism learns a relationship between two stimuli such that the occurrence of one stimulus predicts the occurrence of another.* Information theory would explain that Russ learned to salivate to a tone because he learned a relationship between two stimuli such that the tone (the conditioned stimulus) predicts food (the unconditioned stimulus), resulting in salivation (the conditioned response).

Support for information theory over the stimulus substitution theory comes from a number of findings. For example, classical conditioning occurs best if the neutral stimulus (tone) occurs slightly before the unconditioned stimulus (food). In this sequence, the organism can learn a relationship between two stimuli, such that the tone predicts food. In contrast, if the sequence is reversed, so that the unconditioned stimulus (food) occurs first and is followed by the neutral stimulus (tone), classical conditioning does not usually occur; this reverse sequence is called *backward conditioning.* According to information theory, backward conditioning is not an effective conditioning procedure because the organism cannot learn a relationship between the two stimuli.

After the Concept/Glossary, we'll explore examples of classical conditioning in everyday life.

1. In our example of conditioning Russ the dog, we could have used many different stimuli instead of the tone, as long as these stimuli had two characteristics: they caused some reaction, such as being seen, heard, or smelled, and they did not elicit the unconditioned response. A stimulus that has these two characteristics is called the _____.

2. In classical conditioning, an unlearned, innate, involuntary physiological reflex, such as salivation, that is triggered or elicited by some stimulus is called an _____.

3. In classical conditioning, the stimulus that triggers or elicits the unconditioned response is called the _____.

4. A typical trial in classical conditioning involves first presenting the (a)_____ and then presenting the (b)_____.

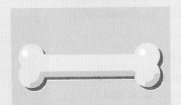

5. On the very first conditioning trial, the neutral stimulus (tone) did not itself elicit the unconditioned response in Russ. However, on the first trial, the presentation of food, which is called the (a)_____, did elicit salivation, called the (b)_____.

6. After a dozen trials that paired the tone with the food, you noticed that as soon as the tone was presented, Russ salivated. Because the tone itself elicited a response similar to that elicited by the unconditioned stimulus (food), the tone is called the (a)_____. The salivation elicited by the tone alone is called the (b)_____.

7. During classical conditioning there is a tendency for a stimulus similar to the original conditioned stimulus to elicit a response similar to the conditioned response. This tendency is called _____.

8. During classical conditioning, an organism learns to make a particular response to some stimuli but not to others; this phenomenon is called _____.

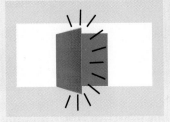

9. If a conditioned stimulus is repeatedly presented *without* the unconditioned stimulus, there is a tendency for the conditioned stimulus to no longer elicit the conditioned response. This phenomenon is called _____.

10. The tendency for the conditioned response to reappear even though there are no further conditioning trials is called _____.

11. According to Pavlov's traditional explanation, classical conditioning occurs because of _____, which means that the conditioned stimulus bonds to the unconditioned stimulus. Through this bond, or association, the conditioned stimulus elicits the conditioned response by substituting for the unconditioned stimulus.

12. The modern explanation of classical conditioning, which is called _____ theory, states that the organism learns a relationship between stimuli such that one stimulus predicts the occurrence of a second.

Answers: 1. *neutral stimulus;* 2. *unconditioned response (UCR);* 3. *unconditioned stimulus (UCS);* 4. *(a) neutral stimulus, (b) unconditioned stimulus (UCS);* 5. *(a) unconditioned stimulus (UCS), (b) unconditioned response (UCR);* 6. *(a) conditioned stimulus (CS), (b) conditioned response (CR);* 7. *generalization;* 8. *discrimination;* 9. *extinction;* 10. *spontaneous recovery;* 11. *stimulus substitution;* 12. *information.*

Classical Conditioning All Around Us

Learned Food Aversion in Humans

Why does Fred hate cherry pie?

Shortly after Fred had a piece of cherry pie at the fair, he rode the Tilt-a-Whirl and became extremely nauseous; he hates cherry pie to this day. What Fred experienced is a powerful form of classical conditioning called **learned food aversion,** *in which a neutral stimulus is paired with an unpleasant response, such as nausea or vomiting* (Andrykowski & Otis, 1990).

Compared to other examples of classical conditioning, learned food aversion is unusual in two ways. First, it may be acquired in a single trial and may last for weeks, months, and even years. Second, a considerable interval of time may occur between tasting some substance and experiencing nausea/vomiting.

Learned food aversion is a common experience among college students. They reported having developed at least one learned food aversion (often to alcoholic drinks) after a single trial, and the aversion lasted an average of four to five years (Logue, Ophir, & Strauss,1981; Rozin, 1986).

Why won't Fred eat cherry pie again?

Classical conditioning made Fred hate cherry pie.

Learned Food Aversion in Animals

Let's see how the two characteristics of learned food aversion—the fact that it can be acquired in one trial and that it lasts a long time—explain a number of remarkable behaviors in animals.

Classical conditioning reduced sheep killing by coyotes.

Can learned food aversion reduce sheep killing?

John Garcia and his colleagues (1974) baited grazing areas with pieces of sheep flesh laced with a chemical (lithium chloride) that causes coyotes to become nauseated and ill. Coyotes that had acquired learned food aversion in this way showed an estimated 30%–60% reduction in sheep killing (Gustavson et al., 1976).

Classical conditioning alerts rats to bait poison.

Why do rats learn to avoid bait poison?

In areas where rats are a problem, their extermination with bait poison is often difficult. What happens is that some rats eat the bait poison but only enough to become sick, not die. As a result, the rats acquire learned food aversion to that particular bait poison and avoid it in the future. Thus, rat exterminators must regularly change their bait poison to overcome rats' learned food aversion to the previous bait.

Why do bluejays stop eating monarch butterflies?

Bluejays feast on butterflies, but they learn to avoid monarch butterflies, which have a distinctive coloring pattern and contain a chemical that, when ingested, makes bluejays sick. Through learned food aversion, the birds associate monarch butterflies with being sick and thus avoid eating them. Many animals, such as monarch butterflies, cause learned food aversion to help them ward off predators.

Classical conditioning protects monarchs from predators.

Now let's turn to other common examples of classical conditioning.

Experiencing Two Events

Unpleasant events such as learned food aversion are good but rather grim examples of classical conditioning. Let's turn to some pleasant situations that also involve classical conditioning.

Does the smell of baby powder elicit pleasant emotions?
If you are or were a parent, you probably used baby powder when you changed diapers. Months or years later, the odor of baby powder will usually bring back warm emotions and fond memories of your smiling infant. Through classical conditioning, baby powder became a conditioned stimulus with the ability to elicit a number of conditioned responses, such as warm emotions and memories of your child.

Do you salivate at the thought of your favorite food?
Just as Pavlov's dog was conditioned to salivate at the sound of a bell, we often salivate at the thought of eating our favorite foods. For example, if right now you vividly imagine eating a favorite food, you will probably salivate within a few seconds. In this case, the conditioned stimulus is not an actual object but a vivid mental image that has acquired the ability to elicit the conditioned response, salivation.

Does a certain song elicit romantic feelings?
Many couples have a special song that becomes romantically associated with their relationship. When this song is heard by one in the absence of the other, it can elicit strong emotional and romantic feelings. In this case, a song becomes a conditioned stimulus with the ability to elicit the conditioned responses, romantic and emotional feelings.

According to the information theory of classical conditioning, these are situations in which we learned a predictable relationship between two stimuli. Creating a relationship between stimuli is one of the primary goals of advertising. Let's compare advertising and classical conditioning.

Advertising and Classical Conditioning

Manufacturers spend billions of dollars each year pairing stimuli in advertisements such as the one shown here. This kind of advertising is based on a principle of learning, called the law of association, that dates from the time of Aristotle. The **law of association** *states that if two events (stimuli) occur close together in time, these events will be associated in our minds so that in the future the thought of one will remind us of the other.* If we compare the law of association with Pavlov's stimulus substitution explanation of classical conditioning, we find one similarity and one difference. The *similarity* is that both the law of association and Pavlov's stimulus substitution theory involve presenting two events (stimuli) close together in time. The *difference* is that in the law of association, any connection between the two events actually occurs in the person's mind and cannot be observed by the researcher.

In classical conditioning, the connection between the two stimuli is controllable and the result is a conditioned response, which is observable and easily measured. Thus, Pavlov's classical conditioning procedure made it possible for psychologists to observe learning taking place rather than having to assume it was occurring in people's minds. Thus, Pavlov's discovery of classical conditioning put learning on an observable basis and gave a great boost to the science of psychology.

Now that you understand the importance of Pavlov's work, we'll end our discussion with a real-life situation that involves classical conditioning.

APPLYING/ EXPLORING: CHEMOTHERAPY AND CONDITIONED NAUSEA

Just an hour earlier, Michelle had received her second chemotherapy treatment for breast cancer. Now she was feeling nauseated, a common side effect of the powerful anticancer drugs used in chemotherapy. Her nausea, which was accompanied by severe vomiting, would last for 6 to 12 hours. In Michelle's case, the medication she had been given to control the nausea was not working.

About a week later, Michelle arrived at the clinic for her third chemotherapy session and took her customary seat in the waiting room. As she looked around, she recognized the painting on the wall, the nurse behind the desk, and the magazines on the table. Michelle was

Why did Michelle become nauseous?

Michelle developed conditioned nausea as a result of her chemotherapy treatments.

talking to another patient, trying to keep her mind off the chemotherapy, when she began to feel nauseated. She had accepted the fact that chemotherapy made her nauseated (Carey & Burish, 1988). But why would simply being in the waiting room have the same effect?

Step 1 Selecting Stimuli and Response

The sights, smells, and thoughts in the waiting and treatment rooms are initially *neutral stimuli.*

+

Chemotherapy is the *unconditioned stimulus,* which elicits nausea and vomiting.

→

The *unconditioned response* is nausea and vomiting, which is elicited by chemotherapy, the unconditioned stimulus.

Step 2 Establishing Conditioning
As neutral stimuli (sights, smells, and thoughts in the waiting room) are paired with the unconditioned stimulus (chemotherapy), the neutral stimuli become conditioned stimuli capable of eliciting the conditioned response (nausea).

Step 3 Testing for Conditioning
When Michelle enters the waiting and treatment rooms, she encounters conditioned stimuli that elicit nausea, the conditioned response.

Michelle, like 25%–35% of patients receiving chemotherapy, had developed *conditioned nausea,* a nauseous feeling that develops through classical conditioning and occurs in anticipation of the actual treatment (Bernstein, 1991). The stimuli and response in the development of conditioned nausea are identified in the box on page 210.

Once established, conditioned nausea is very difficult to treat or control with medication. Conditioned nausea during chemotherapy appears to develop in ways similar to learned food aversions (Bernstein, 1991).

Treatment with Systematic Desensitization

Because antinausea medication was not effective for her, Michelle tried a nondrug treatment called systematic desensitization. **Systematic desensitization,** *which is based on principles of classical conditioning, is a method for pairing a relaxation response with stimuli or situations that elicit anxiety.* This procedure has three steps, as shown on the right.

Michelle is using classical conditioning to develop new associations between relaxation and situations that elicit anxiety. By associating relaxation with each stressful situation in the hierarchy, she reduces the stress, fear, and anxiety associated with conditioned stimuli. You can think of systematic desensitization as a method for changing conditioned stimuli back to neutral stimuli.

Systematic desensitization has been found to be significantly more effective than psychotherapy or relaxation alone in reducing conditioned nausea (Morrow, 1986). Notice that both the cause and treatment of conditioned nausea are based on the principles of classical conditioning.

Systematic Desensitization

1. Michelle is taught to *relax* by tensing and relaxing sets of muscles, beginning with muscles in her toes and continuing up to the muscles in her forehead. She practices intentional relaxation for several weeks before going to the next step.

2. Michelle makes up a list of 7 to 12 stressful situations associated with chemotherapy treatment. She arranges her list of stressful situations in a *hierarchy* from the least to the most stressful. For example, the least stressful situation would be driving to the clinic, entering the clinic, or sitting in the waiting room. The most stressful situation would be receiving an injection, feeling nausea, and vomiting.

Most stressful
9. Vomiting
8. Feeling nausea
7. Receiving injection
6. Being prepared for injection
5. Entering treatment room
4. Being called by nurse
3. Sitting in waiting room
2. Entering clinic
1. Driving to clinic
Least stressful

3. Michelle puts herself into a deeply relaxed state and then vividly imagines the least stressful situation, driving to the clinic. She is told to *remain in a relaxed state while imagining this situation.* If she becomes stressed, she is told to stop imagining the situation and return instead to a relaxed state. Once she is sufficiently relaxed, she again imagines driving to the clinic. If she can imagine driving to the clinic while remaining in a relaxed state, she proceeds to the next stressful situation. She then imagines entering the clinic, while remaining in a relaxed state.

Summary/Self-Test

THREE APPROACHES TO LEARNING

1. A relatively permanent change in behavior that results from experience is a definition of _____; one of its important functions is to help us adapt and adjust to our environments.

2. Psychologists have used three approaches to study learning. One approach had its beginning in Pavlov's well-known experiment in which a bell was sounded and then food was placed in a dog's mouth. Today, Pavlov's procedure for establishing conditioned reflexes is called _____.

3. A second approach to studying learning grew out of Thorndike's observations of cats learning to escape from a box. To explain a cat's goal-directed behavior of hitting a latch to get food, Thorndike formulated a principle of learning called the (a)_____. This law states that if certain random actions are followed by a pleasurable consequence or reward, such actions are strengthened and will likely occur in the future. Today, the law of effect has become part of the second approach to studying learning, called (b)_____.

4. A third approach is learning through observation or imitation, which occurs inside your head. This relatively newer approach, which involves mental processes without any external rewards, is called _____.

■ *As a psychologist, how would you study your friend's problem of being overweight?*

ESTABLISHING CLASSICAL CONDITIONING

5. Suppose you wanted to classically condition your roommate to salivate to the sight of a psychology textbook. One procedure for establishing classical conditioning would be to present two stimuli close together in time. The presentation of the two stimuli is called a *trial*. In our example, a typical trial would involve first presenting a psychology textbook, initially called the (a)_____, which does not elicit salivation. A short time later, you would present a piece of brownie, called the (b)_____ stimulus, which elicits salivation. Salivation, an innate, automatic, and involuntary physiological reflex, is called the (c)_____.

6. After giving your roommate about a dozen trials, you observe that as soon as you show him the psychology text, he begins to salivate. Because the sight of the psychology textbook itself elicits salivation, the psychology text has become a (a)_____. The roommate's salivation to the sight of the psychology book, presented alone, is called the (b)_____. You know that classical conditioning is established when the neutral stimulus becomes the (c)_____ and elicits the (d)_____. Compared to the unconditioned response, the conditioned response is usually similar in appearance but smaller in amount or magnitude.

■ *How do you explain why your heart pounds when you hear the words, "There will be a test next time"?*

OTHER CONDITIONING CONCEPTS

7. During classical conditioning there is a tendency for a stimulus similar to the original conditioned stimulus to elicit a response similar to the conditioned response. This tendency is called _____. Generally, the response will be stronger or larger the more similar the new stimulus is to the original conditioned stimulus.

8. During classical conditioning, an organism learns to make a particular response to some stimuli but not to others; this phenomenon is called _____.

9. If a conditioned stimulus is repeatedly presented without the unconditioned stimulus, there is a tendency for the conditioned stimulus to no longer elicit the conditioned response; this phenomenon is called (a)_____. For example, if you repeatedly presented a psychology text to your roommate without giving him a piece of brownie, your roommate's salivation to the psychology text would disappear. If four days later you again presented the psychology text to your roommate without giving him a brownie, he would show salivation, the conditioned response. This reoccurrence of the conditioned responses after it had been extinguished is called (b)_____.

■ *How do you explain the fact that a person becomes anxious when he hears the sound of a dentist's drill but has no such reaction when he uses a electric hand drill?*

CLASSICAL CONDITIONING: TWO EXPLANATIONS

10. According to Pavlov's traditional explanation, classical conditioning occurs because a bond or association forms between the conditioned stimulus and unconditioned stimulus so that the conditioned stimulus eventually substitutes for the unconditioned stimulus. Pavlov's explanation is called (a)_____. According to the modern explanation of classical conditioning, an organism learns a relationship between two stimuli such that the occurrence of one stimulus predicts the occurrence of another. This explanation is called (b)_____.

■ *Every time you open the refrigerator door, your cat runs into the kitchen and waits to be fed. How would the old and new views of classical conditioning differ in explaining your cat's behavior?*

CLASSICAL CONDITIONING ALL AROUND US

11. A powerful form of classical conditioning occurs in real life when a neutral stimulus is paired with an unpleasant response, such as nausea or vomiting. The result of this pairing is called _____. This form of classical conditioning is unusual in two ways: (1) it may be acquired in a single trial and may last a relatively long period of time,

and (2) there may be a considerable lapse of time between the presentations of the two stimuli.

12. Advertising makes use of an old principle of learning stating that if two events (stimuli) occur close together in time, these events will be associated in our minds so that the thought of one will in the future remind us of the other. This principle is called the _____.

13. The *difference* between the law of association and classical conditioning is that according to the law of association the pairing of two events actually occurs in the person's mind and cannot be observed by the researcher. In classical conditioning, the pairing of two stimuli can be controlled and results in a learning response, called the_____, that can be both observed and measured.

■ *Describe a situation from your own life that involved classical conditioning.*

APPLYING/EXPLORING: CHEMOTHERAPY AND CONDITIONED NAUSEA

14. During chemotherapy for cancer, some patients develop nausea in anticipation of the actual treatment. This is called (a)_____ and is elicited by various stimuli in the waiting and treatment rooms. A nondrug treatment for this problem, based on the principles of classical conditioning, involves pairing a relaxation response with anxiety-provoking situations; the treatment is called (b)_____.

■ *How could we classically condition cigarette smokers to stop smoking?*

MODULE 12
OPERANT CONDITIONING
AND COGNITIVE LEARNING

How do you train an 1800-pound movie star?
Very carefully. Twelve-year-old Bart weighs in at over 1800 pounds; when he stands up, he towers almost ten feet. Bart is a brown Kodiak bear (cousin to the grizzly), one of the world's largest land-dwelling carnivores. With one swipe of his massive 12-inch paw, Bart can demolish anything in his path. Yet there was big Bart, sitting peacefully on his haunches, cradling a stuffed teddy bear in his arms.

Sitting, cradling a teddy bear, and nuzzling it were just some of the 45 behaviors that trainer Doug Seus taught Bart, who, along with a bear cub, starred in the movie *The Bear.*

In the movie, Bart finds and befriends a small bear cub. Bart even

How was Bart trained to be a movie star?

shares a meal with the cub, something that would never occur in the wild, where an adult bear would surely kill and eat a cub. Each time Bart performed a behavior on cue, the trainer gave him an affectionate back scratch, an ear rub, or a juicy apple or pear. For example, when the trainer raised his arms high in the air, it was the signal for Bart to sit and hold the teddy bear. After correctly performing this behavior, Doug would give Bart his reward. After Bart learned to perform all these behaviors with a stuffed teddy bear, a live bear cub was substituted and the scene was filmed for the movie. (adapted from *Los Angeles Times Calendar*, October 22, 1989)

What's Coming

Training Bart to perform different kinds of behaviors on cue is a dramatic example of a kind of learning called operant conditioning. In this module we'll examine operant conditioning as well as a different kind of learning, cognitive learning.

Operant Conditioning

Operant conditioning *(also called instrumental conditioning) is a kind of learning in which the consequences that follow some behavior increase or decrease the likelihood of that behavior occurring in the future.* In operant conditioning an organism acts, or "operates," on the environment in order to change the likelihood of the response occurring again. For example, Bart acts or operates on his environment by picking up the teddy bear. The consequence that follows is a reward that Bart likes. The occurrence of the reward (in many cases, an apple) increases the chance that Bart will again pick up the teddy bear.

Basic Ideas: Thorndike and Skinner

Because operant conditioning includes ideas from Thorndike's law of effect (which we discussed in Module 11), we'll review it first. We'll then go on to study B. F. Skinner's approach to operant conditioning, as it was Skinner's genius that made operant conditioning a major force in psychology.

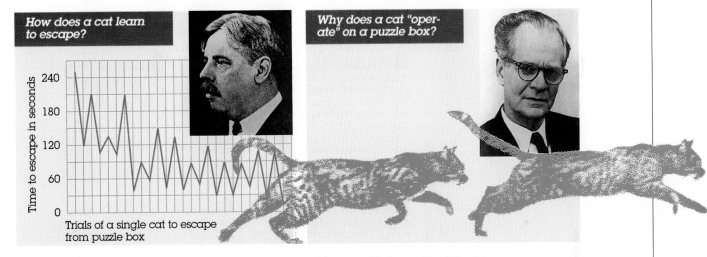

How does a cat learn to escape?

Trials of a single cat to escape from puzzle box

Why does a cat "operate" on a puzzle box?

Thorndike's Law of Effect

As you may remember, in the early 1900s Thorndike studied how a cat learns, through random trial and error, to escape from a puzzle box and get rewarded with a fish. A graph showing a typical cat's escape time is shown here. Notice that on the first trial the cat needed over 240 seconds to escape and get the fish. However, by the 24th trial the cat escaped the box in about 30 seconds. Thorndike discovered that a cat learns to spend more time around the latch and gets better and better at hitting the latch and getting the fish. To explain how a cat's random trial-and-error behaviors gradually become efficient goal-directed behaviors—hitting the latch, escaping the box, getting the fish—Thorndike formulated the *law of effect,* which as we saw in Module 11 states that behaviors followed by positive consequences are strengthened, while behaviors followed by negative consequences are weakened. Notice that Thorndike focused on the consequences of goal-directed behavior rather than on physiological reflexes as Pavlov did. Thorndike's ideas were further developed and expanded by B. F. Skinner.

Skinner and Operant Conditioning

B. F. Skinner devoted more than 50 years to developing a new area of learning that he called *operant conditioning.* Skinner saw organisms "operating" on their environments to obtain rewards, and he coined the term operant conditioning to describe this process. He reasoned that Pavlov's conditioning is not very useful in understanding the role of learning, because much of learning does not involve physiological reflexes. Instead, Skinner believed that Thorndike's law of effect is more useful, since it explains how organisms are rewarded or reinforced for making particular responses and adapting to their environments. Beginning in the late 1930s, Skinner focused on the consequences of behavior and on the principles underlying the law of effect. His genius will become clear as we explain his principles of operant conditioning.

Operant Conditioning

Comparison: Classical Versus Operant Conditioning

It is often difficult to clearly see the differences between classical and operant conditioning. We'll use Bart as a subject to show the primary differences between these two types of conditioning.

Subject: Bart, a giant Kodiak bear.

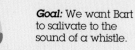

Classical Conditioning

Goal: We want Bart to salivate to the sound of a whistle.

1 The *response* is an *involuntary* physiological reflex, such as salivation.

2 The involuntary response is *elicited* or triggered by the unconditioned stimulus, an apple.

3 The *pairing* of the neutral stimulus (whistle) with the unconditioned stimulus (apple) is important. Through this pairing, Bart learns a relationship between the stimuli: the whistle is followed by an apple. The whistle (neutral stimulus) becomes the *conditioned stimulus* that elicits the *conditioned response,* salivation.

4 Notice that in classical conditioning, the unconditioned stimulus is presented *before the unconditioned response.* The unconditioned stimulus *elicits* the response (salivation) in Bart.

Operant Conditioning

Goal: We want Bart to hold a teddy bear.

1 The *behavior* is a *voluntary* response, holding a teddy bear.

2 The behavior is voluntarily performed or *emitted* by Bart. By holding the teddy bear, Bart acts or "operates" on his environment.

3 The *consequence* of Bart's behavior is important. Each time Bart holds the teddy bear, he receives an apple.
The apple is a *reward* or *reinforcer* and increases the likelihood that Bart will perform the behavior in the future.

4 Notice that in operant conditioning, the reinforcer occurs *after the desired behavior* (as, for instance, after Bart holds the teddy bear). Bart must *emit* some behavior before a reinforcer will occur.

Because Bart is too mighty to safely condition in a laboratory, we'll take you instead to Skinner's laboratory at Harvard University and explain operant conditioning using much smaller and safer subjects.

The Skinner Box

Imagine that you are looking over Skinner's shoulder as he places a white rat into a box that is empty except for a lever jutting out from one side and an empty food cup below and to the side of the lever. Forever after, and apparently to Skinner's dismay, this kind of experimental box will be called a **Skinner box.** In addition to the lever and food cup, the Skinner box contains devices to record the animal's lever presses and the delivery of food pellets. The Skinner box is a very efficient way to study learning.

The Skinner box is standard equipment in many animal laboratories.

Operant Conditioning Procedure

As you watch, Skinner explains that the rat is a good subject for operant conditioning because it can use its front paws to manipulate objects, such as a lever, and it has a tendency to explore its environment, which means that it will find the lever. Skinner goes on to explain three factors involved in operantly conditioning a rat to press a lever:

1 The rat has not been fed for some hours so that it will be active and more likely to eat the food reward. A hungry rat tends to roam restlessly about, sniffing at whatever it finds.

2 The *goal* is to condition the rat to press the lever. By pressing the lever, the rat "operates" on its environment; thus, this response is called an ***operant response.***

3 Skinner explains that a naive rat does not usually waltz over and press the lever. In conditioning a rat to press a lever, Skinner will use a shaping procedure. During **shaping,** *the experimenter reinforces behaviors that lead up to or approximate the desired behavior.* For example, shaping might involve reinforcing a rat when it initially faces or simply moves toward the lever.

Rat is reinforced for facing lever.

Rat is reinforced for approching lever.

Rat is reinforced only for pressing lever.

Shaping Procedure. Now that you have been prepared to know what to look for, Skinner picks up a white rat and places it into the experimental box. The box is lit and the rest of the room is dark, so that the rat will not be distracted by seeing humans in the room. Skinner waits and watches. The rat wanders around the back of the box. As it turns and faces the lever, Skinner releases a food pellet into the food cup. The rat hears the pellet drop and approaches the food cup. It discovers the pellet and eats it. The rat moves about the box some more, and as soon as it again turns and faces the lever, Skinner releases another pellet.

Skinner decides to wait longer and reinforces the rat only when it moves toward the lever. This plan pays off, because the rat soon faces and then moves toward the lever. Only then does Skinner release another pellet. After eating the pellet, the rat wanders a bit but soon returns to the lever and actually sniffs it. A fourth pellet immediately drops into the cup and the rat eats it. When the rat places one paw on the lever, a fifth pellet drops into the cup. Now the rat rears up on its back feet, sniffs the lever, and puts its front paws on it. This downward motion presses the lever and causes release of another pellet. Within a relatively short time, the rat is putting its paws on the lever, pressing down, and getting food pellets.

Skinner explains that in shaping, the *reinforcer* should follow *immediately* after the desired behavior. In this way, the rewarding consequences will come to be associated with the desired behavior and not with some other behavior that just happens to intervene. Skinner tells how he once delivered the food too late; by then, the rat was facing *away* from the lever, and it took quite a while to get the rat to give up this "wrong" behavior. Depending on the rat and the experience of the trainer, it usually takes from five minutes to an hour to train a rat to press a lever.

What Is CACOB? Five words—**consequences are contingent on behavior**—summarize the essentials of operant conditioning. CACOB means that the consequences (reinforcers) are dependent or contingent on an organism emitting some behavior. In the example from Skinner's lab, the consequences (getting food pellets) were dependent or contingent on the rat emitting a particular behavior (pressing the lever).

Because of their importance, we'll take a closer took at some consequences (reinforcers).

A Closer Look at Reinforcers

Which five words describe the essence of operant conditioning?

As you may remember, the essence of operant conditioning is summed up in the phrase "consequences are contingent on behavior." The word *consequences* refers to what happens after the occurrence of a behavior. In operant conditioning, there are two kinds of consequences—reinforcement and punishment—that are contingent on behavior. **Reinforcement** *is a consequence that increases the likelihood of a behavior occurring again.* **Punishment** *is a consequence that decreases the likelihood of a behavior occurring again.* For example, if you call home and ask for money and your parents send money, your calling and asking for money is reinforced and you'll probably repeat that behavior. On the other hand, if you ask for money and your parents give you a stern warning about overspending and refuse to send money, your calling and asking for money is punished, and you'll probably not ask again anytime soon.

> ## "Consequences are contingent on behavior."
>
> **Why are these five words important?**

Positive and Negative Reinforcement

Although the term *reinforcement* suggests a positive consequence, you'll see that reinforcement can be either positive or negative.

Positive Reinforcement

When is an apple a reinforcer?

Immediately after performing certain behaviors, the trainer gave Bart an apple to increase the likelihood of Bart's repeating that behavior. The ripe apple, one of Bart's favorite treats, is an example of a positive reinforcer.

A **positive reinforcer** *is a pleasant stimulus that increases the likelihood of a response occurring again.* If you call your parents and ask for money, their sending money is a positive reinforcer that will increase the chances of your calling again.

Negative Reinforcement

When is an aspirin a reinforcer?

Training an 1800-pound ten-foot-tall bear is a difficult task that sometimes gives the trainer a headache. If the trainer takes two aspirin and the headache goes away, the trainer is likely to take aspirin for future headaches. In this case, the behavior of taking aspirin is followed by the removal of the headache, an unpleasant stimulus.

Negative reinforcement *is the removal of an unpleasant stimulus, thereby increasing the likelihood of a response occurring again.* In the case of the trainer, the removal of the headache is the *negative reinforcer* because it increases the likelihood of the preceding behavior, taking an aspirin.

Remember that both positive and negative reinforcers *increase* the frequency of the responses they follow. Let's look closer at the concept of negative reinforcement, as it is a difficult one. In *negative reinforcement,* some response is followed by the removal of an unpleasant stimulus. For example, if you park in legal spaces, you avoid getting parking tickets (unpleasant stimuli). The avoidance of parking tickets is a negative reinforcer that increases the likelihood that you will park in legal spaces in the future.

How does negative reinforcement differ from punishment? You'll see that they differ greatly and have opposite effects on behavior.

Punishment Versus Negative Reinforcement

In the early 1980s, as part of the navy's crackdown on the use of illegal drugs it dismissed all officers and senior enlisted personnel caught with drugs, levied heavy fines on lower-ranking first offenders, and booted them out for subsequent violations. After the crackdown, urine analysis tests showed that the use of illicit drugs dropped from an estimated 35% to only 3.7% (*Los Angeles Times,* November 28, 1983).

As you may recall, *punishment* is a consequence that decreases the likelihood of a behavior occurring again. The navy's crackdown on illicit drugs primarily used punishment, in the form of heavy fines or immediate dismissal following a positive urine test for illegal drugs. This policy greatly decreased the use of illegal drugs in the navy. As this use demonstrated, *punishment is most effective when it immediately follows the unwanted behavior.*

Negative reinforcement increases the likelihood of exercising to avoid becoming overweight and getting discharged.

In contrast to punishment, which *decreases* the likelihood of a behavior occurring again, negative reinforcement *increases* the likelihood of a behavior occurring again. An example of negative reinforcement in the navy would be exercising to keep one's weight below the established guidelines and thus avoiding being discharged. Not being discharged for being overweight is a negative reinforcer, as it increases the likelihood of exercising.

During a typical day, you encounter dozens of obvious reinforcers, such as food and water, but what kinds of reinforcers are grades, compliments, or money?

Punishment decreases the likelihood of using illegal drugs in the navy.

Primary Versus Secondary Reinforcers

Suppose that you study an average of two hours a day but want to increase your study time to four hours by using positive reinforcement. You might use either a primary or secondary reinforcer.

Primary Reinforcers

Would food increase your study time?
If you allowed yourself to have lunch only after you had studied for four hours that morning, you would be using a primary reinforcer. A **primary reinforcer** *is a stimulus, such as food, water, or sex, that is innately satisfying and requires no learning on the part of the subject to become pleasurable.* For example, Bart's trainer used ripe apples and pears in conditioning the bear.

Secondary Reinforcers

Would money increase your study time?
If you gave yourself $50 each time you met the four-hour study goal, you would be using a secondary reinforcer. A **secondary reinforcer** *is any stimulus that has acquired its reinforcing power through experience; secondary reinforcers are learned, such as by being paired with primary reinforcers.* Money, grades, and hugs are examples of secondary reinforcers, because their value is learned or acquired through experience.

You may have received a high grade on a paper, a compliment on your appearance, laughter following one of your jokes, praise for an answer you gave in class, or thanks from another student for helping with a problem. In each example, your behavior was reinforced with a secondary reinforcer. In some halfway houses, individuals with behavioral problems are given *tokens* when they perform a constructive behavior. For example, after making their bed, cleaning their room, or going to class, individuals receive a token—a secondary reinforcer—that they can turn in later for some valued treat or object (Carden & Fowler, 1984). In such settings, as well as in our own lives, many behaviors are increased or maintained by secondary reinforcers.

We may not always be aware of the reinforcers in our lives because, as you'll see, they don't necessarily occur every time you emit a behavior.

Schedules of Reinforcement

Although B. F. Skinner is best known for his work with rats and pigeons, he was also interested in applying operant conditioning principles to the classroom. His concern about improving teaching methods led to his invention of the teaching machine (Skinner, 1954).

The teaching machine, which took several forms, was essentially a boxlike device with a small window. A small bit of information or a question appeared in the window; the student was to respond by pressing one of several keys. Students received immediate feedback or reinforcement for their answers. Early teaching machines were programmed to quiz students in beginning arithmetic. As students worked their way through addition, subtraction, and multiplication, they were immediately reinforced for their answers. Present-day computer programs that allow students to interact with material are modern take-offs on Skinner's teaching machine.

Skinner's concern with how often reinforcements are presented and how these schedules affect behavior became a major study of operant conditioning. There are a number of **schedules of reinforcement,** *the various ways that reinforcers occur after the performance of some behavior.* We'll begin with two general schedules: continuous and partial reinforcement.

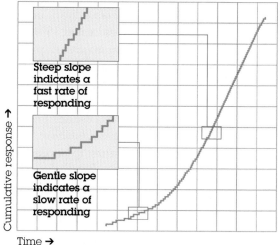

Steep slope indicates a fast rate of responding

Gentle slope indicates a slow rate of responding

Cumulative response ↑

Time →

A cumulative record (shown here) indicates the rate of responding. As paper moves slowly and continuously to the left, each response causes a pen to move up one notch. Slow responding causes the pen to notch up gradually, resulting in a gentle slope. Fast responding causes the pen to notch up more quickly, resulting in a steep slope.

Two Basic Schedules

Continuous Reinforcement

Skinner believed that the advantage of the teaching machine was that it would tirelessly reinforce the student after answering each question. This is an example of **continuous reinforcement**, *in which each and every target behavior is reinforced.* In the real world, relatively few of our behaviors are on a continuous reinforcement schedule.

Continuous reinforcement is often used in the initial stages of operant conditioning because it results in rapid learning of the behavior.

Partial Reinforcement

In a typical classroom, a teacher has time to reinforce only some, but not all, desired behaviors. This is an example of **partial reinforcement**, *in which behaviors are reinforced only some of the times that they occur.*

Once a behavior is learned, a partial reinforcement schedule is more effective in maintaining the behavior over the long run.

As we explain the four schedules of partial reinforcement, notice how differently they affect behavior.

Partial Reinforcement: Four Different Schedules

On a **fixed-ratio schedule** *reinforcement occurs after a fixed number of nonreinforced behaviors.* For example, a pigeon is reinforced after each six pecks. A factory worker is paid by the piece, such as packing a box of carrots.

Effect. A fixed-ratio schedule is often used in assembly lines because it results in fast rates of work—the more work completed, the more the worker is paid (reinforcement).

Steep slope indicates rapid response rate (reinforcers indicated by blips).

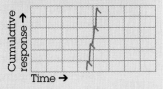

On a **variable-ratio schedule** *reinforcement occurs after a variable number of nonreinforced behaviors.* For example, a pigeon is reinforced after 12, 6, 8, and 2 pecks, with an average of 7 pecks. A slot machine pays off after an average of 85 pulls but at a variable number of pulls.

Effect. The variable-ratio schedule produces a high rate of responding because the subject (pigeon or slot machine player) doesn't "know" which response will finally produce the payoff.

Steep slope indicates rapid, steady response rate (reinforcers indicated by blips).

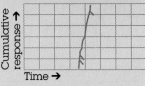

On a **fixed-interval schedule** *reinforcement occurs following the first response that occurs after a fixed interval of time.* For example, a pigeon is reinforced for the first peck that occurs after three minutes. Surfers get a big wave to ride (the reinforcer) every 30 seconds.

Effect. A fixed-interval schedule results in slow responding at first, but as the time for the reinforcer draws near, the response rate greatly accelerates.

Gradual slope indicates slower responding with long pauses after each reinforcer (blips).

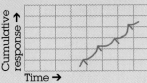

On a **variable-interval schedule** *reinforcement occurs following the first response after a variable amount of time has gone by.* For example, a pigeon is reinforced for the first response that occurs after intervals of 12, 6, 8, and 2 minutes, with an average interval of 7 minutes. A bus arrives (the reinforcer) at your stop at an average of 7 minutes late, but at variable intervals. This reinforces your arriving just a few minutes late.

Effect. A variable-interval schedule results in a more regular rate of responding than does a fixed-interval schedule.

Gradual slope indicates slower responding without pauses after reinforcers (blips).

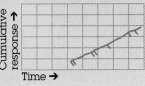

Skinner demonstrated that partial reinforcement, even as few as one reinforcer for an average of 200 responses, would keep a pigeon pecking at a key in a Skinner box. He believed that many of our own behaviors, such as studying for exams, working at a job, or being affectionate in a relationship, are maintained on schedules of partial reinforcement.

Now that you understand the importance of reinforcers, we'll show how they work in two real-life situations.

Examples of Operant Conditioning

Child Training

Imagine that you are a parent of two-year-old Sheryl, who is ready to begin toilet training. In the book *Toilet Training in Less Than a Day* (Azrin & Foxx, 1974), two behavioral psychologists describe how parents can use operant conditioning principles to accomplish this task in a short period of time. Let's see how you might use these techniques with Sheryl (assuming that she is physically mature enough for toilet training).

Can toilet training be made easy?

Steps for Toilet Training

1. Before training begins, you put all of Sheryl's toys away so she will not be distracted. Then you give her a large glass of apple juice so she will have to urinate soon.

2. Identify the *target behavior* (goal), which is for Sheryl to urinate in the toilet.

3. Select *reinforcers,* which can be candy, verbal praise, or a hug. Each time Sheryl performs or emits a desired behavior, you immediately reinforce her. The reinforcer increases the likelihood that the behavior will be repeated.

4. Just as Skinner used the shaping procedure in conditioning a rat to press a lever, you can use a similar *shaping procedure* in conditioning Sheryl to use the toilet. Each time Sheryl performs a behavior that leads to the target behavior (using the toilet), give her a candy, verbal praise, or a hug. For instance, when Sheryl says that she has to go potty, say, "That's great." When Sheryl enters the bathroom, give her a candy. When she lowers her pants by herself, say, "You're doing really good." After Sheryl urinates into the toilet, give her a big hug.

Bear Training

Exactly how was Bart, who is relatively tame and used to humans, operantly conditioned to hold a teddy bear?

Steps for Holding a Teddy Bear

1. The *target behavior* is for Bart to sit and hold a teddy bear.

2. For a *reinforcer,* the trainer used an apple, a pear, or a vigorous back scratch or ear rub.

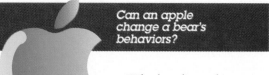

Can an apple change a bear's behaviors?

3. The *shaping procedure* involved reinforcing Bart for performing behaviors that led up to the desired behavior. Immediately after Bart performed the behavior, he was given a reinforcer. (Sometimes the trainer tossed an apple or pear to Bart, who has great hands.) Initially, the trainer reinforced Bart for sniffing, touching, or picking up the teddy bear. Later, the trainer reinforced Bart only if he sat up and held the teddy bear, the desired behavior.

Whether the goal is to condition a rat to press a lever, a child to use the potty, or a bear to hold a teddy bear, the same principles of operant conditioning apply.

Principles of Operant Conditioning

Skinner believed and demonstrated that our daily lives are filled with examples of operant conditioning, some more obvious than others. For example, many of us have been operantly conditioned to put money into a vending machine to obtain a soda; call our parents to get money; study hard to get a good grade on an exam; practice long hours to win at sports; or risk fear of rejection and ask someone for a date. One reason that we perform these behaviors again and again is that they have been reinforced.

During the conditioning procedure, other things are going on that we'll look at next.

Other Conditioning Terms

You may remember these three terms—generalization, discrimination, and extinction—from our discussion of classical conditioning in Module 11. As you'll see here, these terms are also used in operant conditioning.

Generalization

In the wild, a male Kodiak bear would not tolerate the presence of a cub and would probably kill and eat it. Luckily, Bart's trainer saw a way around that. To be on the safe side, he conducted the initial conditioning with a stuffed teddy bear. After Bart had learned to hold the teddy bear, the trainer substituted a live cub, and Bart transferred or generalized his response to the cub. This is an example of **generalization,** *in which the animal or person emits the same response to similar stimuli.* (Recall that in *classical conditioning,* generalization is the tendency for a stimulus similar to the original conditioned stimulus to elicit a response similar to the conditioned response.)

Young children show wonderful examples of generalization. For instance, a young child may call any male "Daddy." This mislabeling occurs because the child, who has been reinforced for saying "Daddy" in the presence of her real father, generalizes her response to other, similar stimuli. As quickly as possible, parents teach their child to discriminate between the father and other mature males.

Bart generalized from a teddy bear to a live cub.

Discrimination

Why didn't Bart take commands from the movie director?

Bart performed his trained behaviors only when signaled by his trainer and not by the director. This is an example of **discrimination,** *in which a response is emitted in the presence of a stimulus that is reinforced and not in the presence of unreinforced stimuli.* Young children learn to discriminate between stimuli when their parents reinforce them for saying "Daddy" in the presence of their real fathers and do not reinforce them for calling strangers "Daddy." (Recall that in *classical conditioning* discrimination is the tendency for some stimuli but not others to elicit a particular response.)

One problem with Bart was that he would repeatedly pick up and hold the teddy bear to receive a juicy pear. To control this problem, the trainer used a cue—raising his arms in the air—to signal that only then would Bart receive a pear for his behavior. This is an example of a **discriminative stimulus,** *which is a cue that a behavior will be reinforced.* If you watch trained animals perform, pay close attention to the trainer and you will probably be able to identify the discriminative stimuli (whistle, hand signal) used to signal the animal that the next behavior will be reinforced.

Bart discriminated between his trainer and other humans.

Without being reinforced, Bart stopped holding the teddy bear.

Extinction

What happened to Bart's trained behaviors?

After filming ended, Bart continued to perform his trained behaviors—for a while. Because these behaviors were no longer reinforced, they gradually diminished and ceased. This is an example of **extinction,** *which is a decrease in emitting a behavior because it is no longer reinforced.* Bart also showed **spontaneous recovery,** *the spontaneous performance of the behavior without it being reinforced.* As you will recall, both extinction and spontaneous recovery also occur in classical conditioning.

Now that you have read about Bart, you can see him in action by renting a copy of the movie *The Bear* (human actors have only 657 words of dialogue).

We'll explain some other applications of operant conditioning in the Applying/ Exploring section. Now, let's go on to cognitive learning, the third approach that psychologists use to study learning.

1. The kind of learning in which the consequences that follow some behavior increase or decrease the likelihood of that behavior occurring in the future is called (a)_____. This name was chosen by B. F. Skinner to signify that an organism (b)_____ on the environment in order to change the likelihood of the response occurring again.

2. In operant conditioning, the organism voluntarily performs or (a)_____ a behavior. Immediately following an emitted behavior, the occurrence of a (b)_____ *increases* the likelihood of that behavior occurring again.

5. If the occurrence of some response is increased because it is followed by a pleasant stimulus, the stimulus is called a (a)_____. An increase in the occurrence of some response because it is followed either by the removal of an unpleasant stimulus or by avoiding the stimulus is called (b)_____.

6. A stimulus, such as food, water, or sex, that is innately satisfying and requires no learning to become pleasurable is a (a)_____. A stimulus, such as grades or praise, that has acquired its reinforcing power through experience and learning is a (b)_____.

3. Because an organism may not immediately emit the desired behavior, a procedure is used to reinforce behaviors that lead to or approximate the final, target behavior. This procedure is called _____.

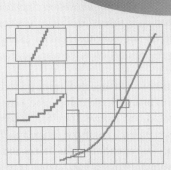

7. The various ways that reinforcers occur after a behavior has been emitted is referred to as (a)_____ of reinforcement. For example, if each and every target behavior is reinforced, it is called a (b)_____ schedule of reinforcement. If behaviors are not reinforced each time they occur, it is called a (c)_____ schedule of reinforcement.

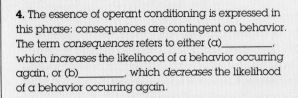

4. The essence of operant conditioning is expressed in this phrase: consequences are contingent on behavior. The term *consequences* refers to either (a)_____, which *increases* the likelihood of a behavior occurring again, or (b)_____, which *decreases* the likelihood of a behavior occurring again.

8. When an organism emits the same response to similar stimuli, it is called (a)_____. When a response is emitted in the presence of a stimulus that is reinforced and not in the presence of unreinforced stimuli, it is called (b)_____. A decrease in emitting a behavior because it is no longer reinforced is called (c)_____. If an organism performs a behavior without it being reinforced, it is called (d)_____.

Answers: 1. (a) operant conditioning, (b) operates; 2. (a) emits, (b) reinforcement or reinforcer; 3. shaping; 4. (a) reinforcement, (b) punishment; 5. (a) positive reinforcer, (b) negative reinforcer; 6. (a) primary reinforcer, (b) secondary reinforcer; 7. (a) schedules, (b) continuous, (c) partial; 8. (a) generalization, (b) discrimination, (c) extinction, (d) spontaneous recovery.

Cognitive Learning

Do you hate bugs?

Learning to detest bugs from watching someone's fearful reaction is an example of cognitive learning, the third approach that psychologists use to study learning. Recall from Module 11 that *cognitive learning* is a kind of learning that involves mental processes, such as attention and memory, and may not involve any external rewards or require the person to perform any observable behaviors. Although interest in cognitive learning was "reborn" in the 1960s, its roots extend back to the work of Wundt in the late 1800s and that of psychologist Edward Tolman in the 1930s. Today the concepts of cognitive learning have become popular in explaining animal and human behavior (Schwartz & Reisberg, 1991). We'll learn about various aspects of cognitive learning, including observational and insight learning, but first let's compare three different views on cognitive learning.

Three Viewpoints

B. F. Skinner—Against. Eight days before his death, B. F. Skinner was honored by the American Psychological Association (APA) with the first APA Citation for Outstanding Lifetime Contribution to Psychology. In his acceptance speech to over 1,000 friends and colleagues, Skinner spoke of how psychology was splitting between those who were studying feelings and cognitive processes and those who were studying observable behaviors. Repeating a thought he had expressed many times before, Skinner said, "As far as I'm concerned, cognitive science is the creationism [downfall] of psychology" (Vargas, 1991, p. 1).

Skinner's severe criticism of cognitive processes and mental events caused many in the audience to gasp and only a few to applaud (Vargas, 1991). Apparently, many in the audience, as well as throughout psychology today, believe that cognitive processes are not psychology's creationism (or, as Skinner implied, a step backward in knowledge). Instead, they believe that cognitive processes are a useful approach to understanding learning and behavior.

Edward Tolman—In Favor. In the 1930s, about the same time that Skinner was emphasizing observable behaviors, Tolman was exploring hidden mental processes. For example, he would place rats individually in a maze, such as the one shown above, and allow each rat time to explore the maze with no food present. Then, with food present in the maze's food box, he would retest the rat to see which path it took. The rat learned very quickly to take the shortest path. Next, Tolman blocked the shortest path to the food box. The first time the rat encountered the blocked shortest path, it selected the next shortest path to the food box. According to Tolman (1948), the rat selected the next shortest path because it had developed a cognitive map of the maze. A **cognitive map** *is a mental representation of the layout of an environment.*

In addition, Tolman showed that rats learned the layout of a maze without being reinforced, a position very different from Skinner's. Tolman's emphasis on cognitive processes in learning is continued today by Albert Bandura.

Albert Bandura—In Favor. Although Bandura began as a behaviorist in the Skinnerian tradition, he has gradually and almost entirely shifted to a cognitive approach. In many of his studies, Bandura (1986) has focused on how humans learn through observation. For example, Bandura would say that a child can learn to hate spiders simply by observing the behaviors of someone who exhibits a great dislike of spiders. This is an example of **observational learning,** *which is a form of learning that develops through watching and does not require the observer to perform any observable behavior or receive a reinforcer.* Just as Tolman found that learning occurred while rats were exploring, Bandura found that humans learned while observing and that much of human learning takes place through observation. Observational learning, which emphasizes cognitive processes, is 180 degrees from Skinner's position, which emphasizes observable, noncognitive behaviors.

We'll next describe one of Bandura's best-known studies on observational learning, which is one form of cognitive learning.

Cognitive Learning

Observational Learning

In a classic study, Bandura (1965) and his colleagues demonstrated the form of cognitive learning called observational learning.

Procedure. In one part of the room, preschool children were involved in their own art projects. In another part of the room, an adult got up and, for the next 10 minutes, kicked, hit, and yelled ("Hit him! Kick him!") at a large, inflated Bobo doll. Some children watched the model's aggressive behaviors. Later, each child was subjected to a mildly frustrating situation and then placed in a room with toys, including the Bobo doll. Without the child knowing, researchers observed the child's behaviors.

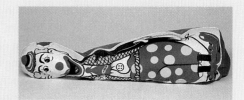

Results. Children who had observed the model's aggressive attacks on the Bobo doll also kicked, hit, and yelled ("Hit him! Kick him!") at the doll. Through observational learning alone, these children had learned the model's aggressive behaviors and were now performing them. In comparison, the children who had not observed the model's aggressive behaviors did not hit or kick the Bobo doll after they had been mildly frustrated.

Conclusion. Why did children kick the Bobo doll? Bandura's point is that children learned to perform specific aggressive behaviors simply by watching a live model. Observational learning can also occur by watching models on film or even from a set of verbal instructions.

Another interesting finding of the Bobo doll studies was that children may learn by observing but then not perform the observed behavior. This is an example of the learning-performance distinction.

Learning Versus Performance

Can you learn behaviors but not perform them?

In another experiment a group of children watched a movie in which someone hit and kicked a Bobo doll. However, after hitting and kicking the doll, the person was punished by being soundly criticized and spanked. Next, each child was left alone in a room filled with toys, including a Bobo doll.

As the experimenters watched each child through a one-way mirror, they found that more boys than girls imitated the model and performed aggressive behaviors on Bobo. But not all the children imitated the model's aggressive behaviors.

However, when each of these children was offered a reward (a sticker or some fruit juice) for *imitating* the model's behavior, different results were obtained. Now all of the children imitated the model's aggressive behaviors.

We will focus on the girls' imitated aggressive behaviors, as their results were similar to but more dramatic than those for the boys. Bandura (1965) found that the girls had actually learned the model's aggressive behaviors through observation but that some did not perform these behaviors until they were reinforced for doing so (Bandura, 1965). This is an example of the **learning-performance distinction:** *learning may occur but may not always be measured by or immediately evident in performance.*

Young children often demonstrate the learning-performance distinction in a way that embarrasses their parents. A young child may overhear a "dirty" word but will not immediately repeat the word in the presence of a parent. Then, when a neighbor comes to visit, the child gleefully repeats the word, showing that it was learned through observation. Knowing about the learning-performance distinction should make parents more careful of what they say around their children.

Based on the Bobo doll study and others, Bandura developed a theory of observational learning that we'll examine next.

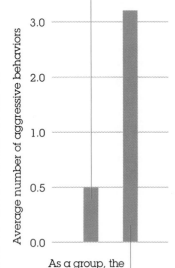

As a group, girls imitated less than 0.5 aggressive behaviors after they watched a model who was punished for performing aggressive behaviors.

Average number of aggressive behaviors

3.0
2.0
1.0
0.5
0.0

As a group, the same girls imitated over 3.0 aggressive behaviors after being promised a reward for imitating the model's behaviors.

Bandura's Theory of Observational Learning

Would you pick up this spider?

Just as Tolman believed that rats gather information and form cognitive maps about their environments through exploring, Bandura believes that humans gather information about their environments and the behaviors of others through observation. Many factors influence this process. For instance, some people are more interesting to watch than others and may therefore have a stronger effect: Those who are warm or powerful are more attention getting than those who are cold and weak.

To explain how observational learning occurs, Bandura (1986, 1989) suggests that four mental processes are in operation. We will illustrate these four processes by using an example of a four-year-old girl observing her mother's reaction to a large spider.

Four Processes Necessary for Observational Learning

1 Attention. The observer must pay attention to what the model says or does. The young girl must see her mother's reaction to the spider before she can imitate the reaction. In the case of the girl on the right, the mother may have watched the spider with interest and said that spiders do a lot of good by eating bothersome insects and that they are not usually dangerous.

2 Memory. The observer must code the information in a way that it can be retrieved and used later. The girl on the right codes both the image of her mother's interested facial expression and the mother's comments about spiders doing good. What has the girl on the left coded? How we code and retrieve information is the topic of Chapter 7.

3 Motor control. The observer must be able to use the coded information to guide his or her own actions and thus imitate the model's behavior. Each girl has developed sufficient muscle control to imitate the mother's facial expression, but she may not know enough language to repeat her mother's comments.

4 Motivation. The observer must have some reason, reinforcement, or incentive to perform the model's behaviors. For example, the girl on the right may want to show her playmate a spider and imitate her mother's interested expression.

This young girl imitates her mother's fear of spiders.

This young girl imitates her mother's interest in spiders.

Bandura maintains that all four mental processes need to operate before observational learning occurs. From personal experience, I have learned that all four processes need to be operating before imitation is possible. Dozens of times I have really attended to, carefully memorized, and been greatly motivated to ski through deep powder, but I have always lacked process number 3, the motor control.

In a later section, we'll compare Bandura's theory of observational learning with a popular method of teaching very young children to play the violin. But for now we'll turn to another kind of cognitive learning, one that is often described as the "ah ha" feeling.

Cognitive Learning

Insight Learning

About the same time that Thorndike in America was studying the trial-and-error learning of cats escaping from a puzzle box, Wolfgang Köhler in Germany was studying how chimpanzees learned to obtain bananas that were out of reach. As you know, Thorndike concluded that cats learn to escape through a process of trial and error. In contrast, Köhler believed that chimps could solve problems through a process of **insight**, *which is a mental process marked by the sudden occurrence of a solution.* We'll introduce you to Köhler's star chimp, Sultan, who seemed to solve difficult problems in an "insightful" way.

How did Sultan get the banana?

Köhler (1925) hung a banana from the ceiling in a room that had a box placed off to one side. The banana was too high for Sultan to grab by reaching or jumping. When Sultan first entered the room, he paced restlessly for about five minutes. Then he seized the box, moved it toward the banana, climbed onto the box, and jumped at and seized the banana. On his second try, Sultan quickly moved the box directly beneath the banana and jumped up to get it.

Köhler then made the problem more difficult by raising the height of the banana but provided several boxes that could be stacked. Again, Sultan solved the problem by dragging the boxes underneath the banana, stacking them, climbing to the top, and snatching the banana.

What intrigued Köhler about Sultan's problem-solving behavior was that it seemed to differ greatly from the random trial-and-error behavior of

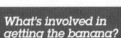

What's involved in getting the banana?

Thorndike's cats. Before Sultan arrived at a solution, he might pace about, sit quietly, or vainly grasp at the out-of-reach banana. Then, all of a sudden, he seemed to hit on the solution and immediately executed a complicated set of behaviors, such as stacking boxes, to get the banana. Köhler believed that Sultan's sudden solution to a problem was an example of insight, a mental process quite different from what Thorndike had observed in the random trial-and-error learning of cats.

Köhler was careful to point out many differences between chimp and human insight. One major difference is that humans can think through the problem with the aid of complex language, while chimps are limited to a more basic language composed of gestures and sounds.

Critics of Köhler's insight studies pointed out that he did not explain how chimps solved problems; rather, he simply described the process. Köhler replied that his studies on insight were more a way to study problem solving than an explanation of what was happening in the chimp's head. The significance of Köhler's work was that it represented a method for studying learning that was different from either classical conditioning or random trial-and-error learning.

Köhler's study of insightful problem solving, Bandura's theory of observational learning, and Tolman's idea of cognitive maps represent three kinds of cognitive learning. An underlying idea that runs through all kinds of learning is that animals and humans learn some things easier than others. This idea brings up an important biological factor.

Biological Factors in Learning

In discussing an organism's capacity for classical, operant, or cognitive learning, we must also consider **biological factors**, *which are innate tendencies that may either facilitate or inhibit certain kinds of learning.* For example, psychologists have tried many times to teach chimpanzees to speak like humans, but all such attempts have failed (Hayes & Hayes, 1951). One reason is the biological restraints imposed by the structure of the chimps' vocal apparatus and the organization of their brain. **Biological restraint** *refers to the limits placed on learning by the structure of the organism's body and brain.* Because of biological restraints resulting from the structure of the human body, we find it impossible to learn to fly like birds. Just as biological factors can inhibit learning, they can also facilitate learning.

Prepared Learning

Why do rats more easily learn by taste than by sight?

After a single taste of a substance that causes nausea, a rat learns to avoid that substance in the future. Learning that involves taste/smell occurs quickly, because a rat's chemical senses have evolved into a complex system for gathering information about its environment. In comparison to its taste/smell system, a rat's visual system is relatively poor. As a result, a rat acquires learned taste aversion more easily if the stimulus is associated with taste/smell than if it is associated with visual cues. A rat's capacity to learn quickly and efficiently with the sense of taste/smell is an example of **prepared learning,** *which is the innate tendency of animals to be equipped to recognize, attend to, and store certain cues over others.* Here's another interesting example of prepared learning.

Why do newly born goslings follow almost any object?

Goslings, chickens, and ducks have inherited tendencies to follow a moving object that they encounter soon after birth. This tendency to follow is called imprinting. **Imprinting** *refers to a set of inherited responses that are elicited by certain stimuli in a newborn animal's environment.* Through imprinting, a young chick, duck, or gosling usually establishes social attachments to members of its species. However, these animals will also imprint on other moving stimuli, such as a human or a basketball.

According to James Gould and Peter Marler (1987), a rat's learned taste aversion to taste/smell cues and a chick's imprinting to a moving stimulus are more easily learned because animals are preprogrammed or prepared for learning. Another example of prepared learning is the fact that a chickadee, with its tiny bird brain, can remember the locations of hundreds of hidden seeds, while humans can't seem to remember more than a dozen. All these examples indicate that prepared learning, which develops through natural selection, facilitates learning. As you will see in Module 16, prepared learning may also occur in humans, as shown by our capacity to acquire language.

Young geese are innately prepared to follow moving objects. Here they follow the famous naturalist Konrad Lorenz.

1. A kind of learning that involves mental processes, such as attention and memory, and that may not require any external rewards or the performance of any observable behaviors is referred to as _____.

2. Tolman studied the behavior of rats that were allowed to explore a maze without any reward given. When food was present, rats quickly learned to select the next shortest path if a previously taken path was blocked. Tolman said the rats had developed a mental representation of the layout of their environment, which he called a _____.

3. Although an organism may learn a behavior through observation or exploration, the organism may not immediately demonstrate or perform the newly learned behavior. This phenomenon is known as the _____ distinction.

4. According to Bandura, one form of cognitive learning that develops through watching and that does not require the observer to perform any observable behavior or receive a reinforcer is called _____ learning.

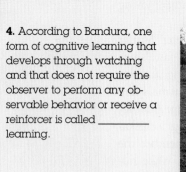

5. Bandura's theory of observational learning involves four mental processes. The observer must pay (a)_____ to what the model says or does. The observer must then code the information and be able to retrieve it from (b)_____ to use it at a later time. The observer must be able to use the coded information to guide his or her (c)_____ in performing and imitating the model's behavior. Finally, the observer must be (d)_____ to perform the behavior, which involves some reason, reinforcement, or incentive.

6. In Köhler's study of problem solving in chimps, he identified a mental process marked by the sudden occurrence of a solution, which he termed _____.

7. Köhler's study of insightful problem solving, Bandura's theory of observational learning, and Tolman's idea of cognitive maps represent three kinds of _____ learning.

8. Learning may be either facilitated or inhibited by the structure of the organism's brain and body, which is referred to as (a)_____. When learning is inhibited by biological factors, it is called (b)_____.

9. The innate tendency of animals to be equipped to recognize, attend to, and store certain cues over others is referred to as (a)_____. An example of this tendency is observed in young geese who are preprogrammed to follow objects immediately after birth. This tendency in newborn birds is called (b)_____.

Answers: 1. cognitive learning; 2. cognitive map; 3. learning-performance; 4. observational; 5. (a) attention, (b) memory, (c) motor control, (d) motivated; 6. insight; 7. cognitive; 8. (a) biological factors, (b) biological restraint; 9. (a) prepared learning, (b) imprinting.

Eastern Teacher, Western Researcher

How do you teach a 3-year-old to play a violin?

In the 1940s, Japanese violinist and teacher Shinichi Suzuki developed a remarkably successful method for teaching violin to very young children. Called the *Suzuki method*, it was brought to the United States in the mid-1960s and has generated incredible enthusiasm among children, parents, and music teachers ever since. One knowledgeable music writer has called the Suzuki method one of the most important innovations in teaching strings in the last half of the 20th century (Lamb, 1990).

The basic principles of the Suzuki method closely follow the four mental processes proposed—decades later—by Bandura. It is interesting to note that Suzuki developed his principles from actually working with and teaching young children and that Bandura arrived at his four mental processes from psychological research.

Comparing Learning Principles: Teacher Suzuki and Researcher Bandura

1 Attention. *Bandura states that the observer must pay attention to what the model says.* Similarly, Suzuki advises parents to teach violin information only when the child is actually looking at and watching the parent. Parents are told to stop teaching and wait if the child rolls on the floor, jumps up and down, walks backward, or talks about unrelated things.

The recommended age for starting a child with the Suzuki method is 3 for girls and 4 for boys. Parents are cautioned, however, that the attention span of the 3- to 4-year-old child is extremely limited, usually from 30 seconds to at most several minutes at a time.

2 Memory. *Bandura says that the observer must code the information in a way that it can be retrieved and used later.* Similarly, Suzuki has parents present information in ways that a young child can code. Because a 3- to 4-year-old child does not have fully developed verbal skills, little time is spent giving verbal instructions. Instead, the child is given violin information through games and exercises. For example, children are taught how to hold the violin, use the bow, and press the strings by first playing games with their hands. Children are taught how to read music (notes) only when they have reached a certain stage of technical skill at playing the violin.

3 Motor control. *Bandura says the observer must be able to use the information to guide his or her own actions and thus imitate the model's behavior.* Similarly, Suzuki suggests that children start at the earliest age that they can physically perform the required movements and imitate their parents and teachers. The reason that girls start earlier than boys is that girls physically mature earlier. As you have probably guessed, 3- and 4-year-olds start with miniature violins and move up to bigger ones as they develop physically and technically.

4 Motivation. *Bandura says that the observer must have some reason, reinforcement, or incentive to perform the model's behaviors.* Similarly, Suzuki emphasizes that the most important role of the parent is to constantly reward and reinforce the child for observing and "doing what Mommy or Daddy is doing." Suzuki recommends several ways to keep motivation high in young children: be an active and interested model for the child, play violin games that are fun for the child, avoid games or lessons that involve competition, and *never* push the child beyond the level that he or she is capable of reaching (Slone, 1985).

As you can judge, the basic principles of the Suzuki method are quite similar to Bandura's four mental processes. Parents and teachers who have used the Suzuki method report great success (Lamb, 1990).

APPLYING/ EXPLORING: APPLICATIONS OF OPERANT CONDITIONING

At the beginning of Chapter 1, we discussed the case of 5-year-old Patrick, who was diagnosed as being autistic. As you may remember, autistic children have mental retardation that ranges from extreme to moderate. Autistic children may not like to be held, rarely make eye contact or any sounds, have poorly developed language skills, do not play with their peers, and often perform unusual repetitive behaviors, such as rocking back and forth for long periods of time.

The cause of autism is unknown, but mental health experts do know that, without treatment, Patrick and others like him will probably continue to be unresponsive and uncommunicative and will remain severely retarded for the rest of their lives.

Using Behavior Modification

What is behavior mod?

Since the early 1970s, Ivar Lovaas of the University of California at Los Angeles has treated autistic children using a method called **behavior modification** or, more colloquially, "behavior mod." His procedures are based on operant conditioning principles. Using a behavior modification program developed by Lovaas, specially trained therapists and parents worked with 19 autistic children, all under 4 years old, on a one-to-one basis for 40 hours each week, every week, for two years. Lovaas reasoned that the earlier the training was begun, the longer it lasted, and the more intense it was, the

Behavior modification programs have been successfully used in classroom settings.

better the chance that the children would learn appropriate behavior patterns.

We'll give you a specific example to show how closely Lovaas's training program follows the principles of operant conditioning (adapted from Lovaas, 1981).

The Program

As you can see in the example on the left, the parent or therapist literally follows the principles of operant conditioning: *selecting* a specific target behavior, *shaping* the behavior, and using positive *rein-*

Dr. Lovaas's Training Program

Goal. Training the child to make eye contact. The *target behavior* is getting the child to make eye contact following the command, "Look at me."

Step 1. Have the child sit in a chair facing you. Give the command "Look at me" every five to ten seconds. When the child makes a correct response of looking at you, say "Good looking," and simultaneously reward the child with food.

Step 2. Continue until the child repeatedly follows the command "Look at me." Then gradually increase the duration of the child's eye contact from one second to periods of two to three seconds.

---

forcers of praise and food, which are given *immediately* after the child *emits* the desired behavior.

Using this intensive behavior modification program, the therapists and parents attempted to train the 19 autistic children to make eye contact; to stop their incessant rocking; to respond to verbal requests, such as "Wash your hands"; and gradually to play with toys, interact with peers, speak, and engage in preschool tasks such as reading and writing.

Results

After two years in this special program, some of the autistic children were able to enter and successfully complete first grade in public school. To avoid any possible biases, neither the school administrators nor the individual teachers were told that any of the children were autistic. Of the 19 autistic children, 9 (47%) achieved normal intellectual and educational functioning as shown by their normal-range IQ scores and successful performances in the first grade. None of these 9 children was recognized by teachers as being autistic.

However, even with such intensive training, 8 (40%) of the children remained mildly retarded, and 2 (10%) remained profoundly retarded and were assigned to classes for retarded children. In comparison, in a control group of autistic children who received only minimal treatment, only 2% achieved normal intellectual and educational functioning, while 45% remained mildly retarded and 53% remained severely retarded.

Lovaas (1987) concluded that without intensive behavioral modification treatment, autistic children will continue to show severe behavioral deficits.

In addition to behavioral modification, other approaches use the ideas of operant conditioning to change people's physiological responses and behaviors.

Biofeedback

In some cases, therapy for back pain, headache, high blood pressure, or stomach distress may include **biofeedback**, *which is a process of learning to control (increase or decrease) some physiological response, such as muscle activity or temperature.*

How do I get rid of muscle tension?
Biofeedback may be used to help treat recurring headaches, some of which are caused by muscle tension. Through video or audio (bio)feedback, a person is made aware of the muscle tension in the forehead. For example, attached to this client's forehead are small sensors that detect activity in the large muscle that stretches across the forehead. She is trying to relax her forehead muscle by imagining relaxing scenes, thinking relaxing thoughts, or actually tensing and relaxing the muscle itself. The *target behavior* is a de-

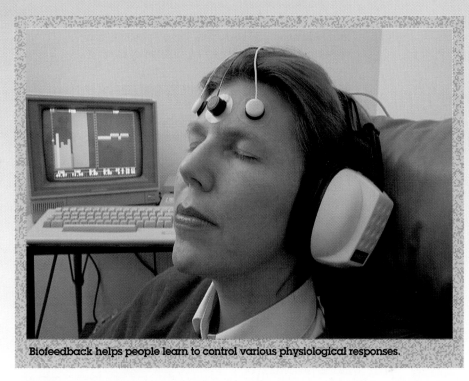
Biofeedback helps people learn to control various physiological responses.

crease in the forehead's muscle tension. To reach this target behavior, the client practices or *shapes* his own physiological responses. A decrease in muscle tension is signaled by a decrease in an audio signal, which acts as a *reinforcer.* After a number of these sessions, the client learns to decrease muscle tension. As you can see, biofeedback is based on the principles of operant conditioning. Biofeedback is most often used in conjunction with other forms of medical treatment or psychotherapy.

An Effective Punishment: Time Out

Although punishment can decrease the occurrence of undesirable behaviors, a poorly chosen punishment may exaggerate a behavioral problem. For example, spanking is not too effective in controlling undesirable aggression in children because the punishment itself provides a model of aggressive behavior that the child may later imitate.

How can a parent discipline an aggressive child?
An effective form of punishment for controlling undesirable and aggressive behaviors in children is called time out. **Time out** *is a procedure that decreases undesirable behaviors by removing all reinforcements.* During time out, the child stays in a room, usually alone, without any games, books, or other amusements that could serve as rewards. Time out, which is a mild punishment, is a form of extinction because it eliminates any reinforcement of an unwanted behavior (Brantner & Doherty, 1983). Experts say that time out is most effective when combined with teaching the child alternative desired behaviors.

You will find many other applications of operant conditioning in later chapters. For example, in Chapter 9 we'll discuss controlling weight; in Chapter 14, reducing stress; and in Chapter 16, treating phobias.

Summary/Self-Test

OPERANT CONDITIONING

1. A kind of learning in which the consequences that follow some behavior increase or decrease the likelihood of that behavior occurring again is called _____.

2. To explain how random trial-and-error behaviors of cats became goal-directed behaviors, Thorndike formulated the _____, which says that behaviors are strengthened by positive consequences and weakened by negative consequences.

3. Skinner used the term *operant conditioning* to describe how organisms _____ on their environments to obtain rewards. He believed that Pavlov's conditioning, which involves physiological reflexes, is not very useful in understanding other forms of learning.

4. If you compare classical and operant conditioning, you will find the following differences. In classical conditioning, the response is an involuntary (a)_____ that is elicited by the (b)_____. In operant conditioning the response is a voluntary (c)_____ that is performed or (d)_____ by the organism. In classical conditioning, the unconditioned stimulus is presented at the beginning of a trial and elicits the (e)_____. In operant conditioning, the organism emits a behavior that is immediately followed by a (f)_____.

5. Suppose you wished to operantly condition your dog, Bingo, to sit up. The procedure would be as follows. You would give Bingo a treat, which is called a (a)_____, after he emits a desired behavior. Because it is unlikely that Bingo will initially sit up, you will use a procedure called (b)_____, which is a process of reinforcing those behaviors that lead up to or approximate the final desired behavior—sitting up. Immediately after Bingo emitted a desired behavior, you would give him a (c)_____.

6. The essence of operant conditioning can be summed up as follows: the reinforcer or consequence is (a)_____ on the organism (b)_____ some behavior.

■ *How would you operantly condition a rude friend to be more likeable?*

A CLOSER LOOK AT REINFORCERS

7. In operant conditioning, the term *consequences* refers to what happens after the occurrence of a behavior. If a consequence increases the likelihood of a behavior occurring again, it is called a (a)_____. If a consequence decreases the likelihood of a behavior occurring again, it is called a (b)_____.

8. If the occurrence of some response is increased because it is followed by a pleasant stimulus, the pleasant stimulus is called a (a)_____. If the occurrence of some response is increased because it is followed either by the removal of an unpleasant stimulus or by avoiding the stimulus, the unpleasant stimulus or the avoidance of the stimulus is called a (b)_____. Both positive and negative reinforcements (c)_____ the frequency of the response they follow. In contrast, punishment is a consequence that (d)_____ the likelihood of a behavior occurring again.

■ *Using operant conditioning terms, how would you explain the behavior of someone who goes to the dentist for regular teeth cleaning and checkups?*

SCHEDULES OF REINFORCEMENT

9. The stimuli of food, water, and sex, which are innately satisfying and require no learning to become pleasurable, are called (a)_____. The stimuli of praise, money, and hugs have acquired their reinforcing properties through experience; these stimuli are called (b)_____.

10. If you were reinforced every time you performed a good deed, you would be on a (a)_____ schedule. This schedule is often used at the beginning of operant conditioning because it results in a rapid rate of learning. If your good deeds were not reinforced every time, you would be on a (b)_____ schedule. This schedule is more effective in maintaining the target behavior in the long run. There are four kinds of partial reinforcement schedules.

■ *How would you explain the schedules of reinforcement for your following behaviors: eating, studying, going to the movies, dating?*

OTHER CONDITIONING TERMS

11. If an organism emits the same response to similar stimuli, it is called (a)_____. If a response is emitted in the presence of a reinforced stimulus but not in the presence of unreinforced stimuli, it is called (b)_____. If an organism is no longer reinforced, it will stop emitting this behavior, which is an example of (c)_____. However, even without being reinforced, an organism may perform the behavior, which is an example of (d)_____.

■ *The first time you visit your 2-year-old niece, she takes one look at you and starts to cry. What happened?*

COGNITIVE LEARNING

12. The kind of learning that involves mental processes, such as attention and memory, and may not involve any external rewards or require the person to perform any observable behaviors is called (a) _____. According to Tolman, rats developed a mental representation of the layout of their environment, which he called a (b)_____.

13. Bandura studied a form of cognitive learning that develops through observation and does not require the observer to perform any observable behavior or receive a reinforcer: this is called (a)_____. Bandura theorized that four processes—attention, memory, motor control, and motivation—are necessary for observational learning to take place. If an observer learns a behavior through observation but does not immediately perform the behavior, this is an example of the (b)_____ distinction.

14. During his studies of problem solving in chimpanzees, Köhler used the term _____ to describe a mental process marked by the sudden occurrence of a solution.

■ *Why did psychologists get interested in cognitive learning?*

BIOLOGICAL FACTORS IN LEARNING

15. The innate tendencies that may either facilitate or inhibit an organism's capacity to learn are called (a)_____. The limits placed on learning by the inherited structure of an organism's body and brain is referred to as (b)_____. On the other hand, the facilitation of learning resulting from the innate tendency of organisms to be equipped to recognize, attend to, and store certain cues over others is referred to as (c)_____. The innate tendency of newborn birds to follow a moving object that they encounter soon after birth is called (d)_____.

■ *No matter how much you train, your dog can always run longer and faster. Why is that?*

CULTURAL DIVERSITY: EASTERN TEACHER AND WESTERN RESEARCHER

16. Bandura's theories of observational learning can be seen at work in a system for teaching children to play the violin, called the _____.

■ *Why do the same principles of learning work in very different cultures?*

APPLYING/EXPLORING: APPLICATIONS OF OPERANT CONDITIONING

17. Using principles of operant conditioning to change human behavior is referred to as (a)_____. Using these same principles to help individuals learn to control (increase or decrease) some physiological response, such as muscle activity or temperature, is called (b)_____. An effective form of punishment for controlling undesirable or aggressive behaviors in children is called (c)_____, which is a procedure that decreases undesirable behaviors by removing all reinforcements.

■ *If you were getting a lot of tension headaches, how could behavior modification or biofeedback help you?*

Answers: 1. operant conditioning; 2. law of effect; 3. operate; 4. (a) reflex, (b) unconditioned stimulus, (c) behavior, (d) emitted, (e) unconditioned response; 5. (a) reinforcer, (b) shaping, (c) reinforcer; 6. (a) dependent, (b) emitting; 7. (a) reinforcer, (b) punishment; 8. (a) positive reinforcer, (b) negative reinforcer, (c) increase, (d) decreases; 9. (a) primary reinforcers, (b) secondary reinforcers; 10. (a) continuous reinforcement, (b) partial reinforcement; 11. (a) generalization, (b) discrimination, (c) extinction, (d) spontaneous recovery; 12. (a) cognitive learning, (b) cognitive map; 13. (a) observational learning, (b) learning-performance; 14. insight; 15. (a) biological factors, (b) biological restraint, (c) prepared learning, (d) imprinting; 16. Suzuki method; 17. (a) behavior modification, (b) biofeedback, (c) time out.

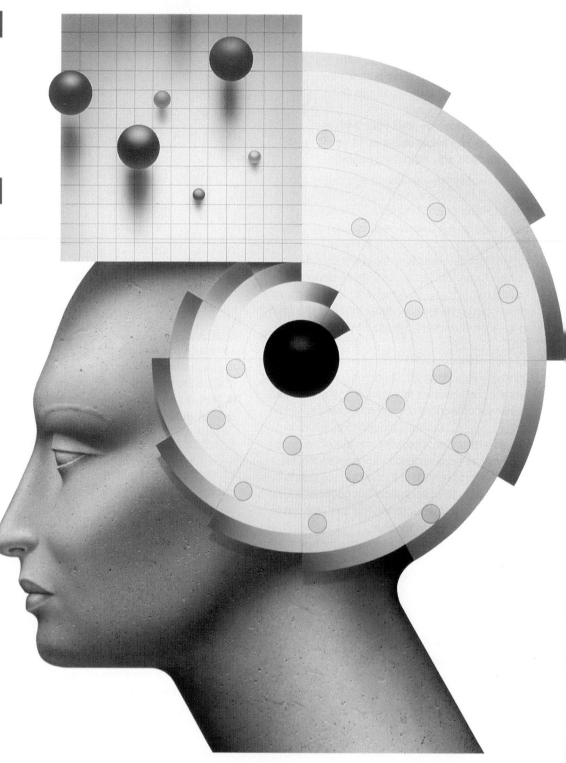

Chapter *Seven*
MEMORY

MODULE 13
KINDS OF MEMORY

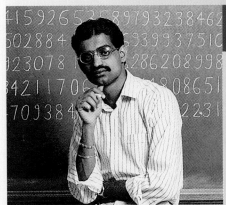

Could anyone memorize 30,000 numbers?

In 1981 Rajan Mahadevan attended the International Congress on Yoga and Meditation and recited, from memory, the first 10,000 digits of pi, the mathematical symbol for the ratio between the diameter and the circumference of a circle. Although many of us know pi as 3.14, this is a rounded off version of a number that actually goes on forever with no known pattern.

A year later, Rajan again stood before a packed house and recited the first 10,000 digits of pi. Then, after pausing to have a soda, he continued. He recited 20,000 digits, 25,000 digits, 30,000 digits—and did not err until the 31,812th digit. This feat took 3 hours and 44 minutes and earned him a place in the *Guinness Book of World Records*.

Rajan did not make an error until he reached the 31,812th digit.

After his record-setting memory performance, Rajan left his native India and, at age 23, entered Kansas State University. There he encountered Professor Charles Thompson, who has made the study of memory his specialty.

When Thompson gave Rajan simple memory tests, such as recalling a string of random numbers, Rajan was able to repeat a string of 50 numbers after a single hearing (most of us can repeat an average of 10 random numbers). Within a few months, Thompson applied for a grant to study the workings of Rajan's memory. It turns out that Rajan is one of the half-dozen people in the world known to have such gargantuan memory powers.

Despite Rajan's unbelievable ability to memorize numbers, he seems to be worse than average at recalling faces, and he constantly forgets where he put his keys. (adapted from the *Los Angeles Times,* July 12, 1989)

When psychologists study Rajan's extraordinary ability to recall long strings of numbers, they are studying **memory**, *the ability to retain information over time through the processes of encoding, storing, and retrieving.* As Rajan memorizes a string of numbers, he is using three processes:

1 *Encoding.* How Rajan places new information into memory is called *encoding.* There are numerous ways to encode information, such as making associations between new and already learned material. For instance, Rajan encodes the number 111 by associating it with Admiral Nelson, who had one eye, one arm, and one leg.

2 *Storing.* Once information is encoded into memory, it can be *stored* in various ways. As we have seen, one way that Rajan stores information is by constantly making associations between new and old information.

3 *Retrieving.* After information is both encoded and stored, Rajan wants to remember or *retrieve* such information at a later date. One way that Rajan retrieves information is by recalling a string of associations.

What's Coming

In this module, we'll look at the characteristics of three kinds of memory—sensory, short term, and long term—and how we encode, store, and retrieve information. In the next module, we'll examine how memory is organized, why we forget, and the biological bases for memory.

Let's begin by defining the basic processes of memory.

Three Kinds of Memory

We often talk about memory as though it were a single thing. In fact, memory is a complicated process that is usually divided into three main types: sensory, short term, and long term. To illustrate these three types of memory, let's examine what happens as you hear a song.

Sensory Memory

If you were to walk through a fair on a summer's day, you would be surrounded by thousands of wondrous sounds, sights, and smells, many of which would reach your sensory memory. **Sensory memory** *refers to an initial process that holds environmental information in its "raw" form for a brief period of time, from an instant to several seconds.*

For example, suppose there is a jazz group playing at the fair. When the sounds from the saxophone first reach your ears, they are held in sensory memory for a second or two. During that brief time, you are able to recognize the stimuli as sounds and decide whether to pay attention to them.

If you do not pay attention to the raw information in sensory memory, it automatically disappears without a trace. However, if you do pay attention, the information is transferred into a longer-lasting memory called short-term memory.

Short-Term Memory

Of the thousands upon thousands of bits of visual and auditory information that reach your eyes and ears, only a relatively small percentage last beyond the few seconds of sensory memory. However, if you attend to information in sensory memory, it is automatically transferred into short-term memory. **Short-term memory**, *also called working memory, has a limited capacity— seven to eight items—and a short duration— 2 to 30 seconds—which can be lengthened if you rehearse or work on the information.* For instance, if you attend to the saxophone sounds in sensory memory, they will be transferred into short-term memory, where they will remain for about 30 seconds if you do not attend further. If you think about the song or try to memorize the tune, it will remain for a longer period of time. However, the song will disappear after this relatively short time unless it is transferred into permanent storage, called long-term memory.

Long-Term Memory

As you rehearse, think about, or study the information in short-term memory, that information will usually be transferred into long-term memory. **Long-term memory** *refers to the process of storing almost unlimited amounts of information over a long period of time.*

You store the melodies and words of your favorite songs, terms and concepts you need for exams, friends' faces from the past, and yesterday's conversations in your long-term memory. Theoretically, all the information in long-term memory is available for retrieval. From personal experience, however, you know that you cannot always retrieve everything you know; even simple things such as song titles, names of artists, or common words sometimes slip your mind. This gap in memory, which we will discuss in Module 14, is due to the fact that retrieving information from long-term memory involves a number of factors.

Now that you are familiar with the three kinds of memory, we will look at each one in more detail.

Sensory Memory: Recording

The man in the photo at the right is using drumsticks with miniature lights attached to their ends. Although he moves the drumsticks in an up and down motion, you see a continuous circle of light.

Iconic memory turns normally jerky movements of drumsticks into smooth circles of light.

How can you see a memory?

The reason that you see a continuous circle is that the many separate images of the drumsticks' positions are held briefly in your visual sensory memory, or iconic memory. **Iconic** (eye-CON-ick) **memory** *is the sensory memory process that holds visual information for about a quarter of a second.* Because many continuous but separate images are held briefly in iconic memory, you see the outline of a continuous circle rather than separate movements of the drumsticks.

Somewhat like the jerky movement of drumsticks, our eyes normally jerk back and forth about four times a second as they fixate on different points. Iconic memory makes our world appear stable and calm despite our eyes' darting movements.

How can you hear a memory?

Most of us have experienced auditory sensory memory, or echoic memory. **Echoic** (ee-KOO-ick) **memory** *is the sensory memory process that holds auditory information for one or two seconds.* Suppose you are busy taking notes and the professor asks you a question. You stop taking notes and ask, "Would you repeat the question?" As soon as you have said

How do you remember movement?

that, you realize that you can recall the exact words of the professor's question. You can remember these words because they are still in echoic memory, which may last as long as two seconds. Echoic memory also allows you to hold speech sounds long enough to identify the sounds as words (Norman, 1982).

You can think of sensory memory as having three functions:

1 Sensory memory prevents you from being overwhelmed by thousands and thousands of incoming stimuli. Unless you pay attention, all incoming information simply fades away in a second or two.

2 Sensory memory gives you the moment or two that you need to determine whether the incoming data should be processed further.

3 Visual sensory memory, or iconic memory, makes your visual world seem smooth and continuous despite frequent blinks and eye movements. Auditory sensory memory, or echoic memory, holds speech sounds long enough so you can recognize the sounds as words (Norman, 1982).

The moment that you pay attention to information in sensory memory, that information is automatically transferred into short-term memory.

What did you say?

Oh, yes. Now I remember.

Short-Term Memory: Working

Check the text to find out why most telephone numbers are only seven digits long.

Imagine looking up a telephone number for takeout pizza. After finding it, you repeat it as you dial the seven-digit number. After ordering your favorite pizza and hanging up, you realize that you have already forgotten the number. From this example, we can identify two features of short-term memory: limited duration and limited capacity.

Two Features of Short-Term Memory

Limited Duration. The telephone number that you look up and dial will remain in short-term memory for a brief time, usually from 2 to 30 seconds. After that, it will fade from memory. However, if you repeat the number to yourself, you can prolong its duration in short-term memory.

The experience of repeating the number, which is almost like hearing an inner voice, is called maintenance rehearsal. **Maintenance rehearsal** *is the intentional repeating of information so that it remains longer in short-term memory.* Maintenance rehearsal is a practical way of increasing the duration of short-term memory.

Although maintenance rehearsal can greatly extend the amount of time that information remains in short-term memory, such rehearsal does not necessarily increase the chances of recalling the information at a later date. That's the reason that no matter how often we repeat a telephone number to ourselves, we may not be able to recall it days later.

The capacity of short-term memory is about seven items or bits.

Limited Capacity. One reason telephone numbers world-wide are generally limited to seven digits is that the capacity of short-term memory is about seven items or bits. George Miller (1956) described this phenomenon in a well-known paper titled "The Magical Number Seven, Plus or Minus Two." Miller discovered that most people can hold only about seven bits (plus or minus two) in short-term memory.

We can verify the capacity of short-term memory with a **memory span test,** *which measures the total number of digits that one can repeat back in correct order after a single hearing.* When students take the memory span test in class, they make few errors when asked to repeat seven or eight digits, make some errors with a list of eight or nine digits, and make many errors when repeating a list that is longer than nine digits.

An efficient way to hold more items in short-term memory is through a process called chunking. **Chunking** *is combining separate items of information into a larger unit or chunk and then remembering chunks of information rather than individual items.* For example, to remember the 11 numbers of the long-distance phone number 1-800-555-1212, you could create four chunks—1, 800, 555, 1212—and remember the 11 numbers as four chunks. Chunking is a useful method of increasing the capacity of short-term memory.

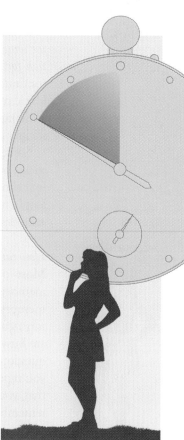

An item will remain in short-term memory for a brief time, usually from 2 to 30 seconds. After that, it will fade from memory.

How does he remember 11131217351802?

A Professional Chunker. One of the interesting things about Rajan's prodigious memory for numbers is his ability to chunk. For instance, in about two minutes he memorized 36 random numbers (in a block of 6 x 6) written on a blackboard. He was able to repeat the numbers forward and backward and to state those in any individual row, column, or diagonal.

When asked about his method for memorizing numbers, he replied that he automatically arranged the numbers into chunks and gave the chunks a name. For example, here's how he chunked the first 14 numbers: 11131217351802. He chunked 111 and named it "Nelson" because Admiral Nelson had one eye, one arm, and one leg; he chunked 312 and named it the "area code of Chicago"; he chunked 1735 and named it "29" because Ben Franklin was 29 in 1735; and he chunked 1802 as "plus 2" because John Adams occupied the White House in 1800. When Rajan wants to recall the numbers, he does so by remembering a string of associations: Nelson, area code of Chicago, Ben Franklin, and John Adams. As Rajan explains, he doesn't know why he makes particular associations; they just come to him.

Short-Term Memory Short-Circuited

Let's return to our pizza-ordering example for a moment. Imagine that you've just looked up the pizza shop's number and then someone asks you a question. Once you answer the question, no matter how simple it is, you're likely to find that when you go to dial, you've forgotten the pizza shop's number. This is an example of losing information in short-term memory because of interference. **Interference** *results when new information overwrites or interferes with the previous information in short-term memory.* According to some researchers, interference is the primary reason why information is forgotten from short-term memory (Zechmeister & Nyberg, 1982). Of course, one way to prevent interference is to use maintenance rehearsal (or to write down the information).

> Don't talk to me while I'm using my short-term memory.

What if there were only sensory and short-term memory?

If you were to spend two hours interviewing Norman on Monday, on Tuesday he would not remember your visit or your name. If you ask Norman what he did yesterday, he will remember almost nothing. Norman can carry on a simple conversation, but if he has to answer the phone in the middle of a conversation, when he returns he will not remember what you were talking about. He doesn't watch television too often because the commercial interruptions cause him to forget what the show is about. Norman's mother does all the cooking because if Norman puts something on the stove to cook, he usually forgets about it (adapted from Kaushall, Zetin, & Squire, 1982).

When he was 22, Norman had a one in a million accident. A fencing sword entered his nose, penetrated his brain, and destroyed an important brain area (part of the thalamus) involved in memory. Since that day, Norman has lost much of his ability to store permanent memories—that is, to transfer information from short-term into long-term memory. Having only short-term memory has tragic consequences for Norman. He cannot make new friends, start a new relationship, move to a different place, or begin a new job, since he remembers most things for only about 20 to 30 seconds, the duration of his short-term memory. Without the ability to add to his long-term memory, Norman's life has become an endless series of unconnected events.

We'll return to Norman's memory problems a little later. For now, let's examine how information is transferred into long-term memory.

An injury to the brain destroyed Norman's ability to store events in long-term memory.

Long-Term Memory: Storing

As you have just seen, when Norman lost an area of his brain, he also lost most of his ability to transfer information into long-term memory. Long-term memory stores enormous quantities of information for long periods of time.

To illustrate the process of transferring information into long-term memory, imagine strolling through the park on a summer's day. Around you are children yelling, dogs barking, jugglers juggling, and people talking. Among all these thousands of incoming auditory and visual stimuli are the notes of a familiar song. Suddenly, you pay attention to that particular auditory information—familiar notes. We'll trace the path these notes take to reach your long-term memory.

Steps in the Memory Process

1 *Sensory memory.* For a very brief period environmental information is held in sensory memory: iconic memory lasts about 1/4 second; echoic memory lasts 1–2 seconds. If you *do not pay attention* to the information in sensory memory, it disappears forever. If you *do pay attention,* such as by focusing on the familiar notes, that information is automatically transferred to short-term memory.

2 *Attention.* This is the process for *controlling* the transfer of information from sensory memory to short-term memory.

3 *Short-term memory.* Once information is in short-term memory, you have time for *further analysis.* However, if you do not pay attention, think about, or rehearse the song any further, the unrehearsed material will disappear from short-term memory in 2–30 seconds. If you further rehearse the material, such as by humming, singing along, or talking about the song and forming associations, information in short-term memory will be transferred or *encoded* into long-term memory.

4 *Encoding.* Encoding *is the process that controls the transfer of information from short-term memory into long-term memory.* Encoding may involve deliberate effort, such as rehearsing, taking notes, or making associations between new and old information. Encoding may occur almost automatically, such as when something interests you. Because of your attention, interest, and thinking about this song, it may be encoded into long-term memory with little effort.

5 *Long-term memory.* Once information is placed or encoded in long-term memory, it may remain for your lifetime. Later, if you were to describe hearing the song to a friend, you would be retrieving the information from long-term memory and placing it back into short-term memory. This is an example of information being retrieved with little effort and almost automatically. In other cases (such as trying to remember who you were with when you first heard a particular song), you may have to search long and hard with deliberate effort to retrieve information from long-term memory. The fact that information is encoded in long-term memory does not guarantee that such information can always or easily be retrieved or remembered.

6 *Retrieving.* Retrieving *is the process for selecting information from long-term memory and transferring it back into short-term memory.* Retrieval may occur almost automatically or may require extensive searching. When we talk about remembering, we usually mean retrieving.

The last time I heard this song I was in New York

By knowing the difference between short-term and long-term memory and how information is transferred between them, we can explain a classic finding in memory research.

Primacy Versus Recency

If you tried to remember a list of items, would you best remember the first items, middle ones, or the last ones? The answer to this question provides a wonderful demonstration of the difference between short-term and long-term memory.

Will you remember the first or the last?
Please read and try to remember the following list of animals:

giraffe, bear, elephant, fly, deer, elk, parrot, gorilla, wolf, robin, snail, turtle, shark, ant, butterfly

Immediately after reading the list, write down (in any order) as many names as you can. As you recall names from the list, there will be a definite pattern to those that you remember. Let's look at this pattern.

giraffe, bear, elephant, fly, deer, elk, parrot, gorilla, wolf, robin, **snail, turtle, shark, ant, butterfly**

Primacy effect. In studies using lists like this one, subjects more easily recalled the *first* five or six items because subjects had more time to rehearse the first words that were presented. As a result of rehearsing, these first names were transferred to and stored in *long-term memory*, from which they were easily recalled. **The primacy effect** *refers to better recall of items at the beginning of a list.*

Subjects did not recall many items from the middle of the list because they did not have much time to rehearse them. When trying to remember items from the middle of the list, their attention and time was split between trying to remember the previous terms and trying to rehearse new ones. Less rehearsal meant that fewer middle names were stored in long-term memory; more interference meant that fewer names remained in short-term memory.

Recency effect. Subjects more easily recalled the *last* five or six items because they were still available in short-term memory and could be "read" off a mental list. **The recency effect** *refers to better recall of items at the end of a list.*

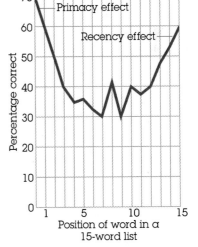

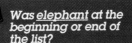
Was elephant at the beginning or end of the list?

You can see evidence for the *primacy-recency effect* in the accompanying graph. Subjects tended to remember best the first items (primacy effect) and the last items (recency effect) from a list of 15 words (adapted from Glanzer & Cunitz, 1966). The primacy-recency effect proved to be important in developing a model for how memory works, demonstrating the existence of the two different kinds of memory processes that we now call short-term and long-term memory (Atkinson & Shiffrin, 1968).

So far we have explained the differences between short- and long-term memory and the transfer of information between them. Now let's examine the kinds of information that are stored in long-term memory.

Long-Term Memory: Storing

Long-Term Memories: Three Kinds

One of the intriguing findings in patients with brain damage is that some memory functions are lost while others are spared. For example, brain damage may interfere with remembering new factual information when one reads a newspaper but not interfere with remembering motor skills when one plays tennis. From his work on patients with brain damage, researcher Larry Squire (1987) proposed that three kinds of information are stored in long-term memory.

### Episodic Information	### Semantic Information	### Procedural Information

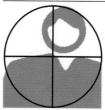

What did you have for breakfast? **Episodic** (ep-ih-SAW-dik) **information** *is knowledge about one's personal experiences.* It includes such events as getting a good grade, seeing a particular movie, eating your favorite breakfast, or recording activities in a diary. You can answer the question "What did you do today?" by recalling episodic information from long-term memory.

Since his injury, Norman has had great difficulty remembering personal events. He forgets that his mother has cooked his dinner and placed it in the refrigerator and instead goes out to eat. He cannot remember conversations or how to drive to a new location. In short, Norman has lost most of his ability to place episodic information into long-term memory.

Who was the last president of the United States to be assassinated? **Semantic** (sah-MANT-ic) **information** *is general knowledge, book learning, facts, and definitions of words.* When you answer exam questions such as "Who was the last president to be assassinated?" or "What is classical conditioning?" you are recalling semantic information from long-term memory.

Since his injury, Norman has had great difficulty remembering general information. For example, he recognizes the word *Watergate* but cannot remember that it signifies political intrigue and the eventual resignation of President Nixon. Norman's difficulty in acquiring general and factual knowledge since his injury indicates that he has lost most of the ability to transfer semantic information into long-term memory. (*Answer:* John F. Kennedy, November 22, 1963.)

Can you still play tennis after many years? **Procedural information** *is knowledge about performing motor skills or knowledge acquired through classical conditioning.* Even if you have not played tennis for years, you can pick up a racket and still remember how to hit a ball by recalling procedural information. An interesting feature of procedural information is that trying to explain how we perform some skill often interferes with our performance. See what happens when you try to explain how you tie your shoelaces while doing it. You'll become confused and resort to "letting your fingers" do the tying while keeping your mouth shut.

After his injury, Norman was tested on mirror drawing, a task that required him to look at an object in a mirror and draw it by reversing his hand movements. With practice over several days, Norman improved at mirror drawing. This improvement indicated that he was able to transfer procedural knowledge into long-term memory. Yet even though his mirror-drawing performance improved, Norman was never able to remember that he had done mirror drawing the previous day.

Through extensive testing, researchers discovered that Norman's brain injury had interfered primarily with transferring episodic and semantic information into long-term memory. However, as shown by his improvement at mirror drawing, Norman had retained the ability to transfer procedural information into long-term memory (Squire, 1987). Data from other patients with brain damage and memory problems support the idea of three kinds of information—episodic, semantic, and procedural—stored in long-term memory (Shimamura, 1989).

After the Concept/Glossary, we'll examine more closely how various kinds of information are transferred or encoded into long-term memory.

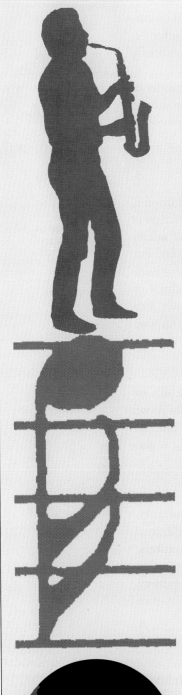

1. The initial step in memory is a process that holds visual and auditory information in its "raw" form for a very brief period of time, from an instant to several seconds; this process is called _____.

2. Memory that holds "raw" visual information for up to a quarter of a second is called (a)_____. Memory that holds "raw" auditory information for up to several seconds is called (b)_____. The process for controlling the transfer of information from sensory memory to the next memory process is (c)_____.

6. Three kinds of information are stored or encoded in long-term memory. One kind is knowledge that results from personal experiences, which is called (a) _____ information. A second kind of information that is encoded in long-term memory is general knowledge, facts, or definitions of words; this knowledge is called (b) _____ information. A third kind of information encoded in long-term memory is knowledge about how to perform motor skills or knowledge acquired through classical conditioning; this knowledge is called (c) _____ information.

3. The kind of memory that has a limited capacity of about seven items (plus or minus two) and a short duration (2 to 30 seconds) for unrehearsed information is called (a)_____. One way to increase this memory capacity is by combining separate pieces of information into larger units, which is called (b)_____. One way to increase the duration of this memory is by repeating the information, which is called (c)_____.

7. The better recall of items at the beginning of a list is called the (a)_____ effect. The better recall of items at the end of a list is called the (b)_____ effect.

8. The process for selecting information from long-term memory and transferring it back into short-term memory is _____.

4. The kind of memory that can store almost unlimited amounts of information over a long period of time is _____.

5. The process for controlling the transfer of information from short-term memory into long-term memory is called _____, which may be automatic or may involve deliberate effort.

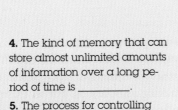

Answers: 1. sensory memory; 2. (a) iconic memory, (b) echoic memory, (c) attention; 3. (a) short-term memory, (b) chunking, (c) maintenance rehearsal; 4. long-term memory; 5. encoding; 6. (a) episodic, (b) semantic, (c) procedural; 7. (a) primacy, (b) recency; 8. retrieval.

Encoding: Transferring Information

We have described two people with very different memories: Norman, whose brain injury prevents the transfer or encoding of certain information (episodic and semantic) into long-term memory, and Rajan, who is incredibly skilled at encoding information (semantic, especially numbers) into long-term memory. Although we have briefly discussed encoding, this process is so important that it deserves a closer look.

As you may remember, *encoding* refers to the process for controlling the transfer of information from short-term memory into long-term memory. We can illustrate the two kinds of encoding processes—automatic and effortful—by discussing some of our everyday experiences.

Learning how to rollerskate is encoded automatically.

Automatic Encoding

Why did I remember our entire conversation?

One reason we so easily remember personal conversations is that such information is encoded automatically into long-term memory. **Automatic encoding** *is the transfer of information from short-term into long-term memory without any effort and usually without any awareness.* Automatic encoding occurs for a number of reasons. For example, our personal experiences and conversations, which are examples of *episodic information,* are usually interesting, hold our attention, and fit with hundreds of previous associations. Because personal experiences are encoded automatically into long-term memory, we can easily recall lengthy conversations, movie plots, clothes we bought, or food we ate.

Personal conversations are encoded automatically.

Why do I remember how to rollerskate after all these years?

Learning how to to perform various motor skills, such as rollerskating, riding a bike, or playing tennis, involves *procedural information,* which is encoded automatically. As we discussed earlier, Norman learned how to mirror draw even though he did not remember doing so, because mirror drawing is procedural information that is also encoded automatically.

Why do sports fans remember all those statistics?

You may know some avid sports fans who can remember an amazing number of sport-related facts, seemingly without effort. One reason we easily remember factual information (semantic information) such as sports statistics, stock market numbers, recipes, or prices of items in the supermarket is that it is personally interesting to us, has many previous associations, and thus is encoded automatically into long-term memory. On the other hand, encoding factual information from classes and textbooks often requires considerable effort. Let's see why.

Learning material from textbooks requires effortful encoding.

Effortful Encoding

Why did it take so long to learn about operant conditioning?

One reason it takes a relatively long time to learn unfamiliar or complicated material, which is *semantic information,* is that we lack interest, may not concentrate, or have difficulty making associations. For all these reasons, learning unfamiliar semantic information from lectures and textbooks involves time and hard work, which is part of effortful encoding. **Effortful encoding** *involves the transfer of information from short-term into long-term memory either by working hard to repeat or rehearse the information or by making associations between new and old information.* We'll examine several methods of effortful encoding that have proved to be effective and may be helpful in your studies.

Strategies of Effortful Encoding

Let's examine several encoding strategies and their effectiveness.

Maintenance Rehearsal

As you already know, a common strategy to keep information in short-term memory is to use *maintenance rehearsal,* which is simply repeating or rehearsing the information. This method, which "maintains" or keeps information alive in short-term memory, is primarily for increasing the duration of short-term memory. However, maintenance rehearsal is not very effective for encoding information into long-term memory, because it involves too little thinking about, visualizing, or making new associations with this information.

1113121735
1113121735
1113121735
1113121735
1113121735

Rajan's primary method of encoding is to use elaborative rehearsal.

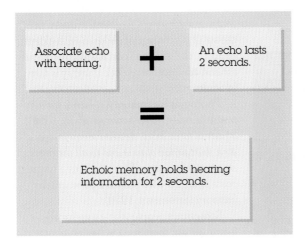

Associate echo with hearing.

+

An echo lasts 2 seconds.

=

Echoic memory holds hearing information for 2 seconds.

What's a good way to remember the definition of *echoic memory*?

Elaborative Rehearsal

A more effective way to encode information into long-term memory is a process called **elaborative rehearsal,** *which involves associating the new information with previous information that you already know.* The word *elaborative* refers to thinking about, elaborating on, or making new associations with the new, unfamiliar information and old, familiar information. For example, students who used elaborative rehearsal to remember a list of words (such as by associating words with cars) were significantly better at later recognizing the words than were students who just looked at the words (Fisk & Schneider, 1984). One reason elaborative rehearsal is more effective than maintenance rehearsal is that by "elaborating" you are actually thinking about, making associations with, and creating cues for the material that will help you remember it in the future.

When we examine Rajan's method of encoding random strings of numbers, we find that he makes great use of elaborative rehearsal. For example, he elaborates or creates an association between number 111 and "Nelson" (Admiral Nelson had one eye, one arm, and one leg), between the number 312 and "area code of Chicago," and between the number 1735 and "39" because Ben Franklin was 39 in 1735.

You can use elaborative rehearsal to encode the definition of *echoic memory.* You might notice that this phrase contains the word *echo,* which you can associate with hearing. Further, you could associate an echo with lasting two seconds. By making these two associations, you have our definition of echoic memory as holding hearing information for several seconds. Because of these associations you are more likely to encode the definition of echoic memory in a way that you can easily retrieve for a future exam.

Imagery

Besides making associations with words or numbers, you can make associations with images. ***Distinctive associations,*** particularly those made with visual images, can serve as good memory aids. Researchers Mark McDaniel and Gilles Einstein (1986) asked students to remember three words—*dog, bicycle,* and *street*—using either bizarre associations, such as "The dog rode the bicycle down the street," or common associations, such as "The dog chased the bicycle down the street." They found that bizarre associations made the words more distinctive and thus easier to remember. Researchers suggest that it is the distinctiveness of associations, rather than their bizarreness, that leads to better recall of information (Kroll, Schepler, & Angin, 1986). Because visual associations can improve encoding, we are using this strategy throughout this book.

So far we have explained the common strategies for encoding information into long-term memory. Now, we'll examine some special cases of encoding information.

APPLYING/ EXPLORING: UNUSUAL MEMORY ABILITIES

There are many stories—some true, some exaggerated—of people claiming to have special memory abilities. You already know about Rajan's supermemory and his feat of memorizing over 30,000 numbers. Let's look at some other interesting cases of unusual memory abilities.

Eidetic and Photographic Memory

Look at the picture below from Rudyard Kipling's *The Jungle Book* for a few minutes. Can you hold the details of this picture before your mind's eye for several minutes?

When you close your eyes, what do you see? This test was given to an 11-year-old girl. After the picture was removed, without hesitation she described the picture in great detail as follows:

Ground is dark greenish brown, then there's a mama and a little leopard and there's a native sitting against him. Then there's a pool with a crab coming out . . . with a fish in it, and I think there are turtles walking in front and a porcupine down near the right. There's a tree that separates a cow in half. The cow's brown and white, and there's something up in the tree—I can't see the bottom right-hand corner. There's a sun with a lot of rays on it near the top on the right . . . eight rays . . . the porcupine has a lot of bristles on it . . . the right is disappearing. I can still see that cow that's divided by the tree . . . Oh, there's a crocodile or alligator in the right-hand corner . . . It's very faint . . . It's gone. (Haber, 1980, p. 72)

What is unusual about her description is not only the amount of detail but the fact

Eight-year-old Jamil memorized the entire Koran.

that she seems to be examining a visual image of the drawing that lingers before her eyes. This image is not held in iconic memory (visual sensory memory) because it lasts longer than a quarter of a second. Research suggests that about 5% of children between the ages of 6 and 12 have this distinctive type of visual memory, called eidetic imagery. **Eidetic** (eye-DET-ick) **imagery** *is the ability to examine a picture or page for 10 to 30 seconds and then retain a detailed visual image of the material for several minutes.* In the small percentage of children with eidetic imagery, the ability almost always disappears around adolescence; eidetic imagery is rare in adults.

Photographic memory, *which is similar to eidetic imagery but occurs in adults, is the ability to form sharp, detailed visual images after a short period of time and recall the entire image at a later date.* There are only a few reports of adults who possess a photographic memory (Stromeyer, 1970).

Sometimes people with exceptional memories are mislabeled as having photographic memories. For example, 8-year-old Jamil Moghul memorized all 77,934 words of the Koran, the Moslem holy book. Jamil accomplished this feat by beginning at age 5 and studying five to six hours a day. Yet neither Jamil (77,934 words) nor Rajan (31,811 numbers) claims to have photographic memories. Rather, both have incredible abilities to encode information using elaborative rehearsal.

Special Memory Abilities of Savants

Unusual and startling memory abilities are found in some mentally retarded individuals, who are called savants. **Savants** (saw-VONTS) *are people who are usually severely to mildly mentally retarded but who have an unusual ability to remember, calculate, draw, or perform musically.* A savant might be able to quickly add an enormous string of numbers, calculate the day of the week for any date, or play a melody after hearing it only once. For example, Gloria can play and sing a song she has heard only once, can remember over a thousand songs, and can converse in a half-dozen languages. However, she does not know how much change she will get back when paying a quarter for something that costs a dime.

In the movie *Rain Man*, Dustin Hoffman played a character based on a real-life autistic savant who could outperform a pocket calculator. When asked, savants usually have no idea how they accomplish feats that far surpass the memory abilities of most "normal" individuals.

Although few of us can match the memories of savants, many of us have experienced the next kind of memory.

Flashbulb Memory—Revised

What were you doing when the space shuttle Challenger *exploded?*
Many individuals can answer this question in great detail, a phenomenon that has been called flashbulb memory. **Flashbulb memories** *are vivid recollections, usually in great detail, of dramatic or emotionally charged incidents* (Brown & Kulik, 1977). Flashbulb memories usually deal with events that are extremely surprising, are emotionally arousing, or have very important consequences.

For example, when people were questioned about what they were doing when they heard that President Reagan had been shot, 94% could recall the exact details even seven months later (Pillemer, 1984).

As you can see in the table below, the top five flashbulb memories of college students involved a car accident, a college roommate, high school graduation and prom, and a romantic experience, all of which are emotionally charged events (Rubin & Kozin, 1984).

Initially, flashbulb memories were claimed to represent a special kind of memory that was complete, accurate, vivid, and immune to forgetting (Brown & Kulik, 1977). Since then, several studies have investigated these claims and reported that flashbulb memories are subject to both inaccuracies and forgetting (Christianson, 1989; McCloskey, Wible, & Cohen, 1988; Neisser, 1991). These researchers conclude that flashbulb memories are not a separate, special kind of memory but result from "ordinary" memory processes.

Gloria can remember over 1,000 songs but cannot make change for a quarter.

Examples of Flashbulb Memories

Cues	Percent*
A car accident you were in or witnessed	85
When you first met your college roommate	82
The night of your high school graduation	81
The night of your senior prom (if you went or not)	78
An early romantic experience	77
A time you had to speak in front of an audience	72
When you got your college admissions letter	65
Your first date—the moment you met him/her	57
The day President Reagan was shot in Washington	52
The night President Nixon resigned	41
The first time you flew in an airplane	40
The moment you opened your SAT scores	33
Your 17th birthday	30
The day of the first space shuttle flight	24
The last time you ate a holiday dinner at home	23
Your first college class	21
When you heard that President Sadat of Egypt was shot	21
When you heard that the Pope had been shot	21
The first time your parents left you alone for some time	19
Your 13th birthday	12

*Percent of students in memory experiment who reported that events on experimenter's list were of "flashbulb" quality.

Summary/Self-Test

THREE KINDS OF MEMORY

1. The study of memory, which is the ability to retain information over time, includes three separate processes. The first process, which is placing information in memory, is called (a)_____. The second process, which is filing information in memory, is called (b)_____. The third process, which is commonly referred to as remembering, is called (c)_____.

2. Although we think of memory as being a single event, it is really a complex sequence that is separated into three different kinds of memory. The initial memory process that holds raw information for up to several seconds is called _____. During this time, you have the chance to identify or pay attention to new information. If you do not pay attention, the new information disappears in a second or two.

3. If you pay attention to information in sensory memory, this information is automatically transferred into a second kind of memory process, called _____ memory, which has a limited capacity and a short duration.

4. If you rehearse or think about information in short-term memory, that information will usually be transferred or encoded into the third, more permanent kind of memory process, called

_____.

■ *You see an ambulance speeding by and it reminds you of your father's heart attack and trip to the hospital. Can you explain this memory process?*

SENSORY MEMORY: RECORDING

5. Visual sensory memory, known as (a)_____ memory, lasts about a quarter of a second. Auditory memory, known as (b)_____ memory, may last as long as two seconds. Sensory memory has many functions, such as preventing you from being overwhelmed by too much incoming information and giving you time to identify the incoming data and pay attention to it.

■ *Why doesn't the world disappear for the short period of time when your eyes are completely closed during blinking?*

SHORT-TERM MEMORY: WORKING

6. If you pay attention to information in sensory memory, it is automatically transferred to short-term memory, which has two main characteristics. The first is that unrehearsed information will disappear after 2 to 30 seconds, indicating that short-term memory has a limited (a)_____. The second characteristic is that short-term memory can hold only about seven items (plus or minus two), indicating that short-term memory has a limited (b)_____. You can increase the length of time that information remains in short-term memory by intentionally repeating the information, which is called (c)_____. You can considerably increase the capacity of short-term memory by combining separate items of information into larger units, which is called (d)_____.

■ *Describe what your life would be like if you had only sensory and short-term memory.*

LONG-TERM MEMORY: STORING

7. Let's follow the progress of information from the time it enters sensory memory to its storage in long-term memory. For an instant to several seconds, incoming raw information is held in (a)_____. If you do not pay attention to this information, it disappears forever; if you pay attention, that information is automatically transferred to short-term memory. The transfer of information from sensory memory to short-term memory is controlled by the process of (b)_____.

8. If information in short-term memory is not (a)_____, it will disappear in 2–30 seconds. If you rehearse or think about information in short-term memory, it may be transferred into long-term memory. The transfer of information from short-term into long-term memory is controlled by a process called (b)_____. In some cases, information is transferred automatically; in other cases, this transfer process may require deliberate effort.

9. Once information is placed or encoded into long-term memory, it may remain for your lifetime. The process of selecting information from long-term memory and transferring it back into short-term memory is called _____. The fact that information has been encoded into long-term memory does not guarantee that such information can always or easily be remembered or retrieved at a later date.

10. One demonstration of the existence of and difference between short-term and long-term memory is observed in the order that subjects remember items from a multiple-item list. Subjects tend to have better recall of items at the beginning of a list; this tendency is called the (a)_____ effect and involves long-term memory. Subjects tend to have better recall of items at the end of the list; this tendency is called the (b)_____ effect and involves short-term memory. The order in which subjects recall items from a long list is called the (c)_____ effect.

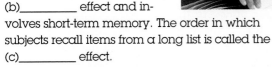

11. Evidence from patients with brain damage indicates the existence of three kinds of information stored in long-term memory. One kind of information includes knowledge about one's personal experiences, called (a)_____ information. A second kind of information is general knowledge, book learning, facts, and definitions of words, which is called (b)_____ information. A third kind of information stored in long-term memory is knowledge about performing motor skills or knowledge acquired through classical conditioning, which is called (c)_____ information.

■ *Your friend claims that all that information he learns the night before an exam is easy to recall because of the recency effect. What's your friend's problem?*

ENCODING: TRANSFERRING INFORMATION

12. There are two processes for transferring or encoding information into long-term memory. Most episodic and procedural information is trans-ferred from short-term into long-term memory without any effort, and usually without any awareness, through a process called (a)_____ encoding. Much of semantic information is transferred from short-term to long-term memory by deliberate attempts to repeat, rehearse, or make associations. Together, these deliberate attempts are referred to as (b)_____ encoding.

13. There are two kinds of effortful encoding that vary in their effectiveness. Encoding by simply repeating or rehearsing the information is called (a)_____. This method is not very effective for encoding information into long-term memory because it involves too little thinking about, visualizing, or making new associations with the information. Encoding by thinking about and associating new information with previous information is called (b)_____. Besides making associations with words or numbers, another method of elaborative rehearsal is to make associations with (c)_____. One reason that visual images enhance encoding is that they create distinctive associations.

■ *Why can your grandmother easily remember the prices of her favorite foods in the supermarket but can't remember her car's license number?*

APPLYING/EXPLORING: UNUSUAL MEMORY ABILITIES

14. The ability of certain children to examine a picture or page for 10–30 seconds and then retain a detailed visual image of the material for several minutes is called (a)_____ memory. In adults, the ability to form sharp, detailed visual images after a short period and recall the entire image at a later date is called (b)_____ memory. Some mentally retarded individuals have unusual and startling memory abilities; such individuals are called (c)_____. Memories that are vivid recollections, usually in great detail, of dramatic or emotionally charged incidents are called (d)_____.

■ *If you could have one unusual memory ability, which one would you choose and how would it make your life different?*

MODULE 14
REMEMBERING AND FORGETTING

What would you remember?

It was about nine at night when you entered the campus building, climbed one flight of stairs, and began walking down the long hallway. You had just finished your psychology paper and were going to slip it under the instructor's office door.

Everything happened very quickly.

From about the middle of the dimly lit hallway a man in a brown leather jacket jumped out from behind a half-opened door and ran at you. Instinctively, you threw out your hands and tried to ward off the on-coming threat. With a quick motion the man grabbed your white shoulder purse, but the strap was wrapped around your arm. The man pushed you down, and with a violent jerk he loosened the strap and got the purse.

The man rose and, for just an instant, your eyes met. He pointed at you with a menacing gesture and said, "Don't move or make a sound." Then he checked the hallway, stepped around you, and was gone. (adapted from Buckout, 1980)

A 12-second filmed sequence with a storyline similar to this one was shown on television. In the TV film, the assailant's face was on the screen for several seconds. Then the viewers were asked to watch a lineup of six men and then to call the TV station and identify which was the assailant. Of the more than 2,000 viewers who called in, only 200 identified the correct man; 1,800 selected the wrong one (Buckout, 1980).

Why did so many people identify the wrong man, even though his face appeared on the screen for several seconds? Before we answer this question, let's see how many details of the opening story you remember.

Without looking back, try to answer the following questions:

1. What color was the mugger's coat? _____

2. What color and type was the student's purse? _____

3. Besides the purse, what else was the student carrying? _____

4. The mugger's exact words were "Don't make a sound." *true or false?*

5. When thrown down, the student yelled out, "Stop!" *true or false?*

6. Of the 2,000 viewers who called in, only 200 identified the correct assailant. *true or false?*

What's Coming

In this module, we'll examine why you probably had more difficulty answering questions 1, 2, and 3 and less trouble answering questions 4, 5, and 6. We'll also explore how your memory is organized, why you forget, and ways to improve your memory.

Ways to Remember

Can you name these four men?
As you try to retrieve the names that go with these well-known faces from long-term memory, you are using a process called recall. **Recall** *is retrieving previously learned information without the aid of any external cues.* In this case, you must search your long-term memory to recall the names of these four actors. As a student, you use recall to retrieve information for essay exams.

Can you match these men with their names?
Chances are that even if you couldn't recall the names of these men, once we tell you that Bruce Willis, Kurt Russell, Arnold Schwarzenegger, and Sylvester Stallone are pictured, you'll be able to match their names and faces. As you do so, you are using a process called recognition. **Recognition** *is identifying information that you have previously learned.* In this case, you have only to recognize the names and faces (provided, of course, that you previously learned this information). As a student, you use recognition to decide which alternative is correct on multiple-choice tests.

Recall Versus Recognition

Our ability to recognize information is usually better than our ability to recall it, because during recognition we can use memory aids or cues. That's why tests of recall (fill-in or essay tests) are more difficult than tests of recognition (true-false, matching, or multiple-choice tests). The difference between recall and recognition also explains why answering questions 1, 2, and 3 from the "mugging" scene was more difficult than answering questions 4, 5, and 6. When witnesses pick out a person from a police lineup, their task is essentially one of recognition or identification.

The experiment described on the right is one example of research showing that recognition tests are easier than recall tests.

How were subjects able to organize

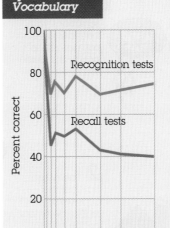

Experiment: Remembering Spanish Vocabulary

Years after people had completed a Spanish course, they were asked to either recall or recognize definitions of Spanish words. Their ability to remember is shown in this graph.

This line shows that subjects were able to correctly recognize or identify a relatively high percentage of Spanish words, even after 50 years.

This line indicates that when subjects were asked to recall a definition of a word, they performed significantly poorer than did subjects who were tested for recognition. Studies such as this show that subjects do perform much better on tests of recognition than on tests of recall (Bahrick, 1984).

Spanish vocabulary in their long-term memory so that they could recognize definitions 50 long years later? How did you organize the names and faces of film stars so that you could recall four famous actors? Psychologists study recognition and recall to find clues about how long-term memory is organized. We'll explore several possibilities.

How Memory Is Organized

Donald Norman was taking a shower in a motel room in Champaign, Illinois, when he suddenly remembered the name of the store in his hometown of San Diego where he could buy trays to hold the slides he used for talks (Norman, 1982). Because Norman is a cognitive psychologist, he was interested in following the sequence of his thinking, beginning with a shower in Illinois and ending in a department store in San Diego.

How do you keep track of all the information stored in memory?

What does taking a shower have to do with memory?

In a more general way, Norman was asking, "How is information organized in long-term memory?" We'll discuss two theories—network theory and schema theory—that suggest how memory may be organized.

Network Theory

Perhaps we store information in a vast spiderweb of interconnected ideas, a concept called network theory. **Network theory** *says that related ideas are stored in separate categories called nodes; connections or associations link the many thousands of nodes that form a gigantic interconnected network* (Anderson, 1985). It may help to think of nodes as cities on a map and the connections or associations between them as roads. Following this analogy, we store new ideas by building new roads between the cities. The thousands of cities (nodes) are interconnected by miles of roads (associations) to form a vast interconnected network. Just as you follow different roads to go from city to city, you follow different associative pathways to go from idea to idea (Schwartz & Reisberg, 1991). Let's see how Donald Norman used network theory to explain his process of remembering.

What's the name of that store?

Here's how Norman traced his own cognitive pathway that began with taking a shower in Champaign, Illinois, and ended with remembering the name of a particular store in San Diego, California. Norman's thoughts followed a chain of personal associations that led from idea to idea, node to node, through his memory network.

3 The smoke detectors had associations with batteries, which are needed to power the detectors.

5 The department store had associations with many items that he bought, including trays for his slides.

4 The batteries had associations with a certain store in San Diego where Norman bought batteries and other items.

2 The house had associations with smoke detectors on the ceilings of the rooms.

6 As Norman thought of buying slide trays, he remembered the store's name.

1 Norman's train of thought began with his remembering a party he had attended earlier at a friend's house.

Norman's train of thought seemed to jump haphazardly from idea to idea, node to node. That's because his thoughts followed paths created by his own personal associations, some of which may seem peculiar to us.

Node: Category and Hierarchy

In following Norman's associations from node to node, it is difficult to determine what exactly is in a node and how nodes are arranged. **Nodes** *are memory areas thought to contain related information organized around a specific topic or category.* For example, if you recall the characteristics of a canary, you do so by searching a category (canary node) that contains related information: can sing, is yellow. If we assume that nodes contain categories of information, we must still determine how these categories are arranged: alphabetically, historically, or according to some other system. According to network theory, some nodes are arranged in a certain order, or *hierarchy,* with concrete ideas at the bottom of the hierarchy and more abstract ideas near the top (Collins & Quillian, 1969). Let's examine the evidence that some nodes may be arranged in a hierarchy.

Does an ostrich have skin?

How do you search your memory to find the answer to this question? According to network theory, you search for a category that contains this information. To find information to answer the question "Does an ostrich have skin?" you begin by searching the lowest category in the hierarchy, which contains more specific information. Then you continue searching up the hierarchy, which becomes increasingly abstract, until you locate information about whether an ostrich has skin.

3 ANIMAL
has skin
can move around
eats
breathes

This category, labeled *animal,* contains information that is more abstract because it applies to all animals: has skin, can move around, eats, breathes. Here's our answer: Because an ostrich is an animal, it has skin.

2 BIRD
has wings
lays eggs
has feathers

You arrive at the second category (node) that is labeled *bird.* This category contains information that is more abstract because it applies in part to ostriches and in part to other birds: has wings, can fly, has feathers. This category (node) tells us nothing about skin, so we keep searching.

1 OSTRICH
long legs
can't fly
is tall

To answer the question "Does an ostrich have skin?" you start with a category or node that contains concrete information that applies only to an ostrich: long legs, can't fly, is tall. This category (node) tells you nothing about skin, so you keep searching.

According to network theory, you can decide the size of an ostrich very quickly because you need search only one category or node. It takes longer to decide whether an ostrich has skin because you must search three separate categories. The time difference required to recall more concrete information versus more abstract information provides evidence that some nodes are arranged in a hierarchy from concrete to abstract.

In other cases, such as recalling more personal or unusual associations, a hierarchical arrangement of categories appears too restrictive and inflexible. For example, information such as "I once rode an ostrich at the zoo" or "An ostrich egg is the size of 13 chicken eggs" may be stored in categories grouped around the ostrich node rather than arranged in a hierarchy. This regrouping of categories demonstrates one way in which cognitive psychologists continue to revise network theory.

One advantage of network theory is that it provides a useful model and starting point for understanding how memory is organized. We're going to compare the network model of memory with a very different model that is based on something called a schema.

How Memory Is Organized

Schemas

Why don't you bring your dog to class?

By the time you enter college you have spent hundreds of hours in various classrooms. Your concept of what's in a classroom and how to behave is called a schema. A **schema** *is a mental model of a concept, event, or object that is based on previous experience.* For example, a "classroom schema" includes information about what's in a classroom (chairs, desks, board, chalk) and how to behave (listen to lectures, take notes, ask questions). Cognitive psychologists use the term *schema* to refer primarily to information about concepts and objects. They use the term ***script*** to refer to a schema that involves events or actions. For instance, your "classroom script" includes events or actions such as taking notes, asking questions, and not taking your dog to class.

What good is a classroom schema?

The advantage of having a classroom schema is that you can enter almost any classroom and know how to behave by remembering or reconstructing the classroom schema (Bartlett, 1932). In addition, you can organize or file information in memory by adding knowledge to your classroom schema or any other schemas.

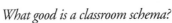

How would you behave in a classroom in Spain, Germany, or England?

As you can see, schemas have two functions:

1 You can recall previous information by reconstructing schemas (and scripts).

2 You can file and organize new information by fitting it into existing schemas (and scripts).

Networks Versus Schemas

Imagine that you went to a party last night and are now attempting to tell a friend what happened. Let's trace two ways of remembering the events, one based on network theory and the other on schema theory.

Network Theory

According to the network theory, memory might be compared to a videotape recording. New information, such as what happened at last night's party, is stored in a particular category (node), which is connected to related categories (friends, recreation, relaxation). If you want to retrieve information about last night's party, you search, find, and replay your mental videotape of last night's party. Your mental videotape of the party remains in long-term memory and can be replayed whenever you choose.

Schema Theory

According to schema theory, memory can be compared to memorizing and storing dozens of "movie scripts" that apply to a variety of situations. For example, because you already have a mental "movie script" or schema for a party, you don't need to mentally videotape everything that happens each time you go to a party. Instead, you need only fit new information into your existing party schema, which probably includes some combination of friends, strangers, music, laughter, and dancing. If you want to retrieve information about last night's party, you reconstruct it by combining your party schema with new information that was fitted in your schema.

According to schema theory, you don't recall exactly what happened at the party but rather reconstruct what happened. During this reconstruction, there is great potential for error from biases and expectations. That's why two people may attend the same party but have different memories of what happened.

Cognitive psychologists think that memories may be organized using some combination of ideas from network theory and schema theory.

Now that you have an idea of how information is organized and filed in long-term memory, let's look at how long memories last.

Lasting Memories

Long-term memory has two remarkable characteristics: it holds almost unlimited amounts of information, and it retains some information for a lifetime. For example, close your eyes for a moment and recall your earliest childhood memory. Researchers have found that our earliest memories are of events that typically occurred in the fourth year of life and are often visual (Kihlstrom & Harackiewicz, 1982). Depending on your current age, the event you remembered occurred 15, 20, 25, 30, or more years ago.

Forgetting Curves

More rigorous tests for how long memories last come from a variety of experiments in which forgetting curves are studied. **Forgetting curves** *measure the amount of previously learned information that subjects can recall or recognize across time.*

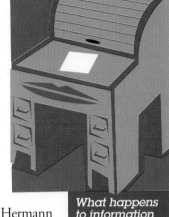

What happens to information we forget?

What good is nonsense?

L U D
Z I B
K O N
M U C
S A R

One of the earliest psychologists to study memory and forgetting was Hermann Ebbinghaus, who used himself as his only subject. He got around the fact that people have better memories for more familiar events by memorizing only three-letter nonsense syllables. He made up and wrote down hundreds of three-letter nonsense syllables on separate cards and arranged these cards into sets of varying length. To the ticking of a metronome, he turned over each card and read aloud each of the three syllables until he had read all the cards in the set. He used only rote memory, and he needed only one or two readings to memorize a set of 7 cards (containing 7 three-letter nonsense syllables) and about 45 readings to memorize a set of 24 cards (Ebbinghaus, 1885/1913).

As the forgetting curve on the left shows, Ebbinghaus was one of the first to demonstrate how quickly we learn and how soon we forget unfamiliar information.

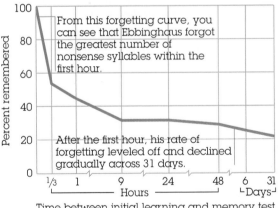

From this forgetting curve, you can see that Ebbinghaus forgot the greatest number of nonsense syllables within the first hour.

After the first hour, his rate of forgetting leveled off and declined gradually across 31 days.

Percent remembered

Time between initial learning and memory test

Can you still remember your high school classmates?

Compared with Ebbinghaus's nonsense syllables, the names and faces of the members of your high school graduating class represent information that is both familiar and interesting. You can see the difference that familiarity and interest make in remembering information by looking at the forgetting curve below. Subjects did better on recognition tests (matching names to faces) than on recall tests (seeing faces and asked to recall the names).

Studies such as this one indicate that familiar or interesting material remains a long time in memory. Even after 47 years, subjects correctly matched about 70% of their high school classmates' names with faces. If you look back to our earlier chart, you'll see that this percentage is similar to subjects' recognition of Spanish words after 50 years. Interestingly, after an extended period of time the recall of Spanish words was higher than the recall of classmates' names.

Now, let's look at some of the reasons for forgetting.

Even after 47 years, subjects were able to correctly match many of their high school classmates' names with faces.

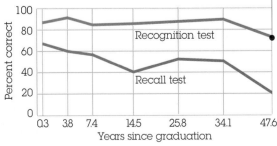

Percent correct

Recognition test

Recall test

Years since graduation

Reasons for Forgetting

Some people can remember almost everything that happened on their 16th birthday, some remember a few things, and others remember almost nothing.

Can you remember your 16th birthday?

Here's an overview of five reasons why you may have forgotten your 16th birthday. Later, we'll focus on three of the reasons.

1 You can't remember your 16th birthday because you haven't thought about it. An early theory of forgetting was the **law of disuse,** *which said that memories fade away and disappear across time if they are not used.* This theory is not widely held today because it is not supported by data. As you know, studies on remembering Spanish vocabulary and names of high school classmates indicate that a relatively high percentage of memories remain after 30–40 years, even if they are not used.

2 You can't remember your 16th birthday because something traumatic happened. According to Sigmund Freud, **repression** *is an unconscious process of forgetting during which information that is threatening to our self-concept or that makes us feel anxious is automatically prevented from reaching consciousness.* Although it is difficult to demonstrate repression with standard experiments, many clinical psychologists report seeing evidence for repression during therapy. As an example, consider the repression that may have occurred in the case of 6-year-old Eileen. She witnessed her father molest and then kill her best friend, 6-year-old Susan, by smashing her skull. When her father discovered that Eileen had seen what happened, he threatened to kill her, too, if she told anyone. When Eileen was 30 years old, she looked into the eyes of her own 6-year-old daughter and suddenly remembered that 24 years earlier her father had molested and murdered Susan. Based primarily on the emergence of Eileen's repressed memories, the jury found the father guilty, and he was sentenced to life imprisonment (*Newsweek,* February 11, 1991). Expert psychologists who testified at the trial disagreed on the reliability of repressed memories and pointed out their potential for distortion. However, the psychologists did agree that repressed memory is a real phenomenon that can be unlocked spontaneously by an unrelated event.

3 You can't remember your 16th birthday because you've had so many others since then. One of the most common reasons for forgetting is **interference,** *which means that other memories may interfere with or prevent retrieval of some particular memory.* Later in this module, we'll discuss two kinds of interference and how they disrupt remembering.

4 You can't remember your 16th birthday because nothing memorable happened. Another common reason for forgetting is **inadequate retrieval cues,** *which means there are too few associations or reminders (retrieval cues) so that memories cannot be retrieved.* Inadequate retrieval cues explain why recall tests are harder than recognition tests: fewer reminders are present during recall. Later, we'll discuss several ways to improve retrieval cues.

5 You can't remember your 16th birthday because you were accidentally hit on the head. Amnesia, *which is loss of memory, may occur after damage to the brain (temporary or permanent) or after severe psychological stress.* For example, striking one's head during a car accident will usually wipe out all memories immediately before and during the accident.

Cognitive psychologists have primarily studied the last three reasons—interference, inadequate retrieval cues, and amnesia. After the Concept/Glossary, we'll discuss these three causes of forgetting in more detail.

1. If you retrieve previously learned information without the aid of any external cues, you are using a process of remembering called (a)_____. If you identify or match information that you have previously learned, you are using a process of remembering called (b)_____.

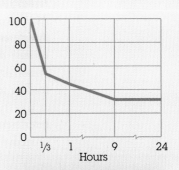

tests

tests

Years since completing course

2. One theory of memory organization says that we file related ideas in separate categories called *nodes*, which are interconnected into a gigantic system. This idea is called _____ theory.

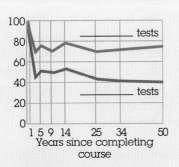

3. According to network theory, some nodes are arranged such that more concrete information is at the bottom and more abstract information is at the top; this order is called a _____.

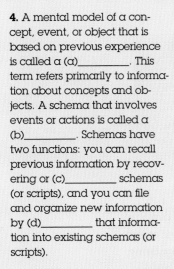

4. A mental model of a concept, event, or object that is based on previous experience is called a (a)_____. This term refers primarily to information about concepts and objects. A schema that involves events or actions is called a (b)_____. Schemas have two functions: you can recall previous information by recovering or (c)_____ schemas (or scripts), and you can file and organize new information by (d)_____ that information into existing schemas (or scripts).

5. A diagram of the amount of previously learned information that subjects can recall or recognize across time is called a _____.

Hours

6. Psychologists have proposed at least five reasons for forgetting. One reason that is no longer held today is that memories fade away and disappear across time if they are not used. This idea is called the _____.

7. One common reason for forgetting is that other memories may interfere with or prevent retrieval of some particular memory; this idea is called (a)_____. Another reason is that a lack of associations or reminders may make it difficult to retrieve a memory; this idea is called (b)_____.

8. According to Sigmund Freud, information that is threatening to our self-concept is automatically driven into our unconscious, from which we cannot retrieve it at will. This process is called _____.

9. A blow to the head may cause a form of forgetting called _____, in which one loses all memories of events that occurred just before or just after being hit.

Answers: 1. (a) recall, (b) recognition. 2. network. 3. hierarchy. 4. (a) schemas, (b) scripts, (c) reconstructing, (d) fitting. 5. forgetting curve. 6. law of disuse. 7. (a) interference, (b) inadequate retrieval cues. 8. repression. 9. amnesia.

MODULE 14: REMEMBERING AND FORGETTING

259

Reasons for Forgetting

Interference

As you've just learned, interference is a common reason for forgetting. According to **interference theory,** *we forget information not because it is lost from storage but rather because other information gets in the way and blocks or interferes with its retrieval.* Personally, unless I take great notes, I have difficulty remembering information after reading several journal articles. As a student, you face a similar problem of interference as you try to recall information after studying several different subjects. What makes interference doubly hard on remembering is that there are two kinds of interference: proactive and retroactive.

With **proactive interference,** *information learned earlier interferes with or disrupts the retrieval of information that was learned later.* The prefix *pro* means "forward," so *proactive* means "acting forward" to disrupt retrieval of newly learned information. Let's see how proactive interference works in a study situation.

proactive

Psychology Information
1. Suppose you study for a test in psychology.

Acts Forward
2. The psychology information already in memory may act "forward" and disrupt information that you study next.

Sociology Information
3. Suppose you next study for a test in sociology. You may experience difficulty in remembering this information because previously learned psychology information disrupts learning of sociology information.

Sociology Exam
4. When you take your sociology exam, you may experience proactive interference from the previously learned psychology information.

With **retroactive interference,** *information learned later interferes with or disrupts the retrieval of information that you learned earlier.* The prefix *retro* means "backward," so *retroactive* means "acting backward" to disrupt retrieval of previously learned information. Let's see how retroactive interference works in a study situation.

retroactive

Psychology Information
1. Suppose you study for a test in psychology.

Sociology Information
2. Next, you study for a test in sociology.

Acts Backward
3. Sociology information going into memory may act "backward" and disrupt previously studied psychology information.

Psychology Exam
4. When you take an exam in psychology, you may experience retroactive interference from recently learned sociology information.

Why did they forget the mugger?
We began this module by asking why only 200 out of 2,000 viewers correctly identified a mugger's face that was shown for several seconds on television. One reason that viewers "forgot" the face is that one or both kinds of interference were operating. If *proactive interference* was operating, previously learned faces acted "forward" to block or disrupt remembering the newly observed mugger's face. If *retroactive interference* was operating, information learned since seeing the mugger's face acted "backward" to block or disrupt remembering the mugger's face.

Besides interference, there is another common reason—inadequate retrieval cues—to explain why we forget.

Inadequate Retrieval Cues and Forgetting

Most of us have had the experience of putting something away and then sometime later being unable to remember where. When students were asked to hide things in common or unusual places, they remembered the locations of more objects hidden in common places than in unusual places (Winograd & Soloway, 1986). One reason students forgot the unusual hiding places was that they had inadequate retrieval cues.

Common Experiences of Forgetting

Where did I put that?

Retrieval cues *are reminders we create when we associate new information with information that we already know.* If you want to hide an item, associate it and the hiding place with a song, film, or even a nursery rhyme that you know well, and you will be more likely to remember the location later.

Because inadequate retrieval cues may lead to forgetting, you will better remember

> *I know it's here someplace.*

concepts, definitions, terms, dates, or formulas if you make associations (elaborative rehearsal) rather than just repeat, read, or underline material (maintenance rehearsal). The more associations you make between new and old information, the better your chances of retrieving that information.

What's her name?

Most of us have also had the frustrating experience of trying to recall the name of a person, song, film, or restaurant that we surely know. This phenomenon, often referred to as the **tip-of-the-tongue phenomenon,** *is the feeling of really knowing something but, despite making a great effort, being unable to recall the information from memory.* One explanation for the tip-of-the-tongue phenomenon is that this information was filed or encoded with inadequate retrieval cues. Later, when you are thinking about something entirely different, the information that was on the tip of your tongue may pop into your head. Perhaps this "forgotten"

> *It's on the tip of my tongue.*

information reappears because you have unknowingly tapped into a retrieval cue.

Who was that man?

The vast majority of viewers who watched the mugging on television may have identi-

> *It happened so fast I didn't get a good look.*

fied the wrong person as the assailant because of *inadequate retrieval cues.* During the fast-paced action in the mugging scene, viewers had little time to concentrate on the mugger's face and to notice any particular features. As a result, they did not have time to associate the mugger's face with particular features or scars and thus forgot his face when later asked to identify it.

An interesting aspect of retrieval cues is that they can come not only from associations but also from your states of mind.

State-Dependent Learning

During the early part of an international bike race, one of the riders fell and broke his collar bone. His ability to remember the events that occurred during this state of physiological arousal will be best whenever he is in a similar state, a phenomenon called state-dependent learning. **State-dependent learning** *means that it is easier to recall information when you are in the same physiological state as when you originally learned that information.* Evidence for state-dependent learning comes from a study in which subjects

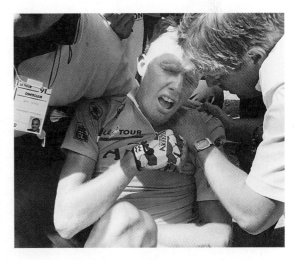

who learned words while using marijuana showed better recall later when tested with marijuana rather than with a placebo (Eich, 1980). Further evidence comes from subjects who learned words in a particular mood and showed better recall if, when they were tested, they were in the same mood (Bower & Mayer, 1989). The results of state-dependent studies indicate that physiological states can serve as cues for retrieval.

Next we'll examine an intriguing memory problem—amnesia—that can have tragic consequences.

This injured bike rider will remember these events better if he is later in a similar state of physiological arousal.

Reasons for Forgetting

Amnesia

Although most people know that amnesia involves a loss of memory, many do not know that the loss may affect only new memories (anterograde amnesia), only old memories (retrograde amnesia), or sometimes both. We'll examine each kind of amnesia in more detail.

Anterograde Amnesia. Every memory researcher knows the unusual and tragic story of a patient identified only by the initials H.M. When H.M. was 27 years old, he underwent radical brain surgery for treatment of his severe and uncontrollable epileptic seizures. He was the first human (and perhaps the last) to have this particular surgical treatment for epilepsy. Neurosurgeons removed the front parts of both temporal lobes and most of an underlying structure, the hippocampus. Although the surgical treatment reduced H.M.'s seizures, it also deprived him of the ability to form new memories, a problem known as anterograde amnesia. **Anterograde amnesia** *is the loss of memory for events and facts that occur after brain damage, although memories formed before the damage remain intact.*

H.M. has severe anterograde amnesia because he has almost no memory for events *after* his surgery but does remember events *before* his surgery. For example, H.M. can remember events and stories from his youth but cannot remember how to get back to his house, because he moved to it after his surgery. H.M.'s brain damage, especially damage to the *hippocampus*, prevents him from transferring most new information from short-term into long-term memory. As a result of this damage, H.M. remembers personal experiences (episodic information) or verbal and factual events (semantic information) only as long as such information remains in short-term memory (15–30 minutes). Once this information leaves short-term memory, H.M. has absolutely no memory of it. For instance, an hour after eating lunch, he can't remember what he ate or even whether he had lunch. When asked to describe his life, H.M. replied that he knows only the moment and not the past. He likens his life to waking from a dream that he never remembers (Milner, 1965).

Although H.M. has learned to solve a motor skills puzzle (see sidebar at left), he has absolutely no memory of solving the puzzle. Researchers conclude that retrograde amnesia usually involves episodic and semantic information while sparing procedural information.

Now, let's turn to anterograde amnesia, which affects previous memories.

Although we speak of H.M. as being unable to form new memories, this is the case primarily for personal experiences (episodic information) and verbal and factual information (semantic information). Surprisingly enough, H.M. does have the ability to form new memories that involve motor skills (procedural information), such as solving a problem called the Tower of Hanoi puzzle.

The puzzle consists of a flat board with three vertical pegs and five wooden blocks of different sizes, each with a hole in the center. To begin, all the blocks are stacked on the left-hand peg. The goal is to move all five blocks to the peg on the right. However, only one block at a time can be moved to a peg, and no block can ever be put on a block smaller than itself.

At the start of the game, H. M. makes a few hesitant moves and then announces, "I'm stuck. It can't be done."

"Yes, it can," says a watching scientist. "Just guess."

H.M. makes a few more moves and then stops again. "I can't do it," he says.

"Of course you can," answers the scientist. "You've done this many times before."

H.M. is incredulous. "I have?" he asks.

H.M. goes on to complete the puzzle in fewer moves than he used on previous attempts (adapted from Cohen & Squire, 1980; McKean, 1983b).

Retrograde Amnesia. If you were in a car accident in which you banged your head and were knocked unconscious, it is unlikely that you will remember anything prior to the blow. The reason is that you suffered retrograde amnesia.

Retrograde amnesia *is a loss of memory for events prior to brain trauma or damage but no loss of memory for events occurring a short time after the brain trauma or damage.* After his accident, Tyson's ability to remember new information returned to normal. Scientists believe that a blow to the head disrupts ongoing memory processes in the brain and prevents the formation or consolidation of memories. *Consolidation* refers to chemical processes or structural changes in the brain that occur while memories are being formed or stored. As we'll explain shortly, one of the hottest research areas in neurobiology is studying how consolidation occurs.

Why don't people remember being in a car accident?

Why do alcoholics develop severe memory problems?

Korsakoff's Syndrome. In some cases, individuals may have both kinds of amnesia. For example, after years of heavy drinking, some alcoholics develop widespread brain damage that usually includes the hippocampus. As a result of this damage, they develop a complex of problems referred to as Korsakoff's syndrome (Shimamura, 1989). **Korsakoff's syndrome** *includes a variety of cognitive and emotional deficits, including an inability to form new memories (anterograde amnesia), an inability to remember events for the past several or more years (retrograde amnesia), deficits in short-term memory, a lack of emotional feelings, and general lack of interest or apathy.* Not all alcoholics develop Korsakoff's syndrome, and there is no treatment for those who do.

Alzheimer's Disease. Another example of individuals developing anterograde and retrograde amnesia is found with Alzheimer's disease, which we discussed in Module 3. **Alzheimer's disease,** *which usually begins after people reach age 50 and is always fatal, results from widespread damage to the brain, including the hippocampus, and produces deterioration in personality, emotions, cognitive processes, and memory.* During the initial stages of Alzheimer's disease, patients have difficulty remembering new information (anterograde amnesia). For instance, they may forget what they read or talked about, or names of people they recently met. As the disease progressively worsens year by year, patients forget more and more of their personal histories as well as information about past events (retrograde amnesia). Toward the end, Alzheimer's patients cannot remember the names of their spouses, children, or friends, which is an extreme example of retrograde amnesia. One reason Alzheimer's disease is so feared is that it gradually destroys all memories, which are among our most treasured possessions.

Alzheimer's disease eventually destroys all memories.

A common thread that runs through all these examples of amnesia is the importance of the hippocampus, which we shall look at next.

The Biological Bases of Memory

Where in your brain do you remember things?
In a landmark paper, researchers Larry Squire and Stuart Zola-Morgan (1991) described how memories are formed in the brain. Their explanation is based on studies of humans with amnesia as well as animals who had amnesia after damage to certain brain areas. Here's their explanation of how the brain forms memories.

Formation of Memories in the Brain

1 *Short-term memory.* Our ability to hold facts or events in short-term memory depends on activity in the surface of the brain, called the *cortex.* The cortex covers both the top and sides of the brain. However, the transfer of information from short-term into long-term memory involves a brain area beneath the cortex of the temporal lobe.

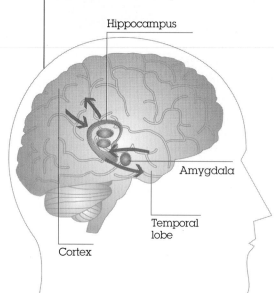

Hippocampus

Amygdala

Temporal lobe

Cortex

2 *Long-term memory.* Our ability to transfer information about facts and events from short-term into long-term memory depends on activity in the *hippocampus,* a curved, finger-shaped structure that lies beneath the cortex in the temporal lobe. The hippocampus is crucial for transferring semantic information (facts) and episodic information (events and personal experiences) from short-term to long-term memory. However, the hippocampus is not necessary for transferring procedural information (motor skills) into long-term memory.

As you remember, damage to H.M.'s hippocampus resulted in anterograde amnesia for facts and events but did not interfere with his memory for motor skills (Tower of Hanoi puzzle). In addition, damage to H.M.'s hippocampus did not disrupt his short-term memory, which indicates that the cortex, not the hippocampus, is necessary for short-term memory.

3 *Recalling old memories.* Our ability to remember facts and events from many months or years ago depends on structures other than the hippocampus, such as areas throughout the cortex. Evidence for this comes from H.M., who had damage to his hippocampus but did not have retrograde amnesia, which means he could remember facts and events from long ago, such as his childhood. Many of our memories, such as of spending holidays with friends, evoke emotional feelings that come from another structure in the temporal lobe.

4 *Adding emotional feelings to memories.* The ability of our memories to evoke emotional experiences depends partly on the activity of the *amygdala,* an almond-shaped structure beneath the cortex in the tip of the temporal lobe. Damage to the amygdala in monkeys results in changes in emotional behavior, such as showing less fear to touching new objects.

One reason Squire and Zola-Morgan's explanation of the brain areas involved in memory is so convincing is that, unlike some previous explanations, it is based on sound research in both humans and animals.

Now that you understand which areas of the brain are involved in memory, let's see what kinds of changes may be taking place that result in forming and storing memories. Most of our knowledge in this area comes from research carried out on a strange-looking animal called a sea slug.

Chemical and Structural Changes

That exotic-looking animal climbing up the side of the next page is a sea slug, an ideal subject for studying memory formation because it has relatively few neurons, only about 20,000, compared to millions in a rat's brain and billions in a human's. The sea slug is able to form and store simple memories, such as those needed in classical conditioning.

In a typical experiment, researchers classically condition a sea slug by presenting a bright light (neutral stimulus) followed closely by an unconditioned stimulus, such as shaking the sea slug's enclosure. The shaking elicits an unconditioned response: the reflexive tensing of the sea slug's muscular foot. After about 150 pairings of the bright light and shaking, the slug will tense its foot (conditioned response) to the onset of the bright light alone (conditioned stimulus). After classical conditioning has occurred, researchers dissect the sea slug's nervous system to search for chemical or structural changes that occurred during the formation of memories necessary for classical conditioning. From studies on sea slugs, on snails, and on tiny pieces of rat brain tissue kept alive in glass dishes, researchers have proposed several biological mechanisms that underlie the formation of memories (Ezzell, 1991).

Mechanisms of Memory

In studying the formation of memories, researchers are especially interested in the activity of neurons, the brain cells specialized to transmit information by releasing chemicals called **neurotransmitters** (see Chapter 2). We'll focus on two biological mechanisms involved in learning and memory: chemical changes and structural changes (Ezzell, 1991).

Molecular and Chemical Changes. The neuron's surface (membrane) contains chemical gates that can be opened or closed by neurotransmitters. If the gates are opened, neural activity is facilitated; if the gates are closed, neural activity is inhibited. Researchers have identified certain *molecules* (protein kinase) in the sea slug that are involved in opening and closing a neuron's chemical gates. Because of their involvement in regulating the chemical gates, researchers believe that these molecules are part of the biological bases of memory (Alkon et al., 1990).

In addition, researchers have discovered that during the formation of some memories, especially long-term memories, new *chemicals* (proteins) are synthesized (Crow et al., 1990). If the synthesis of these proteins is blocked during learning, animals cannot form long-term memories. Thus, researchers believe that the synthesis of new chemicals is also part of the biological basis of memory.

Structural Changes. Besides molecular and chemical changes, researchers also believe that learning and memory involve changes in the physical *structure* of the neuron. For example, as learning occurs, the neuron's structure may change so that the neuron secretes more neurotransmitters. That is, when the same learning situation reoccurs, neurons "remember" the situation by secreting more neurotransmitters. Thus, changes in the structure of neurons are also involved in the biological bases of memory (Ezzell, 1991; Larson & Lynch, 1986).

Because the structure and function of neurons in the sea slug, snail, and rat are similar to those in humans, scientists assume that we learn and form memories through similar molecular, chemical, and structural changes.

Now that you are familiar with the biological bases of memory, we'll discuss several psychological ways to improve your memory.

Closed gates
Open gates

Molecules that open and close chemical gates in neurons may play a role in memory.

The sea slug's simple nervous system is ideal for studying the biological bases of memory.

Mnemonics: Memorization Methods

You may remember the amazing memory record of Rajan (Module 13), which was to recall 31,811 digits accurately. Rajan set this record by using a number of encoding techniques called mnemonics. **Mnemonics (ni-MON-icks)** *are very efficient methods of encoding to improve remembering and prevent forgetting.* We discussed three mnemonic techniques in Module 13 (but without calling them mnemonics): *chunking*, which is putting individual items into a larger group and then encoding the group; *elaborative rehearsal*, which is making associations between new and old information; and *visual imagery*, which uses images to create distinct associations. Here we explain two more mnemonic techniques that are discussed in most books and courses on improving memory.

Method of Loci

If you need to memorize a list of terms, concepts, or names in a particular order, an efficient way is to use the method of loci. The **method of loci (LOW-sigh)** *is an encoding technique that creates visual associations between memorized places and items to be memorized.* Let's use the three steps of the method of loci to memorize the names of five early psychologists: Wilhelm Wundt, William James, John Watson, Sigmund Freud, and Hermann Ebbinghaus.

The method of loci has three steps:

Step 1. Memorize a visual sequence of *places* (*loci* in Latin means "places"), such as places in your apartment where you can store things. Because this list has five psychologists, pick five easily remembered places in your kitchen: sink, cabinet, refrigerator, stove, and closet.

Step 2. Create a vivid *association* for each item to be memorized. For example, picture Wilhelm Wundt hanging from a bridge and saying, "I wundt jump." Imagine William James as a pair of identical twins, one named William and one named James. Think of John Watson as wearing a huge hearing aid and saying "What did you say?" Picture Sigmund Freud lying on a red velvet couch. Imagine Hermann Ebbinghaus living in a strange house built by one mann.

Why is Wundt in the sink? Check the method of loci.

Step 3. Once you have created your list of vivid associations, mentally *put* each psychologist in one place in your kitchen. For example, Wundt goes in the sink, James in the cabinet, Watson in the refrigerator, Freud in the stove, and Ebbinghaus in the closet.

When you want to recall these five psychologists, you take an imaginary stroll through your kitchen and mentally note the image stored in each of your memorized places.

Peg Method

Another useful mnemonic device for memorizing lists is the **peg method,** *which is an encoding technique that creates associations between number-word rhymes and items to be memorized.* The rhymes act like "pegs" on which you hang items to be memorized. Let's use the two steps of the peg method to memorize our five psychologists: Wundt, James, Watson, Freud, and Ebbinghaus.

The peg method has two steps:

Step 1. Memorize a list of **pegwords** (number-word rhymes), such as the following:

one is a **bun**
two is a **shoe**
three is a **tree**
four is a **door**
five is a **hive**
six is **sticks**
seven is **heaven**
eight is a **gate**
nine is a **line**
ten is a **hen**

Step 2. Next, associate each of the items you wish to memorize with one of the pegwords. For instance, imagine Wundt sitting on a hot bun, James with two left shoes, Watson stuck in a tree, Freud behind a closed door, and Ebbinghaus with his head in a beehive.

When you wish to remember the five important early psychologists, you recall your pegs and the image of the psychologist that you hung on each peg.

The major function of these two mnemonic techniques—method of loci and peg method—is to create strong associations that will serve as effective retrieval cues. From our discussion of encoding methods and retrieval cues, you can see a common thread: effective encoding combined with many retrieval cues results in good recall; poor encoding and few retrieval cues leads to forgetting.

Next we'll examine possible cultural influences on whether we are more likely to use verbal or visual retrieval cues.

Aborigines' Memory Cues

You have spent a major part of 12 years of your life in various classrooms. In the academic world, your survival has depended to a large extent on your ability to store or encode enormous amounts of *verbal information*. In stark contrast to your academic world is the harsh, barren desert world of western Australia. Here live Aborigines, who for 30,000 years have followed a seminomadic lifestyle of hunting and gathering. In this desert world the Aborigines' survival depends on finding their way through vast stretches of unmapped country and remembering locations of water, food, and game. Their survival depends to a large extent on their ability to store or encode enormous amounts of environmental or *visual information*.

Psychologist Judith Kearins suggested that Aborigines, who scored low on Western verbal-style intelligence tests, might perform better on tests that took advantage of their ability to encode with visual cues. To test this idea, Kearins placed 20 objects on a board divided into 20 squares. Some objects were natural—stone, feather, leaf; others were manufactured—eraser, thimble, ring. Aborigine and white Australian children were told to study the board for 30 seconds. Then all the objects were heaped into a pile in the center of the board and the children were asked to replace the items in their original locations. Kearins found that the Aborigine children performed significantly better than the white Australian children in placing the objects into their original locations (Kearins, 1981). Kearins concluded that survival of the Aborigines in the harsh desert landscape had encouraged and rewarded their ability to store or encode information using visual retrieval cues. These interesting results suggest that survival needs may shape and reward a particular way of encoding information in memory.

Although we may accurately encode information, there are times when we misremember. One example of a situation in which people may misremember is eyewitness testimony, which we discuss in the following Applying/Exploring section.

Aborigines encode information using primarily visual cues, while Westerners use primarily verbal cues.

APPLYING/ EXPLORING: EYEWITNESS TESTIMONY

Several years ago a series of armed robberies occurred in the Wilmington, Delaware, area. The robber was dubbed the "gentleman bandit" because of his polite manners and well-groomed appearance. The police had few leads on the gentleman bandit until a local citizen informed them that a Roman Catholic priest, Father Bernard Pagano, looked remarkably like the sketch of the robber being circulated in the media. Seven eyewitnesses positively identified Father Pagano as the culprit. At his trial, the case against him seemed airtight. But at the last minute another man, Ronald Clouser, stepped forward and confessed to the robberies. He knew details about the robberies that only the true gentleman bandit could have known. The case against Father Pagano was dropped immediately, and Clouser was charged with the crimes (Rodgers, 1982).

Although eyewitnesses identified Father Pagano . . .

. . . Ronald Clouser later confessed to being the real robber.

Why did people identify the wrong man? As you look at these two photos, you will wonder how this case of mistaken identity could possibly have happened. Ronald Clouser is shorter, 14 years younger, and not nearly as bald as Father Pagano; besides, he has different facial features. Why, then, did seven eyewitnesses say with certainty that Father Pagano was the robber they had seen? One reason involves how the witnesses were questioned. Apparently, before witnesses were questioned and shown photos of the suspects, the police had suggested the possibility that the robber was a priest. Knowing to look for a priest, the witnesses focused on the few similarities Father Pagano had to the real robber. Because Father Pagano was the only suspect wearing a clerical collar, the witnesses concluded that he must be the robber.

Can you identify the person in this photo?
Let's see how good you are at identifying a "suspect" from a photo. Please look closely at the photo below, which shows a well-known person. Next, look at the two photos below it and identify the correct person.

Please make your selection before reading further.

Is the top photo of actor Bruce Willis?   **Is the top photo of actor Sylvester Stallone?**

Answer: See bottom right

This demonstration shows that many of us are susceptible to information that can bias or distort what we see. In this case, the misleading information was our suggestion that the photo was of either Willis or Stallone. As a result, you probably looked for and found similarities between the photo and one of the actors. However, the correct answer, which is shown on the bottom of this page, is neither of these men.

This example, which introduced bias by suggesting an answer, is similar to a clever series of experiments by Elizabeth Loftus and her colleagues. Loftus showed that eyewitnesses sometimes respond to misleading information by misremembering what they saw.

Misinformation and Misremembering

We'll describe several of Loftus's experiments that demonstrate how subjects misremembered what they saw or heard.

Did the car pass the barn?

In one experiment, subjects watched a film of an automobile accident and then were questioned about what they saw. One of the questions contained a false piece of information: "How fast was the red sports car going when it passed the barn while traveling along the country road?" Although there was no barn in the film, 17% of the subjects said they had seen a barn (Loftus, 1975).

How fast was the car traveling?

In another series of experiments, Loftus asked subjects to estimate the speed of two cars involved in an accident. This time only the wording of one verb in the question was changed. Some of the subjects were asked, "How fast were the cars going when they contacted?" For others, the verb *contacted* was replaced with *hit, bumped, collided,* or *smashed.* Subjects increased their estimates of the speed of the cars to match the speed suggested by the verb: *contacted* produced the lowest speed estimate and *smashed* the highest.

Based on many such studies, Loftus and Hoffman (1989) concluded that misleading information introduced during questioning after an event can result in people accepting this misinformation as their own and believing it is true. What is equally interesting and baffling about eyewitness testimony is that a person's confidence in the accuracy of his or her testimony is not a good barometer of whether the person's recollection is true. Researchers found little correlation between confidence and accuracy: subjects who were very confident were no more or less accurate than subjects who were less confident in the accuracy of their recollection (Smith, Womack, & Chen, 1989). In addition, as the case of Father Pagano illustrates, eyewitnesses can be absolutely confident and yet be absolutely wrong.

Cognitive Interview

Although you may have heard that hypnosis is a good method of getting the "truth" from eyewitnesses, several states have placed restrictions on the admissibility of hypnosis-derived testimony in a court of law. The reason for this restriction is that under hypnosis, subjects may be more susceptible to misinformation and to distortions in memory (Geiselman & Machlovitz, 1987).

In trying to improve police interrogation techniques, Geiselman and his colleagues (1986) have developed a questioning procedure called the cognitive interview. In the **cognitive interview,** *witnesses are told to go back in their memory and reconstruct the environment in which the crime occurred.* After asking the witnesses to report everything they can remember, the interrogators then ask them to recall the events in a different order and to envision the crime from a different perspective, such as adopting the role of a prominent character at the scene of the crime. The cognitive interview has proved very useful in police interrogation: detectives trained in cognitive interview techniques obtained 47% more information from victims and suspects than detectives using the "standard" police interrogation method (Fisher, Geiselman, & Amador, 1989). The cognitive interview seems to be very useful for gathering information and preventing forgetting during police interrogation.

Answer: England's Prince Andrew.

contacted
hit
bumped
collided
smashed

Summary/Self-Test

WAYS TO REMEMBER

1. There are two general methods for testing memory. If you are asked to retrieve previously learned information without the aid of external cues, you are using a process of remembering called (a)_____, which is generally more difficult. If you are asked to answer multiple-choice questions, you can identify or match information and use a process of remembering called (b)_____, which is generally less difficult.

■ *Why do many students prefer multiple-choice questions to fill-in questions?*

HOW MEMORY IS ORGANIZED

2. According to one theory of how memory is organized, we file related ideas in separate categories called (a)_____, which are interconnected into a gigantic system. This idea is called the (b)_____ theory. According to this theory, nodes are arranged around a certain topic or category such that more concrete information is at the bottom and more abstract information is at the top; this order is called a (c)_____.

3. According to a second theory of how memory is organized, we have mental models of concepts, events, or objects that are based on previous experience; these mental models are called (a)_____. This term refers primarily to information about concepts and objects, while the term *script* is used for events or actions. Schemas have two functions: you can recall previous information by recovering or (b)_____ schemas (or scripts); you can file and organize new information by (c)_____ that information into existing schemas (or scripts).

■ *Which of your own experiences demonstrate the two theories of how long-term memory is organized?*

LASTING MEMORIES

4. Ebbinghaus demonstrated that nonsense syllables are forgotten relatively quickly, while other studies showed that more relevant information may be remembered for many years. If the amount of previously learned information that subjects can recall or recognize across time is plotted, the graph is called a _____.

■ *Why are you more likely to remember the students from your high school class than the information from your high school history course?*

REASONS FOR FORGETTING

5. There are at least five reasons for forgetting. One of the most common reasons is that other memories may interfere with or prevent retrieval of some particular memory; this idea is called (a)_____. A second reason is that a lack of associations or reminders may make it difficult to retrieve a memory; this idea is called (b)_____. A third reason, put forth by Sigmund Freud, is that information that is threatening to our self-concept is automatically driven into our unconscious, from which we cannot retrieve it at will. This process is called (c)_____. A blow to the head may cause a form of forgetting called (d)_____. A final explanation for forgetting, called the (e)_____ is not widely held today.

6. A common reason for forgetting is not that information is lost from storage but that our retrieval of it is blocked; this blocking is called (a)_____. When earlier-learned information disrupts the retrieval of information that was learned later, it is called (b)_____. In contrast, when later-learned information disrupts the retrieval of information learned earlier, it is called (c)_____.

7. To increase the chances of remembering items from long-term memory, we can create reminders that associate new information with information that we already know; these reminders are called (a)_____. If you file or encode information with inadequate retrieval cues, you may wind up with the feeling of knowing something but being unable to recall it; this is known as the (b)_____.

8. Besides creating retrieval cues, it may also be easier to recall information when you are in the same physiological state as when you originally learned it; this phenomenon is called _____.

9. There are several kinds of amnesia. The loss of memory for events and facts that occur after damage to the brain without affecting memories formed before the damage is called (a)_____ amnesia. A loss of memory for events prior to brain trauma or damage but no loss of memory for events occurring a short time after the brain trauma or damage is called (b)_____.

■ *How many of the five different reasons for forgetting have you experienced?*

THE BIOLOGICAL BASES OF MEMORY

10. Various areas of your brain are involved in different memory processes. Your ability to hold facts or events in short-term memory depends on activity in your (a)_____. Your ability to transfer information about facts and events from short-term into long-term memory depends on activity in your (b)_____. Your ability to experience emotional reactions to memories depends partly on the activity of your (c)_____.

11. Because of their involvement in regulating the opening and closing of chemical gates, certain (a)_____ are thought to be part of the biological bases of memory. Researchers have also discovered that in forming some memories, especially long-term ones, new (b)_____ are synthesized. Researchers also believe that learning and memory involve changes in the physical (c)_____ of the neuron.

■ *If you developed a strange virus that destroyed your hippocampus, what effect would that have on your performance in English, mathematics, and physical education classes?*

MNEMONICS: MEMORIZATION METHODS

12. Techniques that use efficient methods of encoding to improve remembering and prevent forgetting are called (a)_____. The major function of these techniques is to create strong (b)_____ that will serve as effective (c)_____.

13. A method that creates visual associations between memorized places and items to be memorized is called the (a)_____. With another method, one creates associations between number-word rhymes and items to be memorized; this method is called the (b)_____. Additional mnemonic methods, discussed in an earlier module, include (c)_____.

■ *Can you describe a mnemonic method for remembering the five reasons for forgetting?*

CULTURAL DIVERSITY: ABORIGINES' MEMORY CUES

14. Data from Aborigine and white Australian children suggest that survival needs may shape and reward a particular way of (a)_____ information in memory. In the academic world, you are required to store large amounts of (b)_____. However, if you were fending for yourself in the wilds of Australia, you would need to be able to store environmental or (c)_____ to find your way around and survive.

■ *If you had been raised an Eskimo, would you rely on different memory cues than you do now?*

APPLYING/EXPLORING: EYEWITNESS TESTIMONY

15. One reason that eyewitness testimony is often unreliable is that witnesses are (a)_____ to suggestions, meaning that their responses may be influenced by information they are given. Eyewitnesses may accept misleading information and therefore (b)_____ what they saw. Eyewitnesses may be especially susceptible to misinformation when they are under (c)_____.

16. A method used to improve witness recall is the (a)_____. In this method, witnesses are told to go back in their memories and (b)_____ the environment in which the crime occurred. They are then asked to (c)_____ the events in a different order or from a different perspective.

■ *If you were on a jury, what kinds of things should you consider when evaluating eyewitness testimony?*

Chapter *Eight*
INTELLIGENCE, THOUGHT, AND LANGUAGE

MODULE 15
INTELLIGENCE

Clarence Thomas is sworn in as a justice of the United States Supreme Court.

How can a brother and sister be so different?

Clarence Thomas was born in 1948 in Pin Point, Georgia, a dirt-poor town with no roads or sewers. Forty-three years later, he was confirmed as a justice of the United States Supreme Court. He had overcome poverty, a broken home, and terrible racial discrimination to rise to the highest court in our nation.

The family of Clarence Thomas had been very poor, and his father abandoned them when Clarence was a toddler. When Clarence was 5, he and his brother were sent to Savannah, Georgia, to live with his grandfather, who made Clarence work hard and drummed into him the value of education. Clarence attended a Catholic grade school for poor black children.

This was a time when blacks were forced to ride in the back of buses, were banned from restaurants, and were made to attend segregated schools and churches—even to use separate public rest rooms. Clarence followed his grandfather's advice and applied himself in school. After high school, he attended and graduated as an honor student from Holy Cross College in Worcester, Massachusetts. He was recruited by Yale Law School, from which he later graduated.

While Clarence was pursuing his education, his sister Emma was taking a different path. Emma Mae Martin, a year older, remained in Pin Point with their mother, who did not instill in Emma the need for education. Although Emma went to Catholic schools for a few years, she did not go to college. Today Emma lives in a small house with her three children in Pin Point and works as a cook in a local hospital. (adapted from *USA Today*, July 26, 1991; *The Washington Post*, September 16–22, 1991)

The story of this particular brother and sister, who share about half their genes but grew up in different environments, illustrates how genetic and environmental factors interact to result in a wide range of physical and psychological traits, including intelligence.

Since the late 1800s, the study of intelligence has been a dominant issue in psychology. When a wide range of people were asked, "What is intelligence?" they generally agreed that intelligence has three aspects: practical *problem-solving skills*, such as reasoning logically, keeping an open mind, and seeing all sides of a problem; *verbal ability*, such as speaking clearly, having a good vocabulary, and reading widely; and *social competence*, such as getting along with others, admitting mistakes, and having a social conscience (Sternberg et al., 1981). Psychologists generally agree that these three aspects are part of intelligence. The measurement of intelligence is part of **psychometrics**, *which is a field that assesses an individual's abilities, skills, beliefs, and personality traits.*

What's Coming

In this module we'll discuss how psychologists measure intelligence, how genetics and environment influence intelligence, and the meaning of IQ scores. In the next module we'll examine thought and language. Let's begin with how psychologists define intelligence.

Approaches to Defining Intelligence

Who is more intelligent—a judge or a golfer?

The answer to this question depends on how we define intelligence. If we focus on academic accomplishments, we would give the nod to Clarence Thomas, who graduated from Yale Law School, was appointed a federal judge, and became a Supreme Court justice. On the other hand, if we emphasize movement skills, we would give the nod to Nancy Lopez, who has earned more than $2 million on the women's pro golf circuit. Let's see how the main approaches psychologists use to define intelligence—psychometrics and information processing— would answer the question of who is more intelligent.

Psychometric Approach—Lumpers

The **psychometric approach** *focuses on measuring or quantifying cognitive factors or abilities that make up intellectual performance.* For example, each of us has a number of cognitive abilities that are different from someone else's and that influence our intellectual performance. These cognitive factors might include verbal comprehension, memory ability, perceptual speed, and reasoning.

The psychologists who follow the psychometric approach either lump these cognitive factors together (*lumpers*) or split them apart (*splitters*) (Weinberg, 1989).

The **lumpers** *define intelligence as a general unified capacity for reasoning, acquiring knowledge, and solving problems.* One lumper, Charles Spearman, has developed a two-factor theory of intelligence. According to Spearman's **two-factor theory,** *everyone has a general intelligence factor, termed* **g,** *as well as specific abilities, labeled* **s.** Spearman believed that how well or poorly one performs on intellectual tasks is dependent on *g* as well as on abilities, *s,* specific to the task. The idea of general intelligence factors is behind using a single measure of intelligence, such as an IQ (intelligence quotient) score, which we'll discuss later in this module.

Would a lumper consider Judge Thomas or golfer Lopez more intelligent?

Because of Clarence Thomas's success in academic settings, we would predict that he would do well on standard IQ tests, which give considerable weight to verbal skills. Although Nancy Lopez has great success on the women's pro golf circuit, we don't know how she would perform on standard IQ tests, which give little weight to movement skills.

Does lumping work?

One advantage of the lumper's approach is that we end up with a single score for intelligence (IQ), which has proved useful in predicting performance in academic settings. Two disadvantages of this approach are that it excludes other kinds of intelligence (movement skills, music skills, insightful skills) and that it does not explain the specific processes involved in intelligence (Mayer, 1983).

Is Clarence Thomas more intelligent than Nancy Lopez?

Psychometric Approach—Splitters

In contrast to lumpers, **splitters** *define intelligence as composed of many separate mental abilities that function more or less independently.* An example of a modern splitter is Howard Gardner (1983), who rejected the idea that intelligence is a single factor that can be measured by a single score, such as IQ scores. According to Gardner's **multiple-factor theory,** *there are at least seven independent aspects of intelligence: verbal skills, math skills, spatial skills, movement skills, musical skills, insight about oneself, and insight about others.* Further, Gardner believes that understanding these aspects of intelligence comes from studying the person in his or her environment and not from results of IQ tests.

Would a splitter consider Judge Thomas or golfer Lopez more intelligent?
According to the multiple-factor theory of intelligence, both Thomas and Lopez show high levels of intelligence. As a successful lawyer and judge, Thomas has demonstrated great verbal skills. As a successful pro golfer, Lopez has shown great movement skills. The multiple-factor theory would not focus on who is more intelligent but rather on how people show different kinds of intelligence.

Does splitting work?
One advantage of the splitters' approach is that people get credit for being intelligent in a number of areas (music, movement, insight) that are not usually included in the traditional IQ score. One disadvantage of this approach is the difficulty in knowing how many ways to split intelligence.

Information-Processing Approach

The information-processing approach studies how people gather information to solve problems or acquire information. The **information-processing approach** *defines intelligence by analyzing the components of the cognitive processes that people use to solve problems.*

An example of this approach is Robert Sternberg's (1985) **triarchic theory,** *which says that intelligence can be divided into three ways of gathering and processing information* (triarchic means three). The first is using *analytical* or *logical thinking skills* that are measured by traditional intelligence tests. The second is using *problem-solving skills* that require creative thinking, the ability to deal with novel situations, and the ability to learn from experience. The third is using *practical thinking skills* that help a person adjust to and cope with his or her sociocultural environment.

Would an information processor consider Judge Thomas or golfer Lopez more intelligent?
According to Sternberg's triarchic theory, Clarence Thomas would probably score high on analytical thinking and problem-solving skills, as shown by his successful strategies for solving legal problems. Nancy Lopez would probably score high on problem-solving and practical skills, as indicated by her successful strategies on the golf course. The information-processing approach would not focus on who is more intelligent but rather on analyzing the different ways that people process and gather information.

Does the information-processing model work?
One advantage of the information-processing approach is that it gives people credit for being intelligent in several ways not measured by traditional intelligence tests. A person with great practical thinking skills, such as being "street smart" or knowing how to deal with others, may not score high on traditional intelligence tests. One disadvantage of the information-processing approach is that few tests are available to measure the various ways that people think and solve problems.

Which approach is most often used to measure intelligence?
According to Richard Weinberg (1989), intelligence testing today is dominated by the psychometric approach and its traditional IQ tests. He believes that Gardner's multiple-factor approach and Sternberg's information-processing approach may eventually result in alternative ways to assess intelligence. One reason the psychometric approach has dominated intelligence testing is that current IQ tests are relatively successful at predicting performance in academic settings.

Now that you understand the different ways of *defining* intelligence, let's examine how psychologists *measure* intelligence.

Measuring Intelligence

Do the smartest people have the largest brains?

Researchers have tried many methods for measuring intelligence. You may remember from Module 4 that in the 1800s Samuel Morton attempted to assess intelligence by measuring the capacity of the skull, while Paul Broca measured brain size.

Both Morton's and Broca's measures of skull and brain size proved to be unreliable and poorly correlated with intelligence (Gould, 1981). From the brains below you can see that Einstein's brain was of average weight and that Anatole France and Walt Whitman managed to write quite well with brains about half the weight of Jonathan Swift's, one of the heaviest on record.

In the late 1800s Francis Galton observed that intelligent people often had intelligent relatives and concluded that intelligence is, to a large extent, biological or inherited. In trying to develop a method of assessing biological intelligence, Galton measured people's skulls and recorded the speed of their reactions to various sensory stimuli. However, his measures proved to be poorly related to intelligence or academic achievement (Gould, 1981).

Average weight of human brain—about 1450 grams

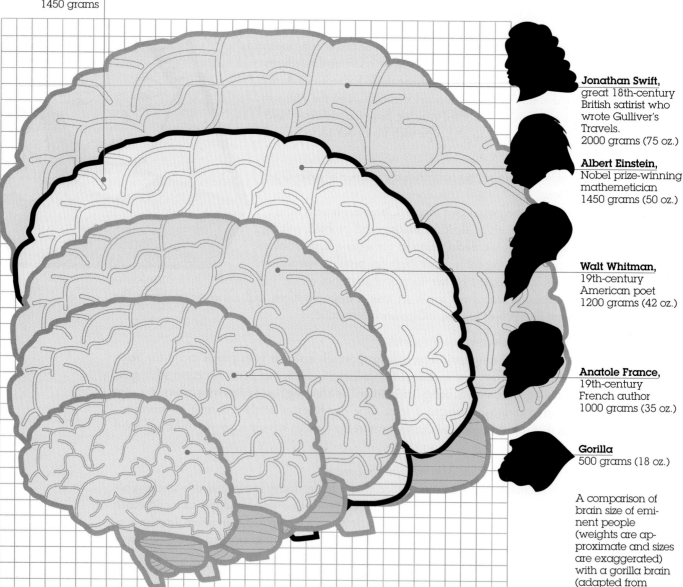

Jonathan Swift, great 18th-century British satirist who wrote Gulliver's Travels. 2000 grams (75 oz.)

Albert Einstein, Nobel prize-winning mathemetician 1450 grams (50 oz.)

Walt Whitman, 19th-century American poet 1200 grams (42 oz.)

Anatole France, 19th-century French author 1000 grams (35 oz.)

Gorilla 500 grams (18 oz.)

A comparison of brain size of eminent people (weights are approximate and sizes are exaggerated) with a gorilla brain (adapted from Gould, 1981).

Binet's Breakthrough

In the early 1900s, a gifted French psychologist named Alfred Binet noted the failures of Broca and Galton to assess intelligence by measuring brain size or reaction time. Instead, Binet believed that intelligence is a collection of mental abilities and that the way to assess intelligence is to measure a person's ability to perform cognitive tasks, such as understanding the meaning of words or being able to follow directions. Binet soon had a chance to put his beliefs to work.

Alfred Binet discounted brain size as a measure of intelligence.

The Paris public schools commissioned Binet and a psychiatrist named Theodore Simon to develop a test to differentiate children of normal intelligence from those who needed special help. In 1905 Binet and Simon succeeded in developing the world's first standardized intelligence test. Their test, the **Binet-Simon Intelligence Scale,** *contained questions that measured vocabulary, memory, common knowledge, and other cognitive abilities.*

Several years later Binet introduced the concept of mental level or mental age. **Mental age** *is a method of estimating a child's intellectual progress by comparing the child's score on an intelligence test to the scores of average children of the same age.* Let's see how Binet measured mental age.

Mental Age: Measure of Intelligence

Binet's test consisted of items arranged in order of increasing difficulty, with different items designed to measure different cognitive abilities. For each item, Binet determined whether an average child of a certain age could answer the question correctly. For example, at age 2 the average child can name certain parts of the body, while at age 10 the average youngster can define abstract words such as *quickly.* Suppose a particular child passed all the items that could be answered by an average 3-year-old but none of the items appropriate for older children. That child would be said to have a mental age of 3. Thus, if a 6-year-old child could answer only questions appropriate for a 3-year-old child, that child would be given a mental age of 3 and would be considered retarded in intellectual development. This idea of a single score that represents mental age helped to popularize Binet's intelligence test.

Terman's Formula for IQ

Soon after Binet developed his test, Lewis Terman and his colleagues at Stanford University in California produced a revised version. One of the significant changes they made was in the final score (Terman, 1916). Terman devised a formula to calculate an intelligence quotient (IQ) score. **Intelligence quotient** *is computed by dividing a child's mental age (MA), as measured by an intelligence test, by the child's chronological age (CA) and multiplying the result by 100.*

Remember that in Binet's test mental age was calculated by noting how many items a child answered that were appropriate to a certain age. For example, if a 4-year-old girl passed the test items appropriate for a 5-year-old, she was said to have a mental age of 5. A child's chronological age is his or her age in months and years. To compute a child's IQ score, Terman used this formula:

$$IQ = \frac{MA}{CA} \times 100$$

To compute the IQ of the child in our example, substitute 5 for MA, 4 for CA, and multiply by 100. You would get: 5/4 = 1.25 × 100 = 125. So the child's IQ is 125. An IQ score computed in this traditional way is called a *ratio IQ,* because the score represents a ratio of mental to chronological age. Today the ratio IQ has been replaced by another method, called the *deviation IQ,* whose computation is too complex to explain. The reason for the switch from ratio IQ to deviation IQ is that deviation IQ scores more accurately reflect test performance as children get older.

Since the 1900s IQ tests have become very popular. We'll examine two of the most widely used tests.

Why might children of different ages have the same IQ scores?

Widely Used IQ Tests

According to the *Guinness Book of World Records,* Marilyn vos Savant's IQ of 228 is the highest on record. She writes a column for the weekly *Parade* magazine.

Which IQ tests are the most popular?

One of the more widely used IQ tests in America today is the **Stanford-Binet.** Developed by Terman and his associates from the original Binet test, it has since been revised several times. It is administered to children and young adults ages 2 through 18 on an individual basis by a trained examiner.

The test consists of a number of items, some *verbal,* such as naming things and understanding instructions, and some *performance,* such as completing a picture or using colored blocks to reproduce a pattern. The items are arranged in order of increasing difficulty and are designated appropriate for certain age levels. A child continues through the series until he or she reaches the age level at which he or she can answer none of the questions.

The most widely used series of IQ tests are the **Wechsler Adult Intelligence Scale–Revised (WAIS–R),** for ages 16 and older, and the **Wechsler Intelligence Scale for Children–Revised (WISC–R),** for children ages 4 to 16. As with the Stanford-Binet, a trained examiner administers the Wechsler scales on a one-to-one basis.

Unlike those in the Stanford-Binet, items on the Wechsler scales are organized into various **subtests.** In the verbal section, for instance, there is a subtest of general information, a subtest of vocabulary, a subtest of verbal comprehension, and so forth. The performance section contains a subtest that involves arranging pictures in a meaningful order, one that requires assembling objects, and one that involves using codes. An individual receives a separate score for each of the subtests; these scores are then combined to yield overall scores for verbal and performance abilities. Finally, the verbal and performance scores are combined to give a single IQ score.

One reason these particular IQ tests are widely used is that they have the two features required of a good psychological test. We'll discuss those features next.

The Wechsler Adult Intelligence Scale–Revised (WAIS–R) is divided into a verbal scale and a performance scale, each with various subtests. Here are some sample items that resemble those on the WAIS–R.

Subtests for the Verbal Scale:

Information
On what continent is France?

Comprehension
Why are children required to go to school?

Arithmetic
How many hours will it take to drive 150 miles at 50 miles per hour?

Similarities
How are a calculator and a typewriter alike?

Digit span
Repeat the following numbers backward: 2, 4, 3, 5, 8, 9, 6.

Vocabulary
What does *audacity* mean?

Subtests for the Performance Scale:

Digit symbol Shown: Fill in:
1 2 3 4   1 4 3 2

Block design
Assemble blocks to match this design.

Picture completion
Tell me what is missing.

Picture arrangement
Put the pictures in the right order.

Object assembly
Assemble the pieces into a complete object.

Two Characteristics of a Good Test

Is handwriting analysis a good test for intelligence?

At many amusement parks you'll find a machine that will describe your personality and intelligence by analyzing a brief sample of your handwriting. Our advice is to save your money, because this kind of test has only one of two characteristics required of a good test.

Reliability

A good psychological test must have two characteristics: reliability and validity. **Reliability** *refers to consistency: a person's score on a test at one point in time should be similar to the score obtained by the same person on a similar test at a later point in time.* If you took the WAIS–R as a senior in high school and then retook the test as a junior in college, your score would be much the same. This is another way of saying that the Wechsler scales, like other standardized IQ tests, are *reliable.* Researchers have found that a person's verbal scores on the WAIS–R are quite stable from age 20 to 74, although there is a considerable drop in performance scores (Kaufman, Reynolds, & McLean, 1989).

Tests of intelligence based on handwriting analysis may actually have good reliability, provided your handwriting remains constant. However, tests that have great reliability but lack validity are useless.

Validity

A good test must also have **validity**, *which means that the test measures what it is supposed to measure.* To a large extent, the validity of an intelligence test depends on the definition of intelligence. If we define intelligence as the ability to perform well in academic settings, then the WAIS–R is a valid test because it predicts academic performance reasonably well. The correlation between IQ score and performance in academic settings ranges from 0.30 to 0.70 (Jensen, 1980). Nevertheless, the cognitive abilities measured by IQ tests do not account for all of a person's performance in academic settings. For instance, when Terman followed the lives of individuals with very high IQs (an average of 151), he discovered that about 30% never finished their college degrees and 2% actually flunked out (Terman & Oden, 1959). According to this study, a high IQ alone does not guarantee academic success, because other personality, motivational, and emotional factors also come into play. Researchers generally agree that *IQ scores alone do not predict whether a person will have a successful career or be effective in solving and adjusting to life's problems* (Zigler & Seitz, 1982).

With regard to handwriting analysis, there is no evidence that such tests actually measure intelligence, so they lack validity. Similarly, many psychological tests in the popular press are relatively useless, as they generally have poor validity.

Changes in IQ Scores Across Time

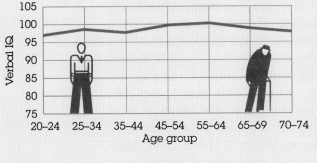

In agreement with previous studies, researchers found little or no decline in verbal IQ across time. That is, scores on verbal subtests remained about the same for individuals in different age groups.

In agreement with previous studies, researchers found a decline in performance IQ across time. That is, scores on performance subtests decreased for older age groups.

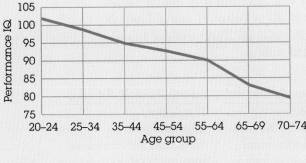

In agreement with previous studies, researchers found a decline in full-scale IQ scores across time. However, this decline is due primarily to a decrease in performance IQ, since verbal IQ remained about the same.

Individuals in seven different age groups (cross-sectional study) were given the WAIS–R. Scores are corrected for level of education (adapted from Kaufman et al., 1989).

Next we'll show you a bell-shaped curve, which nicely describes how IQ scores are distributed throughout the general population.

Distribution of IQ Scores

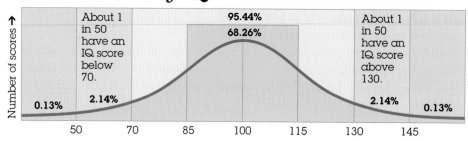

A normal distribution of IQ scores. Over two-thirds of IQ scores fall between 85 and 115.

IQ scores on the Stanford-Binet or WAIS–R have a **normal distribution;** *that is, the scores have a symmetrical arrangement so that the vast majority of scores fall in the middle range and fewer scores fall near the extreme ends of the range.* A normal distribution of IQ scores is represented by the bell-shaped curve above.

One use of IQ scores has been to help identify individuals with mental retardation or those who are gifted or have exceptional skills. However, psychologists caution against using IQ scores as the sole test for either mental retardation or giftedness.

Mental Retardation—One End of the Normal Distribution

An example of an individual with organic retardation is Chris Burke, co-star of the ABC television series *Life Goes On.* Chris has Down syndrome, a genetic defect that results in varying degrees of mental retardation and physical symptoms (slanting eyes, flattened nose, visual problems). Chris has mild mental retardation, has learned an acting skill, and can function very well outside an institution.

As you may remember, Binet originally developed his intelligence test to identify those children who may need special educational help and opportunities. Although IQ tests are used to identify possible cases of mental retardation, they are not the only test. Psychologists have discovered that some individuals who are classified as mentally retarded according to IQ scores are actually functioning very well in society; they are often married and hold steady jobs. For this reason, the notion of social competence has been included in the definition of mental retardation (Matson & Mulick, 1990). **Mental retardation** *is a combination of limited mental ability, usually an IQ of below 70, and difficulty in functioning in everyday life.* Three levels of retardation have been identified.

Mildly Mentally Retarded

These individuals have IQs that range from 50 to 70. With special training and educational opportunities they can learn to read and write, gain social competency, master simple occupational skills, and become self-supporting members of society. About 70% of retarded individuals are in this category.

Moderately Mentally Retarded

These individuals have IQs that range from 35 to 50. With special training and educational opportunities they can learn to become partially independent in their everyday lives, provided they are in a family or self-help setting.

Severely Mentally Retarded

These individuals have IQs that range from 20 to 40. With special training and educational opportunities they can acquire limited skills in taking care of their personal needs. However, because of retarded motor and verbal abilities they require considerable supervision their entire lives.

There are two general causes of mental retardation: **organic retardation** *results from genetic problems or brain damage;* **cultural-familial retardation** *results from greatly impoverished environments with no evidence of genetic or brain damage.* Approximately 5 million Americans have various degrees of mental retardation.

Gifted—The Other End of the Normal Distribution

Charlie

When Charlie was only 4 years old, he liked to browse through magazines in stores. Adults who were also looking at magazines would often glance down at little Charlie and ask, "Do you like to look at pictures?"

Charlie would glance up and reply, "Not especially. I like reading the articles."

The adults would laugh and ask little Charlie to read from an article. To their surprise, Charlie would read fluently.

When Charlie started school at the age of 6, he was far ahead of his classmates. By age 9 he had decided to become a doctor instead of an astronomer or a Standard Oil executive, two professions he had also considered. In high school, Charlie was placed in a special class for very bright students (adapted from Hollingsworth, 1942).

Psychologists describe Charlie as *gifted*.

Michael

Michael is 19 years old, but he has never spoken an intelligible word in his life. He has a habit of rocking his muscular body back and forth in his chair, often with grunting sounds or quick, nervous gestures. One day Michael was handed a scrambled Rubik's cube. On his first try, and in less than 40 seconds, Michael managed to unscramble the Rubik's cube, which involved rotating rows of colors until each side of the cube was a solid color. Solving Rubik's cube is so difficult that many people work on it for days without success. No one knows how Michael solved the puzzle as quickly as he did, because Michael does not speak (adapted from Restak, 1982).

Psychologists describe Michael as *autistic*.

Well-known historical figures (clockwise) Harriet Beecher Stowe, novelist; George Washington Carver, botanist; Se-quo-ya, Native American linguist; and Thomas Jefferson, third president of the United States, would all be described as gifted.

When Charlie was given an IQ test, he scored 180, which placed him in the genius range and in the gifted category. Individuals described as **gifted** *have above-average intelligence, usually IQ scores above 130, as well as some superior talent or skill.* Other examples of gifted individuals include many well-known historical figures, such as Benjamin Franklin, Thomas Jefferson, and Harriet Beecher Stowe. They would be considered gifted because their IQs are estimated to have been 150 or above and because they demonstrated special talents and skills (Cox, 1926).

Michael's ability to solve the Rubik's cube indicates an exceptional talent, but only in that one very limited area. Michael is not considered gifted because his IQ is between 50 and 70, which is in the mildly retarded range. As we discussed in Modules 1 and 13, about 10% of autistic individuals exhibit a geniuslike ability in one tiny area while lacking the basic cognitive and social abilities needed to function in society. Michael's low IQ score places him on one end of the normal distribution, while Charlie's high IQ score places him on the other end.

In some school systems the minimum IQ score for entering accelerated programs is 130–140. The best-known organization of gifted individuals is Mensa, whose members score in the top 2% of the population on IQ tests and generally have IQs of at least 135.

What happens to gifted individuals?

In the early 1920s, Lewis Terman selected a sample of almost 1,500 children with IQs ranging from 130 to 200 (the average was 151). Over the next 35 years, he repeatedly tested these people to see what they had achieved and how they had adjusted. He found that in general they enjoyed health, adjustment, and achievement above that of people with average IQs. For example, 10% to 30% more males obtained advanced degrees compared with men in the general population. About 91% of the Terman sample reported satisfactory mental health, but the remaining 9% had serious emotional problems and in some cases had to be hospitalized (Terman & Oden, 1959). This and other studies indicate that gifted individuals tend to be better adjusted and have fewer emotional problems than the general population (Janos & Robinson, 1985).

Problems with IQ Tests

Binet realized that his intelligence tests could be used in potentially dangerous ways. He cautioned that *intelligence tests do not measure innate abilities or natural intelligence;* rather, they measure an individual's cognitive abilities, which result from both heredity and environment. He also warned that *intelligence tests, by themselves, should not be used to label people* (as, for example, "moron," "average," "genius"); rather, intelligence tests should be used to assess an individual's abilities and used in combination with other information to make academic or placement decisions about people.

History shows that neither of Binet's points was taken seriously. In the early 1900s it became common practice to treat IQ scores as measures of innate intelligence and to use intelligence to label people from moron to genius (Gould, 1981). With IQ labeling came racial and cultural discrimination, some of which continues to this day.

Are IQ tests discriminatory?

Larry, a black child, was assigned to special classes for the educable mentally retarded because he scored below 85 on an IQ test. However, several years later a black psychologist retested Larry and found that his IQ score was higher than originally thought. Larry was taken out of the special classes, which were considered a dead end, and placed in regular classes that allow for more advancement (Kaplan & Saccuzzo, 1982). On the basis of Larry's experience, a class action suit was brought against the San Francisco school system on behalf of all black schoolchildren in the district. The

People from Micronesia demonstrate remarkable navigational skills as they sail long distances, using only information from stars and sea currents. These abilities indicate a high degree of intelligence that might not show up on traditional IQ tests.

suit was based on the finding that although black youngsters made up 27% of all the students enrolled in classes for the mentally retarded, they composed only 4% of the entire school population. Black parents wanted to know why their children were so much more numerous than white children in these special classes. They felt there must be a bias against black children in the selection process.

The federal court of appeals agreed with the black parents and found that IQ tests being used in schools to determine mental retardation were biased against ethnic minorities. The court ruled that California schools could not place minority children in classes for the mentally retarded on the basis of this test alone. The schools must come up with an intelligence test that does not favor whites or else refrain from using a standardized test to identify slow learners.

Increasingly, psychologists and educators believe that *IQ tests should not be used as the primary basis for decisions about a child's educational future.* Instead, IQ scores might be interpreted in the context of each child's total record, including behaviors both inside and outside the classroom (Weinberg, 1989).

Are IQ tests biased?

One major criticism of IQ tests is that they are culturally biased in favor of the white middle class. **Cultural bias** *means that the wording of the questions and the experiences on which they are based are more familiar for members of some social groups than for others.*

For example, consider the adjacent question from an older version of the Wechsler Intelligence Scale for Children.

> "What would you do if you were sent to buy a loaf of bread and the grocer said he did not have any more?"

If you think the answer is "Go to another store," you are correct according to the developers of the Wechsler scale. However, when 200 minority children were asked this same question, 61 said they would go home. Asked to explain their answers, they gave reasonable explanations. Some children answered "Go home" because in their neighborhood there were no other stores. Yet the answer "Go home" would be scored "incorrect," despite its correctness in the child's experience (Hardy et al., 1976). Because minority children often lack the experiences that white, middle-class test developers take for granted, they are often penalized on standardized tests of intelligence.

Are there culture-free IQ tests?

Psychologists have attempted to develop **culture-free tests,** *which do not contain vocabulary, experiences, or social situations that are very different from the cultural experiences of the individual taking the test.* However, the construction of culture-free tests has not been entirely successful (Anastasi, 1988). One solution to using culture-free tests is proposed by the **ecological approach,** *which studies how people solve problems in their usual employment settings.* For example, Sylvia Scribner (1986) and her associates found that dairy workers, bartenders, salespeople, and waitresses regularly solved complex problems in more efficient ways than predicted by standard IQ tests. Another example is a minority student who scores low on an IQ test but shows the ability to function well in his or her environment. Based on ability to function, the child might be placed in regular school classes rather than in a special program for the mentally retarded.

If IQ tests have so many problems, what good are they?

IQ tests can be considered one of many psychological tools used for *assessment* of cognitive skills. Like any assessment tool, IQ tests have the potential for being useful or being misused. Psychologists have found that IQ tests provide reliable information about certain cognitive skills and can be used to make relatively good predictions about people's future academic success. On the other hand, IQ scores are relatively poor for predicting success in a future career or occupation.

IQ tests are misused if they are treated as the *sole* measure of intelligence or *sole* criterion for placement into special classes. Rather, in making decisions about an individual's intelligence or academic future, IQ tests are best used in combination with other information, such as a person's school, medical, and family history as well as ability to function in a variety of social settings. IQ tests are also misused if a teacher or parent lowers expectations and performs fewer helpful behaviors toward a child because of a low IQ score (Rosenthal, 1983).

Because the history of IQ tests indicates that they have been misused, many psychological and legal guidelines are in place to prevent the misuse of IQ tests.

After the Concept/Glossary, we'll discuss how IQ tests have been used to label people and discriminate against them.

1. One approach to measuring intelligence focuses on quantifying cognitive factors or abilities that make up intellectual performance; this is called the (a)_____ approach. This approach encompasses lumpers and splitters. An example of a lumper is Charles Spearman, who formulated a two-factor theory of intelligence: one factor is *g*, or (b)_____; the second factor is *s*, or (c)_____. An example of a splitter is Howard Gardner; his (d)_____ theory identifies seven independent aspects of intelligence: verbal skills, math skills, spatial skills, movement skills, musical skills, insight about oneself, and insight about others.

2. Another approach to measuring intelligence studies how people gather information to solve problems or acquire information; this is called the (a)_____ approach. An example of this approach is Robert Sternberg's (b)_____ theory of intelligence.

3. Binet developed an intelligence test that estimated intellectual progress by comparing a child's score on an intelligence test to the scores of average children of the same age. Binet called this concept _____.

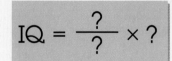

4. Lewis Terman revised Binet's intelligence test and called it the Stanford-Binet. The most significant change made by Terman was to develop a formula to compute a single score that represents a person's (a)_____. This formula is IQ = (b)_____ age divided by (c)_____ age, times (d)_____.

Information: On what continent is France?

Picture completion: Tell me what is missing.

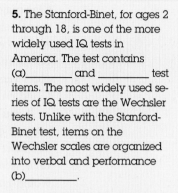

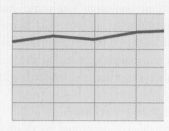

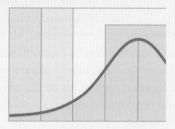

5. The Stanford-Binet, for ages 2 through 18, is one of the more widely used IQ tests in America. The test contains (a)_____ and _____ test items. The most widely used series of IQ tests are the Wechsler tests. Unlike with the Stanford-Binet test, items on the Wechsler scales are organized into verbal and performance (b)_____.

6. A good psychological test has two characteristics. It should be consistent, which is termed (a)_____; and it should measure what it is supposed to measure, which is termed (b)_____.

7. If the pattern of IQ scores can be represented by a bell-shaped curve, the pattern is called a _____. This means that scores have a symmetrical arrangement so that the vast majority fall in the middle range and fewer fall near the extreme ends of the range.

8. If an individual has a combination of limited mental ability, usually an IQ of below 70, and difficulty functioning in everyday life, the individual is said to have some degree of (a)_____. If this condition results from genetic problems or brain damage, it is called (b)_____. If this condition results from a greatly impoverished environment, it is called (c)_____. Individuals who have above-average intelligence, usually IQ scores above 120, as well as some superior talent or skill are called (d)_____.

Answers: 1. (a) *psychometric*, (b) *general intelligence*, (c) *specific abilities*, (d) *multiple-factor*, 2. (a) *information-processing*, (b) *triarchic*; 3. *mental age*; 4. (a) *intelligence quotient or IQ*, (b) *mental*, (c) *chronological*, (d) *100*. 5. (a) *verbal, performance*, (b) *subtests*; 6. (a) *reliability*, (b) *validity*; 7. *normal distribution*; 8. (a) *mental retardation*, (b) *organic retardation*, (c) *cultural-familial retardation*, (d) *gifted*.

IQ Tests and Immigration

The work of several psychologists formed the basis for some of the early immigration laws that controlled the flow of people into the United States.

Lewis Terman:
Used IQ Scores to Measure Innate Intelligence

As you may remember, Lewis Terman was the guiding force behind the Stanford-Binet test. He firmly believed that such tests can measure innate ability and that environmental influences are far less important than inherited ones. One of Terman's goals was to test all children and, based on their IQ scores, sort them into categories of innate abilities. Terman argued that society could use IQ scores (of usually 70 or below) to restrain or eliminate those whose intelligence is too low for an effective moral life (Terman, 1916). He hoped to establish minimum intelligence scores necessary for all leading occupations. For example, he believed that people with IQs below 100 should not be given employment that involves prestige or monetary reward. Those with IQs of 75 or below should be unskilled labor, and those with 75–85 IQs, semiskilled labor. In Terman's world, class boundaries were to be set by innate intelligence, as measured by his Stanford-Binet IQ test (Gould, 1981).

Terman's view that IQ tests measure innate intelligence was adopted by another well-known psychologist, Robert Yerkes.

Immigration laws, some very biased, controlled the flow of 15 million people into America between 1892 and 1943.

Robert Yerkes:
Used IQ Scores to Classify Races

Under Yerkes's direction, over 1.75 million World War I army recruits were given IQ tests. From this enormous amount of data, Yerkes (1921) and his colleagues arrived at three main points:

1. They concluded that the average mental age of white American adults was a meager 13 years, slightly above the classification of a moron. Reasons given for this low mental age were the unconstrained breeding of the poor and feeble-minded and the spread of Negro blood through interracial breeding.

2. They concluded that European immigrants could be ranked on intelligence by their country of origin. The fair peoples of western and northern Europe (Nordics) were most intelligent, while the darker peoples of southern Europe (Mediterraneans) and Slavs of eastern Europe were less intelligent.

3. They stated that Negroes were at the bottom of the racial scale in intelligence.

What happened next was a sad example of how IQ scores have been used for racial discrimination.

Immigration Quotas:
Used IQ Scores as Basis for Laws

Information on Yerkes's intelligence rankings of European races eventually reached members of the United States Congress. Outraged by the "fact" that Europeans of "low intelligence" were being allowed into America, Congressmen sought a way to severely limit the immigration of people from southern and eastern Europe. In writing the Immigration Law of 1924, Congress relied, in part, on Yerkes's racial rankings.

Stephen Jay Gould (1981), a well-known evolutionary biologist, reviewed Yerkes's data and pointed out a number of problems: poorly administered tests, terrible testing conditions, inconsistent standards for retaking tests, written tests given to illiterate recruits (guaranteeing a low score), and no control for educational level or familiarity with the English language. As a result of these problems, Gould concluded that Yerkes's data were so riddled with errors as to render useless any conclusions about racial differences in intelligence.

The Nature-Nurture Question

What is written in the genes?

Beginning in the 1900s and continuing to the present, one question about intelligence has been widely debated. Known as the **nature-nurture question,** *this refers to the relative contributions that genetic factors and environmental factors make to the development of intelligence.*

As you have just seen, some early psychologists believed that intelligence is completely inherited and due entirely to nature. This idea persists in the beliefs of Arthur Jensen (1980), who holds that intelligence is largely inherited. Opposing Jensen's emphasis on nature are psychologists Lewontin, Rose, and Kamin (1984), who emphasize nurture, or environmental effects, on shaping intelligence. There is great interest in the nature-nurture question because emphasizing the effects of nature suggests that intelligence is fixed and unchangeable after birth, whereas emphasizing the effects of nurture suggests that intelligence is more flexible and changeable.

We began this module with the example of Supreme Court Justice Clarence Thomas and his sister, Emma Mae Martin. In an early interview, Thomas was asked why he had turned out so different from his sister—why he had overcome poverty, discrimination, and hardship to make it through law school while his sister had not attended college and remained in relative poverty. Thomas replied, "We come from the same place, have the same genes, same circumstances but were raised by different relatives" (*USA Today,* July 26, 1991, p. 2A). Thomas's answer clearly emphasizes nurture (relatives' influences) over nature (genes). Let's see whether Thomas is right.

One way that researchers study the nature-nurture question is by comparing IQ scores in siblings (brothers and sisters) and in fraternal and identical twins. Like siblings, *fraternal twins*, who develop from separate eggs, have 50% of their genes in common. In comparison, *identical twins* have 100% of their genes in common because they develop from a single egg. If genetic factors contribute to intelligence (IQ scores), then IQ scores of identical twins (same genes) should be more similar than those of fraternal twins (50% of genes in common). If genetic factors contribute little to intelligence, IQ scores of identical twins should be no more similar than those of fraternal twins. Let's examine the results of twin studies.

Twin Studies

When Bouchard and McGue (1981) reviewed the results of over 100 studies on twins, they found that whether reared apart or together, identical twins were more similar in IQ scores than were fraternal twins. Fraternal twins were, in turn, more similar than siblings. For example, the correlation between intelligence scores for identical twins reared together was about .80; in fraternal twins reared together, about .55; and for siblings reared together, about .45. On the basis of twin studies, researchers generally conclude that about 50% of the contribution to intelligence (IQ scores) comes from genetic factors and about 50% comes from environmental factors (McCartney, Marris, & Bernieri, 1990; Plomin, 1989). Additional evidence that environmental factors may hinder or foster intellectual development comes from adoption studies.

How much will genetic factors influence this young girl's intellectual development?

This graph shows the correlation of IQ scores between twins reared together and apart.

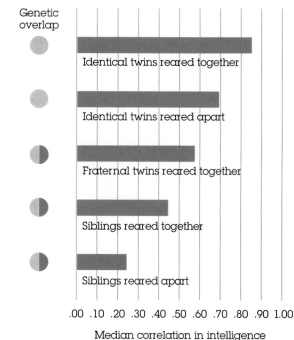

Genetic overlap

Identical twins reared together

Identical twins reared apart

Fraternal twins reared together

Siblings reared together

Siblings reared apart

.00 .10 .20 .30 .40 .50 .60 .70 .80 .90 1.00

Median correlation in intelligence

Adoption Studies

Researchers reasoned that if environmental factors can influence the development of intelligence, then providing environmental opportunities should increase IQ scores. For example, what would happen if lower-class children with limited social-educational opportunities were adopted by upper-class parents and given improved social-educational opportunities? To answer this question, a group of French researchers studied children who had been abandoned as babies by their lower-class parents and adopted during the first 6 months of life into upper-middle-class families. The researchers found that the mean IQ of the adopted children was 14 points higher than that of similar children born and raised in lower-class settings by their natural parents. In addition, the adopted children were four times less likely to fail in school. This study suggests that by improving environmental factors, such as increasing social-educational opportunities, intellectual development (as measured by IQ scores) and performance in the classroom can be improved (Schiff et al., 1982).

In a similar kind of study, researchers observed black children from impoverished environments who were adopted into white middle-class families with many more social-educational opportunities. Researchers found that the IQs of the adopted children were as much as 20 points higher than those of black children who were raised in disadvantaged homes (Scarr & Weinberg, 1976). Adoption studies support the idea that environmental factors (nurture) contribute to intellectual development (as measured by IQ scores).

The Interaction of Nature and Nurture

The general fear is that if genetic factors influence intelligence, then IQ scores may be fixed at birth. In fact, in normal individuals nothing could be further from the truth. Although studies on twins indicate that genetic factors may contribute as much as 50% to development of intelligence, the other 50% comes from one's interaction with the environment. In addition, studies on impoverished children adopted into families with social-educational opportunities indicate that environmental factors also contribute to the development of intelligence.

Richard Weinberg (1989) explains that genes do not fix intelligence; rather, genes only establish a range of possible behaviors that interact with one's environment. Depending on the environment, one's intellectual potential may be hindered or fostered. Psychologists use the term **reaction range** *to indicate the extent that IQ scores may increase or decrease as a result of environmental factors.* Researchers estimate that the reaction range may vary up or down by as much as 20 to 25 IQ points (Zigler & Seitz, 1982). The fact that IQ points may vary so greatly means two things. First, heredity (nature) establishes a very broad range for intellectual development. Second, one's intellectual development depends on the interaction between nature and nurture, between genetic and environmental factors.

The idea that much of intellectual development depends on environmental factors has resulted in programs to help impoverished children. We'll next examine one of the most popular of these programs—Head Start.

Estimates for the amount of genetic influence on IQ scores range from a low of 50% to a high of 70%.

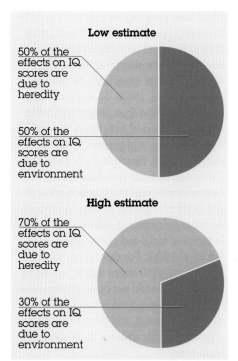

Low estimate

50% of the effects on IQ scores are due to heredity

50% of the effects on IQ scores are due to environment

High estimate

70% of the effects on IQ scores are due to heredity

30% of the effects on IQ scores are due to environment

How much will environmental factors influence this young boy's development?

APPLYING/ EXPLORING: INTERVENTION PROGRAMS

Nancy lives in a lower-class black neighborhood and earns less than $1,500 a year. She has completed only two years of high school and her IQ is 85. She is in her mid-twenties and is pregnant. Given her background and current environment, psychologists would predict that Nancy's child is unlikely to acquire the kind of cognitive skills needed to do well in school. The youngster is a good candidate for an intervention program (Ramey, MacPhee, & Yeates, 1982).

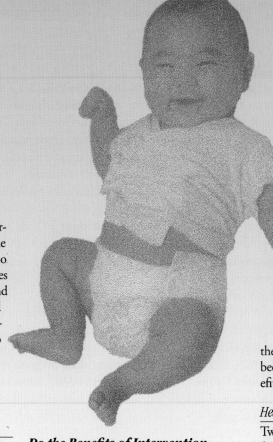

An impoverished environment would put this child at risk for poor intellectual development.

What Is an Intervention Program?

An **intervention program** *creates an environment that offers increased opportunities for intellectual, social, and personality-emotional development.* Perhaps the best-known intervention program is Head Start, which has been running since 1965. In 1989 Head Start enrolled 460,000 3- to 5-year-olds in preschool at a cost of over a billion dollars. Dozens of studies on the effectiveness of Head Start and other intervention programs have focused on some of the questions we discuss here.

Does Head Start Prepare Disadvantaged Children for Grade School?

In answering this question, researchers compared disadvantaged black children who had been in the Head Start program with control children who had not had the benefit of this preschool training. Children who had been in Head Start for a year scored higher on several tests of cognitive ability and social competency (Lee et al., 1990). Similarly, a large evaluation study of Head Start concluded that children in the program showed greater gains than control children in social-emotional development as well as in intellectual skills (McKey et al., 1985).

Do the Benefits of Intervention Programs Last?

One of the original questions asked of intervention programs was whether they could raise the IQ scores of disadvantaged children. In addressing this question, we'll discuss two different intervention programs.

Abecedarian Project

An intervention program called the Abecedarian Project was more intense in time and effort than most Head Start programs (Ramey, MacPhee, & Yeates, 1982). Psychologists identified babies who were at high risk for school failure by being born to mothers with low IQs in disadvantaged environmental settings. With the mothers' permission, these infants spent six or more hours daily, five days a week, in a carefully supervised day care center. The day care continued until the child entered public school. The goal of the program was to teach youngsters from disadvantaged environments the cognitive and social skills needed for success in academic settings.

At the end of the fourth year, children in the Abecedarian Project had IQ scores 12 points higher than control children from disadvantaged environments. However, by the end of the fifth year, the difference in IQ scores was reduced to 7 points. Apparently the disadvantaged children who had not been in the intervention program were benefiting from having started public schooling.

Head Start

Two to three years after leaving Head Start, few if any differences on IQ or other academic scores were found between Head Start children and control groups (Clarke & Clarke, 1989). Despite the fact that differences in IQ scores had faded in several years, the Head Start program showed other important long-term beneficial effects. For example, adolescents who had been in the Head Start program were more likely to be in classes appropriate for their ages rather than to have had to repeat a class, were less likely to show antisocial or delinquent behavior, and were more likely to hold jobs (Zigler & Seitz, 1982). Mothers who had been in the Head Start program reported fewer psychological symptoms, greater feelings of mastery, and greater current life satisfaction (Parker, Piotrkowski, & Peay, 1987). These data indicate that although IQ increases may be transitory, intervention programs offer long-term positive benefits to both the participating children and mothers in terms of social and personal well-being (Holden, 1990). For this reason, Richard Weinberg (1989) warns that IQ scores, by themselves, should not be used to evaluate intervention programs; instead, the personality, motivational, and other psychological adjustments that children make should be considered.

Intervention programs help children develop into their cognitive, social, and emotional "shoes."

What Would Happen if There Were No Intervention Programs?

Psychologists Craig Ramey and Sharon Ramey (1990) make two important points about the usefulness of intervention programs such as Head Start:

1 Intervention programs can reduce the devastating effects that continuing poverty across several generations can have on families and children. These effects include delays in young children's developmental progress, lowered aspirations and increased apathy among older children, and school failure or withdrawal.

2 Intensive intervention programs during the first five years of life are effective in reducing and preventing the significant intellectual dysfunction that may result from continuing poverty and its lack of environmental support.

Without Head Start and other intervention programs, there would be no organized way to rescue children from impoverished environments and help them reach their potentials as human beings.

Do children who attend Head Start programs continue to reap benefits from it as adolescents?

Summary/Self-Test

APPROACHES TO DEFINING INTELLIGENCE

1. Since the late 1800s psychologists have studied intelligence in depth. They generally agree that intelligence has three aspects: (a)_____, _____, and _____. The analysis of intelligence is part of the field of (b)_____, which assesses an individual's abilities, skills, beliefs, and personality traits.

2. The psychometric approach focuses on measuring or quantifying (a)_____ that make up intellectual performance. Those who ascribe to the psychometric approach and group these cognitive factors together are called (b)_____; they define intelligence as a general unified capacity for reasoning, acquiring knowledge, and solving problems.

Intelligence testing today is dominated by the lumpers of the psychometric approach, in part because current IQ tests successfully predict performance in academic and some job settings. According to Spearman's (c)_____ theory of intelligence, everyone has a general intelligence factor, termed (d)_____, as well as specific abilities, labeled (e)_____.

3. Those who view cognitive factors in intelligence individually are called (a)_____; they define intelligence as composed of many separate mental abilities that function more or less independently. According to Gardner's (b)_____ theory, there are at least seven independent aspects of intelligence; these are (c)_____, _____, _____, _____, _____, _____, and _____.

4. The (a)_____ approach studies how people gather information to solve problems or acquire information. An example of this approach is Robert Sternberg's (b)_____ theory of intelligence, which says that intelligence can be divided into three ways of processing information, which are (c)_____, _____, and _____ skills.

■ *Ray Kroc, who started the world-famous McDonald's hamburger chain and built it into a multibillion-dollar business, never finished high school. Do you think he was as intelligent as Albert Einstein?*

MEASURING INTELLIGENCE

5. In trying to measure intelligence, researchers through the years have learned that neither skull size nor brain weight is an accurate predictor of (a)_____. The first intelligence test, called the (b)_____ Intelligence Scale, measured vocabulary, memory, common knowledge, and other cognitive abilities. By comparing a child's score with the scores of average children at the same age, Binet was able to estimate a child's (c)_____. In a later revision of Binet's test, Terman devised a formula to calculate an individual's intelligence quotient. The formula can be written as IQ = (d)_____.

■ *A new intelligence test is based on a very accurate count of all the cells in your brain. Do you think this will prove to be a good test of intelligence?*

WIDELY USED IQ TESTS

6. A good psychological test must have (a)_____ and _____; that is, the test results must be consistent and the test must measure what it is supposed to measure. Three tests in wide use today are the (b)_____, _____, and _____. Each test measures verbal and performance abilities; the Wechsler scales are organized into (c)_____.

■ *Your friend filled out a questionnaire that promised to select the perfect date, yet the date turned out to be awful. What was wrong with the questionnaire?*

DISTRIBUTION OF IQ SCORES

7. Mental retardation is a combination of limited mental ability, usually an IQ of below 70, and difficulty functioning in everyday life. There are two general causes of mental retardation: (a)_____ retardation results from genetic problems or brain damage; (b)_____ retardation results from greatly impoverished environments, with no evidence of genetic or brain damage. At the other end of the normal distribution of IQ scores are those who are considered (c)_____; such people have above-average intelligence, usually IQs above 130, as well as some superior talent or skill.

■ *You are going to hire 25 people for a new business that makes and sells donuts. Would it help in making your hiring decisions if you knew each applicant's IQ score?*

PROBLEMS WITH IQ TESTS

8. Despite Binet's admonitions that intelligence tests should not be used to measure innate abilities or to label people, they have been used in this way, with detrimental effects. One criticism of IQ tests has been that they are _____ in favor of the white middle class. For this and other reasons, psychologists have warned that IQ tests not be used as the primary basis for decisions about a child's educational future.

■ *Most big cities have growing populations of minorities (blacks, Mexican Americans, Asians). Would there be any problem with using IQ scores to place them in grade schools?*

CULTURAL DIVERSITY: IQ TESTS AND IMMIGRATION

9. In contrast to Binet, Terman believed that IQ tests do measure innate intelligence. His view was adopted by Robert Yerkes and ultimately used as a basis for _____.

■ *What convinced members of the United States Congress that IQ scores should be used to influence immigration policy?*

THE NATURE-NURTURE QUESTION

10. The (a)_____ question refers to the relative contributions that genetic and environmental factors make to the development of intelligence. On the basis of twin studies, researchers generally conclude that about (b)_____ of the contribution to intelligence (IQ scores) comes from genetic factors and about (c)_____ comes from environmental factors. Adoption studies support the idea that environmental factors contribute to intellectual development (as measured by IQ scores). The idea that about half of one's in-

tellectual development is dependent on environmental factors has resulted in (d)_____ programs that give impoverished children increased social-educational opportunities.

■ *An upper-class couple is thinking about adopting a child from an impoverished, lower-class unmarried mother. Should the couple be worried that the child's genetic makeup will limit intellectual development?*

APPLYING/EXPLORING: INTERVENTION PROGRAMS

11. An intervention program creates an environment that offers increased opportunities for _____, _____, and _____ development. The data indicate that although IQ increases resulting from intervention programs may be transitory, long-term positive benefits are conferred to both the participating children and their mothers in terms of social and personal well-being.

■ *A newspaper article criticizes Head Start for failing to raise IQ scores and recommends that the program be dropped. What would you reply?*

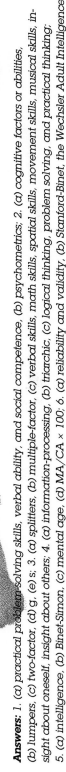

MODULE 16
THOUGHT AND LANGUAGE

Zsofi and Judit discovered that men especially hate to lose to women.

What's in a game?

Judit and Zsofi are two Hungarian sisters, ages 15 and 17, who behave much like average teenagers anywhere when they talk about clothes, boys, and going out. But when they sit down in front of a chess board, their eyes seem to darken, their faces turn serious, and they become highly competitive players. Their father started each girl playing chess at age 4—for as many as six hours a day. Their early training has shown results.

In 1989 Judit was the number one woman player in the world and Zsofi was in the top ten. Unlike some women players who compete in women-only chess matches, Judit and Zsofi have played in mixed male-female tournaments. The sisters have had to put up with open discrimination from male players who generally view women players as inferior. However, as a result of their unbelievable success against men, Judit and Zsofi have challenged long-standing notions about male superiority in chess. At age 12 Judit had done better than any other 12-year-old chess player in history—including former world champion Bobby Fisher and current world champion Gary Kasparov. In fact, Kasparov has remarked that the next world champion may be Judit, provided she can beat Zsofi. Judit may well be on her way to the world championship. In early 1992, her fantastic string of wins earned her the rating of grandmaster, which is the highest rating in chess. (adapted from *Newsweek*, March 27, 1989)

Psychologists are interested in Judit and Zsofi because playing chess involves a number of cognitive abilities, such as thinking, planning, and solving problems, all of which are included in the cognitive approach. As you may remember from Module 1, the **cognitive approach** *studies how we gather, process, and store information, as well as how we think, solve problems, engage in creative activities, and use language.* The topics studied by the cognitive approach are usually included in the concept of *mind,* which refers to the processes of thinking, remembering, perceiving, and using language. Instead of using the concept of mind, psychologists more often use the terms *cognitive processes* or *cognition* when referring to mental processes.

We already discussed several aspects of the cognitive approach when we examined memory and forgetting in Modules 13 and 14. Here we'll explore two more cognitive processes: **thinking**, *which includes forming concepts, solving problems, and engaging in creative activities,* and *language,* which is a special form of communicaton in which an individual learns complex rules to manipulate symbols (words or gestures) that are used to generate an endless number of meaningful sentences.

What's Coming

In the first half of this module, we'll discuss forming concepts, solving problems, and creative thinking. In the second half, we'll focus on the rules, development, and use of language.

Concepts

What is the one thing that these animals share in common?

When Judit began to play chess at age 4, her first task was to learn how each piece moved. In time and with practice, she formed a concept for each piece's movement. A **concept** *is a way to group objects, events, or characteristics on the basis of some common property they all share.* For instance, Judit learned the concept that bishops move diagonally, rooks move forward and backward, but queens can move any direction they please.

*How do you tell a **human** from a **hippopotamus**?*
At this point in your life, you have learned thousands of concepts for objects, events, and characteristics. For example, look at the photos on the left, which show faces that differ in coloring, amount of hair, number of teeth, presence of whiskers, and other features. Despite seeing only the face, you can distinctly identify each animal, knowing whether it is a fox, human, or hippopotamus. You are able to identify them because you have developed a concept for each animal. Similarly, you have developed concepts for identifying fruits, vegetables, rock stars, and American presidents.

Now, take another look at the photos and identify the common property they share. From the position of their mouths, you recognize that each of the animals is yawning. You can identify the facial position because you have a concept for what a yawn is. Your ability to identify these animals and then notice they are yawning illustrates the usefulness of concepts.

Functions of Concepts
Concepts perform two important functions:

1 Concepts allow us to *group things into categories* and thus better organize and store information in memory. You can, for instance, group all three images into one category—yawning animals—and store one concept in memory instead of many separate ones.

2 Concepts allow us to *identify things without relearning.* Once you have a concept for a horse, lion, dog, and fox, you do not have to relearn what they are on each new encounter. In this case, a concept may save your life, since you know which one of these four animals to avoid.

With these two important functions of concepts, we can gather, process, and store information in more efficient ways. Without concepts, our cognitive worlds would consist of unconnected pieces of information whose relationships we would have to relearn constantly.

Because concepts are critical to effective thinking, let's examine how you might have formed a concept for one particular animal.

Forming Concepts

Why does it take only one look at the magnificent creature below to know that it is a tiger? The reason you so easily identify this animal and discriminate it from all others is that you have formed a concept of a "tiger." We'll examine two theories of forming concepts—definitional and prototype—to see which one best describes how we form concepts.

Definitional Theory

How would you find a tiger in the zoo?

According to the **definitional theory,** *you form a concept of an object, event, or characteristic by making a list of the properties that define it.* Suppose your concept of a tiger is a large, catlike animal with enormous teeth and black stripes on yellow-brownish fur. With this concept in mind, you could walk around a zoo until you located such a beast.

Notice that your tiger concept sounds very much like a dictionary definition, which lists the essential properties of the object. According to definitional theory, you formed a concept of a tiger because you made a mental list of the properties that define a tiger. In this case, it seems to work; however, the definitional theory of forming concepts has two serious problems.

Do we form concepts by making up dictionary-like definitions?

ti′ gĕr, *n.; pl.* **ti′ gĕrs** or **ti′ gĕr,** [ME. and OFr. *tigre,* from L. *tigris,* from Gr. *tigris,* from Per. *tighri,* a tiger, from *tighra,* sharp, pointed.]
   1. a large, fierce, carnivorous animal of the cat family, *Felis tigris.* Its coat is bright reddish-yellow or tawny with irregular stripes of black. It has short hair and no mane and is as large or larger than a lion and much more agile.
   2. any of several similar animals, as (a) the South American jaguar; (b) the South African leopard; (c) the Tasmanian tiger or wolf.

How did you know that this is a tiger and not a lion or a very large house cat?

Problems with the Definitional Theory

1 The first problem is the *difficulty in listing all the defining properties* of an object (Rey, 1983). For instance, our list of properties that define a tiger would also apply to some leopards, jaguars, and lions. Similarly, if you were asked to list the defining properties of a dog, your properties would need to include everything from a tiny, hairless chihuahua to a large, hairy sheepdog, from a no-nose bulldog without a tail to a long-nosed collie with a long, flowing tail. Because of the incredible variations in dogs, a list of necessary properties that define a dog would be almost endless.

2 The second problem is that *exceptions always occur and are not included in our list of defining properties.* For example, our list of properties that define a tiger would not apply to albino tigers (black stripes on white fur). Similarly, a list of properties that defined a chair as a four-legged structure in which one sits would not include a three-legged stool or a bean-bag chair.

Because of these problems with the definitional theory, psychologists have developed a second theory—prototype theory—to explain how we form concepts.

Prototype Theory

To understand prototype theory you must first know that a **prototype** *is essentially the average of all the various categories that we have encountered.* For instance, a prototype dog would be of average age, height, weight, and color. Thus, according to **prototype theory,** *we form a concept by constructing an idea of the ideal or prototypic object and then seeing whether a new object matches the prototype.* For example, when we encounter some animal, we automatically compare features of the new animal to our prototype dog. If the features of the new animal match those of our prototype, we conclude that the new object is a dog and not a cat, rabbit, or skunk (Cohen & Murphy, 1984; Rosch, 1978).

Advantages of Prototype Theory

1 With prototype theory, you *do not have to worry about defining all the essential features of an object,* which is often difficult or impossible. Instead, you develop a prototype that has average features. It is easier to develop a prototype dog with average features than to make a list of essential features to cover all dogs.

2 With prototype theory, you *do not have to worry about wide variations or exceptions.* Because a prototype has average features, it automatically includes wide variations and most exceptions. For example, the average features of a prototype dog would apply equally well to a 120-pound St. Bernard as to a 4-pound chihuahua. However, the closer a new object matches your prototype, the more quickly you can identify it. You can quickly decide that a robin is a bird because robins more closely match the prototypical bird, but you need longer to decide that a penguin is a bird because penguins do not as closely match the prototype.

There is now considerable evidence that one of the ways we form concepts involves prototypes, which help us identify things quickly and efficiently (Schwartz & Reisberg, 1991).

Prototype versus Definitional Theory

How do you form a concept of a tiger?

According to definitional theory, you form a concept of "tiger" by making a list of all the essential features that define a tiger. If you meet an animal that has the essential features of a tiger, then you know it is a tiger.

According to prototype theory, you do not form a list of essential features that define a tiger. Instead, you construct an ideal or prototype tiger that is of average everything—height, weight, and color. If you meet an animal that matches your prototype or ideal tiger, then you know the animal is a tiger.

Definitional Theory Concept of tiger is a complete list of exact properties that define a tiger.	*versus*	**Prototype Theory** Concept of tiger is made up of average height, average weight, average teeth, average tail, average stripes.

We have discussed how concepts are useful for identifying objects and saving us from having to relearn the same things over and over. Now let's examine other ways that we use concepts: to solve problems and to think creatively.

Solving Problems

Gary Kasparov defeats Deep Thought, a highly rated computer chess program.

What's my next move?

We spend a considerable part of our time solving problems of all kinds, such as learning a new job, using a computer, putting together unassembled furniture, playing chess, mastering mathematics, or answering test questions. **Problem solving** *involves searching for some rule, plan, or strategy that results in our reaching a certain goal that is currently out of reach.* Although we must use different rules, plans, or strategies, we go through the following three states in solving problems: (1) *the initial state,* which is contemplating the unsolved problem; (2) *the operations state,* which is trying various operations, rules, or strategies to solve the problem; and (3) *the goal state,* which is reaching the solution. Let's begin with how we use certain rules to solve problems.

Two Rules for Solving Problems

We began this module with the story of two Hungarian sisters, Judit and Zsofi, each of whom hopes to become the world chess champion. Close on their heels are other humans and several computers, including a computer program named Deep Thought, which has achieved the highest rating in chess, grandmaster. A chess match between a human and a computer illustrates two kinds of rules—algorithms and heuristics—that are used to solve problems.

Algorithms

We win at games such as chess, checkers, and bridge by following **algorithms** (AL-go-rhythms), *which are rules that, if followed correctly, will eventually lead to a solution.* The first thing you do in learning to play a game is to master its rules or algorithms. Because people vary in their ability to follow and apply algorithms, they differ in their ability to solve problems and win at games. Algorithms are used to handle a variety of problems, such as solve math equations, assemble furniture, or win chess games.

One reason for Deep Thought's great success at chess is a new algorithm that allows it to search up to 30 moves simultaneously instead of the previous 4 moves.

Heuristics

As you gain experience with solving problems, you may use **heuristics** (hyour-RIS-ticks), *which are rules of thumb that reduce the number of operations or allow one to take shortcuts in solving problems.*

One reason that world chess champion Gary Kasparov defeated Deep Thought was that Kasparov compensated for the computer's sizzling speed (analysis of 750,000 moves per second) by using clever shortcuts, or heuristics. Kasparov uses heuristics that allow him to identify a limited number of best moves and search them in great depth.

Common Heuristics

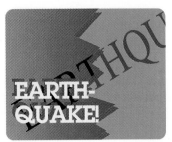

Why do we tend to remember disasters?

We use heuristics to make many kinds of decisions (Smith & Kida, 1991). Psychologists Amos Tversky and Daniel Kahneman (1974, 1983) have discovered a number of heuristics that people use in making everyday decisions.

An example of a common heuristic is the availability heuristic. According to the **availability heuristic,** *we rely on information that is more prominent or easily recalled and overlook other information that is available but less prominent or notable.* For example, you may think that the evening news contained only tragic events, since those are most prominent in your memory. However, if you were asked to think about the newscast, you would recall other, positive events.

When we use the availability heuristic to make a decision, we are essentially using a shortcut. Although heuristics allow us to make quick decisions, they may result in "bad" decisions, since we made them with a limited amount of information.

Sometimes we are not given the rules to solve problems but must develop our own strategies. Let's explore several effective strategies.

Developing Strategies for Solving Problems

Most of us have had the experience of studying a problem that at first seems unsolvable. By studying how people eventually solve problems, psychologists have discovered a number of useful strategies.

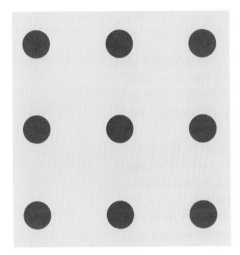

General Problem:	
Write a term paper	

Subgoals:

1 Do library research

2 Take notes

3 Make detailed outline

4 Write paper

Changing One's Mental Set

Try the nine-dot problem you see here. Your task is to connect all nine dots by drawing four straight lines—without lifting your pencil from the paper or retracing any lines. Try to solve it before reading any further.

Could you solve the problem? If, like most people, you failed to solve it, you may be a victim of **functional fixedness,** *which is a mental set characterized by the inability to see an object as having a function different from its usual one.* For instance, you probably have a mental set that a straight line must begin and end on a dot. To solve the nine-dot problem, you need to break out of functional fixedness and think of a line as continuing past the dot. (The solution is on page 300.)

Some people solve this problem in a sudden flash known as insight. **Insight** *is the sudden grasp of a solution after many incorrect attempts.* You can increase your chances of solving problems by insight if you consider the problem from many different viewpoints and unusual angles and and if you decrease your anxiety and concern, which will in turn help you to overcome functional fixedness.

Using Analogies

What plan or strategy could you use to solve the following problem? You have a box of matches, two candles, a piece of string, and several tacks. How would you mount the candle on the wall so that it could be used as a light? (The answer is on page 300.)

You may solve the candle problem in a flash of insight. For most of us, however, the solution may take some thinking. One kind of thinking for solving problems is to use an **analogy,** *which is finding a similarity between the new situation and an old, familiar situation.*

If you use an analogy in the candle problem, here's how your thinking might proceed: "I am familiar with using a shelf to hold a candle on the wall. Which of the objects—candle, string, or box—could serve as a shelf? If I empty the matches, I can tack the box to the wall."

As you gain more experience and knowledge, you become better at using analogies to solve problems. This is one reason that businesses prefer employees with experience: these employees are more likely to use analogies to solve problems.

Forming Subgoals

Suppose you have to write a term paper titled "Creativity and Mental Health." A useful strategy for writing the paper (solving the problem) would be to break the task of writing the paper down into a number of **subgoals,** *which are separate parts that when completed in order will result in a solution.* For example, the first subgoal is doing library research and finding a number of articles on creativity and mental health. The second subgoal is reading the articles and taking notes. The third subgoal is making a detailed outline of the whole paper. A fourth subgoal is using your outline to write the paper. By completing all four subgoals, you will have completed your paper.

The strategy of breaking a general problem down into subgoals accomplishes two things. First, it makes the overall problem easier to work on since you have a series of smaller goals. Second, by having smaller goals, you are more likely to complete the project and less likely to procrastinate.

In some cases, you may want to combine several strategies to solve problems more efficiently. And in many cases, solving problems requires creative thinking, our next topic.

Thinking Creatively

On the one hand, the product of creative thinking can be totally obvious, as in the case of Dr. Seuss's book, *The Cat in the Hat,* which has delighted a generation of kids and grownups. On the other hand, the process of creative thinking can be quite elusive, as you'll discover when we try to define it. We've organized our discussion of creative thinking around five of the most often asked questions.

What is creative thinking?

According to psychologist James Greeno (1989), **creative thinking** *is a combination of flexibility in thinking and reorganization in understanding to produce innovative ideas and solutions.* Well-known products of creative thinking include Michelangelo's Sistine Chapel ceiling, Einstein's theory of relativity, Freud's discovery of psychoanalysis, and Dr. Seuss's rhyming books.

> **What kind of creativity did Dr. Seuss demonstrate?**

Psychologists may also define creative thinking as a type of **divergent thinking,** *which is beginning with a problem and coming up with many solutions* (Guilford, 1967). Examples of divergent thinking include coming up with ways to recycle trash, devising methods for teaching science in schools, and creating ways to advertise a product. The opposite of divergent thinking is **convergent thinking,** *which is beginning with a problem and coming up with the one correct solution.* Examples of convergent thinking include answering multiple-choice questions, solving math problems, and alphabetizing a list.

Can creative thinking be taught?

Based on her research, Teresa Amabile (1985; Amabile, Hennessey, & Grossman, 1986) has described what's needed for creative thinking: being knowledgeable in a particular area, having the ability to concentrate and persist, looking at problems in new ways, and, most important, doing the work for love (which is *intrinsic* motivation) rather than for money or other external rewards (which is *extrinsic* motivation).

Amabile (1985) has outlined a comprehensive program for encouraging creativity in children and adults. This program includes providing a stimulating environment; teaching children how to identify creative thinking; advising parents, educators, and managers to encourage certain nonconforming and unpredictable behaviors that may lead to creative performances; allowing as much freedom as possible in working and completing tasks; and decreasing competition and increasing intrinsic motivation. She believes that the efforts needed to develop and implement this program in a school or a workplace would be more than justified by the accompanying increase in creativity.

Other approaches to encouraging creativity involve training in divergent thinking. One such approach is called **brainstorming,** *which involves a group of people trying to solve a specific problem while following four basic rules:*

1 Do not criticize the suggestions of others.

2 Generate as many ideas as possible.

3 Attempt to be original.

4 Build on others' suggestions.

What traits do creative people have?

In a meeting of internationally known artists and scientists, Harvard Professor David Perkins identified six psychological traits of creative thinkers (Weisburg, 1987):

1. *They have a drive to make sense of or bring order out of chaos.* As discussed in Module 1, Sigmund Freud's psychoanalytic theory, with its emphasis on unconscious feelings and fears, made sense out of the observation that patients could have problems without knowing what caused them.

2. *They have a strong interest in finding and solving unusual problems.* As discussed in Module 12, B. F. Skinner had a great interest in identifying how behavior is dependent on reinforcement.

3. *They believe in objectivity or the need to test creative ideas.* As discussed in Module 12, Albert Bandura hypothesized that humans learn through observation. He tested this idea by studying how children observed and imitated the behaviors of models.

4. *They are not afraid to take risks or live in a novel and uncertain world.* As discussed in Module 1, John Watson took a risk when he declared that psychologists should no longer study mental processes but rather stick entirely to observable behaviors.

5. *They have the ability to change mental directions and consider problems from many angles.* As discussed in Module 1, Abraham Maslow's humanistic approach looked at motivation from many different angles, from psychological needs to the need for achieving personal growth.

6. *They are driven by internal or intrinsic motivation and not by money, reward, or recog-* nition. How many millionaire psychologists can you think of? Creative thinking is sparked by challenges and maintained by the satisfaction of accomplishment.

Perkins believes that these six traits of creative thinking can be taught and encouraged in young children but that conventional schooling does not do so.

The Cat in the Hat was written by Dr. Seuss (Theodor Geisel), who died in 1991.

Is there a relationship between creativity and IQ?

Compared with the general population, creative scientists, writers, and artists generally score above average (120 and higher) on intelligence tests. However, when creative individuals are compared among themselves, there is at best only a modest correlation between creativity and IQ. In other words, those who are generally recognized as creative do tend to have above-average IQ scores, but those with the highest IQs are not necessarily those who are the most creative (Barron & Harrington, 1981).

1. To study how we gather, process, and store information, as well as how we think, solve problems, and engage in creative activities, psychologists use the _____ approach.

2. A way to group objects, events, or characteristics on the basis of some common property is called a _____; grouping objects allows us to better organize and store information in memory and identify things without relearning.

ti′ gĕr, *n.*; *pl.* **ti′ gĕrs** or **ti′ gĕr,** [ME. and OFr. *tigre,* from L. *tigris,* from Gr. *tigris,* from Per. *tighri,* a tiger, from *tighra,* sharp, pointed.]

3. If you form a concept of an object, event, or characteristic by making a list of the properties that define it, you are forming a concept according to the _____ theory.

4. If you form a concept by putting together the average characteristics of an object and then seeing whether a new object matches your average object, you are forming a concept according to the (a)_____ theory. If you develop an idea of a dog of average age, height, weight, and color, you have formed a (b)_____ of a dog.

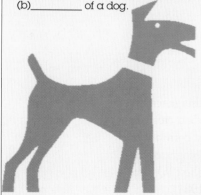

5. If you search for some rule, plan, or strategy that results in your reaching a certain goal that is currently out of reach, you are engaging in an activity called (a)_____. During this activity, you go through three states: contemplating the unsolved problem, which is the (b)_____ state; trying out various operations, rules, or strategies to solve the problem, which is the (c)_____ state; and reaching the solution, which is the (d)_____.

6. Some problems can be solved by following certain rules. If you correctly follow rules that lead to a certain solution, you are using (a)_____. If you follow rules that reduce the number of operations or allow you to take shortcuts in solving problems, you are using (b)_____.

7. Sometimes you use heuristics in making everyday decisions. If you rely on information that is more prominent or easily recalled and overlook other information that is available but less prominent or notable, you are using the _____ heuristic.

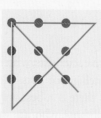

Answers to problems on page 297.

8. There are several effective strategies for solving problems. One strategy is to change your mental set by overcoming (a)_____, which is a type of thinking that prevents people from seeing an object as having a function different from its usual one. A second strategy is to find a similarity between the new situation and an old, familiar situation, which is called using an (b)_____. A third strategy is to break a project down into a number of (c)_____, which are separate parts that when completed will result in a solution.

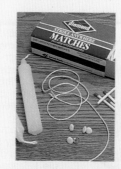

9. If you begin with a problem and come up with many different solutions, you are using (a)_____ thinking, which is one definition of creative thinking. The opposite of this type of thinking is beginning with a problem and coming up with the one correct solution; this is called (b)_____ thinking.

Answers: 1. cognitive; 2. concept; 3. definitional; 4. (a) prototype, (b) prototype; 5. (a) problem solving, (b) initial, (c) operations, (d) goal; 6. (a) algorithms, (b) heuristics; 7. availability; 8. (a) functional fixedness, (b) analogy, (c) subgoals; 9. (a) divergent, (b) convergent.

Language: Basic Rules

Of all the things that humans do, none is more impressive and distinctively human than using language. **Language** *is a special form of communication in which we learn complex rules to manipulate symbols (words or gestures) that can be used to generate an endless number of meaningful sentences.* Notice that language has at least four characteristics: (1) a special form of communication, (2) a set of symbols, (3) complex rules, and (4) the ability to generate an endless number of meaningful sentences.

As we discuss language here and in the Applying/Exploring section, we'll focus on three major questions: What are the rules for language? How is language acquired? Do animals use language like humans?

Why does what you say make sense?
Although there are over 3,000 different languages, they all share four basic language rules. Normally you learn these four rules during childhood. By applying them, you are able to speak so that you make sense.

Four Language Rules

We'll use the word *caterpillar* to explain four rules, many of which a child learns before grade school.

1 The first language rule governs **phonology** (FOE-nal-uh-gee), *which specifies how we make the meaningful sounds that are used by a particular language.* Any English word can be broken down into **phonemes** (FOE-neems), *which are the basic sounds of consonants and vowels.* For example, the various sounds of *c* and *p* represent different phonemes, which are some of the sounds in the word *caterpillar.* How we combine phonemes to form words brings us to the second rule.

2 The second language rule governs **morphology** (MOR-fal-uh-gee), *which specifies how we group phonemes into meaningful combinations of sounds and words.* A **morpheme** (MOR-feem) *is the smallest meaningful combination of sounds in a language.* For example, a morpheme may be a word (such as *cat*), a letter (the -*s* in cats), a prefix (the *un-* in *unbreakable*), or a suffix (the -*ed* in *walked*). The word *caterpillar* is actually one morpheme, and the word *caterpillars* is two (*caterpillar-s*). After we have formed words, we need to arrange them into sentences. To do this, we need the third rule.

3 The third language rule governs **syntax**, or **grammar**, *which specifies how we combine words to form meaningful phrases and sentences.* Now, read the following sentence:

Caterpillars green long and are.

You can see instantly that this sentence is ungrammatical: it violates English rules about the placement of verbs and conjunctions. The correct combination of these words is "Caterpillars are green and long." Although many of us could not list all the rules of syntax, we have learned to automatically follow them when we speak.

4 The fourth language rule governs **semantics** (si-MANT-iks), *which specifies the meaning of words in various contexts.* In the sentence "Did Pat pat a caterpillar?" the word *pat* appears twice. From your knowledge of semantics, you know that the first *Pat* is a noun and the second *pat* is a verb.

How you know that the same word in different contexts may mean different things is an intriguing question. We'll answer it in the next section.

Language: Basic Rules

Understanding Language

If you talk to a 4-year-old, you will soon realize that the child has already learned to use the four language rules, including the complex and difficult rules of grammar. However, it is most unlikely that the child can list the rules that he or she is using to form meaningful sentences. It is also unlikely that most adults can list the grammar rules that they use so proficiently.

The reason we know that young children and adults know the rules of grammar is that they can recognize a sentence with bad grammar. For example, you know that the sentence "The caterpillar crept slowly across the leaf" is correct and that the sentence "The crept leaf caterpillar slowly the across" is meaningless. To make this distinction, you automatically applied the rules of grammar to these two sentences and found that the first followed the rules while the second did not.

In learning about language, you'll read and hear the name of Noam Chomsky (1957) quite frequently. A famous linguist, he explained our ability to interpret the meaning of sentences so quickly and accurately.

How did Seth Kinast, from Hutchinson, Kansas, learn to read over 1,000 books by the age of 3?

Different Structure—Same Meaning

One of the difficult questions that Chomsky addressed was how an idea can be expressed in several different ways, with different grammatical structures, yet mean the same thing. He answered this question by making a distinction between two different structures of a sentence: surface structure and deep structure. A sentence's **surface structure** *is the actual wording of a sentence, as it is spoken.* In comparison, a sentence's **deep structure** *is an underlying meaning that is not spoken but is present in the mind of the listener.*

For example, do the two sentences to the left, which are worded very differently, have similar or opposite meanings?

According to Chomsky, you are able to "look underneath" the different surface structures of the two sentences and recognize that the first sentence "A caterpillar was examined by a happy person" has the same deep structure and therefore the same meaning as the second sentence "A happy person examined a caterpillar."

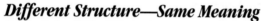

A caterpillar was examined by a happy person. **=** A happy person examined a caterpillar.

Chomsky argues that we learn to shift back and forth between surface and deep structure by applying transforming rules. **Tranformational rules** *are procedures of converting our ideas from surface structures into deep structures and from deep structures back into surface ones.* For example, when you hear the two sentences about the happy person and the caterpillar, you transform the words into their deep structure, which you store in memory. Later, when someone asks what the happy person did, you use transformational rules to convert the deep structure in your memory back into a surface structure, which can be expressed in differently worded sentences.

Most linguists agree that **Chomsky's theory of language,** *which includes the distinction between surface structure and deep structure and transformational rules,* is a remarkable first step in explaining how we produce and understand speech.

Now that you know what language is and about Chomsky's theory for what language means, we can turn to our next major question: How do we acquire a language?

Acquiring Language

Psychologists have discovered a remarkable similarity in the general way children acquire language skills across different languages and cultures (Rice, 1989). How is it possible for children around the world to acquire language at such an early age, in about the same order, and with so little formal training? The answer involves innate and learning factors.

Factors Involved in Language Acquisition

Innate Factors

One reason that children acquire a language involves **innate factors**, *which are genetically programmed physiological and neurological features in the brain and vocal apparatus that facilitate making speech sounds and learning language skills.* Evidence of innate physiological features can be found in our specially adapted vocal apparatus (larynx and pharynx), which allows us to make sounds useful in forming words. Evidence of innate neurological features can be found in the human brain, usually the left hemisphere, which is prewired for language. In fact, as we saw in Module 4, damage to two particular language areas—Broca's and Wernicke's areas—can seriously disrupt the production and understanding of language. Innate neurological factors do not program a child's brain to learn a specific language but rather to acquire the basic, underlying rules of language.

Other evidence for innate factors comes from the idea of a **critical language period**, *which is a period of time from infancy to adolescence when language is easier to learn and a period of time after adolescence through adulthood when language is more difficult to learn.* For example, immigrant children do very well in learning English as a second language, while immigrant adults do less well (Johnson & Newport, 1989). Such data suggest the operation of innate neurological factors that influence language acquisition.

Perhaps the best-known advocate of innate factors is Chomsky (1957, 1980), who maintains that the human brain is genetically preprogrammed so that children can acquire the rules of grammar. Although innate factors are involved in acquiring language, there is also evidence of learning factors.

Why do all children acquire language in much the same way?

Learning Factors

Learning factors, *which involve interactions between the child and his or her environment, such as feedback, reinforcement, observation, and imitation, influence the development of language skills.* The strongest case for learning factors was made by B. F. Skinner (1957), who believed that children acquire language according to the principles of operant conditioning (discussed in Module 12). Just as a rat is shaped to press a lever, a child is shaped to form words and sentences through reinforcement by his or her parents.

Two major criticisms have weakened Skinner's explanation. First, children understand language before they can speak or actually receive feedback and reinforcement. Second, children acquire language rules without receiving feedback and reinforcement for practicing all the possible sentences. For these reasons, operant conditioning principles cannot easily explain language acquisition.

In contrast to Skinner's operant learning approach, many developmental psychologists take a **social learning approach,** *which emphasizes observation, exploration, and imitation in language acquisition.* According to the social learning approach, children have a strong desire to use language to express their needs and to interact socially with their parents, caretakers, and peers. For example, very young children use language as a social tool, such as getting attention, requesting actions, or protesting some event (Rice, 1989). As developmental psychologist Mabel Rice (1989) puts it, each child acquires language through a unique mixture of biological, psychological, social, and environmental factors.

Now that you are familiar with the factors in acquiring language, we can examine the stages that all normal children go through in learning a language.

Language Stages

Although children appear to go through similar stages in acquiring a language, the speed and quality of their language skills interact with a number of *environmental factors,* such as sex of the child, number of children in the family, and socioeconomic level of the child's parents. For example, parents tend to speak more to girls than to boys, they spend more time speaking to firstborns than to laterborns, and those from higher socioeconomic levels tend to encourage greater vocabulary development (McCabe, 1989). Partly because of these environmental factors, there is great variation in the *age* at which a child reaches a particular language stage. There is, however, remarkable similarity in the *order* of stages that a child follows in acquiring language skills. We'll examine the four stages that all children pass through in acquiring language.

Four Stages in Acquiring Language

Dadada

Eat. Go.

1 Babbling. Beginning at about the age of 6 months, a baby begins **babbling,** *or making sounds of one-syllable verbalizations,* such as "dadada" or "bababa." At about 9 months, the babbling sounds come to more and more resemble the vowels and consonants that the child will use later in speaking the language to which he or she is exposed.

Researchers have discovered that by 6 months of age infants have learned to discriminate sounds used in their native language from those used in a foreign language (Kuhl et al., 1992). These exciting findings show that by an early age infants have already become sensitized to sounds of their native languages. By learning language sounds so early, infants are primed for learning their native language.

In *hearing* children, babbling is *oral.* However, in *deaf* children who have been exposed only to the sign language of their deaf parents, babbling is *manual* and not oral. That is, these babies babble by repeating the same hand sign over and over (Petitto & Marentette, 1991). Petitto and Marentette argue that babbling is not tied to speech but rather to the development of language and the processing of different kinds of signals, either spoken or manually signed.

After babbling, the baby begins to form his or her first words.

2 Single word. By about 1 year of age, a child forms **single words,** *which usually refer to what the child can see, hear, or feel.* For instance, the child may refer to objects, such as "Milk" or "Cat," or to simple actions, such as "Eat" or "Go." The child may also say a word in a certain way so that it means much more. For instance, a child may point to an unfamiliar drink and say "Milk" with a rising pitch at the end, indicating "Is that milk?"

As the child learns to say words, parents usually respond by speaking to the child in a specific way called **parentese,** *which includes speaking in a higher than normal voice, emphasizing and stretching out each word, and using very simple sentences.* For over 10 years, psychologist Anne Fernald and her colleagues at Stanford University have traveled around the world, recording child-parent interactions (*Los Angeles Times,* February 17, 1992). She finds that no matter what language parents use, they all use parentese when speaking to their infants. Fernald concludes that parentese has several functions: getting an infant's attention, stimulating infants to make sounds and communicate, and teaching them language.

Next, the child begins to combine words.

3 **Two-word combinations.** At about 2 years of age, a child makes **two-word combinations,** *which are strings of two words that express various actions ("Me play," "See boy") or relationships ("Hit ball,"*

Me play.

"Allgone milk"). Each of the two words provides a hint about what the child is saying. In addition, the relationship between the two words also gives hints about what the child is communicating. For example, "See boy" tells us to look at a specific object; "Daddy shirt" tells us that something belongs to Daddy. The child's new ability to communicate by combining two words and changing their order marks the beginning of learning the rules of grammar.

At this stage, a child may have a vocabulary of more than 50 words, many of which will be used in two-word combinations. Although children usually go through a stage of forming single words and then two-word combinations, there is no three-word stage (Pinker, 1990). Instead, at a certain point the child will begin to form sentences, which gradually increase in length through the fourth year.

4 **Sentences and rules of grammar.** At about 4 years of age, a child is forming sentences that range from three to eight words in length and indicate a growing knowledge of the rules of grammar.

I goed to the zoo.

However, a child's beginning sentences differ from adult sentences. A child's speech is called **telegraphic speech,** *which is a pattern of speaking that omits articles, prepositions, and parts of verbs.* For example, an adult may say, "There is a nice big cat"; the child will use telegraphic speech and say, "There big cat."

By about 4 to 5 years of age, a child has learned the **basic rules of grammar,** *which are the rules for combining nouns, verbs, and adjectives into meaningful sentences.* In learning grammar, children often make errors of **overgeneralization,** *which is applying a grammatical rule to cases where it should not be used.* For example, after a child learns the rule of forming the past tense of many verbs by adding a *d* sound to the end, he or she may overgeneralize this rule and add a *d* to the past tense of irregular verbs (and say, for instance, "I goed to the zoo"). By the time children enter school, they usually have a good grasp of the general rules of their language.

Once a child has learned the rules, language becomes a powerful tool for thinking, which we will turn to next.

Language and Thought

Does our language determine how we think?

By the time a child enters the first grade, he or she has a vocabulary of about 14,000 words. One function of a child's growing supply of words is to facilitate thinking and forming ideas. The obvious link between language and thinking has raised a question of exactly how much our thinking depends on language.

In the 1950s linguist Benjamin Whorf (1956) noticed that Native American Indian languages differ from each other as well as from European languages in their vocabularies and emphasis on different objects and events in their environment. For example, some languages divide colors into two categories; others use twelve. Some languages use verbs with endings that indicate past, present, and future actions; others do not. Based on these observations, Whorf formulated the theory of **linguistic relativity,** *which states that language determines the way people think, and people with different languages think differently.* The most famous example of Whorf's theory of linguistic relativity involves the Eskimos and their words for snow.

How Many Words for Snow?

Eskimos and Americans have about an equal number of words for snow.

Whorf estimated that Eskimos have about seven words for snow (such as terms for falling snow, snow on the ground, snow packed hard like ice, slushy snow, and wind-driven flying snow), while most Americans use just one word, *snow.* Whorf suggested that as a result of their larger vocabulary of snow-related words, Eskimos think differently about snow. Since Whorf's time, the number of snow words attributed to Eskimos has ranged from two dozen to over 100 (Pullum, 1991).

Linguist Laura Martin (1986) discovered that although Eskimos have about a dozen words for snow, the proper comparison is not with just the English word *snow* but with at least ten different English words, including *blizzard, dusting,* and *avalanche.* Even though we now know that Eskimos and Americans have about an equal number of terms for snow, this sheds no light on the question of whether the language of Eskimos results in their thinking differently about snow than Americans do. For an answer to this question, let's examine how individuals who are bilingual (that is, are fluent in two languages) think.

Thinking in Two Languages

Suppose your native language is Chinese but you are also fluent in English. You are asked to read descriptions in either Chinese or English of two different people and then to write impressions of these individuals. You read a Chinese and an English description of a type of person easily labeled in Chinese—"shi gu," one person with strong family ties and much worldly experience—but not easily labeled in English. You read an English and a Chinese description of a type of person easily labeled in English—"artistic" character, one with artistic abilities but very temperamental—but not easily labeled in Chinese. Researchers found that when reading and thinking in Chinese, subjects formed a clearer impression of the shi gu person; when reading and thinking in English they formed a clearer impression of the artistic character (Hoffman, Lau, & Johnson, 1986). These results support the linguistic relativity theory and the idea that your language influences your thinking.

After the Concept/Glossary, we'll examine whether animals can learn to use language like humans do.

When she thinks in Chinese, she may form different impressions than when she thinks in English.

1. A system of symbols that we use in thinking, solving problems, and communicating with others is called _____.

2. There are four rules for learning and using language. How we make the meaningful sounds used by a particular language is covered by the rules of (a)_____. Any English word can be broken down into basic sounds of consonants and vowels, which are called (b)_____.

3. How we group phonemes into meaningful combinations of sounds and words is covered by the rules of (a)_____. The smallest, *meaningful* combination of sounds in a language is called a (b)_____.

4. How we combine words to form meaningful phrases and sentences is specified by the rule of _____.

5. How we know the meaning of words in various contexts is covered by the rule of _____.

6. Chomsky explained that a sentence can be stated in different ways yet have the same meaning. The actual wording of a sentence is called its (a)_____ structure. The underlying meaning of the sentence that is not spoken but is present in the mind of the listener is called the (b)_____ structure. To convert our ideas from surface structures into deep structures and from deep structures back into surface ones is accomplished by using (c)_____ rules.

7. In acquiring language, all children go through the same four stages but at different rates. Beginning at about the age of 6 months, a baby begins making sounds of one-syllable verbalizations, such as "Dadada" or "Bababa," which is called (a)_____. By about 1 year of age, a child forms (b)_____ words, which usually refer to what the child can see, hear, or feel. At about 2 years of age, a child makes (c)_____, which are strings of two words that express various actions ("Me play") or relationships ("Hit ball," "Milk gone"). At about 4 years of age, a child is forming sentences, which range from three to eight words in length and indicate a growing knowledge of the rules of (d)_____.

8. A child's speech is different from an adult's. Children use a pattern of speaking that omits articles, prepositions, and parts of verbs; this pattern is called (a)_____ speech. Another difference is that children often apply a grammatical rule to cases where it should not be used; this error is called (b)_____.

9. One reason all children acquire a language in much the same order is because of genetically programmed physiological and neurological features in the brain and vocal apparatus. These changes are called (a)_____ factors. Interactions between the child and his or her environment, such as feedback, reinforcement, observation, and imitation, are called (b)_____ factors.

10. Whorf's theory of _____ states that language determines the way people think and that people with different languages think differently.

Answers: 1. language; 2. (a) phonology, (b) phonemes; 3. (a) morphology, (b) morpheme; 4. syntax or grammar; 5. semantics; 6. (a) surface, (b) deep, (c) transformational; 7. (a) babbling, (b) single, (c) two-word combinations, (d) grammar or syntax; 8. (a) telegraphic, (b) overgeneralization; 9. (a) innate, (b) learning; 10. linguistic relativity.

APPLYING/ EXPLORING: DO ANIMALS HAVE LANGUAGE?

My dog can respond to a variety of verbal commands ("Sit," "Stay," "Get your Frisbee"); she can also bark to let me know she wants to go out and will carry her food dish when she wants to eat. The obvious question is: Has my dog learned a language? To answer that question, we need to examine the difference between communication and language.

Four Criteria for Language

Communication *is the ability to use sounds, smells, or gestures to exchange information.* As do many animal species, my dog has the ability to communicate. But as we noted earlier, *language* is a special form of communication in which an individual learns complex rules to manipulate symbols (words or gestures) that are used to generate an endless number of meaningful sentences. My dog, who is exceptionally bright, can communicate, but, like most animals, she shows no evidence of using language. So far, humans are the only species to satisfy all four criteria for language.

1 Language, which is a special form of communication, involves learning a set of *abstract symbols* (whether words for spoken language or hand signs for sign language).

2 Language involves using abstract symbols (words or signs) *to express* thoughts or indicate objects and events that may or may not be present.

3 Language involves learning *complex rules* for forming words, phrases, and meaningful sentences.

4 Language involves using the rules *to generate* an endless number of meaningful sentences.

We'll see how close several animals come to satisfying these four criteria for using language.

Dolphins—Responders

In proportion to the size of its body, a dolphin's brain is smaller than the human brain but larger than that of the great apes. Because dolphins have relatively large brains, researchers are particularly interested in how well they communicate.

In the wild, dolphins use two kinds of sounds for communication: clicks, which they use to probe the sea and "see" their environment, and whistles, which they use in dolphin-to-dolphin communication, probably to express emotional state and identify the animal to the group (Ralston, 1989). There is little evidence that dolphins use symbols or apply any rules of grammar in their normal communications.

In testing the ability of dolphins to com-

Louis Herman uses hand signals to tell a dolphin to jump over the person in the pool.

The dolphin carries out the command.

municate, psychologist Louis Herman (1989) of the University of Hawaii has been training dolphins to respond to hand signals or whistles. So far, he has taught two dolphins to respond to approximately 50 such signals. For example, in the top photo above, Herman is signaling "person" "over," which means to jump over the person in the pool. The bottom photo shows the dolphin carrying out the command by jumping over the person.

Based on his research, Herman concluded that dolphins can understand a variety of signals. For example, hand signals for "basket," "right," "Frisbee," "fetch" mean "Go to the Frisbee on the right and take it to the basket." Although dolphins can understand a variety of signals and perform behaviors in sequence, they show little evidence of using abstract symbols or applying rules of grammar to generate meaningful sentences. Thus, dolphins can communicate but show little or no evidence of using language as humans do.

Next, let's turn to the greater apes, which in terms of evolution are the closest animals to humans.

Gorillas and Chimpanzees—Sign Language

Gorillas and chimpanzees have relatively large and well-developed brains (a gorilla's brain weighs about 500 grams; a chimpanzee's, about 400 grams; a human's, about 1400 grams). However, because gorillas and chimpanzees lack the vocal apparatus necessary for making speech sounds, researchers have taught them other forms of language, such as American Sign Language.

Shown here is researcher Francine Patterson using sign language to communicate with Koko the gorilla, who has a vocabulary of about 800 signs. Similarly, Beatrice and Allen Gardner (1975) taught sign language to a chimpanzee named Washoe), who after four years of training had learned about 160 signs. The finding that gorillas and chimps can learn sign language raised the question of whether they use language in the same way as humans. Psychologist Herbert Terrace (1981) analyzed videotapes of chimps using sign language with their trainers. He concluded that the chimps were using signs more as tools to obtain things than as abstract symbols or words, one of the chief characteristics of human language. Further, Terrace found that the chimps were primarily imitating or responding to cues from their human teachers instead of using rules of grammar to initiate or produce new sentences.

As a result of criticisms by Terrace and others, research monies dried up, and researchers were discouraged from pursuing studies on sign language in chimps (Gibbons, 1991). But new findings have again raised the question of language in chimps.

Pygmy Chimp—New Findings

In a series of recent studies, psychologist Sue Savage-Rumbaugh (1991) and colleagues (1986) reported that a pygmy chimp named Kanzi had shown remarkable language skills that surpassed previous data on common chimps. Instead of using sign language, Kanzi "speaks" by touching symbols, each of which stands for a word. For example, Kanzi might signal "Want a drink" by touching the symbol for "drink" or signal "Want to play" by touching two symbols in sequence for "hiding" and "play biting."

Koko, a 19-year-old lowland gorilla, is using sign language to communicate with her human trainer, Francine Patterson.

By the time Kanzi was 6 years old, he had a vocabulary of 90 symbols, and, even more surprising, understood about 200 spoken English words, something that common chimps had failed to master. UCLA psychologist Patricia Greenfield (1991), who has studied Kanzi's language skills in great detail, believes that Kanzi can create sentences that are grammatically correct at about the same level as that of a two-year-old child.

In spite of Kanzi's amazing ability to master language at a level surpassing previous chimps, other researchers caution against deciding that Kanzi is using language like humans do. For example, when psychologists Mark Seidenberg and Laura Petitto (1987) reviewed Kanzi's data, they concluded that the pygmy chimp seemed to be using words more as tools to obtain things than as abstract symbols that stood for some object or event. In addition, Kanzi showed little ability to use rules of grammar to form sentences. Thus, the answer to the question "Is Kanzi using language like hu-

mans?" must await additional data and replication of results by other researchers (Gibbons, 1991). Whatever the final outcome, the interesting findings of Savage-Rumbaugh and her associates have revived interest in the age-old question of whether humans are the only species to fulfill all the criteria for language.

Kanzi, a pygmy chimp, presses a symbol that stands for a word. He also presses words in sequence to form "two-word sentences."

Summary/Self-Test

CONCEPTS

1. A concept is a way to group objects, events, or characteristics on the basis of some common property they all share. Concepts perform two important functions: with them, we can (a)_____ objects and thus better organize and store information in memory, and they allow us to identify things without (b)_____.

■ *If a brain virus destroyed all your concepts, how would your view of the world change?*

FORMING CONCEPTS

2. There are two theories of how you might have formed your concept of a bird and how you form concepts generally. If you form a concept of an object, event, or characteristic by making a list of the properties that define it, you are using (a)_____ theory. If you form a concept by constructing an idea of the ideal or prototypic object and then seeing whether a new object matches that idea, you are using (b)_____ theory.

■ *Why is it difficult to explain to your younger sister that a whale is a mammal and not a fish?*

SOLVING PROBLEMS

3. The process of searching for some rule, plan, or strategy that results in reaching a certain goal that is currently out of reach is called (a)_____. We usually go through three states in solving problems: (b)_____, _____, and _____.

4. We win at games by following rules. If we correctly follow rules that lead to a solution, we are using a set of rules called (a)_____. As you gain experience with solving problems, you may use rules of thumb that reduce the number of operations or allow you to take shortcuts in solving problems; these shortcuts are called (b)_____, of which there are several kinds. If you rely on information that is more prominent or easily recalled and overlook other information that is available but less prominent or notable, you are using the (c)_____ heuristic.

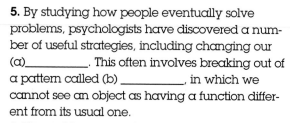

5. By studying how people eventually solve problems, psychologists have discovered a number of useful strategies, including changing our (a)_____. This often involves breaking out of a pattern called (b)_____, in which we cannot see an object as having a function different from its usual one.

6. The sudden grasp of a solution after many incorrect attempts is called (a)_____. Another kind of thinking that is useful in solving problems is to find (b)_____, which are similarities between new situations and familiar situations. Still another useful strategy for solving problems is to break the problem down into a number of (c)_____, which, when completed in order, will result in a solution.

■ *Why is it easier for you to win at checkers if you have several years of experience?*

THINKING CREATIVELY

7. Creative thinking is a combination of flexibility in thinking and reorganization in understanding to produce innovative ideas and solutions. Psychologists also define creative thinking as a type of (a)_____; when using this type of thinking, one begins with a problem and comes up with many different solutions. The opposite, when one begins with a problem and comes up with the one correct solution, is called (b)_____.

■ *Would you teach a class in creative thinking differently in grade school than in college?*

LANGUAGE: BASIC RULES

8. Our most impressive skill is thought to be (a)_____, which is a special form of (b)_____ in which an individual learns complex rules to manipulate symbols (words or gestures) to generate an endless number of meaningful sentences.

9. All of the more than 3,000 known languages share four basic language rules, which are normally learned during childhood. The first language rule governs (a)_____, which specifies how we make meaningful sounds that are used by a particular language. The second language rule governs (b)_____, which specifies how we group phonemes into meaningful combinations of sounds and words. The third language rule governs (c)_____, which specifies how we combine words to form meaningful phrases and sentences. The fourth language rule governs (d)_____, which specifies the meaning of words in various contexts.

10. The linguist Noam Chomsky distinguished between how a sentence is worded, which he called the (a)_____ structure, and the meaning of the sentence, which he called the (b)_____ structure. Procedures for converting our ideas from surface structures into deep structures and from deep structures back into surface ones are called (c)_____.

■ *If you had to give up one of the language rules, which one would you give up? What effect would its loss have on your ability to speak?*

ACQUIRING LANGUAGE

11. One reason children are able to acquire a language with so little formal training derives from genetically programmed physiological and neurological features in the brain and vocal apparatus called (a)_____ factors. An example of this factor is a period of time from infancy to adolescence when language is easier to learn, called the (b)_____. Another reason children are able to acquire a language derives from interactions between the child and his or her environment, which are called (c)_____ factors.

■ *In a tragic case, a child named Genie was raised in near total isolation by her parent, who never spoke to her. When Genie was finally discovered at age 13, do you think she was able to talk?*

LANGUAGE STAGES

12. Around the world, humans acquire language in the same four stages. In the first stage, generally at about the age of 6 months, the infant makes sounds of one-syllable verbalizations; this is called (a)_____. By about 1 year of age, a child forms (b)_____, which usually refer to

what the child can see, hear, or feel. At about 2 years of age, a child makes (c)_____, to express various actions or relationships. At about 4 years of age, a child is forming sentences, which range from three to eight words in length and indicate a growing knowledge of the (d)_____.

13. A child's beginning sentences differ from adult sentences. A child's speech is called (a)_____ because it omits articles, prepositions, and parts of verbs. In learning the rules for combining nouns, verbs, and adjectives into meaningful sentences, children often apply a grammatical rule to cases where it should not be used. This type of error is called (b)_____. The social learning approach emphasizes observation, exploration, and imitation in language acquisition.

■ *How would you program a robot to acquire language in the stages that humans follow?*

LANGUAGE AND THOUGHT

14. Whorf has suggested that language determines the way people think and that people with different languages think differently. This is called the theory of _____.

■ *What kinds of problems could result from having the heads of countries speak through translators at international conferences?*

APPLYING/EXPLORING: DO ANIMALS HAVE LANGUAGE?

15. Many animal species have the ability to use sounds, smells, or gestures to exchange information; this is the ability to (a)_____. The question that researchers are trying to answer in their experiments with animals is whether animals can use a special form of communication called (b)_____. For us to say that an animal truly uses language, we must be able to demonstrate that the animal has learned complex rules to manipulate symbols (words or gestures) that are used to generate an endless number of meaningful sentences. Despite work and research with animals ranging from dolphins to pygmy chimpanzees, no one has yet demonstrated nonhumans using the four criteria for language.

■ *What would you tell your friend who says that his parrot uses language because it speaks perfect English and also understands dozens of commands?*

Chapter *Nine*
MOTIVATION AND EMOTION

MODULE 17
MOTIVATION

Mark Wellman, a paraplegic, pulls himself to the top of a 2,200-foot peak.

Why would a paraplegic climb a mountain?

On a cool September morning, two men began to climb a nearly vertical slope rising over 2,200 feet from the floor of Yosemite National Park. Because of the slope's crumbly granite, fewer than 30 people have completed this particular route up Half Dome, Yosemite's well-known landmark. What made this climb even more difficult was that one of the men, Mark Wellman, is a paraplegic. Some years ago on a different climb, Mark fell 50 feet into a crevice, hurt his back, and was paralyzed from the waist down. Mark now climbs with his friend Mike Corbett, who takes the lead and sets the supports. Because Mark's legs are paralyzed, he climbs by using the supports to pull himself up inch by inch.

Mark figured that by doing the equivalent of 5,000 pull-ups, each of which would raise him about six inches, he could climb the 2,200 feet in seven days. By the end of day seven, however, Mark and Mike were only a little more than halfway up the slope and were feeling exhausted. They had to sleep by hanging in sleeping bags anchored to the sheer granite wall.

By the end of day nine, the top was still several thousand pull-ups away. By day ten, Mark was becoming exhausted as his arms strained to raise his body's weight up the vertical face. By day twelve the men were almost out of food and water. Finally, on day thirteen, six days later than planned, Mark pulled himself up the last six inches and over the top of Half Dome. When Mark was asked later why he still climbed and risked further injury, he said, "Everyone has their own goals . . . Never underestimate a person with a disability." (adapted from *Los Angeles Times,* September 19, 1991, p. A3)

Reporters who questioned Mark about why he risked his life to climb were really asking about his motivation. **Motivation** *refers to the various physiological and psychological factors that cause us to act in a specific way at a particular time.* When you are motivated, you usually show three characteristics: you are *energized* to do something, you *direct* your energies toward a specific goal, and you have differing *intensities* of feelings about reaching that goal. We can observe these three characteristics in Mark's behavior: he was energized to perform 5,000 pull-ups, he directed his energy toward climbing a certain slope, and he felt intensely about reaching that goal. Psychologists study many kinds of motivation, from eating and drinking to achieving good grades to climbing mountains.

What's Coming

In this module we'll discuss how psychologists study motivation and focus on specific examples of biological and social needs; in the next module we'll discuss the theories and functions of emotions.

Let's begin with various approaches psychologists use to explain motivation.

Approaches to Motivation

For thirteen days, sightseers on the Yosemite valley floor watched Mark pull himself up the granite face of Half Dome. As you might have, many asked, "Why is he doing it?" To understand Mark's behavior, we'll discuss four approaches—instincts, needs and drives, incentives, and beliefs/expectations—that psychologists use to explain motivation.

Instincts—Innate Factors

At the beginning of the 1900s, William McDougall (1908) claimed that humans have a number of *instincts, or innate tendencies or biological forces that determine behavior.* Initially, McDougall listed about a half-dozen instincts, such as flight, repulsion, curiosity, pugnacity, and self-abasement. By the 1920s, psychologists had proposed over 6,000 instincts to encompass every kind of human motivation.

Does Mark have an instinct for climbing?

In the 1920s, Mark's desire to climb mountains would probably have been explained in terms of an instinct for climbing. Because so many behaviors were explained by instincts, the concept of instinct had turned into a label or description rather than an explanation of how and why a person engages in a specific behavior. In time the concept of human instincts received intense criticism for its lack of explanatory usefulness, and psychologists looked elsewhere to explain human motivation. In abandoning the use of instincts to explain human motivation, psychologists developed several new concepts. However, a revised definition of instinct continues to be a useful concept in explaining animal behavior.

Animals do have **instincts** or **fixed action patterns**, *which are innate biological forces that predispose an animal to behave in a fixed way in the presence of a specific environmental condition.* For example, in the above photo, the baboon is innately predisposed to behave in a fixed way (opens mouth, stares, rises on hind feet) in the presence of a specific environmental condition (a threatening stimulus).

Ethologists *study instincts or fixed action patterns as well as how animals adjust to their natural environments.* In Module 12, we discussed ethologist Konrad Lorenz, whose well-known work on imprinting in birds is an excellent example of an instinct or fixed action pattern. As you may remember, soon after birth many birds become attached to or imprinted on the first thing (animal, human, or object) they encounter, and they continue to interact with that thing as if it were their caretaker. The work of ethologists points out that biological factors, which exercise considerable influence over animal behaviors, may also play a role in human motivation, especially with respect to eating, drinking, and sexual activity.

Needs and Drives—Internal Factors

By the 1930s the concept of human instinct was dead and buried, and in its place were new concepts—needs and drives—to explain human motivation.

A **need** *is a biological state in which the organism lacks something essential for survival, such as food, water, or oxygen.* The need produces a **drive**, *which is a state of arousal during which the organism engages in behaviors to reduce the need.* Once the need is satisfied, the body returns to a more balanced state. *The tendency of the body to return to and remain in a more balanced state is called* **homeostasis.** If we combine these three concepts—need, drive, and homeostasis—we arrive at the drive-reduction theory. According to **drive-reduction theory,** *a need results in a drive, which in turn arouses the organism to engage in behaviors to reduce the need and return the body to homeostasis.* As an example, not eating for a period of time causes a need for food, which produces a *drive* to reduce the food need. In turn, the drive energizes the person to act, perhaps by raiding the refrigerator, thereby reducing the need and returning the body to homeostasis.

According to drive-reduction theory, drives motivate us to engage in a wide variety of behaviors to reduce *biological* needs. For example, psychologists might refer to an organism as having a hunger drive or a thirst drive. In addition, drives motivate us to engage in a wide variety of behaviors to reduce *psychological* needs. For example, psychologists might refer to an organism as having a curiosity, a social, or an exploratory drive.

Does Mark have a need to climb?

It is unlikely that Mark climbs to satisfy biological needs, because climbing is not necessary for his survival and may in fact threaten it. It is more likely that he climbs to satisfy a variety of psychological needs, such as needs to explore, to prove his physical fitness, or to create excitement.

Needs and drives are processes that we assume are going on inside Mark's body. Let's look at some factors outside the body that also influence motivation.

Incentives—External Factors

Incentives *are external stimuli, reinforcers, goals, or rewards that may be positive or negative and that motivate one's behavior.* Unlike drives and needs, which are assumed to occur inside the body, incentives are external rewards, such as a college degree, a house, money, or praise, that occur outside the body.

Does Mark climb to obtain incentives?

One of the many reasons Mark climbs may be to obtain incentives, such as recognition in the form of national press coverage, invitations for speaking, and monies ($100,000) from corporate sponsors that he donates to helping others with disabilities. However, incentives alone seem unlikely explanations for Mark's motivation to engage in a life-threatening behavior. Several cognitive factors—beliefs or expectations—are probably also involved in Mark's motivation. Before we explain the cognitive factors, let's compare incentives and drive-reduction theory.

Two kinds of motivation are not fully explained by drive-reduction theory. First, what motivates us to continue performing the same behavior after our need is already met? For example, why might we eat a dessert after complaining of being stuffed, or buy more clothes when our closet is already full? Incentive theory answers this question: we are motivated to perform a behavior, even though our immediate needs are met, in order to obtain positive stimuli (desserts, clothes), rewards (college degree), or objects (home or apartment).

Second, why do we engage in risky behaviors that increase arousal (such as mountain climbing and various sports) and that in fact throw homeostasis out of balance? According to the idea of incentives, one reason we are motivated to perform risky, arousing, and even life-threatening behaviors is that we wish to obtain positive incentives (such as praise, recognition, and rewards).

Besides the influence of needs, drives, and incentives on human motivation, cognitive psychologists believe that certain cognitive factors are also involved.

Beliefs/Expectations—Cognitive Factors

Beginning in the 1960s, psychologists such as Albert Bandura (1986), Richard deCharms (1980), and Bernard Weiner (1986) began to apply cognitive ideas to help explain human motivation. As a result, they made an important distinction between extrinsic and intrinsic motivation. **Extrinsic motivation** *influences us to perform*

behaviors to reduce biological needs or obtain various incentives. In contrast, **intrinsic motivation** *influences us to perform behaviors because the behaviors themselves are personally rewarding or because we are following our personal goals, beliefs, or expectations.* Intrinsic motivation explains why people spend hundreds of hours volunteering their services, working at hobbies, or playing amateur sports: these activities are personally enjoyable and rewarding. Intrinsic motivation emphasizes *self-determination,* which combines the feeling that we are behaving according to our chosen expectations and goals with the belief that we are in control of the situation. The concept of intrinsic motivation provides a quite different way of explaining human motivation.

Did Mark climb because of personal satisfaction?

Besides the reasons offered by the theories of needs/drives and incentives, the concept of intrinsic motivation suggests several other explanations for Mark's dangerous climb: climbing itself was rewarding, climbing allowed him to be in control of the situation, and climbing was a way for him to fulfill his own personal beliefs and expectations. As Mark said, "Everyone has their own goals."

Explaining Human Motivation

It is likely that the complete understanding of Mark's motivation for climbing may involve all these aspects: needs or drives, incentives, and beliefs or expectations. Because human motivation is so varied and complex, one or more explanations may be required. For example, students may study because they want to reduce their anxiety (needs and drives), to get a degree and potentially a good job (incentives), or to fulfill their personal goals (beliefs or expectations). Thus, depending on the particular behavior, psychologists may rely on one or more explanations.

One interesting question about human motivation is how we choose which physiological or psychological need to satisfy or which behavior to engage in. We discuss one of the better known answers to this question next.

Biological and Social Needs

How many needs do I have?

The next time you go to an amusement park, look at the activities that people are engaged in to see whether you can identify which needs they are satisfying. One popular activity is eating, which fulfills one of our basic biological needs. **Biological needs** *are physiological requirements that are critical to our survival and physical well-being.* As listed on the left, there are perhaps a half dozen biological needs, some of which are food, water, sex, oxygen, and sleep.

How do we strike a balance between satisfying our biological and social needs?

Human Biological Needs
Food
Water
Sex
Oxygen
Sleep
Avoidance of pain

Human Social Needs
Achievement—need to excel
Affiliation—need for social bonds
Nurturance—need to nourish
Autonomy—need for independence
Dominance—need to influence
Order—need for orderliness
Play—need for fun
Exhibition—need to make an impression

You will also notice people holding hands, waiting in lines, comforting one another, showing affection, screaming, crying, or laughing together, all related to social needs. **Social needs** *are needs that are acquired through learning and experience.* There are a limited number of biological needs but dozens of social needs, depending on one's learning and experiences. As listed on the left, social needs include the needs to achieve, form friendships, be independent, have fun, and nourish others (Murray, 1938).

In some cases the distinction between biological and social needs is blurred. For example, we may eat or drink not only to satisfy biological needs but to make social contact as well. Similarly, we may engage in sex for reproduction, which is a biological need, or to express love and affection, which is a social need. Even if needs overlap, we have only so much time and energy to satisfy a relatively large number of biological and social needs. This condition leaves us with a problem: How do we decide which needs to satisfy first?

Satisfying Our Needs

As you may remember from Module 1, Abraham Maslow was one of the founders of the humanistic approach in psychology. Maslow was particularly interested in human motivation, especially in how we go about choosing which biological or social need to satisfy. For example, should you study late for an exam and satisfy your social need to achieve, or should you go to bed at your regular time and satisfy your biological need for sleep? To answer this question, Maslow (1970) proposed that we satisfy our needs in a certain order, or hierarchy. **Maslow's hierarchy of needs** *is an ascending order or hierarchy with biological needs at the bottom and social needs at the top, indicating that we first satisfy our biological needs before satisfying our social needs.* Maslow hypothesized that after satisfying those needs at the bottom level of the hierarchy, we advance up the hierarchy to satisfy the needs at the next level. However, if we are at a higher level and basic needs are not satisfied, we may come back down the hierarchy.

Maslow's Hierarchy of Needs

According to Maslow's hierarchy of needs, we need to satisfy our biological needs before we can turn our attention and energy to fulfilling our personal and social needs. Thus, we begin at the bottom of the hierarchy, with physiological needs, and then work our way toward the top. As the needs at one level are met, we advance to the next level. For example, if our physiological needs at level 1 are satisfied, we advance to level 2 and work on satisfying our safety needs. Once our safety needs are satisfied, we advance to level 3, and so forth, up the needs hierarchy.

Maslow believed that we satisfy our biological and social needs in this order.

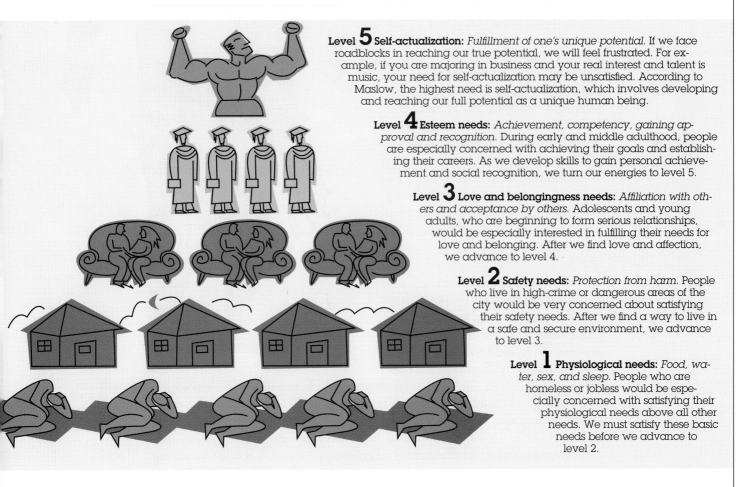

Level 5 Self-actualization: *Fulfillment of one's unique potential.* If we face roadblocks in reaching our true potential, we will feel frustrated. For example, if you are majoring in business and your real interest and talent is music, your need for self-actualization may be unsatisfied. According to Maslow, the highest need is self-actualization, which involves developing and reaching our full potential as a unique human being.

Level 4 Esteem needs: *Achievement, competency, gaining approval and recognition.* During early and middle adulthood, people are especially concerned with achieving their goals and establishing their careers. As we develop skills to gain personal achievement and social recognition, we turn our energies to level 5.

Level 3 Love and belongingness needs: *Affiliation with others and acceptance by others.* Adolescents and young adults, who are beginning to form serious relationships, would be especially interested in fulfilling their needs for love and belonging. After we find love and affection, we advance to level 4.

Level 2 Safety needs: *Protection from harm.* People who live in high-crime or dangerous areas of the city would be very concerned about satisfying their safety needs. After we find a way to live in a safe and secure environment, we advance to level 3.

Level 1 Physiological needs: *Food, water, sex, and sleep.* People who are homeless or jobless would be especially concerned with satisfying their physiological needs above all other needs. We must satisfy these basic needs before we advance to level 2.

One advantage of Maslow's hierarchy is that it integrates biological and social needs into a single framework and sets up a priority for satisfying various needs. One problem with Maslow's hierarchy is that researchers have found it difficult to verify whether his particular order of needs is accurate or to actually measure some of his needs, especially self-actualization (Geller, 1982). Despite the criticisms of Maslow's hierarchy, it remains a useful reminder of the number and complexity of human needs.

To give you a sample of what's involved in human motivation, in the next sections we will focus on three different needs. We'll select two biological drives or needs—hunger and sex—from Maslow's level 1 and one social need—achievement—from Maslow's level 4. Psychologists have studied these three particular needs in great detail.

Hunger

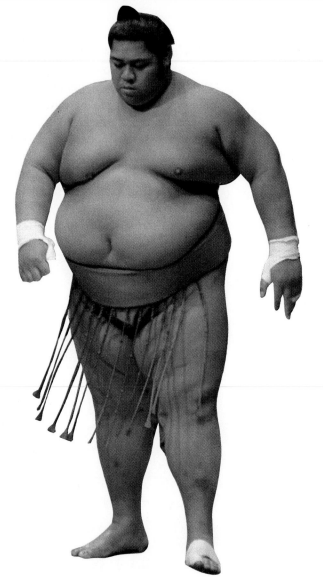

Why would someone want to weigh 580 pounds?

His nickname is Meat Bomb but in Japan he is known as Konishiki. Born in Hawaii, he is one of the first non-Japanese to reach the top ranks of the Japanese sumo wrestlers. Konishiki, who stands six feet, one inch tall and weighs 580 pounds, outweighs his opponents by 100 pounds. Just looking at Konishiki raises two general questions about eating and weight. First, when, where, and how much does Konishiki eat? In other words, where do Konishiki's cues for either feeling hungry and starting to eat or feeling full and stopping come from? For instance, does he feel hungry when his stomach growls? Second, why does Konishiki weigh so much in a country where most people weigh relatively little? That is, which genetic and environmental factors influence his weight? Let's begin with the question of where feelings of being hungry and full come from.

To maintain his 580 pounds, Konishiki must eat for reasons other than hunger.

Do you feel hungry or full?

Hunger is considered a biological drive because eating is critical to our survival. However, satisfying our hunger drive, such as when, where, and how much we eat, is influenced by two different kinds of cues: biological and learned. *Biological cues for hunger* come from a variety of physiological changes in blood chemistry and signals from body organs and the brain that occur either before or after we eat. *Learned cues for hunger* come from associations that we make between eating and various stimuli in our environment. For example, we may learn to eat at a certain time (lunchtime), when engaging in certain activities (watching television), or when encountering certain stimuli (the smell or sight of food).

The powerful influence of learned cues is clearly shown by the observations that humans are the only animals that may eat when they are completely full and have no biological need for food or that will starve themselves to lose weight when their weights are in the normal range. Judith Rodin (1992) found that about half the men and women in America report being dissatisfied with their weight, which is a critical component of body image. **Body image** *refers to one's perception of and satisfaction with one's body.* As shown in the accompanying table, dissatisfaction with body image has increased among both men and women. Rodin suggests that body image has taken on increased significance because today's society emphasizes looks, appearance, and thinness.

Let's begin our discussion of hunger with a closer look at biological cues for eating.

People Dissatisfied with Weight		
	Men	**Women**
1972	35%	48%
1987	41	55

Biological Cues for Hunger
Why don't we see fat animals?

We rarely see fat animals in the wild because their hunger drive is regulated by biological cues; animals eat only as much as their bodies require. In modern societies, we often see overweight humans because their hunger drive is regulated by both biological and learned cues. That is, people may eat because their bodies need nutrients or because of various learned cues.

There are two kinds of biological cues for hunger: **peripheral cues** *are those that come from body organs;* **central cues** *are those that come from the brain.* Much of the evidence for peripheral and central cues for hunger comes from research on animals, primarily rats. Researchers assume that many of the same biological cues identified in animals also apply to humans.

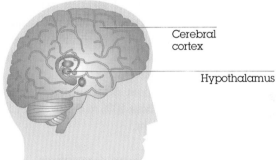

Peripheral Cues

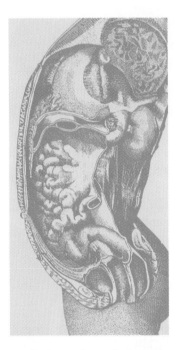

I'm hungry. One of the major peripheral cues for being hungry is a drop in the level of nutrients in the blood. For example, when the stomach is empty, there is a drop in the level of glucose (sugar) in the blood. This glucose drop is detected by the liver, which sends that information to the brain. The stomach's noises and growls are not necessary cues for being hungry. In fact, researchers have discovered that people still feel hungry after their stomachs have been surgically removed for some medical problem (Lytle, 1977).

Remember that in addition to these peripheral cues, there are also learned cues for being hungry, such as the time of day, and social-cultural cues, such as seeing your friends eating.

I'm full. There are two major peripheral cues for feeling full. One set of cues comes from the amount of *food* in the stomach and from stretching of the stomach's walls. Another set of cues comes from the release of a *hormone* (CCK, or cholecystokinin) when food enters the intestines or when the liver detects an increasing level of nutrients in the bloodstream.

Because the stomach, intestines, and liver send information about glucose and other nutrients to the brain, the brain must have areas that respond to these signals. Let's examine the central or brain cues for feeling hungry or full.

Central Cues

I'm hungry. Located in the lower middle of the brain is a particular group of cells, collectively called the hypothalamus, that are involved in feeling hungry and full. For the sake of understanding, we have greatly simplified the explanation of the hypothalamus's functions.

One part of the hypothalamus, the **lateral hypothalamus**, *is involved in feeling hungry and beginning to eat.* For example, rats begin eating when the lateral hypothalamus is electrically stimulated and stop eating if the lateral hypothalamus is destroyed. In addition, there are cells in the lateral hypothalamus that increase or decrease their activity depending on the blood level of glucose, and these cells are apparently involved in the motivation of eating. All this evidence points to the lateral hypothalamus as having a role in feeling hungry and starting to eat.

I'm full. Another part of the hypothalamus, the **ventromedial hypothalamus,** *is involved in feeling full and stopping eating.* For example, rats stop eating when the ventromedial hypothalamus is electrically stimulated and greatly overeat if the ventromedial hypothalamus (and adjacent areas) is destroyed. All this evidence points to the ventromedial hypothalamus (and adjacent areas) as having a role in feeling full and stopping eating.

We can conclude that feelings of being hungry or feeling full result from a combination of peripheral and central cues, as well as from the influence of learned and social-cultural cues.

Now that you understand some of the cues for starting and stopping eating, we'll look at the factors that influence our body weight.

Body Weight

If you look around your college campus, you will see hundreds of students' bodies of varying sizes and weights. We'll examine two groups of factors—inherited and learned—that influence body weight.

Inherited Factors That Influence Body Weight

Inherited factors are those that one is born with and that are controlled by instructions in one's genes. Evidence for inherited factors comes from studies on adopted children and identical twins. One set of researchers found that the weights of adopted adults were strongly correlated with the weights of their biological parents and not with those of their adopted parents (Stunkard et al., 1990). Other researchers reported that the weights of identical twins separated soon after birth and reared in adopted families were much more alike than the weights of fraternal twins reared apart (Bouchard et al., 1990). Based on these findings, researchers have concluded that inherited factors contribute about 60% and environmental factors contribute about 40% to our tendency for a particular body weight.

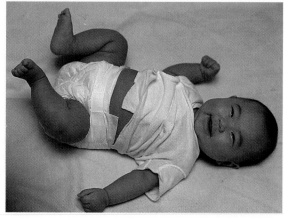

Which specific factors do we inherit?

So far, psychologists have identified three inherited factors that contribute to regulation of weight: fat cells, metabolic rate, and set points.

We inherit different numbers of **fat cells,** *which store body fat.* Normally, the number of fat cells does not increase, except in cases of obesity. Fat cells greatly enlarge if you are storing fat (gaining weight) and shrink if you are giving up fat (losing weight).

We also inherit different **rates of metabolism**, *which is a process that governs how efficiently our bodies break food down into energy and how quickly our bodies burn that energy.* An individual with a low metabolic rate burns less energy and is likely to store any excess energy as fat; a person with a high metabolic rate burns more energy and is less likely to have excess energy to store as fat. Because of differing metabolic rates, people can consume the same number of calories and maintain, lose, or gain weight.

We probably inherit a **set point or range,** *which is a level of body weight (ratio of fat to lean) that remains relatively constant;* any attempt to change that level is met with resistance. Evidence for a set point comes from animals, which were found to change their metabolic rates to prevent weight loss or gain when they were underfed or overfed (Keesey, 1986). Similarly, when humans are underfed (dieting), their metabolic rates decrease and thus work to prevent weight loss. Psychologists think that we probably have a *range* within which our body weight is regulated and beyond which our body resists changes (Brownell & Wadden, 1991).

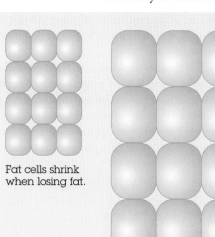

Fat cells shrink when losing fat.

Fat cells expand when storing fat.

What kind of inherited factors will influence this baby's adult weight?

Being of normal
weight or over-
weight is influenced
but not fixed by in-
herited factors.

Why does sumo wrestler Konishiki weigh nearly 600 pounds?
One reason Konishiki weighs three to four times as much as most Japanese males may
be heredity, such as having a larger number of fat cells, a lower metabolic rate, or a
higher set point.

Is my weight fixed by inherited factors?
Although inherited factors are important in regulating the accumulation of body fat, a
number of environmental factors can balance or compensate for the influence of
inherited factors. For example, a person can compensate for a large number of
inherited fat cells by eating less fat (butter, cheese, animal fat), which is twice as high in
calories as protein (fish, chicken) or carbohydrates (vegetables, grains, and fruits). In
addition, a person can compensate for inheriting a low metabolic rate by exercising,
which raises metabolic rate.

    Next let's examine some learned factors that are important in regulating weight.

Body Weight

Learned Factors That Influence Body Weight

Psychological Factors. Psychological factors include learning to associate various psychological states or feelings with eating and food, such as eating more or less

because of stress, depression, anxiety, or unhappiness or being more or less responsive to the sight and smell of food. For example, Judith Rodin (1984) found that someone who is extraresponsive to external food cues will eat an entire bowl of potato chips at one sitting, while a less responsive person will not. Thus, being extraresponsive to food cues may contribute to being overweight. In the Applying/Exploring section, we'll discuss how other psychological factors, such as mood swings, contribute to eating disorders.

Social-Cultural Factors. Social-cultural factors are values and beliefs that we acquire from our particular environments. According to American weight charts, being 20% over the recommended range of weights is considered overweight in our culture and 30% over is considered obese. Konishiki would therefore be considered obese by American standards. This acceptance of what we would consider obe-

Sometimes people eat when stressed.

sity is an example of how social-cultural standards influence our perception of weight.

For an example closer to home, consider obesity in women in the United States. Obesity rates vary widely, depending on a woman's social class: about 30% of lower-class women are obese, 18% of middle-class women, and 5% of upper-class women (Sobal & Stunkard, 1989). It seems that social-cultural pressures to be thin are greater in the middle and upper classes.

As another example, a fat baby is considered a healthy baby in some cultures. However, accumulating fat during infancy and childhood may have long-lasting effects on body weight. For instance, Leonard Epstein (1986) reported that 40% of American children who were obese at age 7 developed into obese adults. It is now clear that fat accumulated early in life is difficult to lose and contributes to maintaining large stores of fat as a teenager and adult.

Women of upper socioeconomic classes have many social pressures to be thin.

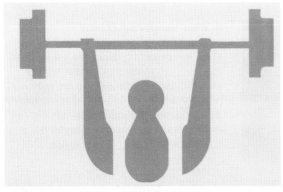

Physical exercise is one of the few proven ways to raise one's metabolic rate.

Physical Factors. Physical factors, such as amount of exercise and activity, are important in controlling one's weight. Researchers commonly find that over-weight individuals, both children and adults, are less physically active than people of normal weight (Kolata, 1986; Stern, 1984). Being less physically active contributes to having a lower rate of metabolism, which in turn results in burning less energy and storing excess energy as fat. On the other hand, vigorous exercise raises metabolic rates for many hours and even days. Claude Bouchard and Angelo Tremblay (1987) found that ten moderately obese women who spent five hours a week doing aerobic exercises (dancing, running, swimming) significantly increased their metabolic rates. For this reason, effective diet plans recommend both reducing intake of calories and increasing physical exercise.

Conclusion. As recently as the late 1970s, researchers thought a single primary factor, amount of calories, regulated body weight. Psychologists now recognize that body weight results from an interaction of all the factors we've discussed (Rodin, 1984). For example, because of inherited factors, identical twins remain remarkably close in weight until early puberty. After puberty, their weights may differ, apparently because the twins are reacting to a number of environmental pressures (Price & Gottesman, 1991). Hunger is considered a biological drive, but notice the number of psychological and social-cultural pressures that influence where, when, and how the hunger drive is satisfied.

After a quick review, we'll turn to a second biological need, sexual behavior, which is also influenced by many psychological and social-cultural factors.

Identical twins may differ in weight because of various environmental factors.

1. Physiological or psychological factors that cause us to act in a specific way at a particular time are included in the definition of _____ .

6. When we perform behaviors to reduce biological needs or obtain various incentives, we are acting under the influence of (a)_____ motivation. When we perform behaviors because they are personally rewarding or because we are following our personal goals, beliefs, or expectations, we are acting under the influence of (b)_____ motivation.

2. Innate biological forces that predispose an animal to behave in a fixed way in the presence of a specific environmental condition are called _____ .

7. The ascending order or hierarchy with biological needs at the bottom and social needs at the top is _____ . This idea assumes that we first satisfy our biological needs before satisfying our social needs.

3. Needs that are not critical to your survival but that are acquired through learning and socialization, such as the needs for achievement or affiliation, are called (a)_____ needs. Needs that are critical to your survival and physical well-being, such as food, water, and sex, are called (b)_____ needs.

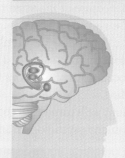

8. Cues for hunger that come from a variety of physiological changes in blood chemistry and signals from body organs and the brain are called (a)_____ cues. Cues for hunger that come from associations we make between eating and various stimuli in our environment are called (b)_____ cues.

4. A biological need produces a state of arousal during which the organism engages in behaviors to reduce the need. This state of arousal is called a (a)_____ . Once a need is satisfied, the body returns to a more balanced state, called (b)_____ . This sequence of need-drive-homeostasis is described by the (c)_____ theory.

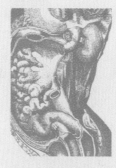

9. There are two kinds of biological cues for hunger. A drop in the level of nutrients in the blood is an example of a (a)_____ cue. Cues that come from the hypothalamus are an example of (b)_____ cues. The part of the hypothalamus that is involved in feeling hungry is called the (c)_____ and the part that is involved in feeling full is called the (d)_____ .

5. External stimuli, reinforcers, goals, or rewards that may be positive or negative and that motivate one's behavior are called _____ .

10. At least four factors are involved in regulation of weight. Factors that we are born with and that are controlled by instructions in our genes, such as number of fat cells and rate of metabolism, are called (a)_____ . Factors that result from learning or personality traits and that influence responsiveness to food are called (b)_____ . Factors that involve values and beliefs that we acquire from our particular society are called (c)_____ . Factors that increase the rate of metabolism are (d)_____ .

Answers: 1. *motivation.* 2. *instincts.* 3. (a) *social,* (b) *biological.* 4. (a) *drive,* (b) *homeostasis,* (c) *drive-reduction.* 5. *incentives.* 6. (a) *extrinsic,* (b) *intrinsic;* 7. *Maslow's hierarchy of needs.* 8. (a) *biological,* (b) *learned.* 9. (a) *peripheral,* (b) *central,* (c) *lateral hypothalamus,* (d) *ventromedial hypothalamus.* 10. (a) *inherited,* (b) *psychological,* (c) *social-cultural,* (d) *physical.*

Sexual Behavior

Why does the word sex *always get your attention?*

No other biological or social need generates as much interest or controversy as sex. Sex is considered a biological need because it is critical to the long-term survival of our species. However, like hunger, sex is heavily influenced by social-cultural factors. For example, surveys report that the kind, frequency, and length of sexual interactions varies greatly in different parts of American culture as well as in different countries of the world.

In many animals, including lions, sexual behavior is almost totally controlled by hormones.

We're going to examine four general questions about human sexual behavior: (1) What is the basis for sexual motivation? (2) How do social-cultural factors influence sexual behavior? (3) What is the current thinking about homosexuality? (4) What do we know about AIDS?

To answer our question about sexual motivation, we ask you to imagine being a lion.

Hormones: Lions Versus Humans

If you were a lion, your sexual motivation would be almost totally regulated by sex hormones. **Sex hormones** *are chemicals, secreted by glands, that circulate in the bloodstream and influence the brain, other body organs, and behaviors.* Human sexual motivation, on the other hand, depends primarily on psychological factors and is less regulated by hormones. There are two kinds of sex hormones: **androgens,** *the major category of male sex hormones secreted by the testes,* and **estrogens,** *the major category of female sex hormones secreted by the ovaries.* The secretion of these hormones is controlled by the hypothalamus in the brain. When certain parts of the hypothalamus are destroyed in animals, secretion of sex hormones ceases, and generally so does their sexual motivation.

In humans, at puberty the hypothalamus of the male triggers the *continuous release* of androgens, influencing the development of secondary sexual characteristics (facial and pubic hair, muscle growth, and so on). In the female, the hypothalamus triggers a *cyclical release* of estrogens, influencing the development of secondary sexual characteristics (breasts, pubic hair) and the menstrual cycle. Thus, the hypothalamus of males, which causes continuous secretion of sex hormones, functions differently from the hypothalamus of females, which causes cyclical secretion of hormones (DeVries, 1990). Now, let's examine how sex hormones influence motivation and behavior.

Motivation: Lions Versus Humans

If a female lion stopped secreting estrogens, her sexual behavior would cease. Similarly, if a male lion stopped secreting androgens, his sexual behavior would cease. In lions and many animals, the rise and fall in levels of sex hormones, especially in females, is the major influence on sexual motivation.

The female lion becomes sexually receptive only at a certain time in her hormonal cycle; at all other times she rejects sexual advances. One cue that the female lion is sexually receptive is that she secretes pheromones. **Pheromones** *are chemicals that have distinctive odors, which in turn attract other animals of the species.*

In contrast to the situation with lions and other animals, there is no convincing evidence that pheromones are important in human sexual behavior (Quadagno, 1987). Further, there is little correlation between levels of sex hormones and *sexual motivation* in humans, provided hormonal levels are within the normal range (Harvey, 1987). For example, androgen levels normally rise and fall throughout the day, but these variations are poorly correlated with sex drive in males. Similarly, estrogens drop to low levels after menopause, but the effects on women's sexual motivation are variable: there may be a decrease, no change, or even an increase in motivation (Leiblum, 1990).

These findings suggest that in normal adult humans, *psychological factors,* such as one's beliefs, expectations, or concerns about sex, exert the major influence on sexual motivation. As a result, psychological factors can greatly influence sexual arousal and orgasm, which we will examine next.

Sexual Behavior

Human Sexual Response

Four Stages of Sexual Response

In the 1950s, two researchers, William Masters and Virginia Johnson, studied physiological changes that occurred when volunteers engaged in masturbation and intercourse. Today Masters and Johnson's research is recognized as the first comprehensive and scientific study of the physiological changes during arousal and orgasm. Their research led to an understanding of human sexual physiology and provided a basis for developing techniques to treat sexual problems.

Based on their laboratory research, Masters and Johnson (1966) divided the sexual response pattern into four stages: *excitement, plateau, orgasm,* and *resolution.* We will describe this four-stage model here, since it is a good introduction to the sexual response pattern. It is important to remember, however, that individuals vary greatly in their sexual response patterns.

Since Masters and Johnson's original description of the sexual response pattern, other researchers have noted considerable variability in this pattern (Kaplan, 1974). For this reason, you should view their four-stage sequence as a general description rather than as the "correct" human sexual response.

Now let's examine how social-cultural factors influence sexual behavior.

Excitement. The **excitement phase** *is marked by increased muscle tension, a moderate increase in heart rate and blood pressure, and increased blood flow to the genitals.* In this stage, females experience vaginal lubrication; males experience erection.

Plateau. With continued arousal, one may reach the **plateau phase,** *which is indicated by increased muscle tension, further increases in heart rate and blood pressure, and increased blood flow to genitals.* No single response marks this phase, which may last for only a few seconds or continue for much longer. Some persons report that the experience of continued arousal during the plateau phase results in a more intense orgasmic experience.

Orgasm. Continued sexual stimulation during the plateau phase may cause an **orgasm,** *which is usually defined as a combination of physiological responses and psychological feelings.* The *physiological responses* for males and females include involuntary muscle spasms; great increases in heart rate (up to 180 beats per minute), blood pressure, and breathing; and rhythmic contractions of the muscles in the anal-genital area. A male's orgasm is accompanied by ejaculation, in which semen is expelled by strong rhyth-mic muscle contractions. A female may experience increased lubrication during orgasm.

After many years of research, Joseph Bohlen (1986) has found little association between physiological responses and duration or intensity of orgasmic feelings. He concluded that physiological responses are the basis for the orgasmic experience but that psychological feelings, which take place in the brain, are the actual orgasmic experience. The *psychological feelings* that accompany orgasm are characterized by intense pleasure. Helen Singer Kaplan (1986) notes that because psychological feelings so greatly influence the orgasmic experience, what goes on in our brains during sex is probably more important than what goes on in our genitals.

Resolution. Following orgasm is the **resolution phase,** *which involves a gradual release of muscle tension and a return to normal heart rate, blood pressure, and breathing.* One major difference between males and females is that following orgasm males usually experience a period of time, called a **refractory period,** during which additional stimulation cannot produce orgasm. According to Masters and Johnson, females do not experience a refractory period, and continued stimulation may result in another orgasm.

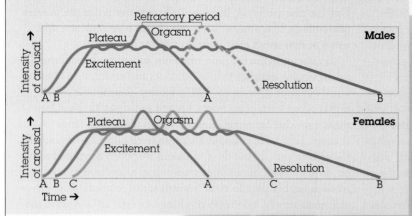

Social-Cultural Influences on Sexual Behavior

As society's general attitudes vary between liberal and conservative, a corresponding variation occurs in attitudes toward sexual behavior. For example, the liberal attitudes of the 1970s were translated into a more permissive attitude toward sexual behavior. In fact, that decade is commonly referred to as the sexual revolution. To illustrate this point, John Earle and

Philip Perricone (1986) reported that in 1970, 1975, and 1981, the percentage of women who had engaged in premarital sex was 35%, 45%, and 52%, respectively, and the corresponding percentages for males were 40%, 61%, and 62%.

By the mid-1980s, two related factors had slowed and perhaps stopped the 1970s sexual revolution. One factor, as we'll see a bit later in the chapter, was a fear of the life-threatening disease AIDS. A second factor was that society in general became politically and socially more conservative, ushering in a correspondingly more conservative attitude toward sexual activity. For example, one study reported that at the height of the 1970s sexual revolution, 51% of college females reported being sexually active at least once a month, but by the mid-1980s the number had dropped to 37% (Gerrard, 1987). In the early 1990s, indications are that the conservative attitudes toward sexual behavior are continuing (Robinson et al., 1991).

Society's double standard influences . . .

Decisions about Being Sexual. Whether one chooses to become sexually active is a personal decision. Although high school and college students report pressure from their peers to be sexually active, there is nothing unusual or abnormal about choosing to delay, limit, or not engage in sexual activity. For example, one survey of college students reported that 47% of females and 38% of males had never engaged in intercourse (Darling & Davidson, 1986). Similarly, a 1991 nationally representative survey reported that 22% of American adults had not engaged in sexual intercourse during the previous year (Smith, 1991). Any decision to be or not be sexually active is based on the interaction between at least three factors: *biological drive, personal values and beliefs,* and *social-cultural pressures.* One social-cultural pressure is known as the double standard.

The Double Standard. For the past 50 years, almost every survey of sexual activity has found the same difference between males and females: males report being sexually active at an earlier age than females and engaging in sexual behaviors more frequently (Abler & Sedlacek, 1989). One factor that accounts for this male-female difference is the existence of a **double standard for sexual behavior:** *the set of beliefs, values, and expectations that subtly encourage males to be sexually active while at the same time discouraging the same behavior in females.* For example, sexually active high school and college males often boast of their sexual conquests and receive approval and encouragement from their peers. In contrast, similar levels of sexual activity in high school and college females would result in ruined reputations and increased criticism from peers.

. . . the sexual behavior of men and women differently.

Although the double standard has changed in some respects (which is reflected, for instance, in the increased frequency of sexual intercourse among college women over the past 30 years), the changes have not necessarily been matched with increased psychological satisfaction. For example, 80% of college men reported being satisfied with their sexual experiences and almost always reaching orgasm; in comparison, only 28% of college women reported being psychologically satisfied with their sexual experiences, and the majority did not reach orgasm during intercourse (Darling & Davidson, 1986). These findings indicate the importance of psychological factors, such as attitudes, feelings, and beliefs, in achieving sexual satisfaction and happiness in a relationship.

Approximately 90% of the American population express their sexuality in *heterosexual* (with the opposite sex) relationships. Next we'll discuss the approximately 10% who are homosexual, either gay or lesbian.

Sexual Behavior

Homosexual Behavior

One question that has puzzled society for at least 2,000 years is "Why does someone develop a homosexual preference?" About 10% of the population are *homosexual* (gay or lesbian), which means having a preference for relations with the same sex. Of this 10%, a small percentage consider themselves *bisexual*, which means having a preference for relations with both sexes. Researchers believe that homosexuality results from a complex interaction between biological and social-learning factors (Bell et al., 1981; Money, 1987).

Why do some people develop a homosexual preference?

Where does one's sexual preference come from?

Drawing on over 40 years of research on sexual behavior, John Money (1987) hypothesized a two-step process for the development of sexual preference, whether heterosexual or homosexual.

Money's Two-Step Process

Step 1 Biological factors. Before birth, the developing embryo (months 1–2) and fetus (months 3–9) are influenced by **prenatal hormones.** Money believes that prenatal hormones act on the brain and create a *predisposition* for either a heterosexual preference or a homosexual preference.

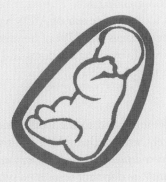

Step 2 Social-learning factors. After birth, social-learning factors, such as the influence of parents and peers, facilitate or inhibit the predisposition for sexual preference.

What biological and social-learning factors might influence a homosexual preference?

Biological Factors

Two recent studies suggest that biological factors may influence sexual preference.

The first was conducted by neurobiologist Simon LeVay (1991) of the Salk Institute, who studied the *hypothalamus,* which is known to regulate sexual behavior in animals and which controls secretion of sex hormones in humans. LeVay found that a tiny area of the hypothalamus in homosexual men was less than half the size of that in heterosexual men. However, this study shows only that there is an association or correlation between size of a particular brain area and sexual preference, so we do not know what caused what. We can say only that LeVay's study suggests a possible role of the hypothalamus in sexual preference.

The second study compared *genetic influence* on sexual preference in 56 pairs of identical twins (who share the same genes), 54 pairs of fraternal twins (share half their genes), and 57 pairs of adoptive brothers (who share no genes). Researchers Michael Bailey and Richard Pillard (1991) found that homosexual preference occurred among *both* brothers in 52% of identical twins, 22% of fraternal twins, and 11% of adoptive brothers. Because both identical twins reported a significantly higher percentage of homosexual preference, Bailey and Pillard suggest that genes play an important role in shaping sexual preference.

However, we must view the results of both studies with caution until their results have been replicated.

Social-Learning Factors

Allan Bell and his associates (1981) at the Kinsey Institute for Sex Research surveyed, interviewed, and compared a large sample of homosexuals and heterosexuals. Based on their findings, Bell believes that social-learning factors are more important than biological factors in the development of sexual preference.

Let's examine one potential social-learning factor. One of the major predictors of developing a homosexual preference is how frequently a child or adolescent engages in **cross-gender behaviors,** *which are behaviors that are more typical or stereotypic of the opposite sex.* A boy would be engaging in cross-gender behaviors if he played social games with girls rather than baseball with his peers. Bernard Zuger (1989) found that of 48 boys who engaged in cross-gender behaviors, 35 (73%) developed a homosexual preference. Some researchers conclude that the more that individuals engage in cross-gender behaviors, the more likely they are to experience homosexual feelings and engage in homosexual behavior (Green, 1987). However, the association between engaging in cross-gender behaviors and developing a homosexual preference is a correlation and, as such, does not indicate cause and effect.

Much of the current data on developing a sexual preference fit in with Money's two-step process, which suggests an interaction between biological and social-learning factors.

Next we'll discuss AIDS, which is of great concern to everyone but particularly to those who are sexually active, whether homosexual, bisexual, or heterosexual.

Sexual Behavior

AIDS: Acquired Immune Deficiency Syndrome

On June 5, 1981 the United States Centers for Disease Control issued a brief report describing five gay men in Los Angeles with a rare form of pneumonia; in time, this pneumonia was determined to be one symptom of AIDS. In 1991, only ten years later, over 125,000 Americans had died from AIDS. AIDS has spread to over 130 countries and has resulted in a global total of 1.5 million cases.

Surveys of homosexuals and heterosexuals indicate that fear of AIDS has greatly altered sexual habits. For example, 29% of heterosexuals and 87% of homosexuals in Los Angeles County changed their habits, primarily by using condoms and limiting their number of partners (*Los Angeles Times*, August 17, 1991).

What does HIV-positive mean?

As basketball star Earvin "Magic" Johnson demonstrated to the world, one can be HIV-positive yet be symptom-free and relatively healthy. Being **HIV-positive** *means that one has been exposed to HIV (human immunodeficiency virus) but may actually be symptom-free.* After initial exposure, the virus may lie dormant (causes no symptoms) for an average of seven to eight years before being reactivated. Once active, the virus progressively destroys the immune system, making the patient vulnerable to life-threatening infections and diseases. When the symptoms of AIDS are diagnosed, a person has an average life expectancy of about one year (May, Anderson, & Blower, 1989).

In 1992 the Centers for Disease Control in Atlanta, Georgia, considered changing the definition of AIDS. At present, someone is considered to have AIDS if the person is HIV-positive and has physical symptoms that result from a breakdown in the immune system. The new definition of AIDS being considered would include individuals who are HIV-positive but show relatively few symptoms. One reason for changing the definition is to allow individuals who are HIV-positive but have no symptoms to get medical treatment. Under the current definition, Magic Johnson is HIV-positive but does not have AIDS. Under the proposed definition, Magic Johnson might be classified as having AIDS.

Computer-generated model of the AIDS virus.

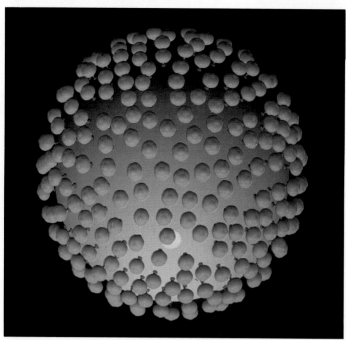

What is the definition of HIV-positive?

How does one get AIDS?

The HIV virus survives best in blood tissues and some bodily fluids, such as semen and vaginal fluids. Thus, AIDS is transmitted through sexual contact (exposure to semen or vaginal fluid); by sharing needles for drugs, tattooing, or ear-piercing; by having had a blood transfusion before 1985 (when a test was developed to detect the HIV virus); or from an infected mother to her unborn child.

The HIV virus cannot survive in air, in water, or on things that people touch. For that reason, there are almost no reports of family members, roommates, or health care workers getting AIDS through casual contact, such as touching, hugging, or coming in contact with sweat or tears of someone with AIDS.

Who is at risk for AIDS?

The groups at greatest risk for AIDS in the United States are currently considered to be homosexual or bisexual men, intravenous drug users, and prostitutes. In other countries, such as those in Africa, the group at greatest risk is heterosexual couples, who transmit the virus through sexual intercourse (May, Anderson, & Blower, 1989). In the United States, the risk of AIDS among heterosexual couples has been gradually increasing, from 0.5% of couples in 1981 to almost 7.0% in 1991.

How does one protect against getting AIDS?

Because AIDS can be spread through sexual contact, the surest way to avoid AIDS is to be celibate—that is, to not have sexual contact. If a person does engage in sex with someone whose HIV status is unknown, techniques for safer sex should be used. That means using condoms so that no semen, vaginal fluid, or blood is exchanged between partners. Over-the-counter spermicides that contain nonoxynol-9 are thought to provide additional protection against the virus (Francis & Chin, 1987).

Does Magic Johnson have AIDS?

In 1991 Earvin "Magic" Johnson, basketball star of the Los Angeles Lakers, stunned the nation with his announcement of being HIV-positive. At that time he was symptom-free, but if no cure is found, he will most likely develop AIDS, which is fatal.

Is there a treatment or cure for AIDS?

As of this writing, there is no cure for AIDS. Several drugs, such as AZT, appear to prolong survival among AIDS patients, but they cause side effects (nausea, headaches). Researchers are working on a vaccine for AIDS, but progress has been slow and difficult (Haverkos, 1989).

Up to this point we have discussed sex and hunger, both basic biological needs that are also influenced by learning, social, and cultural factors. Now we turn to a social need—achievement—that explains why we set goals and work hard to reach them.

Achievement

Why did they succeed in school?

In many high schools across the United States, black males tend to have relatively low grade point averages and relatively high dropout rates. Exceptions to this general finding are Darryl, Wayne, and Hollis, three black male students who were recently honored for their academic achievement in high school (*Los Angeles Times*, June 28, 1991). One explanation for their academic success is that they had a **need for achievement,** *a desire to set challenging goals and to persist in pursuing those goals in the face of obstacles, frustrations, and setbacks.* The need for achievement ranks high in Maslow's hierarchy of needs (level 4) and is an acquired social need. We're going to examine two questions about the need for achievement: How is it measured? How does it relate to failure?

Measuring Achievement

Psychologists David McClelland and John Atkinson used the Thematic Apperception Test (TAT) to measure need for achievement. The **TAT** *is a personality test that consists of asking subjects to look at pictures of people in ambiguous situations and to make up stories about what is happening in the pictures.* For example, one TAT card shows a younger woman gazing off into space and an older woman at her shoulder. This card may trigger stories about things that bother us. McClelland and Atkinson identified achievement themes (setting goals, competing, overcoming obstacles) in the TAT stories of hundreds of subjects and scored the themes in terms of high or low need for achievement (Atkinson, 1958; McClelland et al., 1953).

To test need for achievement, a person makes up a story about a picture like this one, part of the TAT test.

What traits go along with a high need for achievement?

When these researchers studied the *personality characteristics* of people with a high need for achievement, they found that such individuals persist longer at tasks, show better performance on exams, set challenging but realistic goals, and are attracted to jobs that require initiative (Atkinson & Raynor, 1974; Koestner & McClelland, 1990; McClelland, 1985). These characteristics apply to Darryl, Wayne, and Hollis, who set challenging academic goals, studied hard to earn good grades, and overcame negative pressure from peers who viewed school as a waste of time.

If we consider one side of a coin to be a need for achievement, the opposite side can be considered a fear of failure.

Fear of Failure

Atkinson (1964) believed that to understand achievement motivation, we must examine not only a person's need for achievement but also his or her *fear of failure.* Atkinson hypothesized that just as people vary in their need for achievement, they also vary in their motivation to avoid failure. For example, a fear of failure motivates students to study just enough to avoid failing exams but not enough to get good grades or set higher academic goals. In contrast, a need for achievement motivates students to set higher goals and study hard to get good grades. Atkinson thought that individuals motivated primarily by a fear of failure would never do as well, work as hard, or set goals as high as those who were motivated primarily by a need for achievement.

Making Excuses

How do individuals who are motivated by a fear of failure explain their poor performances but retain a good self-image? If students get good grades on exams, they usually attribute their good performances to their abilities, such as studying hard. However, if they get poor grades, they may make up excuses, such as the test being too difficult, tricky, or unfair. Jones and Berglas (1978) call this the **self-handicapping strategy**, *which is a tendency to make up an excuse for one's failure.*

What are our most popular excuses?
Some of the more popular excuses or self-handicapping strategies revolve around concerns about health (missing sleep, having a cold), drug usage (too much partying, having a hangover), or chance/fate (bad luck, "How could it happen to me?"). One reason we use self-handicapping strategies is that they keep our positive self-image intact while allowing us to do poorly (Berglas, 1989). One disadvantage of using self-handicapping strategies is that they may prevent us from taking personal responsibility and steps to correct the situation.

To understand achievement motivation, we need to consider the interaction of at least three factors—need for achievement, fear of failure, and making excuses or using self-handicapping strategies. The combination of these three factors helps us understand why some people work harder and achieve more than others.

Now let's look at another aspect of motivation, one that helps explain why people jump out of balloons or donate blood.

How do we explain the fact that Darryl, Wayne, and Hollis overcame discouragement from some of their peers and became model high school students?

Intrinsic Motivation

Why would someone jump out of a balloon?

One reason people will jump out of a balloon attached only by a stretchable (bungee) cord has to do with intrinsic motivation. As you may remember from our earlier discussion, ***intrinsic motivation*** refers to performing some behavior without receiving any external rewards because the behavior itself is personally rewarding, or because we are acting on some personal goal, belief, or expectation. According to Edward Deci and Richard Ryan (1980), people are intrinsically motivated because of an underlying need to demonstrate their competency and to show that they can gain the upper hand or master a situation. For example, people may jump out of a balloon and bounce in space because that behavior is personally rewarding or because they wish to show they can master the situation. Similarly, intrinsic motivation helps explain why people donate blood, do volunteer work, or engage in hobbies: the behavior or activity itself is personally rewarding.

Intrinsic motivation is one reason that people will jump out of a balloon attached only by a stretchable bungee cord.

Should we pay people to donate blood?

What do you think would happen if people were suddenly paid for doing something they did from intrinsic motivation, such as giving blood? According to Mark Lepper and colleagues, people would donate less blood because of the overjustification effect (Lepper & Greene, 1978). The **overjustification effect** *is a decrease in our enjoyment or desire to perform some intrinsically motivating behavior if we are given an external reward for performing that behavior.* For example, if volunteers donate blood because they are intrinsically motivated, paying them for donating blood would decrease their desire and motivation for making future donations. Similarly, if we were to pay people for engaging in hobbies, the overjustification effect predicts that they would enjoy their hobbies less and would be less motivated to engage in them in the future.

What's interesting about the overjustification effect?

The overjustification effect is an interesting phenomenon for two reasons. First, it contradicts one of the basic principles of learning—namely, that rewards increase the likelihood of performing some behavior—since, according to the overjustification effect, giving external rewards for a behavior that is intrinsically motivating actually *decreases* rather than increases our likelihood of performing that behavior in the future. Second, the overjustification effect is an interesting example of how cognitive processes, such as beliefs, values, and expectations, influence human motivation.

We have seen that cognitive factors play an important role in understanding intrinsic motivation and explaining the overjustification effect. In the Applying/ Exploring section, we'll examine the role of cognitive factors in interfering with hunger and in causing eating problems.

1. Chemicals that are secreted by glands that circulate in the bloodstream and influence the brain, other body organs, and sexual behaviors are called (a)_____. There are two kinds of these hormones; the major category of male sex hormones is (b)_____. The major category of female sex hormones is (c)_____.

2. Chemicals that have distinctive odors that in turn attract other animals of the species are called _____. In contrast to their effects on animals, there is no convincing evidence that such odor chemicals are important in human sexual behavior.

3. The secretion of sex hormones is controlled by a particular area of the brain called the (a)_____. At puberty, this area of the male brain triggers the (b)_____ secretion of androgens; this area of the female brain triggers the (c)_____ secretion of estrogens.

4. Based on their laboratory research, Masters and Johnson divided the sexual response pattern into four stages: (a)_____, (b)_____, (c)_____, and (d)_____.

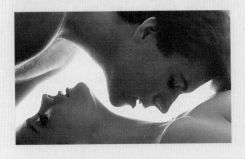

5. A set of beliefs, values, or expectations that subtly encourages males to be sexually active while discouraging sexual activity in females is referred to as the _____.

6. John Money hypothesized a two-step process for the development of sexual preference, whether heterosexual or homosexual. In step 1 the developing embryo (months 1–2) and fetus (months 3–9) are influenced in the womb by (a)_____. Money believes that these hormones act on the brain and create a (b)_____ for a heterosexual preference or a homosexual preference. In step 2 the hypothesized predisposition for the development of a sexual preference is facilitated or inhibited by (c)_____ factors.

7. One of the major predictors of developing a homosexual preference is how frequently a child or adolescent engages in behaviors that are more typical or stereotypic of the opposite sex. These behaviors are called _____.

8. In 1992 the definition of AIDS was anyone who had the _____ virus in his or her body and also had physical symptoms.

9. A desire to set challenging goals and to persist in meeting those goals in the face of obstacles, frustrations, and setbacks is defined as the need for (a)_____. Atkinson hypothesized that just as people vary in their need for achievement, people also vary in their motivation to avoid (b)_____.

10. The strategy of making up excuses to explain one's failure is called the _____ strategy.

11. Experiencing a decrease in our enjoyment of or desire to perform some intrinsically motivating behavior when given an external reward is called the _____ effect.

Answers: 1. (a) sex hormones, (b) androgens, (c) estrogens; 2. pheromones; 3. (a) hypothalamus, (b) continuous, (c) cyclical; 4. (a) excitement, (b) plateau, (c) orgasm, (d) resolution; 5. double standard; 6. (a) prenatal hormones, (b) predisposition, (c) social-learning; 7. cross-gender; 8. HIV; 9. (a) achievement, (b) failure; 10. self-handicapping; 11. overjustification.

APPLYING/ EXPLORING: EATING PROBLEMS

What is my normal weight?

You can answer this question by consulting a standard weight table, which gives a range of normal weights for various heights and body builds. The figures given in these tables are based on mortality data, which take into account the survival rates of people of varying weights. Individuals are considered overweight if their weight is 20% over the recommended weight in these tables; they are considered obese if their weight is 30% over the recommended weight. Being overweight or obese leads to increased health risks and reduced survival rates. For instance, obese women have a 300% greater risk of developing heart disease than do women of normal weight (Manson et al., 1990).

Failure and Success in Dieting

About 27% of American women and 24% of American men are overweight, and most of them go on diets to try to shed those extra pounds. For example, television talk-show host Oprah Winfrey went on a well-publicized diet, lost 67 pounds, and said she was finally cured of overeating. However, one year later she had regained all her lost weight and then some, for a total of 84 pounds. Estimates are that, like Oprah, about 90% of people who diet and lose 25 pounds or more gain the weight back in a year.

Theodore VanItallie, a weight-loss specialist at St. Luke's Hospital, cautions other overweight people not to be discouraged by Oprah's experience. He points out that dieting is only part of the solution to reaching normal weight and reducing health risks.

Before: Oprah Winfrey weighed 190 pounds, considered overweight for her height and frame.

After dieting: Oprah lost 67 pounds.

One year later: Oprah had gained back 84 pounds and weighed about 200 pounds.

The other part is making a strong commitment to a long-term maintenance program, which includes learning sensible eating habits, engaging in regular exercise, and perhaps reducing tension, stress, and anxiety. As Oprah admitted, "I didn't do whatever the maintenance program was. I thought I was cured. And that's just not true. You have to find a way to live in the world with food" (*People*, January 14, 1991, p. 84). As we discussed earlier in this module, there are four general factors—inherited, psychological, social-cultural, and physical—that influence body weight. Maintaining a normal, healthy weight requires taking all four factors into consideration.

Unlike Oprah, many other overweight individuals, including television and sports personalities, have dieted, lost weight, and kept it off a year later. The message is that learning not to overeat is difficult but is attainable with a good diet program.

Eating Disorders

There are a number of psychological and social-cultural pressures on modern American women to be thin, and these pressures may contribute to eating disorders (Striegel-Moore et al., 1989). We'll examine two kinds of eating disorders—bulimia nervosa and anorexia nervosa—whose symptoms are more serious than those associated with eating problems (overeating).

Bulimia Nervosa

Bulimia nervosa (boo-LEE-me-ah ner-VOH-sah), previously called bulimia, *is characterized by a minimum of two binge-eating episodes per week for at least three months; fear of not being able to stop eating; regularly engaging in vomiting, use of laxatives, or rigorous dieting and fasting; and exces-*sive concern about body shape and weight (American Psychiatric Association, 1987). Current estimates are that about 1% of the American population suffer from bulimia nervosa and that 90% of bulimics are adolescent and young white women (Fairburn, Phil, & Beglin, 1990).

Risk Factors. Researchers have identified a number of psychological factors that make a woman at risk for bulimia nervosa. For example, women are more at risk if they live in a culture where the dominant sentiment is "Fat is bad and thin is good," if they have high levels of perceived stress and negative feelings about their weight and attractiveness, and if they experienced bouts of depression, anxiety, and mood swings (Striegel-Moore et al., 1989). Although physical and metabolic changes have been reported, it is difficult to determine whether they are the cause or result of bulimia nervosa (Devlin et al., 1990).

Treatment. Two general kinds of treatment are used for bulimia nervosa. One involves cognitive-behavior therapy, in which emphasis is placed on substituting positive thoughts for negative ones and changing specific eating habits and patterns. A second method, generally less preferred because of unwanted side effects, is the use of antidepressant drugs (Mitchell, 1991). Individuals with bulimia nervosa may need continued support and therapy to deal with their psychological problems.

Anorexia Nervosa

Anorexia nervosa (an-uh-REX-see-ah ner-VOH-sah) *is a serious eating disorder characterized by maintaining body weight 15% or more below normal, having an intense fear of* gaining weight or becoming fat, starving one-self to remain thin, and having a disturbed body image *(American Psychiatric Association, 1987). Anorexics are almost exclusively female (90%), white (99%), and 15 to 24 years old (60%), and they come from the two highest socioeconomic classes (75%) (Murray, 1986). Contrary to reports in the popular press, anorexia nervosa, as defined by these symptoms, is a relatively rare disorder, occurring in only about .001% of females (Szmukler, 1985).

Causes. According to Hilde Bruch (1982), anorexia nervosa arises from a number of psychological problems, such as increased feelings of dependency and decreased feelings of identity and self-assertion. Although hormonal and neurochemical changes have been reported in anorexics, it is difficult to determine whether these changes contributed to or resulted from the self-starvation (Fava et al., 1989).

Treatment. Treatment for anorexics first involves encouraging weight gain, usually through behavior modification (Module 12), then dealing with psychological problems through therapy. Working out these problems may require several years of therapy. Even after treatment, only about half of anorexics maintain normal body weight with only mild psychological symptoms (Yates, 1990).

Eating problems, such as overeating, bulimia nervosa, and anorexia nervosa, point out how various personality and psychological factors can influence, change, and even override hunger, one of our basic biological drives.

The Carpenters were a brother and sister singing duo of the 1970s. A number of personal problems probably contributed to Karen's developing anorexia nervosa, which she struggled with until she died of a heart attack at age 32.

Summary/Self-Test

APPROACHES TO MOTIVATION

1. The combined physiological and psychological factors that cause you to act in specific ways at particular times is referred to as motivation. When motivated, you usually exhibit three characteristics: you are (a)_____ to do something, you (b)_____ your energies toward a specific goal, and you have different (c)_____ of feelings about reaching that goal.

2. Psychologists use four approaches to explain motivation. The earliest of these approaches, now used only with respect to animals, concerns innate biological forces, called (a)_____ or _____, that predispose an animal to behave in a fixed way under certain conditions. A theory that encompasses biological and psychological needs is (b)_____. According to this theory, a need results in a drive, by which we are motivated to engage in activities to return to a more balanced state, called (c)_____. Because this theory does not explain why we continue to perform after our needs are met or why we perform risky behaviors, another theory was developed. According to this theory, external rewards, called (d)_____, motivate our behavior. Cognitive psychologists distinguish between extrinsic and intrinsic motivations. Intrinsic motivation empha-

sizes the idea that we behave according to our chosen expectations and goals and believe that we are in control of the situation; this concept is referred to as (e)_____.

■ *Joe is working hard to get good grades in college because he wants to go to graduate school. What are the various ways we can explain Joe's motivation?*

BIOLOGICAL AND SOCIAL NEEDS

3. Food, water, and sleep are examples of (a)_____ needs. In comparison, needs that are acquired through learning and socialization are called (b)_____ we satisfy our needs in ascending order, with biological needs first and social needs later; this order is referred to as the (c)_____. In Maslow's hierarchy, needs are divided into five levels: biological, safety, love and belongingness, esteem, and self-actualization.

■ *What would your life be like if you won a lottery and were guaranteed $1 million a year for the next 30 years?*

HUNGER

4. In satisfying your biological need for food, you are influenced by two main kinds of cues. Cues arising from physiological changes in your blood chemistry and signals from your body organs and brain are called (a)_____. Those cues arising from your body organs are called (b)_____; those from your brain are called (c)_____. In contrast, cues coming from the associations you make between eating and environmental stimuli are called (d)_____.

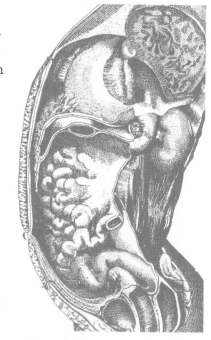

■ *A recent poll indicated that 55% of teenage girls believe that they are overweight, but only 13% actually are (USA Today, October 21, 1991). Is there something wrong with these girls' hunger need?*

BODY WEIGHT

5. The four general factors that influence your body weight are inherited, psychological, social-cultural, and physical factors. Inherited factors include your number of (a)_____ cells, your rate of (b)_____, and your ratio of fat to lean, called the (c)_____.

■ *A mother explains that her son is overweight because it runs in the family. Is the mother right?*

SEXUAL BEHAVIOR

6. The secretion of sex hormones, primarily (a)_____ for men and (b)_____ for women, is controlled by the portion of the brain called the (c)_____. Assuming that hormone levels are within the normal range, there is little correlation between levels of sex hormones and sexual motivation in humans. Instead, (d)_____, such as beliefs, expectations, or concerns, exert the major influence on human sexual motivation.

7. Based on research by Masters and Johnson, human sexual response is generally divided into four stages, called (a)_____, (b)_____, (c)_____, and (d)_____.

8. According to Money's two-step process, sexual preference is influenced by (a)_____ and _____ factors. In the first step, biological factors, such as (b)_____ hormones, influence the developing embryo and fetus. In the sec-

ond step, social-learning factors, which include the influence of parents and peers, interact with the biological factors to result in one's sexual preference.

9. Individuals who are HIV-positive have been exposed to the _____ but may actually be symptom-free. However, people who are HIV-positive almost always develop AIDS. Currently, there is no cure for AIDS, so prevention, through celibacy or safer sex practices, is particularly critical.

■ *If someone were troubled by low sexual desire, would it be possible to increase his or her desire with injections of sex hormones?*

ACHIEVEMENT

10. High in Maslow's need hierarchy is a desire to set challenging goals and persist in meeting them. This desire is called the (a)_____. To fully understand achievement motivation, one must also understand its corollary, (b)_____.

■ *Some college sophomores experience a drop in motivation for studying, attending classes, and staying in college. What are some explanations for these "sophomore blues"?*

INTRINSIC MOTIVATION

11. The desire to perform some behavior without receiving any external rewards is due to (a)_____ motivation. Reduction of this kind of motivation by the addition of external rewards is called the (b)_____.

■ *Carol was so good at helping other students with statistics that she was offered a paid job as a tutor. What might happen to her motivation as a result?*

APPLYING/EXPLORING: EATING PROBLEMS

12. Eating problems demonstrate how personality and psychological factors can override the basic biological hunger drive. An eating disorder characterized by binging, fear of not being able to stop eating, and regularly purging the body is known as (a)_____. Another disorder in which one starves to remain thin and has a disturbed body image is called (b)_____.

■ *An ad promises that you can "lose weight easily and quickly without dieting or exercise by practicing self-hypnosis." What questions would you have about this ad?*

MODULE 18
EMOTION

What's it like to be attacked by a 12-foot, 3,000-pound great white shark?

What's that thing clamped on my leg?

It was a warm Monday morning in July as Eric waited on his surfboard. So far, most of the waves had been short and choppy, and he was becoming discouraged. He stuck it out for about an hour and then decided to quit. He was paddling back to shore when suddenly the back of his board went down and the front jerked up. At the same time he was being pulled off his board by some enormous thing clamped onto his left leg.

When he looked back at his leg, he saw it clamped in huge jaws filled with rows of white teeth. A burst of fear gave him strength to pry his leg out of the creature's jaws. But just as Eric pulled his leg out, the shark opened its mouth and grabbed both his arms. "Next thing I knew," said Eric, "I'd managed to get my right arm free. My adrenaline was flowing. I raised my hand and hit with a hammerblow so violently that I pulled a bunch of muscles in my upper arm." Eric's blows distracted the shark, which released him, turned, and swam away. The entire encounter, according to Eric's estimate, lasted no more than 10 seconds.

Once free of the shark, Eric got back onto his surfboard and paddled toward shore. He was trailing blood and growing weak when he reached the beach. Now that he was safe, he felt the most fear: "It occurred to me I might die."

Eric's left arm was open to the bone from wrist to shoulder, his right forearm had a four-inch bite out of it, and his left leg was in shreds. Surgeons worked on Eric for ten hours, using 400 stitches and 200 surgical staples to mend his wounds.

It will be some time before Eric returns to the Blood Triangle, a surfing area where great white sharks are said to feed. (adapted from San Francisco *Chronicle*, July 3, 1991, July 4, 1991; *People*, July 29, 1991, pp. 32–34)

During and following the shark attack, Eric experienced a number of emotions. An **emotion** *is a feeling made up of three components: conscious or subjective experience, physiological arousal, and overt behavior.* We can identify these three components in Eric's experience with the shark: his cognitive component was thinking of what to do; his physiological component was increased heart rate and a rush of adrenaline; and his overt behavior component was hitting the shark and paddling toward shore.

Although we think of emotions as being separate experiences, they are often intertwined with and give rise to motivations. For example, Eric's fear gave him the strength to hit the shark and swim back to shore.

Just as we experience many kinds of motivations to many different degrees, we feel many kinds of emotions with varying intensities. Emotions play such a major role in our lives that it is impossible to imagine a day without feeling dozens of positive and negative emotions.

What's Coming

In this module we'll discuss three major questions about emotions. First, how many emotions are there? Second, where do emotions come from? And third, what is the function of emotions? To answer the first question, let's return to surfing in the Blood Triangle.

Basic Emotions

How many emotions did you feel today?

If you were to surf in the Blood Triangle as Eric did, you might feel excitement, fear, apprehension, or terror during your time in the water and relief or happiness afterward. From our many emotional experiences, psychologists have tried to construct a list of basic emotions. According to Andrew Ortony and Terence Turner (1990), **basic emotions** *are those that are either recognized in most cultures or help the species survive by motivating behaviors or signaling physiological needs and psychological moods.* We'll discuss which emotions may be basic and explain their functions.

Pleasant

Love

Joy

Surprise

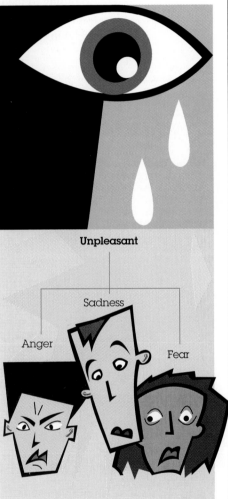

Unpleasant

Sadness

Anger

Fear

Hierarchy of Basic Emotions

Researchers have used a number of approaches to construct a list of basic emotions. Philip Shaver and his colleagues (1987) asked students to rate 213 words according to whether they could be labeled as emotions. At one extreme, all said that *love, anger,* and *hate* are definitely emotions; at the other extreme, all said that *intelligence, carefulness,* and *practicality* are not. By analyzing the students' ratings of the emotion words, Shaver organized emotions into a hierarchy.

At the top of the hierarchy are two broad classes of emotions: *pleasant* and *unpleasant.* Next in the hierarchy are six basic emotions: *love, joy, surprise, anger, sadness,* and *fear.*

Shaver noted that the six basic emotions identified in his study are similar to lists of basic emotions compiled by other researchers. For example, other researchers usually list from four to eight basic emotions, which may include *anger, disgust, anxiety, happiness, sadness, joy, shame,* and *surprise* (Oatley & Johnson-Laird, 1987; Plutchik, 1980).

One reason researchers try to identify basic emotions is that such a list would help explain our complex emotional experiences, such as why people in cultures around the world recognize the same emotional expressions. Although there is some agreement on which emotions are basic, the exact number of such emotions remains undecided. One thing researchers agree on is that emotions are important to the physical and psychological well-being of the individual as well as to the survival of our species.

Next, let's turn to what causes an emotion.

Peripheral Theories

Do emotions come from our bodies?

Imagine swimming in the ocean on a sunny day and suddenly seeing a black fin cut the surface of the blue water. You would immediately experience several emotions, including fear. To explain what causes an emotion such as fear, we'll examine two **peripheral theories** *that emphasize changes in the body.* We'll also discuss several **cognitive theories** *that emphasize cognitive factors.* Let's begin with two peripheral theories of emotions: James-Lange theory and facial feedback theory.

James-Lange Theory

According to the **James-Lange theory**, *emotions result from specific physiological changes in our bodies, and each emotion has a different physiological basis.* This theory was proposed (separately) in the late 1800s by two psychologists, William James and Carl Lange.

Three Steps in the James-Lange Theory

1 We perceive a *stimulus*, such as a shark, in our environment. The perception affects the autonomic nervous system, one part of which (the sympathetic division) causes physiological arousal.

2 The autonomic nervous system (sympathetic division) causes a specific pattern of *physiological arousal*, such as increases in heart rate, blood pressure, and breathing, and other changes. The theory assumes a different pattern of physiological arousal for each emotion.

3 Each pattern of physiological arousal is interpreted by the brain as a different *emotion*. According to the James-Lange theory, the sight of a shark causes a specific pattern of physiological arousal, which you experience and then interpret as fear. Notice that the James-Lange theory emphasizes a pattern of physiological arousal as the major cause of emotions.

There are two major criticisms of the James-Lange theory. First, different emotions do not necessarily cause different kinds of physiological arousal. For instance, anger, fear, and sadness seem to share similar physiological patterns of arousal (Ekman, Levenson, & Friesen, 1983). Second, people whose spinal cords have been severed at the neck are deprived of most of the feedback from their autonomic systems, yet they experience emotions. People without autonomic feedback do, however, often report that emotions are reduced in intensity (Linton & Hirt, 1979). Psychologists generally agree that different kinds of physiological arousal do not cause different emotions. Instead, physiological arousal may increase the *intensity* of emotions. For instance, if you were experiencing fear and also noticed that your heart was pounding and your mouth was dry, these physiological responses might further increase the intensity of your fear.

Now let's examine a second peripheral theory of how emotions might be caused.

Facial Feedback Theory

According to **facial feedback theory**, *sensations or feedback from the movement of facial muscles and skin are interpreted by your brain and result in an emotion.* This theory originated with Charles Darwin, who believed that each emotion has its own innate pattern of facial muscle movement. Two prominent modern supporters of the hypothesis of the facial feedback theory, Carroll Izard (1981) and Silvan Tomkins (1981), believe that under certain conditions feedback from facial muscles and skin can result in feeling distinct emotions.

Researchers have asked two questions about facial feedback theory. First, does specific facial feedback give rise to or initiate specific emotions, such as happiness, sadness, or fear? There is little evidence to support this contention (Winton, 1986). Second, how does facial feedback contribute to our emo-

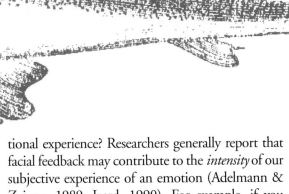

tional experience? Researchers generally report that facial feedback may contribute to the *intensity* of our subjective experience of an emotion (Adelmann & Zajonc, 1989; Izard, 1990). For example, if you smile when you are happy, feedback from the muscles involved in smiling may enhance or intensify your feelings of happiness.

In addition, researchers report that facial feedback may contribute to our *mood*, or overall emotional feeling. Subjects who have been asked to hold a smile later report being in a better mood than those asked to hold a frown. And compared with control subjects, people holding a smile report that cartoons are funnier, that pleasant scenes produce more positive feelings (Laird, 1974; Zuckerman et al., 1981), and that electric shocks are less painful (Lanzetta, Cartweight-Smith, & Kleck, 1976). Although researchers have not confirmed Darwin's original theory of facial muscles determining emotions, they have found that facial feedback does influence the intensity of our emotions and our moods.

Now that you are familiar with the peripheral theories of emotions, let's discuss a very different approach to emotions—cognitive theory.

Three Steps in the Facial Feedback Theory

1 We perceive a *stimulus,* such as a shark, in our environment. The perception results in movement of the muscles and skin of the face.

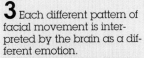

2 Specific *feedback* from the muscles and skin of the face is interpreted by the brain and gives rise to an emotional experience.

3 Each different pattern of facial movement is interpreted by the brain as a different emotion.

According to the facial feedback theory, the sight of a shark causes a specific pattern of facial movement. In turn, feedback from the face is interpreted and experienced as a different emotion, in this case fear. Notice that the facial feedback theory emphasizes feedback from facial muscles and skin as the major cause of emotions.

Cognitive Appraisal Theory

According to **cognitive appraisal theory**, *interpreting or appraising a situation as having a positive or negative impact on our lives results in a subjective feeling that we call an emotion.* The current cognitive appraisal theory of emotions can be traced back to the work of Stanley Schachter and Jerome Singer (1962), who were the first to demonstrate the importance of cognitive factors in emotions. We'll briefly describe their well-known experiment.

Three Steps in the Schachter-Singer Cognitive Theory

2 **Interpreting or appraising situational cues.** After the injections, subjects were placed in different *situations*—a happy one or an angry one. In the "happy" situation a confederate of the researchers created a happy atmosphere in the room where the subject waited by laughing and throwing paper airplanes around. In the "angry" situation, another confederate created an angry atmosphere in the room by complaining about filling out a long questionnaire.

1 **Being physiologically aroused.** Schachter and Singer *injected* some of their subjects with a hormone, epinephrine (adrenaline), that causes physiological arousal (increased heart rate and blood pressure). They told these subjects that the injections were vitamins and did not tell them that they would feel the effects of physiological arousal (increased heart rate).

Some subjects were in a "angry" setting.

→ "I feel angry."

3 **Identifying the emotion.** Subjects did not know that their physiological arousal was due to the injections. Instead, they interpreted their states of arousal as being due to happy or angry emotions based on their appraisals of the situations they were in. For example, subjects in the happy situation often reported feeling happy, while those in the angry situation often reported feeling angry.

Injections with hormone . . .

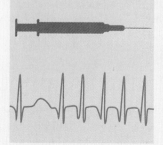

Some subjects were in a "happy" setting.

→ "I feel happy."

. . . causes physiological arousal.

According to **Schachter and Singer's cognitive theory,** *a stimulus causes physiological arousal* (step 1). *The arousal* itself does not cause any particular emotion but *creates the need for an explanation* of some kind. The person interprets or appraises the situational cues for an explanation of the aroused feeling (step 2). Finally, the person's *appraisal of the situational cues results in a subjective feeling or an emotion* (step 3).

In light of subsequent research, Schachter and Singer's theory has undergone two general revisions. First, Schachter and Singer originally proposed that some kind of physiological arousal was needed to start a person searching for an emotional explanation. Today researchers recognize that emotions may occur *without physiological arousal* (Lazarus, 1991). For example, suppose a friend walked up to you and said, "I just saw somebody back into your car and drive away." Your appraisal of that situation would most certainly make you feel angry, even before your physiological arousal kicked in.

A second revision in Schachter and Singer's theory concerns the importance of environmental or situational cues in labeling emotions. Today researchers argue that emotions may result not only from situational or environmental cues but also from our own *cognitive processes*, such as thoughts, interpretations, and appraisals (Lazarus, 1991).

Schachter and Singer's original idea that cognitive processes are involved in forming emotions has developed into the current and popular cognitive appraisal theory of emotions. Today many researchers recognize the role of cognitive processes in forming emotions; the big question, however, is whether emotions or thoughts come first.

Which Comes First: Feeling or Thinking?

One of the interesting questions about emotion is whether we can experience emotions without thinking about them. This is the **primacy question**, *which asks whether we can experience an emotion without any thought or whether we must engage in some kind of thinking or appraising before we can experience an emotion.* This questions has been hotly debated.

I'm feeling.

I'm thinking.

Primacy question:
Can you feel before you think?
Do you need to think before you can feel?

Feeling Before Thinking

What happens when you win a million dollars?
Imagine that you have just won a million dollars. At the moment you get the news, you feel incredibly happy. This emotional experience, which apparently occurs without any conscious thought, demonstrates that feeling occurs before thinking, that emotions precede cognitions.

The chief spokesperson for this position is Robert Zajonc (1984), who believes that feelings and thoughts, or emotions and cognitions, are separate processes that run on parallel tracks and are practically independent of each other. Although Zajonc does not deny that cognitions may sometimes precede emotions, he emphasizes the separateness of the two. However, many examples that Zajonc uses to demonstrate that feelings occur before thinking (such as reactions to seeing a snake, being in an accident, or recognizing a loved one) involve situations that occur very rapidly and allow little room for thinking. Zajonc's point is that feelings or emotions can occur first, before any thinking or appraising.

Thinking Before Feeling

What happens when you get jealous?
Imagine seeing a couple who, for some reason, remind you of your own relationship. As you think about your relationship, you remember a situation when you became jealous. As you continue thinking, you begin to feel jealous all over again. This type of emotional experience, which occurs after a relatively long thought process, demonstrates that thinking occurs before feeling, that cognitions precede emotions.

The chief spokesperson for this position is Richard Lazarus (1991), who takes a hard line in stating that thinking always precedes feelings, that cognitions always precede emotions. He explains that for an emotion to occur, it is necessary, at some level, to think about or appraise the situation. However, many examples that Lazarus uses to demonstrate that thinking occurs before feelings (such as being jealous, worrying about something, or feeling lonely) involve situations that develop over time and allow plenty of room for appraisal. Lazarus suggests that we are aware of our thinking or appraising if it is at a conscious level but may not be aware of our thinking if it occurs at a subconscious level.

Is there an answer to the primacy question?

You may have noticed that Zajonc and Lazarus use different kinds of emotional experiences to make their points. To show that feeling occurs before thinking, Zajonc emphasizes instantaneous emotional reactions, such as those triggered by seeing a snake. To show that thinking occurs before feelings, Lazarus emphasizes more complex, slower-developing emotional reactions, such as feeling jealous. Although the debate on the primacy question is not settled, it has sparked interest in the various ways that our emotional experiences may arise.

So far we have discussed emotions in general. Now we'll examine a particular emotion—happiness.

Happiness

How would you feel if you won the lottery?

Tony said, "You pick three numbers and I'll pick three. We'll split the five-buck fee." His friend nodded OK and added, "And we'll split the winnings." Each one filled in three numbers on the ticket. A few days later they won the lottery. As Tony showed people the winning ticket, he smiled and laughed and felt his heart pounding. He couldn't stop thinking about all the things his millions would buy (adapted from *Los Angeles Times,* October 10, 1987).

This family of lottery winners collected $22 million.

We can use Tony's emotional experience of happiness to review some of the things we know about emotions. We know that an emotion has *three components:* the *physiological component* is Tony's rapid heart rate; the *overt behavior component* is his smile and laughter; the *cognitive component* is his thinking about what he will do. We know that emotion and motivation are closely linked: Tony is motivated to show his ticket to all his friends and plan how to spend his money. We know that thinking about or appraising a situation can greatly influence an emotional experience: thinking about buying a new car increases Tony's happiness, whereas thinking about a large chunk of his winnings going to taxes causes him concern. Thus, Tony's emotional experience of winning the lottery illustrates the theoretical concepts we have discussed.

Now we turn to another intriguing question about emotions (specifically the emotion of happiness): How long does an emotion last?

What's the long-term emotional reaction to winning?

Philip Brickman and his associates (1978) interviewed lottery winners 1 to 12 months after they had won large sums of money. As might be expected, the majority reported positive changes, such as financial security, more leisure time, and earlier retirement. However, when asked to rate their current happiness, lottery winners, on average, turned out to be no happier than nonwinners. Brickman has an explanation for these curious findings.

Why doesn't happiness last?

According to Brickman's ***adaptation level theory,*** lottery winners become accustomed or habituated to the pleasures of having a great deal of money. With the passage of time, lottery winners take for granted having money, and as a result, they don't appreciate money as much and it contributes less to their level of happiness.

Brickman's adaptation level theory also explains why initially we may be very happy over obtaining an A in a course, buying a new car, getting a much-wanted job, or having a new relationship. With time, however, we have a tendency to take these pleasures for granted, so they give us less happiness. Brickman's adaptation level theory illustrates how other factors, such as taking things for granted, affect our emotional experience.

Now that we have covered the basics of emotions, let's turn to their functions.

Functions of Emotions

Emotions have three main functions: (1) they help us adapt and survive; (2) they motivate and arouse us, and (3) they help us send social signals.

Emotions Help Us Adapt and Survive

Emotions are important to the *survival* of individuals and our species. For example, crying alerts others that we may be in pain or discomfort; showing disgust may signal the presence of poisonous or rotten food. Feeling angry or afraid may help us survive a dangerous situation, perhaps by escaping from an assailant. Feeling happy may motivate social activity, bring peace of mind, and provide a chance to relax and enjoy life; being in love fosters social interactions.

There is, however, a darker side to emotions that may lead to problems at a personal or interpersonal level. In Chapter 13 we'll discuss how emotions may result in physical and psychological problems, and in Chapter 16 we'll look at antisocial emotions, such as aggression and anger.

Emotions Motivate and Arouse

As was mentioned earlier, emotions and motivation are closely linked. Emotions can *motivate* new behaviors. We may, for example, feel upset and thus work harder to reach our goals. On the other hand, emotions can *disrupt* behaviors (as they might if you are so worried during an exam that you have difficulty thinking clearly).

In fact, there is a relationship between the physiological arousal that accompanies an emotion and our performance on tasks. According to the **Yerkes-Dodson law**, *performance on a task depends on the amount of physiological arousal and the difficulty of the task. For many tasks, moderate arousal helps performance; for new or difficult tasks, low arousal is better; and for easy or well-learned tasks, high arousal may facilitate performance.*

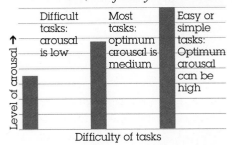

Difficult tasks: arousal is low

Most tasks: optimum arousal is medium

Easy or simple tasks: Optimum arousal can be high

Level of arousal ↑

Difficulty of tasks

The Yerkes-Dodson law predicts that high arousal would interfere with your performance on a difficult exam, while low to medium arousal would result in better performance. The fact that emotions lead to physiological arousal is the basis for the so-called lie detector test, which we'll discuss in the Applying/Exploring section.

Emotions Express Social Signals

The facial expressions that accompany emotions serve as social signals that *communicate* physiological needs and psychological moods. In fact, we often judge someone's psychological mood from his or her facial expression. In some cases, our facial expressions (looking worried or angry) are clearer and more true indicators of our psychological mood than our words ("There's nothing wrong!").

Researchers have found that many facial expressions, such as those of happiness, anger, sadness, fear, disgust, and surprise, are recognized as emotional expressions by people in widely varying cultures (Ekman & Friesen, 1975; Izard, 1977). For example, an open mouth, widened eyes, and raised eyebrows indicate surprise; a scowl indicates anger; and a smile indicates happiness.

Although the same emotional expressions are recognized with remarkable reliability around the world, different cultures encourage or discourage the expression of some emotions more than others. We'll examine cultural influences on emotional expressions after the Concept/Glossary section.

Each of these faces communicates a different social message.

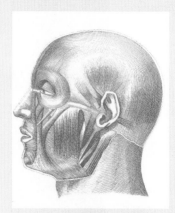

1. Feelings that include a mixture of three components—subjective experience, physiological arousal, and overt behavior—are called (a)_____. Those that are recognized in most cultures or that help the species survive by motivating behavior or signaling our physiological needs and psychological moods are referred to as (b)_____.

2. According to the _____ theory, emotions result from specific physiological changes in our bodies, and each emotion has a different physiological basis. One criticism of this theory is that researchers have not identified a different physiological response pattern to match each emotion.

3. A second theory says that feedback from the movement of facial muscles and skin are interpreted by your brain and result in an emotion. This is the (a)_____ theory. Researchers found that facial muscles and skin do not initiate emotions but rather contribute to their (b)_____.

4. A third theory says that interpreting or appraising a situation as having a positive or negative impact on our lives results in a subjective feeling that we call an emotion. This is the _____ theory. One criticism of this theory is that some emotions occur instantaneously, with very little time for appraisal.

"I feel happy."

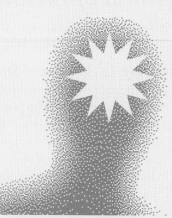

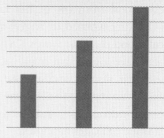

5. Can you experience an emotion without thinking, or must you engage in some kind of thinking or appraisal before you experience an emotion? This is the _____ question. Although debate on this question is not settled, it has sparked interest in the various ways that our emotional experiences may arise.

6. Some months after winning a lottery, winners rate themselves no happier than nonwinners. One explanation for this finding is Brickman's _____ theory. According to this theory, after some time we become accustomed or habituated to certain pleasures; as a result, we no longer appreciate those pleasures as much and they make us less happy.

7. One function of emotions is to help us (a)_____ to our present environments, such as recovering from an accident. A second function of emotions is to (b)_____ behavior, such as feeling happy and seeking out new friends. A third function of emotions is to signal our (c)_____ with our emotional expressions.

8. Your performance on a task depends on the amount of physiological arousal and the difficulty of the task. For many tasks moderate arousal helps performance, for new or difficult tasks, low arousal is better, and for easy or well-learned tasks high arousal may facilitate performance. This relationship between arousal and performance is known as the _____.

Answers: 1. (a) emotions, (b) basic emotions; 2. James-Lange; 3. (a) facial feedback, (b) intensity or mood; 4. cognitive appraisal; 5. primacy; 6. adaptation level; 7. (a) adapt, (b) motivate, (c) physiological need or psychological mood; 8. Yerkes-Dodson law.

Expression and Intensity of Emotions

Does a smile mean "happiness" around the world?

If you were to travel around the world, would you be able to correctly identify people's emotional states from their facial expressions? To answer this question, researchers asked individuals in ten cultures (including those in the United States, Brazil, Chile, Japan, and Argentina) to look at photos of various facial expressions, such as those expressing surprise, anger, happiness, disgust, and sadness, and identify the emotion. What is remarkable is that individuals in these very different cultures generally agreed with the pairings of expressions and emotions as shown here (Ekman et al., 1987).

Although it is true that many emotional expressions are shared and recognized across cultures, it is also true that cultures have unique gestures and differ in their

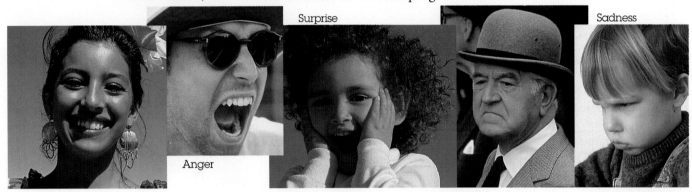

Surprise

Anger

Happiness

Disgust

Sadness

Peoples in different cultures recognized the same emotional expressions.

expression of emotional intensity. One explanation for this difference among cultures is the idea of **display rules,** *which are specific cultural rules that govern the expression and control of emotional expression in specific situations* (Ekman & Friesen, 1969). For example, in some European cultures, males may greet each other with a kiss to the cheek or lips. This male gesture of greeting is not observed in most Western cultures. Other examples are found in the dramatic differences between Americans and Japanese in expressing emotional intensity.

How intense are emotions?

Imagine being shown photos of emotional expressions and being asked to judge, on a scale of 1 to 10 (least to most), the intensity of the emotional expressions. This is what researchers did when they showed photos of five emotional expressions—surprise, anger, happiness, disgust, and sadness—to a group of Japanese and a group of Americans (Matsumoto & Ekman, 1989). Each group looked at two sets of photos: one depicted a

Americans rated happiness as the most intense of six emotions.

Japanese rated disgust as the most intense of six emotions.

Japanese showing five facial emotional expressions and the other depicted a Caucasian showing the same five expressions. The Japanese and Americans were asked to rate the intensity of each

emotional expression in each set. The Japanese gave significantly lower ratings of emotional intensity to all five emotional expressions compared to the higher ratings of the Americans. These results indicate that the display rules of Japan discourage the expression of intensity, while those of America encourage the showing of emotional intensity. In fact, these results match our stereotypes of Japanese displaying low emotional intensity in public while Americans exhibit more intensity.

Which emotion is most intense? Of the five emotions—surprise, anger, happiness, disgust, and sadness—which do you think the Japanese and Americans rated as the most intense? The Japanese rated disgust first, followed by happiness, anger, surprise, and sadness. In comparison, Americans identified happiness as the most intense of the five emotions, followed by anger, disgust, surprise, and sadness. This study illustrates how cultures may differently influence how people perceive the intensity of emotions.

As you may remember, an emotion has three components: overt behavior (smiling), cognitive process (thinking about being happy), and physiological arousal (increasing heart rate). We're going to return to the physiological component because it is the basis for what is often called the lie detector test.

APPLYING/ EXPLORING: THE LIE DETECTOR TEST

Can you tell the truth and fail the test? Floyd was surprised to see two police officers at his door. He was even more surprised when they showed him a warrant and arrested him for the armed robbery of a liquor store. The case against Floyd was weak, since none of the witnesses could positively identify Floyd as the robber. Soon after his arrest, the prosecutor offered to drop all charges if Floyd agreed to take, and passed, a lie detector exam. Floyd jumped at the chance to prove his innocence and took the test. He failed the lie detector exam but insisted that he had not lied and that he be allowed to take a second one, which he also failed. Eventually Floyd was tried, found guilty, and sent to prison. He served several years behind bars before his lawyer was able to track down the real robbers (*Los Angeles Times,* December 22, 1980).

The problems Floyd had with lie detector tests raise two questions. First, how does this test detect lies? Second, how reliable are lie detector tests?

Three Steps in the Lie Detector Test

1 **Recording physiological responses.**
The modern lie detector is a small machine, called a polygraph, that resembles a suitcase crammed with instruments. The **polygraph** *measures a person's heart rate, blood pressure, respiration, and galvanic skin response (better known as sweating).* When we experience an emotion, these physiological changes occur automatically and without any conscious effort. For example, if you are feeling some emotion, such as being nervous, upset, anxious, happy, or guilty after telling a lie, you will normally and automatically experience a variety of physiological changes. The basis for the lie detector test is the fact that physi-

ological arousal occurs automatically as a part of many emotions and that it is difficult to suppress or control these physiological changes.

2 **Asking neutral and critical questions.**
The examiner told Floyd that he would ask two kinds of questions—neutral and critical—and that Floyd should answer with only a yes or a no. As Floyd answered the neutral and critical questions, the polygraph machine simultaneously recorded his heart rate, blood pressure, respiration, and galvanic skin response.

An examiner is using a polygraph machine to record a client's physiological responses when answering questions.

If Floyd is like most people, answering a critical question with a lie would make him feel an emotion, such as guilt about lying or fear about being caught. Floyd's emotion is automatically accompanied by increases in heart rate, blood pressure, respiration, and galvanic skin response (sweating). The polygraph machine measures only physiological changes that accompany emotional experiences such as fear, guilt, nervousness, or worry. For this reason the "lie detector" test is misnamed: it essentially measures physiological arousal rather than lying, per se.

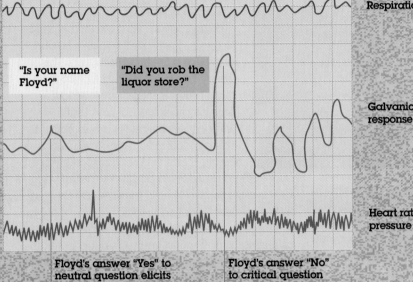

Neutral questions are designed not to elicit any emotional responses and are used to establish a baseline of normal physiological activity.

Critical questions are designed to elicit emotional responses if the person is lying.

"Is your name Floyd?"

"Did you rob the liquor store?"

Respiration

Galvanic skin response

Heart rate/blood pressure

Floyd's answer "Yes" to neutral question elicits relatively flat physiological responses.

Floyd's answer "No" to critical question elicits a big change in galvanic skin response.

Reliability of Lie Detector Tests

If Floyd was innocent, why did he fail two lie detector exams? Many emotions besides guilt from lying can cause increased physiological arousal. For example, the mention of a liquor store may have caused Floyd to feel nervous about a drinking problem or worry about his having stolen something from a store as a child. Remember that a lie detector test records only physiological arousal and does not detect lying itself.

There is much debate about how often polygraph examiners make correct decisions; estimates range from 65% to 95% of the time. This means that, depending on the ability of the examiner, from 5% to 35% of the time the examiner will fail to detect a lie or will accuse an innocent person of lying (Iacono & Patrick, 1986). In addition, examiners are more likely to identify truthful people as liars than the reverse. Because of this kind of error, one researcher suggests that innocent people should be careful about taking a lie detector test because of the risk of being erroneously labeled a liar (Shenour, 1990).

3 Interpreting physiological responses. The examiner decides whether the client is lying or telling the truth by comparing the differences between physiological responses to neutral and critical questions. In Floyd's case, he answered "No" to a number of critical questions, such as "Did you rob the liquor store?" but he showed a great increase in heart rate, blood pressure, respiration, and galvanic skin response. As a result of the difference between Floyd's answers and his increased physiological responses, the examiner decided that Floyd was lying and was, in fact, involved in the robbery. However, we know that, in truth, Floyd did not commit the robbery. This brings up the question of reliability, which is addressed in the above box.

Is lie detector evidence admissible in court? Because of their potential for error, evidence from lie detector tests is not permitted in most courts of law and cannot be a requirement for civilian employment. Sometimes the mere threat of a lie detector test will elicit a confession of a crime. Although lie detector tests have been used for over 60 years, there is still no agreement on their usefulness or reliability.

One curious and little-known fact about lie detector tests is that they are primarily used in the United States and are almost unknown in the rest of the civilized world (Shenour 1990).

Summary/Self-Test

BASIC EMOTIONS

1. Those emotions that help the species survive or that signal physiological and psychological needs are called basic emotions. Emotions can be divided into two broad classes, pleasant and unpleasant, which can be further divided into the six basic emotions of _____, _____, _____, _____, _____, and _____. Although researchers agree that basic emotions do exist, they do no always agree on the exact number of such emotions. The reason researchers study basic emotions is that these emotions are important to the physical and psychological well-being of the individual as well as to the survival of our species.

■ *Your airplane crash-lands in the jungles of South America and you are rescued by a native tribe. How will you communicate your needs and wishes?*

PERIPHERAL THEORIES

2. Several theories explain what causes emotions. Theories that emphasize changes in the body are called (a)_____ theories. One such theory states that emotions result from specific physiological changes in our bodies and that each emotion has a different physiological basis. The major criticism of this theory, called the (b)_____ theory, is that different emotions do not always cause different patterns of physiological arousal. According to another peripheral theory, sensations or feedback from the movement of facial muscles and skin are interpreted by your brain and result in an emotion. One criticism of this theory, called the (c)_____ theory, is that facial skin and muscles do not initiate emotions. The general conclusion is that periph-

eral theories—James-Lange and facial feedback—do not satisfactorily explain the initiation of emotions but do explain differences in the (d)_____ of emotions.

■ *Jennifer comes home from the dentist with one side of her face numb from anesthetic. She goes to a horror movie and finds it only half as frightening as her roommate does. What's going on?*

COGNITIVE APPRAISAL THEORY

3. According to Schachter and Singer's theory of emotions, a stimulus causes physiological arousal, which creates a need for an explanation. As a result, the person (a)_____ the situational cues and arrives at a feeling or emotion. This theory has been revised to recognize that emotions may occur without physiological arousal and that (b)_____ processes are important. These modifications have resulted in a theory that says that interpreting or appraising a situation as positive or negative results in a subjective feeling that we call an emotion; this theory is called the (c)_____ theory.

4. Researchers explain that some emotions, such as feeling happy when you see your partner, involve little thinking; however, other emotions, such as feeling jealous when seeing your partner with someone else, involve a complex thought process. The interesting question of whether you can experience an emotion without any thought or whether you must first engage in thought or appraisal is called the _____ question.

■ *Someone accidentally backs into Chris's car but just hits the bumper and doesn't do any damage. How would you explain why Chris became so angry?*

HAPPINESS

5. An emotion such as happiness has three components: feeling a change in heart rate is the (a)_____; smiling or laughing is the (b)_____; and thinking about what is happening is the (c)_____.

6. The intensity of an emotion, such as feeling happy because something wonderful occurred, may be strong on the first occasion but may decrease on future occasions. The idea that we grow accustomed to the emotional situation and

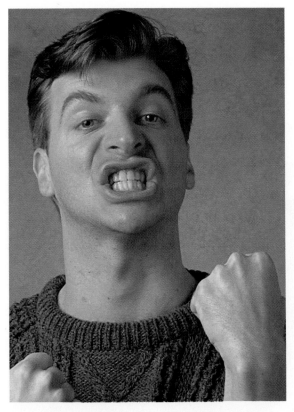

no longer feel the emotion so strongly is called the _____ theory.

■ *Kelly is really excited about having received a high grade on her paper. How long do you think her happiness will last?*

FUNCTIONS OF EMOTIONS

7. As a general rule, emotions are considered helpful to our survival, as individuals and as a species. The other functions of emotions include the ability to (a)_____ new behaviors and to (b)_____ our physiological needs and psychological moods.

8. Depending on the situation, the physiological arousal that accompanies an emotion can help or hinder performance; this relationship between arousal and performance is known as the _____ law. According to this law, moderate arousal helps performance on many tasks, but for new or difficult tasks, low arousal is better.

■ *The zookeeper is telling students that emotions serve many of the same functions in animals as they do in humans. Would you agree?*

CULTURAL DIVERSITY: EXPRESSION AND INTENSITY OF EMOTIONS

CULTURAL DIVERSITY: EXPRESSION AND INTENSITY OF EMOTIONS

9. Researchers have found that many (a)_____ expressions, such as surprise, anger, and happiness, are shared and recognized in a variety of cultures. Despite these similarities, there are also differences. One reason cultures may differ in their emotional gestures or emotional intensity is that they have different (b)_____ rules. An example is the finding that Americans rate emotions as being more intense than Japanese do.

■ *Do you think there is any truth to the stereotypes of Italians being emotional, Britishers showing a stiff upper lip, Germans being serious, and Americans doing what they feel?*

APPLYING/EXPLORING: THE LIE DETECTOR TEST

10. An instrument that measures a person's heart rate, blood pressure, respiration, and galvanic skin response is called a (a)_____. This instrument, which is commonly referred to as a lie detector, essentially measures a person's

(b)_____ arousal to an emotional situation, such as feeling guilt about telling a lie, feeling nervous or upset about a situation, or feeling embarrassed. To determine whether a person is telling the truth or a lie, the examiner compares the person's physiological arousal to neutral and critical questions. The error rate for interpretation of results from polygraph tests is high enough (5% to 35%) that evidence from these tests is not admitted in most courts of law.

■ *The professor announces that someone cheated on the last test. He intends to identify the cheater by asking everyone to take a lie detector test. Would you take the test?*

Answers: 1. love, joy, surprise, anger, sadness, fear; 2. (a) peripheral, (b) James-Lange, (c) facial feedback, (d) intensity; 3. (a) appraises or interprets, (b) cognitive, (c) cognitive appraisal; 4. primacy; 5. (a) physiological component, (b) overt behavior, (c) cognitive component; 6. adaptation level; 7. (a) motivate, (b) communicate; 8. Yerkes-Dodson; 9. (a) emotional, (b) display; 10. (a) polygraph, (b) physiological.

Chapter *Ten*
CHILD DEVELOPMENT

Oliviero Toscani for BENETTON

MODULE 19
INFANCY

What's smaller and cuter than a pound of butter? Madeline was delivered by emergency cesarean section, but since she had spent only 27 weeks instead of the normal 36 to 40 weeks in the womb, she weighed less than a pound of butter—a tiny 9.9 ounces. The doctor could hold her in the palm of one hand. Premature infants do not usually survive if they weigh less than a pound or are born before 24 weeks' gestation because they have no lung tissue. However, at 27 weeks Madeline was fully formed and is the smallest newborn ever to have survived.

Madeline spent her first months in intensive care, where all her bodily functions were carefully monitored. She also battled two bouts of pneumonia and had surgery for an eye problem. When she finally went home at the end of four months, she had to be given oxygen four times a day to aid her tiny lungs. The doctors told the parents that they would just have to wait and hope because no one knew whether Madeline would make it.

The parents did wait and hope, and Madeline grew into a spunky child who at 2 years of age weighed a relatively enormous 12 pounds, 10 ounces (normal for a 2-year-old ranges from 22 to 33 pounds). At 2 her mental development appeared normal and she had spoken her first words, including a loud "Out," when she wanted to leave her crib. Madeline's parents have been so pleased about her progress that each day seems like a miracle to them. (adapted from *People Special,* Fall 1991)

Madeline's survival, growth, and development are of interest to **developmental psychologists,** *who study biological, emotional, cognitive, and social development across the life span, from infancy through late adulthood.* For instance, developmental psychologists would be interested in Madeline's *biological changes,* which involve genetic, hormonal, and nutritional influences on the body, brain, and nervous system. They would also be interested in her *emotional changes,* which involve feelings and affective reactions to a variety of situations and stimuli. They would study her *cognitive changes,* which include processing, storing, and retrieving information. And they would be interested in her *social changes,* which include developing a unique personality and interacting with other people. Although we will discuss the biological, emotional, cognitive, and social changes separately, remember that they are closely interwoven so that one affects the others, that they often occur simultaneously, and that they result in a tremendous accomplishment, a human being.

What's Coming

In this module, we'll discuss fetal growth, capacities of the newborn, and motor and emotional development in infants. In the next module we'll examine cognitive and social changes during childhood. Let's begin with major issues and methods in developmental psychology.

Issues and Approaches

What could you paint at age 9?

For a few moments Yani Wang kneels quietly before a large piece of rice paper spread on the floor. Then she picks up a brush, dips it in ink, and begins painting. She paints one playful monkey, then another and another until they are scampering across 35 feet of paper. Yani, who lives in China, is a child art prodigy who began painting at age 3. So far, she has completed over 10,000 wondrous paintings. When she visited the United States at age 16, she seemed extremely shy, said that she doesn't like rock 'n' roll, and never paints sad pictures (adapted from *Los Angeles Times*, November 2, 1991).

Yani's amazing talent was recognized by the Smithsonian Institution in Washington, D.C., which made her the youngest person ever to have a solo painting exhibition. We can use Yani to illustrate two major issues that developmental psychologists study: nature versus nurture and continuity versus stages.

This is part of a 35-foot-long hand-scroll that Yani Wang painted when she was 9 years old.

Nature Versus Nurture

The nature-nurture issue is one of the oldest questions in developmental psychology. *Nature* refers to the influence of inherited or genetic factors on development; *nurture* refers to the influence of learning and experience. The **nature-nurture question** *asks how each factor influences and contributes to a person's biological, emotional, cognitive, and social development.*

How does the nature-nurture issue apply to Yani Wang?
As a child prodigy, Yani showed an incredible talent at a very early age: she began painting beautifully when she was only 3 years old. In the case of child prodigies, the influence of nature is clearly evident, since their extraordinary skill occurs with the barest minimum of learning and experience. However, even in the case of child prodigies, there is an interaction between nature and nurture. In Yani's case, her "natural" skills have improved under the guidance of her father, who is also an artist. The influences of nature and nurture *interact* and interweave and are often difficult to separate. For this reason, developmental psychologists do not ask, "Which is more important, nature or nurture?" but rather "How do nature and nurture interact in a person's development?"

In recent years, researchers have answered some of the nature-nurture questions with well-designed studies on identical and fraternal twins. Researchers have reported significant genetic influences on a variety of behaviors, including IQ scores, personality traits, and mental health (Bouchard et al., 1990; Plomin, 1990). We'll discuss more of these findings in Chapter 11.

Continuity Versus Stages

Continuity *refers to a person's physical, emotional, cognitive, and social development occurring in a gradual and progressive fashion across the life span.* **Stages** *refers to a person's development occurring in distinct steps or discrete stages across the life span.*

How does the continuity versus stage issue apply to Yani?
An example of continuous development would be Yani's learning to walk, which involved a slow, gradual process of learning to crawl, then to stand, balance on two feet, and finally walk. An example of development by stages would be the discrete stages Yoni went through as she learned to think in abstract terms. These stages, which were described by French psychologist Jean Piaget, are discussed later in this module.

As you will see, some developmental psychologists emphasize continuity and others emphasize stages; some emphasize nature and others emphasize nurture.

Next we'll examine the methods that psychologists use to study development across the life span.

Issues and Approaches

Methods for Studying Development

One problem faced by developmental psychologists is how to study changes that may occur over long periods of time, such as from infancy to adolescence or adulthood. To solve this problem, researchers use three different methods: cross-sectional, longitudinal, and case study methods. A fourth method, the cross-cultural approach, is illustrated in the cross-cultural sections throughout this text.

Yani painting at age 14.

Madeline smiling at age 2.

Case Study Method. In the **case study method** *a single individual's physical, emotional, cognitive, or social processes is studied in great depth across time.* Essentially, the case study method is using the longitudinal method to study a single individual (or each individual in a small group). Jean Piaget used the case study method when he traced the cognitive changes in his own children across time. One advantage of the case study method is that it allows us to study and analyze the thoughts, emotions, and behaviors of a single individual in greater depth than is otherwise possible. One disadvantage is that the data obtained from a single individual may be unique and not applicable to others.

What would the case study method tell us about Yani?

The fact that Yani was a child prodigy sets her apart from most other children and raises many questions about her development. With the case study method, we could study what effects her amazing talent at such an early age has on later emotional, cognitive, and social development.

What would the case study method tell us about Madeline?

The fact that Madeline was born very prematurely and spent many months in intensive care makes her early environment different from that of infants born after full term. With the case study method, psychologists could observe how Madeline's premature birth affected her later physical, personal, and social development.

Next we'll explain two other popular methods for studying development.

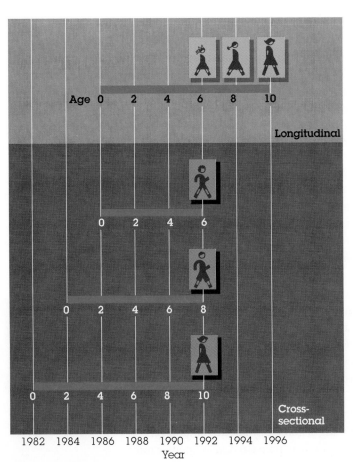

Age 0 2 4 6 8 10

Longitudinal

0 2 4 6

0 2 4 6 8

0 2 4 6 8 10

Cross-sectional

1982 1984 1986 1988 1990 1992 1994 1996
Year

In a longitudinal study, the same children are tested when they are 6, 8, and 10 years old. In a cross-sectional study, three different groups of 6-, 8-, and 10-year-old children are tested.

Cross-Sectional and Longitudinal Methods. In the **cross-sectional method**, *several groups of different-aged individuals are studied at the same time.* For example, suppose we were interested in the effects of age on memory. We could study this problem by testing different age groups (6-year-olds, 8-year-olds, 10-year-olds, and so on) all at the same time.

One advantage of the cross-sectional method is that it allows us to immediately compare any developmental differences, such as changes in memory, across many different age groups. One disadvantage of the cross-sectional approach is that it cannot tell us how the same individuals change or develop across time.

In the **longitudinal method**, *the same group of individuals is studied repeatedly at many different points in time.* For instance, you could study the effects of age on memory by selecting a group of 6-year-olds and then repeatedly testing this same group at ages 8, 10, and so on.

One advantage of the longitudinal method is that it allows us to focus on the same subjects as they grow older and chart developmental patterns or determine how specific characteristics affect later development. Disadvantages of the longitudinal method are that researchers must wait many years for their subjects to grow older, and subjects may drop out of the study for various reasons (relocation, illness, death). Despite the difficulties with the longitudinal method, many researchers prefer it over the cross-sectional method because it allows them to trace continuity or stability in the same subjects across time.

How could we study the effects of premature birth on Madeline's memory development? To study the effects of premature birth on Madeline's memory development, we could use either the cross-sectional or the longitudinal method. With the cross-sectional method, we would select different-aged groups of individuals who had been born prematurely and who were normal term. Then we would give memory tests to all the groups at the same time and compare those who had been premature infants with those who were normal term. If we used the longitudinal method, we would select a group of premature infants and a group of normal-term infants and repeatedly test each group at different points across time. With the longitudinal method, we would be able to trace the development of Madeline's memory and compare her with individuals who were delivered after a normal term—but we would need many years for our research.

Now that you are familiar with some of the issues and methods of developmental psychology, we'll return to the very beginning of Madeline's story, to her life in the womb.

Prenatal Development

Madeline's remarkable story is loaded with interesting questions: Why was her body perfectly formed? How was she able to survive outside the womb? At what point in prenatal development does a fetus take on human characteristics? The **prenatal period** *extends from conception to birth, a period of about nine months.* It is divided into three phases: the germinal, embryonic, and fetal periods. In examining the prenatal period, we'll unravel one of the great puzzles of science—the beginning of a human being.

Germinal Period

The first step toward conception is for a sexually mature female to experience **ovulation,** *which is the release of an ovum or egg cell from her ovaries.* In most cases, only a single ovum is released during ovulation, but sometimes two ova are released. **Fraternal twins,** *which result from the release and fertilization of two ova, are no more genetically alike than any other two children of the same parents.* On the other hand, **identical twins,** *which result from a single ovum that splits into two parts after fertilization, are genetically exactly alike.*

Before we continue to follow the ovum, let's take a moment to explore this idea of genetic similarity that we see in twins. Assuming that you are not an identical twin, one reason that you have developed into a unique human being is due to chromosomes and genes. **Chromosomes** *are strands of chemicals found in all human cells; there are 23 such strands inside each ovum and sperm.* The chemical strand that makes up each chromosome is further divided into microscopic pieces called genes. **Genes,** *which are composed of deoxyribonucleic acid (DNA), form a chemical code that contains the equivalent of approximately 1 million pages of typed instructions.* The remarkable development of a single cell into a human being is guided by about 100,000 genes.

Early in prenatal development, a number of genetic errors can be identified if they are present. **Amniocentesis** (AM-nee-oh-sen-TEE-sis), *which is done between weeks 14 and 20 of pregnancy, involves inserting a long needle through the mother's abdominal muscles into the amniotic fluid surrounding the fetus.* By analyzing the fetal cells thus withdrawn, doctors can identify a number of genetic problems. One example is **Down syndrome,** *which results from an extra 21st chromosome and causes abnormal physical traits (a fold of skin at the corner of each eye, a wide tongue, heart defects) and abnormal brain development, resulting in degrees of mental retardation.* In addition to Down syndrome, more than 100 other inherited genetic disorders can now be identified.

Now let's return to the path of the ovum. After being released, it begins a long journey down the woman's fallopian tube to her uterus. What happens next depends on whether or not sperm are present.

A single sperm has penetrated an ovum's membrane.

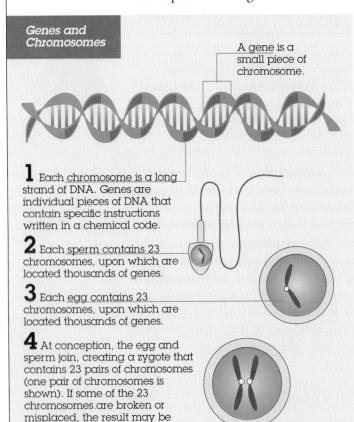

Genes and Chromosomes

A gene is a small piece of chromosome.

1 Each chromosome is a long strand of DNA. Genes are individual pieces of DNA that contain specific instructions written in a chemical code.

2 Each sperm contains 23 chromosomes, upon which are located thousands of genes.

3 Each egg contains 23 chromosomes, upon which are located thousands of genes.

4 At conception, the egg and sperm join, creating a zygote that contains 23 pairs of chromosomes (one pair of chromosomes is shown). If some of the 23 chromosomes are broken or misplaced, the result may be genetic errors and problems.

How does conception take place?

If no sperm are present, there can be no fertilization and the ovum, together with the lining of the uterus, is sloughed off in the process called *menstruation*. If, however, sperm have been deposited in the vagina, they make their way to the uterus and into the fallopian tubes in search of an ovum. **Conception (or fertilization)** *occurs if one of the sperm penetrates the ovum's outside membrane.* After the ovum has been penetrated by a single sperm, its outside membrane changes and becomes impenetrable to the millions of remaining sperm (100 to 500 million sperm may be deposited with each act of intercourse).

The fertilized egg is a single cell called a **zygote.** We each began as a zygote, which is smaller than the dot in the letter *i*. After about a week, a zygote has divided over and over into about 150 cells. After two weeks, it has become a mass of cells and attaches itself to the wall of the uterus.

The two-week period following conception is called the **germinal period.** After the germinal period comes the embryonic period, during which the zygote changes into a multicelled organism with humanlike characteristics.

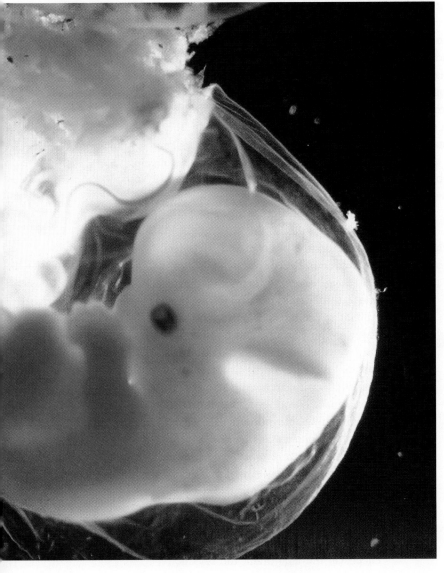

This 6-week-old embryo is about a half-inch long and floats in fluids that act like a cushion.

Embryonic Period

How long before the organism develops body organs?

The **embryonic period** *spans the 2 to 8 weeks that follow conception; during this period, cells divide and begin to differentiate into bone, muscle, and body organs.* At about 21 days after conception, the beginnings of the spinal cord and eyes appear; at about 24 days, cells differentiate to what will become part of the heart; at about 28 days, tiny buds appear that will develop into arms and legs; and at about 42 days, features of the face take shape.

Toward the end of the embryonic period, the organism has developed a number of body organs, such as the heart. The embryo is only about an inch long but already has the beginnings of major body organs and limbs and begins to look very human indeed. After this phase of development, the embryo enters the fetal period.

Prenatal Development

Fetal Period

The embryonic period is followed by the **fetal period**, *which is a time of development that begins two months after conception and lasts for about seven months.* At the end of the fetal period, usually 38 to 42 weeks after conception (or roughly nine months), birth occurs and the fetus becomes a newborn.

What happens during the fetal period?
It is during this period that the fetus develops vital organs, such as lungs, and physical characteristics that are distinctively human. For example, at about six months a fetus has eyes and eyelids that are completely formed, a fine coating of hair, relatively well-developed external sex organs, and lungs that are beginning to function. As you may remember, Madeline was delivered prematurely at about six months. Although she was extremely tiny (9.9 ounces), she was able to survive because her lungs were already formed. A six-month-gestation fetus begins to show irregular breathing and, for this reason, can survive if born prematurely.

What effect do drugs have in the fetal period?
Because the fetus experiences rapid body growth and development of the nervous system, it is highly vulnerable to the effects of drugs and other harmful agents. The blood supply of the mother and the blood supply of the fetus are connected by an organ called the *placenta*. The placenta acts like a filter, allowing oxygen and nutrients to pass through while keeping out some toxic or harmful substances. Certain viruses and many drugs, including nicotine, caffeine, marijuana, cocaine, and heroin, do, however, pass from the placenta into the fetus's blood vessels.

A number of chemicals are **teratogens** (from the Greek word *tera,* for "monster"), *or damaging agents that cause birth defects;* these agents are studied by those in the field of teratology. We'll discuss a number of teratogens, including some of the more commonly used legal and illegal drugs, as well as other factors that affect fetal growth and development.

Alcohol. Alcohol is one of the drugs that can cross the placenta and affect fetal development. Recent research has shown that *social drinking* (defined as having one to three drinks per day) during pregnancy can produce newborns who show lower levels of arousal and body control than those whose mothers did not drink; many of these newborns also have learning problems later on (Streissguth, Sampson, & Barr, 1989). Even more serious is **fetal alcohol syndrome (FAS)**, *which is caused by heavy maternal drinking during pregnancy and results in a combination of physical and psychological defects.* FAS is the leading cause of mental retardation in the United States and causes retarded physical growth and interference with brain development. Because of alcohol's effects on the fetal brain, the FAS newborn shows a variety of motor and learn-

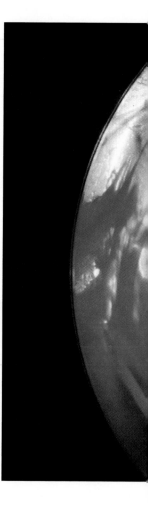

This chart shows the periods during which body organs are most vulnerable to damage by toxic agents.

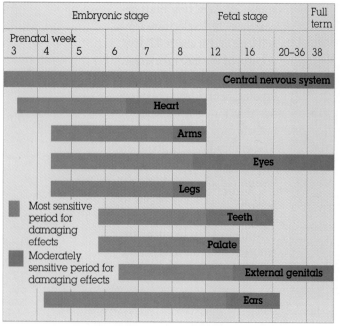

	Embryonic stage					Fetal stage			Full term
Prenatal week									
3	4	5	6	7	8	12	16	20–36	38

Central nervous system
Heart
Arms
Eyes
Legs
Teeth
Palate
External genitals
Ears

■ Most sensitive period for damaging effects

■ Moderately sensitive period for damaging effects

This 22-week-old fetus is a girl. She is about 10 inches long, looks much like a newborn, but lacks some vital organs, such as lungs.

ing problems, such as difficulty in sucking and weak reflexes (Driscoll, Streissguth, & Riley, 1990). In addition, the effects of FAS continue into adolescence and adulthood, as indicated by low IQ scores and a tendency to be easily distracted and to misperceive social cues (Streissguth et al., 1991).

Because of the serious and preventable effects of drinking alcohol during pregnancy, many state and local governments have required that signs be posted in bars and on alcohol containers to warn women about the dangers of drinking during pregnancy.

Tobacco. Smoke from cigarettes affects fetal development by decreasing blood flow through the umbilical cord to the fetus and by increasing carbon dioxide in the blood. As a result, women who smoke heavily during pregnancy have a higher rate of stillbirths and premature births and have babies who weigh significantly less at birth (Barr et al., 1990; Rush & Callahan, 1989). These data warn women against smoking during pregnancy.

Cocaine and Heroin. Infants exposed to cocaine prenatally have been found to have a number of problems that increase with the dose used by the mother. These problems include premature birth, lower birth weight, and smaller head circumference; in addition, these infants have to go through drug withdrawal after birth (Neuspiel & Hamel, 1991). Cocaine has also caused fetal strokes, blindness, and partial paralysis.

The use of heroin during pregnancy can cause similar problems. Prenatal exposure to heroin results in higher rates of premature birth, lower birth weight, and having to go through drug withdrawal after birth (Fulroth, Phillips, & Durand, 1989).

Cocaine or heroin should not be used during pregnancy. In addition, pregnant women are warned against the use of marijuana, which may affect fetal development.

Birth and Delivery

About 38 to 42 weeks after conception, birth occurs. A woman's labor averages 14 hours for the birth of her first child and about 8 hours for her second child. To reduce the anxiety, pain, and use of drugs during delivery, a number of childbirth education programs have been developed. The goal of these programs is to involve the mother in the birth process instead of treating her like a passive patient. One of the better-known programs, the Lamaze method, requires the mother to take a series of classes to prepare for childbirth. In these classes, the mother is taught how to control her breathing (often with her partner's assistance) as one way to divert her attention from the pain of labor and how to use her muscles to aid in the delivery process. First-time mothers who had participated in any of several different childbirth education programs reported being more satisfied with the delivery process when fewer medical/obstetrical interventions were used (Kyman, 1991).

From the time of birth until approximately 1 month of age, a child is considered a **newborn,** or **neonate.** Let's examine the newborn's abilities.

WARNING: ALCOHOL MAY BE HAZARDOUS TO YOUR HEALTH AND TO THE HEALTH OF YOUR UNBORN CHILD

Generally, drugs of all kinds should be avoided during pregnancy.

The Newborn

What can an infant do in the first weeks of life?
One moment a fetus is in the warm, quiet, fluid-cushioned world of the womb; the next moment, it is in the cold, noisy, bright world of the delivery room. The newborn shown on this page has already lost the reddish, wrinkled appearance he had on delivery. His major body organs (heart, lungs, kidneys) have begun to function as he struggles to survive on his own. During the coming months, he will show rapid development of perceptual and motor responses.

Let's first examine the newborn's sensory and perceptual responses. Newborns can't tell us in words what they perceive of the world, so we must determine what they can see, hear, smell, taste, and feel by observations and various conditioning procedures (see Module 6).

Vision

Visual acuity *is the ability to see fine details.* A newborn's visual acuity is about 20/600 versus a normal human 20/20. This means that a newborn can see at 20 feet what an adult (with perfect vision) can see at 600 feet. An acuity of 20/600 is below that required to read the big E on the eye chart. By age 6 months, this acuity improves to 20/100, and by 3–4 years of age, acuity has reached that of an adult.

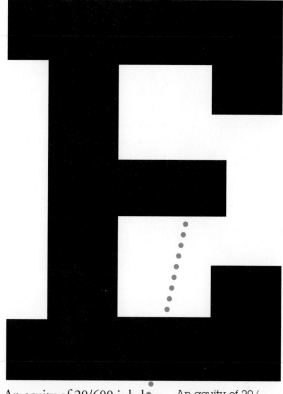

An acuity of 20/600 is below that required to read the big E on the eye chart.

 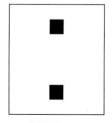

Preferred pattern

Preferred face

Patterns. If 1-month-old infants are shown two patterns, they will consistently look longer at the more complex pattern. These longer looking times are interpreted to mean that the infant can discriminate between patterns.

Faces. The evidence is controversial as to whether newborns can tell their mothers' face from that of strangers (Bushnell & Mullin, 1989). But by about 5 weeks of age, infants can distinguish their parent's face. As for patterns, they also prefer looking at the regular face over the scrambled face shown here (Field et al., 1984).

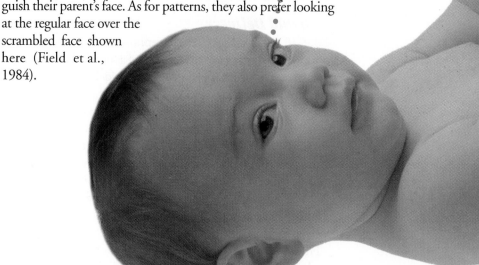

Depth Perception. Researchers have not yet devised a way to determine whether newborns have depth perception. But in a well-known study, Eleanor Gibson and Richard Walk (1960) studied whether infants have depth perception by observing whether they would crawl off a visual "cliff." The **visual cliff** *is a glass tabletop with a checkerboard patterned surface on one side; on the other side is clear glass with a checkerboard pattern several feet below, creating the illusion of a clifflike drop to the floor.* As you see here, an infant is placed on the checkerboard pattern side and is encouraged to creep off the "cliff." Six-month-old infants hesitate when they reach the clear glass "dropoff," indicating that they have developed depth perception.

This infant is being tested on the visual cliff.

Other Senses

As you have just seen, infants have relatively good vision. Similarly, an infant's other senses, especially hearing, are also well developed. Let's examine the other senses of the newborn.

Hearing. The ability to hear a wide range of sounds is well developed in newborns. One-month-old infants have very keen hearing and can discriminate small sound variations, such as the difference between *bah* and *pah*. By 6 months, infants have developed the ability to make all the sounds that are necessary to learn the language in which they are raised.

Touch. Newborns also have a well-developed sense of touch and will turn their head when lightly touched on the cheek. Touch will also elicit a number of reflexes, such as grasping and sucking.

Smell. Do newborns have a good sense of smell? Researchers used a classical conditioning procedure to determine whether 1-day-old infants could discriminate between a citrus and a floral odor. The citrus odor was paired with stroking, which produced head turning. Later, the citrus odor alone—and not the floral odor—produced head turning. Researchers concluded that newborns are capable of classical conditioning as well as of discriminating between odors (Sullivan et al., 1991). The data fit well with earlier reports that 6-week-old infants can smell the difference between their mother and a stranger (Macfarlane, 1975).

Taste. Newborns have an inborn preference for both sweet and salt. To see how researchers determined this, look back to Module 6.

The perceptual abilities of newborns are relatively good and develop very quickly. Within a short period, infants develop a wide range of sensory and perceptual abilities that form the basis for acquiring the emotional, cognitive, and social processes that we will discuss in the rest of this chapter.

The Newborn

Risks to the Newborn

After birth, an infant faces a number of potential environmental risks. We're going to focus on the two relatively serious risks of malnutrition and lead poisoning.

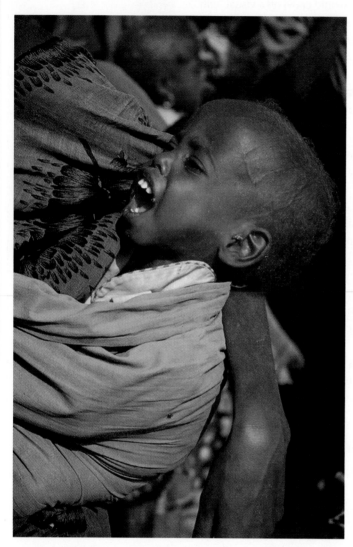

In many parts of the world, children suffer from malnutrition.

Malnutrition. According to surveys, 40%–60% of children around the world (including in the United States) suffer from mild to moderate undernutrition, and 3%–7% are severely malnourished (Galler, 1984). Although a newborn's brain has most of its neurons, it lacks many of the connections between neurons and many of the supporting cells that contribute to neural functioning. For the brain to develop properly, the infant's diet must contain an adequate supply of protein. If an infant's diet is low in protein over a long period of time, physical growth and brain development will be retarded and the infant may suffer from behavioral and cognitive deficits. If, however, malnutrition and protein deficiency are detected early, intervention programs providing good nutrition, health care, and education can reverse some of the problems caused by malnutrition (Lozoff, 1989).

Lead Poisoning. The development of the infant's brain can also be harmed by exposure to toxic substances. For example, there is evidence that children who live in lower socioeconomic environments have much higher than normal levels of lead in their blood. In these environments, lead comes primarily from breathing air with a high concentration of auto exhaust fumes and from eating chips of old paint that has peeled off walls. Researchers report that low to high levels of lead can result in retarded brain development and in behavioral and cognitive deficits (Needleman & Gatsonis, 1990; Thomson et al., 1989). These data were the major reason that the Environmental Protection Agency banned lead in paint and gasoline.

Now let's examine an infant's remarkable physical growth that makes grandparents say, "My, how you've grown!"

Animal Model for Malnutrition. One group of rats, labeled Control, was fed a regular diet and showed a normal growth curve. Another group of rats, labeled Experimental, were fed a reduced amount of food from birth to day 30. After day 30, however, the experimental group was given a normal amount of food. As shown here, rats in the experimental group failed to reach normal body weight even after getting normal amounts of food. This animal model shows that early malnutrition can reduce future body weight (Adapted from Bedi et al., 1980)

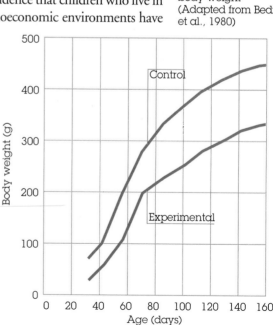

Motor Development

Why does the head grow faster than the feet?

Motor development *is the acquisition of the muscular control necessary for coordinated physical activity.* It follows two general principles. The first is the **cephalocaudal principle,** *which means that parts of the body closer to the head* (cephalo *in Greek means "head"*) develop before the parts closer to the feet (caudal *in Greek means "tail"*). For example, as infants learn to crawl, they first do so by using their more developed arms and only later their feet. The second factor governing motor development is the **proximodistal principle,** *which means that parts closer to the center of the infant's body* (proximo *in Latin means "near"*) develop before parts farther away (distal *in Latin means*

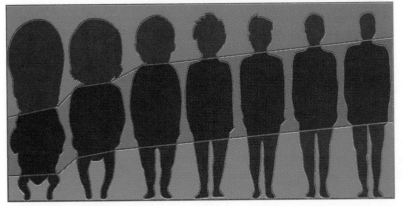

2 months   5 months   New-   2 years   6 years   12 years   25 years
(fetus)   (fetus)   born

Earlier development of body parts near the head before parts near the feet illustrates the cephalocaudal principle.

"far"). For example, in reaching for objects, infants first use their more developed arms and then their fingers, whose control develops later.

Much of the sequence in developing early motor skills is governed by a process known as maturation. **Maturation** *is development that occurs in a sequential and orderly fashion because of a genetic plan.* A child's first step is a good example of maturation, since it has been preceded by the development and control of many sets of muscular activities. The sequence of motor development and control that results in walking is, to a major extent, controlled by maturation.

In most cases, development occurs because of an interaction between the effects of maturation (nature) and those of experience/learning (nurture). For example, if a child were confined to a crib and deprived of motor learning experiences, his or her first step would most probably occur later than normal. In the early stages of motor development, maturation seems to be the major force guiding development. In later stages of motor development—as, for instance, in learning to ski, play baseball, or dance—learning/experience seems to be the major force.

Sitting up alone—average 5.5 months (range 4.5–8.0 months)

Crawling—average 10 months (range 7.0–12.0 months)

Norms for Development

At what age should an infant begin to walk?

In observing their fast-growing infants, parents often note the key points in motor development, such as when infants first sit up, crawl, or walk. **Norms for development** *refer to the average age at which individuals perform various kinds of skills or exhibit abilities or behaviors.* Some examples of norms for development for stages in walking are shown here. Because norms for development represent *average ages* rather than *absolute ages,* parents should not be disturbed if their infant's motor progress does not match the norms.

After the Concept/Glossary, we'll discuss emotional development.

Walking holding on—average 9.2 months (range 7.3–13.0 months)

Walking alone—average 12.1 months (range 11.5–14.5 months)

Emotional Development

Why do babies cry?

Emotions help individuals survive by signaling physiological needs and psychological moods and by motivating behaviors. (For more information, you may want to look back to Module 18.) For instance, the loud piercing cry of a newborn is a powerful communication that often signals discomfort or distress and that certainly gets the attention of parents or caretakers.

As a newborn, this little girl had a limited range of emotional expressions. At 9 months, however, she can show many emotions, including anger, surprise, sadness, fear, and social smiling.

To study the range of emotions in very young infants, Carroll Izard and his colleagues (1987) videotaped the expressions of infants as they were exposed to emotion-producing stimuli, such as seeing a stranger approach, hearing a balloon pop, tasting lemon juice, and receiving a regularly scheduled shot. The researchers found that newborns had a limited repertoire of emotional expressions, which included only *interest, startle, distress, disgust,* and *neonatal smile* (a sort of half-smile that appears spontaneously for no apparent reason). We have no way of knowing what, if any, inner feelings accompany a newborn's emotional expressions. Over the next two years, infants develop a wide range of emotional expressions and feelings, including *social smiling* (age 4–6 weeks); *anger, surprise,* and *sadness* (age 3–4 months); *fear* (age 5–7 months); *shame* and *shyness* (age 6–8 months); and *contempt* and *guilt* (age 24 months).

Based on a lifetime of studying emotions, Carroll Izard (1987) has hypothesized that *emotional development* in infants is a two-step process. The first step involves the biological capacity of infants to produce, imitate, and discriminate among emotional expressions. The second step involves *feedback* from the parents' (or caregivers') emotions or moods that influences and alters the infants' behaviors and emotional expressions. For example, if an infant who is exploring looks up and sees her father smiling, the infant may continue to explore. On the other hand, if the exploring infant sees her father frowning, she may stop exploring and return to her father's side. According to Izard, emotional development is an interaction between infants' biological capacity to express emotions (nature), and their responsiveness to their environments (nurture). We'll discuss two interesting studies that relate to the nature-nurture interaction in emotional development.

Temperament

Why are some babies so smiley?

Some infants fuss very little, play contentedly, and seldom cry. Others fret much of the time, react badly to new situations, and frequently cry. A general emotional difference among infants is called temperament. **Temperament** *refers to a characteristic mood, level of energy, and reaction to new objects, situations, or people.* You can think of an infant's temperament as an emotional beginning point from which a wide range of specific emotional feelings, expressions, and reactions will develop. If you have observed a baby brother or sister or are a parent with babies of your own, you already know that even very young infants differ greatly in temperament.

Three researchers, Stella Chess, Alexandar Thomas, and Herbert Birch, carried out a longitudinal study on infant temperament. They interviewed mothers with 2- to 3-month-old infants, then observed them repeatedly over the next seven years. The researchers rated each infant on nine components of temperament, including activity level, attention span, fussiness, and mood. Based on these ratings, they were able to divide the infants into four categories.

1. *Easy babies,* who made up 40% of the sample, were happy and cheerful, had regular sleeping and eating habits, and adapted quickly to new situations.

2. *Slow-to-warm-up babies,* who made up 15% of the sample, were more withdrawn, were moody, and tended to take longer to adapt to new situations.

3. *Difficult babies,* who made up 10% of the sample, were fussy, fearful of new situations, and more intense in their reactions. During the course of the seven-year study, difficult babies developed more serious emotional problems than the easy or slow-to-warm-up babies.

4. *No-single-category babies,* who made up 35% of the sample, had a variety of traits and could not be classified into one of the other three categories.

The researchers found that the vast majority of infants developed distinct temperaments in the first 2 to 3 months of life. Because of this finding, they emphasized the effects of nature, as nurture had very little chance to operate (Thomas & Chess, 1977).

We'll discuss a recent study that more clearly shows the large influence of nature, or inherited tendencies, on temperament.

Emotional Development

Temperamental Factors in Human Development

Psychologists Jerome Kagan and Nancy Snidman (1991) were interested in two questions: How strong is nature's influence on temperament? How stable is temperament across time? To answer these questions, they completed a remarkable longitudinal study in which they observed fear reactions in 94 infants at 2, 4, 9, 14, and 21 months of age. They defined fear by the amount of motor activity, fretting, or crying that the infants showed when presented with novel objects and sounds. Based on the amount of fear expressed, each infant was classified into one of four groups that ranged from low to high fear.

Results. The first question Kagan and Snidman asked was whether very young infants already have a distinctive temperament—in this case, a clearly observable fear response. They found that 23% could be classified as high-fear responders and 37% as low-fear responders. (The remaining infants were classified in between.) Thus, a relatively large percentage of the 4-month-old infants already had a well-developed fear response (either high or low). The second question was whether this particular temperament was stable from 4 to 20 months of age. Although the high-fear temperament tended to persist, some of the infants did change from high to low fear between 4 and 21 months, and 2 of 31 changed from low to high fear. Generally, infants who showed high fear at 4 months continued to show high fear at 9, 14, and 21 months. Similarly, infants who showed low fear at 4 months continued this pattern throughout testing.

Very young infants were found to have distinctive temperaments.

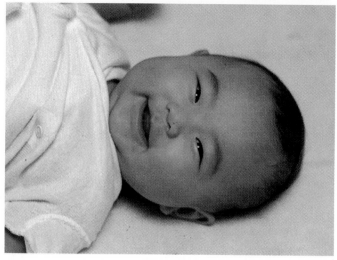

Conclusions. Kagan and Snidman concluded that there are at least two distinct temperaments, which they call inhibited (shy) and uninhibited (outgoing). These two temperaments are relatively stable across time, probably involve the excitability of various brain areas, and are partially under genetic control, or influence of nature. The researchers caution that although genetically influenced temperaments may have a potent influence on behavior, temperament is not necessarily fixed and unchangeable. Some of the infants (5 out of 20) did change from high to low fear groups, indicating that early temperament may be influenced by nurture (learning/experience).

Now we'll turn to another aspect of emotional behavior, the attachment of an infant to his or her parent or caregiver.

1. Studying development across the life span by observing separate groups of different-aged individuals is an example of the (a)_____ method. Studying development across the life span by observing the same group of individuals repeatedly at many different points in time is an example of the (b)_____ method. Studying an individual's physical, emotional, cognitive, or social processes in great depth across the life span is an example of the (c)_____ method.

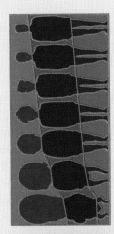

2. Conception occurs when a single sperm penetrates the ovum's outer membrane. The newly fertilized cell is called a (a)_____. The period of two weeks that follows conception and is marked by the zygote dividing into many cells is called the (b)_____ stage. The next period of development, which lasts from the second through the eighth week after conception, is called the (c)_____ period: during this period cells divide and begin to differentiate into bone, muscle, and body organs.

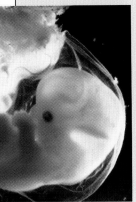

3. Inside each ovum and sperm are 23 strands called (a)_____, which are composed of deoxyribonucleic acid (DNA). Each long strand is divided into individual pieces of DNA that contain chemical instructions and are called (b)_____, whose total number in humans is about 100,000.

4. The developmental period that begins two months after conception and lasts for about seven months is called the (a)_____ period. During this period, various drugs can retard development. Agents that can cause birth defects are called (b)_____. If a pregnant woman drinks heavily, the result is a combination of physical and psychological defects called the (c)_____. One drug that increases the rate of stillbirths, premature births, and lower birth weight is (d)_____. Two drugs that cause premature birth, lower birth weight, and the necessity of going through drug withdrawal after birth are (e)_____ and _____.

5. The fact that newborns have some visual acuity and good senses of touch, hearing, smell, and taste indicates that they have relatively well-developed (a)_____. Newborns face a number of risks, including a lack of protein, which is an example of (b)_____, and the buildup of toxic substances, such as (c)_____, in the bloodstream.

6. The acquisition of muscular control necessary for coordinated physical activity, which is called (a)_____ development, follows two general principles. The principle that parts of the body closer to the head develop before the parts closer to the feet is the (b)_____ principle. The principle that parts closer to the center of the infant's body develop before parts farther away is called the (c)_____ principle.

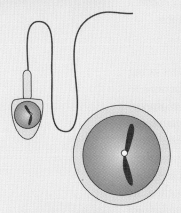

7. Development that occurs in a sequential and orderly fashion because of a genetic plan is called (a)_____. This is demonstrated in a child's first step, since it has been preceded by the development and control of many sets of muscular activities. The average ages at which individuals perform various kinds of skills or exhibit abilities or behaviors are called (b)_____ for development.

8. A characteristic mood, level of energy, and reaction to new objects, situations, or people is a person's _____.

Answers: 1. (a) *cross-sectional,* (b) *longitudinal,* (c) *case study.* 2. (a) *zygote,* (b) *germinal,* (c) *embryonic;* 3. (a) *chromosomes,* (b) *genes;* 4. (a) *fetal,* (b) *teratogens,* (c) *fetal alcohol syndrome,* (d) *tobacco or nicotine,* (e) *cocaine, heroin.* 5. (a) *senses,* (b) *malnutrition,* (c) *lead;* 6. (a) *motor,* (b) *cephalocaudal,* (c) *proximodistal;* 7. (a) *maturation,* (b) *norms;* 8. *temperament.*

Attachment

How do an infant and parent form a bond?

If you've ever watched the interactions between a caring parent and a young infant, you know that the parent spends a great deal of time touching, kissing, holding, changing, feeding, caressing, and responding to the infant's needs. This early parent-infant interaction is thought to be the basis for **attachment,** *which is a close emotional bond between the infant and his or her parent or caregiver.* (We'll use the terms *parent* and *caregiver* interchangeably.)

The original work and much of attachment theory has come from Mary Ainsworth (1989). She believes that attachment behavior evolved through a process of natural selection because it gives the infant a better chance of surviving. For instance, attachment keeps the caregiver close to the infant, which means that the infant is better cared for and protected. Let's look at some questions about attachment.

When does attachment occur and how does it develop?

Ainsworth believes that attachment is a gradual process that begins in the newborn and continues through infancy. At about 1 month, an infant will begin to direct her smile toward another person; this behavior is called *social smiling.* In addition to crying, social smiling is another powerful signal that facilitates forming an attachment with the parent (Lamb, 1984). At about 6 months, an infant begins to give her parents a happy greeting (smiling, holding out arms) when they reappear after a short absence. These behaviors all contribute to attachment.

As the infant develops a closer attachment to her parents, she also shows more distress when her parents leave. **Separation anxiety** *is an infant's distress, as indicated by loud protests, crying, and agitation, whenever the infant's parents temporarily leave.* According to Ainsworth, separation anxiety is a clear sign that the infant has become attached to one or both parents. By the end of the first year, an infant usually shows a close attachment to her parents as well as to one or more other family members.

How does a parent bond with an infant?

Are there different kinds of attachment?

Ainsworth (1979) developed a method for studying infants' reactions to being separated from and then reunited with their mothers. She then used these reactions to indicate the kind or quality of the infants' attachment. **Secure attachment** *is characteristic of infants who use their caregiver as a safe home base from which they can wander off and explore their environments.* When placed in an unfamiliar room containing many interesting toys, securely attached infants tend to explore freely as long as their caregiver looks on. If the caregiver leaves, most of the infants cry. On the caregiver's return, securely attached infants happily greet the caregiver and are easily soothed. In contrast, **insecure attachment** *is characteristic of infants who avoid or show ambivalence toward their caregivers.* For example, insecurely attached infants may cling and want to be held one minute and squirm and push away the next minute. The more sensitive the caregiver is to the infant's needs, the more secure seems to be the infant-caregiver attachment.

What are the long-term effects of early attachment?

The kind of attachment—secure or insecure—may affect a child's later behaviors. For example, the more secure the infant's attachment, the better he or she copes with the stress of attending kindergarten (Sroufe, Fox, & Pancake, 1983). In addition, a more secure attachment in infancy may increase the chances of forming better emotional bonds in later relationships (Ainsworth, 1989).

Parenting and Emotions

According to Theodore Dix (1991), parenting is essentially an emotional experience because it involves more affection, joy, anger, and worry than most other endeavors. Because of the importance of emotions in raising children, Dix believes that emotion is at the heart of both effective and ineffective parenting. Based on his review of the literature, Dix draws four conclusions about the importance of emotion in parenting.

Good parenting is characterized by warm emotions.

1 *Strong emotions* are common in raising children, being aroused an average 3 to 15 times an hour. Parents report high levels of anger with their children and need to find ways to deal with this anger. Parents also report about two and a half times more positive than negative interactions with their children. Thus, parenting is closely intertwined with both positive and negative emotions.

2 The *kinds of emotions* that parents display greatly affect the child's later adjustment, happiness, and success. For example, parents who give poor emotional support or generate a hostile environment generally raise children who are distressed and have adjustment problems. In contrast, parents who provide good emotional support and warmth generally raise children who are better adjusted and happier. Thus, good parenting is closely associated with a warm emotional environment.

3 The parents' *occupations, marital relations, and other stressors* greatly influence the emotions that they show their children. For instance, parents with high levels of stress experience more negative emotions that are often translated into harsh and inconsistent discipline of their children. Good parenting involves dealing with one's own problems and keeping these problems from causing negative interactions with children.

4 *Long-term and intense negative emotions* in parents are a sign of family dysfunction and a distressed family environment. For instance, the display of negative emotions is prominent in the history of parents who abuse their children and of mothers who have aggressive boys. Bad parenting is characterized by a predominance of negative emotions, whereas good parenting is characterized by a predominance of positive emotions.

According to Dix, the one single factor that reflects the health of the parent-child relationship is its emotional quality. Emotional quality also predicts children's poor or good mental and social adjustments.

Next we'll discuss an important issue for thousands of working parents and for society at large: day care for children.

APPLYING/ EXPLORING: QUESTIONS ABOUT DAY CARE

Helen explains her problem. "I'm recently divorced, have a good job, and best of all I have Sarah, who's my terrific 7-month-old daughter." Her faces takes on a worried look as she continues, "I would like to stay home and take care of Sarah, but I really don't have a choice. I need to work full time to support us." She pauses for a moment and then asks something that's been really bothering her, "Do you think it's okay to put Sarah in day care?"

For many parents, like Helen, day care is not so much an option as a necessity. In fact, about half of America's infants today have mothers who are employed, and a large percentage of these children will be placed in day care (U.S. Bureau of the Census, 1986). We'll examine a number of questions about the effects of day care on an infant's emotional, social, and cognitive development.

Close to 60% of mothers in the United States with children under 6 are on the job and need quality day care for their children.

Emotional Development

How does day care affect later emotional development?

One debate about day care is whether it can lead to later emotional problems. This issue revolves around the interpretation of the *quality* of the infant-mother attachment. As you may remember, insecure attachments are thought to interfere with forming secure relationships and secure attachments are hypothesized to lead to better emotional relationships.

In looking at all the studies on attachment, Clarke-Stewart (1989) found that mothers who were employed full time were more likely to have infants who formed insecure attachments (36% of infants). In comparison, mothers who worked part time or who were unemployed were less likely to have infants who formed insecure attachments (29% of infants). Researchers do not dispute the finding that working mothers are somewhat more likely to have infants who form insecure attachments. What they dispute is whether insecure attachments formed in infancy will give rise to later emotional insecurities (Caruso, 1990).

According to Jay Belsky (1989), we should be concerned about infants who spend 20 hours a week in day care during their first year, because these infants are more likely to form insecure attachments. He believes that insecurely attached infants interpret their mothers' absence as rejection and that their feelings of rejection will result in later emotional insecurities.

According to Clarke-Stewart (1989), Belsky's interpretation may be correct, but at this point it is highly speculative because it is not supported by data. Clarke-Stewart points out that no one knows what effects insecure attachment has on later emotional development because no one has followed the emotional development of insecurely attached infants through childhood, adolescence, and adulthood. She stresses the fact that other measures of security, self-confidence, and emotional adjustment reveal no differences between infants who were and were not in day care. Clarke-Stewart concludes: "At the present time, in my view, it is not appropriate to interpret the difference [in attachment] as suggesting that these children are emotionally insecure"

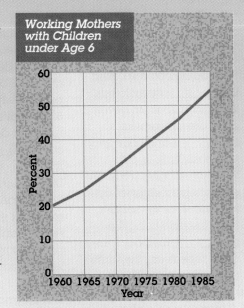

Working Mothers with Children under Age 6

(1989, p. 268). Thus, while it is possible that insecure infant-mother attachments may result in later emotional insecurities, there is little hard evidence that this actually happens.

Social Development

Does day care result in social problems?

Similar to the studies on emotional problems, studies on social problems associated with day care have found varying effects (Clarke-Stewart, 1989). Some researchers found that children who spent their first year in day care were later observed to be more aggressive with their peers and less obedient with their parents. Other researchers found no social, behavioral, or aggressive problems in children who had been in day care during their first year.

Clarke-Stewart (1989) interprets the findings of increased aggressiveness in day-care children not to be a sign of maladjustment. Rather, she thinks that children who have been in day care are more independent, more likely to think on their own, and less likely to comply with rules and wishes of adults. As a result, they seem to be more aggressive but are rather more independent, confident, and self-assured.

Intellectual Development

Does day care retard intellectual development?

Researchers have consistently found that children who attended infant day care are, on the average, advanced in intellectual de-

velopment (Clarke-Stewart, 1989). For example, children who were in day care generally score higher on intelligence tests and generally show intellectual, language, and perceptual development either equal to or surpassing that of children who remain at home with their mothers. However, longitudinal studies of children who have been in day care show that their intellectual advancement is short term and disappears when they enter school.

Clarke-Stewart concludes that quality day care centers may not retard the emotional, social, or intellectual development of a child. How, then, do we determine what is quality day care?

What are the signs of a good day care center?

Sandra Scarr and her colleagues (1990) have identified at least three signs of quality day care:

1 The *ratio* of caregivers to infants should be 1 to 4—that is, one staff member for every four infants. A small staff-to-infant ratio means more time for education, social interactions, and cognitive stimulation.

2 The *training and education* of caregivers is important. Caregivers with more child-related education show greater responsiveness, more positive emotions, and a better ability to provide stimulating experiences. Such caregivers are better able to recognize and respond to a baby's signals.

3 The *stability* of the day care and caregivers is also important; it helps infants and children develop stable relationships. Children who experience many changes in day care or caregivers show slower development in social and language skills.

Scarr concludes that, for children, the most pressing issue is quality care; for parents, the most pressing issues are affordability and availability of consistent and dependable child care. Scarr remarks that, for many parents, it is easier to purchase a quality car or refrigerator than to buy good child care.

Summary/Self-Test

ISSUES AND APPROACHES

1. Those who study biological, emotional, cognitive, and social development across the life span from infancy through late adulthood are called

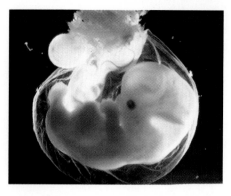

(a)_____ psychologists. Two major issues in development are nature versus (b)_____ and continuity versus (c)_____.

2. If psychologists study several groups of different-aged individuals at the same time, they are using the (a)_____ method. If they study repeatedly the same group of individuals at many different points in time, the are using the (b)_____ method. If they study a single individual's physical, emotional, cognitive, or social processes in great depth across time they are using the (c)_____ method. If they study cultural differences and similarities in development they are using the (d)_____ method.

■ *How would you find out whether being an identical twin has any effect on how fast or slow a child learns to talk?*

PRENATAL DEVELOPMENT

3. The time from conception to birth is called the (a)_____ period. This period is divided into three parts. The two-week period that immediately follows conception is called the (b)_____ period; it is marked by the zygote dividing into many cells. The period that includes the 2 to 8 weeks after conception, during which cells divide and begin to differentiate into bone, muscle, and body organs, is called the (c)_____ period. The period of development that begins two months after conception and lasts for about seven months is called the (d)_____ period. At the end of this period, usually 38 to 42 weeks after conception (or roughly nine months), birth occurs and the fetus becomes a newborn.

4. One reason that you have developed into a unique human being is your genetic heritage, contained in the ovum and sperm. There are 23 strands of chemicals inside each ovum and sperm; each of these strands is called a

(a)_____. The chemical strand that makes up each chromosome is further divided into microscopic pieces called (b)_____; these are composed of deoxyribonucleic acid and form a chemical code containing the equivalent of approximately 1 million pages of typed instructions.

5. The development of the fetus can be interrupted or damaged by a variety of toxic agents, called (a)_____, which cause malformation of the brain or body and result in birth defects. Drugs, including alcohol, nicotine, cocaine, and heroin, can cause problems in prenatal development. For example, heavy drinking during pregnancy can cause a combination of physical and psychological deficits called (b)_____, the leading cause of mental retardation in the United States.

■ *A pregnant woman remarks that she doesn't have to worry about ingesting chemicals that would affect her unborn child since her blood supply and that of the fetus are separate. What would you reply?*

THE NEWBORN

6. The newborn comes into the world with relatively well-developed sensory and perceptual responses. For example, the newborn can see but has poor ability to see details, which is called (a)_____. Six-month-old infants will not crawl off the visual cliff, indicating that they have developed (b)_____ perception. Newborns have good hearing, touch, and smell and an inherited preference for sweet and salt tastes.

7. If a newborn does not receive an adequate diet, he or she may suffer from (a)_____ and develop behavioral and cognitive deficits. In addition, if infants are exposed to automobile exhaust or paint chips, some of which contains (b)_____, they may have maldeveloped brains as well as behavioral and cognitive deficits.

■ *One parent tells the other that their 2-week-old infant can already tell the difference between them. Can there be any truth to this?*

MOTOR DEVELOPMENT

8. Motor development, which is the acquisition of the muscle control required for coordinated physical activity, follows two general principles.

The principle that parts of the body closer to the head develop before those closer to the feet is called the (a)_____ principle. The principle that parts closer to the center of the body develop before those farther away is called the (d)_____ principle.

9. Development that occurs in a sequential and orderly fashion because of a genetic plan is called (a)_____. The average age at which individuals perform various kinds of skills or exhibit abilities or behaviors is reflected in (b)_____.

■ *A father wants his son to grow up to be a great baseball player, so he is already playing baseball with his 3-year-old son. Will this help?*

EMOTIONAL DEVELOPMENT

10. Signals that infants use to indicate physiological needs and psychological moods and to motivate parents' behaviors are called (a)_____. Newborns have a limited range of emotional expressions that include interest, startle, distress, disgust, and neonatal smile. According to Carroll Izard, the first step in emotional development involves infants' (b)_____ capacity to produce, imitate, and discriminate among emotional expressions. The second step involves (c)_____ from the parents' (or caregivers') emotions or moods that influences and alters the infants' behaviors and emotional expressions.

11. An infant's characteristic mood, level of energy, and reaction to new objects, situations, or people is referred to as _____, which is considerably influenced by nature or inherited tendencies.

■ *Marcie and Jeff love their 6-month-old son but find that he is easily irritated and frightened. What should they do?*

ATTACHMENT

12. The close emotional bond between infant and parent or caregiver is called (a)_____. This bond is formed, in part, by the infant's responses, which include crying and social smiling. As the infant develops a closer attachment to her parents, she also shows more distress when her parents leave. An infant's distress, as indicated by loud protests, crying, and agitation,

whenever her parents temporarily leave is called (b)_____.

13. There are two kinds of attachment. Infants who use their caregiver as a safe home base from which they can wander off and explore their environments are said to be (a)_____ attached. This kind of attachment may contribute to better emotional bonds later in life. Infants who avoid or show ambivalence toward their caregivers are said to be (b)_____ attached. For example, these infants may cling and want to be held one minute and squirm and push away the next minute.

14. Theodore Dix offers four conclusions about the importance of emotion in parenting. First, strong (a)_____ occur an average of 3 to 15 times an hour in child-parent interaction. Second, the kinds of emotions that parents display greatly affect the child's later (b)_____. Third, the occupations, marital relations, and other stressors of the (c)_____ greatly influence the emotions that parents show their children. Fourth, long-term and intense negative emotions in parents are a sign of family (d)_____.

■ *Every time Amy's parents temporarily leave, she becomes very upset. Is this normal behavior?*

APPLYING/EXPLORING: QUESTIONS ABOUT DAY CARE

15. The effects of day care on children's emotional, social, and intellectual development are under study. Research indicates that infants who spend 20 hours a week in day care during their first year are more likely to form (a)_____ attachments, but the effects of such attachment on later development are not yet known. Other researchers have found no social, intellectual, behavioral, or aggressive problems in children who had been in day care during their (b)_____ year.

■ *A company is setting up a day care center for the children of its employees. What should they do to have a quality center?*

MODULE 20 CHILDHOOD

A 3-year-old child is fooled by a sponge that looks like a rock.

Can you squeeze a rock?

"What do you think this is?" asks the researcher.

Three-year-old Sam looks at the object in the researcher's hand and confidently answers, "A rock."

The researcher hands the rock to Sam and tells him to squeeze it.

Sam takes the rock and squeezes it really hard. He lets out an "Ohhh!" as he easily squashes the rock between his tiny fingers. Sam looks at the squeezed rock and then at the researcher.

The researcher smiles and asks, "Is that thing in your hand really and truly a sponge or it is really and truly a rock?"

Sam looks at the thing in his hands carefully and then holds it up for the researcher to see. Sam answers very proudly, "It's a rock."

The researcher puts the sponge/rock on the table and next shows Sam a glass of milk. "What color is this milk?"

Sam points at the glass and says, "White."

The researcher puts a yellow filter in front of the glass of milk so that the glass of milks looks yellow. The researcher asks Sam, "Is this glass of milk really and truly white or is it really and truly yellow?"

For just a moment Sam seems confused and then shouts, "It's yellow!" (adapted from Flavell, *Psychology Today,* January 1986)

Like most 3-year-olds, Sam has trouble distinguishing between an object's appearance and its reality. For instance, the appearance of the sponge/rock leads him to say that it is a rock even though he could squeeze it. Similarly, the appearance of yellow milk leads him to say that milk is yellow even though he earlier saw a glass of white milk. Sam's problem distinguishing between appearance and reality will disappear as his cognitive processes develop. By the time he is 5 or 6 years old, he will have learned that a rocklike sponge is actually a sponge and that a glass of milk behind a yellow filter is still white. This ability to distinguish appearance from reality is just one of the interesting cognitive changes that occurs during childhood.

What's Coming

In the first part of this module we'll examine **cognitive development,** *or how a person gains an understanding of his or her world through experience and learning.* In the second part, we'll discuss **social development,** *or how a person develops social relationships and a sense of self and becomes a social being.* We'll begin with the best-known theory of cognitive development, Piaget's theory.

Cognitive Development

Piaget's Theory of Cognitive Development

The work of Jean Piaget, who was both a biologist and psychologist, led to the development of a major theory of cognitive development. From the 1920s to his death in 1980, Piaget (1929) studied how children solved problems in their natural settings, such as cribs, sandboxes, and playgrounds. In some cases, Piaget used a combination of case study and longitudinal methods when he observed how his own children solved problems. For example, he discovered that a 7-month-old infant perceives, thinks, and interacts with his world very differently than a 4-, 10-, or 14-year-old child does.

Piaget's work led to the current view that children are actively involved in their own cognitive development. By *active involvement,* Piaget meant that children are constantly striving to understand what they encounter, and in such encounters they form their own guesses or hypotheses about how the world works.

It is easier to understand Piaget's idea of active involvement if you imagine 3-year-old Sam playing with the sponge/rock. Without realizing it, Sam is trying to understand the things in his world. According to Piaget, Sam's understanding comes about primarily by interacting with his environment, such as by squeezing, throwing, and manipulating the sponge/rock. Piaget believed that children gain an understanding of things in their world through two processes: assimilation and accommodation.

Assimilation

Can you squeeze a rock?

Assimilation *is the process of incorporating new information or experience into existing knowledge.* For example, at age 5 or 6, if Sam is given an object that looks exactly like a rock, he will first try to fit the object into his existing knowledge of rocks. However, since the object has none of the traits of a rock except appearance but does have the traits of a sponge, he will assimilate the new object as a sponge.

We assimilate things in different ways depending on our amount of existing knowledge. For instance, a sponge/rock might be assimilated by an infant as something to suck, by a toddler as something to throw, by an adolescent as something to use for playing tricks, and by an adult as something for cleaning up spilled water. The assimilation of new information leads to the next process—accommodation.

Accommodation

Can sponges look like rocks?

Accommodation *is the change that occurs in existing knowledge or experience as a result of assimilating some new information.* For example, because of Sam's experience with sponge/rocks, he learns that some objects may look like rocks but may not be rocks. The process of having to accommodate or change existing knowledge because of new information is one way that mental growth occurs.

As an infant or child is actively involved with his or her environment, more chances for assimilation and accommodation occur, resulting in different kinds of cognitive growth and development.

We'll next examine the stages of cognitive development that Piaget described.

Cognitive Development

Piaget's Stages of Cognitive Development

According to Piaget, infants and children make big gains in reasoning, thinking, and understanding through active involvement and the processes of assimilation and accommodation. As a result of these processes, infants and children proceed through a series of four reasoning or cognitive stages. Each of **Piaget's cognitive stages** *is thought to be qualitatively different from the previous one because each new stage represents the development of some new reasoning or thinking ability.* In addition, Piaget believed that each successive cognitive stage is more advanced because it involves a qualitatively different way of thinking or reasoning.

Piaget's hypothesis that cognitive development occurs in stages was one of his unique contributions to developmental psychology. Although he believed that people all go through the same four cognitive stages, he acknowledged that they may go through the stages at different rates. As we examine Piaget's stages in detail, we'll imagine Sam developing from a newborn to age 14.

Stage 1: Sensorimotor Stage

What's in my world?

During the **sensorimotor stage** *(from birth to about age 2), infants interact with and learn about their environments by relating their sensory experiences (such as hearing and seeing) to their motor actions.* As a newborn, Sam's primary way of interacting with the world is through reflexive responses, such as sucking and grasping. By 5 months, Sam has developed considerable voluntary muscle control, such as reaching out, grasping a toy, and bringing it to his mouth.

If his toy is in plain view, 5-month-old Sam looks at it.

Where did the toy monkey go?

If 5-month-old Sam is shown a toy, he looks at and tries to grab it. However, if a screen is placed in front of the toy, Sam looks away. He doesn't push the screen away to get at the toy because, at this point, Sam behaves as if things that are out of sight no longer exist. However, beginning at around 9 months, Sam learns that things out of sight still exist and are worth looking for.

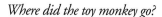

A 1-year-old infant explores the world by sensory and motor means.

When Sam is about 9 months old, he looks for a toy that is out of sight because he is learning a new concept—object permanence. **Object permanence** *refers to the understanding that objects or events still continue to exist even if they can no longer be heard, touched, or seen.* The concept of object permanence develops slowly. At the end of the sensorimotor period (about age 2), the infant will search long and hard for lost or disappeared objects, indicating a fully developed concept of object permanence. At the end of this period 2-year-old Sam can think about things that are not present as well as form simple plans for solving problems, such as searching for things.

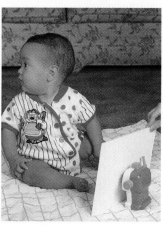

If his toy is covered, Sam behaves as if it no longer exists.

Stage 2: Preoperational Stage

When does a shoebox become a "car"?

During the **preoperational stage** *(from about 2 to 7 years old), children learn to use symbols, such as words or mental images, to think about things that are not present and to help them solve simple problems.* For instance, Sam can talk about things that are not physically present, he can represent things by drawing, and he can pretend, such as pretending a shoebox is a car. Although Sam uses and manipulates symbols in speech and play, his thinking has a number of interesting limitations that make it different from an adult's.

Piaget used the term *preoperational* to mean that children's thinking at this stage is characterized by their inability to perform operations. An **operation** *is the ability of mentally transforming, manipulating, or reversing an event or action.* For example, one reason 3-year-old Sam can't distinguish a sponge/rock from a real rock is that he can't perform the operations involved in logical thinking. Sam sees a sponge/rock and calls it a rock because he is deceived by appearance. If he could think logically, he would conclude that even though a sponge/rock looks like a rock, it is still a sponge. Piaget developed a number of clever methods to test for a child's ability to perform operations (think logically). He discovered that children between 2 and 7 think preoperationally—that is, they cannot perform some basic operations that involve logical thinking.

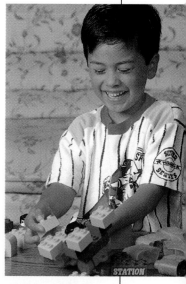

By 5 years old Sam is good at pretending that blocks are cars, houses, or animals.

Egocentric Thinking

"Me want cookie, " says 4-year-old Sam.

As Sam reaches into the cookie jar, father says, "Now remember, just one cookie."

"OK," replies Sam as he grabs and pulls out as many cookies as his tiny hand will hold.

This father-son conversation illustrates a particular kind of preoperational thought known as egocentric thinking. **Egocentric** (ee-goh-SEN-trick) **thinking** *refers to seeing and thinking of the world only from your own viewpoint and having difficulty appreciating someone else's viewpoint.* When Sam wants a cookie, he tries to get as many as he can, without considering his father's rule about taking only one cookie at a time. Piaget used the term *egocentric thinking* not to mean that children are selfish but rather to mean that preoperational children are incapable of looking at the world from another's viewpoint or way of thinking.

Conservation

The term **conservation** *refers to the fact that the amount of a substance remains the same even though its shape changes.* Conservation means that a long, thin stick of gum has the same amount as one rolled into a ball. Can a preoperational child master the concept of conservation?

1 Five-year-old Sam watches as his mother fills two short, wide glasses with equal amounts of milk.

2 Next Sam sees his mother pour the milk from one short, wide glass into a tall, thin glass. Mother asks, "Does one glass have more?"

3 Sam points to the tall, thin glass as having more, even though he saw his mother pour the milk from a short, wide glass.

Sam thinks there is more milk in the tall, thin glass because it looks like more. Children at the preoperational stage cannot master the concept of conservation, which develops during the next stage.

Cognitive Development

Stage 3: Concrete Operations Stage

Does a short, wide glass hold the same amount as a tall, thin glass?

During the **concrete operations stage** *(from about 7 to 11 years), children can perform a number of logical mental operations on concrete objects (ones that are physically present).* These mental operations include the ability to classify objects according to some dimension, such as height or length, and the ability to figure out relationships between objects, such as larger and smaller. Piaget calls this stage "concrete" operations because children at this level can easily figure out relationships between objects provided the objects are "concrete," or physically present.

By the time he is 10 years old, Sam has mastered a number of mental concepts, including that of classification.

In the preoperational stage, Sam had not mastered the concept of conservation. In comparison, in the concrete operations stage, Sam can watch a liquid being poured from a short glass into a tall glass and correctly answer that the amount of liquid remains the same. Similarly, Sam thinks that when a ball of clay is flattened, the amount of clay is the same even if the shape changes. Preoperationally, Sam could divide objects, such as puppies, into categories based only on one category, such as color. In comparison, Sam can now classify puppies according to two categories, such as color and size.

At the preoperational stage 5-year-old Sam watched a ball of clay flattened and said that the flattened piece was bigger.

At the concrete operations stage, 10-year-old Sam watched a ball of clay flattened and said that it was the same amount.

Compared to preoperational thinking, concrete operational thinking is characterized by grasping the concepts of conservation and classification. However, at this stage, children still have difficulty figuring out relationships among imaginary or hypothetical objects and situations, which brings us to Piaget's fourth stage.

Stage 4: Formal Operations Stage

Is Mary taller than Susan?

During the **formal operations stage** *(from about 12 years old through adulthood), adolescents and adults develop the ability to think about and solve abstract problems in a logical manner.* Piaget believed that it is during the formal operations stage that adolescents develop thinking and reasoning typical of adults. For example, 14-year-old Sam can solve the following problem:

Susan is shorter than Janice.

Janice is shorter than Mary.

Is Mary shorter or taller than Susan?

High school senior Michael Agney scored a perfect 1600 on his Scholastic Aptitude Tests. His exceptional reasoning is an example of skills characteristic of the formal operations stage.

Sam would reason that Mary is taller than Susan. His solution indicates that he has learned to solve abstract problems in a systematic, logical manner. In comparison, when Sam was at the concrete operations stage, he could only guess at the solution, since he lacked the ability to think hypothetically or solve abstract problems.

Once adolescents reach the formal operations stage, they encounter exciting new worlds of abstract ideas and hypothetical concepts. For example, they can discuss abstract ideas, such as justice, democracy, and love, as well as examine hypothetical situations, such as "What if there were no more wars?" The logical, systematic, and abstract thinking abilities characteristic of the formal operations stage open a world of new ideas and possibilities. If you were not at the formal operations stage, you would find most college classes difficult to understand.

Evaluation of Piaget's Theory

If we were to squeeze Piaget's theory into three essential ideas, they would be:

1 Children progressively develop reasoning abilities through active involvement with their environment.

2 Children use accommodation and assimilation to develop reasoning abilities.

3 Specific kinds of reasoning abilities and specific kinds of cognitive limitations are characteristic of different ages.

After more than 25 years of intensive research, psychologists generally agree that Piaget's theory deserves some support and some criticism (Halford, 1989).

Criticisms and Support

One hallmark of Piaget's theory is that children go through four stages, during which they develop qualitatively different ways of thinking and reasoning. However, researchers have found that children may solve certain kinds of problems at stages earlier than Piaget proposed if the problems are simplified or presented in different ways. For example, preoperational children can solve some hypothetical problems, such as who is taller or shorter than whom, if the problems are repeated many times. According to Piaget, preoperational children should not be able to solve these simple hypothetical problems. Because children have knowledge and skills that would not be predicted from Piaget's stages, researchers now believe that Piaget's stages of cognitive development are not as rigid as he originally proposed (Carey, 1990).

A second hallmark of Piaget's theory is that children are actively involved, through accommodation and assimilation, in their own cognitive development. Many developmental psychologists agree with Piaget that cognitive changes occur through interactions with the environment and that children are active rather than passive participants in their cognitive development (Carey, 1990).

Many of Piaget's ideas have stood the test of time.

Conclusions

Some of Piaget's ideas and parts of his overall theory have not been supported by subsequent research. Nevertheless, many developmental psychologists admire Piaget's work and give him credit for almost singlehandedly launching the study of cognitive development. And, as we have noted, many of his ideas have stood the test of time (Bidell & Fischer, 1989).

Today two major changes have occurred in the study of cognitive development. First, psychologists divide cognitive development into separate areas of memory, problem solving, creativity, and social interactions. For each of these areas, they note a flexible schedule for change and growth that is affected by both a person's age and the quality of his or her environment (Carey, 1990). Second, greater emphasis is placed on how a child's social and environmental interactions affect his or her cognitive development. For example, researchers have reported that factors in a child's home environment, such as responsiveness of parents to children's needs and availability of stimulating play materials, are strongly related to cognitive development (Bradley et al., 1989). In addition, different cultural experiences can result in variations in both the age at which cognitive skills begin to appear and the order in which these skills are acquired (Bidell & Fischer, 1989). Such studies indicate how children's environmental and social worlds affect their interactions and subsequent cognitive development.

For the sake of simplicity, we have discussed cognitive development as if it proceeds independently. In fact, cognitive development is intertwined with social development, which we'll examine next.

Social Development

How does an infant develop into a social being?

Why did Delia turn out so well?
During infancy, Delia had at least two major problems that had the potential to retard her social development. First, she was born to an unwed 17-year-old mother who had problems of her own and who showed little interest in raising Delia. Second, during Delia's early years, her mother continued to be indifferent, withdrawn, and immature, and her father was rarely around. Shortly after Delia's first birthday, she was sent to live with her grandparents, who loved her dearly. When she was 7, Delia and her younger brother were adopted by the grandparents. Before and after her adoption, Delia had only fleeting contacts with her mother, who remained indifferent to her. Despite financial troubles, the grandparents took over the role of mother and father and raised Delia in a warm and caring home environment (Werner & Smith, 1982).

This real-life example of Delia illustrates the complexity of social development. **Social development** *refers to how a person develops relationships with others, develops a sense of self, and becomes a social being.* The reason we know so much about Delia is that she was one of over 600 children who researchers followed from birth to the age of almost 20. Before we tell you how Delia developed socially, let's examine three theories of social development, each of which emphasizes a different aspect.

Three Theories of Social Development

Freud's Psychosexual Stages

Sigmund Freud hypothesized five **psychosexual stages,** *or developmental periods during which a child's primary goal is to satisfy desires associated with innate biological needs, such as those involving sex and aggression.* The satisfaction of these needs is a source of potential conflict between the child, who wants immediate gratification, and the **5 PERIODS** parents, who place restrictions on when, where, and how the child's needs should be satisfied. Freud believed that interactions between parent and child over satisfying these psychosexual needs, such as during breastfeeding or toilet training, greatly influence the child's social development and future social interactions.

What is the importance of Delia's first five years? According to Freud, Delia's first five years would be most important in setting down patterns for later social interactions. Freud's theory of psychosexual stages is part of his larger psychoanalytic theory of personality, which we'll discuss in Chapter 13.

Erikson's Psychosocial Stages

Erik Erikson identified eight **psychosocial stages,** *or developmental periods during which an individual's primary goal is to satisfy desires associated with inborn social needs, such as developing trust, autonomy, or initiative.* Erikson hypothesized that from infancy through adulthood, we proceed through these stages, each **8 STAGES** of which is related to a different problem that needs to be resolved. If we successfully deal with the potential problem inherent in each psychosocial stage, we develop positive personality traits and are better able to solve the problem at the next stage. However, if we do not successfully handle the problem, we may become anxious, worried, or troubled and develop social or personality problems.

Are Delia's sexual or social needs more important? Unlike Freud, Erikson believed that psychosocial needs deserve the greatest emphasis and that social development continues throughout one's lifetime. Thus, Erikson would emphasize Delia's *psychosocial needs* and downplay the importance of sexuality in the first five years.

Bandura's Social Cognitive Theory

Albert Bandura's **social cognitive theory** *emphasizes the importance of learning through imitation, observation, and reinforcement in the development of social skills, interactions, and behaviors.* Unlike Freud's emphasis on satisfying innate biological needs or Erikson's emphasis on satisfying inborn social needs, **LEARNING** social cognitive theory stresses how learning affects the behavior of people in social situations.

How important is learning to Delia's social development? According to Bandura, learning has a major impact on Delia's social development.

Erikson's Psychosocial Stages

What problems does Delia face as she develops socially?

As Delia proceeds from infancy through adulthood, Erikson suggested, she will go through eight psychosocial stages, each of which presents a particular kind of problem. By solving a psychosocial problem at one stage, Delia develops or adds a personality/social trait that will help her deal with a new problem at the next stage. Let's look at Delia's progression through the first four stages.

Psychosocial Stages

Stage 1 Trust Versus Mistrust

Period: Early infancy—birth through first year.
Potential problem: Delia comes into the world as a helpless infant who needs much care and attention. If her caregiver is responsive and sensitive to her needs, Delia will develop what Erikson calls *basic trust*, which makes it easier for her to trust people later in life. If Delia's caregiver neglects her needs, Delia may view her world as uncaring, may learn to become mistrustful, and may have difficulty dealing with the second stage. Fortunately, the insensitivity and unresponsiveness of Delia's own mother has been compensated for by the sensitivity and care of her grandmother.

Stage 2 Autonomy Versus Shame and Doubt

Period: Late infancy—1 to 3 years.
Potential problem: As Delia begins walking, talking, and exploring, she is bound to get into trouble with the wishes of her grandparents. Thus, this second stage is a battle of wills between the caregivers, who wish to control their infant, and Delia, who wishes to do whatever she chooses. If the caregivers encourage and support Delia's autonomy, she will develop a sense of independence or autonomy. If the caretakers disapprove of or punish Delia's explorations, she may develop a feeling that independence is bad and feel shame and doubt.

Stage 3 Initiative Versus Guilt

Period: Early childhood—3 to 5 years.
Potential problem: As a preschooler, Delia has developed a number of cognitive and social skills that she is expected to use to meet the challenges in her small world. Some of these challenges involve assuming responsibility and making plans. If the caregivers encourage initiative, Delia will develop the ability to plan and initiate new things. However, if they discourage initiative, she may feel uncomfortable or guilty and may develop a feeling of being unable to plan her future.

Stage 4 Industry versus Inferiority

Period: Middle and late childhood—5 to 12 years.
Potential problem: Delia's grade school years are an exciting time, filled with participating in school, playing games with other children, and working to complete projects. If Delia can direct her energy into working at and completing tasks, she will develop a feeling of industry. If she has difficulty applying herself and completing homework, she may develop a feeing of inferiority and incompetence.

Evaluation of Erikson's Theory

It is possible to squeeze Erikson's theory of psychosocial stages into three intriguing ideas:

1. Each psychosocial stage is like a thermometer, with one end representing a positive trait and the other end a negative trait. If the person resolves the conflict nearer the positive end, he or she has a greater likelihood of developing a positive trait. On the other hand, if the person resolves the conflict nearer the negative end, he or she has a greater likelihood of developing a negative trait.

2. Each stage builds on the others; thus, resolving the conflict at one stage lays the groundwork for successfully meeting the challenge and solving the conflict at the next stage.

3. Because social development continues throughout one's life, Erikson believed that it is possible to compensate at a later stage for some unresolved problem left over from an earlier stage.

Many psychologists agree with Erikson that psychosocial conflicts, which are based on interpersonal and environmental interactions, are important and contribute to later social-emotional development.

Now, we'll turn to an idea that fits in with this last point—namely, that it is possible to compensate for earlier problems.

According to Erikson, children develop the ability to plan through the initiation of new activities.

Vulnerability and Resiliency

Children of Kuaui represent an ethnic mixture.

Delia was part of a study of 600 children from a small rural community on the Hawaiian island of Kuaui. In this study, conducted by psychologist Emmy Werner (1989), the children were followed from birth to almost 20. Like Delia, all the children were exposed to numerous life stresses, including problems during their mother's pregnancy, family instability, mental and financial difficulties of parents, and a lower social class environment with less stimulation than others. How these life stressors affect children brings up the issue of vulnerability and resiliency. **Vulnerability** *refers to psychological or environmental difficulties that make children more at risk for developing later personality, behavioral, or social problems.* On the other hand, **resiliency** *refers to various personality, family, or environmental factors that compensate for increased life stresses so that expected problems do not develop.*

In Delia's group of 600 children, about 200 showed increased vulnerability and later developed serious behavioral or learning problems. However, the most remarkable finding is that over 400 of the children showed resiliency and developed into competent and autonomous young adults (Werner, 1989; Werner & Smith, 1982). Let's look at what might cause this discrepancy.

Reasons for Resiliency

Children like Delia are called resilient, or stress-resistant. These children defy expectations because they develop into well-adapted individuals in spite of serious life stressors (Luthar & Zigler, 1991). For example, despite having an insensitive, unresponsive young unwed mother and no active father, Delia at age 20 had developed adequate self-esteem, high achievement motivation, a fair degree of insight into her life, and realistic plans for the future.

Werner (1989) has identified at least three factors that characterize children who are resilient—that is, who cope successfully with numerous life stresses:

1 Some useful *dispositional traits,* or dominant genetic or temperamental characteristics that are present early on. For example, Werner reported that from birth to age 2, resilient children had more positive dispositional traits, such as being more active, cuddly, affectionate, smiley, and socially responsive. Because of these characteristics, the infants elicited and received a great deal of attention, which in turn led to an affectionate bond between infant and caregiver.

2 A number of *family factors,* such as family size or presence of substitute caregivers. For example, Werner found that resilient children came from families with four or fewer children, so they had more opportunity for care, attention, and adequate bonding. In addition, resilient children usually had a substitute caregiver who compensated for the natural mother's lack of interest.

3 *Outside emotional support,* such as from classmates and friends. Resilient children were usually well liked and had a number of classmates, neighbors, and elders who provided counsel and emotional support. For example, many resilient children mentioned a favorite teacher who had become a friend, supporter, and confidant.

Studies on resilient children make three important points. First, the occurrence of a traumatic emotional event in childhood does not necessarily lead to later social-emotional problems. Second, some early emotional trauma may be offset by some other positive experience. Third, the early years of childhood are not necessarily the most important.

Studies on resilient children question Freud's belief that the first five years are most important and support Erikson's view that early problems may be compensated for by later positive experiences.

After the Concept/Glossary, we'll discuss a related aspect of social development—gender roles.

1. How a person gains an understanding of his or her world through experience and learning is referred to as _____ development.

2. Piaget believed that children are actively involved in understanding their world through two basic processes. The process of incorporating new information or experience into existing knowledge is called (a)_____. The change that occurs in existing knowledge or experience as a result of assimilating some new information is called (b) _____.

3. Piaget's theory of cognitive development includes four stages, each of which is characterized by the development of particular kinds of reasoning The first stage, during which infants learn about their environments by relating their sensory experiences (such as hearing and seeing) to their motor actions, is called the (a) _____ stage. The second stage, during which infants learn to use symbols to think about things that are not present and to help them solve simple problems, is called the (b) _____ stage. The third stage, during which children learn to perform a number of logical mental operations on objects that are physically present, is called the (c) stage. The fourth stage, during which adolescents and adults develop the ability to think about and solve abstract problems in a logical manner, is called the (d) _____ stage.

4. The process through which a person develops social relationships, develops a sense of self, and becomes a social being is called _____ development.

5. According to Freud's theory of social development, children go through five developmental periods, which he called _____ stages. During these stages, a child's primary goal is to satisfy desires associated with innate biological needs.

6. According to Albert Bandura's social cognitive theory, a person's social skills, interactions, and behaviors are greatly influenced by _____ through imitation, observation, and reinforcement.

7. According to Erik Erikson, a person goes through eight developmental periods during which the primary goal is to satisfy desires associated with inborn social needs. Each of these eight periods is called a _____ stage, during which the person works to resolve a potential problem. A successful resolution of the potential problem leads to the development of positive personality traits, while the unsuccessful resolution results in developing social or personality problems.

8. Increased risk for a child to develop later personality, behavioral, or social problems because of early life stresses is called (a) _____. Compensation for early life stresses through positive personality, family, or environmental factors, which reduce the risks of developing psychological or behavioral problems, is called (b) _____.

Answers: 1. *cognitive*; 2. (a) *assimilation*, (b) *accommodation*; 3. (a) *sensorimotor*, (b) *preoperational*, (c) *concrete operations*, (d) *formal operations*; 4. *social*; 5 *psychosexual*; 6. *learning*; 7. *psychosocial*; 8. (a) *vulnerability*, (b) *resiliency*.

Gender Role Development

The one question everyone asks about a newborn is, "Is it a girl or a boy?" In a relatively short time, the infant begins developing traditional or stereotypic girl or boy behaviors, called gender roles. **Gender roles** *are the expectations of parents, peers, and society of how we should think or behave because we are male or female.* Gender roles have a relatively powerful effect on how we behave, think, and act. For example, it is only in the last few years that women have managed to make inroads in work and occupational settings that have in the past been viewed as traditionally male.

We're going to discuss two related questions about gender roles: How are gender roles acquired, and can gender roles be changed?

Acquiring Gender Roles

When do you know whether you're a boy or a girl?
Between the ages of 2 and 3, most children learn to label themselves as boys or girls and can classify others as being the same sex or a different sex. By the time they are 3, American children know the traditional expectations of how gender roles relate to toys, clothes, games, and tools. From ages 4 to 5, children develop a clear idea of which occupations are for men and which are for women. And by the relatively early age of 5, children have already learned the thoughts, expectations, and behaviors that accompany their particular gender role (Biernat, 1991).

How children acquire gender roles is explained by two related theories: social learning theory and cognitive developmental theory.

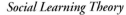

Social learning theory offers one explanation of how this young girl develops stereotypic female thoughts and behaviors.

Social Learning Theory

According to **social learning theory,** *soon after the infant's birth, parents or caregivers expect, treat, and reward different kinds of behaviors in boys than in girls.* Essentially, the theory is based on the idea that parents socialize boys differently than girls and this contributes to different gender roles.

Research supports this idea that different kinds of socialization leads to different gender roles. For example, researchers wondered whether parents subtly socialize boys and girls differently by buying them different kinds of toys. Rather than interviewing parents, researchers actually visited homes and observed the kinds of toys that parents had bought for their infants. The researchers discovered that parents bought more sports equipment, tools, and cars/trucks for boys and more dolls and child's furniture for girls (Pomerleau et al., 1990). This is a case of parents differentially socializing traditional gender roles by buying traditional boy toys or girl toys.

In a related study, researchers reported that mothers encouraged talking in girls more than in boys, that fa-thers discouraged boys from using female kinds of toys or games, and that both parents encouraged boys to act out but ignored girls if they acted out (Fagot & Hagan, 1991). This is a case of parents rewarding or discouraging behaviors depending on whether they matched traditional gender roles.

Are we what we learn?
In reviewing the literature on differential socialization, two psychologists reported that parents are more likely to encourage achievement in and use more disciplinary measures on boys; are more likely to show warmth toward and encourage dependence in girls; and generally reward boys and girls for conforming to traditional play activities and household chores (Lytton & Romney, 1991). They concluded that there is some, but not overwhelming, evidence that parents differentially socialize boys and girls.

One criticism of social learning theory is that it neglects how children's cognitive abilities interact with acquiring gender roles. We'll next examine an explanation of gender roles that is supported by cognitive developmental theory.

Cognitive Developmental Theory

According to **cognitive developmental theory**, *mental processes must be sufficiently developed for children to learn and understand the rules underlying gender roles, and children learn male rules or female rules through active involvement with their environments.* In this view, children actively process information that results in their learning gender rules, such as which behaviors are "correct" for girls and "wrong" for boys or vice versa. Based on these rules, children form mental images of how they should act; these mental images are called gender schemas. **Gender schemas** *are sets of information and rules organized around how either a male or a female*  *should think and behave* (Bem, 1985). For instance, the traditional gender schema for "being a boy" includes rough-and-tumble play, sports, and exploring; the traditional gender schema for "being a girl" includes playing with dolls, expressing emotions, and being dependent.

Are we what we think?

In cognitive developmental theory, a child is considered an active participant in acquiring gender roles. Once children have developed their gender schemas, they have a mental image of how to behave in various situations as well as a way to organize new information. Research on gender schemas indicates that, to some extent, we are what we think (Liben & Signorella, 1987).

Changes in Gender Roles

Can a boy be both assertive and sensitive?

The answer to this question highlights one of several major changes in gender roles, involving the definitions of masculinity and femininity. Up to the 1970s, masculinity and femininity were considered to represent opposite poles of a continuum, such that someone who rated high on one pole had to be low on the other. For instance, a high score on traditional scales of masculinity would include being high in assertiveness and low in sensitivity, which is traditionally considered to be a female trait.

Cognitive theory offers another explanation of how this young boy develops stereotypic male thoughts and behaviors.

Sandra Bem (1985) questioned the traditional two-pole masculine-feminine idea and introduced the concept of androgyny. **Androgyny** (an-DRAW-gin-knee) *means that masculine and feminine traits can both be present in the same individual.* According to Bem, an androgynous child would have both the stereotypic female trait of sensitivity as well as the stereotypic male trait of assertiveness. An advantage of being androgynous is that one is not restricted to a stereotypic masculine or feminine role but rather is able to develop traits from both gender roles.

Should a girl plan a career in science?

Another major change in gender roles relates to careers. Up to the 1980s, considerable societal, business, and media pressures were brought upon individuals to conform to traditional careers and occupations. For instance, stereotypic male careers included doctors, lawyers, plumbers, and scientists; stereotypic female careers included nurses, secretaries, receptionists, and salesclerks. Today television commercials continue to portray men in high-status occupations significantly more often than women and to show women in the home or without occupations (Lovdal, 1989).

During the past decade, legal, governmental, and business pressures have opened up stereotyped careers to both sexes. Thus we now see men and women in nontraditional careers, such as male nurses, schoolteachers, salesclerks, and chefs and female doctors, plumbers, scientists, and lawyers. Today, boys and girls have considerably more flexibility in planning future careers in science, business, and industry than they did a decade or two ago.

Gender Roles Around the World

How similar are gender roles in Australia, Japan, Peru, and the United States?

To answer that question, let's look closely at a recent study. Researchers tested hundreds of 5-, 8-, and 11-year-old children in 24 countries to determine whether relatively young children in these countries had already developed beliefs about which characteristics are associated with males and which with females (Williams & Best, 1990).

Method

Younger children (5- and 8-year-olds) were told stories like the one below and then asked whether the person in the story was more like a man than a woman.

Older children (11-year-olds) were given a list of 300 adjectives and asked to

One of these people is always pushing other people around and getting into fights. Which person gets into fights?

indicate which were more likely to be associated with males and which with females. Unlike 5- and 8-year-old children, 11-year-old children were able to understand the meanings of the adjectives and indicate their preferences.

Results

Across the 24 countries, relatively young children showed remarkable similarities and some interesting differences in characteristics that they associated with gender roles.

Children's perception of male gender role: strong, aggressive, dominant, independent, coarse, loud, boastful.

Children's perception of female gender role: emotional, weak, appreciative, excitable, gentle, meek, submissive.

Similarities

Most 5-year-old children associated being strong, aggressive, and dominant with males and being gentle and affectionate with females. By 8 years of age, children had learned that being weak, emotional, appreciative, excitable, gentle, softhearted, meek, and submissive was associated with females, while being disorderly, cruel, coarse, adventurous, independent, ambitious, loud, and boastful was associated with males. By 11 years of age, children had learned to associate being talkative and complaining with females and being confident, steady, and jolly with males. Thus, children in all 24 countries were well aware of gender roles by the age of 5, and the extent of this awareness increased with age.

Differences

Across countries, interesting differences occurred in children's perception of gender roles. In the United States, Canada, Peru, Ireland, and England, children were similar or typical in the characteristics they associated with males or females. In Germany, Japan, Pakistan, Venezuela, and India, children were dissimilar or atypical in the characteristics they associated with males or females. For example, in Germany, children associated being adventurous, confident, jolly, and steady with females, while in most other countries these characteristics were typically associated with males. In Japan, children associated being dominant and steady with females, while in other countries these characteristics were typically associated with males.

Conclusions

Based on their study, Williams and Best (1990) concluded that knowledge of gender roles develops in a generally similar way at a similar time in many different countries.

Besides gender roles, psychologists also study other kinds of gender differences, which we'll examine next.

Gender Differences

According to Carol Jacklin (1989), a much respected researcher on gender characteristics, speculation about differences between females and males has become a national preoccupation and a potential source for discrimination. We'll examine some of the most frequently asked questions about gender differences.

Are there gender differences in math abilities?

In the early 1980s, two researchers reported that, on a standardized test of *mathematical ability,* gifted boys consistently scored higher than gifted girls (Benbow & Stanley, 1980). This finding included the suggestion that a difference in math ability might be due to biological or inherited factors. The media highlighted the suggestion of biological differences and raised questions about women pursuing careers in math.

After a half-dozen years of intense study, other researchers offered three environmental explanations for the differences in math scores (Eccles & Jacobs, 1986). According to this research, girls did less well on math tests because

1. Girls developed math anxiety that interfered with performance.

2. Parents discouraged girls from taking math.

3. Girls perceived little value in taking or doing well in high school math classes.

Based on these kinds of findings, researchers urge the media to be more careful in reporting results that have the potential for promoting discrimination (Jacklin, 1989).

Are there gender differences in verbal abilities?

Although previous reviews found that girls perform better on *verbal tasks* than boys, for some reason this verbal difference has disappeared over the last ten years (Hyde & Lynn, 1988). With regard to intellectual abilities, Jacklin (1989) concludes that tests of intellectual ability have differentiated girls and boys less and less over the last few decades.

Are there gender differences in play and aggression?

In an earlier review of gender differences, researchers found that boys tended to show more rough-and-tumble play and more aggressive behavior than girls (Maccoby & Jacklin, 1974). In her more recent review, Maccoby (1989) confirms this general finding. Perhaps related to their different kinds of play is the finding that boys and girls choose to play in separate or segregated groups (Maccoby, 1989). *Segregated play groups* form as early as nursery school and continue to the sixth grade. These groups are encouraged both by children, who tease each other for playing with the "wrong" group, and by parents, who encourage like-gender play groups. Besides these gender differences, researchers report few if any other social-emotional or personality differences.

What can we conclude about gender differences?

In general, studies on gender differences tell us that relatively few exist and that those that have been identified are relatively minor. More important, these studies provide little justification for many existing stereotypes that boys and girls, men and women, think and behave as they do because of inherited differences in abilities (Hogrebe, 1987).

As these children grow up, will they show differences based on gender?

Next we'll examine a tragic topic—child abuse—that, unfortunately, affects both genders.

APPLYING/ EXPLORING: CHILD ABUSE

What 10-year-old Karen remembered most about her mother was all the beatings. Her mother would get angry over the tiniest thing, grab something handy, and start hitting. Karen remembered being beaten with high-heeled shoes, with her father's belt, even with a potato masher. When Karen was 8, her mother beat her so hard that Karen's legs turned black and blue. Karen hurt so bad that she threatened her mother with telling the police. Her mother replied in an angry voice, "Go ahead. They won't believe you and they'll put you in the darkest prison." (adapted from *Time*, September 5, 1983)

Similar to Karen's experience, an estimated 500,000 children are physically abused each year in the United States (National Center on Child Abuse and Neglect, 1988). **Child abuse** *includes inadequate care, neglect, or acts of the parent that put the child in danger or that cause physical harm or in-* jury *or involve sexual molestation.* We'll focus on three questions: Why do parents abuse their children? Are some children more likely to be abused? What are the treatments for child abuse?

This self-portrait was drawn by an abused child.

Why do some parents abuse their children? Being abused or maltreated as a child does put an individual at risk for becoming an abusive parent. However, rather than the 90% figure often reported in the popular press, Joan Kaufman and Edward Zigler (1989) conclude that about 30% of abused children actually become abusive parents. Thus, although an abused child is at risk for becoming an abusive parent, a number of *compensatory factors* can prevent the abused child from repeating the abuse when he or she becomes a parent. Some of these factors include having a history of positive attachment to a caregiver, resolving not to repeat the abuse, having an awareness of one's early abusive experiences, experiencing fewer stressful live events than the abusive parents did, and having a supportive spouse or good social supports (Kaufman & Zigler, 1989).

The path from being abused to becoming an abusive parent is neither direct nor inevitable and can be reversed by these compensatory factors.

Abusive parents are likely to have a wide range of personal and caregiving problems. Parents who abuse are more likely to be young, poorly educated, and socially isolated and to have serious marital problems and numerous life stresses. Because they have few friends or healthy social contacts, abusive parents have few good role models or the social-emotional support needed to deal with multiple life stresses. Sometimes child abuse is only one symptom of a violent family pattern, which may also include violent interactions between husband and wife (Parke & Salby, 1983). In addition, researchers found that abusive mothers had a number of specific problems involving caregiving: they did not know how to develop social relationships, did not understand how to meet a child's needs, and had no knowledge of what it meant to be a good caregiver (Pianta, Egeland, & Erickson, 1989). Thus, abusive parents must deal with these multiple personal, social, and caregiving problems.

Parent-Child Interactions

Are some children more likely to be abused? Just as certain personal, social, and caregiving problems increase the risk for parents to become abusers, certain physical and psychological characteristics of children place them at risk for being abused. Researchers found that infants are at risk for abuse if they have a difficult temperament (are fussy, irritable, or dependent), have a serious illness during the first year, have a mental or physical handicap, or are generally difficult to care for and provide few rewards for the parent (Pianta, Egeland, & Erickson, 1989). Thus, some children have characteristics that may elicit maltreatment from parents who would not abuse otherwise normal children.

However, an infant's or child's characteristics alone rarely result in maltreatment. Rather, maltreatment results from the interactions between the child's characteristics and those of his or her parent. Parent-child interactions involve the **principle of bidirectionality,** *which says that a child's behaviors influence how his or her parents respond, and in turn the parents' behaviors influence how the child responds* (Maccoby, 1984).

Physically abused children have more depressed symptoms, lower self-esteem, and greater hopelessness about the future than do nonabused children (Allen & Tarnowski, 1989).

Researchers emphasize that child abuse results from an interaction between the child's problematic traits, which may elicit maltreatment, and the parents' social-emotional and caregiving problems, which make it difficult for parents to meet their child's needs (Pianta, Egeland, & Erickson, 1989). Thus, one goal of treatment for child abuse is to change parent-child interactions from negative to positive experiences.

Treatment Approaches

What are the treatments for child abuse? A number of therapeutic programs, which use some combination of personal therapy and behavioral modification, have proven relatively successful in decreasing child abuse (Azar & Siegel, 1990; Olds & Henderson, 1989). In general, treatment for child abuse involves at least two goals.

1. Overcoming the parent's personal problems. Abusive parents need help in learning about and developing social relationships, which lead to positive parent-child attachment. Abusive parents also need training in caregiving, which involves learning how to meet the physical, social, and emotional needs of their children. Dealing with personal problems, some of which may result from the parent's own abuse as a child, usually requires long-term professional therapy.

2. Changing parent-child interactions. Abusive parents need to learn more positive ways of interacting with their children. Researchers have found that abusive parents are less likely to use behaviors such as smiling, praising, and touching and are more likely to use behaviors such as threatening, disapproving, and showing anger (Reid, Taplin, & Lorber, 1981). Behavior modification techniques, discussed in Module 12, have been used to help parents learn to reduce the negative interactions (Azar & Siegel, 1990). This form of treatment includes helping the parent identify specific situations that trigger abuse, modeling how to reward appropriate behaviors, using time-out periods instead of physical punishment and threats, and learning how to settle problems and arguments through negotiation rather than violence.

Many social agencies offer free services to those in need of counseling and help. There is also a free National Child Abuse Hotline number: 800-422-4453.

Summary/Self-Test

1. How a person gains an understanding of the world through experience and learning is called _____ development.

2. The work of biologist and psychologist (a)_____ led to the current view that children participate in their own cognitive development by active involvement. He believed they do so by two processes. The process of incorporating new information or experience into existing knowledge is called (b)_____. The change that occurs in one's knowledge or experiences as a result of assimilating some new information is called (c)_____.

3. Piaget divided cognitive development into four stages. In the first, lasting from birth to about age 2, infants interact with and learn about their environments by relating their sensory experiences to their motor actions; this is called the (a)_____ stage. A significant development of this stage is the concept that objects or events continue to exist even if they cannot be heard, touched, or seen; this is called (b)_____. In the second stage, lasting from about age 2 to age 7, children learn to use symbols to think about things that are not present and to help them solve simple problems; this is the (c)_____ stage. A limitation in this stage is the tendency to think of the world only from one's own viewpoint, called (d)_____ thinking. The third stage, which lasts from about ages 7 to 11, is called the (e)_____ stage. During this stage, children can perform a number of logical mental operations on concrete objects (ones that are physically present). These mental operations include the ability to classify objects according to some dimension, such as height or length, and being able to

figure out relationships between objects, such as larger and smaller. The idea that the amount of a substance remains the same even in different shapes, known as (f)_____, is mastered during the third stage. During the fourth and last stage, which lasts from about age 12 through adulthood, one develops the ability to think about and solve abstract problems logically; this is called the (g)_____ stage.

4. Each of Piaget's cognitive stages is thought to be qualitatively different from the previous one, because each new stage represents the development of some new _____ ability.

5. There are two hallmarks of Piaget's theory. The first is that children go through four (a)_____, during which they develop qualitatively different ways of thinking and reasoning. A second hallmark is that children are actively involved in their own cognitive development through the two processes of (b)_____ and _____.

■ *Why does a 1-year-old child like playing the game of peek-a-boo, but a 7-year-old thinks the game is silly?*

6. How a person develops social relationships, develops a sense of self, and becomes a social being is called (a)_____ development. Three theories of such development each emphasize a different aspect. According to Freud, a person goes through five developmental periods, called (b)_____ stages, during which the primary goal is to satisfy innate biological needs. In contrast, Erikson divided development into eight developmental periods in which the primary goal is to satisfy inborn social needs; he called these (c)_____ stages. Bandura emphasizes the importance of learning through imitation, observation, and reinforcement; this is called (d)_____ theory.

7. The first four of Erikson's eight stages involve the resolution of a potential social problem between the child and his or her environment. In stage 1, the infant deals with resolving issues surrounding trust versus (a)_____. In stage 2, the toddler must resolve issues surrounding autonomy versus shame and (b)_____. In stage 3, the younger child deals with issues of initiative versus (c)_____. In stage 4, the older child deals with issues that involve industry versus (d)_____.

■ *A father who is going through a divorce is worried about the effects on his 3-year-old son. What would Freud and Erikson say about this situation?*

VULNERABILITY AND RESILIENCY

8. Psychological or environmental difficulties may put children more at risk for later personality, behavioral, or social problems; these are a measure of the child's (a)_____. Certain factors, such as dispositional traits, family factors, and outside emotional support, contribute to the child's (b)_____ and may compensate for life stresses so that problems do not develop later.

■ *We sometimes hear about an individual who overcame tremendous hardships as a child and developed into a mature and responsible adult. How might this happen?*

GENDER ROLE DEVELOPMENT

9. Expectations of how we should think or behave because we are male or female are called (a)_____. One theory says that these roles develop because parents or caregivers expect, treat, and reward different kinds of behaviors depending on the child's sex; this is the (b)_____ theory. Another theory says that children learn male or female rules through active involvement with their environments; this is the (c)_____ theory. This theory includes the idea that there are sets of information and rules that are organized around how either a male or female should think and behave; these rules are called (d)_____.

10. Over the years modifications have occurred in the definitions of femininity and masculinity. The newer definition says that the same individual might have both traits that have been tradi-

tionally thought of as female and those that have been traditionally thought of as male, a situation termed _____.

■ *Suppose a mother and father make a deliberate attempt to eliminate gender differences in raising their fraternal twins, a boy and girl. Do you think the boy and girl will develop gender roles?*

CULTURAL DIVERSITY: GENDER ROLES AROUND THE WORLD

11. Although children's perceptions of gender roles show some variation across countries and cultures, it appears that their _____ of gender roles develops in a generally similar way at similar times.

■ *Why do you think that young boys and girls around the world develop relatively similar gender roles?*

APPLYING/EXPLORING: CHILD ABUSE

12. Inadequate care, neglect, or acts of the parent that put the child in danger or that cause physical harm or injury or involve sexual molestation is a definition of (a)_____. Parents who were abused as children are at (b)_____ for abusing their own children. According to the principle of (c)_____, the child's behaviors influence how the parents respond and the parents' behaviors influence how the child responds. Two goals of treatment to stop or prevent child abuse are to help parents overcome their personal problems and to change parent-child interactions from negative to positive.

■ *If one were abused as a child, what kinds of problems might one face as a parent?*

Answers: 1. cognitive; 2. (a) Jean Piaget, (b) assimilation, (c) accommodation; 3. (a) sensorimotor, (b) object permanence, (c) preoperational, (d) egocentric, (e) concrete operations, (f) conservation, (g) formal operations; 4. reasoning or thinking; 5. (a) stages, (b) assimilation, accommodation; 6. (a) social, (b) psychosexual, (c) psychosocial, (d) social cognitive; 7. (a) mistrust, (b) doubt, (c) guilt, (d) inferiority; 8. (a) vulnerability, (b) resiliency; 9. (a) gender roles, (b) social learning, (c) cognitive developmental, (d) gender schemas; 10. androgyny; 11. knowledge; 12. (a) child abuse, (b) risk, (c) bidirectionality.

Chapter *Eleven*
ADOLESCENCE AND ADULTHOOD

MODULE 21
ADOLESCENCE

"I will eventually become President. In 2017. I think. I've figured it out. I don't want people to think, 'She's just a kid. She doesn't know what's ahead of her.' I know the presidency will not come easy to me. I'm black, first of all, and I'm a woman. I want to be a lawyer, then work my way up in politics, become like mayor, then senator, then governor . . .

"I know people will look into my past and say, 'Years ago, she did this, she did that, blah, blah blah.' The worst thing I've ever done is to steal two little 5-cent Bazooka gums from a 7-Eleven when I was 9. I don't think they'll count that against me . . .

"Sometimes people just expect me to make trouble because I'm 'one of the black kids.' Do not label me as anything. Label me as individual . . .

What are my plans?

Branndi is a 12-year-old adolescent with great plans for the future.

"I want everyone to know that some 12-year-olds really do think seriously about the future. I want to be a role model. I'm glad I was born black. I want to tell others, 'Stay in there because you can do just as much good as any other person.'"

Besides talking like a philosopher, Branndi is a fun-loving adolescent who likes rap music, hanging out at the mall with her friends, and movies like *House Party 2.* She is an above-average student, likes to write fairy tales for children, and sings in the youth choir at the neighborhood church. (*Los Angeles Times*, December 22, 1991, pp. E-1, E-12)

At age 12, Branndi is just beginning adolescence. **Adolescence** *is a developmental period, lasting from about ages 12 to 18, that marks the end of childhood and the beginning of adulthood; it is a transitional period of considerable biological, cognitive, and social changes.* While it is true that adolescents go through remarkable changes, experts now believe that adolescence is not necessarily marked by great psychological turmoil. For instance, about the same percentage (10% to 20%) of adolescents experience severe emotional problems as adults do. Researchers are no longer searching for what should occur (great emotional problems) but rather are studying what actually occurs: how adolescents change, adapt, and grow (Powers, Hauser, & Kilner, 1989). In this module we'll use Branndi as an example of how teenagers change.

What's Coming
This module discusses the biological, social, and cognitive changes that occur during adolescence. The next module focuses on the changes that occur during adulthood and aging.

Let's begin with the most significant biological change that Branndi is experiencing—puberty.

Biological Changes: Puberty

What's happening to my body?

Puberty *refers to the biological changes, such as sexual maturity and body growth, that occur during adolescence.* The sequence of changes is similar across all cultures. On this page and the next, we'll outline the major biological and physical changes that occur during puberty. These changes begin at about age 9 for girls and age 10 for boys and continue through age 17.

Girls During Puberty

Why was I taller than the boys in junior high school?

Girls experience three major biological and physical changes during puberty.

1 A major physical change is a surge in *physical growth,* marked by an increase in height that starts on average at 9.6 years. This growth spurt begins about 6 to 12 months before the onset of breast development.

2 A major biological change is the development of *female sexual maturity,* which primarily involves the onset of menarche. **Menarche** *is the first menstrual period; it is a signal that ovulation may have occurred and that the girl may have the potential to conceive and bear a child.* In the United States, menarche occurs on average at 12.5 years, about 2.5 years after the beginning of breast development. For reasons of diet, exercise, and genes, age of menarche varies with society and country.

The onset of menarche is triggered by an area of the brain called the the *hypothalamus,* which stimulates the pituitary to produce hormones that travel throughout the bloodstream. These hormones stimulate the ovaries to greatly increase production of female hormones. **Estrogen,** *one of the major female hormones, shows up to an eightfold increase and stimulates development of both primary and secondary sexual characteristics.*

3 Estrogen stimulates the development of **female secondary sexual characteristics,** *which include growth of pubic hair and development of breasts.* On average, the onset of secondary sexual characteristics begins at 10.5 years (the range is from age 9 to age 18) and continues for about 4.5 years.

Normally, girls experience the biological and physical changes of puberty about 2 years earlier than boys (at 10.5 versus 12.5 years).

Early Versus Late Maturing. Girls who go through puberty early (often called early maturing) do not have the psychological or social advantages that have been reported for adolescent boys. Early-maturing girls may be more shy and introverted, rate lower on social skills, and tend to be less involved in social activities than their later-maturing classmates (Siegel, 1982). The psychological differences between early- and late-maturing girls do, however, decrease with age.

Sexual Behavior

In 1990 the Centers for Disease Control (CDC) in Atlanta surveyed the sexual behavior of over 11,000 American high school students (grades 9–12). Adolescents of both sexes reported that much of the pressure to become sexually active comes from peers.

Boys During Puberty

Why did my voice crack during adolescence?

Boys experience three major biological and physical changes during puberty, beginning at about age 10.

1 A major biological change is the development of *male sexual maturity,* which includes growth of the genital organs—testes and penis—and production of sperm. The onset of genital growth begins at around 11.5 years (the range is from age 9 to age 16) and continues for approximately 3 years. The production and release of sperm begins between 12 and 14 years of age.

The increase in genital growth and production of sperm is triggered by the hypothalamus, which stimulates the male pituitary gland. The pituitary in turn triggers the testes to increase production of testosterone—up to an eighteenfold increase. **Testosterone,** *which is the major male hormone, stimulates growth of genital organs and development of secondary sexual characteristics.*

2 Testosterone triggers the development of **male secondary sexual characteristics,** *which include the growth of pubic hair, development of muscles, and a change in voice.* These changes usually occur between 12 and 16 years of age, but there is a wide range in their development.

3 A major physical change is a spurt in physical growth, especially height, generally at 13 to 14 years of age.

Boys tend to lag about two years behind girls in experiencing the biological and physical changes associated with puberty.

Early Versus Late Maturing. Generally, boys who go through puberty later (late maturing) are found to be lacking in self-confidence and self-esteem and to be anxious and tense, more dependent on their parents, and less highly regarded by peers. In comparison, boys who go through puberty earlier (early maturing) are found to be more confident, relaxed, and socially responsible, and they are more popular and highly regarded by their peers. However, when researchers followed early- and late-maturing boys into their 30s, many of the earlier differences simply disappeared (Siegel, 1982).

Girls. According to the CDC survey, 48% of high school girls reported having had sexual intercourse (*Los Angeles Times,* January 4, 1992). About half of these sexually active girls reported not using contraceptives.

In 1989 the birth rate for teenage mothers reached its highest level in 15 years. Among girls ages 15 to 17, 36.5 out of every 1,000 had a baby (*USA Today,* December 13–15, 1991). This increase in birth rate is consistent with reports that teenage girls are more sexually active today than in the past.

Boys. Among high school boys, 61% reported having had sexual intercourse. Black students reported higher rates (72%) than whites (52%) or Hispanics (53%). Of the male teens who are sexually active, generally about half report not using contraceptives during their first intercourse. In addition, a relatively high percentage of teen males are estimated to continue the practice of not using contraceptives during sexual intercourse (Brooks-Gunn & Furstenberg, 1989).

The lack of responsible contraceptive use among sexually active teenagers contributes to two major problems: the transmission of sexually transmitted diseases, including AIDS, and the growing percentage of births among unwed teenage girls. Both of these problems have persuaded a number of high schools to either consider opening or actually open on-site health clinics, which counsel and distribute contraceptives in addition to the other services they provide.

Sex Information. A primary source of information about sex, relationships, and contraceptives is parents. However, surveys of over 8,000 teenagers during the past dozen years reveal that fewer than 15% received meaningful sex education from their parents (Gordon, 1986). For this reason, many psychologists, educators, and public health professionals point out the need for parent-teen communication about the issues surrounding sex and relationships. In addition, many elementary schools and the majority of high schools have now instituted programs on sex education (Hofferth & Hayes, 1987).

Along with biological and physical changes during puberty, adolescents are faced with a number of personality, social, and cognitive changes and moral dilemmas. Let's begin with how teenagers discover their identities.

Personality and Social Development

Who am I?

We began this module with Branndi's description of herself. She said that she likes being black, dislikes being labeled, thinks everyone can accomplish something good, and hopes someday to become a lawyer, a city mayor, and then president of the United States. The process that Branndi is going through in finding her identity, fulfilling her hopes, and realizing her dreams is part of personality and social development.

A challenge for all adolescents is finding an **identity** or **self**, *which is how one describes oneself and includes one's values, goals, traits, interests, and motivations.* In general, girls achieve developmental milestones, such as finding an identity, earlier than boys, a difference that declines with age (Cohn, 1991). How adolescents develop their identities involves one of Erikson's psychosocial stages.

Branndi is discovering her identity during adolescence.

Erikson's Psychosocial Stage 5

As you may recall from Module 20, Erik Erikson (1982) proposed that, across our life span, we proceed through eight *psychosocial stages,* each of which presents a particular kind of problem. What is significant about each stage is how we resolve the psychosocial problem. According to Erikson, being successful in resolving the problem leads to developing a healthy personality or social trait. Conversely, being unsuccessful in resolving the problem leads to developing an unhealthy personality or social trait that may lead to future personality problems. Of Erikson's eight stages, stage 5, which involves finding one's identity, is characteristic of adolescence.

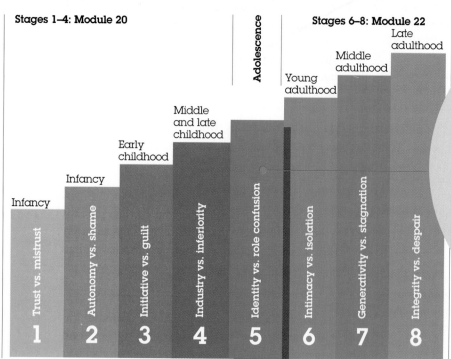

Stages 1–4: Module 20

Stages 6–8: Module 22

Adolescence

- Infancy — 1 Trust vs. mistrust
- Infancy — 2 Autonomy vs. shame
- Early childhood — 3 Initiative vs. guilt
- Middle and late childhood — 4 Industry vs. inferiority
- Adolescence — 5 Identity vs. role confusion
- Young adulthood — 6 Intimacy vs. isolation
- Middle adulthood — 7 Generativity vs. stagnation
- Late adulthood — 8 Integrity vs. despair

Stage 5: Identity Versus Role Confusion
Period: Adolescence
Potential problem: Adolescents need to leave behind the carefree, irresponsible, and impulsive behaviors of childhood and develop the more purposeful, planned, and responsible behaviors of adulthood. If adolescents successfully resolve this problem, they will develop a sense of confidence and a positive, healthy identity. With a positive identity, they can function in ways that benefit themselves and society. On the other hand, if they are unsuccessful in resolving the problem, they will experience *identity confusion,* which results in their having low self-esteem. They may then become unstable or socially withdrawn.

The process of finding one's identity continues through adolescence and into adulthood. Many factors influence identity development, including being exposed to varying and even conflicting values; receiving both positive and negative feedback from peers, parents, and siblings; and having to deal with many kinds of social interactions.

To illustrate the development of identity, we'll focus on one component of self—self-esteem.

Patterns of Self-Esteem

Self-esteem *is how much one likes oneself and includes feelings of worth, attractiveness, and social competence.* In adolescents, self-esteem is greatly influenced by two factors: physical appearance, which is especially important for girls, and acceptance by one's peers, which is a measure of popularity (Harter, 1990). During adolescence, dramatic changes can occur in self-esteem. For example, in one study, self-esteem was assessed in 128 adolescent boys and girls at the beginning, middle, and end of junior high (grades 6 through 9). In this and other longitudinal studies, researchers identified three patterns of how self-esteem develops (Bower, 1991; Harter, 1990; Hirsch & Dubios, 1991):

1 A large percentage (60%–65%) of adolescents *maintain a strong sense of self-esteem or show a small increase in self-esteem* through junior high. These individuals do well in school, develop rewarding friendships, and participate in social activities.

2 A small percentage (10%–15%) of adolescents have a *chronically low self-esteem* that continues through junior high school. Researchers believed that the personal and social problems that contribute to this low self-esteem have been present for some time.

3 A slightly larger percentage (20%–25%) of adolescents may show dramatic *reversals in self-esteem*, especially from high to low. The researchers hypothesized that one reason for this decrease in self-esteem may relate to the kind of support and discipline used by parents, which we'll discuss later in this module. It is encouraging to note that many adolescent boys and girls who show lowered self-esteem during adolescence recover to a higher level of self-esteem during their early adult years.

Appearance and popularity greatly influence self-esteem in adolescents.

Researchers also found a *gender difference* in levels of self-esteem, with girls more likely to report lower self-esteem during adolescence. Some of the reasons that girls have lower levels are greater concerns than boys about personal appearance, more dissatisfaction with their weight, more problems associated with becoming sexually mature, less confidence in their academic abilities, and fewer aspirations to professional careers (Bower, 1991). Thus, maintaining or achieving high levels of self-esteem is more difficult for adolescent girls than for boys.

Conclusions. Adolescence is a time when a girl or boy becomes intent on discovering her or his identity, a process that continues into early adulthood. Adolescents are likely to experience conflicting values, contradictory goals, and both positive and negative feedback. Adolescents who develop a negative identity and low level of self-esteem may have problems later on, such as eating disorders in females and delinquency in males (Harter, 1990). On the other hand, adolescents who develop a positive identity and high level of self-esteem are likely to continue as mentally healthy adults who achieve their goals.

One reason adolescence is a time for making great strides in developing identity is the simultaneous development of abstract cognitive processes. Next we'll focus on cognitive changes during adolescence and indicate how they promote development of identity.

Cognitive Changes

For Branndi, adolescence marks the beginning of a new kind of thinking.

Why is my head spinning with new ideas?
"I don't believe in the Pledge of Allegiance. I don't say it because they're telling a lie—'liberty and justice for all.' . . . My first step into politics will be mayor. I write lots of letters to Tom Bradley [mayor of Los Angeles] about things like animal rights. But he just sent me, you know, one of those typed things. I don't think it's right . . . I'm very outspoken. I worry about things—sex, rape, and stuff like that. . . . I believe in God. I believe God let's awful things happen to teach us a lesson. . . ." (*Los Angeles Times*, December 22, 1991, p. E-13)

After reading Branndi's words, you will agree that she is wonderfully outspoken and holds strong opinions on issues both concrete and abstract. During adolescence, one of the most significant changes in cognitive development is the ability to think about abstract issues, such as liberty and justice. Twelve-year-old Branndi's reasoning indicates that she is entering Piaget's fourth cognitive stage.

Piaget's Cognitive Stages

Piaget hypothesized that cognitive development occurs in four distinct stages. Each *cognitive stage* is thought to be qualitatively different from and more advanced than the previous one because each stage represents the development of some new reasoning or thinking ability. Although we discussed all four stages in Module 20, we'll return to stage 4 here because it is so relevant to adolescent thinking.

Stages 1–3: Module 20

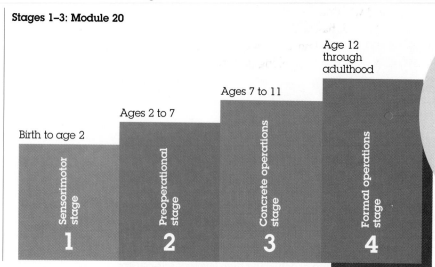

Birth to age 2 — **Sensorimotor stage 1**

Ages 2 to 7 — **Preoperational stage 2**

Ages 7 to 11 — **Concrete operations stage 3**

Age 12 through adulthood — **Formal operations stage 4**

Stage 4: Formal Operations
The formal operations stage, the last of Piaget's four cognitive stages, extends from about age 12 through adulthood. During this stage, adolescents and adults develop the abilities to think about hypothetical concepts, to consider an issue from another's viewpoint, and to solve abstract problems in a logical manner.

The Importance of Formal Operations

One reason adolescents can think about and discuss abstract concepts such as liberty, animal rights, and God is that they have entered the stage of formal operations. **Formal operations** *include the abilities to think about abstract concepts, to consider issues from another's viewpoint, and to solve abstract problems.* As the newly developed thinking abilities of formal operations take hold, adolescents are able to reflect on and critically consider their beliefs, attitudes, values, and goals. For instance, adolescents' top five concerns, listed here, indicate their wide range of interests.

The same cognitive changes that open the adolescent's mind to new worlds of ideas, values, and insights also bring about changes in his or her personal and social worlds. Specifically, we'll discuss how the ability to think abstractly affects how adolescents describe themselves and plan for the future and how the ability to take another's viewpoint affects social interactions. So that you can appreciate the style of adolescent thinking, we'll use examples written by high school students.

Taking Another's Viewpoint

Marcy: "My father is just about the most important person in my life. I may not act so appreciative of him all the time, but I really am. I can confide in him completely and tell him things not too many teenagers can tell their parents." (*Los Angeles Times Magazine,* May 31, 1987, p. 19)

Marcy has developed the capacity to consider her father's viewpoint, whereas a child who is totally self-centered would not. The ability to take another's viewpoint is characteristic of formal operational thinking. Because of this ability, adolescent-parent interactions become more give-and-take, involving more discussion and more mutual sharing (Paikoff & Brooks-Gunn, 1991). However, adolescent thinking still reflects a high degree of self-concern, or egocentric thinking.

Using Egocentric Thinking

Stephanie: "Slowly but surely, we start talking about how the previous week has been. We'll usually discuss the hardships and struggles first. Annoyances such as a fight with someone I care a lot about, or being completely ignored by someone that I am attracted to." (*Los Angeles Times Magazine,* May 31, 1987, pp. 37–38)

Stephanie's intense concern with every aspect of her daily life is one example of egocentric thinking. **Adolescent egocentric thinking** *is the belief that everyone is as totally preoccupied with the adolescent's appearance, thoughts, and feelings as he or she is and the belief that he or she is invincible* (Elkind, 1978). Because they are so preoccupied with their own concerns, adolescents feel as if they are under a harsh spotlight that points out all their flaws. One result of adolescent egocentric thinking is to exaggerate all these concerns, which can lead to problems. Thinking they are invincible, adolescents may take life-threatening risks, such as drinking and driving, being reckless and showing off, or attempting suicide.

Thinking Abstractly

Richard: "It's scary to think that I'll be out on my own in the real world very soon. I am just a kid trying to survive in high school, get good grades, have fun, and still stay a gentleman. I've got problems just like the next person, and I don't expect all of my questions to be answered." (*Los Angeles Times Magazine,* May 31, 1987, p. 38)

Richard's ability to look at himself differently arises from a new capacity to think abstractly, which is characteristic of formal operations. With the development of *abstract thinking,* adolescents' descriptions of themselves shift from the concrete, such as things they are doing, to the more abstract, such as their feelings and psychological states (Harter, 1990). For example, adolescents often describe themselves in abstract terms, such as being friendly, making mistakes, and hurting people. Thus, being able to think abstractly gives adolescents a new way of looking at and describing themselves.

Planning for the Future

Jessica: "This year has been the most difficult of my life. I still haven't decided what I'm going to do with my future, and graduation is just three months away. I always wanted to go to the university, so that's what I'm going to do . . ." (*Los Angeles Times Magazine,* May 31, 1987, p. 37)

Jessica's decision to go to college is an example of planning for the future, which is characteristic of formal operational thinking. Adolescents think about and make plans for their careers, lifestyles, relationships, and families. In thinking about their futures, boys tend to be more optimistic and girls more pessimistic, because girls feel a conflict between achieving a career and having a family. For most adolescents, planning for the future extends only to what can be accomplished by age 30 (Nurmi, 1991).

The abstract and logical thinking abilities of adolescents have a direct bearing on the development of moral reasoning, our next topic.

"Jennifer Capriati turned 16 Sunday, but life recently for the millionaire tennis phenom has not been sweet. The bubbliness displayed two years ago, when she became the youngest U.S. player to turn professional, has been replaced by a business-like rebelliousness. . . . 'Am I a rebellious little kid?' she asks rhetorically. 'I'm sure I have a little of that in me like every kid. I guess that goes with growing up. Do I give my parents a tough time? Sometimes I'm tough for them; sometimes they're tough for me.'" (*USA Today,* March 30, 1991, p. C-1)

Moral Development

Would you steal to save a dying friend?

"Suppose your best friend is dying of cancer. You hear of a chemist who has just discovered a new wonder drug that could save her life. The chemist is selling the drug for $10,000, many times more than it cost him to make. You try to borrow the full amount, but can get only $5,000. You ask the chemist to sell you the drug for $5,000 and he refuses. Later that night, you break into the chemist's laboratory and steal the drug. Should you have done that?" (adapted from Kohlberg, 1969)

Did you decide that it would be all right to steal the drug to save the life of your dying friend? If you did, how did you justify your moral decision? Lawrence Kohlberg and associates (1984) presented similar dilemmas to individuals who were asked to explain their moral decisions. Based on such studies, Kohlberg developed a theory to explain moral development.

Kohlberg's Theory of Moral Reasoning

Kohlberg's theory has two distinct features. First, he classifies moral reasoning into three distinct levels—preconventional, conventional, and postconventional. Second, he suggests that everyone progresses through the levels in order, from lowest to highest. However, not everyone reaches the higher levels of moral development.

Now let's examine the three levels in more detail.

I **The preconventional level,** *which represents Kohlberg's lowest level of moral reasoning, has two stages. At stage 1, moral decisions are based primarily on fear of punishment or the need to be obedient; at stage 2, moral reasoning is guided most by satisfying one's self-interests, which may involve making bargains.* For example, individuals at stage 1 might say that you should not steal the drug because you'll be caught and go to jail. Individuals at stage 2 might say that you can steal the drug and save your best friend, but in return you'll have to give up some freedom by going to jail. Most children are at the preconventional level.

II **The conventional level,** *which represents an intermediate level of moral reasoning, also has two stages. At stage 3, moral decisions are guided most by conforming to the standards of others we value; at stage 4, moral reasoning is determined most by conforming to laws of society.* Individuals at stage 3 might say that you should steal the drug since that is what your family would expect you to do. Individuals at stage 4 might say that you should not steal the drug because of what would happen to society if everybody took what they needed. Many adolescents and adults are at this level.

III **The postconventional level,** *which represents the highest level of moral reasoning, has one stage. At stage 5, moral decisions are made after carefully thinking about all the alternatives and striking a balance between human rights and laws of society.* Individuals at stage 5 might say that one should steal the drug because life is more important than money. (Stage 6, which appeared in earlier versions of Kohlberg's theory, has been omitted in later versions because too few people had reached it.) Some, but not all, adults reach the postconventional level.

Evaluating Kohlberg's Theory

Does everyone go through all five stages in the same order?

Kohlberg hypothesized that everyone goes through the five stages in sequence. That is, you begin at stage 1 and cannot reach stage 4 without going through stages 2 and 3. To evaluate this idea, one researcher reviewed 45 studies conducted in 27 cultures. The studies used moral dilemmas similar to the one about stealing the drug, but they were adapted to the particular culture. What was the conclusion? The vast majority of these studies supported Kohlberg's assumption that individuals progress through the stages in order but that not everyone reaches the higher stages (Snarey, 1987).

How much does moral reasoning reflect actual moral behavior?

Many college students are at the higher stages of moral reasoning, yet repeated surveys indicate that a certain percentage of college students engage in blatantly immoral behaviors, such as cheating on exams. Kohlberg (1984) recognized the problem of whether moral reasoning is reflected in actual moral behavior. He concluded that the match is less than perfect but that there are moderate levels of correlation between moral reasoning and moral behavior. Thus, one serious criticism of Kohlberg's stages is that they are not necessarily reflected in an individual's moral behavior.

Are there gender differences in moral reasoning?

Psychologist Carol Gilligan has questioned whether Kohlberg's theory, which was based on research with male subjects, accurately reflects the moral reasoning of females. To study possible gender differences in moral reasoning, Gilligan presented moral dilemmas to women. Here's one such example: "Janice said, 'I didn't want to. I hadn't planned to. I was in shock when I found out.' Two weeks earlier, Janice had been told that she was pregnant. Now she was talking to a counselor about whether to have the baby or have an abortion."

Gilligan (1982) asked women who had been in Janice's situation how they had reached their moral decision about whether to continue their pregnancy or have an abortion. She discovered that in making moral decisions, women talked more about care issues, which she labeled a care orientation. A **care orientation** *is making moral decisions based on issues of caring, on avoiding hurt, on how things affect their interpersonal relationships, and on concerns for others.* In contrast, she pointed out that the subjects in Kohlberg's studies used more of a **justice orientation**, *which is making moral decisions based more on issues of law and equality.*

Lawrence Kohlberg

In studies of moral reasoning in adolescents and young adults of both sexes, Gilligan (1987) found that females tended to use more of a care orientation in making moral decisions, while males tended to use more of a justice orientation. Studies on Gilligan's care-justice distinction in moral reasoning have found it to be a consistent tendency for women and men in moral reasoning. However, studies also show that women may favor the care orientation but at times also use the justice orientation. Similarly, men may favor the justice orientation but at times use the care orientation (Boldizar, Wilson, & Deemer, 1989; Galotti, Kozberg, & Farmer, 1991). After a decade of studies, researchers report a slight gender difference in moral reasoning, with women being more care oriented and men being more justice oriented.

After the Concept/Glossary, we'll discuss how parental influences also affect cognitive, social, and moral development.

1. A period of transition between childhood and adulthood (ages 12 to 18) that involves considerable biological, cognitive, and social changes is known as _____.

2. During adolescence a number of biological and physical changes occur. These changes signal a time known as (a)_____. During this time, females experience their first menstrual cycle, which is called (b)_____.

Piaget's
Stages
Age 12
through
adulthood

? stage

4

5. Piaget hypothesized that cognitive development is made up of four distinct stages of reasoning, with each stage qualitatively different from and more advanced than the previous one. According to Piaget, adolescents are at the _____ stage, which involves the ability to think about hypothetical concepts, consider an issue from another's viewpoint, and solve abstract problems in a logical manner.

6. Thinking that is characteristic of formal operations helps adolescents describe themselves in (a)_____ terms, better understand their parents' points of (b)_____, and plan for their (c)_____.

7. The belief that everyone else is as totally preoccupied with the adolescent's appearance, thoughts, and feelings as the adolescent is and the belief that he or she is invincible are referred to as _____.

3. According to Erik Erikson, across our lifetimes we proceed through eight (a)_____, each of which presents a particular kind of personality or social problem. For adolescents, stage 5 is most relevant and involves (b)_____ versus _____.

8. The idea that moral reasoning can be classified into three distinct levels and that everyone goes through the levels in order is (a)_____ theory of moral development. The three levels of moral reasoning, which are arranged in order from lowest to highest, are (b)_____, (c)_____, and (d)_____.

Erikson's
Stages
Adolescence

? vs. ?

5

4. One's identity has many aspects. The aspect that involves how much we like ourselves and our feelings of worth, attractiveness, and social competence is called _____.

9. Carol Gilligan has proposed two orientations for making moral decisions. The one slightly favored by women is called the (a)_____ orientation, which is making moral decisions based on issues of caring and on how things affect interpersonal relationships. The one slightly favored by men is called the (b)_____ orientation, which is making moral decisions based more on issues of law and equality.

Answers: *1* adolescence; *2* (a) puberty, (b) menarche; *3.* (a) psychosocial stages, (b) identity, role confusion; *4.* self-esteem; *5.* formal operations; *6.* (a) abstract, (b) view, (c) futures; *7.* adolescent egocentric thinking; *8.* (a) Kohlberg's, (b) preconventional, (c) conventional, (d) postconventional; *9.* (a) care, (b) justice.

Styles of Parenting

How strict were your parents?

For just a minute, think about the rules your parents laid down for you as an adolescent and your response to those rules. Or, if you are a parent, think about the rules that you have laid down for your own children and how they respond to them. For instance, when teenagers were asked how they responded to their parents' rules, here's what two replied:

Ida (age 17)
"I live in a strict Italian home. Sometimes my parents are really, really great, but their rules for me are absolutely ridiculous. So I get around them. My friends will tell you I'm a good kid. I don't drink. I don't do drugs. I don't smoke. But my parents think that, if I've gone out on a Friday night and I ask to go on Saturday, too, I'm asking for the world . . . So I lie a lot. . . . A lot of people know I do this, but nobody yells at me for it because I'm a good kid, and my parents' rules are so ridiculous."

Christopher (age 18)
"My parents never make their punishments stick. Like, I'll get my Jeep taken away for a week, and I'll get it back within six hours. Why? Because my parents hate to see their kids unhappy, and I know it, so I play right into it. They'll punish me by not letting me go out, so I'll walk around the house, slam the door occasionally, this, that . . . and after a while this just plays on them, and they feel bad, and they let me out." (*Parade Magazine*, July 14, 1991, pp. 6–7. Reprinted with permission from Parade. Copyright © 1991.)

After reading these two descriptions, you can see that Ida's parents are the opposite of Christopher's. How do such different styles of parenting affect development? To answer this question, psychologist Diana Baumrind (1991) has been carrying out a longitudinal study that involves observations of parent-child and parent-adolescent interactions. She has identified a number of parenting styles, of which we'll focus on three.

1. Authoritarian parents *attempt to shape, control, and evaluate the behavior and attitudes of their children in accordance with a set standard of conduct, usually a standard that comes from religious or respected authorities.* For these parents, obedience is a virtue, and they punish and use harsh discipline to keep the adolescent in line with their rules. This parenting style seems to describe Ida's parents. Boys from authoritarian families are found to be relatively hostile, while girls are found to be relatively dependent and submissive. This description fits Ida, who admits to problems with being independent.

2. Authoritative parents *attempt to direct their children's activities in a rational and intelligent way; they are supportive, loving, and committed, encourage verbal give-and-take, and discuss their rules and policies with their children.* Authoritative parents value being expressive and independent, but are also demanding. The children of such parents tend to be competent. In addition, girls are achievement oriented and boys are friendly and cooperative.

3. Permissive parents *are less controlling and behave with a nonpunishing and accepting attitude toward their children's impulses, desires, and actions; they consult with their children about policy decisions, make few demands, and tend to use reason rather than direct power.* This parenting style seems to describe Christopher's parents. Girls with such parents are less socially assertive, and both boys and girls are less achievement minded.

How parents interact with their adolescents will influence the adolescents' sense of competence and independence.

Baumrind concludes that, in general, parents who are more demanding have adolescents with fewer behavioral problems, such as using illicit drugs or acting out. In addition, each parenting style is associated with certain kinds of adolescents. Authoritarian parents tend to have adolescents who are conforming and have low self-esteem. Authoritative parents have adolescents who tend to be competent. Permissive parents tended to have adolescents who have more autonomy and self-esteem. Thus, parenting styles have very different effects on many aspects of adolescents' development.

APPLYING/EXPLORING: TEENAGE SUICIDE

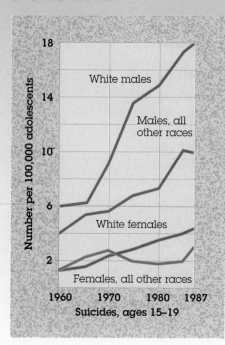

Number per 100,000 adolescents

White males

Males, all other races

White females

Females, all other races

18

14

10

6

2

1960   1970   1980   1987

Suicides, ages 15–19

What is the third leading cause of death for teenagers? Suicides for teenagers ages 15–19 quadrupled from about 2 per 100,000 in 1950 to about 10 per 100,000 in 1990. In this age group, suicide is now the third leading cause of death. Based on a survey of over 11,000 teenagers, the Centers for Disease Control estimate that about 1 million American teenagers attempted suicide during 1990 (*Los Angeles Times,* September 20, 1991). As seen in the graph on the left, white teenage boys continue to have the highest suicide rates.

We'll focus on the two most-asked questions about teenage suicide: What factors are related to teenage suicide? What steps can be taken to prevent teenage suicide? We'll use four real-life examples to illustrate how complex the causes are.

In a span of five weeks, four teenage boys committed suicide in the small southern town of Sheridan, Arkansas (adapted from *People,* May 21, 1990, pp. 56–59):

March 28, 1990
Raymond, 17 years old

According to the police chief, Ray had threatened to kill himself in the past, but the threats were considered teenage histrionics. He had a drinking problem, had been arrested for drunken driving, and had been sent to a rehabilitation center for several weeks. Prior to Ray's shooting himself, however, his life seemed to be improving, and he had made plans to go to college. A suicide note to his girlfriend said, "Don't blame yourself. It's nobody's fault."

April 30, 1990
Tommy, 16 years old

His teenage peers considered Tommy a clown, but his best friend, Rhonda, didn't believe that. She thought Tommy's clever wit and clowning were a mask for his insecurity. On April 29, Tommy called Rhonda, which he did regularly, and told her that he was going to kill himself. Certain he would not carry out his threat, she made him promise to come to school the next day. Tommy came to school, and in one of his classes he got up and stated that he had two things to say. He said that he loved Rhonda, although they had never dated. "The other thing," he said, "is this." He pulled out a pistol and shot himself.

April 30, 1990
Thomas, 19 years old

Thomas was a straight-A student who liked to read, listen to oldies, and hunt and fish. He did not drink, smoke, or swear. He lived too far out of town to have many buddies. His father had died when he was 9. Two years earlier, his grandfather, who had terminal cancer, committed suicide with a pistol to his head. Tommy Smith had shot himself in the afternoon, and that very night Thomas did the same. In his suicide note he said, "Where shall I begin? I really don't know. It's hard to say what's going on anymore. A long time now I have felt like I am on the edge and slipping fast. I guess I've finally slipped over the edge."

April 31, 1990
Jerry, 17 years old

Jerry's suicide was the last of the four and the most troubling. He was popular, gregarious, good-looking, and so deeply religious that he was nicknamed "preacher boy." The night after Tommy's suicide he told his mother, "I can't understand how anyone would commit suicide—that was the coward's way." That same night he called his girlfriend and said, "I love you. I'll talk to you tomorrow." The next day he stayed home from school, and around noon he shot himself in the head. The family insists that Jerry's death was accidental.

As will become clear, there are factors in the lives of Raymond, Tommy, Thomas, and Jerry that are representative of suicide victims in general.

What factors are related to teenage suicide? These four suicide victims illustrate many of the following major factors related to teenage suicide (de Wilde et al., 1992; Hoberman & Garfinkel, 1989; Shafii, 1989):

1 Long before committing suicide, adolescents have usually experienced various psychological problems and behavioral symptoms. The most common *psychological problems* include depression, feelings of helplessness, and drug-related problems, such as Raymond's alcohol problem. Usually these problems have persisted for some time. The most common *behavioral symptoms* include decline in school performance; social isolation and withdrawal; intense difficulties with parents, siblings, and peers; and antisocial behavior. For example, Thomas's suicide note says, "A long time now I have felt like I am on the edge and slipping fast."

2 In most cases, there are *precipitators* of suicide, such as events, feelings, or situations. Common precipitators are problems with relationships, bouts of depression, drinking, or relatively common stressors, such as dating, parents, and school. A precipitating event for Jerry may have been the earlier suicide of Tommy.

3 A high percentage of victims either *expressed the wish to die* to family or friends or made a *threat to commit suicide.* This was true for both Raymond and Tommy. The most common method of suicide for males is by gun, which was used by all four boys in our examples.

After interviewing the family and friends of suicide victims, researcher Mohammed Shafii (1989) concluded that some recent personal crisis is merely the last event in a long history of serious, chronic emotional and behavioral problems. Shafii suggests that one reason family and friends are surprised by a suicide is that the victim's problems have too long been denied, been neglected, or gone unrecognized. Recognizing signs of impending suicide is part of all prevention programs.

Sometimes the problems of one who commits suicide have been denied, neglected, or not recognized.

What steps can be taken to prevent teenage suicide?

Mary Rotheram (1987) has proposed a model to help identify those youths who may be at risk for suicide. The *at risk factors* include being male, having a history of antisocial behavior, having a close friend or family member who committed suicide, frequently using drugs and alcohol, feeling depressed, and previously attempting suicide. She considers a youth to not only be at risk but to be in *imminent danger* of committing suicide if he or she has current thoughts about or plans for suicide or exhibits five or more of the at risk factors.

If a youth is judged to be in imminent danger of committing suicide, Rotheram recommends that a counselor take the following four steps. First, the youth should be requested to make a written promise not to engage in suicidal behavior for a specified period of time, such as two weeks. Second,

since youths in imminent danger are typically unable to see anything good or positive about themselves, the counselor needs to help the youth recognize and praise his or her strengths and focus on the good things in the environment as opposed to the unpleasant things. Third, although suicide attempts frequently follow arguments or breakups, youths typically deny how upset they are at the time of such events. The counselor should help the youth recognize and assess the intensity of his or her feelings. Fourth, the counselor should help the youth make a detailed plan for the kind of help to seek when negative feelings intensify.

Rotheram asserts that these four steps have proved useful in helping many teens overcome thoughts of suicide. In addition, most large cities have community hot lines for counseling individuals who are thinking about committing suicide.

Summary/Self-Test

BIOLOGICAL CHANGES: PUBERTY

1. The transitional developmental period of considerable biological, cognitive, and social changes that lasts from about age 12 to 18 and marks the end of childhood and the beginning of adulthood is called _____. Although it is true that young people go through remarkable changes during this time, experts now believe that this period is not necessarily marked by great psychological turmoil.

2. The biological and physical changes that occur during adolescence are a part of going through a period called (a)_____. These changes occur in similar sequence across all cultures. During this period, girls and boys experience three major biological and physical changes; the changes for girls tend to start about two years earlier than those for boys. For both girls and boys, one of these changes is the development of (b)_____ maturity. For girls, this includes the first menstrual cycle, called (c)_____; this is a signal that (d)_____ may have occurred and that the girl has the potential to become pregnant. For boys, it includes the production of sperm. These changes in girls and boys are controlled by a portion of the brain called the (e)_____. A second change is the development of (f)_____ sexual characteristics. A third change is a surge in (g)_____ growth, especially height.

3. The lack of responsible contraceptive use among sexually active teenagers has led to the transmission of _____, including AIDS, and a rise in teenage pregnancy.

■ *Imagine that you are the parent of a young teenager. What advice would you give about getting through puberty?*

PERSONALITY AND SOCIAL DEVELOPMENT

4. How you describe yourself, including your values, goals, traits, interests, and motivations, is a function of your sense of your (a)_____, which is part of the problem to be faced in stage 5 of Erikson's eight (b)_____ stages. One

who is unsuccessful in resolving the problems of this stage will experience (c)_____, which results in low self-esteem and may make one socially withdrawn.

5. How much you like yourself is a function of your _____, which includes your feelings of worth, attractiveness, and social competence. In adolescents, self-esteem is influenced particularly by physical appearance and acceptance by peers.

■ *Sharon, who is 16 years old, seems to have far less self-esteem than her friend Brian, who is the same age. Why might this be so?*

COGNITIVE CHANGES

6. One of Piaget's four (a)_____ stages is particularly relevant to adolescents. This stage, in which individuals develop the ability to think about hypothetical concepts, consider an issue from someone else's perspective, and solve abstract problems, is called (b)_____.

7. The belief, shared by many adolescents, that others are as preoccupied with the adolescent's appearance as he or she is, is one aspect of _____. Another aspect of this type of thinking is the belief that the adolescent is invulnerable; this belief often leads to taking life-threatening risks, from reckless driving to suicide attempts.

■ *Suppose you caught a strange virus that totally wiped out all the reasoning abilities characteristic of formal operations. How would your life change?*

MORAL DEVELOPMENT

8. According to Kohlberg's theory, moral reasoning can be classified into three distinct levels, and everyone progresses through the levels in order; some, but not all, adults reach the highest levels. The first level, called (a)_____, has two stages. In stage 1, moral decisions are determined primarily through fear of punishment, while at stage 2 they are guided by satisfying one's self-interest. The second level, called (b)_____, also has two stages. In the first of these, stage 3, people conform to the standards of others they value; in stage 4 they conform to the laws of society. In the third level, called (c)_____, moral decisions are made after thinking about all the alternatives and striking a balance between human rights and the laws of society.

9. There seem to be gender differences in moral reasoning. Women may tend to make moral decisions based on issues of caring, on avoiding hurt, on how things affect their interpersonal relationships, and on concerns for others; this is termed the (a)_____ orientation. In contrast, men may tend to rely on issues of law and equality, called the (b)_____ orientation.

■ *Is there any reason to suspect that a female judge would hand out different sentences than a male judge?*

STYLES OF PARENTING

10. Parenting styles affect many aspects of adolescents' development. Parents who attempt to shape, control, and evaluate the behavior and attitudes of their children in accordance with a set standard of conduct, usually a standard that comes from religious or respected authorities. are termed (a)_____. Parents who attempt to direct their children's activities in a rational and intelligent way, who are supportive, loving, and committed, who encourage verbal give-and-take, and who discuss their rules and policies with their children are called (b)_____. Parents who are less controlling, who behave with a nonpunishing and accepting attitude toward their children's impulses, desires, and actions, and who tend to use reason rather than direct power are called (c)_____. In general, parents who are more demanding have adolescents with fewer behavioral problems, such as using illegal drugs or acting out.

■ *As a parent, what do you think is the best approach for disciplining teenagers?*

11. A number of factors have been found to be related to teenage suicide. Before committing suicide, adolescents usually show psychological problems such as depression, feelings of helplessness, or drug-related problems and difficulties in (a)_____, such as falling grades, social isolation and withdrawal, difficulties with family and peers, and antisocial behavior. Usually there are events that precede suicide, which are called (b)_____; these may include problems with relationships or bouts of depression or drinking.

12. One model used to identify youths who may commit suicide identifies factors that make the individual _____ for suicide, such as being male, having a history of antisocial behavior, and being depressed. A youth is considered to be in imminent danger of committing suicide if he or she has current thoughts about or plans for suicide or exhibits five or more of the at risk factors.

■ *Why do friends of suicide victims often say, "I'm really surprised. I never suspected that he would do it"?*

Answers: 1. adolescence; 2. (a) puberty, (b) sexual, (c) menarche, (d) ovulation, (e) hypothalamus, (f) secondary, (g) physical; 3. sexually transmitted diseases; 4. (a) identity or self, (b) psychosocial, (c) identity confusion; 5. self-esteem; 6. (a) cognitive, (b) formal operations; 7. adolescent egocentric thinking; 8. (a) preconventional, (b) conventional, (c) postconventional; 9. (a) care, (b) justice; 10. (a) authoritarian, (b) authoritative, (c) permissive; 11. (a) behavior, (b) precipitators; 12. at risk.

MODULE 22
ADULTHOOD

I changed a lot between being a prom queen and my 40th birthday.

What's in store for a prom queen?

I remember standing on stage in front of all the students. I was thinking "Can this really happen to me?" The next minute everyone was applauding and shouting my name, "Susan, Susan." It was my junior year of high school and I had been elected prom queen. It was like being in a fairy tale.

I cried at my high school graduation. I felt sad about leaving all my friends. At the same time I was excited about going away to college and being on my own. I considered myself a very sensible, logical, and level-headed person. So what did I do? I began seriously dating a guy who was my opposite. He was a fun-loving, kidding-around, cocky-type person. I met him in January, got engaged in February, and was married in September. What had love done to my sensible head?

As I look back over my five years of marriage, I now realize that it was okay but not great. It was great to have two wonderful children. It wasn't great to have to move a lot because of my husband's job. The worst thing was that when I was pregnant the second time, I found out that my husband was having an affair. We got divorced soon after my daughter was born. It was hard being single again. Here I was with two children and no job. How many times can you start over? Thank God my parents helped me.

And then everything got worse. My 12-year-old son developed a brain tumor. He was in and out of the hospital, suffering through surgery, chemotherapy, recovery, and relapse. Several years later, he died. How does one prepare for the death of one's child? Without help from my parents and friends, I would never have survived.

I'm almost 40 now. My daughter and I are doing pretty well. I think about getting married again. I don't know if I will. You see, I also like my independence. Come back and see me when I'm 70 and I'll tell you what happened. (adapted from Wallechinsky, 1986)

Like Susan in her youth, some of you are just beginning your adult years by going to college and preparing for your career. Some of you are already adults and have returned to college to finish degrees or perhaps start new careers. Like Susan, each of you has dreams of what you would like to achieve in the next 20 years. Susan dreamt of finishing college, getting married, and having a family, all of which she did. However, she did not figure on a divorce, having to support herself and her children, and her son's dying of a brain tumor, all before she was 40 years old. This snapshot of Susan's life illustrates some of the joys, challenges, frustrations, achievements, and stresses of adulthood.

What's Coming

In the first part of this module we'll discuss the physical changes as well as the cognitive, personality, and social changes of adulthood. In the second part we'll focus on the challenges and problems facing adults. Let's begin with a question that extends from adolescence well into adulthood: How much of me will change and how much will remain the same?

Consistency Versus Change

Each of us goes through three major developmental periods marked by significant physical, cognitive, personality, and social changes. We have already discussed two of these periods: infancy/childhood (Modules 19 and 20) and adolescence (Module 21). Now we look at the third period, adulthood. Throughout these developmental periods, researchers are interested in which things change and which ones remain the same.

As you may remember, researchers use two main methods to answer questions about change and consistency. In **longitudinal studies,** *the same group of people are tested repeatedly across many years.* For instance, the same group of adolescents would be tested at ages 15, 25, 35, and 55. In **cross-sectional studies,** *many groups of people of different ages are tested at the same time.* This means that one group of 15-year-olds, one of 25-year-olds, one of 35-year-olds, and one of 55-years-olds would all be tested at the same time. In assessing developmental changes, researchers prefer longitudinal studies because they show how the same individuals change or remain the same across time.

The Big Picture: Adolescence to Middle Adulthood

What kind of adult will I become?

One answer to this question comes from D. Eichorn (1981) and his associates, who completed a longitudinal study of 248 individuals from birth through adulthood. Their findings illustrate continuity and change between adolescence, ages 14 to 18, and middle adulthood, ages 36 to 48.

"Will I change as much as you?"

Cognition. Eichorn found a correlation between adolescent and adult IQ scores of about .80. This high correlation means that IQ scores were relatively stable across 30 years. However, about half the subjects showed as much as a 10-point increase or decrease, which indicates room for change.

Personality Traits. Subjects showed considerable consistency in certain personality traits, such as impulse control and introversion-extraversion. For example, individuals who acted impulsively or were extraverted during adolescence tended to behave that way as adults. Subjects showed considerable changes in other personality traits, such as levels of self-esteem, which indicate that some personality traits are more variable across time.

Mental Health. Males who had been responsible and intellectually competent adolescents were likely to become mentally healthy adults. Females who were intellectually competent adolescents and did not develop stereotypic feminine traits of dependency and unassertiveness were likely to become mentally healthy adults. However, the correlations between mental health in adolescence and in adulthood were only moderate, which indicates that this time period involves considerable change.

Major Concerns and Stresses. Adolescents were primarily concerned about their physical appearance, finding their identity, and sex. In contrast, adults were primarily concerned about getting married, starting a family, and reaching their career goals. Thus, concerns and stresses undergo major changes between adolescence and middle adulthood.

Longitudinal studies such as Eichorn's tell us that the passage from adolescence to middle age involves an interesting combination of consistency and change. Now that you have the big picture, we'll examine these consistencies and changes in more detail. Let's begin with some of the most obvious changes.

Physical Changes

We will all experience **normal aging**, *which is a gradual and natural slowing of our physical and psychological processes from middle through late adulthood.* In addition, some of us will experience **pathological aging**, *which may be caused by genetic defects, physiological problems, or diseases, all of which accelerate the aging process.* One goal of the study of aging, which is called *gerontology*, is to separate the causes of normal aging from those of pathological aging.

We'll examine four related questions about aging: Why do our bodies age? How does aging change our bodies? How can we slow aging? How long can we expect to live?

Why do our bodies age?

Normal aging is explained by two theories, each of which emphasizes a different mechanism (Gibbons, 1990).

Wear and Tear

According to the **wear and tear theory**, *our bodies age because of naturally occurring problems or breakdowns in the body's cells.* These cellular changes may include a build-up of waste products that interferes with the cell's functioning; a breakdown in the immune system, which destroys the body's defenses against toxic agents; or an increased number of errors in the genetic mechanism (DNA code), which interferes with cell structure and function. Briefly, according to the wear and tear theory, cells become less efficient with age and less able to repair themselves; as a result, aging occurs.

Biological Limit

According to **biological limit theory**, *our bodies age because there is a biological limit on the number of times that cells can divide and multiply; after that limit is reached, cells begin to die and aging occurs.* Although this idea was first proposed over 30 years ago, new data from humans and animals support the biological limit theory (Goldstein, 1990). Currently, researchers are working to uncover possible genetic switches that turn off a cell's ability to divide and multiply.

Researchers suggest that normal aging is likely a combination of both the wear and tear theory and the biological limit theory (Gibbons, 1990).

Facial changes occur with normal aging.

Pathological Aging

One example of pathological aging is **Alzheimer's disease,** *whose symptoms include a progressive loss of memory and cognitive abilities, deterioration in personality, inability to recognize family and close friends, and eventual death.* Alzheimer's disease, which affects 5%–15% of people over the age of 65, is now the nation's fourth major cause of death (about 100,000 people per year). A person with Alzheimer's has a life expectancy of about seven years.

Another tragic example of pathological aging is a rapid-aging syndrome called progeria. **Progeria** (pro-JER-ee-ah) *is a rare and incurable disease that causes aging at ten times the normal rate; it is apparently caused by a genetic abnormality and reduces life expectancy to about 13 years.* Progeria so aged Alicia, shown to the right, that her 11-year-old body resembled that of an 80-year-old: she was bald and wrinkled and had failing eyesight, poor hearing, trouble breathing, and poor appetite.

Researchers hope that by studying progeria, which causes rapid aging, they will find clues to mechanisms that regulate normal aging.

Alicia, only 11 years old, had a disease that aged her body at ten times the normal rate.

How does aging change our bodies?

Early adulthood. The finding that most athletes peak in their 20s indicates that this is a period of *maximum physical ability and capacity*. For example, tennis champions reach their peak at about 25 years, baseball players are best at about 27, Olympic runners at about 25, and Olympic swimmers at about 20 (Schulz & Curnow, 1988). Like most superathletes, we reach our peak physical ability in our early to middle twenties.

Middle adulthood. In our 30s and 40s, we usually gain weight, primarily because we are less active. By the late 40s, there is a slight decrease in a number of physiological responses, including heart rate, lung capacity, muscle strength, and kidney function.

Late adulthood. In our 50s and 60s, we may experience a gradual decline in height because of loss of bone, a further decrease in output of lungs and kidneys, an increase in skin wrinkles, and a deterioration in joints. Sensory organs become less sensitive, resulting in less acute vision, hearing, and taste. The heart, which is a muscle, becomes less effective at pumping blood, which may result in as much as a 35% decrease in blood flow through the coronary arteries. A general decrease occurs in both number and diameter of muscle fibers, which may explain some of the slowing in motor functions that usually accompanies old age (Stevens-Long, 1984).

Very late adulthood. In our 70s and 80s, we undergo further decreases in muscle strength, bone density, speed of nerve conduction, and output of lungs, heart, and kidneys.

How can we slow aging?

You probably know some older people who act young and some middle-aged individuals who act old. This points out the difference between **chronological age,** *which is age in years,* and **functional age,** *which is how old one acts and feels and is a combination of physical, psychological, and social factors that affect attitudes toward life, social roles, and quality of life.* The effects of chronological aging can be retarded and functional age improved if individuals eat the right foods, exercise, and involve themselves in personal and social activities (Rowe & Kahn, 1987). For example, there are three communities (in Russia, Pakistan, and Ecuador) where more inhabitants than expected live to be 100. The secret of their longevity seems to be that they eat a diet low in calories and animal fats, rarely become obese, use alcohol and tobacco in moderation, maintain a high level of physical activity and fitness, and feel actively involved and useful in their communities (Fries & Crapo, 1981).

How long can we expect to live?

For individuals born in the United States in 1990, the life expectancy is 72 years for males and 78 years and 10 months for females. Researchers estimate that even if we could eliminate most heart disease, cancer, and diabetes—major causes of death in aging adults—the life expectancy in the United States would not go much beyond 85 years old (Olshansky, Carnes, & Cassel, 1990). Thus, human life expectancy may be about 85 years, which represents both a practical limit (influenced by future ability to control diseases) and a biological limit (determined by genes and cell life) (Barinaga, 1991). The entire population of the United States will age significantly in the next few decades, as individuals 65 years and older are expected to rise from their current 12% of the population to about 20% in the year 2030.

Now let's turn to cognitive changes in adulthood.

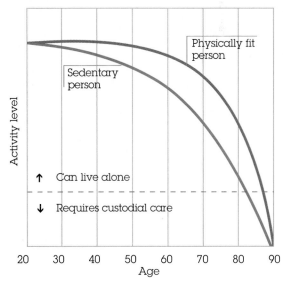

Exercise does not necessarily increase longevity, but it does improve the quality of life by helping people keep fit and independent.

Cognitive Changes

She was talking about her new autobiography, *Me: Stories of My Life,* for which she was reportedly paid $4.5 million. The "she" is well-known and former movie star Katharine Hepburn. Here's a sample of Hepburn's keen and witty 84-year-old mind.

"It's none of your business how much they paid me," she says, establishing right off the bat her renowned candor, which borders on crustiness but carries no malice. "But they paid me so much I want the book to sell, so I'm talking to you. . . .

"Women's brains are just as good as men's. They could accomplish practically everything a man could accomplish. I mean, they can write, they can paint, they can play tennis so goddamn good. . . .

"There are things I now feel I have a perfect right to do, or can do," she says, jutting out that chin as if to invite a swipe. "So I do them."

Hepburn leads a very active life that includes swimming in Long Island Sound all year round, traveling, biking, painting, writing, and talking. (adapted from *Los Angeles Times,* September 1, 1991, p. E-1)

Judging from her witty, clever, and thoughtful interview, you would have difficulty identifying problems often reported by older people, such as forgetting words, repeating things, or getting off the subject. In the past, psychologists focused more on the cognitive processes that decline with age. Currently, researchers emphasize that while some cognitive processes may decline, others grow (Adams, 1991). We'll examine both the decline and growth in cognitive processes in adulthood.

Decline in Cognitive Processes

Although Katharine Hepburn's interview indicates a generally bright, quick mind, testing her in a research setting would most likely reveal slowing in the following three cognitive processes:

Changes in Cognitive Processes

Reaction time, *which is the time required to respond to some stimulus (visual or auditory), slows with increasing age.* For instance, 20- to 29-year-old subjects were fastest in pressing a button when a light appeared, while subjects 60 and above were slowest (Wilkinson & Allison, 1989). Researchers are convinced that the decline in speed of performance in older adults results from slowing in mental processing rather than decreased motor (hand movements) or sensory abilities (Bashore, Osman, & Heffley, 1989).

Perceptual speed, *which is the time required to identify a particular sensory stimulus from many others and respond to this stimulus, decreases.* For instance, in a set period of time, subjects were given a list of words and were instructed to find and cancel (draw a line through) all words that contained the letter *a.* Twenty-five-year-old subjects canceled an average of 52 words; 67-year-old subjects cancelled 48 words, significantly fewer (Schaie, 1989). Researchers believe that slower perceptual speed in older adults results from slower encoding or retaining of information (Salthouse et al., 1990).

The ability to memorize and recall a list of words, objects, or events decreases. For example, 20-year-olds memorized and recalled significantly more words than 60-year-olds did. Older adults appear to have more difficulty in encoding or storing lists of information, as well as a greater difficulty in reliably retrieving or recalling specific information from such lists (Howe, 1988).

Now that you know which cognitive processes slow with age, let's examine those that get better.

Growth in Cognitive Processes

Research suggests that Katharine Hepburn could more easily memorize lines for a movie at age 25 but that at age 84 she is better able to discuss the meaning of life. Young adults are superior at memorizing and recalling hundreds of details, whereas mature adults are superior at interpreting the meaning and significance of information (Labouvie-Vief, 1990). This young-old difference between memorization and interpretation indicates that we process and use information in different ways at different stages in our lives.

For example, imagine that you're given a short story to read and are told that you should read it only once and will be asked questions about it later. After you have read the story, you are asked to write a summary of what you have just read. It turns out that the kind of summary you write will depend greatly on your age. Here are three story summaries from two age groups (Adams, 1991, p. 333):

Older people lose the capacity to memorize details but develop the ability to interpret information.

13-Year-Old
Once there was a stream. The stream made a journey and was stopped by a desert. When the stream tried to pass the desert it was absorbed by the sand. A voice said that the wind had to carry the stream over the desert. The stream doubted it but later agreed to let the wind carry him over. The wind carried the stream over and the stream never forgot what the voice said.

65-Year-Old
The essence of the story is that in order to accomplish one's goals, one sometimes has to sacrifice one's individuality and join forces with others moving in similar directions.

70-Year-Old
Do not be afraid to venture out of your original and present form for you will also retain your true identity.

As you compare these summaries, notice that the young person's summary essentially delineates the details of the story with no interpretation or analysis. In contrast, the older persons' summaries are relatively short, give few exact details, and essentially focus on the meaning of the story.

These different summaries illustrate different strategies in processing information between young and mature adults. Young adults excel at encoding (storing) and recalling vast amounts of details with little attempt at interpretation or analysis. On the other hand, mature adults excel at interpreting information and grasping the underlying meaning, but at the cost of sacrificing much of the detail. A *major cognitive change* is that mature adults lose much of the ability to store and recall huge amounts of detail but gain the ability to interpret information and identify its meaning.

Some have suggested that memory in mature adults might be improved with exercise. Let's see if that's true.

Exercise and Memory

Exercise improves aerobic capacity in older adults but leads to little improvement in memory.

Aging leads to declines in physical functions, such as a decrease in aerobic capacity (heart/lung output), as well as declines in psychological functions, such as storing and recalling information. Researchers hypothesized that an improvement in aerobic capacity (which would result in more oxygen to the brain) might lead to an improvement in memory. Although most studies report that exercise increases aerobic capacity 10% to 30%, few studies report corresponding increases in reaction times or in encoding or recalling information in mature adults (Clarkson-Smith & Hartley, 1989; Madden et al., 1989; Stones & Kozma, 1989). Thus, there is little support for the idea that improving aerobic capacity improves memory. However, there is much data showing that exercise/aerobic programs greatly improve physiological functioning at all stages of adulthood.

Next we'll examine the challenges and problems that most adults encounter over the life cycle.

Stages of Adulthood

We began this module with the story of Susan, who encountered a series of challenges and problems as she progressed through adulthood. Like Susan, most adults encounter challenges. These challenges can be viewed as being based in psychosocial problems or in real-life problems. According to Erikson, we have to resolve different **psychosocial problems,** *whose resolution leads to developing positive or negative personality traits.* According to Daniel Levinson, we have to solve **real-life problems,** *whose solutions lead to achieving personal happiness and reaching one's goals.*

Erikson's Psychosocial Stages

We have discussed Erikson's first five psychosocial stages in previous modules. Here we'll explain the last three stages, which deal with the challenges of adulthood.

Stage 6: Intimacy Versus Isolation	*Stage 7: Generativity Versus Stagnation*	*Stage 8: Integrity Versus Despair*
Period: Young adulthood	*Period:* Middle adulthood	*Period:* Late adulthood
Potential problem: Young adulthood is a time for finding intimacy by developing loving and meaningful relationships. On the positive side, we can find *intimacy* in caring relationships. On the negative side, without intimacy we will have a painful feeling of *isolation* and our relationships will be impersonal.	*Potential problem:* Middle adulthood is a time for helping the younger generation develop worthwhile lives. On the positive side, we can achieve *generativity* through raising our own children. If we do not have children of our own, we can achieve generativity through close relationships with children of friends or relatives. Generativity can also be achieved through mentoring at work and in helping others. On the negative side, a lack of involvement leads to a feeling of *stagnation,* of having done nothing for the younger generation.	*Potential problem:* Late adulthood is a time for reflecting on and reviewing how we met previous challenges and lived our lives. On the positive side, if we can look back and feel contented about how we lived and what we accomplished, we will have a feeling of satisfaction or *integrity.* On the negative side, if we reflect and see a series of crises, problems, and bad experiences, we will have a feeling of regret and *despair.*

Erikson's stage theory points out potential psychosocial problems across our lifetimes. If we resolve these problems in a positive way, we will likely develop healthy personality traits; if we resolve them in a negative way, we are likely to develop unhealthy personality traits. Erikson emphasized that no single stage is all important and that unresolved problems at earlier stages can be compensated for by successful resolutions at later stages.

In comparison to Erikson's stages, which emphasize psychosocial challenges, Levinson's stages focus more on real-life problems.

Levinson's Real-Life Stages

From the time Susan entered college, she faced a number of problems, such as leaving home, dating, getting married, having children, getting divorced, finding a job, and coping with the death of her son. Similar to Erikson, Daniel Levinson (1978, 1986) believes that adults pass through a series of stages, each of which presents a different problem to be solved. However, in contrast to Erikson's emphasis on psychosocial problems, Levinson's focus is on how adults deal with and solve real-life problems. Here's a summary of the stages he outlined.

Early Adult Transition (ages 17–22) The problem is to *develop a sense of independence* by separating from our family and trying out different lifestyles. This is the time when we formulate our grand dreams about what we hope to achieve.

Entering the Adult World (ages 22–28) The problem at this stage is to *explore and acquire the many adult roles* that we need to be happy and successful in our careers, relationships, and social situations.

Age-Thirty Transition (ages 28–33) The problem at this stage is to *re-evaluate earlier career choices and make decisions about our goals.* If we make the right career and goal decisions, we lay the groundwork for a productive and satisfying future.

Settling Down (ages 33–40) Here the problem is to *develop a feeling of success in the major areas of our lives,* including career, intimate relationships, and personal goals. If we reach our goals in the time we set, we will feel successful and happy.

Midlife Transition (early 40s) The problem at this stage is to *evaluate life goals and commitments,* knowing there is only a limited amount of time left to reach them. The feeling that time is running out may contribute to what is often called the midlife crisis.

Entering Middle Adulthood (middle 40s) Here the problem is to *learn to live with previous decisions,* such as by becoming more committed to one's family or career.

Conclusions and Criticisms

Both Erikson and Levinson stress the idea that adulthood involves a series of predictable stages and that personality development, happiness, and achievement hinge on how we handle the problems specific to each of the stages.

There are two major criticisms of stage theories:

1. These theories describe an average person going through an average life. They do not take into account how educational level, family and social environments, and physical and mental health may change the way we respond to challenges.

2. Because Levinson's original data came entirely from interviews with a relatively small sample of middle-aged men, his stages may not apply to all men or to all women.

In a review of relevant studies, researchers reported that women do indeed differ from men in their goals and dreams (Roberts & Newton, 1987). For example, women's goals involved both having careers and relationships, while men's goals emphasized careers. Thus, in their current form, Levinson's stages are more representative of men.

In spite of these criticisms, stage theories do provide a useful framework in which to view complex human behavior over a long span of time.

One of the major challenges faced by women and men is the development of gender roles, which we will examine next.

Elton John survived many real-life problems, including drug abuse, to reach his dream of being a successful and happy rock star.

Personality Development: Gender Roles

How can a woman win?

It is an 11-day race for survival across 1,130 frostbitten miles, mountain ranges, blizzards, and frozen seas. Only two people have won the Alaska Iditarod dogsled race four times. One is a man—Rick Swenson—and the other is a woman—Susan Butcher. The first time the men called her win a fluke. The second time the men said it was easier for a woman to win because she weighed less. The third time the men said that there should be two races, one for men and one for Susan Butcher. The fourth time some men accused her of drugging her dogs to make them go faster, a charge that showed their resentment but held no merit (*Los Angeles Times,* April 29, 1990).

Butcher's four wins elicited an enormous amount of male hostility because she had upset the difference between traditional male and female gender roles. If men are the strongest, bravest, and most daring athletes, how do you explain Susan Butcher?

As this example illustrates, many people take gender roles seriously and get upset if others stray from the traditional roles. **Gender roles** *refer to behaving in expected ways because one is male or female.* Initially established during childhood and adolescence, these roles are shaped by the expectations and pressures of parents, peers, and society. Because gender roles interrelate with mental health, relationships, achievement, and social interactions, they are closely tied to personality development. We'll discuss a number of questions about gender roles to determine what they are, how they've changed, and what advantages they might hold.

What are the traditional gender roles for adult males and females?

College students from around the world were asked to select adjectives that they associated most with female and male gender roles. Their top selections are listed below (Williams & Best, 1990).

The students agreed remarkably well on which traits are associated with gender roles. This agreement suggests that each culture exerts considerable pressure on its members to conform to gender roles.

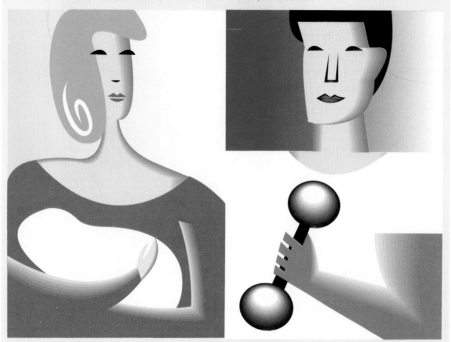

Feminine Gender Role
gentle, affectionate, weak, emotional, appreciative, excitable, softhearted, meek, submissive

Masculine Gender Role
strong, aggressive, dominant, disorderly, coarse, adventurous, independent, ambitious

By winning a man's dogsled race four times, Susan Butcher aroused a lot of resentment among traditional males. She is shown with her champion lead dog, Granite.

How much have gender roles changed in the past 20 years?
Beginning in the 1970s, the women's movement had a significant impact on career and educational opportunities, participation in politics, and family relationships. Thus, we might expect a corresponding change in gender roles. Is this borne out by research?

In 1972, researchers gave a list of 300 adjectives to 50 undergraduate men and 50 undergraduate women and asked them to indicate which adjectives best described women and which best described men. Researchers repeated the study in 1988 and compared the results of the two studies. Feminine and masculine traits selected by young adults in 1972 were quite similar (correlation .90) to those selected by young adults in 1988 (Bergen & Williams, 1991). Thus, this study indicates that traits associated with traditional gender roles have remained remarkably stable. However, what has changed is how psychologists interpret gender roles.

Personality Development: Gender Roles

Traditional Versus Contemporary View

Can I have some traits of each?

The **traditional view of gender roles** *is that masculinity and femininity represent opposite poles of a continuum.* According to this view, someone rated high on one pole has to be low on the other: you cannot possess both male and female traits because they are on opposite ends of the continuum. In contrast, the **contemporary view of gender roles** *is that masculinity and femininity are independent personality variables.* You can therefore possess both masculine and feminine traits. This contemporary view is best represented by the concept of **androgyny,** *the idea that preferred masculine and feminine traits can both be present in the same individual.* According to Sandra Bem (1985), the concept of androgyny means that we are no longer restricted to traditional masculine or feminine roles but rather are able to develop preferred traits from both gender roles. Bem assumes that being androgynous will result in increased flexibility in personal and social interactions as well as better adjustment and mental health. Let's see if her assumptions hold up.

Gender Role and Mental Health

Which role is related to better mental health?

When psychologists, psychiatrists, social workers, and college students were asked to list the traits of a mentally healthy adult, they selected traits that closely matched those of the traditional male gender role (Broverman et al., 1970; Wise & Rafferty, 1982).

Two pieces of evidence support the idea that masculine traits are associated with being mentally healthy. First, men who scored high on traditional male traits (dominant, confident, controlling) were better adjusted than men who scored low. Second, women who rated higher on masculine traits and lower on feminine traits were rated as better adjusted.

Is the male or female role associated with better mental health?

How well adjusted are androgynous men and women?
Researchers found that androgynous men and androgynous women were also rated as well adjusted (O'Heron & Orlofsky, 1990). This finding supports Bem's view that being androgynous is associated with being mentally healthy.

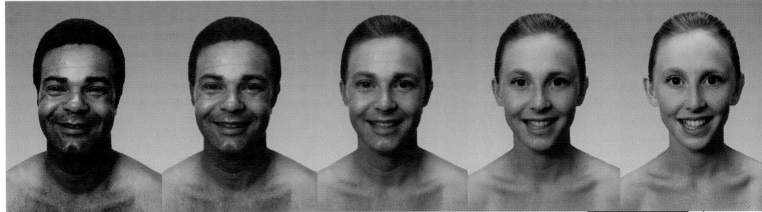

Is androgyny associated with better adjustment?

Which role is seen as having more advantages?
When college students rated the advantages and disadvantages of gender roles, both males and females rated the masculine gender role as having significantly more advantages (Fabes & Laner, 1986). One major advantage of the masculine role is that it seems more powerful and domineering, which would help in settings in which achievement is critical. However, women generally report greater satisfaction and happiness than men, which suggests that traditional feminine traits such as emotional expressiveness have advantages in other areas (Wood, Rhodes, & Whelan, 1989).

How successful are androgynous men and women?
Researchers found that androgynous men and women rated themselves high on achieving success and were rated highly by their peers in achieving success (Dimitrovsky, Singer, & Yinon, 1989). This later finding supports Bem's view that being androgynous is associated with being well adjusted.

From this discussion we can arrive at three conclusions about gender roles:

1 *Traditional masculine traits* are associated with being mentally healthy because they emphasize taking a more active part in solving life's problems. The traditional male gender role may also have advantages in achievement situations.

2 *Traditional feminine traits* may have advantages in forming intimate relationships as well as in achieving greater life satisfaction and happiness.

3 There is some evidence that being *androgynous,* which is a combination of preferred masculine and feminine traits, is associated with good mental health and achieving success.

Gender roles are important in many areas of our lives, especially love and marriage, which we'll examine next.

Social Development: Relationships

How did Susan recognize Mr. Right?

Susan was trying to explain how she fell in love with and married Charlie:

"When I went away to college, I was a very sensible, logical, and level-headed person. That's probably why the first person I dated was very much like me. We had wonderful serious talks, read poetry, discussed philosophy but never had much passion. After we broke up, a friend of mine said that she knew someone who wanted to date me. That friend was Charlie, a fun-loving, arrogant, cocky, abrasive basketball player who was my complete opposite. Well, I dated Charlie and loved his zest for life. We got engaged and about a year later we were married. Oh, yes, I knew we were complete opposites, but I thought that was great and besides, I really loved Charlie. I'm sorry to say that our marriage lasted only five years." (adapted from Wallechinsky, 1986)

Like Susan, about 90% of adults will eventually commit to long-term relationships and marry. We'll examine three questions about relationships: What does it mean to fall in love? How do we select a partner for a long-term relationship? Why do some marriages succeed and others fail?

Love

What does it mean to fall in love?

Psychologists have used a number of approaches to define and measure this magical feeling called love. One such approach is Robert Sternberg's (1986) **triangular theory of love,** *which divides love into three components: passion, intimacy, and commitment.*

Passion *is feeling physically aroused and attracted to someone.* Passion arises quickly and exerts a strong influence on one's judgment. For example, people rate their satisfaction with a first date almost entirely on the basis of physical attraction. People tend to use the passion component to make initial judgments about "being in love" with someone.

Intimacy *is feeling close and connected to someone; it develops through sharing and communicating.* Other ways of promoting intimacy include sharing one's time, self, and possessions; promoting the other person's well-being; offering emotional and material support; and touching, hugging, and being physically intimate.

Commitment *is making a pledge to nourish the feelings of love and to actively maintain the relationship.* Ways of expressing commitment include forming a serious relationship, becoming engaged, getting married, and promising support through difficult times.

Sternberg believes that the kind of love most of us strive for is **complete love,** *which is a balanced combination of all three components—intimacy, passion, and commitment.*

Now that you know something about love, let's look at marriage.

According to Robert Sternberg, love has three components: passion, commitment, and intimacy.

Sternberg uses his triangular theory of love to answer a number of commonly asked questions.

Is there love at first sight?
Love at first sight occurs when we are overwhelmed by passion, without any intimacy or commitment. Sternberg calls this **infatuated love,** *which can arise in an instant, involves a great deal of physiological arousal, and lasts varying lengths of time.* Because there is no intimacy or commitment, infatuated love is destined to fade away.

Why do some people get married after being in love for a very short time?
Sternberg calls this **Hollywood love,** *which is a combination of passion and commitment but without any intimacy.* In Hollywood love, two people make a commitment based on their passion for each other. Unless they develop intimacy over time, the relationship is likely to fail.

Why doesn't romantic love last?
Romantic love, *which is a combination of intimacy and passion,* usually doesn't last because there is no commitment. As soon as the passion dies and the intimacy fades, the individuals no longer feel "in love" and go their separate ways.

Can there be love without sex?
Sternberg calls love without sex **companionate love,** *which is a combination of intimacy and commitment without any sexual passion.* An example of companionate love is a married couple who are committed to each other and share their lives but whose physical attraction has waned.

Marriage

How do we select a partner for a long-term relationship?

The fact that about 90% of adults in the United States marry means that most of us will select a partner for a long-term relationship. However, selecting the right partner seems to be a somewhat difficult and mysterious process. Experts predict that almost one out of every two American marriages will end in divorce (*USA Today*, May 29, 1991).

One way we select our partners is by first forming a *mental list of desirable characteristics* and then looking for someone who matches our list. For instance, the list here, compiled from unmarried college students, is averaged for men and women and in order of preferences. The two primary differences between men and women are pointed out (Buss & Barnes, 1986).

Researchers concluded that college men and women form similar mental lists of desirable traits, but with two major differences: men rank physical attractiveness as more important than women do, and women rank good earning capacity higher than men do.

The dating process provides a way to decide whether someone does or does not possesse the traits on our list. If dating results in mutual agreement over traits, the couple may decide to form a long-term relationship, such as marriage.

Couples who confront conflicts head on report higher levels of marital satisfaction.

Why do some marriages succeed while others fail?

To find out why some marriages work beautifully and others fail, John Gottman and his colleagues (1989, 1991) observed and coded facial and verbal interactions in married couples. Gottman found that one key to a successful marriage is how couples handle conflicts. In successful marriages, couples confront disagreements in an open, straightforward way, often venting their anger and frustration. In marriages that fail, couples suppress conflicts and do not deal with the underlying issues. For example, wives suppress conflicts by acting agreeable and compliant with their husbands. Similarly, husbands avoid conflicts by withdrawing, not listening, and avoiding eye contact with their wives. Gottman found that suppression or avoidance of marital conflicts is a sure road to eventual marital dissatisfaction.

Other researchers report that couples in successful marriages have communication patterns that contain much positive reinforcement and little punishment (Markman, 1981). In addition, couples who can share more experiences report higher levels of marital happiness (Caspi, Herbener, & Ozer, 1992). Finally, women generally report greater satisfaction with marriage than do men (Wood, Rhodes, & Whelan, 1989).

After the Concept/Glossary, we'll see whether "love" is the number-one reason for choosing a marriage partner in all cultures.

Desirable Traits in a Marriage Partner

1 Kind and understanding

2 Exciting personality

3 Intelligent

4 Physically attractive (*more important for men*)

5 Healthy

6 Easygoing

7 Creative

8 Wants children

9 College graduate

10 Good earning capacity (*more important for women*)

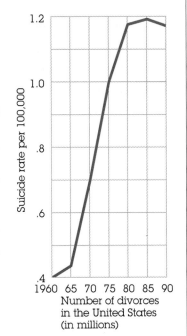

Number of divorces in the United States (in millions)

1. The natural and gradual slowing of physical and psychological processes from middle through late adulthood is called (a)_____ aging. An unnatural acceleration in the aging process caused by genetic defects, physiological problems, or diseases is called (b)_____ aging.

2. Normal aging is explained by two theories. The theory that aging occurs because cells become less efficient and less able to repair themselves is called the (a)_____ theory. The theory that aging occurs because there is a limit on the number of times that cells can divide and multiple is called the (b)_____ theory.

3. Your age calculated according to your birth date is called your (a)_____ age. Figuring your age according to how old you act and feel is called your (b)_____ age.

4. In middle and late adulthood, a decline occurs in three cognitive processes: speed required to respond to some stimulus, which is called (a)_____; speed required to identify and respond to some stimulus, which is called (b)_____; and ability to (c)_____ and _____ a list of words, objects, or events. In middle and late adulthood there is also a growth in one cognitive process, which is the ability to (d)_____ the meaning of something.

5. Two theories divide adulthood into stages. According to Erikson, we encounter a number of different (a)_____ problems, whose resolution leads to developing positive or negative personality traits. According to Levinson, we have to solve a number of different (b)_____ problems, whose solutions lead to achieving personal happiness and reaching our goals.

6. Behaving in certain ways because we are male or female is referred to as having a _____, which is shaped by the expectations and pressures of parents, peers, and society.

7. The idea that masculinity and femininity represent opposite poles of a continuum and that someone rated high on one pole has to be low on the other is the (a)_____ view of gender roles. In comparison, the idea that masculinity and femininity are independent personality variables and that someone can actually possess both masculine and feminine traits is the (b)_____ view of gender roles. This latter view is best represented by the concept of (c)_____, which means that preferred masculine and feminine traits can both be present in the same individual.

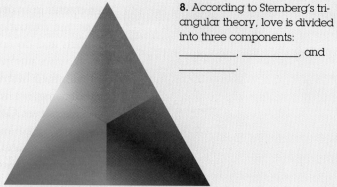

8. According to Sternberg's triangular theory, love is divided into three components: _____, _____, and _____.

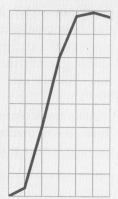

9. One way we select a partner for a long-term relationship is by first forming a mental list of _____ and then looking for someone who matches our list.

10. In successful marriages, couples confront (a)_____ in an open, straightforward way, often venting their anger and frustration, and they use a pattern of (b)_____ that contains much positive reinforcement and little punishment.

Preferences for Partners

How much does your culture influence your choice of a partner?

Imagine being born and raised in a country different from your own—perhaps Nigeria, Germany, China, Iran, Brazil, Japan, France, or India. Now imagine being asked to list, in order, those traits that you consider most desirable in a potential mate. How much would living in a different culture influence how you ordered the desirable traits? To answer this question, researchers surveyed over 9,000 young adults (males and females), all in their 20s, who lived in 33 countries (Buss et al., 1990). Subjects were given a list of 18 traits and were asked to rank them in terms of most to least desirable in a potential mate. Let's look at some of the major findings.

Gender Differences

Do the sexes rank desirable traits differently?

As shown on the right, the lists of desirable traits for males was remarkably similar to that for females. The two lists had a very high correlation of +.87.

For both males and females, the three most desirable traits were mutual attraction (love), dependable character, and emotional stability; the three least desirable were having similar political backgrounds, having similar religious backgrounds, and being chaste (no sexual intercourse). The numerous similarities of male and female lists indicate the powerful influence of culture.

There were, however, differences between the sexes. For instance, males valued physical appearance in a mate more than females did, while females valued earning potential in a mate more than males did. The few differences between males and females indicate the relatively small effects of gender on mate preferences.

1 Mutual attraction—love

2 Dependable character

3 Emotional stability and maturity

4 Pleasing disposition

5 Good health

6 Education and intelligence

7 Sociable

8 Desire for home and children

9 Refinement, neatness

10 Good looks (ranked higher by males)

11 Ambitious and industrious

12 Good cook and housekeeper

13 Good financial prospect (ranked higher by females)

14 Similar education

15 Favorable social status or rating

16 Chastity (ranked higher by males)

17 Similar religious background

18 Similar political background

Male/Female Average Ranking of Desirable Traits

Cultural Differences

Do cultures rank desirable traits differently?

Despite the many similarities among cultures on mate preferences, there were also some interesting differences. On the left are some examples of traits ranked high by different cultures.

In comparing the ranking of desirable traits for potential mates, we find that no country is exactly like another. Each country had its own unique ranking, with African and Asian cultures the most distinct. Researchers concluded that cultures do exert strong influences on the mate preferences of their members (Buss et al., 1990).

Now let's examine changes that occur in sexual behavior with aging.

Highly Ranked Traits for Potential Partners

United States: Love ranked first

Nigeria: Love ranked fourth
Ranked high: good health, refinement/neatness, desire for home and children

China: Love ranked sixth
Ranked high: good health, chastity, domestic skills

Iran: Love ranked third
Ranked high: education, intelligence, ambition, industriousness, chastity

South Africa-Zulu: Love ranked seventh
Ranked high: emotional stability and maturity, dependable character

Sexual Behavior

Does sex change after age 50?

Although a decrease in sexual responsiveness occurs with aging, this decrease need not interfere with sexual activity, provided the individual is in good health.

Women's Sexual Behavior

What are the effects of menopause?

Menopause *occurs in women at about age 50 (between 35 and 60) and involves a gradual reduction in secretion of the major female hormone (estrogen), which in turn results in cessation of both ovulation and the menstrual cycle.* During and immediately after menopause, about 75% of women experience some physical and psychological symptoms.

Older people are still sexual beings, despite popular misconceptions.

Physical Symptoms. Common physical symptoms of menopause include hot flashes, sleep disturbance, and changes in genital organs. The decrease in estrogen levels causes a thinning of the vaginal walls and reduction of lubrication, both of which may make intercourse painful. However, women experience little or no change in the ability to become sexually aroused or to reach orgasm. Potential problems that contribute to painful intercourse may be compensated for by hormone replacement therapy (taking estrogen), by using moisturizing creams, and by having a stimulating sexual partner (Leiblum & Bachmann, 1987).

According to Sandra Leiblum (1990), those women who experienced sexual activity as fulfilling and enriching before menopause will likely continue to enjoy sexual activity after menopause and into late adulthood. On the other hand, women who experienced sexual activity as just tolerable or worse before menopause may gradually discontinue sexual activity after menopause.

Psychological Symptoms. Recent studies report a more positive psychological picture of menopause than found in earlier reports, which were mostly anecdotal. For example, in a five-year longitudinal survey of 2,500 women between the ages of 45 and 55, researchers found that the majority of postmenopausal women reported feeling neutral or expressed relief from the concerns of pregnancy, contraception, and menstruation (McKinlay, McKinlay, & Brambilla, 1987).

Men's Sexual Behavior

Can a grandfather be fertile?

The male hormone testosterone continues to be produced throughout a man's lifetime. Thus, healthy men do not experience a decrease in hormone secretion comparable to what women experience during menopause. However, as men reach late adulthood (60s, 70s, and 80s) they may experience physiological changes that decrease sexual responsiveness. Although men usually have no difficulty in becoming sexually aroused or reaching orgasm, they may require more time and stimulation to do so. Some men worry that a decrease in sexual performance signals the end to their sexuality. However, such is not the case. Additional time, stimulation, and the couple's imaginative sexual activity can usually compensate for any decreases in physiological responsiveness (Masters & Johnson, 1981).

Now let's turn to the influence of careers on our lives.

Social Development: Careers

What am I going to be?

As you may remember from Daniel Levinson's (1978) theory of real-life stages, young adulthood (mid-20s) is the time for formulating a grand dream, which is the ideal job, career, or goal that we hope to reach. The mid-20s to the mid-40s is the time when people usually accomplish their dreams, unless they have decided to change their goals in midlife. We will feel happy and satisfied if we have reached our career goals, usually around our late 40s. On the other hand, we will be unhappy and dissatisfied if we did not reach our goals, did not work as hard as we should have, or found our careers less rewarding than we had hoped. These feelings of dissatisfaction may lead to a *midlife crisis,* which is a sense of failure and disappointment. Estimates are that about 10% of men change jobs during midlife crises.

What brings job satisfaction?

Most people in most kinds of jobs and careers—blue or white collar—report increasing job satisfaction as they grow older, from about age 20 through age 60 (Rhodes, 1983). There are many reasons for increasing job satisfaction, including learning to do the job better, feeling more comfortable, performing the job better, getting promotions, and gaining seniority.

Conversely, losing one's job can produce devastating effects. For example, blue- or white-collar men who had lost their jobs reported feeling anxiety and depression, missing their co-workers' friendship, missing the rewards associated with their jobs, and worrying about not fulfilling their expectations and goals (Liem & Liem, 1988).

With the increasing number of women entering the work force, researchers are studying the psychological effects of jobs on women's life satisfaction. Unlike men, women often have two jobs, one in the home and one in the work world. Researchers found that women who worked outside the home actually reported feeling less, rather than more, stressed. Employed women also said that their jobs gave them opportunities for forming friendships and gaining respect, power, and prestige that were not available to them in their homes (Baruch, Biener, & Barnett, 1987).

Clowns at a reunion. Each year about 2,000 people apply for 50 clown jobs at the Ringling Bros. and Barnum & Bailey Clown College in Venice, Florida. Is this a career for you?

What particular difficulties do women face in the work force?

Women face major difficulties in the work force that men usually do not. The first difficulty is job discrimination based on sex. Historically, fewer job opportunities have been available to women, especially at higher levels of government, business, and academics (Flam, 1991). Related to job discrimination is pay discrimination—women continue to receive lower pay for work similar or equal to that of men.

About 20% of women report that they have been sexually harassed on the job (*Newsweek,* October 21, 1991). The 1986 Supreme Court ruling that sexual harassment violates civil rights has given women a legal way to fight sexual harassment.

We have discussed many events, challenges, and situations that we face as adults. Now we come to the final event of adulthood—death.

APPLYING/ EXPLORING: VIEWS ON DEATH

"I, Marjorie Wantz, want everyone to know that this is my decision and no one else's. After three and a half years, I find I can no longer go on with this pain and agony. I have not been out of this house in three years except to go to Detroit to the doctors. I do not call this living, never getting out—what is it like to go to a grocery store? Or go for a walk? I am glad there is Dr. Kevorkian who can help me. I have begged him to help me for two years, but the last year, I should say 13 months, have been pure hell. No doctor can help me anymore. If God won't come to me, I'm going to find God. I can't stand it any longer." (*USA Today,* October 25–27, 1991, p. 1A.*)

If someone you loved died, how would you deal with it?

Marjorie had a pelvic disease that caused excruciating and unmanageable pain. With Dr. Kevorkian's help and with her husband at her side, Marjorie, age 58, committed suicide at 5:05 on an October morning.

Marjorie's death by suicide illustrates a longstanding moral dilemma: Does a person have the moral right to end his or her life? This question represents one of the major death-related issues in our society today.

Death and Dying

What happens as death grows near?
Until the early 1970s, death was considered too personal and tragic to be a topic for open discussion or research. It was the 1968 publication of Elisabeth Kübler-Ross's book *On Death and Dying* that was the beginning of a much-needed public discussion of

death. Kübler-Ross had interviewed patients who were dying and asked them to describe their feelings. She organized these feelings into five stages: *denial, anger, bargaining, depression,* and *acceptance of death.* Denial is characterized by statements such as "There must be some mistake; it can't be me." As the illness grows more serious, however, a person may next become angry and ask, "Why does it have to be me?" The person may attempt to cope with dying by bargaining with the medical staff or with God. But soon the increasing severity of the illness makes the person realize that he or she will soon lose everything; the result is depression. If a dying person works through the feelings of denial, anger, bargaining, and depression, he or she may show acceptance of impending death (Kübler-Ross, 1968, 1974).

Kübler-Ross's stages have been criticized. Researchers found that not every dying person goes through all five stages or in the same order (Kastenbaum, 1981). However, her work changed our view of death by describing the potential feelings of a dying person and the reactions of his or her family.

Death with Dignity

What if dying takes a long time?
The 1980s saw the growth of a new institution called the hospice, a second major reflection of our changing view of death. A **hospice** *is a place where people may go to die with the least amount of pain and the greatest amount of dignity.* In some cases, hospice workers may help a person die comfortably in his or her own home. The need for hospices, of which there are thousands worldwide, arose because people with terminal illness can be kept alive by modern medicine for months and years. Neither patients nor their families were prepared to deal emotionally, physically, or financially with the prolonged state of dying that resulted (Levy, 1989). Because the number of Americans over 65 will rise dramatically during the next 40 years, the need for hospices is likely to increase.

Death and Moral Rights

Does a person have the moral right to end his or her life?
On July 5, 1989 a Michigan judge granted David Rivlin the right to be disconnected from his respirator. David, a quadriplegic, had been confined to his bed for the previous three years and could not breathe on his own. Before his respirator was disconnected, he said, "It's not that I welcome death; it's just that I welcome it over life" (*People*, August 1989, p. 58).

On March 14, 1991 *The New England Journal of Medicine* published an article by Dr. Timothy Quill, who described how he gave a woman suffering from leukemia a prescription for sleeping pills and told her how many she needed for a lethal dose. A New York grand jury refused to indict Dr. Quill on criminal charges, and his license has not been taken away.

On August 25, 1991 the book *Final Exit*, by Derek Humpry, made the *New York Times* bestseller list. The book is a manual on how to commit suicide.

On October 23, 1991 Dr. Kevorkian helped two people commit suicide. One was Marjorie Wantz. The second was a woman whose body had been destroyed by multiple sclerosis. As of this writing, criminal charges were filed against Dr. Kevorkian but dismissed. However, his medical license has been suspended. At least 27 states have laws

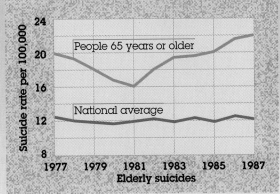

Between 1980 and 1987, the suicide rate among people 65 or older increased 21%, and the trend into the 1990s seems to be continuing (data from *USA Today*, September 16, 1991).

banning assisted suicide by anyone, including doctors, but many of these laws are unclear.

These incidents point out one of the newest concerns over death: Should the medical profession help terminally ill people end their lives? Should a person be allowed to end his or her own life? These questions have produced sharply divided opinions.

No. Opponents say that allowing people to take their own lives opens the door to many potential abuses. For example, making suicide easier may increase the chances that people who are suffering from mental problems or temporary emotional difficulties may take their own lives without exploring other possibilities for living. In addition, the medical profession, which is pledged to keeping people alive, is either flatly opposed to or unsure about helping people who wish to die.

Yes. Proponents explain that each of us has the moral right to end our lives if we find that life has become unbearable for health reasons. For example, a 1975 Gallop poll found that only 41% believed that someone in great pain and with no hope of improvement had the moral right to commit suicide, but by 1990 that percentage had risen to 66% (*Newsweek*, August 16, 1991).

No doubt questions about ending one's life, with or without official medical assistance, will continue to provoke personal, medical, moral, and legal debate in the 1990s.

Marjorie Wantz and Dr. Jack Kervorkian appeared on a Detroit talk show. Marjorie chose to end her life with Dr. Kervorkian's help; he arranged it so that she could inject herself with a lethal drug.

Summary/Self-Test

CONSISTENCY VERSUS CHANGE

1. Researchers use two main methods to answer questions about change and consistency across the lifetime. When they study the same group of people across many years, they use (a)_____ studies. When they study many groups of people of different ages all at the same time, they use (b)_____ studies. Research has shown both continuity and change between adolescence and middle adulthood.

■ *If a psychologist wanted to study your development from the end of adolescence through your 40s, how and what would the psychologist study?*

PHYSICAL CHANGES

2. The gradual and natural slowing of physical and psychological processes from middle through late adulthood is called normal aging and is explained by two theories, each of which emphasizes a different mechanism. According to one theory, our bodies age because of naturally occurring problems or breakdowns in the cells; this theory is called the (a)_____ theory. According to another theory, our bodies age because of a biological limit on the number of times that cells can divide and multiply; after that limit is reached, cells begin to die and aging occurs; this is called the (b)_____ theory.

3. The aging that may be caused by genetic defects, physiological problems, or diseases is called (a)_____. Examples of this type of aging include Alzheimer's disease and (b)_____.

4. Your age in years is called your (a)_____. How old you act and feel results from a combination of physical, psychological, and social factors that affect your attitudes toward life, social roles, and quality of life; these factors add up to your (b)_____.

■ *Although two older persons are exactly the same age, how do you explain why one acts very young and the other acts very old?*

COGNITIVE CHANGES

5. Research indicates a slowing in certain cognitive processes as we age. These declines include a decrease in the time required to respond to an auditory or visual stimulus, called (a)_____; in the time required to identify a particular sensory stimulus and respond to it, called (b)_____; and in the ability to memorize and recall a list. Other cognitive processes may improve with age. Young adults are superior at memorizing and recalling hundreds of details; mature adults are superior at (c)_____ the meaning and significance of information. This difference indicates that we process and use information in different ways at different stages in our lives.

■ *If you overheard a young adult and her grandfather discussing the same movie, what would you notice about their conversation?*

STAGES OF ADULTHOOD

6. The challenges of adulthood are covered in the last three of Erikson's eight (a)_____ stages. According to his theory, in stage 6, young adults face the problems of finding (b)_____ versus _____. In stage 7, middle adults need to help the next generation or perform tasks that leave the world a better place; these problems are called (c)_____ versus _____. In stage 8, older adults reflect on their lives; if they feel positive and contented about how they lived and what they accomplished, they will have a feeling of satisfaction or (d)_____; if not, they will have a feeling of regret and (e)_____.

7. In contrast to Erikson's focus on psychosocial problems, Levinson's theory focuses on how adults resolve _____ problems.

■ *Let's suppose that you are in your mid-20s and are completing a calendar of events for your next 40 years. What kinds of events would you write down?*

PERSONALITY DEVELOPMENT: GENDER ROLES

8. During childhood and adolescence, expectations and pressures of parents, peers, and society shape behaviors that are characteristics of males and females; these behaviors are called (a)_____. The idea that masculinity and femininity represent opposite poles of a continuum is included in the (b)_____ view of gender roles. The view that masculinity and femininity are independent personality variables, such that one person can possess both masculine and feminine traits, ts included in the (c)_____ idea of gender roles. There is evidence that being (d)_____ is associated with good mental health and success.

■ *If you could freely pick and choose from a list of personality traits, what kinds of traits would you choose?*

SOCIAL DEVELOPMENT: RELATIONSHIPS

9. Sternberg has developed a triangular theory of love, dividing it into three components. Feeling physically aroused and attracted to someone is called (a)_____; feeling close and connected to someone, which develops through sharing and communicating, is called (b)_____; making a pledge to nourish the feelings of love and to maintain the relationship is called (c)_____. Sternberg believes that most of us strive for (d)_____, which is a balanced combination of these three components.

10. One way that we select a mate is by developing a _____ list of desirable characteristics and then looking for someone who matches this list.

■ *What are the two or three things that you believe couples should work on changing to make their relationship happier?*

CULTURAL DIVERSITY: PREFERENCES FOR PARTNERS

11. People's lists of desirable traits for a mate are remarkably similar across cultures, although there are some differences in ranking between the genders. The similarities from culture to culture indicate that cultures exert strong _____ on the partner preferences of their members.

■ *How is it possible that in some countries being in love is low on the list of reasons for getting married?*

SEXUAL BEHAVIOR

12. The gradual reduction in secretion of estrogen, which results in cessation of ovulation and the menstrual cycle, is called (a)_____; it occurs in women at about age 50. Although men do not stop producing testosterone as they age, they may experience a decrease in sexual responsiveness due to (b)_____ changes.

■ *Why do you think that many young adults believe their parents no longer have sex?*

SOCIAL DEVELOPMENT: CAREERS

13. Feelings of dissatisfaction with what we have accomplished in our careers may lead to a sense of failure and disappointment, part of what is called a _____ crisis.

14. A job has important benefits to both men and women. However, women face major difficulties in the work force that men usually do not because of various forms of _____ at their job.

■ *If you saw a photograph of all the leaders of the world governments, what would be strange about this photo?*

APPLYING/EXPLORING: VIEWS ON DEATH

15. Kübler-Ross interviewed patients who were dying and had them describe their feelings. She classified their feelings into five stages: _____, _____, _____, _____, and _____.

16. A place where people may go to die with the least amount of pain and the greatest amount of dignity is called a _____. Because of changes in medical science and the aging population, the number of such places is expected to increase—as are questions about the rights of the terminally ill to end their own lives.

■ *If your grandfather were dying of incurable stomach cancer and wanted to end his life before the pain became too bad, what would you tell him?*

Chapter *Twelve*
PERSONALITY

MODULE 23
FREUDIAN AND HUMANISTIC THEORIES

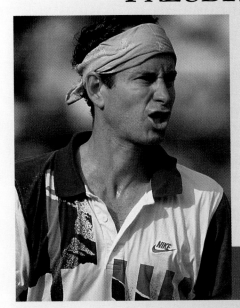

Why does this pro tennis player have outbursts on the court?

His career winnings total about $11 million.

In 1981 John was an unknown 18-year-old tennis player whose court antics at the Wimbledon Open included breaking rackets, cursing the officials, and sassing the fans. He was officially fined $1,500 for bad behavior. He made the finals but lost the championship match.

In 1982 he returned to England to play at Wembley. In a match that lasted 3½ hours, he continually argued with the umpires, whacked a microphone, and used obscenities. John was fined twice and risked a 21-day suspension for bad behavior. He lost the match.

Between 1982 and 1985, John won a number of major tennis championships that earned him a number-one ranking for three of the four years. However, his bad behavior also continued.

In 1985 a long-time tennis reporter and supporter of the tennis star made an about-face. The reporter wrote that John was making being a bully a career and that John's whims did not give him the right to pick on people who ran the tournaments (Lupica, 1985).

In 1989 John's ranking had fallen to number six, and he was working hard on regaining the top spot. He said that he could no longer afford the fury that marked his play from the mid-1970s through the mid-1980s. "There's no question in my mind that I need control at this point in my life," he said. "I'm 30 years old, I have a wife and two kids, my priorities are different, and my outlook is different" (Flink, 1989, p. 21).

In 1990, after declaring that he was turning over a new leaf, John became the first player in 22 years to get kicked out of a Grand Slam tournament (Australian Open) for numerous counts of misconduct. By now you may have guessed that this tennis player is John McEnroe.

Although I am not a great tennis fan, I have followed John McEnroe's career because his puzzling behaviors provide interesting examples for my lectures on personality. **Personality** *refers to a combination of lasting and distinctive behaviors, thoughts, and emotions that typify how we react and adapt to other people and situations.* McEnroe's behaviors bring to mind a number of questions about personality: When was his personality formed? Why does he show such offensive behavior playing tennis but loving behavior as husband and father? Why did he promise to change only to revert back to his bad habits? Questions such as these are answered in slightly different ways by various theories of personality. A **theory of personality** *is an organized attempt to describe and explain how personalities develop and why personalities differ.*

What's Coming

In this module we'll discuss two contrasting theoretical approaches to personality: Freud's psychodynamic theory, which emphasizes unconscious forces, and humanistic theories, which stress our freedom to choose and develop our potentials.

In the next module, we'll examine two more approaches that emphasize different factors. The first is social learning theory, which stresses the influence of beliefs on behavior; then we'll move to trait theory, which looks at differences among personalities.

Freud's Psychodynamic Theory

Freud's theory of psychoanalysis includes two related theories: a theory of personality development and a method of psychotherapy. We'll focus on Freud's theory of personality here; later, in Module 29, we'll examine his method of psychotherapy. **Freud's psychodynamic theory of personality** *emphasizes the importance of early childhood experiences and the effects of conflicts between conscious and unconscious forces.* (The word *dynamic* refers to mental energy or force.) Freud's theory of personality begins with his model of the human mind and contains one of his most important and controversial assumptions about human behavior.

How the Mind Functions

If we could journey back to the late 1800s, we would find Freud trying to solve a perplexing problem: several of his women patients have developed profound physical symptoms, such as losing all sensations in their hands or control over their legs. What most puzzles Freud, who is a medical doctor, is the absence of any physical causes for these symptoms. In a flash of brilliance, Freud arrives at his controversial assumption about how the mind functions: since there are no neurological causes of these physical symptoms, the causes must be unconscious psychological forces (Westen, 1990). According to Freud, the *functioning of the mind* involves a continuing battle between our conscious thoughts and an equal or even greater unconscious force. Because of its importance, we'll examine this unconscious force more closely.

Conscious Thoughts Versus Unconscious Forces

What did you do Friday night?
You might answer that you and a date went to a party Friday night. According to Freud, you answered this question by recalling conscious thoughts. **Conscious thoughts** *are wishes, desires, or thoughts of which you are aware or can recall at any given moment.* However, Freud theorized that your conscious thoughts are only a small part of your total thoughts, wishes, or desires, most of which are unconscious. **Unconscious forces** *represent wishes, desires, or thoughts that, because of their disturbing or threatening content, we automatically repress.*

Was your date flirting?
Freud suggested that one reason you may not remember threatening events, feelings, or impulses, such as your date flirting with someone else, is that such events are automatically repressed and thus become part of the unconscious force. Although repressed thoughts are unconscious, they may influence your behaviors.

Why did you argue with your date?
You explain to a friend that after the party you got into a big argument with your date over where to stop for a late snack. According to Freud, your argument may represent repressed feelings about your date's flirting, and these repressed feelings provide unconscious motivation. **Unconscious motivation** *is a Freudian concept that refers to the influence of repressed thoughts, desires, or impulses on our conscious thoughts and behaviors.* Freud assumed that our mind functions on two different levels: (1) The conscious level, which includes events, desires, and thoughts of which we are aware; and (2) the unconscious level, which includes events, thoughts, and impulses of which we are not normally aware of but that influence our behaviors.

Freud used the concept of unconscious motivation to solve one puzzle of the mind—why we do or say things that we don't understand. However, Freud's solution creates a second puzzle: How do we discover what is in our unconscious?

Discovering the Unconscious

Why does McEnroe insult and argue with tennis fans and officials?
Here's what John says: "I know I've got a problem. When I walk out there on the court I become a maniac. I'm capable of saying anything. I suppose I didn't care about what I said for so long that now I want to change I can't. Something comes over me, man. It's weird." (Evans, 1990, p. 175)

McEnroe is unable to explain why he has behaved so obnoxiously on the tennis court for over a decade. If his offensive behaviors are due to unconscious forces, then such information has been repressed and cannot be consciously recalled.

To obtain clues about what's in the unconscious, Freud developed three techniques: free association, dream interpretation, and analysis of slips of the tongue (which are now commonly known as Freudian slips).

Free Association. Freud encouraged his patients to relax and to sit back or lie down on his now-famous couch and talk freely about anything. He called this process free associating. **Free association** *is a Freudian technique that encourages clients to talk about any thoughts or images that enter their head; the assumption is that this kind of free-flowing, uncensored talking will provide clues to unconscious material.* Free association was one of Freud's important methodological inventions and one that some therapists still use today to help reveal a client's unconscious thoughts, desires, and wishes.

Dream Interpretation. Freud listened to and interpreted his patients' dreams because he believed that dreams represent the purest form of free association. **Dream interpretation,** *a Freudian technique of analyzing dreams, is based on the assumption that dreams contain underlying, hidden meanings and symbols that provide clues to unconscious thoughts and desires.* Freud distinguished between a dream's **manifest content**—*the plot of the dream at the surface level*—and its **latent content**—*the hidden or disguised meaning of the plot's events.* Simply put, Freud interpreted certain objects (such as sticks and knives) as symbols for male sexual organs and interpreted other objects (such as boxes and ovens) as symbols for female sexual organs. The therapist's task is to look behind the dream's often bizarre disguises and symbols to decipher clues to unconscious material. According to Freud, dreams are a "royal road" into the unconscious.

Freud assumed the existence of unconscious forces underlying personality and developed techniques to uncover them.

Freudian Slips. One of my colleagues was lecturing on the importance of regular health care. She said, "It is important to visit a veterinarian for regular checkups." According to Freud, mistakes like substituting *veterinarian* for *physician* are not accidental but rather "intentional" ways of expressing unconscious desires. **Freudian slips** *are mistakes or slips of the tongue that we make in everyday speech; such mistakes are thought to reflect unconscious thoughts or wishes.* As it turns out, my colleague, who is in very good health, was having serious doubts about her relationship with a person who happened to be a veterinarian.

Freud assumed that free association, dream interpretation, and slips of the tongue share one thing in common: they are mental processes that are the least controlled by our conscious, rational, and logical minds. As a result, he thought, these techniques let uncensored clues slip out and reveal our unconscious wishes and desires.

Freud's view of how the mind functions involves a continuing struggle between conscious thoughts and unconscious forces. Now let's examine how this battle is fought.

Divisions of the Mind

How big is John McEnroe's ego?

After I describe John McEnroe's offensive, obnoxious, and insulting behaviors on the tennis court to my class, I ask students to rank the sizes of his id, ego, and superego. They unanimously agree that McEnroe's id is the biggest, followed by an almost equally large ego, and finally a very tiny superego. Although this exercise might make Freud roll over in his grave, the purpose is to demonstrate that almost everyone knows of Freud's famous threesome. As it turns out, the id, ego, and superego are Freud's very clever answers to a very complicated question: How does the human mind develop?

Id: Seeking Pleasure

Freud believed that mental processes must have a source of energy, which he called the id. The **id,** *which is Freud's first division of the mind to develop, contains two biological drives—sex and aggression—that are the source of all psychic or mental energy; the id's goal is to pursue pleasure and satisfy the biological drives.* The id operates according to the **pleasure principle,** *whose one policy is the satisfaction of drives and avoidance of pain without concern for moral restrictions or society's regulations.* You can think of the id as a spoiled child who operates in a totally selfish, pleasure-seeking way, without regard for reason, logic, or morality. However, following the pleasure principle leads to conflict with others. This conflict results in the development of the ego.

Ego: Functioning in the World

As infants discover restrictions on satisfying their wishes, they learn control through the development of an ego. The **ego,** *which is Freud's second division of the mind, develops from the id during infancy; the ego's goal is to find safe and socially acceptable ways of satisfying the id's desires and to negotiate between the id's wants and the superego's prohibitions.* In contrast to the id's pleasure principle, the ego follows the reality principle. The **reality principle** *has a policy of satisfying a wish or desire only if there is a socially acceptable outlet available.* You can think of the ego as an executive who operates in a reasonable, logical, and socially acceptable way in finding outlets for satisfaction. This ego executive tries to come up with compromise solutions to satisfy the needs of the id and the demands of the superego.

Superego: Playing by the Rules

As children learn the hard lesson that they must follow rules and regulations in satisfying their wishes, they develop a superego. The **superego,** *which is Freud's third division of the mind, develops from the ego during early childhood; the superego's goal is applying the moral values and standards of one's parents or caregivers and society in satisfying one's wishes.* Through interactions with the parents or caregivers, a child develops a superego by taking on or incorporating the parents' or caregivers' standards, values, and rules. The superego's power is in making the person feel guilty if the rules are disobeyed. Because the pleasure-seeking id wants to avoid feeling guilty, it is motivated to listen to the superego. You can think of a superego as a moral guardian or conscience that is trying to control the id's wishes and impulses. Every time I hold open my refrigerator door and ponder its contents, I hear my superego say in a voice that sounds exactly like my mother's, "Close that door and stop letting out all the cold air!"

Conscious Levels

Freud assumed that portions of the mind's three divisions—id, ego, and superego—are unconscious. To help envision this idea, think of the mind as an iceberg.

Ego. Think of the iceberg's tip, which is clearly visible, as the part of the ego that is conscious. Freud said that a relatively large part of the ego's material is conscious, such as information that we have gathered in adapting to our environments. Smaller parts of the ego's material are preconscious and unconscious, such as threatening wishes that have been repressed.

Id. The iceberg's massive under-water bulk, which is hidden from view, represents the id, which Freud assumed is totally unconscious.

Superego. To continue the analogy, think of the super-ego as running vertically through the iceberg. Part of it is visible (and conscious); the rest extends below the water (and is part of the preconscious and the unconscious).

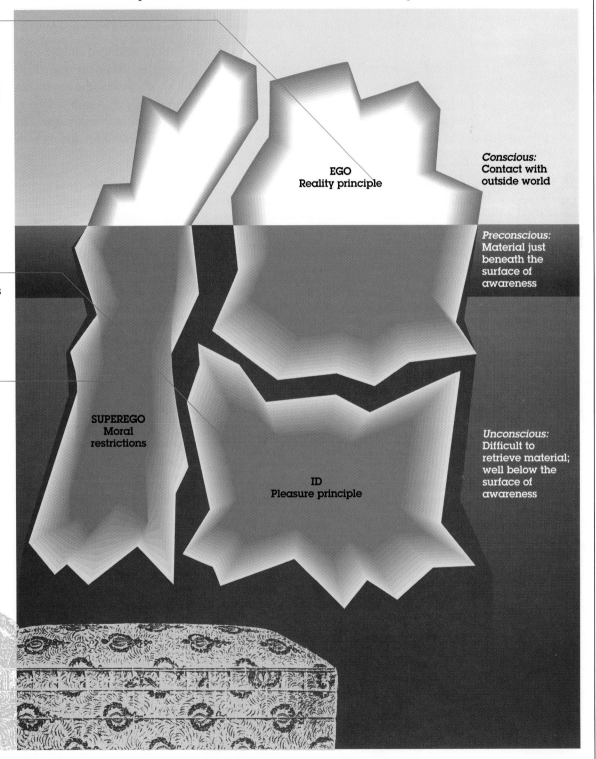

EGO
Reality principle

SUPEREGO
Moral restrictions

ID
Pleasure principle

Conscious:
Contact with outside world

Preconscious:
Material just beneath the surface of awareness

Unconscious:
Difficult to retrieve material; well below the surface of awareness

What happens if the id, ego, and superego disagree?

Divisions of the Mind

Anxiety

Much of the time the three divisions of the mind—id, ego, and superego—work together to satisfy our needs. However, at other times the id, ego, and superego are in conflict over how a need should be satisfied.

What happens if I plan to work but want to go to a movie?
I can think of this situation as a conflict between my pleasure-seeking id and my rule-enforcing superego. Caught in the middle of this id-superego conflict is my ego, which has a peace-keeping goal. If my ego feels threatened by my id's desires, the ego creates a feeling of anxiety. **Anxiety** *is an unpleasant state that is associated with feelings of uneasiness, apprehension, and heightened physiological arousal, such as increased heart rate and blood pressure.* Freud suggested some very interesting mechanisms for dealing with anxiety.

Defense Mechanisms

What happens when I feel anxious about going to a movie instead of working?
On the one hand, my ego can take realistic steps to solve the problem of going to a movie when I should be working. For example, after the movie I can work late into the night, which will reduce my anxiety. On the other hand, my ego can use a variety of defense mechanisms to reduce anxiety. **Defense mechanisms** *are Freudian processes that operate at unconscious levels to help the ego reduce anxiety through self-deception.*

According to Freud, if you should be working but instead go to a movie, you will feel anxious.

Here we'll outline some of the more significant defense mechanisms that Freud identified.

Rationalization *involves making up acceptable excuses for behaviors that cause us to feel anxious.* A student who feels anxious about doing poorly on a test would be rationalizing if he blamed his low test score on the "poorly worded" test questions rather than on the fact that he did not study.

Denial *is refusing to recognize some anxiety-provoking event or piece of information.* A heavy smoker would be using denial if she disregarded the scientific evidence that smoking increases the risk of lung cancer.

Repression *involves pushing unacceptable or threatening feelings or impulses into the unconscious.* You would be repressing envious feelings of your sibling's academic abilities if you shoved them into your unconscious.

Projection *is unconsciously transferring unacceptable traits onto others.* A worker may be projecting if he attributes a quick temper to his boss when in fact it's he himself who has the temper.

Reaction formation *involves turning unacceptable wishes into acceptable behaviors.* A person who feels guilty about engaging in sexual activity may use reaction formation by joining a strict religious group that bans sex.

Displacement *involves transferring feelings from their true source to another source that is safer and more socially acceptable.* If you were angry with a friend, you might displace your anger by picking an argument with a "safer" object, such as a stranger.

Sublimation, *which is a type of displacement, involves redirecting a threatening or forbidden desire, usually sexual, into a socially acceptable one.* For instance, a person might sublimate strong sexual desires by channeling that energy into physical activities.

There are two things to remember about defense mechanisms. First, because defense mechanisms are totally unconscious, a spouse, friend, co-worker, or boss may point out our being defensive, yet we will deny being so. Second, according to Freud, defense mechanisms can be helpful or harmful, depending on how much we rely on them. The occasional use of defense mechanisms is normal and helps reduce anxiety so that we can continue to function as we work on the real causes of our anxiety. But the overuse of defense mechanisms may prevent us from recognizing or working on the real causes. The idea of defense mechanisms continues to be important, as growing experimental evidence indicates that we do indeed use defense mechanisms in the way that Freud theorized (Westen, 1990).

The ego reduces anxiety by using a variety of defense mechanisms.

Development of Personality

How would you describe John McEnroe?

"He is a young man who raises perfectly placed ground strokes to a high art form, only to resort to on-court tantrums that smear his masterpieces like graffiti. His touch and spin are nothing short of magic, capable of enthralling huge and even hostile crowds under high-pressure conditions; but he meets a stranger one-on-one with a bumbling shyness that borders on rudeness. He is blessed with as much natural ability as anyone who ever played his game, but he is cursed with a perpetual pouting expression that seems to deny the very joy that he is capable of producing. Surely it all adds up to a torn and complex character, boiling with talents and emotions that can barely be understood, much less controlled." (*Newsweek,* September 7, 1981, p. 50)

Explaining how McEnroe developed such a complex and often contradictory personality is a challenge, even for a personality theorist. To meet this challenge, we might use Freud's comprehensive theory of personality development. The essence of this theory is a series of five developmental stages, which we'll examine next.

Developmental Stages

According to Freud, personality develops as we pass through a series of psychosexual stages. **Psychosexual stages** *are five developmental periods—the oral, anal, phallic, latency, and genital stages—during which the individual seeks pleasure from different areas of the body associated with sexual feelings.* Freud used the term **erogenous zones** to describe *the body areas that are associated with sexual feelings.*

Before we describe each psychosexual stage, two general points apply to all five stages.

First, each stage is a source of potential *conflict* between the id, which seeks immediate gratification, and the parents, who place restrictions on when, where, and how the gratification can take place. The resolution of this conflict has important implications for the development of the child's personality.

Second, if a strong conflict develops between a child's wanting gratification and the parents' restricting gratification, the result can be fixation. **Fixation,** *which can occur at any stage, refers to a Freudian process through which an individual may be locked into an earlier psychosexual stage because his or her wishes were overgratified or undergratified.* If fixation occurs at the oral stage because of too little gratification, the person goes through life trying to obtain oral satisfaction. If, however, fixation occurs at the oral stage because of too *much* gratification, the person has little motivation to go beyond this stage and continues to seek oral gratification throughout life.

Freud proposed that personality develops as we pass through a series of five psychosexual stages.

1 The **oral stage** *lasts for the first 18 months of life and is a time when the infant's pleasure seeking is centered on the mouth.* Pleasure-seeking activities include sucking, chewing, and biting. Fixation at this stage results in adults who continue to engage in oral activities, such as over-eating, gum chewing, or smoking; oral activities can be symbolic as well, such as being overly demanding or "mouthing off."

2 The **anal stage** *lasts from about age 1½ to age 3 and is a time when the infant's pleasure seeking is centered on the anus and its functions of elimination.* Fixation at this stage results in adults who continue to engage in activities of *retention* or *elimination.* Retention may take the form of being very neat, stingy, or behaviorally rigid. Elimination may take the form of being generous, messy, or behaviorally loose.

3 The **phallic** (FAL-ik) **stage** *lasts from about age 3 to age 6 and is a time when the infant's pleasure seeking is centered on the genitals.* Freud theorized that this stage is particularly important for personality development because of the occurrence of the Oedipus complex (named for Oedipus, the character in Greek mythology who unknowingly killed his father and married his mother). The **Oedipus** (ED-ah-pus) **complex** *is a process in which a child competes with the parent of the same sex for the affections and pleasures of the parent of the opposite sex.* According to Freud, this complex presents different problems for boys and girls.

When a boy discovers that his penis is a source of pleasure, he develops a sexual attraction to his mother. As a result, the boy feels hatred, jealousy, and competition toward his father and has fears of castration. The boy resolves his Oedipus complex by identifying with his father. If he does not resolve the complex, fixation occurs and he may go through life trying to prove his toughness.

When a girl discovers that she does not have a penis, she feels a loss that Freud called *penis envy.* Her loss makes her turn against her mother and develop sexual desires for her father. A girl resolves her Oedipus complex, sometimes called the *Electra complex* (for Electra, a woman in Greek mythology who killed her mother) by identifying with her mother. If this complex is not resolved, fixation occurs and the woman may go through life feeling inferior to men.

According to psychiatrist Bennett Simon (1991) of Harvard Medical School, the idea of the Oedipus complex has waned in popularity and credibility, both within psychoanalysis and within the culture at large. For example, Freud's assertion that the Oedipus complex occurs universally is not supported by data from other cultures (Bower, 1991).

4 The **latency stage,** *which lasts from about age 6 to puberty, is a time when the child represses sexual thoughts and engages in nonsexual activities, such as developing social and intellectual skills.* At puberty, sexuality reappears and marks the beginning of a new stage.

5 The **genital stage** *lasts from puberty through adulthood and is a time when the individual has renewed sexual desires that he or she seeks to fulfill through relationships with other people.* How a person meets the conflicts of the genital stage depends on how crises in the first three stages were resolved. If the individual is fixated at an earlier stage, less energy will be available to resolve conflicts at the genital stage. If the individual successfully resolved conflicts in the first three stages, he or she will have the energy to develop loving relationships and a healthy and mature personality.

Freud believed that a child's first five years are the most important, but as we will see, many of his followers disagreed.

Freud's Followers

Freud's theory was so creative and revolutionary for its time that it attracted a number of followers, who formed the Vienna Psychoanalytic Society. It was not long, however, before theoretical disagreements arose among members of the society as well as later followers. Here's why three influential followers eventually broke with Freud's theory.

Carl Jung

Why did Freud's "crown prince" stop talking?

In 1910 Carl Jung, with the whole-hearted support of Sigmund Freud, became the first president of the Vienna Psychoanalytic Society. Freud said that Jung was to be his "crown prince" and personal successor. However, just four years later Jung and Freud ended their personal and professional relationship and never again spoke to each other.

The main reason for the split was that Jung disagreed with Freud's emphasis on the sex drive. Jung believed the collective unconscious—and not sex—to be the basic force. According to Jung, the **collective unconscious** *consists of ancient memory traces and symbols that are passed on by birth and are shared by all peoples in all cultures.* Jung developed an elaborate theory of personality, called *analytical psychology,* which has influenced not only the field of psychology but also art, literature, and philosophy.

Alfred Adler

Why did one of the society's presidents resign?

Alfred Adler was another contemporary of Freud's who later became president of the Vienna Psychoanalytic Society. However, after Adler voiced his disagreement with Freud at one of the society's meetings, he was so badly criticized that he resigned as president.

Like Jung, Adler disagreed with Freud's theory that humans are governed by biological and sexual urges. Adler proposed instead that humans are motivated by *social urges* and that each person is a social being with a unique personality. Adler formed his own group whose philosophy became known as *individual psychology.* In contrast to Freud, Adler suggested that we are aware of our motives and goals and have the capacity to guide and plan our futures.

Karen Horney

What would a woman say about penis envy?

Karen Horney was trained as a psychoanalyst; her career reached its peak shortly after Freud's death in 1939. For many years, Horney was dean of the American Institute of Psychoanalysis in New York.

Horney strongly objected to Freud's view of women as dependent, vain, and submissive because of biological forces and childhood sexual experiences, such as penis envy. Rather, Horney insisted that the major influence on personality development, whether in women or men, can be found in child-parent *social interactions.* Unlike Freud, who believed that child-parent conflicts are inevitable, Horney theorized that such conflicts are avoidable if the child is raised in a loving, trusting, and secure environment.

Neo-Freudians

Horney is sometimes referred to as a *Neo-Freudian* because she changed and renovated Freud's original theory. Erik Erikson, whose theories we discussed in Chapters 11 and 12, was also a Neo-Freudian. Erikson believed that everyone goes through a series of *psychosocial* stages instead of the *psychosexual* stages proposed by Freud.

Neo-Freudians generally agreed with Freud's basic ideas, such as the importance of the unconscious; the division of the mind into the id, ego, and superego; and the use of defense mechanisms to protect the ego. They mostly disagreed with Freud's emphasis on biological forces, sexual drives, and psychosexual stages. The Neo-Freudians turned the emphasis of Freud's psychodynamic theory away from biological drives toward psychosocial and cultural influences.

Now let's see how Freud's theory has held up over more than 50 years.

Freudian Theory Today

It should not be surprising that some of Freud's concepts, which he formulated over half a century ago, have been revised and changed. Here are some of the major criticisms and revisions of Freud's theory.

How valid is Freud's theory?

Freud's theory is so comprehensive that it can explain almost every behavior—even opposite ones. For example, Freud's theory predicts that fixation at the anal stage may result in a person being at one extreme very messy and at the other extreme very neat. Critics argue that because Freud's theory can explain almost every behavior, his theory is not very useful in making predictions. Followers reply that Freud's theory has proven useful in raising new issues and questions about human behavior. Many psychoanalytic theorists now suggest that, if psychoanalysis is to survive, Freud's theory must undergo a more systematic and experimental analysis (Westen, 1990).

Can Freud's concepts be tested?

Many of Freud's concepts, such as id, ego, and superego, the Oedipus complex, and psychosexual stages, have proved difficult to test under experimental conditions. For example, since the id is a totally unconscious force and represents biological energy, how does one study it? Critics argue that Freudian concepts either are too descriptive or involve unconscious processes that are difficult to verify through experimental methods.

Critics have questioned some of Freud's assumptions.

Are the first five years the most important?

Based on his observations of his patients, Freud concluded that personality development is essentially complete after the first five years. However, several lines of evidence question Freud's assumption.

As you may recall from our discussion of resilient children in Module 20, the occurrence of serious psychological and physical problems during the first five years does not necessarily stunt or inhibit personality development, as Freud predicted. For example, children who had experienced poverty, the death of or separation from their parents, or a poor home life nevertheless developed into healthy, mature adults provided the children had a loving caregiver (Werner, 1989).

In addition, a number of longitudinal studies indicate that personality development is not complete in the first five years but rather continues well into middle adulthood (McCrae & Costa, 1990).

Is there evidence for unconscious forces?

One of Freud's major assumptions was that unconscious forces greatly influence our conscious thoughts and behaviors. According to John Kihlstrom (1987), there is now good evidence that unconscious influences do affect our conscious behaviors, but these influences are not the repressed, threatening desires proposed by Freud. To distance his meaning from Freud's, Kihlstrom uses the term **cognitive unconscious** *to refer to mental processes of which we are unaware but that influence our thoughts and behaviors.* Examples of cognitive unconscious include many practiced motor patterns, such as riding a bike, and automatic thought processes, such as recognizing someone's face. Today, cognitive psychologists see the unconscious as part of a general information-processing system rather than a battleground for the id, ego, and superego (Power & Brewin, 1991).

Freud's theory has had an enormous impact on society, as can be seen in the widespread use of Freudian terms (ego, id, rationalization) in literature, art, media, and our everyday conversations. In addition, Freud's theory has had a great impact on psychology, as seen in how many of his concepts have been incorporated into the fields of personality, development, abnormal psychology, and psychotherapy.

As you now know, Freud emphasized unconscious forces and developed methods to discover these forces. Next, we'll examine several other methods that also try to uncover unconscious forces.

Projective Tests

How would we analyze John McEnroe's personality?
To assist us in analyzing his personality, we could ask McEnroe to describe himself. Chances are that his description would be essentially a list of his conscious wishes, desires, thoughts, and behaviors. However, according to Freud's psychodynamic theory, people's major motivational forces are unconscious, and it takes special techniques to uncover them. In addition to Freud's three techniques for uncovering unconscious motivation (free association, dream interpretation, and interpretation of slips of the tongue), we now add a fourth technique, called the projective test, that was not developed by Freud but that fits with his theory. A **projective test** *involves presenting an ambiguous stimulus and asking the person to describe the stimulus or make up a story about it; the assumption is that the person will project feelings, needs, and motives into his or her responses.* Projective tests are part of **personality assessment,** *which is an area of psychology that involves the description of personality and the identification of personality problems and disorders.*

Examples of Projective Tests
Two of the best-known projective tests are the Rorschach inkblot test and the Thematic Apperception Test.

What do you see?
The **Rorschach (ROAR-shock) inkblot test** *is used to assess personality by showing a person a series of ten inkblots and then asking the person to describe what he or she sees in each.* This test, usually called the Rorschach, was developed in 1912 by a Swiss psychiatrist, Hermann Rorschach. This test is used primarily in the therapeutic setting to assess personality problems of clients.

What's happening here?
The **Thematic Apperception Test (TAT)** *involves showing a person a series of 20 pictures of people in ambiguous situations and asking the person to make up a story about what the people are doing or thinking in each situation.* For example, given the illustration shown here, a person might be asked to make up a story about what the young woman is thinking. The TAT, which was developed by Henry Murray in the 1930s, is used to assess personalities of normal individuals as well as personality problems of clients.

Use of Projective Tests
The most frequent use of projective tests is by therapists in clinical settings. Usually the therapist uses a combination of tests to assess the client's personality problems.

Advantages
One advantage of projective tests such as the Rorschach and the TAT is that they are difficult to fake or bias. Because the stimuli are ambiguous, individuals taking projective tests do not know which are the best, correct, or socially desirable answers. A second advantage is that in responding to ambiguous stimuli individuals may reveal more about their personalities than they consciously intended.

Disadvantages
As we discussed in Module 15, good psychological tests need to have two characteristics—reliability and validity. **Reliability** *means the person should obtain similar scores when taking the test on two different occasions.* **Validity** *means that the test actually measures what it is supposed to measure.* A disadvantage of the Rorschach and TAT is that their ambiguous stimuli make them difficult to score and interpret, which results in relatively low reliability and validity (Anastasi, 1988).

In spite of these disadvantages, experienced clinical psychologists report that projective tests, when used in combination with other assessment techniques, can provide useful information about a client's personality and problems (Anastasi, 1988).

After the Concept/Glossary, we'll discuss a theory of personality that has a highly optimistic view of human nature compared to Freud's more pessimistic view.

1. A combination of lasting and distinctive behaviors, thoughts, and emotions that are typical of how we react and adapt to other people and situations is a definition of _____.

2. Freud's theory of personality, which emphasizes the importance of early childhood experiences and of conflicts between conscious thoughts and unconscious forces, is called the _____ theory.

3. Freud developed three techniques for probing the unconscious. A technique that encourages clients to talk about any thoughts or images that enter their head is called (a)_____; a technique to interpret the hidden meanings and symbols in dreams is called (b)_____. With a third technique, the therapist analyzes the mistakes or (c)_____ that the client makes in everyday speech.

4. Freud considered the mind to have three major divisions. The division that contains the biological drives and is the source of all psychic or mental energy is called the (a)_____. This division operates according to the (b)_____ principle, which demands immediate satisfaction. The division that develops from the id during infancy and whose goal is finding safe and socially acceptable ways of satisfying the id's desires is called the (c)_____. This division operates according to the (d)_____ principle, which involves satisfying a wish only if there is a socially acceptable outlet. The division that develops from the id during early childhood and whose goal is applying the moral values and standards of one's parents and society is called the (e)_____.

5. Conflicts between the id and the super-ego over satisfaction of desires may cause the ego to feel threatened. When threatened, the ego generates an unpleasant state that is associated with feelings of uneasiness, apprehension, and heightened physiological arousal; this unpleasant state is called (a)_____. Freud suggested that the ego may reduce anxiety by using unconscious mechanisms that produce self-deception; these are called (b)_____.

6. Freud proposed that the major influence on personality development occurs as we pass through five developmental periods that he called the (a)_____ stages, each of which results in conflicts between the child's wishes and parents' restrictions. The result of a person's wishes being overgratified or undergratified at any one of these stages is called (b)_____.

7. A personality test that involves presenting an ambiguous stimulus and asking the person to describe or make up a story about the stimulus is called a (a)_____ test. These tests assume that the person will project his or her feelings, needs, and motives into his or her responses. Two examples of these tests are the (b)_____ and _____.

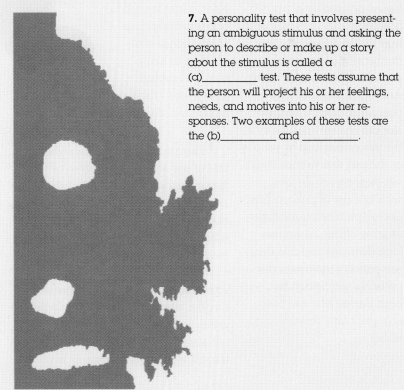

Answers: 1. personality; 2. psychodynamic; 3. (a) free association, (b) dream interpretation, (c) Freudian slips or slips of the tongue; 4. (a) id, (b) pleasure, (c) ego, (d) reality, (e) superego; 5. (a) anxiety, (b) defense mechanisms; 6. (a) psychosexual, (b) fixation; 7. (a) projective, (b) Rorschach inkblot test, Thematic Apperception Test (TAT).

Humanistic Theories

What does it take to win a gold medal?

For Kristi Yamaguchi, it meant giving her whole life to ice skating: spending thousands of hours practicing, entering grueling competitions, struggling with disappointments, and sacrificing her life to reach the final contest—the winter Olympics. Skating to sounds of "Malaguena," Kristi demonstrated such grace, skill, and artistry that she dazzled the audience and impressed the judges. After so many years of preparation, she obtained her lifelong dream: an Olympic gold medal.

Kristi's remarkable display of determination and self-discipline in reaching her potential as a skater perfectly illustrates the basic assumptions of humanistic theories. **Humanistic theories** *emphasize our capacity for personal growth, development of our potential, and freedom to choose our destiny.* Kristi's dedication and struggle to become a champion figure skater highlight the humanistic concept of choosing one's destiny. Humanistic theories reject the determinism of other theories of personality and share three features that distinguish them from other theories:

1 Humanistic theories stress the **phenomenological** (feh-nom-in-no-LODGE-ee-cal) **perspective,** *which means that our perception of the world, whether or not it is accurate, becomes our reality.* For instance, Kristi's phenomenological perspective of her competitive abilities may or may not have been accurate, but because of her belief her perception became her reality. Another example of how phenomenological perspective can change one's reality is the perception held by people in the past that women could not perform certain jobs, such as those of police officer, doctor, plumber, truck driver, or army officer. As women have demonstrated that they can perform these jobs, this particular perception has been proven false and has changed many people's reality.

2 Humanistic theories emphasize the **holistic** (hole-LIS-tick) **view,** *which means that one's personality is more than the sum of its individual parts; instead, one's personality is a unique and total entity that functions as a unit.* For example, the holistic view would explain that Kristi outperformed her competitors because of her unique combination of many traits—discipline, ability, motivation, persistence, desire—rather than any single trait.

3 Humanistic theories highlight the idea of **self-actualization,** *which is the inherent tendency to reach our true potentials.* We would say that in her gold medal–winning performance, Kristi presented a perfect example of reaching a high level of self-actualization. According to humanistic theories, no matter what our skills or abilities, each of us has the capacity for self-actualization and can reach our potentials as students, parents, or teachers.

Kristi Yamaguchi, from Fremont, California, won a gold medal in the 1992 winter Olympics. Her winning performance illustrates the development of one's potential.

The beginning of humanistic theory can be traced to two psychologists—Abraham Maslow and Carl Rogers—who had surprisingly different backgrounds.

Level 5
Self-actualization: Fulfillment of one's unique potential

Level 4
Esteem needs: Achievement, competency, gaining approval and recognition

Level 3
Love and belongingness needs: Affiliation with others and acceptance by others

Level 2
Safety needs: Protection from harm and concern about safety and survival

Level 1
Physiological needs: Hunger, thirst, sex, and sleep

Abraham Maslow and Self-Actualization

How did humanism begin?

We can think of humanism as officially beginning in the early 1960s with the publication of the *Journal of Humanistic Psychology*. One of the major figures behind establishing the journal was Abraham Maslow. Although trained as a behaviorist, Maslow increasingly felt there was too much emphasis on rewards and punishments in psychology and not enough focus on feelings and subjective experiences. Breaking away from behaviorism, Maslow (1968) developed his humanistic theory, which emphasizes our need and capacity for self-actualization.

Which of our many needs must we satisfy first?

Maslow believed that in trying to achieve self-actualization and reach our true potential, we must first satisfy four other types of needs. As you may remember from Module 11, Maslow arranged all human needs into a hierarchy. His **hierarchy of needs** *arranges needs in ascending order, with biological needs at the bottom and social and personal needs at the top; as needs at one level are met, we advance to the next level.* According to Maslow's hierarchy, we must satisfy our biological needs before we can turn our attention and energy to fulfilling our personal and social needs.

Maslow divided needs into two general categories: deficiency and growth needs. **Deficiency needs** *are physiological needs (food, sleep) and psychological needs (safety, belongingness, and esteem) that we try to fulfill if they are not met.* **Growth needs** *are those at the higher levels and include the desire for truth, goodness, beauty, and justice.* According to Maslow, we must satisfy our deficiency needs, in proper sequence, before having the time and energy to satisfy our growth needs and move toward self-actualization.

What exactly is self-actualization?

Maslow (1971) developed his idea of **self-actualization**, *which is fulfilling one's unique human potential,* after studying highly productive, exceptional people. For example, Maslow believed that Abraham Lincoln, Albert Einstein, and Eleanor Roosevelt had been self-actualized. There is no doubt that Maslow would also have considered Martin Luther King, Jr. an example of a self-actualized person.

Characteristics of Self-Actualized Individuals

- Perceive reality accurately

- Are independent and autonomous

- Prefer to have a deep, loving relationship with only a few people

- Focus on accomplishing their goals

- Report *peak experiences,* which are moments of great joy and satisfaction

Martin Luther King, Jr. devoted his life to achieving civil rights for all people. Here he delivers his famous "I Have a Dream" speech at a civil rights rally in Washington, D.C. He was awarded the Nobel prize for peace at age 35. He was gunned down by an assassin's bullet at age 39. King's achievements exemplify the humanistic idea of self-actualization.

Maslow believed that although very few individuals reach the level of self-actualization, everyone has a self-actualizing tendency. This tendency motivates us to become the best kind of person we are capable of becoming.

Humanistic Theories

Carl Rogers: Self Theory

Wasn't he trained in the Freudian tradition?

Carl Rogers, who was initially trained in the psychodynamic approach, was a practicing clinical psychologist for most of his life. He felt that Freud placed too much emphasis on unconscious forces and not enough on the potential for psychological growth. Beginning in the 1960s, Rogers developed his own version of humanistic theory.

Does rock star David Bowie's change in looks reflect his change in self?

Carl Rogers's theory of personality is often called *self theory* because of his emphasis on the self or self-concept. **Self** or **self-concept** *refers to how we see or describe ourselves; it includes how we perceive our abilities, personality characteristics, and behaviors.* According to Rogers (1980), self-concept plays an important role in personality because it influences our behaviors, feelings, and thoughts. For example, if we have a **positive self-concept,** *we will tend to act, feel, and think optimistically and constructively;* if we have a **negative self-concept,** *we will tend to act, feel, and think pessimistically and destructively.*

Sometimes a person may be undecided about what is his or her real self. As we discover our real self, we may undergo a number of changes in personality.

Which is David Bowie's real self?

Through the years, rock star David Bowie has radically changed his looks, clothes, and personal values. For example, Bowie's earlier looks and behaviors might be described as having been on society's fringe. Now, however, Bowie is in his mid-40s and appears to be quite conventional in looks, clothes, and personal values. In fact, he surprised many of his fans with the announcement of his marriage and a strong desire to settle down. Has Bowie finally found his real self?

Which is the real me?

Carl Rogers said that his clients often asked questions related to their selves: "How do I find myself?" "Why do I sometimes feel that I don't know myself?" "Why do I say or do things that aren't really me?" Rogers developed a clever answer to these relatively common and perplexing questions. He said that there are two kinds of selves: there is the **real self,** *which is based on one's actual experiences and represents one's actual self;* and there is the **ideal self,** *which is based on one's hopes and wishes and reflects one's desired self.*

In some cases, the desires and wishes of one's ideal self may contradict the abilities and experiences of the real self. For example, suppose a student's ideal self is a hardworking, responsible student who receives good grades, but the student's real self puts things off to the last minute, studies less than required, and obtains poor grades. According to Rogers, a glaring contradiction between the ideal and real self can result in personality problems. Rogers suggested that we can resolve contradictions between the ideal and real self by paying more attention to our actual experiences, working to have more positive experiences, and paying less attention to the expectations of others. In working out discrepancies between our ideal and real selves, we may undergo changes in looks, clothes, and behavior.

Now that you know what the self is, let's see how it develops.

What is unconditional positive regard?

As we develop from child to teenager to adult, we have a need for being given **positive regard,** *which includes love, sympathy, acceptance, and respect from family, friends, and people important to us.* One type of positive regard, *conditional positive regard,* is dependent on our behaving in certain ways, such as living up to the standards of others. For instance, parents may give a child support, warmth, or approval only if the child does well in school. In this case, the child is receiving conditional positive regard,

Pets are such wonderful companions because they give unconditional positive regard.

based on good academic performance. If children receive primarily conditional positive regard, they will develop a negative self-concept and will feel bad or worthless when they do something that disappoints others.

Rogers believed that the development of a positive self-concept depends on receiving unconditional positive regard. **Unconditional positive regard** *means that others show us love and acceptance despite the fact that we sometimes behave in ways that are different from what they think or value.* For example, parents who show their love and respect even if a child does not always get high grades exhibit unconditional positive regard. Children who receive unconditional positive regard will develop a positive self-concept and will feel good about themselves even when they do something that disappoints others.

Carl Rogers stressed unconditional positive regard.

Did Rogers also emphasize self-actualization?

Similar to Maslow, Rogers emphasized the idea of self-actualization, which he defined as an inherent tendency for reaching a healthy psychological state and achieving self-fulfillment. Rogers saw self-actualization as providing both motivation and direction toward gaining fulfillment and developing our potentials. However, our tendency for self-actualization may be hindered or blocked if we encounter frustrating conditions, such as situational hurdles or personal difficulties. Rogers believed that we will experience the greatest self-actualization if we work to remove situational problems, resolve our personal problems, and receive unconditional positive regard.

Humanistic Theories

Evaluation of Humanistic Theories

Maslow's and Rogers's humanistic theories made three contributions to understanding personality:

1 Humanistic theories stress the belief that human nature is basically good and that we all have an inherent potential for self-fulfillment and self-actualization. These theories contrast with the more pessimistic Freudian belief that we are driven by unconscious forces and biological drives.

Critics reply that there is little scientific evidence for an inherent tendency toward self-fulfillment. They say that the idea of self-actualization is more of a philosophical statement than a scientific explanation.

2 Humanistic theories point out that to understand personality we need to study the whole person rather than focusing on individual pieces or parts.

Critics reply that while holistic concepts, such as self-actualization, may be useful, they have proven difficult to study or verify. Furthermore, it is often useful to break complex phenomenon into individual parts in order to understand the whole.

3 Humanistic theories have had the greatest impact in counseling and clinical settings that have adopted the ideas of personal growth, self-fulfillment, and self-actualization (Ford, 1991).

Critics reply that humanistic theories have had less impact on mainstream psychology because of the difficulty of verifying humanistic concepts.

Maslow hoped that humanistic theories would become a third major force in psychology, along with behavioral and psychoanalytic theories. Although it is too early to judge whether the humanistic approach has achieved Maslow's goal, many of humanism's ideas have been incorporated into approaches for counseling and psychotherapy.

After the Concept/Glossary, we'll discuss an uplifting story of how Indo-Chinese refugee children are overcoming language and cultural difficulties to reach their potentials.

CONCEPT/ GLOSSARY: Humanistic Theories

1. Personality theories that emphasize our capacity for personal growth, the development of our potential, and freedom to choose our destinies are referred to as _____ theories.

2. These theories have three characteristics in common. They take the perspective that our perception of the world, whether or not it is accurate, becomes our reality; this is called the (a)_____ perspective. Humanistic theories see personality as more than the sum of individual parts and consider personality as a unique and total entity that functions as a unit; this is the (b)_____ view of personality. Humanistic theories point to an inherent tendency that each of us has to reach our true potential; this tendency is called (c)_____.

3. The idea that our needs occur in ascending order with biological needs at the bottom and social and personal needs at the top and that we must meet our lower-level needs before we can satisfy higher ones is called (a)_____. Our physiological needs (food, sleep) and psychological needs (safety, belongingness, and esteem) are called (b)_____ needs because we try to fulfill them if they are not met. The highest need of self-actualization, which includes the desire for truth, goodness, beauty, and justice, is called a (c)_____ need.

4. One of the basic concepts of Carl Rogers's theory of personality is (a)_____, or how we see or describe ourselves, which includes how we perceive our abilities, personality characteristics, and behaviors. According to Rogers, it is important that we receive love and acceptance despite the fact that we sometimes behave in ways that are different from what others think or value; this type of acceptance is called (b)_____.

Answers: 1. humanistic; 2. (a) phenomenological, (b) holistic, (c) self-actualization; 3. (a) Maslow's hierarchy of needs, (b) deficiency, (c) growth; 4. (a) self or self-concept, (b) unconditional positive regard.

Personal Values and Achievement

Why did researchers study the boat people?

In the late 1970s and early 1980s, people from Vietnam and Laos were escaping the political and economic chaos that had followed the war in Vietnam. Thousands of Indo-Chinese refugees, many of whom escaped by boat and were therefore known as "boat people," were allowed to resettle in the United States. On their arrival in America, their only possessions were the clothes they wore. They knew virtually no English and had almost no knowledge of Western culture. In spite of horrendous difficulties, refugee children achieved such remarkable academic success that American educators were scratching their heads and asking why. To answer this question, a team of researchers studied Indo-Chinese schoolchildren (Caplan, Choy, & Whitmore, 1992).

Method. The researchers selected a random sample of 200 Indo-Chinese refugee families with a total of 536 school-age children. The children had been in the United States for an average of three and a half years and had attended schools in low-income metropolitan areas where academic environments are usually far from optimal.

Results. The researchers computed the mean grade point average for the 536 children, who were fairly evenly distributed among grades 1 through 12. They found that 27% of the children had a grade point average in the A range, 52% had a GPA in the B range, 17% in the C range, and only 4%, below a grade of C. Equally noteworthy was the children's overall performance in math. Almost 50% of the children earned A's, while another 33% earned B's in this subject. On national math tests, the Indo-Chinese children's average scores were almost three times higher than the national norm. After analyzing all these data, the researchers asked the obvious question.

In Indo-Chinese families, all the members get involved in doing homework. (photo © Jason Goltz)

How did the Indo-Chinese students beat the odds?

The researchers discovered that family values were the reason Indo-Chinese children could solve problems of language and culture and excel in school.

The *primary values* held by Indo-Chinese families are that parents and children have mutual respect and obligation, that family members strive to maintain cooperation and harmony, and that family members are committed to accomplishment and achievement. A clear example of commitment to accomplishment is the amount of time Indo-Chinese children spend doing homework: they average about 3 hours a day. In contrast, American students average about 1¹/₂ hours a day.

Conclusions. The Indo-Chinese children earned great academic success primarily because of personal and cultural values transmitted by their families. The researchers concluded that American parents must become more committed to the education of their children if their children are to succeed in school. It seems, then, that Americans can truly learn from the values of the Indo-Chinese refugees. Besides showing the influence of culture, this example illustrates one of the humanists' basic assumptions—the tendency for self-fulfillment.

Next we'll see how two approaches to personality handle a relatively common problem: shyness.

APPLYING/ EXPLORING: SHYNESS

What's it like to be shy? Tom hated going to parties, but his friends assured him that this one would be fun. When he and his friend arrived, the party was going strong and there were people—mostly strangers—everywhere. As he looked around for something to do, he felt tense and worried. He did not like meeting or talking to strangers because he could not think of anything to say. The more people he saw talking, laughing, and having a good time, the more inadequate and self-conscious he felt. Finally, Tom left the party early and went home feeling like a failure.

Social situations are very threatening to shy people.

Tom's difficulties in this social situation are due to shyness. **Shyness** *is the tendency to feel tense, worried, or awkward in social situations.* About 25% of college students report severe shyness, which means that they frequently feel shy in many different social situations; about 40% of college students report mild shyness, which means that their feelings of shyness are less frequent and do not occur in all social situations (Jones, Briggs, & Smith, 1986; Zimbardo, 1977).

One way in which psychologists measure shyness is with questionnaires. Shy people typically agree with a large percentage of the following questions (Cheek & Buss, 1981):

- I am often uncomfortable at parties and other social gatherings.
- I feel tense when I'm with people I don't know well.
- I feel nervous when speaking to someone in authority.
- I have trouble looking someone right in the eye.
- When conversing I worry about saying something dumb.
- I am more shy with members of the opposite sex.
- I am socially somewhat awkward.
- I feel inhibited in social situations.

Although shyness is relatively easy to measure, its causes are more difficult to determine. We're going to review shyness as it might be interpreted by two different approaches, one based on Freud's psychodynamic theory of personality and one based on current cognitive-behavioral views of personality.

Psychodynamic Approach

Although Freud did not specifically talk about shyness, Donald Kaplan (1972) has applied psychodynamic concepts to this problem. Kaplan is a practicing psychoanalyst whose data come from observations on his clients. According to Kaplan, the symptoms of shyness include both conscious and unconscious feelings of fear and anxiety, which are activated only by social situations. For example, shy people may have conscious fears of having nothing to say and of being misunderstood or ignored, as well as unconscious fears of displaying themselves, being rejected, or losing control. Shy people may deal with these anxieties by using defense mechanisms. Kaplan describes one of his shy clients who reduced his anxiety through *displacement* by changing his fears of being ignored, rejected, or overlooked into opposite feelings of self-righteousness and contempt. Another client reduced her anxiety through *projection* by creating elaborate social fantasies in which she was a successful hostess.

As for the causes of shyness, Kaplan traces them back to unresolved conflicts at one or more of Freud's psychosexual stages. For example, one very shy client reported that his mother constantly fed him so that he would never cry or whimper. As a result, Kaplan suggests that this client's unresolved conflict during the oral stage resulted in his feelings of inadequacy and shyness in later social interactions.

One advantage of the psychodynamic approach is that it provides a rich and complex view of shyness, which takes in conscious and unconscious fears, use of defense mechanisms, and unresolved psychosexual conflicts. However, critics say that the psychodynamic approach to shyness, similar to other Freudian explanations, has proven difficult to verify through research (Cheek & Watson, 1989).

Cognitive-Behavioral Approach

The cognitive-behavioral approach breaks shyness down into three measurable or observable components: emotional, behavioral, and cognitive (Briggs, Cheek, & Jones, 1986; Cheek & Watson, 1989). The emotional component includes blushing, butterflies in the stomach, dry mouth, pounding heart, trembling, and cold or wet hands. The behavioral component includes talking and smiling less, making less eye contact, showing fewer facial expressions, initiating fewer conversations, and having fewer dates and friends. The cognitive component includes excessive worry about being noticeable, paying too much attention to one's negative thoughts, being too critical of oneself, and making primarily negative evaluations of one's actions. According to the cognitive-behavioral approach, shyness can be understood by analyzing the interaction among these three components.

As for the causes of shyness, the cognitive-behavioral approach emphasizes three influences: genetic, cognitive, and behavioral. We touched on the genetic influence on shyness in our earlier discussion of temperament (Module 19). Researchers found that about 25% of infants inherit nervous systems that cause excessive physiological arousal to novel stimuli and that this arousal is associated with being fearful and shy in social situations (Kagan & Snidman, 1991). The cognitive influence on shyness comes from being overly self-consciousness, which leads to worrisome thoughts and irrational beliefs that interfere with functioning. The behavioral influence on shyness involves having too few social and communication skills, which results in being punished over and over for social interactions.

One advantage of the cognitive-behavioral approach is that it breaks shyness down into three measurable or observable components. Critics of this approach point out that its emphasis on observable components may overlook unconscious factors of which the shy person is unaware.

Summary/Self-Test

FREUD'S PSYCHODYNAMIC THEORY

1. The lasting behaviors, thoughts, and emotions that typify how we react and adapt to other people and situations make up our (a)_____. An organized attempt to explain how personalities develop and why they differ is called a (b)_____ of personality.

2. Freud's approach that emphasizes the importance of early childhood experiences and conflicts between conscious and unconscious forces is called a (a)_____ theory of personality. According to Freud, those wishes, desires, or thoughts of which we are aware or that we can readily recall are (b)_____; those that we automatically repress because of their disturbing or threatening content are (c)_____.

3. Freud's technique of encouraging clients to talk about any thoughts or images that enter their heads is called (a)_____. His assumption that dreams provide clues to unconscious thoughts and desires gave rise to his technique of (b)_____. Mistakes that we make in everyday speech that are thought to reflect unconscious thoughts or wishes are called (c)_____.

■ *Two weeks before every big test, Tony plans to study two hours daily, but he always finds some excuse to put off studying until the day before the exam. How would a Freudian explain Tony's behavior?*

DIVISIONS OF THE MIND

4. According to Freud, the biological drives of sex and aggression are the source of all psychic or mental energy and give rise to the development of the (a)_____. Because this division of the mind strives to satisfy drives and avoid pain without concern for moral or social restrictions, it is said to be operating according to the (b)_____. During infancy, the second division of the mind develops from the id and is called the (c)_____. The goal of this second division is to find safe and socially acceptable ways of satisfying the id's desires. The ego follows a policy of satisfying a wish or desire only if a socially acceptable outlet is available; thus it is said

to operate according to the (d)_____. During early childhood the third division of the mind develops from the id and is called the (e)_____. The goal of this division is to apply the moral values and standards of one's parents and society in satisfying one's wishes.

5. When the id, ego, and superego are in conflict, an unpleasant state of uneasiness, apprehension, and heightened physiological arousal may occur; this is known as (a)_____. The Freudian processes that operate at unconscious levels to help the ego reduce anxiety through self-deception are called (b)_____; they can be helpful or harmful, depending on how much we rely on them.

■ *Sheryl, who claims to be sensitive to women's issues, tends to wear sexy clothes around campus. What might a Freudian say about the relationship between her id, ego, and superego?*

DEVELOPMENT OF PERSONALITY

6. The essence of Freud's theory of personality development is a series of five developmental stages, called (a)_____, during which the individual seeks pleasure from different parts of the body. The stage that lasts for the first 18 months of life is called the (b)_____ stage. It is followed by the (c)_____ stage, which lasts until about age 3. The next stage, until about age 6, is called the (d)_____ stage. The stage that lasts from about age 6 to puberty is called the (e)_____ stage; it is followed by the (f)_____ stage, which lasts through adulthood.

7. The resolution of the potential conflict at each stage has important implications for personality. A Freudian process through which individuals may be locked into earlier psychosexual stages because their wishes were overgratified or undergratified is called _____; it can occur at any stage.

■ *You are very neat and your roommate is extremely sloppy. How would Freud's theory explain each of your behaviors?*

FREUD'S FOLLOWERS

8. Jung believed that the basic force is not the sex drive, as Freud believed, but ancient memory traces and symbols shared by all peoples in all cultures, called the (a)_____. According to Adler's philosophy, each person is a social being with a unique personality and is motivated by (b)_____.

9. Those who generally agreed with Freud's basic ideas but disagreed with his emphasis on biological forces, sexual drives, and psychosexual stages are referred to as _____; they turned the emphasis of psychodynamic theory to psychosocial and cultural influences.

■ *For just a few minutes examine your own upbringing, how you were treated by your parents, and what kind of personality you have developed. Which factors in the development of your personality support Freud's theory and which do not?*

PROJECTIVE TESTS

10. Typically a combination of tests are used to assess personality. Tests that involve presenting an ambiguous stimulus and asking the person to describe it are called (a)_____ tests. A test used to assess personality in terms of how one interprets a series of inkblots is called the (b)_____ test. A test in which the subject is to make up a story about people shown in ambiguous situations is called the (c)_____.

■ *Could projective tests be used to determine which students are more likely to cheat on exams?*

HUMANISTIC THEORIES

11. Humanistic theories emphasize our capacity for personal growth, development of our potential, and freedom to choose our (a)_____. They stress that our perception of the world becomes our reality; this is called the (b)_____ perspective. These theories emphasize that one's personality is unique, functions as a unit, and is more than the sum of individual parts; together these ideas make up the (c)_____ view. These theories also highlight the idea of an inherent tendency to reach our true potentials, which is called (d)_____.

12. According to Maslow, our needs are arranged in a hierarchy with (a)_____ at the bottom and (b)_____ at the top.

13. How we see or describe ourselves, including how we perceive our abilities, personality characteristics, and behaviors, is referred to as our (a)_____. According to Carl Rogers, the development of self-concept depends on our interactions with others. If we receive (b)_____

positive regard, even when our behavior is disappointing, we will develop a positive self-concept and tend to act, feel, and think optimistically and constructively.

■ *How would humanistic theories explain why many students change their majors three to five times during their college careers?*

CULTURAL DIVERSITY: PERSONAL VALUES AND ACHIEVEMENT

14. Indo-Chinese children overcame problems of language and culture and excelled in American schools in part because of the _____ held by their families. One of these values was that these children believed they had control over their own destinies.

■ *If you were the principal of a grade school, how might you improve overall student performance?*

APPLYING/EXPLORING: SHYNESS

15. Using Freud's psychodynamic concepts, Kaplan has concluded that shyness includes conscious and unconscious feelings of _____ and _____, which are activated by social situations. In comparison, the cognitive-behavioral approach breaks shyness down into three measurable or observable components: physiological, behavioral, and cognitive.

■ *Carl says that he's always been shy and that's just the way he is. How would a Freudian differ from a cognitive behaviorist in helping Carl deal with his shyness?*

MODULE 24
SOCIAL LEARNING AND TRAIT THEORIES

Charles Dutton says that an insight forever changed his personality and his life.

He had been in and out of reform schools since he was 12 years old. Now he was in prison for manslaughter and illegal possession of a firearm. He was trouble in prison, acting as a ringleader of a riot, for which he was punished with solitary confinement. To pass his time, he took along a book that a friend had given him. It was a book of plays by black authors. He was so moved by the plays that his rage and anger at society were channeled into an intense passion for acting.

At one point he spent more than 60 painful days in the prison hospital after a fellow inmate had plunged an icepick through his neck. During

What changed a convicted felon into a respected actor?

those long days in the hospital, he thought about how his life had almost ended. He decided that it was time to put his life in order and accomplish something worthwhile during his remaining time in prison. He obtained a high school equivalency and then a two-year college degree, read dozens of plays, and even started a prison theater. After his parole, he attended college and got his B.A. in drama. His high point came when he was accepted into Yale drama school.

After Yale, he won several roles in Broadway plays. Two of his performances (in "Ma Rainey's Black Bottom" and "The Piano Lesson") were nominated for Tonys, theater's highest award. By 1992, ex-problem boy, ex-con, ex-prison terrorist Charles Dutton had turned into a very successful actor. He landed a big role in the movie *Alien³* and was starring in *Roc,* his own television series.

Charles says, "Several people asked me, how did I make it? How did I change? . . . The bottom line is discovering one's humanity and realizing we are only on this planet for a couple of seconds in the large scheme of things." (adapted from *Los Angeles Times Magazine,* August 25, 1991, p. 84)

The uplifting story of Charles Dutton illustrates several points about personality. First, the fact that Charles underwent major personality changes following powerful insights points to the influence of cognitive processes in behavior. Second, the apparent differences in Charles's personality over time are remarkable—and lead us to question how we might measure and describe personality traits. These two points are the major focus of the two theories of personality in this module.

What's Coming

In this module we'll explain two approaches to personality, each with a different emphasis. Social learning theory (also called social-cognitive theory) stresses the influence of cognitive, learning, and social processes on personality. Trait theory concentrates on measuring and describing differences among personalities.

We'll begin with social learning theory.

Social Learning Theory

Social learning theory grew out of the research of a number of psychologists, including Julian Rotter (1966), Albert Bandura (1989a), and Walter Mischel (1990). **Social learning theory** *emphasizes the influence of learning, social, and cognitive processes on how we evaluate, interpret, and organize information and apply that information to ourselves and others.* For example, Charles Dutton changed from being a troublesome prisoner to an aspiring actor after several incidents in prison caused him to rethink his values and goals.

We're going to ask two major questions about social learning theory: How do cognitive processes influence our behaviors? And can specific beliefs change how we perceive our world?

How do cognitive processes influence our behaviors?
Albert Bandura (1989a) originally called his theory social learning theory but later changed its name to social-cognitive theory to emphasize cognitive influences. **Bandura's social-cognitive theory** *assumes that personality development, growth, and change are influenced by four distinctively human cognitive processes: highly developed language ability, observational learning, purposeful behavior, and self-analysis.* Let's see how each of these cognitive processes influences personality.

1 Our *highly developed language ability* gives us a powerful tool for processing and understanding information, which is critical to personality development. Insights, thoughts, and ideas help us interpret and evaluate what is important to development and growth and provide guidance and motivation for our actions. For example, if you value education, you will work hard to obtain a college degree.

2 Our capacity for *observational learning,* which is also called *vicarious learning,* is one of the key elements of social learning theory. **Observational learning** *is a form of learning that develops through watching and does not require the observer to perform any observable behavior or receive a reinforcer.* Through observational learning we can acquire a wide range of knowledge that affects personality development.

3 Our capacity for forethought, which is the ability to anticipate events, plan ahead, and set goals, gives our behavior a purpose. *Purposeful behavior* can provide motivation for personality development, growth, and change. For instance, once Charles set the goal of becoming an actor, his personality changed from behaving like an angry convict to behaving like a hopeful actor.

4 Thanks to our capacity for *self-analysis,* we can monitor our own thoughts and actions as well as set or change our goals, values, and personality. For example, after analyzing all the time he had spent in prison, Charles decided that there must be something more, which motivated him to start his education while still in prison.

Bandura's social-cognitive theory identifies four processes that influence personality development.

According to Bandura's social-cognitive theory, these four cognitive processes influence our personality development, growth, and change. To make the relationship between ideas and personality more concrete, we'll focus on three specific beliefs.

Social Learning Theory

Can specific beliefs change how we perceive our world?
Charles Dutton would tell us that two beliefs radically changed his life: realizing that in the bigger picture his life amounted to only a couple of seconds, and deciding to become an actor. The power of beliefs and ideas to change the way that we interpret situations and events is one of the basic assumptions of social learning theories (Messer & Warren, 1990). We're going to examine three beliefs—locus of control, self-efficacy, and delay of gratification—that were developed by three different psychologists.

You will be more successful in college if you believe that you control your own fate.

Locus of Control

How much control do you have over your grades?
This is the kind of question that intrigued Julian Rotter (1990), who developed the concept of locus of control. **Locus of control** *refers to our beliefs concerning how much control we have over situations or rewards.* We are said to have an **internal locus of control** *if we believe that we have control over situations and rewards.* We are said to have an **external locus of control** *if we believe that we do not have control over situations and rewards and that events outside ourselves (fate) determine what happens.*

For example, if you believe that how much you study determines your grades, you have an internal locus of control; if you believe that your grades are determined by things outside you, such as chance, the grade curve, or tricky questions, you have an external locus of control.

There are literally hundreds of studies that report a consistent but relatively low (.20–.30) correlation between locus of control and such variables as mental health and psychological functioning (Lefcourt, 1981). For example, people with an internal locus of control were more likely to take preventive health measures, report less stress, and be less depressed than those with an external locus of control (Stern, McCants, & Pettine, 1982). These findings indicate that a specific belief, such as how much control you believe you have, might change how you perceive your world.

Self-Efficacy

Do you believe that you can get high grades?
According to Albert Bandura (1989b), one reason some students study hard and get higher grades and others study less and get lower grades is related to self-efficacy. **Self-efficacy** *refers to our personal beliefs of how capable we are of exercising control over events in our lives.* For example, saying, "I think that I am capable of getting a high grade in this course" would be a sign of high self-efficacy. We judge self-efficacy by combining four sources of information:

Determining Locus of Control

Here are several items from a scale that Rotter (1966) developed to measure locus of control. For each item, select the alternative (a or b) that is most true for you.

1 (a) No matter how hard you try, some people just don't like you.
(b) People who can't get others to like them don't understand how to get along with others.

2 (a) It is not always wise to plan too far ahead, because many things just turn out to be a matter of good or bad fortune.
(b) When I make plans, I am almost certain I can make them work.

3 (a) In the case of the well-prepared student, there is rarely such a thing as an unfair test.
(b) Often exam questions tend to be so unrelated to course work that studying is really useless.

Internal locus of control is indicated by 1b, 2b, and 3a. Rotter's actual scale consists of 23 items that are similar to these three. Locus of control is considered a continuum, with internal on one end and external on the other. Most of us lie somewhere in between.

1. We use previous experiences of success or failure on similar tasks to estimate how we will do on a new, related task.

2. We compare our capabilities with those of others.

3. We listen to what others say about our capabilities.

4. We use feedback from our bodies about our strength, vulnerability, and capability.

Thus, we exhibit self-efficacy for getting a good grade in a course if we have previous success with getting high grades, if we believe we are as academically capable as others, if our friends say we are smart, and if we do not become too stressed during exams.

Research on self-efficacy indicates that the higher a person's self-efficacy, the more likely that he or she will be successful in changing some behavior or performing well on a task, such as stopping smoking, losing weight, overcoming a phobia, or doing well in school (Bandura, 1989b; Schunk, 1989). These findings indicate that a specific belief, such as self-efficacy, can affect our performance on a variety of tasks.

Delay of Gratification

Can you put off going to a party in order to study?

Walter Mischel (1989) and his colleagues have recast the ideas behind the popular ideas of "willpower" and "self-control" into the concept of delayed gratification. **Delay of gratification** *is voluntarily postponing an immediate reward to persist in completing a task for the promise of a future reward.*

If you had a lot of willpower—if you were good at delaying gratification—you would postpone the immediate reward of going to a party and instead study with the hope of obtaining a larger future reward, a good grade.

A technique that Mischel used to measure delay of gratification was to show children two objects, one less preferred (a single marshmallow) and one more preferred (two marshmallows). The children were told that to obtain the more preferred reward, they had to wait until the experimenter, who had to leave the room, returned after some delay (about 15 minutes). Children were free to end the waiting period by ringing a bell—but then they would get only the less preferred reward. Thus, the child had a real conflict: accept immediate gratification and take the less preferred reward, or delay gratification and obtain the more preferred reward. Researchers found that 4-year-old children differed greatly in the length of time they could delay gratification. This time was, in turn, significantly associated with a number of psychological variables. For example, 4-year-old children who preferred delayed rewards tended to be more intelligent, to have greater social responsibility, and to strive for higher achievement.

You will be more successful in college if you can put off immediate pleasures for the sake of better and future rewards.

More interesting is the fact that when these children were tested at age 14, the same relationships held: those adolescents who had preferred to delay gratification at age 4 were now rated by parents as more competent, more intelligent, and better able to concentrate than those who did not delay gratification. This study makes an important point: the cognitive processes that underlie delay of gratification also affect a number of personal and social behaviors.

These three beliefs—locus of control, self-efficacy, and delay of gratification—influence behavior and thus support the basic assumption of social learning theory.

Social Learning Theory

Evaluation of Social Learning Theory

Social learning theory has made three major contributions to understanding personality:

1 Social learning concepts are based on *objective measurement* and *laboratory research* and thus are less subject to error and bias. As a result, these concepts (locus of control, observational learning, delay of gratification, self-efficacy) can be manipulated, controlled, and experimentally tested.

Critics say that because social learning concepts deal only with particular aspects of learning or cognition, they do not form a complete theory of personality. They argue that a complete theory of personality should also include the influence of childhood and emotional factors.

2 Social learning theory emphasizes specific *learning and cognitive processes*, which are often neglected by other theories. For example, social learning theory describes the steps involved in observational learning and how certain beliefs and ideas influence behavior.

Critics point out that social learning theory generally ignores emotional behavior and genetic influences, two factors that have significant effects on human behavior.

3 Social learning theory's concepts have resulted in the development of several successful programs for changing behavior and personality. We discussed one such program, behavior modification, in Module 12, and we will discuss several more behavioral change programs in Module 30.

Critics argue that therapy programs based on social learning theory may treat only the symptoms and not deeper emotional or unconscious causes. We will discuss this complex issue in Chapter 15.

Critics complain that social learning theory concentrates on pieces of personality and neglects emotional forces. Social learning theorists reply that they have provided objectively measured and carefully researched concepts that not only show how learning and cognitive processes influence behavior but also how these concepts can be used in programs to change behavior and personality.

Next we'll discuss a personality theory that emphasizes describing and assessing differences between personalities.

Nelson Mandela, one of South Africa's respected black leaders, exemplifies one of the basic assumptions of social learning theory: that beliefs and ideas influence behavior. Mandela's lifelong opposition to apartheid resulted in his being imprisoned for 27 years. Finally, in 1990, at the age of 71, he was released and today continues to fight for his belief—an end to apartheid. In the spring of 1992 the great majority of South African whites (68%) supported a referendum to end apartheid. Mandela said, "We are happy indeed" (*Los Angeles Times*, March 19, 1992, p. A-1).

Trait Theory

Do women make better cops?

Officer Kelly patrols an area known for problems with street thugs. Although we may think that the best way to control thugs is with threat or force, Kelly rarely uses either. Kelly is a female cop who readily admits that her physical strength cannot always match that of the macho males she encounters. "Coming across aggressively doesn't work with gang members," Kelly explains. "If that first encounter is direct, knowledgeable, and made with authority, they respond. It takes a few more words but it works" (*Time*, February 17, 1992, p. 70).

Observations on female officers indicate that in many situations they are calmer, are better communicators, are more diplomatic, and use a softer touch than their male counterparts. For example, women officers are rarely charged with use of excessive force, and they are more likely to deal with rape and domestic-violence calls with more empathy and to resolve conflicts without making the victims defensive. Women officers see themselves more as peacekeepers and negotiators, while male officers see themselves as enforcers and crime-fighters. Houston Police Chief Elizabeth Watson, the only woman in the nation to head a major metropolitan force, says, "Women tend to rely more on intellectual than physical prowess." So far women make up only 9% of over 525,000 police officers. However, there is growing evidence that, in some ways, women do make better cops.

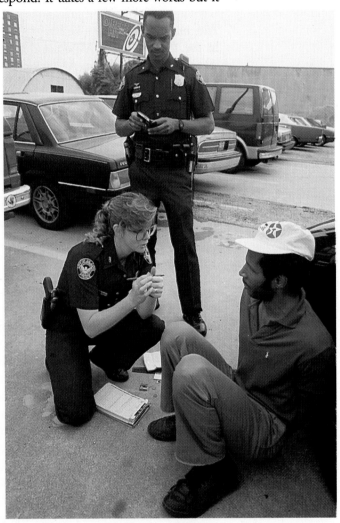

Do female police officers have personality traits different from their male counterparts?

If we were interested in describing the personality differences between female and male police officers, we would find ourselves using trait theory. **Trait theory** *refers to an approach to understanding the structure of personality by measuring, identifying, and analyzing differences in personality.* The basic units of measurement are *traits,* which act like keys in unlocking personality differences. A **trait** *is a relatively stable and enduring tendency to behave in a particular way.* The goal of trait theory is to find the smallest number of traits that can describe all differences of personality.

One method of measuring traits is to give subjects a list of adjectives and ask them to check those that best describe their personalities. For example, some traits of women police officers are compassion, sympathy, and diplomacy, which give them the tendency to act more as peacekeepers and negotiators. Some traits of male officers are assertiveness, aggressiveness, and directness, which give them the tendency to act more as enforcers and crime-fighters.

Let's see how close psychologists are to reaching their goal of identifying the basic traits of human personality.

Trait Theory

Searching for Traits

For over 50 years, one goal of personality researchers was to find a list of traits whose criteria seemed almost mutually exclusive. The list had to be very short, but it also had to be comprehensive enough to describe anyone's personality—whether student, professor, doctor, truck driver, police officer, salesperson, computer programmer, secretary, or zookeeper. The search for the elusive list of traits began in the 1930s—with a dictionary.

How many traits can there be?

In the 1930s Gordon Allport and an associate went through the dictionary and selected every term that could distinguish differences among personalities (Allport & Odbert, 1936). They found about 18,000 terms that dealt with all kinds of personality differences, but of these about 4,500 were considered to fit their definition of personality traits. Allport defined *traits* as stable and consistent tendencies of how an individual adjusts to his or her environment. The advantage of Allport's list was that it was so comprehensive that it could describe anyone's and everyone's personality. The disadvantage was that it was so incredibly long that it was impractical to use in research.

Although Allport's search for and definition of traits set the stage for future research, his alphabetical list of thousands of traits needed to be organized into far fewer traits. This task fell to Raymond Cattell.

Aren't some traits related?

In the 1940s Raymond Cattell (1943) took Allport's list of 4,500 traits and used factor analysis to reduce the list to the most basic traits. **Factor analysis** *is a complicated statistical method that finds relationships among many different or diverse items.* Cattell used factor analysis to search for *relationships* among the hundreds of traits on Allport's list. Cattell reduced the original list to 35 basic traits, which he called *source traits* because he claimed that they could describe all differences among personalities. Although Cattell's achievement was remarkable, his list of 35 traits, and even his further reduction of the list to 16 traits, still proved too long to be practical for research and only moderately useful in assessing personality differences. Obviously, Cattell's list needed more reducing, but that was to take another 30 years.

Can all the traits be reduced to five?

From the 1960s to the early 1990s, about a dozen researchers in several countries used factor analysis to find relationships among lists of adjectives that described personality differences. They identified five traits, now known as the Big Five, and the five-factor model of personality. The **five-factor model** *organizes all personality traits under five categories that are used to describe differences in personality.*

Could you define all the personality differences between this individual . . .

Five-Factor Model Here are examples of adjectives that define each of the five factors (OCEAN).	**Openness to experience** Down to earth— Imaginative Conventional— Original Uncreative— Creative	**Conscientiousness** Negligent— Conscientious Lazy—Hardworking Late—Punctual	**Extraversion** Reserved— Affectionate Quiet—Talkative Loner—Joiner	**Agreeableness** Suspicious—Trusting Irritable—Good-natured Ruthless—Soft-hearted	**Neuroticism** Calm—Worrying Comfortable—Self-conscious Unemotional—Emotional

OCEAN

. . . and this one by using only five traits? (You'll learn their identities later in this module.)

Most researchers agree on the following names for the five factors: *openness to experience, conscientiousness, extraversion, agreeableness,* and *neuroticism.* As a help to remembering these factors, notice that the first letters make the acronym OCEAN.

These five factors can be thought of as supertraits because each factor includes dozens of related traits. For example, conscientiousness includes the traits of being late or punctual, lazy or hardworking, and aimless or ambitious. Data supporting the five-factor model have been replicated in at least three different languages and countries (John, 1990).

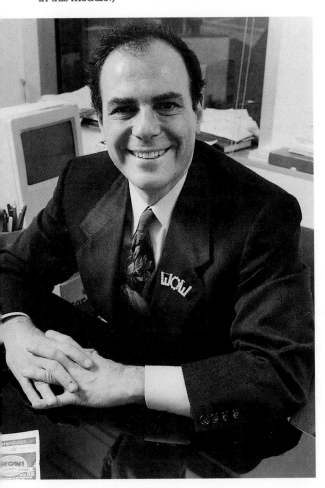

Why does the five-factor model make researchers smile? One reason personality researchers are smiling is that the five-factor model brings them, at last, within reach of their goal: finding a short but exhaustive list of personality traits. Compared with previous lists of personality traits, the five-factor model is the first to organize all personality differences under only five comprehensive categories (McCrae, 1991). This means that questionnaires based on the five-factor model should enable researchers to assess the vast majority of personality differences among individuals, such as female and male police officers. In addition, the five-factor model should lead to more complete and accurate techniques of assessing personality, which is one of the major tasks of therapists, clinicians, and psychologists (Costa, 1991). Although a few researchers suggest caution, there is general agreement that the five-factor model will be a powerful tool for defining differences among personality, which will lead to identifying the structure of personality (Digman, 1990).

Now that we have discussed traits in general, let's look at one of the Big Five traits—extraversion—in more detail.

Questions about Traits

How much do traits tell us?

As you read the two personal ads on the left (which have been adapted from a San Diego newspaper), notice that each writer is essentially seeking a partner with particular personality traits.

We could characterize the "woman seeking man" ad as asking for traits that we commonly associate with introversion and the "man seeking woman" ad as asking for traits that we usually associate with extraversion. British psychologist Hans Eysenck (1990) originally identified introversion-extraversion as one of three dimensions of personality. Today, extraversion is one of the five dimensions of personality known as the Big Five.

Eysenck's Hierarchy of Traits

According to Eysenck, who also used factor analysis to pare down a list of traits, personality traits are arranged in a hierarchy of four levels, each of which provides different kinds of information.

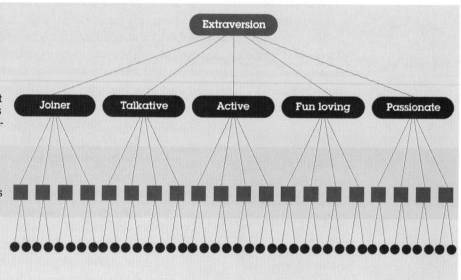

Hierarchy of Traits

Looking at Eysenck's hierarchy, you can see that each level provides a different kind of information. Level 4 provides general knowledge of the person's personality, while level 1 gives specific examples.

4. Higher-order trait. Extraversion represents one of the Big Five traits.

3. Traits. These describe activities that are related, such as all fun-loving activities.

2. Habitual acts or thoughts. These indicate how a person tends to express emotions.

1. Single acts or thoughts. These show specific activity, such as laughing at a joke.

Looking at Eysenck's hierarchy, you can see that each level provides a different kind of information. Level 4 provides general knowledge of the person's personality while level 1 gives specific examples.

What's the best way to describe your personality?

If you were asked to describe your personality, would it be most informative to others to provide very general information (level 4) or more specific information (levels 1–3)? Researchers answered this question by giving subjects information from various levels—general to specific—and then asking them which level provided the most information. Subjects preferred a level of information that was neither too general nor too specific and that would probably be analogous to Eysenck's level 3 (John, Hampson, & Goldberg, 1991). Thus, if you were asked to describe your personality during a job interview, research suggests that your best approach would be to mention traits that are neither too broad nor too specific.

Although traits do indicate a person's tendency to behave in a certain way, questions remain about how reliable or consistent this tendency is across many different situations.

Are traits like X-rays?

In the early 1960s, psychologists generally believed that assessing a person's traits was analogous to taking an X-ray of his or her personality. It followed that once we knew a person's traits, we could predict his or her behavior in many different situations. However, in a famous (infamous) attack on traits, Walter Mischel (1968) blasted the basic assumption of trait theory and said that individuals do not necessarily behave

In one situation—when he is off stage—Michael Jackson appears to be shy, timid, and introverted.

consistently across different situations. We'll describe one of Mischel's studies to show why he challenged the basic assumption of trait theory.

How consistent are traits across situations? Mischel's study questions the basic assumption of trait theory: If traits represent consistent behavioral tendencies, then traits should predict behaviors across many different situations. Here's how Mischel designed a study to test this assumption.

Study. Suppose we ask college students, "How conscientious are you?" If they answer that they are "very conscientious," trait theory would predict that the students would behave conscientiously in many different situations. They would,

In another situation—when he is on stage—Michael Jackson appears to be dynamic, energetic, and extraverted.

for example, attend all classes, go to study sessions, get homework in on time, and keep their rooms neat. To test trait theory's basic assumption of behavioral consistency across situations, Walter Mischel and Philip Peake (1982) observed students' conscientiousness in 19 different conditions.

Results. Students who rated themselves as very conscientious behaved that way day after day in similar situations, but not across all 19 conditions. For example, very conscientious students might clean their rooms daily but not get their homework in on time; or they might attend all their classes but not clean their rooms. Researchers concluded that students behaved with great consistency in the *same* situation but behaved with low consistency across *different* situations. Thus, these results brought into doubt the basic assumption that people behave consistently across different situations.

Implications. Mischel's earlier attack on trait theory and his subsequent research questioned the long-accepted idea of people behaving similarly under different conditions. Mischel started a new controversy by pointing out that predicting a person's behavior must take into account not only the person's traits but also the effects of the situation. This idea became known as **person-situation interaction**, *which means that a person's behavior results from an interaction between his or her traits and a particular situation.* For instance, being in class may bring out your shyness, but being with close friends may bring out your rowdiness.

An end to the person-situation dilemma may be in sight.

Questions about Traits

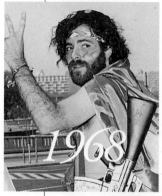

In 1968 Jerry Rubin was a social revolutionary and political activist. His motto was "Don't trust anyone over 30." Rubin's major personality changes occurred before age 30.

1968

1992

In 1992 Jerry Rubin was a well-dressed 53-year-old business-person. He was actively pursuing the very money-making ventures that he condemned in the 1960s. One of his more stable traits has been his flair for promoting ideas and products (*Los Angeles Times*, January 21, 1992).

How can the person-situation dilemma be resolved?

For 20 years debate continued as researchers struggled with the question of how traits can predict an individual's behaviors across situations if the situations also influence the individual's behaviors. According to a thoughtful review by Douglas Kenrick and David Funder (1988), this question may be settled, signaling the end of the person-situation debate. Here's some of their findings.

1 There is good evidence that humans have stable and consistent parts of their personalities, which are called traits. For example, you can easily list many of your best friend's traits because your friend behaves in consistent and stable ways.

2 Accuracy in predicting behaviors across situations will be low if that prediction is based on traits that were measured in very few situations. For instance, your accuracy in predicting an individual's behavior on a camping trip would be low if you had observed her or his behavior in a work situation only.

3 Accuracy in predicting behaviors across situations can be increased if that prediction is based on a larger sample of the individual's behaviors, such as taking observations under a number of different conditions, using many different raters, or observing behaviors under a number of real-life conditions.

Most personality researchers now agree that traits are useful concepts to describe our stable and consistent behavioral tendencies. Yet researchers warn that traits are not useful in predicting behaviors across different situations unless such traits have been assessed by observing a large sample of the person's behaviors.

How consistent are traits across time?

If you are 20, 25, or 30 now, what will your personality be like at 50, 60, and 70? In a longitudinal study, researchers followed men from their early 20s to their early 70s. They found that a number of traits, such as general activity level, sociability, emotional stability, friendliness, and thoughtfulness, showed a high degree of stability across the years. They also found that a few other traits, such as the tendency to be anxious or neurotic, were not as stable across the years because they are affected by levels of stress that may increase through adulthood (Costa, McCrae, & Arenberg, 1983).

When are you most likely to change your personality?

Robert McCrae and Paul Costa, Jr. (1990) reviewed longitudinal studies that focused on personality changes. They found that most changes in personality occur before age 30, because adolescents and young adults are more willing to adopt new values and attitudes or revise old ones. After age 30 adults show fewer personality changes but they do continue to grow in their ideas, beliefs, and attitudes as they respond to changing situations and environments. McCrae and Costa emphasize that although numerous personality traits show remarkable continuity through the middle and later adult years, we should remember that adults continue to grow and change some of their values, beliefs, and attitudes.

One of the newest areas of personality research is the study of genetic or inherited factors, which is our next topic.

Genetic Influences on Traits

Most of us grew up hearing one or both of the phrases "You're acting just like your father" or "You're behaving just like your mother." What we dislike about these phrases is their implied accusation that something is making us blindly follow in our parent's footsteps. The idea of such genetic influences has, during the past decade, resulted in a new area of psychology. This area, called **behavioral genetics**, *focuses on how inherited or genetic factors influence and interact with psychological factors, such as the ways we behave, adapt, and adjust to our environments, to affect behavior and personality.* Many of us have a difficult time accepting the idea of genetic influences because we equate "genetic" with "fixed." The modern way of thinking about genetic factors is that they do not fix behaviors but rather set a *range for behaviors.* For example, genetic factors set a range for our heights and weights. How much we actually grow or weigh will depend on the way that inherited factors interact with environmental ones, such as diet, disease, and exercise. We'll examine recent studies on whether genetic factors also set a range for and influence personality traits. As we discuss the influence of genetic factors on personality traits, please remember that our actual traits result from the interaction between genetic factors and environmental influences.

Why are these two people so incredibly similar?
Jim Lewis and Jim Springer drove the same model of blue Chevrolet, chain-smoked the same brand of cigarettes, owned dogs named Toy, held jobs as deputy sheriff, enjoyed the same woodworking hobby, and had vacationed on the same beach in Florida. When they were given personality tests, they scored almost alike on traits of flexibility, self-control, and sociability. The two Jims are identical twins who were separated four weeks after birth and were reared separately. When reunited at age 39, they were flabbergasted at how many things they had in common (*Time,* January 12, 1987).

Are we seeing coincidence or genetic influence?
The amazing coincidences between the two Jims were highlighted in an ongoing University of Minnesota project on genetic factors. One of the project's major questions is whether similarities between the two Jims are mere coincidence or reflect the influence of genetic factors on personality traits.

Jim Lewis has a dog named Toy.

Jim Springer has a dog named Toy.

Genetic Influences on Traits

Studying Genetic Influences

Method. According to Thomas Bouchard and his colleagues (1990) at the University of Minnesota, their study of genetic influences was the first to compare simultaneously four different groups of twins:

Group 1

Identical twins reared together. Remember that identical twins share *100%* of their genes and thus are genetically identical.

Group 2

Identical twins separated early and reared apart. Because identical twins in this group were reared apart, researchers could study the influence of environment on their personalities. The identical twins in the study were separated very early in life—at an average age of 5 months. They were reared apart and were first reunited as adults at an average age of 41 years.

Group 3

Fraternal twins reared together. Remember that fraternal twins share only *50%* of their genes and thus are no more genetically alike than brothers and sisters.

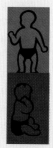

Group 4

Fraternal twins separated early and reared apart. Because fraternal twins in this group were reared apart, researchers could study the influence of environment on their personalities.

Each participant in this study underwent over 50 hours of medical and psychological assessment, including four different tests to measure personality traits.

The measure that researchers use to estimate genetic influences is called heritability. **Heritability** *is a statistical measure that estimates how much of some behavior is due to genetic influences.* For example, you may remember from Module 15 that genetic factors have a considerable influence on IQ scores. The heritability of IQ is a range of 50% to 70%, which means that about 50% to 70% of IQ scores are explained by genetic factors (Bouchard et al., 1990). The question is, what is the heritability estimate for personality traits?

Results. The researchers reported that the correlations for personality traits in identical twins, whether reared apart or together, were larger than those for fraternal twins. Based on these data, the researchers concluded that the heritability of personality traits ranges from 20% to 50%. This heritability score means that about 20% to 50% of the development of personality traits is explained by *genetic influences* and the remaining 50% to 80% is explained by *environmental influences.* For instance, on such personality traits as self-control, tolerance, achievement, extraversion, and flexibility, identical twins reared apart showed correlations about twice that of fraternal twins reared apart.

Genetic factors do not fix behavior in place; rather, genetic factors set a range for behavior.

In addition, the researchers found that whether twins were identical or fraternal, correlations for those twins reared together were similar to those for twins reared apart (Bouchard & McGue, 1990). Researchers say that these results indicate that sharing a common family environment is not a major influence on personality development, since twins raised apart were similar in personality to those raised together. Instead, researchers suggest that the environmental factor important in shaping personality is how each child responds or reacts to his or her environment. Thus, it's not being reared in the same family that is important to personality development; rather, it is how each child reacts to or adjusts in his or her own way to being in that family (Bouchard & McGue, 1990; Plomin, 1990). This finding has questioned a major belief of developmental psychologists who hold that being in a shared family environment greatly influences personality development among the siblings (brothers and sisters). Instead, this research suggests that psychologists need to look more closely at each child's reactions to his or her family environment as a major influence on personality development.

Although these twin studies highlight similarities, Bouchard (1984) emphasizes that each member of a pair of identical twins, whether reared together or apart, has many differences that make her or him a unique human being. For example, while the two Jims show remarkable similarities, they also display unique differences. Jim Lewis says that he is more easygoing and worries less than his identical twin, Jim Springer. When the twins get on a plane, Jim Springer worries about the plane being late, while Jim Lewis says that there is no use worrying (*San Diego Tribune*, November 12, 1987). Bouchard adds that no matter how similar twins were found to be, each twin's fundamental uniqueness has always come through.

Examples of personality traits that were more similar in identical twins, even if raised apart, than in fraternal twins, even if raised together (Tellegen et al., 1988).

Legend:
- Identical twins reared together
- Identical twins reared apart
- Fraternal twins reared together
- Fraternal twins reared apart

Categories: Positive emotionality (extraverted, achievement oriented); Negative emotionality (anxious, angry, alienated); Constraint (inhibited, cautious, conventional)

Conclusion

According to Robert Plomin (1990), a prominent behavioral geneticist, the idea of genes influencing complex human behaviors was unthinkable as recently as 15 years ago. Today, however, after over 30 twin studies involving more than 10,000 pairs of twins, there is convincing evidence that genetic factors exert a considerable influence on many complex human behaviors, including IQ scores, personality traits, and mental health. Yet Plomin warns that genetic influences on human behavior should not be blown out of proportion, because heritability scores generally do not exceed 50%. This means that when explaining human behavior, about 50% or less of the explanation involves genetic factors while the remaining 50% or more involves environmental influences. Thus, we can think of genes as setting a wide range within which human behavior may vary greatly.

Evaluation of Trait Theory

Trait theorists have dealt with three major issues in identifying the structure of personality:

One reason that each member of a couple knows how his or her partner will behave is related to how well each knows the other's traits. Why do you think newlyweds have more difficulty in predicting their partner's behaviors than do couples who have been married longer?

1 *Comprehensive list of traits.* Trait theory assumes that differences between personalities can be described by a short but comprehensive list of traits. The list currently in use is known as the Big Five, or the five-factor model.

Critics of the five-factor model point out that the data for the model came from questionnaires that may be too structured to give real and complete portraits of personalities. As a result, data from questionnaires may paint too simplistic a picture of human personality and may not reflect its depth and complexity.

2 *Consistency across situations.* Trait theory assumes that traits are consistent and stable influences on our behaviors. Researchers generally agree that traits are useful concepts for describing the consistent and stable behaviors that people show. However, we cannot use traits to predict behaviors across different situations.

Critics argue that when traits are measured in one situation, they do not necessarily predict behaviors in different situations. Researchers get around this problem by measuring traits under many different conditions, a method that provides greater accuracy in predicting behaviors across different situations.

3 *Influence of genetic factors.* Observations from over 10,000 pairs of twins indicate that genetic factors significantly influence personality traits. For example, heritability scores range from 20% to 50%, which means that about 20% to 50% of the explanation for traits comes from genetic factors.

Critics point out that genetic factors do not fix personality traits but rather establish a range of behaviors. Critics also warn that inherited factors should not be exaggerated, since about 50%–80% of the explanation for traits comes from environmental factors.

Although there are criticisms of trait theory, at a practical level everyone is thankful for the existence of traits, since they provide consistency and stability in our own lives and in our social interactions with others.

After the Concept/Glossary, we'll compare the major points of the four personality theories that we have discussed in these two modules.

1. The personality theory that emphasizes the influence of learning, social, and cognitive processes on how we evaluate, interpret, and organize information and apply that information to ourselves and others is called _____ theory.

2. An example of the social learning approach is the theory that assumes that personality development, growth, and change are influenced by four distinctively human cognitive processes, which include highly developed language ability, observational learning, purposeful behavior, and self-analysis; this theory is referred to as Bandura's _____ theory.

4. An approach of describing personality by identifying and analyzing ways in which personalities differ is known as _____ theory.

5. A relatively stable and enduring tendency to behave in a particular way is called a _____.

6. The model that organizes all personality traits under five categories that are used to describe differences in personality is called the (a) _____ model. The categories are openness to experience, conscientiousness, extraversion, agreeableness, and neuroticism; you can remember them by the acronym (b) _____.

3. Three different beliefs, based on social learning theory, have been shown to influence behavior. Rotter referred to beliefs in how much control we have over situations or rewards as our (a) _____. According to Bandura, our personal beliefs of how capable we are of exercising control over events in our lives, called (b) _____, affects our performance. Mischel devised ways of measuring our ability to voluntarily postpone an immediate reward to persist in completing a task for the promise of a future reward, which is called (c) _____.

7. Current research supports Hans Eysenck's idea that information about traits is arranged in a _____, with very specific information at the bottom and very general information at the top.

8. The idea that a person's behavior results from an interaction between his or her traits and a particular situation became known as _____ interaction.

9. The field that focuses on how inherited or genetic factors influence and interact with psychological factors is called (a) _____. A statistical procedure that estimates how much of some behavior is due to genetic influences is called (b) _____.

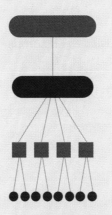

Answers: 1. *social learning;* 2. *social-cognitive;* 3. (a) *locus of control,* (b) *self-efficacy,* (c) *delay of gratification,* 4. *trait* 5. (a) *five-factor* (b) *OCEAN;* 7. *hierarchy;* 8. *person-situation;* 9. (a) *behavioral genetics,* (b) *heritability.*

Four Theories of Personality

| Theorist/Theory | Big Questions |

Sigmund Freud and Psychodynamic Theory

Freud's psychodynamic theory, which he developed in the early 1900s, grew out of his work with patients.

Can McEnroe's disruptive tournament behaviors be due to unconscious forces?

Carl Rogers and Humanistic Theory

Rogers's self theory, which he developed in the 1960s as a reaction to psychodynamic theory, is an example of humanistic theory. His theory grew out of his work with clients in clinical settings.

Did an insight make a major change in Charles Dutton's personality?

Albert Bandura and Social Learning Theory

Bandura's social-cognitive theory, which he developed in the 1970s, is an example of social learning theory. Bandura's theory was based on laboratory research.

Did Kristi Yamaguchi achieve her potential by winning a gold medal at the 1992 winter Olympics?

Hans Eysenck and Trait Theory

Eysenck's hierarchy of traits, which he developed in the 1960s, explains how we organize information about personality into different levels. In the 1990s, trait theory developed the five-factor model, which is based on laboratory research, especially questionnaires and statistical procedures.

Do female police officers have different personality traits and thus behave differently?

Development: The development of personality occurs during the first five years through the resolution of conflicts during the psychosexual stages.

Motivation: Person is driven by unconscious forces, primarily sexual and aggressive biological urges.

Problems: Personality problems develop when conflicts are not resolved during the psychosexual stages.

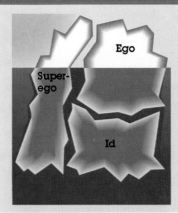

Development: Our self or self-concept develops from our experiences of receiving positive regard. Depending on our experiences, we can develop either a positive or a negative self-concept.

Motivation: Each of us has an inherent tendency to fulfill our potential, which is called self-actualization.

Problems: If we do not receive unconditional positive regard, we may develop a negative self-concept and find our tendency to self-actualization partially blocked.

Development: Our personality develops from four distinctively human cognitive processes: language ability, observational learning, forethought, and self-analysis.

Motivation: Our thoughts, ideas, and beliefs can provide motivation for our behaviors.

Problems: If we have disruptive or faulty beliefs, ideas, and thoughts, we may experience personality problems.

Development: Personality development results from an interaction between inherited and environmental influences.

Motivation: Traits are a tendency to behave in a certain way.

Problems: Personality difficulties may arise from inherited problems and environmental stressors.

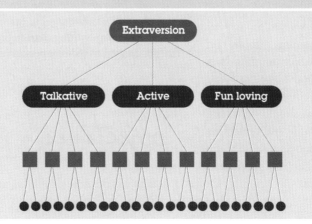

APPLYING/ EXPLORING: MEASURING TRAITS

What do you think about so-and-so?
We usually answer such questions about people by taking on the role of amateur psychologist and identifying and listing a person's traits. Identifying traits is important in our daily lives as we evaluate friends, dates, bosses, and workers. It is also important to companies in selecting and promoting personnel, to clinicians in helping and advising clients, to researchers in explaining personality differences, and to those who write horoscopes and analyze handwriting. Because the need to identify traits is so widespread, it is important to know which methods are the most reliable and valid. As we saw in Module 23, *reliability* refers to obtaining approximately the same score when taking a test on two different occasions separated in time; *validity* refers to a test's accurately measuring what it claims to be measuring.

Let's begin with two popular methods of identifying traits.

Astrology and Graphology

What's your sign?
Horoscopes, which are carried in most newspapers, are a popular method of identifying traits. As you read the following horoscope, note how many things are true for you.

You are bright, sincere, likable, and have a good sense of humor. At times you are too critical of yourself and take the negative comments of others too seriously. You should be careful of acting on impulse and remember to stop and think before making decisions. You tend to trust people and see their good side.

Sagittarius: Nov. 23–Dec. 22: outspoken, loving, independent, warm, outgoing, sportsminded, self-starter

Because horoscopes contain traits that could apply to almost everyone, a majority of readers find truth in this horoscope. Read it carefully, and you'll see that it follows the **Barnum principle** (named after the famous circus owner P. T. Barnum), *which is a strategy for reaching the widest possible audience by phrasing something in such a general way that almost everyone thinks it applies to him or her* (Snyder et al., 1977).

Astrologers claim that they can identify your personality traits by knowing the sign under which you were born. However, researchers report that horoscopes have poor validity because no relationship has been found between the twelve signs of the zodiac and personality traits (Gauguelin, 1982).

Does your handwriting reveal your personality?
The belief that handwriting can reveal personality traits is known as graphology. **Graphology** *is a method that claims to measure personality traits and predict job success by analyzing one's handwriting.* For example, below are some handwriting characteristics that are claimed to indicate personality traits.

The claims that graphology can measure personality traits and predict job success are based primarily on testimonials, which have great potential for error and bias. When evaluated using the scientific method, researchers report that graphology has poor validity because little relationship is found between handwriting characteristics and personality traits or job success (Ben-Shakhar et al., 1986).

We see that two popular methods of identifying traits—astrology and graphology—have poor validity, which means that they do not measure what they claim. Let's now turn to methods that psychologists use to measure traits.

Personality Tests

In this chapter we discussed four approaches to personality. Because each approach emphasizes different personality factors, each uses different methods to assess personality. We discussed some of those methods in the previous module and we'll discuss several more here.

Projective Tests

The psychodynamic approach, which focuses on unconscious factors, uses projective tests that assume subjects will project their unconscious feelings, thoughts, and fears onto unstructured stimuli. We have already discussed two of these tests, the Rorschach inkblot test and the Thematic Apperception Test (TAT).

objectives

Large writing indicates awareness.

from old friends on stressful days!

Small writing shows concentration.

g g y j

Long and heavy strokes reveal determination.

Self-Report Inventories

Unlike psychodynamic theory, trait theory concentrates on more observable personality differences and uses highly structured questions. **Self-report inventories** *are tests with highly structured formats that include objective questions with a limited range of answers.* As an example, on the right is a (very abbreviated) self-report inventory that measures extraversion, one of the Big Five factors (adapted from Wilson, 1978).

A higher score indicates a tendency to be outgoing or extraverted, while a lower score indicates a tendency to be private or introverted. Most of us fall somewhere on a continuum between introversion and extraversion rather than being at the extremes.

Some self-report inventories, such as this one for extraversion, measure a single personality trait. Other inventories measure a number of traits and personality problems.

What's the MMPI?

One of the best-known self-report inventories is the MMPI, or **Minnesota Multiphasic Personality Inventory,** *which consists of 567 statements that describe a wide range of normal and abnormal behavior to which the person answers, "True," "False," or "Cannot say."*

A few statements from the MMPI are given below:

- I do not tire quickly.
- I am worried about sex.
- When I get bored, I like to stir up some excitement.
- I believe I am being plotted against.
- Most people will use somewhat unfair means to gain profit or an advantage rather than to lose it.

The MMPI, which was revised in 1989, assesses a wide range of behaviors, including sexual, religious, political, and social attitudes; health and psychosomatic symptoms; and many well-known neurotic or psychotic

Which of these questions apply to you?

Please answer these questions as honestly as you can.

yes no	1A.	Do you often long for excitement?
yes no	2A.	Are you usually carefree?
yes no	3B.	Do you stop and think things over before doing anything?
yes no	4A.	Would you do almost anything on a dare?
yes no	5A.	Do you often do things on the spur of the moment?
yes no	6B.	Generally, do you prefer reading to meeting people?
yes no	7B.	Do you prefer to have few but special friends?
yes no	8A.	When people shout at you, do you shout back?
yes no	9A.	Do other people think of you as very lively?
yes no	10B.	Are you mostly quiet when you are with people?

Scoring: Count each question followed by an A to which you answered yes. Count each question followed by a B to which you answered no. Add these two numbers.

symptoms (delusions, phobias, sadistic tendencies). Answers on the MMPI are divided into ten behavioral categories or scales, four of which are Depression, Paranoia, Social introversion, and Schizophrenia. The MMPI

is considered to have reasonably good reliability and validity and is most often used in clinical settings; it is also used by some businesses and government agencies that need to screen applicants for high-risk jobs (Anastasi, 1988).

The major *advantages* of self-report inventories are that they are easily administered, have relatively good reliability, and have generally acceptable validity. The major *disadvantages* of self-report inventories are that they cannot predict behaviors in specific situations and that people may bias their results by giving socially desirable or acceptable answers. On the one hand, trait psychologists consider self-report inventories useful in identifying personality differences and the structure of personality. On the other hand, critics from the psychodynamic approach point out that self-report inventories do not expose deeper, hidden, or unconscious personality factors.

Because self-report inventories and projective tests have different advantages and disadvantages, clinical psychologists may use a combination of both to assess a client's personality traits and problems.

Summary/Self-Test

1. Theories that emphasize the influence of learning, social, and cognitive processes on how we evaluate, interpret, and organize information and apply the information to ourselves and others are called (a)_____ theories. Albert Bandura's social-cognitive theory assumes that personality development, growth, and change are influenced by four distinctively human cognitive processes. Our highly developed (b)_____ ability provides us with a tool for processing and understanding information, which is critical to personality development. Our capacity for (c)_____ learning allows us to learn through watching, without observable behavior or a reinforcer. Our capacity for forethought enables us to plan ahead and set goals,

to have (d)_____ behavior. Finally, the fact that we can monitor our thoughts and actions as well as set and change goals and values gives us the capacity for (e)_____.

2. The power of beliefs and ideas to change the way that we interpret situations and events is one of the basic assumptions of social learning theories. Rotter developed a scale to measure our belief about how much control we have over situations or rewards; he called this belief (a)_____. If we believe that we have control over situations and rewards, we are said to have an (b)_____ locus of control. In contrast, if we believe that we do not have control over situations and rewards and that events outside ourselves determine what happens, we are said to have an (c)_____ lo-

cus of control. According to Bandura, our personal beliefs of how capable we are of exercising control over events in our lives is called (d)_____. According to Mischel, our voluntarily postponing an immediate reward to persist in completing a task for the promise of a future reward is called delay of (e)_____.

■ *What kinds of beliefs would make a student invest thousands of dollars and struggle through 4 to 6 years to obtain a college degree?*

3. A relatively stable and enduring tendency to behave in a particular way is called a (a)_____. An approach to understanding the structure of personality by measuring, identifying, and analyzing differences in personality is called (b)_____ theory. In attempting to pare down a list of traits by finding relationships among them, researchers have used a statistical method called (c)_____. The model that organizes all personality traits into five categories is called the (d)_____. These categories, known by the first letters in the word OCEAN, are openness to experience, conscientiousness, extraversion, agreeableness, and neuroticism.

■ *Why is it possible to describe someone's personality differences by using only five categories?*

4. According to Hans Eysenck, traits are arranged in a _____ of four levels, each of which provides different kinds of information about the person. The highest level provides general knowledge of the person's personality; the lowest level provides examples of single acts or thoughts.

5. Mischel questioned the basic assumption of trait theory, saying that if traits represent consistent behavioral tendencies, they should then predict behaviors across many different (a)_____. Instead, he found that people behaved with great consistency in the same situation but behaved with low consistency across different situations. Mischel pointed out that predicting a person's behavior must take into account not only the person's traits but also the effects of the situation; this idea became known as (b)_____ interaction.

■ **Why might a person who married after dating only six months be later surprised by some of his or her partner's behaviors?**

GENETIC INFLUENCES ON TRAITS

6. How inherited or genetic factors influence and interact with psychological factors, such as the ways we behave, adapt, and adjust to our environments, is the focus of the field of behavioral (a)_____. Current thinking about genetic factors is that they do not fix behaviors but rather set a range for behaviors. Researchers estimate genetic influences with a measure that estimates how much of some behavior is due to genetic influences; this measure is referred to as (b)_____. There is evidence that genetic factors influence IQ scores, personality traits, and mental health.

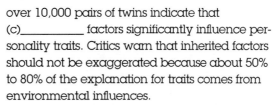

■ **A couple is considering artificial insemination because the husband is sterile. Would it be a good idea to select the donor on the basis of personality characteristics?**

EVALUATION OF TRAIT THEORY

7. Trait theory assumes that differences among personalities can be described by a short but comprehensive list of traits. Critics of the current list that is known as the (a)_____ or _____ point out that the data for the model may paint too simplistic a picture of human personality and may not reflect its depth and complexity. Trait theory assumes that traits are consistent and stable influences on our (b)_____. Critics argue that when traits are measured in one situation, they do not necessarily predict behaviors in other situations. Observations from

over 10,000 pairs of twins indicate that (c)_____ factors significantly influence personality traits. Critics warn that inherited factors should not be exaggerated because about 50% to 80% of the explanation for traits comes from environmental influences.

■ **You are looking for the best possible roommate to share your apartment. Should you select someone who has traits similar or dissimilar to yours?**

APPLYING/EXPLORING: MEASURING TRAITS

8. The ability to obtain approximately the same score when taking a personality test on two different occasions separated in time is a measure of the test's (a)_____. Whether the test accurately measures what it claims to be measuring is its (b)_____. Because the need to identify traits is so widespread, it is important to know which methods are the most reliable and valid. Two methods of identifying traits, astrology and graphology, although popular, show poor validity.

9. Because each approach to personality emphasizes different factors, each uses different methods to assess personality. The psychodynamic approach uses (a)_____ tests to assess personality; the trait approach uses structured formulas with objective questions, called (b)_____. The best-known of these, the Minnesota Multiphasic Personality Inventory (MMPI), consists of statements describing normal and abnormal behaviors. Mental health professionals often use a combination of both projective and self-report inventories to assess personality.

■ **You are going to set up a booth at the fair and charge customers for identifying their personality traits based on their favorite colors. How could you be sure that your customers would agree with your assessments?**

Chapter *Thirteen*
STRESS AND HEALTH

MODULE 25
RESPONDING TO STRESS

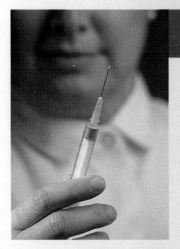

What's the big deal about giving a little blood?

The doctor explains that as part of my physical exam, the nurse will take a couple of samples of my blood. The nurse enters the room, smiles, and says, "This will only take a minute." As she busies herself with the syringe, she asks me to sit on the edge of the examining table and to roll up my sleeve. I slowly roll up my sleeve and look at my bare arm as if it were about to be cut off.

After the nurse tightens a rubber tourniquet around my upper arm, she says in a gentle voice, "Please make a fist and hold it." As the nurse brings the needle to my vein, she says, "You'll feel a tiny prick but it won't hurt." With a swift and practiced movement, she sticks the thin needle into my vein.

I am saying to myself, "This isn't so bad after all."

She pulls the plunger back and I see my blood, which is a deep red color, flow rapidly into the syringe.

I say to myself, "It's almost over."

She removes the first syringe and starts to fill a second.

By now my heart is beating crazily and I have broken out in a fine sweat. I try to distract myself by looking away and thinking about my wonderful fuzzy dog that has the head of a lion and the heart of a true friend.

Now I am floating in space and it is so peaceful. I hear someone calling my name, "Rod, Rod," but I am a million miles away and cannot answer.

When I do come to, the nurse tells me that I fainted and that I should just lie still for several minutes. As I lie there I wonder: "What's the big deal about giving a little blood?"

The big deal concerns what is going on in my head. I have developed an overwhelming fear of seeing blood or seeing an injury, and this fear causes me to faint. Such fear and subsequent fainting is reported by about 15% of the population and is found equally in males and females (Kleinknecht, 1988). Compared with other strong fears (of, for example, snakes, heights, or small spaces), the fear of the sight of blood or injury is one of the few to result in fainting (Ost, 1992).

For some of us, the sight of blood or injury can be considered a cause of great stress. According to Richard Lazarus and Susan Folkman (1984), **stress** *is the feeling we have when we evaluate or appraise a situation as something that overloads or strains our psychological resources.* Throughout both modules in this chapter, we will refer to Richard Lazarus's (1990) well-developed theory of stress.

My fear of the sight of blood and the subsequent response of fainting perfectly illustrate how stress involves an interaction between the mind and the body. First, my mind *appraises* the situation (blood) as a threat. Second, my thoughts are so threatening that they cause an extreme *bodily reaction:* fainting. The study of stress is very much the study of how the mind and body interact.

What's Coming

In this module we'll discuss physiological and psychological responses to stress, the immune system, and development of psychosomatic symptoms. In the next module we'll examine situational, personality, and social factors that help or hinder our coping with stress.

Appraisal

How does stress begin?

As is only too clear, there is no real danger or threat to my survival in giving a sample of blood. Rather, it is my personal appraisal that changes the situation from a common medical practice into a fearful threat. Richard Lazarus (1990), whose theory is widely accepted, sees appraisal as the first of several steps in experiencing stress.

Step 1: Primary Appraisal

An ordinary, nonthreatening situation can be turned into a stressful one through a process called primary appraisal. **Primary appraisal** *refers to our initial, subjective evaluation of a situation in which we balance the environmental demands against our ability to meet them.* There are three kinds of primary appraisals: *irrelevant,* which means the situation does not matter to our well-being; *positive,* which means the situation will enhance or preserve our well-being; and *stressful,* which means the situation has the potential for three kinds of reactions—harm/loss, threat, or challenge. For example, my primary appraisal of giving blood is that it is stressful: I am forced to undergo a medical procedure that I evaluate as being a threat and that I have not learned to manage. We'll focus here on stressful appraisals.

How do you evaluate a stressful situation?

Our first reaction to a potentially stressful situation, such as giving blood, is to determine whether it will cause us harm/loss, threat, or challenge.

Harm/Loss

Appraisal of a situation as involving harm/loss means that you have already sustained some damage or injury. For example, if you have been injured in a car accident, seeing your blood would indicate that you have suffered harm. You would therefore be using a harm/loss appraisal.

Threat

Appraisal of a situation as a threat means that the harm/loss has not yet taken place but you anticipate it in the near future. For instance, if you are asked to give blood and you are one of the 15% of the population with a great fear of the sight of blood, this situation represents a threat to you, and you use a threat appraisal in evaluating the situation. A threat appraisal elicits negative emotions such as fear, anxiety, and anger.

Challenge

Appraisal of a situation as a challenge means that you have the potential for gain or personal growth but also need to mobilize your physical energy and psychological resources to meet the challenging situation. For example, if you were told that giving blood may save the life of another, you would evaluate this situation as a chance for doing good and you would be using a challenge appraisal. A challenge appraisal elicits positive emotions such as eagerness, exhilaration, and excitement.

Primary appraisal may occur with considerable deliberation (as in deciding whether to take a certain job or to go on to graduate school) or may occur quickly and with little deliberation (as in being told of a pop quiz). Not all appraisals are clearcut, however: some may represent a combination of threat and challenge. For instance, if you are about to start an important job, you may feel threatened by the competition and challenged by the chance to prove your talents.

How much do appraisals affect our stress levels?

To demonstrate the importance of appraisal, Lazarus and his colleagues asked subjects to watch a film of a man who had a bloody accident with a power saw. One group of subjects was instructed to identify with the man who had the accident and imagine themselves in his place; another group was instructed to watch the movie from a detached viewpoint by remembering that it was only a movie.

In several such experiments, Lazarus found that subjects who were told to appraise the situation by identifying with the severely injured man had significantly higher levels of physiological arousal and stress than subjects who were asked to use an objective appraisal. Lazarus concluded that in stressful situations, our feelings arise more from our appraisal and our dealing with the situation than from the situation itself. However, when people are asked to identify the cause of their stressful feelings, they usually point to a particular situation and rarely to their appraisals.

Depending on each subject's appraisal, a gory movie scene caused differing levels of stress.

In one survey, Americans rated these situations as major causes of stress, especially anger or impatience. (Respondents could choose more than one response.)

Situation	Percent of respondents rating it stressful
Waiting for someone who is late	65%
Being caught in traffic	63
Waiting in line	61
Waiting in doctor's office	59
Waiting for the government to act	51
Waiting for a repair person	46
Looking for a parking space	42
Waiting for an airplane to take off	26
Waiting for a bus	19

What everyday situations cause you stress?

To see how appraisal works in the real world, read down the list of potential situations on the left and notice two things. First, not all respondents appraised these situations the same way, which means that it is one's appraisal of a situation, and not the situation itself, that causes stress. Second, not everyone appraised each of these situations as stressful, which means that some people have learned to handle such situations or cope with them in ways that are not stressful. After making our primary appraisal, we go to step 2 in the stress process.

Step 2: Secondary Appraisal

What do I do now?

After deciding that we face a threat or a challenge, we make a secondary appraisal. **Secondary appraisal** *refers to deciding what we can do to manage, cope with, or deal with the situation.* For instance, after determing that having blood drawn is a scary threat (primary appraisal), I decided to manage the situation (secondary appraisal) in the future by lying down, which prevents me from fainting. In the next module, you will learn of psychological procedures that I could also use to manage my fainting. I have not invested the time needed to learn these procedures since I have learned to manage by simply lying down. However, if I were a paramedic, police officer, firefighter, or doctor, I would need to learn how to manage my fear of blood and injury—without lying down on the job.

Secondary appraisal, which involves managing the situation, requires coping processes, which we will discuss in the next module. For now we'll look more closely at the physiological responses triggered by a primary appraisal of threat or challenge.

Physiological Arousal

How often do you experience stress?

Take a few moments to estimate how many times you experienced a great deal of stress this week. Almost 60% of Americans report experiencing great stress at least twice a week, and 30% report feeling great stress every day (Louis Harris Poll, *San Diego Union*, September 12, 1987). Given this frequency and the fact that stress causes a significant overload to the body and the mind, you can see why psychologists, doctors, and mental health professionals are concerned about reducing stress.

When we speak in public, most of us feel stressed, which in turn results in many physiological responses.

Fight-or-Flight Response

One of the most consistently reported stressful situations is speaking in public. In fact, the physiological responses most of us experience during public speaking are similar to those we would experience during a car accident, a mugging, or an escape from a threatening situation.

What happens when you must speak in public?

You walk to the front of the room, turn around, and face 35 strangers. In the few minutes before you start to talk, your heart pounds, your mouth becomes dry, your hands sweat, your stomach knots, your muscles tense, and your breathing becomes short and rapid. Your stress level is high and your body is fully aroused.

Public speaking is not a real threat to physical survival. Nevertheless, if you appraise public speaking as a threat, it can trigger the fight-or-flight response similar to that caused by real threats, such as a mugging. The **fight-or-flight response** *is a combination of physiological responses that arouse and prepare the body for action—fight or flight; it can be triggered by physical or psychological situations that are novel, threatening, or challenging.* The fight-or-flight response provides the body with increased energy to deal with threatening situations, whether they are real threats to physical survival or imagined threats to psychological well-being. Thus your body makes no real distinction between escaping from a mugger or speaking in public: both situations can trigger the fight-or-flight response. Many of us experience dozens—or even hundreds—of fight-or-flight responses daily, depending on our levels of stress.

Activation of the Fight-or-Flight Response

Although the fight-or-flight response can be triggered by physical stimuli (noise, heat, cold), in humans it is often initiated by appraisals of threat or challenge. In turn, threat appraisals activate a part of the brain called the *hypothalamus,* which initiates the fight-or-flight response. As you may remember from Module 4, the hypothalamus controls the *autonomic nervous system,* which has two divisions. The *sympathetic division* causes physiological arousal and prepares the body to deal with some emergency, danger, or challenge. The *parasympathetic division* calms the body down, returns it to a more relaxed state, and aids in digestion.

Physiological Symptoms of Stress

As you read through the following list of physiological symptoms associated with stressful feelings, note the ones that you commonly experience. The symptoms are listed in order of frequency as reported by over 1,200 male and female college students (Smith & Seidel, 1982).

- Stomach symptoms: feelings of discomfort, pain, pressure, acid, and churning
- Heart and respiration: pounding heart and short, shallow breaths
- Restless activity: pacing, moving feet, fidgeting
- Muscle tension: trembling, unsteady voice
- Fatigue: feeling tired or exhausted, having little energy
- Headaches: having either tension or migraine headaches
- Perspiring and blushing
- Muscle pain: feeling pain in neck, shoulders, and back
- Skin disorders: having or exaggerating skin blemishes, pimples, oiliness
- Eating problems: either feeling a compulsion to eat or losing one's appetite

Notice that activation of the sympathetic division results in the fight-or-flight response, which has evolved over milllions of years to help us fight or flee in a dangerous situation.

Let's examine exactly what happens during the fight-or-flight response.

Stress: "Oh, no! I have to give a speech!" Threat appraisal activates the hypothalamus.

The **hypothalamus** does two things simultaneously: it triggers the pituitary gland, and it activates the sympathetic division of the autonomic nervous system.

The **pituitary gland** releases ACTH (adrenocorticotropic hormone), which acts on the adrenal cortex.

The **sympathetic division** produces arousal by automatically and simultaneously triggering all of the following responses: increased heart rate, increased blood pressure, rapid and shallow breathing, dilation of pupils, sweaty palms, reduced salivation and dry mouth, muscle tension, trembling voice and shaky hands, reduced stomach and intestinal movement and digestion, and activation of the adrenal medulla.

The **adrenal medulla** is activated by the sympathetic division. It secretes two powerful activating hormones, one of which is epinephrine (adrenaline). These hormones increase heart rate, blood pressure, blood flow to muscles, and release of glucose for use as a source of energy.

The **adrenal cortex** is activated by the ACTH secreted by the pituitary. In turn, the adrenal cortex secretes a group of hormones, called corticoids, that regulate levels of minerals and glucose in the body.

The fight-or-flight response is perfectly organized and automatically executed to cause arousal and prepare the body for action and survival. But what happens if we overuse the fight-or-flight response? As we'll see next, if we keep our body in a continuously aroused state, we may wind up with painful physical symptoms.

Psychosomatic Symptoms

How does your body react to stress?

A million years ago, the fight-or-flight response of our ancestors was triggered by hunting wild animals and escaping predators and enemies. Today, our fight-or-flight response is more often triggered by appraisals of non-life-threatening events, such as worrying about exams, being impatient in traffic, having to wait in lines, getting angry over a putdown, or arguing with someone.

One of the first researchers to recognize that stress triggers the fight-or-flight response was Hans Selye (1956). His pioneering work showed that stress can produce physical symptoms and, in some cases, actual breakdown in body organs.

What happens as the semester comes to an end?

At the end of the semester, Joan feels her level of stress rising: She has too many chapters to read, too many papers to write, too many tests to take, and too little time to do everything. She stays up late, worries a lot, misses sleep, and feels anxious much of the time. Perhaps worst of all are those nagging stomach pains that become more frequent.

General Adaptation Syndrome

Joan's stomach pains are not **hypochondriacal (high-po-con-DRY-e-cal) symptoms,** *or imagined physical ailments,* but real physical symptoms. Their existence illustrates how continuing stressful situations can cause psychosomatic symptoms. **Psychosomatic (SIGH-ko-so-MAH-tik) symptoms** *are real physical symptoms that are caused by psychological factors, such as our reactions to stress.* (The word *psychosomatic* is derived from *psyche,* which means "mind," and *soma,* which means "body").

According to Selye, we develop psychosomatic symptoms because stress evokes the general adaptation syndrome. The **general adaptation syndrome** *consists of a series of three stages—alarm, resistance, and exhaustion—that the body goes through in dealing with stress.* As stress continues, we may develop psychosomatic symptoms, and in extreme cases, we may die.

Let's look at the three stages that Selye identified.

Sometimes we respond to stress by appearing normal on the outside . . . . . . but on the inside, stress is taking its toll.

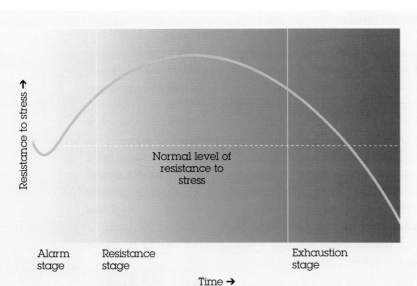

Stages of the General Adaptation Syndrome

Resistance to stress →

Normal level of resistance to stress

Alarm stage   Resistance stage   Exhaustion stage

Time →

1 As Joan worries over how much work she must do, she makes a threat appraisal, which in turn triggers the alarm stage. The **alarm stage** *is our initial reaction to stress and is marked by activation of the fight-or-flight response; in turn, the fight-or-flight response causes physiological arousal.* If the alarm stage is relatively prolonged (perhaps hours), we may experience any number of psychosomatic problems. For example, Joan's worrying has prolonged her alarm reaction, which is interfering with her digestion and causing stomach pains.

With short bursts of stress, our bodies go into and out of the alarm stage (fight-or-flight response) many times during the day. In extreme cases, a person with an unstable heart may die during the alarm stage, usually from cardiac arrest (Morse, Martin, & Moshonov, 1991).

If stress continues, our bodies go into the resistance stage.

2 As the semester ends, Joan is in an almost continual state of stress, and her body goes into the resistance stage. The **resistance stage** *is the body's reaction to continued stress; it is marked by most physiological responses returning to normal levels as the body uses up great stores of energy.* During the resistance stage, Joan may think that her body is functioning normally since, for example, her stomach pains lessen. In fact, Joan's body has returned to almost normal levels of functioning by using up vital reserves of hormones, minerals, and glucose (blood sugar). Joan may feel healthy and energetic, but if stress continues for a longer period of time, her body will go into the exhaustion stage.

3 As the stress of writing papers, completing assignments, and taking exams continues over many months, Joan's body may enter the exhaustion stage. The **exhaustion stage** *is the body's reaction to long-term, continuous stress: it is marked by actual breakdown in internal organs or weakening of the infection-fighting immune system.* During the exhaustion stage, Joan's stomach pains may turn into a full-blown case of ulcers or her weakened immune system may result in her getting a virus, cold, strep throat, or other infection.

In extreme cases, the exhaustion stage may lead to death. This progression helps explain deaths resulting from voodoo curses, which have been reported by many competent researchers. With a voodoo curse, the victim is condemned to eventual death, from which there is no escape. Victims who believe in the power of the curse and are therefore greatly stressed by it apparently lose their "will to live" and die from heart problems or shock (Morse, Martin, & Moshonov, 1991).

Selye's general adaptation syndrome was considered an important discovery because it provided one of the first explanations of how psychosomatic symptoms can develop.

Psychosomatic Symptoms

Prevalence of Psychosomatic Symptoms

Do you have symptoms?

For many years I have presented the list of symptoms on the left to my classes of healthy-looking college students and asked, "How many of you have a psychosomatic symptom from this list?" Generally, in a class of 50 students, about 49 will report one or more of these symptoms, and about 10 to 15 will report two or more symptoms.

The top three psychosomatic symptoms are usually stomach problems, headaches, and back, neck, or shoulder pains.

The second question I ask is, "Since almost everyone has a psychosomatic symptom, how many of you engage in a regular program of reducing stress through relaxing, thinking positive thoughts, or using relaxing images?" Usually, only 2 to 5 students report engaging in a regular stress-reduction program.

These numbers, which have remained constant in my classes for the past ten years, make two points:

1. Many of us who are in generally good health do not recognize that some of our recurring symptoms result from our reactions to stress. Instead, we believe that our health problems are caused by external things. For example, we often attribute stomach and intestinal symptoms to some quality of the food (greasy, spicy) rather than to he fact they we ate when we were stressed. Thus, we need to *take responsibility for those health problems* that could be reduced or controlled by a stress-reduction program.

Common Psychosomatic Symptoms

- Headaches (tension or migraine)
- Stomach problems (pain, ulcers, gas)
- Intestinal difficulties (constipation or diarrhea)
- Fatigue much of the time without doing physical activity
- Recurring bouts of insomnia
- Recurring skin problems or rashes
- Worsening of asthmatic or allergic problems
- Recurring outbreaks of herpes (facial or genital)
- High blood pressure or other cardiovascular difficulties
- Pains in the neck, shoulders, or back
- Grinding teeth during sleep (bruxism)
- Recurring colds or flu
- Eating problems (eating too much or too little)

2. Many or us believe that "as soon as" we finish a semester, get a job, graduate from college, buy a car, start a career, get a new boss, or find a relationship, our stress will decrease and our psychosomatic symptoms will go away. While it is true that some stressors are eliminate with time, experience indicates that another stressor is sure to take its place. Because researchers have now demonstrated a *link between stress and illness,* we cannot fool ourselves into believing that if we just wait, stress will decrease (Steptoe, 1991). For example, doctors estimate that between 75% and 90% of health problems are psychosomatic—that is, stress related.

Here is an example of how some individuals are genetically predisposed to develop psychosomatic problems.

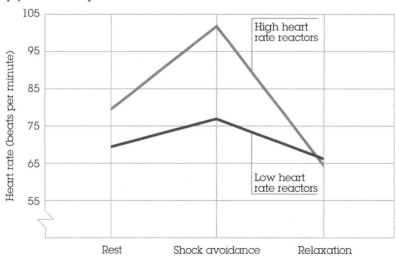

In one study, "high heart rate reactors" were students who were genetically predisposed to responding with a big increase in heart rate to a mild psychological stressor. "Low heart rate reactors" were students who were genetically predisposed to a small or moderate heart rate increase." Although there was no significant difference between the two groups at rest, during a shock avoidance task (a moderate stressor), the high heart rate reactors showed a significantly higher rate increase. Such individuals are at risk for developing future cardiovascular problems, such as high blood pressure (Light & Obrist, 1980).

How do psychosomatic symptoms develop?
Why is it that each of us develops a particular psychosomatic symptom that may or may not be present in another? Let's see why stress may cause headaches in one person and stomach problems in another.

1 Researchers believe that most of us develop psychosomatic symptoms because we have a genetic predisposition for the breakdown of certain organs or because of *nutritional or lifestyle factors,* such as smoking, being overweight, or not exercising. For example, in one study healthy college males were exposed to stressful situations that involved completing a series of mental tasks to avoid an electrical shock. Those students who had parents with hypertension showed significantly higher increases in blood pressure and heart rate. The researchers concluded that students with overresponsive vascular systems had inherited that physical condition from their parents and that these students would be more susceptible to problems of high blood pressure or other cardiac difficulties (Light, 1981; Light & Obrist, 1980). Thus, inherited predispositions, nutrition, or lifestyle factors target certain body organs for future breakdown.

2 The parts of our bodies that are targeted or weakened by inherited predispositions, nutrition, or lifestyle factors will be especially vulnerable during stress. Appraisal of a situation as stressful triggers the fight-or-flight response, which in turn causes heightened physiological arousal. The continuous activation of the fight-or-flight response keeps the body aroused, thus putting strain on those body parts that are already targeted or weakened. After months or years of threat appraisals, our overused fight-or-flight response will likely break down the targeted or weakened part, causing psychosomatic symptoms (Steptoe, 1991).

In the face of continuing stress, we can counterbalance predisposing genetic, nutritional, or lifestyle factors by adopting a reasonable stress reduction program and thus protect against psychosomatic symptoms and breakdown of body parts. We will discuss such programs in the Applying/Exploring sections of this and the next module.

Now we turn to a mysterious and interesting topic—our immune system.

Stress and the Immune System

How could final exams give you a cold?

How often have you gotten a cold, strep throat, or some other infection when final exams are over? Although this common experience suggests that stressful psychological events can influence the immune system, until recently researchers firmly believed the immune system to be a totally independent system. The **immune system** *is the body's defense and surveillance network of cells and chemicals that fight off bacteria, viruses, and other foreign matter.* In the mid-1970s, a psychologist and an immunologist found a clear connection between psychological factors and the immune system (Ader & Cohen, 1975). Through conditioning, they weakened animals' immune systems and made the animals more susceptible to disease. Their discovery laid the foundation for an area of study called psychoneuroimmunology.

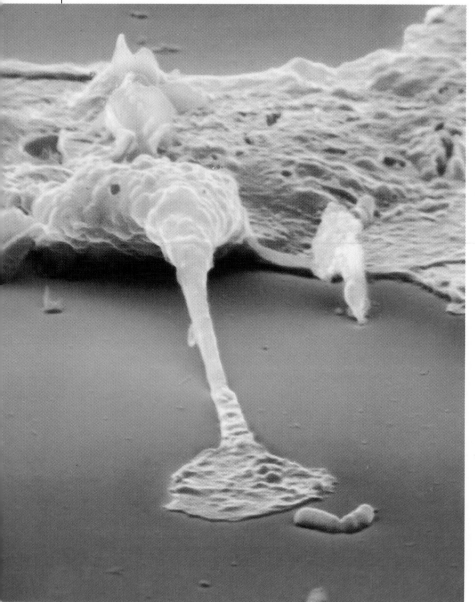

In this remarkable photo, you see an immune system cell (macrophage) sending out a footlike extension to engulf and destroy a bacterial cell (small green cell at the very front).

A New Area

Psycho what?

Psychoneuroimmunology (psycho-neuro-im-you-NAL-a-gee) *is the study of the relationship between the central nervous system, the endocrine system, and psychosocial factors.* The **central nervous system** *consists of the brain and spinal cord;* the **endocrine system** *is the network of glands that secrete hormones.* **Psychosocial factors** *include cognitive reactions to stressful events, the individual's personality traits, and social influences.* The interaction among these three factors can suppress or strengthen the immune system and in turn make the body more or less susceptible to disease and infection. For example, researchers reported that having to take exams suppressed the immune systems of medical students, which explains why students are more susceptible to infections during exam periods (Keicolt-Glaser & Glaser, 1989).

To highlight some of what has been learned through psychoneuroimmunology, we'll look at a recent experiment that studies the common cold.

Evidence for Psychoneuroimmunology

Why didn't you get a cold when your roommate did?

Researchers were faced with a difficult question: Why doesn't everyone who is exposed to a disease virus or bacterium actually get the disease? They tackled this question head on by giving the same amount of cold virus to 394 subjects, all of whom were quarantined for a week. During this period, the researchers checked for symptoms of colds and found that those individuals who reported high levels of psychological stress were twice as likely to develop colds as those who reported low stress levels (Cohen, Tyrrell, & Smith, 1991). The researchers concluded that with every increase in psychological stress, there's an increased likelihood of developing a cold—provided one is exposed to the cold virus. (There is no truth to the folk wisdom that people get colds simply by being cold or damp.)

What makes some people more susceptible to colds?

One reason some individuals are more susceptible to colds lies in the activation of their fight-or-flight responses. Researchers discovered that activating the fight-or-flight response produces two groups of hormones: corticoids and catecholamines (epinephrine or adrenaline is a catecholamine). These two groups of hormones *suppress the immune system,* thus making the body more susceptible to diseases, viruses, and infections (O'Leary, 1990; Cohen & Williamson, 1991).

Can the immune system be conditioned?

The process by which stress or psychological factors can affect the immune system is shown in the following cleverly conceived experiment in which researchers classically conditioned two groups of rats. (To refresh your memory of classical conditioning, please see Module 11.)

Method
On three trials, a light flashed and a fan hummed (conditioned stimuli), then rats were individually injected with a substance (unconditioned stimulus) that caused an allergic reaction (unconditioned response).

On the fourth trial, one group of animals received the regular sequence but the second group received *only* the conditioned stimulus without the injection.

Results
On the fourth trial, the group of animals that received only the conditioned stimulus showed a conditioned response—that is, just the presentation of the light and fan caused the allergic reaction.

The researchers concluded that the brain itself can trigger an allergic reaction in animals and most probably in humans (MacQueen et al., 1989). These findings help explain why some people have allergic reactions to plastic flowers: their physical responses have been conditioned to the sight of flowers.

Conclusion
The fact that immune responses can be conditioned demonstrates a mechanism by which purely psychological or cognitive factors can affect immune function. The ability to condition the immune response suggests the possibility of enhancing it, a goal toward which researchers are currently working (O'Leary, 1990).

After the Concept/Glossary, we'll see how some individuals have learned to control the autonomic nervous system, which is not normally under voluntary control.

1. If we evaluate or appraise a situation as being a threat or a challenge and feel that dealing with the situation strains our psychological resources, we define that feeling as _____.

2. Our initial, subjective evaluation of a situation in which we balance environmental demands against our ability to meet them is referred to as (a)_____, of which there are three kinds: (b)_____, _____, and _____.

3. A stressful primary appraisal has the potential for three kinds of reactions, which are (a)_____, _____, and _____. After making our primary appraisal of a situation, we decide what we can do to manage, cope with, or deal with the situation; this is called (b)_____.

6. A series of three stages—alarm, resistance, and exhaustion—that the body goes through in dealing with stress is referred to as the (a)_____. The alarm stage is our initial reaction to stress and is marked by activation of the (b)_____. The resistance stage is the body's reaction to continued stress and is marked by most physiological responses returning to (c)_____ levels. The exhaustion stage is the body's reaction to long-term, continuous stress and is marked by the actual breakdown or weakening of (d)_____.

4. A combination of physiological responses that arouse and prepare the body for action is referred to as the (a)_____ response. This response begins in a part of the brain, called the (b)_____, which triggers the (c)_____ division of the autonomic nervous system. This response is especially triggered by threat appraisals.

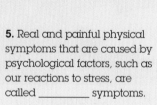

7. The body's defense and surveillance network of cells and chemicals that fight off bacteria, viruses, and other foreign matter is called the _____ system.

8. The study of how three factors—the central nervous system, the endocrine system, and psychosocial factors—interact to affect the immune system is called _____.

5. Real and painful physical symptoms that are caused by psychological factors, such as our reactions to stress, are called _____ symptoms.

7. immune; 8. psychoneuroimmunology.
6. (a) general adaptation syndrome, (b) fight-or-flight response, (c) normal, (d) internal organs or immune system;
challenge, (b) secondary appraisal; 4. (a) fight-or-flight, (b) hypothalamus, (c) sympathetic; 5. psychosomatic;
Answers: *1. stress or stressful; 2. (a) primary appraisal, (b) irrelevant, positive, stressful; 3. (a) harm/loss, threat,*

Tibetan Monks

Where's the heat coming from?

The air temperature was a rather chilly 40°F as the monk wrapped himself in a soaking wet sheet that measured about 40 × 75 inches. The monk began a kind of meditation that can significantly raise body temperature. Within 3 to 5 minutes, his body temperature rose, steam began to rise from the sheet, and the sheet started to dry. After about 45 minutes, the sheet was totally dry, in spite of an air temperature that would require most of us to wear a heavy coat to stay warm. The monk repeated this process two more times, each time drying a wet sheet in 40° temperatures and never once showing any signs of shivering or being cold (Benson et al., 1990).

For about the last dozen years, researcher Herbert Benson and his colleagues have been visiting India to study the physiological changes in monks who possess a remarkable ability to control their autonomic nervous systems. The **autonomic nervous system** *regulates heart rate, breathing, blood pressure, digestion, secretion of hormones, and other functions as well as maintaining the body in a state of optimal balance, or homeostasis.* It functions automatically; we can voluntarily control only a few responses, such as eye blinking and breathing. All other responses of the autonomic nervous system, such as increasing or decreasing heart rate, dilating or constricting blood vessels, and increasing or decreasing oxygen consumption, are not usually under voluntary control.

Can monks control their autonomic nervous system?

Certain Tibetan monks, through various forms of meditation, have learned to exert an amazing amount of control over normally involuntary autonomic responses, including temperature and metabolic rate.

Benson's group of researchers obtained permission from three monks at a monastery in Upper Dharamsala, India, to measure their temperature changes during heat meditation, or g Tummo yoga. The monks sat in the lotus position during meditation, and within a few seconds to a few minutes they had made the temperature of their toes and fingers increase as much as 12° to 15°F with no change in heart rate (Benson et al., 1982). In comparison, most Westerners who practice raising their finger temperature through relaxation or biofeedback average a much smaller 0.25° to 2° increase (Freedman, 1991).

Harvard researcher Herbert Benson measures significant increases in temperature as a Tibetan monk engages in g Tummo (heat) yoga.

What's the heat source?

Benson and others suggest that monks are able to raise temperature by dilating tiny blood vessels that lie near the surface of the skin. The monks' description of how they raise temperature is more interesting: During the practice of g Tum-mo yoga, "wind" is taken from the scattered condition of normal consciousness and is made to enter into the "central channel" inside the body. Then, by dissolving these winds in the central channel, internal heat is ignited (Benson et al., 1982).

Before you attempt to duplicate these considerable physiological feats, bear in mind that these monks have been practicing meditation for over 20 years.

Researchers' interest in altering physiological processes through meditation has a practical application. As we will explain in the Applying/Exploring section, there are a number of psychosomatic symptoms (headaches, intestinal problems, extremely cold fingers or Raynaud's disease, cardiac difficulties) whose treatment usually includes some form of meditation or relaxation.

APPLYING/ EXPLORING: STRESS MANAGEMENT I

How can Tim deal with his fear of blood?
Tim, who was in his early 30s, had a 15-year history of fainting when giving blood, receiving injections, or seeing movies in which people were injured. Other than this problem, he was in excellent health and jogged daily. Tim confessed to having almost daily anxiety, some of which involved worrying about fainting. His first fainting response had occurred at age 15 when he was injured in a sporting activity and required injections and stitches (McGrady & Bernal, 1986).

Let's see how learning to relax helped Tim over his fainting problem.

Learning to Relax

Most stress management programs have two parts: the first involves learning some form of relaxation; the second includes changing one's thoughts and behaviors through cognitive and behavioral techniques. We'll discuss part 1 here and part 2 in the Applying/Exploring section of the next module. In actual practice, however, the client works on both facets simultaneously.

Where is the baseline?
One physiological measure of anxiety is muscle tension. Before beginning a relaxation program for Tim, researchers recorded his muscle tension at baseline, when he was sitting in a reasonably relaxed position (McGrady & Bernal, 1986). Tim thought he was relaxed at the time of the recording, but as shown in the graph on the right, the baseline measure of the tension from muscles in his neck indicated considerable tension there.

Does relaxation work?
Before we describe three kinds of relaxation programs—biofeedback, progressive relaxation, and meditation—please look again at

the graph. Notice that at session 5 (right after two baseline measurements), Tim's muscle tension was relatively high. After he began his biofeedback training, the tension gradually declined, until, by session 35, his muscle tension was very low. Without question, Tim had learned to relax the muscles in his neck; this change reflected relaxation of the body in general.

After undertaking the relaxation program, whenever Tim was required to give blood, receive an injection, or witness an injury, he would practice his relaxation response, along with cognitive and behavioral procedures. He was able, for example, to go in for a dental appointment and received an injection without fainting. Thus, learning to relax was part of the program that helped Tim avoid fainting in the presence of fearful stimuli.

Now let's examine the three different relaxation programs.

Biofeedback, Progressive Relaxation, and Meditation

When told to "calm down," most of us are unable to do so. This is in part because the autonomic nervous system's responses are not under our voluntary control. As a result,

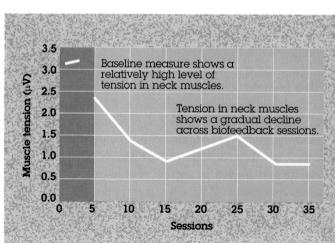

Baseline measure shows a relatively high level of tension in neck muscles.

Tension in neck muscles shows a gradual decline across biofeedback sessions.

we must practice for weeks to learn how to calm down or relax. Relaxing without first practicing would be like playing a great game of tennis the first time you step on the court. There are three techniques you can use to help learn to relax.

Biofeedback

Tim learned to relax using **biofeedback,** *a process of recording and amplifying physiological signals from the body, such as muscle activity, brain waves, or temperature, so that we can learn to increase or decrease them.* In Tim's case, researchers placed several small metal disks on his neck and connected the disks to a machine that measured tiny changes in the muscles' electrical activity. Each time Tim tensed the muscles in his neck, the machine sensed the increased electrical activity and made a high tone. When he relaxed the muscles, the machine sensed the decreased electrical activity and made a low tone. Through his thoughts and mental images, Tim tried to keep the tone low and thus the muscles in his neck, relaxed. After 12 to 30 biofeedback training sessions (about 20 minutes per session), most individuals would be able to calm down when needed, just as Tim was able to do.

Progressive Relaxation

Tim could have learned to calm down by using **progressive relaxation,** *an exercise of tensing and relaxing the major muscle groups of the body until one is able to relax the groups when needed.* For example, Tim would start by tensing and relaxing his toes and then continue up his body, tensing and relaxing the muscles of his calves, thighs, pelvis, stomach, shoulders, arms, hands, neck, face, and forehead. He would repeat the tensing and relaxing exercise for about 20 minutes. After several weeks of regular practice, he would be able to use this exercise to calm down.

Researchers report that progressive relaxation is a very effective way to produce a reduction in muscle tension and overall body relaxation (Lucic et al., 1991).

Meditation

Tim could have learned to relax through several kinds of meditation. For example, he could use **transcendental meditation (TM),** *which involves assuming a comfortable position, closing one's eyes, and repeating and concentrating on a sound to clear one's head of all thoughts (worrisome and otherwise).*

Besides transcendental meditation, there are various forms of Eastern meditation (yoga) as well as a Western version. Herbert Benson, who studied Tibetan monks, has popularized the **relaxation response,** *which involves sitting or lying in a comfortable position while repeating a meaningless sound over and over to rid oneself of anxious thoughts.*

If you were to practice some form of meditation for about 20 minutes a day for six weeks, you would learn to clear your mind of upsetting thoughts and, as a result, calm your body (Benson, 1975).

Which relaxation technique is best?

Some researchers have found progressive relaxation and biofeedback to be equally effective in reducing headaches (Blanchard et al., 1987). After comparing many studies, another researcher concluded that transcendental meditation, biofeedback, and progressive relaxation are about equally effective in reducing anxiety and high blood pressure (Shapiro, 1985). There is now sufficient evidence to show that all three techniques are about equally effective and valuable in helping a person calm down and reduce mild anxiety. Because the three techniques generally produce similar results, which one you choose is not as important as how often you use it.

Summary/Self-Test

APPRAISAL

1. Our initial, subjective evaluation of a situation in which we balance various environmental demands against our ability to meet them is called (a) _____. Deciding what we can do to manage, cope with, or deal with the situation is called (b)_____. The feeling we have when we evaluate or appraise a situation as something that overloads or strains our psychological resources is (c)_____. Lazarus concluded that when we feel stressed, our feelings arise more from our appraisal and our dealing with the situation than from the situation itself.

2. There are three kinds of primary appraisal. Those situations that do not matter to our well-being are called (a)_____; those that will enhance or preserve our well-being are called (b)_____. The third kind, called stressful, have the potential for three different kinds of reactions. One reaction occurs when you have already sustained some damage or injury; this is referred to as (c)_____. A second reaction is that the injury has not yet taken place but you anticipate it in the near future; this is referred to as (d)_____. A third reaction is that you have the potential for gain or personal growth but need to use physical energy and psychological resources; this is referred to as (e)_____. Not all appraisals are clear-cut; some may represent a combination of threat and challenge.

■ *Sue and Mary are happy as roommates except for two problems. Sue gets really mad because Mary leaves dirty clothes lying around, and Mary gets angry because Sue is usually late for everything. Why don't the same things bother Mary and Sue?*

PHYSIOLOGICAL AROUSAL

3. A combination of physiological responses that arouse and prepare the body for action is called the (a)_____ response. This response originally evolved to help us survive dangerous and life-threatening situations and can be triggered by intense physical stimuli (noise, heat, cold). In addition, this response can be triggered by psychological stimuli, such as our (b)_____ of threat or challenge.

4. Threat appraisals activate a part of the brain called the (a)_____; once activated, it does two things simultaneously. It triggers the (b)_____ gland to release ACTH (adrenocorticotropic hormone). ACTH then acts on the adrenal cortex, which secretes hormones that regulate levels of minerals and glucose in the body. The hypothalamus also triggers the (c)_____

division of the autonomic nervous system, which causes physiological arousal. One response of the sympathetic division is to trigger the adrenal (d)_____, which secretes two powerful activating hormones that in turn further increase physiological arousal.

■ *A newspaper article describes how a 96-pound woman was able to push a 4,200-pound car that had drifted back and trapped a young girl between its bumper and the next car. How did this relatively tiny woman accomplish such a powerful feat?*

PSYCHOSOMATIC SYMPTOMS

5. Our psychological reactions to stressful situations can result in real physical symptoms called (a)_____ symptoms. According to Selye, we develop psychosomatic symptoms because the body's response to stress involves going through three stages that he called the (b)_____ syndrome. The first stage involves our initial reaction to stress and is marked by physiological arousal; this is called the (c)_____ stage. The second stage is the body's reaction to continued stress and is marked by most physiological responses returning to normal levels as the body uses up great stores of energy; this is called the (d)_____ stage. The third stage is the body's reaction to long-term, continuous stress and is marked by the actual breakdown in body organs or weakening of the infection-fighting immune system; this is called the (e)_____ stage.

6. Researchers believe that most of us develop particular psychosomatic symptoms because of two factors: a (a)_____ predisposition for the breakdown of certain organs or (b)_____ or _____ factors, such as smoking, being overweight, or not exercising. The continuous activation of the fight-or-flight response keeps the body aroused, thus putting strain on those body parts that are already targeted or weakened. We can protect against psychosomatic symptoms and breakdown of body parts by adopting a reasonable (c)_____ program.

■ *Immediately after Carol ended her three-year relationship with Fred, she came down with the flu. However, three weeks later she felt healthy. How would Hans Selye explain what happened?*

STRESS AND THE IMMUNE SYSTEM

7. The body's network of cells and chemicals that automatically fight off bacteria, viruses, and other foreign matter is known as the (a)_____. The study of the relationship between the central nervous system, the endocrine system, and psychosocial factors is called (b)_____. The interaction among these factors can suppress or strengthen the immune system and, in turn, make the body more or less susceptible to disease and infection.

■ *Why do Gene's allergies act up every time he has to ask his parents for more money?*

CULTURAL DIVERSITY: TIBETAN MONKS

8. Heart rate, breathing, blood pressure, digestion, secretion of hormones, and other functions, including those that maintain the body in a state of optimal balance or homeostasis, are regulated by the _____ system. This system functions automatically; eye blinking and breathing are among the few responses we can control voluntarily. Other responses, such as increasing or decreasing heart rate or oxygen consumption, are not usually under voluntary control. Benson and his colleagues found that monks had learned to use meditation to control their autonomic nervous systems.

■ *The Tibetan monks explain that they warm their bodies by redirecting the "winds of consciousness." How would a Western researcher explain the monks' remarkable temperature increases?*

APPLYING/EXPLORING: STRESS MANAGEMENT I

9. Most stress management programs have two goals: learning to _____ the body and changing thoughts and behaviors through cognitive and behavioral techniques.

10. Recording and amplifying physiological signals from the body and displaying these signals so that we can learn to increase or decrease them is known as (a)_____. An exercise of tensing and relaxing the major muscle groups is called (b)_____. Several different kinds of meditation also relieve muscle tension and stress. One method involves sitting or lying in a comfortable position while repeating a meaningless sound over and over to rid oneself of anxious thoughts; this is called the (c)_____ response. Another approach that involves assuming a comfortable position, closing one's eyes, and repeating and concentrating on a meaningless sound to clear one's head of all thoughts (worrisome and otherwise) is called (d)_____. There is now sufficient evidence to show that all three techniques are about equally effective and valuable in helping a person calm down and reduce mild anxiety. Which technique you choose is not as important as how often you use it.

■ *Terry says that the best way to relax one's body is to follow the ancient meditation techniques that are practiced in Eastern religions. Does the evidence support Terry?*

MODULE 26
COPING WITH STRESS

Sandra's day includes caring for two active children, attending classes, taking exams, doing assignments, and worrying about money, self-esteem, and her future.

How does a 27-year-old single mother with two children succeed in college?

Six-thirty A.M. With a groan Sandra slaps at the alarm, rolls out of bed, and stands grimacing at herself in the bathroom mirror. "Too fat," she thinks as she ducks into the shower. A few minutes later she wakes Jesse, 5, and Caiti, 3, and the morning rush is on. She sits the kids down at the dinette for breakfast, packs their lunches, pops them in the tub, compromises on the temperature for the thousandth time (Jesse likes it "wicked hot," Caiti doesn't). Loads dishwasher, dries the kids, doles out their clothes, finds Jesse's sneakers, reminds him Auntie Erika is picking them up after school today. Scoops up a stack of books, almost forgets the 15-page religion paper she slaved over all weekend. Turns off the TV, bundles up the kids. Out the door.

This is what life is like for Sandra Sullivan, 27-year-old single mother of two, recovering drug addict, former homeless person, surviving without child support, unable to make ends meet without food stamps and welfare, trying against all odds to go to college. And not just any college: She's going to Wellesley, one of the most prestigious women's colleges in the nation.

One day, after some disappointing news about her husband forging a check, Sandra got down on her knees and prayed. In a flash it seemed that her old self had died and she was ready to make a new beginning. She swallowed her pride and made some tough decisions: she left her husband who had been in and out of jobs for five years, quit drugs, and moved with her babies into a homeless shelter. She found a subsidized apartment and went into therapy. When her group told her to quit complaining about finding a decent job, she decided to get more skills by enrolling in a community college. She did well. She applied to Wellesley College under a special program for women over age 24 and was accepted. At first Sandra was elated, and then she was terrified of competing with younger students.

Sandra finished her first semester with two A's and a B-minus. She has lost 35 pounds, and for two and a half years she's been free from drugs. Once the best she hoped for was a job as a nurse's aide. Now she wants to get a Ph.D. in religion. (excerpted and adapted from *Life*, April 1992, pp. 62–65)

For Sandra, every day might be described as a series of nonstop potential stressors. To deal with all these possible problems, she uses a variety of coping techniques. **Coping** *is the cognitive and behavioral efforts that we use to manage a situation that we have appraised as exceeding, straining, or taxing our personal resources* (Lazarus, 1990). These situations may be *external*, such as events in our environment, or *internal*, such as worrisome thoughts or beliefs. When we think of coping, we often think of coping with some specific situations. But as you will learn, two very different situations—problems versus emotions—require our coping skills.

What's Coming

In the first half of this module we'll examine kinds of coping and measurements of stress in our lives. In the second half we'll discuss the personality and social factors that help or hinder our coping.

Coping

How many ways does Sandra cope?

"But sometimes Sandra wondered if it was all worth it. She was often lonely, and once she came down with the flu and missed a week of school . . . She worried about her kids. She wanted to go to Wellesley so her children wouldn't know welfare, but the stress of all the rushing around was hard on them. Caiti often got sick on the way to school; Jesse had taken to calling her Sandra (instead of mom)." (*Life*, April 1992, p. 65)

Sandra is faced with a bundle of problems and will use different methods to live with or change those problems. As part of his theory of stress, Lazarus (1990) has developed definitions of two ways in which we handle problems: problem-focused and emotion-focused coping.

Problem-Focused Coping

With **problem-focused coping**, *we seek information about what needs to be done, change our own behavior, or take whatever action will solve the problem.* For example, in facing exams, Sandra uses problem-focused coping by studying with a friend; to make time for her children, she uses problem-focused coping by taking them to as many activities as she can.

Emotion-Focused Coping

With **emotion-focused coping**, *we make some effort to handle the emotional distress caused by a harm or threat appraisal. These efforts include directing our attention to something else, avoiding thinking about or denying the situation, engaging in positive thinking, or putting some distance between us and the situation.* Unlike problem-focused coping, in which we actually change the situation, environment, or our behavior, emotion-focused coping involves changing only how we think about the situation. For instance, when Jesse called Sandra by her name rather than the more familiar "Mom," Sandra used emotion-focused coping by engaging in positive thinking, such as remembering how much time she spends reading to Jesse.

How does Sandra cope?

Sandra must cope with having to do well in college and make time for her children.

Which method—and when?

The pattern of coping depends on the situation (Lazarus, 1990). In some cases, such as dealing with an exam, we may engage primarily in problem-focused coping by taking actions such as reading and outlining the text, studying our notes, or attending a review session. These actions may keep our anxiety low. In fact, researchers found that students who used problem-focused coping to deal with exams had much lower levels of test anxiety than students who used emotion-focused coping, such as complaining and avoiding studying (Blankstein, Flett, & Watson, 1992). In other cases, such as dealing with the breakup of a relationship, we may engage primarily in emotion-focused coping by regulating our distress through distraction, denial, or positive thoughts about ourselves.

The major factor that influences whether we use primarily problem-focused or emotion-focused coping is how much *control* we have over the situation. If we appraise a situation as being under our control if we take some action, such as studying for an exam to get a good grade, we may use primarily problem-focused coping to deal with the stress. On the other hand, if we appraise the situation as being out of our control—if, for example, the other person ended our relationship—we may use primarily emotion-focused coping to manage our negative emotional state. Finally, in some situations that are frustrating or that involve conflict, such as deciding whether to study through the weekend, we may use both emotion-focused and problem-focused coping.

Now that you know the two ways of coping with stress, let's see how psychologists measure your level of stress.

Major Life Events and Daily Hassles

Few people would disagree that experiencing the death of a close family member, getting divorced or married, being fired from work, or having to move makes an impact on one's life. **Major life events** *are potentially disturbing, troubling, or disruptive situations, both positive and negative, that we appraise as having a significant impact on our lives.*

How are major life events important?
When researchers Thomas Holmes and Richard Rahe (1967) studied the effects of *major life events,* they reasoned that people who face a large number of such events would have to make major adjustments and would in turn feel increasing levels of stress. Because increased stress levels often lead to psychosomatic problems, perhaps facing many life events would be associated with increased illness. Holmes and Rahe and many others have indeed found a modest correlation (.20–.30) between number of major life events and subsequent physical or psychological illness (Maddi, Bartone, & Puccetti, 1987; Schroeder & Costa, 1984).

Take a moment to read through the scale that Holmes and Rahe developed, shown on the right. How many major life events have you experienced during the past year?

Importance of Negative Events

In their original scale, Holmes and Rahe made no distinction between positive events (entering college) and negative events (failing a course). However, other researchers have argued that it is not the accumulation of life events but rather our appraisal of events as positive or negative that is important. These researchers found that negative life events are more important predictors of developing an illness than are positive events (Sarason, Sarason, & Johnson, 1985). These studies tell us that experiencing many major life events, especially negative ones, may ultimately contribute to our becoming ill.

More recently, psychologists have found that not only do major life events affect our lives, but so do daily annoyances that we know as hassles.

Social Readjustment Rating Scale

Life event	Mean value
Death of spouse	100
Divorce	73
Marital separation	65
Jail term	63
Death of close family member	63
Personal injury or illness	53
Marriage	50
Fired at work	47
Marital reconciliation	45
Retirement	45
Change in health of family member	44
Pregnancy	40
Sex difficulties	39
Gain of a new family member	39
Business readjustment	39
Change in financial state	38
Death of a close friend	37
Change to a different line of work	36
Change in number of arguments with spouse	35
Mortgage or loan for major purchase (home etc.)	31
Foreclosure of mortgage or loan	30
Change in responsibilities at work	29
Son or daughter leaving home	29
Trouble with in-laws	29
Outstanding personal achievement	28
Wife begins or stops work	26
Begin or end school	26
Change in living conditions	25
Revision of personal habits	24
Trouble with boss	23
Change in work hours or conditions	20
Change in residence	20
Change in school	20
Change in recreation	19
Change in church activities	19
Change in social activities	18
Mortgage or loan for lesser purchase (car, TV, etc.)	17
Change in sleeping habits	16
Change in number of family get-togethers	15
Change in eating habits	15
Vacation	13
Christmas	12
Minor violations of the law	11

Each number refers to the expected impact that the event would have on one's life, with death of one's spouse having the maximum value of 100. To obtain your score, add the numbers associated with each event you experienced in the last year. The total reflects how much life change you have experienced. In Holmes and Rahe's (1967) original study, a score in the 200s was associated with about a 50% chance of getting an illness, and a score of 300 or above was associated with about an 80% change of developing an illness.

Importance of Hassles

Do those small annoyances get to you?

During the 1970s and 1980s, psychologists were primarily concerned with the association between major life events and illness. However, during the 1990s the focus of research has broadened to include daily annoyances. **Hassles** *are those small, irritating, frustrating events that we face in our daily lives.* Hassles include getting stuck in traffic, running out of time, looking for a parking spot, having too many things to do, experiencing car problems, waiting in line, and on and on.

The major reason researchers have been studying hassles is that they are a better predictor of mood, levels of stress, and getting an illness than major life events are. For example, researchers found that the number of hassles reported by medical students was a better predictor of having a negative mood than was the occurrence of major life events (Wolf, Elston, & Kissling, 1989). Subsequently, researchers reported that hassles were better predictors of psychological symptoms (anxiety, worries, tension) and levels of reported stress than were life events (Kohn, Lafreniere, & Gurevich, 1991; Lu, 1991).

You might say that the flip side of hassles is **uplifts**: *those small, pleasurable, happy, and satisfying experiences that we have in our daily lives.* In an interesting study, subjects reported experiencing a great increase in hassles and a corresponding decrease in uplifts several days before coming down with a cold (Evans & Edgerton, 1991). Thus, there is now considerable support for the idea that daily hassles contribute to negative mood, levels of stress, and illness.

One reason that hassles are such a bother is that they represent frustrating situations, which is our next topic.

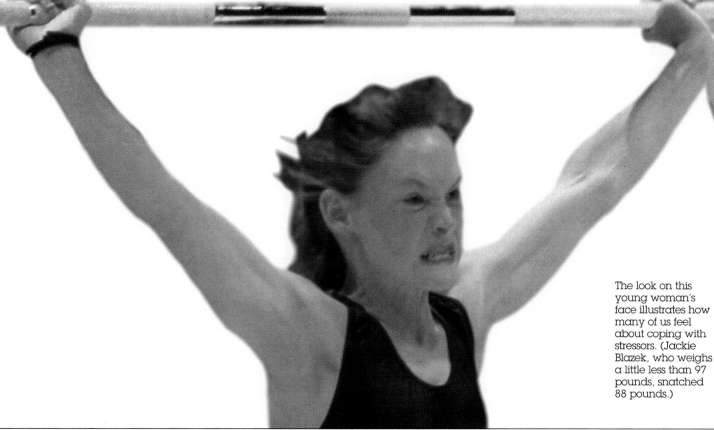

The look on this young woman's face illustrates how many of us feel about coping with stressors. (Jackie Blazek, who weighs a little less than 97 pounds, snatched 88 pounds.)

Situational Stressors

We're going to examine three experiences—frustration, burnout, and cultural differences—that have the potential to cause relatively high levels of stress. However, it is important to remember that our actual level of stress is determined by how we appraise a particular situation.

Frustration

Imagine being in the following situations:

• You miss getting a good grade on an exam because you made several dumb mistakes.

• Your boss insists that you work on a weekend that you were planning to take off.

What these situations have in common is the potential for making you frustrated. **Frustration** *is the feeling that results when your attempts to reach some goal are blocked.* You may not be able to reach a goal because of *personal limitations,* such as making dumb mistakes on an exam or forgetting to set the alarm for an early study session. Or you may not reach a goal because of *social* or *environmental limitations,* such as your boss changing your work schedule or someone damaging your car.

How do you handle making dumb mistakes on exams?

No matter what the cause, your stress levels will be influenced by how you respond to frustration. If your response to frustrating situations is primarily emotional, your levels of stress will increase, because emotional responses trigger the fight-or-flight response and cause increased physiological arousal. Similarly, if you believe that the frustrating situation is uncontrollable or hopeless, your levels of stress will also increase, because lack of control is highly frustrating. These examples indicate the use of *emotion-focused coping,* in which our energy is used to manage our emotions rather than seek a solution to the problem. If, however, we respond to frustrating situations with *problem-focused coping,* our levels of stress will decrease as we remove the causes of the the frustration.

Most of us experience daily frustration. If the frustration extends over a long period of time, we may experience burnout.

Burnout

Imagine being in the middle of your college career and feeling overwhelmed by the demands of facing too many classes, exams, work hours, decisions, and plans coupled with the reality of having too little energy, determination, and time. In this case, you may be experiencing a feeling known as burnout. **Burnout** *refers to feelings of failing, wearing out, or becoming exhausted because of too many demands on one's time and energy.* Burnout does not result from the demands of two or three stressful situations. Rather, burnout occurs when stressful events accumulate over a period of time and result in feelings of emotional exhaustion and impersonal feeling toward others (Green, Walkey, & Taylor, 1991).

How can you avoid burnout?

College counselors report that burnout is a relatively frequent cause of students dropping out of college before obtaining their degrees. Counselors suggest that before students decide to drop out they consider ways to reduce their work and class load so that life and school seem less overwhelming and more manageable (Leafgren, 1989).

Just as burnout has great potential for raising levels of stress, so do situations that involve cultural differences.

Cultural Differences

Imagine being a student from a culture where it is not considered appropriate to ask questions in class, to ask for help or special assistance in mastering material, or to admit to others that you are having difficulties in class. These are examples of cultural stress. **Cultural stress** *refers to difficulties created when the original practices of one's culture are in conflict with the practices of the new, adopted culture.* For example, some students might not take advantage of tutoring services because, in their country or subculture, to do so is admitting to a personal failure. As a result, such students often feel overwhelmed by practices that are common in their adopted culture (Martinez, 1990).

How can you reduce cultural stress?

Minority students who enroll in America's colleges and universities will likely experience cultural stress. Most colleges have a variety of minority programs and counseling services to help students deal with cultural stress—but the very students these programs and services are designed to help must overcome that stress to make use of them.

Certain situations are inherently stressful, such as a young boy saying goodbye to his father.

In addition to stress caused by frustration, burnout, and cultural differences, there is also the stress that comes with conflict.

Conflict

How am I ever going to decide?
Imagine having to make the following decisions:

• You can either go to a great party or see an old and dear friend who is visiting town for just one day.

• You can study for a psychology exam or write a paper for a history class.

• You want to ask a new person for a date but you are afraid of being rejected.

These kinds of situations require difficult decisions that put us into conflict. **Conflict** *is the feeling we experience when we must decide between two or more incompatible choices.* One reason situations involving conflict trigger feelings of stress is that no matter which option you choose, you must give up something else. Let's examine three common kinds of conflicts: approach-approach, avoidance-avoidance, and approach-avoidance.

Approach-approach conflict *involves choosing between two situations that both have pleasurable consequences.* For example, going to a great party and seeing an old and dear friend both involve pleasurable consequences. In some respects, approach-approach conflicts are the least stressful of the three kinds because whichever option we choose, we will experience pleasurable consequences. In other respects, approach-approach conflicts are the most stressful because we must give up a pleasurable consequence.

Avoidance-avoidance conflict *involves choosing between two situations that both have disagreeable consequences.* For instance, you might prefer to avoid studying for a psychology exam—*and* to avoid writing a paper for a history class. In addition, no matter which one you choose, it—and not choosing the other—will have disagreeable consequences and carry the potential to increase your level of stress. As the time to decide in avoidance-avoidance situations grows near, we often change our minds many times. Usually we wait until the last possible minute before making the final decision and deal with the disagreeable consequences.

Approach-avoidance conflict *involves a single situation that has both pleasurable and disagreeable aspects.* A relatively common approach-avoidance conflict is thinking about asking a new person for a date but being afraid of being rejected. Another example is wanting to get a new hairstyle but being afraid that it will not look as good as your current one. In these cases, the approach part involves wanting to ask the person for a date or wanting to change hairstyles, while the avoidance part involves wanting to avoid being rejected or looking bad. Our lives are full of approach-avoidance conflicts that have the potential to increase our levels of stress and influence our moods.

Besides dealing with the stress caused by these types of conflicts, we must deal with the stress that comes from being anxious, which we will examine next.

Anxiety

Why does Sandra feel anxious?

"Sandra was elated but terrified, too. The more she learned about Wellesley, the more she felt the school had made a mistake. She knew she wasn't smart enough to go there. She knew she wouldn't fit in socially." (*Life*, April 1992, p. 65)

Sandra's fears and uncertainties about her ability to compete and do well at Wellesley are causing anxiety. **Anxiety** *is an unpleasant state characterized by feelings of uneasiness and apprehension as well as increased physiological arousal,* such as increased heart rate and blood pressure. We feel anxious when our goals are blocked, when we are in conflict over choosing between two goals, when we feel emotionally exhausted, when we must deal with a different culture, or when we believe the situation is uncontrollable.

Causes of Anxiety

We'll examine three possible causes of anxiety: classical conditioning, observational learning, and unconscious conflict.

Classical Conditioning

Why does walking into the library cause me anxiety?

Each time I enter the library, I can actually feel my heart kick into overdrive and feel a wave of mild anxiety flowing over me. Recall that classical conditioning involves the pairing of a neutral stimulus with an unconditioned stimulus. In my case, the neutral stimulus is walking into the library. It is paired with the unconditioned stimulus: considerable worry over writing a chapter for this book. The unconditioned stimulus—worry—elicits the unconditioned response—anxiety. After repeated pairings of walking into the library (conditioned stimulus) with worry (unconditioned stimulus), the conditioned stimulus (library) acquires the ability to elicit the conditioned response (anxiety). The anxiety I feel when walking into the library is an example of a conditioned emotional response. A **conditioned emotional response** *results when an emotional response is classically conditioned to a previously neutral stimulus.* After they are established, conditioned emotional responses are triggered quickly and automatically by the occurrence of the conditioned stimulus. A conditioned emotional response is highly resistant to extinction.

Observational Learning

Why does seeing a bee cause me great fright?

As you may remember from Module 12, Albert Bandura (1986) showed that many responses, including emotional responses, can be acquired through observational learning. Just to remind you, **observational learning** *is a form of learning that develops through watching and does not require the observer to perform any observable behavior or receive a reinforcer.* In my case, I vividly remember seeing my brother being attacked by a swarm of bees and watching in horror as he ran to escape them. Since that time, the sight of a bee automatically causes me great anxiety, which I learned through observational learning.

Unconscious Conflict

What happens if I plan to write but instead rent a video?

Sigmund Freud suggested a cause of anxiety that is very different from classical conditioning or observational learning. As we discussed in Module 23, Freud hypothesized that the three divisions of the mind—id, ego, and superego—usually work together to satisfy our needs. However, at other times the id, ego, and superego are in conflict over how a need should be satisfied. If the ego feels threatened by the id's desires, the ego creates a feeling of anxiety. Thus, according to Freud's explanation, **anxiety** *arises when there is an unconscious conflict between the id and superego, with the ego caught in the middle; the ego's solution to this conflict is to create a feeling of anxiety.* Freud's idea of unconscious conflict explains why I feel guilty about renting a video instead of writing.

Depending on whether our anxiety arises from classical conditioning, observational learning, or unconscious conflicts, we would use different methods to cope with this feeling.

A common defense mechanism is projection.

Freudian Defense Mechanisms	
Rationalization	Making up acceptable excuses for behaviors that cause us to feel anxious.
Denial	Refusing to recognize some anxiety-provoking event or piece of information.
Repression	Placing unacceptable or threatening feelings or impulses into the unconscious.
Projection	Transferring our unacceptable traits to others.
Reaction formation	Turning unacceptable wishes into acceptable ones.
Displacement	Redirecting an unacceptable feeling from one object toward a safer, more socially acceptable one.
Sublimation	A type of displacement that involves redirecting a threatening or forbidden desire into a socially acceptable one.

Coping with Anxiety

Extinction. Can the anxious feelings learned through classical conditioning or observational learning be changed? In fact, there are a number of *extinction* techniques we can use to reduce our anxiety. In Modules 11 and 12, we discussed several methods to "unlearn" responses, including systematic desensitization and behavior modification. In later modules (29 and 30) we'll discuss additional methods. At this point it is enough to note that all extinction procedures involve actively working to change certain thoughts, behaviors, or physiological responses associated with our anxious feelings. These procedures might be characterized as being *problem-focused conscious coping techniques,* since they represent active attempts to deal with the problem itself.

Freudian Defense Mechanisms. In comparison to conscious, problem-focused coping, Freud's defense mechanisms represent *emotion-focused, unconscious coping techniques.*. As you may remember, **defense mechanisms** *are processes that operate at unconscious levels to help the ego reduce anxiety through self-deception.* On the right is a brief list of Freud's more important defense mechanisms. (For a more complete discussion, refer to Module 23.)

According to Freud, the occasional use of defense mechanisms is normal and helps reduce anxiety so that we can continue to function as we work on the real causes of our problems. Yet we must remember that the overuse of defense mechanisms may prevent us from recognizing or working on the real causes of our anxiety.

Next we'll examine how different kinds of personality variables can help or hinder our coping with anxiety and stress.

Personality Factors

How can a heart surgeon work 15 hours a day, seven days a week?

The door opens. Dr. Michael DeBakey enters and walks quickly to the operating table. His assistants have already opened the patient's chest and removed the diseased heart. With the skill and precision of a master, DeBakey transplants a healthy donor heart into the patient's chest. It takes about an hour. When DeBakey finishes, he leaves the operating suite and goes to the scrub room. He takes off his operating clothes, scrubs down, and puts on clean, sterilized clothes. In a matter of minutes, he enters another operating suite, and the whole process starts over. In a normal working day, DeBakey operates on five to nine patients. He normally spends 15 hours a day, seven days a week in the hospital and performs as many heart operations in one month as most surgeons do in a year. There is one more thing you should know about DeBakey. He is over 80 years old (*San Diego Tribune,* November 27, 1987).

There are two major reasons that Michael DeBakey functions so successfully in such a potentially stressful environment. The first is that he appraises situations as challenges rather than as threats. Challenge appraisals result in more problem-focused coping, which is associated with bringing out positive emotions, such as excitement and eagerness, as well as reducing stress. In comparison, threat appraisals result in more emotion-focused coping, which is associated with negative emotions as well as increased stress.

A second reason DeBakey functions so well is that he has a winning combination of personality factors that help him perform under great stress. Specifically, he has what is known as a hardy personality, which helps people deal with stress.

Hardiness

In a series of experiments, researchers asked why certain people handled potentially stressful situations much better than others (Kobasa, 1982; Kobasa, Maddi, & Kahn, 1982; Kobasa, Maddi, & Puccetti, 1982). They studied the personality characteristics of middle- and upper-level executives and lawyers who had experienced considerable stress in the previous three years. What they discovered was that some of the executives and lawyers became ill while others stayed healthy. Those who stayed healthy in spite of stressful life situations had three personality traits, which taken together the

By himself, Frenchman Gerard D'Aboville rowed 8,000 miles across the Pacific Ocean in 134 days. It would take a hardy personality to survive such a stressful ordeal.

researchers labeled hardiness. **Hardiness** *is a combination of three personality traits—control, commitment, and challenge—that protect or buffer us from the potentially harmful effects of stressful situations and reduce our chances of developing psychosomatic illness.* Research on hardiness explains why some individuals develop psychosomatic problems in potentially stressful situations while others do not.

From what we know of DeBakey, he appears to be the perfect example of a hardy person. His medical reputation shows he has *commitment,* which means he knows and pursues his goals and values. His pursuit of open-heart surgery shows he likes a *challenge,* which means he actively confronts and solves problem situations. His role as head of surgery indicates his desire to be in *control,* which means he believes that his actions directly affect how situations turn out.

Researchers have especially studied control, one of the three traits of hardiness. Let's see why control reduces stress.

Locus of Control and Stress

As we discussed in Module 24, beliefs about whether you control the situation or the situation controls you determine your *locus of control.* If you believe you are basically in control of life's events and that what you do influences what happens, you are said to have an *internal locus of control.* If you believe that chance and luck mostly determine what happens and that you do not have much influence, you are said to have an *external locus of control.* Locus of control should be thought of as a continuum, with internal on one end and external on the other. Most of us lie somewhere along this continuum, rather than being oriented completely toward one or the other (Lefcourt, 1982).

Does what I do really matter?

"No matter how much I study, it never seems to help." This statement is more characteristic of students with an external locus of control. Individuals with an external locus of control tend to believe that there is nothing they can do when things go badly. They use primarily threat appraisals and emotion-focused coping; they experience more negative emotions, higher levels of stress, and more psychosomatic symptoms than those with an internal locus of control. In contrast, individuals whose locus of control is internal tend to use challenge appraisals and problem-focused coping; they experience more positive emotions, lower levels of stress, and fewer psychosomatic symptoms than those whose locus of control is external (Taylor & Cooper, 1989).

An example of the interaction between locus of control and appraisal is shown in the graph. Subjects in the study who perceived situations as uncontrollable felt increased levels of stress and were more likely to develop physical and psychological problems. On the other hand, subjects with an internal locus of control were found to appraise situations as less stressful and were better able to cope (Stern, McCants, & Pettine, 1982). Another study found that cardiac patients with an internal locus of control were more cooperative, were less depressed, and had shorter stays in intensive care than patients with an external locus of control (Cromwell et al., 1977).

From research on locus of control and hardiness, we learn that personality traits influence our appraisals, which may in turn increase or decrease our feelings of stress and our chances of developing illness.

Let's look next at one particular combination of personality traits that has received much scientific and popular attention.

Individuals who thought of themselves as being in control of their lives (high controllability) were found to have significantly fewer illnesses than people who thought they had little control over their lives (low controllability).

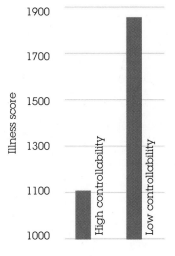

Personality Factors

Type A Personality

In 1974, two doctors published a book, *Type A Behavior and Your Heart*, that startled the medical community (Friedman & Rosenman, 1974). They reported that in addition to the known risk factors associated with coronary heart disease, such as diet, exercise, and smoking, there was a psychological risk factor, which they called Type A behavior.

What does it mean to be called a "Type A"?
According to the original definition, **Type A behavior** referred to a combination of personality traits that included an overly competitive and aggressive drive to achieve, a hostile attitude when frustrated, a habitual sense of time urgency, and a rapid and explosive pattern of speaking (Friedman & Rosenman, 1974). **Type B behavior** was characterized by being easygoing, calm, relaxed, and patient.

Compared to Type B's, Type A's were found to have experienced two to three times as many heart attacks. By 1978 Type A behavior was officially recognized as an independent risk factor for heart disease by a National Institutes of Health panel.

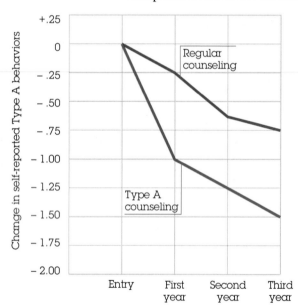

However, at about this same time data began coming in that raised two questions about Type A behavior. First, is Type A behavior really a risk factor, as earlier research had suggested? Second, which personality traits make up Type A behavior? Let's examine these two questions.

Is Type A behavior a risk factor in heart problems?
To determine the connection between Type A behavior and heart problems, researchers analyzed 83 studies on this subject (Booth-Kewley & Friedman, 1987). They concluded that a modest but reliable association exists between Type A personality variables and cardiovascular disease.

One of the strongest cases to be made for Type A behavior being a risk factor comes from a study on changing this behavior. As shown in the graph, a stress management program (described in the Applying/Exploring section for this module) was successful not only in decreasing Type A behaviors but in reducing subsequent heart attacks by half, compared with a control group (Friedman et al., 1984). These studies suggest that Type A behavior is a heart disease risk factor of about the same magnitude as smoking.

Over the course of three years, cardiac patients who received counseling in how to reduce Type A behaviors showed a significantly greater reduction in their Type A behaviors. In addition, only 8.9% of subjects who received Type A counseling experienced another heart attack, compared to 18.9% in the regular counseling group.

Since 1978 a number of large-scale studies had failed to find an association between Type A behavior and coronary heart disease. However, these findings have been questioned. For example, almost all of the studies that found no association between Type A behavior and heart problems used subjects who already had serious heart problems. In comparison, in studies that used subjects who did not already have such problems, researchers reported that 70% of men who developed heart problems were Type A as compared with only 46% of control subjects (Miller et al., 1991). These researchers conclude that Type A behavior has been and continues to be a risk factor for coronary heart disease.

What personality traits reflect Type A behavior?

The popular conception of the Type A person is someone who is hurried, impatient, and a workaholic. Interestingly, some researchers have recently found that coronary disease is not associated with a workaholic attitude and have recommended that this trait be dropped from the Type A behavior pattern (Booth-Kewley & Friedman, 1987). So we now have a truer and more accurate picture of Type A behavior. The revised definition of **Type A personality** *is an individual who frequently expresses one or more negative emotions, such as anger, hostility, or aggression, or who experiences depression.* Further, other researchers have suggested that negative emotions should be considered the distinguishing features of Type A behavior (Matthews & Haynes, 1986). These researchers now agree that a Type A individual is someone who may be described as being depressed, aggressively competitive, easily frustrated, anxious, angry, or some combination of these traits.

Besides Type A behavior, is there a single trait or combination of traits that put one at risk for headaches, ulcers, asthma, or rheumatoid arthritis?

The Disease-Prone Personality

Although the exact cause of headaches, ulcers, asthma, and rheumatoid arthritis is unknown, doctors estimate that 30% to 50% of these maladies are caused by psychological factors. Is it possible that certain personality traits, such as anxiety, depression, and anger, contribute to developing these symptoms? When researchers analyzed 101 studies to answer this question, they found that the relationship between a personality trait (such as anxiety, depression, anger, or hostility) and one of the diseases is low but comparable to that reported for other medical risk factors (Friedman & Booth-Kewley, 1987).

Do worriers get ulcers and anxious types get headaches?

Contrary to the popular notion that worriers get ulcers and anxious types get headaches, the researchers discovered a **disease-prone personality:** *a trait or a combination of traits—such as anxiety, anger, hostility, aggression, and depression—associated with a particular disease.* The importance of depression in disease was also suggested by the results in another study. In a 20-year follow-up study, researchers found that men who had scored high on a depression scale had a higher incidence of cancer and death from cancer than men who had scored low (Persky, Kempthorne-Rawson, & Shekelle, 1987). This means that the frequent expression of certain negative personality traits puts one at risk for developing a number of disorders, just as being a smoker puts one at risk for developing coronary heart disease.

In conclusion, there is convincing research pointing to the influence of personality variables on the development of physical problems, including coronary heart disease, headaches, rheumatoid arthritis, and asthma. The specific traits range from depression to anger and hostility.

Just as personality factors can influence health, so, too, can social factors, which we'll discuss next.

Social Factors

Why were there so few heart attacks in this community?

"There was something curious about the town of Roseto, Pennsylvania. Only one Rosetan man in 1,000 died of a heart attack, compared with a national rate of 3.5 per 1,000; the rates for women were even lower. Rosetans also had lower rates for ulcers and emotional problems compared with the rest of the United States and their neighboring towns. This was very puzzling, because the men and women of Roseto were relatively obese. They also ate as much animal fat, smoked as much, and exercised as little as residents of the other towns. 'One striking feature did set Roseto apart from its neighbors,' says Stewart Wolf, vice president for medical affairs at St. Luke's Hospital in Bethlehem, Pennsylvania, and a principal investigator of the Roseto phenomenon. 'We found that family relationships were extremely close and mutually supportive. This cohesive quality extended to neighbors and to the community as a whole.'" (Greenberg, 1978, p. 378)

As Rosetan families prospered, they moved into the countryside, and their social support system began to break down. With the breakdown in social supports came an increase in heart attacks, especially in younger men. The study on Rosetan families suggests the importance of social support in dealing with stress. **Social support** *refers to human relationships that have a lasting and positive impact on our lives; social support helps us mobilize our resources so that we can control or minimize the effects of stressful situations.* Others may help us deal with stress by assisting with a task, lending money, solving problems, and giving attention, affection, or love. Social support from others may also help us cope with stress by raising our self-esteem, confidence, and feelings of self-worth, which in turn promote and maintain psychological adjustment. Apparently, it is not the number of friends we have that matters in coping with stress. Rather, it is the quality of our friendships that is important in receiving social support (Gove, Hughes, & Style, 1983).

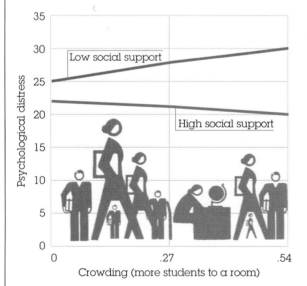

High levels of social support helped students cope with crowded living conditions.

Social Support and Symptoms of Stress

Generally, individuals with strong social support report fewer neurotic and depressive symptoms than people with little or no social support (Duck & Silver, 1990). This finding suggests that family and friends help us cope with stressful situations. For example, as shown in this graph, college students with strong social support were better able to cope with overcrowded living conditions than students with weak social support (Lepore, Evans, & Schneider, 1991). Similarly, researchers reported that higher social support was associated with lower blood pressure in a random sample of over 1,400 males and females (Bland et al., 1991). After reviewing a decade of literature on social support, researchers concluded that it contributes to our well-being, both physically and psychologically (Cohen & Wills, 1985). Among other benefits, social support protects or buffers us from potentially harmful situations by changing our appraisals, improving our self-esteem, providing us with information, and changing our coping patterns. All of these factors give us more reason to be thankful for our families and our good friends.

After the Concept/Glossary, we'll discuss behavioral and cognitive components of stress management.

1. The cognitive and behavioral efforts that we use to manage a situation that we have appraised as exceeding, straining, or taxing our personal resources is referred to as (a)_____. Seeking information about what needs to be done, changing our own behavior, or taking whatever action will solve the problem is referred to as (b)_____ coping. Making some effort to deal with the emotional distress caused by a harm or threat appraisal is referred to as (c)_____ coping.

5. We can become anxious if an emotional response is classically conditioned to a previously neutral stimulus; this procedure results in a (a)_____ response. If we become anxious through watching and do not perform any observable behavior or receive a reinforcer, this is called (b)_____ learning. If we become anxious because of unconscious conflicts between the id and superego, this is (c)_____ explanation of anxiety.

2. Potentially disturbing, troubling, or disruptive situations, both positive and negative, that we appraise as having considerable impact on our lives are called (a)_____ events. Small, irritating, frustrating events that we face in our daily lives are called (b)_____.

6. A combination of three personality traits—control, commitment, and challenge—that protect or buffer us from the potentially harmful effects of stressful situations and reduce our chances of developing psychosomatic illness is referred to as _____.

3. The feeling that results when our attempts to reach some goal are blocked is called (a)_____. The feeling of failing, wearing out, or becoming exhausted because of too many demands from a stressful work environment is called (b)_____. The difficulties created when the original practices of one's culture are in conflict with the practices of the new, adopted culture is referred to as (c)_____.

4. There are three general kinds of conflict. A single situation that has both pleasurable and disagreeable aspects is called (a)_____ conflict; choosing between two options that both have pleasurable consequences is called (b)_____ conflict; choosing between two options that both have disagreeable consequences is called (c)_____ conflict.

7. An individual who frequently expresses one or more negative emotions, such as anger, hostility, or aggression, or who experiences depression fits into the revised definition of (a)_____. Individual personality traits or a combination of traits, such as anxiety, anger, hostility, aggression, and depression, associated with a particular disease is called the (b)_____ personality.

8. Some human relationships have a lasting and positive impact on our lives and help us mobilize our resources so that we can control or minimize the effects of stressful situations. These human relationships are called _____.

Answers: *1. (a) coping, (b) problem-focused, (c) emotion-focused. 2. (a) major life, (b) hassles; 3. (a) frustration, (b) burnout, (c) cultural stress; 4. (a) approach-avoidance, (b) approach-approach, (c) avoidance-avoidance; 5. (a) conditioned emotional, (b) observational, (c) Freud's; 6. hardiness; 7. (a) Type A behavior, (b) disease-prone; 8. social support.*

APPLYING/ EXPLORING: STRESS MANAGEMENT II

How do you cope with an upcoming exam? During your college career, you will take literally dozens of exams, each one a potential stressor. You can use exam situations as oportunities to practice stress management and to improve your coping skills for future problems. With this in mind, let's look at a stress management program that was developed by two clinical psychologists to improve the coping skills of Type A's (Roskies & Avard, 1982). The five steps of this program—self-observation, appraisal, coping, dealing with unavoidable stressors, and practice—can be used by anyone and for any stressor.

Step 1 Self-Observation

The stress management program begins with observing and recording your stress-related thoughts, behaviors, and symptoms for two weeks. This can be done easily by keeping a daily diary. Your goal is to identify daily hassles, negative self-statements ("I'll never pass that exam"), and pyschosomatic symptoms.

Before you dismiss the importance of observing yourself, consider a study by Featherstone and Beitman (1983). They found that migraine sufferers were far more likely to improve with treatment if they were aware of how much their own thoughts and behaviors contributed to their problem. Migraine sufferers who denied the impact of their thoughts and behaviors rarely improved, even though they were receiving treatment.

After the two weeks of self-observation, you should be more aware of the types of appraisals that you are using, your negative self-statements, built-up body tension, feelings of anxiety, and psychosomatic symptoms. Once you know yourself much better, you are ready to begin changing your thoughts and behaviors.

Step 2 Appraisal

Most potentially stressful situations have both threatening and challenging aspects; however, we usually focus more on one than the other. For instance, students facing exams who make more of a challenge appraisal, such as striving to get a good grade, are more likely to take some direct action to deal with the situation itself, such as developing a study program or organizing a review session. Students who make more of a threat appraisal, such as feeling they will do poorly or feeling their self-esteem is jeopardized, are more likely to focus on negative emotions like anxiety and fear (Krantz, 1983). Responses to these negative emotions may take the form of complaining, using drugs, or seeking pleasurable escape activities.

In emphasizing the importance of appraisal, Lazarus (1990) reminds us that

• A threat appraisal will increase your feelings of stress; a challenge appraisal will decrease these stressful feelings. Because most situations include threat and challenge appraisals, your goal is to focus more on the challenging than on the threatening aspects.

• Work at changing a threatening appraisal into a more challenging one, as challenge appraisals elicit positive emotions, such as excitement and eagerness, while threatening appraisals elicit negative emotions, such as anxiety and fear.

Coping involves juggling our resources to deal with stressors.

• Your appraisal of a situation influences your kind of coping. For example, researchers who studied the coping patterns of married couples reported that challenge appraisals were related to using more problem-focused coping. This means that people who use challenge appraisals are more likely to deal with the causes of their problems (Folkman et al., 1986).

Let's examine the ways that you can change a threat appraisal to more of a challenge.

Step 3 Coping

In coping with an upcoming exam, you might use a number of techniques. One technique for changing exams from threats to challenges is to substitute positive self-statements for negative ones. Specifically, on one side of a sheet of paper write your negative self-statements, then next to them write the positive ones that you can substitute.

For example, on one side you might have these negative self-statements:

"I'll never do well on the exam."
"There's no time to study."
"I'm not smart enough."
"I'm never going to learn all this stuff."

On the other side you should have positive self-statements that replace the negative ones:

"I bet I can do OK on the exam."
"I'll think of ways to make time to study."
"I've got plenty of ability."
"I can do better than last time."

Another technique is to reduce your emotional reactions (fear, anxiety, tension) by regularly engaging in a relaxation exercise (as explained in Module 25). You can also reduce your emotional reactions by substituting confidence-building positive thoughts for negative emotional thoughts.

Or you might change a threat to a challenge by asking for social support from friends or family. Social support may take the form of good advice, friendly encouragement, or comforting thoughts. It might even include help with studying, whether through a study group or with someone quizzing you.

Remember, many situations involve both threat and challenge appraisals. As a result you will need to use a combination of emotion-focused and problem-focused coping techniques.

Step 4 Dealing with Unavoidable Stressors

Exams are an unavoidable fact of college life. Besides exams, many other unavoidable situations increase our stress levels and chances of developing psychosomatic symptoms. In such situations, people often say, "There's nothing I can do about it." But there are a number of things you *can* do about stressful and unavoidable situations (Lazarus, 1990). When you cannot avoid a situation, you must work instead on changing your appraisal of it. Remember that subjects who watched a film of a bloody accident were able to alter their levels of stress and physiological arousal by changing their self-appraisal from one of involved participant to one of objective observer. You can change your appraisal of exams by thinking that exams are ways of evaluating what you have learned rather than torture instruments that threaten your self-esteem and confidence.

Researchers have discovered that thinking about unavoidable stressful situations provokes stress that is as great as or greater than engaging in the actual events. Thinking about the event causes what is called *anticipatory stress*. Researchers reported that students' blood pressure was just as high on the days immediately preceding a test as on test day itself (Sausen et al., 1992). This finding indicates that the sooner you begin coping with the situation (problem-focused coping), the better your chances of reducing anticipatory stress.

Step 5 Practice

Researchers unanimously agree that a stress management program works best if you follow all of its steps. Improving your ability to manage stress requires effort—and practice. Keep in mind that just as learning to play tennis takes many weeks of practice, so, too, does learning more effective coping techniques.

Is it worth the effort? A stress management program similar to the one just described helped Type A individuals reduce their Type A behaviors and lower their risk of heart attacks (Friedman et al., 1984; Roskies & Avard, 1982). You decide what it might do for you.

Summary/Self-Test

COPING

1. The cognitive and behavioral efforts we use to manage a situation that we have appraised as exceeding, straining, or taxing our personal resources are known as (a)_____. When we seek information about what needs to be done, change our own behavior, or take whatever action will solve the problem, we use (b)_____ coping. When we use our energies to deal with emotional distress caused by a harm or threat appraisal, we are using (c)_____ coping. The major factor that influences which method of coping we use is how much control we feel we have over the situation.

■ *Susan has decided to break up with her boyfriend. What kinds of problems will she face? How should she cope?*

MAJOR LIFE EVENTS AND DAILY HASSLES

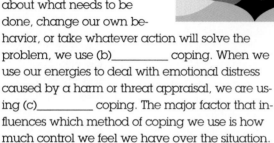

2. Situations that are potentially disturbing, troubling, or disruptive and that we appraise as having an impact on our lives are called (a)_____ events. These may be positive or negative; negative life events are more important predictors of developing an illness than are positive events. Even better predictors of illness are the small, irritating events called (b)_____.

■ *Harold explains that there have been no major problems in his life but he keeps having outbreaks of cold sores. What's going on?*

SITUATIONAL STRESSORS

3. The feeling that results when our attempts to reach some goal are blocked is called (a)_____. If we respond to this feeling primarily with emotion-focused coping, our levels of stress will increase because emotions trigger the (b)_____ response. If, however, we respond to frustration with (c)_____ coping, our levels of stress will decrease as we remove the causes of the frustration.

4. Feelings of failing, wearing out, or becoming exhausted because of too many demands on our time and energy are referred to as _____. One consequence of this feeling is to raise our levels of stress.

5. When we must decide between two or more incompatible choices, we are in (a)_____, which can include at least three possibilities. If we must choose between two options with pleasurable consequences, we experience (b)_____ conflict. If we must choose between two options that both have disagreeable consequences, we are in (c)_____ conflict. If a single situation has both pleasurable and disagreeable aspects we are in (d)_____ conflict.

6. The difficulties created when the original practices of one's culture are in conflict with the practices of the new, adopted culture are referred to as _____.

■ *Nancy wants to drop out of college and get a job. What do you think led up to her decision? What kind of conflict is she in?*

ANXIETY

7. An unpleasant state in which we have feelings of uneasiness and apprehension as well as increased physiological arousal is called (a)_____. This feeling has at least three sources. One source is classical conditioning of an emotional response to a previously neutral stimulus; the result is called a (b)_____ response, which is highly resistant to extinction. A second source of anxiety is a form of learning that develops through watching and does not require any observable behavior or reinforcer; this kind of learning is called (c)_____ learning. According to Freud, a third source of anxiety arises when the id and superego disagree, resulting in an (d)_____ conflict; the ego's solution to this conflict is to create a feeling of anxiety.

8. Procedures we use to reduce our anxiety by actively working to change certain thoughts, behaviors, or physiological responses are examples of (a)_____ coping techniques. In contrast, Freudian processes that operate at unconscious levels to help the ego reduce anxiety through self-deception, called (b)_____, represent unconscious, emotion-focused coping techniques.

■ *When Mark goes to parties, he always feels a little anxious. What could be causing his feelings?*

PERSONALITY FACTORS

9. Three personality traits protect or buffer us from the potentially harmful effects of stressful situations and reduce our chances of developing psychosomatic symptoms. These three traits are (a)_____, _____, and _____; taken together, researchers call these traits (b)_____.

10. If you believe that what you do influences what happens, you are said to have an (a)_____ of control. In contrast, if you believe that chance and luck mostly determine what happens and that you do not have much influence, you are said to have an (b)_____ of control. People with an external locus experience more negative emotions, higher levels of stress, and more psychosomatic symptoms than those whose locus of control is internal.

11. Two doctors originally defined an overly competitive and aggressive drive to achieve, a hostile attitude when frustrated, a habitual sense of time urgency, and a rapid and explosive pattern of speaking as personality traits of a (a)_____ individual. Those who were easygoing, calm, relaxed, and patient were characterized as (b)_____. Studies suggest that Type A behavior is a heart disease risk factor of about the same magnitude as smoking. The definition of Type A behavior has been revised and now refers to an individual who frequently expresses one or more negative (c)_____, such as anger, hostility, or aggression, or who experiences depression.

12. Doctors estimate that 30%–50% of maladies such as headaches, ulcers, asthma, and rheumatoid arthritis are caused by psychological factors. These disorders are associated with individual personality traits or a combination of traits, such as anxiety, anger, hostility, aggression, and depression; such personality traits contribute to what is known as _____ personality.

■ *Jose is starting a new business and wants to hire employees who can handle a lot of stress. What traits should he be looking for? Could he spot a Type A personality?*

SOCIAL FACTORS

13. Human relationships that have a lasting and positive impact on our lives and that help us gather and use our resources so that we can control or minimize the effects of stressful situations are called _____.

■ *This is Greg's first year in college and his first time away from his family and hometown friends. What are some reasons that he is doing poorly in his classes and personal life?*

APPLYING/EXPLORING: STRESS MANAGEMENT II

14. Two clinical psychologists developed a stress management program to improve the coping skills of people with Type A personalities. The program, which anyone can use, begins with observing and recording your behaviors, negative self-statements, and psychosomatic symptoms. This process is called (a)_____ and helps you become aware of the types of appraisals that you use. One goal is to improve your ability to change a threatening appraisal into a (b)_____ one, since such appraisals decrease feelings of stress.

15. One technique for changing a threat to a challenge is to substitute (a)_____ self-statements for negative ones. Another is to reduce emotional reactions (fear, anxiety, tension) by regularly engaging in (b)_____ exercises. Or you might change a threat to a challenge appraisal by asking for social support from friends or family.

16. Thinking about unavoidable stressful situations causes what is called _____ and provokes stress that is as great as or greater than engaging in the actual events. Thus, the sooner we begin coping with a situation, the better our chances of reducing stress.

■ *Maria's parents tell her that they are getting divorced. What advice would you give Maria?*

Chapter *Fourteen*
DISORDERS

MODULE 27
DISORDERS I

His eyes are hazel, placid, almost vacant and his appearance is neither sinister nor scary. Until the day he was caught, his neighbors considered him an "average Joe." But over a period of three years, Jeffrey Dahmer planned and carried out the murders of 15 young men, while 5 more potential victims managed to escape.

How did a mass murderer go unnoticed?

In a very real sense Dahmer led two different lives. In public, Dahmer seemed like a harmless, quiet guy who held down a job in a chocolate factory. However, in private, Dahmer would con potential victims into coming to his apartment, where he would drug them, commit sexual acts, and then kill and mutilate them.

Although no two serial killers are alike, Dahmer fits the typical pattern. Serial killers are almost always young, white males who are quite intelligent and often come from broken homes; they may have been physically or sexually abused during childhood, and they have serious personality defects, such as low self-esteem and a lifelong sense of loneliness. Over half of serial killers have mutilated their victims (Hickey, 1991). John Douglas, investigative chief at the FBI's National Center for Analysis of Violent Crime, adds that serial killers are obsessed with control, manipulation, and dominance and often con their victims into agreeing to their requests.

Dahmer's defense was that he was legally insane when he committed the murders. However, the jury rejected Dahmer's plea of insanity and agreed with the prosecution that Dahmer was legally sane. The jury found Dahmer guilty on 15 counts of murder and characterized him as a con man who killed for his own selfish interests. On February 17, 1992 a Milwaukee County judge sentenced 31-year-old Dahmer to 15 consecutive life terms. (adapted from *Newsweek*, August 5, 1991 and February 3, 1992; *San Diego Union-Tribune*, February 17, 1992)

Jeffrey Dahmer, convicted of murdering 15 young men, appeared harmless in everyday life.

Some psychiatrists testified for the defense that Dahmer was insane; others testified for the prosecution that he was sane. The **legal definition of insanity** *is not knowing the difference between right and wrong.* This is very different from how the term *insanity* is used by mental health professionals, who prefer the term *mental disorders.* But because the definition of mental disorders must take into account so many factors (genetic, behavioral, cognitive, and environmental), it is often surrounded with controversy. A general definition of **mental disorder** *is a prolonged or recurring problem that seriously interferes with an individual's ability to live a satisfying personal life and function in society.*

What's Coming

In this module, we'll discuss three approaches to understanding mental disorders, the definitions of mental disorders, and some specific examples of mood and other disorders, including phobias. In the next module, we'll discuss mood and personality disorders as well as the disorder responsible for the hospitalization of most psychiatric patients: schizophrenia. Let's begin with the various approaches that are used to define, explain, and treat abnormal behaviors.

Three Approaches

How we view mental disorders has changed greatly since the Middle Ages. At that time, mental disorders were thought to be the result of demons or devils who made the person do strange and horrible things. In the 1500s, mental disorders were thought to involve witches and witchcraft, and a number of people were burned at the stake for that reason.

Today there are three approaches to understanding and treating mental disorders: medical, psychoanalytic, and cognitive-behavioral. As you can guess, each emphasizes different factors.

Understanding and treating mental disorders such as that of Jeffrey Dahmer would involve the three approaches discussed below.

Medical Model Approach

According to the **medical model approach,** *mental disorders are likened to diseases and, as such, have symptoms that can be diagnosed and treated.* Just as drugs are used to treat diseases, a major part of the treatment of mental disorders involves the use of **psychoactive drugs,** *which affect patients' minds and behaviors.*

One advantage of the medical model is that it focuses attention on the body and nervous system in search of possible causes of mental disorders. For example, as you will learn in this chapter, neurotransmitter malfunctions and genetic factors have been found to be involved in certain forms of depression and schizophrenia. Thus, as suggested by the medical model, defects in the chemistry or structure of the brain may contribute to mental disorders.

One disadvantage of the medical model is that mental disorders do not always have clearly defined symptoms or causes. Thus, the medical model may not always be applicable to psychological problems.

Under the medical model, those with mental disorders are treated as *patients* with *illnesses.* Psychiatrists are medical doctors and therefore more likely to follow the medical model than are clinical psychologists, who are not medical doctors.

Psychoanalytic Approach

According to the **psychoanalytic approach,** *the causes of mental disorders lie in unconscious conflicts or in problems with unresolved conflicts at one or more of Freud's psychosexual stages.* As you remember from Module 23, Sigmund Freud divided the mind into three functions: the id or pleasure seeker, the superego or conscience, and the ego or rational peacekeeper. If these three divisions are in conflict, the result is anxiety. To deal with anxiety, the ego uses various defense mechanisms; overusing these defense mechanisms can create additional problems. In addition, Freud believed that various personality problems could result from the unsuccessful resolution of conflicts during the psychosexual stages of early childhood.

According to Freud, treatment of mental disorders centers on the therapist helping the *patient* identify and resolve these *unconscious conflicts.*

Cognitive-Behavioral Approach

The **cognitive-behavioral approach** *uses a combination of information from cognitive processes and learning-conditioning factors to understand and treat mental disorders.* The *cognitive* part of this approach grew out of research to apply what we know about cognitive processes to psychological problems. The *behavioral* part of this approach grew out of research to apply what we know about classical and operant conditioning to psychological problems.

According to the cognitive-behavioral approach, people do not have mental illness but rather have learned maladaptive ways of responding to or thinking about themselves and their environments. In contrast to the medical model, which treats patients who have illnesses, the cognitive-behavioral approach treats *clients* who have *problems.*

Throughout this module and the next, we'll see ways in which these approaches are used. For now, let's examine the various ways of defining what is abnormal.

What Is Abnormal Behavior?

There is no doubt that Jeffrey Dahmer's murder and mutilation of 15 young men indicates severe mental disorder and extremely abnormal behavior. In other cases, it is more difficult to decide what is abnormal. In fact, there are several approaches to defining what is abnormal. To see the differences, consider the case of 54-year-old Richard Thompson.

The City of San Diego evicted Thompson and all his belongings from his home. His belongings included shirts, pants, dozens of shoes, several Bibles, a cooler, a toolchest, lawn chairs, a barbecue grill, tin plates, bird cages, two pet rats, and his self-fashioned bed. For the previous nine months, Thompson's home had been a downtown storm drain (sewer). Because the city does not allow people to live in sewers, Thompson was forbidden to return. Although Thompson has lived in several care centers and mental hospitals, he prefers the privacy and comfort of the sewer (*San Diego Tribune*, April 16, 1986).

The question is, are Thompson's behaviors—including living in the sewer—abnormal? We can take three approaches in answering this question.

Richard Thompson lived happily in a San Diego sewer until he was evicted by the city.

Statistical Frequency

According to the **statistical frequency approach,** *a behavior may be considered abnormal if it occurs infrequently in relation to the behaviors of the general population.* By this definition, living in a sewer would be considered abnormal. However, so would getting a Ph.D., raising orchids, being president, or living in a monastery, since relatively few people engage in these behaviors. As these last examples demonstrate, the statistical frequency definition of abnormality has limited usefulness.

Deviation from Social Norms

According to the **social norms approach,** *a behavior is considered abnormal if it deviates greatly from accepted social norms.* Because Thompson greatly deviated from society's norms when he decided to live in a sewer, his behavior would be considered abnormal. However, definitions of abnormality based solely on deviations from social norms run into problems when social norms change with time. For example, 30 years ago smoking was considered a sign of a mature, sophisticated person; today it is looked on as a serious health risk. Thirty years ago, a woman who was thin was considered to be ill; today many women strive to be thin. Thus, we see that defining abnormality on the basis of social norms can be risky, as these norms may and do change over time.

Maladaptive Behavior

According to the **maladaptive behavior approach,** *a behavior may be defined as abnormal if it interferes with the individual's ability to function as a person or in society.* For example, being terrified to go out in public, hearing voices that dictate dangerous acts, feeling compelled to wash one's hands for hours on end, drinking so much alcohol that it interferes with personal interactions, starving oneself to the point of death, and committing mass murder would all be considered maladaptive and, in that sense, abnormal. However, Thompson's seemingly successful adaptation to living in a sewer may not be maladaptive for him and certainly has no adverse consequences to society. Of the three definitions discussed here, most mental health professionals would agree that the maladaptive definition is perhaps the most useful.

Now that we have a reasonably useful definition of abnormal behaviors, let's explore how such behaviors are classified.

Diagnosing and Classifying Mental Disorders

Arnold was flying with a friend in a private plane when they had to make an emergency landing. The landing was very dangerous and the plane flipped over, but Arnold was not seriously injured. Now whenever Arnold thinks about flying, he feels a pressure in his chest, has difficulty breathing, and begins sweating. Arnold has difficulty even going to an airport to pick someone up.

Arnold's symptoms are so clear-cut that most mental health professionals would agree that his problem is a *phobia*—in his case, a great fear of flying. (We'll learn more about phobias later in this module.) In the next case, the symptoms are not so clear-cut and the problem is more difficult to pinpoint.

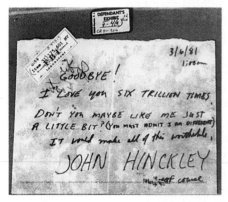

John Hinckley wrote several love letters to actress Jodie Foster.

Why did he shoot the president?

After John Hinckley, Jr., saw the movie *Taxi Driver*, he began collecting guns and became obsessed with Jodie Foster, who was a teenager when she starred in that movie. He called her several times, but she refused to meet him. The relationship that he had dreamed about went absolutely nowhere. In a final love letter, Hinckley indicated he was going to do something to impress Foster and make her understand how much he loved her. Several days later, Hinckley waited in a Washington crowd for President Ronald Reagan to appear. As Reagan emerged from a building, Hinckley opened fire, wounding the president and three other men (*Los Angeles Times*, February 14, 1983).

Assessment Methods

Psychiatrists examined Hinckley soon after his arrest. They used the three major methods of assessing abnormal behavior— clinical interviews, psychological tests, and neurological exams—to diagnose Hinckley's mental disorder.

Clinical Interviews. A number of psychiatrists conducted *clinical interviews* with Hinckley that lasted for many hours. In these interviews they tried to establish a good rapport and create a trusting environment so that he would reveal very private information about himself.

The clinical interview can provide an enormous amount of information about a person's background and current problems. It is important to bear in mind, however, that in all likelihood the person will give different information to different psychiatrists, who may interpret the information in different ways. For example, Hinckley apparently revealed certain of his fantasies to some psychiatrists and not to others. In spite of these potential problems, the clinical interview is perhaps the primary technique used to assess abnormal behavior (Leckman et al., 1982).

Psychological Tests. Hinckley was given a number of *psychological tests*, including projective tests such as the Rorschach inkblot test and personality inventories such as the MMPI. To refresh your memory of these tests, you may want to look back to Modules 23 and 24.

Neurological Examinations. Hinckley was given a number of *neurological tests* to check for possible brain damage. These tests included evaluation of reflexes, motor coordination, brain waves, and brain structures. Because some abnormal behaviors may be caused by tumors, diseases, or infections of the brain, neurological tests are necessary before these causes can be ruled out.

Aftermath of a shooting: President Ronald Reagan, who was shot in the chest, has already been rushed to the hospital for surgery. On the ground (front center) is press secretary James Brady, who was shot in the head. John Hinckley is being held against the wall on the far right (out of sight).

What was the diagnosis?

After their assessments, the psychiatrists agreed that the following behaviors displayed by Hinckley were abnormal: he had long periods of great anxiety, was socially withdrawn, lived in a fantasy world, was obsessed with Jodie Foster, and had attempted murder to demonstrate his love and devotion. Given these symptoms, the next question is how to classify or identify Hinckley's exact problem. Compared to the relatively straightforward symptoms of a phobia, John Hinckley's symptoms are much more complex and difficult to classify.

In Hinckley's widely publicized trial, psychiatrists for the prosecution maintained that he had mental problems but was not suffering from a serious mental disorder. Psychiatrists for the defense presented evidence that Hinckley did not know right from wrong at the time of the shootings because he was suffering from a serious mental disorder: schizophrenia. Here are the opinions of three of these expert witnesses (adapted from *Los Angeles Times*, May 14–15, June 22, July 10, 1982):

John J. Hopper, a psychiatrist in private practice, had treated John Hinckley for four months before the shooting. Hopper said he saw no evidence that would have predicted Hinckley's later violent act. Hopper described Hinckley as a typical socially underdeveloped young man who had anxiety spells but no serious psychotic behaviors, such as thought disorders, that occur with schizophrenia.

William T. Carpenter, a University of Maryland psychiatrist, disagreed with Hopper. In the months after the shooting, he interviewed Hinckley for 45 hours and felt Hinckley was driven by an inner world of fantasies. According to Carpenter, Hinckley believed that by shooting Reagan he could achieve a magical union with Jodie Foster. Carpenter diagnosed Hinckley as suffering from schizophrenia.

Sally Johnson, a staff psychiatrist at the federal corrections institution at Butner, North Carolina, interviewed Hinckley 57 times after the shooting. She said that Hinckley had an adolescent admiration for, not an obsession with, Jodie Foster. She diagnosed Hinckley as having a personality disorder but said that he functioned too well to have schizophrenia.

Why do psychiatrists sometimes disagree?

After literally hundreds of hours of assessment, these psychiatrists and others agreed that Hinckley had displayed abnormal behaviors, but they disagreed on the exact nature of his disorder. As we've seen, one of the psychiatrists diagnosed Hinckley as having schizophrenia while another diagnosed him as having a personality disorder.

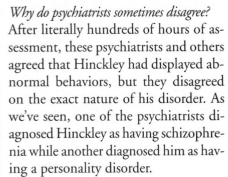

The diagnosis of schizophrenia, like the diagnosis of a phobia or any other mental problem, depends on the presence of certain symptoms. However, an individual may, as in Hinckley's case, show some of the symptoms usually associated with a condition but not others. When this happens, the diagnosis is difficult to make and mental health professionals may disagree.

One reason diagnoses are important is that they have significant implications for therapy. Different kinds of abnormal behaviors are treated with different kinds of psychotherapy and different kinds of drugs. In trying to reach agreement on the kind of problem that a client has, mental health professionals use a set of guidelines that we'll examine next.

Diagnosing and Classifying Mental Disorders

Diagnostic and Statistical Manual of Mental Disorders (DSM)

How do we classify mental disorders?

"I think that person is crazy."

"He must have been insane to do that."

"How could any rational person think that way?"

There have always been people who thought or behaved very differently; one problem has been how to classify their behaviors. Because of a need to develop a uniform system, the American Psychiatric Association (APA) prepared the *Diagnostic and Statistical Manual of Mental Disorders* (DSM-I). Published in 1962, this document described 60 mental disorders. Since 1962 the APA has revised the classification system and published a new edition every few years. The DSM-II was published in 1968 and contained general descriptions of mental problems based on Sigmund Freud's concepts of *psychoses* (severe mental disorders such as schizophrenia) and *neuroses* (less severe forms of psychological conflict and anxiety). Major changes were made in the DSM-III, which was published in 1980. The DSM-III dropped Freudian terminology and instead listed specific criteria for more than 150 disorders, based primarily on expert opinion rather than on systematic evidence. The revised third edition (DSM-III-R) was published in 1987 and included over 250 disorders. The DSM-IV is expected to be published in 1993 and will emphasize a classification system based more on research and evidence than on expert opinion (Frances et al., 1990).

How is the DSM used?

To know which symptoms are characteristic of which mental disorders, most mental health professionals use the **DSM-III-R,** *which defines a mental disorder by assessing an individual's symptoms on five different* **axes,** *or separate dimensions.* In brief form, these axes are as follows:

Axes 1 and 2 include all categories of mental disorders.	**Axis 3** includes all physical disorders and conditions.	**Axis 4** refers to the severity of the condition, the presence of other health problems, and the amount of environmental stress.	**Axis 5** refers to the overall psychological, social, and occupational functioning of the individual based on functioning.

Based on these five axes, the mental health professional arrives at a diagnosis of the person's mental disorder. Because the DSM-III-R lists specific behavioral criteria for a diagnosis, it is expected to be more reliable than previous diagnostic systems.

There are three advantages to a good system of classifying mental disorders: (1) Mental health professionals use the classification system to communicate with one another and discuss their clients' problems. (2) Researchers use the classification system to study and explain mental disorders. (3) Therapists use the classification system to design their treatment program to best fit their clients' problems.

Thus, classification of mental disorders has important implications for discussion, research, and treatment of mental disorders.

Classification According to the DSM-III-R

Here is a list of some of the major categories described in the DSM-III-R. We'll discuss a number of these categories in this chapter (adapted from American Psychiatric Association, 1988).

Axis I: Major Clinical Syndromes

1. Disorders usually first evident in infancy, childhood, or adolescence

This category includes disorders that arise before adolescence, such as attention deficit disorders, bulimia, anorexia, enuresis, and stuttering.

2. Organic mental disorders

These disorders are temporary or permanent dysfunctions of brain tissue caused by diseases or chemicals. Examples are delirium, dementia, and amnesia.

3. Psychoactive substance use disorders

This category refers to the maladaptive use of drugs and alcohol. Mere consumption and recreational use of such substances are not disorders. This category requires an abnormal pattern of use, as with alcohol abuse and cocaine dependence.

4. Schizophrenic disorders

The schizophrenias are characterized by psychotic symptoms (for example, grossly disorganized behavior, delusions, and hallucinations) and by over six months of behavioral deterioration.

5. Delusional disorders

These disorders, of which paranoia is the most common, are characterized by persecutory delusions in the absence of other psychotic symptoms. In general, delusional patients are less impaired than schizophrenics.

6. Mood disorders

The cardinal feature is emotional disturbance. Patients may, or may not, have psychotic symptoms. These disorders include major depression, bipolar disorder, dysthymic disorder, and cyclothymic disorder.

7. Anxiety disorders

These disorders are characterized by physiological signs of anxiety (for example, palpitations) and subjective feelings of tension, apprehension, or fear. Anxiety may be acute and focused (panic disorder) or continual and diffuse (generalized anxiety disorder).

8. Somatoform disorders

These disorders are dominated by somatic symptoms that resemble physical illnesses. These symptoms cannot be accounted for by organic damage. There must also be strong evidence that these symptoms are produced by psychological factors or conflicts. This category includes somatization and conversion disorders and hypochondriasis.

9. Dissociative disorders

These disorders all feature a sudden, temporary alteration or dysfunction of memory, consciousness, identity, and behavior, as in depersonalization disorder, psychogenic amnesia, and multiple personality.

10. Psychosexual disorders

Psychological factors play major etiological roles in all of these disorders. There are three basic types: gender identity disorders (discomfort with identity as male or female), paraphilias (preference for unusual acts to achieve sexual arousal), and sexual dysfunctions (impairments in sexual functioning).

Axis II: Personality and Developmental Disorders

Personality disorders

These disorders are patterns of personality traits that are longstanding, maladaptive, and inflexible and involve impaired functioning or subjective distress. Examples include borderline, schizoid, and passive-aggressive personality disorders.

Specific developmental disorders

These are disorders of specific developmental areas that are not due to another disorder. Examples include mental retardation, autism, and reading, writing, and arithmetic disorders.

(Adapted with permission from the *Diagnostic and Statistical Manual of Mental Disorders*, third edition, revised. Copyright 1987 American Psychiatric Association.)

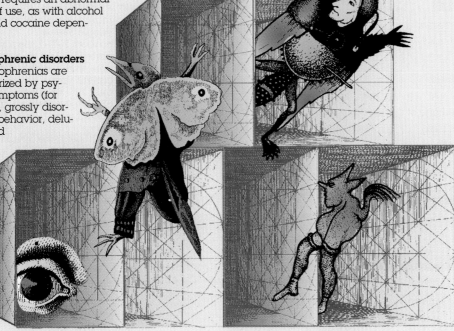

Classifying mental disorders is often difficult because symptoms do not always fit into one category.

You may be surprised to learn that the terms *neurosis* and *psychosis* do not appear in the DSM-III-R. In recent years psychiatrists and psychologists have moved away from the psychoanalytic or Freudian terms to those based on more specific, observable symptoms, as well as on research and scientific evidence.

Before we discuss some of the specific symptoms of the disorders, let's consider how prevalent psychological problems are.

Diagnosing and Classifying Mental Disorders

Frequency of Mental Disorders

As part of a $15 million study, researchers conducted 19,000 interviews to determine what percentage of Americans age 18 and older had mental disorders. Using the DSM-III-R classification system, researchers asked people about their symptoms and then used these symptoms to classify the disorders (Robins & Regier, 1991). All the questions were carefully spelled out to make the interviews reliable across five sites (New Haven, Connecticut; Baltimore, Maryland; St. Louis, Missouri; Durham, North Carolina; and Los Angeles, California). Here's what the researchers found (Robins & Regier, 1991).

How many Americans have mental disorders?

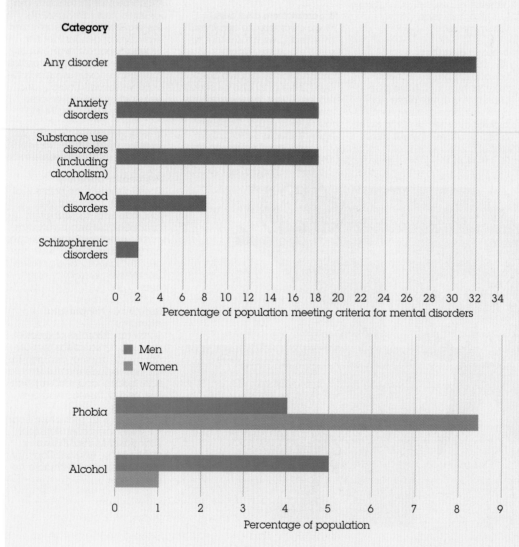

- About 32% of the sample reported having had at least one mental disorder during their lifetime. The most common disorders reported were anxiety disorders and substance use disorders.
- Taking all mental disorders together, men had had more disorders over their lifetime than women did. In addition, younger people had more than older, blacks more than whites, and the undereducated more than the well educated.
- People under 45 had twice as many mental disorders as people over 45.
- About 20% of the sample reported having an active disorder—that is, a disorder in the current year. Of these people, only 19% reported seeking and obtaining treatment during the current year.

- Although the overall rate for all active mental disorders was approximately the same (20%) for men and women, there were differences within classifications. Women reported more problems with phobias and depression, while men reported more problems with substance abuse, especially of alcohol.

This study is important because it gives us the first reasonably accurate report of the frequency of specific mental disorders in the United States. These results will help set policy to reduce the burden of mental illness, such as by encouraging people to seek treatment and by providing earlier and more adequate treatment.

Next we'll examine a number of specific mental disorders, beginning with anxiety.

Anxiety Disorders

Fred was quite visibly distressed during the initial therapy interview, gulping before he spoke, sweating, and continually fidgeting in his chair. His repeated requests for water to quench a never-ending thirst were another indication of his extreme nervousness. At first Fred spoke only of his dizziness and problems with sleeping. However, it soon became clear that he had nearly always felt tense. He admitted to a long history of having difficulties interacting with others, difficulties that led to his being fired from two jobs. He constantly worried about all kinds of possible disasters that might happen to him (Davison & Neale, 1990).

Anxiety disorders make people feel like they are under the gun, like something terrible is about to happen.

Why was Fred upset and sweating?

As we'll see, Fred was suffering from an anxiety disorder. Such disorders are divided into generalized anxiety disorders, panic attacks, phobias, and obsessive-compulsive disorders. We will begin with Fred's particular problem and then explain the other disorders.

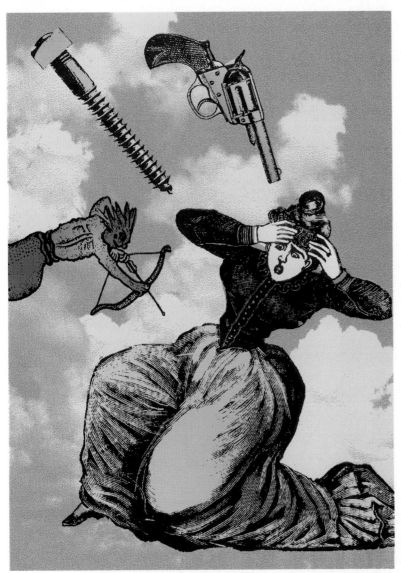

Generalized Anxiety Disorder

Fred was suffering from **generalized anxiety disorder**, *which is characterized by a chronic and pervasive feeling of anxiety in many life situations, a feeling of general apprehension, worry about impending disasters, and extreme sensitivity to criticism.* Physical symptoms may include sweating, flushing, pounding heart, diarrhea, clammy hands, headaches, muscle tension, and muscle aches. Psychological symptoms frequently include attacks of nervousness or persistent nervousness, fatigue, restlessness, irritability, and insomnia. It is estimated that about 4% of the population suffer from generalized anxiety disorder, which makes this a relatively common problem.

What is the treatment?

Generalized anxiety disorder is commonly treated with some form of psychotherapy (discussed in Chapter 15) or with drugs. The drugs most frequently prescribed are tranquilizers, such as Valium and Librium (Salzman, 1991). These drugs belong to a group known as the ***benzodiazepines*** (ben-zoh-die-AS-ah-peens). In moderate doses, the benzodiazepines are not usually physically addicting. In higher doses, however, these drugs are addicting, which means that a person would suffer withdrawal symptoms if the drug were stopped. In a six-year follow-up of people who had been treated for generalized anxiety disorder with drugs and psychotherapy, 68% were either recovered or less impaired than untreated controls (Noyes et al., 1980).

Anxiety Disorders

Panic Disorder

Karen went down the street to Antoine's Beauty Shop to have her hair set. As she was sitting under the dryer, a sudden feeling swept over her. She thought she was losing her mind. Her heart started beating fast. Her legs felt weak. Her body trembled. It was the most incredible feeling of fear. She wanted to scream, to run out of there. Karen got up with all the pins in her hair, slapped a $5 bill on the counter, and ran all the way home (*Los Angeles Times*, December 13, 1981).

The symptoms that accompany panic disorder can be very frightening, and some victims think that they are having a heart attack.

Why did Karen run home?

Karen is one of 4 to 10 million Americans who suffer from panic disorder or panic attack. During **panic disorder,** *a person usually experiences a combination of physiological symptoms, such as a pounding heart, labored breathing, dizziness, and sweating, and psychological symptoms, such as great apprehension, terror, and feelings of impending doom.*

According to the DSM-III-R, panic disorders are distinct and separate from generalized anxiety and various types of phobias. The causes of panic disorder are not completely understood. It may be due to an inherited neurochemical abnormality that results in sudden surges of physiological arousal and fear. Or it may be the result of psychological factors, such as conditioning and irrational beliefs (McNally, 1990).

How serious is panic disorder?

People who suffer from panic disorders (75% of whom are women) have an increased risk of alcohol and other drug abuse, an increased incidence of suicide, decreased social functioning, and decreased marital happiness; about a third also suffer from depression (Markowitz et al., 1989). Thus, panic disorder is assocated with a decreased quality of life. Studies in the United States, Puerto Rico, Austria, Switzerland, and Germany indicate that panic disorder is prevalent in about 1%–2% of the population (Amering & Katschnig, 1990).

How is it treated?

Panic disorders are treated with a combination of benzodiazepines or antidepressants and psychotherapy. Successful treatment may require from 3 to 8 months of drug therapy and psychotherapy (Ballenger, 1991). Panic attacks may also occur with some phobias, our next topic.

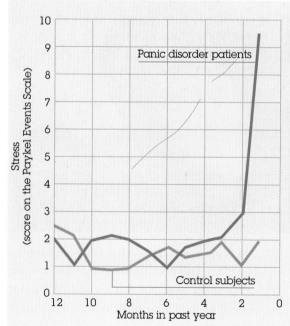

What role does stress play in panic disorder?

A dramatic increase in stress was seen in those who developed panic disorder compared with a control group of hospital patients. These data suggest that stress may trigger panic disorder (Faravelli & Pallianti, 1989).

Phobia

Fear trapped Rose in her house for years. If she thought about going outside to do her shopping, pain raced through her arms and chest. She grew hot and perspired. Her heart beat rapidly and her legs felt like rubber. She said that thinking about leaving her house caused stark terror, sometimes lasting for days. This 39-year-old mother of two is one of millions of Americans suffering from an intense fear of public places called agoraphobia (*Los Angeles Times*, October 19, 1980).

Why couldn't Rose leave her house?

Rose has a type of *phobia*, which is the most common kind of mental disorder. A **phobia** (FOE-bee-ah) *is an anxiety disorder characterized by an intense and irrational fear that is out of all proportion to the danger elicited by the object or situation.* Individuals who have phobias usually go to great lengths to avoid the object or situation that triggers the intense fear.

DSM-III-R divides phobias into three categories: simple, social, and agoraphobia.

• **Simple phobias** *are usually triggered by common objects, situations, or animals, such as a fear of heights, snakes, or bugs.*

• **Social phobias** *are brought on by the presence of other people; someone with a social phobia may not be able to make public speeches or eat in a restaurant.*

• **Agoraphobia** *is a fear of open or public places, such as being out on a public street or in a shopping center; it is much more common in women than in men.*

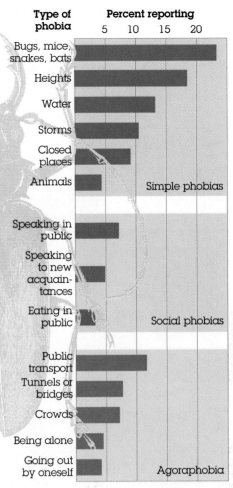

Simple phobias, such as fear of snakes, bugs, and heights, are the most frequently reported (Eaton, Dryman, & Weissman, 1991).

Although many of us have irrational fears, the difference between a normal irrational fear and a phobia is one of degree. Individuals who have phobias usually go to great lengths to avoid the object or situation that triggers the intense fear.

Some phobias appear to be learned through classical conditioning. To determine how phobias begin, researchers questioned 91 subjects. About 75% reported that their phobia began with a conditioning experience in which some object or situation was associated with a fearful, painful, or traumatic experience (Merckelbach et al., 1989). However, the remaining 25% could not recall a conditioning experience, which suggests that there are other ways to acquire a phobia besides conditioning.

Can it be treated?

After a phobia is established, it is extremely persistent and may continue for years. For example, agoraphobics may avoid leaving their homes for years at a time. It appears that their condition is maintained by one of the principles of operant conditioning: negative reinforcement. With *negative reinforcement* a behavior is reinforced by the removal or avoidance of an aversive stimulus. The agoraphobic is able to avoid the aversive stimulus (going out in public) by staying at home. In other words, the fear is never allowed to be extinguished.

Support for this idea comes from research on the treatment of phobias, as one of the most effective treatments involves *exposure* to the feared stimulus (Franklin, 1989). We'll discuss treatment for phobias in the Applying/Exploring section, after we look at more disorders.

Anxiety Disorders

Obsessive-Compulsive Disorders

Why was Shirley late for school?

Shirley was an outgoing, popular high school student with average grades. Her one problem was being late for school almost every day. Before she could leave the house in the morning, she had to be very sure that she was clean, so she needed to take showers that lasted two hours. She also spent a long time dressing because each act of dressing, such as putting on her stockings, underclothes, skirt, and blouse, had to be counted

Constant hand washing is a common ritual in obsessive-compulsive individuals.

and repeated precisely 17 times. When asked about her washing and counting, she said she knew that it was crazy but that it was something that she just had to do and couldn't explain why. She said that she had struggled against this problem for three years but had no success stopping her washing and counting (Rapoport, 1988).

Shirley would be diagnosed as having an obsessive-compulsive disorder. As the name implies, an **obsessive-compulsive disorder** *consists of obsessions and compulsions.* **Obsessions** *are persistent, recurring irrational thoughts that a person is unable to control and that interfere with normal functioning.* **Compulsions** *are irresistible impulses to perform some ritual over and over even though the ritual serves no rational purpose.* Shirley's obsession was her need to be clean and careful about dressing. Her compulsions were the excessive length of her showers and the need to count her acts of dressing precisely 17 times.

Obsessive-compulsive behaviors interfere with normal functioning and make social interactions difficult. Only five years ago this disorder was considered relatively rare, but now it is known to affect about 3% of the population, making it the fourth most common psychiatric disorder after phobia, substance abuse, and major depression (Rasmussen & Eisen, 1990).

What is the treatment?

Shirley's compulsive behaviors are thought to be one way that she reduces or avoids anxiety—in her case, anxiety associated with being dirty. Based on this idea, many successful treatment programs involve exposing the person to the very situations or objects he or she is attempting to avoid. If exposure therapy does not work, a relatively new drug, clomipramine, is used. This antidepressant drug is used in combination with exposure therapy. For example, exposure therapy did not work in Shirley's case because she refused to cooperate with the therapist and insisted that she had to continue her washing and counting rituals. But after she had taken clomipramine for about three weeks, her urges to wash and count faded sufficiently so that she could cooperate with her psychotherapist in further reducing her strange behaviors (Rapoport, 1988).

In a six-year follow-up study of treatment that had combined self-exposure therapy and clomipramine, researchers found that about 80% of the clients had maintained their improved status of reducing their rituals from five hours to about one hour a day (O'Sullivan et al., 1991).

Next we'll examine real physical symptoms that have no physical causes.

Somatoform Disorders

Just as the more than 500 students from various schools began to give a choir and orchestra concert, there was an outbreak and rapid spread among them of headaches, dizziness, weakness, abdominal pain, and nausea. About half the students—but no one in the audience—developed one or more of these symptoms. Those students who became ill were most often those who saw someone near them take ill. Chorus members from one school, particularly girls in the soprano section, experienced the highest rate of symptoms. Younger members reported more symptoms than older members, and girls (51%) reported more symptoms than boys (41%). At first, someone thought that a gas line had broken (Small et al., 1991).

Purely psychological factors can make people ill or can result in physical symptoms.

Why did all these students suddenly become ill?
There was no ruptured gas line; rather, an unusual case of one of the somatoform disorders had occurred. **Somatoform** (so-MA-toe-form) **disorders** *involve the appearance of real physical symptoms that are not under voluntary control, have no known physical causes, and are believed to be caused by psychological factors.* The ancient Greeks believed that unusual or unexplained physical symptoms were caused in women by the displacement of the uterus. In the Middle Ages, somatoform disorders were attributed to evil spirits or the devil.

The students at the concert probably experienced a kind of somatoform disorder called a conversion disorder. In a **conversion disorder** (formerly called hysteria), *the bodily organs and senses are healthy but the person reports physical problems.* Anxiety or emotional conflicts are turned into (converted to) symptoms that influence physical functioning in some way. For example, individuals may report paralysis or blindness when in fact their limbs or eyes have no physical or structural damage. Usually the symptoms of a conversion disorder are associated with psychological factors, are brought on by stressful situations, and effectively remove the person from the threatening situation.

The students reported headaches and nausea although there were no physical causes. The conditions for *mass conversion disorder* (often called *mass hysteria*) include being in a relatively confined area; being under some stress; watching someone, usually a leader, become sick; and hearing rumors of impending disaster (Herbert, 1982). Most of these conditions were met at the concert.

Another kind of somatoform disorder is **somatization disorder,** *in which an individual has multiple physical symptoms (at least 12 to 14) that have no physical causes but that are triggered by psychological problems or distress.* This disorder is most frequently reported in less educated women who use health services frequently and who also tend to have many hospitalizations and surgeries (Robins & Regier, 1991). Somatization disorders, though relatively rare (1.3 in 1000), are exceedingly interesting. Why is it that individuals with no physical damage develop multiple physical problems? Apparently, they do so to help them cope with a stressful situation or to obtain wanted attention.

After the Concept/Glossary, we'll discuss an anxiety disorder that seems to occur only in Japan.

1. A prolonged or recurring problem that seriously interferes with the ability of an individual to live a satisfying personal life and function in society is called a _____.

2. There are three approaches to studying mental disorders. Viewing mental disorders as diseases is using the (a)_____ approach. Looking for the causes of mental disorders in unconscious conflicts or problems with unresolved conflicts is using the (b)_____ approach. Combining information from cognitive processes and learning-conditioning factors to understand mental disorders is using the (c)_____ approach.

4. There are four kinds of anxiety disorders. If a person has a chronic and pervasive feeling of anxiety in many life situations, experiences general apprehension, worries about impending disasters, and is extremely sensitive to criticism, he or she has a (a)_____. A combination of physiological symptoms, such as a pounding heart, labored breathing, dizziness, and sweating, and psychological symptoms, such as great apprehension, terror, and feelings of impending doom, is called a (b)_____. An intense and irrational fear that is out of all proportion to the danger elicited by the object or situation is a (c)_____. If a person has obsessions, which are persistent, recurring irrational thoughts, and compulsions, which are irresistible impulses to perform some ritual over and over, he or she has an (d)_____.

3. There are three definitions of abnormality. If a behavior occurs infrequently in the general population, this is the (a)_____ definition. If a behavior deviates greatly from accepted social norms, this is the (b)_____ definition. If the behavior interferes with the individual's ability to function as a person or in society, this is the (c)_____ definition, which is used by most mental health professionals.

5. The appearance of real physical symptoms that are not under voluntary control, have no known physical causes, and are believed to be caused by psychological factors is a _____ disorder. This disorder is subdivided into conversion and somatization disorders.

Answers: 1. *mental disorder*; 2. (a) *medical model*, (b) *psychoanalytic*, (c) *cognitive-behavioral*; 3. (a) *statistical*, (b) *social norms*, (c) *maladaptive*; 4. (a) *generalized anxiety disorder*, (b) *panic disorder*, (c) *phobia*, (d) *obsessive-compulsive disorder*; 5. *somatoform*.

A Japanese Disorder

Is there a mental disorder found only in one culture?

There is a psychiatric disorder that is relatively common in Japan but is found in no other culture. The disorder, called **taijin kyofusho** or **TKS**, *is a specific social phobia characterized by a morbid fear of offending others through one's awkward social or physical behavior.* For example, a person with TKS would have a fear of eye-to-eye contact, fear of blushing, fear of giving off an offensive odor, fear of having an unpleasant or tense facial expression, or fear of having trembling hands (Kirmayer, 1991).

Although many Westerners are also concerned about offending others, staring, having offensive body odors, or blushing, TKS is different in that it is a *morbid* fear—in other words, a real phobia. People with TKS behave as if they have a phobia by trying voluntarily to stop these symptoms; since that usually fails, they try to avoid social situations and interactions altogether.

We know that some physical factors, such as blushing easily, having offensive odors, or being quickly aroused, may contribute to TKS. However, physical factors cannot answer the following questions: Why is TKS a common disorder in Japan and no other culture, why it is reported more frequently in men than in women, and why does it begin primarily around adolescence and rarely after age 40? All these questions point to the influence of powerful cultural factors in the development and mainte- nance of TKS.

In Japan, some people develop a phobia about of- fending others through social inter- actions.

Cultural Influences

The Japanese culture places great emphasis on the appropriate way to conduct oneself in public. For example, from a very early age Japanese children are encouraged to have a strong sense of responsibility for the feelings of others. To emphasize the impor- tance of proper behavior in public, mothers often use threats of abandonment, ridicule, and embarrassment as punishment. Through this process of socialization, the child is encouraged to be aware of the impact of his or her social interactions on family members. That is, any loss of face that a person shows in social interactions reflects badly on the person's family and social group.

Social Customs

In Japan, individuals are taught to recognize and are expected to know the needs and thoughts of others by reading nonverbal behaviors and not by asking directly, which is considered very rude. One method of such communication is through eye contact and reading another's facial expressions. Westerners often use direct eye contact to show interest, to convey confidence, or to intensify a point in social interactions. However, Japanese people who make too much eye contact are likely to be viewed as insensitive to others, unpleasantly bold, or aggressive. In fact, Japanese children are taught to fix their gaze at the level of the neck of people with whom they are in conversations. Thus, the development of a morbid fear of offending others through one's inappropriate social behaviors is deeply rooted in Japanese customs (Kirmayer, 1991).

TKS is so common in Japan that there are special clinics for treating it. These clinics enjoy the same popularity as weight clinics do in the United States. Although TKS does resemble some Western-type social phobias, its symptoms are specific to the cultural concerns and social customs of the Japanese (Kirmayer, 1991).

The prevalence of TKS in Japan—and nowhere else—points to the powerful influence that culture may have on the development of mental disorders. Next we'll see how some of the phobias that are common in this country are treated.

APPLYING/ EXPLORING: TREATING PHOBIAS

How do you get rid of agoraphobia?

"I began visiting Marge at her home," Ross (the therapist) said. "At the first session, she was terrified that I'd try to drag her out. She sat there in tears, saying over and over again, 'Are you going to make me go out? Are you going to make me go out?' I kept saying no. Finally, at the end of the session, I asked her if she would like to walk me to my car, which was parked right out front. For 20 minutes she put her foot out the apartment door, then back in again. Finally, she broke down, cried and ran out to my car."

During the next session, Ross was able to coax Marge into walking to the mailbox on the corner. Gradually, the territory was expanded to two blocks. Then a store. Ross would walk down the street—first side by side with Marge, then in front of her, then behind. . . . Today, Marjorie Goff is training to be a paralegal at the George Washington University Institute of Law and Aging. . . . But there are still shaky moments, fading tinges of the old fear. One day she was walking down the street to work and started having a panic attack, but she knows now that the surge of fear lasts only 20 seconds. "Any other time, I would have run back home," she said. "But I didn't turn around. I just kept going. I kept going. I kept going." (*Los Angeles Times,* December 13, 1981, p. C3)

Behavioral Treatment: Exposure

It is most unlikely that Marge's agoraphobia (fear of open spaces) would have extinguished without treatment. The treatment she received has proven effective because it involves *live* or *in vivo* exposure to the feared situation. In Marge's case, the therapist actually accompanied her as she gradually confronted the feared situations. In other cases, clients learn how to confront their feared situations on their own.

Researchers compared the reduction in fear among agoraphobics who received their in vivo exposure instructions from a psychiatrist, a self-help book, or a computer program (Ghosh & Marks, 1987). In all three situations, the agoraphobics were not simply told to confront their feared situation. Rather, they were instructed to do *all* of the following:

• Identify each of several feared situations.

• Confront each target situation one by one.

• Practice each confrontation regularly for hours at a time.

• Record panic level in special diaries.

• Anticipate and deal with setbacks.

• Get partners or close friends to help and provide support.

The participants in this study had been agoraphobics for an average of nine years. They had complained of the phobia being a handicap in their everyday lives and reported nearly always avoiding certain situations and experiencing strong fear if they could not. After ten weeks of treatment, all three groups showed a significant improvement. All reported no longer avoiding the situations that once caused them to panic, and they felt only slight anxiety when involved in these situations. When evaluated

Individuals with social phobias have an intense fear that everyone is noticing them and criticizing what they are doing.

six months later, subjects reported continued reductions in avoidance and fear. The researchers concluded that agoraphobia can be treated successfully with in vivo exposure, even when the instructions are given by a self-help book or computer program.

Treatment with Drugs

The previous behavioral study, as well as many others, found that the behavioral treatment of agoraphobia results in a success rate similar to that reported for treatment with drugs. A program using drugs, such as antidepressants, is often used in combination with a behavioral treatment. However, one problem with such programs is the high dropout rate due to the unpleasant side effects of the medications (Noyes, Chaudry, & Domingo, 1986).

Today individuals have the choice of three treatments that have proven successful in reducing the fear and anxiety of agoraphobia: behavioral treatment, treatment with drugs, or a treatment that combines behavioral and drug therapy. As we'll see next, the *social phobias*, which include speaking in public, speaking to new acquaintances, and eating in public, can be treated by a method that is similar to the behavioral technique used for agoraphobia.

Cognitive-Behavioral Treatment

Individuals with social phobias have an intense fear of being exposed to public scrutiny and of doing something that will be humiliating or embarrassing. About 2%–3% of American men and women have social phobias. Researchers used a cognitive-behavioral treatment program consisting of four components (Heimberg et al., 1990):

1 The researchers *explained* that social phobias involve learned social anxiety. They discussed how one's thoughts and physiological arousal can magnify the phobic feelings and thus cause the person to deal with the fear primarily by avoiding the situation.

2 The researchers *exposed* the subjects to their fears by simulating the situation. For example, some of the subjects feared presenting material to their co-workers, making a classroom presentation, or initiating a conversation with the opposite sex. Therapists simulated these situations in group meetings and played the role of the audience.

3 The researchers had subjects *record* their thoughts immediately before and after being exposed to the simulated fear situation. Thoughts were analyzed and divided into positive ones, which helped the person deal with the situation, and negative ones, which hindered the subject's response by worsening the fears.

4 Finally, the researchers asked subjects to *complete* homework assignments. Subjects were asked to imagine themselves in feared situations and then to analyze their thoughts before and after to separate positive from negative thoughts. In addition, subjects were asked to eliminate negative thoughts by substituting positive ones.

This cognitive-behavioral treatment program proved significantly more successful than general instructions given to a control group of subjects. Subjects in the cognitive-behavioral program showed less fear of their social phobias, had reduced anxiety, made fewer negative statements, and made more positive statements. The researchers concluded that the cognitive-behavioral program was very successful in helping people overcome social phobias. The elements of this treatment program could be used to treat other phobias as well.

Summary/Self-Test

THREE APPROACHES

1. A prolonged or recurring problem that seriously interferes with an individual's ability to live a satisfying personal life and function in society is a _____. This definition takes into account genetic, behavioral, cognitive, and environmental factors, all of which may contribute to a mental disorder.

2. One approach to understanding and treating mental disorders looks at psychological problems like diseases, and a major part of the treatment involves the use of psychoactive drugs. This approach is called the (a)_____ model. An approach that looks for the causes of mental disorders in unconscious or unresolved conflicts is the (b)_____ approach. An approach that uses a combination of information from cognitive processes and learning-conditioning factors to understand and treat mental disorders is the (c)_____ approach. According to this approach, people do not have mental illness but rather have learned maladaptive ways of responding to or thinking about themselves and their environments.

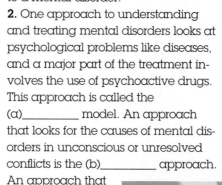

3. If a behavior is considered abnormal because it occurs infrequently in the general population, we are using a definition based on (a)_____ frequency. If a behavior is considered abnormal because it deviates greatly from what's acceptable, we are using a definition based on (b)_____. If a behavior is considered abnormal because it interferes with an individual's ability to function as a person or in society, we are using a definition based on (c)_____ behavior.

■ *You would like to understand why some parents abuse their children. What kind of information would each of the three approaches provide?*

DIAGNOSING AND CLASSIFYING MENTAL DISORDERS

4. One of the primary methods of obtaining information about a person's background and current problems is through the (a)_____. This method has two potential disadvantages: the client may give different information to different therapists, and each therapist may interpret answers in different ways, reflecting their own biases. Another method of obtaining information is to ask the client to take (b)_____ tests, such as the Rorschach inkblot test and the Minnesota Multiphasic Personality Inventory (MMPI). In some cases, brain damage is ruled out as a cause of the client's problems through (c)_____ tests.

5. In trying to diagnose and reach agreement on the kind of problem a client has, mental health professionals currently use a set of guidelines developed by the American Psychiatric Association, called the (a)_____, abbreviated as DSM-III-R. These guidelines define a mental disorder by assessing an individual's symptoms on five different dimensions, or (b)_____. A good system of classifying mental disorders helps with communication or discussion, research, and treatment or therapy.

■ *Why do mental health professionals spend so much time and effort classifying mental disorders?*

ANXIETY DISORDERS

6. A type of anxiety disorder characterized by a chronic and pervasive feeling of anxiety, a feeling of general apprehension, worry about impending disasters, and extreme sensitivity to criticism is called (a)_____ disorder. This relatively common disorder is often treated with some form of psychotherapy and/or drugs. If a person has a combination of physiological symptoms, such as a pounding heart, labored breathing, dizziness, and sweating, and psychological symptoms, such as great apprehension, terror, and feelings of impending doom, the person probably has a (b)_____. These disorders are distinct and separate from generalized anxiety and various types of phobias. Panic attacks may be due to an inherited neurochemical abnormality or to psychological factors, such as conditioning, stress, and irrational beliefs. These disorders are usually treated with some combination of psychotherapy and benzodiazepines or antidepressants. A third anxiety disorder characterized by an intense and irrational fear that is out of all proportion to the danger elicited by the object or situation is called a (c)_____.

7. DSM-III-R divides phobias into three categories. Those that are triggered by common objects, situations, or animals (such as snakes or heights) are called (a)_____ phobias. Those that are brought on by the presence of other people are called (b)_____. A fear of open or public places, such as being out on a public street or in a shopping center, is called (c)_____. It appears that some phobias are learned through classical conditioning. Once established, phobias are extremely persistent and may continue for years.

8. Persistent, recurring irrational thoughts that a person is unable to control and that interfere with normal functioning are called (a)_____. Irresistible impulses to perform some ritual over and over even though the ritual serves no rational purpose are called (b)_____. A disorder that consists of both of these behaviors and that interferes with normal functioning is called (c)_____ and is now the fourth most common psychiatric disorder after phobia, substance abuse, and major depression. Treatment includes exposure and drugs.

■ *If you were going to select astronauts to go on a three-month mission into space, how would you be sure of identifying those with anxiety disorders?*

SOMATOFORM DISORDERS

9. The appearance of real physical symptoms that are not under voluntary control, have no known physical causes, and are believed to be caused by psychological factors are the hallmarks of _____ disorders.

10. In one type of somatoform disorder, the bodily organs and senses are healthy but the person reports physical problems that effectively remove him or her from a stressful situation. This disorder was formerly called hysteria but is now called (a)_____. In another somatoform disorder, an individual has at least 12 to 14 physical symptoms that have no physical causes but that are triggered by psychological problems or distress; this is called (b)_____.

■ *Imagine you are a doctor who has just examined a woman who claims to have numerous physical and painful problems. How do you convince her that there are no physical causes for her problems?*

CULTURAL DIVERSITY: A JAPANESE DISORDER

11. A social phobia found in Japan that is characterized by a morbid fear of offending others through one's awkward social or physical behavior is called taijin kyofusho, or _____. This phobia appears to result from cultural and social influences unique to Japan.

■ *What kinds of cultural factors in the United States might contribute to causing major depression?*

APPLYING/EXPLORING: TREATING PHOBIAS

12. There are a number of methods of treatment for people with phobias. A treatment that has been successful in treating fear of open spaces or agoraphobia involves the actual (a)_____ to the feared situation. This is an example of the (b)_____ treatment of agoraphobia and results in a success rate similar to that reported for treatment with drugs. Often, behavioral and drug treatments are used together.

13. Social phobias, such as of speaking or eating in public, can be treated by a method that is similar to the behavioral technique used for agoraphobia. The treatment for social phobias that includes having the clients doing homework and imagining the feared situation is called _____ treatment.

■ *You are terrified about taking a class in public speaking. What kind of program could you develop to help you decrease your phobia?*

Answers: 1. mental disorder; 2. (a) medical, (b) psychoanalytic, (c) cognitive-behavioral; 3. (a) statistical, (b) social norms, (c) maladaptive; 4. (a) interview, (b) psychological, (c) neurological; 5. (a) Diagnostic and Statistical Manual of Mental Disorders—Revised, (b) axes; 6. (a) generalized anxiety, (b) panic attack or disorder, (c) phobia; 7. (a) simple, (b) social phobias, (c) agoraphobia; 8. (a) obsessions, (b) compulsions, (c) obsessive-compulsive disorder; 9. somatoform; 10. (a) conversion disorder, (b) somatization disorder; 11. TKS; 12. (a) exposure, (b) behavioral; 13. cognitive-behavioral.

MODULE 28
DISORDERS II

What was his depression like?

William Styron, famous writer, describes his five-year battle with depression and his eventual recovery in his book *Darkness Visible*.

To those who have been there, lived through it and dared to talk about it, the very word seems quite inadequate. *Depression* suggests an indentation, a rut in the road or a hole in the earth. It recalls foul moods, bad days, fights with the family, economic decline.

"It's such a catch-all phrase," said William Styron, the novelist and survivor of what he would prefer to call madness—depression that nearly cost his life. For such a major illness, Styron said, *depression* is a "true wimp of a word." . . .

This is how it felt to William Styron, the Pulitzer prize–winning author of *Lie Down with Darkness, The Confessions of Nat Turner, Sophie's Choice,* and other books and plays. At his year-round home in Roxbury, Connecticut, five years ago Styron's family watched helplessly when he moaned and shouted from his bed.

"My head is exploding!" Styron cried. "My head is exploding!"

The next day he entered the psychiatric unit of Yale–New Haven Hospital for the treatment he believes saved his life. . . .

This is what happened. Five years ago, at 60, Styron's body and mind staged a revolt. A legendary drinker, a man who had been able to consume alcohol "abundantly, almost mercilessly," Styron became unable to imbibe even the slightest quantity of alcoholic spirits. . . .

Styron's mood darkened. His body became stooped, like a very old man. On Martha's Vineyard, he responded indifferently to the friends and fellowship he had previously treasured. "I felt a kind of numbness," Styron writes. "But more particularly, an odd fragility, as if my body had actually become frail."

With this sense of physical debilitation came "an immense and aching solitude." Styron could no longer concentrate. "The act of writing became more and more difficult and exhausting, stalled and then finally ceased," he writes. (*Los Angeles Times,* August 28, 1990, pp. E-1, E-2)

Styron's bout with major depression is an example of a **mood disorder**, *which is a prolonged emotional state that affects almost all of a person's thoughts and behaviors.* Most of us have experienced a continuum of moods, with depression on one end and elation on the other. DSM-III-R lists two categories of mood disorders: **depressive disorders,** *which are marked by prolonged periods of depression,* and **bipolar disorder,** *which is characterized by swings between depression and an extreme elation called mania.*

What's Coming

In the first part of this module, we'll discuss depressive, personality, and sexual disorders. In the second part, we examine one of the more perplexing mental disorders, schizophrenia. We'll begin with depressive disorders such as Styron experienced.

Mood Disorders

How would someone who recovered describe depression?
"Depression is a disorder of mood, so mysteriously painful and elusive in the way it becomes known to the self—to the mediating intellect—as to verge close to being beyond description. It thus remains nearly incomprehensible to others who have not experienced it in its extreme mode, although the gloom, 'the blues' which people go through occasionally and associate with the general hassle of everyday existence are of such prevalence that they do give many individuals a hint of the illness in its catastrophic form." (Styron, 1990, p. 7)

Major Depression

Styron listed some of the symptoms of his depression: his voice changed to that of a faint whisper; he lost his sexual desires; he ate only to survive; he was exhausted but could sleep for only a few hours, never dreaming; he was suicidal and thought about writing suicide notes; he lost all interest in writing; and he found no joy in visiting and talking to best friends. Styron's list is much like the list of symptoms for major depression given in DSM-III-R. **Major depression**, which is also called **unipolar depression**, *is the most common form of mood disorder; the symptoms include sad, dejected mood, problems with appetite and weight, difficulties in sleeping, loss of energy, lack of interest and pleasure in usual activities, negative self-concept, and recurring thoughts of death or suicide.* Almost 6.5% of the population has reported major depression, with women (7.0%) reporting significantly more episodes than men (2.6%).

In unipolar depression, individuals have only bouts of depression.

Dysthymic Disorder

The other depressive disorder is **dysthymic** (dis-THY-mick) **disorder**, *which is characterized by being chronically depressed but with periods of normal mood lasting for a few days or weeks but never more than a month or two.* Individuals with dysthymic disorder may also have symptoms of dejected mood, lack of pleasure in normal activities, and problems with sleeping and appetite. However, the symptoms in dysthymic disorder are not as serious as those seen in major depression.

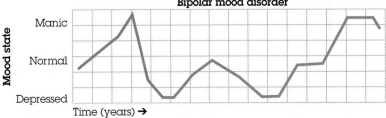

In bipolar depression, individuals alternate between bouts of depression and mania.

Bipolar Disorder

Less than 1% of the population suffers from *bipolar disorder,* formerly called *manic-depressive illness;* the symptoms include periods of depression that may suddenly lift and are followed immediately by periods of **mania** (MAY-nee-ah), *in which the person exhibits exaggerated energy, enthusiasm, and elation.* During the manic period, individuals may undertake countless activities and make hundreds of plans, only some of which can be carried out.

It is quite rare to experience mania without depression, but it does occur. Mania experienced without depression has the following symptoms: extraordinary increase in activity level at work, socially, or sexually; unusual talkativeness; decreased need for sleep; inflated self-esteem; and reckless activities, such as unrestrained spending.

Now that you know the symptoms, let's look at two possible causes of depression.

Mood Disorders

Causes of Depression

You read Styron's description of his depression. Now let's see what he thought triggered it.

"After I began to recover in the hospital it occurred to me to wonder—for the first time with any really serious concern—why I had been visited by such a calamity . . . The very number of hypotheses is testimony to the malady's all but impenetrable

Feeling depressed is like being caught in a spiderweb.

mystery. As for that initial triggering mechanism—which I have called the manifest crisis—can I really be satisfied with the idea that abrupt withdrawal from alcohol started the plunge downward? What about other possibilities—the dour fact, for instance, that at about the same time I was smitten I turned 60, that hulking milestone of mortality. Or could it be that a vague dissatisfaction with the way in which my work was going . . . Unresolvable questions, perhaps." (Styron, 1990, p. 78)

Two popular theories—a biological theory and a cognitive theory—attempt to answer the "unresolvable question" of why about 15 million Americans in any given year experience severe depression.

Biological Theory

Is it something in one's brain, body, or genes?
Although researchers agree that there are many causes of depression, an underlying genetic or biological factor may be common to all. The **biological theory of depression** *emphasizes underlying genetic or biological factors that predispose a person to experiencing depression.*

If one identical twin has a mood disorder, the chance that the other twin does is over 60%. In comparison, the relationship in fraternal twins is only about a 15% chance. These data suggest a genetic predisposition for depression (Moldin, Reich, & Rice, 1991).

Researchers have also discovered that an excess secretion of stress hormones occurs in about 50% of cases of major depression, which suggests that depression may be triggered by maladaptive responses to stress (Post, 1991). Finally, the majority of drugs used to treat depression act on systems of neurotransmitters called *monoamines* (mon-no-A-means), suggesting that malfunction of this monoamine system contributes to depression.

Researchers believe that a certain percentage of the population may be predisposed to depression and that one of the predisposing factors is biological (Holden, 1991).

Cognitive Theory

Is it something in one's thoughts?
If stress is a trigger for depression, why is it that many people who are exposed to stressful events do not become depressed (Monroe & Simons, 1991)? This fact suggests that it is not the event itself but rather how we interpret the event that is important.

The cognitive aspects of how we interpret stressful events were emphasized by Aaron Beck (1967). Beck, a psychiatrist, noticed that his depressed patients had pessimistic views of their lives and futures and that these attitudes distorted and changed their everyday experiences into negative events. According to **Beck's cognitive theory of depression**, *individuals become depressed and stay depressed because of errors in thinking; namely, they interpret and distort whatever happens to them as catastrophes, hopeless situations, or reasons for self-blame.* Beck believes that depressed individuals' faulty reasoning makes them see a distorted world and future. Beck's theory has received general support, although not all depressed individuals distort everything into negative experiences (Davison & Neale, 1990). One advantage of Beck's theory is that it can be tested and points to the importance of cognition in depression.

Now let's look at the treatments for mood disorders.

Treatment of Mood Disorders

Cathy's first complaints were physical. She couldn't sleep, and she lost her appetite as well as 15 pounds. She moved slowly and talked in a monotone. She lost all sexual interest in her husband. After this went on for three months, she made herself see a therapist. She told the therapist, "No matter what I do, there's no joy, no pleasure. Just a treadmill of duty and guilt. I'm exhausted. What's the point of continuing?" (Rosenfeld, 1985).

Psychotherapy and antidepressant drugs help people break out of their depression.

The question of how depression such as Cathy's should be treated was the subject of a six-year, $10 million research program conducted by the National Institute of Mental Health (Elkin et al., 1989). The clients, 70% of whom were women, suffered from varying degrees of major depression. The primary question was whether psychotherapy was as effective as drug therapy in treating major depression. To answer this question, clients were randomly assigned to one of four groups: two different psychotherapy groups, one drug group, and one placebo group. Let's examine the results.

Psychotherapy

The first psychotherapy group received **cognitive-behavior therapy,** *which attempts to correct a person's distorted views and pessimistic beliefs about the self and the world.* For instance, one goal of this therapy is to change Cathy's belief that she is a failure. This therapy is based on Aaron Beck's cognitive theory of depression.

The second psychotherapy group received **interpersonal therapy,** *which examines how conflicts with others and disturbed relationships affect depression.* For example, one goal of this therapy would be to help Cathy resolve conflicts in trying to be a perfect lawyer, wife, mother, and lover.

The researchers found that, generally, clients in either form of psychotherapy did moderately well—not as well as the drug group but much better than the placebo group. However, on closer analysis the researchers noted that for the less severely depressed clients, psychotherapy was as effective as drugs. Thus, for some types of depression, the researchers concluded that psychotherapy may be as effective as antidepressant drugs (Hollon, Shelton, & Loosen, 1991).

Drugs for Depression

The third group received a commonly used **antidepressant drug,** *one of a group of drugs known as* **tricyclics,** *which raise the level of certain neurotransmitters, called monoamines.* According to the **monoamine theory of depression,** *depression results when the activity of monoamines is extremely low and mania results when the levels are extremely high.*

The fourth group received a placebo (a sugar pill with no medicinal value). The drug and placebo groups received minimal supportive therapy.

The clients who received antidepressant drugs showed the quickest and best improvement; those who received placebos showed the poorest improvement. As we mentioned, however, drugs were more effective for the severely depressed. For less severely depressed clients, drugs and psychotherapy were equally effective.

Antidepressants may take four to six weeks before they begin working. Even then, only about 70% of those taking them show any improvement; the remaining 30% receive no benefit from the drugs. Another disadvantage of antidepressant drug therapy is that some of the drugs have unwanted side effects (such as weight gain and lethargy), which sometimes cause clients to drop out of treatment. The fact that a relatively new antidepressant, Prozac, has fewer side effects than some of the older antidepressants has contributed to its popularity.

For clients with extreme depression that is not helped by drugs, the treatment is usually electroconvulsive therapy, which we'll discuss next.

Mood Disorders

Electroconvulsive Therapy

One of the most controversial treatments for major depression may be used when a patient does not improve on antidepressant drugs. This treatment, **electroconvulsive therapy,** or **ECT,** *involves placing electrodes on the skull and administering a mild electrical current to the brain that results in a seizure.* Usually the patient receives a series of six to ten such treatments at the rate of three per week.

Can seizures help?

Although it is not known exactly why ECT is effective in the treatment of depression, it is known that the seizures are effective in reducing depressive symptoms. If antidepressants fail, ECT is the most effective treatment remaining for severe depression (Pearlman, 1991).

As shown in the graph on the right, eight of nine seriously depressed patients who did not respond to antidepressants showed a rather dramatic reduction in depressive symptoms after ECT and remained symptom-free after one year (Paul et al., 1981).

There is no evidence that using modern ECT procedures causes physical damage to the brain. However, it should be kept in mind that it may be difficult to measure slight or moderate brain damage.

Electroconvulsive therapy causes seizures in the brain.

One serious side effect of ECT is possible memory impairment; there may be a persistent loss of memory for events experienced during the weeks of treatment, as well as events before and after treatment. However, following ECT treatment, there is a gradual improvement in memory functions. One group of researchers report that long-term impairment of memory following ECT was minimal and returned to pretreatment levels within six months (Calev et al., 1991). In spite of this finding, about 50% of patients given ECT reported poor memory three years after treatment. In these cases, it is not known whether the impairment was caused by the ECT or by the longstanding depression (Squire & Slater, 1983).

A National Institute of Mental Health panel of experts gave a cautious endorsement to the use of ECT as a treatment of last resort for some types of severe depression. The panel added that the patient should be informed as fully as possible of the potential risks (Holden, 1985).

Now that you know the treatment options for one kind of depression (unipolar), let's examine the treatment for bipolar depression.

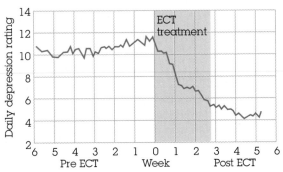

Patients suffering from severe depression had their symptoms significantly reduced with ECT.

Lithium Treatment

An individual with bipolar disorder suffers from mood swings that shift from periods of deep depression to periods of high elation or mania. **Lithium** (LITH-ee-um), *a natural mineral salt, is the most used treatment for bipolar disorder, especially mania.* Studies in four countries, including the United States, have shown that lithium is effective in preventing mood swings in about 64% of patients with bipolar disorder; in contrast, only 21% of those treated with placebos showed significant improvement (Murray, 1986). Lithium has also been found to be effective in treating individuals with mania—that is, manic episodes without the depression. Exactly how lithium affects the brain's neurotransmitter systems to reduce manic episodes in mania and mood swings in bipolar disorder is unclear.

Next we'll look at personality disorders and a person who seems to feel no guilt.

Personality Disorders

Can a person steal and feel no guilt?

As an adolescent, Jim had stolen money from his mother's purse. Later he was charged with raping a young woman he had picked up at the local skating rink. He was sentenced to five years at a reform school but received an immediate parole. After several parole violations he was sentenced to one year at the reform school. When he returned to his hometown a year later, he continued to get into trouble with the law (Davison & Neale, 1990).

Theodore "Ted" Bundy looked like the boy next door. However, before he was executed in 1989, this psychopath admitted to having brutally killed 28 women, from Washington to Florida.

Jim has all the signs of having a personality disorder. A **personality disorder** *involves inflexible and maladaptive traits that cause significantly impaired functioning in one's personal and social life.* Jim's specific personality disorder is **antisocial personality,** *which is characterized by a failure to conform to social norms in many areas of the person's life (work, family, interpersonal relationships).* Antisocial personality, or being a psychopath, usually begins in childhood with a variety of behavioral problems at home and school and continues into adult life.

Psychopaths usually show a complete disregard for obligations, unabashed lying, total lack of guilt or remorse, impulsiveness, reckless behavior, and failure to learn from experience (Lewis, 1991). Antisocial personality is more common among men (4.5%) than among women (0.8%) (Robins, Tipp, & Przybeck, 1991).

Besides antisocial personality, the DMS-III-R lists many other personality disorders, including **paranoid,** *being excessively suspicious;* **schizoid,** *being very self-absorbed and socially withdrawn;* **narcissistic,** *having an exaggerated sense of self-importance;* and **passive-aggressive,** *always indirectly resisting what others ask or expect.*

Where do we look for the causes?

Currently, research on antisocial personality looks to neurochemical and behavior factors for the root of this disorder.

Neurochemical Factors

When parents brought their children to a clinic because of serious behavior problems, they were asked to describe the child's earlier behaviors. Some parents reported that their child had always had behavioral problems. For example, from infancy on the youngster displayed temper tantrums, became furious when frustrated, bullied other children, did not respond to punishment, and was generally unmanageable. The fact that these behavioral problems appeared at such an early age and are so difficult to change suggest that there may be an underlying neurochemical imbalance that contributes to developing an antisocial personality (Lewis, 1991).

Behavioral Factors

One researcher followed up on more than 500 cases of children who had been referred to a clinic for behavioral problems (Robins, 1966). The former problem children who had become psychopaths as adults had originally been brought to the clinic because of aggressive and antisocial behaviors, such as truancy, theft, disobeying their parents, and frequent lying with no signs of remorse. Some had had parents who became rejecting and hostile toward them, and this hostile attitude elicited more behavioral problems. Thus, a vicious circle was set in motion that reinforced the child's antisocial behaviors and kept him on the road to psychopathy (Millon, 1981).

The treatment outcome for psychopaths is not very promising. They are mistrusting, irresponsible, and guiltless and learn little from past mistakes. They may challenge and provoke their therapists. Most therapists are pessimistic about modifying the behavior of psychopathology, whether it occurs in teenagers or adults (Millon, 1981).

The next disorder we'll examine—schizophrenia—is one of the most tragic and difficult to understand.

Schizophrenia

How does a person lose touch with reality?

About 1% of the population suffer from **schizophrenia** (skit-suh-FREE-knee-ah), *a serious mental disorder that includes a number of symptoms, such as loss of contact with reality and problems of thought, attention, perception, motor behavior, and emotion.* Of the inpatients in mental hospitals, about 30% are there because of schizophrenia; this percentage is the highest of any mental disorder (Robins & Regier, 1991). The incidence of schizophrenia is approximately the same for women and men. We'll discuss two major forms of schizophreina—acute and chronic—which are serious mental disorders with enormous personal, medical, and financial costs.

Acute Schizophrenia

In **acute schizophrenia,** *problems develop suddenly, without any previous history of mental disorder.* People with acute schizophrenia, like the patient described next, have a relatively good chance for recovery.

Can a fire alarm become a message from God?

When a fire alarm went off in school, 29-year-old Jeanette knew that it was a message from God. This message was the key to solving her own personal problems as well as having worldwide implications. She came home and told her husband that God had sent her a message. When her husband asked her questions about the message, her answers made little sense. The next morning Jeanette was admitted to a hospital for treatment. She remained in the hospital for 13 days, receiving antipsychotic medication. After her symptoms decreased, she was released. For the next six years, she continued to take antipsychotic medication and received psychotherapy as an outpatient. She is currently symptom-free, is writing a book about her experience, and is serving on two mental health boards (*Los Angeles Times,* June 21, 1984).

Chronic Schizophrenia

In **chronic schizophrenia,** *individuals have a long history of schizophrenia and less chance of recovery than those with acute schizophrenia.* Consider the case of Barry, a patient with chronic schizophrenia, who is being interviewed by a therapist:

Therapist: How old are you?

Barry: Why I am centuries old, sir.

Therapist: How long have you been here?

Barry: I've been now on this property on and off for a long time. I cannot say the exact time because we are absorbed by the air at night, and they bring back people. They kill up everything; they can make you lie; they can talk through your throat.

Therapist: Who is this?

Barry: Why, the air.

Therapist: What is the name of this place?

Barry: This place is called a star.

Therapist: Who is the doctor in charge of your ward?

Barry: A body just like yours, sir. They can make you black and white. I say good morning, but he just comes through there. At first it was a colony. They said it was heaven. . . . I was sent by the government to the United States to Washington to some star, and they had a pretty nice country there. Now you have a body like a young man who says he is of the prestigitis? (White, 1932, p. 228)

Barry was diagnosed as having chronic schizophrenia. His problems developed over several years and his treatment was not successful. Individuals with chronic schizophrenia have a much poorer chance of recovery than those with the acute form.

Now let's examine why Jeanette's and Barry's symptoms match those of schizophrenia.

Symptoms of Schizophrenia

How do doctors identify persons with schizophrenia?

Jeanette's and Barry's cases illustrate the range of symptoms that occur in schizophrenia. In fact, no two patients have exactly the same set of symptoms, but they all share some symptoms in common. According to DSM-III-R, the diagnosis of schizophrenia should involve the symptoms listed to the left.

The creators of the DSM-III-R diagnostic system hope to make diagnosis more accurate by requiring that the symptoms exist for at least six months and that patients have a combination of the symptoms. Different combinations of symptoms are used to identify different subcategories of schizophrenia.

Subcategories of Schizophrenia

DSM-III-R lists several types of schizophrenia, including paranoid, disorganized, and catatonic.

Paranoid schizophrenia *is characterized by delusions, such as thoughts of being persecuted by others or thoughts of grandeur.* For example, a paranoid schizophrenic may think that the crowd of people waiting in line at a movie theater is plotting to kidnap him. Many paranoid schizophrenics have delusions of grandeur, such as believing they are famous people.

Disorganized schizophrenia *is characterized by bizarre ideas, often about one's body (bones melting), confused speech, childish behavior (giggling for no apparent reason, making faces at people), great emotional swings (fits of laughing or crying), and often extreme neglect of personal appearance and hygiene.*

Catatonic schizophrenia *is characterized by periods of wild excitement or periods of rigid, prolonged immobility; sometimes the person assumes the same frozen posture for hours on end.* One reaction will usually predominate. Between 1900 and 1979, the number of cases of catatonic schizophrenia has decreased, probably because of the use of antischizophrenic drugs.

Differentiating between types of schizophrenia can be difficult, since some symptoms, such as disordered thought processes and delusions, are shared by all types.

Next, we'll look at the causes of schizophrenia.

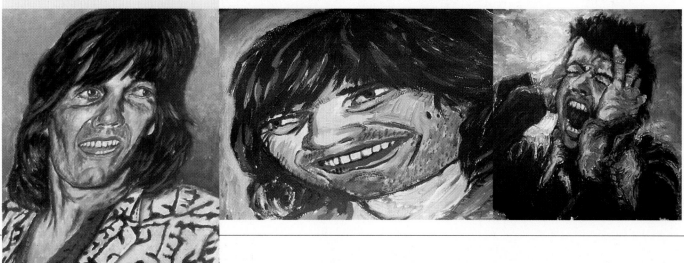

Artist Andy Wilf painted these self-portraits across a number of years when he was having serious drug problems. They illustrate possible schizophrenic symptoms.

Schizophrenia

Causes of Schizophrenia

What was unusual about these four girls?

By the time the Genain quadruplets were young adults, they had all developed schizophrenic symptoms. At their 51st birthday party, their symptoms had decreased, but there was still room for improvement (Mirsky & Quinn, 1988).

In 1930 the birth of four identical baby girls (quadruplets) was a rare occurrence (1 in 16 million) and received great publicity. By the time the girls had reached high school, all four were labeled "different." They sometimes broke light bulbs, tore buttons off their clothes, complained of bones slipping out of place, and had periods of great confusion. By young adulthood all four were diagnosed as schizophrenic. The similar and shared disorders of these girls, the Genain quadruplets, point to a genetic factor in schizophrenia (Mirksy & Quinn, 1988).

We'll look at genetic factors and two other causes being considered as relevant to schizophrenia: brain and environment.

Genetic Factors. In a dramatic fashion, the Genain quadruplets illustrate that schizophrenia runs in families. The graph gives the **concordance rates for schizophrenia,** *or likelihood of being schizophrenic if another person is.* Statistically, if one brother or sister (sibling or fraternal twin) is schizophrenic, there is only about a 10%–14% chance that the other will be also. In comparison, if one identical twin (remember: identical twins share 100% of their genes) is schizophrenic, there is about a 48% chance that the other twin will be also. In the case of the Genain quadruplets, however, the concordance rate was 100, meaning that if one was schizophrenic, so were all (Gottesmann, 1991).

These findings indicate that a person may inherit a *predisposition* for schizophrenia. However, researchers have been unable to find the gene or genes involved in transmission of schizophrenia (Onstad et al., 1991). One way that genes could be involved in a predisposition for schizophrenia is by altering factors in the brain, which we'll study next.

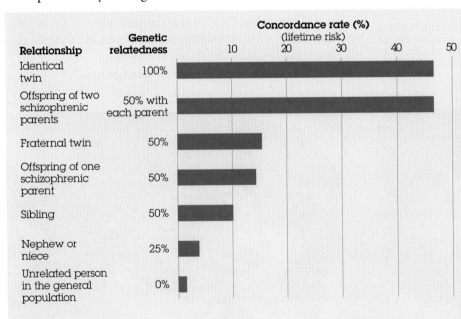

Relationship	Genetic relatedness	Concordance rate (%) (lifetime risk)
Identical twin	100%	████████████████████ (~48)
Offspring of two schizophrenic parents	50% with each parent	████████████████████ (~46)
Fraternal twin	50%	██████ (~17)
Offspring of one schizophrenic parent	50%	██████ (~16)
Sibling	50%	████ (~10)
Nephew or niece	25%	██ (~4)
Unrelated person in the general population	0%	█ (~1)

The concordance rate refers to the likelihood of being schizophrenic if another person is. For example, if one identical twin is schizophrenic, there is a 48% chance that the other twin will be, too (Holzman & Matthysse, 1990).

Brain Factors. One of the puzzling questions about schizophrenia is how many of the symptoms result from changes to or defects in the brain itself. During the past ten years, remarkable advances in methods for studying the living brain (see Module 4 for information on PET, MRI, and CAT) have allowed researchers to study and compare the brains of people with and without schizophrenia.

Is the brain of a person with schizophrenia different?
Today more than ever before, researchers have renewed hope of identifying neurological causes or factors related to schizophrenia (Berquier & Ashton, 1991). We'll review some of the major findings.

Dopamine Receptors

One clue to changes in the brain comes from the fact that the majority of antipsychotic drugs work by decreasing the activity of dopamine (DOPE-ah-mean), one of the brain's neurotransmitters. This finding supports the **dopamine theory of schizophrenia**, *which holds that abnormalities in the dopamine system are involved in producing some symptoms of schizophrenia.* For example, using positron emission tomography (PET) researchers found that schizophrenics had a higher number of dopamine receptors than nonschizophrenics (Wong et al., 1986).

Ventricle Size

Four fluid-filled holes, called ventricles, are located in various areas of the brain. The fluid in these ventricles provides nutriments to the brain. A small but consistent finding is that the ventricles in the brains of people with schizophrenia, as well as other disorders, such as Parkinson's, are relatively larger than those in brains of normal people (Cleghorn, Zipursky, & List, 1991).

Frontal Lobe

We know that the frontal lobe is involved in many important cognitive, emotional, and personality behaviors. Researchers have reported that schizophrenics show decreased metabolic activity in the frontal lobes (Clegborn, Zipursky, & List, 1991). This decreased frontal lobe activity is consistent with many of the symptoms seen in schizophrenics.

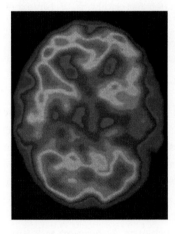 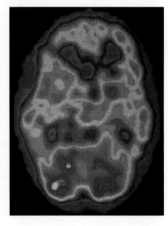

The brain of a normal subject (left) shows more activity in the frontal lobe (top of photos) during a cognitive task than does the brain of a schizophrenic (right). Blue and green indicate little activity; orange shows increased activity (Rubin et al., 1991).

Environmental Factors. The fact that the concordance rate for schizophrenia for identical twins is only about 48% raises a number of questions. Why wouldn't identical twins—who have 100% of the same genes—have a concordance rate of 100%?

There is evidence that *environmental factors,* especially stress, contribute to the development of schizophrenia. Stressful factors include a wide variety of life events that range from having hostile parents or poor social relations to losing a parent or having career or personal problems (Rosenthal, 1980). According to the **diathesis** (die-ATH-uh-sis) **stress theory of schizophrenia**, *some people have a genetic or neurological predisposition, called diathesis, that interacts with life stressors to result in the onset and development of schizophrenia.* This theory assumes that an inherited predisposition for schizophrenia may be triggered by stressful family relationships and other negative life experiences (Fowles, 1992).

Now let's look at the treatment for schizophrenia.

Schizophrenia

Treatment

What kind of drug was Jeanette given?

Earlier in this module, you read of Jeanette, who had the delusion that the fire alarm was a message from God. When she was admitted to the hospital and diagnosed as schizophrenic, she was probably given an **antipsychotic drug** *to reduce the level of dopamine and thus reduce the bizarre hallucinations, confusion, and delusions that are common with schizophrenia.* One generally used antipsychotic is from a family of drugs called *phenothiazines* (pheen-no-THIGH-ah-zines); one commonly used one goes by the trade name Thorazine. The fact that phenothiazines decrease schizophrenic symptoms by reducing dopamine supports the dopamine theory of schizophrenia (Davis et al., 1991). But the fact that some patients do not improve when given phenothiazines or suffer relapses while taking them suggests that the dopamine theory is not the entire answer.

A person may remain on antipsychotic drugs for a long period of time. As an example, Jeanette, whose schizophrenia was acute, was on them for six years. Individuals with chronic schizophrenia remain on antipsychotic drugs for much of their lives.

What's it like to be on antipsychotic drugs?

Here is how one person who took Thorazine described his experience:

"Thorazine has lots of unpleasant side effects. It makes you groggy, lowers your blood pressure, making you dizzy and faint when you stand up too quickly. If you go out in the sun your skin gets red and hurts like hell. It makes muscles rigid and twitchy. On Thorazine everything's a bore. You can read comic books and *Reader's Digest* forever. The weather is dull, the flowers are dull, nothing's very impressive." (Vonnegut, 1976, pp. 252–253)

As this description indicates, antipsychotic drugs not only affect schizophrenic symptoms, they also have a number of side effects, such as generally dulling the emotions and decreasing motivation.

Why is he twitching?

One of the serious side effects of phenothiazines, which are prescribed to about 3 million people in the United States each year, is the appearance of unwanted motor function. This motor function, called **tardive dyskinesia** (TARD-if dis-cah-KNEE-zee-ah), *involves the appearance of slow, involuntary, and uncontrollable rhythmic movements and rapid twitching of the mouth and lips, as well as unusual movements of the limbs.* Tardive dyskinesia often develops after several months of taking antipsychotic drugs such as phenothiazines. The risk of developing it rises the longer the patients remain on antipsychotics.

According to an American Psychiatric Association task force report, about 20% of patients taking antipsychotics develop some tardive dyskinesia; about 10% suffer moderate to severe symptoms (Bower, 1991). About 30% of patients with tardive dyskinesia will experience a reduction in symptoms if they are taken off antipsychotic drugs. However, in the remaining patients tardive dyskinesia may persist even when the drug therapy is stopped. Currently there is no effective treatment for tardive dyskinesia (Wojcik et al., 1991).

Do schizophrenic symptoms continue to worsen?

Researchers followed 40 patients with schizophrenia and tested them at admission and then 2, 5, and 11 years later. The researchers reported that the seriousness of patients' symptoms generally reached a plateau at about 5 years and did not worsen after that (Carpenter & Strauss, 1991). Thus, contrary to popular belief, schizophrenic symptoms do not necessarily worsen across a patient's lifetime but rather reach a plateau and then generally remain about the same.

In a related study, researchers followed 58 schizophrenics for 2 to 12 years and reported that only about 20% showed a good outcome, while the remaining showed poor outcomes—that is,

Antipsychotic drugs help patients escape from or deal with their schizophrenic symptoms.

their symptoms reached a plateau in from 5 to 7 years and then persisted even though they were maintained on antipsychotic drugs. In addition, the researchers reported that about 78% of the group suffered a relapse, which means that their original serious symptoms returned; about 38% attempted suicide, and about 24% also suffered from a major mood disorder (Breier et al., 1991).

According to one researcher, the outcomes of long-term follow-up studies over the last two decades indicate the following (McGlashan, 1988):

• Schizophrenia can be a chronic disorder that frequently disables a person for a lifetime.

• The average outcome of schizophrenia is worse than that of other major mental disorders.

• Schizophrenia is associated with an increased risk for suicide, physical illness, and death.

• Schizophrenic symptoms, although disabling and long-lasting, do not get progressively worse but reach a plateau in 5 to 7 years.

• The outcome of schizophrenia is varied. Generally, about 20% of schizophrenics recover, about 60% continue to suffer some behavior impairment although their symptoms reach a plateau, and about 20% do not recover at all.

As you can see, the current treatment for schizophrenia helps only about 20% of the patients to recover completely, keeps about 60% from getting worse, and does not help the remaining 20% much at all. One reason we do not have a cure for schizophrenia is that we do not yet understand all its causes.

Next we'll discuss a disorder that is a little hard to believe.

Dissociative Disorders

Multiple personality is different from schizophrenia.

Nancy was alone in her kitchen smoking a cigarette. "Go ahead and finish it," she heard Alice say. "It'll be the last one you'll have." Nancy withdrew as if behind a curtain. When she returned, she was standing on a bench with a telephone cord wrapped around her neck. Shocked, she suddenly realized that what her therapist had been telling her must be true. She was sharing her body with someone else. In fact, Nancy eventually learned she was living with an "inner family" of 13 personalities, each with a name and a purpose. They included the Actress, a promiscuous flirt; the Nun, a righteous moralist; the Kid, a mischievous 5-year-old; Marsha, who faints under stress; and Richard, the gatekeeper who directs their comings and goings. There was also Alice, a suicidal personality who didn't care that if she killed herself Nancy would die, too (*Los Angeles Times*, January 29, 1985).

Nancy has a dissociative disorder, in which part of her memory or personality is split off, or dissociated. A **dissociative disorder** *is characterized by a a split or breakdown in a person's normally integrated consciousness, identity, or motor behavior.* There are three dissociative disorders: psychogenic amnesia, psychogenic fugue, and multiple personality.

Psychogenic amnesia *occurs when a person is suddenly unable to recall important personal information, usually after some stressful incident.* For example, a woman may forget who she is following some traumatic event, such as being physically or sexually abused.

Psychogenic fugue *occurs when a person not only loses all memory of personal and other events but suddenly leaves home and moves to a new place and assumes a new identity.* Every now and then we hear of individuals discovered wandering around, not knowing who they were, where they came from, or the names of family members. Such people may be experiencing psychogenic fugue.

Multiple personality *is the presence of two or more distinct personalities within a single individual.* The personalities are usually quite different and quite complex, the original personality is seldom aware of the existence of the others, and each personality takes its turn at being in control. Nancy's case is an example of multiple personality. It is an extremely rare phenomenon, with only 300 cases reported in the world literature, and at least 79 occurring between 1971 and 1980 (Fahy, 1988). Researchers do not know why there was an "epidemic" of multiple personality cases in the 1970s. The majority of cases have been reported in North America, with very few in India and almost none in Britain (Modestin, 1992).

What do we know about multiple personality?

When it comes to multiple personality, females with the disorder outnumber males eight to one. In the vast majority of multiple personality cases, the individual had experienced severe psychological or physical abuse or sexual trauma during early childhood. Apparently, other personalities arose as a defense against or way to cope with this trauma (Putnam et al., 1986).

One interesting finding is that different brain-wave patterns have been recorded in individuals who suffer from multiple personality. Researchers initially thought that these patterns were indicative of which personality was in control at the moment (Putnam, 1982). But it was later found that the patterns are most probably caused by differences in emotional states. Different brain-wave patterns also occur in normal individuals who simply vary their mood, concentration, and muscle tension (Coons, Milstein, & Marley, 1982). Multiple personality disorder should not be confused with schizophrenia.

After the Concept/Glossary, we'll discuss ways of treating mild depression.

1. A prolonged emotional state that affects almost all of a person's thoughts and behaviors is called a _____ disorder.

2. The most common form of mood disorder includes sadness, dejection, problems with appetite and weight, difficulties in sleeping, loss of energy, lack of interest and pleasure in usual activities, negative self-concept, and recurrent thoughts of death or suicide; it is called _____.

3. A depressive disorder that is characterized by being chronically depressed but with periods of normal mood lasting for a few days or weeks but never more than a month or two is called _____.

4. A mood disorder that includes periods of depression that may suddenly lift and are followed immediately by periods of exaggerated energy, enthusiasm, and elation, called (a)_____, is (b)_____.

5. The theory of depression that emphasizes underlying genetic or biological factors that predispose a person to experiencing depression is the (a)_____ theory. Another theory of depression that holds that individuals become depressed and stay depressed because of errors in thinking is (b)_____ theory.

6. Drugs that raise the level of certain neurotransmitters, called monoamines are (a)_____ drugs. The theory holding that depression results when the activity of monoamines is extremely low and mania results when the levels are extremely high is called the (b)_____ theory.

7. One treatment for major depression when antidepressant drugs fail is placing electrodes on the skull and administering a mild electrical current to the brain; this procedure is called _____.

8. A disorder that involves inflexible and maladaptive traits that cause significantly impaired functioning in one's personal and social life is called a _____ disorder. One example of this disorder is antisocial personality, or psychopathy.

9. A serious mental disorder that includes such symptoms as loss of contact with reality and problems of thought, attention, perception, motor behavior, and emotion is _____.

10. A split or breakdown in a person's normally integrated consciousness, identity, or motor behavior is (a)_____. The presence of two or more distinct personalities within a single individual is called (b)_____.

APPLYING/ EXPLORING: MILD DEPRESSION

"I've got the sophomore blues," said Harold. "At first I was excited about going off to college and being on my own. Now all I feel is the pressure to study, get good grades, and scrape up enough bucks to pay my rent. I've lost interest in my classes and I'm not doing well on exams. I'll be lucky to pass my courses this semester. To make matters worse, I find myself complaining about every little thing. I don't enjoy things the way I used to. I can tell that my friends just don't want to be around me when I'm like this. I want to do something to get out of this depressed mood, but I don't know where to start."

Harold is suffering from mild depression. Before trying to get over being depressed, people like Harold should know what kinds of things keep them depressed. Psychologists have come up with three general hypotheses about what maintains mild depression (Hokanson & Butler, 1992; Hokanson et al., 1989).

1 Depressed individuals have social behaviors that are deficient or cause problems in social interactions. For example, some depressed college students were found to be overdependent, while others were competitive, aggressive, and mistrustful.

2 Friends and roommates react negatively to the depressed individual's behaviors. They become hostile and progressively less happy and thus give the depressed person less and less social support.

3 The depressed individual's social behaviors turn off friends and roommates, which in turn maintains and deepens the individual's depressed state and keeps the cycle of depression going.

The task for the mildly depressed individual is to break out of this vicious cycle by engaging in more normal social behaviors that do not elicit hostility or turn off friends and roommates. Psychologists offer a number of suggestions for helping people take steps to overcome mild depression. They recommend focusing on positive events, giving yourself credit, and taking action as ways to help break out of the vicious cycle of mild depression. Let's explore these three recommendations.

Focus on Positive Events

Harold is stuck in a rut of noticing and remembering primarily negative things, constantly complaining, and getting little pleasure in normal daily events, such as watching television, eating out, or talking to friends. Researchers have found that depressed individuals have a tendency to select and remember unhappy or depressing thoughts and events. For example, when asked to remember a list containing both depressed and nondepressed words, depressed individuals better remembered more depressed words, while nondepressed individuals better remembered more nondepressed ones (Derry & Kuiper, 1981). In addition, depressed individuals have

Psychologists have three suggestions for breaking out of the vicious cycle of mild depression.

more difficulty remembering good things about themselves than bad things and take a more pessimistic view of life (Dykman et al., 1989). These findings suggest that unless Harold alters his behavior, he will continue to focus on the negative aspects of his life and have a harder time overcoming his depression.

How can I focus on positive events?

The first step in breaking out of the vicious cycle of mild depression is to substitute recalling depressing things with making a daily list of positive events, conversations, and self-statements (Rehm, 1982). For instance, depressed individuals who make, read, and remember a daily list of pleasant events begin to focus more on the positive and to improve their daily mood.

Give Yourself Credit

Harold is not taking credit for anything that he is doing in his life, however small the activity—such as going to class and taking

notes. In other words, he attributes his failures to his personal deficiencies and does not credit himself for his successes. After reviewing many studies, researchers concluded that people who were depressed were more likely to attribute their failures to faults within themselves and more likely to explain their successes by pointing to luck or chance (Sweeney, Anderson, & Bailey, 1986). Like Harold, depressed people are caught in a vicious cycle. The more they blame themselves for their failures and credit their successes to luck or chance, the more depressed they feel.

How can I take more credit for what I do?

Harold needs to blame himself less for his failures and credit himself more for his successes. He could do so by monitoring and writing down negative self-statements, such as "I'm passing my classes through luck." Then he would make up a list of positive self-statements, such as "I wouldn't be here

unless I was smart." By substituting positive for negative self-statements, he would learn to take more credit for his successful behaviors and begin to feel better about himself (Rehm, 1982).

Take Some Action

Harold said, "I want to get out of this depressed mood but I don't know how." In addition to following the two suggestions just described—focusing on positive events and giving himself some credit—he can start an exercise program.

How can engaging in an exercise program help?

Researchers compared the effects of aerobic exercise, relaxation training, and no treatment on a group of depressed college women. After ten weeks, the exercise group showed significantly less depression than the other two groups (McCann & Holmes, 1984). In a related study, researchers found that mildly depressed subjects showed a significant improvement whether they took part in ten weeks of cognitive therapy, ten weeks of running, or ten weeks of combimed cognitive therapy and running (Fremont & Craighead, 1987). In reviewing studies on exercise and depression, other researchers concluded that there is reason for cautious optimism on the potentially helpful effects of exercise in overcoming depression (Simons et al., 1985).

Psychologists find that by taking all three suggestions—focusing on positive events, giving oneself credit, and taking some action—individuals can break out of the vicious cycle of mild depression.

Summary/Self-Test

MOOD DISORDERS

1. A prolonged emotional state that affects almost all of a person's thoughts and behaviors is called a (a)_____ disorder. Disorders marked by prolonged periods of depression are (b)_____ disorders.

2. Sad, dejected mood, problems with appetite and weight, difficulties in sleeping, loss of energy, lack of interest or pleasure in usual activities, and recurrent thoughts of suicide are the hallmarks of (a)_____ depression, which is the most common form of mood disorder. Chronic depression with periods of normal mood lasting for a few days or weeks but never more than a month or two is called (b)_____ disorder.

3. The disorder characterized by periods when a person exhibits exaggerated energy, enthusiasm, and elation is called (a)_____. This disorder is rarely experienced without depression. More commonly, periods of elation follow periods of depression and this cycle, formerly called manic-depressive illness, is now called (b)_____ disorder.

4. One popular theory of depression that emphasizes underlying genetic or biological factors that predispose a person to experiencing depression is called the (a)_____ theory of depression. According to another theory, when the activity of certain neurotransmitters called monoamines is extremely low, depression results; when the levels are extremely high, mania results. This is called the (b)_____ theory of depression. According to another theory of depression, individuals become depressed and stay depressed because of errors in thinking; this is Beck's (c)_____ theory of depression.

5. A form of therapy that attempts to correct a person's distorted views and pessimistic beliefs about the self and the world is referred to as (a)_____ therapy. A form of therapy in which one examines how conflicts with others and disturbed relationships affect depression is called (b)_____ therapy.

6. The group of drugs used to treat depression, called _____, are particularly useful in treating severe depression. However, they have a number of unwanted side effects, including weight gain and lethargy. Side effects sometimes cause clients to drop out of treatment.

7. Those whose extreme depression is not helped by drugs may have a mild electrical current administered to the brain to cause a seizure; this treatment is called _____. A serious side effect of this treatment is possible memory impairment.

8. The most popular treatment for bipolar depression is a natural mineral salt called _____, which is effective for a majority of patients. It is also effective in treating individuals who have manic episodes without depression.

■ *A student is brought into the health clinic after attempting suicide. What are some of the questions the mental health professional will ask?*

PERSONALITY DISORDERS

9. Inflexible and maladaptive traits that cause significantly impaired functioning in one's personal and social life are the signs of a (a)_____ disorder. One such disorder is reflected in a failure to conform to social norms in many areas of life from childhood on; this is called (b)_____ personality or psychopathy. Researchers are investigating neurochemical and behavioral factors as the root of this disorder.

10. DMS-III-R lists ten other personality disorders, including ones in which the subject is excessively suspicious, or (a)_____; is very self-absorbed and socially withdrawn, or (b)_____; has an exaggerated sense of self-importance, or is (c)_____; and always indirectly resists what others ask or expect, called being (d)_____.

■ *A teenager is arrested by police for maliciously breaking car windows. The teenager says that he is very sorry and will never to it again. How would you determine whether this teenager is a psychopath?*

SCHIZOPHRENIA

11. The mental disorder that accounts for the highest percentage of inpatients in mental hospitals and includes such symptoms as loss of contact with reality and problems of thought, attention, perception, motor behavior, and emotion is called (a)_____. Patients whose problems develop suddenly, without any previous history of mental disorder, have (b)_____ schizophrenia; their chances for recovery are relatively good. In contrast, individuals who have a long history of schizophrenia, called (c)_____ schizophrenia, have significantly less chance of recovery.

12. DSM-III-R lists four categories of schizophrenia. Schizophrenia that includes delusions, such as thoughts of being persecuted, is called (a)_____. A form that includes bizarre ideas, confused speech, childish behavior, great emotional swings, and neglect of personal appearance and hygiene is called (b)_____. Periods of wild excitement or rigid, prolonged immobility may indicate (c)_____.

13. The concordance rate for schizophrenia indicates the likelihood that a person may inherit a _____ for schizophrenia.

14. One theory of schizophrenia finds support in the fact that schizophrenics have been shown to have a higher number of (a)_____ receptors than nonschizophrenics. There is also evidence that environmental factors, especially stress, contribute to the development of schizophrenia. An inherited predisposition for schizophrenia may be triggered by stressful family relationships and other negative life experiences; this is the (b)_____ theory of schizophrenia.

15. To reduce the bizarre hallucinations, confusion, and delusions common with schizophrenia, patients are often given (a)_____ drugs. A family of drugs called phenothiazines decrease schizophrenic symptoms by reducing levels of the neurotransmitter dopamine; this supports the (b)_____ theory of schizophrenia. A serious side effect of this treatment is the appearance of unwanted motor function (such as slow, involuntary, and uncontrollable rhythmic movements and rapid twitching of the mouth and lips), called (c)_____.

■ *Why do you think that drugs and not psychotherapy is the treatment of choice for schizophrenia?*

DISSOCIATIVE DISORDERS

16. A split or breakdown in a person's normally integrated consciousness, identity, or motor behavior is referred to as a (a)_____ disorder, of which there are three types. If a person is suddenly unable to recall important personal information, usually after some stressful incident, the person has psychogenic (b)_____. If a person loses all memory of personal and other events and suddenly leaves home, moves to a new place, and assumes a new identity, this person has psychogenic (c)_____. If there are two or more distinct personalities within a single individual, this is (d)_____. In the vast majority of these cases, the individual had experienced severe psychological or physical abuse or sexual trauma during early childhood. Apparently, other personalities arose as a way to cope with this trauma.

■ *What factors might have contributed to the great increase in cases of multiple personality seen in the 1970s?*

APPLYING/EXPLORING: MILD DEPRESSION

17. Psychologists have three general hypotheses about what maintains mild depression. Depressed individuals have deficits or problems with (a)_____ behaviors, which in turn cause problems in social interactions. Friends and roommates react negatively to the depressed individual's behaviors and provide progressively less social (b)_____. The depressed individual's social behaviors turn off friends and roommates, thus maintaining and deepening the individual's (c)_____ state. Psychologists suggest that mildly depressed individuals can break out of this vicious cycle by focusing on positive events, giving themselves credit, and taking action, such as starting an exercise program.

■ *Why is it difficult for people to break out of the vicious cycle of mild depression?*

Chapter *Fifteen*
THERAPIES

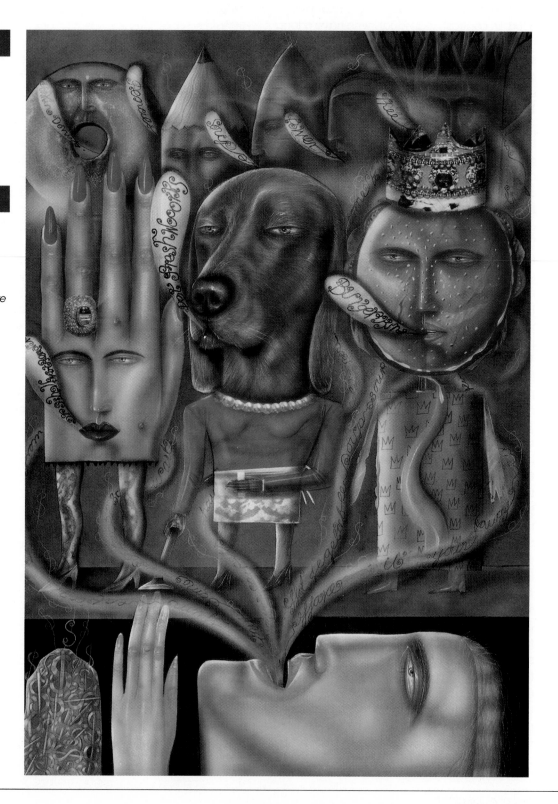

MODULE 29
THERAPY I

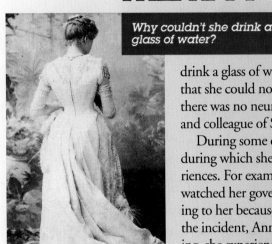

Why couldn't she drink a glass of water?

The treatment of Anna O.'s strange symptoms lead to the development of psychoanalysis.

During the time that Anna O. was caring for her dying father, she developed a number of symptoms that came and went. These symptoms included not being able to drink a glass of water, having a squint in both eyes that at times was so bad that she could not see, and developing a paralysis in her right arm although there was no neurological cause. Anna's doctor was Joseph Breuer, a friend and colleague of Sigmund Freud.

During some of his visits, Breuer would find Anna in a trancelike state during which she would talk uninhibitedly and recall many of her past experiences. For example, Anna related a childhood incident in which she had watched her governess's dog drink out of a glass. The experience was disgusting to her because she disliked both the governess and the dog. At the time of the incident, Anna had shown no emotional reaction. But during her retelling, she experienced emotional reactions that had been inhibited, and for the first time in many weeks she was able to drink a glass of water without feeling disgust.

Subsequently, Breuer used hypnosis to help Anna recall other troublesome past experiences. According to his account, as Anna recalled each past, traumatic experience, a physical symptom associated with that trauma would vanish. For example, she told of sitting by her father's sickbed and having a horrifying vision of a snake attacking him. She could not reach out and stop the snake because her arm had fallen asleep from hanging over the chair. As Anna relived the powerful guilt feelings arising from not being able to protect her father, the paralysis of her right arm disappeared. (adapted from Breuer & Freud, 1895/1955)

Whether the symptoms disappeared as easily as Breuer's telling indicates, we cannot know—in part because Anna was treated in the 1880s. But we do know that Anna's treatment can be considered the beginnings of Freud's system of psychoanalysis, one form of psychotherapy. Every form of **psychotherapy** *shares three characteristics: verbal interaction between therapist and client(s); the development of a supportive relationship during which a client can bring up and discuss traumatic or bothersome experiences that may have led to current problems; and analysis of the client's experiences and/or suggested ways for the client to deal with or overcome his or her problems.* Psychotherapies have multiplied over the years. By 1985 there were about 450 distinct forms of psychotherapy (Karasu, 1986). Despite this number, all psychotherapies developed from two or three basic forms, which we will discuss in this chapter.

What's Coming

In this module we'll examine the historical background of therapy, various types of therapists, and the granddaddy of all therapies, Freud's psychoanalysis. In the next module we'll discuss three popular forms of psychotherapy: behavior therapy, cognitive therapy, and humanistic therapy.

Let's begin with an overview of the field so that you can appreciate the development of psychotherapy.

Historical Background

Today we take for granted the treatment of many mental disorders with some form of psychotherapy that may or may not be combined with drug therapy. However, up until the 1800s serious mental disorders were handled in a way that was primitive and in many cases cruel. It was not until the discovery of psychoactive drugs in the 1950s that serious mental disorders were treated with more humane methods.

Crueler Times

Why did the public buy tickets?

From the 15th to 17th centuries, people who today would probably be diagnosed as schizophrenics were considered insane and called lunatics. They were primarily confined to asylums or hospitals for the mentally ill where there was little or no treatment. Instead, patients might be placed in a hood and straightjacket, padlocked to a cell wall, swung back and forth until they were quieted, strapped into a chair, or locked in handcuffs. The patients' chains were long enough to allow them to eat a mushy gruel out of bowls but did not always permit them to lie down at night. Other treatments involved withdrawing huge amounts of blood (as much as six quarts over a period of months) or frightening the patients, such as convincing them that they were about to die.

Even as late as the 1800s, some hospitals sold tickets so that the public could view the mentally disordered and their pathetic behaviors.

Reform Movement

How did one woman change the system?

In the 1800s a Boston schoolteacher named Dorothea Dix began to visit the jails and poorhouses where most of the mental patients in the United States were kept. Dix publicized the terrible living conditions and the lack of reasonable treatment of mental patients. Her work was part of the *reform movement* or *moral treatment movement,* which led to building huge hospitals for the humane treatment of mental patients. However, these mental hospitals soon became overcrowded, the public lost interest, funds became tight, and treatment became scarce.

Imagine a huge room filled with hundreds of mental patients, in various states of dress or undress, acting out their symptoms with little or no supervision, and you have an accurate view of the inside of these mental hospitals. The wretched conditions and inhumane treatment of patients persisted up until the 1950s.

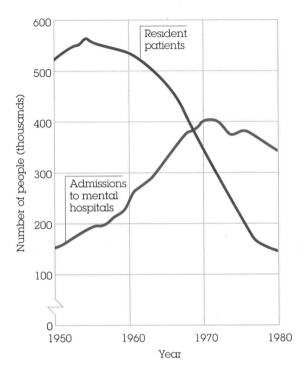

Deinstitutionalization

Was it a good idea?

The 1950s were marked by the development and use of antipsychotic drugs, which decreased serious mental symptoms. For the first time many mental patients were able to return to more normal functioning and, in some cases, to leave the mental hospitals. After antipsychotic drugs came to be widely used in treatment, mental hospitals began to let patients out, to *deinstitutionalize* them. The term **deinstitutionalization** *refers to the release of mental patients from mental hospitals and their return to the community.* As the graph shows, in 1955 there were 550,000 patients in mental hospitals; by 1980, after deinstitutionalization, there were about 150,000 patients in mental hospitals. This drop is all the more remarkable given the rise in overall population over that 25-year span.

The goal of deinstitutionalization—to get patients back into the community—has been only partly realized. Some former mental patients do live in halfway houses that provide help and support in bridging the transfer from mental hospitals to the community. However, there are not enough halfway houses to accommodate all the patients who have been deinstitutionalized. As a result, a relatively large number of former mental patients now roam our streets as the homeless and receive little or no treatment.

The Mental Health System Today

How far have we come?

In a number of topnotch private mental hospitals, patients receive many kinds of excellent therapy. However, there still remain a number of large state mental hospitals without enough staff or funds to provide a high level of treatment. Some of these large hospitals use drugs more to control the patients than as part of an overall treatment program (Okin, 1983).

The mental health profession has a way to go in providing adequate care to all mental patients (whether in state hospitals or on the streets) who are in need of continued help, support, and treatment.

So far we have focused on the treatment of those patients with serious mental disorders. However, many people have mental disorders that do not require hospitalization. Instead, many of these clients seek treatment in individual psychotherapy sessions that often take place in private offices or in **community mental health centers** *that offer low-cost or free mental health care to members of the surrounding community.* The services offered by the community mental health center may include psychotherapy, support groups, or telephone crisis counseling.

Let's look at the various kinds of mental health professionals who provide care for mental disorders.

Therapists and Approaches

Are there different kinds of psychotherapists?

Several kinds of professionals conduct psychotherapy: psychiatrists, clinical psychologists, social workers, psychiatric nurses, and counselors. Some receive more training in psychotherapy techniques than others. Let's look at the training required for each of three major groups of psychotherapists.

Becoming a therapist requires a considerable investment in time, money, and commitment. Therapists differ in their training and emphasis.

How do I become a psychiatrist?

If you wanted to be a **psychiatrist**, *you would first be trained as a physician; after receiving an M.D., degree, you would go on to a psychiatric residency, which involves additional training in pharmacology, neurology, psychopathology, and psychotherapeutic techniques.* Psychiatrists who receive additional training in psychoanalytic institutes are called *psychoanalysts*.

Psychiatrist	Clinical psychologist	Counseling psychologist
M.D. with psychiatric residency	Ph.D. with clinical experience	Ph.D. with counseling experience
B.S.	B.S. or B.A.	

How do I become a clinical psychologist?

If you wanted to be a **clinical psychologist**, *you would complete a Ph.D. program in clinical psychology, which includes one year of work in a clinical setting; this usually requires four to six years of work after obtaining a bachelor's degree.* Clinical psychologists who receive additional training in psychoanalytic institutes can also use psychoanalysis.

How do I become a counseling psychologist?

If you wished to become a **counseling psychologist**, *you would need to complete a Ph.D. program in psychology or education, including work in a counseling setting; this usually requires about four to six years after obtaining a bachelor's degree.* This training is similar to that of clinical psychologists but places less emphasis on research and the experimental method and more emphasis on practice in the real world. Counseling psychologists, who function in such settings as schools, colleges, industry, and private practice, generally deal more with problems of living than with the mental disorders that are treated by clinical psychologists.

How do psychiatrists and clinical psychologists differ?

Although there are similarities in the training of psychiatrists and clinical psychologists, there are also many differences. Here are a few:

- Psychiatrists receive extensive training in medicine and drugs and less training in basic psychology and the experimental method. Clinical psychologists receive less training in medicine and drugs and extensive training in basic psychology, psychotherapy techniques, and the experimental method.

- Psychiatrists tend to view psychological disorders as diseases and to treat them with drugs. Clinical psychologists are more likely to view psychological disorders as learned problems and to treat them with psychotherapy.

- Psychiatrists tend to study the effects of drugs on mental disorders; clinical psychologists tend to study the effects of psychotherapy on mental disorders.

- When psychiatrists do use therapy, they tend to use psychoanalytical and psychodynamic approaches. Clinical psychologists tend to use a wider variety of techniques, including behavior and cognitive therapies.

Approaches

Which approaches are being used today?

If you were to become a therapist, you would have a number of approaches from which to choose. When therapists were asked why they had chosen a certain approach, they answered that personal satisfaction was the primary reason (Garfield, 1980). Apparently, therapists choose a particular approach both because of its presumed effectiveness and because it suits their personalities.

In one study psychologists were asked, "Which approach do you use in therapy?" Their answers are given in the table to the right. The majority of those surveyed agreed that the days of a single approach, or one school dominating the field, were drawing to a close (Smith, 1982). In fact, the most widely used approach is **eclectic** (ee-KLEK-tik), *in which the psychotherapist combines features from several schools of thought.* For example, a therapist might use elements of psychoanalysis, such as looking for underlying problems; behavior therapy, such as specifying behavioral goals; cognitive therapy, such as changing irrational beliefs; and person-centered therapy, such as providing a supportive environment.

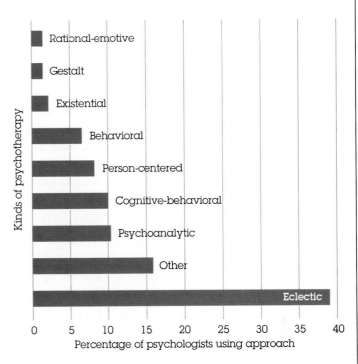

Of 450 kinds of therapies, these are the most popular (Smith, 1982).

This survey indicates a dramatic shift in the general methods of psychotherapy. In the 1940s and 1950s most mental health professionals were trained in the psychoanalytic approach and in the general method of long-term psychoanalysis. In more recent decades, however, with the discovery of antipsychotic drugs and the rise of cognitive-behavior therapy, the popularity of psychoanalysis has declined in favor of *short-term* therapies (Garfield, 1981). Before we discuss some of the more widely used contemporary psychotherapies, let's see how effective psychotherapy is.

Effectiveness

Is psychotherapy more effective than just waiting for problems to go away with time? To determine the effectiveness of psychotherapy, researchers used meta-analysis to evaluate almost 400 studies on psychotherapy. **Meta-analysis** *is a powerful statistical procedure that determines the effectiveness of some treatment (in this case psychotherapy) across many studies.* The researchers found that psychotherapy was generally more effective in treating problems than was doing nothing or waiting for the problem to go away (Smith & Glass, 1977). A large number of studies now show that approximately 66% of clients who seek psychotherapy experience at least some improvement, although only a small percentage show great improvement. The remaining 33% of the clients do not improve or, in a small number of cases, actually get worse. Even so, for many mental disorders psychotherapy is an effective treatment (Goldfried, Greenberg, & Marmar, 1990).

Now, let's return to the beginnings of psychotherapy and Freud's psychoanalytic approach, which we'll study in some detail because of its enormous influence through the years.

Traditional Psychoanalysis

What were Freud's three major discoveries?

Freud's theory of psychoanalysis *includes two related theories: a theory of personality development and a method of psychotherapy.* We explained Freud's theory of personality in Module 23; here we'll examine his method of psychotherapy.

At the core of **psychoanalysis** *is the idea that each of us has an unconscious part whose existence, activities, and thoughts are hidden behind a barrier that we cannot voluntarily remove and that our unconscious conflicts can result in psychological and physical symptoms.* Psychoanalysis comes under the general heading of **insight therapy,** *whose goal is to help the patient both become aware of and understand the causes of his or her problem.*

For ten years Freud worked in isolation as the world's only psychoanalyst. From 1902 onward, a number of young doctors and interested laypersons gathered around Freud to learn the principles and practice of psychoanalysis. They learned the three foundations of Freud's approach:

1 Freud believed that because *unconscious conflicts* give rise to psychological and physical symptoms, treatment should involve helping the patient become aware of and gain insight into his or her unconscious conflicts and repressed thoughts.

2 Freud developed *three techniques*—free association, dream interpretation, and analysis of slips of the tongue—that he believed provides clues to unconscious conflicts and repressed thoughts.

3 Freud found that at some point during therapy the patient would react to the therapist as a substitute parent, lover, sibling, or friend and, in the process, project or *transfer* strong emotions onto the therapist.

Freud developed three techniques—free association, dream interpretation, and analysis of slips of the tongue—to reveal unconscious conflicts and desires.

Let's look at Freud's psychoanalytic process in more detail.

Techniques

How did Freud uncover the unconscious?

Freud used the techniques of free association, dream interpretation, and analysis of slips of the tongue to treat neuroses or neurotic symptoms such as phobias, anxieties, and obsessions. Freud saw **neuroses** *as maladaptive thoughts and actions that indicate feelings of anxiety arising from some unconscious thought or conflict.*

Free Association

Freud encouraged patients to relax, sit back, or lie down on his now-famous couch and talk freely about anything, which he called free associating. **Free association** *is a technique that encourages clients to talk about any thoughts or images that enter their heads; the assumption is that this kind of free-flowing, uncensored talking will provide clues to unconscious material.*

For example, here is how Freud described a session with one of his most famous patients, later named the Rat Man (a 29-year-old lawyer who was obsessed with the idea that rats would destroy his father and lover): "The next day I made him [Rat Man] pledge himself to submit to the one and only condition of the treatment—namely, to say everything that came into his head even if it was *unpleasant* to him, or seemed *unimportant* or *irrelevant* or *senseless.* I then gave him leave to start his communications with any subject he pleased." (Freud, 1909/1949, p. 297; italics Freud's)

Free association was one of Freud's important methodological discoveries and one that psychoanalysts still use today to probe a client's unconscious thoughts, desires, and conflicts.

Dream Interpretation

Freud listened to and interpreted his patients' dreams because he believed that dreams represent the purest form of free association. **Dream interpretation** *is a psychoanalytic technique based on the assumption that dreams contain underlying, hidden meanings and symbols that provide clues to unconscious thoughts and desires.* For example, here is one of the best-known dreams in psychoanalytic literature. This dream was told to Freud by a patient who was later named Wolf Man (Buckley, 1989). Wolf Man, who was 23 years old when he entered therapy with Freud, had a phobia of wolves and other animals:

"I dreamt that it was night and that I was lying in my bed. Suddenly the window opened of its own accord, and I was terrified to see that some white wolves were sitting on the big walnut tree in front of the window. There were six or seven of them. The wolves were quite white, and looked more like foxes or sheep-dogs, for they had big tails like foxes and they had their ears pricked like dogs when they are attending to something. In great terror, evidently of being eaten up by the wolves, I screamed and woke up . . . I was 3, 4, or at most 5 years old at the time. From then until my 11th or 12th year I was always afraid of seeing something terrible in my dreams." (Freud 1909/1949, p. 498)

Freud's interpretation of this dream was that the young boy was "transformed" into a wolf and had witnessed his parents' sexual intercourse (looking through the bedroom window). Later, sexual fears created unconscious conflicts and resulted in a phobia of wolves and other animals. In general, the psychoanalyst's task is to look behind the dream's often bizarre disguises and symbols and follow Freud's lead in deciphering clues to unconscious material.

Freudian Slips

Sooner or later each of us makes a Freudian slip, which can often be embarrassing. **Freudian slips** *are slips of the tongue that we make in everyday speech; such mistakes are thought to reflect unconscious thoughts or wishes.* For example, once when I was lecturing on the brain I said, "Your bank is critically involved in thinking" when I had meant to say, "Your brain." At the time I was worried about borrowing money from the bank. Freud would say that slips of the tongue can be embarrassing because they reflect unconscious thoughts that we would prefer not to know or have revealed.

These psychoanalytic techniques help bring unconscious thoughts and conflicts to the surface so that the patient can deal with them and thereby reduce his or her symptoms. Next we'll explore how these techniques are put to use.

Traditional Psychoanalysis

A Psychoanalytic Session

What does the analyst do?

To give you a sense of what goes on in psychoanalysis, here is a brief excerpt from an actual session:

"Henry is in his mid-forties and is well advanced in treatment, As he arrives, he casually mentions his somewhat late arrival at the analyst's office. Without his mentioning, his late arrival might have gone unnoticed.

"'You will think it is a resistance,' Henry remarked sarcastically, 'but it was nothing of the kind. I had hailed a taxi that would have gotten me to the office on time. However, the traffic light changed just before the cab reached me, and someone else got in instead. I was so annoyed that I yelled "F___ you!" after the cab driver.'

"A brief pause ensued, followed by laughter as Henry repeated 'F___ you!'—this time clearly directed to the analyst.

"The analyst interpreted this interaction to mean that the cabbie had represented the analyst in the first place. Henry's anger at the analyst was relieved by the opportunity to 'curse out' the analyst (cabbie).

"After another brief pause, it was the analyst who broke the silence and injected his first and only interpretation of the 50-minute session. He asserted that Henry seemed to be angry about a previously canceled therapy session.

"Henry was furious over the interpretation. 'Who are you that I should care about missing that session?' he stormed.

"Henry paused again, and then reflected more tranquilly, 'My father, I suppose.'

"This time it was the word *father* that served as the switch word to a new line of thought.

"'My father was distant, like you,' he began. 'We never really had a conversation.'" (adapted from Lipton, 1983)

What does the analyst do?

This brief excerpt from a psychoanalytic session illustrates some of the basic features of psychoanalysis. Notice that the patient is encouraged to free associate and the analyst makes few comments. When the analyst does comment, he interprets or analyzes something the patient says, such as the meaning of the anger at the cab driver. By analyzing the client's free associations, the analyst hopes to bring up clues to the client's unconscious conflicts that are causing problems.

The main thrust of psychoanalysis is to help the patient remove barriers that prevent unconscious conflicts from rising to the surface.

Problems During Therapy

One of Freud's important observations was that as therapy proceeds, two problems arise: transference and resistance. Both of these problems need to be resolved before therapy can proceed.

Transference

Notice that Henry projected onto the therapist certain negative traits of his father ("My father was distant, like you"). The therapist in effect served as a "substitute father," toward whom Henry could direct the anger and hostility he felt toward his real father. **Transference** *is the process by which the patient feels toward the therapist the conflict-ridden emotions felt toward someone important in the patient's life.* Freud believed that the main portion of therapy involves transference and working through the transference—that is, resolving the emotional feelings that have been transferred to the therapist. Understanding the process of transference is considered one of Freud's greatest achievements.

In therapy, transference occurs when the patient is close to connecting his or her current problems with unconscious conflicts that involve some important person in the patient's life. At this point, the patient feels strong emotions that are transferred to the therapist, who becomes a substitute for the important person. If the feelings involved in transference are not worked out, therapy will be stalled. The analyst helps the patient deal with these feelings so that therapy may proceed.

Thus, one of the cornerstones of psychoanalysis is analysis of transference: it helps the patient understand how he or she might have misperceived, misinterpreted, and related to some past event or situation. By working through transference, the patient can evaluate his or her unrealistic impulses and anxieties and see the past in a more realistic way. The patient reinterprets the past in a more mature fashion and comes to understand and work out his or her unconscious conflicts.

Resistance

Psychoanalysts recognize that working out transference is one of the two essential requirements for improvement in patients' mental health. The other essential requirement is that patients achieve insight into the causes of their problems. However, working out transference and achieving insight are long, difficult processes, in part because the patient has so many defenses against admitting repressed thoughts and feelings into consciousness. These defenses lead to resistance. **Resistance** *is characterized by the patient's reluctance to work through feelings or to recognize unconscious conflicts and repressed thoughts.* Resistance may show up in many ways: patients may cancel or come late for sessions, may refuse to talk about certain problems, may argue continually, or may criticize the analyst. However, the occurrence of resistance is one sign that therapy is uncovering critical unconscious material. The analyst must use tact and patience in getting the client to accept threatening interpretations and in breaking down resistance. A necessary role of the analyst is to overcome the patient's resistance so that the therapy can proceed and stay on course.

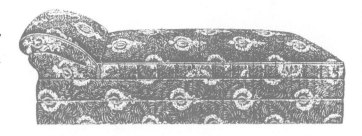

Once patients succeed in gaining insight and working out transference, and once the analyst has succeeded in breaking down their resistance, patients are well on their way to solving their problems.

Psychoanalysis Today

In 1989 the 50th anniversary of Sigmund Freud's death was marked by a series of articles in the *Psychoanalytic Quarterly* on the future of psychoanalysis. One author commented that the question "Is there a future for American psychoanalysis?" would never have been debated in the heyday of analysis in the 1950s (Kirsner, 1990). However, the decline of psychoanalysis was discussed in the 1960s, taken seriously in the 1970s, and judged to be very real in the 1980s and 1990s. According to one psychoanalyst, here are some reasons for the decline of psychoanalysis and questioning of its future (Kirsner, 1990):

• Drugs are now used to treat problems formerly dealt with in psychoanalysis.

• There are more analysts but fewer patients than before. This is due in part to the fact that patients who go into psychoanalysis must commit themselves to several sessions every week and must be able to afford to do so for several years. In addition, psychoanalysis is less appropriate for patients with serious mental disorders, such as schizophrenia, but rather is used primarily with those who have a less severe problem, such as general anxiety, phobia, compulsion, or a personality or relationship problem.

• Because of their earlier success, psychoanalysts became too isolated in their "ivory towers." As a result, they neglected to reach out into the community and to have good programs for education at universities and medical schools.

• Psychoanalysts have been very slow to analyze their own profession in terms of education—how to train analysts—as well as research into what goes on during analysis, how it can be made more effective, and how it can be improved.

• A number of competing therapies are equally effective but less costly (in terms of time and money) than psychoanalysis.

This last point is particularly significant. We'll examine some of these other therapies in depth in the next module. For now, let's see how psychoanalysis itself and its proven successes may have contributed to its own decline.

Many concepts of psychoanalysis, such as the search for unconscious conflicts, dream interpretation, and working through transference, have been incorporated into other approaches, such as the psychodynamic approach.

Psychoanalysis reached the height of its popularity in the 1950s.

How is the psychodynamic approach related?

The **psychodynamic approach** *assumes that symptoms are signs of more basic underlying problems, that transference needs to be worked out, and that the primary role of the therapist is to interpret and clarify the patient's behaviors.* It is thus similar to traditional psychoanalysis. However, psychodynamic therapists take a much more active role in interpreting and clarifying client problems and suggesting solutions. Another difference is that the psychodynamic approach has grown in popularity as the psychoanalytic approach has declined.

How is dynamic psychotherapy related?

Dynamic psychotherapy, or **short-term dynamic therapy,** *is one method of the psychodynamic approach; it is essentially a shortened version of psychoanalysis.* Dynamic psychotherapy shares many of the features of psychoanalysis: using face-to-face interaction; going over the client's feelings and fantasies; breaking down the client's defenses and resistances; focusing on interpretations that help the client resolve unconscious conflicts; building up the client's confidence and self-esteem; working through transference problems; and preparing the client for the termination of therapy.

Although dynamic psychotherapists place great importance on analyzing behaviors and working through transference, unlike the traditional psychoanalysts they take very active roles in the process, freely challenging the client's beliefs. What really sets dynamic psychotherapy apart from psychoanalysis is that it occurs in a maximum of 25 to 30 sessions (compared with an average of 600 sessions spread over two years for traditional psychoanalysis).

Unlike traditional psychoanalysis, which is rarely evaluated for its effectiveness, dynamic psychotherapy has proven effective for the treatment of stress and bereavement disorders, late life depression, and adjustment, affective, and personality disorders (Svartberg & Stiles, 1991). Thus, for many disorders short-term dynamic psychotherapy has become a real alternative to long-term psychoanalysis.

Since the 1960s, psychoanalysis has declined in popularity.

Where does psychoanalysis stand?

One analyst concludes that although psychoanalysis has fallen on difficult times, it is still the best therapy around for understanding a person's unconscious or inner world by examining transference and resistances (Kirsner, 1990). Although psychoanalysis has declined in popularity over the last decade, many of its concepts, such as the importance of unconscious thoughts, interpretation of dreams, working out transference, and overcoming resistance, have been incorporated into many other forms of psychotherapy.

After the Concept/Glossary, we'll discuss a very old and primitive form of "psychotherapy."

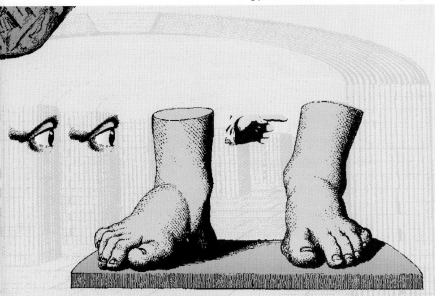

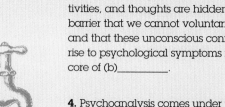

1. A process that involves a verbal interaction between therapist and client and that leads to the development of a supportive relationship during which a therapist may analyze or suggest ways for the client to deal with and overcome his or her problems is called _____.

2. If you first trained as a physician and then went into a psychiatric residency, which involves additional training in pharmacology, neurology, psychopathology, and psychotherapeutic techniques, you would be a (a)_____. If you completed a Ph.D. program in psychology, which includes one year of work in a clinical setting, you would be a (b)_____. If you completed a Ph.D. program in psychology or education, which includes work in a counseling setting, you would be a (c)_____.

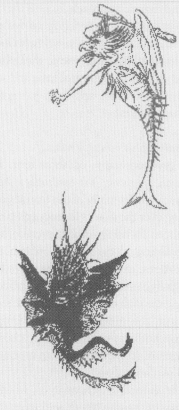

3. Freud's theory of psychoanalysis includes two related theories: a theory of personality development and a method of (a)_____. The idea that each of us has an unconscious part whose existence, activities, and thoughts are hidden behind a barrier that we cannot voluntarily remove and that these unconscious conflicts give rise to psychological symptoms is at the core of (b)_____.

4. Psychoanalysis comes under the general heading of _____ therapy, whose goal is to help the patient become aware of and understand the causes of his or her problem.

5. Freud used psychoanalysis to treat phobias, anxieties, and obsessions. These are examples of _____, or maladaptive thoughts and actions that indicate feelings of anxiety arising from some unconscious thought or conflict.

6. A psychoanalytic technique that encourages clients to talk about any thoughts or images that enter their heads is called _____. The assumption is that this kind of free-flowing, uncensored talking will provide clues to unconscious material.

7. A psychoanalytic technique based on the assumption that dreams contain underlying, hidden meanings and symbols that provide clues to unconscious thoughts and desires is called _____.

8. Mistakes that we make in everyday speech that are thought to reflect unconscious thoughts or wishes are called

_____.

9. The process of projecting onto the therapist all the conflict-ridden emotions felt toward someone important in the patient's life is called (a)_____. The patient's reluctance to work through feelings or recognize unconscious conflicts and repressed thoughts is called (b)_____.

10. An approach that assumes that symptoms are signs of more basic underlying problems, that transference needs to be worked out, that the primary role of the therapist is to interpret and clarify the patient's behaviors, but in which the sessions are limited is called _____.

Answers: 1. psychotherapy; 2. (a) psychiatrist, (b) clinical psychologist, (c) counseling psychologist; 3. (a) psychotherapy, (b) psychoanalysis; 4. insight; 5. neuroses; 6. free association; 7. dream interpretation; 8. slips of the tongue or Freudian slips; 9. (a) transference, (b) resistance; 10. psychodynamic approach.

A Healer

Why do the local people go to the healer?

Putu, a young unmarried woman about 20 years old, lived with her family in a small village on the beautiful island of Bali. Putu's family had made her break off a relationship with someone she loved and become engaged to another man whom she did not love. Since this new engagement, Putu had lost all interest in things around her, ate very little, and did not take part in normal activities or engage in conversations. The young woman was taken to the local nurse, who gave her an injection of multivitamins for general apathy. The injection did not help, and the nurse recommended that the family take Putu to a local healer, or *balian* (Connor, 1982).

Western therapists would have treated Putu's depression with some form of psychotherapy or, if it was severe, some combination of therapy and drugs. However, in Bali, Putu was said to be the victim of witchcraft and thus required the services of a balian.

The family took the depressed Putu to a well-respected balian, who massaged her neck. The balian pointed out a small pulsation that indicated the presence of an evil wind spirit, placed in Putu's body by the rejected lover. The balian said that she would mix special medicine and that the evil spirit would be exorcised. The balian then asked Putu to stand in the midst of healing smoke. After about 40 minutes the evil wind spirit left Putu's body and entered small male and female rice effigies, which were broken and thrown away. Then Putu's body was purified with holy water. During the course of the afternoon, Putu began to talk, show interest in food and things around her, and generally to get over her former apathy. For two more weeks, Putu stayed with the balian, who continued to perform purification ceremonies and drive away the evil wind spirits.

It is interesting to compare the assumptions underlying Western psychotherapy with the approach used by the healers of Bali. Western psychotherapy assumes that the major cause of a problem is something the person feels, thinks, or did. In contrast, balians assume that the cause of the problem is an evil spirit that has been cast by someone else. Although their assumptions, beliefs, and rituals are very different from those of Western psychotherapists, balians seem to have success rates similar to those reported by psychotherapists. Are these successes due to the rituals themselves, or to the support and trust developed between the balian and the person being helped? That's a question to keep in mind as you learn more about psychotherapy and how people are helped with their problems.

The healers of Bali, called balians, use rituals to drive out evil spirits and treat psychological problems.

APPLYING/ EXPLORING: SEEKING PSYCHOTHERAPY

Why don't more people with problems seek psychotherapy?

Over their lifetimes, about one-third of all Americans will develop a mental disorder for which they may need professional help. However, of those people, only about one out of three actually seek professional help (Robins, Tipp, & Przybeck, 1991). Besides economic reasons, many people do not seek professional help because they feel embarrassed, think there is a stigma attached to being in therapy, or are frightened because they don't know what happens in psychotherapy.

We'll focus on three major questions about psychotherapy: Why is psychotherapy effective? What skills does a therapist need? How do I choose a therapist?

For therapy to work, a therapist should be compassionate, helpful, and supportive.

For therapy to work, a client should make a commitment in terms of time, money, and energy.

Why is psychotherapy effective?
According to well-known psychotherapy researcher Hans Strupp (1989), there are four requirements for psychotherapy to be effective:

1 *Therapist.* Depending on the particular kind of therapy, the therapist must be personally able and professionally trained to listen, question, support, and interpret the client's thoughts and behaviors.

2 *Client.* The client must be internally motivated. That is, the client should be eager and willing to work hard and make the necessary changes for resolving his or her problems.

3 *Partnership.* The client and therapist need to form a helping and supportive partnership. Having such a partnership will further trust between client and therapist, which in turn will provide continued support for the client.

4 *Commitment.* The client must be at a point in his or her life where all the conditions are present for change. These conditions include the client being motivated, having or finding financial resources, making a time commitment, and being open to making major changes.

These four requirements are called nonspecific factors. **Nonspecific factors in psychotherapy** *are conditions common to many different kinds of therapies, including a verbal interaction between therapist and client, a motivated client, the formation of a supportive therapist-client relationship, and a program to work out the client's problems.* Because nonspecific factors are common to many different kinds of therapies, the specific kind of therapy may not be as important as the skill of the therapist.

What skills does a therapist need?
According to Strupp (1989), there are two skills the therapist should have in order to be effective. The first and foremost skill is the ability *to create an accepting and compassionate atmosphere.* Such an atmosphere has in itself great healing value because, for many individuals, it is a new and gratifying experience to be accepted and listened to in a respectful manner. In fact, many people who seek psychotherapy have previously suffered from a lack of significant others and have received little help, support, and guidance in their times of need. The accepting and compassionate atmosphere of psychotherapy helps the client talk about troublesome thoughts or actions, recall unpleasant experiences, and perhaps relive traumatic events. The therapist creates this compassionate atmosphere partly by consistently and diligently using his or her energies to listen to the client, to understand the client's personal experiences, and to talk to the client in language that makes sense.

The second skill the therapist needs is the ability *to deal with the client's feelings* that will be projected onto the therapist. In other words, the therapist must be skilled at dealing with and helping the client work through transference. The client responds emotionally as if the therapist were a stand-in parent, lover, friend, or sibling from the past; these projected emotional feelings can be very powerful. The therapist must have the skill to hold his or her ground and not be manipulated by the client while at the same time helping the client work out these emotional feelings.

How do I choose a therapist?
Just as we ask others for advice about choosing a medical doctor, we can ask friends, psychology professors, or our medical doctors to recommend a therapist. In addition, most universities and colleges have counseling centers that make recommendations. Many larger cities also have community mental health programs that can provide recommendations.

Finally, knowing about what goes on in psychotherapy and what skills a therapist needs can be a help in choosing a therapist. If, in the initial interview, you do not like the therapist's manner and feel that you do not trust the therapist, you should voice these feelings. The therapist will discuss your feelings, and if they cannot be resolved to your satisfaction, the therapist will usually recommend a number of other therapists for your consideration.

Summary/Self-Test

1. Up until the 1800s, mental disorders were handled in a way that was very primitive and in many cases cruel. In the 1800s Dorothea Dix publicized the terrible living conditions and the lack of reasonable treatment of mental patients in the United States. Her work was part of the reform or _____ treatment movement, which led to building huge mental hospitals for the humane treatment of mental patients.

2. The 1950s were marked by the discovery and use of (a)_____ drugs, which allowed many mental patients to regain some normal functioning. As a result of these drugs, mental patients were released from mental hospitals and sent back into the community, a process called (b)_____. People with mental disorders that do not require hospitalization often seek treatment in individual psychotherapy sessions, which may be provided in private offices or in community mental health centers.

■ *What were the driving forces in changing the treatment of mental patients over the past centuries?*

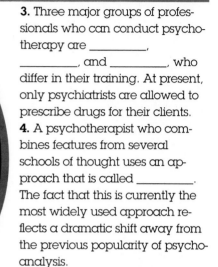

3. Three major groups of professionals who can conduct psychotherapy are _____, _____, and _____, who differ in their training. At present, only psychiatrists are allowed to prescribe drugs for their clients.

4. A psychotherapist who combines features from several schools of thought uses an approach that is called _____. The fact that this is currently the most widely used approach reflects a dramatic shift away from the previous popularity of psychoanalysis.

5. A large number of studies show that approximately 66% of clients who seek psychotherapy show improvement; the remaining clients do not improve or, in a very small number of cases, actually get worse. Even so, for many mental disorders, _____ is an effective treatment.

■ *The word on campus is that a professor in sociology is a great therapist. How can this be since she isn't trained in psychotherapy?*

6. Helping the client become aware of and understand the causes of his or her problems is the goal of insight therapy. Freud developed one of the first forms of insight therapy, which he called (a)_____. At the core of psychoanalysis is the idea that psychological and physical symptoms rise from unconscious (b)_____ that a person cannot voluntarily uncover.

7. Freud developed three techniques that he believed provide clues to unconscious conflicts and repressed thoughts. A technique that encourages clients to talk about any thoughts or images that enter their heads is called (a)_____; it was one of Freud's important methodological discoveries and one that psychoanalysts use today to probe a client's unconscious thoughts, desires, and conflicts. His technique of analyzing dreams, called (b)_____, is based on the assumption that dreams contain underlying, hidden meanings and symbols that provide clues to unconscious thoughts and desires. Freud would say that mistakes we make in everyday speech can be embarrassing because they reflect unconscious thoughts that we would prefer not to know or have revealed; these are called (c)_____.

8. During the course of therapy, a patient will project conflict-ridden emotions onto the therapist; this process is called (a)_____. Freud's explanation of this process was one his major contributions. By working through transference the patient can evaluate his or her unrealistic impulses and anxieties and see the past in a more realistic way. Working through transference is one of the two essential requirements for improvement in psychoanalysis; the other is that the patient achieves (b)_____ into the causes of his or her problem.

9. Psychoanalysis may be long and difficult, in part because the patient has so many defenses against admitting repressed feelings and thoughts. A patient's reluctance to work through feelings or recognize unconscious conflicts and repressed thoughts is called _____.

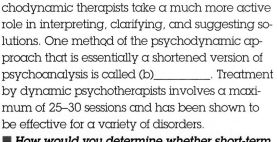

■ *Would it be possible to write a computer program to be a Freudian analyst? How good would your computer/analyst be?*

PSYCHOANALYSIS TODAY

10. Some of the factors that contributed to the decline in psychoanalysis's popularity included the fact that many problems formerly dealt with in psychoanalysis can now be successfully treated with _____. Further, a number of competing therapies are equally effective but less costly than psychoanalysis in both time and money.

11. A therapy approach that assumes that symptoms are signs of more basic underlying problems, that transference needs to be worked out, and that the primary role of the therapist is to interpret and clarify the patient's behaviors is called the (a)_____ approach. This approach is similar to traditional psychoanalysis, but psy-

chodynamic therapists take a much more active role in interpreting, clarifying, and suggesting solutions. One method of the psychodynamic approach that is essentially a shortened version of psychoanalysis is called (b)_____. Treatment by dynamic psychotherapists involves a maximum of 25–30 sessions and has been shown to be effective for a variety of disorders.

■ *How would you determine whether short-term dynamic therapy, which takes a fraction of the time of psychoanalysis, is as effective as psychoanalysis?*

CULTURAL DIVERSITY: A HEALER

12. Western psychotherapy assumes that the major cause of a problem is something the person feels, thinks, or did. In contrast, healers of Bali assume that the cause of the problem is an evil spirit cast by someone else. Since balians seem to have success rates similar to those reported by psychotherapists, it appears that many different kinds of _____ can help people overcome their problems.

■ *Do psychoanalysts use rituals that are analogous to the rituals used by the Bali healers?*

APPLYING/EXPLORING: SEEKING PSYCHOTHERAPY

13. Conditions that are common to many different kinds of therapies are called _____ factors. These factors include verbal interaction between therapist and client, an internally motivated client, the formation of a supportive therapist-client relationship, and a program to work out the client's problems. Because nonspecific factors are common to many different kinds of therapies, the specific kind of therapy may not be as important as the skill of the therapist.

■ *Jason has a drug problem and has lost interest in college. His parents want him to go into psychotherapy but Jason wants to get better on his own. What would you recommend?*

MODULE 30
THERAPY II

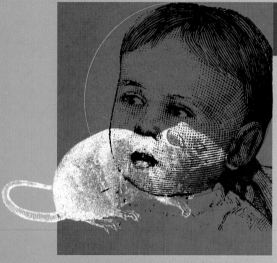

Why was Albert afraid of a white rat?

How could an infant be made to fear a white rat? The answer introduces one of the most famous infants in psychology.

Little Albert was about 9 months old when he was presented with a number of objects to see which ones he might fear. For example, he was suddenly and successively shown a white rat, a rabbit, a dog, a monkey, several masks, cotton wool, and burning newspapers. At no time did Albert show fear of these objects.

Next, Albert was tested with a loud sound. As one experimenter stood in front of and distracted Albert, another stood behind him and struck a steel bar a sharp blow with a hammer that made a very loud sound. Albert started violently, his breathing was checked, and his arms were raised in characteristic manner. On the third occasion of the loud sound, Albert broke into a sudden crying fit, indicating that the stimulus had elicited fear.

When Albert was about 11 months old, he was tested again. This time he was seated on a table as a white rat was suddenly taken from a basket and presented to him. Albert began to reach for the rat, but as he touched the animal the steel bar was struck immediately behind his head. The boy jumped violently and fell forward, burying his face in the mattress. He was brought back ten days later for further testing. During this session, the pairing of the rat and noise was repeated about five times. Then the rat was presented alone, without the loud sound. The instant the rat appeared, Albert began to cry. The experimenter, John Watson, concluded, "This was as convincing a case of a completely conditioned fear response as could have been theoretically pictured." (adapted from Watson & Rayner, 1920)

And so reads the case of Little Albert, one of the most famous infants in the history of psychology. We do know that Albert was conditioned to fear a white rat and that his fear was generalized to similar objects, such as a white rabbit, a dog, a fur coat, and cotton wool, but not to dissimilar objects, such as wood blocks. The conditioning of Little Albert's emotional responses raised new questions about the development of emotional disorders. For example, if emotional responses could be conditioned, perhaps they could also be extinguished. In a sense, the case of Little Albert laid some of the groundwork for behavior therapy. **Behavior therapy,** *which is based on classical and operant conditioning, emphasizes treatment of specific behaviors and working toward specific goals without focusing on mental events or underlying unconscious factors.* Behavior therapy, which began in the 1950s, remains popular today.

What's Coming

In the first part of this module we'll discuss behavior therapy and cognitive therapy. In the second part we'll examine person-centered therapy.

Let's see what happens in behavior therapy.

Behavior Therapy

As you read the following interaction between a client and a therapist, notice the hallmarks of behavior therapy, which focuses on identifying and changing specific behaviors.

Client: The basic problem is that I have the tendency to let people step all over me. I don't know why, but I just have difficulty in speaking my mind.

Therapist: So you find yourself in a number of different situations where you don't respond the way you would really like to. And if I understand correctly, you would like to learn how to behave differently.

Client: Yes. But you know, I have tried to handle certain situations differently, but I just don't seem to be able to do so.

Therapist: Well, maybe you've tried to do too much too fast in the past, and consequently weren't very successful. Maybe a good way to look at the situation is to imagine yourself at the bottom of a staircase, wanting to get to the top. It's probably too much to ask to get there in one gigantic leap. Perhaps a better way to go about changing your reaction in these situations is to take it one step at a time.

Client: That would seem to make sense, but I'm not sure if I see how it could be done.

Therapist: Well, there are probably certain situations in which it would be less difficult for you to assert yourself, such as telling your boss that he forgot to pay you for the past four weeks.

Client (*laughing*): I guess in that situation, I would say something. Although I must admit, I would feel uneasy about it.

Therapist: But not as uneasy as if you went in and asked him for a raise.

Client: No. Certainly not.

Therapist: So, the first situation would be low on the staircase, whereas the second would be higher up. If you can learn to handle easier situations, then the more difficult ones would present less of a problem. And the only way you can really learn to change your reactions is through practice.

Client: In other words, I really have to go out and actually force myself to speak up more, but taking it a little bit at a time?

Therapist: Exactly. And as a way of helping you carry it off in the real-life situations, I think it would be helpful if we reviewed some of these situations and your reactions to them beforehand. In a sense, going through a dry run. It's safer to run through some of these situations here, in that it really doesn't "count" if you don't handle them exactly as you would like to. Also, it can provide you an excellent opportunity to practice different ways of reacting to these situations, until you finally hit on one which you think would be best.

Client: That seems to make sense. (adapted from Goldfried & Davison, 1976)

A behavior therapist would focus on helping a client learn to be more assertive and not be walked on.

What happens in behavior therapy?
Instead of letting the client free associate, which is a major technique of psychoanalysis, the behavior therapist moves quickly to discuss a program for behavior change. The emphasis in behavior therapy is on modifying observable behaviors. The therapist focuses on a specific problem—in this case, the client's unassertiveness—and discusses specific goals with the client—in this case, learning to be assertive or to speak up. The therapist helps the client change problem behaviors, first in less threatening situations and then in more threatening ones.

Let's see how a behavior therapist might treat a phobia.

Behavior Therapy

Treatment of Phobias

Jack was a high school senior who wanted to be an ambulance driver. But he had one serious problem: he passed out at the sight or discussion of blood. He had been afraid of blood for years and had fainted about 20 times in science and biology classes. He even felt queasy when bloody accidents or operating-room scenes were shown on television. He worried that his supervisor would find out about his phobia and not let him try out for ambulance driver. Other than that, he was happy at school, rarely became depressed, and was generally easygoing. His only real problem was this phobia of blood (Yule & Fernando, 1980).

Some therapies for phobias might require years of treatment; for instance, a psychoanalyst would search for unconscious conflicts causing the phobia. In contrast, behavior therapists would take a direct approach to the treatment, requiring from 5 to 30 sessions. Behavior therapists have developed a number of powerful and effective phobia treatment techniques that involve exposing the client to the feared stimulus (Rachman, 1990). Let's follow Jack through one particular technique—desensitization.

Desensitization. Behavior therapists assume that Jack's phobia was acquired through a conditioning process and that it can therefore be "unconditioned." At the heart of the unconditioning process is exposure to the feared object. **Desensitization** *is a technique of behavior therapy in which the client is gradually exposed to the feared object while simultaneously practicing relaxation.* Desensitization involves three steps:

1 *Relaxation.* Jack learned to practice a form of relaxation, in his case progressive relaxation. This involves tensing and relaxing various muscle groups, beginning with the toes and working up to the head. By tensing and relaxing various muscle groups, he learned how to put himself into a relaxed state. Learning progressive relaxation required several weeks with at least one 20-minute session every day.

2 *Stimulus hierarchy.* Next Jack made up a **stimulus hierarchy:** *a list of feared stimuli, arranged in order from least to most feared.* With the help of his therapist, Jack made a stimulus hierarchy of various situations associated with blood. A rating of 1 indicated that he felt "not at all scared" if confronted by this stimulus, while a rating of 10 indicated that he would probably feel "about to pass out." Here is Jack's hierarchy:

Rating	Situation
1	Seeing the word *blood*
1	Small cut on own finger
5	Bad cut on own finger
5	Watching heart operation on TV
5	Needle being put into arm
6	Seeing someone being cut in school
7	Blood from own finger dripping on floor
9	Unable to stop blood on own
10	Needle drawing blood out

Notice that the items in this hierarchy are ranked in a way that provides gradual exposure to the feared stimulus, blood.

3 After successfully completing steps 1 and 2, Jack was ready to combine relaxation while simultaneously imagining the feared stimuli in his hierarchy.

Desensitization training began when Jack put himself into a relaxed state and then imagined the first or least-feared item in his hierarchy, seeing the word *blood.* He tried to remain in a relaxed state while vividly imagining the word *blood.* He repeated this procedure until he felt no tension or anxiety in this situation. At this point, he went on to the next item in his hierarchy. Jack repeated the procedure of pairing relaxation with images of each feared item until he reached the last and most feared item.

If Jack became anxious at any point, he immediately stopped imagining that item. For example, suppose Jack became anxious while imagining a needle being put into his arm. In this case, he went back to the immediately preceding item, watching a heart operation on TV, and repeated the procedure. If he remained relaxed while imagining watching a heart operation on TV, he went on to the next item again. Jack continued desensitization training until he could imagine all the stimuli in his hierarchy without becoming anxious.

Through the desensitization program described here, Jack's blood phobia was treated in five one-hour sessions. A follow-up five years later indicated that Jack was still free of his blood phobia, had not developed any substitute symptoms, and was training to be an ambulance driver (Yule & Fernando, 1980).

Desensitization appears to be most effective if, instead of just imagining the items on his list, the client is gradually exposed to the actual situations, such as drawing blood. Such treatment is called *in vivo desensitization* (the phrase *in vivo* is Latin for "in real life").

Jack's fear of blood would be considered a simple phobia, for which desensitization has proved to be very effective. Social phobias, agoraphobia, dental phobias, and phobias accompanied by panic attacks are more difficult to treat and may require 20 to 30 sessions. However, as shown in the graph, many of these phobia have also been successfully treated with some form of exposure therapy (Hafner, 1983). Of course, the success of desensitization is not guaranteed; a small percentage of people with phobias fail to benefit from the treatment or benefit to only a small degree (Klein et al., 1983). Psychologists believe that exposure to the feared stimulus is critical and that desensitization is one way of bringing about the exposure (Marks, 1991). Another technique of exposure is called flooding.

Clients with agoraphobia, symptoms of panic attacks, and anxiety were treated with twelve hours of exposure—going out in public—over a two-week period. A year after completing treatment, clients reported a significant reduction in agoraphobia, panic attacks, and anxiety.

Flooding. During desensitization, Jack was gradually exposed to his feared stimulus, blood. **Flooding** *is another technique of behavior therapy in which the client is immediately and directly exposed to the most feared stimulus.* In Jack's case, flooding might involve having him hold a container of blood.

During a flooding session, which may last several hours, Jack would be asked either to imagine a needle drawing blood from his arm or to hold an actual container of blood, called *in vivo flooding.* During flooding, Jack is encouraged to experience the fear and not try to escape it. Because Jack will experience intense fear and anxiety during flooding, this procedure requires the guidance and support of a trained therapist. Flooding has been shown to be an effective treatment for phobias (Wilson, 1982).

Now let's see how behavior therapy has fared.

Why would someone hold a container of blood?

Flooding is a treatment for phobia that involves exposure to the most feared stimulus.

Behavior Therapy

Behavior Therapy Today

How well does behavior therapy work?

The number of journals, articles, therapists, and societies devoted to behavior therapy indicates that it remains popular today (Martin, 1991). Let's examine the advantages and criticisms of behavior therapy.

Behavior therapy focuses on changing behaviors to help a client escape from his or her maze of problems.

Advantages

Some advantages of behavior therapy stem from the fact that it has a strong experimental foundation: the principles of behavior therapy grew out of laboratory research on learning and conditioning. One such principle, an emphasis on changing observable behaviors, is one of behavior therapy's major advantages over other approaches (Reiss & Bootzin, 1985). A second advantage is behavior therapy's emphasis on evaluating the effectiveness of its techniques. For example, in this and previous chapters we have described a variety of specific behavior therapy techniques for changing behavior, including self-observation, goal setting, self-reinforcement, modeling, role playing or practicing new behaviors, desensitization, and flooding. In some cases, these techniques provide yet another advantage in that they may be used in self-help programs without the assistance of a therapist. For more serious problems or additional support, the aid and help of a therapist may be needed.

Another advantage is behavior therapy's wide application. Initially confined to treating a narrow range of problems, behavior therapy applications have expanded dramatically to include problems with weight, social skills, depression, negative emotions, sexual dysfunction, and stress management. In addition, behavior therapy is now used in individual, marital, and group settings, as well as in combination with drug therapies. Just as important, behavior therapy has been shown to be more effective in treating problems than placebos are (Clum & Bowers, 1990). At the heart of behavior therapy is a single idea: the best way to deal with behavioral problems is to change behavior.

Criticisms

Therapists who prefer a more psychodynamic approach criticize behavior therapy because it does not examine underlying factors. Consider the problem of a student with failing grades. Poor grades may simply indicate lack of academic skills or excessive test anxiety, which is probably what a behavior therapist would concentrate on. In such cases, simply treating the symptoms may solve the problem. However, failing grades may also reflect the presence of some more basic conflict, such as dealing with achievement pressures from parents or being unhappy with one's career choice. In these cases, treating the symptoms does not address underlying problems that are contributing to current difficulties (Wachtel, 1982).

Behavior therapists are also criticized for neglecting the therapist-client relationship (Goldfried, 1982). For example, the fact that a client misses sessions, misunderstands instructions, or does not complete homework assignments might be interpreted by a psychodynamic therapist as a sign of transference or resistance, whereas a behavior therapist might ignore these behaviors. Psychodynamic therapists argue that behavior therapists should be more aware of signs of transference and resistance that may interfere with the treatment's progress.

Especially during the past decade, behavior therapy has been criticized for neglecting cognitive behaviors, such as maladaptive thought patterns and irrational beliefs, that may significantly influence behavior (Rachman, 1991). These criticisms have resulted in a relatively recent approach, called cognitive therapy, that we will discuss next.

Cognitive Therapy

When can thinking be dangerous?

As you read the following interaction between a cognitive therapist and a client, notice how the client tries to avoid admitting that her thoughts influence her feelings. The client is a 26-year-old graduate student who has bouts of depression.

Client: I agree with the descriptions of me but I guess I don't agree that the way I think makes me depressed.

Therapist: How do you understand it?

Client: I get depressed when things go wrong. Like when I fail a test.

Therapist: How can failing a test make you depressed?

Client: Well, if I fail I'll never get into law school.

Therapist: So failing the test means a lot to you. But if failing a test could drive people into clinical depression, wouldn't you expect everyone who failed the test to have a depression? . . . Did everyone who failed get depressed enough to require treatment?

Client: No, but it depends on how important the test was to the person.

Therapist: Right, and who decides the importance?

Client: I do.

Therapist: And so, what we have to examine is your way of viewing the test (or the way that you think about the test) and how it affects your chances of getting into law school. Do you agree?

Client: Right.

Therapist: Do you agree that the way you interpret the results of the test will affect you? You might feel depressed, you might have trouble sleeping, not feel like eating, and you might even wonder if you should drop out of the course.

Client: I have been thinking that I wasn't going to make it. Yes, I agree.

Therapist: Now what did failing mean?

Client: (*tearful*): That I couldn't get into law school.

Therapist: And what does that mean to you?

Client: That I'm just not smart enough.

Therapist: Anything else?

Client: That I can never be happy.

Therapist: And how do these thoughts make you feel?

Client: Very unhappy.

Therapist: So it is the meaning of failing a test that makes you very unhappy. In fact, believing that you can never be happy is a powerful factor in producing unhappiness. So, you get yourself into a trap—by definition, failure to get into law school equals "I can never be happy." (Beck et al., 1979, pp. 145–146)

Cognitive therapists assume that our heads contain irrational thoughts that influence our feelings and behaviors.

This excerpt points out a major technique of cognitive therapy—that of helping a client observe and record her thoughts or cognitions. After a client realizes how much thoughts or cognitions influence feelings, the next step is to change the distorted thoughts. **Cognitive therapy** *makes three assumptions: (1) our thoughts shape our emotions and our actions; (2) our beliefs and assumptions shape how we perceive and interpret events; and (3) our distorted thoughts can lead to a variety of disorders.* In contrast to the behavior therapist, who focuses on modifying behaviors, the cognitive therapist focuses on modifying thoughts or cognitions. We'll examine two popular forms of cognitive therapy: Ellis's rational-emotive therapy and Beck's cognitive therapy.

Cognitive Therapy

Ellis's Rational-Emotive Therapy

Do you have irrational beliefs?

Read the sentences on the right (adapted from Ellis, 1970) that describe ways of thinking and feeling and indicate how true each one is for you. Assign each a number from 1 to 5, with 1 indicating that the statement has no application to you and 5 indicating that it has great application.

According to Albert Ellis (1992), these statements reflect various kinds of *irrational beliefs* that may lead to biased and distorted thinking and emotions. Ellis developed a form of cognitive therapy called rational-emotive therapy (RET). **Rational-emotive therapy** *assumes that our irrational interpretations of our experiences, not the experiences themselves, cause problems, such as negative feelings.* Ellis uses humorous names to label common irrational beliefs. For example, *musturbation* is the irrational belief that we must act in some particular way; *awfulization* is the tendency to exaggerate how awful something is. Ellis is known for his directness in therapy and for showing how thoughts influence emotions, which he calls the ABC theory of emotions.

Ellis's ABC Theory of Emotions

A = Activating event

B = Belief triggered by activating event

C = Emotional feeling resulting from belief

____ **1.** It is very important to me to be loved or approved of by almost everyone I meet.
____ **2.** I believe I should be competent at everything I attempt.
____ **3.** I become more upset than I should when things are not the way I want them to be.
____ **4.** My past history is an important determinant of my present behavior. I believe that once something strongly affects my life, it will always affect my behavior.
____ **5.** I become more upset than I should about other people's problems and disturbances.

According to the **ABC theory of emotions,** *A is the activating event in the environment, B is the belief that the event triggers, and C is the emotional feelings resulting from that belief.* For example, in the case of the graduate student, Ellis would say that A is the event of failing a test, B is the belief of not getting into law school, and C is the feeling of depression and unhappiness. In therapy with this client, Ellis might first point out the irrational belief that one must do well on every exam in graduate school. The next step would be to help the client get rid of this belief so that she doesn't keep thinking about it. Finally, Ellis would give the client homework to catch herself thinking irrational beliefs and to work at changing these irrational beliefs.

What is rational-emotive therapy's impact?

Researchers have demonstrated that rational-emotive therapy is effective in treating a variety of disorders (Lyons & Woods, 1991). Ellis's approach not only contributed to the development of cognitive therapy, but many of his ideas about the effects of irrational beliefs have been incorporated into other approaches.

Beck's Cognitive Therapy

When was the last time you made one of the following statements?

"I'm a failure."

"Nothing ever goes right for me."

"Most people don't like me."

"People always criticize me."

"No matter how hard I study it doesn't help."

"I'm worthless."

"No one loves me."

These kinds of statements were typically made by depressed clients whom Aaron Beck was treating in psychoanalytically oriented therapy. Beck discovered that although his clients often made these statements, they were only dimly aware of making them. However, when he drew attention to them, the clients responded by making a whole string of related negative statements. These initial observations on the prevalence of negative statements in mental disorders provided the basis for Beck's cognitive therapy (Beck, 1991). **Beck's cognitive therapy** *assumes that we have automatic thoughts (thoughts that we typically say to ourselves without much notice) and that negative automatic thoughts color and distort how we perceive and interpret things, thus influencing our behaviors and feelings.*

Beck has identified a number of specific maladaptive thoughts that contribute to various symptoms, such as anxiety and depression. For example, thinking "I'm a failure" after doing poorly on one test is an example of *overgeneralization,* which is making blanket judgments about yourself based on a single incident. Thinking "Most people don't like me" is an example of *polarized thinking,* which is sorting information into one of two categories, good and bad. Thinking "People always criticize me" is an example of *selective attention,* which is focusing on one detail so much that you do not notice other events, such as being complimented. Beck believes that maladaptive thought patterns cause a distorted view of oneself and one's world, which in turn may lead to various emotional problems. Thus, the primary goals of cognitive therapy are to identify and change maladaptive thoughts.

How effective is cognitive therapy?
Numerous studies have shown the effectiveness of cognitive therapy in treating a number of disorders, especially depression (Beck, 1991). For example, in one large study cognitive behavior modification and an antidepressant drug were compared to see their relative effectiveness in treating major depression. Clients in cognitive therapy were told how their maladaptive thoughts and irrational beliefs can result in feelings of depression and were instructed in self-monitoring of their thoughts and beliefs. Therapists helped the clients recognize maladaptive patterns, such as overgeneralization and polarized thinking, and to substitute rational responses. The clients were also given homework assignments that involved practicing new thought patterns on their own. The results? Depressive symptoms were significantly reduced by both cognitive therapy and antidepressant drugs. A significant difference was that fewer clients dropped out of the cognitive therapy group than from the drug group; clients' reasons for dropping out were often related to the drug's side effects (Elkin et al., 1989). These data indicate that cognitive therapy can be as effective as antidepressant drugs in treating some forms of depression.

Cognitive therapy has also been used effectively to treat panic attacks, generalized anxiety disorders, eating disorders, and couples' problems (Beck, 1991). According to Beck, cognitive therapy has successfully challenged the giants in the field, psychoanalysis and behavior therapy.

What irrational beliefs guide your behavior?

Humanistic Therapy

What's different about the humanistic approach?

As we discussed in Chapter 12, the **humanistic approach** *assumes that each individual has great freedom in directing his or her future, a large capacity for achieving personal growth, a considerable amount of intrinsic worth, and an impressive number of talents to achieve self-fulfillment.* Humanists believe that you have control of your fate and are free to become whatever you are capable of being. Those who ascribe to this approach disagree with the theory behind psychoanalysis, which emphasizes how unconscious fears and feelings influence or control one's destiny. Humanists also disagree with behavior therapy, which stresses how the environment determines or manipulates one's behaviors.

The humanistic approach emphasizes the positive side of human nature, along with its creative and constructive tendencies and its focus on building caring relationships. This concept of human nature is the most distinctive feature of the humanistic approach and sets it far apart from the behavioral and psychoanalytic approaches (DeCarvalho, 1990). One form of humanistic therapy was developed by Carl Rogers, who called it client-centered therapy but then changed the name to person-centered therapy.

Person-Centered Therapy

Carl Rogers, as a practicing therapist, initially used a psychoanalytic approach. However, he grew disillusioned with this approach because of its deterministic and pessimistic view of human nature and its overemphasis on unconscious forces and biological instincts. Rogers made a 180-degree change from psychoanalysis and developed person-centered therapy. **Person-centered therapy** *assumes that each person has an actualizing tendency, which is a tendency to develop one's full potential; the therapist's task is to show compassion and positive regard in helping the client reach his or her potential.*

What happens in person-centered therapy?

Let's see what happens in person-centered therapy. In this case, the client is a mother who is having problems letting her daughter be independent.

Client: I'm having a lot of problems dealing with my daughter. She's 20 years old; she's in college; I'm having a lot of trouble letting her go . . . And I have a lot of guilt feelings about her; I have a real need to hang on to her.

Rogers: A need to hang on so you can kind of make up for the things you feel guilty about—is that part of it?

Client: There's a lot of that . . . Also, she's been a real friend to me, and filled my life . . . And it's very hard with a lot of empty places now that she's not with me.

Rogers: The old vacuum, sort of, when she's not there.

Client: Yes, yes. I also would like to be the kind of mother that could be strong and say, you know, "go and have a good life," and it's really hard for me to do that.

Rogers: It's very hard to give up something that's been so precious in your life, but also something that I guess has caused you pain when you mentioned guilt.

Client: Yeah, and I'm aware that I have some anger toward her that I don't always get what I want. I have needs that are not met. And, uh, I don't feel I have a right to those needs. You know . . . she's a daughter; she's not my mother—though sometimes I feel as if I'd like her to mother me . . . It's very difficult for me to ask for that and have a right to it.

Rogers: So it may be unreasonable, but still, when she doesn't meet your needs, it makes you mad.

Client: Yeah. I get very angry, very angry with her.

(*pause*)

Rogers: You're also feeling a little tension at this point, I guess.

Client: Yeah, yeah. A lot of conflict . . .

Rogers: A lot of pain.

Client: A lot of pain.

Rogers: A lot of pain. Can you say anything more what that's about? (Rogers, 1989)

Notice in this excerpt that Rogers avoids giving any directions, advice, or disapproval. Instead, Rogers shows the client that he understands what the client is feeling. One technique for showing understanding is *restating* (often called reflecting) the client's concerns. This shows the client that the therapist is actively listening to and understanding what the client is saying. This reflection of the client's feelings is one of the basic techniques of the person-centered approach.

Why did Rogers develop person-centered therapy?
A number of reasons were behind Rogers's development of this therapy. He was not only dissatisfied with the assumptions and goals of psychoanalysis but disagreed with the role the therapist took in traditional psychoanalysis. Specifically, he objected to the expert role the therapist played and the assumption that the therapist—and not the client—was responsible for the client's progress. Rogers turned this assumption around and said that clients themselves have the capacity for change and are responsible for change. He changed the role of the therapist from that of an all-knowing and analyzing expert to a helper or facilitator. Although Rogers downplayed the importance of the therapist, he did believe that the therapist's characteristics fostered growth and change.

What characteristics should a therapist have?
Rogers believed that certain characteristics of the therapist are necessary and sufficient to bring about the client's change. The therapist needs to have empathy, positive regard, and genuineness. *Empathy* is the ability to understand what the client is saying and feeling. *Positive regard* is the ability to communicate caring, respect, and regard for the client. *Genuineness* is the ability to be real and nondefensive in interactions with the client. Rogers and his followers assumed that a therapist with these three characteristics would be able to help a client change and grow.

Person-centered therapists help clients open the doors to their full potentials.

Are empathy, positive regard, and genuineness critical to the success of therapy? One way to answer this question is to determine whether these characteristics tend to be associated with successful resolution of clients' problems. A number of studies have shown that these three characteristics are not always related to successful outcomes (Garfield, 1980), which indicates that therapist characteristics are not sufficient to bring about change as Rogers assumed. Person-centered therapy does result in successful treatment, but the success appears to be because of nonspecific factors it shares with other psychotherapeutic approaches (Garfield, 1980).

What impact has person-centered therapy had?
In the 1940s and 1950s Carl Rogers's ideas had a great impact on psychotherapy. His person-centered therapy is called a *humanistic* therapy because he placed so much emphasis on the client's own potential and ability to change. We can see this developed in several later forms of therapy, including the group approach called "encounter groups."

Studies show that person-centered therapy is effective in treating a variety of problems and is also used in counseling settings. Two frequent results of successful person-centered therapy are increased self-esteem and greater openness to experience (Raskin & Rogers, 1989). Although person-centered therapy is less popular today than it was in the 1950s and 1960s, many of Rogers's techniques have been adopted by therapists who use an eclectic approach.

After the Concept/Glossary we'll compare the four types of therapies that we have discussed.

1. A therapy based on classical and operant conditioning that emphasizes treatment of specific behaviors and working toward specific goals without focusing on mental events or underlying unconscious factors is called _____ therapy.

2. One technique of behavior therapy in which the client is gradually exposed to the feared object while simultaneously practicing to relax during each exposure is called (a)_____. Another technique of behavior therapy in which the client is immediately and directly exposed to the most feared stimulus is called (b)_____

3. One type of therapy makes three assumptions: our thoughts shape our emotions and our actions; our beliefs and assumptions shape how we perceive and interpret events; and our distorted thoughts can lead to a variety of disorders. This is called _____ therapy.

4. There are several variations of cognitive therapy. The therapy of Albert Ellis assumes that our irrational interpretations of our experiences, not the experiences themselves, cause problems, such as negative feelings. This is called (a)_____ therapy. Along with this therapy Ellis developed a theory of emotions in which A is the activating event in the environment, B is the belief that the event triggers, and C is the emotional feelings resulting from that belief. This is called the (b)_____ theory of emotions.

5. Another variation of cognitive therapy assumes that we have negative automatic thoughts that color and distort how we perceive and interpret things and that influence our behaviors and feelings. This is called _____ therapy.

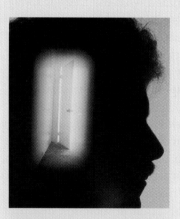

6. An approach that assumes that each individual has great freedom in directing his or her future, a large capacity for achieving personal growth, a considerable amount of intrinsic worth, and an impressive number of talents to achieve self-fulfillment is called the _____ approach.

7. A humanistic therapy developed by Carl Rogers assumes that each person has an actualizing tendency and the therapist's task is to show compassion and positive regard in helping the client reach his or her potential. Rogers called this (a)_____ therapy. Rogers also assumed that empathy, positive regard, and genuineness, which are (b)_____ of the therapist, are important to bringing about change and growth in the client.

Answers: 1. behavior; 2. (a) desensitization, (b) flooding; 3. cognitive; 4. (a) rational-emotive, (b) ABC; 5. Beck's cognitive; 6. humanistic; 7. (a) person-centered, (b) characteristics.

Psychotherapy: A Review

In these two modules we have discussed four therapies: psychoanalysis, behavior therapy, cognitive therapy, and person-centered therapy. Let's review their different assumptions and techniques.

Psychoanalysis

History. The granddaddy of all therapies, psychoanalysis was developed in the late 1800s and early 1900s by Sigmund Freud.

Basic assumption. Emotional problems are caused by underlying unconscious conflicts.

Techniques. The psychoanalyst's techniques for uncovering unconscious conflicts are free association, dream interpretation, and interpretation of slips of the tongue. Freud was the first to recognize the importance of transference and resistance during therapy. The patient overcomes his or her problems by bringing up and dealing with unconscious conflicts.

Behavior Therapy

History. Developed in the 1950s from laboratory research on operant and classical conditioning, behavior therapy was a reaction against psychoanalysis's emphasis on unconscious and unobservable conflicts.

Basic assumption. Emotional problems are learned and can be unlearned.

Techniques. The behavior therapist's techniques include desensitization, flooding, role playing, and modeling. The client overcomes his or her problems through changing behavior.

Cognitive Therapy

History. Developed in the late 1970s and early 1980s, cognitive therapy was partly a reaction against psychoanalysis's focus on hidden conflicts and behavior therapy's emphasis on observable behaviors.

Basic assumption. Irrational thoughts and beliefs color our feelings and actions, distort our perceptions, and result in various problems.

Techniques. The cognitive therapist's techniques include recognizing irrational thoughts and replacing them with positive ones. The client deals with his or her problems by gradually substituting positive thoughts for distorted ones.

Person-Centered Therapy

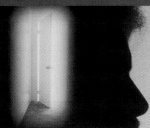

History. Developed in the 1940s by Carl Rogers, person-centered therapy was a reaction against psychoanalysis's focus on the expert role of the therapist.

Basic assumption. The client has the capacity to actualize and reach his or her full potential and the client, not the therapist, is responsible for change.

Techniques. The person-centered therapist's techniques include reflecting the client's concerns and showing three characteristics: empathy, positive regard, and genuineness. The client deals with his or her problems through growth and change in an understanding and supportive therapeutic environment.

Why are such different therapies effective?

At first glance it is somewhat astonishing that four therapies with such different assumptions and techniques can all be relatively effective. There are differences in effectiveness, however, and certain therapies are recommended for certain disorders. For example, behavior therapy is useful for treating phobias and obsessive-compulsive disorders, while cognitive therapy is effective for overcoming depression (Goldfried, Greenberg, & Marmer, 1990). One reason for the effectiveness of all therapies is that they share the same basic underlying characteristics, or nonspecific factors. As mentioned earlier, nonspecific factors include verbal interactions, a supportive and trusting relationship between therapist and client, and the creation of an accepting atmosphere in which the client feels comfortable to admit problems and work on change.

Next we'll examine some specific cognitive techniques that have proven effective in dealing with a variety of problems.

APPLYING/ EXPLORING: COGNITIVE TECHNIQUES

One trademark of cognitive therapy is that the client is given *homework,* which focuses on first identifying irrational thoughts and beliefs and then changing them. We'll examine several typical homework assignments that can be carried out on one's own or that can be accomplished with the help and support of a therapist.

Thought Stopping

How can Carol stop thinking about her ex-boyfriend?

Carol was depressed because she couldn't stop thinking about her former boyfriend, Fred. She thought about Fred almost every day, and her thinking triggered a chain of other negative thoughts: "I feel that I am a failure. I feel ugly and useless. I keep thinking about not being able to have a relationship. I feel really depressed and I don't want to do anything." (Martin, 1982)

Carol has a relatively common problem: the inability to stop thinking about something that bothers and upsets her. Let's look at a cognitive technique for stopping troublesome thoughts, which has three steps:

1 *Self-monitoring.* As with all cognitive procedures, the first step is **self-monitoring,** *which is observing one's own behavior without making any changes.* In Carol's case it meant that for one week she wrote down all depressing thoughts about Fred that lasted for more than a couple of minutes. In addition, the therapist asked Carol to bring in pictures of herself that showed her in pleasurable activities. These pictures would provide cues for thinking rational thoughts.

2 *Thought stopping.* Each time Carol began to experience a disturbing thought, she would stop what she was doing, clasp her hands, close her eyes, silently yell "Stop!" to herself, and silently count to 10. This was the *thought-stopping procedure.*

3 *Thought substitution.* After counting silently to 10, she would open her eyes and take five photographs out of her purse. She would look at each photograph and read what she had written on the back. For example, one photograph showed her about to board an airplane for a trip. On the back she had written, "I'm my own boss. My life is ahead of me. I can do what I want to do." Carol would then think about the trip and how much she liked to travel. She would do the same for all five photographs.

This thought-substituting procedure took from 1 to 2 minutes. After that, she would return to whatever she had been doing.

One technique for getting rid of bothersome thoughts is thought stopping.

One technique for helping Rose over her phobia of public places is thought substitution.

Irrational Thoughts	Rational Thoughts
• I am much safer if I stay at home.	• Rarely has anything bad happened when I have gone out.
• I feel more protected if I do not have to walk through crowds.	• I have never been harmed by a crowd of people.
• I think something awful will occur if I go to a supermarket.	• Thousands of people go to supermarkets and do their shopping unharmed.
• I can't bear the thought of going to a movie theater.	• Many people enjoy going to movies.

During Carol's first week of self-monitoring, she thought about Fred constantly and spent from 15 minutes to an hour each day crying. However, after using the thought-stopping and thought-substituting procedures for eight weeks, Carol had reduced the time thinking about Fred to the point that she rarely cried or was depressed. A follow-up interview four months after therapy revealed that Carol was no longer having problems thinking about Fred, was no longer depressed, had developed no new symptoms, and had a new boyfriend (Martin, 1982). This and similar studies indicate that thought-stopping techniques can be effective in turning off annoying thoughts (Logan, 1985).

Thought Substitution

How can Rose change her thinking and go out in public?

For many years Rose was trapped in her house because of her intense fear or phobia of public places, which is called agoraphobia. If she even thought about going outside

to do her shopping, she felt pain in her arms and chest, she began to perspire, her heart beat rapidly, and her feet felt like rubber. However, after cognitive therapy, she overcame her agoraphobia.

As part of the overall therapy program, a cognitive therapist asked Rose a number of questions to identify her irrational thoughts. For example, she may have overgeneralized, thinking, "The last time I went out I was terrified; it's sure to happen again." Or Rose may have engaged in polarized thinking: "All my happiness is right here in this house; nothing outside could give me any pleasure." Her thinking might have been distorted by selective attention, such as remembering all those activities outside the house that terrified her and forgetting all those activities that she had once found pleasurable, such as shopping and going to movies.

Rose was asked to make a list of all her irrational thoughts on one side of a sheet of paper. Then, next to each irrational thought, she was asked to write down a rational response that could be substituted for the irrational one. Here are some examples:

There are three steps to thought substitution, a very powerful technique for changing one's feelings and behaviors.

1 Through self-monitoring, write down as many irrational thoughts as possible. If you are in a habit of thinking irrational thoughts, it may require special attention to identify them.

2 Next to the column of irrational thoughts, compose a matching list of rational thoughts. The rational thoughts should be as specific as possible.

3 Begin to practice substituting rational thoughts for irrational ones. Each time you make a substitution, give yourself a mental reward or a pat on the back.

Cognitive therapists assume that irrational thoughts and beliefs are the primary causes of emotional and behavioral problems. Therapeutic homework, such as thought stopping and thought substituting, helps the client practice rational living.

Summary/Self-Test

BEHAVIOR THERAPY

1. Therapy that emphasizes treatment of specific behaviors and working toward specific goals without focusing on mental events or underlying unconscious factors is known as _____ therapy. This form of therapy is based on classical and operant conditioning principles.

2. A technique of behavior therapy in which the client is gradually exposed to the feared object while simultaneously practicing relaxation is called (a)_____. As part of this technique, the client must prepare a list of feared stimuli, arranged in order from least to most feared; this is called a (b)_____ hierarchy. Another technique is for the client to be gradually exposed to the actual situations; this treatment is called (c)_____ desensitization.

3. A technique of behavior therapy in which the client is immediately and directly exposed to the most feared stimulus is called _____; it has been shown to be an effective treatment for phobias. Because clients experience intense fear and anxiety during this procedure, it requires the guidance and support of a therapist.

4. Behavior therapy's emphasis on changing observable _____ and its wide applications are two of its major advantages. However, behavior therapy is criticized for neglecting the maladaptive thought patterns and irrational beliefs that may significantly influence behavior.

■ *Charlie says that he has so much test anxiety that he can't think straight. If you were a behavior therapist, what would you recommend?*

COGNITIVE THERAPY

5. Cognitive therapists, who focus on modifying thoughts or cognitions, make three assumptions: our thoughts shape our emotions and our actions; our beliefs and assumptions shape how we perceive and interpret events; and our distorted thoughts can lead to a variety of _____.

6. A form of cognitive therapy that was developed by Albert Ellis assumes that our irrational interpretations of our experiences—rather than the experiences themselves—cause problems. His therapy is called (a)_____. Ellis's ideas about how thoughts influence emotions are summarized in his (b)_____ theory of emotions.

7. A basic assumption of Beck's cognitive theory is that our (a)_____ negative thoughts color and distort how we perceive and interpret things, thus influencing our behaviors and feelings. For example, making blanket judgments about yourself based on a single incident is called (b)_____. Sorting information into one of two categories is (c)_____. Focusing on one detail so much that you do not notice other events is using (d)_____. Beck believes maladaptive thought patterns such as these cause a distorted view of oneself and one's world, which in turn may lead to various emotional problems.

8. Cognitive therapy has been shown to have approximately the same effectiveness as _____ drugs in treating major depression. Cognitive therapy has also been used effectively to treat panic attacks, generalized anxiety disorders, eating disorders, and couples' problems.

■ *Carol is so shy that she can enjoy herself at parties only by drinking alcohol—often too much. If you were a cognitive therapist, what would you recommend?*

HUMANISTIC THERAPY

9. The approach that emphasizes the positive side of human nature, along with its creative and constructive tendencies and its focus on building caring relationships, is the _____ approach. Those who subscribe to this approach believe that you have control of your fate and are free to become whatever you are capable of being.

10. The form of humanistic therapy developed by Carl Rogers assumes that each person has a ten-

dency to develop his or her full potential, called the (a)_____ tendency. Rogers originally called his approach client-centered therapy but then changed its name to (b)_____ therapy. A basic technique of this approach is to restate or (c)_____ the client's concerns and feelings.

11. Rogers downplayed the importance of the therapist but believed that the therapist's characteristics do foster growth and change. The therapist needs to have the ability to understand what the client is saying and feeling, a trait called (a)_____; the ability to communicate caring, respect, and regard for the client, called (b)_____; and the ability to be real and nondefensive in interactions with the client, called (c)_____.

■ *Dave is thinking about dropping out of college because he is tired of school, having lost all his motivation and interest. If you were a person-centered therapist, what would you recommend?*

PSYCHOTHERAPY: A REVIEW

12. Developed by Sigmund Freud in the late 1800s and early 1900s, the basic assumption of _____ is that emotional problems are caused by underlying unconscious conflicts. Techniques used in this approach are free association, dream interpretation, and interpretation of slips of the tongue.

13. In reaction to psychoanalysis's emphasis on unconscious conflicts, a therapy was developed based on learning principles; it was called _____ therapy. Its basic assumption is that emotional problems are learned and can be unlearned. Its techniques include desensitization, flooding, role playing, and modeling.

14. A therapy that developed in reaction to psychoanalysis's focus on hidden conflicts and behavior therapy's emphasis on observable behaviors is called (a)_____ therapy. Its basic assumption is that irrational thoughts and beliefs color our feelings and actions, distort our perceptions, and result in various problems. Its techniques include recognizing (b)_____ thoughts and replacing them with positive ones.

15. In the 1940s Carl Rogers developed (a)_____ therapy in reaction to psychoanalysis's focus on the expert role of the therapist. Rogers's basic assumption is that the client is responsible for change and has the capacity to (b)_____ and reach his or her full potential. Techniques include reflecting the client's concerns as well as showing the characteristics of empathy, positive regard, and genuineness.

16. Despite their different assumptions and techniques, each of these four therapies can be relatively effective; however, certain therapies are recommended for certain disorders. All the therapies share the same basic underlying characteristics, called _____. These include verbal interactions, a supportive and trusting relationship between therapist and client, and the creation of an accepting atmosphere in which the client feels comfortable to admit problems and work on change.

■ *Janice has a problem with relationships and is thinking about seeking professional help. Which of the four therapies would you recommend?*

APPLYING/EXPLORING: COGNITIVE TECHNIQUES

17. One trademark of cognitive therapy is that the client is given homework, which focuses on first identifying (a)_____ thoughts and beliefs and then changing them. Observing one's behavior without making any changes is called (b)_____ and is the first step in changing one's behavior or thoughts. Two effective techniques for changing one's thoughts, feelings, and behaviors are thought stopping and thought substitution.

■ *Frank has very low confidence and self-esteem but doesn't want to go into therapy. What could he do on his own to raise his levels of confidence and esteem?*

Answers: 1. behavior; 2. (a) desensitization, (b) stimulus, (c) in vivo; 3. flooding; 4. behaviors; 5. disorders; 6. (a) rational-emotive therapy (RET), (b) ABC; 7. (a) automatic, (b) overgeneralization, (c) polarized thinking, (d) selective attention; 8. antidepressant; 9. humanistic; 10. (a) actualizing, (b) person-centered, (c) reflect; 11 (a) empathy, (b) positive regard, (c) genuineness; 12. psychoanalysis; 13. behavior; 14. (a) cognitive, (b) irrational; 15. (a) person-centered, (b) actualize; 16. nonspecific factors; 17. (a) irrational, (b) self-monitoring.

Chapter *Sixteen*
SOCIAL PSYCHOLOGY

MODULE 31
SOCIAL COGNITION

Fran Conley says that for too long she put up with sexism from male colleagues.

In 1975 Fran Conley reached her goal of becoming a board-certified neurosurgeon. At the time, she was one of only two female board-certified neurosurgeons in the United States. Yet despite her exceptional accomplishments, Conley has had to put up with sexist attitudes from male colleagues. For example, she said that as a young neurosurgeon, she was repeatedly propositioned by fellow doctors in front of others, primarily for effect. Conley admits that she tolerated this kind of behavior because she wanted to advance in her profession and be accepted by her colleagues. She believed that once she became a full professor and had sufficient status in her profession, the sexist treatment would cease. She was mistaken.

Even after Conley had achieved the status of a full professor at Stanford Medical Center, the sexism continued. For instance, whenever Conley disagreed with male colleagues, they would jokingly attribute her lack of agreement to a difficult menstrual period. But when male colleagues disagreed, it was viewed as an honest difference of opinions.

Conley described how she is still treated by one of her male colleagues: He walks in during surgery and asks in front of her surgical team, "How's it going, honey?" For a neurosurgeon of Conley's caliber to be called "honey" in front of her operating team is an obvious sign of disrespect and continued sexism.

Finally, on September 1, 1991, Conley had her fill of sexist treatment. She startled Stanford Medical Center by resigning her position as neurosurgeon and professor.

As a postscript to this story, Conley has stayed on to help battle sexism at Stanford Medical Center, which has since appointed a committee on sexual harassment and gender insensitivity—and has censured two top doctors. (adapted from *Los Angeles Times,* June 7, 1991 and *San Francisco Examiner,* June 28, 1992)

The story of Fran Conley illustrates many of the topics of **social psychology,** *a broad field that studies how our thoughts, feelings, perceptions, and behaviors are influenced by interactions with others.* A branch of social psychology is **social cognition,** *the study of how people perceive, store, and retrieve information about social interactions.* Social psychologists study how we form impressions and perceive others, how we form attitudes and stereotypes, how we evaluate social interactions, and why sexism exists—all of which are involved in Fran Conley's story.

What's Coming

In this module we'll examine person perception, social information, attitudes, and persuasion. In the next module we'll discuss a variety of social behaviors, including behavior in groups, helping, and aggression.

Let's begin with an aspect of social cognition that is important in all our social interactions: first impressions and perceptions of others.

Person Perception

How do we form first impressions?

The millions of people who spend time in Disney theme parks are likely to form the impression that all the park employees are well groomed, neat, and nicely dressed. One reason for this impression is a 15-page manual titled "The Disney Look," which carefully spells out the rules for dress and grooming. For example, male employees cannot wear beards or mustaches, and female employees cannot wear eyeliner, nor can they wear pants without a jacket. The use of corporate dress codes is one way to positively influence first impressions, which is part of person perception.

Person perception *involves making judgments about the traits of others through social interactions and gaining knowledge from social perceptions.* The flip side of person perception is image management: how we present ourselves, make impressions, and try to influence others' perceptions of us. Researchers have found that in making first impressions we primarily use three characteristics: sex (physical features), race, and clothing style (Stangor et al., 1992). "The Disney Look" manual is an attempt to regulate one of the three major characteristics, clothing style.

What's your first impression of this person?

What's involved in perceiving people?

Look at the photo of the college student on the right, then write down your impressions. They might include: male, Asian, neatly dressed, friendly, intelligent. Notice that person perception involves not only interpreting obvious information based on what we see, such as sex, race, and clothing, but also making judgments on what we infer, such as the person's personality traits. Here are some of the factors involved in person perception (Fiske & Taylor, 1991):

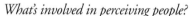

1 *Hidden characteristics.* One of the real challenges in person perception is to make judgments about things we cannot observe, such as personality traits, based on what we *can* observe, such as physical appearance. For example, you probably judged the student in the photo to be friendly, based on his physical appearance.

2 *Two-way process.* Person perception is often a two-way process. This means that our perceptual processes are being distracted and perhaps influenced by thoughts and that, at the same time, we are also being perceived by and making impressions on others.

3 *Seeking causes.* When we perceive people we try to explain why they look, dress, or behave a certain way. We are not satisfied with simply observing how someone looks or behaves but also want to explain why he or she is looking or behaving that way.

4 *Social consequences.* How we perceive someone usually has immediate social consequences. For example, if you perceive a stranger as friendly and warm, you may strike up a conversation, which you would not do if you perceived the stranger as aloof and cold. Similarly, being perceived *by* someone has social consequences. Thus, you would behave differently if you were being perceived by future in-laws than by fellow students.

After reading this list of factors, you may have the impression that person perception is a difficult task. However, you constantly engage in person perception and do so rather effortlessly. One reason person perception seems effortless is that you are aided by a wealth of social information stored in your memory. Let's look at how stored social information can bias person perception.

What's your first impression of this person?

Stereotypes

How biased are our perceptions?

Harry Duh was born in Taiwan and grew up in predominantly white Tallmadge, Ohio. As part of a class project, Harry dressed up as what he called an "Asian nerd" and looked similar to the person in the photo on the left. Harry wanted to study racial stereotyping on his campus. **Stereotypes** *are widely held beliefs that people have certain traits because they belong to a particular group.* Stereotypes tend to be applied uniformly to all members of the group, tend to be extreme, and can be positive or negative. The most common stereotypes are based on sex, ethnic group, or occupation. For example, Harry grew up in a community where the ethnic stereotypes were of whites being superior, beautiful, and strong and of Asians being inferior, ugly, and weak.

Negative stereotypes are often accompanied by prejudice and discrimination. **Prejudice** *refers to an unfair, biased, or intolerant attitude toward another group of people.* An example of prejudice is believing that Asians are inferior, ugly, and weak. **Discrimination** *refers to specific unfair behaviors exhibited toward members of a group.* An example of discrimination is not renting to Asians.

The reactions of both white and fellow Asian students toward Harry when he was dressed as an Asian nerd were quite similar. They teased him, giggled, and jeered behind his back (*San Diego Union*, March 12, 1992). These fellow students apparently acted on two negative stereotypes: the nerd stereotype and the Asian stereotype. Harry's experience illustrates that sometimes we form impressions based on stored social information, specifically stereotypes, that bias and distort our social perceptions.

How do stereotypes influence person perceptions?

Researchers have found that stereotypes have a double effect on person perception (Zarate & Smith, 1990). First, we use information based on a stereotype of a group to make inferences about a specific person in that group. This means that if we have a stereotype of men as independent, we will infer that a particular man is independent. Second, our stereotype activates other social information in long-term memory. This means that other social information related to men, such as being competitive and unemotional, will be activated and applied to our perception of a specific man.

As shown in the graph, in the United States the common stereotypes for men include being independent and competitive and for women include being warm and emotional (Deaux et al., 1985). If we possess these stereotypes, they will bias our perceptions of specific men and women. In turn, our biased perceptions will reinforce and maintain our original stereotypes (Hamilton & Sherman, 1989). Because stereotypes tend to reinforce themselves, they are persistent and resistant to change.

Stereotypes represent an organized form of social knowledge that social psychologists call a *schema*, which is our next topic.

This graph shows some of the common sex stereotypes of men and women.

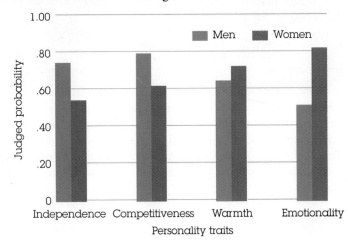

Schemas

How do I filter out irrelevant social information?

Imagine shaking hands with a stranger and then having a five-minute conversation. During those five minutes you are bombarded by many thousands of social stimuli, including the person's sex, race, clothing style, words, tone of voice, facial expressions, eye movement, posture, and countless other social cues. Researchers emphasize the impossibility of attending to, storing, or recalling every stimulus in our social interactions (Kenrick, 1990). Instead we use mental portraits or schemas to help us make sense of our social worlds. As you learned in Chapter 7, **schemas** *are cognitive structures that represent an organized collection of knowledge about people, events, and concepts.* Let's see how a schema helps a customs official do his or her job.

Whom should a customs official search?

Suppose you are a customs official charged with preventing illegal items from entering this country. What kinds of people would you search? After years of experience, customs officials have developed a "smuggler" schema: someone who hesitates before answering, gives short answers, avoids eye contact with the official, and shifts posture (Kraut & Poe, 1980). The smuggler schema reflects the three functions of schemas:

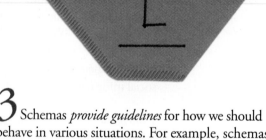

When do schemas act like filters?

1 Schemas help us *select* relevant information from a tremendous amount of incoming social information. For example, we pay attention to only a small amount of information during a social interaction.

2 Schemas help us *interpret* and make sense of social information. In a conversation, for example, we use schemas to process the enormous amount of social information that comes in quickly.

3 Schemas *provide guidelines* for how we should behave in various situations. For example, schemas help keep us from doing embarrassing things in social situations.

There are three major types of social schemas: person, role, and event schemas.

Person Schemas

Person schemas *include our judgments about the traits that we and others possess.* Person schemas vary from sketchy to detailed. If person schemas are sketchy, such as after meeting a stranger, we may use information from related schemas to fill in the missing blanks. Person schemas that contain general information about people who have membership in groups are stereotypes.

Role Schemas

Role schemas *are based on the jobs people perform or the social positions they hold.* If someone tells us her occupation, such as a college professor, we can fairly accurately reconstruct what she does. The reason we often ask, "What do you do?" is so we can use our role schemas to provide information about the person. Role schemas encourage us to develop beliefs and expectations about people so that we can sort them into cognitive pigeonholes.

Event Schemas

Event schemas, also called **scripts**, *contain behaviors that we associate with familiar activities, events, or procedures.* For example, the script for a sporting event is to sing the national anthem before the game starts. The script for a psychology class is to file in, sit down, and be silent. We know not to use a sporting event script in a psychology class. Event schemas help us know what to expect and how to behave in related situations.

Schemas Influence Social Interactions

The advantage of schemas is that they help us organize complex stimuli, seek out relevant information, fill in missing information, and make predictions about how we and others should behave in various situations. The disadvantage of schemas is that they restrict what we attend to, store, and recall and thus cause us to overlook information (Taylor & Crocker, 1981). However, without schemas our social lives would be so complex and overwhelming that we would rarely engage in social interactions.

Let's look more closely at two particular features of schemas.

Schemas Influence Memory

Each of us has our own person schema, which is called a *self schema.* When researchers studied the self schemas of individuals, they identified some as having a feminine self schema (they listed traditional feminine traits) and others as having more of a masculine self schema (they listed a combination of masculine and feminine traits). Thee researchers asked subjects of both types to look at a list of 60 adjectives, some traditionally feminine and some traditionally masculine. The researchers found that individuals with feminine self schemas recalled more feminine than masculine adjectives and remembered more examples of past feminine behaviors than masculine ones. Similar results were reported for persons having masculine self schemas (Markus et al., 1982). These data indicate that self schemas act like spotlights that focus our attention and, as a result, influence what we remember.

Schemas Resist Change

Once schemas are formed, they are highly resistant to change. This is because we generally select and attend to information that supports our schemas and discount information that is inconsistent with them (Sherman, Judd, & Park, 1989). For example, if your parents think of you as somewhat irresponsible, they will notice situations that support this schema, such as your failure to phone when you said you would. At the same time they may overlook events that show you are responsible, such as being on time for all your classes.

Now let's apply what we know about schemas to male-female interactions, specifically cases of sexism.

Schemas and Sexism

We began this module with the story of neurosurgeon Fran Conley, who had resigned because of repeated instances of sexist treatment from her male colleagues. Conley said, "The most frustrating part of this whole thing is that most of the harassment is an attitude where male faculty members are in this time warp; they believe in male superiority and female subservience" (*Los Angeles Times,* June 7, 1991, p. A-3). It appears that in Conley's case some of her male colleagues have sexist schemas by which they perceive women, even neurosurgeons, to be in inferior and subservient roles. The data in the graph indicate that this schema is not confined to Conley's colleagues.

The relatively widespread existence of sexist schemas is indicated by the results of a survey of federal employees and by complaints made to the EEOC (Equal Employment Opportunity Commission).

We already know that sexist schemas have a powerful influence on attention and memory and are highly persistent. Thus, changing sexist schemas will require some intervention, since they are likely to persist and reinforce themselves. The appointment of a Stanford Medical Center committee on sexual harassment and gender insensitivity is a start in replacing sexist schemas with equitable ones.

Once psychologists became aware of schemas, the next step was naturally to try to explain them. Explaining social behavior is one of the most intriguing areas of social cognition.

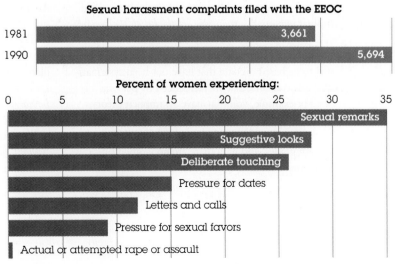

Sexual harassment complaints filed with the EEOC

| 1981 | 3,661 |
| 1990 | 5,694 |

Percent of women experiencing:

0   5   10   15   20   25   30   35

- Sexual remarks
- Suggestive looks
- Deliberate touching
- Pressure for dates
- Letters and calls
- Pressure for sexual favors
- Actual or attempted rape or assault

Attribution

Is there anything unusual about this umpire?

After 13 seasons and 2,000 games in the minor leagues, this umpire was passed over for promotion to the major leagues and released. An evaluation report by the Office for Umpire Development claimed that this umpire's work had "deteriorated in areas of enthusiasm and execution," even though earlier in the season the rating had been "better than average." What is unusual about this umpire is that she is a woman. Pam Postema claims the reason that she was passed over for promotion and released was

What are two possible explanations for why this umpire was not promoted?

that she was a woman. She has filed a sex discrimination suit against professional baseball. As Pam says, "Baseball wasn't ready for a woman umpire no matter how good she was" (*People*, May 5, 1992).

Most sports fans would have an opinion or explanation as to why Pam Postema was not promoted to the major leagues, where there are no women umpires. In a practical sense, the sports fans' readiness to explain behavior makes them amateur social psychologists. Whether amateur or professional, we all rely on the two theories we describe next.

Implicit Personality Theories

The idea that people function like amateur social psychologists was formally stated by Fritz Heider, a famous social psychologist. He said that people behave like *naive scientists* because, even though they lack formal training, they try to explain behaviors in their everyday lives (Heider, 1958). Heider claimed that, like scientists, naive scientists rely on theories. These theories, called **implicit personality theories,** *are the beliefs that we rely on when we analyze the behavior of others.*

Compared to real scientific theories, implicit theories tend to be based on data that have not been systematically collected and that are influenced by personal biases. For example, you may have an implicit theory about how smart attractive people are, why people endanger their lives by drinking and driving, how students get high grades, and why there are no women umpires in the major leagues.

Attribution Theory

Naive scientists and social psychologists also try to understand behavior through **attribution,** *the process by which we determine causes for and explain people's behavior.* For instance, two explanations, or attributions, about Pam Postema not being promoted are that she was not a very good umpire or that she was a woman. **Attribution theory** *is a collection of formal theories that attempt to explain the process of attribution.*

Psychologists have reasoned that, when finding causes for behavior, we have essentially two types of explanations. We can attribute behavior to **disposition,** *or the internal characteristics of the person performing the behavior* (such as that Pam did not have the personal skills to be a good umpire), or we can attribute the behavior to the **situation,** *or the circumstances or context of that behavior* (such as that the major leagues are not ready for a woman umpire).

Factors That Influence Attributions

Is the explanation dispositional or situational?

How do we decide whether Pam was passed over for promotion because of dispositional or situational factors? To answer this question, we can turn to a model developed by psychologist Harold Kelley (1967). Kelley developed a logical model that can be used to decide whether the explanation of a behavior should be attributed to the internal characteristics of the person (dispositional) or to the demands of the environment (situational). According to his **covariation principle,** *we should look for factors that change, or covary, along with the behavior we are trying to explain.* Kelley proposed that in deciding between dispositional and situational explanations, we should look for three factors: consensus, consistency, and distinctiveness.

Was it her disposition or the situation?

Consensus. We should look for **consensus,** *which means determining whether other people engage in the same behavior in the same situation.* With respect to Pam's situation, we should ask whether she calls balls and strikes, makes decisions, and controls the game with the same degree of firmness and accuracy as other umpires. If the answer is no, then we are more likely to attribute her lack of promotion to her disposition, since her skills are less polished. However, if the answer is yes, we are more likely to attribute her lack of promotion to the *situation*—namely, that the major leagues are not willing to have a woman umpire.	**Consistency.** We should look for **consistency,** *which means determining whether the person engages in this behavior every time he or she is in a particular situation.* If Pam makes good decisions in one game and poor decisions in another game, she is not consistent and we are likely to attribute her lack of promotion to her disposition. If Pam is consistent and makes good decisions in every game, then we are likely to attribute her lack of promotion to the situation, or the major league's position on women umpires.	**Distinctiveness.** We should look for **distinctiveness,** *which means determining how differently the person behaves in one situation when compared to other situations.* If Pam makes good decisions in calling balls and strikes and good decisions in calling players out or safe, we would conclude that her umpiring behavior is not distinctive and that her lack of promotion should not be attributed to her disposition but rather to the situation. However, if Pam makes good decisions behind the plate and poor decisions in the field, her umpiring behavior is distinctive and probably should be attributed to her disposition rather than the situation.

High consistency
Low consensus
Low distinctiveness

↓

Dispositional attribution

High consistency
High consensus
High distinctiveness

↓

Situational attribution

Why was Pam fired?

According to Kelley, you will attribute Pam's firing to the *situation*—that is, to the major league's position on women umpires—if there is consensus (her skills are as good as others'), consistency (she makes good decisions through every game), and distinctiveness (she was the only umpire with a good record who was fired).

If we took the time to heed Kelley's three factors and covariation principle, we would be more accurate in deciding whether an explanation is a dispositional or situational attribution. However, as you will see, we rarely have or take such time and thus tend to make errors in attribution.

Attribution

Biases and Errors in Attribution

Why do I make the wrong attributions?

When you read about Kelley's covariation principle, you might have asked, "Do we really go through all that every time we make an attribution?" This is a good question, and the answer is probably no.

Careful attribution takes time and effort. According to the **cognitive miser model**, *people feel they must conserve time and effort by taking cognitive shortcuts* (Taylor, 1981). For example, some social psychologists believe that we tend to underuse agreed upon information and instead prefer to rely on our own self-generated estimates of "what most people would do" in a given situation (Kassin, 1979).

Many such shortcuts and biases have been identified in the attribution process (Fiske & Taylor, 1991). Let's look at three of the most common ones: the fundamental attribution error, the actor-observer effect, and self-serving bias.

Why did this person have an accident?

Why did you get an A on the exam?

Fundamental Attribution Error

According to the **fundamental attribution error,** *we tend to attribute the cause of a behavior to a person's disposition and overlook the demands of the environment or situation* (Ross, 1977). We make the fundamental attribution error when we explain behavior by choosing dispositional causes over situational ones. Examples of fundamental attribution errors include believing that people who get in car accidents are careless, that students who do poorly on an exam are not very smart, and that actors who play tough guys are really tough.

Actor-Observer Effect

The **actor-observer effect** *occurs when we, as actors, attribute our own behavior to situational factors but as observers attribute the behaviors of others to their dispositions.* We fall victim to the actor-observer effect when we attribute our being in a car accident to the situation (a dangerous intersection) but attribute others being in a car accident to their dispositions (they are careless drivers). The actor-observer effect can be lessened when people are asked to imagine themselves in the position of the person they are observing. In one study, people became more sensitive to situational factors that might bring about suicidal behavior when they were asked to imagine themselves as the suicidal person (Goggin & Range, 1986).

Self-Serving Bias

According to the **self-serving bias,** *we attribute success to our disposition and failure to the situation.* That is, the actor-observer effect breaks down when we make attributions after engaging in successful behaviors. According to the self-serving bias, if we get an A on an exam, we tend to attribute our success to our personality traits or disposition (hard work). However, if we get a D on an exam, we attribute our failure to the situation (bad questions). Thus, according to the self-serving bias, we make different and opposite attributions depending on whether we have done well or poorly.

Although our attributions can be a problem when they cause errors in person perception, attributions can also be an advantage when they help us change our behaviors. Let's examine a case in which attributions helped students raise their grades.

Attributions and Grades

How can freshmen get better grades?
The following study provides an example of how attributions helped college freshmen improve their grades and stay in college.

Hypothesis. Researchers chose as their target group college freshmen who were concerned about their academic performance (Wilson & Linville, 1982). The researchers theorized that incoming college students have fears about whether they can handle the work and would be particularly susceptible to attributions about their problems. If freshmen attribute the causes of their academic problems to relatively permanent conditions, they will have little expectation of improvement and lowered motivation, and their chances of improving will be low. This is in part because their attributions cause additional worrying and anxiety, making it even more difficult for them to study. However, if freshmen attribute the causes of their academic problems to temporary conditions, they can develop expectations of improving, work harder, and show improvement. In this study the researchers tried to change students' attributions about academic problems from permanent to temporary ones.

Method. Freshmen who were having academic problems read a booklet about previous freshmen who had similar academic problems but showed improvement later in college. In addition, these subjects watched videotapes of previous students, who described very convincingly how their grade point averages had risen after their freshman year. Next, the subjects were asked to write down all the reasons they could think of why grade point averages might increase after the freshman year. Another group of freshmen with academic problems did not receive any of this information and served as a control group.

Results. As shown in the graph, freshmen who were encouraged to attribute their problems to temporary conditions showed a significant improvement in grade point averages one year after the completion of this study. In addition, only 5% of them dropped out of college, while 25% of those in the control group dropped out. These data suggest two things: (1) it is possible to change students' attributions and, as a result, their expectations about performance, and (2) changing students' attributions and expectations can actually improve grade point averages. As this study illustrates, attributions play a very important role in influencing behaviors.

One of the most active areas of social cognition has been how we form and change attitudes.

What you think can change your grades.

Freshmen who attributed their academic problems to temporary factors had better academic performance and dropped out less than did control students.

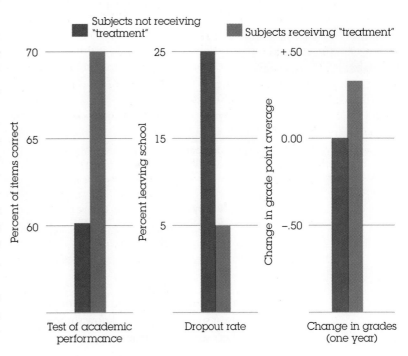

Attitudes

Can your attitudes get you fired?

The letter read: "Terri . . . it is our decision to terminate your employment as an airport sales agent . . . for insubordination." Terri's insubordination was that she had refused to wear makeup (lipstick, eyeliner) as specified in Continental Airlines's new 45-page appearance code manual. Terri had never worn makeup in her 11 years in the airline industry and no one had ever complained before. Her attitude was that she was doing a good job without wearing makeup, so why should she start now. Terri stuck to her attitude and was fired. However, several weeks later Continental announced that it had changed its mind, apologized to Terri, and allowed her to keep her job without having to wear makeup (*Los Angeles Times,* May 27, 1991).

Terri's story introduces the concept of attitude, which has long been an important topic in social psychology. An **attitude** *is any belief or opinion that includes a positive or negative evaluation of some target* (an object, person, or event) *and that predisposes us to act in a certain way toward the target.* Many definitions of the term *attitude* exist, but they all share certain ideas in common:

• An attitude is *evaluative:* it involves likes and dislikes. That is why attitudes are often expressed in terms of negatives and positives.

• An attitude is *targeted:* there is always an object of this evaluation. For instance, Terri dislikes wearing makeup.

• An attitude *predisposes* us to behave in a certain way. This means that we approach some targets and avoid others because of corresponding positive or negative attitudes. Terri's attitude toward wearing makeup predisposed her to fight against wearing it, even to the point of losing her job.

Components of Attitudes

If you closely examine Terri's attitude you will discover that it has three components: cognitive, affective, and behavioral.

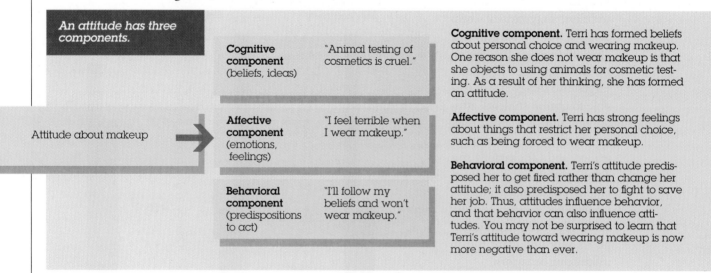

An attitude has three components.

Attitude about makeup

Cognitive component (beliefs, ideas)
"Animal testing of cosmetics is cruel."

Affective component (emotions, feelings)
"I feel terrible when I wear makeup."

Behavioral component (predispositions to act)
"I'll follow my beliefs and won't wear makeup."

Cognitive component. Terri has formed beliefs about personal choice and wearing makeup. One reason she does not wear makeup is that she objects to using animals for cosmetic testing. As a result of her thinking, she has formed an attitude.

Affective component. Terri has strong feelings about things that restrict her personal choice, such as being forced to wear makeup.

Behavioral component. Terri's attitude predisposed her to get fired rather than change her attitude; it also predisposed her to fight to save her job. Thus, attitudes influence behavior, and that behavior can also influence attitudes. You may not be surprised to learn that Terri's attitude toward wearing makeup is now more negative than ever.

The link between attitude and behavior is one that has intrigued social psychologists because it suggests that if we know someone's attitude we can predict that person's behavior. Let's see if this is true.

Attitudes and Behavior

What can we predict from attitudes?

In a general way, attitudes may be used to predict behavior, but there are some cases in which those predictions will be wrong. For example, surveys indicate that most people have positive attitudes toward maintaining our health. However, we cannot always predict from this attitude whether individuals will actually watch their diets, exercise, refrain from smoking, and not drink and drive. How is it possible for someone with a positive attitude toward health to take health risks? The explanation is that *general attitudes* seem to be only slightly related to specific behaviors (Ajzen, Timko, & White, 1982). Thus, your general attitude toward health is not a very good predictor of whether or not you will exercise.

However, measuring an individual's attitude toward the *target behavior* itself—exercising—does predict relatively well how he or she would respond if offered this choice. Studies indicate that attitudes are related to and generally predict behaviors, provided that the attitudes focus directly on the target behaviors we want to know about (Ajzen, Timko, & White, 1982).

Because each of us has literally hundreds of attitudes, you may be curious about their functions.

Your attitude toward women in the armed forces serves one or more of four functions.

Functions of Attitudes

In Terri's case, her attitudes toward restrictions on personal choice and use of makeup had a number of functions. We'll examine four general functions (Tesser & Shaffer, 1990).

1 Attitudes have a **utilitarian function**: *they are convenient guidelines for interpreting and categorizing objects and events and deciding whether to approach or avoid them.* For example, if you have a positive attitude toward rock music, you will categorize it as something to seek out by buying records and going to concerts. In Terri's case, her negative attitude toward makeup resulted in her categorizing cosmetics as something she wished to avoid.

2 Attitudes have a **defensive function**: *they can decrease our anxiety or increase our self-esteem.* If you have a negative attitude toward chemistry class, you will not be bothered as much by getting a low grade as you would if you valued or majored in chemistry. In Terri' case, her negative attitude toward cosmetics apparently boosts her self-esteem and makes her feel good about not using these products.

3 Attitudes have a **social-adjustive function**: *they help us adjust to or fit in better with a new group.* For instance, if you were to join a sorority or fraternity, you might quickly adopt the attitudes of the group to fit in better. On the other hand, attitudes also help one stand out from the group. In Terri's case, she was the only ticket agent who refused to go along with the rules on makeup and thus stood out from the group.

4 Attitudes have a **value-expressive function**: *they help us define and stand up for beliefs and values that we consider central to ourselves.* For example, people have strong attitudes about politics, religious practices, and college education, and these attitudes go to the core of the person. In Terri's case, she had strong attitudes about animal rights and the misuse of animals in cosmetic testing that made her shun the use of makeup.

An attitude can serve only one function or it can serve more than one. In attempting to change or alter an attitude, it is helpful to know what function it is serving. How to change attitudes is our next topic—and one in which advertisers and politicians are particularly interested.

Persuasion

Bill Clinton, Democratic candidate for president in 1992, used a number of methods to persuade voters.

What makes a political candidate popular?

Political candidates spend much of their time and money persuading people to vote for them. As we examine what politicians do and say, we'll introduce you to the psychology of persuasion.

Two Routes to Persuasion

If you wanted to direct a political campaign, you should know that there are two ways or routes—central and peripheral—for persuading voters (Petty & Cacioppo, 1986). Each route uses a different method and appeals to different voters.

Central Route

The **central route for persuasion** *presents information with strong arguments, analyses, facts, and logic.* The central route assumes that the audience is interested enough in the issues to think carefully about them. A

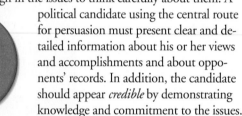

political candidate using the central route for persuasion must present clear and detailed information about his or her views and accomplishments and about opponents' records. In addition, the candidate should appear *credible* by demonstrating knowledge and commitment to the issues.

Politicians should choose the central route when they are trying to persuade voters who have a high need for cognition or a high need to know the facts and issues (Cacioppo & Petty, 1982). The central route of persuasion works with people who think about and analyze the issues. For example, jury members with a high need for cognition will want to carefully review written arguments prior to being given evidence (Kassin & Reddy, 1990).

However, not all voters can be persuaded by the central route. For some a peripheral route for persuasion proves the better method.

Peripheral Route

The **peripheral route for persuasion** *emphasizes emotional appeal, focuses on personal traits, and generates positive feelings.* The peripheral route assumes that not all voters will be motivated to devote sufficient time, energy, and thought to digesting the issues. Politicians choosing the peripheral route for persuasion will use bands, banners, parties, and personal appearances to generate excitement and create a positive attitude toward the candidate. In addition, the candidate should appear energetic, should be well dressed, and should speak with enthusiasm. An audience with a low need to know spends less time analyzing the issues and is better persuaded via the peripheral route. Research shows that people will overestimate the degree of similarity between their position on an issue and that of a candidate if they like the candidate (Carlson, 1990).

In a very literal sense, the peripheral route is more concerned with style and the central route is more concerned with substance.

Which route should politicians choose?

These two routes to persuasion remind us that, in order to change someone's attitude, we must consider the *component* we wish to address with our persuasion. A central route works primarily on the cognitive component, while a peripheral route works primarily on the affective or feeling component. Researchers generally find that the central route produces more enduring results, while the peripheral route produces more transient results (Ford & Smith, 1991). In practical terms, a political candidate usually combines the central and peripheral routes to reach the greatest number of voters.

Whether the central or peripheral route is used, a number of specific elements are important in persuasion.

Elements of Persuasion

In 1989 some 17,000 patients were waiting for organs to become available for transplant. However, only one in three patients would actually receive organs because of a lack of donors. Although there is a sufficient pool of potential donors available, only about 15% to 20% sign donor cards. To increase the availability of organs for transplant, psychologists and medical health personnel are studying ways of persuading people to sign donor cards.

What would persuade you to sign an organ donor card?

The identification of elements involved in persuasion was begun in the 1950s by the Yale Communication Program, which is still considered one of the best models (Hovland, Janis, & Kelley, 1953). As we explain the communication program, we'll show how it applies to persuading people to sign organ donor cards.

Yale Communication Program

The Yale Communication Program focuses on key elements in persuasion. We'll examine three of these elements: the source, the message, and the audience.

Source. One element in persuading someone involves the *source of the message:* we are more likely to believe sources who appear trustworthy, have expertise and credibility, are attractive, or appear similar to us. For example, at criminal trials, defense attorneys and prosecutors often call in expert witnesses because such sources have expertise and credibility and are likely to persuade the jury. In addition, similarity and attractiveness are widely used in advertising to persuade consumers to purchase specific products.

Who should present the idea of organ donation?
Good sources of messages concerning organ donations can be either a competent and sympathetic medical care worker or a friend or colleague who has signed an organ donation card.

Message. Another element of persuasion involves the *content of the message.* If the persuader is using the *central route,* the messages will contain convincing and understandable facts. If the facts are complicated, a written message is better than a spoken one (Chaiken & Eagly, 1976).

If the persuader is using the *peripheral route,* the messages will be designed to arouse emotion, sentiment, and loyalty. One type of message that uses the peripheral route is the *fear appeal.* Could we, for example, change people's attitudes toward smoking by showing them blackened lungs? There is no simple answer to this question. We do know that the more fearful people are, the more likely they are to be persuaded. We also know that a message high in fear appeal will not be particularly persuasive unless accompanied by a clear message on how to avoid the feared outcome (Rogers, 1983).

Some messages are better presented as *one-sided*—that is, you present only the message that you want accepted. Other messages are better presented as *two-sided*—that is, you include both the message and rebuttals against potential disagreements.

What should the organ donation message be?
Researchers found that a two-sided message proved significantly more persuasive in getting people interested in organ donor cards than did a one-sided message (Ford & Smith, 1991).

Audience. A number of *characteristics of the audience* determine a message's effectiveness. Audiences high in a need for cognition are best addressed via the central route; those low in the need for cognition are best persuaded by the peripheral route.

In persuading an audience, we want to know whether the audience is initially on our side. If we are making a proenvironmental speech to a business group or a pro-military speech to peace activists, we will structure our message differently than when speaking to people who already agree with us.

What does the audience believe about donation?
As with other topics, if the audience initially agrees with the idea you are presenting (in this case, the reasons to sign an organ donor card), you can use a one-sided argument; if the audience initially disagrees, it is better to use a two-sided argument.

Remember: When choosing the best method for persuasion, you must consider the source, the message, and the audience.

Sometimes our attitudes do not match our behaviors, such as believing in the importance of living a healthful life but never exercising. How we deal with such inconsistencies is important enough to have its own theory.

Attitude Change

What made a neo-Nazi skinhead reform?

At one time, Gregory Withrow was an out-and-out hatemonger who belonged to the White Aryan Resistance, the Ku Klux Klan, the Skinheads, and the American Nazi Party. His goal was "the complete and total extermination of all nonwhites from the the face of the American continent." He preached hatred and bashed and robbed Japanese tourists in San Francisco. Then he met Sylvia, who completely rejected Gregory's white supremacist notions. As Gregory grew to love Sylvia, he found himself caught between her disapproval of his Nazi values and his years of preaching hate. Gregory finally resolved his personal dilemma by renouncing his previous white supremacist values and abandoning the hate organizations. He now speaks against hate and racism (*Los Angeles Times*, June 14, 1989).

Gregory Withrow changed from a hate-filled neo-Nazi to a spokesperson against racism.

Initially, Gregory maintained consistency among his beliefs, attitudes, and behaviors by preaching hate, joining racist organizations, and bashing nonwhites. However, coming in contact with Sylvia's nonviolent values gave him pause and created inconsistencies in his beliefs. Gregory's inconsistencies were extreme, but we all face inconsistencies among beliefs, attitudes, and behaviors. For example, you may believe you are a good student but behave inconsistently by cutting classes or not studying for exams. One explanation for how we deal with inconsistencies is offered by the theory of cognitive dissonance.

Cognitive Dissonance

According to one theory, inconsistencies among beliefs and behaviors cause cognitive dissonance. Leon Festinger (1957) defines **cognitive dissonance** *as a state of unpleasant psychological tension that motivates us to reduce our inconsistencies and return to a more consistent state.* There are two main ways to reduce cognitive dissonance—that is, to make our beliefs and attitudes consistent with our behavior.

1 We can reduce cognitive dissonance by *adding new beliefs* or *changing old beliefs* and making them consistent with our behavior. In Gregory's case, cognitive dissonance was created by the conflict between Sylvia's nonviolent values and his own racist and hate-filled beliefs. To decrease his cognitive dissonance, Gregory renounced his hate beliefs so that his attitudes became consistent with his behavior (love of Sylvia). In addition, Gregory added new beliefs and behaviors, such as becoming a spokesperson for the Anti-Defamation League, whose goal is the reduction of racial tension.

2 We can reduce cognitive dissonance by engaging in **counterattitudinal behavior,** *which involves taking a public position counter to our private attitude.* An example of how counterattitudinal behavior works is a classic study by Festinger & Carlsmith (1959). In this study, subjects were asked to do an extremely boring task, such as turn pegs in a board. At the end of the task, the experimenter asked the subjects to help out by telling the next group of subjects how interesting the task was. For lying about the task—that is, engaging in counterattitudinal behavior—some subjects received $1 and some received $20. Sometime later, another experimenter asked the original subjects how much they liked the boring task. Based on common sense, we would predict that subjects who were paid $20 would think the boring task was actually rather interesting. However, just the reverse happened. Subjects paid just $1 showed a more favorable attitude to the boring task than those who paid $20.

Predictions of Cognitive Dissonance

The results of this counterattitudinal study actually turned out just as Festinger and Carlsmith had predicted, based on cognitive dissonance theory. Subjects had to resolve an inconsistency between doing a boring task and telling others that it was interesting. Those who were paid $20 for lying resolved their inconsistency easily: they had been well paid for lying, so felt little cognitive dissonance. However, those subjects who were paid only $1 had no good reason for lying. They experienced cognitive dissonance because they had engaged in a boring task but said that it was interesting. To resolve their cognitive dissonance, they ended up convincing themselves that the task was somewhat interesting.

In this experiment, we see that cognitive dissonance was reduced by engaging in counterattitudinal behavior, which is believing one thing but saying another. This study explains why we sometimes come to believe our own lies to resolve our inconsistencies. However, the changes observed in counterattitudinal behavior may occur for another reason.

Self-Perception Theory

Perhaps the reason people come to believe their own lies after engaging in counterattitudinal behavior is not to reduce cognitive dissonance but because of self-perception. According to Daryl Bem's (1967) **self-perception theory**, *we first observe or perceive our own behavior and then infer attitudes from the behavior.* Bem would explain that subjects paid only $1 for lying would observe their behavior and conclude that they would never lie for $1 so the task must have actually been interesting.

At first glance, both cognitive dissonance theory and self-perception theory seem to be similar, since they both indicate that if we say something it must be true. However, each theory points to different reasons. According to cognitive dissonance theory, the belief "if I say it, it must be true" occurs because we are trying to reduce the inconsistency in our beliefs and behaviors. In comparison, according to self-perception theory, concluding that "if I say it, it must be true" simply reflects a way of explaining our own behaviors.

Self-perception theory has challenged cognitive dissonance theory and added another dimension to explaining counterattitudinal behavior. Self-perception theory has also challenged the traditional assumption that the road between attitudes and behaviors is always one direction—that attitudes give rise to behavior. For example, you believe that you are religious so you attend church. According to Bem, the reverse may also occur—behavior may influence attitudes. For instance, after attending church you believe that you are a religious person. We now know that Bem was right in his suggestion that behavior can influence attitudes.

After the Concept/Glossary we'll look at the incredible change in American attitudes toward the Russians in the last few years.

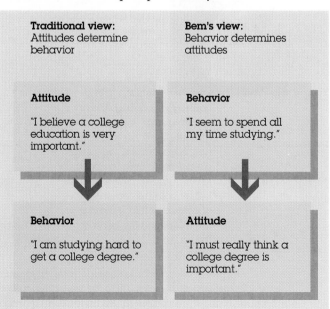

Traditional view: Attitudes determine behavior	Bem's view: Behavior determines attitudes
Attitude	**Behavior**
"I believe a college education is very important."	"I seem to spend all my time studying."
↓	↓
Behavior	**Attitude**
"I am studying hard to get a college degree."	"I must really think a college degree is important."

1. A broad field that studies how our thoughts, feelings, perceptions, and behaviors are influenced by interactions with others is called (a)_____. A major branch of this field that studies how people perceive, store, and retrieve information about social interactions is called (b)_____.

2. Making judgments about the traits of others through social interactions and gaining knowledge from our social perceptions is called _____.

3. Widely held beliefs that people have certain traits because they belong to a particular group are known as (a)_____. An unfair, biased, or intolerant attitude toward another group of people is called (b)_____. Specific unfair behaviors exhibited toward members of a group is known as (c)_____.

4. Cognitive structures that represent an organized collection of knowledge about people, events, and concepts are called _____.

5. The process by which we find causes for people's behavior is known as (a)_____. If we attribute behavior to the internal characteristics of a person, we are attributing the behavior to (b)_____. If we attribute behavior to the circumstances or context of that behavior, we are attributing the behavior to the (c)_____.

6. If we attribute the cause of a behavior to a person's disposition and overlook the demands of the environment or situation, we are committing the (a)_____ error. If we attribute our own behavior to situational factors but the behaviors of others to their disposition, we are committing the (b)_____ error. If we attribute success to our disposition and failure to the situation, we are using the (c)_____ bias.

Cognitive

Affective

Behavioral

7. Beliefs or opinions that include a positive or negative evaluation of some target (object, person, or event) and that predispose us to act in a certain way toward the target are called _____.

8. If we persuade by presenting information with strong arguments, analyses, facts, and logic, we are using the (a)_____ route. If we persuade voters by emphasizing emotional appeals, focusing on the personal traits of the candidate, and generating positive feelings, we are using the (b)_____ route.

9. A state of unpleasant psychological tension that motivates us to reduce our inconsistencies and return to a more consistent state is called (a)_____. If we take a public position that is counter to our private attitude, we are engaging in (b)_____ behavior.

10. If we first observe or perceive our own behavior and then infer our attitudes from our behavior, we are behaving according to _____ theory.

Answers: 1. (a) *social psychology,* (b) *social cognition;* 2. *person perception;* 3. (a) *stereotypes,* (b) *prejudice,* (c) *discrimination;* 4. *schemas;* 5. (a) *attribution,* (b) *disposition,* (c) *situation;* 6. (a) *fundamental attribution,* (b) *actor-observer,* (c) *self-serving;* 7. *attitudes;* 8. (a) *central,* (b) *peripheral;* 9. (a) *cognitive dissonance,* (b) *counterattitudinal;* 10. *self-perception.*

604   *CHAPTER 16: SOCIAL PSYCHOLOGY*

Attitudes Toward Russians

The Soviet Union lasted 74 years, from 1917 to 1991. During this time, the U.S. government, public officials, and media fostered negative attitudes toward Russians. For example, one of the famous anti-Russian slogans of the 1960s was "Better dead than Red." In 1983 President Ronald Reagan called Russia "the evil empire." Suddenly, in the early 1990s, we find that the Soviet Union no longer exists, Communism is outlawed, and the feared secret police (KGB) are disbanded. Let's see how these developments are changing the American people's attitudes toward Russians.

Attitudes and Behavior

For most of the Soviet Union's existence, the American attitude was that the Soviets were a terrible threat to our security, lives, and happiness. We can identify three components in this attitude. The *cognitive component* was a belief that Russia was a threat to our existence and security. The *affective component* was a combined feeling of dislike, distrust, and hatred toward the Soviets. The *behavioral component* was a tremendous buildup in defensive weapons and high-tech intelligence. Is it any wonder that a survey of American and Russian adolescents in the late 1980s (Tudge et al., 1991) reported that 54% of Americans and 88% of Russians were very worried about nuclear war? Let's see how these attitudes were formed.

A worker takes down a statue of Lenin after the Communist party fell.

Persuasion

We know that the *central route for persuasion* involves the use of information, analysis, and logic and that this route is best for individuals with a high need for cognition. The press coverage of the Soviet Union prior to the late 1980s included information on how much money the Soviets were spending on weapons, how many nuclear warheads they possessed, and the strength and readiness of their army. We know that the *peripheral route for persuasion* involves the use of photos, emotional appeals, and threats. Many of us have vivid memories of photos of Soviet nuclear missiles and gigantic parades of soviet weaponry. We can see that our attitudes toward the Soviet Union were formed by information via the central and peripheral routes.

Attitude Change

The new Russia has caused many Americans to feel cognitive dissonance because the old evil Soviet empire is now being treated like a new-found friend. As you know, one way to resolve cognitive dissonance is to change our beliefs. This is currently being accomplished as our government leaders and the American press discuss the economic struggles of the Russian people in sympathetic and friendly tones.

We may also be changing our attitudes toward Russians because of self-perception. According to Bem's self-perception theory, we look at the American government giving aid to the Soviets and we say to ourselves, "We would not be aiding our enemies, so the Russians must now be our friends." Thus, both cognitive dissonance and self-perception theory explain the amazing turnabout in our attitudes toward the Russian people.

We've seen how attitudes can affect our view of a whole nation. Next we'll look at how attitudes can apply to our perception of individuals—specifically, how attitudes apply to attractive people.

APPLYING/ EXPLORING: MAKING AN IMPRESSION

It is no secret that each of us is concerned about how others perceive, talk about, and evaluate us. We spend a considerable amount of time selecting clothes or putting on makeup and behaving so that others will see us as interesting and attractive. Political candidates have expensive advisers who help them make good impressions. Among the first things you learn about interviewing for a job are ways to make good first impressions. These are all examples of impression management. **Impression management**, which is also called **self-presentation**, *refers to our attempts to regulate and control, sometimes consciously and sometimes without awareness, information that we present to others* (Schlenker & Weigold, 1992). The major reason we are concerned about making a good first impression is that it will greatly influence how others perceive, evaluate, and treat us. We are always engaging in impression management, with or without conscious awareness, as we adjust our behaviors to suit different situations and audiences.

There are two major reasons we try hard to impress people.

At one time concern about making an impression was considered a way to manipulate others and was primarily useful in business, politics, or advertising. Today, however, impression management is considered something that we all do whenever we interact with others. Each of us has a personal agenda or role schema that includes what we want to accomplish in social interactions and plans for going about it (Schlenker & Weigold, 1992). Impression management has become an important and legitimate area of social psychology.

Motivation

What motivates us to make good impressions? In business, politics, and advertising, the motivation to make a good impression is usually financial or material—making deals, getting votes, or selling products. In our personal interactions, there are two major motives—self-esteem and self-consistency—that guide and influence our making impressions.

1 Self-esteem. A major motive for making good impressions is to enhance and maintain our self-esteem (Leary & Kowalski, 1990). By enhancing our self-esteem we feel good, look good to others, make better adjustments, have better mental health, and experience superior personal functioning (Brown, 1991). In general, performing behaviors that enhance self-esteem generate positive feelings, while performing behaviors that diminish self-esteem generate negative feelings.

2 Self-consistency. Another motive for creating impressions is to receive feedback that reinforces our self-concepts and gives us a feeling of self-consistency (Swann, 1990). For example, we get a feeling of self-consistency if people give us positive feedback and if we behave in ways that people judge to be appropriate.

Success or Failure

What kind of impression do you make?
If you work very hard at making good impressions, how successful will you be? Researchers find that when people expect to make good impressions and then work hard at it, they usually succeed. In contrast, when people expect to perform poorly and then work hard at making good impressions, they usually fail, because their concentration creates anxiety and interferes with their performance (Schlenker & Weigold, 1992). One way to improve our ability to make good impressions is to practice the required social skills, such as conversing, talking in a natural tone, asking questions, making eye contact, and smiling.

Another way to make a good first impression is to be born attractive.

Greta Garbo, the great film star of the 1930s, died in 1992. Her face was considered one of the most attractive ever.

Does attractiveness matter?
You may not be surprised to learn that physically attractive people create more-favorable impressions than less attractive people do. The reason is that attractiveness has a significant positive effect on social judgment across many social situations. Physically attractive people are considered to be more responsive, interesting, sociable, intelligent, kind, strong, outgoing, and poised and are more likely to be recommended for job promotions (Cunningham, 1987; Dion, Berscheid, & Walster, 1972; Morrow & McElroy, 1990). One of the most widely cited conclusions from research on physical attractiveness is the phrase "What is beautiful is good" (Dion, Berscheid, & Walster, 1972). Most researchers agree that the beautiful-is-good stereotype is a relatively strong and general phenomenon (Eagly & Ashmore, 1991).

What's attractive?
One group of researchers showed undergraduate women photos of males and asked them to identify attractive facial features. What women found attractive were large eyes, prominent cheekbones and a large chin, a big smile, and high-status clothing (Cunningham, Barbee, & Pike, 1990).

Are women and men able to agree on what is attractive? To answer this question, researchers created male and female faces by averaging many individual faces to create a single face. Subjects were than asked to select the most attractive face from a group that included not only individual faces but faces created from averaging 16 or 32 individual faces. In all cases, whether the faces were of males or females, subjects agreed that the averaged faces were more attractive. Researchers concluded that we favor prototypic faces that have characteristics close to the mean of the faces found in the general population (Langlois & Roggman, 1990).

It appears that we can all practice skills to make good impressions but that attractive people have an inside track.

Summary/Self-Test

PERSON PERCEPTION

1. How our thoughts, feelings, perceptions, and behaviors are influenced by interactions with others is studied in the field of (a)_____ psychology. A branch of this field studies how people perceive, store, and retrieve information about social interactions; this branch is called social (b)_____.

2. Making judgments about the traits of others through social interactions and gaining knowledge from our social perceptions is part of person (a)_____. This process is aided by a wealth of social information that is stored in our memories. However, some memories can bias our perceptions. Widely held beliefs that people have certain traits because they belong to a particular group are called (b)_____. Those that are negative are often accompanied by an unfair, biased, or intolerant attitude toward another group of people, called (c)_____, and by specific unfair behaviors exhibited toward members of a group, called (d)_____.

■ *Mark says that he doesn't make snap judgments about people but waits to get to know them better. Do you think Mark is doing what he says?*

SCHEMAS

3. Cognitive structures that represent an organized collection of knowledge about people, events, and concepts are called _____. They help us select relevant information from a tremendous amount of incoming social information, help us interpret and make sense of social information, and provide guidelines for how we should behave in different situations. These functions point to some of the advantages of schemas; the disadvantage is that they may cause us to overlook information.

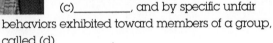

4. Social schemas that include our judgments about the traits that we and others possess are called (a)_____ schemas. Those that are based on the jobs people perform or the social positions they hold are called (b)_____ schemas. Those that contain behaviors that we associate with familiar activities, events, or procedures are called (c)_____ schemas, or scripts.

■ *What would happen to your social interactions if you had to form new schemas each time you met someone?*

ATTRIBUTION

5. Even people with no formal training behave like naive scientists when they try to explain behaviors in their everyday lives. The beliefs that we rely on as naive scientists when we analyze the behavior of others are called (a)_____ personality theories. A collection of formal theories that attempt to explain the process by which we find causes for people's behavior is called (b)_____ theory. If we attribute behavior to the internal characteristics of the person performing the behavior, we are using (c)_____ explanations; if we attribute behavior to the circumstances or context of that behavior, we are using (d)_____ explanations.

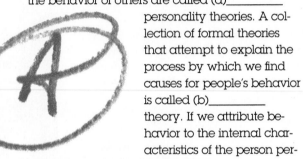

6. Harold Kelley proposed that in deciding between dispositional and situational explanations, we should look for factors that change along with the behavior we are trying to explain; this is called the _____ principle. To decide between dispositional and situational explanations, we should look for consensus, consistency, and distinctiveness.

7. An error that we make by attributing the cause of a behavior to a person's disposition and overlooking the demands of the environment or situation is the (a)_____ attribution error. If we attribute our own behavior to situational factors but others' behaviors to their dispositions, we fall prey to the (b)_____ effect. If we attribute success to our disposition and failure to the situation, we use the (c)_____ bias.

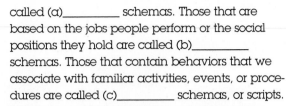

■ *What's the best way to avoid making errors in explaining your friend's behavior?*

ATTITUDES

8. Beliefs or opinions that include a positive or negative evaluation of an object, person, or event and that predispose us to act in a certain way are called (a)_____. General attitudes are convenient guidelines for interpreting and categorizing objects and events and deciding whether to approach or avoid them; in this case they serve a (b)_____ function.

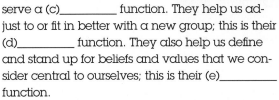

They can decrease our anxiety or increase our self-esteem; in this case they serve a (c)_____ function. They help us adjust to or fit in better with a new group; this is their (d)_____ function. They also help us define and stand up for beliefs and values that we consider central to ourselves; this is their (e)_____ function.

■ *If Nancy's attitude is that recycling things is good for the planet, what could you predict about her behavior?*

PERSUASION

9. A method of persuasion that presents information with strong arguments, analyses, facts, and logic is the (a)_____ route, which works primarily on the cognitive component. Another route emphasizes emotional appeal, focuses on personal traits, and generates positive feelings; this is called the (b)_____ route. This route works primarily on the affective or feeling component.

10. One element in persuasion is those to be persuaded, or the audience. People who appear trustworthy, have expertise and credibility, and are attractive or appear similar to those to be convinced are more likely to be believed as (a)_____ of information. If the audience initially agrees with the idea you are presenting, a (b)_____ argument is preferred; if the audience initially disagrees, it is better to use a (c)_____.

■ *You are going to run for president of the student body. What kind of campaign should you run?*

ATTITUDE CHANGE

11. A state of unpleasant psychological tension that motivates us to reduce our inconsistencies and return to a more consistent state is called cognitive (a)_____. One way to reduce this tension is to make our beliefs and attitudes consistent with our behavior by adding new beliefs or changing old beliefs. Taking a public position that is counter to our private attitude is called (b)_____ behavior. According to Daryl Bem's theory, we first observe or perceive our own behavior and then infer attitudes from that behavior; this is called (c)_____ theory.

■ *Your boss thinks women can't do a man's work. What would make him change his attitude?*

CULTURAL DIVERSITY: ATTITUDES TOWARD RUSSIANS

12. The belief that Russia was a threat to our existence and security, feelings of distrust and hatred toward the Soviets, and the buildup in defensive weapons reflected the three components of attitudes, which are (a)_____, (b)_____, and (c)_____.

■ *What are the major factors in changing our attitudes toward minorities?*

APPLYING/EXPLORING: MAKING AN IMPRESSION

13. Attempts to regulate and control information that we present to others are called self-presentation, or (a)_____ management. How others perceive, evaluate, and treat us is greatly influenced by their first impressions of us. In business, politics, and advertising, the motivation to make a good impression is usually financial or material. In personal interactions, the two major motives are (b)_____ and _____.

14. Attractiveness has a significant positive effect on social _____. The beautiful-is-good stereotype is a relatively strong and general phenomenon.

■ *Harold says that he doesn't worry about making a good impression but just is himself. Is Harold doing what he says?*

Answers: 1. (a) social, (b) cognition; 2. (a) perception, (b) cognition; 3. schemas; 4. (a) person, (b) role, (c) event; 5. (a) implicit, (b) attribution, (c) dispositional, (d) situational; 6. covariation; 7. (a) fundamental, (b) actor-observer, (c) self-serving; 8. (a) attitudes, (b) utilitarian, (c) defensive, (d) social-adjustive, (e) value-expressive; 9. (a) central, (b) peripheral; 10. (a) sources, (b) one-sided, (c) two-sided argument; 11. (a) dissonance, (b) counterattitudinal, (c) self-perception; 12. (a) cognitive, (b) affective, (c) behavioral; 13. (a) impression, (b) self-esteem, self-consistency; 14. judgment.

MODULE 32
SOCIAL BEHAVIOR

What's he really like?

As he walked up to the podium to receive his award, he looked neither right nor left. He approached the microphone with the same enthusiasm as a convicted man approaching the gallows. When he reached the podium, he stopped in front of the microphone and said in a soft, rather high voice, "Thank you." That was all he said. Giving a very uncomfortable smile, he turned and left the stage.

His friends and family describe him as a serious and sensitive person who is primarily interested in his work. On first meeting he seems bashful and reserved and rarely makes eye contact.

When he began to have success as a 17-year-old and should have been enjoying life and looking forward to a promising future, he seemed on the verge of hopelessness and despair. "People hurt each other over and over and over again," he said bleakly. "I spend a lot of time being sad. I'm just sad a lot." In his autobiography, he said, "I'm one of the loneliest people in the world. I'm a shy person. It's true. Everybody has many facets to them and I'm no different. When I'm in public, I often feel shy and reserved.

"It's different when I'm on stage, however. When I perform, I lose myself. I'm in total control on that stage. I don't think of anything. I know what I want to do from the moment I step out there and I love every minute of it. I'm actually relaxed on stage. Totally relaxed."

On stage, spotlights pick out his dazzling black jacket, his black shoes and white socks. When the music starts his body moves to the beat with such rhythm and ferocity that he turns into pure energy and becomes the ultimate performer. Nobody can sing and dance and completely captivate the audience like Michael Jackson. (adapted from Jackson, 1988, pp. 277–278; Taraborrelli, 1991, p. 169)

What is unusual about Michael Jackson is that in private he behaves in a way totally opposite of how he acts on stage. The private Michael is shy and bashful; the on-stage Michael is brash and confident. In his on-stage behavior, Michael is responding to a number of **social forces,** *which refer to demands, pressures, judgments, requests, and expectations that arise from the presence of other people.* For example, we behave differently if we are in the company of our boss, our in-laws, a blind date, a stranger, someone we do not like, or neighborhood children. We respond differently to requests from a roommate, salesclerk, police officer, bully, mother, or teacher. Thus, depending on which social forces are operating, we adjust our behaviors and responses appropriately. Without realizing, we are constantly responding and adjusting our behaviors to many different social forces.

What's Coming

In this module, we'll discuss the difference between the public and private self, different forms of social influence, effects of being in a group, helping behavior, and aggression. Let's begin with a closer look at the public versus private self.

Public Versus Private Self

Have you ever laughed at a joke you didn't think was funny?
Most people know how to laugh on cue, making a storyteller feel good by pretending a joke was funny even when it wasn't. Similarly, perhaps you have told a white lie to fit in with a group. Both of these examples illustrate the difference between our public and private self. As it turns out, people respond differently depending on their concern for their public or private selves.

Self-Monitoring

According to psychologist Mark Snyder (1974), how much we laugh at jokes that aren't funny or tell white lies to make us look good depends on how much our behavior is influenced by the demands of social situations. Snyder has identified two patterns of responding: high self-monitoring and low self-monitoring.

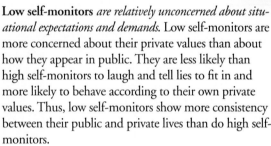

Why might someone tell a white lie to fit in?

High self-monitors *constantly monitor their behavior to make sure that it is consistent with the demands of a given situation.* High self-monitors are very concerned about how they appear in public. For example, they laugh at jokes they don't think are funny and may tell more white lies to fit in. High self-monitors show less consistency between their public and private lives than do low self-monitors. At first glance it may appear that high self-monitors are overly worried about how they appear in public and are too willing to overlook their private values. An advantage, however, is that high self-monitors show particular sensitivity to the situations, feelings, and wishes of others.

Low self-monitors *are relatively unconcerned about situational expectations and demands.* Low self-monitors are more concerned about their private values than about how they appear in public. They are less likely than high self-monitors to laugh and tell lies to fit in and more likely to behave according to their own private values. Thus, low self-monitors show more consistency between their public and private lives than do high self-monitors.

How do we use self-monitoring?
The self-monitoring concept has numerous implications. For example, when males are examining information about a potential date, high self-monitors spend more time studying photographs, whereas low self-monitors spend more time looking at personality information (Snyder, Berscheid, & Glick, 1985). When rating advertisements, high self-monitors tend to rate image-oriented ads more favorably; low self-monitors rate product quality–oriented ads more favorably (Snyder & DeBono, 1985). These studies indicate that depending on our degree of self-monitoring, we respond and behave differently to social forces. In addition, self-monitoring explains how much consistency there will be between our public and private lives.

Self-Handicapping

Let's imagine that you must make a class presentation but think that your fear of public speaking will result in a poor presentation. One way to protect your public image is through self-handicapping. **Self-handicapping** *is deliberately constructing obstacles or handicaps that will protect one's sense of self-esteem from public failure* (Jones & Berglas, 1978). For example, researchers found that subjects protected their self-esteem from public failure and negative evaluations of others through such self-handicaps as inadequate preparation or practice and use of performance-altering drugs such as alcohol (Kimble, Funk, & DaPolito, 1990). These studies indicate that if we have doubts about our self-esteem, we may use self-handicapping strategies to protect our public self from negative evaluations.

We have seen that self-handicapping and self-monitoring are ways of adjusting to social influences. Let's examine three common forms of social influence.

Social Influences

Why did these people commit mass suicide?

The congregation consisted of nurses, clerks, teachers, truck drivers, longshoremen, professionals, and students. They listened to the promises of the Reverend Jim Jones and followed him into the jungle of Guyana, where he founded a settlement named Jonestown. Reports began to leak out that some of the Jonestown residents were being held against their will. U.S. Congressman Leo D. Ryan from California, accompanied by journalists, went to Jonestown to investigate. Fearing that the investigators would destroy his commune, Jones had his men attack the party as they were about to leave. Several were killed, but others escaped. After the attack, Jones set into motion a planned mass suicide. Over 900 adults and children were persuaded or forced to drink a cyanide-laced fruit punch. Jones told his followers that by taking their lives now, they would win peace in the hereafter. He walked among them, embracing them and saying that he'd see them in the next life (*Los Angeles Times*, November 18, 1983).

The Jonestown suicide is an extreme and tragic case of conformity and obedience to a person in authority.

Most of us are horrified that over 900 men, women, and children would obey an order to kill themselves. Although what happened at Jonestown is an extreme example, some of the reasons these people obeyed are similar to the reasons we commonly obey people in authority and conform to group and social pressures. We'll examine how social forces bring about conformity and obedience. Let's begin with conformity.

Conformity

The followers of Jim Jones conformed in a number of ways: they followed him to Guyana, they worked in the commune, and they agreed on a set of religious beliefs. **Conformity** *refers to any behavior you perform because of group pressure, even though that pressure might not involve direct requests.* For example, we conform by wearing clothes in style, using similar slang phrases, and buying the latest hit CDs. Let's see how conformity has been studied.

What was Asch's experiment?

In a classic experiment, Solomon Asch (1958) studied the influence of group pressures to conform. Imagine that you are part of Asch's study. How do you think you might behave?

Procedure. You are seated at a round table with five others and have been told that you are taking part in a visual perception experiment. Your group is shown a straight line and then is instructed to look at three more lines of different lengths and pick out the line equal in length to the original one. The three choices are different enough that it is not hard to pick out the correct one. Each person at the round table identifies his choice out loud, with you answering next to last. When you are ready to answer, you will have heard four others state their opinions. What you do not know is that these four other people are the experimenter's accomplices. On certain trials, they will answer correctly, making you feel your choice is right. On other trials, they will deliberately answer incorrectly, much to your surprise. In these cases you will have heard four identical incorrect answers before it is your turn to answer.

You will almost certainly feel some pressure to conform to the others' opinion. Will you give in?

Results. Out of 50 subjects in Asch's experiment, 75% conformed on some of the trials, but no one conformed on all the trials; 25% never conformed. These data indicate that the desire to have your attitudes and behaviors match those of others in a group can be a powerful force. Asch's results have been replicated in recent times (Larsen, 1990).

Compliance

Were the subjects just pretending?

One interpretation of Asch's data is that subjects were not really changing their beliefs but rather just pretending to go along with the group. For example, when subjects in Asch's experiment privately recorded their answers, conforming drastically declined. This decline indicated that subjects were conforming but not really changing their beliefs, which is one kind of *compliance.* **Compliance** *is a kind of conformity in which we give in to social pressure in our public responses but do not change our private beliefs.* For example, you may conform to your instructor's suggestions on rewriting a paper although you do not agree with the suggestions. In this case, you would be complying with someone in authority.

One particular technique of compliance is used by many salespeople. Those in sales soon learn that if they can get the customer to comply with a small request (get a foot in the door), the customer is more likely to comply with a later request to buy the product. The **foot-in-the-door technique** *relies on the increased probability of compliance to a second request if a person complies with a small, first request.* The request may be sales related, as we've said, or may be in social contact, as in asking a friend for a favor. A review of 15 years of research on the foot-in-the-door technique indicates that it is a small but repeatable finding (Beaman et al., 1983).

Next we'll examine a kind of compliance that we know as obedience.

Is this line similar in length to lines 1, 2, or 3?

1 2 3

These are the kinds of lines used in Asch's study on conformity.

Good salespeople are masters at getting us to comply with their suggestions to buy their products.

Social Influences

Obedience

How many times did you obey today?

Chances are you have a long history of obeying speed laws, parking signs, traffic lights, smoking restrictions, parental requests, instructors' assignments, and doctors' orders. **Obedience** *refers to behavior performed in response to an order given by someone in a position of authority.*

With your history of obeying, let's see how you might behave in one of the most famous experiments in social psychology: the Milgram experiment on obedience.

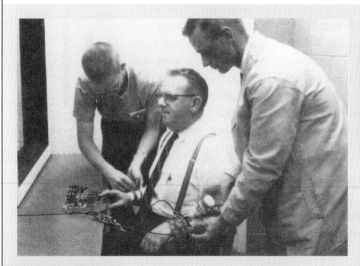

Milgram's Experiment

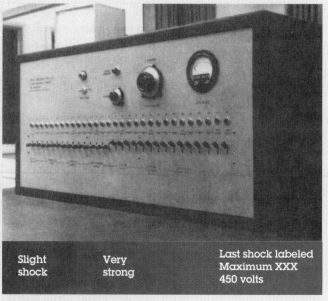

| Slight shock | Very strong | Last shock labeled Maximum XXX 450 volts |

Marking on shock generator ranged from slight to very strong to maximum XXX 450 volts.

Would you punish a learner for making errors?

You have volunteered for a study on the effects of punishment on learning (Milgram, 1963). After arriving in the laboratory at Yale University, you are selected to be the "teacher" and another volunteer is to be the "learner." What you don't know is that the learner is actually an accomplice of the experimenter. You watch as the learner is strapped into a chair and has electrodes placed on his wrists. The electrodes are attached to a shock generator in the next room. You and the researcher then leave the learner's room and go into an adjoining room.

The researcher gives you a list of questions to ask the learner over an intercom, and the learner is to signal his answer on a panel of lights in front of you. For each wrong answer, you are to shock the learner, and you are to increase the intensity of the shock by 15 volts for each succeeding wrong answer. In front of you is the shock machine, with 30 separate switches that indicate increasing intensities. The first switch is marked "15 volts, Slight Shock," and the last switch is marked "XXX 450 volts, Danger: Severe Shock." You begin to ask the learner questions, and as he misses them, you administer stronger and stronger shocks.

What would you do if the subject stopped answering?

After receiving 300 volts, the learner pounds on the wall. After 315 volts, he pounds again and then stops answering your questions. You don't know that this is all an act and that the learner is not actually being shocked, so you plead with the researcher to stop the experiment. The researcher tells you to continue asking questions and that if the learner fails to respond, you should treat it as a wrong answer and deliver the next level of shock. Would you continue to follow the researcher's orders? How far would you go?

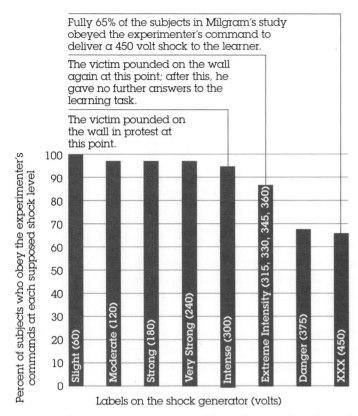

Fully 65% of the subjects in Milgram's study obeyed the experimenter's command to deliver a 450 volt shock to the learner.

The victim pounded on the wall again at this point; after this, he gave no further answers to the learning task.

The victim pounded on the wall in protest at this point.

Percent of subjects who obey the experimenter's commands at each supposed shock level

Slight (60)
Moderate (120)
Strong (180)
Very Strong (240)
Intense (300)
Extreme Intensity (315, 330, 345, 360)
Danger (375)
XXX (450)

Labels on the shock generator (volts)

How many subjects obeyed an inhumane order?

When Stanley Milgram conducted these experiments in the early 1960s, they demonstrated what no one had imagined. Psychiatrists who had been asked to predict how many people would deliver the full range of shocks, including the last 450 volts, estimated that only 0.1% of the population would do so. Members of the general public asked the same question predicted that only 2% would deliver the 450 volts. To the horror and dismay of many, including Milgram, 65% of the subjects delivered the full range of shocks. Numerous replications conducted in various parts of the world have obtained similar results (Meeus & Raaijmakers, 1989).

The results of these experiments helped answer a question people had asked since World War II: Why had Germans obeyed Hitler's commands? And why did the Jonestown members follow the suicide orders of Jim Jones? Milgram's experiments clearly demonstrated that a large percentage of people will obey orders, even if they are unreasonable, and that situations have a powerful effect on obedience.

Why did Milgram's subjects obey?

Psychologists have suggested several reasons that so many subjects in Milgram's experiment obeyed to the end, even though they believed they were inflicting severe pain on someone else. One of the main reasons is that people have learned to follow the orders of *authority figures,* whether they are religious leaders, army commanders, doctors, scientists, or parents. Interestingly, in one of his follow-up studies Milgram (1974) found that it is less difficult for people to defy an authority figure they do not have to deal with face to face. Perhaps this helps explain why many people do not follow their doctor's orders.

People also obey because they have *learned to follow orders* in their daily lives, whether it be in traffic, on the job, or in personal interactions. It is thought that obeying minor orders increases the probability of later obeying major ones.

Were Milgram's experiments ethical?

Although the Milgram experiments provided important information about obedience, it is unlikely that they could be conducted today. This is because all experiments, especially those with the potential for causing psychological or physical harm, are now carefully screened by research committees, a practice that did not exist at the time of Milgram's research. These committees determine whether proposed experiments on animals or humans have the potential for psychological or physical harm and whether these potential damaging effects can be eliminated or counteracted (see Module 2). Although scientists disagree over whether Milgram's experiments were ethical, they agree that Milgram's findings dramatically changed our view about how much people will obey.

We have now seen that the effects of three kinds of social influences—conformity, compliance, and obedience—may depend on the presence of other people. Let's further examine the influence of groups on behavior.

Group Dynamics

As human beings we spend much of our time in various kinds of **groups,** *which are collections of two or more people who interact and share some common attribute or purpose.* When we are with a group, whether family, friends, co-workers, or professional colleagues, we come under its influence, which may be subtle or obvious. Let's begin with why we form groups.

Group Membership

Standing before the judge was a 13-year-old boy who had murdered another boy by smashing his skull with a rock. What disturbed the judge almost as much as the murder was the behavior shown by the 13-year-old's circle of friends. They had known about the murdered body in the park for months but had refused to tell a single adult. Why were they silent about a murder? Had they no consciences?

Why did the boys remain silent?

Why would a group of young teenagers maintain a conspiracy of silence about something as serious as a murder? Rather than answering this question by saying the teens had no conscience, social psychologists would point to the powerful influence of group membership and of such forces as group cohesion and group norms. **Group cohesion** *is group togetherness, which is determined by how much group members perceive that they share common attributes.* **Group norms** *are the formal or informal rules about how group members should behave.* For example, the group norms of the 13-year-old's circle of friends required them to protect their members—and thus keep silent about a murder.

Should students study in groups?

Many students form study groups because they believe two or more heads are better than one. Successful study groups are **task oriented:** *the members have specific duties to complete.* In such groups, students may divide up the overall task, work on parts individually, and then share their work with their group. In comparison, unsuccessful study groups are **socially oriented:** *the members are primarily concerned about fostering and maintaining social relationships among the members of the group.* A socially oriented study group may be fun but provides little help on exams.

Why do we form groups?

In his hierarchy of human motivation, humanistic psychologist Abraham Maslow identified *the need for love and belonging* as fundamental to human happiness (Maslow, 1954; see also Module 17). One way to satisfy this need is through membership in a group that helps people develop a sense of identity. For instance, in high school you were defined, in part, by the groups to which you belonged—the teams you played for, the clubs you joined, the friends you associated with. Our need for belonging carries into adulthood as we join community and business organizations. Maslow's theory provides *motivational reasons* for forming groups: they satisfy our need to belong.

At about the same time that Maslow published his work on the hierarchy of motivation, Leon Festinger's (1954) social comparison theory offered another reason for joining groups. According to **social comparison theory,** *we are driven to compare ourselves to others who are similar to us so that we can measure the correctness of our attitudes and beliefs.* Festinger's theory provides *cognitive reasons* for forming groups: they help us create our social reality by allowing us to compare our social selves with others like us.

An additional reason for forming groups is being able to accomplish things in groups that we simply cannot do alone. In fact, groups can be so important that members are willing to make considerable sacrifices for the group in terms of time, effort, and money. Perhaps you've seen this in a volunteer organization—or even in your study group.

Group Behaviors

The presence of others may cause you to behave very differently than you would if you were alone. As you will see, the presence of others may facilitate or inhibit behavior, may lead to antisocial behaviors, or may result in refusal to help.

Social Facilitation and Inhibition

If a runner has a history of successful competition, he may turn in a better performance in front of a large crowd due to **social facilitation,** *which is an increase in performance in the presence of a crowd.* In contrast, if a runner has a spotty history in competition, he may turn in a worse performance in front of a large crowd because of **social inhibition,** *which is a decrease in performance in the presence of a crowd.* Whether we show facilitation or inhibition depends partly on our previous experience. Generally, the presence of others will facilitate well-learned, simple, or reflexive responses but will inhibit new, unusual, or complex responses.

Deindividuation in Crowds

During the Los Angeles riots of 1992, people were arrested for looting, setting fires, and beating others. These behaviors may not have occurred if these people were not in a **crowd,** *which is a large group of persons most of whom are unacquainted.* Because individuals cannot be identified easily in a crowd, they are more likely to take on antisocial roles, such looting and burning. **Deindividuation** *refers to the increased tendency for subjects to behave irrationally or perform antisocial behaviors when there is less chance of being personally identified.*

For example, researchers found that subjects are more likely to express verbal and physical hostility (delivering shocks) if there is less chance of being personally identified (Mann, Newton, & Innes, 1982). One researcher thinks that deindividuation occurs because self-awareness, guilt, shame, or fear is reduced by the anonymity of being in a crowd (Zimbardo, 1970). According to this idea, if our guilt and self-awareness are reduced, we are less controlled by internal standards and therefore more willing to take on a deviant or antisocial role (Prentice-Dunn & Rogers, 1982).

The Bystander Effect

As a person lies unconscious on the sidewalk, hundreds of people walk by without helping. Why does this happen? One reason is the **bystander effect,** *which inhibits an individual from taking some action because of the presence of others.* Data from over 50 studies indicate that 75% of people offer assistance when alone, but fewer than 53% do so when in a group (Latané & Nida, 1981). There are two explanations for the bystander effect.

According to the **informational influence theory,** *we use the reactions of others to judge the seriousness of the situation.* If other bystanders are taking no action, we conclude that no emergency exists and do nothing.

According to the **diffusion of responsibility theory,** *the presence of others makes one feel less personal responsibility and inhibits taking action.* Thus, an individual may feel less responsibility to help when in a group than when alone (Latané, 1981).

Besides influencing a number of behaviors, the presence of others also influences how we make decisions, which we'll examine next.

Group Dynamics

Group Decisions

Social psychologists have studied how being in a group influences decision making. In doing so, they discovered two interesting phenomena: group polarization and groupthink.

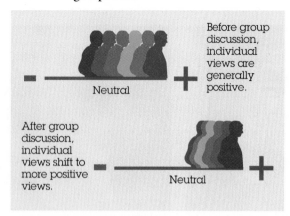

Before group discussion, individual views are generally positive.

After group discussion, individual views shift to more positive views.

What's most important is that we stick together.

Group Polarization

A young lawyer is trying to decide which of two job offers to accept. The first offer is from a large, well-established firm that promises more security, financial opportunities, and prestige. However, it has a poor record as an equal employer of women and currently has no women partners. The second offer is from a small, recently established firm that can promise little security or prestige. However, this firm is doing well and has an excellent record in promoting women as partners. Which offer should the lawyer accept?

Using dilemmas such as this, a researcher compared the recommendations from individuals in a group with those made by the group after it had engaged in discussion (Pruitt, 1971). The finding? The group arrived at more risky recommendations than did individuals. This phenomenon became known as the *risky shift.*

Researchers later discovered that the direction of a group's risky shift depends on how conservative or liberal the group was to begin with. If a group's members are initially more conservative, group discussion will shift its recommendation to an even more conservative one. If a group's members are initially more liberal, group discussion will shift its recommendation to an even more liberal one.

The group's shift to a more extreme position is called *polarization.* **Group polarization** *refers to group discussion reinforcing the majority's point of view and shifting that view to a more extreme direction.* Whether this polarization is in a liberal or conservative direction depends on the initial leanings of the group's members.

Groupthink

In 1962 President John F. Kennedy took the world to the brink of nuclear war when he ordered the invasion of Cuba. This invasion, which occurred at the Bay of Pigs, was a terrible decision and a well-remembered failure. Psychologist Irving Janis (1982) analyzed group decision-making processes involved in bad decisions like the Bay of Pigs and other disasters and concluded that part of the fault lay in something called groupthink. **Groupthink** *occurs when group discussions emphasize cohesion and agreement over critical thinking and making the best decisions.*

Groupthink has a number of clearly defined characteristics: discussions are limited, few alternatives are presented, and there is increased pressure to conform. For example, the group usually has a member that Janis calls a *mindguard,* whose job it is to discourage ideas that might be a threat to the group's unity. In addition, groupthink results in viewing the world in very simple terms: there is the *ingroup,* which includes only the immediate members of the group, versus the *outgroup,* which includes everyone who is not a part of the group. Adoption of the ingroup-outgroup attitude strengthens groupthink by emphasizing protection of the group over making the best decisions.

Psychologists suggest several ways to avoid groupthink. One is to allow the group's members to express differing opinions without being considered threatening to the group. A second is to make sure that communication and gathering of information are kept open and unbiased.

We have seen how the presence of others influences a variety of social and cognitive behaviors. Next we'll discuss two other social behaviors, helping and aggression.

Helping

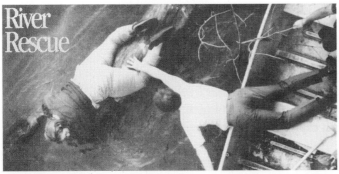

River Rescue

A member of the Minnesota Boat Club rescues a woman from a floating log after she fell into the Mississippi River.

What would you do if you saw a serious accident?

About 60 people had gathered around a serious car crash in a downtown area. They were talking about the accident and pointing at the victims, but no one was helping. One of the victims was a woman, obviously pregnant and unconscious. One person in the crowd, Ken Von, came forward and tried to save the woman with cardiopulmonary and mouth-to-mouth resuscitation that he had learned by watching television. He kept her alive until paramedics arrived (*San Diego Tribune*, September 9, 1983).

Ken's quick action is an example of helping or prosocial behavior. **Prosocial behavior** *is any behavior that benefits others or has positive social consequences.* One form of helping is **altruism,** *or doing something, often at a cost or risk, for reasons other than the expectation of a material or social reward.* Ken's helping may be described as altruistic, since he expected no external reward. Helping occurs not only in emergencies but in a variety of social situations, such as giving someone directions or contributing to a charitable cause.

Studies suggest three different motivations for helping: empathy, personal distress, and norms and values:

• We may help because we feel *empathy*—that is, we identify with what the victim must be going through.

• We may help because we feel *personal distress*—that is, we have feelings of fear, alarm, or disgust from seeing a victim in need.

• We may help because of our *norms* and *values*—that is, we may feel morally bound or socially responsible to help those in need.

Many of those who watched the car crash experienced some of these motivations. Why was it that only Ken Von took action? Let's examine two models that explain how Ken made his decision to help.

Decision Stage Model

According to the **decision stage model**, *we go through five stages in deciding to help* (Latané & Darley, 1970): (1) we *notice* the situation; (2) we *interpret* it as one in which help is needed; (3) we *assume personal responsibility;* (4) we *choose a form of assistance;* and (5) we *carry out* that assistance. Onlookers who did not help may have reached stage 3 and decided at that point that it was not their responsibility. The advantage of this model is that it explains why people may fail to help even though they recognize the situation as an emergency.

Arousal-Cost-Reward Model

According to the **arousal-cost-reward model**, *we make decisions to help by calculating the costs and rewards of helping* (Piliavin et al., 1982). For example, seeing an accident may cause us an unpleasant emotional *arousal* that we want to reduce. In deciding how to reduce these unpleasant feelings, we calculate the *costs* and *rewards* of helping. For instance, those who decided not to help may have felt that the costs of helping, such as getting involved in a potentially dangerous situation, outweighed the rewards.

The arousal-cost-reward model and the decision stage model are not mutually exclusive: elements of each may be present in making decisions about helping. It is possible, for instance, that other onlookers to the car crash might have helped but saw gasoline leaking and decided that the risk of being trapped in a fire while helping victims of the crash was too great.

The opposite of prosocial behavior is aggression, the causes of which are of great interest to social psychologists.

Aggression

How does a child become an aggressive adult?

Tony was always starting fights in grade school, was always getting into trouble as a teenager, and was arrested several times before he reached age 21. Researchers have found that boys such as Tony, aggressive at age 8, have a good chance of being aggressive at age 30 (Eron et al., 1987). **Aggressive behavior** *is any act that is intended to do physical or psychological harm.* We'll examine four major theories—biological, frustration-aggression, social learning, and cognitive—that explain aggressive behavior.

Biological Theory

According to the **biological theory**, *behaviors such as aggression are influenced by genetic, physiological, and hormonal factors.* These factors are more dominant in animals than in humans. Much of the data for the biological theory come from *ethologists,* who study animal behavior in natural settings. For example, animals have evolved signals to stop fights and avoid injury. A wolf shows submission and prevents a fight by rolling over on its back. This submissive posture acts as an *innate releaser* to inhibit aggression. Evidence such as this shows that genetic and biological factors play a dominant role in regulation of aggressive behavior in animals.

There is also evidence that biological factors influence aggression in humans. For example, the correlation of aggressive behaviors in identical twins reared apart is significantly higher (.33) than in fraternal twins reared apart (.04) (Plomin, Chipuer, & Loehlin, 1990). Data from both twin and adoption studies indicate a biological component for aggressive behavior in humans (DiLalla & Gottesman, 1991). However, in humans aggressive behavior results from an interaction between biological and environmental factors. Let's look at a common environmental factor—frustration.

Frustration-Aggression Hypothesis

The idea that frustration plays a major role in aggression was proposed more than 50 years ago by a group of researchers at Yale University (Dollard et al., 1939). According to the **frustration-aggression hypothesis**, *when our goals are blocked, we become frustrated and respond with anger and aggression.* However, researchers soon discovered that although frustration may lead to aggression, the link between the two is not absolute. Leonard Berkowitz (1989) reviewed the research on the frustration-aggression hypothesis and concluded that (1) frustration doesn't always lead to aggression, (2) social rules may inhibit aggression, (3) frustration may result in behaviors others than aggression, and (4) cognitive factors can override aggression. Thus, according to the **modified frustration-aggression hypothesis**, *frustration may lead to aggression but a number of situational and cognitive factors may override the aggressive response.*

One cognitive factor that may lead to aggression involves what we learn through observation.

What does a baseball manager do when frustrated?

What does a wolf do to prevent a fight?

Why was Tony always getting arrested?

Social Learning Theory

According to Bandura's (1986) **social learning theory,** *behavior, including aggressive behavior, may be learned and maintained through interactions with one's environment, such as through observation, imitation, and reinforcement.* Data in support of social learning theory come from both laboratory and naturalistic studies. A classic laboratory study by Bandura (1965) found that children who observed a model's aggressive behaviors later performed similar aggressive behaviors (see Module 12). In a more naturalistic study, Leonard Eron and his associates (1987) reported that children who were exposed to aggressive models of parents, such as parents using physical punishment, showed increased aggression with their peers. According to Eron (1990), the individual most likely to behave aggressively and violently is one who has been programmed through observing and imitating adult role models.

A popular and pervasive source of adult models engaged in aggressive behaviors is television. Researchers have concluded that watching violent television programs has a small but significant effect on causing aggression in children (Friedrich-Cofer & Huston, 1986).

Another factor that contributes to aggressive behavior is cognitive programs.

Cognitive Theory

Some individuals are aggressive throughout their lives because of cognitive factors. According to the **cognitive theory,** *social behaviors such as aggression are controlled by cognitive programs that are stored in memory and used as guides for behavior and social problem solving* (Eron, 1990). According to cognitive theory, children learn **scripts,** *which are cognitive programs of how to behave in certain situations.* For example, a boy may learn that he can get his way by fighting and thus learns a fighting script. The more the fighting script is reinforced, the more likely the boy will continue to behave aggressively. Once a script is learned and stored, it is readily available to be recalled in similar situations. As a result, an individual behaves aggressively because aggressive scripts serve as guidelines and ways of solving social problems. The availability of aggressive scripts explains why aggressive behavior may persist and be difficult to change.

How does a child learn to be a bully?

What do children learn from watching television?

We have focused on four theories used to explain aggression, but no one theory holds all the answers. In fact, researchers suggest that, at the human level, all four theories play some part (Eron, 1990).

One particularly humiliating, terrifying, and degrading form of aggression is sexual aggression, which we'll examine next.

Aggression

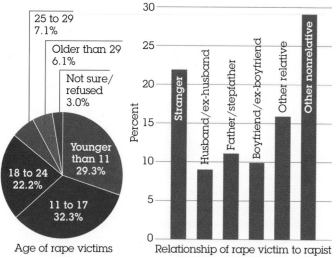

25 to 29
7.1%

Older than 29
6.1%

Not sure/
refused
3.0%

Younger
than 11
29.3%

18 to 24
22.2%

11 to 17
32.3%

Age of rape victims

Most rape victims are under age 18 and were raped by someone they knew.

Relationship of rape victim to rapist

(Bar graph, Percent 0–30)

Stranger | Husband/ex-husband | Father/stepfather | Boyfriend/ex-boyfriend | Other relative | Other nonrelative

Sexual Aggression

According to a National Victim Center poll, 683,000 adult women were forcibly raped in the United States in 1990. As shown in the graph, 61% of rape victims were under 18 years of age, and in almost 80% of cases the victim knew the rapist (*Rape in America*, National Victim Center, 1992). Let's look at some of the reasons that men rape.

Most researchers agree that the primary motivation for rape is not sexual but rather a combination of aggression, power, and control (Darke, 1990). For example, in interviews with ten convicted rapists, nine stated that sex was of secondary importance in motivating their assaults. Rather, these rapists stressed that either anger or the need to dominate was the most important factor to them (Levine & Koenig, 1980).

Recent surveys have shown that sexual aggression in the form of date rape is relatively common. For example, a national survey of approximately 3,000 male and 3,000 female college students found that about 27% of the college females had experienced either rape or attempted rape. About 8% of the college males reported committing or attempting rape (Koss, Gidyez, & Wisniewski, 1987). One contributing factor to rape is erroneous beliefs that men hold about women.

Rape Myths

As you read the following statements, guess which ones rapists agree with.

• Healthy women cannot be raped against their will.

• Women often falsely accuse men of rape.

• Rape is primarily a sex crime committed by sex-crazed maniacs.

• Only bad girls get raped.

• If a girl engages in necking or petting and she lets things get out of hand, it is her own fault if her partner forces sex on her.

All of these statements, called **rape myths**, *are examples of the kinds of misinformed beliefs that are frequently held by rapists* (Burt, 1980).

Although researchers have found that belief in rape myths is more common among men who have raped, rape myths are also held by college males. One survey of male college students reported that from 17% to 75% of the students agreed with one or more of nine rape myths (Giacopassi & Dull, 1986). The association between rape myths and rapists suggests that these erroneous social beliefs contribute to sexual aggression. In our society, it is estimated that during their lifetime 20%–30% of women will be victims of some type of sexual aggression. Researchers are currently starting a number of rape prevention programs at college campuses to both prevent rape and stop the perpetuation of rape myths (Gray et al., 1990).

After the Concept/Glossary, we'll examine ways of reducing and controlling aggression.

Kinds of Rapists

Keeping in mind that the primary motivation is aggression, power, or control, Gail Abarbanel, director of the Santa Monica Rape Treatment Center, describes four kinds of rapists (*Los Angeles Times*, February 24, 1984):

▪ The *power rapist*, who commits 70% of all rapes, is not out to hurt physically but to possess. His acts are premeditated and are often preceded by rape fantasies. He may carry a weapon, not to hurt but to intimidate the victim.

▪ The *sadistic rapist* accounts for fewer than 5% of rapes, but he is the most dangerous because for him sexuality and aggression have become fused, and using physical force is arousing and exciting.

▪ For the *anger rapist*, rape is an impulsive, savage attack of uncontrolled physical violence. The act is of short duration, accompanied by abusive language, and the victim usually suffers extensive physical trauma, such as broken bones and bruises.

▪ The *acquaintance or date rapist* knows his victim and uses varying amounts of verbal or physical coercion to force his partner to engage in sexual activities.

1. The demands, pressures, judgments, requests, and expectations that arise from the presence of other people are referred to as _____ forces.

2. Individuals who constantly review their behavior to make sure it is consistent with the demands of a given situation are called high (a)_____. Individuals who are relatively unconcerned about situational expectations and demands are called low (b)_____.

3. If we deliberately construct obstacles or handicaps that will protect our sense of self-esteem from public failure, we are engaging in _____.

1   2   3

4. Any behavior we perform because of group pressure, even if that pressure involves no direct requests, is called (a)_____. A kind of conformity in which we give in to social pressure in our public responses but do not change our private beliefs is called (b)_____. Any behavior performed in response to an order given by someone in a position of authority is called (c)_____.

5. A collection of two or more people who interact and share some common attribute or attributes is called a (a)_____. Togetherness, which is determined by how much group members perceive that they share common attributes, is called group (b)_____.

6. An increase in performance in the presence of a crowd is called social (a)_____; a decrease in performance in the presence of a crowd is called social (b)_____. An increased tendency for individuals to behave irrationally or perform antisocial behaviors if there is less chance of being personally identified is called (c)_____. Being socially inhibited to take some action because of the presence of others is called the (d)_____ effect.

7. The phenomenon by which group discussion reinforces the majority's point of view and shifts that view to a more extreme direction is called group (a)_____. Emphasizing group cohesion and agreement over critical thinking and making the best decisions is called (b)_____.

8. Any behavior that benefits others or has positive social consequences is called (a)_____ behavior. One form of helping that involves doing something, often at a cost or risk, for reasons other than the expectation of a material or social reward is called (b)_____.

9. Any act that is intended to do physical harm and that involves biological, social learning, and cognitive factors is called _____.

Answers: 1. *social;* 2. (a) *self-monitors,* (b) *self-monitors;* 3. *self-handicapping;* 4. (a) *conformity,* (b) *compliance,* (c) *obedience;* 5. (a) *group,* (b) *cohesion;* 6. (a) *facilitation,* (b) *inhibition,* (c) *deindividuation,* (d) *bystander;* 7. (a) *polarization,* (b) *groupthink;* 8. (a) *prosocial,* (b) *altruism;* 9. *aggression.*

APPLYING/ EXPLORING: CONTROLLING AGGRESSION

Aggression is a serious individual and social problem. We'll focus here on programs designed to reduce and control individual aggression. All of the programs assume that aggression is primarily a learned response and that it can be controlled or unlearned.

Catharsis

An especially popular method for reducing and controlling aggression has been **catharsis,** *which drains off or releases emotional tension.* Freud theorized that engaging in aggressive behavior can get rid of pent-up emotions and thus be helpful. However, most research does not support Freud's conclusion about the usefulness of catharsis. For example, researchers measured the levels of aggression in fans before and after a football game. On the basis of catharsis, we would predict that the losing fans who showed the most aggression during the game should have the lowest levels after the game. Instead, researchers found that both losing and winning fans showed increased levels of aggression at the end of the game (Goldstein, 1989).

Another drawback to the use of catharsis is that, as researchers report, it is difficult to find appropriate people on whom to vent cathartic aggression, since these people feel obliged to aggress back (Tavris, 1982).

Anger Control in Children

Often anger or a bad temper triggers a child's aggressive behavior. If children could learn to control their anger, they could curb their aggression. One group of researchers has developed an anger control program to treat aggressive children (Lochman & Curry, 1986).

Central to this program is the idea that aggressive children have social-cognitive deficits. For example, aggressive children do not know how to stop themselves from thinking in aggressive ways or to overcome their belief that other children, not them, are acting aggressively. In this program, a child with a bad temper would be taught the following:

1 The child learns specific rules. For example, no matter how angry the child gets, he or she must not hit, yell, or kick. The child receives special reinforcement for obeying these rules.

2 The child learns to use self-statements to inhibit impulsive behavior. These include "Count to ten before acting," "I'll be sorry later," and "I can stop myself."

3 The child learns to use alternate, nonaggressive solutions when frustrated. These might be hand clapping, scribbling on a sheet of paper, or tensing and relaxing muscles.

4 The child learns through observation and imitation of students who had bad tempers but have used this program to control their temper.

This anger control program has been shown to be effective for reducing aggression. For example, after being in the program for 18 weeks, grade school children showed significant reductions in aggression

(as rated by their parents) and in disruptive and aggressive classroom behaviors, as well as increases in self-reported self-esteem (Lochman & Curry, 1986). Now let's see what kind of program works for adults.

Anger Control in Adults

Although Margaret is good at selling computer software, she becomes angry at clients and at herself if she loses a sale. She has developed a pattern of taking out her anger on her husband. As a result, their marriage is in trouble.

Researchers have developed an anger control program for people like Margaret, whose quick tempers lead to problems (Deffenbacher et al., 1987). These researchers use a program that combines cognitive relaxation and social skills training. We'll follow Margaret through this program to see how it works.

During the first two weeks of this program, Margaret practices progressive relaxation and monitors when, where, and why she becomes angry. During the next six sessions, she imagines events that make her angry, such as losing a sale, and then reduces her anger by relaxing. She is then told to continue monitoring events that make her angry outside the sessions and to reduce her anger by relaxing rather than taking it out on her husband. In addition, she is taught to minimize interpersonal anger by developing better listening and communications skills, such as learning how to ask questions, seek clarifications, and check for understanding.

The researchers found that five weeks after finishing this program clients report significant reductions both in suppressing an-

Psychologists have developed a number of successful programs for controlling aggression.

ger and in coping better with potentially angering situations.

Avoiding Date Rape and Sexual Aggression

According to researchers, one way to avoid sexual aggression on a date is to know the risk factors (Muehlenhard & Linton, 1987). These factors include the man initiating the date, paying all the expenses, and driving; miscommunication about sex; heavy alcohol or drug use; "parking"; and the man's acceptance of traditional sex roles, interpersonal violence, and rape myths. The length of time the partners know each other is not a major factor in date rape.

One of the problems in avoiding date rape is that men who are guilty of this act do not fit the stranger-in-the-dark-alley stereotype. Women are less likely to recognize what is happening and more likely to blame themselves or be blamed by others for arousing the man. To prevent sexual aggression, the researchers suggest that women avoid the risk factors associated with date rape, learn to recognize the cues very early, and clearly put a stop to unwanted sexual advances.

The common method men use to obtain unwanted sex is to just do it, even if the woman has said no. For this reason,

Muehlenhard and Linton counsel women to use a strategy of increasing forcefulness, going from direct refusal to vehement verbal refusal and, if necessary, physical force. However, when women were presented with sexual situations and asked whether they could refuse comfortably, only 60% said they could. This means that 40% of respondents would seem to be at risk for sexual aggression on dates. The researchers suggest that women take assertiveness training if they foresee having a problem saying no.

Even though anger and aggression may be difficult to control, programs and education can help people reduce and avoid aggressive behaviors.

Summary/Self-Test

PUBLIC VERSUS PRIVATE SELF

1. The demands, pressures, judgments, requests, and expectations that arise from the presence of other people are called (a)_____ forces. We respond differently to requests from various people, adjusting our behaviors and responses appropriately. People who constantly review their behaviors to make sure that they are consistent with the demands of a given situation are called high (b)_____. Those who are relatively unconcerned about situational expectations and demands, called low (c)_____, are more concerned about their private values than how they appear in public.

2. Deliberately constructing obstacles or handicaps that will protect your sense of self-esteem from public failure is called _____.

■ *Ken says that he behaves the same way whether he's with his best friend or in a group of strangers. Is Ken right?*

SOCIAL INFLUENCES

3. Any behavior you perform because of group pressure is called (a)_____. Giving in to social pressure in your public responses but not changing your private beliefs is called

(b)_____. A technique that relies on the increased probability of meeting a second request if you comply with a small, first request is called the (c)_____.

4. A behavior performed in response to an order given by someone in a position of authority is called _____. In his experiments, Stanley Milgram demonstrated that a large percentage of people will obey orders, even those that are unreasonable. The main reasons that people obey is that they have learned to follow the orders of authority figures and follow orders in their daily lives.

■ *Carol says that the best way to stop students from cheating is to appeal to their honesty. Is Carol mistaken?*

GROUP DYNAMICS

5. A collection of two or more people who interact and share some common attribute or attributes is called a (a)_____. How much group members perceive that they share common attributes determines group cohesion. The formal or informal rules about how group members should behave are called group (b)_____ .

6. Humanistic psychologist Abraham Maslow identified *the need for love and belonging* as fundamental to human happiness. One way to satisfy this need is through membership in a group. Maslow's theory provides (a)_____ reasons for forming groups. According to Leon Festinger's social comparison theory, we compare ourselves to others who are similar to us so that we can measure the correctness of our attitudes and beliefs. His theory provides (b)_____ reasons for forming groups. An additional reason for forming groups is being able to accomplish things that we simply cannot do alone.

7. An increase in performance in the presence of others is called social (a)_____; a decrease in performance in the same circumstances is called social (b)_____.

8. A large group of persons, most of whom are unacquainted, is called a (a)_____. Because people cannot be identified easily in a crowd, they are more likely to take on antisocial roles, which is called (b)_____.

9. If one is inhibited from taking some action because of the presence of others, it may be due to the (a)_____ effect, for which there are two explanations. According to one theory, we use the reactions of others to judge the seriousness of the situation; this is the (b)_____ influence theory. The idea that the presence of others makes us feel less personal responsibility and inhibits our taking action is the basis of the diffusion of (c)_____ theory.

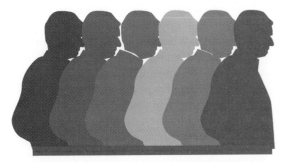

10. The phenomenon of a group arriving at a more risky decision than its individuals would is known as the (a)_____. The direction in which this change is made depends on how conservative or liberal the group is at the start. Group discussion reinforcing the majority's point of view and shifting that view to a more extreme direction is called (b)_____. The phenomenon of group discussions tending to emphasize cohesion and agreement over critical thinking and making the best decisions is called (c) _____.

■ *Members of a campus fraternity discussed whether to ban drinking alcohol in their rooms. Why might their decision surprise you?*

HELPING

11. Any behavior that benefits others or has positive social consequences is called (a)_____ behavior. A form of helping that involves doing something, often at a cost or risk, for reasons other than the expectation of a material or social reward is called (b)_____.

12. Studies on helping suggest three different motivations. We may help because we identify with what the victim must be going through—that is, we feel (a)_____. We may help because we have feelings of fear, alarm, or disgust from seeing a victim in need; this is called (b)_____ distress. Or we may feel morally bound or socially responsible to help those in need because of our (c)_____.

13. Two different models explain how we make our decisions to help. The model that frames our decision as a five-stage process is called the (a)_____ model. According to another model, we make decisions to help by calculating the costs and rewards of helping; this is called the (b)_____ model.

■ *How would you go about developing a program to increase altruism in your community?*

AGGRESSION

14. Any act that is intended to do physical or psychological harm is termed (a)_____ behavior. Four major theories are used to explain this behavior in humans. Saying that aggressive behaviors are influenced by genetic, physiological, and hormonal factors points to the (b)_____ theory. According to another theory, frustration may lead to aggression, but a number of situational and cognitive factors may override the aggressive response; this is called the modified (c)_____ hypothesis. Aggressive behavior may be learned and maintained through interactions with one's environment; this is the basis of the (d)_____ theory. According to another theory, social behaviors such as aggression are controlled by cognitive programs that are stored in memory and used as guides for behavior and social problem solving; this is called the (e)_____ theory of aggression.

15. The primary motivation for rape is not (a)_____ but a combination of aggression, power, and control. Rapists have been classified into four types: power, sadistic, anger, and acquaintance/date. The misinformed beliefs that are frequently held by rapists and that are contributing factors to rape are called (b)_____.

■ *One of your friends says, "Getting angry and being aggressive is just part of human nature." What would you reply?*

APPLYING/EXPLORING: CONTROLLING AGGRESSION

16. Freud theorized that draining off or releasing emotional tension, known as _____, could get rid of pent-up emotions and thus reduce and control aggression; however, most research does not support this conclusion. A child's aggressive behavior may be due to social-cognitive deficits and can often be curbed if the child learns to control his or her anger. Methods of teaching anger control in adults combine cognitive, relaxation, and social skills training.

■ *Suppose you have always had a quick temper and get angry at little things. What could you do to control your anger?*

APPENDIX
STATISTICS IN PSYCHOLOGY

DESCRIPTIVE STATISTICS
Frequency Distributions
Measures of Central Tendency
Measures of Variability

INFERENTIAL STATISTICS
Chance and Reliability
Tests of Statistical Significance

Descriptive Statistics

Do numbers speak for themselves?
Suppose you are curious about how many people are capable of being hypnotized. You read up on how to induce hypnosis and put together a list of five things that people under hypnosis have been known to do, such as feeling no pain when a finger is pricked, being unable to bend an arm when told that the arm will remain stiff, and acting like a young child when told to regress to infancy.

You next persuade 20 people to participate in a little test. You attempt to hypnotize them and then ask them to do each of the things on your list. Of your 20 subjects, 2 follow none of your suggestions, 4 follow only one, 7 go along with two suggestions, 4 go along with three, 2 go along with as many as four, and only 1 follows all five.

The next day a friend asks you how your study worked out. How would you make generalizations about your findings?

To answer this type of question, psychologists rely on *statistics.* Although you often hear that numbers "speak for themselves," this is not really true. Numbers must be sorted, organized, and presented in a meaningful fashion before they tell us much. **Statistics,** *then, are the tools researchers use to analyze and summarize large amounts of data.*

If the very word *statistics* brings to mind complex formulas you think you could never master, you may be surprised to realize how much you already use statistics in your everyday life. When you hear that a ball player has a batting average of .250 and you know this means he has gotten a hit 1 in every 4 times at the plate, you are using statistics. When you understand that a rise in the median income means that people, on average, are earning more money, you are understanding statistics. When you know that scoring in the 90th percentile on a final exam means you did better than 9 out of 10 of your classmates, you are showing a grasp of statistics. These are all examples of **descriptive statistics**—*numbers used to present a collection of data in a brief yet meaningful form.* One important part of descriptive statistics is presenting distributions of measurements and scores.

Frequency Distributions

Individual differences show up in everything that can be measured. There are no measurements—whether of height, heart rate, memory capability, shyness, or political opinion—that do not show individual variation. When we measure a sample of people regarding some trait, the **frequency distribution** *is the range of scores we get and the frequency of each one.* Frequency distributions are often presented in graphic form so their patterns can be seen at a glance. We'll discuss two of these distributions, normal and skewed.

What is a normal distribution?
For many traits in a large population, the frequency distribution has a characteristic pattern. For instance, if you measured the height of 500 students chosen at random from your school, you would find a few very short people and a few very tall people, while the height of the majority of students would be somewhere in the middle. Height, like weight, IQ, years of education, and many other characteristics, has what is known as a *normal distribution.* When graphed, a normal distribution produces what is called a **normal curve**: *the curve tapers off equally on either side of a central high point,* as shown in Figure A.1. This characteristic bell shape shows that most of the measurements fall near the center, with as many falling to one side as to the other. When you measure a trait that is distributed normally throughout a population, your measurements should produce an approxi-

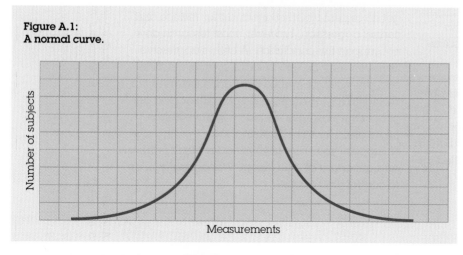

Figure A.1:
A normal curve.

Number of subjects

Measurements

mately normal curve, provided that your sample is large enough.

What is a skewed distribution?
Not all traits are distributed normally. There are also **skewed distributions** *in which more data fall toward one side of the scale than toward the other.* When plotted on a graph, skewed distributions do not have a symmetrical shape. Instead, they have a "tail" on one end, which shows that relatively fewer frequencies occur on that side of the horizontal scale. When the tail is on the right, as in Figure A.2, we say the distribution is skewed to the right, or has a *positive skew* (there are fewer frequencies at the higher end of the horizontal scale). When the tail is on the left, as in Figure A.3, we say the distribution is skewed to the left, or has a *negative skew* (there are fewer frequencies at the lower end of the horizontal scale).

The data you collected about susceptibility to hypnosis present a skewed distribution. If you plotted them on a graph, with score along the horizontal axis and number of people along the vertical one, the curve would be skewed to the right. This would show at a glance that more people in the sample fell at the low end of your hypnotic susceptibility scale than fell at the high end.

In fact, your sample is fairly representative of the general population. About twice as many people are poor hypnotic subjects as are excellent ones. But note that to be assured of obtaining the true distribution in a large population, you would usually have to test quite a large representative sample.

Measures of Central Tendency

Suppose you want to summarize in a few words the average height of people, the typical susceptibility to hypnosis, or the most common performance on an IQ test. For this you would need another kind of descriptive statistic, called a ***measure of central tendency.*** There are three measures of central tendency: the mean, the median, and the mode. Each is a slightly different way of describing what is "typical" within a given distribution.

Mean. The **mean** *is the arithmetic average of all the individual measurements in a distribution.* Suppose that ten students in a semi-

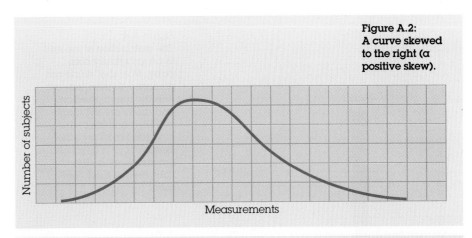

**Figure A.2:
A curve skewed
to the right (α
positive skew).**

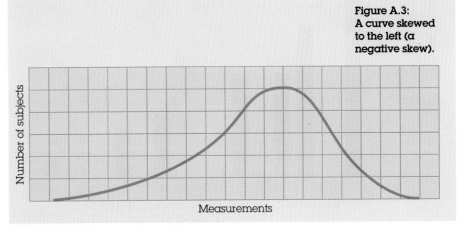

**Figure A.3:
A curve skewed
to the left (α
negative skew).**

nar take an exam. Their scores are 98, 96, 92, 88, 88, 86, 82, 80, 78, and 72. You find the mean by adding all the scores and dividing the sum by the total number of scores. In this case, the sum of all the scores is 860; dividing this by 10 gives a mean of 86.

Median. The **median** *is the score above and below which half the scores in the distribution fall.* If you took our ten test results and arranged them in order from highest to lowest, the median would be the point right in the middle, between the fifth and sixth scores on the list. That would be 87.

Mode. The **mode** *is the most frequent measurement in a distribution,* the one that occurs most often. In this group of scores, the mode is 88.

In the example just given, the mean, median, and mode are very close together, but this is not always true. In some distributions, particularly those that are strongly skewed, these three measures of central tendency

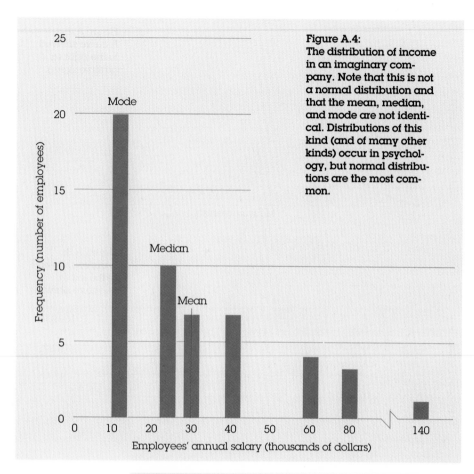

Figure A.4:
The distribution of income in an imaginary company. Note that this is not a normal distribution and that the mean, median, and mode are not identical. Distributions of this kind (and of many other kinds) occur in psychology, but normal distributions are the most common.

may be quite far apart. In such cases, all three of the measures may be needed to give a complete understanding of what is "typical."

For instance, look at the graph in Figure A.4, which shows the distribution of income in an imaginary company. The mean income of its 50 employees is $30,600 a year. But look at the distribution. The president of the company earns $140,000, three other executives earn $80,000, and another four earn $60,000 a year. There are also six lower-level managers at $40,000, six salespeople at $30,000, and ten foremen at $25,000. The rest of the employees, the 20 people who keep the company records and run the machines, earn only $12,000 each. Thus, the mean of $30,600 does not really give a full indication of what is "typical" at this firm.

A better measure of central tendency in this instance is probably the median, or $25,000. It tells us that half the people at the company earn no more than this amount. Also revealing is the mode, or most common salary; it is only $12,000 a year. As you can see, the mean, median, and mode can provide us with very different figures.

Measures of Variability

If you get an A in a course and are told that the grades ranged from A to F, you will feel a greater sense of accomplishment than if the grades ranged only from A to B. Why this difference in how you perceive a grade? The answer is that it is often important to take into account the extent to which scores in a distribution are spread out. In other words, it is often informative to have a **measure of variability,** *an indication of how much scores vary from one another.* On a graph, scores that vary greatly produce a wide, flat curve; scores that vary little produce a curve that is narrow and steep. Figure A.5 illustrates these two patterns.

The **range,** *or two most extreme scores at either end of a distribution,* is one measure of variability. Another measure, the **standard deviation,** *shows how widely all the scores in a distribution are scattered above and below the mean.* If scores cluster closely around the mean, the standard deviation will be small; if scores are dispersed widely from the mean, the standard deviation will be large. Thus, the standard deviation is an indication of

Figure A.5:
At left, a distribution with a great deal of variability. At right, a distribution with little variability.

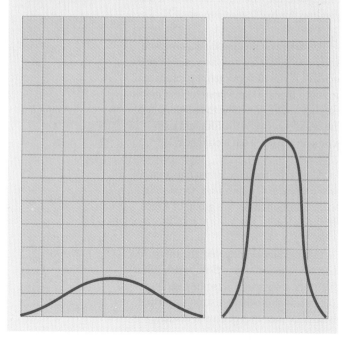

How to Find the Standard Deviation

Finding the standard deviation of a distribution is not difficult, although it is tedious without the aid of a calculator. To compute the standard deviation follow these five steps:

1. Determine the mean of all the measurements in the distribution.
2. Subtract the mean from each measurement and square the difference. (Squaring the difference eliminates the negative signs that result when dealing with measurements that fall below the mean.)
3. Add the squares together.
4. Divide the sum of the squares by the number of measurements.
5. Take the square root of the value you obtained in step 4. This figure is the standard deviation.

how representative the mean is. If the standard deviation is small, we know that the mean is representative of most scores in the distribution. Conversely, if the standard deviation is large, we know that many scores are quite far from the mean.

Figure A.6 shows that the standard deviation divides a normal curve into several portions, each of which has a certain percentage of the total distribution. As you can see,

68.2% of all scores fall somewhere between the mean and one standard deviation to either side of it. If you move two standard deviations to either side of the mean, you will take in 95.4% of all the scores in the distribution. Finally, 99.8% of all the scores will fall between the mean and three standard deviations from it. Only a scant 0.2% fall beyond three standard deviations.

Knowing the mean and the standard deviation of any normal distribution allows you to determine just how "average" any given score is. For instance, suppose you take a difficult test consisting of 100 questions and receive a score of 80. How well did you perform? If you learn that the mean is 60 and the standard deviation is 8, you know that your score of 80 is very good indeed. The overwhelming majority of people—95.4%—scored no better than 76, or 2 standard deviations above the mean. Thus, relative to what most others have done, an 80 is excellent. By the same token, a 40 is not very good at all; 95.4% of people scored 44 or higher on this test. Thus, if you received a 40 you are near the bottom of the distribution and had better start studying much harder.

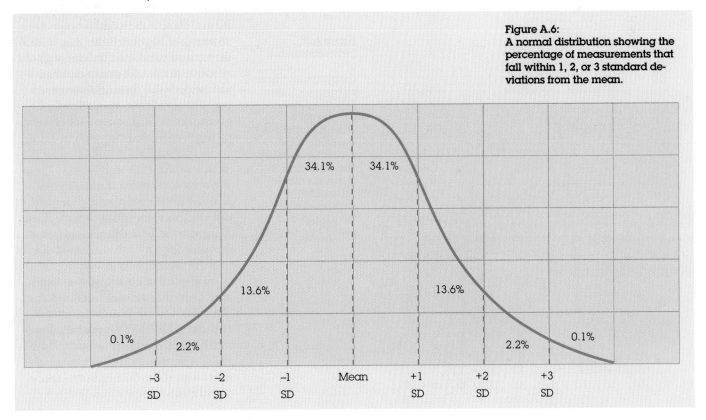

Figure A.6:
A normal distribution showing the percentage of measurements that fall within 1, 2, or 3 standard deviations from the mean.

Inferential Statistics

Can scientists be 100% certain?
In the mid-1970s many Americans were puzzled to learn that a distinguished panel of scientists could not determine with absolute certainty whether the artificial sweetener called cyclamate posed a risk of cancer. The scientists announced that based on months of research, costing millions of dollars, they could be only 95% sure that cyclamate was safe. Why this remaining margin of doubt? Why can't a team of highly skilled researchers, backed by government funds, manage to tell us absolutely if a substance is hazardous to our health?

Chance and Reliability

No one can totally eliminate the influence of chance on scientific findings. Even when you randomly select groups of subjects there is always the possibility that, just by chance, those groups will differ slightly in ways that affect your experiment. This is why scientists must rely on statistics to tell them the likelihood that a certain set of results could have happened purely by chance. If this likelihood is small—5% or less—the researchers are justified in rejecting the chance explana-

tion and in concluding instead that their findings are probably reliable. *Reliable* means that the investigators would probably obtain similar results if they repeated their study over and over with different groups of subjects.

Determining the reliability of experimental findings is a major way in which psychologists use inferential statistics. **Inferential statistics** *are a set of procedures for determining what conclusions can be legitimately inferred from a set of data.* These procedures include what are called *tests of statistical significance.* Tests of statistical significance were used to determine the 95% certainty of the finding that cyclamate is safe to eat. Different tests of statistical significance are needed for different kinds of data.

Tests of Statistical Significance

Suppose you are an educational psychologist who has put together a special program to raise the IQ levels of children with learning disabilities. You expose one group of children with learning deficits to the special program and another group, with equal learning deficits, to the standard curriculum. At the end of a year you give all the subjects an IQ test. Those in the special program score an average of 10 points higher than those in the standard curriculum. Is this enough of a difference to reject the chance explanation and conclude that the program was a success? The most frequent procedure for answering questions like this is a test of statistical significance called the t-*test.*

What is a t-*test?*
The **t-test** *is an estimate of reliability that takes into account both the size of the mean difference and the variability in distributions.* The *greater* the mean difference and the *less* the variability, the less the likelihood that the results happened purely by chance.

Imagine that the results of your experiment looked like the ones in Figure A.7. The mean IQs of the two groups differ by 10 points: 75 for the experimental subjects and 65 for the controls. But look at the variability in the two distributions; there is almost none. All the children in the experimental group received a score within 5

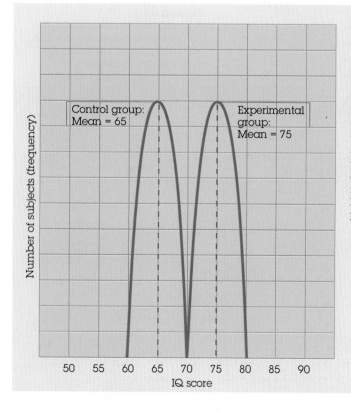

Figure A.7:
In this distribution of IQ scores, the control group has a mean of 65; the experimental group, a mean of 75. When distributions in a study show this little variability and no overlap between the two curves, they are not very likely to have happened purely by chance.

Control group: Mean = 65

Experimental group: Mean = 75

Number of subjects (frequency)

50   55   60   65   70   75   80   85   90

IQ score

points of 75; all the children in the control group received a score within 5 points of 65. It seems that some genuine effect is at work here. The IQ patterns in the two groups are distinctly different and are not the kinds of differences usually caused by chance.

Unfortunately, the results of most experiments are not this clear-cut. Far more often, the distributions look more like those in Figure A.8. In this figure, you can see that the mean difference in scores is still 10 points, but now there is a sizable amount of variability in the two groups. In fact, some of the experimental subjects are doing no better than some of the controls, while some of the controls are scoring as high as some of those in the experimental program. Is a mean difference of 10 points in this case large enough to be considered reliable?

When should you use a t-*test?*
The *t*-test also considers how many subjects are included in the study. You should not put much faith in a comparison of educational programs that tries out each approach on only two or three children. There is too much chance that such samples are not representative of the larger population from which they are drawn. Let's say that in the hypothetical experiment we have been describing, you included 100 randomly selected children in

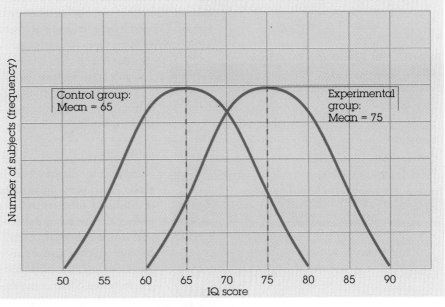

Figure A.8:
In this much more likely set of distributions than the one in Figure A.7, the mean is still 65 for the control group and 75 for the experimental group. But now the variability of the distributions is substantially greater. There is also substantial overlap between the two curves. Is the mean difference in this case statistically significant? A *t*-**test can provide the answer.**

each of the two groups. It is much less likely that samples of this size would be biased enough to distort the research's findings.

To learn the steps involved in actually performing the *t*-test, please read the accompanying box.

How to Perform the t-Test

The *t*-test is an estimate of how reliable the difference between two means is. To determine the likelihood that the outcome occurred by chance, you first need to know the size of the mean difference (mean 1 minus mean 2). In general, the larger the mean difference, the less likely that it happened by chance alone. You also need to know the **variance** within each group, *which is a measure of the variability within the two distributions.* In general, the lower the variance, the less likely that chance alone caused the results. Finally, you need to know how many subjects are in the random samples. In general, the larger the samples, the less the likelihood of a purely chance explanation.

To calculate the *t*-test just follow these steps:
1. Determine the mean of the scores for each group and subtract one from the other.
2. Go back to the box on standard deviation and work through that calculation for each of your distributions, stopping at step 4. This gives you the variance of each distribution.
3. Add the two variances.
4. Add the total number of subjects minus 2 (in our example 200 − 2 = 198).
5. Divide the summed variances by the number obtained in step 4 and take the square root.
6. Divide the mean difference between the two groups by the square root from step 5.
If the samples add up to more than 50 individuals, any value of *t* over 2 is statistically reliable more than 95% of the time.

Table A.1: The Format of a 2 × 2 Table

Talk heard	Signed up for clinic	Didn't sign up	Row total
Fear tactics			100
No fear tactics			100
Column totals			200 (grand total)

Table A.2: Study Results in Our Example

Talk heard	Signed up for clinic	Didn't sign up	Row total
Fear tactics	60	40	100
No fear tactics	40	60	100
Column totals	100	100	200 (grand total)

Analysis of Variance

Not all data lend themselves to a *t*-test, however. Often researchers want to compare the mean scores of more than two groups, or they want to make comparisons among groups that are classified in more than one way. (For instance, does age or sex have an effect on how much children benefit from our special educational program?) In such cases another test of statistical significance is needed. This test is called an *analysis of variance,* or *ANOVA* for short. An analysis of variance is rather like a more complex *t*-test. To learn more about the ANOVA technique, consult any introductory statistics text.

Chi-Square

Sometimes the data psychologists collect do not consist of sets of scores with means or averages. Instead, the researchers have recorded who does what, or who falls into which of several categories. For instance, psychologists have found that chess players are more apt to be introverts than they are to be extraverts. Is this just a chance association? To answer such questions, statisticians often use the **chi** (ky) **square,** *a test of statistical significance.*

Suppose you are a psychologist and you want to study the usefulness of fear tactics in changing people's behavior. You randomly select 200 habitual smokers who are willing to participate in an experiment. You expose half to a 20-minute talk on the known health hazards of smoking, complete with graphic illustrations of diseased lungs and hearts. You expose the rest to a 20-minute talk on the history of tobacco. After the talks, the members of each group are given the opportunity to sign up for a free "quit smoking" clinic. Some people from each group sign up for the clinic; some do not. The easiest way to present their choices is with a 2 × 2 table, like the one set up in Table A.1.

Table A.2 shows how the distribution worked out in your study. Of the 100 subjects in your experimental group (the ones exposed to the fear tactic), 60 signed up for the quit-smoking clinic and 40 did not. Of the 100 subjects in the control group, 40 signed up for the free clinic and 60 did not. Is this difference in the distribution of choices statistically significant?

The chi-square estimates the reliability of such a difference by comparing it with the expected distribution if people had made their decisions purely by chance—for instance, by the toss of a coin. If chance had been the deciding factor, the same number of people would be expected to sign up for the clinic in each of the two groups. The accompanying box gives a step-by-step description of how to do the chi-square calculation.

How to Calculate Chi-Square

Chi-square ($x2$) is an estimate of how sure we can be that a distribution of events or of people did not happen just by chance. In our example, chi-square calculates the *expected* number of people that a chance distribution would place in each of the categories represented by the four cells in the table. This expected number is then compared with the actual *observed* number of people in each of these categories, shown by cells (the data presented in Table A.2). If the difference between the expected and observed numbers is large enough, the distribution is not likely to have happened by chance alone.

Here are the steps in making the chi-square calculation:

1. Figure out how many people, by chance alone, would be likely to fall into the upper-left cell. To do this, multiply the first row total by the first column total (100×100) and divide by the grand total (200). The expected number is 50.

2. Subtract the expected number (50) from the observed number in the upper-left cell (60). The difference is 10 ($60 - 50 = 10$). Square the difference to eliminate negative signs ($10 \times 10 = 100$) and divide the result by the expected number: $100 \div 50 = 2$.

3. Repeat steps 1 and 2 for each of the four cells. In this example the expected values are the same for each cell, but that won't always be true.

4. Add the four values you get from calculating the difference between the expected and observed number for each cell. This is the chi-square.

The reliability of the chi-square value must be looked up in a table. In this example, the fear tactic subjects signed up for the clinic so much more often than the control subjects did that this distribution could have occurred by chance only two times in a hundred.

Summary/Self-Test

DESCRIPTIVE STATISTICS

1. The tools that researchers use to analyze and summarize large amounts of data are called (a)_____. Numbers that are used to present a collection of data in a brief yet meaningful form are (b)_____ statistics, which are often used to present distributions of measurements and scores. The range of scores and the frequency of each one is called the (c)_____; this is often presented in graphic form so the patterns can be seen at a glance.

2. When graphed, a normal distribution produces a curve that tapers off equally on either side from a central high point; this is called a (a)_____ curve. This curve has the characteristic shape of a (b)_____ and shows that most of the measurements fall near the center, with as many falling to one side as to the other. However, not all traits are distributed normally. If more data fall toward one side of the scale than toward the other, it is called a (c)_____ distribution. Such distributions do not have symmetrical shapes when plotted; instead, they have a "tail" on one end. When there are fewer frequencies at the higher end of the horizontal scale (the tail is on the right), we say the distribution is skewed to the right or has a

(d)_____ skew. When there are fewer frequencies at the lower end of the horizontal scale (the tail is on the left), we say the distribution is skewed to the left or has (e)_____ skew.

3. Ways of describing what is "typical" within a given distribution are called measures of (a)_____. The arithmetic average of all the individual measurements in a distribution is the (b)_____. The score above and below which half the scores in the distribution fall is the (c)_____. The measurement that occurs most often in a distribution is the (d)_____.

4. The extent to which scores in a distribution are spread out, or how much scores vary from one another, is the measure of (a)_____. The two most extreme scores at either end of a distribution indicate the range. The measure of variability that shows how widely all the scores in a distribution are scattered above and below the mean is called the (b)_____.

■ *Under what circumstances would you prefer that your professor not use a curve for grading your exams?*

INFERENTIAL STATISTICS

5. Because the influence of chance on scientific findings cannot be completely avoided, procedures are necessary for determining what conclusions can be properly inferred from a set of data; these procedures are called (a)_____ statistics. If the likelihood

that the results could have occurred purely by chance is small, researchers can reject the chance explanation and conclude that their findings are probably (b)_____; that is, they would probably obtain similar results if they repeated the study over and over with different groups.

6. Different kinds of data require different tests of statistical significance. An estimate of reliability that takes the size of the mean difference and the variability in distributions into account is called the (a)_____; it estimates how reliable the difference between two means is. In general, the larger the difference between (b)_____, the less likely that it happened by chance alone.

7. A measure of the variability within two distributions is called the (a)_____. In general, the lower the variance, the less likely that chance alone caused the results. An analysis of variance, or (b)_____, test is similar to, but more complex than, the *t*-test.

8. How sure we can be that a distribution of events or of people did not happen just by chance is measured by another test of statistical significance, called the _____.

■ *How might you use tests of statistical significance to determine the usefulness of the values of your results on working memory span?*

GLOSSARY

ABC theory of emotions According to Albert Ellis, a sequence that occurs when people experience emotions, in which A is the activating event in the environment, B is the belief that the event triggers, and C is the emotional feelings resulting from that belief.

absolute threshold The lowest level of stimulus energy needed in order for that stimulus to be detected. Because this level varies depending on the person and certain other conditions, absolute threshold is today defined as the intensity level that a person detects 50% of the time.

achievement motivation *See* need for achievement

accommodation In Piaget's theory, the change that occurs in existing knowledge or experience as a result of assimilating some new information. In vision, the process by which the muscles of the eye adjust the lens to help focus on close or far objects.

action potential A sudden reversal in the polarity of a neuron's membrane, causing the inside of the axon to reverse its charge and become positive, thereby generating a tiny electrical current.

actor-observer effect The tendency we have, as the actors, to attribute our own behavior to situational factors but as observers to attribute the behaviors of others to their dispositions.

acupuncture An ancient Oriental procedure for relief of pain, in which small needles are inserted into various points on the body, often far removed from the site of the pain.

acute schizophrenia A form of schizophrenia in which problems develop suddenly, without any previous history of mental disorder.

adaptation The ability of an organism to change its responses based on new sensory or perceptual experiences. In sense organs, a decrease in responding with prolonged or continuous stimulation.

adaptive theory A theory suggesting that sleep evolved as a survival mechanism, since it prevented early humans and animals from wasting energy and exposing themselves to the dangers of nocturnal predators.

addiction A physiological need for a drug in order to function normally.

adolescence A developmental period, lasting from about ages 12 to 18, that marks the end of childhood and the beginning of adulthood.

adolescent egocentric thinking The belief that everyone is as totally preoccupied with the adolescent's appearance, thoughts, and feelings as he or she is and the belief that he or she is invincible.

afferent neurons Neurons that carry information from the senses to the spinal cord; also called sensory neurons.

aggressive behavior Any act that is intended to do physical or psychological harm.

agnosia A disorder in which one can receive bits of sensory information but cannot assemble these bits into a meaningful pattern or image.

agoraphobia A fear of open or public places, such as being out on a public street or in a shopping center.

alarm stage In the general adaptation syndrome, our initial reaction to stress, marked by activation of the fight-or-flight response, which in turn causes physiological arousal.

alcoholism A problem in which a person has drunk heavily for a long period of time, is addicted to and has an intense craving for alcohol, and has problems in two or three major life areas (such as social, personal, financial).

algorithms Rules that, if followed correctly, will eventually lead to a solution.

all-or-none law The fact that once a nerve impulse starts in a small segment at the very beginning of the axon, it continues full strength to the very end.

altruism Doing something, often at a cost or risk, for reasons other than the expectation of a material or social reward.

Alzheimer's disease A disorder that usually begins after people reach age 50 and is always fatal; it results from widespread damage to the brain, including the hippocampus, and produces deterioration in personality, emotions, cognitive processes, and memory.

amnesia Loss of memory; it may occur after damage to the brain (temporary or permanent) or after severe psychological stress. *See also* anterograde amnesia; retrograde amnesia

amniocentesis A diagnostic procedure in which a long needle is inserted through the mother's abdominal muscles into the amniotic fluid surrounding the fetus and cell samples are collected.

amplitude The distance from the bottom to the top of a sound wave or a brain wave.

anal stage The second of Freud's psychosexual stages; it lasts from about age 1 1/2 to age 3 and is a time when the infant's pleasure seeking is centered on the anus and its functions of elimination.

analogy Finding a similarity between a new situation and an old, familiar situation.

androgens The major category of male sex hormones secreted by the testes.

androgyny The presence of both masculine and feminine traits in the same individual.

animal model Testing animals on a behavioral task or physiological condition that closely approximates some human problem, disease, or condition.

anorexia nervosa A serious eating disorder characterized by maintaining body weight 15% or more below normal, having an intense fear of gaining weight or becoming fat, starving oneself to remain thin, and having a disturbed body image.

anterograde amnesia The loss of memory for events and facts that occur after damage to the brain but intact memory for events that occurred before the brain damage.

antidepressant drugs A group of drugs used to combat depression.

antipsychotic drugs Drugs used to reduce the level of dopamine and thus reduce the bizarre hallucinations, confusion, and delusions common with schizophrenia.

antisocial personality A personality disorder characterized by a failure to conform to social norms in many areas of the person's life (work, family, interpersonal relationships); also called psychopathy.

anxiety An unpleasant state associated with feelings of uneasiness, apprehension, and heightened physiological arousal, such as increased heart rate and blood pressure.

aphasia Loss of the ability to use or understand words.

approach-approach conflict Having to choose between two situations that both have pleasurable consequences.

approach-avoidance conflict The conflict that arises in a single situation that has both pleasurable and disagreeable consequences.

approaches to understanding behavior Viewpoints on psychology that each have a different focus or perspective that may involve a different method or technique.

arousal-cost-reward model The idea that we make decisions of whether to help by calculating the costs and rewards of helping.

assimilation The process of incorporating new information or experience into existing knowledge.

association areas Brain areas involved in adding meaning or associations to sensory stimuli.

attachment A close emotional bond between an infant and his or her parent or caregiver.

attitude Any belief or opinion that includes a positive or negative evaluation of some target (an object, person, or event) and that predisposes us to act in a certain way toward the target.

attribution The process by which we determine causes for and explain people's behavior.

attribution theory A collection of formal theories that attempt to explain the process of attribution.

auditory nerve A band of fibers that carries impulses from the cochlea to the brain, resulting in the perception of sounds.

authoritarian parents Parents who attempt to shape, control, and evaluate the behavior and attitudes of their children in accordance with a set standard of conduct, usually a standard that comes from religious or respected authorities.

authoritative parents Parents who attempt to direct their children's activities in a rational and intelligent way.

automatic encoding The transfer of information from short-term into long-term memory without any effort and usually without any awareness.

automatic processes Activities that require little awareness, minimal attention, and do not interfere with other activities.

autonomic nervous system That portion of the peripheral nervous system that regulates heart rate, breathing, blood pressure, diges-

tion, secretion of hormones, and other functions as well as maintaining the body in a state of optimal balance or homeostasis.

availability heuristic A rule of thumb by which we rely on information that is more prominent or easily recalled and overlook other information that is available but less prominent or notable.

avoidance-avoidance conflict Choosing between two situations that both have disagreeable consequences.

axon A single threadlike structure that extends from and carries signals away from the cell body.

babbling Making sounds of one-syllable verbalizations.

Bandura's social-cognitive theory A personality theory that assumes personality development, growth, and change are influenced by four distinctively human cognitive processes: highly developed language ability, observational learning, purposeful behavior, and self-analysis. *See also* social-cognitive theory

Barnum principle A strategy for reaching the widest possible audience by phrasing something in such a general way that almost everyone thinks it applies to him or her.

basic emotions Emotions that are either recognized in most cultures or help the species survive by motivating behaviors or signaling physiological needs and psychological moods. The six basic emotions have been identified as love, joy, surprise, anger, sadness, and fear.

basic rules of grammar The rules for combining nouns, verbs, and adjectives into meaningful sentences.

basilar membrane A membrane within the cochlea that contains the auditory receptors, or hair cells.

Beck's cognitive theory of depression The idea that individuals become depressed and stay depressed because of errors in thinking.

Beck's cognitive therapy A form of psychotherapy based on the assumption that negative automatic thoughts color and distort how we perceive and interpret things, thus influencing our behavior.

behavior therapy A form of psychotherapy based on classical and operant conditioning; it emphasizes treatment of specific behaviors and working toward specific goals without focusing on mental events or underlying unconscious factors.

behavioral approach An approach in psychology that studies how organisms learn new behaviors and change or modify existing behaviors in response to influences from their environments; it emphasizes the objective, scientific analysis of observable behaviors.

behavioral genetics A field of psychology that focuses on how inherited or genetic factors influence and interact with psychological factors, such as the ways we behave, adapt, and adjust to our environments, to affect behavior and personality.

Binet-Simon Intelligence Scale One of the first IQ tests; it contained questions that measured vocabulary, memory, common knowledge and other cognitive abilities.

biofeedback A process of recording and amplifying physiological signals from the body, such as muscle activity, brain waves, or temperature, so that one can learn to increase or decrease them.

biological factors Innate tendencies that may either facilitate or inhibit certain kinds of learning.

biological limit theory The idea that our bodies age because there is a biological limit on the number of times that cells can divide and multiply; after that limit is reached, cells begin to die and aging occurs.

biological needs Physiological requirements that are critical to our survival and physical well-being.

biological restraints The limits placed on learning by the structure of the organism's body and brain.

biological theory The idea that behaviors such as aggression are influenced by genetic, physiological, and hormonal factors.

biological theory of depression The idea that underlying genetic or biological factors predispose a person to experiencing depression.

bipolar disorder A mood disorder characterized by swings between depression and mania.

blind spot The point at which the optic nerve exits the eye; at this point the retina has neither rods nor cones.

body image One's perception of and satisfaction with one's body.

brain A physical structure composed of membranes, fluids, and chemicals.

brainstorming A method of problem solving in which a group of people do not criticize each other's suggestions, try to generate as many ideas as possible, attempt to be original, and build on what others propose.

Broca's aphasia An inability to speak in fluent sentences while retaining the ability to understand written or spoken words; it is caused by damage to Broca's area.

Broca's area An area in the frontal lobe necessary for producing and arranging words into meaningful sentences.

bulimia nervosa An eating disorder characterized by a minimum of two binge-eating episodes per week for at least three months; fear of not being able to stop eating; regularly engaging in vomiting, use of laxatives, or rigorous dieting and fasting; and excessive concern about body shape and weight.

burnout Feelings of failing, wearing out, or becoming exhausted because of too many demands on one's time and energy.

bystander effect Inhibition of an individual from taking some action because of the presence of others.

care orientation Making moral decisions based on issues of caring, on avoiding hurt, on how things affect one's interpersonal relationships, and on concerns for others.

case study A method of research in which a single individual's physical, emotional, cognitive, or social processes are studied in great depth across time.

catatonic schizophrenia A type of schizophrenia characterized by periods of wild excitement or periods of rigid, prolonged immobility.

catharsis Engaging in activities that drain off or release emotional tension.

cell body For neurons, relatively large, egg-shaped structure that provides fuel, manufactures chemicals, and maintains the entire neuron in working order; also called the soma.

central cues Hunger cues that come from the brain.

central nervous system The brain and spinal cord.

central route for persuasion Presenting information with strong arguments, analyses, facts, and logic.

cephalocaudal principle The fact that parts of the body closer to the head (*cephalo* in Greek means "head") develop before the parts closer to the feet (*caudal* in Greek means "tail").

cerebellum A region of the brain that serves as a coordination center for voluntary movements and balance.

chi-square A test of statistical significance that calculates the expected number of people that chance distribution would place into various categories, for comparison against the actual observed number of people in each category.

child abuse Inadequate care, neglect, or acts of the parent that put the child in danger or that cause physical harm or injury or involve sexual molestation.

Chomsky's theory of language A theory of how language is acquired that includes the distinction between surface structure and deep structure and transformational rules.

chromosomes Strands of DNA found in all human cells; they carry the organism's genes.

chronic schizophrenia A form of schizophrenia in which individuals have a long history of the disease—and less chance of recovery than with acute schizophrenia.

chronological age Age in years.

chunking A process of combining separate items of information into a larger unit or chunk and then remembering chunks of information rather than individual items.

circadian rhythm A daily rhythm in the body, such as the sleep-wake cycle.

classical conditioning A kind of learning in which a neutral stimulus acquires the ability to produce a response that was originally produced by a different stimulus.

clinical psychologist A psychologist who has a Ph.D., has specialized in the subarea of clinical psychology, and has spent an additional year in a supervised therapy setting to gain experience in diagnosing and treating a wide range of abnormal behaviors.

closure A principle of perception that says that we have a tendency to fill in missing parts of a figure and see the figure as complete.

cochlea The coiled, fluid-filled apparatus of the inner ear.

cognitive appraisal theory The idea that interpreting or appraising a situation as having a positive or negative impact on our lives results in a subjective feeling that we call an emotion.

cognitive approach An approach to psychology that emphasizes how we gather, process, and store information, as well as how we think, solve problems, engage in creative activities, and use language.

cognitive-behavior therapy A method of psychotherapy that uses a combination of information from cognitive processes and learning-conditioning factors to understand and treat mental disorders; it attempts to correct a person's distorted views and pessimistic beliefs about the self and the world.

cognitive development How a person gains an understanding of his or her world through experience and learning.

cognitive developmental theory The idea that, in gender role learning, mental processes must be sufficiently developed for children to learn and understand the rules underlying gender roles, and that children learn male rules or female rules through active involvement with their environments.

cognitive dissonance A state of unpleasant psychological tension that motivates us to reduce our inconsistencies and return to a more consistent state.

cognitive interview A method for obtaining more accurate information from eyewitnesses; they are told to go back in their memory and reconstruct the environment in which the crime occurred.

cognitive learning A kind of learning that involves mental processes, such as attention and memory, and may not involve any external rewards or require the person to perform any observable behaviors.

cognitive map A mental representation of the layout of an environment.

cognitive miser model The idea that in making attributions people feel they must conserve time and effort by taking cognitive shortcuts.

cognitive psychologists Psychologists who study how we process, store, and retrieve information.

cognitive theory In social psychology, the idea that social behaviors such as aggression are controlled by cognitive programs that are stored in memory and used as guides for behavior and social problem solving.

cognitive therapy A type of psychotherapy based on three assumptions: (1) our thoughts shape our emotions and our actions, (2) our beliefs and assumptions shape how we perceive and interpret events, and (3) our distorted thoughts can lead to a variety of disorders.

cognitive unconscious Mental structures and processes of which we are unaware but that influence our conscious thoughts and behaviors.

collective unconscious According to Jung, ancient memory traces and symbols that are passed on by birth and are shared by all peoples in all cultures.

color blindness The inability to distinguish between two or more shades in the color spectrum.

commitment Making a pledge to nourish the feelings of love in a relationship and to actively maintain the relationship.

communication The ability to use sounds, smells, or gestures to exchange information.

community mental health centers Government-sponsored centers that offer low-cost or free mental health care to members of the surrounding community.

companionate love A combination of intimacy and commitment without any sexual passion.

complete love A balanced combination of intimacy, passion, and commitment.

compliance A kind of conformity in which we give in to social pressure in our public responses but do not change our private beliefs.

compulsions Irresistible impulses to perform some ritual over and over even though the ritual serves no rational purpose.

computerized axial tomography (CAT) A technique used to study the structure of the living brain; it measures the amount of radiation absorbed by brain cells.

concept A way to group objects, events, or characteristics on the basis of some common property they all share.

conception Fertilization of an ovum by a sperm.

concordance rates for schizophrenia Statistics that indicate the likelihood of being schizophrenic if another person is.

concrete operations stage According to Piaget, a cognitive developmental stage (from about age 7 to 11), during which children can perform a number of logical, mental operations on concrete objects (ones that are physically present).

conditioned emotional response A feeling that results when an emotional response is classically conditioned to a previously neutral stimulus.

conditioned response (CR) A response elicited by the conditioned stimulus, similar to the unconditioned response.

conditioned stimulus (CS) A formerly neutral stimulus that has acquired the ability to elicit a response that was previously elicited by the unconditioned stimulus.

conduction deafness Deafness caused by wax in the auditory canal, injury to the tympanic membrane, or malfunction of the ossicles.

cones Photoreceptors that contain chemicals called opsins, which are activated in bright light and allow us to see color.

conflict The feeling we experience when we must decide between two or more incompatible choices.

conformity Any behavior you perform because of group pressure, even though that pressure might not involve direct requests.

confounding A type of experimental error that occurs when behaviors are linked and tangled up with each other.

conscious thoughts Wishes, desires, or thoughts of which you are aware or can recall at any given moment.

consciousness Different levels of awareness of one's thoughts and feelings, as well as of other internal and external stimuli and events.

consensus In making attributions, determining whether other people engage in the same behavior in the same situation.

conservation The fact that the amount of a substance remains the same even though its shape changes.

consistency In making attributions, determining whether the person engages in a particular behavior every time he or she is in a certain situation.

contemporary view of gender roles The idea that masculinity and femininity are independent personality variables.

continuity The idea that a person's physical, emotional, cognitive, and social development occur in a gradual and progressive fashion across the life span. In perception, the tendency to perceive a series of points or lines along a smooth or continuous path.

continuous reinforcement Conditioning in which each and every target behavior is reinforced.

control group In an experiment, the group that undergoes everything the experimental group does, except receive the treatment.

controlled processes Activities that require full awareness, alertness, and concentration to reach some goal and that interfere with other ongoing activities.

conventional level In Kohlberg's model of moral development, an intermediate level of moral reasoning, which has two stages. At stage 3, moral decisions are guided most by conforming to the standards of others we value. At stage 4, decisions are based on law and order.

convergence The tendency of both eyes to move inward to focus on a near object, which serves as a cue to depth. Also, the extent to which ganglion cells synapse with rods and cones in the eye; rods have a great deal of convergence, while cones have very little.

convergent thinking Beginning with a problem and coming up with the one correct solution.

conversion disorder A type of somatoform disorder in which the bodily organs and senses are healthy but the person reports physical problems.

coping The cognitive and behavioral efforts that we use to manage a situation that we have appraised as exceeding, straining, or taxing our personal resources.

cornea The rounded, transparent covering over the front of the eye.

correlation A method used to describe the extent of linkage or relationship between the occurrence of two or more events.

correlation coefficient A number used to describe the strength of a relationship between two variables.

cortex A thin layer of cells that essentially covers the entire surface of the forebrain.

counseling psychologist A psychologist who has completed a Ph.D. program in psychology or education, including work in a counseling setting, and who deals more with problems of living than with mental disorders.

counterattitudinal behavior Taking a public position counter to one's private attitude.

covariation principle The idea that we should look for factors that change, or covary, along with a behavior we are trying to explain.

creative thinking A combination of flexibility in thinking and reorganization in understanding to produce innovative ideas and solutions.

critical language period A period of time from infancy to adolescence when language is easier to learn and a period of time after adolescence through adulthood when language is more difficult to learn.

critical period In early development, a period during which the brain cells of humans or other animals are especially vulnerable to changes or restrictions in sensory experience.

cross-cultural approach An approach to psychology that studies the similarities and differences in psychological and social functioning of individuals in different cultures and ethnic groups.

cross-gender behaviors Behaviors that are more typical or stereotypic of the opposite sex.

cross-sectional method A research approach in which several groups of different-aged individuals are studied at the same time.

crowd A large group of persons, most of whom are unacquainted.

cultural bias In testing, the situation that occurs when the wording of the questions and the experiences on which they are based are

more familiar for members of some social groups than for others.

cultural influences Persuasive pressures that encourage members of a particular society to conform to shared values.

cultural stress Difficulties created when the original practices of one's culture are in conflict with the practices of the new, adopted culture.

cultural-familial retardation Mental retardation that results from greatly impoverished environments, with no evidence of genetic or brain damage.

culture-free tests Tests that do not contain vocabulary, experiences, or social situations that are very different from the cultural experiences of the individual taking the test.

dark adaptation The process of adapting from bright light to dim light.

decibels Units of measure for describing the loudness of sounds.

decision stage model A model that describes five stages in deciding whether to help someone in distress: (1) we notice the situation, (2) we interpret it as one in which help is needed, (3) we assume personal responsibility, (4) we choose a form of assistance, and (5) we carry out this assistance.

deep structure According to Chomsky, a sentence's underlying meaning that is not spoken but is present in the mind of the listener.

defense mechanisms Processes that operate at unconscious levels to help the ego reduce anxiety through self-deception.

deficiency needs Physiological needs (food, sleep) and psychological needs (safety, belongingness, and esteem) that we try to fulfill if they are not met.

definitional theory The idea that we form a concept of an object, event, or characteristic by making a list of the properties that define it.

deindividuation The increased tendency for people to behave irrationally or perform antisocial acts when they are in a crowd.

deinstitutionalization The release of mental patients from mental hospitals and their return to the community.

delay of gratification Voluntarily postponing an immediate reward to persist in completing a task for the promise of a future reward.

dendrites Branchlike extensions of a neuron that arise from the cell body.

denial Refusing to recognize some anxiety-provoking event or piece of information.

dependency *See* psychological dependency

dependent variables Aspects of the behavior of experimental subjects that are expected to change as a result of conditions manipulated by the experimenter.

depressive disorders Mood disorders marked by prolonged periods of depression.

descriptive statistics Numbers used to present a collection of data in a brief yet meaningful form.

desensitization A technique of behavior therapy in which the client is gradually exposed to the feared object while simultaneously practicing relaxation.

developmental approach An approach to studying perception in which psychologists examine the normal development of perceptual processes through infancy and childhood.

developmental psychologists Psychologists who study biological, emotional, cognitive, and social development across the life span, from infancy through late adulthood.

developmental psychology A branch of psychology that focuses on moral, social, emotional, and cognitive development during the life span.

diathesis stress theory of schizophrenia The idea that some people have a genetic or neurological predisposition, called diathesis, that interacts with life stressors to result in the onset and development of schizophrenia.

dichromats People who have trouble distinguishing red from green because their eyes have just two kinds of cones.

diffusion of responsibility theory The idea that the presence of others makes one feel less personal responsibility and inhibits taking action in a helping situation.

discrimination In classical conditioning, learning to make a particular response to some stimuli but not to others. In operant conditioning, the learning that has occurred when a response is emitted in the presence of a stimulus that is reinforced and not in the presence of unreinforced stimuli. In social psychology, specific unfair behaviors exhibited toward members of a group.

discriminative stimulus A cue that a behavior will be reinforced.

disease-prone personality A trait or a combination of traits—such as anxiety, anger, hostility, aggression, and depression—associated with a particular disease.

disorganized schizophrenia A type of schizophrenia characterized by bizarre ideas, often about one's body (bones melting), confused speech, childish behavior (giggling for no apparent reason, making faces at people), great emotional swings (fits of laughing or crying), and often extreme neglect of personal appearance and hygiene.

displacement Transferring feelings from their true source to another source that is safer and more socially acceptable.

display rules Specific cultural rules that govern the expression and control of emotional expression in specific situations.

disposition In making attributions, the internal characteristics of the person performing a behavior.

dissociative disorder A psychological disorder characterized by a split or breakdown in a person's normally integrated consciousness, identity, or motor behavior.

distinctiveness In making attributions, determining how differently the person's reaction is in one situation when compared to other situations.

divergent thinking Beginning with a problem and coming up with many solutions.

dopamine theory of schizophrenia The idea that abnormalities in the dopamine system are involved in producing some symptoms of schizophrenia.

double standard for sexual behavior The set of beliefs, values, and expectations that subtly encourage males to be sexually active while at the same time discouraging the same behavior in females.

Down syndrome A genetic disorder that results from an extra 21st chromosome and causes abnormal physical traits (a fold of skin at the corner of each eye, a wide tongue, heart defects) and abnormal brain development, resulting in degrees of mental retardation.

dream interpretation A psychoanalytic technique based on the assumption that dreams contain underlying, hidden meanings and symbols that provide clues to unconscious thoughts and desires.

drive A state of arousal during which the organism engages in behaviors to reduce a need.

drive-reduction theory The idea that a need results in a drive, which in turn arouses the organism to engage in behaviors to reduce the need and return the body to homeostasis.

DSM-III-R The revised third edition of the *Diagnostic and Statistical Manual of Mental Disorders,* published by the American Psychiatric Association. It provides a method for diagnosing a mental disorder by assessing an individual's symptoms on five axes, or dimensions.

dynamic psychotherapy A psychodynamic approach to therapy that is essentially a shortened version of psychoanalysis.

dysthymic disorder A mood disorder characterized by being chronically depressed but with periods of normal mood lasting for a few days or weeks but never more than a month or two.

eardrum A thin, taut membrane at the end of the ear canal that moves in and out in response to sound wave patterns; also called the tympanic membrane.

echoic memory The sensory memory process that holds auditory information for several seconds.

eclectic therapy An approach to psychotherapy in which the therapist combines features from several schools of thought.

ecological approach An approach to assessing intelligence in which researchers study how people solve problems in their usual employment settings.

ECT *See* electroconvulsive therapy

efferent neurons Neurons that carry information away from the spinal cord and are involved in producing some response in muscles or organs; also called motor neurons.

effortful encoding The transfer of information from short-term into long-term memory either by working hard to repeat or rehearse the information or by making associations between new and old information.

ego Freud's second division of the mind, which develops from the id during infancy; the ego's goal is to find safe and socially acceptable ways of satisfying the id's desires and to negotiate between the id's wants and the superego's prohibitions.

egocentric thinking Seeing and thinking of the world from only your viewpoint and having difficulty appreciating someone else's viewpoint. *See also* adolescent egocentric thinking

eidetic imagery The ability to examine a picture or page for 10 to 30 seconds and then retain a detailed visual image of the material for several minutes.

elaborative rehearsal Associating new information with previous information that you already know.

Electra complex *See* Oedipus complex

electroconvulsive therapy (ECT) A procedure used to treat depression in which electrodes are placed on the patient's skull and a mild electrical current is administered to the brain, resulting in a seizure.

embryonic period The prenatal period that spans the two to eight weeks that follow conception.

emotion A feeling made up of three components: conscious or subjective experience, physiological arousal, and overt behavior.

emotion-focused coping Making some effort to handle the emotional distress caused by a harm or threat appraisal. These efforts include directing our attention to something else, avoiding thinking about or denying the situation, engaging in positive thinking, or putting some distance between us and the situation.

encoding The process for controlling the transfer of information from short-term memory into long-term memory.

endocrine system The network of glands that secrete hormones.

endorphins Naturally occurring chemicals in the body that have the same pain-reducing properties as morphine.

episodic information Knowledge about one's personal experiences.

erogenous zones Body areas that are associated with sexual feelings.

ESP *See* extrasensory perception

estrogens The major category of female sex hormones secreted by the ovaries.

ethologists Scientists who study instincts or fixed action patterns as well as how animals adjust to their natural environments.

event schemas Social schemas that contain behaviors that we associate with familiar activities, events, or procedures; also called scripts.

excitement phase The first phase of the sexual response cycle; it is marked by increased muscle tension, a moderate increase in heart rate and blood pressure, and increased blood flow to the genitals.

exhaustion stage In the general adaptation syndrome, the body's reaction to long-term, continuous stress; it is marked by actual breakdown in internal organs or weakening of the infection-fighting immune system.

experiment A procedure for delivering a treatment, observing its effects on behavior, and analyzing the results using statistical procedures. *See also* laboratory experiment

experimental approach In perceptual research, a method in which psychologists either restrict or experimentally change an organism's sensory experience and then assess effects on later perceptual processes.

experimental group In an experiment, the group that will receive the treatment.

experimental psychologists Psychologists whose research includes areas of sensation, perception, learning, motivation, and emotion.

external locus of control The belief that one does not have control over situations and rewards and that events outside oneself (fate) determine what happens.

extinction A decrease in emitting a conditioned behavior because it is no longer associated with an unconditioned stimulus or is no longer reinforced.

extrasensory perception (ESP) A group of psychic experiences that involve perceiving or sending information (images) outside normal sensory processes or channels.

extrinsic motivation Outside forces that influence us to perform behaviors to reduce biological needs or obtain various incentives.

facial feedback theory The idea that sensations or feedback from the movement of facial muscles and skin are interpreted by your brain and result in an emotion.

factor analysis A complicated statistical method that finds relationships among many different or diverse items.

farsightedness A visual acuity problem in which distant objects are clear but near objects are blurry; it is often caused by the eyeball being too short.

fat cells Cells that store body fat.

female secondary sexual characteristics Sexual characteristics unrelated to reproduction that develop during adolescence, including growth of pubic hair and development of breasts.

fetal alcohol syndrome (FAS) A combination of physical and psychological defects caused by heavy maternal drinking during pregnancy.

fetal period A time of prenatal development that begins two months after conception and lasts for about seven months.

fight-or-flight response A combination of physiological responses that arouse and prepare the body for action; it can be triggered by physical or psychological situations that are novel, threatening, or challenging.

figure-ground principle Our tendency to automatically identify a figure, which has more detail, standing out against a background, which has less detail.

five-factor model An approach to personality that organizes all traits under five categories that are used to describe differences in personality.

fixation A Freudian process through which an individual may be locked into an earlier psychosexual stage because his or her wishes were overgratified or undergratified.

fixed action pattern *See* instincts

fixed-interval schedule A schedule of reinforcement in which a reinforcement occurs with the first response following a fixed interval of time.

fixed-ratio schedule A schedule of reinforcement in which a reinforcement occurs after a fixed number of nonreinforced behaviors.

flashbulb memories Vivid recollections, usually in great detail, of dramatic or emotionally charged incidents.

flavor What we experience when we combine the sensations of taste and smell.

flooding A technique of behavior therapy in which a phobic client is immediately and directly exposed to his or her most feared stimulus.

foot-in-the-door technique A method of persuasion that relies on the increased probability of compliance to a second request if a person complies with a small, first request.

forebrain The largest division of the brain, involved in a vast array of responses, including initiating movements and receiving sensations, as well as in behaviors that we characterize as most "human," such as thinking, talking, creating, and imagining.

forgetting curves Graphs indicating the amount of previously learned information that subjects can recall or recognize across time.

formal operations The abilities to think about abstract concepts, to consider issues from another's viewpoint, and to solve abstract problems.

formal operations stage In Piaget's cognitive developmental stages, the stage from about 12 years old through adulthood, in which individuals develop the ability to think about and solve abstract problems in a logical manner.

fovea An area near the center of the retina where cones are highly concentrated and that provides sharp, detailed vision.

fraternal twins Twins that result from the release and fertilization of two ova; they are no more genetically alike than any other two children of the same parents.

free association A psychoanalytic technique that encourages clients to talk about any thoughts or images that enter their head, with the expectation that this kind of free-flowing talk will provide clues to unconscious motivation.

frequency distribution The range of scores we get and the frequency of each one when

we measure a sample of people regarding some trait.

frequency speed The number of sound waves that occur within one second.

frequency theory In explaining pitch perception, the idea that low-frequency sound waves are transformed directly into rate of impulses, as long as the sound waves are 1,000 cycles or less.

Freud's psychodynamic theory of personality A personality theory that emphasizes the importance of early childhood experiences and the effects of conflicts between conscious and unconscious forces. *See also* psychoanalytic approach

Freudian slips Mistakes or slips of the tongue that we make in everyday speech; they are thought to reflect unconscious thoughts or wishes.

frontal lobe A relatively large cortical area in the front part of the brain that is involved in many of our social-emotional behaviors, such as behaving normally in social and emotional situations, maintaining a healthy personality, and making and carrying out plans.

frontal lobotomy An operation in which the front part of the frontal lobe is cut away and thus separated from the rest of the brain.

frustration The feeling that results when one's attempts to reach some goal are blocked.

frustration-aggression hypothesis The idea that when our goals are blocked, we become frustrated and respond with anger and aggression. *See also* modified frustration-aggression hypothesis

functional age How old one acts and feels, based on a combination of physical, psychological, and social factors that affect attitudes toward life, social roles, and quality of life.

functional fixedness A mental set characterized by the inability to see an object as having a function different from its usual one.

functionalism A school of psychological thought that emphasized the study of the function, use, and adaptability of the mind to one's changing environment.

fundamental attribution error The tendency to attribute the cause of a behavior to a person's disposition and to overlook the demands of the environment or situation.

g General intelligence factor, as identified by Spearman.

gender roles The expectations of parents, peers, and society of how we should think or behave because we are male or female.

gender schemas Sets of information and rules organized around how either a male or a female should think and behave.

general adaptation syndrome According to Selye, a series of three stages—alarm, resistance, and exhaustion—that the body goes through in dealing with stress.

generalization In classical conditioning, the tendency for a stimulus that is similar to the original conditioned stimulus to elicit a response that is similar to the conditioned response. In operant conditioning, the tendency to emit the same response to similar stimuli.

generalized anxiety disorder A psychological disorder characterized by a chronic and pervasive feeling of anxiety in many life situations, a feeling of general apprehension, worry about impending disasters, and extreme sensitivity to criticism.

genes The chemical blueprints for the development of an organism and the functioning of its cells; they are carried on the chromosomes in every living cell.

genital stage The final stage in Freud's psychosexual stages, which lasts from puberty through adulthood and is a time when the individual has renewed sexual desires that he or she seeks to fulfill through relationships with other people.

germinal period The two-week period following conception.

Gestalt approach An older theoretical approach that emphasized the idea that perception is more than the sum of its parts and that studied how sensations are assembled into meaningful perceptual experiences.

gifted Individuals who have above-average intelligence, usually IQ scores above 130, as well as some superior talent or skill.

glial cells Cells in the nervous system that have at least three functions: they provide scaffolding to guide the growth of developing neurons and support mature neurons, they wrap themselves around neurons and form a kind of insulation to prevent interference from other electrical signals, and they release chemicals that influence a neuron's growth and function.

grammar *See* basic rules of grammar; syntax

graphology A method that claims to measure personality traits and predict job success by analyzing one's handwriting.

group cohesion Group togetherness, which is determined by how much group members perceive that they share common attributes.

group norms The formal or informal rules about how group members should behave.

group polarization The phenomenon that occurs when group discussion reinforces the majority's point of view and shifts that view to a more extreme direction.

groups Collections of two or more people who interact and share some common attribute or purpose.

groupthink Poor group decision making that occurs when group discussions emphasize cohesion and agreement over critical thinking and making the best decisions. With groupthink discussions are limited, few alternatives are presented, and there is increased pressure to conform.

growth needs According to Maslow, higher-levels needs that are not essential to existence, such as the desire for truth, goodness, beauty, and justice.

hallucinations Sensory experiences without any stimulation from the environment.

hallucinogens Drugs that act on the brain (and body) to produce perceptual, sensory, and cognitive experiences that are not occurring in reality.

hardiness A combination of three personality traits—control, commitment, and challenge—that protect or buffer us from the potentially harmful effects of stressful situations and reduce our chances of developing psychosomatic illness.

hassles Those small, irritating, frustrating events that we face in our daily lives.

hemispheres The two main halves of the brain.

heritability A statistical measure that estimates how much of some behavior is due to genetic influences.

heuristics Rules of thumb that allow one to take shortcuts in solving problems.

hierarchy of needs *See* Maslow's hierarchy of needs

high self-monitors Individuals who constantly monitor their behavior to make sure that it is consistent with the demands of a given situation.

hindbrain An area at the base of the brain that is involved in sleeping, waking, coordinating body movements, and regulating vital reflexes (heart rate, blood pressure, and respiration).

HIV-positive Referring to someone who has been exposed to HIV (human immunodeficiency virus) but may actually be free of AIDS symptoms.

holistic view An approach holding that one's personality is more than the sum of its individual parts; instead, one's personality is a unique and total entity that functions as a unit.

Hollywood love In Sternberg's terminology, a combination of passion and commitment but without any intimacy.

homeostasis The tendency of the autonomic nervous system to maintain the body's internal environment in a balanced state of optimum functioning.

hormones Chemicals secreted by glands of the endocrine system that affect organs, muscles, and glands throughout the body.

hospice A place where people may go to die with the least amount of pain and the greatest amount of dignity.

humanistic approach An approach to psychology and psychotherapy that assumes that each individual has great freedom in directing his or her future, a large capacity for achieving personal growth, a considerable amount of intrinsic worth, and an impressive number of talents to achieve self-fulfillment.

hypnosis An altered state of awareness, attention, and alertness, during which a person is usually much more open to suggestions of a hypnotist or therapist.

hypochondriacal symptoms Imagined physical ailments.

hypothesis An educated guess about some phenomenon that is stated in very precise or concrete language to rule out any confusion or error in the meaning of its terms.

iconic memory The sensory memory process that holds visual information for about a quarter of a second.

id In Freud's personality structure, the first division of the mind to develop, containing two biological drives—sex and aggression—that are the source of all psychic or mental energy. The id's goal is to pursue pleasure and satisfy the biological drives.

ideal self Self-concept based on one's hopes and wishes and reflecting one's desired self.

identical twins Twins that result from a single ovum that splits into two parts after fertilization; they are genetically exactly alike.

identity How one describes oneself, including one's values, goals, traits, interests, and motivations.

illusion A distorted perception of reality that occurs when perceptual processes are tricked.

immune system The body's defense and surveillance network of cells and chemicals that fight off bacteria, viruses, and other foreign matter.

implicit personality theories The beliefs that we rely on when we analyze the behavior of others.

impression management Our attempts to regulate and control, sometimes consciously and sometimes without awareness, information that we present to others; also called self-presentation.

imprinting A set of inherited responses that are elicited by certain stimuli in a newborn animal's environment.

inadequate retrieval cues Too few associations or reminders so that memories cannot be retrieved.

incentives External stimuli, reinforcers, goals, or rewards that may be positive or negative and that motivate one's behavior.

independent variable In an experiment, something the researcher controls or manipulates.

infatuated love Love that often arises instantly, involves a great deal of physiological arousal, and lasts varying lengths of time.

inferential statistics A set of procedures for determining what conclusions can be legitimately inferred from a set of data.

information theory of classical conditioning An explanation for how classical conditioning works: an organism learns a relationship between two stimuli, such that the occurrence of one stimulus predicts the occurrence of another.

information-processing approach An approach to intelligence that defines it by analyzing the components of the cognitive processes that people use to solve problems.

informational influence theory A theory suggesting that we use the reactions of others to judge the seriousness of a helping situation.

innate factors In language, genetically programmed physiological and neurological features of the brain and vocal apparatus that facilitate making speech sounds and learning language skills.

insanity *See* legal definition of insanity

insecure attachment A pattern characteristic of infants who avoid or show ambivalence toward their caregivers; they may cling and hold on one minute but squirm and push away the next minute.

insight The sudden grasp of a solution after many incorrect attempts.

insight therapy Any type of psychotherapy whose goal is to help the patient both become aware of and understand the causes of his or her problem.

insomnia Difficulty in going to sleep and staying asleep throughout the night.

instincts Innate biological forces that predispose an animal to behave in a fixed way in the presence of a specific environmental condition; also called fixed action patterns.

intelligence quotient (IQ) A number that is computed by dividing a child's mental age (MA), as measured by an intelligence test, by the child's chronological age (CA) and multiplying the result by 100.

interference A cause of forgetting that occurs when previous or new information interferes with or prevents retrieval of some particular memory.

interference theory The idea that we forget information not because it is lost from storage but rather because other information gets in

the way and blocks or interferes with its retrieval.

internal locus of control The belief that one has control over situations and rewards.

interpersonal therapy A type of psychotherapy that examines how conflicts with others and disturbed relationships affect depression.

intervention program A program for disadvantaged children that creates an environment that offers increased opportunities for intellectual, social, and personality-emotional development.

interviews A research method in which psychologists ask questions, which range from open-ended to very structured, about behaviors and attitudes, usually in one-to-one situations.

intimacy Feeling close and connected to someone; it develops through sharing and communicating.

intrinsic motivation Performing behaviors because they are personally rewarding or because we are following our personal goals, beliefs, or expectations.

introspection A method of research used by the structuralists, who asked subjects to look inward and observe and report on the workings of their minds.

IQ *See* intelligence quotient

iris A circular muscle that surrounds the pupil and controls the amount of light that enters the eye.

James-Lange theory The idea that emotions result from specific physiological changes in our bodies and that each emotion has a different physiological basis.

just noticeable difference An increase or decrease in the intensity of a stimulus that a person can just manage to detect.

justice orientation Making moral decisions based primarily on issues of law and equality.

Korsakoff's syndrome An alcohol-related disorder that includes a variety of cognitive and emotional deficits: an inability to form new memories (anterograde amnesia), an inability to remember events for the past several or more years (retrograde amnesia), deficits in

short-term memory, a lack of emotional feelings, and general lack of interest, or apathy.

laboratory experiment A research method in which psychologists study behavior in a controlled environment that permits the careful manipulation of some treatment and the measurement of the treatment's effects on behavior.

laboratory setting The research setting used if psychologists answer questions by studying individuals under systematic and controlled conditions, with many of the real-world influences eliminated.

language A special form of communication in which we learn complex rules to manipulate symbols (words or gestures) that can be used to generate an endless number of meaningful sentences.

latency stage In Freud's psychosexual stages, a middle stage that lasts from about age 6 to puberty. It is a time when the child represses sexual thoughts and engages in nonsexual activities, such as developing social and intellectual skills.

latent content The hidden or disguised meaning of a dream's events.

lateral hypothalamus Any area of the hypothalamus involved in feeling hungry and beginning to eat.

law of association A principle stating that if two events (stimuli) occur close together in time, these events will be associated in our minds so that, in the future, the thought of one will remind us of the other.

law of disuse The idea that memories fade away and disappear across time if they are not used.

law of effect The principle that behaviors followed by positive consequences tend to be strengthened or repeated, while behaviors followed by negative consequences are weakened and tend not to be repeated.

learned food aversion A dislike for a particular food that occurs when a neutral stimulus (the food) is paired with an unpleasant response, such as nausea or vomiting.

learning A relatively permanent change in behavior (both mental events and overt behaviors) that results from experience.

learning factors In language development, interactions between the child and his or her environment, such as feedback, reinforcement, observation, and imitation, that influence the development of language skills.

learning-performance distinction The idea that learning may occur but may not always be measured by or immediately evident in performance.

legal definition of insanity Not knowing the difference between right and wrong.

lens A transparent oval structure in the eye whose curved surface functions to bend and focus light waves into an even narrower beam.

light adaptation The process of adapting from dim to bright light.

limbic system A group of interconnected brain structures that are involved in many motivational and emotional behaviors.

linguistic relativity The idea that language determines the way people think and that people with different languages think differently.

lithium A natural mineral salt used in the treatment of bipolar disorder, especially mania.

localization of function The idea that specific functions or tasks reside in various specialized areas of the brain.

locus of control Our beliefs concerning how much control we have over situations or rewards. *See also* external locus of control; internal locus of control

long-term memory A system that stores enormous quantities of information for very long periods of time.

longitudinal method A research design in which the same group of individuals is studied repeatedly at many different points in time.

loudness Our perception of the height or amplitude of sound waves.

low self-monitors Individuals who are relatively unconcerned about situational expectations and demands in social interactions.

lumpers Theorists who define intelligence as a general unified capacity for reasoning, acquiring knowledge, and solving problems.

magnetic resonance imaging (MRI) A technique for studying the structure of the living brain in which computers and magnetic fields are used to obtain a high-resolution image of the brain; sometimes referred to as nuclear magnetic-resonance imaging (NMR).

maintenance rehearsal The intentional repeating of information so that it remains longer in short-term memory.

major depression The most common form of mood disorder, characterized by a sad, dejected mood, problems with appetite and weight, difficulties in sleeping, loss of energy, lack of interest in formerly pleasurable activities, a negative self-concept, and recurring thoughts of death and suicide; also called unipolar disorder.

major life events Potentially disturbing, troubling, or disruptive situations, both positive and negative, that we appraise as having a significant impact on our lives.

maladaptive behavior approach Defining abnormal behavior as anything that interferes with the individual's ability to function as a person or in society.

male secondary sexual characteristics Sexual characteristics unessential to reproduction that develop during adolescence, such as the growth of pubic hair, development of muscles, and a change in voice.

mania Exaggerated energy, enthusiasm, and elation.

manifest content The plot of a dream at the surface level.

Maslow's hierarchy of needs An arrangement of needs or motives in ascending order, with biological needs at the bottom and social needs at the top, indicating that we first satisfy our biological needs before satisfying our social needs.

maturation Development that occurs in a sequential and orderly fashion because of a genetic plan.

MDMA A drug (also called "Ecstasy") that closely resembles both amphetamine and a natural hallucinogen that is found in nutmeg.

mean The arithmetic average of all the individual measurements in a distribution.

measure of variability An indication of how much scores in a distribution vary from one another.

median The score above and below which half the scores in a distribution fall.

medical model approach An approach to defining abnormality in which mental disorders are likened to diseases and, as such, have symptoms that can be diagnosed and treated.

medulla An area in the hindbrain that controls vital reflexes, such as respiration, heart rate, and blood pressure.

memory span test A test that measures the total number of digits that one can repeat back in correct order after a single hearing.

memory The ability to retain information over time through the processes of encoding, storing, and retrieving.

menarche The first menstrual period.

menopause A gradual reduction in secretion of the major female hormone (estrogen), which in turn results in cessation of both ovulation and the menstrual cycle.

mental age A method of estimating a child's intellectual progress by comparing the child's score on an intelligence test to the scores of average children of the same age.

mental disorder A prolonged or recurring problem that seriously interferes with an individual's ability to live a satisfying personal life and function in society.

mental retardation A combination of limited mental ability, usually an IQ of below 70, and difficulty in functioning in everyday life.

meta-analysis A powerful statistical procedure that determines the effectiveness of some treatment (such as psychotherapy) across many studies.

method of loci A memory encoding technique that creates visual associations between memorized places and items to be memorized.

midbrain The smallest division of the brain; it makes connections with the hindbrain and forebrain and alerts the forebrain to incoming sensations.

mind Mental activities, such as feeling, thinking, learning, imagining, and dreaming.

Minnesota Multiphasic Personality Inventory (MMPI) A self-report inventory consisting of 567 statements that describe a wide range of normal and abnormal behaviors to which the person answers "True," "False," or "Cannot say."

mnemonics Techniques that use very efficient methods of encoding to improve remembering and prevent forgetting.

mode The most frequent measurement in a distribution.

modified frustration-aggression hypothesis The idea that frustration may lead to aggression but that a number of situational and cognitive factors may override the aggressive response.

monoamine theory of depression The idea that depression results when the activity of monoamines is extremely low and that mania results when the levels are extremely high.

monochromats Individuals who have total color blindness; their world looks like a black-and-white movie.

monocular cues Visual depth cues that are produced by signals from a single eye; they most commonly result from how objects are positioned in the environment.

mood disorder A prolonged emotional state that affects almost all of a person's thoughts and behaviors.

morpheme The smallest meaningful combination of sounds in a language.

morphology How we group phonemes into meaningful combinations of sounds and words.

motion parallax A depth cue created by the fact that near objects appear to move faster relative to far ones.

motivation The various physiological and psychological factors that cause us to act in a specific way at a particular time.

motor cortex A strip of cortex located on the back edge of the frontal lobe that is involved in the initiation of all voluntary movements.

motor development The acquisition of the muscular control necessary for coordinated physical activity.

motor homunculus A diagram of a distorted body, showing the location of the body's parts along the motor strip in the somatosensory cortex.

multiple-factor theory The idea that here are at least seven independent aspects of intelligence: verbal skills, math skills, spatial skills,

movement skills, musical skills, insight about oneself, and insight about others.

multiple personality The presence of two or more distinct personalities within a single individual.

myelin sheath A tubelike structure of fatty material that wraps around and insulates an axon.

narcissistic personality Having an exaggerated sense of self-importance.

narcolepsy A relatively rare condition that includes irresistible attacks of sleepiness and often muscle paralysis (cataplexy), which are commonly triggered by laughing.

naturalistic setting A research setting in which psychologists gather information by observing individuals' behaviors in their environments, without attempting to change or control the situations.

nature-nurture question The relative contributions that genetic factors and environmental factors make to a person's biological, emotional, cognitive, and social development.

nearsightedness A visual acuity problem in which near objects are clear but distant objects appear blurry.

need for achievement A desire to set challenging goals and to persist in pursuing those goals in the face of obstacles, frustrations, and setbacks.

need A biological state in which the organism lacks something essential for survival, such as food, water, or oxygen.

negative reinforcement The removal of an unpleasant stimulus, resulting in an increased likelihood of the response occurring again.

negative self-concept A poor sense of self that tends to make one act, feel, and think pessimistically and destructively.

neglect syndrome A perceptual disorder caused by brain damage in which the person essentially neglects everything on the left side.

nerves Stringlike bundles of axons and dendrites that are held together by connective tissue.

network theory The idea that related ideas are stored in separate memory categories that are called nodes.

neural deafness Deafness caused by damage to the auditory receptors (hair cells), which prevents the triggering of impulses, or by damage to the auditory nerve, which prevents impulses from reaching the brain.

neurons Cells that have specialized extensions for the reception and transmission of electrical signals.

neuroses According to Freud, maladaptive thoughts and actions that indicate feelings of anxiety arising from some unconscious thought or conflict.

neurotransmitters Chemicals that transmit information between neurons.

neutral stimulus A stimulus that causes some reaction, such as being seen, heard, or smelled, but does not produce the reflex being tested.

night blindness Difficulty seeing at night, often the result of vitamin A deficiencies.

night terrors Sleep disruptions that occur during delta sleep and usually start with a piercing scream, followed by sudden waking in great distress.

nightmares Dreams that contain emotionally charged images that provoke fear and anxiety, all of which may be vividly remembered.

nodes In the network approach to memory, "areas" thought to contain related information that is organized around a specific topic or category.

non-REM sleep Stages 1–4 of sleep, in which rapid eye movement does not occur; it makes up about 80% of sleep time.

nonspecific factors in psychotherapy Conditions common to many different kinds of therapies, including a verbal interaction between therapist and client, a motivated client, the formation of a supportive therapist-client relationship, and a program to work out the client's problems.

normal aging A gradual and natural slowing of our physical and psychological processes from middle through late adulthood.

normal curve A graph of a frequency distribution in which the curve tapers off equally on either side of a central high point.

normal distribution A frequency distribution curve in which the scores have a symmetrical arrangement so that the vast majority fall in the middle range and fewer fall near the extremes of the range.

norms for development The average age at which individuals perform various kinds of skills or exhibit abilities or behaviors.

NREM sleep *See* non-REM sleep

obedience Behavior performed in response to an order given by someone in a position of authority.

object permanence The understanding that objects or events still continue to exist even if they can no longer be heard, touched, or seen.

observational learning A form of learning that develops through watching and does not require the observer to perform any observable behavior or receive a reinforcer.

obsessions Persistent, recurring irrational thoughts that a person is unable to control and that interfere with normal functioning.

obsessive-compulsive disorder An anxiety disorder that consists of obsessions and compulsions.

occipital lobe Two lobes at the back of the brain cortex that contain areas involved in vision.

Oedipus complex According to Freud, a process in which a child competes with the parent of the same sex for the affections and pleasures of the parent of the opposite sex; called the Electra complex in females.

olfaction The sense of smell.

operant conditioning A kind of learning in which the consequences that follow some behavior increase or decrease the likelihood of that behavior occurring in the future.

operation According to Piaget, the ability of mentally transforming, manipulating, or reversing an event or action.

opiates Depressant drugs, derived from the opium poppy (morphine, heroin, codeine) that reduce pain and produce euphoria.

opponent-process theory A theory of color vision suggesting that ganglion cells in the retina and cells in the thalamus respond to two pairs of colors: red-green or blue-yellow.

optic nerve The bundle of neural fibers that carries visual impulses from the eyes to the brain.

oral stage The first of Freud's five psychosexual stages, lasting the first 18 months of life; it is a time when the infant's pleasure seeking is centered on the mouth.

organic retardation Mental retardation that results from genetic problems or brain damage.

orgasm The combination of pleasurable physiological and psychological experiences that accompany ejaculation in males and sexual climaxing in females.

ossicles Three small bones in the middle ear.

oval window A thin, taut membrane between the middle ear and the inner ear.

overgeneralization Applying a grammatical rule to cases where it should not be used.

overjustification effect A decrease in our enjoyment or desire to perform some intrinsically motivating behavior if we are given an external reward for performing that behavior.

ovulation The release of an ovum or egg cell from a female's ovaries.

panic disorder A combination of physiological symptoms, such as a pounding heart, labored breathing, dizziness, and sweating, and psychological symptoms, such as great apprehension, terror, and feelings of impending doom.

paranoid personality disorder Being excessively suspicious.

paranoid schizophrenia A type of schizophrenia characterized by delusions, such as thoughts of being persecuted by others or thoughts of grandeur.

parasympathetic nervous system The segment of the autonomic nervous system that returns the body to a calmer, relaxed state after mobilization and that is involved in digestion.

parentese Speaking in a higher than normal voice, emphasizing and stretching out each word, and using very simple sentences.

parietal lobes Lobes in the upper middle of the brain cortex that contain a region (the somatosensory cortex) where feeling sensations are processed.

Parkinson's disease A disorder characterized by movement problems that occurs when neurons in an area of the forebrain, called the basal ganglia, do not receive a sufficient supply of the neurotransmitter dopamine.

partial reinforcement A schedule for delivery reinforcement in which behaviors are not reinforced each time that they occur.

passion Feeling physically aroused and attracted to someone.

passive-aggressive personality disorder Always indirectly resisting what others ask or expect.

pathological aging Acceleration of the aging process, which may be caused by genetic defects, physiological problems, or diseases.

PCP (phencyclidine) A psychoactive drug that acts as a sedative, because it reduces activity, and as an analgesic, because it reduces pain.

peg method A memory encoding technique that creates associations between number-word rhymes and items to be memorized.

perception The experience of a meaningful pattern or image that your brain assembles from thousands of individual sensations; a perception is normally changed, biased, colored, or distorted by one's unique set of experiences.

perceptual adaptation Changing behaviors in response to new sensory experiences.

perceptual constancy The tendency to perceive sizes, colors, brightness, and shapes as remaining the same even though they are constantly changing.

perceptual sets Learned expectations that automatically add information or feelings to our perceptions and thus change or bias our perceptions.

perceptual speed The time required to identify a particular sensory stimulus from many others and respond to this stimulus.

perfect negative correlation coefficient The correlation coefficient achieved when an increase in one event is always matched by a decrease in a second event (or vice versa).

perfect positive correlation coefficient The correlation coefficient achieved when an increase in one event is always matched by an increase in a second event.

peripheral cues Hunger cues that come from body organs.

peripheral nervous system All the nerves outside the brain and spinal cord.

peripheral route for persuasion Approaches to persuasion that emphasize emotional appeal, focus on personal traits, and generate positive feelings.

peripheral theories Theories of emotion that emphasize changes in the body.

permissive parents Parents who are less controlling and behave with a nonpunishing and accepting attitude toward their children's impulses, desires, and actions.

person-centered therapy A psychotherapeutic approach that assumes that each person has an actualizing tendency, which is a tendency to develop one's full potential; the therapist's task is to show compassion and positive regard in helping the client reach his or her potential.

person perception Making judgments about the traits of others through social interactions and gaining knowledge from social perceptions.

person schemas Our judgments about the traits that we and others possess.

personality A combination of lasting and distinctive behaviors, thoughts, and emotions that typify how we react and adapt to other people and situations. *See also* theory of personality

personality and social psychology The study of social interactions, stereotypes, prejudices, attitudes, conformity, group behaviors, aggression, development of personality, personality change, and abnormal behaviors.

personality assessment An area of psychology that involves the description of personality and the identification of personality problems and disorders.

personality disorder Any psychological disorder characterized by inflexible and maladaptive traits that cause significantly impaired functioning in one's personal and social life.

phallic stage In Freud's psychosexual stages, the stage that lasts from about age 3 to age 6; it is a time when the infant's pleasure seeking is centered on the genitals.

phenomenological perspective The idea that our perception of the world, whether or not it is accurate, becomes our reality.

pheromones Chemicals that have distinctive odors, which in turn attract other animals of the species.

phobia An anxiety disorder characterized by an intense and irrational fear that is out of all proportion to the danger elicited by the object or situation.

phonemes The basic sounds of consonants and vowels.

phonology Rules of how we make the meaningful sounds that are used by a particular language.

photographic memory The ability to form very sharp and detailed visual images after a short period of time and recall the entire image at a later date.

photoreceptors Cells, such as rods and cones, that can absorb light waves.

physiological/neurological responses Changes in the body, such as blood pressure, heart rate, and hormonal secretions, as well as in the brain, such as electrical and chemical changes.

physiological psychologists Psychologists who answer questions about how our genetic makeup and nervous system interact with our environments and influence our behaviors.

Piaget's cognitive stages A series of stages identified by Piaget in which each stage is thought to be qualitatively different from the previous one because it represents the development of some new reasoning or thinking ability.

pitch The highness or lowness of a sound, based on the speed or frequency of its sound waves.

place theory The theory that the brain perceives the pitch of a sound by receiving information about where on the basilar membrane a given sound wave vibrates the most.

plateau phase The second stage of the sexual response cycle, indicated by increased muscle tension, further increases in heart rate and blood pressure, and increased blood flow to the genitals.

pleasure principle According to Freud, the principle according to which the id operates: the satisfaction of drives and avoidance of pain without concern for moral restrictions or society's regulations.

polygraph A device that measures a person's heart rate, blood pressure, respiration, and galvanic skin response, all as means to determine whether the person is lying or telling the truth.

pons A bridge that connects the spinal cord with the brain and parts of the brain with one another.

positive regard Love, sympathy, acceptance, and respect from family, friends, and people important to us.

positive reinforcer A pleasant stimulus that increases the likelihood of the response occurring again.

positive self-concept A good sense of our self, such that we will tend to act, feel, and think optimistically and constructively.

positron emission tomography (PET) A technique used to study the function of the brain by measuring the brain cells' absorption of radioactive substances.

postconventional level According to Kohlberg, the highest level of moral reasoning, in which moral decisions are made after carefully thinking about all the alternatives and striking a balance between human rights and laws of society.

preconventional level Kohlberg's lowest level of moral reasoning, at which moral decisions are based primarily on fear of punishment or the need to be obedient.

prejudice An unfair, biased, or intolerant attitude toward another group of people.

prenatal period The period from conception to birth, about nine months.

preoperational stage In Piaget's cognitive developmental stages, the stage from about 2 to 7 years old, when children learn to use symbols, such as words or mental images, to think about things that are not present and to help them solve simple problems.

prepared learning The innate tendency of animals to be equipped to recognize, attend to, and store certain cues over others.

primacy effect Better recall for items at the beginning of a list.

primacy question The question of whether we can experience an emotion without any thought or whether we must engage in some kind of thinking or appraising before we can experience an emotion.

primary appraisal Our initial, subjective evaluation of a situation in which we balance the environmental demands against our ability to meet them. There are three kinds of primary appraisals: irrelevant, positive, and stressful.

primary auditory cortex An area in the temporal lobe where electrical impulses are transformed into sensations of simple, rather meaningless sounds and tones of different pitches and loudness.

primary reinforcer A stimulus, such as food, water, or sex, that is innately satisfying and requires no learning on the part of the subject to become pleasurable.

primary visual cortex A small area, located at the back of each occipital lobe, that receives sensory information from visual receptors in the eyes and transforms that information into visual sensations.

principle of bidirectionality The idea that a child's behaviors influence how his or her parents respond, and in turn the parents' behaviors influence how the child responds.

principles of organization Rules that specify how we (our brains) organize separate pieces or elements into meaningful perceptions.

proactive interference Interference with learning that occurs when information learned earlier interferes or disrupts retrieval of information learned later.

problem-focused coping Seeking information about what needs to be done, changing our own behavior, or taking whatever action will solve the problem.

problem solving Searching for some rule, plan, or strategy that results in our reaching a certain goal that is currently out of reach.

procedural information Knowledge about performing motor skills or knowledge acquired through classical conditioning.

progeria A rare and incurable disease that causes aging at ten times the normal rate.

progressive relaxation An exercise of tensing and relaxing the major muscle groups of the body until one is able to relax the groups whenever needed.

projection Unconsciously transferring unacceptable traits onto others.

projective test Presenting an ambiguous stimulus and asking the person to describe the stimulus or make up a story about it.

prosocial behavior Any behavior that benefits others or has positive social consequences.

prototype A general concept of what something is like; the average of all the various categories that we have encountered.

prototype theory The idea that we form a concept by constructing an idea of the ideal or prototypic object and then seeing whether a new object matches the prototype.

proximity The tendency to group objects that are physically close together.

proximodistal principle The fact that parts closer to the center of an infant's body (*proximo* in Latin means "near") develop before parts farther away (*distal* in Latin means "far").

psychiatrist A medical doctor who has spent several years in clinical training, which includes diagnosing possible physical and neurological causes of abnormal behaviors and treating these behaviors, often with prescription drugs.

psychoactive drugs Drugs that affect the nervous system and, as a result, may alter consciousness and awareness, influence sensations and perceptions, and modify moods and cognitive processes.

psychoanalysis A method of psychotherapy based on the idea that each of us has an unconscious part whose existence, activities, and thoughts are hidden behind a barrier that we cannot voluntarily remove and that our unconscious conflicts can result in psychological and physical symptoms.

psychoanalytic approach An approach to understanding behavior that focuses on how hidden or unconscious feelings and fears influence one's motivation, thoughts, and behaviors, as well as the development of later personality traits and psychological problems.

psychobiological approach An approach to psychology that examines how our unique genetic makeups and nervous systems interact with our environments to influence learning, personality, emotions, memories, coping techniques, and other traits and abilities.

psychodynamic approach An approach to psychotherapy that assumes that symptoms are signs of more basic underlying problems, that transference needs to be worked out, and that the primary role of the therapist is to interpret and clarify the patient's behaviors.

psychogenic amnesia A dissociative disorder that occurs when a person is suddenly unable to recall important personal information, usually after some stressful incident.

psychogenic fugue A dissociative disorder that occurs when a person not only loses all memory of personal and other events but suddenly leaves home and moves to a new place and assumes a new identity.

psychological dependency The strong psychological need or desire to use a drug to deal with some situation or problem.

psychologist Someone who has completed four to five years of postgraduate education and obtained a Ph.D. in psychology.

psychology The systematic, scientific study of behaviors and mental processes.

psychometric approach An approach to studying intelligence that focuses on measuring or quantifying cognitive factors or abilities that make up intellectual performance.

psychometrics A field that assesses an individual's abilities, skills, beliefs, and personality traits.

psychoneuroimmunology The study of the relationship between the central nervous system, the endocrine system, and psychosocial factors.

psychosexual stages According to Freud, five developmental periods—the oral, anal, phallic, latency, and genital stages—during which the individual seeks pleasure from different areas of the body that are associated with sexual feelings. In each period the child's primary goal is to satisfy desires associated with innate biological needs, such as those involving sex and aggression.

psychosocial factors Factors that affect reaction to stress, include cognitive reactions, personality traits, and social influences.

psychosocial stages According to Erikson, eight developmental periods during which an individual's primary goal is to satisfy desires associated with inborn social needs, such as developing trust, autonomy, or initiative.

psychosomatic symptoms Real physical symptoms that are caused by psychological factors, such as our reactions to stress.

psychotherapy Approaches to treating psychological problems that involve three elements: verbal interaction between therapist and client(s); the development of a supportive relationship during which a client can bring up and discuss traumatic or bothersome experiences that may have led to current problems; and analysis of the client's experiences and/or suggested ways for the client to deal with or overcome his or her problems.

puberty The biological changes, such as sexual maturity and body growth, that occur during adolescence.

punishment A consequence that decreases the likelihood of a behavior occurring again.

pupil A round opening at the front of the eye.

questionnaires A method of research in which subjects are asked to read a list of written questions and then mark specific answers.

random selection A research design such that each subject in a sample population, such as all students on a college campus, has an equal chance of being selected to participate in the experiment.

range The two most extreme scores at either end of a distribution.

rape myths Misinformed beliefs about women and rape often held by rapists.

rapid eye movement sleep *See* REM sleep

rates of metabolism How efficiently our bodies break food down into energy and how quickly our bodies burn that energy.

rational-emotive therapy An approach to psychotherapy that assumes that our irrational interpretations of our experiences, not the experiences themselves, cause problems, such as negative feelings.

rationalization Making up acceptable excuses for behaviors that cause us to feel anxious.

reaction formation Turning unacceptable wishes into acceptable behaviors.

reaction range The extent that IQ scores may increase or decrease as a result of environmental factors.

reaction time The time required to respond to some stimulus (visual or auditory); it slows with increasing age.

real self That aspect of self-concept based on one's actual experiences and representing one's actual self.

reality principle According to Freud, the principle on which the ego operates: satisfying a wish or desire only if there is a socially acceptable outlet available.

recall Retrieving previously learned information without the aid of any external cues.

recency effect The better recall of items at the end of a list.

recognition Identifying information that you have previously learned.

reflex An unlearned, involuntary reaction to a stimulus.

reinforcement A consequence that increases the likelihood of a behavior occurring again.

relaxation response A physiological response induced by sitting or lying in a comfortable position while repeating a meaningless sound over and over to rid oneself of anxious thoughts.

reliability The extent to which a test is consistent: a person's score on the test at one point in time should be similar to the score obtained by the same person on a similar test at a later point in time.

REM (rapid eye movement) sleep The stage of sleep during which one's eyes move raidly back and forth behind closed eyelids; dreams usually occur during this stage.

repair theory A theory of sleep suggesting that activities during the day deplete key factors in one's brain or body that are replenished or repaired by sleep.

representative heuristic A rule of thumb in which we classify or judge the likelihood of some event by comparing it with our mental image or representation of that event.

repression Pushing unacceptable or threatening feelings or impulses into the unconscious.

resiliency Various personality, family, or environmental factors that compensate for increased life stresses so that expected problems do not develop.

resistance In psychotherapy, especially psychoanalysis, the patient's reluctance to work through feelings or to recognize unconscious conflicts and repressed thoughts.

resistance stage The second stage in the general adaptation syndrome, during which the body returns to apparent normal functioning as a reaction to continued stress, but doing so uses up great stores of energy.

resolution phase In the sexual response cycle, the gradual release of muscle tension and return to normal heart rate, blood pressure, and breathing following orgasm.

reticular formation A brain area that alerts and arouses the forebrain to incoming sensory information.

retina A thin film lining the back of the eye that contains several layers of cells that perform transduction—that is, change light waves into impulses.

retinal disparity Depth perception resulting from the fact that the two eyes are separated by several inches, so that each eye actually receives a slightly different image.

retrieval cues Reminders that we create when we associate new information with information that we already know.

retrieving The process for selecting information from long-term memory and transferring it back into short-term memory.

retroactive interference Memory interference that occurs when information learned later interferes with or disrupts the retrieval of information that you learned earlier.

retrograde amnesia A loss of memory for events prior to brain trauma or damage but no loss of memory for events occurring a short time after the brain trauma or damage.

reuptake The action by which neurotransmitters are removed from a synapse through reabsorption.

rods Photoreceptors that contain a chemical called rhodopsin that is activated by small amounts of light.

role schemas Social schemas based on the jobs people perform or the social positions they hold.

romantic love A combination of intimacy and passion; it usually doesn't last because there is no commitment.

Rorschach inkblot test A projective test used to assess personality by showing a person a series of ten inkblots and then asking the person to describe what he or she sees in each.

s Specific abilities, as defined by Spearman.

savants Severely to mildly mentally retarded or autistic individuals who have an unusual ability to remember, calculate, draw, or play music.

Schachter and Singer's cognitive theory A three-step theory of emotion in which (1) a stimulus causes physiological arousal, (2) the arousal creates the need for an explanation of some kind, and (3) the person's interpretation or appraisal of the situational cues results in a subjective feeling of an emotion.

schedules of reinforcement The various ways that reinforcers occur after some behavior is performed.

schemas Cognitive structures or mental models that represent an organized collection of knowledge about people, events, and concepts.

schizoid A personality disorder in which one is self-absorbed and socially withdrawn.

schizophrenia A serious mental disorder that includes a number of symptoms, such as loss of contact with reality and problems of thought, attention, perception, motor behavior, and emotion.

scientific method A set of rules and procedures on how to study, observe, or conduct experiments and minimize the effects of error, bias, and chance occurrences.

scripts Cognitive programs of how to behave in certain situations.

secondary appraisal Deciding what we can do to manage, cope with, or deal with a threat or challenge.

secondary reinforcer Any stimulus that has acquired its reinforcing power through experience.

secondary sexual characteristics *See* female secondary sexual characteristics, male secondary sexual characteristics

secure attachment Characteristic of infants who use their caregiver as a safe home base from which they can wander off and explore their environments.

self or **self-concept** How we see or describe ourselves; it includes how we perceive our abilities, personality characteristics, and behaviors.

self-actualization The inherent tendency to reach our true potentials.

self-efficacy Our personal beliefs of how capable we are of exercising control over events in our lives.

self-esteem How much one likes oneself; it includes feelings of worth, attractiveness, and social competence.

self-fulfilling prophecy Making a prediction or statement about a future behavior and then acting, usually unknowingly, to fulfill it.

self-handicapping Deliberately constructing obstacles or handicaps that will protect one's sense of self-esteem from public failure.

self-handicapping strategy A tendency to make up an excuse for one's failure.

self-monitoring In cognitive therapy, observing one's own behavior without making any changes.

self-perception theory The idea that we first observe or perceive our own behavior and then infer attitudes from the behavior.

self-presentation *See* impression management

self-report inventories Tests with highly structured formats that include objective questions with a limited range of answers.

self-serving bias Attributing success to our disposition and failure to the situation.

semantic information General knowledge, book-learning, facts, and definitions of words.

semantics A field that specifies the meaning of words in various contexts.

semipermeable Pertaining to membranes, the ability to selectively regulate the flow of chemical particles.

sensation Our first awareness of some outside stimulus.

sensorimotor stage The first stage in Piaget's cognitive developmental stages, lasting from birth to about age 2; at this stage infants interact with and learn about their environments by relating their sensory experiences (such as hearing and seeing) to their motor actions.

sensory experience A psychological experience of some physical stimuli, which occurs after impulses are processed by the brain.

sensory homunculus A distorted diagram of the body showing the location of the body's parts along the sensory strip in the somatosensory cortex.

sensory memory An initial process that holds environmental information in its "raw" form for a brief period of time, from an instant to several seconds.

separation anxiety An infant's distress, as indicated by loud protests, crying, and agitation, whenever the infant's parents temporarily leave.

set point or range A level of body weight (ratio of fat to lean) that remains relatively constant.

sex hormones Chemicals, secreted by glands, that circulate in the bloodstream and influence the brain, other body organs, and behaviors.

shaping In operant conditioning, reinforcing behaviors that lead up to or approximate the desired behavior.

short-term memory Working memory, which has a limited capacity and a short duration of 2 to 30 seconds, which can be lengthened if you rehearse or work on the information.

shyness The tendency to feel tense, worried, or awkward in social situations.

similarity In perception, our tendency to group elements together that appear similar.

simple phobias Irrational fears triggered by common objects, situations, or animals, such as a fear of heights, snakes, or bugs.

simplicity In perception, our tendency to organize stimuli in the simplest way possible.

single-word stage The stage in language development when children utter single words, usually referring to what they can see, hear, or feel.

situation In making attributions, the circumstances or context of a behavior.

skewed distributions Distributions in which more data fall toward one side of the scale than toward the other.

Skinner box An experimental apparatus used in operant conditioning, it has a lever, food cup, and devices to record the animal's bar presses and the delivery of food pellets.

sleepwalking Walking or carrying out behaviors in one's sleep, such as dressing, eating, performing bathroom functions, and even driving a car.

social-adjustive function Pertaining to behaviors that help us adjust to or fit in better with a new group.

social cognition The study of how people perceive, store, and retrieve information about social interactions.

social-cognitive theory An approach that emphasizes the importance of learning through imitation, observation, and reinforcement in the development of social skills, interactions, and behaviors. *See also* Bandura's social-cognitive theory

social comparison theory The idea that we are driven to compare ourselves to others who are similar to us so that we can measure the correctness of our attitudes and beliefs.

social development How a person develops relationships with others, develops a sense of self, and becomes a social being.

social facilitation An increase in performance in the presence of a crowd.

social forces Demands, pressures, judgments, requests, and expectations that arise from the presence of other people.

social inhibition A decrease in performance in the presence of a crowd.

social learning theory An approach that emphasizes the influence of learning, social, and cognitive processes on how we evaluate, interpret, and organize information and apply that information to ourselves and others.

social needs Needs that are acquired through learning and experience.

social norms approach In defining abnormality, the idea that behavior is considered abnormal if it deviates greatly from accepted social norms.

social phobias Irrational fears brought on by the presence of other people.

social psychology A broad field that studies how our thoughts, feelings, perceptions, and behaviors are influenced by interactions with others.

social support Human relationships that have a lasting and positive impact on our lives.

socially oriented Pertaining to groups in which the members are primarily concerned about fostering and maintaining social relationships.

sociocognitive theory The idea that hypnosis works by creating powerful pressures that make subjects want to conform and, as a result, want to perform behaviors suggested by the hypnotist.

somatic nervous system A network of ropelike nerves that are connected either to sensory receptors or to muscles that you can move voluntarily, such as muscles in your limbs, back, neck, and chest.

somatization disorder A somatoform disorder in which an individual has multiple physical symptoms (at least 12 to 14) that have no physical causes but that are triggered by psychological problems or distress.

somatoform disorders Psychological disorders that involve the appearance of real physical symptoms that are not under voluntary control, have no known physical causes, and are believed to be caused by psychological factors.

somatosensory cortex The area of the brain that receives sensations, such as touch, pain, and temperature, from receptors in the skin and joints.

special process theory The idea that a hypnotized individual is in a special state (trance) and, as a result, hypnotic behaviors are different from normal waking behaviors.

splitters Psychologists who define intelligence as composed of many separate mental abilities that function more or less independently.

spontaneous recovery The tendency for a conditioned response to reappear even though there are no further conditioning trials.

stages Development occurring in distinct steps or discrete stages across the life span.

standard deviation A statistic indicating how widely all the scores in a distribution are scattered above and below the mean.

standardized tests Psychological tests that have been given to hundreds of people and have been shown to reliably measure thought patterns, personality traits, emotions, or behaviors.

state-dependent learning The idea that it is easier to recall information when you are in the same physiological state as when you originally learned that information.

statistical frequency approach In defining abnormality, the idea that a behavior may be considered abnormal if it occurs infrequently in relation to the behaviors of the general population.

statistics Methods researchers use to analyze and summarize large amounts of data.

stereotypes Widely held beliefs that people have certain traits because they belong to a particular group.

stimulants Drugs, such as cocaine, amphetamine, coffee, and nicotine, that increase activity in the nervous system and result in heightened alertness, arousal, and euphoria and decreased appetite and fatigue.

stimulus hierarchy In desensitization therapy, a list of feared stimuli, arranged in order from least to most feared.

stimulus substitution A bond or association that forms between a conditioned stimulus and an unconditioned stimulus so that the conditioned stimulus eventually substitutes for the unconditioned stimulus.

stress The feeling we have when we evaluate or appraise a situation as something that overloads or strains our psychological resources.

strict behaviorism A behaviorist approach that emphasizes observable behaviors, the importance of environmental reinforcers, and the exclusion of mental processes.

structuralism An early school of psychological thought that emphasized the study of conscious elements—sensations, images, and feelings—of the normal human mind. Structuralists argued that we could understand how perceptions were formed by breaking them down into smaller and smaller units and then analyzing these basic units.

subgoals In solving problems, dealing with separate parts that when completed in order will result in a solution.

sublimation A type of displacement that involves redirecting a threatening or forbidden desire, usually sexual, into a socially acceptable one.

superego Freud's third division of the mind, which develops from the ego during early childhood; its goal is applying the moral values and standards of one's parents or caregivers and society in satisfying one's wishes.

surface structure According to Chomsky, the actual wording of a sentence, as it is spoken.

survey A research technique in which information is obtained by asking many individuals to answer written or oral questions.

sympathetic nervous system The portion of the autonomic nervous system triggered by threatening or challenging physical or psychological stimuli; it increases the body's physiological arousal.

synapse An infinitely small space (20–30 billionths of a meter) between neurons, over which chemical messages are transmitted.

syntax How we combine words to form meaningful phrases and sentences.

systematic desensitization Based on principles of classical conditioning, a method for pairing a relaxation response with stimuli or situations that elicit anxiety.

t-test A test of statistical significance that takes into account both the size of the mean difference and the variability in distributions.

taijin kyofusho (TKS) Unique to Japan, a specific social phobia characterized by a morbid fear of offending others through one's awkward social or physical behavior.

tardive dyskinesia A disease associated with use of antipsychotic drugs such as phenothiazines; it involves the appearance of slow, involuntary, and uncontrollable rhythmic movements and rapid twitching of the mouth and lips, as well as unusual movements of the limbs.

task oriented Pertaining to groups in which the members have specific duties to complete.

taste buds Structures on the tongue that contain the receptors for tasting.

TAT *See* Thematic Apperception Test

telegraphic speech A pattern of speaking that omits articles, prepositions, and parts of verbs.

temperament An infant's characteristic mood, level of energy, and reaction to new objects, situations, or people.

temporal lobe A segment of the brain located directly below the parietal lobe that is critical to hearing and speech.

teratogens Damaging agents that cause birth defects.

terminal buttons Bulblike swellings at the ends of axons that store neurotransmitters.

testimonial A statement in support of a particular viewpoint based on personal experience.

testosterone The major male hormone, which stimulates growth of genital organs and development of secondary sexual characteristics.

Thematic Apperception Test (TAT) A personality test that consists of asking subjects to look at pictures of people in ambiguous situations and asking the subjects to make up stories about what is happening in the pictures.

theory of personality An organized attempt to describe and explain how personalities develop and why personalities differ.

thinking Forming concepts, solving problems, and engaging in creative activities.

threshold A point above which a stimulus is perceived and below which it is not perceived.

time-out A procedure that decreases undesirable behaviors by removing all reinforcements.

tip-of-the-tongue phenomenon The feeling of really knowing something but, despite making a great effort, being unable to recall the information from memory.

tolerance The body's reaction to regular drug use, whereby the person has to take larger doses of the drug to achieve the same behavioral effect.

touch The skin senses, which include pressure, temperature, and pain.

traditional view of gender roles The idea that masculinity and femininity represent opposite poles of a continuum.

trait A relatively stable and enduring tendency to behave in a particular way.

trait theory An approach to understanding the structure of personality by measuring, identifying, and analyzing differences in personality.

transformational rules According to Chomsky, procedures of converting ideas from surface structures into deep structure and from deep structures back into surface ones.

transcendental meditation (TM) A type of meditation that involves assuming a comfortable position, closing one's eyes, repeating and concentrating on a sound to clear one's head of all thoughts (worrisome and otherwise).

transduction The process by which a sense organ changes or transforms particular physical stimuli into impulses.

transference In psychotherapy, the process by which the patient feels toward the therapist the conflict-ridden emotions felt toward someone important in the patient's life.

triangular theory of love Sternberg's theory of love, which divides it into three components: passion, commitment, and intimacy.

triarchic theory The idea that intelligence can be divided into three ways of gathering and processing information (*triarchic* means "three").

trichromatic theory The idea that cones in the retina are most responsive to three primary colors—blue, green, and red—from which all other colors can be mixed.

tricyclics A group of antidepressant drugs.

two-factor theory Spearman's suggestion that everyone has a general intelligence factor, termed *g*, as well as specific abilities, labeled *s*.

two-word combinations In language development, strings of two words that express various actions ("Me play," "See boy") or relationships ("Hit ball," "Allgone milk").

Type A personality Characteristic of an individual who frequently expresses one or more negative emotions, such as anger, hostility, or aggression, or who experiences depression.

unconditional positive regard Showing someone love and acceptance despite the fact that he or she sometimes behaves in ways that are different from what we think or value.

unconditioned response (UCR) An unlearned, innate, involuntary, physiological reflex that is elicited by the unconditioned stimulus.

unconditioned stimulus (UCS) A stimulus that triggers or elicits some physiological reflex, such as salivation.

unconscious forces Wishes, desires, or thoughts that, because of their disturbing or threatening content, we automatically repress.

unconscious motivation The influence of repressed thoughts, desires, or impulses on our conscious thoughts and behaviors.

unipolar disorder *See* major depression

uplifts Those small, pleasurable, happy, and satisfying experiences that we have in our daily lives.

validity The extent to which a test measures what it is supposed to measure.

variable-interval schedule A schedule of reinforcement delivery in which reinforcement occurs on the first response after a variable amount of time has gone by.

variable-ratio schedule A schedule of reinforcement delivery in which a reinforcement occurs after an variable number of nonreinforced behaviors.

variance A measure of the variability within two distributions.

ventromedial hypothalamus An area of the hypothalamus involved in feeling full and stopping eating.

vestibular organs Three archlike structures in the inner ear that provide feedback on your body's position in space.

visual acuity The ability to see fine details.

visual agnosia Difficulty in assembling simple visual sensations into more complex, meaningful images.

visual cliff A glass tabletop with a checkerboard patterned surface on one side, used to test depth perception in infants.

volley theory In explaining pitch perception, the idea that at above 1,000 cycles per second, neurons fire in volleys and the brain "adds" volleys and creates the sensation of a low-pitched sound.

vulnerability Psychological or environmental difficulties that make children more at risk for developing later personality, behavioral, or social problems.

wear and tear theory The idea that our bodies age because of naturally occurring problems or breakdowns in the body's cells.

Weber's law A psychophysics law stating that the amount of increase in intensity of a stimulus needed to produce a just noticeable difference grows in proportion to the intensity of the initial stimulus.

Wernicke's aphasia Difficulty in understanding spoken or written words and in putting words into meaningful sentences, as a result of injury to Wernicke's area in the brain.

Wernicke's area An area located in the left temporal lobe that plays a role in understanding speech and speaking in coherent sentences.

withdrawal symptoms Painful physical and psychological symptoms that occur when an addicted person stops taking a drug.

Yerkes-Dodson law The principle that performance on a task depends on the amount of physiological arousal and the difficulty of the task. For many tasks, moderate arousal helps performance.

zygote A fertilized egg.

REFERENCES

Abler, R. M., & Sedlacek, W. E. (1989). Freshman sexual attitudes and behaviors over a 15-year period. *Journal of College Student Development, 30,* 201–209.

Adams, C. (1991). Qualitative age differences in memory for text: A life-span developmental perspective. *Psychology and Aging, 6,* 323–336.

Adelmann, P. K., & Zajonc, R. B. (1989). Facial efference and the experience of emotion. *Annual Review of Psychology, 40,* 249–280.

Ader, R., & Cohen, N. (1975). Behaviorally conditioned immunosuppression. *Psychosomatic Medicine, 37,* 333–340.

Aguayo, A. J. (1985). Capacity for renewed axonal growth in the mammalian central nervous system. In A. Bignami, F. E. Bloom, C. L. Bolis, & A. Adelyoe (Eds.), *Central nervous system plasticity and repair.* New York: Raven Press.

Ainsworth, M. D. S. (1979). Infant-mother attachment. *American Psychologist, 34,* 932–937.

Ainsworth, M. D. S. (1989). Attachments beyond infancy. *American Psychologist, 44,* 709–716.

Ajzen, I., Timko, C., & White, J. B. (1982). Self-monitoring and the attitude-behavior relation. *Journal of Personality and Social Psychology, 42,* 426–435.

Alcock, J. E. (1987). Parapsychology: Science of the anomalous or search for the soul? *Behavioral and Brain Sciences, 10,* 563–643.

Alkon, D. L., Ikeno, H., Dworkin, J., McPhie, D. L., Olds, J. L., Lederhendler, I., Matzel, L., Schreirs, B. G., Kuzirian, A., Collin, C., & Yamoah, E. (1990). Contraction of neural branching volume: An anatomic correlate of Pavlovian conditioning. *Proceedings of the National Academy of Sciences, 87,* 1611–1614.

Allen, D. M., & Tarnowski, K. J. (1989). Depressive characteristics of physically abused children. *Journal of Abnormal Child Psychology, 17,* 1–11.

Allport, G. W. (1937). *Personality: A psychological interpretation.* New York: Holt.

Allport, G. W., & Odbert, H. S. (1936). Trait-names: A psycho-lexical study. *Psychological Monographs, 47* (Whole No. 211).

Amabile, T. M. (1985). Motivation and creativity: Effects of motivational orientation on creative writers. *Journal of Personality and Social Psychology, 48,* 393–399.

Amabile, T. M., Hennessey, B. A., & Grossman, B. S. (1986). Social influences on creativity: The effects of contracted-for reward. *Journal of Personality and Social Psychology, 50,* 14–23.

American Psychiatric Association. (1987). *Diagnostic and statistical manual of mental disorders* (3rd ed., rev.). Washington, DC: Author.

American Psychiatric Association. (1952/1968/1980). *Diagnostic and statistical manual of mental disorders* (1st ed., 2nd ed., 3rd ed.). Washington, DC: Author.

American Psychological Association. (1981). Ethical principles of psychologists. *American Psychologist, 36,* 633–638.

Amering, M., & Katschnig, H. (1990). Panic attacks and panic disorder in cross-cultural perspective. *Psychiatric Annals, 20,* 511–516.

Anastasi, A. (1988). *Psychological testing* (6th ed.). New York: Macmillan.

Anderson, J. R. (1985). *Cognitive psychology and its implications* (2nd ed.). New York: W. H. Freeman.

Andreasen, N. C. (1987). Creativity and mental illness: Prevalence rates in writers and their first-degree relatives. *American Journal of Psychiatry, 144,* 1288–1292.

Andreasen, N. C. (1988). Brain imaging: Applications in psychiatry. *Science, 239,* 1381–1388.

Andrykowski, M. A., & Otis, M. L. (1990). Development of learned food aversions in humans: Investigation in a "natural laboratory" of cancer chemotherapy. *Appetite, 14,* 145–158.

Annis, H. M. (1990). Relapse to substance abuse: Empirical findings within a cognitive-social learning approach. *Journal of Psychoactive Drugs, 22,* 117–124.

Armstrong, S. M. (1989). Melatonin: The internal Zeitgeber of mammals? *Pineal Research Reviews, 7,* 157–202.

Asch, S. E. (1958). Effects of group pressure upon modification and distortion of judgments. In E. E. Maccoby, T. M. Newcomb, & E. L. Hartley (Eds.), *Readings in social psychology* (3rd ed.). New York: Holt, Rinehart & Winston.

Atkinson, J. W. (Ed.). (1958). *Motives in fantasy, action and society.* Princeton, NJ: Van Nostrand Reinhold.

Atkinson, J. W. (1964). *An introduction to motivation.* Princeton, NJ: Van Nostrand Reinhold.

Atkinson, J. W., & Raynor, J. O. (Eds.). (1974). *Motivation and achievement.* Washington, DC: V. H. Winston.

Atkinson, R. C., & Shiffrin, R. M. (1968). Human memory: A proposed system and its control processes. In K. W. Spence & J. T. Spence (Eds.), *The psychology of learning and motivation: Advances in research and theory* (vol. 2). New York: Academic Press.

Attias, J., Gordon, C., Ribak, J., Binah, O., & Arnon, R. (1987). Efficacy of transdermal scopolamine against seasickness: A 3-day study at sea. *Aviation, Space and Environmental Medicine, 58,* 60–62.

Attie, I., & Brooks-Gunn, J. (1989). Development of eating problems in adolescent girls: A longitudinal study. *Developmental Psychology, 25,* 70–79.

Azar, S. T., & Siegel, B. R. (1990). Behavioral treatment of child abuse. *Behavior Modification, 14,* 279–300.

Azrin, N. H., & Foxx, R. M. (1974). *Toilet training in less than a day.* New York: Simon & Schuster.

Bahrick, H. P. (1984). Semantic memory content in permastore: Fifty years of memory for Spanish learned in school. *Journal of Experimental Psychology: General, 113,* 1–29.

Bahrick, H. P., Bahrick, P. O., & Wittlinger, R. P. (1975). Fifty years of memory for names and faces. *Journal of Experimental Psychology: General, 104,* 54–75.

Bailey, J. M., & Pillard, R. C. (1991). A genetic study of male sexual orientation. *Archives of General Psychiatry, 48,* 1089–1096.

Ballenger, J. C. (1991). Long-term pharmacologic treatment of panic disorder. *Journal of Clinical Psychiatry, 52,* 18–23.

Bandura, A. (1986). *Social foundations of thought* and *action: A social cognitive theory.* Englewood Cliffs, NJ: Prentice-Hall.

Bandura, A. (1989). Human agency in social cognitive theory. *American Psychologist, 44,* 1175–1184.

Bandura, A. (1989a). Social cognitive theory. In R. Vasta (Ed.), *Annals of child development* (vol. 6). Greenwich, CT: JAI Press.

Bandura, A. (1989b). Regulation of cognitive processes through perceived self-efficacy. *Developmental Psychology, 25,* 729–735.

Bandura, A. (1965). Influence of models' reinforcement contingencies on the acquisition of imitative responses. *Journal of Personality and Social Psychology, 1,* 589–596.

Barinaga, M. (1991). How long is the human lifespan? *Science, 254,* 936–938.

Barr, H. M., Streissguth, A. P., Darby, B. L., & Sampson, P. D. (1990). Prenatal exposure to alcohol, caffeine, tobacco, and aspirin: Effects on fine and gross motor performance in 4-year-old children. *Developmental Psychology, 26,* 339–348.

Barron, F., & Harrington, D. M. (1981). Creativity, intelligence, and personality. *Annual Review of Psychology, 32,* 439–476.

Bartlett, F. C. (1932). *Remembering: A study in experimental and social psychology.* Cambridge: Cambridge University Press.

Baruch, G. K., Biener, L., & Barnett, R. C. (1987). Women and gender in research on work and family stress. *American Psychologist, 42,* 130–136.

Bashore, T. R., Osman, A., & Heffley, E. F., III. (1989). Mental slowing in elderly persons: A cognitive psychophysiological analysis. *Psychology and Aging, 4,* 235–244.

Baumrind, D. (1991). Effective parenting during the early adolescent transition. In P. A. Cowan & E. M. Hetherington (Eds.), *Advances in family research.* Hillsdale, NJ: Erlbaum.

Beaman, A. L., Cole, C. M., Preston, M., Lkentz, B., & Steblay, N. M. (1983). Fifteen years of foot-in-the-door research. *Personality and Social Psychology Bulletin, 9,*181–196.

Beatty, M. J., & Behnke, R. R. (1991). Effects of public speaking trait anxiety and intensity of speaking task on heart rate during performance. *Human Communication Research, 18,* 147–176.

Beck, A. T. (1967). *Depression: Clinical, experimental, and theoretical aspects.* New York: Harper & Row.

Beck, A. T. (1991). Cognitive therapy: A 30-year retrospective. *American Psychologist, 46,* 368–375.

Beck, A. T., Rush, A. J., Shaw, B. F., & Emery, G. (1979). *Cognitive therapy of depression.* New York: Guilford Press.

Bedi, K. S., Thomas, Y. M., Davies, C. A., & Dobbing, J. (1980). Synapse-to-neuron ratios of the frontal and cerebellar cortex of the 30-day-old and adult rats undernourished during early postnatal life. *Journal of Comparative Neurology, 193,* 49–56.

Bell, A. P., Weinberg, M. S., & Hammersmith, S. K. (1981). *Sexual preference: Its development in men and women.* Bloomington: Indiana University Press.

Belsky, J. (1989). Infant-parent attachment and day care: In defense of the Strange Situation. In J. S. Lande, S. Scarr, & N. Gunzenhauser (Eds.), *Caring for children: Challenge to America.* Hillsdale, NJ: Lawrence Erlbaum.

Bem, D. (1967). Self-perception: An alternative interpretation of cognitive dissonance phenomena. *Psychological Review, 74,* 183–200.

Bem, S. L. (1985). Androgyny and gender schema theory: Conceptual and empirical integration. In T. B. Sonderegger (Ed.), *Nebraska symposium on motivation.* Lincoln: University of Nebraska Press.

Ben-Shakhar, G., Bar-Hillel, M., Bilu, Y., Ben-Abba, E., & Flug, A. (1986). Can graphology predict occupational success? Two empirical studies and some methodological ruminations. *Journal of Applied Psychology, 71,* 645–653.

Benbow, C. P., & Stanley, J. C. (1980). Sex differences in mathematics ability: Fact or artifact? *Science, 210,* 1262–1264.

Benson, H. (1975). *The relaxation response.* New York: Morrow.

Benson, H., Lehmann, J. W., Malhotra, M. S., Goldman, R. F., Hopkins, P. J., & Epstein, M. D. (1982). Body temperature changes during the practice of g Tum-mo yoga. *Nature, 295,* 234–235.

Benson, H., Malhotra, M. S., Goldman, R. F., Jacobs, G. D., & Hopkins, P. J. (1990). Three case reports of the metabolic and electro-encephalographic changes during advanced Buddhist meditation techniques. *Behavioral Medicine, 16,* 90–95.

Bergen, D. J., & Williams, J. E. (1991). Sex stereotypes in the United States revisited: 1972–1988. *Sex Roles, 24,* 413–423.

Berglas, S. (1989). Self-handicapping behavior and the self-defeating personality disorder. In R. C. Curtis (Ed.), *Self-defeating behaviors: Experimental research, clinical impressions, and practical implications.* New York: Plenum Press.

Berkowitz, L. (1989). Frustration-aggression hypothesis: Examination and reformulation. *Psychological Bulletin, 106,* 59–73.

Bernstein, D. A., & Kleinknecht, R. A. (1982). Multiple approaches to the reduction of dental fear. *Journal of Behavior Therapy and Experimental Psychiatry, 13,* 287–292.

Bernstein, I. L. (1991). Aversion conditioning in response to cancer and cancer treatment. *Clinical Psychology Review, 11,* 185–191.

Berquier, A., & Ashton, R. (1991). A selective review of possible neurological etiologies of schizophrenia. *Clinical Psychology Review, 11,* 645–661.

Bidell, T. R., & Fischer, K. W. (1989). Commentary. *Human Development, 32,* 363–368.

Biernat, M. (1991). Gender stereotypes and the relationship between masculinity and femininity: A developmental analysis. *Journal of Personality and Social Psychology, 61,* 351–365.

Bjorklund, A., & Stenevi, U. (1979). Reconstruction of the nigrostriatal dopamine pathway by intracerebral nigral transplants. *Brain Research, 177,* 555–560.

Blackmore, S. (1985). Unrepeatability: Parapsychology's only finding. In B. Shapin & L. Coly (Eds.), *The repeatability problem in parapsychology.* New York: Parapsychology Foundation.

Blackmore, S. (1987a). Where am I?: Perspectives in imagery and the out-of-body experience. *Journal of Mental Imagery, 11,* 53–66.

Blackmore, S. (1987b). The elusive open mind: Ten years of negative research in parapsychology. *The Skeptical Inquirer, 11,* 244–255.

Blakemore, C. (1977). *Mechanics of the mind.* London: Cambridge University Press.

Blanchard, E. B., Andrasik, F., Guarnieri, P., Neff, D. F., & Rodichok, L. D. (1987). Two-, three-and four-year follow-up on the self-regulatory treatment of chronic headache. *Journal of Consulting and Clinical Psychology, 55,* 257–259.

Bland, S. H., Krough, V., Winkelstein, W., & Trevisan, M. (1991). Social network and blood pressure: A population study. *Psychosomatic Medicine, 53,* 598–607.

Blankstein, K. R., Flett, G. L., & Watson, M. S. (1992). Coping and academic problem-solving ability in test anxiety. *Journal of Clinical Psychology, 48,* 37–46.

Bohlen, J. (1986). Quoted in: W. Gallagher, The etiology of orgasm. *Discover,* 51–59.

Boldizar, J. P., Wilson, K. L., & Deemer, D. K. (1989). Gender, life experiences, and moral judgment development: A process-oriented approach. *Journal of Personality and Social Psychology, 57,* 229–238.

Booth-Kewley, S., & Friedman, H. S. (1987). Psychological predictors of heart disease: A quantitative review. *Psychological Bulletin, 101,* 343–362.

Bootzin, R. R., & Nicassio, P. N. (1978). Behavioral treatments for insomnia. In M. Hensen, R. M. Eisler, & P. M. Miller (Eds.), *Progress in* behavior modification (vol. 6). Orlando, FL: Academic Press.

Bouchard, C., & Tremblay, A. (1987). Quoted in: G. Kolata, Metabolic catch-22 of exercise regimens. *Science, 236,* 146–147.

Bouchard, C., Trembley, A., Despres, J. P., Nadeu, A., Lupien, P. J., et al. (1990). The response to long-term overfeeding in identical twins. *New England Journal of Medicine, 322,* 1477–1482.

Bouchard, T. J., Jr. (1984). Twins reared together and apart: What they tell us about human diversity. In S. W. Fox (Ed.), *Individuality and determinism: Chemical and biological bases.* New York: Plenum Press.

Bouchard, T. J., Jr., & McGue, M. (1981). Familial studies on intelligence: A review. *Science, 212,* 1055–1059.

Bouchard, T. J., Jr., & McGue, M. (1990). Genetic and rearing environmental influences on adult personality: An analysis of adopted twins reared apart. *Journal of Personality, 58,* 263–292.

Bouchard, T. J., Jr., Lykken, D. T., McGue, M., Segal, N. L., & Tellegen, A. (1990). Sources of human psychological differences: The Minnesota study of twins reared apart. *Science, 250,* 223–228.

Bower, B. (1989). The diagnostic dilemma. *Science News, 135,* 120–122.

Bower, B. (1991). New report offers antipsychotic guidelines. *Science News, 139,* 293.

Bower, B. (1991). Oedipus wrecked. *Science News, 140,* 248–250.

Bower, B. (1991). Teenage turning point. *Science News, 139,* 184–186.

Bower, G. H., & Mayer, J. D. (1989). In search of mood-dependent retrieval. *Journal of Social Behavior and Personality, 4,* 121–156.

Bradley, R. H., Caldwell, B. M., Rock, S. L., Barnard, K. E., Gray, C., Hammond, M. A., Mitchell, S., Siegel, L., Ramey, C. T., Gottfried, A. W., & Johnson, D. L. (1989). Home environment and cognitive development in the first 3 years of life: A collaborative study involving six sites and three ethnic groups in North America. *Developmental Psychology, 25,* 217–235.

Brantner, J. P., & Doherty, M. A. (1983). A review of timeout: A conceptual and methodological analysis. In S. Axelrod & J. Apsche (Eds.), *The effects of punishment on human behavior.* Orlando, FL: Academic Press.

Brecher, E. M. (1972). *Licit and illicit drugs.* Boston, Little, Brown.

Breier, A., Schreiber, J. L., Dyer, J., & Pickar, D. (1991). National Institute of Mental Health longitudinal study of chronic schizophrenia. *Archives of General Psychiatry, 48,* 239–253.

Bremer, T. A., & Wittig, M. A. (1980). Fear of success: A personality trait or a response to occupation deviance and role overload? *Sex Roles, 6,* 27–46.

Breuer, J., & Freud, S. (1895; reprinted 1955).

Studies on hysteria. In J. Strachey (Ed. and Trans.), *The standard edition of the complete psychological works of Sigmund Freud.* London: Hogarth.

Brickman, P., Coates, D., & Janoff-Bulman, R. (1978). Lottery winners and accident victims: Is happiness relative? *Journal of Personality and Social Psychology, 36,* 917–927.

Briggs, M. H. (1984). *Recent vitamin research.* Boca Raton, FL: CRC Press.

Briggs, S. R., Cheek, J. M., & Jones, W. H. (1986). Introduction. In W. H. Jones, J. M. Cheek, & W. H. Jones (Eds.), *Shyness: Perspectives on research and treatment.* New York: Plenum Press.

Broca, P. (1861). In S. J. Gould, *The mismeasure of man.* New York: Norton, 1981.

Brooks-Gunn, J., Furstenberg, F. F., Jr. (1989). Adolescent sexual behavior. *American Psychologist, 44,* 249–257.

Broverman, I. K., Broverman, D. M., Clarkson, F. E., Rosenkrantz, P. S., & Vogel, S. R. (1970). Sex-role stereotypes and clinical judgments of mental health. *Journal of Consulting and Clinical Psychology, 34,* 1–7.

Brown, J. D. (1991). Accuracy and bias in self-knowledge. In C. R. Snyder & D. R. Forsyth (Eds.), *Handbook of social and clinical psychology.* New York: Pergamon Press.

Brown, P. (1985). *The transfer of care: Psychiatric deinstitutionalization and its aftermath.* London: Routledge & Kegan Paul.

Brown, R., & Kulik, J. (1977). Flashbulb memories. *Cognition, 5,* 73–99.

Brownell, K. D. (1991). Dieting and the search for the perfect body: Where physiology and culture collide. *Behavior Therapy, 22,* 1–12.

Brownell, K. D., & Wadden, T. A. (1991). The heterogeneity of obesity: Fitting treatments to individuals. *Behavior Therapy, 22,* 153–177.

Brubaker, R. G., Prue, D. M., & Rychtarik, R. G. (1987). Determinants of disulfiram acceptance among alcohol patients: A test of the theory of reason action. *Addictive Behaviors, 12,* 43–51.

Bruch, H. (1982). Anorexia nervosa: Therapy and theory. *American Journal of Psychiatry, 139,* 1531–1538.

Bryden, M. P., George, J., & Inch, R. (1990). Sex differences and the role of figural complexity in determining the rate of mental rotation. *Perceptual and Motor Skills, 70,* 467–477.

Buckley, P. (1989). Fifty years after Freud: Dora, the Rat Man, and the Wolf-Man. *American Journal of Psychiatry, 146,* 1394–1403.

Buckout, R. (1980). Nearly 2,000 witnesses can be wrong. *Bulletin of the Psychonomic Society, 16,* 307–310.

Burisch, M. (1984). Approaches to personality inventory construction. *American Psychologist, 39,* 214–227.

Burt, M. R. (1980). Cultural myths and supports for rape. *Journal of Personality and Social Psychology, 38,* 217–230.

Bushnell, I. W. R., & Mullin, J. T. (1989). Neonatal recognition of the mother's face. *British Journal of Developmental Psychology, 7,* 3–15.

Buss, D. M., & Barnes, M. (1986). Preferences in human mate selection. *Journal of Personality and Social Psychology, 50,* 559–570.

Buss, D. M., Abbott, M., Angleitner, A., Asherian, A., Biaggio, A., Blanco-Villasenor, A., Bruchon-Schweitzer, A., Ch'U, H. Y., Czapinski, J., Deraad, B., Ekehammar, B., Lohamy, N. E., Fioravanti, M., Georgas, J., Gjerde, P., Guttman, R., Hazan, F., Iwawaki, S., Janakiramaiah, H., Khosroshani, F., Kreitler, S., Lachenicht, L., Lee, M., Liik, K., Little, B., Mika, S., Moadel-Shahid, M., Moane, G., Montero, M., Mundy-Castle, A. C., Niit, T., Nsenduluka, E., Pienkowski, R., Pirttila-Backman, A. M., De Leon, J. P., Rousseau, J., Runco, M. A., Safir, M. P., Samuels, C., Sanitioso, R., Serpell, R., Smid, N., Spencer, C., Tadinac, M., Todorova, E. N., Troland, Z. K., Van Den Brande, L., Van Heck, G., Van Langenhove, L., & Yang, K. S. (1990). International preferences in selecting mates. *Journal of Cross-Cultural Psychology, 21,* 5–47.

Cacioppo, J. T., & Petty, R. E. (1982). The need for cognition. *Journal of Personality and Social Psychology, 42,* 116–131.

Cain, W. S. (1977). Differential sensitivity for smell: "Noise" at the nose. *Science, 195,* 796–798.

Calev, A., Nigal, D., Shapira, B., Tubi, N., Chazan, S., Ben-Yehuda, U., Kugelmass, S., & Lerer, B. (1991). Early and long-term effects of electroconvulsive therapy and depression on memory and other cognitive functions. *The Journal of Nervous and Mental Disease, 179,* 526–533.

Cannon, D. S., Baker, T. B., & Wehl, C. K. (1981). Emetic and electric shock alcohol aversion therapy: Six- and twelve–month follow-up. *Journal of Consulting and Clinical Psychology, 49,* 360–368.

Cannon, D. S., Baker, T. B., Gino, A., & Nathan, P. E. (1986). Alcohol-aversion therapy: Relation between strength of aversion and abstinence. *Journal of Consulting and Clinical Psychology, 54,* 825–830.

Caplan, N., Choy, M. H., & Whitmore, J. K. (1992). Indochinese refugee families and academic achievement. *Scientific American, 266,* 36–42.

Caplan, P. J., MacPherson, G. M., & Tobin, P. (1985). Do sex-related differences in spatial abilities exist? *American Psychologist, 40,* 786–799.

Carden, L. K., & Fowler, S. A. (1984). Positive peer pressure: The effects of peer monitoring on children's disruptive behavior. *Journal of Applied Behavior Analysis, 17,* 213–227.

Carey, M. P., & Burish, T. G. (1988). Etiology

and treatment of the psychological side effects associated with cancer chemotherapy: A critical review and discussion. *Psychological Bulletin, 104,* 307–325.

Carey, S. (1990). Cognitive development. In D. N. Osherson & E. E. Smith (Eds.), *An invitation to cognitive science, vol. 3: Thinking.* Cambridge, MA: MIT Press.

Carlson, J. M. (1990). Subjective ideological similarity between candidates and supporters: A study of party elites. *Political Psychology, 11,* 485–492.

Carlson, N. R. (1991). *Physiology of behavior.* Boston: Allyn and Bacon.

Carpenter, W. T., & Strauss, J. S. (1991). The prediction of outcome in schizophrenia IV: Eleven-year follow-up on the Washington IPSS cohort. *The Journal of Nervous and Mental Disease, 179,* 517–525.

Cartwright, R. (1988, July–August). Quoted in *Psychology Today.*

Caruso, D. A. (1990). Infant day care and the concept of developmental risk. *Infant Mental Health Journal, 11,* 358–364.

Caspi, A., Herbener, E. S., & Ozer, D. J. (1992). Shared experiences and the similarity of personalities: A longitudinal study of married couples. *Journal of Personality and Social Psychology, 62,* 281–291.

Cattell, R. B. (1943). The description of personality: Basic traits resolved into clusters. *Journal of Abnormal and Social Psychology, 38,* 476–506.

Cattell, R. B. (1965). *The scientific analysis of personality.* Baltimore: Penguin.

Chaiken, S., & Eagly, A. H. (1976). Communication modality as a determinant of message persuasiveness and message comprehensibility. *Journal of Personality and Social Psychology, 34,* 605–614.

Cheek, J. M., & Buss, A. H. (1981). Shyness and sociability. *Journal of Personality and Social Psychology, 41,* 330–339.

Cheek, J. M., & Watson, A. K. (1989). The definition of shyness: Psychological imperialism or construct validity. *Journal of Social Behavior and Personality, 4,* 85–95.

Chen, G., Li, S., & Jiang, C. (1986). Clinical studies on neurophysiological and biochemical basis of acupuncture analgesia. *American Journal of Chinese Medicine, 14,* 86–95.

Cho, A. K. (1990). Ice: A new dosage form of an old drug. *Science, 249,* 631–634.

Chomsky, N. (1957). *Syntactic structures.* The Hague: Mouton.

Chomsky, N. (1980). The linguistic approach. In M. Piatelli-Palmarini (Ed.), *Language and learning.* Cambridge, MA: Harvard University Press.

Christianson, S. (1989). Flashbulb memories: Special, but not so special. *Memory & Cognition, 17,* 435–443.

Clarke, A. M., & Clarke, A. D. B. (1989). The later cognitive effects on early intervention. *Intelligence, 13,* 289–297.

Clarke-Stewart, K. A. (1989). Infant day care. *American Psychologist, 44,* 266–273.

Clarkson-Smith, L., & Hartley, A. A. (1989). Relationships between physical exercise and cognitive abilities in older adults. *Psychology and Aging, 4,* 183–189.

Cleghorn, J. M., Zipursky, R. B., & List, S. J. (1991). Structural and functional brain imaging in schizophrenia. *Journal of Psychiatry and Neuroscience, 16,* 53–74.

Cloninger, C. R. (1987). Neurogenetic adaptive mechanisms in alcoholism. *Science, 236,* 410–416.

Clum, G. A., & Bowers, T. G. (1990). Behavior therapy better than placebo treatments: Fact or artifact? *Psychological Bulletin, 107,* 110–113.

Cohen, B., & Murphy, G. L. (1984). Models of concepts. *Cognitive Science, 8,* 27–58.

Cohen, D. B. (1979). *Sleep and dreaming: Origins, nature and functions.* New York: Pergamon Press.

Cohen, N. J., & Squire, L. R. (1980). Preserved learning and retention of pattern analyzing skill in amnesia: Association of knowing how and knowing that. *Science, 210,* 207–209.

Cohen, S., Tyrrell, D. A. J., & Smith, A. P. (1991). Psychological stress and susceptibility to the common cold. *New England Journal of Medicine, 325,* 606–612.

Cohen, S., & Williamson, G. M. (1991). Stress and infectious disease in humans. *Psychological Bulletin, 109,* 5–24.

Cohen, S., & Wills, T. A. (1985). Stress, social support, and the buffering hypothesis. *Psychological Bulletin, 98,* 310–357.

Cohn, L. D. (1991). Sex differences in the course of personality development: A meta-analysis. *Psychological Bulletin, 109,* 252–266.

Coleman, R. M., Miles, L. E., Guilleminault, C. C., Zarcone, V. P., Jr., Van den Hoed, J., & Dement, W. C. (1981). Sleep-wake disorders in the elderly: A polysomnographic analysis. *Journal of the American Geriatrics Society, 29,* 289–296.

Coles, M. G. H. (1989). SPR Presidential Address, 1988. Modern mind-brain reading: Psychophysiology, physiology, and cognition. *Psychophysiology, 26,* 251–269.

Collins, A. M., & Quillian, M. R. (1969). Retrieval time from semantic memory. *Journal of Verbal Learning and Verbal Behavior, 8,* 240–247.

Connor, L. (1982). In A. J. Marsella & G. M. White (Eds.), *Cultural conceptions of mental health and therapy.* Boston: D. Reidel Publishing.

Coons, P. M., Milstein, V., & Marley, C. (1982). EEG studies of two multiple personalities and a control. *Archives of General Psychiatry, 39,* 823–825.

Coren, S., & Ward, L. M. (1989). *Sensation and perception* (3rd ed.). San Diego: Harcourt Brace Jovanovich.

Costa, P. T., Jr. (1991). Clinical use of the five-factor model: An introduction. *Journal of Personality Assessment, 57,* 393–398.

Costa, P. T., Jr., McCrae, R. R., & Arenberg, D. (1983). Recent longitudinal research of personality and aging. In K. W. Schaie (Ed.), *Longitudinal studies of adult psychological development.* New York: Guilford Press.

Courchesne, E., Yeung-Courchesne, R., Press, B. A., Hesselink, J. R., & Jernigan, T. L. (1988). Hypoplasia of cerebellar vermal lobules VI and VII in autism. *The New England Journal of Medicine, 318,* 1349–1354.

Cox, C. M. (1926). *Genetic studies of genius, Vol. II: The early mental traits of three hundred geniuses.* Stanford, CA: Stanford University Press.

Craik, F. I. M., & Tulving, E. (1975). Depth of processing and the retention of words in episodic memory. *Journal of Experimental Psychology: General, 104,* 268–294.

Cromwell, R. L., Butterfield, E. C., Brayfield, F. M., & Curry, J. J. (1977). *Acute mycocardial infarction.* St. Louis, MO: Mosby.

Cross, G. M., Morgan, C. W., Mooney, A. J., Martin, C. A., & Rafter, J. A. (1990). Alcoholism treatment: A ten-year follow-up study. *Alcoholism: Clinical and Experimental Research, 14,* 169–173.

Crow, T. J., & Forrester, J. (1990). Inhibition of protein synthesis blocks long-term enhancement of generator potentials produced by one-trial *in vivo* conditioning in Hermissenda. *Proceedings of the National Academy of Sciences, 87,* 4490–4494.

Cunningham, M. R. (1987). Measuring the physical in physical attractiveness: Quasi-experiments on the sociobiology of female facial beauty. *Journal of Personality and Social Psychology, 50,* 925–935.

Cunningham, M. R., Barbee, A. P., & Pike, C. L. (1990). What do women want? Facialmetric assessment of multiple motives in the perception of male facial physical attractiveness. *Journal of Personality and Social Psychology, 59,* 61–72.

Czeisler, C. A., Johnson, M. P., Duffy, J. F., Brown, E. N., Ronda, J. M., & Kronauer, R. E. (1990). Exposure to bright light and darkness to treat physiological maladaptation to night work. *The New England Journal of Medicine, 322,* 1253–1259.

Czeisler, C. A., Kronauer, R. E., Allan, J. S., Duffy, J. F., Jewett, M. E., Brown, E. N., & Ronda, J. M. (1989). Bright light induction of strong (Type O) resetting of the human circadian pacemaker. *Science, 244,* 1328–1333.

Darke, J. L. (1990). Sexual aggression. In W. L. Marshall, D. R. Laws, & H. E. Barbaree (Eds.), *Handbook of sexual assault: Issues, theories, and treatment of the offender.* New York: Plenum Press.

Darling, C. A., & Davidson, J. K., Sr. (1986). Coitally active university students: Sexual behaviors, concerns, and challenges. *Adolescence, 21*, 403–419.

Davanloo, H. (Ed.). (1980). *Short-term dynamic psychotherapy.* New York: Jason Aronson.

Davis, G. E., Blaker, S. N., Engvall, E., Varon, S., Manthorpe, M., & Gage, F. H. (1987). Human amnion membrane serves as a substratum for growing axons in vitro and in vivo. *Science, 236*, 1106–1109.

Davis, K. L., Kahn, R. S., Ko, G., & Davidson, M. (1991). Dopamine in schizophrenia: A review and reconceptualization. *American Journal of Psychiatry, 148*, 1474–1486.

Davis, M. H., & Stephan, W. G. (1980). Attributions for exam performance. *Journal of Applied Social Psychology, 10*, 235–248.

Davison, G. C., & Neale, J. M. (1990). *Abnormal psychology* (3rd ed.). New York: Wiley.

De Vries, G. J. (1990). Sex differences in neurotransmitter systems. *Journal of Neuroendocrinology, 2*, 1–13.

de Wilde, E. J., Kienhorst, I. C. W. M., Kiekstra, R. F. W. D., & Wolters, W. H. G. (1992). The relationship between adolescent suicidal behavior and life events in childhood and adolescence. *American Journal of Psychiatry, 149*, 45–51.

Deaconson, R. F., O'Hair, D. P., Levy, M. R., Lee, M. B. F., Schuenerman, A. L., & Condon, R. E. (1988). Sleep deprivation and resident performance. *Journal of the American Medical Association, 260*, 1721–1727.

Deaux, K., Winton, W., Crowley, M., & Lewis, L. L. (1985). Level of categorization and content of gender stereotypes. *Social Cognition, 3*, 145–167.

DeCarvalho, R. J. (1990). A history of the "Third Force" in psychology. *Journal of Humanistic Psychology, 30*, 22–44.

deCharms, R. (1980). The origins of competence and achievement motivation in personal causation. In L. J. Fyans, Jr. (Ed.), *Achievement motivation.* New York: Plenum Press.

Deci, E. L., & Ryan, R. M. (1980). The empirical exploration of intrinsic motivational processes. In L. Berkowitz (Ed.), *Advances in experimental social psychology* (vol. 13). Orlando, FL: Academic Press.

Deffenbacher, J. L., Story, D. A., Stark, R. S., Hogg, J. A., & Brandon, A. D. (1987). Cognitive-relaxation and social skills interventions in the treatment of general anger. *Journal of Counseling Psychology, 34*, 171–176.

Deregowski, J. B. (1980). *Illusions, patterns and pictures: A crosscultural perspective.* Orlando, FL: Academic Press.

Derry, P. A., & Kuiper, N. A. (1981). Schematic processing and self-reference in clinical depression. *Journal of Abnormal Psychology, 90*, 286–297.

Devlin, M. J., Walsh, T., Kral, J. G., Heymsfield, S. B., Pi-Sunyer, F. X., & Dantzic, S. (1990). Metabolic abnormalities in bulimia nervosa. *Archives of General Psychiatry, 47*, 144–148.

Digman, J. M. (1990). Personality structure: Emergence of the five-factor model. *Annual Review of Psychology, 41*, 417–440.

DiLalla, L. F., & Gottesman, I. I. (1991). Biological and genetic contributions to violence—Widoms' untold tale. *Psychological Bulletin, 109*, 125–129.

Dimitrovsky, L., Singer, J., & Yinon, Y. (1989). Masculine and feminine traits: Their relation to suitedness for and success in training for traditionally masculine and feminine army functions. *Journal of Personality and Social Psychology, 57*, 839–847.

Dion, K. K., Berscheid, E., & Walster, E. (1972). What is beautiful is good. *Journal of Personality and Social Psychology, 24*, 285–290.

Dix, T. (1991). The affective organization of parenting: Adaptive and maladaptive processes. *Psychological Bulletin, 110*, 3–25.

Dobie, T. G., May, J. G., Elder, S. T., & Kubiyz, K. A. (1987). A comparison of two methods of training resistance to visually-induced motion sickness. *Aviation, Space and Environmental Medicine, 58*, A34–A41.

Dollard, J., Doob, L. W., Miller, N. E., Mower, O. H., & Sears, R. R. (1939). *Frustration and aggression.* New Haven, CT: Yale University Press.

Driscoll, C. D., Streissguth, A. P., & Riley, E. P. (1990). Prenatal alcohol exposure: Comparability of effects in humans and animal models. *Neurotoxicology and Teratology, 12*, 231–237.

Duck, S., & Silver, R. C. (Eds.). (1990). *Personal relationships and social support.* Beverly Hills, CA: Sage.

Dykman, B. M., Abramson, L. Y., Alloy, L. B., & Hartlage, S. (1989). Processing of ambiguous and unambiguous feedback by depressed and nondepressed college students: Schematic biases and their implications for depressive realism. *Journal of Personality and Social Psychology, 56*, 431–445.

Eagly, A. H., & Ashmore, R. D. (1991). What is beautiful is good, but . . . : A meta-analytic review of research on the physical attractiveness stereotype. *Psychological Bulletin, 110*, 109–128.

Earle, J. R., & Perricone, P. J. (1986). Premarital sexuality: A ten-year study of attitudes and behavior on a small university campus. *Journal of Sex Research, 22*, 304–310.

Eaton, W. W., Dryman, A., & Weissman M. M. (1991). Panic and phobia. In L. N. Robins & D. A. Regier (Eds.), *Psychiatric disorders in America: The epidemiological catchment area study.* New York: Free Press.

Ebbinghaus, H. (1885; reprinted 1913). *Memory: A contribution to experimental psychology* (H. A. Ruger & C. E. Bussenius, Trans.). New York: Teachers College Press.

Eccles, J. S., & Jacobs, J. E. (1986). Social forces shape math attitudes and performance. *Signs, 11*, 367–389.

Eich, E. (1980). The cue-dependent nature of state-dependent retrieval. *Memory and Cognition, 8*, 157–173.

Eichorn, D. H., Clausen, J. A., Haan, N., Honzik, M. P., & Mussen, P. H. (Eds.). (1981). *Present and past in middle life.* Orlando, FL: Academic Press.

Eijkman, E. G. J., Jongsma, H. J., & Vincent, J. (1981). Two-dimensional filtering oriented line detectors and figural aspects as determinants of visual illusions. *Perception Psychophysics, 29*, 352–358.

Ekman, P., & Friesen, W. V. (1969). The repertoire of nonverbal behavior: Categories, origins, usage, and coding. *Semiotica, 1*, 49–98.

Ekman, P., & Friesen, W. V. (1975). *Unmasking the face.* Englewood Cliffs, NJ: Prentice-Hall.

Ekman, P., Levenson, R. W., & Friesen, W. V. (1983). Autonomic nervous system activity distinguished among emotions. *Science, 361*, 1208–1210.

Ekman, P., Friesen, W. V., O'Sullivan, M., Chan, A., Diacoyanni-Tarlatzis, I., Heider, K., Krause, R., LeCompte, W. A., Pitcairn, T., Ricci-Bitti, P. E., Scherer, K., Tomita, M., & Tzavaras, A. (1987). Universals and cultural differences in the judgments of facial expressions of emotions. *Journal of Personality and Social Psychology, 53*, 712–717.

Elkin, I, Shea, M. T., Watkins, J. T., Imber, S. D., Sotsky, S. M., Collins, J. F., Glass, D. R., Pilkonis, P. A., Leber, W. R., Docherty, J. P., Fiester, S. J., & Parloff, M. B. (1989). NIMH treatment of depression collaborative research program: 1: General effectiveness of treatments. *Archives of General Psychiatry, 46*, 971–982.

Elkind, D. (1978). Understanding the young adolescent. *Adolescence, 13*, 127–134.

Elkins, R. L. (1991). An appraisal of chemical aversion (emetic therapy) approaches to alcoholism treatment. *Behavior Research Therapy, 29*, 387–413.

Ellis, A. (1970). *The essence of rational psychotherapy: A comprehensive approach to treatment.* New York: Institute for Rational Living.

Ellis, A. (1992). My early experiences in developing the practice of psychology. *Professional Psychology: Research and Practice, 23*, 7–10.

Epstein, L. (1986). Quoted in: G. Kolata, Obese children: A growing problem. *Science, 232*, 20–21.

Erikson, E. H. (1963). *Childhood and society.* New York: Norton.

Erikson, E. H. (1968). *Identity, youth, and crisis.* New York: Norton.

Erikson, E. H. (1982). *The life cycle completed: Review.* New York: Norton.

Eron, L. D. (1990). Understanding aggression.

Bulletin of the International Society for Research on Aggression, 12, 5–9.

Eron, L. D., Huesmann, L. R., Dubow, E., Romanoff, R., & Yarmel, P. W. (1987). Aggression and its correlates over 22 years. In D. H. Crowell, I. M. Evans, & C. R. O'Donnell (Eds.), *Childhood aggression and violence: Sources of influence, prevention, and control.* New York: Plenum Press.

Estes, W. K. (1990). Introduction, *Principles of Psychology: 1890–1990. Psychological Science, 1,* 149–150.

Evans, P. D., & Edgerton, N. (1991). Life-events and mood as predictors of the common cold. *British Journal of Medical Psychology, 64,* 35–44.

Evans, R. (1990). *McEnroe: Taming the talent.* New York: Steven Greene Press.

Eysenck, H. J. (1990). Biological dimensions of personality. In L. A. Previn (Ed.), *Handbook of personality.* New York: Guilford Press.

Ezzell, C. (1991). Memories might be made of this. *Science News, 139,* 328–330.

Fabes, R. A., & Laner, M. R. (1986). How the sexes perceive each other: Advantages and disadvantages. *Sex Roles, 15,* 129–143.

Fagot, B. I., & Hagan, R. (1991). Observations of parent reactions to sex-stereotyped behaviors: Age and sex effects. *Child Development, 62,* 617–628.

Fahy, T. A. (1988). The diagnosis of multiple personality disorder: A critical review. *British Journal of Psychiatry, 153,* 597–606.

Fairburn, C. G., Phil, M., & Beglin, S. J. (1990). Studies of the epidemiology of bulimia nervosa. *American Journal of Psychiatry, 147,* 401–408.

Fantz, R. L., & Yeh, J. (1979). Configurational selectives: Critical for development of visual perception and attention. *Canadian Journal of Psychology, 33,* 277–287.

Faravelli, C., & Pallianti, S. (1989). Recent life events and panic disorders. *American Journal of Psychiatry, 146,* 622–626.

Farb, P., & Armelagos, G. (1980). *Consuming passions.* Boston: Houghton Mifflin.

Fava, M., Copeland, P. M., Schweiger, U., & Herzog, D. B. (1989). Neurochemical abnormalities of anorexia nervosa and bulimia nervosa. *American Journal of Psychiatry, 146,* 963–970.

Featherstone, H. J., & Beitman, B. D. (1983). "Daily" common migraine: Psychosocial predictors of outcomes of medical therapy. *Headache, 23,* 110–112.

Fernandez, E., & Turk, D. C. (1989). The utility of cognitive coping strategies for altering pain perception: A meta-analysis. *Pain, 38,* 123–135.

Festinger, L. (1954). A theory of social comparison processes. *Human Relations, 7,* 117–140.

Festinger, L. (1957). *A theory of cognitive dissonance.* Palo Alto, CA: Stanford University Press.

Festinger, L., & Carlsmith, J. M. (1959). Cognitive

consequences of forced compliance. *Journal of Abnormal and Social Psychology, 58,* 203–210.

Field, T. M., Cohen, D., Garcia, R., & Greenberg, R. (1984). Mother-stranger face discrimination by the newborn. *Infant Behavior and Development, 7,* 19–25.

Fiore, M. C., Novotny, T. N., Pierce, J. P., Giovino, G. A., Hatziandreu, E. J., Newcomb, P. A., Surawicz, T. S., & Savis, R. M. (1990). Methods used to quit smoking in the United States. *Journal of the American Medical Association, 263,* 2760–2765.

Fisher, R. P., Geiselman, R. E., & Amador, M. (1989). Field test of the cognitive interview: Enhancing the recollection of actual victims and witnesses of crime. *Journal of Applied Psychology, 74,* 722–727.

Fishman, S. (1988). *A bomb in the brain.* New York: Charles Scribner's Sons.

Fisk, A. D., & Schneider, W. (1984). Memory as a function of attention, level of processing, and automatization. *Journal of Experimental Psychology: Learning, Memory, and Cognition, 10,* 181–197.

Fiske, S. T., & Taylor, S. E. (1991). *Social cognition.* New York: McGraw-Hill.

Flam, F. (1991). Still a "chilly climate" for women? *Science, 252,* 1604–1606.

Flavell, J. H. (1986, Jan.). Really and truly. *Psychology Today.*

Flink, S. (1989, May). McEnroe: Coming around again. *World Tennis.*

Folkman, S., Lazarus, R. S., Dunkel-Schetter, C., DeLongis, A., & Gruen, R. J. (1986). Dynamics of a stressful encounter: Cognitive appraisal, coping and encounter outcomes. *Journal of Personality and Social Psychology, 50,* 992–1003.

Ford, J. G. (1991). Rogers's theory of personality: Review and perspectives. *Journal of Social Behavior and Personality, 6,* 19–44.

Ford, L. A., & Smith, S. W. (1991). Memorability and persuasiveness of organ donation message strategies. *American Behavioral Scientist, 34,* 695–711.

Foulkes, D. (1983). Cognitive processes during sleep: Evolutionary aspects. In A. Mayes (Ed.), *Sleep mechanisms and functions.* Wokingham, Eng.: Van Nostrand Reinhold.

Fowles, D. C. (1992). Schizophrenia: Diathesis-stress revisited. *Annual review of Psychology, 43,* 303–336.

Frances, A., Pincus, H. A., Widiger, T. A., Davis, W. W., & First, M. B. (1990). *DSM-IV:* Work in progress. *American Journal of Psychiatry, 127,* 1439–1448.

Francis, D. P., & Chin, J. (1987). The prevention of acquired immunodeficiency syndrome in the United States. *Journal of the American Medical Association, 257,* 1357–1366.

Franklin, J. A. (1989). A 6–year follow-up of the effectiveness of respiratory retraining, in-situ isometric relaxation, and cognitive modification

in the treatment of agoraphobia. *Behavior Modification, 13,* 139–167.

Freedman, R. R. (1991). Physiological mechanisms of temperature biofeedback. *Biofeedback and Self-regulation, 16,* 95–115.

Fremont, J., & Craighead, L. W. (1987). Aerobic exercise and cognitive therapy in the treatment of dysphoric moods. *Cognitive Therapy and Research, 11,* 241–251.

Freud, S. (1900; reprinted 1980). *The interpretation of dreams* (J. Strachey, Ed. and Trans.). New York: Avon.

Freud, S. (1909; reprinted 1949). Notes upon a case of obsessional neurosis. In *Collected papers* (vol. 3) (Alix and James Strachey, Trans.). London: Hogarth.

Frezza, C., Di Padova, C., Pozzeto, G., Terpin, M., Baraono, E., & Lieber, C. S. (1990). Higher blood alcohol levels in women: The role of decreased gastric alcohol dehydrogenase activity and first-pass metabolism. *The New England Journal of Medicine, 322,* 95–99.

Friedman, H. S., & Booth-Kewley, S. (1987). The "disease-prone personality." *American Psychologist, 42,* 539–555.

Friedman, M., & Rosenman, R. (1974). *Type A behavior and your heart.* New York: Knopf.

Friedman, M., Thoresen, C. E., Gill, J. J., Powell, L. H., Ulmer, D., Thompson, L., Price, V. A., Rabin, D. D., Breall, W. S., Dixon, T., Levy, R., & Bourg, E. (1984). Alteration of Type A behavior and reduction in cardiac recurrences in postmyocardial infarction patients. *American Heart Journal, 108,* 237–248.

Friedman, S., & Stevenson, M. (1980). Perception of movements in pictures. In M. Hagen (Ed.), *Perception of pictures, vol. 1: Alberti's window: The projective model of pictorial information.* Orlando, FL: Academic Press.

Friedrich-Cofer, L., & Huston, A. C. (1986). Television violence and aggression: The debate continues. *Psychological Bulletin, 100,* 364–371.

Fries, J. F., & Crapo, L. M. (1981). *Vitality and aging.* New York: W. H. Freeman.

Fujita, S. (1990). Surgical treatment of obstructive sleep apnea: UPPP and linguoplasty (laser midline glossectomy). In C. Guilleminault & M. Partinen (Eds.), *Clinical research and treatment.* New York: Raven Press.

Fulroth, R., Phillips, B., & Durand, D. J. (1989). Perinatal outcome of infants exposed to cocaine and/or heroin in utero. *American Journal of Diseases of Children, 143,* 905–910.

Furumoto, L. (1989). The new history of psychology. In I. S. Cohen (Ed.), *The G. Stanley Hall lecture series* (vol. 9). Washington, DC: American Psychological Association.

Furumoto, L., & Scarborough, E. (1986). Placing women in the history of psychology. *American Psychologist, 41,* 35–42.

Gage, R. H., Bjorklund, A., Stenevi, U., Dunnett, S. B., & Kelly, P. A. T. (1984). Intrahippocampal septal grafts ameliorate learning impairments in aged rats. *Science, 225,* 533–536.

Galler, J. R. (Ed.). (1984). *Human nutrition: A comprehensive treatise, vol. 5: Nutrition and behavior.* New York: Plenum Press.

Galotti, K. M., Kozberg, S. F., & Farmer, M. C. (1991). Gender and developmental differences in adolescents' conceptions of moral reasoning. *Journal of Youth and Adolescence, 20,* 13–30.

Garcia, J., Hankins, W. G., & Rusiniak, K. W. (1974). Behavioral regulation of the milieu interne in man and rat. *Science, 185,* 824–831.

Gardner, B. T., & Gardner, R. A. (1975). Evidence for sentence constituents in the early utterances of child and chimpanzee. *Journal of Experimental Psychology: General, 104,* 244–267.

Gardner, H. (1976). *The shattered mind.* New York: Vintage Books.

Gardner, H. (1983). *Frames of mind: The theory of multiple intelligences.* New York: Basic Books.

Gardner, M. (1981). *Science: Good, bad, and bogus.* Buffalo, NY: Prometheus.

Garfield, S. L. (1980). *Psychotherapy: An eclectic approach.* New York: Wiley.

Garfield, S. L. (1981). Psychotherapy: A 40-year appraisal. *American Psychologist, 36,* 174–183.

Gauguelin, M. (1982). Zodiac and personality: An empirical study. *The Skeptical Inquirer, 6,* 57–65.

Gawin, F. H. (1991). Cocaine addiction: Psychology and neurophysiology. *Science, 251,* 1580–1586.

Gazzaniga, M. S. (1983). Right hemisphere language following brain bisection. *American Psychologist, 39,* 525–537.

Gazzaniga, M. S. (1985). *The social brain.* New York: Basic Books.

Gehringer, W. L., & Engel, E. (1986). Effect of ecological viewing conditions on the Ames' distorted room illusion. *Journal of Experimental Psychology: Human Perception and Performance, 12,* 181–185.

Geiselman, R. E., Fisher, R. P., MacKinnon, D. P., & Holland, H. L. (1986). Enhancement of eyewitness memory with the cognitive interview. *American Journal of Psychology, 99,* 385–401.

Geiselman, R. E., & Machlovitz, H. (1987). Hypnosis memory recall: Implications for forensic use. *American Journal of Forensic Psychology, 5,* 37–47.

Geller, L. (1982). The failure of self-actualization theory: A critique of Carl Rogers and Abraham Maslow. *Journal of Humanistic Psychology, 22,* 56–73.

Gerrard, M. (1987). Sex, sex guilt, and contraceptive use revisited: The 1980s. *Journal of Personality and Social Psychology, 52,* 975–980.

Gershon, E. S. (1989). Recent developments in genetics of manic depressive illness. *Journal of Clinical Psychiatry, 50* (Supplement), 4–7.

Ghosh, A., & Marks, I. M. (1987). Self-treatment of agoraphobia by exposure. *Behavior Therapy, 18,* 3–16.

Giacopassi, D. J., & Dull, R. T. (1986). Gender and racial differences in the acceptance of rape myths within a college population. *Sex Roles, 15,* 63–75.

Gibbons, A. (1990). Gerontology research comes of age. *Science, 250,* 622–625.

Gibbons, A. (1991). Deja vu all over again: Chimp-language wars. *Science, 251,* 1561–1562.

Gibson, E. J., & Walk, R. (1960). The visual "cliff." *Scientific American, 202,* 64–71.

Gilligan, C. (1982). *In a different voice: Psychological theory and women's development.* Cambridge, MA: Harvard University Press.

Gilligan, C. (1987). Adolescent development reconsidered. In C. E. Irwin, Jr. (Ed.), *Adolescent social behavior and health.* San Francisco: Jossey-Bass.

Gillin, J. C., & Byerley, W. F. (1990). The diagnosis and management of insomnia. *The New England Journal of Medicine, 322,* 239–248.

Glanzer, M., & Cunitz, A. R. (1966). Two storage mechanisms in free recall. *Journal of Verbal Learning and Verbal Behavior, 5,* 351–360.

Glass, C. R., & Shea, C. A. (1986). Cognitive therapy for shyness and social anxiety. In W. H. Jones, J. M. Cheek, & W. H. Jones (Eds.), *Shyness: Perspectives on research and treatment.* New York: Plenum Press.

Glass, G. V., & Kliegl, R. M. (1983). An apology for research integration in the study of psychotherapy. *Journal of Consulting and Clinical Psychology, 31,* 28–41.

Glenberg, A. M., Sanocki, T., Epstein, W., & Morris, C. (1987). Enhancing calibration of comprehension. *Journal of Experimental Psychology: General, 116,* 119–136.

Goggin, W. C., & Range, L. M. (1986). Actor-observer differences in the perception of suicide. *Journal of Social and Clinical Psychology, 4,* 101–106.

Goldfried, M. R. (1982). Resistance and clinical behavior therapy. In P. Wachtel (Ed.), *Resistance: Psychodynamic and behavioral approaches.* New York: Plenum Press.

Goldfried, M. R., & Davison, G. C. (1976). *Clinical behavior therapy.* New York: Holt, Rinehart & Winston.

Goldfried, M. R., Greenberg, L. S., & Marmar, C. (1990). Individual psychotherapy: Process and outcome. *Annual Review of Psychology, 41,* 659–688.

Goldstein, A. P. (1989). Aggression reduction: Some vital steps. In J. Groebel & R. A. Hinde (Eds.), *Aggression and war: Their biological and social bases.* Cambridge, Eng.: Cambridge University Press.

Goldstein, S. (1990). Replicative senescence: The human fibroblast comes of age. *Science, 249,* 1129–1133.

Gordon, S. (1986, Oct.). What kids need to know. *Psychology Today.*

Gottesmann, I. I. (1991). *Schizophrenia genesis: The origins of madness.* New York: W. H. Freeman.

Gottman, J. M. (1991). Predicting the longitudinal course of marriages. *Journal of Marital and Family Therapy, 17,* 3–7.

Gottman, J. M., & Krokoff, L. J. (1989). Marital interaction and satisfaction: A longitudinal view. *Journal of Consulting and Clinical Psychology, 57,* 47–52.

Gould, J. L., & Marler, P. (1987). Learning by instinct. *Scientific American, 256,* 74–85.

Gould, S. J. (1981). *The mismeasure of man.* New York: Norton.

Gove, W. R., Hughes, M., & Style, C. B. (1983). Does marriage have positive effects on the psychological well-being of the individual? *Journal of Health and Social Behavior, 24,* 122–131.

Gray, M. D., Lesser, D., Quinn, E., & Bounds, C. (1990). The effectiveness of personalizing acquaintance rape prevention: Programs on perception of vulnerability and/or reducing risk-taking behavior. *Journal of College Student Development, 31,* 217–220.

Green, B. (1987). *The "sissy boy syndrome" and the development of homosexuality.* New Haven, CT: Yale University Press.

Green, D. E., Walkey, F. H., & Taylor, A. J. W. (1991). The three-factor structure of the Maslach burnout inventory: A multicultural, multinational confirmatory study. *Journal of Social Behavior and Personality, 6,* 453–472.

Greenberg, J. (1978). The Americanization of Roseto. *Science News, 113,* 378–382.

Greenfield, P. (1991). Quoted in: A. Gibbons, Deja vu all over again: Chimp-language wars. *Science, 251,* 1561–1562.

Greeno, J. G. (1989). A perspective on thinking. *American Psychologist, 44,* 134–141.

Greenwald, A. G., Spangenberg, E. R., Pratkanis, A. R., & Eskenazi, J. (1991). Double-blind tests of subliminal self-help audiotapes. *Psychological Science, 2,* 119–122.

Gregory, R. L. (1974). Recovery from early blindness: A case study. In R. L. Gregory (Ed.), *Concepts and mechanisms of perception.* London: Gerald Duckworth.

Guida, F. V., & Ludlow, L. H. (1989). A cross-cultural study of test anxiety. *Journal of Cross-cultural Psychology, 20,* 178–190.

Guilford, J. P. (1967). *The nature of human intelligence.* New York: McGraw-Hill.

Gustavson, C. R., Kelly, D. J., Sweeney, M., & Garcia, J. (1976). Prey-lithium aversion I: Coyotes and wolves. *Behavioral Biology, 17,* 61–72.

Guthrie, R. V. (1976). *Even the rat was white.* New York: Harper & Row.

Haber, N. R. (1980, Nov.). Eidetic images are not just imaginary. *Psychology Today.*

Hafner, R. J. (1983). Behaviour therapy for agoraphobic men. *Behavior Research and Therapy, 21,* 51–56.

Halford, G. S. (1989). Reflections on 25 years of Piagetian cognitive developmental psychology, 1963–1988. *Human Development, 32,* 325–357.

Hall, C. S., & Van de Castle, R. L. (1966). *The content analysis of dreams.* New York: Appleton-Century-Crofts.

Halpern, D. F. (1986). *Sex differences in cognitive abilities.* Hillsdale, NJ: Lawrence Erlbaum.

Hamilton, D. L., & Sherman, S. J. (1989). Illusory correlations: Implications for stereotype theory and research. In D. Bar-Tal, C. R. Graumann, A. W. Kruglanski, & W. Stroebe (Eds.), *Stereotyping and prejudice: Changing conceptions.* New York: Springer-Verlag.

Hardy, J. B., Welcher, D. W., Mellits, E. D., & Kagan, J. (1976). Pitfalls in the measurement of intelligence: Are standardized intelligence tests valid for measuring the intellectual potential of urban children? *Journal of Psychology, 94,* 43–51.

Harris, G., Thomas, A., & Booth, D. A. (1990). Development of salt taste in infancy. *Developmental Psychology, 26,* 534–538.

Harter, S. (1990). Self and identity development. In S. S. Feldman & G. R. Elliott (Eds.), *At the threshold: The developing adolescent.* Cambridge, MA: Harvard University Press.

Harvey, S. M. (1987). Female sexual behavior: Fluctuations during the menstrual cycle. *Journal of Psychosomatic Research, 31,* 101–110.

Hauri, P. (1982). *The sleep disorders.* Kalamazoo, Ml: Upjohn Company.

Haverkos, H. W. (1989). AIDS update: Prevalence, prevention, and medical management. *Journal of Psychoactive Drugs, 21,* 365–370.

Hayes, K. J., & Hayes, C. H. (1951). The intellectual development of a home-raised chimpanzee. *Proceedings of the American Philosophical Society, 95,* 105–109.

Hayes, S. C., Munt, E. D., Korn, Z., Wulfert, E., Rosenfarb, I., & Zettle, R. D. (1986). The effect of feedback and self-reinforcement instructions on studying performance. *Psychological Record, 36,* 27–37.

Heider, F. (1958). *The psychology of interpersonal relations.* New York: Wiley.

Heimberg, R. G., Dodge, C. S., Hope, D. A., Kennedy, C. R., & Zollo, L. J. (1990). Cognitive behavioral group treatment for social phobia: Comparison with a credible placebo control. *Cognitive Therapy and Research, 14,* 1–23.

Helzer, J. E., Canino, G. J., Yeh, E., Bland, J. R. C., Lee, C. K., Hwu, H., & Newman, S. (1990). Alcoholism—North America and Asia. *Archives of General Psychiatry, 47,* 313–319.

Herbert, W. (1982). An epidemic in the works. *Science News, 122,* 188–190.

Herman, L. (1989, April). Quoted in: S. Chollar, Conversations with the dolphins. *Psychology Today.*

Hickey, E. W. (1991). *Serial murderers and their victims.* Pacific Grove, CA: Brooks/Cole.

Hilgard, E. R. (1977). *Divided consciousness: Multiple controls in human thought and action.* New York: Wiley.

Hilgard, E. R. (1979). Divided consciousness in hypnosis: The implications of the hidden observer. In E. Fromm & R. E. Shor (Eds.), *Hypnosis: Developments in research and new perspectives* (2nd ed.). New York: Aldine.

Hirsch, B. J., & Dubois, D. L. (1991). Self-esteem in early adolescence: The identification and prediction of contrasting longitudinal trajectories. *Journal of Youth and Adolescence, 20,* 53–72.

Hirsch, H. V., & Spinelli, D. N. (1970). Visual experience modifies distribution of horizontally and vertically oriented receptive fields in cats. *Science, 168,* 869–871.

Hoberman, H. M., & Garfinkel, B. D. (1989). Completed suicide in youth. In C. R. Pfeffer (Ed.), *Suicide among youth: Perspectives on risk and prevention.* Washington, DC: American Psychiatric Press.

Hobson, J. A. (1988). *The dreaming brain.* New York: Basic Books.

Hobson, J. A., & McCarley, R. W. (1977). The brain as a dream state generator: An activation-synthesis hypothesis of the dream process. *American Journal of Psychiatry, 134,* 1335–1348.

Hofferth, S. L., & Hayes, C. D. (Eds.). (1987). *Risking the future: Adolescent sexuality, pregnancy, and childbearing, vol. 2: Working papers and statistical reports.* Washington, DC: National Academy Press.

Hoffman, C., Lau, I., & Johnson, D. R. (1986). The linguistic relativity of person cognition: An English-Chinese comparison. *Journal of Personality and Social Psychology, 51,* 1097–1105.

Hogrebe, M. C. (1987). Gender differences in mathematics. *American Psychologist, 42,* 265–266.

Hokanson, J. E., & Butler, A. C. (1992). Cluster analysis of depressed college students' social behaviors. *Journal of Personality and Social Psychology, 62,* 273–280.

Hokanson, J. E., Rubert, M. P., Welker, R. A., Hollander, G. R., & Hedeen, C. (1989). Interpersonal concomitants and antecedents of depression among college students. *Journal of Abnormal Psychology, 98,* 209–217.

Holden, C. (1985). A guarded endorsement for shock therapy. *Science, 228,* 1510–1511.

Holden, C. (1987). Is alcoholism treatment effective? *Science, 236,* 20–22.

Holden, C. (1990). Head Start enters adulthood. *Science, 247,* 1400–1402.

Holden, C. (1991). Depression: The news isn't depressing. *Science, 254,* 1450–1452.

Hollingworth, L. S. (1942). *Children above 180 IQ.* Yonkers, NY: World Book.

Hollon, S. D., Shelton, R. C., & Loosen, P. T. (1991). Cognitive therapy and pharmacotherapy for depression. *Journal of Consulting and Clinical Psychology, 59,* 88–99.

Holmes, T. H., & Rahe, R. H. (1967). The social readjustment rating scale. *Journal of Psychosomatic Research, 11,* 203–218.

Holzman, P. S., & Matthysse, S. (1990). The genetics of schizophrenia: A review. *Psychological Science, 1,* 279–286.

Honorton, C. (1985). Meta-analysis of psi ganzfeld research: A response to Hyman. *Journal of Parapsychology, 49,* 51–91.

Hoon, E. F., Hoon, P. W., Rand, K. H., Johnson, J., Halls, N. R., & Edwards, N. B. (1991). A psycho-behavioral model of genital herpes recurrence. *Journal of Psychosomatic Research, 35,* 25–36.

Hopson, J. L. (1986, June). The unraveling of insomnia. *Psychology Today.*

Hovland, C. I., Janis, I. L., & Kelley, H. H. (1953). *Communication and persuasion: Psychological studies of opinion change.* New Haven, CT: Yale University Press.

Howe, M. L. (1988). Measuring memory development in adulthood: A model-based approach to disentangling storage-retrieval contributions. In M. L. Howe & C. J. Brainerd (Eds.), *Cognitive development in adulthood.* New York: Springer-Verlag.

Hsu, F., Anantharaman, T., Campbell, M., & Nowatzyk, A. (1990). A grandmaster chess machine. *Scientific American, 263,* 44–50.

Hubel, D. H., & Wiesel, T. N. (1962). Receptive fields, binocular interaction and functional architecture in the cat's visual cortex. *Journal of Physiology, 160,* 106–154.

Hubel, D. H., & Wiesel, T. N. (1979). Brain mechanisms of vision. *Scientific American, 241,* 150–162.

Huesmann, L. R., Gruder, C. L., & Dorst, G. (1987). A process model of posthypnotic amnesia. *Cognitive Psychology, 19,* 33–62.

Humphry, D. *Final exit.* Eugene, OR: Hemlock Society.

Hyde, J. S., & Linn, M. C. (1988). Are there sex differences in verbal abilities? A meta-analysis. *Psychological Bulletin, 104,* 53–69.

Hyman, R. (1985). The ganzfeld psi experiment: A critical appraisal. *Journal of Parapsychology, 49,* 3–49.

Hyman, R., & Honorton, C. (1986). A joint communique: The psi ganzfeld controversy. *Journal of Parapsychology, 50,* 351–364.

Iacono, W. G., & Patrick, C. J. (1986). What psychologists should know about lie detection. In A. Hess & I. Weiner (Eds.), *Handbook of forensic psychology.* New York: Wiley.

Izard, C. E. (1977). *Human emotions.* New York: Plenum Press.

Izard, C. E. (1981). Differential emotions theory and the facial feedback hypothesis of emotion activation: Comments on Tourangeau and Ellsworth's "The role of facial response in the experience of emotion." *Journal of Personality and Social Psychology, 40,* 350–354.

Izard, C. E. (1987, May). Quoted in: R. J. Trotter, You've come a long way, baby. *Psychology Today*.

Izard, C. E. (1990). Facial expressions and the regulation of emotions. *Journal of Personality and Social Psychology, 58,* 487–498.

Izard, C. E., Hembree, E. A., & Huebner, R. R. (1987). Infants' emotional expressions to acute pain: Developmental change and stability of individual differences. *Developmental Psychology, 23,* 105–113.

Jacklin, C. N. (1989). Female or male: Issues of gender. *American Psychologist, 44,* 127–133.

Jackson, M. (1988). *Moonwalk*. New York: Doubleday.

Jamison, K. R. (1989). Mood disorders and patterns of creativity in British writers and artists. *Psychiatry, 52,* 125–134.

Janis, I. L. (1982). *Groupthink* (2nd ed.). Boston: Houghton Mifflin.

Janos, P. M., & Robinson, N. M. (1985). Psychosocial development in intellectually gifted children. In F. D. Horowitz & M. O'Brien (Eds.), *The gifted and the talented*. Washington, DC: American Psychological Association.

Jensen, A. R. (1980). *Bias in mental testing*. New York: Free Press.

John, O. P. (1990). The "big five" factor taxonomy: Dimensions of personality in the natural language and in questionnaires. In L. A. Previn (Ed.), *Handbook of personality*. New York: Guilford Press.

John, O. P., Hampson, S. E., & Goldberg, L. R. (1991). The basic level in personality-trait hierarchies: Studies of trait use and accessibility in different contexts. *Journal of Personality and Social Psychology, 60,* 348–361.

Johnson, B., Mayberry, W. E., & McGlynn, F. D. (1990). Exploratory factor analysis of sixty-item questionnaire concerned with fear of dental treatment. *Journal of Behavior Therapy and Experimental Psychiatry, 21,* 199–203.

Johnson, D. (1990). Animal rights and human lives: Time for scientists to right the balance. *Psychological Science, 1,* 213–214.

Johnson, J. S., & Newport, E. L. (1989). Critical period effects in second language learning: The influence of maturational state on the acquisition of English as a second language. *Cognitive Psychology, 21,* 60–99.

Johnson, R. C., & Nagoshi, C. T. (1990). Asians, Asian-Americans, and alcohol. *Journal of Psychoactive Drugs, 22,* 45–52.

Jones, D. R., Levy, R. A., Gardner, L., Marsh, R. W., & Patterson, J. C. (1985). Self-control of psychophysiologic response to motion stress: Using biofeedback to treat airsickness. *Aviation, Space and Environmental Medicine, 56,* 1152–1157.

Jones, E. (1953). *The life and work of Sigmund Freud*. 3 vols. New York: Basic Books.

Jones, E., & Berglas, S. (1978). Control of attributions about the self through self-handicapping strategies: The appeal of alcohol and the role of underachievement. *Personality and Social Psychology Bulletin, 4,* 200–206.

Jones, W. H., Briggs, S. R., & Smith, T. G. (1986). Shyness: Conceptualization and measurement. *Journal of Personality and Social Psychology, 51,* 629–639.

Kagan, J., & Snidman, N. (1991). Temperamental factors in human development. *American Psychologist, 46,* 856–862.

Kagitcibasi, C., & Berry, J. W. (1989). Cross-cultural psychology: Current research and trends. *Annual Review of Psychology, 40,* 493–531.

Kamarck, T., & Jennings, J. R. (1991). Biobehavioral factors in sudden cardiac death. *Psychological Bulletin, 109,* 42–75.

Kaplan, D. M. (1972). On shyness. *International Journal of Psycho-Analysis. 53,* 439–453.

Kaplan, H. (1974). *The new sex therapy*. New York: Brunner/Mazel.

Kaplan, H. (1986, Feb.). Quoted in: W. Gallagher, The etiology of orgasm. *Discover*.

Kaplan, R. M., & Saccuzzo, D. P. (1982). *Psychological testing*. Pacific Grove, CA: Brooks/Cole.

Karasu, T. B. (1986). The psychotherapies: Benefits and limitations. *American Journal of Psychotherapies, 40,* 324–342.

Kassin, S. M. (1979). Consensus information, prediction, and causal attribution: A review of the literature and issues. *Journal of Personality and Social Psychology, 37,* 1966–1981.

Kastenbaum, R. (1981). *Death, society and human experience* (2nd ed.). St. Louis, MO: Mosby.

Kaufman, A. S., Reynolds, C. R., & McLean, J. E. (1989). Age and WAIS–R intelligence in a national sample of adults in the 20 to 74 age range: A cross-sectional analysis with educational level controlled. *Intelligence, 13,* 235–253.

Kaufman, J., & Zigler, E. (1989). The intergenerational transmission of child abuse. In C. Cicchetti & V. Carlson (Eds.), *Child maltreatment: Theory and research on the causes and consequences of child abuse and neglect*. Cambridge, Eng.: Cambridge University Press.

Kaushall, P., Zetin, M., & Squire, L. R. (1982). A psychosocial study of chronic, circumscribed amnesia. *The Journal of Nervous and Mental Disease, 169,* 383–389.

Kearins, J. M. (1981). Visual spatial memory in Australian Aboriginal children of desert regions. *Cognitive Psychology, 13,* 434–460.

Keesey, R. E. (1986). A set-point theory of obesity. In K. D. Brownell & J. P. Foreyt (Eds.), *Handbook of eating disorders: Physiology, psychology, and treatment of obesity, anorexia and bulimia*. New York: Basic Books.

Keith, S. J., Regier, D. A., & Rae, D. S. (1991). In L. N. Robins & D. A. Regier (Eds.), *Psychiatric disorders in America*. New York: Free Press.

Kelley, H. H. (1967). Attribution theory in social psychology. In D. Levine (Ed.), *Nebraska symposium on motivation* (vol. 15). Lincoln: University of Nebraska Press.

Kenrick, D. T. (1990). A biosocial perspective on mates and traits: Reuniting personality and social psychology. In D. M. Buss & N. Cantor (Eds.), *Personality psychology*. New York: Springer-Verlag.

Kenrick, D. T., & Funder, D. C. (1988). Profiting from controversy. *American Psychologist, 43,* 23–34.

Kiecolt-Glaser, J. K., & Glaser, R. (1989). Psychoneuroimmunology: Past, present, and future. *Health Psychology, 8,* 677–682.

Kiester, E., Jr. (1980, May–June). Images of the night. *Science 80*.

Kihlstrom, J. F. (1987). The cognitive unconscious. *Science, 237,* 1445–1452.

Kihlstrom, J. F., & Harackiewicz, J. M. (1982). The earliest recollection: A new survey. *Journal of Personality, 50,* 134–148.

Kimble, C. E., Funk, S. C., & DaPolito, K. L. (1990). The effects of self-esteem certainty on behavioral self-handicapping. *Journal of Social Behavior and Personality, 5,* 137–149.

King, F. A., Yarbrough, C. J., Anderson, D. C., Gordon, T. P., & Gould, K. G. (1988). Primates. *Science, 240,* 1475–1482.

Kinsey, A. C., Pomeroy, W. B., & Martin, C. E. (1948). *Sexual behavior in the human male*. Philadelphia: Saunders.

Kirk, M. S. (1972, March). Head-hunters in today's world. *National Geographic*.

Kirmayer, L. J. (1991). The place of culture in psychiatric nosology: Taijin kyofusho and DSM-III-R. *The Journal of Nervous and Mental Disease, 179,* 19–28.

Kirsner, D. (1990). Is there a future for American psychoanalysis? *Psychoanalytic Review, 77,* 175–200.

Klein, D. B., Zitrin, C. M., Woerner, M. G., & Ross, D. C. (1983). Treatment of phobias. *Archives of General Psychiatry, 40,* 139–145.

Kleinknecht, R. A. (1988). Specificity and psychosocial correlates of blood/injury fear and fainting. *Behaviour Research and Therapy, 26,* 303–309.

Klesges, R. C. (1983). An analysis of body image distortions in a nonpatient population. *International Journal of Eating Disorders, 2,* 37–41.

Klinger, E. (1987, Oct.). The power of daydreams. *Psychology Today*.

Kobasa, S. C. (1982). Commitment and coping in stress resistance among lawyers. *Journal of Personality and Social Psychology, 42,* 707–717.

Kobasa, S. C., Maddi, S. R., & Kahn, S. (1982). Hardiness and health: A prospective study. *Journal of Personality and Social Psychology, 42,* 168–177.

Kobasa, S. C., Maddi, S. R., & Puccetti, M. C.

(1982). Personality and exercise as buffers in the stress-illness relationship. *Journal of Behavioral Medicine, 5,* 391–404.

Koestner, R., & McClelland, D. C. (1990). Perspectives on competence motivation. In L. A. Previn (Ed.), *Handbook of personality.* New York: Guilford Press.

Kohlberg, L. (1969). Stage and sequence: The cognitive-developmental approach to socialization. In D. A. Goslin (Ed.), *Handbook of socialization theory and research.* Chicago: Rand McNally.

Kohlberg, L. (1984). *The psychology of moral development: Essays on moral development* (vol. 11). San Francisco: Harper & Row.

Kohler, I. (1962). Experiments with goggles. *Scientific American, 206,* 62–86.

Köhler, W. (1925). *The mentality of apes* (E. Winter, Trans.). New York: Harcourt, Brace & World. (Original German edition 1917)

Kohn, P. M., Lafreniere, K., & Gurevich, J. (1991). Hassles, health, and personality. *Journal of Personality and Social Psychology, 61,* 478–482.

Kolata, G. (1986). Obese children: A growing problem. *Science, 232,* 20–21.

Koss, M. P., Gidycz, C. A., & Wisniewski, N. (1987). The scope of rape: Incidence and prevalence of sexual aggression and victimization in a national sample of higher education students. *Journal of Consulting and Clinical Psychology, 55,* 162–170.

Kozel, N. J., & Adams, E. H. (1986). Epidemiology of drug abuse: An overview. *Science, 234,* 970–974.

Krantz, S. E. (1983). Cognitive appraisals and problem-directed coping: A prospective study of stress. *Journal of Personality and Social Psychology, 44,* 638–643.

Kraut, R. E., & Poe, D. (1980). Behavioral roots of person perception: The deception judgments of customs inspectors and laymen. *Journal of Personality and Social Psychology, 38,* 784–798.

Kreitler, S., Kreitler, H., & Carasso, R. (1987). Cognitive orientation as predictor of pain relief following acupuncture. *Pain, 28,* 323–341.

Kroll, N. E. A., Schepeler, E. M., & Angin, K. T. (1986). Bizarre imagery: The misremembered mnemonic. *Journal of Experimental Psychology: Learning, Memory and Cognition, 12,* 42–53.

Kronauer, R. E. (1989). Quoted in *Science, 244,* 1257.

Krueger, J. M., Pappenheimer, J. R., & Karnovsky, M. L. (1982). Sleep-promoting effects of muramyl peptides. *Proceedings of the National Academy of Science, 79,* 6102–6106.

Kübler-Ross, E. (1968). *On death and dying.* New York: Macmillan.

Kübler-Ross, E. (1974). *Questions and answers on death and dying.* New York: Macmillan.

Kuhl, P. K., Williams, K. A., Lacerda, F., Stevens, K. N., & Lindblom, B. (1992). Linguistic expe-

rience alters phonetic perception in infants by 6 months of age. *Science, 255,* 606–608.

Kyman, W. (1991). Maternal satisfaction with the birth experience. *Journal of Social Behavior and Personality, 6,* 57–70.

LaBerge, S. (1988). The psychophysiology of lucid dreaming. In J. Gackenbach & S. LaBerge (Eds.), *Conscious mind, sleeping brain: Perspectives on lucid dreaming.* New York: Plenum Press.

Labouvie-Vief, G. (1990). Modes of knowledge and the organization of development. In M. L. Commons, C. Armon, F. A. Richards, & J. Sinnott (Eds.), *Beyond formal operations: 2. The development of adolescent and adult thinking and perception.* New York: Praeger.

Laird, J. D. (1974). Self-attribution of emotion: The effects of expressive behavior on the quality of emotional experience. *Journal of Personality and Social Psychology, 29,* 475–486.

Lamb, M. E. (1984). Social and emotional development in infancy. In M. M. Bornstein & M. E. Lamb (Eds.), *Developmental psychology: An advanced textbook.* Hillsdale, NJ: Lawrence Erlbaum.

Lamb, N. (1990). *Guide to teaching string* (5th ed.). Dubuque, IA: William C. Brown.

Langlois, J. H., & Roggman, L. A. (1990). Attractive faces are only average. *Psychological Science, 1,* 115–121.

Lanzetta, J. T., Cartwright-Smith, J., & Kleck, R. E. (1976). Effects of nonverbal discrimination on emotional experience and autonomic arousal. *Journal of Personality and Social Psychology, 33,* 354–370.

Larsen, K. S. (1990). The Asch conformity experiment: Replication and transhistorical comparisons. *Journal of Social Behavior and Personality, 5,* 163–168.

Latané, B. (1981). The psychology of social impact. *American Psychologist, 36,* 343–356.

Latané, B., & Darley, J. M. (1970). *The unresponsive bystander: Why doesn't he help?* New York: Appleton-Century-Crofts.

Latané, B., & Nida, S. (1981). Ten years of research on group size and helping. *Psychological Bulletin, 89,* 308–324.

Lauber, J. K., & Kayten, P. J. (1988). Sleepiness, circadian dysrhythmia, and fatigue in transportation system accidents. *Sleep, 11,* 503–512.

Lazarus, R. S. (1990). Psychological stress in the workplace. *Journal of Social Behavior and Personality, 6,* 1–13.

Lazarus, R. S. (1991). Cognition and motivation in emotion. *American Psychologist, 46,* 352–367.

Lazarus, R. S., & Folkman, S. (1984). *Stress, appraisal, and coping.* New York: Springer.

Lazarus, R. S., Opton, E. M., Nomikos, M. S., & Fankin, N. O. (1965). The principle of short-circuiting of threat: Further evidence. *Journal of Personality, 33,* 622–635.

Leafgren, A. (1989). Health and wellness programs.

In M. L. Upcraft & J. N. Gardner (Eds.), *The freshman year experience.* San Francisco: Jossey-Bass.

Leary, M. R., & Kowalski, R. M. (1990). Impression management: A literature review and two-component model. *Psychological Bulletin, 107,* 34–47.

Leckman, J. F., Sholomskas, D., Thompson, D., Belanger, A., & Weissman, M. M. (1982). Best estimate of lifetime psychiatric diagnosis. *Archives of General Psychiatry, 39,* 879–883.

Lee, V. E., Brooks-Gunn, J., Schnur, E., & Liaw, F. R. (1990). Are Head Start effects sustained? A longitudinal follow-up comparison of disadvantaged children attending Head Start, no preschool, and other preschool programs. *Child Development, 61,* 495–507.

Lefcourt, H. M. (1982). *Research with the locus of control concept* (vol. 1). New York: Academic Press.

Leiblum, S. R. (1990). Sexuality and the midlife woman. *Psychology of Women Quarterly, 14,* 495–508.

Leiblum, S. R., & Bachmann, G. (1987). The sexuality of the climacteric woman. In B. Eskin (Ed.), *The menopause: Comprehensive management.* New York: Yearbook Publications.

Lepore, S. J., Evans, G. W., & Schneider, M. L. (1991). Dynamic role of social support in the link between chronic stress and psychological distress. *Journal of Personality and Social Psychology, 61,* 899–909.

Lepper, M. R., & Greene, D. (1978). *The hidden costs of reward: New perspectives on the psychology of human motivation.* Hillsdale, NJ: Erlbaum.

LeVay, S. (1991). A difference in hypothalamus structure between heterosexual and homosexual. *Science, 253,* 1034–1036.

Levine, S., & Koenig, J. (Eds.). (1980). *Why men rape: Interviews with convicted rapists.* Toronto: Macmillan.

Levinson, D. J. (1978). *The seasons of a man's life.* New York: Knopf.

Levinson, D. J. (1986). A conception of adult development. *American Psychologist, 39,* 3–13.

Levitan, A. A. (1991). Hypnosis in the 1990s—and beyond. *American Journal of Clinical Hypnosis, 33,* 141–149.

Levy, C. D., & Carter, D. B. (1989). Gender schema, gender constancy, and gender-role knowledge: The role of cognitive factors in preschoolers' gender-role stereotype attributions. *Developmental Psychology, 25,* 444–449.

Levy, J. (1983). Language, cognition and the right hemisphere. *American Psychologist, 39,* 538–541.

Levy, J. (1985, May). Right brain, left brain: Fact and fiction. *Psychology Today.*

Levy, J., & Trevarthen, C. (1976). Metacontrol of hemispheric function in human split-brain patients. *Journal of Experimental Psychology: Human Perception and Performance, 2,* 299–312.

Levy, J., Trevarthen, C., & Sperry, R. W. (1972).

Perception of bilateral chimeric figures following hemispheric deconnection. *Brain, 95,* 61–68.

Levy, J. A. (1989). The hospice in the context of an aging society. *Journal of Aging Studies, 3,* 385–399.

Lewis, C. E. (1991). Neurochemical mechanisms of chronic antisocial behavior (psychopathy). *The Journal of Nervous and Mental Disease, 179,* 720–727.

Lewontin, R. C., Rose, S., & Kamin, L. (1984). *Not in our genes: Biology, ideology and human nature.* New York: Pantheon.

Lewy, A. J., Wehr, T. A., Goodwin, F. K., Newsome, D. A., & Markey, S. P. (1980). Human sleep: Its duration and organization depend on its circadian phase. *Science, 210,* 1264–1268.

Lhermitte, J., Chain, F., Escourolle, R., Ducarne, B., & Pillon, B. (1972). Etude anatomoclinique d'un cas de prosopagnosie. *Review Neurology* (Paris), *126,* 329–346.

Liben, L. S., & Signorella, M. L. (Eds.). (1987). *Children's gender schemata.* San Francisco: Jossey-Bass.

Liem, R., & Liem, J. H. (1988). Psychological effects of unemployment on workers and their families. *Journal of Social Issues, 44,* 87–105.

Light, K. C. (1981). Cardiovascular responses to effortful active coping: Implications for the role of stress in hypertension development. *Psychophysiology, 18,* 216–225.

Light, K. C., & Obrist, P. A. (1980). Cardiovascular reactivity to behavioral stress in young males with and without marginally elevated causal systolic pressure: A comparison of clinic, home and laboratory measures. *Hypertension, 2,* 802–808.

Lindvall, O., Brundin, P., Widner, H., Rehncrona, S., Gustavii, B., Frackowiak, R., Leenders, K. L., Sawle, G., Rothweel, J. C., Marsden, C. D., & Bjorklund, A. (1990). Grafts of fetal dopamine neurons survive and improve motor function in Parkinson's disease. *Science, 247,* 574–577.

Linton, J. C., & Hirt, H. (1979). A comparison of predictions from peripheral and central theories of emotion. *British Journal of Medical Psychology, 52,* 11–15.

Lipton, S. D. (1983). A critique of so-called standard psychoanalytic technique. *Contemporary Psychoanalysis, 19,* 35–52.

Lochman, J. E., & Curry, J. F. (1986). Effects of social problem-solving training and self-instruction training with aggressive boys. *Journal of Clinical Child Psychology, 15,* 159–164.

Loeb, G. E. (1985, Feb.). The functional replacement of the ear. *Scientific American,* 104–111.

Loftus, E. F. (1975). Leading questions and the eyewitness report. *Cognitive Psychology, 7,* 560–572.

Loftus, E. F., & Hoffman, H. G. (1989). Misinformation and memory: The creation of new memories. *Journal of Experimental Psychology: General, 118,* 100–104.

Logan, G. D. (1985). On the ability to inhibit simple thoughts and actions, II: Stop-signal studies on repetition priming. *Journal of Experimental Psychology: Learning, Memory, and Cognition, 11,* 675–691.

Logue, A. W., Ophir, I., & Strauss, K. E. (1981). The acquisition of taste aversions in humans. *Behavior Research and Therapy, 19,* 319–335.

Lovaas, O. I. (1981). *Teaching developmentally disabled children.* Baltimore: University Park Press.

Lovaas, O. I. (1987). Behavioral treatment and normal educational and intellectual functioning in young autistic children. *Journal of Consulting and Clinical Psychology, 55,* 3–9.

Lovdal, L. T. (1989). Sex role messages in television commercials: An update. *Sex Roles, 21,* 715–724.

Lozoff, B. (1989). Nutrition and behavior. *American Psychologist, 44,* 231–236.

Lu, L. (1991). Daily hassles and mental health: A longitudinal study. *British Journal of Psychology, 82,* 441–447.

Lucic, K. S., Steffen, J. J., Harrigan, J. A., & Steubing, R. C. (1991). Progressive relaxation training: Muscle contraction before relaxation? *Behavior Therapy, 22,* 249–256.

Ludwig, A. M. (1989). Reflections on creativity and madness. *American Journal of Psychotherapy, 43,* 4–14.

Lupica, M. (1985, May). Taking the bully by the horns. *World Tennis.*

Luthar, S. S., & Zigler, E. (1991). Vulnerability and competence: A review of research on resilience in childhood. *American Journal of Orthopsychiatry, 61,* 6–22.

Lyons, L. C., & Woods, P. J. (1991). The efficacy of rational-emotive therapy: A quantitative review of the outcome research. *Clinical Psychology Review, 11,* 357–369.

Lytle, L. D. (1977). Control of eating behavior. In R. J. Wurtman & J. J. Wurtman (Eds.), *Nutrition and the brain* (vol. 2). New York: Raven Press.

Lytton, H., & Romney, D. M. (1991). Parents' differential socialization of boys and girls: A meta-analysis. *Psychological Bulletin, 109,* 267–296.

Maccoby, E. E. (1984). Socialization and developmental change. *Child Development, 55,* 317–328.

Maccoby, E. E. (1989). Gender and relationships. *American Psychologist, 45,* 513–520.

Maccoby, E. E., & Jacklin, C. N. (1974). *The psychology of sex differences.* Palo Alto, CA: Stanford University Press.

Macfarlane, A. J. (1975). Olfaction in the development of social preferences in the human neonate. *CIBA Foundation Symposium, 33,* 103–117.

MacQueen, G., Marshall, J., Perdue, M., Siegel, S., & Biennenstock, J. (1989). Pavlovian conditioning of rat mucosal mast cells to secrete rat mast cell protease II. *Science, 243,* 83–85.

Madden, D. J., Blumenthal, J. A., Allen, P. A., & Emery, C. F. (1989). Improving aerobic capacity in healthy older adults does not necessarily lead to improved cognitive performance. *Psychology and Aging, 4,* 307–320.

Maddi, S. R., Bartone, P. T., & Puccetti, M. C. (1987). Stressful events are indeed a factor in physical illness: Reply to Schroeder and Costa (1984). *Journal of Personality and Social Psychology, 52,* 833–843.

Mann, L., Newton, J. W., & Innes, J. M. (1982). A test between deindividuation and emergent norm theories of crowd aggression. *Journal of Personality and Social Psychology, 42,* 260–272.

Manson, J. E., Colditz, G. A., Stampfer, M. J., Willett, W. C., & Rosner, R. (1990). A prospective study of obesity and risk of coronary heart disease in women. *New England Journal of Medicine, 322,* 882–889.

Marcos, L. R., Cohen, N. L., Nardacci, D., & Brittain, J. (1990). Psychiatry takes to the streets: The New York City initiative for the homeless mentally ill. *American Journal of Psychiatry, 147,* 1557–1561.

Markman, H. J. (1981). Prediction of marital distress: A 5-year follow-up. *Journal of Consulting and Clinical Psychology, 49,* 760–762.

Markowitz, J. S., Weissman, M. M., Ouellette, R., Lish, J. D., & Klerman, G. L. (1989). Quality of life in panic disorder. *Archives of General Psychiatry, 46,* 984–992.

Marks, D., & Kammann, R. (1980). *The psychology of the psychic.* Buffalo, NY: Prometheus.

Marks, I. (1991). Self-administered behavioural treatment. *Behavioural Psychotherapy, 19,* 42–46.

Markus, H., Crane, M., Bernstein, D. A., & Siladi, M. (1982). Self-schemas and gender. *Journal of Personality and Social Psychology, 42,* 38–50.

Markus, H., Hamill, R., & Sentis, K. P. (1987). Thinking fat: Self-schemas for body weight and the processing of weight relevant information. *Journal of Applied Social Psychology, 17,* 50–71.

Martin, G. L. (1982). Thought-stopping and stimulus control to decrease persistent disturbing thoughts. *Journal of Behavior Therapy and Experimental Psychiatry, 13,* 215–220.

Martin, L. (1986). Eskimo words for snow: A case study in the genesis and decay of an anthropological example. *American Anthropologist, 88,* 418–423.

Martin, P. R. (1991). Theoretical and empirical foundations of behavior therapy. In P. R. Martin (Ed.), *Handbook of behavior therapy and psychological science.* New York: Pergamon Press.

Martinez, J. L. (1990, March). *Acculturation among Hispanic Americans.* Symposium presented at the meeting of the American Psychological Society, Dallas, TX.

Maslow, A. H. (1954). *Motivation and personality.* New York: Harper & Row.

Maslow, A. H. (1968). *Toward a psychology of being* (2nd ed.). New York: Van Nostrand.

Maslow, A. H. (1970). *Motivation and personality* (2nd ed.). New York: Harper & Row.

Maslow, A. H. (1971). *The farther reaches of human nature.* New York: Viking Press.

Masters, W. H., & Johnson, V. E. (1966). *Human sexual response.* Boston: Little, Brown.

Masters, W. H., & Johnson, V. E. (1981). Sex and the aging process. *Journal of the American Geriatrics Society, 19,* 385–389.

Matsnev, E. I., Kuz'min, M. P., & Zakharova, L. N. (1987). Comparative assessment of vestibular, optokinetic, and optovestibular stimulation in the development of experimental motion sickness. *Aviation, Space and Environmental Medicine, 58,* 954–957.

Matson, J. L., & Mulick, J. A. (Eds.). (1990). *Handbook of mental retardation* (2nd ed.). Elmsford, NY: Pergamon.

Matsuda, L. A., Lolait, S. J., Brownstein, M. J., Young, A. C., & Bonner, T. I. (1990). Structure of a cannabinoid receptor and functional expression of the cloned cDNA. *Nature, 346,* 561–564.

Matsumoto, D., & Ekman, P. (1989). American-Japanese cultural differences in intensity ratings of facial expressions of emotion. *Motivation and Emotion, 13,* 143–157.

Matthews, K. A., & Haynes, S. G. (1986). Type A behavior pattern and coronary disease risk. *American Journal of Epidemiology, 123,* 923–960.

Maugh, T. M. (1982). Sleep-promoting factor isolated. *Science, 216,* 1400.

May, R. M., Anderson, R. M., & Blower, S. M. (1989). The epidemiology and transmission dynamics of HIV-AIDS. *Daedalus, 118,* 163–201.

Mayer, R. E. (1983). *Thinking, problem solving, cognition.* New York: W. H. Freeman.

McCabe, A. E. (1989). Differential language learning styles in young children: The importance of context. *Developmental Review, 9,* 1–20.

McCann, I. L., & Holmes, D. S. (1984). Influence of aerobic exercise on depression. *Journal of Personality and Social Psychology, 46,* 1142–1147.

McCartney, K., Marris, M. J., & Bernieri, F. (1990). Growing up and growing apart: A developmental meta-analysis of twin studies. *Psychological Bulletin, 107,* 226–237.

McClelland, D. C. (1985). *Human motivation.* Glenview, IL: Scott, Foresman.

McClelland, D. C., Atkinson, J. W., Clark, R. W., & Lowell, E. L. (1953). *The achievement motive.* New York: Appleton-Century-Crofts.

McCloskey, M., Wible, C. G., & Cohen, N. J. (1988). Is there a special flashbulb-memory mechanism? *Journal of Experimental Psychology: General, 117,* 171–181.

McCrae, R. R. (1991). The five-factor model and its assessment in clinical settings. *Journal of Personality Assessment, 57,* 399–414.

McCrae, R. R., & Costa, P. T., Jr. (1990). *Personality in adulthood.* New York: Guilford Press.

McDaniel, M. A., & Einstein, G. O. (1986). Bizarre imagery as an effective memory aid: The importance of distinctiveness. *Journal of Experimental Psychology: Learning, Memory and Cognition, 12,* 54–65.

McDougall, W. (1908). *Social psychology.* New York: Putnam.

McGlashan, T. H. (1988). A selective review of recent North American long-term follow-up studies of schizophrenia. *Schizophrenia Bulletin, 14,* 515–542.

McGrady, A. V., & Bernal, G. A. A. (1986). Relaxation based treatment of stress induced syncope. *Journal of Behavior Therapy and Experimental Psychiatry, 17,* 23–27.

McKean, K. (1983, Nov.). Memory. *Discover.*

McKey, R. H., Condelli, L., Granson, H., Barrett, B., McConkey, C., & Plantz, M. (1985). *The impact of Head Start on children, families and communities.* Final report of the Head Start Evaluation, Synthesis, and Utilization Project. Washington, DC: CSR.

McKinlay, J. B., McKinlay, S. M., & Brambilla, D. (1987). The relative contributions of endocrine changes and social circumstances to depression in mid-aged women. *Journal of Health and Social Behavior, 28,* 345–363.

McNally, R. J. (1990). Psychological approaches to panic disorder: A review. *Psychological Bulletin, 108,* 403–419.

Meeus, W. & Raaijmakers, Q. (1989). Obedience to authority in Milgram-type studies: A research review. *Zeitschrift fur Sozialpsychologie, 20,* 70–85.

Melzack, R., & Wall, P. D. (1965). Pain mechanisms: A new theory. *Science, 150,* 971–979.

Merckelbach, H., de Ruitter, C., van den Hout, M. A., & Hoekstra, R. (1989). Conditioning experiences and phobias. *Behaviour Research and Therapy, 27,* 657–662.

Mesirow, K. H. (1984). *Report on animal research survey.* Paper presented at the American Psychological Association, Toronto.

Messer, S. B., & Warren, S. (1990). Personality change and psychotherapy. In L. A. Previn (Ed.), *Handbook of personality.* New York: Guilford Press.

Milgram, S. (1963). Behavioral study of obedience. *Journal of Abnormal and Social Psychology, 67,* 371–378.

Milgram, S. (1974). *Obedience to authority.* New York: Harper & Row.

Millan, M. J. (1986). Multiple opioid systems and pain. *Pain, 27,* 303–347.

Miller, G. (1956) The magical number seven, plus or minus two: Some limits on our capacity for information processing. *Psychological Review, 48,* 337–442.

Miller, T. Q., Turner, C. W., Tindale, R. S.,

Posavac, E. J., & Dugoni, B. L. (1991). Reasons for the trend toward null findings in research on Type A behavior. *Psychological Bulletin, 110,* 469–485.

Millon, T. (1981). *Disorders of personality.* New York: Wiley.

Milner, B. (1965). Memory disturbance after bilateral hippocampal lesions. In P. Milner & S. Glickman (Eds.), *Cognitive processes and the brain.* Princeton, NJ.: Van Nostrand.

Mirsky, A. F., & Quinn, O. W. (1988). The Genain quadruplets. *Schizophrenia Bulletin, 14,* 595–612.

Mischel, W. (1968). *Personality and assessment.* New York: Wiley.

Mischel, W. (1990). Personality dispositions revisited and revised: A view after three decades. In L. A. Previn (Ed.), *Handbook of Personality.* New York: Guilford Press.

Mischel, W., & Peake, P. K. (1982). Beyond deja vu in the search for cross-situational consistency. *Psychological Review, 89,* 730–755.

Mischel, W., Shoda, Y., & Rodriguez, M. L. (1989). Delay of gratification in children. *Science, 244,* 933–937.

Mitchell, D. (1980). The influence of early visual experience on visual perception. In C. Harris (Ed.), *Visual coding and adaptability.* Hillsdale, NJ: Lawrence Erlbaum.

Mitchell, J. E. (1991). A review of the controlled trials of psychotherapy for bulimia nervosa. *Journal of Psychosomatic Research, 35,* 23–31.

Modestin, J. (1992). Multiple personality disorder in Switzerland. *American Journal of Psychiatry, 149,* 88–92.

Moffitt, A., Hoffmann, R., Mullington, J., Purcell, S., Pigeau, R., & Wells, R. (1988). Dream Psychology. In J. Gackenbach & S. LaBerge (Eds.), *Conscious mind, sleeping brain: Perspectives on lucid dreaming.* New York: Plenum Press.

Moldin, S. O., Reich, T., & Rice, J. P. (1991). Current perspectives on the genetics of unipolar depression. *Behavior Genetics, 21,* 211–242.

Money, J. (1987). Sin, sickness or status? *American Psychologist, 42,* 384–399.

Monroe, S. M., & Simons, A. D. (1991). Diathesis-stress theories in the context of life stress research: Implications for the depressive disorders. *Psychological Bulletin, 110,* 406–425.

Moody, R. A. (1976). *Life after life.* Harrisburg PA: Stackpole Books.

Moore-Ede, M. C., & Czeisler, C. A. (1984). *Mathematical models of the circadian sleep-wake cycle.* New York: Raven Press.

Morgan, M. (1985). Self-monitoring of attained subgoals in private study. *Journal of Educational Psychology, 77,* 623–630.

Morris, R. A. (1989). The admissibility of evidence derived from hypnosis and polygraphy. In D. C. Raskin, *Criminal investigation and evidence.* New York: Springer.

Morrow, G. R. (1986). Effect of the cognitive hierarchy in the systematic desensitization treatment of anticipatory nausea in cancer patients: A component comparison with relaxation only, counseling, and no treatment. *Cognitive Therapy and Research, 10,* 421–446.

Morrow, P. C., & McElroy, J. C. (1990). The effects of physical attractiveness and other demographic characteristics on promotion decisions. *Journal of Management, 16,* 723–736.

Morse, D. R., Martin, J., & Moshonov, J. (1991). Psychosomatically induced death: Relative to stress, hypnosis, mind control, and voodoo: Review and possible mechanisms. *Stress Medicine, 7,* 213–232.

Mower, G. D., Christen, W. G., & Caplan, C. J. (1983). Very brief visual experience eliminates plasticity in the cat visual cortex. *Science, 221,* 178–180.

Muehlenhard, C. L., & Linton, M. A. (1987). Date rape and sexual aggression in dating situations: Incidence and risk factors. *Journal of Counseling Psychology, 34,* 186–196.

Murray, H. A. (1938). *Explorations in personality.* New York: Oxford University Press.

Murray, J. B. (1986). New psychoactive drugs. *Genetic, Social and General Psychology Monographs, 112,* 429–453.

Murray, J. B. (1986). Psychological aspects of anorexia nervosa. *Genetic, Social and General Psychology Monographs, 112,* 5–40.

Musto, D. F. (1991). Opium, cocaine and marijuana in American history. *Scientific American, 265,* 40–47.

Myers, D. G. (1981, Aug.). The psychology of ESP. *Science Digest.*

Nadol, J. B., & Eddington, D. E. (1988). Treatment of sensorineural hearing loss by cochlear implantation. *Annual Review of Medicine, 39,* 491–502.

Naitoh, P. (1976). Sleep deprivation in human subjects: A reappraisal. *Waking and Sleeping, 1,* 53–60.

Nash, M. (1987). What, if anything, is regressed about hypnotic age regression? A review of the empirical literature. *Psychological Bulletin, 102,* 42–52.

Nathans, J., Piantanida, T. P., Eddy, R. L., Shows, T. B., & Hogness, D. S. (1986a). Molecular genetics of inherited variation in human color vision. *Science, 232,* 203–210.

Nathans, J., Thomas, D., & Hogness, D. S. (1986b). Molecular genetics of human color vision: The genes encoding blue, green, and red pigments. *Science, 232,* 193–202.

National Center on Child Abuse and Neglect. (1988). *Study of national incidence and prevalence of child abuse and neglect: 1988.* (Contract 105-85-1702). Washington, DC: U.S. Department of Health and Human Services.

National Institute on Drug Abuse. (1990). *National household survey on drug abuse: Population estimates 1990.* Rockville, MD: Author.

Needleman, H. L., & Gatsonis, C. A. (1990). Low-

level lead exposure and the IQ of children. *Journal of the American Medical Association, 263,* 673–678.

Neill, J. R., & Ludwig, A. M. (1980). Psychiatry and psychotherapy: Past and future. *American Journal of Psychotherapy, 34,* 39–50.

Neisser, U. (1991). A case of misplaced nostalgia. *American Psychologist, 46,* 34–36.

Neubuerger, O. W., Miller, S. I., Schmitz, R. E., Matarazzo, J. D., Pratt, H., & Hasha, N. (1982). Replicable abstinence rates in an alcoholism treatment program. *Journal of the American Medical Association, 248,* 960–963.

Neuspiel, D. R., & Hamel, S. C. (1991). Cocaine and infant behavior. *Developmental and Behavioral Pediatrics, 12,* 55–64.

Newcomb, M. D., & Bentler, P. M. (1989). Substance use and abuse among children and teenagers. *American Psychologist, 44,* 242–248.

Nicassio, P., & Bootzin, R. (1974). A comparison of progressive relaxation and autogenic training as treatments for insomnia. *Journal of Abnormal Psychology, 83,* 253–260.

Norman, A. B., Lehman, M. N., & Sanberg, P. R. (1989). Functional effects of fetal striatal transplants. *Brain Research Bulletin, 22,* 163–172.

Norman, D. A. (1982). *Learning and memory.* New York: Freeman.

Nottebohm, F. (1989). From bird song to neurogenesis. *Scientific American, 260,* 74–79.

Noyes, R., Jr., Chaudry, D. R., & Domingo, D. V. (1986). Pharmacologic treatment of phobic disorders. *Journal of Clinical Psychiatry, 47,* 445–452.

Noyes, R., Jr., Clancy, J., Hoenk, P. R., & Slymen, D. J. (1980). The prognosis of anxiety neurosis. *Archives of General Psychiatry, 37,* 173–178.

Nurmi, J. (1991). How do adolescents see their future? A review of the development of future orientation and planning. *Developmental Review, 11,* 1–59.

Oatley, K., & Johnson-Laird, P. N. (1987). Towards a cognitive theory of emotions. *Cognition and Emotion, 1,* 29–50.

O'Heron, C. A., & Orlofsky, J. L. (1990). Stereotypic and nonstereotypic sex role trait and behavior orientations, gender identity, and psychological adjustment. *Journal of Personality and Social Psychology, 58,* 134–143.

Ojehagen, A., & Berglund, M. (1989). Changes of drinking goals in a two-year out-patient alcoholic treatment program. *Addictive Behaviors, 14,* 1–9.

Okin, R. L. (1983). On the future of state hospitals: Should there be one? *American Journal of Psychiatry, 140,* 577–581.

Olds, D. L., & Henderson, C. R., Jr. (1989). The prevention of maltreatment. In C. Cicchetti & V. Carlson (Eds.), *Child maltreatment: Theory and research on the causes and consequences of child abuse and neglect.* Cambridge, Eng.: Cambridge University Press.

O'Leary, A. (1990). Stress, emotion, and human immune function. *Psychological Bulletin, 108,* 363–382.

Olshansky, S. J., Carnes, B. A., & Cassel, C. (1990). In search of Methuselah: Estimating the upper limits to human longevity. *Science, 250,* 634–640.

Onstad, S., Skre, I., Torgersen, S., & Kringlen, E. (1991). Twin concordance for DSM-III-R schizophrenia. *Acta Psychiatrica Scandinavica, 83,* 395–401.

Orne, M. T., & Evans, F. J. (1965). Social control in the psychological experiment: Antisocial behavior and hypnosis. *Journal of Personality and Social Psychology, 1,* 189–200.

Ortony, A., & Turner, T. J. (1990). What's basic about basic emotions. *Psychological Review, 97,* 315–331.

Ost, L. (1992). Blood and injection phobia: Background and cognitive, physiological, and behavioral variables. *Journal of Abnormal Psychology, 101,* 68–74.

O'Sullivan, G., Noshirvani, H., Marks, I., Monteiro, W., & Lelliott, P. (1991). Six-year follow-up after exposure and clomipramine therapy for obsessive-compulsive disorder. *Journal of Clinical Psychiatry, 52,* 150–155.

Paikoff, R. L., & Brooks-Gunn, J. (1991). Do parent-child relationships change during puberty? *Psychological Bulletin, 110,* 47–66.

Palfai, T., & Jankiewicz, H. (1991). *Drugs and human behavior.* Dubuque, IA: William C. Brown.

Parke, R. B., & Salby, R. G. (1983). Aggression: A multi-level analysis. In P. H. Mussen (Ed.), *Handbook of child psychology* (vol. 4). New York: Wiley.

Parker, F. L., Piotrkowski, C. S., & Peay, L. (1987). Head Start as a social support for mothers: The psychological benefits of involvement. *American Journal of Orthopsychiatry, 57,* 220–233.

Parker, G. (1982). Researching the schizophrenogenic mother. *The Journal of Nervous and Mental Disease, 170,* 452–462.

Parks, T. E., & Coss, R. G. (1986, Oct.). Prime illusion. *Psychology Today.*

Paul, D. B., & Blumenthal, A. L. (1989). On the trail of Little Albert. *Psychological Record, 39,* 547–553.

Paul, S. M., Extein, I., Calil, H. M., Potter, W. Z., Chodoff, P., & Goodwin, F. K. (1981). Use of ECT with treatment-resistant depressed patients at the National Institute of Mental Health. *American Journal of Psychiatry, 138,* 486–489.

Payne, K. (1989, Aug.). Elephant talk. *National Geographic.*

Pearlman, C. (1991). Electroconvulsive therapy: Current concepts. *General Hospital Psychiatry, 13,* 128–137.

Persky, V. W., Kempthorne-Rawson, J., &

Shekelle, R. B. (1987). Personality and risk of cancer: 20-year follow-up of the Western Electric study. *Psychosomatic Medicine, 49,* 435–449.

Petitto, L. A., & Marentette, P. F. (1991). Babbling in the manual mode: Evidence for the ontogeny of language. *Science, 251,* 1493–1496.

Petrie, K., Conaglen, J. V., Thompson, L., & Chamberlain, K. (1989). Effect of melatonin on jet lag after long haul flights. *British Medical Journal, 298,* 705–707.

Petty, R. E., & Cacioppo, J. T. (1981). *Attitudes and persuasion: Classic and contemporary approaches.* Dubuque, IA: William C. Brown.

Piaget, J. (1929). *The child's conception of the world.* New York: Harcourt, Brace.

Pianta, R., Egeland, B., & Erickson, M. F. (1989). The antecedents of maltreatment: Results of the mother-child interaction research project. In C. Cicchetti & V. Carlson (Eds.), *Child maltreatment: Theory and research on the causes and consequences of child abuse and neglect.* Cambridge, Eng.: Cambridge University Press.

Piccione, C., Hilgard, E. R., & Zimbardo, P. G. (1989). On the degree of stability in measured hypnotizability over a 25-year period. *Journal of Personality and Social Psychology, 56,* 289–295.

Piliavin, J. A., Dovidio, J. F., Gaertner, S. L., & Clark, R. D. (1982). Responsive bystanders: The process of intervention. In V. J. Derlega & J. Grzelak (Eds.), *Cooperation and helping behavior.* Orlando, FL: Academic Press.

Pillemer, D. B. (1984). Flashbulb memories of the assassination attempt on President Reagan. *Cognition, 16,* 63–80.

Pinker, S. (1990). Language acquisition. In D. N. Osherson & L. Howard (Eds.), *An invitation to cognitive science, vol. 1: Language.* Cambridge, MA: MIT Press.

Plomin, R. (1989). Environment and genes. *American Psychologist, 44,* 105–111.

Plomin, R. (1990). The role of inheritance in behavior. *Science, 248,* 183–188.

Plomin, R., Chipuer, H. M., & Loehlin, J. C. (1990). Behavioral genetics and personality. In L. A. Pervin (Ed.), *Handbook of personality theory and research.* New York: Guilford Press.

Plutchik, R. (1980). A general psychoevolutionary theory of emotion. In R. Plutchik & H. Kellerman (Eds.), *Emotion: Theory, research, and experience:, vol. 1: Theories of emotion.* New York: Academic Press.

Pomerleau, A., Bolduc, D., Malcuit, G., & Cossette, L. (1990). Pink or blue: Environmental gender stereotypes in the first two years of life. *Sex Roles, 22,* 359–367.

Portal, J. (1988). Patterns of eye-hand dominance in baseball players. *New England Journal of Medicine, 319,* 655–656.

Posner, M. I., Petersen, S. E., Fox, P. T., & Raichle, M. E. (1988). Localization of cognitive operations in the human brain. *Science, 240,* 1627–1631.

Post, R. (1991). Quoted in: C. Holden, Depression: The news isn't depressing. *Science, 254,* 1450–1452.

Power, K. G., Jerrom, D. W. A., Simpson, R. J., Mitchell, M. J., & Swanson, V. (1989). A controlled comparison of cognitive-behaviour therapy, diazepam and placebo in the management of generalized anxiety. *Behavioural Psychotherapy, 17,* 1–14.

Power, M., & Brewin, C. R. (1991). From Freud to cognitive science: A contemporary account of the unconscious. *British Journal of Clinical Psychology, 30,* 289–310.

Powers, S. L., Hauser, S. T., & Kilner, L. A. (1989). Adolescent mental health. *American Psychologist, 44,* 200–208.

Prentice-Dunn, S., & Rogers, R. W. (1982). Effects of public and private self-awareness on deindividuation and aggression. *Journal of Personality and Social Psychology, 43,* 505–513.

Pressley, M., Snyder, B. L., Levin, J. R., Murray, H. G., & Ghatala, E. S. (1987). Perceived readiness for examination performance (PREP) produced by initial reading of text and text containing adjunct questions. *Reading Research Quarterly, 22,* 219–236.

Price, R. A., & Gottesman, I. I. (1991). Body fat in identical twins reared apart: Roles for genes and environment. *Behavior Genetics, 21,* 1–7.

Prochaska, J. O., & Norcross, J. C. (1983). Contemporary psychotherapists: A national survey of characteristics, practices orientations, and attitudes. *Psychotherapy: Theory, Research and Practice, 20,* 161–173.

Pruitt, D. G. (1971). Choice shifts in group discussion: An introductory review. *Journal of Personality and Social Psychology, 20,* 339–360.

Pullum, G. K. (1991). *The great Eskimo vocabulary hoax.* Chicago: University of Chicago Press.

Putnam, F. W. (1982, Oct.). Traces of Eve's faces. *Psychology Today.*

Putnam, F. W., Guroff, J. J., Silberman, E. K., Barban, L., & Post, R. M. (1986). The clinical phenomenology of multiple personality disorder: Review of 100 recent cases. *Journal of Clinical Psychiatry, 47,* 285–293.

Quadagno, D. M. (1987). Pheromones and human sexuality. *Medical Aspects of Human Sexuality, 21,* 149–154.

Quill, T. E. (1991). Death and dignity. *New England Journal of Medicine, 324,* 691–694.

Rabkin, S. W., Boyko, E., Shane, F., & Kaufert, J. (1984). A randomized trial comparing smoking cessation programs utilizing behavior modification, health education or hypnosis. *Addictive Behaviors, 9,* 157–173.

Rachman, S. (1990). The determinants and treatment of simple phobias. *Advances in Behaviour Research and Therapy, 12,* 1–30.

Rachman, S. J. (1991). The medium-term future. *Behavioural Psychotherapy, 19,* 3–5.

Rakic, P. (1985). Limits of neurogenesis in primates. *Science, 227,* 1054–1055.

Ralph, M. R., Foster, R. G., Davis, F. C., & Menaker, M. (1990). Transplanted suprachiasmatic nucleus determines circadian period. *Science, 247,* 975–978.

Ralston, J. (1989, April). Quoted in: S. Chollar, Conversations with the dolphins. *Psychology Today.*

Ramachandran, V. S., & Anstis, S. M. (1986). The perception of apparent motion. *Scientific American, 254,* 102–109.

Ramey, C. T., MacPhee, D., & Yeates, K. O. (1982). Preventing developmental retardation: A general system model. In D. K. Detterman & R. J. Sternberg (Eds.), *How and how much can intelligence be increased.* Norwood, NJ: Ablex Publishing.

Ramey, C. T., & Ramey, S. L. (1990). Intensive educational intervention for children of poverty. *Intelligence, 14,* 1–9.

Rao, K. R., & Palmer, J. (1987). The anomaly called psi: Recent research and criticism. *Behavioral and Brain Sciences, 10,* 539–643.

Rapoport, J. L. (1988). The neurobiology of obsessive-compulsive disorder. *Journal of the American Medical Association, 260,* 2888–2890.

Raskin, N. J., & Rogers, C. R. (1989). Person-centered therapy. In R. J. Corsini & D. Wedding (Eds.), *Current psychotherapies* (4th ed.). Itasca, IL: F. E. Peacock.

Rasmussen, S. A., & Eisen, J. L. (1990). Epidemiology of obsessive-compulsive disorder. *Journal of Clinical Psychiatry, 51,* 10–13.

Redmond, D. E., Jr., Naftolin, F., Collier, T. J., Leranth, C. C., Robbins, R., Sladek, C. D., Roth, R. H., & Sladek, J. R., Jr. (1988). Cryopreservation, culture, and transplantation of human fetal mesencephalic tissue into monkeys. *Science, 242,* 768–771.

Rehm, L. P. (1982). Self-management in depression. In P. Karoly & F. H. Kanfer (Eds.), *Self-management and behavior change.* New York: Pergamon Press.

Reid, J. B., Taplin, P. S., & Lorber, R. (1981). A social interactional approach to the treatment of abusive families. In R. B. Stuart (Ed.), *Violent behavior: Social learning approaches to prediction, management and treatment.* New York: Brunner/Mazel.

Reiss, S., & Bootzin, R. R. (Eds.). (1985). *Theoretical issues in behavior therapy.* Orlando, FL: Academic Press.

Relman, A. S. (Ed.). (1982). *Marijuana and health.* Washington, DC: National Academy Press.

Rescorla, R. A. (1987). A Pavlovian analysis of goal-directed behavior. *American Psychologist, 42,* 119–129.

Rescorla, R. A. (1988). Pavlovian conditioning. *American Psychologist, 43,* 151–160.

Restak, R. (1982, May). Islands of genius. *Science 82.*

Rey, G. (1983). Concepts and stereotypes. *Cognition*, 15, 237–262.

Reyneri, A. (1984, April). The nose knows, but science doesn't. *Science 84*.

Rhodes, S. R. (1983). Age-related differences in work attitudes and behavior: A review and conceptual analysis. *Psychological Bulletin, 93*, 328–367.

Rice, M. L. (1989). Children's language acquisition. *American Psychologist, 44,* 149–156.

Richardson, P. H., & Vincent, C. A. (1986). Acupuncture for the treatment of pain: A review of evaluative research. *Pain, 24,* 15–40.

Roan, S. (1991). A prized fighter. *Los Angeles Times,* February 26.

Robbins, P. R., & Houshi, F. (1983). Some observations on recurrent dreams. *Bulletin of the Menninger Clinic, 47,* 262–265.

Roberts, P., & Newton, P. M. (1987). Levinsonian studies of women's adult development. *Psychology and Aging, 2,* 154–163.

Robins, L. N., & Regier, D. A. (Eds.). (1991). *Psychiatric disorders in America.* New York: Free Press.

Robins, L. N., Tipp, J., Przybeck, T. (1991). Antisocial personality. In L. N. Robins, & D. A. Regier (Eds.), *Psychiatric disorders in America.* New York: Free Press.

Robinson, I., Ziss, K., Ganza, B., & Katx, S. (1991). Twenty years of the sexual revolution, 1965–1985: An update. *Journal of Marriage and the Family, 53,* 216–220.

Rock, I., & Palmer, S. (1990). The legacy of Gestalt psychology. *Scientific American, 263,* 84–90.

Rodgers, J. E. (1982, June). The malleable memory of eyewitnesses. *Science 82*.

Rodin, J. (1984, Dec.). Quoted in: E. Hall, A sense of control. *Psychology Today.*

Rodin, J. (1992, Jan./Feb.). Body mania. *Psychology Today.*

Rogers, C. R. (1959). A theory of therapy, personality and interpersonal relationships, as developed in the client-centered framework. In S. Koch (Ed.), *Psychology: A study of a science* (vol. 3). New York: McGraw-Hill.

Rogers, C. R. (1980). *A way of being.* Boston: Houghton Mifflin.

Rogers, C. R. (1989). Quoted in: N. J. Raskin & C. R. Rogers, Person-centered therapy. In R. J. Corsini & D. Wedding (Eds.), *Current psychotherapies* (4th ed.). Itasca, IL: F. E. Peacock.

Rosch, E. (1978). Principles of categorization. In E. Rosch & B. B. Lloyd (Eds.), *Cognition and categorization.* Hillsdale, NJ: Lawrence Erlbaum.

Rosenfeld, A. H. (1985, June). Depression: Dispelling despair. *Psychology Today.*

Rosenthal, D. (1980). Genetic aspects of schizophrenia. In H. M. Van Praag (Ed.), *Handbook of biological psychiatry,* Part III. New York: Marcel Dekker.

Rosenthal, R. (1983). Experimenter effects in laboratories, classrooms, and clinics. In J. Murray &

P. R. Abramson (Eds.), *Bias in psychotherapy.* New York: Praeger.

Roskies, E., & Avard, J. (1982). Teaching healthy managers to control their coronary-prone (Type A) behavior. In K. R. Blankstein & J. Polivy (Eds.), *Advances in the study of communication and affect* (vol. 7). New York: Plenum Press.

Ross, L. (1977). The intuitive psychologist and his shortcomings: Distortions in the attribution process. In L. Berkowitz (Ed.), *Advances in experimental social psychology* (vol. 10). New York: Academic Press.

Rotheram, M. J. (1987). Evaluation of imminent danger for suicide among youth. *American Journal of Orthopsychiatry, 57,* 102–110.

Rotter, J. B. (1966). Generalized expectancies for internal versus external locus of control of reinforcement. *Psychological Monographs: General and Applied, 80*(Whole No. 609).

Rotter, J. B. (1990). Internal versus external control of reinforcement: A case history of a variable. *American Psychologist, 45,* 489–493.

Rowe, J. W., & Kahn, R. L. (1987). Human aging: Usual and successful. *Science, 237,* 143–149.

Rowland, L. W. (1939). Will hypnotized persons try to harm themselves or others? *Journal of Abnormal and Social Psychology, 34,* 114–117.

Rozin, P. (1986). One-trial acquired likes and dislikes in humans: Disgust as a U.S. food predominance, and negative learning predominance. *Learning and Motivation, 17,* 180–189.

Rubin, D. C., & Kozin, M. (1984). Vivid memories. *Cognition, 16,* 81–95.

Rubin, P., Holm, S., Friberg, L., Videbech, P., Andersen, H. S., Bendsen, B. B., Stromoso, N., Larsen, J. K., Lassen, N. A., & Hemmingsen, R. (1991). Altered modulation of prefrontal and subcortical brain activity in newly diagnosed schizophrenia and schizophreniform disorder. *Archives of General Psychiatry, 48,* 987–995.

Rush, D., & Callahan, K. R. (1989). Exposure to passive cigarette smoking and child development. *Annals of the New York Academy of Sciences, 562,* 74–100.

Salthouse, T. A., Legg, S., Palmon, R., & Mitchell, D. (1990). Memory factors in age-related differences in simple reasoning. *Psychology and Aging, 5,* 9–15.

Salzman, C. (1991). The APA task force report on benzodiazepine dependence, toxicity, and abuse. *American Journal of Psychiatry, 148,* 151–152.

Sarason, I. G., Sarason, B. R., & Johnson, J. H. (1985). Stressful life events' measurement, moderators and adaptation. In S. R. Burchfield (Ed.), *Stress: Psychological and physiological interactions.* New York: Hemisphere.

Sarbin, T. R., & Coe, W. C. (1972). *Hypnosis: A social psychological analysis of influence communication.* New York: Holt, Rinehart & Winston.

Sausen, K. P., Lovallo, W. R., Pincomb, G. W., & Wilson, M. R. (1992). Cardiovascular responses to occupational stress in male medical students: A paradigm for ambulatory monitoring studies. *Health Psychology, 11,* 55–60.

Savage-Rumbaugh, S. (1991). Quoted in: A. Gibbons, Deja vu all over again: Chimp-language wars. *Science, 251,* 1561–1562.

Savage-Rumbaugh, S., McDonald, K., Sevcik, R. A., Hopkins, W. D., & Rubert, E. (1986). Spontaneous symbol acquisition and communicative use by pygmy chimpanzees (*Pan paniscus*). *Journal of Experimental Psychology: General, 115,* 211–235.

Scarr, S., & McCartney, K. (1988). Far from home: An experimental evaluation of the mother-child home program in Bermuda. *Child Development, 59,* 531–543.

Scarr, S., Phillips, D., & McCartney, K. (1990). Facts, fantasies and the future of child care in the United States. *American Psychological Society, 1,* 26–35.

Scarr, S., & Weinberg, R. A. (1976). IQ test performance of black children adopted by white families. *American Psychologist, 31,* 726–739.

Schab, F. R. (1991). Odor memory: Taking stock. *Psychological Bulletin, 109,* 242–251.

Schachter, S., & Singer, J. (1962). Cognitive, social and physiological determinants of emotional state. *Psychological Review, 69,* 379–399.

Schaie, K. W. (1989). Perceptual speed in adulthood: Cross-sectional and longitudinal studies. *Psychology and Aging, 4,* 443–453.

Scharf, M. B., & Fletcher, K. A. (1989). GHB—New hope for narcoleptics? *Biological Psychiatry, 26,* 329–330.

Schiff, M., Duyme, M., Dumaret, A., & Tomkiewicz, S. (1982). How much could we boost scholastic achievement and IQ scores? A direct answer from a French adoption study. *Cognition, 12,* 165–196.

Schlenker, B. R., & Weigold, M. F. (1992). Interpersonal processes involving impression regulation and management. *Annual Review of Psychology, 43,* 133–168.

Schroeder, D. H., & Costa, P. T., Jr. (1984). Influence of life events stress on physical illness: Substantive effects or methodological flaws? *Journal of Personality and Social Psychology, 46,* 853–863.

Schuckit, M. A. (1990, Aug.). Are there dangers to marijuana? *Drug Abuse & Alcoholism Newsletter.* Vista Hill Foundation.

Schulz, R., & Curnow, C. (1988). Peak performance and age among superathletes: Track and field, swimming, baseball, tennis, and golf. *Journal of Gerontology, 43,* 113–120.

Schunk, D. H. (1989). Self-efficacy and cognitive skill learning. In R. Vasta (Ed.), *Annals of child development* (vol. 6). Greenwich, CT: JAI Press.

Schwartz, B., & Reisberg, D. (1991). *Learning and memory.* New York: Norton.

Schwartz, R. H., Gruenewalk, P. J., Klitzner, M.,

& Fedio, P. (1989). Short-term memory impairment in cannabis-dependent adolescents. *American Journal of Diseases of Children, 143,* 1214–1219.

Scribner, S. (1986). Thinking in action: Some characteristics of practical thought. In R. J. Sternberg & R. K. Wagner (Eds.), *Practical intelligence: Nature and origins of competence in the everyday world.* Cambridge, Eng.: Cambridge University Press.

Seidenberg, M. S., & Petitto, L. A. (1987). Communication, symbolic communication, and language: Comment on Savage-Rumbaugh, McDonald, Sevcik, Hopkins, and Rupert (1986). *Journal of Experimental Psychology: General, 116,* 279–287.

Selkoe, D. J. (1990). Deciphering Alzheimer's disease: The amyloid precursor protein yields new clues. *Science, 248,* 1058–1060.

Selye, H. (1956). *The stress of life.* New York: McGraw-Hill.

Senden, M. von. (1960). *Space and sight: The perception of space and shape in the congenitally blind before and after operation* (P. Heath, Trans.). New York: Free Press.

Sewitch, D. E. (1987). Slow wave sleep deficiency insomnia: A problem in thermodown regulation at sleep onset. *Psychophysiology, 24,* 200–215.

Shafii, M. (1989). Completed suicide in children and adolescents: Method of psychological autopsy. In C. R Pfeffer (Ed.), *Suicide among youth: Perspectives on risk and prevention.* Washington, DC: American Psychiatric Press.

Shapiro, C. M. (1981). Growth hormone sleep interaction: A review. *Research Communications in Psychology, Psychiatry and Behavior, 6,* 115–131.

Shapiro, D. H., Jr. (1985). Clinical use of meditation as a self-regulatory strategy: Comments on Holmes's conclusions and implications. *American Psychologist, 40,* 719–722.

Shaver, P., Schwartz, J., Kirson, D., & O'Connor, C. (1987). Emotion knowledge: Further exploration of a prototype approach. *Journal of Personality and Social Psychology, 52,* 1061–1086.

Shenour, E. A. (1990). Lying about polygraph tests. *Skeptical Inquirer, 14,* 292–297.

Shimamura, A. P. (1989). Disorders of memory: The cognitive science perspective. In F. Boller & J. Grafman (Eds.), *Handbook of neuropsychology* (vol. 3). Amsterdam: Elsevier Science Publishers.

Sidtis, J. J., Volpe, B. T., Wilson, D. H., Rayport, M., & Gazzaniga, M. S. (1981). Variability in right hemisphere language function after callosal section: Evidence for a continuum of generative capacity. *Journal of Neuroscience, 1,* 323–331.

Siegel, O. (1982). Personality development in adolescence. In B. B. Woman (Ed.), *Handbook of developmental psychology.* Inglewood Cliffs, NJ: Prentice-Hall.

Siegel, R. K. (1989). *Intoxication.* New York: Dutton.

Silberner, J. (1986). Hypnotism under the knife. *Science News, 129,* 186–187.

Simon, B. (1991). Is the Oedipus complex still the cornerstone of psychoanalysis? Three obstacles to answering the question. *Journal of the American Psychoanalytic Association. 39,* 641–668.

Simons, A. D., McGowan, C. R., Epstein, L. H., & Kupfer, D. J. (1985). Exercise as a treatment for depression: An update. *Clinical Psychology Review, 5,* 553–568.

Skinner, B. F. (1954). The science of learning and the art of teaching. *Harvard Educational Review, 24,* 86–97.

Skinner, B. F. (1957). *Verbal behavior.* New York: Appleton-Century-Crofts.

Skinner, B. F. (1989). The origin of cognitive thought. *American Psychologist, 44,* 13–18.

Slater, W. H., Graves, M. F., & Piche, G. L. (1985). Effects of structural organizers on ninth-grade students' comprehension and recall of four patterns of expository text. *Reading Research Quarterly, 20,* 189–202.

Slone, K. C. (1985). *They're rarely too young . . . and never too old "to twinkle!"* Ann Arbor, MI: Shar Publications.

Small, G. W., Propper, M. W., Randolph, E. T., & Spencer, E. (1991). Mass hysteria among student performers: Social relationship as a symptom predictor. *American Journal of Psychiatry, 148,* 1200–1205.

Smith, D. (1982). Trends in counseling and psychotherapy. *American Psychologist, 37,* 802–809.

Smith, J. C., & Seidel, J. M. (1982). The factor structure of self-reported physical stress reactions. *Biofeedback and Self-regulation, 7,* 35–47.

Smith, J. F., & Kida, T. (1991). Heuristics and biases: Expertise and task realism in auditing. *Psychological Bulletin, 109,* 472–489.

Smith, M. L., & Glass, G. V. (1977). Meta-analysis of psychotherapy outcome studies. *American Psychologist, 32,* 752–760.

Smith, M. C., Womack, W. M., & Chen, A. C. N. (1989). Hypnotizability does not predict outcome of behavioral treatment in pediatric headache. *American Journal of Clinical Hypnosis, 31,* 237–241.

Smith, V. L., Kassin, S. M., & Ellsworth, P. C. (1989). Eyewitness accuracy and confidence: Within- versus between-subjects correlations. *Journal of Applied Psychology, 74,* 356–359.

Snarey, J. (1987). Cross-cultural universality of social-moral development: A critical review of Kohlbergian research. *Psychological Bulletin, 97,* 202–232.

Snyder, C. R. (1974). Why horoscopes are true: The effects of specificity on acceptance of astrological interpretations. *Journal of Clinical Psychology, 30,* 577–580.

Snyder, C. R., Shenkel, R. J., & Lowery, C. R. (1977). Acceptance of personality interpretations: The "Barnum effect" and beyond. *Journal of Consulting and Clinical Psychology, 45,* 104–114.

Snyder, M. (1974). Self-monitoring of expressive behavior. *Journal of Personality and Social Psychology, 30,* 526–537.

Snyder, M., Berscheid, E., & Glick, P. (1985). Focusing on the exterior and the interior: Two investigations of the initiation of personal relationships. *Journal of Personality and Social Psychology, 48,* 1427–1439.

Snyder, M., & Debono, K. G. (1985). Appeals to images and claims about quality: Understanding the psychology of advertising. *Journal of Personality and Social Psychology, 49,* 586–597.

Sobal, J., & Stunkard, A. J. (1989). Socioeconomic status and obesity: A review of the literature. *Psychological Bulletin, 105,* 260–275.

Spanos, N. P. (1986). Hypnotic behavior: A social-psychological interpretation of amnesia, analgesia, and the "trance logic." *Behavioral and Brain Sciences, 9,* 449–502.

Spanos, N. P. (1988). Author's response. *Behavioral and Brain Sciences, 11,* 714–717.

Spanos, N. P., Lush, N. I., & Gwynn, M. I. (1989). Cognitive skill-training enhancement of hypnotizability: Generalization effects and trance logic responding. *Journal of Personality and Social Psychology, 56,* 795–804.

Spanos, N. P., Menary, E., Brett, P. J., Cross, W., & Ahmed, Q. (1987). Failure of posthypnotic responding to occur outside the experimental setting. *Journal of Abnormal Psychology, 96,* 52–57.

Sperry, R. W. (1943). Effect of 180 degree rotation of the retinal field on visuomotor coordination. *Journal of Experimental Zoology, 92,* 263–277.

Sperry, R. W. (1974). Lateral specialization in the surgically separated hemisphere. In R. O. Schmitt and F. G. Worden (Eds.), *The neurosciences: Third study program.* Cambridge, MA: MIT Press.

Sperry, R. W. (1982). Some effects of disconnecting the cerebral hemispheres. *Science, 217,* 1223–1226.

Springer, S. P., & Deutsch, G. (1989). *Left brain, right brain* (3rd ed.). New York: W. H. Freeman.

Squire, L. R. (1987). *Memory and the brain.* New York: Oxford University Press.

Squire, L. R., & Slater, P. C. (1983). Electroconvulsive therapy and complaints of memory dysfunction: A prospective three-year follow-up study. *British Journal of Psychiatry, 142,* 1–8.

Squire, L. R., Slater, P. C., & Miller, P. L. (1981). Retrograde amnesia and bilateral electroconvulsive therapy. *Archives of General Psychiatry, 38,* 89–95.

Squire, L. R., & Zola-Morgan, S. (1991). The medial temporal lobe memory system. *Science, 253,* 1380–1386.

Sroufe, L. A., Fox, N. E., & Pancake, V. R. (1983). Attachment and dependency in developmental perspective. *Child Development, 54,* 1615–1627.

Stampi, C. (1990). Quoted in: C. Holden, Briefings. *Science, 249,* 244–245.

Stangor, C., Lynch, L., Duan, C., & Glass, B. (1992). Categorization of individuals on the basis of multiple social features. *Journal of Personality and Social Psychology, 62,* 207–218.

Steptoe, A. (1991). The links between stress and illness. *Journal of Psychosomatic Research, 35,* 633–644.

Stern, G. S., McCants, T. R., & Pettine, P. W. (1982). Stress and illness: Controllable and uncontrollable life events' relative contributions. *Personality and Social Psychology Bulletin, 8,* 140–143.

Stern, J. S. (1984). Is obesity a disease of inactivity? In A. J. Stunkard & E. Stellar (Eds.), *Eating and its disorders.* New York: Raven Press.

Sternberg, R. J. (1985). Human intelligence: The model is the message. *Science, 230,* 1111–1118.

Sternberg, R. J. (1986). A triangular theory of love. *Psychological Review, 93,* 119–135.

Sternberg, R. J., Conway, B. E., Ketron, J. L., & Bernstein, M. (1981). People's conceptions of intelligence. *Journal of Personality and Social Psychology, 41,* 37–55.

Stevens-Long, J. (1984). *Adult life.* Palo Alto, CA: Mayfield.

Stones, M. J., & Kozma, A. (1989). Age, exercise, and coding performance. *Psychology and Aging, 4,* 190–194.

Streissguth, A. P., Sampson, P. D., & Barr, H. M. (1989). Neurobehavioral dose-response effects of prenatal alcohol exposure in humans from infancy to adulthood. *Annals of the New York Academy of Sciences, 562,* 145–158.

Streissguth, A. P., Aase, J. M., Clarren, S. K., Randels, S. P., LaDue, R. A., & Smith, D. F. (1991). Fetal alcohol syndrome in adolescents and adults. *Journal of the American Medical Association. 265,* 1961–1967.

Striegel-Moore, R. H., Silberstein, L. R., Frensch, P., & Rodin, J. (1989). A prospective study of disordered eating among college students. *International Journal of Eating Disorders, 8,* 499–509.

Stromeyer, C. F., III (1970, Nov.). Eidetikers. *Psychology Today.*

Strupp, H. H. (1980). Success and failure in time-limited psychotherapy. *Archives of General Psychiatry, 37,* 595–603.

Strupp, H. H. (1989). Psychotherapy. *American Psychologist, 44,* 714–724.

Stunkard, A. J., Harris, J. R., Pederson, N. L., & McClearn, G. E. (1990). The body-mass index of twins who have been reared apart. *The New England Journal of Medicine, 322,* 1483–1487.

Styron, W. (1990). *Visible darkness.* New York: Vintage Books.

Sullivan, R. M., Taborsky-Barba, S., Mendoza, R., Itano, A., Leon, M., Cotman, C. W., Payne, T. R., & Lott, I. (1991). Olfactory classical

conditioning in neonates. *Pediatrics, 87,* 511–518.

Svartberg, M., & Stiles, T. C. (1991). Comparative effects of short-term psychodynamic psychotherapy: A meta-analysis. *Journal of Consulting and Clinical Psychology, 39,* 704–714.

Sweeney, P. D., Anderson, K., & Bailey, S. (1986). Attributional style in depression: A meta-analytic view. *Journal of Personality and Social Psychology, 50,* 974–991.

Swets, J. A., & Bjork, R. A. (1990). Enhancing human performance: An evaluation of "New Age" techniques considered by the U. S. Army. *American Psychological Society, 1,* 85–96.

Szmukler, G. I. (1985). The epidemiology of anorexia nervosa and bulimia. *Journal of Psychiatric Research, 19,* 143–153.

Szyfelbein, S. K., Osgood, P. F., & Carr, D. B. (1985). The assessment of pain and plasma B-endorphin immunoactivity in burned children. *Pain, 22,* 173–182.

Taraborrelli, J. R. (1991). *Michael Jackson: The magic and the madness.* New York: Birch Lane Press.

Tavris, C. (1982). *Anger: The misunderstood emotion.* New York: Simon & Schuster.

Taylor, H., & Cooper, C. L. (1989). The stress-prone personality: A review of the research in the context of occupational stress. *Stress Medicine, 5,* 17–27.

Taylor, S. E. (1981). The interface of cognitive and social psychology. In J. Harvey (Ed.), *Cognition, social behavior, and the environment.* Hillsdale, NJ: Erlbaum.

Tellegen, A., Lykken, D. T., Bouchard, T. J., Jr., Wilcox, K. J., & Segal, N. L. (1988). Personality similarity in twins reared apart and together. *Journal of Personality and Social Psychology, 54,* 1031–1039.

Tenenbaum, S. J., Kurtz, R. M., & Bienias, J. L. (1990). Hypnotic susceptibility and experimental pain reduction. *American Journal of Clinical Hypnosis, 33,* 40–49.

Terenius, L., & Wahlstrom, A. (1975). Morphine-like ligand for opiate receptors in human CSF. *Life Sciences, 16,* 1759–1764.

Terman, L. M. (1916). *The measurement of intelligence.* Boston: Houghton Mifflin.

Terman, L. M., & Oden, M. H. (1959). *The gifted group at mid-life* (vol. 5). Stanford, CA: Stanford University Press.

Terrace, H. S. (1981). A report to an academy, 1980. *Annals of the New York Academy of Sciences, 364,* 94–114.

Tesser, A., & Shaffer, D. R. (1990). Attitudes and attitude change. *Annual Review of Psychology, 41,* 479–523.

Thomas, A., & Chess, S. (1977). *Temperament and development.* New York: Brunner/Mazel.

Thompson, S. (1990). Putting a big thing into a little hole: Teenage girls' accounts of sexual initiation. *Journal of Sex Research, 27,* 341–361.

Thomson, G. O. B., Raab, G. M., Hepburn, W. S., Hunter, R., Fulton, M., & Laxen, D. P. H. (1989). Blood-lead levels and children's behaviour—Results from the Edinburgh lead study. *Journal of Child Psychology and Psychiatry and Allied Disciplines, 30,* 515–528.

Toch, H. H., & Schulte, R. (1961). Readiness to perceive violence as a result of police training. *British Journal of Psychology, 52,* 389–393.

Tolman, E. C. (1948). Cognitive maps in rats and men. *Psychological Review, 55,* 189–208.

Tomkins, S. S. (1981). The quest for primary motives: Biography and autobiography of an idea. *Journal of Personality and Social Psychology, 41,* 306–329.

Tudge, J., Chivian, E., Robinson, J., Andreyenkov, V., & Popov, N. (1991). American and Soviet adolescents' attitudes toward the future: The relationship between worry about nuclear war and optimism. *International Journal of Mental Health, 19,* 58–84.

Turnbull, C. (1961). Some observations regarding the experiences and behavior of the Bambuti pygmies. *American Journal of Psychology, 74,* 304–308.

Tversky, A., & Kahneman, D. (1974). Judgment under uncertainty: Heuristics and biases. *Science, 185,* 1124–1131.

Tversky, A., & Kahneman, D. (1983). Extensional versus intuitive reasoning: The conjunction fallacy in probability judgment. *Psychological Review, 90,* 293–315.

Ulrich, R. E. (1991). Animal rights, animal wrongs, and the question of balance. *Psychological Science, 2,* 197–201.

U.S. Bureau of the Census. (1986). *Estimates of the population of the U.S. by age, sex, and race, 1980–1985 (Current Population Reports, Series P-25, No. 985).* Washington, DC: U. S. Government Printing Office.

U.S. Department of Health and Human Services. (1982). *The health consequences of smoking: Cancer: A report of the Surgeon General.* Rockville, MD: Author.

Valenstein, E. S. (1986). *Great and desperate cures.* New York: Basic Books.

Vargas, J. S. (1991). B. F. Skinner—The last few days. *Journal of the Experimental Analysis of Behavior, 55,* 1–2.

Vollhardt, L. T. (1991). Psychoneuroimmunology: A literature review. *American Journal of Orthopsychiatry, 6,* 35–47.

Vonnegut, M. (1976). *The Eden express.* New York: Bantam.

Wachtel, P. L. (1982). What can dynamic therapies contribute to behavior therapy? *Behavior Therapy, 13,* 594–609.

Wadden, T. A., & Anderton, C. H. (1982). The

clinical use of hypnosis. *Psychological Bulletin, 91,* 215–243.

Wallechinsky, D. (1986). *Midterm report.* New York: Viking.

Warga, C. (1987, Aug.). Pain's gatekeeper. *Psychology Today.*

Watson, J. B., & Rayner, R. (1920). Conditioned emotional reactions. *Journal of Experimental Psychology, 3,* 1–14.

Webb, W. B. (1983). Theories in modern sleep research. In A. Mayes (Ed.), *Sleep mechanisms and functions.* Wokingham, Eng.: Van Nostrand Reinhold.

Weinberg, R. A. (1989). Intelligence and IQ. *American Psychologist, 44,* 98–104.

Weiner, B. (1986). *An attributional theory of motivation and emotion.* New York: Springer-Verlag.

Weisburd, S. (1987). The spark. *Science News, 132,* 298–300.

Werner, E. E. (1989). Children of the garden island. *Scientific American, 260,* 106–111.

Werner, E. E., & Smith, R. S. (1982). *Vulnerable but invincible.* New York: McGraw-Hill.

Westen, D. (1990). Psychoanalytic approaches to personality. In L. A. Previn (Ed.), *Handbook of personality.* New York: Guilford Press.

Wever, R. A. (1989). Light effects on human circadian rhythms: A review of recent Andechs experiments. *Journal of Biological Rhythms, 4,* 161–185.

White, W. A. (1932). *Outlines of psychiatry* (13th ed.). New York: Nervous and Mental Disease Publishing Company.

Whorf, B. (1956). *Language, thought, and reality.* New York: Wiley.

Wilkinson, R. T., & Allison, S. (1989). Age and simple reaction time: Decade differences for 5,325 subjects. *Journal of Gerontology: Psychological Sciences, 44,* 29–35.

Williams, J. E., & Best, D. L. (1990). *Measuring sex stereotypes* (vol. 6, rev. ed.). Newbury Park, CA: Sage Publications.

Williamson, D. A., Kelley, M. L., Davis, C. J., Ruggiero, L., & Blouin, D. S. (1985). Psychopathology of eating disorders: A controlled comparison of bulimic, obese, and normal subjects. *Journal of Consulting and Clinical Psychology, 53,* 161–166.

Wilson, G. D. (1978). Introversion/extroversion. In H. London & J. E. Exner (Eds.), *Dimensions in personality.* New York: Wiley.

Wilson, G. T. (1982). Adult disorders. In G. T.

Wilson & C. M. Franks (Eds.), *Contemporary behavior therapy.* New York: Guilford Press.

Wilson, G. T. (1991). Chemical aversion conditioning in the treatment of alcoholism: Further comments. *Behaviour Research and Therapy, 29,* 415–419.

Wilson, T. D., & Linville, P. W. (1982). Improving the academic performance of college freshmen: Attribution therapy revisited. *Journal of Personality and Social Psychology, 42,* 367–376.

Winograd, E., & Soloway, R. M. (1986). On forgetting the locations of things stored in special places. *Journal of Experimental Psychology: General, 115,* 366–372.

Winson, J. (1990). The meaning of dreams. *Scientific American, 263,* 86–96.

Winton, W. M. (1986). The role of facial response in self-reports of emotion: A critique of Laird. *Journal of Personality and Social Psychology, 50,* 808–812.

Wise, E., & Rafferty, J. (1982). Sex bias and language. *Sex Roles, 8,* 1189–1196.

Wojcik, J. D., Falk, W. E., Fink, J. S., Cole, J. O., & Gelenberg, A. J. (1991). A review of 32 cases of tardive dystonia. *American Journal of Psychiatry, 148,* 1055–1059.

Wolf, T. M., Elston, R. C., & Kissling, G. E. (1989). Relationship of hassles, uplifts, and life events to psychological well-being of freshman medical students. *Behavioral Medicine, 15,* 37–45.

Wong, D. F., Wagner, H. N., Jr., Tune, L. E., Dannals, R. F., Pearlson, G. D., Links, J. M., Tamminga, C. A., Broussolle, E. P., Ravert, H. T., Wilson A. A., Toung, J. K. T., Malat, J., Williams, A., O'Tuama, L. A., Snyder, S. H., Kuhar, M. J., & Gjedde, A. (1986). Positron emission tomography reveals elevated D2 dopamine receptors in drug-naive schizophrenics. *Science, 234,* 1558–1563.

Wood, W., Rhodes, N., & Whelan, M. (1989). Sex differences in positive well-being: A consideration of emotional style and marital status. *Psychological Bulletin, 106,* 249–264.

Woolfolk, R. L., & McNulty, T. E. (1983). Relaxation treatment for insomnia: A component analysis. *Journal of Consulting and Clinical Psychology, 51,* 495–503.

Yates, A. (1990). Current perspectives on the eating disorders, II: Treatment, outcome, and research directions. *Journal of the American Academy of Child and Adolescent Psychiatry, 29,* 1–9.

Yerkes, R. M. (1921). *Psychological examining in the United States Army.* Washington, DC: Memoirs of the National Academy of Sciences, No. 15.

Yule, W., & Fernando, P. (1980). Blood phobia—beware. *Behavior Research and Therapy, 18,* 587–590.

Zahn, T. P., & Rapoport, J. L. (1987). Autonomic nervous system effects of acute doses of caffeine in caffeine users and abstainers. *International Journal of Psychophysiology, 5,* 33–41.

Zaidel, E. (1983). A response to Gazzaniga. *American Psychologist, 39,* 542–546.

Zajonc, R. B. (1984). On the primacy of affect. *American Psychologist, 39,* 117–123.

Zarate, M. A., & Smith, E. R. (1990). Person categorization and stereotyping. *Social Cognition, 8,* 161–185.

Zechmeister, E. G., & Nyberg, S. E. (1982). *Human memory.* Pacific Grove, CA: Brooks/Cole.

Zigler, E., & Seitz, V. (1982). Social policy and intelligence. In R. J. Sternberg (Ed.), *Handbook of human intelligence.* Cambridge, Eng.: Cambridge University Press.

Zimbardo, P. G. (1970). The human choice: Individuation, reason and order versus deindividuation, impulse and chaos. In W. J. Arnold & D. Levine (Eds.), *Nebraska symposium on motivation.* Lincoln: University of Nebraska Press.

Zimbardo, P. G. (1977). *Shyness: What it is, what to do about it.* Reading, MA: Addison-Wesley.

Zucker, R. A., & Gomberg, E. S. (1986). Etiology of alcoholism reconsidered. *American Psychologist, 41,* 783–793.

Zuckerman, B., Frank, D. A., Hingson, R., Amaro, H., Levenson, S. M., Kayne, H., Parker, S., Vinci, R., Aboagye, K., Fried, L. E., Cabral, H., Timperi, R., & Rauchner, H. (1989). Effects of maternal marijuana and cocaine use on fetal growth. *New England Journal of Medicine, 320,* 762–768.

Zuckerman, M., Klorman, R., Larrance, D. T., & Speigel, N. H. (1981). Facial, autonomic, and subjective components of emotion: The facial feedback hypothesis versus the externalizer-internalizer distinction. *Journal of Personality and Social Psychology, 41,* 929–944.

Zuger, B. (1989). Homosexuality in families of boys with early effeminate behavior: An epidemiological study. *Archives of Sexual Behavior, 18,* 155–166.

NAME INDEX

Hayes, K. J., 229
Hayes, S. C., 19
Haynes, S. G., 509
Heffley, E. F., 416
Heider, F., 594
Heimberg, R. G., 533
Henderson, C. R., 393
Hennessey, B. A., 298
Herbener, E. S., 425
Herbert, V., 22
Herbert, W., 529
Hering, E., 96
Herman, L., 308
Hickey, E. W., 517
Hilgard, E. R., 179, 181
Hirsch, B. J., 401
Hirsch, H. V., 144
Hirt, H., 342
Hoberman, H. M., 408
Hobson, J. A., 172
Hofferth, S. L., 399
Hoffman, C., 306
Hoffman, H. G., 269
Hogrebe, M. C., 391
Hokanson, J. E., 550
Holden, C., 197, 288, 538, 540
Hollingsworth, L. S., 281
Hollon, S. D., 539
Holmes, D. S., 551
Holmes, T. H., 500
Holzman, P. S., 544
Honorton, C., 155
Hoon, E. F., 6
Hopson, J. L., 174
Horney, K., 444
Houshi, F., 171
Hovland, C. I., 601
Howard, R., 11
Howe, M. L., 416
Hubel, D. H., 69, 94, 144
Huesmann, L. R., 180
Hughes, M., 510
Huston, A. C., 621
Hyde, J. S., 391
Hyman, R., 155

I

Iacono, W. G., 351
Innes, J. M., 617
Izard, C. E., 343, 347, 368

J

Jacklin, C. N., 391
Jackson, M., 610
Jacobs, J. E., 391
James, W., 12, 13, 342
Janis, I. L., 601, 618
Jankiewicz, H., 190, 196
Janos, P. M., 281
Jennings, J. R., 6

Jensen, A. R., 279, 286
Jiang, C., 119
John, O. P., 465, 466
Johnson, B., 204
Johnson, D. R., 37, 306
Johnson, J. H., 500
Johnson, J. S., 303
Johnson, R. C., 195
Johnson, V. E., 326, 428
Johnson-Laird, P. N., 341
Jones, D. R., 112
Jones, E., 184, 186, 333, 611
Jones, W. H., 455
Jongsma, H. J., 135
Jung, Carl, 444

K

Kagan, J., 370, 455
Kagitcibasi, C., 10
Kahn, R. L., 415
Kahn, S., 506
Kahneman, D., 296
Kamarck, T., 6
Kamin, L., 286
Kammann, R., 154
Kaplan, D. M., 455
Kaplan, H. S., 326
Kaplan, R. M., 282
Karasu, T. B., 555
Karnovsky, M. L., 169
Kassin, S. M., 596
Kastenbaum, R., 431
Katschnig, H., 526
Kaufman, A. S., 279
Kaufman, J., 392
Kaushall, P., 241
Kayten, P. J., 163
Kearins, J. M., 267
Keesey, R. E., 320
Keicolt-Glaser, J. K., 490
Kelley, H. H., 595, 601
Kempthorne-Rawson, J., 509
Kenrick, D. T., 468, 592
Kida, T., 296
Kiester, E., Jr., 171
Kihlstrom, J. F., 161, 257, 445
Kilner, L. A., 397
Kimble, C. E., 611
King, F., 37
Kinsey, A. C., 26
Kirk, M. S., 114
Kirmayer, L. J., 531
Kirsner, D., 564, 565
Kissling, G. E., 501
Kleck, R. E., 343
Klein, D. B., 575
Kleinknecht, R. A., 204, 481
Klesges, R. C., 149
Klinger, E., 160
Kobasa, S. C., 506

Koenig, J., 622
Koestner, R., 332
Koffka, K., 13
Kohlberg, L., 404, 405
Kohler, I., 146
Köhler, W., 13, 228
Kohn, P. M., 501
Kolata, G., 323
Koss, M. P., 622
Kowalski, R. M., 607
Kozberg, S. F., 405
Kozel, N. J., 190
Kozin, M., 249
Kozma, A., 417
Krantz, S. E., 512
Kraut, R. E., 592
Kreitler, H., 119
Kreitler, S., 119
Kroll, N. E. A., 247
Kronauer, R. E., 163
Krueger, J. M., 169
Kübler-Ross, E., 430–431
Kuhl, P. K., 304
Kuiper, N. A., 550
Kulik, J., 249
Kurtz, R. M., 180
Kyman, W., 363

L

LaBerge, S., 173
Labouvie-Vief, G., 417
Lafreniere, K., 501
Laird, J. D., 343
Lamb, M. E., 372
Lamb, N., 231
Laner, M. R., 423
Lange, C., 342
Langlois, J. H., 607
Lanzetta, J. T., 343
Larsen, K. S., 613
Latané, B., 617, 619
Lau, I., 306
Lauber, J. K., 163
Lazarus, R. S., 344, 345, 481, 482–483, 498, 499, 512, 513
Leafgren, A., 502
Leary, M. R., 607
Leckman, J. F., 520
Lee, V. E., 288
Lefcourt, H. M., 460, 507
Leiblum, S. R., 325, 428
Lepore, S. J., 510
Lepper, M. R., 334
LeVay, S., 329
Levenson, R. W., 342
Levine, S., 622
Levinson, D. J., 419, 429
Levitan, A. A., 182
Levy, J. A., 81, 83, 431
Lewis, C. E., 541

Lewontin, R. C., 286
Lewy, A. J., 169
Lhermitte, J., 147
Li, S., 119
Liben, L. S., 389
Liem, J. H., 429
Liem, R., 429
Light, K. C., 488, 489
Lilly, J., 160
Lindvall, O., 56, 57
Linton, J. C., 342
Linton, M. A., 625
Linville, P. W., 597
Lipton, S. D., 562
List, S. J., 545
Lochman, J. E., 624
Loeb, G. E., 111
Loehlin, J. C., 620
Loftus, E. F., 269
Logan, G. D., 585
Logue, A. W., 208
Loosen, P. T., 539
Lorber, R., 393
Lorenz, K., 314
Lovaas, O. I., 232–233
Lovdal, L. T., 389
Lozoff, B., 366
Lu, L., 501
Lucic, K. S., 495
Ludlow, L. H., 10
Lupica, M., 435
Lush, N. I., 179
Luthar, S. S., 386
Lynn, M. C., 391
Lyons, L. C., 578
Lytle, L. D., 319
Lytton, H., 388

M

McCabe, A. E., 304
McCann, I. L., 551
McCants, T. R., 460, 507
McCarley, R. W., 172
McCartney, K., 286
McClelland, D. C., 332
McCloskey, M., 249
Maccoby, E. E., 391, 393
McCrae, R. R., 445, 465, 468
McDaniel, M. A., 247
McDougall, W., 314
McElroy, J. C., 607
Macfarlane, A. J., 365
McGlashan, T. H., 547
McGrady, A. V., 494
McGue, M., 286, 471
Machlovitz, H., 269
McKean, K., 262
McKey, R. H., 288
McKinlay, J. B., 428
McKinlay, S. M., 428

SUBJECT INDEX

Anger rapists, 622
"Animal brain," 80
Animal magnetism, 179
Animal model, 30
Animals
    dreaming in, 171
    language in, 308–309
    learned food aversion in, 208
    problem-solving behavior in, 228
    research using, 30, 37
Animal training, operant conditioning and, 222
Anorexia nervosa, 337
ANOVA, 634
Anterior pituitary, 79
Anterograde amnesia, 262
Anticipatory stress, 513
Antidepressants, 539
    for treating phobias, 533
Antipsychotic drugs, 71, 546
    deinstitutionalization and, 557
Antisocial personality, 541
Anxiety, 504–505. *See also* Stress
    coping with, 505
    defined, 440
    muscle tension and, 494
Anxiety disorders, 523, 524, 525–528
APA. *See* American Psychiatric Association,
        American Psychological Association
Apes, communication among, 309
Apparent motion, 13, 138
Appraisal
    changing, 513
    fight-or-flight response and, 489
    locus of control and, 507
    of major life events, 500
    stress and, 482–483
    stress management and, 512
Approach-approach conflict, 503
Approach-avoidance conflict, 503
Arousal-cost-reward model, 619
Artificial intelligence, 17
Asch, Solomon, 613
Asian American Psychological Association, 11
Assertiveness training, 625
Assimilation, 379
Association, law of, 209
Association areas, 75, 94, 108
    damage to, 148
Association of Black Psychologists, 11
Astrology, 476
Atmospheric perspective, 133
Attachment, in infants, 372–373
Attention
    memory and, 238, 242
    role in observational learning, 227, 231
Attention disorders, 543
Attitudes, 598–599
    behavior and, 598, 599, 605
    changing, 602–603, 605
Attractiveness, importance of, 607

Attribution, 594–597
    bias and error in, 596
    changing, 597
    factors that influence, 595
Attribution theory, 594
Auditory association areas, 75
Auditory canal, 106
Auditory nerve, 107
Auditory receptors, 111
Auditory sensory memory, 239
Authoritarian parents, 407
Authoritative parents, 407
Authority figures, 615
Autism, 3, 6, 281
    treating, 232–233
Automatic encoding, 246
Automatic processes, 160
Autonomic nervous system, 62–63
    emotion and, 342
    hypothalamus and, 80
    stress and, 484
    voluntary control of, 493
Autonomy versus shame and doubt stage, 385
Availability heuristic, 296
Aversion, learned, 208
Aversive conditioning, 197
Avoidance-avoidance conflict, 503
Axes, defined, 522
Axon, 44
    resting state of, 49
    structure and function of, 48–50
Axon membrane, 48

B

Babbling stage, 304
Backward conditioning, 206
Balian healers, 567
Bandura's social-cognitive theory, 384, 459
Bandura's theory of observational learning, 227
Barnum principle, 476
Basal ganglia, 57
Basic emotions, 341
Basilar membrane, 107
Beautiful-is-good stereotype, 607
Behavior, 4
    abnormal, 519, 520–521
    approaches to understanding, 5
    attitudes and, 599
    biological bases of, 40–83
    controlling, 4
    effect of neurotransmitters on, 52
    emotional, 80
    emotion and, 347
    gender roles and, 388
    hypnosis and, 183
    influence of cognitive processes on, 459
    moral reasoning and, 405
    prediction of, 28
    problem-solving, 228
    settings for studying, 31
    sexual, 325–331

social-emotional, 70, 71
    trial-and-error, 215
    use of traits in predicting, 467–468
Behavioral approach, 5, 7, 9, 13
Behavioral component of attitudes, 598, 605
Behavioral factors, in personality disorders, 541
Behavioral genetics, 469
Behavioral problems, suicide and, 409
Behaviorism, 7, 13
Behavior modification
    in treating anorexia nervosa, 337
    in treating child abuse, 393
    uses for, 232–233
Behavior therapy, 572, 573–576
    advantages and criticisms of, 576
    review of, 583
Beliefs, perception and, 24
Belongingness needs, 317, 449
Benzodiazepines, 525
Bias
    in attribution, 596
    beliefs and, 31
    in experiments, 36
    in IQ testing, 282–283
    in perception, 24, 126, 127, 151, 591
    in study methods, 23
    in testimonials, 24
Biased sample, 26
Bidirectionality, principle of, 393
Bilingualism, 306
Binet-Simon Intelligence Scale, 277
Binocular cues, 131
Biofeedback, 233, 494–495
Biological clocks, 162
Biological cues, for hunger, 318, 319
Biological drives, 438
Biological factors, 229
    in motivation, 314
    in sexual preference, 329
Biological intelligence, 276
Biological limit theory of aging, 414
Biological needs, 314, 316–317
Biological restraint, 229
Biological theory
    of aggression, 620
    of depression, 538
Biopsy, 124
Bipolar disorder, 536, 537
    lithium treatment for, 540
Birth defects, 362–363
Bisexuality, 328
Blackmore, Susan, 155
Blind spot, 91, 98
Blood alcohol level (BAL), 197
"Boat people" studies, 453
Body image, 149, 318
Body temperature, sleep-wake cycle and, 169
Body weight, 320–323
Brain, 64–83
    control centers of, 68–75
    development of neurons in, 43

Brain (*continued*)
divisions of, 64–66
evolution of, 68
language areas of, 303
organization of, 80–81
racial myths about, 67
regulation of, 79
relationship to mind, 42
research on, 82–83
sensations and, 127
substance of, 42
techniques for studying, 76–77
Brain activity, physical movement and, 41
Brain damage, 65
diagnosing, 76–77
effect on memory, 241, 244
effect on perception, 147
treatment of, 54
Brain death, 161
Brain defects, 518, 545
Brain disorders, neurotransmitters and, 52
Brain hemispheres, 64, 81, 82–83
Brain size, intelligence and, 276
Brainstorming, 298
Brain tissue transplant, 52
Brain waves, amplitude and frequency of, 164
Brightness constancy, 134
Broca's aphasia, 74
Broca's area, 74
Bulimia nervosa, 337
Burnout, 502
Bystander effect, 617

C

CACOB (Consequences are contingent on behavior), 217, 218
Caffeinism, 188
Calkins, Mary, 11
Cancer detection, 123, 124
Careers
gender stereotypes in, 389
in psychology, 15
social development and, 429
Care orientation, 405
Case studies, 23, 24–25
Case-study approach, 31, 143, 358
Cataracts, 90
Catatonic schizophrenia, 543
Catecholamines, 491
Categorizing of concepts, 293
Catharsis, 624
CAT scan, 76
Causation, versus correlation, 28
Cause-effect relationships, in perceptual processes, 143
CCK, 319
Cell body, 44
Centers for Disease Control (CDC), 399
Central cues, 319
Central nervous system, 54, 60, 61–63
psychoneuroimmunology and, 490

Central route for persuasion, 600, 605
Central tendency, measures of, 629–630
Cephalocaudal principle, 367
Cerebellum, 6, 66
Challenge appraisal, 482, 484
stress management and, 512
Child abuse, 392–393
Childbirth, 363
Child development, 355–375
Childhood, 378–393
anger control in, 624
cognitive development in, 379–383
gender role development in, 388–390
mental disorders in, 523
social development in, 384–385
vulnerability and resiliency during, 386
Child-parent social interactions, 444
Child prodigies, 356, 357
Child training, operant conditioning and, 222
Chi-square, 634
Cholecystokinin (CCK), 319
Chromosomes, 360
Chronic schizophrenia, 542
Chronological age, 415
Chunking, 240, 241, 266
Cigarette smoking
effect on fetal development, 363
hypnosis and, 183
nicotine addiction and, 189
studies of, 28
Circadian rhythm, 162, 163
Clairvoyance, 154
Classical conditioning, 202–210
advertising and, 209
anxiety and, 504
examples of, 203–204, 208–209
explanations for, 206
versus operant conditioning, 216
Clinical interviews, 520
Clinical psychologists, 15, 558
Clomipramine, 528
Closure principle, 129
Cocaine, 184, 186–187
effect on fetal development, 363
Cochlea, 107
nerve impulses from, 108
Cochlear implant, 111
Coding of information, 227
Cognition, 292
lifetime changes in, 413
Cognitive appraisal theory of emotion, 344–345
Cognitive approach, 5, 6, 292
Cognitive-behavioral approach
to mental disorders, 518
to shyness, 455
Cognitive-behavior therapy
in treating depression, 539
in treating bulimia nervosa, 337
in treating phobias, 533
Cognitive component of attitudes, 598, 605

Cognitive development, 378
in adolescence, 402–403
Piaget's theory of, 379–383, 402
Cognitive development theory, gender-role acquisition and, 389
Cognitive dissonance, 602–603
predictions of, 603
Cognitive interviews, 269
Cognitive learning, 202, 225–228
Cognitive map, 225
Cognitive miser model, 596
Cognitive processes
changes in, 416–417
emotion and, 345
influence on behaviors, 459
influence on motivation, 315, 334
Cognitive psychologists, 12, 17, 161
Cognitive stages, 380–383, 402
Cognitive theory, 344–345
aggression and, 621
depression and, 538
Cognitive therapy, 577–579
review of, 583
Cognitive unconscious, 161, 445
Colds
curing, 23
susceptibility to, 491
Collective unconscious, 444
Color blindness, 97, 99
Color constancy, 134
Color signals, 96
Color vision, 95–97
theories of, 96
Coma, 63, 65
vegetative, 161
Commitment, defined, 424
Communication, 308
parent-teen, 399, 403
Community mental health centers, 557
Companionate love, 424
Complementary afterimages, 99
Complete love, 424
Compliance, 613
Compulsions, 528
Computer-generated reality, 138–139
Computerized axial tomography (CAT), 76
Conception, 360–361
Concepts, 293–295
forming, 294–295
functions of, 293
Concordance rates for schizophrenia, 544
Concrete operations stage, 382
Conditional positive regard, 451
Conditioned emotional response, 504
Conditioned nausea, 210–211
Conditioned reflex, 202
Conditioned response (CR), 203, 204, 210
Conditioned stimulus (CS), 203, 204, 210
Conditioning. *See also* Classical conditioning; Operant conditioning
aversive, 197

backward, 206
concepts in, 203–205
of emotional responses, 572
of the immune system, 491
phobias and, 527
types of, 202
Conduction deafness, 111
Cones, 91, 92, 96
Conflict, stress and, 503
Conformity, 612–613
Confounded causes, 24
Conscious mind, 439
Consciousness, 159
levels of, 160–161
loss of, 65
states of, 159–197
study of, 12
Conscious thoughts, 436
Consensus, attribution and, 595
Consequences, types of, 218
Consequences are contingent on behavior
(CACOB), 217, 218
Conservation, defined, 381
Consistency, attribution and, 595
Consolidation, defined, 263
Contemporary view of gender roles, 422
Continuity, defined, 357
Continuity principle, 129
Continuity versus stages issue, 357
Continuous reinforcement, 220
Continuum of consciousness, 160–161
Contraceptives, teenage use of, 399
Control
of behavior, 4
coping and, 499
Control group, 33
Controlled processes, 160
Conventional level of moral reasoning, 404
Convergence, 92
test for, 131
Convergent thinking, 298
Conversion disorder, 529
Coping, 498–513
with anxiety, 505
stress management and, 513
types of, 499
Cornea, 89
Corpus callosum, 82
Correlation, 27–28
prediction and, 28
versus causation, 28
Correlation coefficient, 27
Cortex, 68, 69–75
short-term memory and, 264
thalamus and, 80
Cortical cells, 94
Corticoids, 485, 491
Counseling, in schools, 15
Counseling psychologists, 558
Counterattitudinal behavior, 602, 603
Covariation principle, 595

Creative thinkers, traits of, 299
Creative thinking, 298–299
Critical period, 144
language, 303
Cross-cultural approach, 5, 10
Cross-gender behaviors, 329
Cross-sectional studies, 359, 413
Crowd, defined, 617
Cultural bias, 283
Cultural-familial retardation, 280
Cultural stress, 502
Culture
alcoholism rates and, 195
emotional expression and, 349
mate preferences and, 427
perception and, 152–153
phobias and, 531
retrieval cues and, 267
taste and, 114
Culture-free tests, 283
Curare, 51

D

Dahmer, Jeffrey, 517
Dark adaptation, 92
Date rape, 622
avoiding, 625
Dating process, 425
Day care, 374–375
Daydreaming, 160
Deafness, 111
language acquisition and, 304
Death, 430–431
DeBakey, Michael, 506–507
Debriefing, 36
Decibels, 104, 108
Decision stage model, 619
Deep structure of language, 302
Defense mechanisms, 440–441
anxiety reduction and, 505, 518
shyness and, 455
Defensive function of attitudes, 599
Deficiency needs, 449
Definitional theory, 294
versus prototype theory, 295
Deindividuation, 617
Deinstitutionalization, 557
Delay of gratification, 461
Delinquency, self-esteem and, 401
Delta waves, 165
Delusional disorders, 523
Dendrites, 44
Denial, 440
anxiety reduction and, 505
Dentistry, use of hypnosis in, 182
Deoxyribonucleic acid (DNA), 360
Dependent variable, 32, 33
Depressants, 196–197
effect on the brain, 66
Depression, 536
causes of, 538

cognitive therapy in treating, 79
disease and, 509
major, 537
overcoming, 550–551
Depressive disorders, 536
Depth perception, 131–133
effect of culture on, 152
in infancy, 143, 365
Descriptive statistics, 628–631
Desensitization training, 574–575
Designer drugs, 192
Development
methods for studying, 358–359
norms for, 367
Developmental approach, 143
Developmental disorders, 523
Developmental periods, consistency versus change
in, 413
Developmental psychologists, 355
Developmental psychology, 16
issues and approaches in, 356–359
Developmental stages, 357
Deviation IQ, 277
Diabetes, 79
Diagnoses, importance of, 521
Diagnostic and Statistical Manual of Mental Disorders
(DSM), 522–523
Diathesis stress theory of schizophrenia, 545
Dichromats, 97
Diet, aging and, 415
Dieting, 336–337
Diffusion of responsibility theory, 617
Disadvantaged children, intervention programs and,
288–289
Discrimination, 591
in conditioning, 205, 223
in employment, 429
gender and, 391
in intelligence testing, 282, 285
Discriminative stimulus, 223
Disease, depression and, 509. *See also* Illness
Disease-prone personality, 509
Disorganized schizophrenia, 543
Displacement, 441
anxiety reduction and, 505
shyness and, 455
Display rules, 349
Dispositional attribution, 594–595, 596
Dispositional traits, 386
Dissociative disorders, 523, 548
Distinctive associations, as memory aids, 247
Distinctiveness, attribution and, 595
Divergent thinking, 298
Dix, Dorothea, 556
DNA, 360
Dolphins, communication among, 308
Dopamine, 57, 185
Dopamine theory of schizophrenia, 545, 546
Double-blind technique, 36
Double standard for sexual behavior, 327
Down syndrome, 360

Freudian slips, 437, 560, 561
Freudian techniques, 561
Freudian theory, 161, 172, 384, 435, 436–446, 560–563
   criticisms and revisions of, 445
   followers of, 444–445
Frontal lobe, 69, 70–72
   schizophrenia and, 545
Frontal lobotomy, 71
Frustration, 502
Frustration-aggression hypothesis, 620
Functional age, 415
Functional fixedness, 297
Functionalism, 12, 13
Fundamental attribution error, 596
Future, planning for, 403

G
Gage, Phineas, 71
Galton, Francis, 276
Ganglion cells, 91, 92, 96
Gate control theory, 118
Gender differences, 391
   in mate preferences, 427
   in moral reasoning, 405
   in perception, 150
   in self-esteem, 401
Gender role development, 388–390
Gender roles, 388, 420–423
   advantages and disadvantages of, 423
   changes in, 421
   mental health and, 422–423
   traditional versus contemporary views of, 422
Gender schemas, 389
Gender stereotypes, 389, 391
General adaptation syndrome, 486–487
General anesthesia, 65
General goals, 18
Generalization, 205
   in operant conditioning, 223
Generalized anxiety disorder, 525
Generativity versus stagnation stage, 418
Genes, 360
Genetic factors
   in body weight, 320–321
   in IQ, 470
   in perception, 142, 143, 144–145, 148
   in personality and intellect, 6, 286–287
   in schizophrenia, 544
   in sexual preference, 329
   in temperament, 370
   in traits, 469–471
Genetic problems, identifying, 360
Genetic risk factors, 195
Genital stage, 443
Genuineness, 581
Germinal period, 360–361
Gerontology, 414
Gestalt approach, 13
Gestalt principles of organization, 128, 129
Gestalt psychology, 128

Giftedness, 281
Glial cells, 42, 43
Goal-directed behavior, 215
Goals
   of information gathering, 23
   of studying, 18
Goal state of problem solving, 296
Gonads, 79
Grammar, 301
   basic rules of, 305
Graphology, 476
Gratification, delay of, 461
Group behaviors, 617
Group cohesion, 616
Group decisions, 618
Group dynamics, 616–618
Group norms, 616
Group polarization, 618
Groups, defined, 616
Group therapy, for drug abuse, 197
Groupthink, 618
Growth hormone, 79, 165, 170
Growth needs, 449

H
Hair receptors, 116
Halfway houses, 557
Hallucinations, 191
Hallucinogens, 191–192
Handwriting analysis, 279, 476
Happiness, 346
Hardiness, 506–507
Harm/loss appraisal, 482
Hassles, effect on health, 500, 501
Headaches, relaxation techniques and, 495
Head Start program, 288–289
Health
   daily hassles and, 500, 501
   major life events and, 500
   personality factors and, 508–510
   stress and, 480–512
Hearing, 102–112
   in newborns, 365
   range of, 105
   role of temporal lobe in, 74
Heart disease
   risk factors for, 508
   smoking and, 189
Heat meditation, 493
Helping behavior, 619
Hemispheres of the brain, 64, 81
   research on, 82–83
   specialization of, 83
Hepburn, Katharine, 416
Heredity. *See* Genetic factors
Heritability, 470
Heroin, 193
   effect on fetal development, 363
Heterosexual relationships, 327
Heuristics, 296
Hidden observer, 181

Hierarchy of needs, 316–317, 449
Hierarchy of traits, 466
High blood pressure, relaxation techniques and, 495
High self-monitors, 611
Hinckley, John, Jr., 520–521
Hindbrain, 64, 66
Hippocampus, 80
   long-term memory and, 264
   results of damage to, 262
Hispanic Journal of Behavioral Science, 11
Hispanics, 11
HIV-positive, defined, 330
Holistic skills, right hemisphere and, 83
Holistic view, 448
Hollywood love, 424
Homelessness, 31
Homeostasis, 63, 314
Homosexual behavior, 328, 329
   AIDS risk and, 331
Hormone replacement therapy, 428
Hormones, 79
   depression and, 538
   prenatal, 329
   sexual motivation and, 325
Hospices, 431
Howard, Ruth, 11
Humanistic approach, 5, 9
Humanistic theories of personality, 435, 448–452, 474–475
Humanistic therapy, 580–581
Human nature, 9
Hunger, 318–319
Hypnosis, 31, 32–34, 178, 179–183, 555
   applications of, 182–183
   behaviors under, 180
   explanations of, 181
   misinformation and, 269
Hypnotic analgesia, 180
Hypochondriacal symptoms, 486
Hypothalamus, 79, 80
   effect on sexual behavior, 329
   fight-or-flight response and, 484, 485
   role in hunger, 319
   role in menstruation, 398
   sexual motivation and, 325
Hypothesis, defined, 32

I
Iconic memory, 239, 242
Id, 438, 439
Ideal self, 450
Identical twins, 286, 360
Identification, 293
Identity, defined, 400
Identity versus role confusion stage, 400
Illness
   hassles and, 501
   major life events and, 500
   personality factors and, 508–510
   stress and, 488
Illusions, 135–136

Image management, 590
Image perception, effect of culture on, 152
Imagery, 247
Imagined perception, 180
Imitation, 7
    role in learning, 226
Immigration, IQ tests and, 285
Immune system, 490–491
Implicit personality theories, 594
Impossible figures, 136
Impression management, 606–607
Imprinting, 229
Impulsive behavior, control of, 624
Inadequate retrieval cues, 258, 261
Incentives, 315
Independent variable, 32, 33
Individual psychology, 444
Indo-Chinese students, studies of, 453
Industrial/organizational psychologists, 15
Industry versus inferiority stage, 385
Infancy, 355
    abuse during, 393
    attachment in, 372–373
    emotional development in, 368–370
    motor development in, 367
    risks during, 366
Infatuated love, 424
Inferential statistics, 632–634
Information
    coding of, 227
    encoding, storing, and retrieving, 237
Informational influence theory, 617
Information gathering, 23, 26
Information-processing approach, 275
Information theory of classical conditioning, 206
Ingroup-outgroup attitude, 618
Inhibitory neurotransmitter, 51
Initial state of problem solving, 296
Initiative versus guilt stage, 385
Innate factors, in language acquisition, 303
Inner ear, 107
Insanity, legal definition of, 517
Insecure attachment, 372, 375
Insight, 297
Insight learning, 228
Insight therapy, 560–563
Insomnia, 174
    caffeine and, 188
Instincts, 314
Instrumental conditioning. *See* Operant
    conditioning
Insulin, 79
Integrity versus despair stage, 418
Intellectual development, day care and, 375
Intelligence, 273–289
    approaches to defining, 274–275
    artificial, 17
    aspects of, 273
    biological, 276
    brain size and, 67
    measuring, 276–283

nature-nurture question and, 286–287
    racial differences in, 285
Intelligence quotient (IQ), 274
    computing of, 277
    creativity and, 299
    environment and, 287
    heritability of, 470
Intelligence quotient (IQ) scores, 28
    distribution of, 280–281
Intelligence tests, 277–283
    immigration and, 285
    problems with, 282–283
Interference
    defined, 241
    memory and, 258
Interference theory, 260
Internal locus of control, 460, 507
Interpersonal therapy, as a treatment for depression,
    539
Interposition, 132
Interpretation skills, effect of aging on, 417
Intervention programs, 288–289
Interviews, 30
Intimacy, defined, 424
Intimacy versus isolation stage, 418
Intrinsic motivation, 298, 315, 334
Introspection, 12, 13
Invisible light waves, 88, 89
In vivo desensitization, 575
In vivo exposure, 532–533
In vivo flooding, 575
Involuntary response, 216
Ions, 49
IQ. *See* Intelligence quotients
Iris, 89

J

Jackson, Michael, 610
James-Lange theory, 342
Jet lag, 163
Job discrimination, 429
Job satisfaction, 429
Johnson, Earvin "Magic," 330, 331
Jordan, Michael, 62
Journal of Black Psychology, 11
Journal of Humanistic Psychology, 9
Justice orientation, 405
Just noticeable difference, 125

K

Kevorkian, Jack, 430, 431
Kinsey report, 26
Korsakoff's syndrome, 263

L

Laboratory experiments, 30
Laboratory settings, 31
    effects of, 34
Lamaze method, 363
Language, 292, 301–309
    acquiring, 303–305

among animals, 308–309
    Chomsky's theory of, 302
    criteria for, 308
    personality development and, 459
    rules of, 301–302
    thought and, 306
Language acquisition stages, 304–305
Language skills, 83
Latency stage, 443
Latent content of dreams, 437
Lateral hypothalamus, hunger and, 319
Law of association, 209
Law of disuse, 258
Law of effect, 202, 215
L-dopa, 56
Lead poisoning, 366
Learned cues, for hunger, 318
Learned factors
    body weight and, 322–323
    in language acquisition, 303
Learned food aversion, 208
Learned taste aversion, 229
Learning, 201–233. *See also* Observational learning
    approaches to, 202
    biological factors in, 229
    cognitive, 225–228
    defined, 201
    effect on perception, 142, 149–150
    prepared, 229
Learning-performance distinction, 226
Learning principles, comparing, 231
Left hemisphere, 64, 72
    stroke in, 74
Lens, 89
Lesbianism, 328
Librium, 525
Lie detector test, 347, 350–351
Life expectancy, 415
Light, primary colors of, 95
Light adaptation, 92
Light and shadow depth cue, 133
Light waves, 88
    pathway through the eye, 89
Limbic system, 80
Linear perspective, 132
Linguistic relativity, 306
Lithium treatment, 540
Lobes of the brain, 69
Lobotomy, 71
Local anesthetic, 50
Localization of function, 81
Locus of control, 460
    stress and, 507
Logical thinking, 275
Longevity. *See also* Aging
    exercise and, 415
Longitudinal studies, 359, 413
Long-term memory, 238, 242–244, 257
    hippocampus and, 264
    kinds of information stored in, 244
Loudness, 108

Peripheral nervous system, 60, 61–63
Peripheral route for persuasion, 600, 605
Peripheral theories of emotion, 342–343
Permissive parents, 407
Personal distress, prosocial behavior and, 619
Personality, 435–455
    brain damage and, 71
    changes in, 468
    humanistic theories of, 435, 448–452, 474–475
    implicit theories of, 594
    psychology of, 16
    review of theories of, 474–475
    social learning theory of, 458, 459–462
    stress and, 506–509
    trait theory of, 463–472
Personality assessment, 446
Personality development
    in adolescence, 400–401
    in adulthood, 420–423
    language and, 459
    psychosexual stages of, 422–443
Personality disorders, 523, 541–549
Personality tests, 476–477
Personality traits. *See also* Traits; Trait theory of
    personality
    heritability of, 470
    lifetime changes in, 413
    Type A behavior and, 509
Personal values, achievement and, 453
Person-centered therapy, 580–581
    review of, 583
Person perception, 590–591
Person schemas, 592
Person-situation debate, 468
Person-situation interaction, 467
Persuasion, 600–601
Pessimism, depression and, 551
PET scan, 77, 545
Peyote cactus, 192
Phallic stage, 443
Phencyclidine (PCP), 192
Phenomenological perspective, 448
Phenothiazines, 546
Pheromones, 325
Phi phenomenon, 13, 139
Phobias, 520, 527
    cultural influences on, 531
    treating, 532–533, 574–575
Phonemes, 301
Phonology, 301
Photographic memory, 248
Photoreceptors, 91
Physical appearance, self-esteem and, 401
Physical changes, in adulthood, 414–415
Physical factors, effect on body weight, 323
Physiological needs, 317, 449
Physiological/neurological responses, 30
Physiological processes, altering through meditation, 493
Physiological psychologists, 17

Physiological responses
    interpreting, 351
    recording, 350
Piaget's theory of cognitive development, 379–383, 402
Pineal gland, 163
Pitch, 105, 110
Pituitary gland, 79
    fight-or-flight response and, 485
    role in sexual maturity, 398, 399
Placenta, 362
Place theory, 110
Plateau phase, 326
Play, gender differences in, 391
Pleasure principle, 438, 439
Polarized thinking, 79, 585
Police investigations, use of hypnosis in, 182
Polygraph, 350
Pons, 66, 169
Positive correlation coefficient, 27
Positive ions, 49
Positive regard, 451, 581
Positive reinforcement, 218, 232
Positive self-concept, 450
Positive self-statements, 513
Positive thinking, 7
Positron emission tomography (PET), 77, 545
Postconventional level of moral reasoning, 404
Posterior pituitary, 79
Posthypnotic amnesia, 180
Posthypnotic suggestion, 180
Poverty, intervention programs and, 288–289
Power rapists, 622
Practical thinking skills, 275
Precognition, 154
Preconventional level of moral reasoning, 404
Prediction
    correlation and, 28
    as a goal of psychology, 4
Preferred eye, 98
Prejudice, 591. *See also* Bias
Prenatal development, 360–363
Prenatal hormones, 329
Prenatal period, 360–363
Preoperational stage, 381
Prepared learning, 229
Primacy effect, 243
Primacy question, 345
Primary appraisal, 482–483
Primary auditory cortex, 74, 108
Primary olfactory cortex, 115
Primary reinforcers, 219
Primary values, 453
Primary visual cortex, 75, 94
Principles of Psychology (James), 12
Prisms, 88
Privacy, for experimental subjects, 36
Private self, 611
Proactive interference, 260
Problem-focused coping, 499, 502, 505
Problem solving, 296–297

Problem-solving behavior, 228
Problem-solving skills, 273, 275
Procedural information, 244, 246
Procrastination, 19
Progeria, 414
Progressive relaxation, 174, 494–495
Prohibition, 196–197
Projection, 441
    anxiety reduction and, 505
    shyness and, 455
Projective tests, 446, 476
Prosocial behavior, 619
Prosopagnosia, 147
Prototype, defined, 295
Prototype theory, 295
Proximity principle, 129
Proximodistal principle, 367
Prozac, 539
Psilocybin, 191
Psi phenomena, 155
Psychiatrists, 15, 558
    disagreement among, 521
Psychic powers, 154–155
Psychoactive drugs, 185–193, 518
    mental disorders associated with, 523
Psychoanalysis, 555
    present-day, 564–565
    problems during, 563
    review of, 583
    techniques of, 561
    theory of, 560–563
    traditional, 560–563
    typical session in, 562
Psychoanalysts, 558
Psychoanalytic approach, 5, 8, 9, 13, 518
Psychobiological approach, 5, 6, 12
Psychobiologists, 17
Psychodynamic approach, 565
    to shyness, 455
Psychodynamic theory of personality, 435, 436–446, 474–475
Psychogenic amnesia, 548
Psychogenic fugue, 548
Psychokinesis, 155
Psychological dependency, 184, 190
Psychological disorders. *See* Mental disorders
Psychological experiments, ethics and, 615
Psychological factors
    sexual motivation and, 325
    in sexual satisfaction, 327
Psychological needs, 314
Psychological problems, suicide and, 409
Psychological tests, 17, 30
    for assessing abnormal behavior, 520
    characteristics of, 279
    reliability and validity of, 446, 476
Psychologists, 15
Psychology
    analytical, 444
    careers in, 15
    defined, 4

Psychology (*continued*)
    early approaches to, 12–13
    goals of, 4
    minorities in, 11
    modern approaches to, 5–10
    research in, 16–17, 23–37
    rise and fall of approaches to, 13
    subareas of, 16–17
    women in, 11
"Psychology as a Behaviorist Views It," 13
Psychology of Women Quarterly, 11
Psychometric approach, 274
Psychometrics, 17, 273
Psychoneuroimmunology, 490–491
Psychopaths, 541
Psychoses, 522, 523
Psychosexual disorders, 523
Psychosexual stages, 384, 422–443, 475
Psychosocial factors, 490
Psychosocial problems, 418
Psychosocial stages, 384, 385, 400, 418, 444
Psychosomatic illness, 507
Psychosomatic symptoms, 486–489
Psychotherapists
    characteristics of, 581
    choosing, 569
    kinds of, 558
    skills needed by, 569
Psychotherapy, 555–585. *See also* Psychoanalysis
    approaches to, 558–559
    behavior therapy, 573–576
    cognitive therapy, 577–579, 584–585
    dynamic, 565
    effectiveness of, 559, 569
    historical background of, 556–557
    humanistic therapy, 580–581
    nonspecific factors in, 569, 583
    review of, 583
    seeking, 568–569
    as a treatment for depression, 539
Puberty, 398–399
Public self, 611
Punishment, 218
    effective, 233
    versus negative reinforcement, 219
Pupil, 89
Purkinje cells, 66
Purposeful behavior, 459
Pygmy chimps, language mastery in, 309

Q
Questionnaires, 30
Quinlan, Karen Ann, 63, 161

R
Racial myths, about brain size, 67
Racism, in intelligence testing, 282, 285
Randi, James, 154
Random selection, 33
Range, defined, 630
Rape, 622

Rapid eye movement sleep. *See* REM sleep
Rate of impulses, 108, 110
Ratio IQ, 277
Rational-emotive therapy (RET), 578
Rationalization, 440
    anxiety reduction and, 505
"Raw" sensations, 126
Reaction formation, 441
    anxiety reduction and, 505
Reaction range, 287
Reaction time, effect of aging on, 416
Readiness potential, 41, 55
Reality, changing nature of, 139. *See also* Perception
Reality principle, 438, 439
Real-life problems, 418
Real-life stages, 419
Real motion, 138
Real self, 450
Recall, 253
    tests of, 257
Recency effect, 243
Receptors, 45, 51–52
    auditory, 111
    effect of drugs on, 185, 188
    olfactory, 115
    for pain, 118
    for touch, 116
Recognition, 253
    tests of, 257
Red-green color deficit, 99
Reflection of feelings, 581
Reflexes, 46
Refractory period, 326
Reinforcement, 218
    schedules of, 220–221
Reinforcers, 216, 217, 218–219
Relative size, depth perception and, 132
Relaxation
    in biofeedback, 233
    in treating phobias, 574
    stress management and, 513
    systematic desensitization and, 211
    techniques of, 494–495
Relaxation response, 495
Reliability, of psychological tests, 279, 446, 476
REM rebound, 167
REM sleep, 165–167
    characteristics of, 167
    over the life cycle, 169
    neurotransmitters and, 169
Repair theory, 170
Repressed memory, 258
Repression, 440
    anxiety reduction and, 505
Research
    animals in, 37
    in psychology, 16–17, 23–37
    techniques in, 30
Resiliency, defined, 386
Resistance, in psychoanalysis, 563
Resistance stage, 487

Resolution phase, 326
Resting state of an axon, 49
Restricted-experience studies, 144–148
RET (rational-emotive therapy), 578
Retardation, levels of, 280
Reticular formation, 65, 169
Retina, 89
    function of, 91–92
Retinal disparity, 131
Retrieval cues, 258, 261
Retrieval of information, 237, 242
Retroactive interference, 260
Retrograde amnesia, 262, 263
Reuptake, 185
Rewards, 216
Rhodopsin, 91, 92
Right hemisphere, 64, 65, 72, 83
Right-to-die issue, 430–431
Risk-taking behavior, in adolescence, 403
Risky shift, 618
Rods, 91, 92
Role schemas, 592
Romantic love, 424
Rorschach inkblot test, 446, 476
Rotating figures, 150
Russians, American attitudes toward, 605

S
Sadistic rapists, 622
Safety needs, 317, 449
Salamander experiment, 145
Sample population, 33
Sanchez, George, 11
Savants, 249
Schedules of reinforcement, 220–221
Schemas, 591, 592–593
Schema theory, 256
Schizoid personality, 541
Schizophrenia, 28, 30, 521, 542–547
    causes of, 544–545
    symptoms and subcategories of, 543
    treatment of, 546–547
Schizophrenic disorders, 523
School psychologists, 15
Scientific method, 23
    steps in, 32–35
Scripts, 256, 592, 621
Secondary appraisal, 483
Secondary reinforcers, 219
Secondary sexual characteristics, 398, 399
Secure attachment, 372, 375
Sedatives, 185
Segregated play groups, 391
Seizures, 82
Selective attention, 79, 585
Self
    defined, 400
    public versus private, 611
Self-actualization, 317, 448, 449, 451, 475
Self-analysis, personality and, 459

Self-concept, 450
    weight and, 149
Self-consistency, impression management and, 607
Self-determination, 315
Self-efficacy, 460–461
Self-esteem
    in adolescence, 401
    impression management and, 607
    protecting, 611
Self-fulfilling prophecy, 24, 25, 36
Self-handicapping, 333, 611
Self-hypnosis, 160
Self-image, self-handicapping strategy and, 333
Self-monitoring, 584, 611
Self-observation, stress management and, 512
Self-perception theory, 603
Self-presentation, 606–607
Self-reinforcement, 19
Self-report inventories, 477
Self schema, 593
Self-serving bias, 596
Self-statements
    impulsive behavior and, 624
    stress management and, 513
Self theory, 450–451
Semantic information, 244, 246
Semantics, 301
Semipermeable membrane, 48
Sensations, 127
    versus perception, 126–127
Sense organs, 127
    adaptation in, 87
Senses, 87–155
    hearing, 102–112
    in newborns, 364–365
    smell, 115
    taste, 113–114
    touch, 116–119
    vision, 87–99
Sensorimotor stage, 380
Sensory experiences, 87
    restriction of, 144–148
Sensory homunculus, 73
Sensory memory, 238, 242
    functions of, 239
Sensory neurons, 46
Sentence structure, 302
Separation anxiety, 372
Serial killers, 517
Serotonin, 169
Set point, defined, 320
Settings, for studying behavior, 31
Sex
    as a biological drive, 438
    job discrimination based on, 429
    love without, 424
Sex hormones, 325
Sex information, 399
Sexist schemas, 593
Sexual activity, coffee drinking and, 27, 28

Sexual aggression, 622
    avoiding, 625
Sexual behavior, 325–331
    in adolescence, 399
    decisions about, 327
    effect of aging on, 428
    social-cultural influence on, 326–327
Sexual development, 79
Sexual harassment, 429
Sexually transmitted diseases, 399
Sexual maturity, 398–399
Sexual motivation, hormones and, 325
Sexual preference, 329
Sexual response, stages of, 326
Sexual revolution, 326
Shape constancy, 134
Shaping procedure, 217, 222, 232
Short-term dynamic therapy, 565
Short-term memory, 238, 242
    cortex and, 264
    features of, 240
    interference and, 241
Short-term therapies, 559
Shyness, 454–455
Similarity principle, 129
Simple phobias, 527
Simplicity principle, 129
Single-word stage, 304
Situational attribution, 594–595, 596
Situational stressors, 502
Size constancy, 134
    effect of culture on, 152
Skewed distribution, 629
Skin, structure of, 116
Skinner box, 216–217, 221
Sleep
    causes of, 169–170
    levels of, 161
    measuring, 164
    problems with, 174–175
    reasons for, 170
    rhythms of, 162–163
    role of pons in, 66
    stages of, 165–167
Sleep apnea, 174
Sleep deprivation, 170
Sleep spindles, 165
Sleep-wake cycle, 65
Sleepwalking, 166, 175
Smell, 115
    effect on taste, 113
    in newborns, 365
Smoking. See Cigarette smoking
Social-adjustive function of attitudes, 599
Social behavior, 610–625
Social cognition, 589–625
Social-cognitive theory, 384, 458, 459, 474–475
Social comparison theory, 616
Social competence, 273

Social-cultural factors
    body weight and, 322
    influence on sexual behavior, 326–327
Social development, 378, 384–385
    in adolescence, 400–401
    in adulthood, 424–429
    careers and, 429
    day care and, 375
Social drinking, 362
Social facilitation, 617
Social factors, stress and, 510
Social forces, 610
Social influences, 612–615
Social inhibition, 617
Social interactions, schemas and, 593
Social learning approach, 7
    to language acquisition, 303
Social-learning factors, in sexual preference, 329
Social learning theory, 458, 459–462, 474–475
    aggression and, 621
    evaluation of, 462
    gender-role acquisition and, 388
Socially oriented groups, 616
Social needs, 316–317
Social norms approach, 519
Social phobias, 527, 531
    treating, 533
Social psychology, 16, 588–625
Social Readjustment Rating Scale, 500
Social signals, emotions as, 347
Social smiling, 372
Social support, 510
    stress management and, 513
Social urges, 444
Sociocognitive theory, 181
Sodium ion, 49
Sodium pump, 49
Somatic nervous system, 61
Somatization disorder, 529
Somatoform disorders, 523, 529
Somatosensory cortex, 73, 116
Somnambulism, 175
Sounds, direction of, 109
Sound waves, 103, 106
    frequency of, 110
Source traits, 464
Spatial-perceptual skills
    gender differences in, 150
    right hemisphere and, 83
Special process theory, 181
Speech, 82
    problems with, 74
Spinal cord, 61
    treatment of damage to, 54
Split-brain research, 82–83
Splitters, 274–275
Spontaneous recovery, 205, 223
Standard deviation, 630–631
Standardized tests, 30
Stanford-Binet IQ test, 278
Stanford Hypnotic Susceptibility Scale, 179

PHOTO CREDITS

Front Matter

iii: Photo by Craig McClain, construction by Floyd Fronius, after a concept by Vladimir Chaika; **vii:** Robert Estall Photographs © Angela Fisher & Carol Beckwith; **viii:** © Murrae Haynes/Picture Group; **xi:** Sam Abell © 1991 National Geographic Society; **xii:** (left to right, top to bottom) © Runk/Schoenberger from Grant Heilman; Craig McClain; From *The Mentality of Apes,* by Wolfgang Koehler, Routledge & Kegan Paul. Reproduced by permission of International Thomason Publishing Services, Ltd.; Craig McClain; Thomas McAvoy, Life Magazine © Time Warner, Inc.; **xiii:** © Benn Mitchell/The Image Bank; **xxv:** (top) NASA; (bottom) © Michel Tcherevkoff/The Image Bank; **xxvi:** (top) © Zig Leszcynski/Animals Animals; (center) Robert Estall Photographs © Angela Fisher & Carol Beckwith; **xxvii:** (top) © 1988 Louie Psihoyos/Matrix; (bottom) © Jim Tuten/Black Star; **xxviii:** (top) © 1990 Stanislaw Fernandes; (bottom) © Laurie Rubin/Tony Stone Worldwide; **xxix:** (top) © 1985 Rob Lewine; (bottom) Oliviero Toscani for Benetton; **xxx:** (top) © Mark Seliger; (bottom) Photo by 3045-Gamma-Liaison; **xxxi:** (top) Tony Stone Worldwide; (center) © Will Cormier; **xxxii:** (top) "Giving Good Voice" by Janet Wooley. Reproduced by Special Permission of PLAYBOY Magazine. Copyright © 1991 by PLAYBOY; (bottom) © Jeffrey Rotman.

Chapter One

2: NASA; **3 and 4:** Kirk McKoy/Los Angeles Times photo; **6:** (top right) © Biophoto Associates/Science Source/Photo Researchers, Inc.; (bottom left) © 1992 Louis Psihoyos/Matrix; **7:** (bottom) Vince Compagnore/Los Angeles Times photo; (right) Courtesy, B. F. Skinner; **8:** National Library of Medicine; **9:** William Carter; **10:** Craig McClain; **11:** (center) Courtesy, Margaret Clapp Library Archives, Wellesley College, photo by Patridge; (top right) Courtesy, Dr. Robert Guthrie Collection; (bottom right) The Institute of Texan Cultures, San Antonio; **12–13:** (left to right) Courtesy, Archives of the History of American Psychology, University of Akron, Akron, Ohio 44304; National Library of Medicine, Bethesda, MD; Brooks/Cole Collection; Archives of the History of American Psychology, University of Akron; FPG International; **14:** (top to bottom, left to right) Kirk McKoy/Los Angeles Times photo; © 1992 Louis Psihoyos/Matrix; Vince Compagnore/Los Angeles Times photo; Craig McClain; **16–17:** (left to right) © Dan McCoy/Rainbow; © Yada Classen/Jeroboam, Inc.; © Sepp Seitz 1978/Woodfin Camp & Associates; © Doug Menuez/Reportage; Bettmann Archive; © Joel Gordon 1988; **18:** © Mimi Forsyth/Monkmeyer Press Photo Service; **19:** © Henley and Savage/Tony Stone Worldwide/Chicago, Ltd.; **20:** © Biophoto Associates/Science Source/Photo Researchers, Inc.; **21:** © Joel Gordon 1988; **22:** UPI/Bettmann; **23:** Craig McClain; **24:** © Joe McDonald/Animals Animals; **25:** Craig McClain; **26:** (top) © Joel Gordon 1990; (bottom) Craig McClain; **27:** © Ron Chapple 1987/FPG International; **28:** Courtesy, Dr. Richard Parker, Deaconess Hospital; **29:** (top to bottom, left to right) Craig McClain; © Joe McDonald/Animals Animals; Craig McClain; © Joel Gordon 1990; © Ron Chapple 1987/FGP International; **31:** © Ray Stubblebine (taken for the *Los Angeles Times*); **32:** Craig McClain; **33:** © Stacy Pick 1988/Stock, Boston; **34:** (bottom left) © Richard Laird 1988/FPG International; (bottom right) © Will & Deni McIntyre/Photo Researchers, Inc.; **35:** © Ray Stubbebine (taken for the *Los Angeles Times*); **36:** Craig McClain; **37:** Courtesy of the Foundation for Biomedical Research; **38:** (left) © Joe McDonald/Animals Animals; (right) Craig McClain.

Chapter Two

40: © Michel Tcherevkoff/The Image Bank; **42, 47:** © John D. Cunningham/Visuals Unlimited; **50:** © Schmid-Langsfeld/The Image Bank; **51:** © Borys Malkin/Anthro-Photo; **52:** © Ira Wyman/Sygma; **54:** Larry Salzman/AP/Wide World Photos; **55:** Dave B. Fleetham ©/Visuals Unlimited; **58:** © John Cunningham/Visuals Unlimited; **59:** (top) © Borys Malkin/Anthro-Photo; (bottom) Dave B. Fleetham ©/Visuals Unlimited; **60:** Craig McClain; **61:** © Dana Fineman/Sygma; **62:** © Focus on Sports; **63:** (center left) AP/Wide World Photos; (bottom) Craig McClain; **65:** (top) © Will & Deni McIntyre/Photo Researchers, Inc.; (bottom) © Russell Cheyne/Allsport USA; **66:** © John Dominis/Index Stock Photography, Inc.; **68:** Photo by Ed Kashi. Reprinted by permission from *Psychology Today* Magazine. Copyright © 1984 (Sussex Publishers, Inc.); **69:** (top) © Robert D. Terry, M.D., Neurosciences Education and Research Foundation, University of California, San Diego; (bottom) Craig McClain; **70:** © Richard Laird/FPG International; **71:** Courtesy Warren Museum, Harvard Medical School; **72–73:** Sculpture by Jonathan Parker, photos by Craig McClain; **74:** © Ed Lettau 1991/FPG International; **75:** Craig McClain; **76:** (center right) Courtesy, Boston University Radiology Department; (right) Craig McClain; **77:** (left) © Dan McCoy/Rainbow; (bottom) Courtesy, Phelps and Mazziotta, UCLA, Laboratory of Nuclear Medicine; **78:** (top right) © Focus on Sports; **79:** (center left) © Paul Berger/Tony Stone Worldwide; **84:** © Dana Fineman/Sygma;

Chapter Three

86: (clockwise from top left) © Larry Lefever from Grant Heilman; © Zig Leszcynski/Animals Animals; © Elyse Lewin/The Image Bank; © Michael Dick/Animals Animals; **88–90:** Craig McClain; **91:** John Odam; **92 and 93:** © Arthur Tress/Photo Researchers, Inc.; **95:** Craig McClain;

97: Micky Lawler; 99: (bottom) *Ishihara Tests for Colour Blindness*, courtesy of Graham-Field, Inc., Hauppauge, NY. Reproduced with permission; 100: Craig McClain; 101: (left) Craig McClain; (right) Mickey Lawler; 102: © Erich Hartmann/Magnum Photos; 103: (right) © 1989 Tony Freeman/Photo Edit; (left) © Thomas Hoepker/Magnum Photos; 104: (top, shuttle) Courtesy, NASA; (bottom, forest) Grant Heilman/Grant Heilman Photography; 105: © Bob Self/Florida Times-Union/Silver Image; 109: (left) © Richard Hutchings/Photo Researchers, Inc.; (right) © Mark Richards/PhotoEdit; 110: (left) © M. P. Kahl/DRK Photo; (right) © A. Glauberman/Photo Researchers, Inc.; 112: © David W. Hamilton/The Image Bank; 114: (left) © Malcolm S. Kirk; (center) Guy Mary-Rousseliere © National Geographic Society; (right) © Danielle Pellegrini/Photo Researchers, Inc.; 115: Photograph © 1989 by Jonathan Levine, All rights reserved; 116 and 117: © Stephen Green-Armytage 1986/Stock Market; 119: (top) © Lawrence Fried/Magnum Photos; (bottom) © 1987 P. R. Miller/Focus on Sports; 120: © Erich Hartmann/Magnum Photos; 121: Guy Mary-Rousseliere © National Geographic Society.

Chapter Four

122: Robert Estall Photographs © Angela Fisher & Carol Beckwith; 123 and 124: © Howard Sochurek/Stock Market; 125: Al Francekevich/The Stock Market; 126: Custom Medical Stock; 127: (top left and bottom right) Micky Lawler; (bottom left) Deborah Ivanoff; 128: (bottom left) Georges Seurat, "A Sunday on La Grande Jatte–1884," oil on canvas, 1884–86, 207.6 × 308 cm. Helen Birch Barlett Memorial Collection, 1926.224, detail: #23. Photograph © 1992, The Art Institute of Chicago. All rights reserved; (bottom right) Georges Seurat, "A Sunday on La Grande Jatte–1884," oil on canvas, 1884–86, 207.6 × 308 cm. Helen Birch Barlett Memorial Collection, 1926.224. Photograph © 1992, The Art Institute of Chicago. All rights reserved; 130: (center left) Micky Lawler; (bottom) Georges Seurat, "A Sunday on La Grande Jatte–1884," oil on canvas, 1884–86, 207.6 × 308 cm. Helen Birch Barlett Memorial Collection, 1926.224, detail #23. Photograph © 1992, The Art Institute of Chicago. All rights reserved; 131: (left) Random House photo by Charlotte Green; (right) Photo courtesy Nikon Inc., photography © Jerry Friedman; (bottom) Craig McClain; 132: (left) © Ellen Schuster/The Image Bank; (right) © Pete Turner/The Image Bank; (bottom) © Bob Daemmrich/Stock, Boston; 133: (top to bottom) © Rohan/Tony Stone Worldwide; © Michael S. Yamashita/Woodfin Camp & Associates; © Richard Pasley/Stock, Boston; Jackie Estrada; 135: (top left) Courtesy, Field Museum of Natural History, photographer: Diane Alexander-White, Ron Testa,

Neg. #GN-85079; (right) Craig McClain; (bottom) Courtesy, Professor Peter Thompson, York, England; 136: © E. Nagele/FPG International; 137: (top to bottom) Photo Courtesy Nikon Inc., photography © Jerry Friedman; Random House photo by Charlotte Green; © Pete Turner/The Image Bank; © Rohan/Tony Stone Worldwide; 138: Courtesy VPL, photo by Sydney Stein; 139: (top) © Tony Freeman/PhotoEdit; (bottom, masks) © Walter Wick, Mask by Willa Shallit; 140: © Al Francekevich/The Stock Market; 142: Jackie Estrada; 143: (left) © Enrico Ferorelli; (right) Craig McClain; 144: © Jane Burton/Bruce Coleman, Inc.; 146: (left) Courtesy, Cleveland State University, photo by Chuck Humel; (right) © David Lissy 1986/Focus on Sports; 147 and 148: Craig McClain; 149: © Mark Hanauer; 151: © 1991 Jim Amentler; 152: (top left) © Ken Novak/Tony Stone Worldwide/Chicago, Ltd.; (bottom left) © Norvia Behling/Animals Animals; (right) © Cannon-Bonventre, K./AnthroPhoto; 153: © Mark Hanauer; 154: © Dana Fineman/Sygma; 156: (left) © Jane Burton/Bruce Coleman, Inc.; (right) © David Lissy 1986/Focus on Sports; 157: © Ken Novak/Tony Stone Worldwide/Chicago, Ltd.

Chapter Five

158: © 1988 Louie Psihoyos/Matrix; 159: © Murrae Haynes/Picture Group; 160–161: (left to right) © Diana Digiacomo/Focus on Sports; © 1990 Tony Freeman/PhotoEdit; Craig McClain; George F. Mobley, NGP in "Incredible Machine 1986," National Geographic, p. 344; John Odam; © Cesar Paredes/Stock Market; Neil Leifer/Sports Illustrated, © Time Warner; 162: © Tom Ives; 163: AP/Wide World Photos; 164: (top) Art Resource, NY; (bottom left) San Diego Tribune/Tom Kurtz; (bottom right) © Jeffrey Sylvester/FPG International; 167: (top right) Illustration by Cary Henrie. Reprinted with Permission from *Psychology Today* Magazine. Copyright © 1987 (Sussex Publishers, Inc.); 168: © Diania Digiacomo/Focus on Sports; 170: © Fran Heyl Associates; 171: Craig McClain; 173: (top) © James D. Wilson/Woodfin Camp & Associates; (bottom) Craig McClain; 174: © Paul Buddle; 175: (top left) © Dan McCoy/Rainbow; (right) © 1988 Louis Psihoyos/Matrix; 176: John Odam; 177–179: Craig McClain; 180: (left) Craig McClain; (top right) © Michael Salas/The Image Bank; (bottom right) © Myrleen Ferguson/PhotoEdit; 182: Courtesy, Rainbow Babies and Children's Hospital, University Hospitals of Cleveland, Dr. Howard Hall. Photo © Joe Glick; 183: (top left and right) Craig McClain; (bottom left) © Myrleen Ferguson/PhotoEdit; 186: (left) © D. & I. MacDonald/Third Coast Stock Source; (right) Courtesy, National Library of Medicine, Bethesda, MD; (coca leaves) The Granger Collection, New York; 187: (top and

center) Craig McClain; (bottom) © Drug Enforcement Administration; 188-189: Craig McClain; 190: (top) © Bill Pierce/Rainbow; (bottom) Craig McClain; 191: (top) AP/Wide World Photos; (bottom) © Joy Spurr/Bruce Coleman, Inc.; 192: Craig McClain; 193: (top right) © Alan Oddie/PhotoEdit; (left) Craig McClain; 195: © Richard Kalvar/Magnum Photos; 196: Craig McClain; (center, handwriting samples) Courtesy, Joseph E. Seagram & Sons, Inc.; 197: Illustration by Marc Yankus. Reprinted with permission from *Psychology Today* Magazine. Copyright © 1988 (Sussex Publishers, Inc.); 199: Craig McClain.

Chapter Six

200: © Jim Tuten/Black Star; 201 and 202: Craig McClain; 208: (top to bottom, left to right) © Janice Fullman/The Picture Cube; © Barry L. Runk/From Grant Heilman; Courtesty, Professor Stuart Ellins, California State University, San Bernardino; Runk/Schoenberger/From Grant Heilman; 209: (left to right) Courtesy, Johnson & Johnson; © Michael Stuckey/Comstock; Courtesy, Wurlitzer; 210: © Benn Mitchell/The Image Bank; 213: (top) © Janice Fullman/The Picture Cube; (bottom) © Michael Stuckey/Comstock; 214: © George Frey; 215: (left) Brooks/Cole Collection; (right) Courtesy, B. F. Skinner; 216: (top) © George Frey; (bottom) © Sepp Seitz/Woodfin Camp & Associates; 221: (clockwise from top left) © Andy Sacks/Tony Stone Worldwide; © Michael P. Gadomski/Photo Researchers, Inc.; © Norman Mosallem/Tony Stone Worldwide; © Vince Cavataio/Allsport Photographic Ltd./USA; 222: © Peter Southwick/Stock, Boston; 223: (top right) © Stephen J. Krasemann/DRK Photo; (bottom right) © George Frey; 224: (top left) © Peter Southwick/Stock, Boston; (bottom) © Stephen J. Krasemann/DRK Photo; 225: (left) Courtesy B. F. Skinner; (center) Brooks/Cole Collection; (left) Courtesy, Albert Bandura; 226: Craig McClain; 227: (top) © Runk/Schoenberger from Grant Heilman; (bottom left and right) Craig McClain; 228: (left) Craig McClain; (right) From *The Mentality of Apes*, by Wolfgang Koehler, Routledge & Kegan Paul. Reproduced by permission of International Thomason Publishing Services, Ltd.; 229: Thomas McAvoy, *Life* Magazine © Time Warner, Inc.; 230: (top to bottom, left to right) © Runk/Schoenberger from Grant Heilman; Craig McClain; From *The Mentality of Apes*, by Wolfgang Koehler, Routledge & Kegan Paul. Reproduced by permission of International Thomason Publishing Services, Ltd.; Thomas McAvoy, *Life* Magazine © Time Warner, Inc.; 231: © Hiroji Kubota/Magnum Photos; 232: © Richard Hutchings/Photo Researchers, Inc.; 233: © Dan McCoy/Rainbow; 235: © Runk/Schoenberger from Grant Heilman.

Chapter Seven

236: © 1990 Stanislaw Fernandes; **237:** Chris Assaf/ © The Washington Post; **238:** Craig McClain; **239:** © 1991 Peter Menzel; **241:** Chris Assaf/© The Washington Post; **243:** © Stephen J. Krasemann/ DRK Photo; **246:** (top left) © 1989 Tony Freeman/ PhotoEdit; (top right) Vince Compagnore/Los Angeles Times Photo; (bottom) © Henley and Savage/Tony Stone Worldwide; **248:** (top) AP/ Wide World Photos; (bottom) Courtesy Prof. Ralph Norman Haber; **249:** Ken Hively/Los Angeles Times Photo; **250:** © Stephen J. Krasemann/DRK Photo; **251:** Ken Hively/Los Angeles Times Photo; **253:** © Alan Berliner/Gamma-Liaison; **258–260:** Craig McClain; **261:** Laurent Rebours/AP/Wide World Photos; **263:** (top) © Brett H. Froomer/The Image Bank; (center left) Craig McClain; (bottom) © Ira Wyman/Sygma; **265:** © Gary McDonald/ McDonald Associates; **267:** Sam Abell © 1991 National Geographic Society; **268:** UPI/Bettmann; **269:** (top left) Rex Features, London; (bottom left) © Alan Berliner/Gamma-Liaison(bottom right) © RDR Productions 1988/Rex Features, Ltd.; **270:** Craig McClain.

Chapter Eight

272: © Laurie Rubin/Tony Stone Worldwide; **273:** © Wally McNamee/Woodfin Camp & Associates; **274:** (top left) © Martin Simon/SABA; (bottom left) © Ken Levine/Allsport, USA; **277:** (top) Bettmann Archive; **278:** Photograph reproduced by permission; **280:** Courtesy of Marian Burke; **281:** Bettmann Archive; **282:** © Rick Smolan/Stock, Boston; **284:** (left) Bettmann Archive; (right) Courtesy of Marian Burke; **285:** UPI/Bettmann; **286:** © Loren Santow/Tony Stone Worldwide; **287:** © Myrleen Ferguson/PhotoEdit; **288:** © Laura Dwight/Peter Arnold; **289:** © Jacques Chenet/ Woodfin Camp & Associates; **290:** Bettmann Archive; **291:** © Laura Dwight/Peter Arnold, Inc.; **292:** © Nigel Eddis; **293:** (top) © Stephen J Krasemann/DRK Photo; (center) © M. P. Kahl/ DRK Photo; (bottom) Craig McClain; **294:** © Belinda Wright/DRK Photo; **296:** © Nigel Eddis; **297:** Craig McClain; **299 and 300 (right):** From *The Cat in the Hat* by Dr. Seuss. Copyright © 1957 by Dr. Seuss. Copyright renewed 1985 by Theodor S. Geisel and Audrey S. Geisel. Reprinted by permission of Random House, Inc.; **300:** (top left and center) © Nigel Eddis; (top right and bottom) Craig McClain; **302:** © Chris Oschner-Hutchinson News/Sipa Press; **303:** (left, top to bottom) © Jose Hzel 1989 Contact Press/Woodfin Camp & Associates; © Roland et Sabrina Michaud/ Woodfin Camp & Associates; © Kal Muller/ Woodfin Camp & Associates; (right) © Jim Pickerell 1990/Stock, Boston; **304:** (left) © John Coletti/Stock, Boston; (right) © Stephen Swinburne/Stock, Boston; **305:** (left) © Michal

Heron/Woodfin Camp & Associates; (right) © Mimi Forsyth/Monkmeyer Press Photos; **306:** © Alon Reininger 1985/Contact Press/Woodfin Camp & Associates; **307:** (top to bottom) © John Coletti/Stock, Boston; © Michal Heron/Woodfin Camp & Associates; © Jim Pickerell 1990/Stock, Boston; **308:** Ed Kaski © 1989 *Psychology Today* Magazine (Sussex Publishers, Inc.); **309:** (top) © Ronald H. Cohn/The Gorilla Foundation; (bottom) © Michael Nichols/Magnum Photos; **310:** Craig McClain.

Chapter Nine

312: © 1985 Rob Lewine; **313:** © Jay Mather/ Sygma; **314:** (left) John Dominis LIFE Magazine © 1967 Time Warner, Inc.; (right) © Michael Melford/The Image Bank; **315:** (left) Courtesy, Richard Sjoberg; (right) © Mike Malyszko/Stock, Boston; **318:** © Kim Newton/Woodfin Camp & Associates; **320:** © Laura Dwight/Peter Arnold, Inc.; **321:** © Mark Hanauer; **322:** (left) Craig McClain; (bottom) © Marc Grimberg/The Image Bank; **323:** © John Ficara/Woodfin Camp & Associates; **324:** (left, top to bottom) © Jay Mather/ Sygma; John Dominis *Life* Magazine © 1967 Time Warner, Inc.; © Michael Melford/The Image Bank; Courtesy, Richard Sjoberg; (top right) © Mike Malyszko/Stock, Boston; **325:** © George B. Shaller/ Bruce Coleman, Inc.; **326:** (background photo) © Sam Zamember/The Image Bank; **328:** (background photo) © Herbert Lotz; (inset) © Deborah Davis/PhotoEdit; **330:** Division of Computer Research & Technology, National Institute of Health/Science Photo Library/Photo Researchers, Inc.; **331:** Damian Strohmeyer/Sports Illustrated © Time Warner Inc.; **332:** Reprinted by permission of the publishers from *The Thematic Apperception Test,* by Henry A. Murray, Cambridge, Mass.: Harvard University Press, © 1971 by Henry A. Murray; **333:** Bruce K. Huff/Los Angeles Times Photo; **334:** Mel Meleon/Los Angeles Times Photo; **335:** (top left) © George B. Shaller/Bruce Coleman, Inc.; (top right) Division of Computer Research & Technology, National Institute of Health/Science Photo Library/Photo Researchers, Inc.; (bottom, left to right) © Sam Zamember/The Image Bank; © Herbert Lotz; Bruce K. Huff/Los Angeles Times Photo; **336:** (left and right) UPI/Bettmann; (center) AP/Wide World Photos; **337:** (left) UPI/Bettmann; (right) AP/Wide World Photos; **340 and 343:** © Marty Snyderman; **344:** (top) © Topham/OB/ The Image Works; (bottom) © Don Smetzer/Tony Stone Worldwide; **345:** © Don Smetzer/Tony Stone Worldwide; **346:** Frankie Ziths/AP/Wide World Photos; **347:** (top) © David Pollack/The Stock Market; (center) © Burt Glinn/Magnum Photos; (bottom) © Myrleen Ferguson/PhotoEdit; **348:** (top left) © Myrleen Ferguson/PhotoEdit; (top right) Frankie Ziths/AP/Wide World Photos;

(bottom right) David Pollack/The Stock Market; **349:** (left to right) © David Ball/The Picture Cube; © Topham/OB/The Image Works; © Renee Lynn/ Photo Researchers, Inc.; © Burt Glinn/Magnum Photos; © Ray Ellis/Photo Reseachers, Inc.; **350:** © Brian Seed/Tony Stone Worldwide; **352:** © Myrleen Ferguson/PhotoEdit; **353:** (top) David Pollack/The Stock Market; (center) © Burt Glinn/ Magnum Photos; (bottom) © David Ball/The Picture Cube.

Chapter Ten

354: Oliviero Toscani for Benetton; **355:** © Harry Benson; **356:** "A Hundred Monkeys," by Wang, Yani. Collection of the artist. [Photo courtesy of the Nelson-Atkins Museum of Art]; **358:** (top) Courtesy, Nelson-Atkins Museum of Art; (bottom) © Harry Benson; **360:** (left) © Francis Leroy/ BioCosmos/Science Photo Library/Photo Researchers, Inc.; **361:** © Petit Format/Nestle/ Science Source/ Photo Researchers, Inc.; **363:** © Boehringer Ingelheim International GmbH, photo: Lennart Nilsson, **364–365:** (bottom) © Larry Keenan/The Image Bank; **365:** (top) © Enrico Ferorelli; **366:** © L. Stone/Sygma; **367:** (clockwise from top left) © Laura Dwight; © Ichi/ The Stock Market; © Laura Dwight; © Laura Dwight; **368-369:** (background) © Gabe Palmer/ The Stock Market; **368:** © Janeart Ltd/The Image Bank; **370:** (top) © A. Glauberman/Photo Researchers, Inc.; (bottom) © Laura Dwight/Peter Arnold, Inc.; **371:** (top to bottom, left to right) © Harry Benson; © Petit Format/Nestle/Science Source/Photo Researchers, Inc.; © Boehringer Ingelheim International GmbH, photo: Lennart Nilsson; © Laura Dwight; **373:** © Bob Daemmrich/Stock, Boston; **374:** © Nancy Brown/ The Image Bank; **376:** © Petit Format/Nestle/ Science Source/Photo Researchers, Inc.; **377:** © Bob Daemmrich/Stock, Boston; **378:** © Walter Wick; **380:** (left, top and bottom) Craig McClain; (right) © Mark E. Gibson/The Stock Market; **381:** Craig McClain; **382:** (all top photos) Craig McClain; (bottom left) Eileen Simpson/AP/Wide World Photos; **383:** © Yves DeBraine/Black Star; **384:** © Kory Addis/The Picture Cube; **385:** © Peter Beck/The Stock Market; **386:** © Mike Teruya, Free Spirit Photography; **387:** (top to bottom, left to right) © Walter Wick; © Yves DeBraine/Black Star; © Kory Addis/The Picture Cube; © Peter Beck/ The Stock Market; © Mike Teruya, Free Spirit Photography; **388:** © Bob Daemmrich/Stock, Boston; **389:** © Charles Gupton/Stock, Boston; **390:** (top) © Steve Winn/Anthro-Photo; (bottom) © Lila AbuLughod/Anthro-Photo; **391:** (top) © Gabe Palmer/The Stock Market; (bottom) © Cliff Feulner/The Image Bank; **392:** Private collection; **394:** (left) © Mark E. Gibson/The Stock Market; (bottom) © Peter Beck/The Stock Market; **395:** © Lila AbuLughod/Anthro-Photo.

Chapter Eleven

396: © Mark Seliger; 397: Tammy Lechner/Los Angeles Times Photo; 398: © Mark Seliger; 400, 402: Tammy Lechner/Los Angeles Times Photo; 403: Peter Brooker/Rex Features, London; 405: Courtesy, Lawrence Kohlberg; 406: (top left) © Mark Seliger; (center left) Tammy Lechner/Los Angeles Times Photo; (center right) Courtesy, Lawrence Kohlberg; 407: © Frank Siteman/Stock, Boston; 410: © Mark Seliger; 411: © Frank Siteman/Stock, Boston; 412: H. Armstrong Roberts; 413: © Harry Benson; 414: (left 3 photos) © Nathan Benn/Woodfin Camp & Associates; (right) © Paul Howell/Gamma-Liaison; 416: (top) Bettmann Archive; (bottom) UPI/Bettmann; 417: (left) © Bob Daemmrich/Stock, Boston; (right) © Del Mulkey/Photo Researchers, Inc.; 418: (left to right) © Bob Daemmrich/Stock, Boston; © John Lei/Stock, Boston; © B. Barbey/Magnum Photos; 419: Jorgensen/Rex Features, London; 421: © Bill Roth, Anchorage Daily News/Gamma-Liaison; 423: © 1992 Gryphon Software Corp., San Diego, California; 425: © Tom Moran 1991; 426: (top left 3 photos) © Nathan Benn/Woodfin Camp & Associates; (right) © Bill Roth, Anchorage Daily News/Gamma-Liaison; (bottom left) UPI/Bettmann; 428: © Michael Abramson/Woodfin Camp & Associates; 429: © Henry Groskinsky; 430: © Martin Simon/SABA; 431: © Dennis Cox/SABA; 432: H. Armstrong Roberts; 433: © Michael Abramson/Woodfin Camp & Associates.

Chapter Twelve

435: © Dan Smith/Allsport; 437: National Library of Medicine, Bethsada; 441: © O. Franken/Sgyma; 444: (left to right) National Library of Medicine; Courtesy, Adler School of Professional Psychology. Reproduced by permission of Kurt Adler; Courtesy, Association for the Advancement of Psychoanalysis; 446: (right) Reprinted by permission of the publishers of *The Thematic Apperception Test,* by Henry A. Murray, Cambrige, MA; Harvard University Press, © 1971 by Henry A. Murray; 447: © O. Franken/Sygma; 448: Photo by 3045-Gamma-Liaison; 449: © Bob Adelman/Magnum Photos; 450: (top) © Nancy Moran/Sygma; (bottom) © Francois Lochon/Gamma-Liaison; 451: (left) © Jose Azel/Contact Press Images/Woodfin Camp & Associates; (right) Doug Land, A Landmark Photo/Courtesy; 452: © Steve Schapiro/Gamma-Liaison; 453: © Jason Goltz; 458: © James Hamilton/Sygma; 460: © Henley & Savage/Tony Stone Worldwide; 461: © Roy Morsch/The Stock Market; 462: © Nils Jorgensen/RDR Productions/Rex Features, London; 463: © Ann States/SABA; 464: UPI/Bettmann; 465: Axel Koester/Los Angeles Times photo; 467: (left) © Rex Features, Ltd.; (right) © Eugene Aderbari/RDR Productions/Rex Features, London; 468: (top) UPI/Bettmann; (bottom) Axel Koester/Los Angeles Times Photo; 469: © Michael Nichols/Magnum Photos; 473: (top right) UPI/Bettmann; (bottom left) © Henley & Savage/Tony Stone Worldwide; 474: (top to bottom left to right) National Library of Medicine, Bethsada; Doug Land, A Landmark Photo/Courtesy; Courtesy, Albert Bandura; Photo by Mark Gerson/Courtesy, Dr. H. J. Eysenck; © Dan Smith/Allsport; © James Hamilton/Sygma; Photo by 3045-Gamma-Liaison; © Ann States/SABA; 475: © Jose Azel/Contact Press Images/Woodfin Camp & Associates; 478: © Eugene Aderbari/RDR Produtions/Rex Features, London.

Chapter Thirteen

480: Tony Stone Worldwide; 481–483: Craig McClain; 490: © Boehringer Ingelheim International GmbH, photo Lennart Nilsson; 493: Photo by Dr. John W. Lehmann, courtesy of Dr. Herbert Benson, Mind/Body Medical Institute; 497: © Boehringer Ingelheim International GmbH, photo Lennart Nilsson; 498–499: Arlene Gottfried, Life Magazine © 1992 The Time Inc. Magazine Company; 501: Lars Gelfan/Sports Illustrated; 502: Jeff Tuttle, The Wichita Eagle, Kansas; 506: © Dominique Aubert/Sygma; 511: (top to bottom, left to right) Arlene Gottfried, Life Magazine © 1992 The Time Inc. Magazine Company; Lars Glefan/Sports Illustrated; Jeff Tuttle, The Wichita Eagle, Kansas; © Dominique Aubert/Sygma; 514: Lars Glefan/Sports Illustrated.

Chapter Fourteen

516: © Will Cormier; 517: UPI/Bettmann; 518: © Henrik Drescher; 519: San Diego Tribune/Rick McCarthy; 520: UPI/Bettmann; 521: © Sebastiao Salgado, Jr./Magnum Photos; 526, 528: Craig McClain; 530: (top left) © Henrik Drescher; (bottom left) San Diego Tribune/Rick McCarthy; 531: AP/Wide World; 534: UPI/Bettmann; 535–536: AP/Wide World Photos; 538–540: Craig McClain; 541: © George Kochaniec, Jr./Sygma; 543: Courtesy, Ulrike Kantor Gallery; 544: Courtesy of Dr. Allan F. Mirsky, National Institute of Mental Health; 545: Courtesy of Dr. Pia Rubin, Department of Psychiatry, Bispebjerg Hospital; 548: Craig McClain; 549: (top left) AP/Wide World Photos; (center right) © George Kochaniec, Jr./Sygma; (all other photos) Craig McClain; 552: Craig McClain.

Chapter Fifteen

554: "Giving Good Voice" by Janet Wooley. Reproduced by Special Permission of *Playboy* Magazine. Copyright © 1991 by Playboy; 555: Culver Pictures; 556: (background photo) Mary Evans Picture Library, London; (inset) Photo by Ken Smith of painting in Harrisburg State Hospital; 557: © Bernard Gotfryd/Woodfin Camp & Associates; 566: Culver Pictures; 567: © Roger Dashow/Anthro-Photo; 570: Photo by Ken Smith of painting in Harrisburg State Hospital; 575–577, 581–583, 586: Craig McClain.

Chapter Sixteen

588: © Jeffrey Rotman; 589: © James Wilson/Woodfin Camp & Associates; 590–591: Craig McClain; 594–595: © Robert Johnson/Gamma-Liaison; 596: © K. Scholz/Superstock; 598: AP/Wide World Photos; 599: © Lori Grinkler/Contact Press/Woodfin Camp & Associates; 600: AP/Wide World Photos; 602: Photo by A. L. Wendroff, courtesy of the Anti Defamation League of B'nai B'rith, San Francisco and Gregory Withrow; 604: (top to bottom , left to right) Craig McClain (2 photos); © Robert Johnson/Gamma-Liaison; © K. Scholz/Superstock; Photo by A. L. Wendroff, courtesy of the Anti Defamation League of B'nai B'rith, San Francisco and Gregory Withrow; 605: East News/Sipa Press; 606: © Dan McCoy/Rainbow; 607: Clarence S. Bull/Kobal Collection; 608: Craig McClain; 609: AP/Wide World Photos; 610: © Rex Features USA Ltd; 612: © Washington Post 1978 Frank Johnston/Woodfin Camp & Associates; 614: Copyright © 1965 by Stanley Milgram. From the film *Obedience,* distributed by New York University Film Library and Pennsylvania State University, PCR; 617: (left to right) © Bill Ross/Woodfin Camp & Associates; Reuters/Bettmann; © Dan Miller/Woodfin Camp & Associates; 619: John Doman, St. Paul Pioneer Press, AP/Wide World Photos; 620–621: (left to right) © Zig Leszcynski/Animals Animals; AP/Wide World Photos; © Michael Newman/PhotoEdit; Craig McClain; 623: (top right) © Bill Ross/Woodfin Camp & Associates; (bottom right) John Doman, St. Paul Pioneer Press, AP/Wide World Photos; 626: © Bill Ross/Woodfin Camp & Associates.

FIGURE CREDITS

Chapter Three

92: Drawing adapted from *Biopsychology,* by J. P. L. Pinel, 1990, p. 171. Allyn & Bacon, Boston.

Chapter Four

150: (top) Adapted from *Sensation and Perception,* Third Edition, by Stanley Coren and Lawrence M. Ward, copyright © 1989 by Harcourt Brace Jovanovich, Inc., reprinted by permission of the publisher; **169:** (bottom) Based on painting by Davis Meltzer in © copyrighted material from National Geographic Society. Redrawn by permission.

Chapter Five

185: Graph based on information from the National Institute on Drug Abuse, 1990; **195:** Graph adapted from data in "Alcoholism—North America and Asia," by J. E. Helzer, G. J. Canino, E. Yeh, J. R. C. Bland, C. K. Lee, H. Hwu, & S. Newman, 1990, *Archives of General Psychiatry, 47,* p. 314.

Chapter Seven

249: Adapted from "Vivid Memories," by D. C. Rubin and M. Kozin, 1984, *Cognition, 16,* 81–95. Copyright © 1984 by Elsevier Science Publishers BV. Adapted by permission; **257:** Data from "Fifty Years of Memory for Names and Faces," by H. P. Bahrick, P. O. Bahrick, & R. P Wittlinger, 1975, *Journal of Experimental Psychology: General, 104,* 54–75.

Chapter Eight

279: Adapted from "Age and WAIS-R: A Cross-Sectional Analysis with Educational Level Controlled," by A. S. Kaufman, C. R. Reynolds, J. E. McLean, 1989, *Intelligence, 13,* pp. 246, 247. Copyright © 1989 by Ablex Publishing Company. Adapted by permission; **286:** Adapted from "Familial Studies of Intelligence: A Review," by T. J. Bouchard & M. McGue, 1981, *Science, 212,* 1055–1059. Copyright © 1981 by the Association for the Advancement of Science. Adapted by permission; **287:** Adapted from *Psychology: Themes and Variations,* 2nd ed., by Wayne Weiten, 1992, p. 320. Brooks/Cole Publishing Co. Copyright © 1989, 1992 by Wadsworth, Inc.

Chapter Ten

362: Adapted from a figure in *The Developing Human: Clinically Oriented Embryology,* by Keith L. Moore, 4th ed., Philadelphia, W. B Saunders Co., 1988. Adapted by permission; **364:** (patterns and faces) Adapted from *Sensation and Perception,* Third Edition, by Stanley Coren and Lawrence M. Ward, copyright © 1989 by Harcourt Brace Jovanovich, Inc., reprinted by permission of the publisher; **375:** Adapted from data in *Handbook of Labor Statistics,* August 1989, U.S. Department of Labor, Bureau of Labor Statistics.

Chapter Eleven

407: Reprinted with permission from *Parade.* Copyright © 1991; **408:** (graph) Data from U.S. Department of Health and Human Services; **415:** (graph bottom right) *Newseeek,* 5/13/91, p. 61, Source, "The Health Connection." Reprinted with permission; **425:** (graph bottom right) Data from National Center for Health Statistics; **430:** Copyright 1991, *USA Today.* Reprinted with permission; **431:** (graph) Data from National Center for Health Statistics, John L. McIntosh, Indiana University.

Chapter Twelve

465: Adapted from "The Five-Factor Model and Its Assessment in Clinical Settings," by R. R. McCrae, 1991, *Journal of Personality Assessment, 57,* p. 402; **471:** Adapted from "Personality Similarity in Twins Reared Apart and Together," by A. Tellegen, D. T. Lykken, T. J. Bouchard Jr., K. Wilcox, N. I. Segal, & S. Rich, 1988, *Journal of Personality and Social Psychology, 54* (6), 1031–1039. Copyright © 1988 by the American Psychological Association. Adapted by permission; **477:** Self-report inventory questions adapted from "Introversion/Extroversion," by G. D. Wilson, 1978. In *Dimensions in Personality,* H. London & J. E. Exner (Eds.). John Wiley & Sons.

Chapter Thirteen

483: (list) Data from *USA Today,* August 19, 1987, p. 4D; **487:** Adapted from *The Stress of Life,* by Hans Selye, p. 121, 1956. Copyright © 1956 by McGraw-Hill, Inc. Adapted by permission; **498 and 499:** (text about Sandra) Sasha Nyary, *Life* Magazine © 1992 The Time Inc. Magazine Company. Reprinted with permission; **500:** Reprinted with permission from *Journal of Psychosomatic Research, 11,* 213–218, by T. H. Holmes & R. H. Rahe in "The Social Readjustment Rating Scale," 1967, Pergamon Press Ltd. Oxford, England; **504:** (text about Sandra) Sasha Nyary, *Life* Magazine © 1992 The Time Inc. Magazine Company. Reprinted with permission; **507:** (graph) From "Stress and Illness," by G. S. Stern, T. R. McCants, & P. W. Pettine, 1982, *Personality and Social Psychology Bulletin, 6,* 140–145. Copyright © 1982 by the Society for Personality and Social Psychology, Inc. Reprinted by permission of Sage Publications, Inc.; **508:** (chart) Adapted from

"Alteration of Type A Behavior and Reduction in Cardiac Recurrences in Postmyocardial Infarction Patients," by M. Friedman, et al., 1984, *American Heart Journal, 108,* 237–248. Reprinted by permission of The C. V. Mosby Company; **510:** (graph) From "Dynamic Roles of Social Support in the Link Between Chronic Stress and Psychological Distress," by S. J. Lepore, G. W. Evans, & M. L. Schneider, 1991, *Journal of Personality and Social Psychology, 61,* p. 905. Copyright © 1991 by the American Psychological Association. Reprinted by permission.

Chapter Fourteen

521: Psychiatrist's profiles on Hinckley adapted from *Los Angeles Times,* 5/14/82, 5/15/82, 6/22/92, 7/10/92; **523:** Adapted with permission from the *American Psychiatric Association: Diagnostic and Statistical Manual of Mental Disorders, Third Edition, Revised,* Washington, D.C., American Psychiatric Association, 1987; **526:** Adapted from "Recent Life Events and Panic Disorders," by

C. Faravelli and S. Pallanti, 1989, *American Journal of Psychiatry, 146,* 622–626. Copyright © 1989 by the American Psychiatric Association. Adapted by permission; **527:** Adapted from *Psychology: Themes and Variations,* 2nd ed., by Wayne Weiten, 1992, p. 514, after data from Eaton, Dryman, & Weissman, 1991. Brooks/Cole Publishing Co. Copyright © 1989, 1992 by Wadsworth, Inc.

Chapter Fifteen

557: (graph) Data taken from *The Transfer of Care: Psychiatric Deinstitutionalization and Its Aftermath,* by P. Brown, 1985, p. 51. Routledge & Kegan Paul; **559:** From "Trends in Counseling and Psychotherapy," by D. Smith, 1982, *American Psychologist, 37,* 802–809. Copyright © 1982 by the American Psychological Association. Reprinted by permission; **575:** Adapted from "Behavior Therapy for Agoraphobic Men," by R. J. Hafner, 1983, *Behavior Research and Therapy, 21,* 51–56. Copyright © 1983 by Pergamon Press Ltd. Reprinted by permission.

Chapter Sixteen

591: Adapted from "Level of Categorization and Content of Gender Stereotypes" by K. Deaux, W. Winton, M. Crowley, & L. L. Lewis, 1985, *Social Cognition, 3,* 145–167. Copyright © 1985 by Guilford Publications, Inc. Adapted by permission; **593:** (graph) Adapted from *Newsweek,* 10/21/91, p. 36. EECO, Merit Systems Protection Board. Used with permission; **597:** Adapted from "Improving the Academic Performance of College Freshman," by T. D. Wilson & P. W. Linville, 1982, *Journal of Personality and Social Psychology, 42,* 367–376. Copyright © 1982 by the American Psychological Association. Adapted by permission; **615:** (graph) Adapted from "Behavioral Study of Obedience," by S. Milgram, 1963, *Journal of Abnormal and Social Psychology, 67,* 371–378; **622:** Data from *Rape Report,* produced by the National Victim Center, Ft. Worth, TX. Used by permission of the National Victim Center.

TO THE OWNER OF THIS BOOK:

I'd like to ask you a small favor. I have worked very hard to make this book readable and stimulating and would like to know if I have succeeded. Would you take a few minutes to fill out this form and tell me your reactions to this textbook? I will use your comments, suggestions, and criticisms to improve the next edition of *Introduction to Psychology*.

School: _____

Your instructor's name: _____

1. What did you like most about *Introduction to Psychology?* _____

_____

_____

2. What did you like least about the book? _____

_____

3. Were all the chapters or modules assigned for you to read?   Yes _____   No _____

   (If not, which ones were omitted?) _____

4. Did you use the Concept/Glossary sections?   Yes _____   No _____

   Did you find them useful?   Yes _____   No _____

5. How interesting and informative did you find the Cultural Diversity sections, which told you about behaviors in other cultures?

_____

_____

6. Did you use the Summary/Self-Test sections?   Yes _____   No _____

   Did you find them useful?   Yes _____   No _____

7. How interesting and informative did you find the Applying/Exploring sections? _____

_____

_____

8. In the space below (or in a separate letter) please make any other comments that you have about the book. (For example, did you like the way that photos and figures were integrated with the text?) I would really like to hear from you.

_____

_____

_____

_____

Many thanks for taking the time to fill out this request.

Best wishes,
Rod Plotnik

OPTIONAL

Your name: _____   Date: _____

May Brooks/Cole, my publisher, quote you in promotion for *Introduction to Psychology* or in future publishing ventures?

Yes _____   No _____

FOLD HERE

BUSINESS REPLY MAIL

FIRST CLASS   PERMIT NO. 358   PACIFIC GROVE, CA

POSTAGE WILL BE PAID BY ADDRESSEE

ATT: Rod Plotnik

**Brooks/Cole Publishing Company
511 Forest Lodge Road
Pacific Grove, California 93950-9968**

FOLD HERE